Epidemiology and Prevention of Cardiovascular Diseases

A Global Challenge

Darwin R. Labarthe, MD, MPH, PhD
James W. Rockwell Professor of Public Health
School of Public Health
The University of Texas Houston
Health Science Center
Houston, Texas

AN ASPEN PUBLICATION®
Aspen Publishers, Inc.
Gaithersburg, Maryland
1998

The author has made every effort to ensure the accuracy of the information herein. However, appropri⁻⁺ information sources should be consulted, especially for new or unfamiliar procedures. It is the responsibility of every practitioner to evaluate the appropriateness of a particular opinion in the context of actual clinical situations and with due considerations to new developments. The author, editors, and publisher cannot be held responsible for any typographical or other errors found in this book.

Library of Congress Cataloging-in-Publication Data

Labarthe, Darwin.
Epidemiology and prevention of cardiovascular diseases:
a global challenge/Darwin R. Labarthe.
p. cm.
Includes bibliographical references and index.
ISBN 0-8342-0659-5
1. Cardiovascular system—Diseases—Prevention.
2. Cardiovascular system—Diseases—Epidemiology.
3. Cardiovascular system—Diseases—Etiology. I. Title.
[DNLM: 1. Cardiovascular Diseases—epidemiology.
2. Cardiovascular Diseases—prevention & control.
WG 120 L113e 1998]
RA645.C34L33 1998
614.5'91—dc21
DNLM/DLC
for Library of Congress
97-45221
CIP

Orders: (800) 638-8437
Customer Service: (800) 234-1660

About Aspen Publishers • For more than 35 years, Aspen has been a leading professional publisher in a variety of disciplines. Aspen's vast information resources are available in both print and electronic formats. We are committed to providing the highest quality information available in the most appropriate format for our customers. Visit Aspen's Internet site for more information resources, directories, articles, and a searchable version of Aspen's full catalog, including the most recent publications:
http://www.aspenpub.com
 Aspen Publishers, Inc. • The hallmark of quality in publishing
 Member of the worldwide Wolters Kluwer group.

Editorial Services: Jane Colilla
Library of Congress Catalog Card Number: 97-45221
ISBN: 0-8342-0659-5

Printed in the United States of America

1 2 3 4 5

This book is dedicated to all whose work is reflected here and to all who will contribute to advances in the understanding of cardiovascular diseases and reduction of the public health burden they represent throughout the world.

Table of Contents

Foreword

The role of public health and its concepts, methods, and values have recently received increased recognition by policy makers and those responsible for the financing and delivery of health care. The unique contribution of epidemiology in acquiring the scientific basis for appropriate policy and decision making has also been widely acknowledged. Books are being written and courses developed to prepare students and practitioners of public health to respond to this increased demand and to provide them with the necessary skills and knowledge to do so. The generalist public health professional of the future will need to have a broad understanding of public health issues and critical insights into diverse public health topics in order to relate intelligently to the various segments of the health care sector.

This book, *Epidemiology and Prevention of Cardiovascular Diseases: A Global Challenge*, is notable for the breadth of topics it covers, the wealth of knowledge about risk factors that it presents, and its national and international perspective. The book will enable readers to become versed in current and future problems in the cardiovascular disease field, as well as to understand the means for preventing and controlling these conditions in this country and elsewhere. It is an excellent up-to-date reference and text for courses on the subject.

Morbidity and mortality from cardiovascular diseases are at their peak in industrialized nations, and these conditions have now begun to threaten the developing world in a similar fashion. The global orientation of this book, as well as its population and individual approaches, offers important lessons in prevention and control that could provide the basis for policies to prevent this epidemic from spreading in developing countries.

This volume is written by an internationally renowned author. Careful in the selection of topics, this distinguished author has provided in-depth information and critical analysis of conditions and their risk factors. He has authoritatively covered current issues and provided a glimpse of the future, giving the generalist public health student the proper perspective for anticipating the future. He has crafted a comprehensive and readable text by balancing and integrating the diverse subject matter, with emphasis on prevention and policy implications.

Michel A. Ibrahim, MD, PhD
Professor of Epidemiology
The University of North Carolina
School of Public Health

Preface

The primary goal of this book is to provide teachers and students of the subject with a current and comprehensive collection of relevant materials synthesized from the unifying perspective of a single author. A further goal emerged in course, that of documenting evidence of the unique and fundamental contributions of epidemiology, especially in the past 50 years, toward understanding the nature of cardiovascular diseases and the means of their prevention. It was an ambitious and perhaps presumptuous project from the start and became more so with growing appreciation of its necessary scope. Its progress was stimulated by the continuing need for the final product and was buoyed by signs of widening recognition that cardiovascular diseases truly represent a global public health challenge—a theme especially elevated to a new prominence by the Fourth International Conference on Preventive Cardiology convened in Montreal in 1997. Coverage of this subject could never be exhaustive, and work in this field is far from finished, but the time arrived when publication seemed justified on the basis of progress toward the stated goals. This book can now be viewed and evaluated by others who, it is hoped, will find it useful.

Readers may be students of epidemiology and public health, other health professionals, or others interested in an account of cardiovascular diseases and their epidemiologic investigation up to the present time. Knowledge of technical terms and concepts is not assumed. For the more demanding reader, extensive illustrations and citations to original, sometimes early, sources are provided. Materials from sources outside the United States are presented often, although most illustrations are from material more familiar to US readers. Early sources are emphasized in many illustrations because they are least often encountered through literature searches bounded by only the most recent years, and much of what we know about this subject was not discovered as recently as is sometimes thought. This book is not a history of the field, but it is presented with a historical perspective.

The primary focus of this book is on the epidemiology and prevention of the atherosclerotic and hypertensive diseases—the conditions that predominate among the cardiovascular diseases in most industrialized countries and threaten to do so in developing countries throughout the world. When the results of decades of epidemiologic, clinical, and laboratory investigation are considered, the causation of these conditions appears to be highly intricate. At the same time, however, a few causal factors of major importance have been recognized for nearly four decades. These include high blood cholesterol concentration, high blood pressure, their underlying determinants—especially broad social patterns of dietary imbalance and physical inactivity—and cigarette smoking. Knowledge of even these long-established causal factors and determinants has yet to be applied fully toward prevention of their associated disease outcomes, much less to prevention of these major factors themselves.

Concepts of prevention of cardiovascular diseases are considered both at the level of whole communities or societies (the population-wide strategy) and at the level of individuals (the high-risk strategy). The evolution of policies and recommendations for cardiovascular disease prevention in the latter half of the 20th century clearly reflects this duality, and more effective implementation of public health interventions is needed at both levels. This is especially true if the majority of the world's population is to be spared the full onslaught of the coronary heart disease epidemic that has already afflicted most industrialized countries.

Other cardiovascular diseases, such as rheumatic fever, rheumatic heart disease, and Chagas' disease still predominate in large areas of the world. Principles of their prevention are also well established but are insufficiently implemented to achieve the full potential for public health benefit. Still other conditions, specifically congenital heart disease and Kawasaki disease, remain so little understood as to their causation that only very limited preventive measures are currently available.

The foremost public health challenge in relation to cardiovascular diseases is the application of current knowledge toward their prevention. This task is a major obligation for epidemiologists and other health professionals. At the same time, new questions inviting etiologic research continue to arise, such as those concerning the potential linkage between discoveries at the molecular level and patterns of actual risk and disease occurrence in populations. Finally, as always, the need remains for epidemiologic monitoring of populations to assess the changing natural history of cardiovascular diseases, their determinants, and the impact of public health interventions. Consistent with these observations, two main themes are addressed

throughout the book. First, epidemiology has made fundamental and decisive contributions to the understanding of causation and the potential for prevention of these diseases. Second, much remains to be learned about cardiovascular diseases, and the greater part of the challenge of prevention remains to be met.

The book is organized into five parts. Part I provides a public health perspective on cardiovascular diseases, including their definition and scope (Chapter 1) and an overview of the contributions of 20th century epidemiology (Chapter 2). Part II addresses the atherosclerotic and hypertensive diseases in two sections. The first of these reviews the nature and occurrence of the major conditions within this broad category—atherosclerosis, coronary heart disease, stroke, and others (Chapters 3 though 6). The second section reviews the main determinants of the occurrence of these conditions. This largest section of the book addresses many of the factors in the causation of the atherosclerotic and hypertensive diseases in a sequential approach. As background for the chapters that follow, some general aspects of age, sex, race, and heredity are presented first (Chapter 7). Following review of two of the especially prominent determinants—dietary imbalance (Chapter 8) and physical inactivity (Chapter 9)—conditions largely considered to be intermediate outcomes of these behavioral patterns are addressed: fatness, overweight, and central adiposity; adverse blood lipid profile; high blood pressure; and glucose intolerance, insulin resistance, and diabetes (Chapters 10 through 13). Next, additional behavioral factors are considered—smoking and other tobacco use (Chapter 14) and alcohol consumption (Chapter 15). A discussion of hemostatic dysfunction, which may result from many of the foregoing influences, follows (Chapter 16). Adverse psychosocial patterns (Chapter 17) and other personal characteristics (Chapter 18) complete the series of chapters addressing factors that operate at the individual, as well as the societal, level. Social conditions, which may underlie or transcend these personal factors, are then reviewed (Chapter 19). Closing the discussion of these numerous factors is a chapter devoted to synthesis of the foregoing material into a coherent understanding of causation of the atherosclerotic and hypertensive diseases (Chapter 20).

Part III concerns the application of knowledge of the causation of these diseases in public health efforts to achieve their prevention and control. Multifactor primary prevention trials are first reviewed (Chapter 21) to illustrate the experience of both individual and community-wide levels of intervention to modify risks and rates of adverse outcomes. Parallel with the research reviewed throughout the preceding chapters, prevention policies have undergone significant evolution (Chapter 22). The special implications of this knowledge and of intervention policies for certain population groups—identified by age, sex, race or ethnicity, heredity or genotype, and socioeconomic level—are then discussed in this last chapter devoted specifically to the atherosclerotic and hypertensive diseases (Chapter 23).

In Part IV, other major cardiovascular diseases are reviewed. They are selected for their dominance as sources of cardiovascular morbidity and mortality in many countries—rheumatic fever and rheumatic heart disease (Chapter 24), and Chagas' disease and other cardiomyopathies (Chapter 25)—or for their continued challenges to epidemiologic investigation to establish their causes and means of prevention—congenital heart disease (Chapter 26) and Kawasaki disease (Chapter 27). In addition to the atherosclerotic and hypertensive diseases, these other conditions serve to broaden the perspective on cardiovascular diseases as a global public health challenge, with significant need for both effective intervention and further epidemiologic research. Part V brings together many of the implications of Parts I through IV for public health action (Chapter 28) and for advancement of epidemiologic research on the cardiovascular diseases (Chapter 29).

This book will have achieved the author's goals if it facilitates learning and enhances both professional commitment and societal investment in the epidemiology and prevention of the major cardiovascular diseases throughout the world.

Acknowledgments

Merrily Labarthe is foremost in deserving immense gratitude for her many contributions to this project, not only as its tireless bibliographer and librarian, but also for her boundless enthusiasm and timely inspiration from beginning to end.

Technical assistance in the permissions process, acquisition of certain materials, photo reproduction of illustrative material, and execution of original artwork were contributed in turn by Ruth Firsching (whose tenacity and diligence were surpassing), Mary Carroll, Sandra Acholonu, Dottsie Nat, Fran Holden, and Henry Fung.

Contributions of critical points of information were made by Patty Borhani, Elizabeth Barrett-Connor, Rory Collins, Leonard Cook, Jeffrey Cutler, Jack Farquhar, Nancy Haase, Millicent and Ian Higgins, George Howard, William Kannel, Thomas Kottke, Ian MacMahon, Henry McGill, Porfirio Nordet, Judith Ockene, Anthony Orencia (bibliographic work for Chapter 26), Kenneth R. Pelletier, Geoffrey Rosenthal, Richie Sharrett, Jeremiah Stamler, Elaine Stone, Jack Strong, and Thomas Thom.

Reviewers of the draft text are acknowledged for their comments, especially Aaron Folsom, whose meticulous review and extensive suggestions to a great extent improved the final product.

The needed research could not have been accomplished without the extraordinary resources and the able and willing support of staff of The University of Texas Houston School of Public Health Library and the Houston Academy of Medicine Library. Aspen Publishers provided significant support for this project and highly skilled editorial assistance for which gratitude is well deserved.

Finally, The University of Texas Houston Health Science Center program of faculty development leave is recognized for the opportunity it provided the author to plan and initiate the project, and School of Public Health students, faculty, and staff are due thanks for their patience, indulgence, and interest throughout the project.

PART I

Cardiovascular Diseases: A Public Health Perspective

CHAPTER 1

Cardiovascular Diseases: A Global Public Health Challenge

SUMMARY

Cardiovascular diseases, as defined in this book, comprise the major disorders of the heart and the arterial circulation supplying the heart, brain, and peripheral tissues. Their common occurrence in most populations and the attendant mortality, loss of independence, impaired quality of life, and social and economic costs are compelling reasons for public health concern. The epidemiology and prevention of these diseases involve the understanding of their causes, identification of means of prevention, and monitoring of populations to assess the changing burden of these diseases and the measurable impact of interventions to control them. Together, the cardiovascular or circulatory diseases have figured prominently in the large shifts among causes of death, especially in industrial societies, during the 20th century. During this period they have become the dominant cause of death in many countries. The theory of "epidemiologic transition" predicts that such shifts will also occur in developing countries as a result of both increasing proportions of these populations attaining older ages and concurrent social changes. Major demographic change consistent with this prediction is already taking place, and there is also some evidence of changing patterns of disease to support the forecast. The conditions selected for detailed consideration in this book are those that are especially common globally, constitute particularly serious problems for large regions of the world, or pose special challenges to epidemiology in identifying causes and establishing means of their prevention.

THE EPIDEMIOLOGY AND PREVENTION OF CARDIOVASCULAR DISEASES: DEFINITION AND SCOPE

The cardiovascular diseases, or diseases of the heart and blood vessels, comprise many conditions that vary widely in their particular manifestations and in their impact on health. Because the terminology is not strictly standardized, it is important to note several conventions adopted here. Tables or figures from other sources use the terms found in the original source, with explanation where needed. For example, CVD may refer to cardiovascular disease, meaning specifically disease of the heart or its blood supply, or to cerebrovascular disease, affecting the arterial supply to the brain. A major condition of the heart, coronary heart disease, may be abbreviated as CHD, IHD (ischemic heart disease), or CAD (coronary artery disease). In general, the term *cardiovascular diseases* here will refer to the full spectrum of conditions, including stroke or cerebrovascular disease, except where otherwise indicated.

These conditions vary in the extent to which they compromise normal circulatory function; some cardiovascular conditions such as heart attack or stroke are often rapidly fatal, while cases of rheumatic heart disease usually persist for long periods and share with surviving cases of heart attack and stroke prolonged illness and disability. The personal and social costs of such conditions justify substantial efforts both to understand their causes and to devise practical means of prevention. This is especially true of conditions that occur with the greatest frequencies in the population as a whole. For such conditions, monitoring their frequencies of occurrence is a third important task, both to estimate the current and future population burden of these conditions and to gauge the effectiveness of interventions against them.

Epidemiology and prevention embrace these three tasks—understanding causation, devising means of intervention, and monitoring the frequency of occurrence of important conditions that are common in the population. It may be unnecessary to add the term *prevention*, as many readers would consider this implicitly as part of epidemiology. For others, however, omission of this term might imply a much more limited view of the role of epidemiology than is intended here, and it is therefore included prominently. The function of monitoring may be less readily recognized by some as an inherent aspect of epidemiology. However, the essential contribution of the monitoring function of epidemiology should become apparent from much of the discussion in this book.

The Cardiovascular Diseases—An International Classification

What, then, is the scope of cardiovascular diseases? Definition and classification of the cardiovascular diseases, as with other conditions, have evolved with changing concepts of disease and take many forms, in part due to different purposes. In epidemiology, special value attaches to a classification that is standardized and in common use in many or most hospitals, medical practices, states, countries, and regions of the world. In this way some confidence is justified that reference to the same condition in different information sources corresponds to the same reality. The leading source of such a classification for use throughout the world is the World Health Organization publication, now in its 10th revision, the *International Statistical Classification of Diseases and Related Health Problems* (ICD 10).[1] Published in 1992, the ICD 10 presents the category of Diseases of the Circulatory System as shown in Exhibit 1–1.

Each three-character code in this classification has an alphabetic initial followed by two digits. The alpha code for this category is the

---

Exhibit 1–1 Diseases of the Circulatory System (I00–I99)

I00–I02	Acute rheumatic fever
I05–I09	Chronic rheumatic heart diseases
I10–I15	Hypertensive diseases
I20–I25	Ischemic heart diseases
I26–I28	Pulmonary heart disease and diseases of pulmonary circulation
I30–I52	Other forms of heart disease
I60–I69	Cerebrovascular diseases
I70–I79	Diseases of arteries, arterioles, and capillaries
I80–I89	Diseases of veins, lymphatic vessels, and lymph nodes, not elsewhere classified
I90–I95	Other and unspecified disorders of the circulatory system

Note: Classification excludes congenital malformations, transient cerebral ischemic attacks and related syndromes, and certain others.

letter *I*, with blocks of digits from 00–02 to 90–95 that distinguish 10 classes. Within a block, each two-digit code corresponds to a distinct subset of that class. Greater detail can be provided by use of an additional decimal place. For example, for "ischemic heart diseases" (I20–I25) the code I21 identifies acute myocardial infarction, or heart attack; codes I21.1 through I21.4 represent the anatomic location of the damage within the heart, and I21.9 is used for cases where location is not specified. Thus a case record, whether in the form of a death certificate or a hospital discharge summary, can potentially be coded in a consistent way, and cases with the same code can be collected and treated statistically as representing the same kind of circulatory event. The validity of such analyses depends, of course, on the quality of information available and the nosologic coding procedures applied.

The conditions listed in Exhibit 1–1 are those judged by the drafters of the ICD 10 to be classified best as diseases of the circulatory system. Not all of the conditions identified in Exhibit 1–1 are addressed in this book (specifically parts of codes I80–I89, diseases of the veins and lymphatic vessels and lymph nodes, and I90–I95, "other"). Two categories not included in Exhibit 1–1 do receive attention: (1) congenital malformations or birth defects of the heart and major blood vessels and (2) transient cerebral ischemic attacks or "light strokes," which for present purposes are considered to belong with the cerebrovascular diseases or circulatory conditions affecting the brain. Classification of these conditions is addressed in their respective chapters. In the terms used conventionally to refer to the conditions addressed in subsequent chapters, the cardiovascular diseases to be discussed are atherosclerotic and hypertensive diseases and selected venous system disorders (essentially I10–I15, I20–I25, I26, I60–I69, parts of I70–I79, I80–I89, and G45) in Chapters 3–20, rheumatic heart disease (I00–I02, I05–I09) in Chapter 24, Chagas' disease and other cardiomyopathies (parts of I30–I52) in Chapter 25, congenital heart disease (Q20–Q28) in

Chapter 26, and Kawasaki disease (M30.3) in Chapter 27.

In the chapters specific to a given condition, further detail of the ICD 10 codes will be noted, and earlier ICD codes will be referenced as needed. This is because ICD 10 has only recently been introduced; the data currently available on the conditions of interest therefore represent one or another of the previous versions, each of which was current for only about a decade. The use of ICD 10 as the present framework provides an orientation to the future for the benefit of those who will address the issues discussed here in the years ahead.

THE BASIS OF PUBLIC HEALTH CONCERN WORLDWIDE

The Magnitude of the Problem

Why do the cardiovascular diseases, taken together, warrant epidemiologic attention? The answer lies in part in the very large proportion of deaths, throughout the world, attributed to cardiovascular conditions. Figure 1–1 presents the percentages of deaths due to cardiovascular diseases (CVDs) in the world as a whole (23%) and separately in developing countries (16%) and industrial countries (48%) in 1980.[2] Although such estimates are subject to some reservations—especially for the developing countries—there is substantial support for the view that cardiovascular diseases are becoming more prominent as a health problem of developing countries. In fact, the proportion of all deaths worldwide occurring in these populations is so great that the majority of cardiovascular deaths also occurs in developing countries.

Changing Patterns of Mortality in the United States

Within an industrialized nation such as the United States, the prominence of heart disease among causes of death has risen sharply

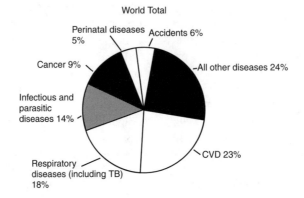

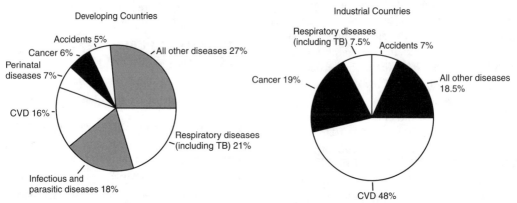

Note: CVD, cardiovascular disease; TB, tuberculosis. Of the total deaths 78% are in developing countries.

Figure 1–1 Relative Contributions of Cardiovascular Death to Total Mortality in Developing and Industrial Countries and the World, 1980. *Source:* From *Disease Control Priorities in Developing Countries*, edited by DT Jamison et al. Copyright © 1993 The International Bank for Reconstruction and Development/The World Bank. Used by permission of Oxford University Press, Inc.

throughout most of the 20th century, as shown for the period 1900–1970 in Figure 1–2.[3] The importance of this early analysis of mortality in the United States is its contribution to a theory of population-wide changes in patterns of disease formulated in the 1970s, discussed below. The figure serves well even now to illustrate the changes in death rates, or the numbers of deaths per 100,000 population per year, due to several categories of causes over several decades. The relative shift for heart disease resulted from both an absolute increase in the rate of heart disease deaths (from a little more than 100 deaths to about 400 deaths per 100,000 population) and concurrent major decreases in other causes

of death, especially in tuberculosis and other infectious diseases. Even before the 1920s, heart disease and stroke together exhibited mortality greater than that from any other category. Today they still account for more than 40% of all deaths in the United States, as described in subsequent chapters.[4]

Such vast shifts in causes of death stimulate strong epidemiologic interest, because they must reflect profound changes in the factors that influence health and disease. Factors that are identified or confirmed through their association with such trends may constitute clues to causation or point to potential interventions. But, as will be seen, major increases in disease

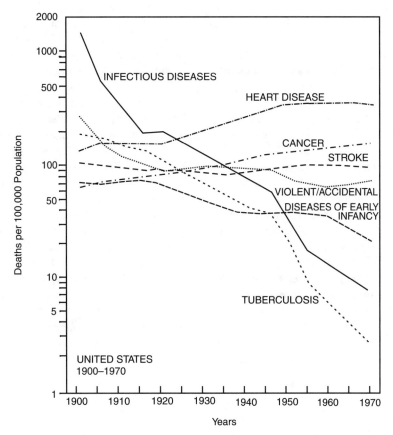

Figure 1–2 Secular Trends for Cardiovascular Disease and Other Cause-Specific Death Rates in the United States, 1900–1970. Courtesy of the Population Reference Bureau, Inc., Washington, DC.

occurrence have generally proved difficult to explain in retrospect. The same is true of the trends toward disappearance of very common diseases, long after the fact. But the United States is not unique in its 20th-century experience (indicated in Figure 1–2), and such changes in patterns of mortality may be repeated in many countries in the future. This creates the possibility of observing such changes—to the extent they may escape effective control measures—as they actually unfold in the future in a number of populations. The likelihood of this is suggested both by epidemiologic theory and by a number of observations illustrated in the following section.

The Epidemiologic Transition and Developing Countries

The theoretical basis for this view is that of the "epidemiologic transition," formulated by Omran in an analysis of long-term patterns of mortality in human societies and first published in 1971.[5] Omran distinguished three stages of progression, historically over centuries, in the dominant patterns of mortality: the "age of pestilence and famine," the "age of receding pandemics," and the "age of degenerative and manmade diseases." In a later development of the theory, others have proposed a fourth stage, the "age of delayed degenerative diseases."[6] These four stages of the epidemiologic transition are characterized with reference to the frequencies of circulatory diseases, as percentages of all causes of death, in Table 1–1.[2] The shift from very low to much higher frequencies of circulatory diseases as causes of death is much like that demonstrated in Figure 1–2. These changing proportions of death due to circulatory conditions are expected even if the absolute rates of death from these causes decline, for other causes are likely to decrease more rapidly.

As shown in Table 1–1, under this theory circulatory diseases increase from a minor proportion of all deaths in the first stage to become the predominant cause in the third; finally, they may decrease slightly in relative importance, though still perhaps representing the largest single category of deaths. Characteristic shifts also occur in the predominance of particular forms of circulatory disease over the successive phases: first, solely rheumatic heart disease and cardiomyopathies; second, these and also hy-

pertensive heart disease and hemorrhagic stroke; third, all forms of stroke plus ischemic heart disease; and fourth, the latter causes persisting but occurring at older ages and as a slightly reduced proportion of all deaths.

In the United States and other countries undergoing industrialization in the 19th and 20th centuries, this epidemiologic transition is already far advanced into the third or fourth stage. Developing countries, however, are typically in the first or second stage. The prospect of further transition in these countries, perhaps more rapid transition in some features than in the already-industrialized countries, is suggested by changes underway in recent decades. Thus Dodu, of the World Health Organization Cardiovascular Diseases Unit in Geneva, wrote in 1988 of the emergence of cardiovascular diseases in developing countries.[7] He presented data (Figure 1–3), based on Omran's work, to show that the percentage of deaths due to cardiovascular diseases (and cancer) in a popula-

Table 1–1 The Epidemiologic Transition

Phase of Epidemiologic Transition	Deaths from Circulatory Disease (%)	Circulatory Problems	Risk Factors
Age of pestilence and famine	5–10	Rheumatic heart disease; infectious and deficiency-induced cardiomyopathies	Uncontrolled infection; deficiency conditions
Age of receding pandemics	10–35	As above, plus hypertensive heart disease and hemorrhagic stroke	High-salt diet leading to hypertension; increased smoking
Age of degenerative and man-made diseases	35–55	All forms of stroke; ischemic heart disease	Atherosclerosis from fatty diets; sedentary lifestyle; smoking
Age of delayed degenerative diseases	Probably under 50	Stroke and ischemic heart disease[a]	Education and behavioral changes leading to lower levels of risk factors

Note: Omran introduced the concept of epidemiologic transition with discussion of phase 1, 2, and 3. Olshansky and Ault added the concept of a fourth phase.

a. At older ages. Represents a smaller proportion of deaths.

Source: From *Disease Control Priorities in Developing Countries*, edited by DT Jamison et al. Copyright © 1993 The International Bank for Reconstruction and Development/The World Bank. Used by permission of Oxford University Press, Inc.

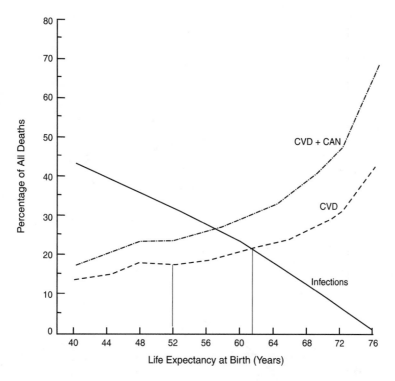

Figure 1–3 Percentages of Deaths Due to Cardiovascular Diseases (CVD), Cancer (CAN), and Infections, in Relation to Life Expectancy at Birth. *Source*: Percentage of All Dealths Due to Various Causes at Different Levels of Life Expectancy at Birth, *Cardiology*, © 1988. Reproduced with permission of S Karger AG, Basel.

tion increases as life expectancy at birth increases. This would be anticipated because cardiovascular disease death rates are very much higher for successively older age groups in adulthood. Thus, as shown by Dodu, when the average person attains age 61 or 62 cardiovascular diseases are expected to predominate over infectious diseases as a cause of death.

Dodu further demonstrated, as in Figure 1–4, that life expectancy at birth increased sharply in developing regions of the world in the third quarter of the 20th century. Further, this increase has been projected to continue, so that by the year 2000 even Africa will attain an average life expectancy at birth of nearly 60 years. This value will be slightly exceeded by that for the population of South Asia but far exceeded by East Asia and Latin America. This changing demographic picture alone, influenced partly by

recession of infectious diseases as a cause of neonatal and infant mortality, leads to an expectation of an increasing proportion of deaths from circulatory diseases, in accordance with the theory of epidemiologic transition. As a concrete example, Dodu cited the experience of Singapore, where in 30 years (1948–1979) life expectancy increased from about 40 years to 70 years, and cardiovascular diseases shifted from only 5% to more than 30% of all deaths.

Economic Considerations

Public health concern about cardiovascular diseases is worldwide, in part because of the high frequency of occurrence of these diseases as a cause of death, both on a continuing basis in industrialized countries and as a serious prospect

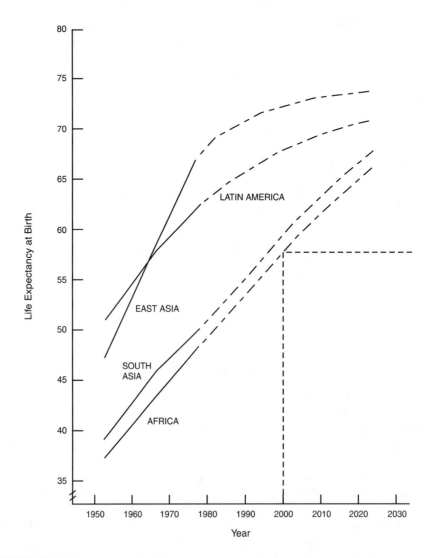

Figure 1–4 Life Expectancy in Relation to Calendar Time, by Region of the World, 1950–2030. *Source*: Life Expectancy at Birth (Both Sexes) by Region Medium Variant 1950–2025 as Assessed in 1980, *Cardiology*, © 1988. Reproduced with permission of S Karger AG, Basel.

in developing countries. In addition, among the personal and social costs of cardiovascular diseases, both fatal and nonfatal, their economic costs are increasingly important. In the United States, for example, the cost of medical care alone for cardiovascular diseases has been variously estimated as approximately $100 billion[4] or several times that amount.[2] The higher estimate, which includes indirect costs such as loss of productivity, would correspond to more than 3% of the US gross national product—a huge economic burden. The persistence of this economic circumstance in industrialized countries and the prospect of its emergence as an increasing problem for developing countries lend importance to intensified efforts to control the cardiovascular diseases in populations throughout the world.

RATES OF OCCURRENCE IN SELECTED POPULATIONS AND CHANGES IN RECENT DECADES

Regional Variation in Mortality from Diseases of the Circulatory System

The status of the major regions of the world with respect to mortality from circulatory system diseases late in the 20th century is summarized in Table 1–2.[2] For the total world population and for each geographic/economic area distinguished by the World Bank, Table 1–2 indicates the 1985 data on the total number of deaths (in thousands), the percentage of the total due to circulatory diseases, and the death rate (per 100,000 population, adjusted for differences between regions in age composition) for all circulatory diseases and for two of the component categories, ischemic heart disease and cerebrovascular disease.

The percentages of deaths from circulatory diseases are highest for the industrial economies, both market economics such as the United States (46%) and nonmarket ones such as the countries of the former Soviet Union (47%), and one-half to one-quarter as high for the remaining four regions (10–22%). The actual mortality rate is highest for the industrial nonmarket economies (357 per 100,000). This observation indicates that the populations of these countries are especially in need of effective interventions to reduce the already-high toll of circulatory diseases. This impression is reinforced by the comparatively high mortality from both ischemic heart disease and cerebrovascular disease in the industrial nonmarket economies.

In other regions the death rates for total circulatory diseases are lower and rather similar (222–273 per 100,000), except in Asia, which has the lowest rate (195 per 100,000). This implies that the relatively lower percentages of circulatory deaths in the nonindustrial regions reflect a relative excess of deaths from noncirculatory causes. That is, the rise of circulatory diseases appears to have outpaced the recession of pandemics in these regions, and thus mortality is currently high for both of these broad categories of disease. The more-specific categories of ischemic heart disease and cerebrovascular disease exhibit patterns similar to those for total

Table 1–2 Estimated Mortality from Circulatory System Diseases, World Bank, 1985

Region	Deaths (Thousands)	Total Deaths (%)	Age-Standardized Death Rate (per 100,000 Population)[a]		
			Total	Ischemic Disease	Cerebrovascular Disease
Industrial market economies	3,355	46	235	99	59
Industrial nonmarket economies	2,220	47	357	164	106
Latin America and the Caribbean	691	22	222	69	57
Sub-Saharan Africa	756	10	273	85	74
Middle East and North Africa	602	14	250	82	68
Asia	3,841	17	195	46	91
Total	11,465	23	243	84	81

a. Rates are standardized using the 1985 world age structure.

Source: From *Disease Control Priorities in Developing Countries*, edited by DT Jamison et al. Copyright © 1993 The International Bank for Reconstruction and Development/The World Bank. Used by permission of Oxford University Press, Inc.

circulatory mortality, with the highest mortality in the industrial nonmarket region (164 and 106 per 100,000, respectively). Asia is again exceptional, in this instance by having the lowest mortality for ischemic heart disease of any region (46 per 100,000) and the highest for cerebrovascular disease (91 per 100,000) outside the industrial nonmarket region.

The Variable Dynamics of Cardiovascular Mortality

As of the late 20th century, marked differences in mortality from circulatory and other causes are demonstrable in populations comprising the several regions of the world defined in broad economic and geographic terms. The mortality pattern of a particular national population, such as the absolute and relative rise of heart disease mortality in the United States shown in Figure 1–2, has been seen to evolve throughout much of this century. But even within one to two decades populations may dif-

fer strikingly in both direction and rate of change in heart disease mortality, as shown in Figures 1–5 and 1–6.

In these figures, data on heart disease mortality (excluding rheumatic heart disease) from 1970–1974 to 1984–1987 for 27 countries reporting to the World Health Organization are compared for both men and women dying at ages from 45 to 64 years.[8] For men, the differences among populations range from a decrease of nearly 50% for Australia to an increase of about 40% for Poland and (the former) Yugoslavia. For women, the maximum decrease (also for Australia) was similar to that for men, but the greatest increase (for Czechoslovakia) was less, about 15%. (All four countries with increasing rates for men or women were industrialized nonmarket countries in the World Bank classification discussed above.)

These differences over time among populations in the change in mortality are of even greater epidemiologic interest than a major shift in the pattern of mortality within a particular

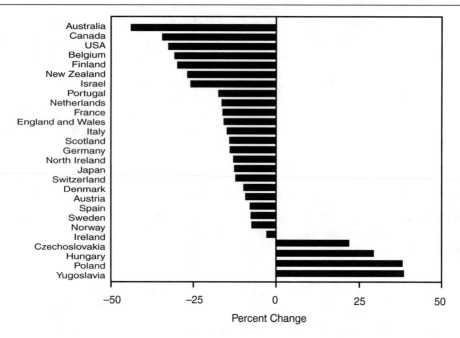

Figure 1–5 Percent Change in Heart Disease Mortality, by Country, 1970–74 to 1984–87, for Men Aged 45–64. *Source:* Reprinted from National Heart, Lung and Blood Institute, National Institutes of Health, Bethesda, Maryland.

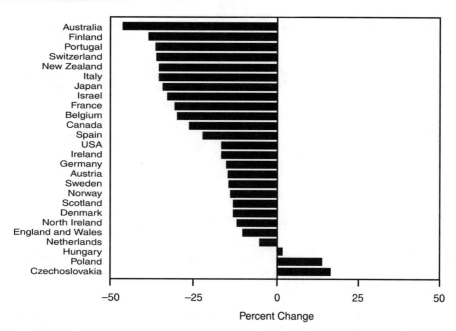

Figure 1–6 Percent Change in Heart Disease Mortality, by Country, 1970–74 to 1984–87, for Women Aged 45–64. *Source:* Reprinted from National Heart, Lung and Blood Institute, National Institutes of Health, Bethesda, Maryland.

population over time because of the added dimension of variation between populations. Such data greatly expand the possibilities for useful comparative investigation, with the opportunity for deeper insight into both the causes of these large population changes and the potential for prevention or control of the underlying epidemic processes.

CURRENT RATES OF MAJOR CARDIOVASCULAR DISEASES IN THE UNITED STATES AND ELSEWHERE

US Mortality and Morbidity in the Early 1990s

The continuously evolving pattern of mortality in a population is reflected in the relative frequencies of various component conditions at any given time, these frequencies resulting from many concurrent influences that may have acted over decades or longer. Figure 1–2 demonstrates this point with respect to heart disease

and other broad categories, if the frequencies of death by cause are viewed vertically at any selected year between 1900 and 1970. An analogous picture of the main components *within* the cardiovascular diseases can be gleaned from various sources of information for the United States as of the early 1990s, as shown in Table 1–3.[4]

The American Heart Association provides an annual report on the occurrence of cardiovascular diseases in the United States based on the most recent data available. The 1997 update includes the numbers of deaths from particular cardiovascular conditions reported in national vital statistics and projected to either 1993 or 1994, as available, and estimates of the "prevalence" of each condition, expressed as the numbers either of affected persons or of hospital discharges, for the total US population. (Because these estimates are not expressed as the percentage or other fraction of the population, and because hospital discharges may count the same person more than once in a single year,

Table 1–3 Frequencies of Major Types of Cardiovascular Diseases in the United States as of the Early to Mid-1990s

Condition[a]	Deaths[b]	Prevalence[c]
Coronary heart disease (410–414)	487,490	13,670,000**
Stroke (430–438)	154,350	3,890,000**
Arrhythmias (426–427)	43,431	4,462,000**
Heart failure (428)	41,819	4,780,000**
High blood pressure (401–404)	38,130	50,000,000**
Cardiomyopathy (425)	26,214	50,000*
Valvular heart disease (424)	15,200	76,000*
Congenital heart defects (745–747)	5,540	960,000**
Rheumatic fever/rheumatic heart disease (390–398)	5,540	1,380,000**
All cardiovascular diseases[d]	954,720	57,490,000**

a. Conditions are listed in descending order by number of deaths in the U.S. population; numeric codes are from the International Classification of Diseases (9th Rev.).

b. Deaths are the numbers reported for either 1993 or 1994.

c. Figures indicate either the number of hospital discharges reported for 1993 or 1994 (*) or the estimated number of affected persons in the population in 1996 (**).

d. "All cardiovascular diseases" includes deaths not tabulated above. The total prevalence is based on the estimated number of persons affected, not hospitalizations, and takes into account the occurrence of multiple conditions in the same person.

Source: Data from *1997 Heart and Stroke Statistical Update*, American Heart Association, Dallas, Texas.

these counts are not estimates of prevalence in the usual technical sense of the term in epidemiology.) Deaths are enumerated from national vital statistics, and prevalence is estimated by projections from the National Health and Nutrition Examination Surveys or from hospital discharge data. The conditions, identified by their respective codes under ICD 9, are listed in Table 1–3 in descending order by the numbers of deaths reported annually.

Coronary heart disease is by far the dominant condition with respect to reported deaths (almost one-half million), with stroke deaths occurring about one-fourth as frequently. More than one-half of the nearly 1 million cardiovascular disease deaths are due to coronary heart disease. About one-100th as many deaths are due to congenital heart defects, or to rheumatic heart disease, as to coronary heart disease in the United States today. In between are arrhythmias, heart failure, high blood pressure, cardiomyopathy, and valvular heart disease, with deaths ranging from approximately 15,000 to 40,000.

The numbers of persons in the United States projected as being affected by cardiovascular conditions is large, nearly 60 million, corresponding to nearly one-fourth of all Americans. Examination of Table 1–3 makes it clear that by far the largest single contributor to this count is high blood pressure (50 million individuals). Considerations in the interpretation of this fact are addressed in Chapter 12, including the caution that the estimate is based on single-occasion screening measurements and not on confirmed, persistent high blood pressure. The next largest contributor is coronary heart disease (more than 13 million individuals). Comment is provided in a later chapter (Chapter 4) for this count also, which increased substantially between 1994 and 1995 due to reclassification to include persons reporting characteristic chest pain and not only survivors of nonfatal heart attacks. For arrhythmias, cardiomyopathy, and valvular heart disease, the caution noted above concerning hospital discharge data applies: To the extent that affected patients are hospitalized more than once in the year, the count will be inflated above the number of individuals affected. This may be likely for disturbances of the heart rhythm and heart failure, for example.

The importance of these prevalence figures is that they indicate, depending on the method of enumeration, either the number of persons who continue to live with the condition, perhaps having disability or incurring substantial medical care costs, or the frequency of hospitalizations to be expected for the condition at this stage in the history of cardiovascular diseases in this country. They also underscore the fact that mortality data, which have been considered alone up to this point in the discussion, do not provide a complete picture of the cardiovascular diseases and that therefore information of other kinds is needed to assess fully their importance in the population.

Some Contrasting Circumstances in Other Countries

Corresponding information could be compiled for many other countries, or could be presented for subgroups of particular interest within the US population. For the conditions emphasized in subsequent chapters, more detailed information on prevalence and other measures of disease occurrence are presented as an indication of the similarities and differences within and among countries or regions in the distributions of these conditions. One example can serve to demonstrate the limitation of the US experience in seeking a more global view of cardiovascular diseases: The prevalence of rheumatic heart disease is estimated to be less than 0.05 persons per 1000 population in the United States and other industrial countries, whereas it is 5 per 1000 or greater (ie, at least 100 times as high) in one or more countries each in the areas of Africa, Latin America, Asia, and the Pacific.[9]

CONCLUSION

The cardiovascular diseases, or circulatory system diseases, of greatest public health concern for any country are those of the highest frequency now or potentially in the decades ahead. Particular conditions among the cardiovascular diseases, such as ischemic heart disease, are important both as common causes of death and as causes of illness and disability among those who live with the disease. In addition, special challenges to epidemiology are to identify causes and establish means of prevention, such as for congenital heart disease or Kawasaki disease. On grounds such as these, the several conditions selected for emphasis in this book were chosen. The major condition, based on the considerations discussed above, is the category of atherosclerotic and hypertensive diseases, which are discussed in Parts II and III.

REFERENCES

1. World Health Organization. *International Statistical Classification of Diseases and Related Health Problems*: *Tenth Revision*. Geneva, Switzerland: World Health Organization; 1992; 1.

2. Pearson TA, Jamison DT, Trejo-Gutierrez J. Cardiovascular disease. In: Jamison DT, Mosley WH, Measham AR, Bobadilla JL, eds. *Disease Control Priorities in Developing Countries*. Oxford, England: Oxford University Press; 1993; 577–594.

3. Omran AR. Epidemiologic transition in the United States: the health factor in population change. *Popul Bull*. 1977;32:1–42.

4. *1997 Heart and Stroke Statistical Update*. Dallas, Tex: American Heart Association; 1996.

5. Omran AR. The epidemiological transition: a theory of the epidemiology of population change. *Milbank Q*. 1971;49:509–538.

6. Olshansky SJ, Ault AB. The fourth stage of the epidemiologic transition: the age of delayed degenerative diseases. *Milbank Q.* 1986;64:355–391.

7. Dodu SRA. Emergence of cardiovascular diseases in developing countries. *Cardiol.* 1988;75:56–64.

8. Thom TJ, Epstein FH, Feldman JJ, Leaverton PE, et al. *Total Mortality and Mortality from Heart Disease, Cancer and Stroke from 1950 to 1987 in 27 Countries: Highlights of Trends and Their Interrelationships among Causes of Death.* Bethesda, Md: National Heart, Lung and Blood Institute, National Institutes of Health, Public Health Service, US Dept of Health and Human Services; 1992. NIH publication 92-3088.

9. Michaud C, Trejo-Gutierrez J, Cruz C, Pearson TA. Rheumatic heart disease. In: Jamison DT, Mosley WH, Measham AR, Bobadilla JL, eds. *Disease Control Priorities in Developing Countries.* Oxford, England: Oxford University Press; 1993; 221–232.

CHAPTER 2

Causation and Prevention of Cardiovascular Diseases: An Overview of the Contributions of 20th-Century Epidemiology

SUMMARY

The epidemiologic research of the past several decades has advanced understanding of major cardiovascular diseases to the point where their prevention is largely within reach. This is true for the atherosclerotic and hypertensive diseases, rheumatic fever and rheumatic heart disease, and Chagas' disease, for example. Implementation of well-established preventive strategies for these diseases has lagged behind the acquisition of knowledge. Fully effective implementation of these strategies awaits action by knowledgeable and committed health professionals who can help to mobilize the needed resources. For other conditions, such as most of the cardiomyopathies, congenital heart disease, and Kawasaki disease, prevention depends to a large extent on knowledge yet to be developed through further research. Even in the areas of established intervention policies, however, much remains to be learned from their application in diverse settings, even while continuing research on causes and mechanisms identifies new avenues for prevention or improvements on current interventions. The global public health challenge of addressing the cardiovascular diseases is considerable, as are the opportunities for effective public health action.

INTRODUCTION

The first of two central themes of this book is a retrospective one—that concurrent with the recent history of cardiovascular diseases, outlined broadly in Chapter 1, epidemiology has made fundamental and decisive contributions to the understanding of causation and the potential for prevention of these diseases. This has been an achievement mainly of the latter half of the 20th century. The second theme is prospective —that much remains to be learned and the greater part of the challenge of prevention remains to be met. This challenge continues in the United States and in other industrialized countries and is arising with new urgency elsewhere. Of special concern are developing and historically nonmarket economies, where atherosclerotic and hypertensive diseases are already increasing sharply in frequency or are projected to do so in the immediate future.

What is known today offers a sound scientific basis for current preventive strategies. Wider implementation of these strategies depends on informed and committed health professionals and policy makers and a more knowledgeable public. Similarly, continued and expanded support for further epidemiologic research requires professional, political, and public recognition of the needs and opportunities for further progress in the understanding and control of these diseases. Among the highest research priorities are identification of causal factors potentially important for specific high-risk subsets of the population and demonstration and evaluation of prevention programs to assess their effectiveness in diverse populations. If the perspective offered here contributes to recognition of these challenges and the requirements for addressing them, the purposes of the book will have been achieved.

The brief synopsis that follows presents a current picture of cardiovascular diseases of particular public health importance from the perspective of the two themes noted above. It also introduces some subthemes developed further in subsequent chapters.

THE GLOBAL PERSPECTIVE

Popular reference to the "global village" has become commonplace and perhaps trite, although the social and political realities underlying this concept are profound. To approach a scientific field expressly in a global context therefore risks appearances of either superficiality or presumptuousness. However, with respect to the cardiovascular diseases the validity of a global view is readily apparent, especially in the work of Keys since the 1940s[1] and illustrated more recently by Dodu and by Strasser,[2,3] among other examples. Forces of demographic change increase the population size at ages where rates of atherosclerotic and hypertensive diseases are highest, and this demographic process is compounded by economic, social, and behavioral changes that foster adverse trends in factors underlying the occurrence of these diseases. These diseases are therefore seen as looming even larger as potential health and economic burdens in developing countries than they have become in industrialized countries in the present century.

But even rheumatic fever and rheumatic heart disease, historically the major forms of cardiovascular disease in the United States until their near disappearance in terms of newly arising cases by the 1970s, have exhibited local resurgence in the United States, which suggests a need for vigilance regarding the progress in the natural history of this disease elsewhere in the world. Kawasaki disease is principally a Japanese phenomenon, having occurred in outbreaks of tens of thousands of cases over an interval of only a few months in Japan. But it is also more common than rheumatic fever/rheumatic heart disease in the United States. The main epidemiologic features of both rheumatic fever/rheumatic heart disease and Kawasaki disease are unexplained and underscore the potential importance of understanding these diseases in countries where they are not currently so prominent. The cardiomyopathies are a heterogeneous class of conditions presumed to have different causes, but some aspects of pathogenesis may be common to several of the underlying diseases. Knowledge of the natural history of cardiomyopathies in one region may be directly relevant to local forms of the disease elsewhere. Congenital heart disease, occurring throughout the world, remains largely enigmatic in its causation and prevention, and therefore knowledge gained in any one population may be applicable in others, subject to appropriate confirmation of findings across populations.

For these reasons, and because wider application of communications technology is putting health professionals around the globe in closer contact, both interest and opportunity exist for greater commonality of knowledge about cardiovascular diseases and other health concerns on a global basis. The flow of both information and potential health benefits will depend less on relative economic status between parties than on their mutual past and current experience with cardiovascular diseases. Many countries can gain from the previous experience of industrialized countries with atherosclerotic and hypertensive diseases. Conversely, the United States and other industrialized countries stand to gain substantially from lessons to be learned through interventions carried out in developing countries. For example, in recent community intervention studies in the United States, benefits have been difficult to evaluate due to generally favorable secular trends in the risk factors, whereas in contrasting settings that have adverse secular trends in these factors, experience of preventive programs could strengthen the evidence for the effectiveness of community intervention strategies. In consequence, greater impetus would be expected for intervention in relatively disadvantaged US populations that have especially high mortality or high risk.

It is important for public health globally that a broad view of mutual needs and opportunities be recognized. To foster that global view, attention is given in this book to cardiovascular diseases that have significant impact in one or another region of the world, though not necessarily at present in industrialized countries. While disproportionate reliance is placed on US data and circumstances for illustration throughout the book, greater balance is needed in the future so that data from other countries and regions are equally accessible and familiar to those working in this area. The work of Wielgosz and of Lopez in the World Health Organization and investigators in a number of developing countries, as recently reported in *World Health Statistics Quarterly*, is particularly important in this connection.[4]

THE MAJOR CARDIOVASCULAR DISEASES

Atherosclerotic and Hypertensive Diseases

The term *atherosclerotic and hypertensive diseases* is awkward but identifies a meaningful set of distinct but closely related conditions, including coronary heart disease, stroke, peripheral arterial disease, aortic aneurysm, congestive heart failure, and others. The importance of the atherosclerotic and hypertensive diseases is most obvious in countries experiencing an epidemic occurrence of these diseases in recent decades. The pattern in the United States and elsewhere of sharply declining age-adjusted mortality from coronary heart disease in the

past two to three decades has been heralded often as evidence of a triumph of public health measures, which it may well be in significant part. But other measures of public health achievements reveal a more complex process in which total numbers of deaths from coronary heart disease remain as high as at the peak of the mortality rates; congestive heart failure is becoming much more prevalent as a late consequence of nonfatal coronary heart disease; and the numbers of cardiovascular procedures, hospitalizations, and physician visits continue to rise. In addition, final mortality data for 1993, the most recent year available, indicate higher rates for Black and White women and men in the United States than in 1992.[5] Thus total cardiovascular disease mortality rates may have begun to increase once again, as of the early 1990s, a change as unpredicted as the major reversal of the trend from its continuous rise up to the late 1960s.

Distributions and Determinants

Wide geographic variations in rates and trends of mortality from coronary heart disease and stroke have been shown for countries reporting to the World Health Organization (WHO) since the early 1950s[6] and for incidence and case fatality from coronary heart disease by the WHO MONICA Project in the mid-1980s.[7] The latter project, the most extensive international collaboration in cardiovascular epidemiologic research to date, will soon report on joint trends in coronary event rates, risk factors, and treatment in the 39 contributing populations in four continents. Still, major areas of the world lack basic vital statistics systems to permit reliable estimation of cause-specific mortality, much less trends, so the available data remain limited chiefly to industrialized countries. The Sino-MONICA centers in the People's Republic of China are a major exception.

Among the lessons from these observations is the conclusion that environmental factors must constitute a major influence on population rates of coronary heart disease, whatever the underlying genetic determinants, for such rapid changes in rates to occur. The argument for preventability gains credence from this fact, as it does from data on populations migrating from low- to high-rate areas, which rapidly exhibit rates near or even exceeding those of the new population setting. Extensive epidemiologic investigations of the effects of migrations of Japanese to the United States and South Asians to the United Kingdom support this view.

Rose emphasized, as the first priority for public health with its responsibility to whole populations, the importance of factors influencing population rates of coronary heart disease in contrast to individual risks within a population.[8] The singular contribution of the Seven Countries Study to epidemiologic understanding of coronary heart disease at the population level brings significant credit to Keys, the study founder and director.[9] The paramount relation of dietary fats and cholesterol, the added contribution of blood pressure, and the dependence of the role of smoking on population patterns of diet and blood cholesterol concentration are among the major conclusions on determinants of incidence and mortality from coronary heart disease. Noteworthy in addition is the impact of this more than 30-year project in stimulating two generations of investigators in Europe, North America, and Japan to collaborate in cardiovascular epidemiology, as the vanguard of a research community growing steadily throughout the world especially since the mid-1970s.

Among the many studies of individual risks of coronary events within local populations, those constituting the US National Pooling Project, especially those included in the pooled analysis (the studies in Framingham, Massachusetts; Albany, New York; Chicago, Illinois; and Tecumseh, Michigan), provided evidence strongly supporting the roles of blood cholesterol concentration, blood pressure, and smoking as determinants of individual risks for first major coronary events. The demonstration of a 20-fold gradient in risk from the joint effects of these three factors awaited the follow-up of more than 360,000 men screened as candidates for the Multiple Risk Factor Intervention Trial,

a large enough cohort to be subclassified into 50 categories of risk.[10]

Beyond these three major factors and their underlying determinants—dietary imbalance, physical inactivity, and marketing of commercial tobacco products—many other factors have been associated with risks of coronary events or with stroke and other manifestations of atherosclerosis or hypertension. The discussion of these factors in Chapters 7–20, concerning the main determinants of atherosclerotic and hypertensive diseases, begins with attention to age, sex, race, and heredity, fundamental personal characteristics long recognized as influencing health in general and also associated with many of the specific factors causing these diseases. Aspects of these specific factors are discussed in the context of their epidemiologic investigation, including conceptual and methodologic issues. The interrelated factors of dietary imbalance, physical inactivity, overweight/fatness/central adiposity, adverse blood lipid profile, high blood pressure, and insulin resistance and diabetes are reviewed in turn to illustrate a great wealth of epidemiologic knowledge of these factors as well as issues for further investigation. Studies of smoking behavior, alcohol consumption, hemostatic dysfunction, and adverse psychosocial patterns are similarly reviewed. Brief attention to dietary antioxidants, homocystinemia, and vascular and endothelial factors completes discussion of individual or personal factors. Finally, social conditions are reviewed as major determinants of atherosclerotic and hypertensive diseases, including culture change or cultural mobility, occupational status and social class, and social conditions in fetal and neonatal life.

The extensive, though not exhaustive, consideration of factors involved in causation of the atherosclerotic and hypertensive diseases leads to review of epidemiologic concepts of causation as they have evolved from the 1950s. The view that a single agent must be identified that accounts wholly for the occurrence of these diseases is inappropriate and fails to recognize the true complexity of these multifaceted disease processes at levels from their dynamic occurrence in whole populations to their cellular and molecular aspects. The problem of multifactorial causation that characterizes these diseases is approached by distinguishing between causation as it reflects scientific understanding and as it provides a basis for preventive action. In the first sense, the continuing expansion of knowledge makes an open framework for causal relations most useful so that new evidence can always be accommodated. In the second sense, those elements of the causal complex that offer greatest practical applicability for preventive strategies can be selected on a rational basis and tested for their effectiveness through community intervention trials or demonstrations, as needed.

Prevention and Control

Because of the complex causation of atherosclerotic and hypertensive diseases, multiple factors have been addressed in relation to their prevention since at least the late 1950s.[11] Much experience has been gained in implementation of interventions based on either single or multiple factors. Parallel with the development of specific interventions, such as dietary and pharmacologic approaches to adverse blood lipid profiles, conceptual development has shaped the current theory of prevention of these diseases. The observation that in populations with high rates of coronary mortality, low risk is concentrated in a small proportion of the population has led to the view that population-wide intervention is necessary to achieve a substantial impact on incidence or mortality rates for this disease.[12] The resulting distinction between the population-wide and the high-risk strategies has assumed a fundamental place in policy development and preventive practice.

Studies of intervention on single factors and their impact on disease occurrence are addressed in the factor-specific chapters in Part II to examine their contributions to understanding the roles of these respective risk factors and the potential place of each in a comprehensive prevention policy. Separately, in Part III, multifactor interventions are reviewed as they have been evaluated in both high-risk and population-wide approaches. Part III recognizes the public health perspective on multifactor intervention as the preferred approach to addressing this complex health problem. The rationale for this approach includes both the recognition that causation of atherosclerotic and hypertensive disease reflects the joint operation of multiple factors and that the underlying behaviors of dietary imbalance, physical inactivity, and tobacco use contribute to risks of other chronic diseases also. Effective intervention would therefore have public health benefits even beyond those measured by reduced frequency of coronary heart disease, stroke, and other cardiovascular conditions.

An obvious consideration in implementation of disease prevention and control, apart from the interventions themselves, is the target population. Because populations often differ in characteristics relevant to intervention—such as income, education, access to services, language, and culture—special concern arises about populations unlikely to be reached effectively by programs not designed with these characteristics in view. Group differences in age, sex, and race or ethnicity raise questions also about the applicability of the evidence for certain causal factors and the appropriateness of interventions even if they are presented in ways tailored to the intended target population. Health research policies of the US government have recognized the need for greater inclusion of women and minorities in clinical and population-based research, reflecting this concern. As participation by more diverse groups expands, it will become clearer whether group-specific tailoring of interventions is as necessary as might be argued, or at what levels of implementation such special provisions are needed. The potential role of genetic characterization of individuals regarding disease risks and choice of interventions is problematic and will be best incorporated as an adjunct to high-risk intervention policies and not adopted in place of population-wide public health recommendations.

Rheumatic Fever and Rheumatic Heart Disease

Acute rheumatic fever and rheumatic heart disease, while traceable backward for centuries in clinical case descriptions, were characterized by Jones in 1944 as only recently attaining public health importance.[13] Epidemiologic study of these conditions had begun at least as early as the 1890s. Laboratory and clinical work on the nature of the group A beta-hemolytic *Streptococcus*, which is the agent of this disease, set the stage for further epidemiologic investigation that intensified during the Second World War because of the occurrence of epidemic streptococcal sore throat in military camps and the need to devise preventive strategies for this condition. Recently published accounts from the Armed Forces Epidemiological Board in the United States document much of this work.[14] Availability of penicillin permitted intervention to interrupt progression from acute streptococcal pharyngitis to acute rheumatic fever or later stages of progression or recurrence.

In the United States, it became the standard of practice to obtain throat cultures for bacteriologic diagnosis of sore throat in children so that those with positive results could receive prophylactic penicillin treatment. By the 1970s this policy came into question due to several concerns. Many infections, perhaps one-half, were asymptomatic and therefore not detected or treated to prevent acute rheumatic fever. Intervention was therefore unavoidably incomplete. Many positive cultures, again perhaps one-half, were from carriers of the organism who were not infected and thus not at risk of progression to rheumatic fever. In such cases, treatment was not only unnecessary but was often ineffective. Also, by this time the incidence of acute rheumatic fever had declined greatly, and therefore policies based on past circumstances needed reconsideration in any case. More recently, focal resurgence of acute rheumatic fever in the United States has aroused renewed concern about this disease and its potential for larger-scale emergence due to changing characteristics of the agent or other still-unknown factors.

Globally, the problem of acute rheumatic fever and rheumatic heart disease became a focus of attention within the World Health Organization in the mid-1950s. The Cardiovascular Disease Unit of the WHO subsequently contributed significantly to work in this area and fostered studies of intervention in many countries.[15] Based on epidemiologic considerations and resource availability, WHO recommendations for secondary prevention have been adopted in many countries with especially high burdens of rheumatic heart disease. In these programs, screening of school populations for a history of acute rheumatic fever or rheumatic heart disease leads to long-term penicillin prophylaxis against progression or recurrence of disease. Primary prevention of rheumatic fever, by treatment of culture-positive cases of sore throat, has been deemed impractical in most settings in such countries. Despite knowledge of effective preventive measures, the disease continues to be a major health problem and the leading cardiovascular disease problem in many countries.

Chagas' Disease and Other Cardiomyopathies

The cardiomyopathies are a heterogeneous group of conditions in which cardiac function is compromised with resulting disability or death. Specific causes are known for only a few of these diseases. The example of Chagas' disease is reviewed in greatest detail, given the extensive knowledge of its causation and prevention. The specific causal agent, *Trypanosoma cruzi*, and a number of insect vectors, species of the Triatomid bugs, are widely distributed throughout Central and South America where the disease is endemic. Epidemiologic features of special importance are the pattern of transmission by Triatomids in the peridomestic setting of rural populations, transportation of the vector into urban areas with population movements from impoverished farming regions, and contamination of urban-area blood supplies with mounting risks of infection through transfusions. Effective community-wide programs have been demonstrated in rural areas in which insecticide spraying and monitoring for residual Triatomids have been conducted. Screening of blood donors by use of health and residential histories and, if necessary, treatment of collected blood units can control transfusion-related infection. In this example of the cardiomyopathies, a specific agent, a well-characterized epidemiologic picture of the disease process, and successfully demonstrated interventions offer promise of effective control. However, many factors work against the potential for control: agricultural policies, continued poverty of rural farmers, persistent migration from rural to urban areas, and programs of clearing forested areas for new (perhaps transient) settlements, thereby creating new habitats for the disease vectors. Accordingly, Chagas' disease continues as a dominant form of cardiovascular disease in endemic areas and challenges to prevention persist.

Congenital Heart Disease

The epidemiology and prevention of congenital heart disease overlap with those of other congenital defects and share many of the same limitations: issues of classification, standardization of approaches to case ascertainment, and evaluation of extrinsic exposures that might point to preventive actions. A framework for prevention based on current understanding of these defects includes policies of avoidance of known or suspected hazardous exposures (tobacco, alcohol, certain pharmaceuticals), protection of potentially pregnant women from rubella infection, and counseling of parents of an affected offspring regarding the risks of recurrent defects in subsequent offspring. Diagnostic and surgical treatment facilities are regionally organized to some extent, so necessary services can be concentrated effectively. A recently emerging aspect of the epidemiology of congenital heart disease has been the survival of increasing numbers of affected children into adulthood and therefore to reproductive age. In consequence, the potential need for prophylaxis against bacterial endocarditis due to persistent anatomical or surgical defects arises. In addition, the question of heritability of the defects and risk to offspring of affected individuals becomes an issue. Although important avenues of prevention are available, they remain only partially effective given the still-limited knowledge of the causation of these defects. Much remains to be accomplished in investigation of the epidemiology of these conditions.

Kawasaki Disease

The importance of Kawasaki disease is more immediately apparent in Japan than elsewhere, given the principal occurrence of the disease there.[16] However, the fact of its unexpected appearance as a newly discovered disease only in the 1960s, its occurrence in other countries (eg, the United States, where it exceeds rheumatic heart disease in incidence), and its elusive causation broaden interest and concern about this disease considerably. Affecting children two years old or younger as the primary risk group, the disease progresses through several stages of clinical and pathological development. In a small proportion of cases, the coronary arteries become involved in an inflammatory process that can culminate in obstructive or hemorrhagic lesions and death. With no firm knowledge of its causation, intervention is limited currently to treatment of the acute case. Preventive strategies are needed but must await further epidemiologic and other studies to establish meaningful approaches.

ACHIEVING THE POTENTIAL FOR PREVENTION

Part V addresses the status of prevention of the major cardiovascular diseases, the prospects for more effective public health action, and the need to advance epidemiologic research toward that goal.

Implementation of Prevention Policies

The currently available strategies for prevention of the atherosclerotic and hypertensive diseases, rheumatic heart disease, and Chagas' disease reflect decades of epidemiologic and other research and offer the potential for substantial impact against these diseases. However, implementation of these strategies is limited by several identifiable obstacles. These can be viewed as operating at the levels of both population-wide and high-risk individual interventions. Most of these obstacles can be addressed by knowledgeable and committed health professionals with adequate resources much more effectively than they have been to date.

Advancement of Epidemiologic Research

Concurrent with broader implementation of intervention strategies based on current knowledge, epidemiologic research is needed to continue the identification and elucidation of causal factors and, no less importantly, to monitor the changing natural history of the major cardiovascular diseases and the impact of preventive programs against them. Each of the three core functions of public health—assessment, policy development, and assurance—rests on contributions from epidemiology, which must be adequately supported to serve these functions.[17] Biomedical and community health research needs to be recognized as part of the spectrum of research for which government and private support are needed and should be given increased emphasis. Epidemiology is viewed as unique in addressing health phenomena at the population level and also linking observations in laboratory and patient-oriented investigation with their potential public health applications. This view of epidemiology and the implications for prevention of cardiovascular diseases are illustrated extensively by the recent task force report to the US National Heart, Lung and Blood Institute.[18] The report outlines broad research priorities, resource requirements, and specific research questions to be pursued in the decade or more ahead. Although other conditions are addressed, the primary topic is the atherosclerotic and hypertensive diseases and their complications, with a newly emphasized focus: prevention of the risk factors in the first place. This concept is a notable advance from concentration on the prevention of cardiovascular events to prevention of the factors producing them. Detection and management of already-present risk factors is only part of the preventive task, from this point of view. Effective prevention and needed research must address the causes of the risk factors themselves and evaluate interventions to prevent the emergence of adverse blood lipid profiles, high blood pressure, habitual tobacco use, and other factors.

CONCLUSION

The extensive contributions of 20th-century epidemiology to the understanding and potential for prevention of major cardiovascular diseases throughout the world are addressed throughout this book. The significant public health challenge is to apply effectively the knowledge already gained and to continue to learn from that application the strengths and weaknesses of currently proposed strategies. Integrating new knowledge from laboratory and clinical investigation and from epidemiologic studies into the growing complex of causation and applying this knowledge to develop concepts of and approaches to intervention are important tasks for epidemiology, preventive cardiology, and public health. The chapters that follow are intended to foster that integration and application by knowledgeable and committed health professionals who share the view that cardiovascular diseases represent both a global public health challenge and a commensurate opportunity.

REFERENCES

1. Keys A. From Naples to Seven Countries—a sentimental journey. *Prog Biochem Pharmacol*. 1983; 19:1–30.

2. Strasser T. Reflections on cardiovascular diseases. *Interdisc Sci Rev*. 1978;3:225–230.

3. Dodu SRA. Emergence of cardiovascular diseases in developing countries. *Cardiol*. 1988;75:56–64.

4. Wielgosz AT. Cardiovascular disease mortality in the developing countries: introduction [with 8 additional articles]. *World Health Stat Q*. 1993;46:89–150.

5. *1997 Heart and Stroke Statistical Update*. Dallas, Tex: American Heart Association; 1996.

6. Thom J, Epstein H, Feldman J, Leaverton PE, et al. *Total Mortality and Mortality from Heart Disease, Cancer and Stroke from 1950 to 1987 in 27 Countries: Highlights of Trends and Their Interrelationships among Causes of Death*. Bethesda, Md: National Heart, Lung and Blood Institute, National Institutes of Health, September 1992. NIH publication 92-3088.

7. World Health Organization MONICA Project. Myocardial infarction and coronary deaths in the World Health Organization MONICA Project. Special Report. *Circ*. 1994;90:583–612.

8. Rose G. Sick individuals and sick populations. *Int J Epidemiol*. 1985;14:32–38.

9. Keys A. *Seven Countries: A Multivariate Analysis of Death and Coronary Heart Disease*. Cambridge, Mass: Harvard University Press; 1980.

10. Stamler J. Established major coronary risk factors. In: Marmot M, Elliott P, eds. *Coronary Heart Disease Epidemiology: From Aetiology to Public Health*. Oxford, England: Oxford University Press; 1992; 35–66.

11. White PD, Wright IS, Sprague HB, Katz LN, et al. *A Statement on Arteriosclerosis: Main Cause of "Heart Attacks" and "Strokes."* New York: National Health Education Committee, Inc.; 1959.

12. Rose G. Strategy of prevention: lessons from cardiovascular disease. *Br Med J*. 1981;282:1847–1851.

13. Jones TD. The diagnosis of rheumatic fever. *JAMA*. 1944;126:481–484.

14. Denny FW Jr, Houser HB. History of the Commission on Streptococcal and Staphylococcal Diseases. In: Woodward TE, ed. *The Armed Forces Epidemiological Board: The Histories of the Commissions*. Washington, DC: Borden Institute, Office of the Surgeon General, Department of the Army, United States of America; 1994; 259–382.

15. World Health Organization. *Joint WHO/ISFC Meeting on Rheumatic Fever/Rheumatic Heart Disease Control, with Emphasis on Primary Prevention*. September 7–9, 1994; Geneva. WHO/CVD/94.1. Geneva, Switzerland: World Health Organization; 1994.

16. Kawasaki T, Kosaki F, Okawa S, Shigematsu I, et al. A new infantile acute febrile mucocutaneous lymph node syndrome (MLNS) prevailing in Japan. *Pediatr*. 1974; 54:271–276.

17. Remington RD. Role of organized public health in cardiovascular disease prevention. In: Marmot M, Elliott P, eds. *Coronary Heart Disease Epidemiology: From Aetiology to Public Health*. Oxford, England: Oxford University Press; 1992; 515–524.

18. National Heart, Lung and Blood Institute. *Report of the Task Force on Research in Epidemiology and Prevention of Cardiovascular Diseases*. Washington, DC: National Institutes of Health, Public Health Service, US Dept of Health and Human Services; 1994.

PART II

Atherosclerotic and Hypertensive Diseases: Distributions and Determinants

CHAPTER 3

Atherosclerosis

SUMMARY

Atherosclerosis is a pathological condition occurring widely throughout the arterial circulation, with clinical manifestations especially in the heart, brain, aorta, and lower extremities. It is the underlying condition in the occurrence of myocardial infarction (heart attack), cerebrovascular accident (stroke), aortic aneurysm, and peripheral arterial disease of the lower extremities. A major component of atherosclerosis research since long before the 20th century has been the study of autopsy material. Recent technology has permitted clinical investigation through angiographic examination of patients with overt disease and now through use of magnetic resonance imaging (MRI) in clinical studies and ultrasound for measurement of atherosclerotic lesions of the carotid artery in large population studies. Through autopsy studies, atherosclerosis has been found in populations throughout the world, with evidence of early-stage lesions within childhood. Studies of US military casualties in Korea and Vietnam indicated unexpectedly severe coronary atherosclerosis in some young soldiers who had been without symptoms of coronary heart disease. Recent evidence indicates strong correlations between the extent and severity of atherosclerosis in adolescents and young adults and the presence of characteristics such as adverse blood lipid profile, high blood pressure, and cigarette smoking. Treatment of adults with drugs, surgery, and behavioral interventions to lower cholesterol concentrations has been shown by serial angiographic examination to result in delayed progression and even regression of existing atherosclerotic lesions. Public health recommendations have been proposed to promote desirable behavior patterns beginning in childhood and thereby prevent atherosclerosis from early in life.

ATHEROSCLEROSIS: A PATHOLOGICAL CLOSE-UP

Atherosclerosis refers to the consistency of material typically found at postmortem examination in abnormal areas or lesions on the inner, or luminal, surface and in the wall of large- to medium-diameter arteries throughout the body. It is a descriptive term for the pathological mushy areas (atheromata), often encrusted or hardened (sclerosed) by deposition of calcium, which weaken the arterial wall and intrude into the lumen or channel of the vessel, restricting or obstructing blood flow past the lesion. The fully developed lesion, or atherosclerotic plaque, is now regarded as the basis of a dynamic process in which rapid changes may occur, precipitating either transient or fixed interruption of blood flow and a resulting variety of clinical appearances among cases of acute coronary heart disease syndromes.

Figure 3–1 presents a microscopic view of such a lesion, from a fatal case of myocardial infarction, seen within a cross section of a coronary artery.[1] The detailed appearance of the lesion at this magnification is markedly different from that of a normal artery. The clear area at the upper right within the artery is what remains of its lumen or blood-carrying channel. This is greatly reduced by the dark-staining thrombus or blood clot immediately to the left and by the adjacent material within the arterial wall. This region of the wall contains not only dead tissue but crystals of cholesterol, shalelike in appearance, which are an essential component of the atherosclerotic plaque.

Studies of atherosclerosis in populations living under widely varying conditions were undertaken more than three decades ago, after development of carefully standardized techniques for postmortem collection and examination of specimens of the aorta and coronary arteries. More recently, the location and extent of atherosclerotic lesions have been investigated clinically, in patients suspected of having atherosclerosis, by injection of radiopaque dye into specific regions of the arterial circulation, such as in coronary angiography. This technique has advanced to permit measurement of change in size of atherosclerotic lesions—reduced rates of progression or actual regression—in response to treatment, as in trials of therapy for existing coronary atherosclerosis.[2] Because of obvious ethical and other considerations, however, these procedures are generally inapplicable in population studies, which require less direct methods of examination.

More recently, ultrasound reflectance, a noninvasive and lower-cost technology, has been validated for estimating arterial wall thickness as an indicator of underlying atherosclerosis. This technique is now being used, for example, in a population study of some 15,800 healthy

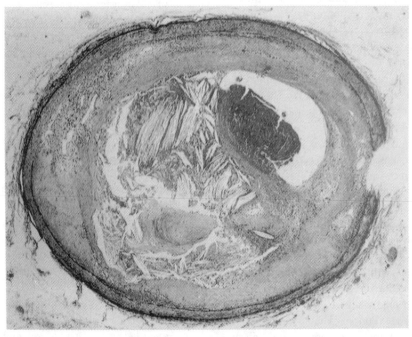

Figure 3–1 Light Micrograph of a Histological Section of a Complicated Atherosclerotic Plaque from Human Coronary Artery with Attached Mural Thrombus. Note mural thrombus protruding into narrowed lumen of artery. At base of the area of necrosis is a site of accumulation of inflammatory cells. This is often seen with mural thrombosis. *Source*: Reproduced with permission from RW St Clair, Biology of Atherosclerosis, in TA Pearson et al, *Primer in Preventive Cardiology*, © 1994, American Heart Association.

American adults, the Atherosclerosis Risk in Communities (ARIC) Study.[3] By this technique of blood vessel examination, through an ultrasound transducer and sensor applied over the easily accessible carotid artery in the neck, measurements to the scale of tenths of a millimeter are possible. The technique is capable of detecting atherosclerotic lesions as represented by variations in wall thickness or lumen diameter in these arteries. Thus epidemiologic investigation of atherosclerosis, at this stage of progression, is no longer limited to postmortem samples or highly selected cases of known or clinically suspected arterial disease but can be extended to the general, living population. Other noninvasive imaging techniques such as MRI, ultra-fast computed tomography (UFCT), and positron-emission (PET) scanning have had little or no application to date in epidemiology

(though an exception with regard to UFCT is discussed below). The potential value of more practical noninvasive techniques for population studies of atherosclerosis is readily apparent.

DIVERSITY OF THE CLINICAL MANIFESTATIONS OF ATHEROSCLEROSIS

Atherosclerosis is a systemic disorder, in that it occurs in large- and medium-diameter vessels throughout the arterial tree. For this reason its clinical appearance may relate to any of several different regions of the circulation, for example, the heart, brain, lower extremities, or aorta, as indicated in Figure 3–2.[4] (This schematic view of the varied manifestations of atherosclerosis above the "clinical horizon" has been published in several versions, since the 1950s, among

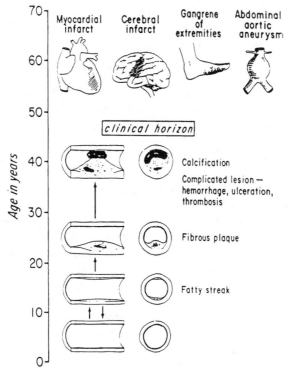

Figure 3–2 Schematic View of the Development of Atherosclerosis. *Source*: Reprinted with permission from HC McGill Jr, JC Geer, and JP Strong, The Natural History of Human Atherosclerotic Lesions, in *Atherosclerosis and Its Origin*, M Sandler and G Bourne, eds, p 42, © 1963, Academic Press.

which this is one of the most recent.) No single cardiovascular condition, such as coronary heart disease, reflects the full extent to which atherosclerosis contributes to disease, disability, and death in a population. Accordingly, among the conditions identified in Exhibit 1–1 by ICD 10 codes, all those from I10 through I79 and some in the category I95 through I99 are potential consequences of atherosclerosis. Thus the epidemiology of atherosclerosis is not strictly comprehensive but has been approached mainly in relation to its most common discrete clinical manifestations, such as coronary heart disease, stroke, peripheral arterial disease, and atherosclerosis of the aorta.

Recently, however, the Cardiovascular Health Study (CHS) of adults aged 65 years and older investigated a composite index of subclinical atherosclerosis, which indicates the value of a broader approach.[5] A detailed examination included carotid ultrasound, echocardiography, electrocardiography, a measure of blood pressure differences between arm and ankle reflecting obstruction in lower extremity arterial supply, and responses to questionnaires indicating impairment of either coronary or lower extremity arterial blood flow. More than one-third of participants had subclinical (inapparent) signs or symptoms of atherosclerosis in the absence of any clinically recognized disease. Because only one-quarter to one-third of men and women had clinical disease, the additional detection of subclinical disease among the remainder of the population indicated that atherosclerosis was more than twice as prevalent as could be determined by clinical evidence alone.

RESEARCH ON THE MECHANISMS OF ATHEROGENESIS

The question of how atherosclerosis develops has been investigated at least since the mid-19th century. A recent overview by Stamler is the basis for the following highlights of the early research.[6] The work by Virchow in the latter half of the 19th century established atherosclerosis as a distinct pathological entity in which

the "mush" was identified as fatty (lipid) material, specifically including cholesterol. In clinical research that followed, a variety of diseases characterized by prolonged high blood concentrations of cholesterol were found to produce severe premature atherosclerosis, linking this pathological phenomenon with blood lipid concentrations.

Early in the 20th century the accidental discovery was made that experimental manipulation of the diet of rabbits, by feeding them animal products, produced atherosclerosis. Subsequent animal experiments indicated that long-term dietary changes with only small cholesterol supplements would also produce this condition. Further animal studies included observations suggesting cellular processes in which the arterial wall was invaded by migrating cells that were especially high in cholesterol content. The laboratory research data suggesting that development of atherosclerosis was dependent on diet were reinforced in the mid-1930s by many reports on "geographical pathology," that is, studies that linked differences among populations in the frequency of occurrence of atherosclerosis with differences in their typical diets.

In the period immediately following the Depression and Second World War, laboratory and clinical research on atherosclerosis expanded rapidly and included biochemistry, biophysics, pathology, and cell biology. Mechanisms of lipid metabolism and transport were investigated intensively, and research continues to generate significant advances in understanding of this aspect of atherogenesis. (This research is addressed in Chapter 11.)

By the mid-1970s, studies in vascular biology had also contributed much to refinement of concepts of atherogenesis. Three distinct but possibly complementary hypotheses were suggested to explain this process, principally the "response-to-injury" hypothesis, attributed in its original formulation to Virchow.[7,8] Briefly, the "injury" of the endothelial cells that form the inner surface of the artery has come to be thought of as a late stage of the atherosclerotic lesion, not the initiating process. An earlier step in atherogenesis appears to be the adhesion of blood monocytes to the arterial endothelium, migration of these cells into the intimal layer, and subsequent concentration of lipid in these cells, a process facilitated by the oxidation of lipids carried by low density lipoproteins. In a second phase of development, fatty streaks that have formed beneath the endothelium may be altered by migration of smooth muscle cells from the media into the intimal layer of the arterial wall, where factors stimulating cellular proliferation may produce a marked multiplication of these cells. Then, in the later progression of the raised lesions so produced, the long-hypothesized endothelial cell dysfunction and damage may occur from viral infection, elevated blood lipid concentrations, or many other plausible causes. Platelet adherence to damaged endothelial cells then leads to local thrombosis (blood clot formation), with occlusion of the artery and the resulting signs and symptoms of impaired or obstructed blood flow to the tissues beyond.[1] Further laboratory studies continue to elaborate on this concept of atherogenesis, which still requires confirmation in some aspects, including the relation of this process to clinical manifestations of atherosclerosis (see below).

A separate and more-limited line of investigation supports the concept that atherosclerosis originates with viral infection.[9] Members of the herpesviruses (herpes simplex virus, Epstein-Barr virus, cytomegalovirus, and herpes zoster virus) have been of particular interest on the basis of observations in both animals and humans, including the suggestion that risk of reocclusion of the coronary artery following angioplastic surgery to relieve stenosis may be associated with such viral infection.[10] The widespread occurrence of these viruses and high incidence of infection early in life add to epidemiologic interest in this concept, which also deserves further investigation. How this might be linked with evidence for other processes involved in atherosclerosis remains to be established. Bacterial infection has also been invoked as a factor in the progression of atherosclerosis, with growing interest in apparent associations between infection with *Chlamydia pneumoniae* or *Helicobacter pylori*, for example, and presence of coronary heart disease.[10,11]

Another aspect of atherogenesis, noted above, is the sometimes dynamic nature of the atherosclerotic plaque. Progression of plaque formation through a series of plaque types (based on their pathologic description) is now considered to explain the development of acute clinical symptoms of coronary heart disease, discussed further in Chapter 4.[12] Briefly, an advanced atherosclerotic plaque, or atheroma, may undergo changes due to chronic inflammation, which tends to soften the material within its fibrous cap.[13] This leads to predisposition to rupture or cracking (fissuring) of the covering of the plaque and a chain of events that includes local formation of blood clots. These either heal and add to growth of the plaque or become large enough to obstruct blood flow. Whether or not the inflammatory process within the plaque is dependent on systemic infection or other chronic inflammatory condition as the stimulus is not yet resolved, though some indications suggest this is the case.

EPIDEMIOLOGY OF ATHEROSCLEROSIS, INCLUDING ITS GEOGRAPHIC DISTRIBUTION

The presence of atherosclerosis as a human disease has been well recognized, as noted above, since the mid-19th century. Many accounts indicate the presence of this disease from antiquity, and examination of well-preserved human remains from ancient China and Egypt has revealed atherosclerosis in the coronary arteries.[14,15] This does not establish that atherosclerosis was epidemic in ancient times, as it has become more recently; it can be presumed that those whose remains were so carefully prepared for burial were members of particularly affluent, and possibly high-risk, strata of those early societies.

In the past 50 years, important insights about patterns of occurrence of atherosclerosis have resulted from pathological studies. A detailed account of work up to the mid-1950s was presented by Holman and colleagues in 1958, the source of the original version of Figure 3–2.[16] The concept advanced at that time was based on a large series of autopsies in persons 1–40 years of age, at Charity Hospital of Louisiana in New Orleans, as well as previous reports from as early as 1911. The essential observation was that the earliest lesions of atherosclerosis, the fatty streaks, appear commonly in the first decade of life. These can progress to fibrous plaques and more-advanced lesions with age at different rates in different population groups, such as its more gradual progression in Blacks than in Whites in New Orleans, up to the time of Holman's review.

Holman suggested that factors responsible for the initiation of fatty streaks differ from the factors leading to their gradual conversion, over perhaps 15 years or more, to advanced lesions. In addition, a rapid increase during puberty in the percentage of aortic surface involved with fatty streaks was taken as evidence that hormonal changes, rather than diet, were the major determinant of progressive atherogenesis. (This interpretation is discussed further in subsequent chapters.)

In 1953 a report of postmortem examinations among US military casualties in Korea revealed atherosclerosis of the coronary arteries in the majority of young men examined, typically in their early 20s.[17] Lesions were visible at autopsy in the coronary arteries of 77.3% of the 300 cases studied; complete occlusion of one or more coronary arteries was found in 3.0% of cases. (Presumably these occlusive lesions had evolved very gradually, and therefore from much earlier ages, with development of collateral circulation to protect against myocardial ischemia.)

An analogous investigation was conducted 18 years later among US military casualties in Vietnam,[18] based on postmortem coronary angiography to detect atherosclerosis. The resulting estimate of the frequency of "some degree" of coronary atherosclerosis was 45% among the 105 examinations performed, and "apparently severe atherosclerosis" in 5%. This was thought to represent a decrease in prevalence relative to the observations in Korea two decades earlier, but subsequent reinvestigation of materials from the Korean War casualties indicated that the two results were consistent, at least in the frequency of severe lesions.[19] These studies reinforce the view presented in Figure 3–2 that important development of atherosclerosis has already occurred before age 20 in a substantial proportion of US population groups, as found in young military personnel and both Black and White residents of New Orleans.

The occurrence of atherosclerosis in other, more diverse populations has also been studied. A landmark investigation of the epidemiology of atherosclerosis was the International Atherosclerosis Project (IAP), in which, altogether, 23,207 sets of coronary arteries and aortas were collected in 14 countries, from 1960 to 1965.[20] The materials were from autopsy examinations of males and females from 10 to 69 years of age at death. Dissected and prepared under a common protocol locally, the materials were examined grossly and microscopically by teams of pathologists in a central laboratory. One measure of the extent of atherosclerosis was the percentage of the surface area of the intimal surface of the artery that was covered by raised atherosclerotic lesions, that is, by fibrous plaques and complicated or calcified lesions.

This measure of the extent of atherosclerosis in the aorta (abdominal and thoracic aorta combined) and coronary arteries (three coronary arteries combined) was presented for each of 19 race-location groups in the IAP. Subjects were decedents at 25 to 64 years of age, excluding those dying of conditions related to atherosclerosis. For New Orleans Whites, for example, the percentage surface involvement for males was greatest, somewhat greater than 20% and more than twice the percentage for females, for coronary artery involvement. For Bantus in Durban, South Africa, by contrast, the corresponding percentages of surface involvement for both males and females were much less, only about

8%. Atherosclerosis in the aorta was not consistently more extensive among males than among females; for the coronary arteries, the extent was almost without exception greater among males. Large population differences can thus occur in the extent of atherosclerosis. It differs in different regions of the circulation, such as aorta versus coronary arteries, even between males and females in the same population. In addition, among men in the age groups of 45–54 and 55–64 years, the relative ranks of nine population groups by extent of raised lesions in the coronary arteries corresponded closely with their ranks by mortality rates for coronary heart disease.

Marked progression of the presence of atherosclerotic plaques by age is indicated by selected results from the IAP combined with those from several populations studied under a protocol of the World Health Organization (WHO) to indicate the marked progression of the presence of atherosclerotic plaques with age.[21] A composite curve for five cities studied under the WHO protocol shows increases in the proportion of persons with atherosclerotic plaques from less than 15% at age 20 to 100% at ages 50 and above for Malmo, Sweden, and four Eastern European cities (vessel and lesion type not specified) (Figure 3–3). Among persons not dying of atherosclerosis-related causes, the percentages of those (males and females combined) with fibrous plaques in the left anterior descending coronary artery are indicated, by age, for several of the IAP locations. The wide variation in the extent of such lesions at the earliest age level shown is remarkable, as is the steep increase in all populations to peaks from 50% to nearly 100% of persons being affected. That more than 30% of the population is affected by age 20 indicates that the process often culminating in death due to myocardial infarction or stroke in middle or late adulthood has commonly begun well before the earliest adult years. By inference, whatever factors determine the rate of progression of atherosclerosis must also operate early.

EARLY DEVELOPMENT OF ATHEROSCLEROSIS AND ITS RELATION TO THE MAJOR CARDIOVASCULAR DISEASE RISK FACTORS

The work reviewed above has provided a strong impetus to further investigation of the onset and progression of atherosclerosis from childhood through early adulthood. In particular, interest has developed in determining whether factors predictive of the later clinical manifestations of atherosclerosis are related to its early progression. A challenge for epidemiologic study of this question has been to obtain information for the same individuals about both the presence and extent of atherosclerosis, based on postmortem examination, and the presence of factors before death that might be predictive of the nature and extent of the disease.

Two approaches have been used to conduct such investigations. First, a study of the occurrence in childhood of factors related to atherosclerotic and hypertensive diseases was conducted by Berenson and others in Bogalusa, Louisiana, beginning in the 1970s and ultimately including several thousand children of school age at first examination. In 1986 the investigators first reported that 35 study participants had died and undergone autopsy examinations including standardized examination of the heart, coronary arteries, and aorta.[22] By 1992 an update included a total of 62 decedents with such data available.[23] Because these decedents had been examined in previous surveys, the earlier measurements of blood lipids, blood pressure, and height/weight index could be analyzed in relation to the extent of atherosclerosis present at autopsy. The extent of such involvement was substantially greater in the aorta than in the coronary arteries. In general, for males, previously measured factors and the degree of fatty streak involvement in both the aorta and coronary arteries were associated in ways consistent with their relation to adult atherosclerosis. The results

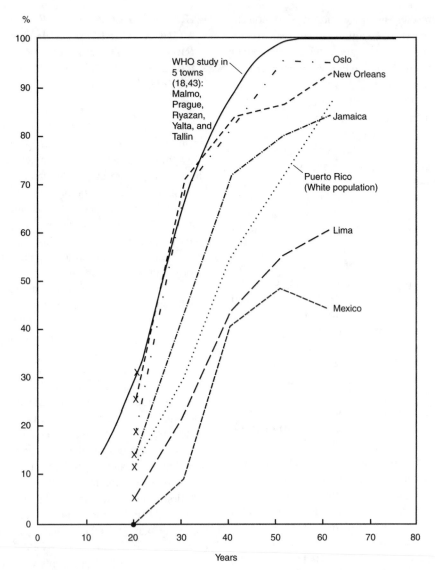

%

Figure 3–3 The Extent of Atherosclerosis by Age, from the WHO Project and the International Atherosclerosis Project. Derived from autopsy studies prevalence rates at age 20 (X). *Source*: Reprinted with permission from *TRS 678*, p 35, World Health Organization.

were similar for Whites and Blacks, although few results were statistically significant in the smaller group of Blacks and females were too few in number for separate analysis. These findings and others described in the report add to the view that factors that could potentially be controlled in childhood, such as blood lipids and blood pressure, contribute importantly to the earliest development of atherosclerosis and offer potential avenues of prevention.

The second approach to study of such factors in relation to atherosclerosis at early ages is to obtain information about them at the time of death. This approach has been applied in a large, multicenter study in the United States, the Pathobiological Determinants of Atherosclerosis (PDAY) Study. The first major report of this study presented results for 390 males with postmortem examinations at ages from 15 to 34 years.[24] Figure 3–4, taken from that report, demonstrates the relation of percentage surface area of the abdominal aorta involved with all lesions to blood lipid concentrations and to smoking status as determined from blood tests for thiocyanate, a marker for cigarette smoking. Taking these data into account allows derivation of a statistical prediction of the extent of abdominal aortic atherosclerosis for males at each year of age in relation to these factors. For the group with unfavorable blood lipids who were smokers, the surface involvement was above 30% at age 15 and 50% or greater at age 34; by contrast, for the group with favorable blood lipids who were not smokers, the corresponding percentages of surface involvements were about

10% at age 15 and less than 25% at age 34. Once again, it appears that a close link exists between these factors and the extent of early atherosclerosis.

More recent data from the PDAY Study are shown in Figure 3–5.[25] The upper panels show the extent of surface area involved with fatty streaks in the abdominal aorta (A) and right coronary artery (C), for men (open bars) and women (solid bars), by five-year age groups. The lower panels refer to raised lesions in the corresponding vessels. In these comparisons, variations in blood lipids and smoking have been taken into account, so the sex differences seen cannot be due to these factors. Relative to males, females had more-extensive fatty streaks but a similar extent of raised lesions in the aorta and had a similar extent of fatty streaks but fewer raised lesions in the coronary artery, at all ages. Thus sex differences in development of atherosclerosis that are apparent among teens

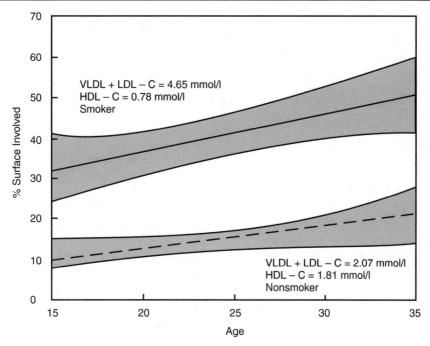

Figure 3–4 The Extent of Atherosclerosis by Age in Relation to Blood Lipids and Smoking, from the PDAY Study. *Source*: Reprinted with permission from *Journal of the American Medical Association*, Vol 264, p 3022, Copyright 1990, American Medical Association.

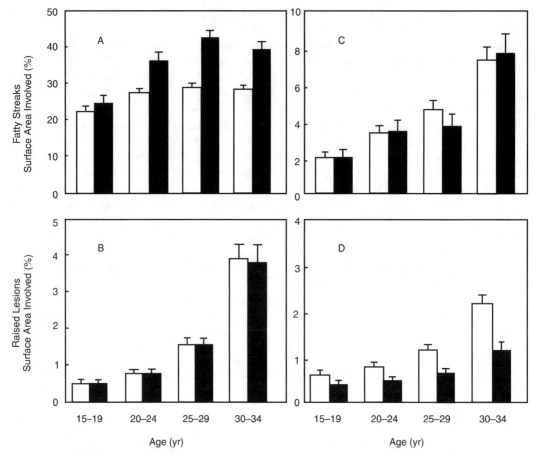

Figure 3–5 Extent of Fatty Streaks and Raised Lesions in the Abdominal Aorta (A and B) and Right Coronary Artery (C and D) in Men (□) and Women (■) Aged 15–34 Years, from the PDAY Study. All values are adjusted for race, VLDL + LDL cholesterol and HDL cholesterol concentrations, and smoking. In the abdominal aorta, women have more extensive fatty streaks than men but equally extensive raised lesions. In contrast, in the right coronary artery, women have equally extensive fatty streaks but less raised lesions. Standard error (⊤) is indicated. *Source*: Reprinted with permission from HC McGill Jr, et al, *Arteriosclerosis, Thrombosis and Vascular Biology*, Vol 17, p 98, © 1997, American Heart Association.

and young adults are not explained by differences in blood lipids or smoking behavior.

It is of interest that a previous comparative study of the pathology of atherosclerosis in the United States and Japan showed substantially less-extensive involvement of the aorta and coronary arteries in men in Tokyo than Black or White men in New Orleans, all autopsied at ages 25 to 44 years.[26] Notably, the differences between New Orleans Whites and Japanese men was not in fatty streaks but in the percent-

age of the surface area of either aorta or coronary arteries with raised lesions. This finding accords with long-recognized differences in the rates of coronary heart disease death in Japan relative to that in the United States and most other industrialized countries. When a study of pathology of the aorta and coronary and cerebral arteries in relation to premortem factors such as blood lipids and blood pressure was undertaken in Japan, medical records were used as the source of information on these factors.[27]

The extent of more advanced atherosclerotic lesions was quite limited in the aorta, but in the coronary and especially the cerebral arteries, fibrous plaques constituted a much-increased proportion of the lesions found. The extent of lesions in the aorta was primarily related to the age at death; in the coronary arteries, age, cholesterol, and blood pressure were all significantly related; and in the cerebral arteries, blood pressure was strongly and singularly related to a statistically significant degree. This report adds to the other insights to the epidemiology of atherosclerosis, in part by emphasis on the contrasting appearance of this disease in different regions of the circulation. Further, it indicates that factors thought to accelerate the development of atherosclerosis even in its early stages relate differently to the disease in these different anatomic locations.

One further observation on the relation between factors measured in childhood and the development of atherosclerosis is based on the long-term follow-up of children examined in school and recontacted as young adults in their early 30s in the Muscatine Study organized by Lauer and colleagues.[28] This project in Iowa began in the 1970s and has recently included examination by ultra-fast CT scan of the coronary arteries to detect calcified coronary lesions. The results support those already described, indicating that factors such as weight/height index, blood lipids, and blood pressure measured in the school years predict the finding of such lesions as early as the early 30s.

TREATMENT AND PREVENTION OF ATHEROSCLEROSIS

Because atherosclerosis in any individual is regarded mainly as a localized disease—chiefly in the coronary, cerebral, or peripheral arteries or the aorta—the question of whether treatment reduces the risk of complications, recurrence, or death due to atherosclerosis becomes a question related to one or another of these specific conditions. In its earliest phases, atherosclerosis is both clinically "silent" (inapparent) and undetectable by currently available noninvasive examination procedures, such as ultrasound reflectance. It is presently unknown whether this or other techniques will become sufficiently sensitive to measure change in the earliest lesions, such as the small fibrous plaques observable at autopsy in teens, in response to measures aimed at preventing atherosclerosis near the beginning of the process. Accordingly, studies are not yet available to indicate whether practical interventions have a measurable effect on the actual onset or progression of early atherosclerosis.

During late stages of the disease, however, regression of lesions has been clearly demonstrated in clinical trials of medical, surgical, and behavioral intervention. By 1992, for example, 10 studies of the effect of cholesterol reduction with one or another method of angiographic evaluation had indicated that reduction of cholesterol concentrations by approximately 40% resulted in significant benefit in terms of the reduced progression, or even regression, of the atherosclerotic lesions.[29]

Despite the lack of direct evidence of effects on early development of atherosclerosis, preventive recommendations have been made with the expectation that their implementation in childhood would have the benefit of avoidance or delay of the progressive change in atherosclerotic lesions that is the basis for later clinical manifestations. In an expert committee report from the World Health Organization in 1990, for example, encouragement was given to the development of national policies in support of improvements in habits of diet and physical activity, as well as the elimination of tobacco use in childhood and youth.[30] These and other such recommendations have to date undergone limited evaluations for their effect on blood lipids, blood pressure, and weight/height indices but none with respect to atherosclerosis itself. Much could be gained in prevention of atherosclerosis if more-sensitive methods for measurement of early lesions were developed.

REFERENCES

1. St. Clair RW. Biology of atherosclerosis. In: Pearson TA, Criqui MH, Luepker RV, Oberman A, Winston M, eds. *Primer in Preventive Cardiology*. Dallas, Tex: American Heart Association; 1994; 11–24.

2. Blankenhorn DH. Prevention or reversal of atherosclerosis: review of current evidence. *Am J Cardiol*. 1989; 63:38H–41H.

3. Bond MG, Barnes RW, Riley WA, Wilmoth SK, et al for the ARIC Study Group. High resolution B-mode ultrasound scanning methods in the Atherosclerosis Risk in Communities Study (ARIC). *Neuroimaging*. 1991;1:68–73.

4. Strong JP. The natural history of atherosclerosis in childhood. In: Williams CL, Wynder EL, eds. *Hyperlipidemia in Childhood and the Development of Atherosclerosis*. New York: Annals of the New York Academy of Sciences; 1991; 9–15.

5. Kuller L, Borhani N, Furberg C, Gardin J, et al. Prevalence of subclinical atherosclerosis and cardiovascular disease and association with risk factors in the Cardiovascular Health Study. *Am J Epidemiol*. 1994;139: 1164–1179.

6. Stamler J. Established major coronary risk factors. In: Marmot M, Elliott P, eds. *Coronary Heart Disease: From Aetiology to Public Health*. Oxford, England: Oxford Medical Press; 1992; 35–66.

7. Ross R, Glomset JA. The pathogenesis of atherosclerosis. First of two parts. *N Engl J Med*. 1976;295:369–377.

8. Ross R, Glomset JA. The pathogenesis of atherosclerosis. Second of two parts. *N Engl J Med*. 1976;295: 420–425.

9. Benditt EP, Barrett T, McDougall JK. Viruses in the etiology of atherosclerosis. *Proc Natl Acad Sci*. 1983; 80:6386–6389.

10. Epstein SE, Speir E, Zhou YF, Guetta E, et al. The role of infection in restenosis and atherosclerosis: focus on cytomegalovirus. *Lancet*. 1996;348:S13–S17.

11. Patel P, Mendall MA, Carrington D, Strachan DP, et al. Association of *Helicobacter pylori* and *Chlamydia pneumoniae* infections with coronary heart disease and cardiovascular risk factors. *Br Med J*. 1995;311:711–714.

12. Stary HC, Chandler AB, Dinsmore RE, Fuster V, et al. A definition of advanced types of atherosclerotic lesions and a histological classification of atherosclerosis. A report from the Committee on Vascular Lesions of the Council on Arteriosclerosis, American Heart Association. *Arteriosclerosis Thromb Vasc Biol*. 1995;15:1512–1531.

13. Moreno PR, Shah PK, Falk E. Determinants of rupture of atherosclerotic coronary lesions. In: Willich SN, Muller JE, eds. *Triggering of Acute Coronary Syndromes: Implications for Prevention*. Dordrecht, the Netherlands: Kluwer Academic Publishers; 1996; 267–283.

14. Hall AJ. A lady from China's past. *National Geographic*. 1974;45:661–681.

15. Sandison AT. Degenerative vascular disease in the Egyptian mummy. *Med Hist*. 1962;6:77–81.

16. Holman RL, McGill HC, Strong JP, Geer JC. The natural history of atherosclerosis. *Am J Pathol*. 1958; 34:209–235.

17. Enos WF, Holmes RH, Beyer J. Coronary disease among United States soldiers killed in action in Korea. *JAMA*. 1953;152:1090–1093.

18. McNamara JJ, Molot MA, Stremple JF, Cutting RT. Coronary artery disease in combat casualties in Vietnam. *JAMA*. 1971;216:1185–1187.

19. Virmani R, Robinowitz M, Geer JC, Breslin PP, et al. Coronary artery atherosclerosis revisited in Korean War combat casualties. *Arch Pathol Lab Med*. 1987; 111:972–976.

20. Tejada C, Strong JP, Montenegro MR, Restrepo C, et al. Distribution of coronary and aortic atherosclerosis by geographic location, race, and sex. *Lab Invest*. 1968;18:509–526.

21. Report of a WHO Expert Committee. *Prevention of Coronary Heart Disease*. Geneva, Switzerland: World Health Organization; 1982. WHO Technical Report Series 678.

22. Newman WP III, Freedman DS, Voors AW, Gard PD, et al. Relation of serum lipoprotein levels and systolic blood pressure to early atherosclerosis. *N Engl J Med*. 1986;314: 138–144.

23. Berenson GS, Wattigney WA, Tracy RE, Newman WP III, et al. Atherosclerosis of the aorta and coronary arteries and cardiovascular risk factors in persons ages 6 to 30 years and studied at necropsy (the Bogalusa Heart Study). *Am J Cardiol*. 1992;70:851–858.

24. Pathobiological Determinants of Atherosclerosis in Youth (PDAY) Research Group. Relationship of atherosclerosis in young men to serum lipoprotein cholesterol concentrations and smoking. *JAMA*. 1990;264: 3018–3024.

25. McGill HC Jr, McMahan CA, Malcom GT, Oalmann MC, et al, PDAY Research Group. Effects of serum lipoproteins and smoking on atherosclerosis in young men and women. *Arteriosclerosis, Throm Vasc Biol*. 1997;17:95–106.

26. Ishii T, Newman WP III, Guzman MA, Hosoda Y, et al. Coronary and aortic atherosclerosis in young men from Tokyo and New Orleans. *Lab Invest*. 1986; 54:561–565.

27. Tanaka K, Masuda J, Imamura T, Sueishi K, et al. A nation-wide study of atherosclerosis in infants, children and young adults in Japan. *Atherosclerosis*. 1988; 72:143–156.

28. Mahoney LT, Burns TL, Stanford W, Thompson BH, et al. Coronary risk factors measured in childhood and young adult life are associated with coronary artery calcification in young adults: the Muscatine Study. *J Am Coll Cardiol*. 1996;27:277–284.

29. Blankenhorn DH. Lipoproteins and the progression and regression of atherosclerosis. *Cardiovasc Rev Rep*. 1992;13:52–56.

30. WHO Expert Committee on Prevention in Childhood and Youth of Adult Cardiovascular Diseases. *Prevention in Childhood and Youth of Adult Cardiovascular Diseases: Time for Action*. Geneva, Switzerland: World Health Organization; 1990. Technical Report Series 792.

CHAPTER 4

Coronary Heart Disease

SUMMARY

Coronary heart disease is the major component of cardiovascular morbidity and mortality in much of the industrialized world and is anticipated to become so in many developing countries in the decades ahead. Because the initial event is often rapidly fatal to the affected individual, and because risks of recurrence and death among survivors are high, prevention of first coronary events through interventions at both the individual and the population-wide level are advocated. Several long-term epidemiologic studies were undertaken in the United States and other countries beginning in the late 1950s, drawing on current concepts of the disease and stimulating development of standard methods for diagnosis and classification of cases. These studies documented differences in mortality and incidence between populations as well as differences in risks among individuals within populations. Long-term trends based on vital statistics demonstrate the rise and fall of the vast epidemic curve of coronary heart disease mortality in the United States throughout the 20th century. Shorter-term but also striking trends in such rates are evident among many populations. The World Health Organization (WHO) MONICA Project is the largest undertaking to date in cardiovascular epidemiology and is evaluating the determinants of changes in incidence, case-fatality, and overall mortality from coronary heart disease in 38 populations in 21 countries. From both the knowledge gained to date and the remaining gaps in that knowledge, major issues in coronary heart disease are identified that require attention from public health professionals if further progress toward prevention of epidemic coronary heart disease is to be achieved.

CLINICAL COURSE OF THE INDIVIDUAL CASE

The Coronary Arteries

Coronary heart disease is one of several terms referring to atherosclerosis of the arteries supplying the myocardium, or muscle of the heart. These arteries are illustrated in Figure 4–1[1]. The arteries are named descriptively after their typical anatomic configuration. At the lower right of the figure (corresponding to the lower left of the subject's chest) is the apex of the heart. At the top and left side of the figure is the base of the heart. From the base, the principal arteries extend distally toward the apex and can be imagined to form a crown (corona) around the main muscle mass comprising the left and right ventricles, the pumps to the systemic arterial circulation and to the lungs, respectively. Insufficiency of myocardial blood supply (ischemia) results from reduction of

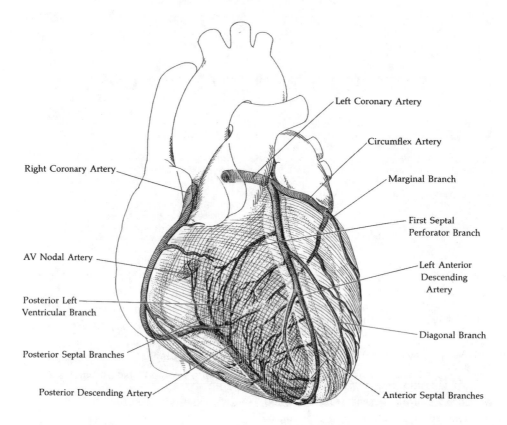

Figure 4–1 The Coronary Arteries—A Schematic View. *Source*: Hutter A, Scientific American Medicine, Dale DC, Federman DD, eds. 5 Cardiovascular Medicine, Subsection IX © 1996 Scientific American, Inc. All rights reserved.

blood flow through one or more of these coronary arteries or their branches.

Because myocardial cells are dependent on a continuous or, during exertion, an increased supply of oxygen and nutrients and removal of metabolic products through the coronary circulation, they undergo injury and death if blood flow is interrupted and not restored within minutes. Unless emergency treatment is instituted to minimize it, the extent of the injury often widens, with increased risk of complications or death. Typical symptoms experienced by the victim include pain described as pressing, stabbing, or crushing and located especially beneath the sternum or breastbone or in the jaw, arms, or mid-back, often accompanied by sweating, faintness, and a sense of impending death. Por-

tions of the electrophysiologic conducting system that controls the rate and rhythm of cardiac contraction pass through the septum or wall between the right and left atria and ventricles. Especially if the area of ischemia includes the septum, an abrupt disturbance of cardiac rhythm may result with loss of effective pumping action of the heart, resulting in immediate collapse and sudden death unless resuscitation is successfully applied.

Course of the Individual Case

Some common features of the course of the individual case of an acute coronary event are shown schematically in Figure 4–2. Four phases of the process are depicted from the perspective

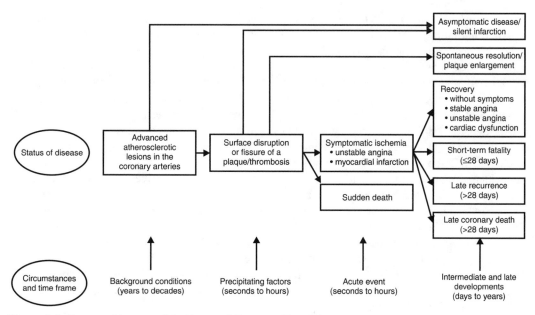

Figure 4–2 Common Features of the Course of Coronary Heart Disease

of its biological and clinical progression, and for each phase the status of disease and time frame are noted. First, against a background of progressive atherogenesis over many years or several decades, described in the preceding chapter, advanced atherosclerotic lesions develop in the coronary arteries. Second, under the current concept of the acute coronary event, one or more of several potential precipitating factors leads to disruption of an advanced atherosclerotic lesion or plaque, either at its endothelial surface or by fissuring into deeper levels of the lesion.[2] Stimuli to thrombosis at the site of the plaque may produce only minor aggregation of blood platelets, with spontaneous resolution of the resulting small clot and some enlargement of the plaque. At the other extreme, a large occlusive clot may form and persist for several hours or longer, producing acute symptoms (unstable angina), myocardial infarction, or sudden death. If the acute event is not rapidly fatal, several short- or long-term outcomes are possible: recovery, with or without symptoms or residual cardiac dysfunction; short-term fatality

(often defined as occurring within 28 days of clinical onset); later recurrence as a new episode (defined as symptoms present after a 28-day period from onset of an earlier event); or late coronary death, occurring more than 28 days (and up to many years) following the onset of the first event. Asymptomatic disease, or "silent" infarction, is another late outcome shown in Figure 4–2. This represents a circumstance in which evidence of myocardial infarction may be found only on special examination, perhaps arising through the same process as described here, and in which, for reasons not well understood, no history of chest pain can be elicited.

Recently, characteristics of the "vulnerable plaque" that predispose it to disruption, the precipitating factors triggering this process, and the consequent "acute coronary syndromes" including "sudden cardiac death" have received detailed attention in published reports and reference works in the field.[2–6] Sudden cardiac death is a common outcome of this process and a prominent focus of attention, though definition of the term has been controversial. A recently proposed definition is the following: "a natural death due to cardiac causes, heralded by the abrupt loss of consciousness within 1 hour of the onset of acute symptoms. Preexisting heart disease may or may not have been known to be present, but the time and mode of death are unexpected."[5(p 742)] Study of sudden death has been impeded by lack of a consistent definition. In the past a 24-hour criterion was often used, and evidence of prior cardiac disease sometimes excluded cases from the definition. Some previous expert opinion was opposed to attempts to define the condition at all.[6] As currently defined, however, sudden cardiac death may represent 50% of all cardiovascular deaths in the United States. The other acute outcomes, now classified as unstable angina, non–Q wave and Q-wave infarction (referring to specific electrocardiographic findings) include potential additional deaths that may occur within 28 days of onset (conventionally the limit for inclusion in calculation of case fatality) and later-occurring deaths, as well as long-term nonfatal outcomes. Especially for unstable angina, there is a need for standardized definition and criteria to render reports of this condition comparable.

Several aspects of the acute-stage process are particularly noteworthy from an epidemiologic perspective. First, this phase of the disease, which evolves in a time frame of seconds to hours, is a very late development in relation to the long-standing process of atherogenesis. Prevention of atherosclerosis may be opportune throughout much of the life span, whereas effective intervention within seconds, minutes, or even hours of the onset of an acute coronary event poses often insurmountable practical obstacles. Thus prevention of either irreversible myocardial damage or sudden death requires strategies long in advance of this phase for a large proportion of those who may be at risk. Second, investigation of precipitating or triggering factors is in progress at multiple levels, including both extrinsic factors (eg, physical activity, psychological factors and emotional states, and physiological aspects of circadian variation) and intrinsic factors (especially physical and biochemical aspects of the plaque, blood coagulation, and blood vessel contractility or spasm). Third, current studies of interventions to provide long-term protection or acute-phase control of the processes leading to acute coronary syndromes are accompanied by study of community-based intervention to reduce the delay between onset of symptoms and access to emergency care so that new acute-phase interventions can be received in time to be effective. Although this area of research has promise of being valuable for settings in which rapid access to care is practicable, the extent of its potential impact on the epidemic process has yet to be assessed and it will be of little benefit in many areas of the world where both access and treatment resources are limited.

BACKGROUND OF EPIDEMIOLOGIC INVESTIGATION

In his detailed historical account of coronary heart disease, Liebowitz traced to Egyptian and Greek antiquity clinical observations that in retrospect are inferred to indicate cases of this disease.[7] (Chapter 3 includes reference to an ancient case in a mummified Chinese woman, also.) Progress in understanding the clinical and pathological characteristics of coronary heart disease continued only very gradually until the 19th century. The publication in 1896 of Osler's *Lectures on Angina Pectoris and Allied States* provided numerous case descriptions representing a wide spectrum of manifestations of coronary ischemia, including accounts of cases in persons of note from the 18th century and others compiled from his own practice.[8] (Osler commented on the rarity of this condition in hospital practice but noted that it was much more commonly observed in private consultation and especially in wealthy patients.) As of 1900, the accumulated clinical and pathological knowledge of coronary atherosclerosis and angina pectoris did not yet include full recognition of the link between the acute thrombosis of a coronary artery and the occurrence of myocardial infarction. This understanding was advanced especially by Herrick, whose publications in 1912 and 1919 are now recognized as classic descriptions of pathologic and electrocardiographic findings in acute myocardial infarction.[7]

The first half of the 20th century saw developments essential for the later emergence of epidemiologic studies: clear recognition of the clinical and pathological entity and commonly applicable diagnostic procedures, including electrocardiography. Insights from "geographical pathology," in which observations made independently in different populations around the world could be contrasted, indicated variations in the frequency of coronary atherosclerosis in relation to dietary patterns. Keys' account of the genesis of the Seven Countries Study (discussed below) indicates the contribution of such observations from China, Java, the Netherlands, and wartime Scandinavia and Germany.[9]

By the 1950s and early 1960s a remarkable series of epidemiologic studies had begun, some of which continue to the present. Examples include the Seven Countries Study, in which 16 groups of men, more than 12,000 in all, were examined in one of the seven participating countries under the leadership of Keys and his local colleagues[10]; the Ni-Hon-San Study of nearly as many men of Japanese ancestry in Japan, Hawaii, and the San Francisco Bay Area, organized after analysis of vital statistics showed striking gradients across the three populations in mortality from coronary heart disease and (oppositely) stroke[11,12]; the Framingham Study and other community- or employment-based studies of more than 8000 men collectively[13]; and other studies in the United States and elsewhere. The goal of these studies was to identify factors that could explain either differences in rates of occurrence of coronary heart disease between populations or differences in risks of coronary events among individual members of a population.

Accounts of the organization and implementation of these early studies are rich sources of insight into the formative period of contemporary cardiovascular epidemiology. For example, in 1951 Dawber, Meadors, and Moore described the background of the Framingham Study.[14] This included the exercise of sample size estimation, which was instructively imaginative, albeit primitive by present conventions. The authors' concern about the potential for successful follow-up over a 20-year period, while revolutionary, underestimated the study's longevity by more than 25 years (thus far). A second example includes a series of three reports, from personal anecdotes of a key field investigator (Blackburn), to a scientific update after 35 years' experience in the Seven Countries Study.[15-17] These, too, offer unique perspectives on this pioneering study of international contrasts in coronary heart disease rates and their determinants.

The early results of these studies led to many clinical trials and community interventions to test the ability to modify one or more of the factors identified and thereby to control or prevent coronary heart disease. Some major examples, addressed in subsequent chapters, are studies of diet (eg, the Diet-Heart Feasibility Study), high blood pressure (Hypertension Detection and Follow-Up Program), blood cholesterol concentrations (Lipid Research Clinics—Coronary Primary Prevention Trial), or multiple factors in individual participants (World Health Organization European Collaborative Trial of Multifactorial Prevention of Coronary Heart Disease and Multiple Risk Factor Intervention Study). Whole communities became subjects of intervention to modify risk-related behavior (diet, physical activity, cigarette smoking, and others) in North Karelia, Finland; in California, Minnesota, and Rhode Island; and in numerous studies elsewhere (see Chapter 21).

Concurrent with these studies on prevention of coronary heart disease and the continuing observational studies, all in adult populations, other investigations were undertaken as early as the 1970s to clarify the essential factors in the early onset and progression of the underlying process of atherosclerosis. As reviewed in Chapter 3, these studies reconfirmed the long-standing evidence for extensive atherosclerosis in the coronary arteries of some individuals in adolescence and early adulthood. It was further established that factors related to the occurrence of atherosclerosis and coronary heart disease in adulthood (eg, adverse blood lipid profile, high blood pressure, and smoking) are also related to the nature and extent of atherosclerosis in childhood and adolescence.

This research has been progressive with respect to its development from the earliest observational to the most recent experimental studies. It would be erroneous, however, to conclude that only experimental epidemiologic studies are now needed to advance understanding of coronary heart disease and its prevention. The fundamental methods of observational epidemiology continue to be applied to new questions, in new populations, and under circumstances often changed dramatically from those studied earlier in this half-century of investigation. The remainder of this chapter addresses the application of these methods to the study of the occurrence of coronary heart disease in diverse populations and over extended periods of time. Subsequent chapters (Chapters 7–20) address the many factors identified as contributing to the explanation of its occurrence and offering avenues of prevention.

POPULATION STUDIES: DEFINITION AND CLASSIFICATION, DIAGNOSTIC ALGORITHMS, AND CRITERIA

The undertaking of population studies of coronary heart disease in the 1950s and 1960s led to the need to standardize definitions and classification for improved comparability of data across studies. To determine the presence or absence of coronary heart disease among participants in general population surveys, information about participants' personal health history was needed. In addition, electrocardiographic examination was needed both to supplement the history and, because myocardial infarction can occur without symptoms, to detect previous silent infarction should the usual abnormalities

persist. Methods were developed for standardized history taking by interview or questionnaire (the London School of Hygiene or Rose questionnaire), and an objective procedure was devised for coding and classifying electrocardiographic findings (the Minnesota code). These essential tools for epidemiologic studies were incorporated in a more comprehensive guide, *Cardiovascular Survey Methods*, first published in 1968 through the auspices of the Cardiovascular Disease Unit of the World Health Organization.[18] These methods were suitable for discriminating between already-established (and surviving) cases and noncases of coronary heart disease and served both to estimate its prevalence (ie, the affected proportion of the population at large) and to identify those still free of the disease who constituted a "population at risk" or cohort of persons for long-term observation to identify predictors of first-time coronary events occurring in the future.

Further methodologic development was required to standardize the diagnosis of acute coronary events for investigations such as hospital-based myocardial infarction case registers, community surveillance of newly occurring cases, and trials in which new events were the end point for evaluating intervention effects. The acute changes in the electrocardiogram during the process of myocardial infarction and the abrupt appearance in the blood of increasing concentrations of enzymes released from damaged myocardial cells were added to the diagnostic criteria. In addition, a more-detailed classification was developed to recognize various levels of confidence in the diagnosis or particular characteristics of the acute event.

A detailed algorithm for diagnosis and classification of acute coronary heart disease was formulated by Gillum and colleagues, under the auspices of the Criteria and Methods Committee of the Council on Epidemiology and Prevention of the American Heart Association.[19] Its wide adoption is illustrated by the WHO MONICA (*MONI*toring Trends and Determinants in *CA*rdiovascular Disease) Project, in which 38 centers in 21 countries are conducting a decade-long study of coronary events. The diagnostic elements for coronary heart disease are summarized in Exhibit 4–1 and incorporate the foregoing methodologic developments.[20] These are presented in greater detail, including specific electrocardiographic criteria, in a more recent report.[21] Events, whether fatal or nonfatal, are classified as "definite" or "possible" on the basis of the severity or completeness of the findings; the possibility of successful resuscitation from cardiac arrest is recognized; and provision is made for those fatal cases in which the rapid time course or other factors preclude the collection of the requisite data for classification as definite or possible infarction. (The continuing evolution of study methods in this and many other aspects of cardiovascular epidemiology can be followed through the *Annotated Bibliography of Epidemiologic Methods of Cardiovascular Research*, also prepared by the Criteria and Methods Committee of the Council on Epidemiology and Prevention, American Heart Association, and maintained currently at www.fhcrc.org/~cvdeab/ on the Internet.

Much of the comparative information on the occurrence of coronary heart disease, both between populations and over extended periods of time, has been based on mortality data, as reflected in national vital statistics. These data are collected under the system of the International Classification of Diseases (ICD) codes. Currently, the classification of coronary heart disease events and conditions is organized in the Tenth Revision (ICD 10) as indicated in Exhibit 4–2.[22] Angina pectoris (I20) is further subclassified under the ICD code into four categories: unstable angina, angina pectoris with documented spasm of the coronary arteries, other forms, and unspecified. Acute myocardial infarction (I21) is subclassified in accordance with the site of infarction and its extent, whether transmural (affecting the full thickness of the myocardial wall) or only subendocardial (limited to a few millimeters from the interior surface of the heart chamber). Subsequent myocardial infarction (I22) refers to recurrent events and is subclassified only by location. Certain current complications (I23) are conditions such as cardiac rupture or development of a defect in the interatrial or interventricular septum—not concurrent with the acute infarction but developing as a late complication. Other acute ischemic heart disease (I24) include conditions

---

Exhibit 4–1 Summary of Diagnostic Elements and Classification Scheme for Fatal and Nonfatal Coronary Heart Disease Events in Population Studies

Diagnostic elements

- electrocardiogram (up to four per acute attack)
- myocardial enzymes
- history of chest pain (including time of onset)
- necropsy evidence

Classification of events

- definite infarction
- possible infarction
- ischemic cardiac arrest (resuscitated)
- fatal cases with insufficient data
- no myocardial infarction

Source: Data from World Health Organization MONICA Project Principal Investigators, The World Health Organization MONICA Project (Monitoring Trends and Determinants in Cardiovascular Disease): A Major International Collaboration, *Journal of Clinical Epidemiology* Vol 41, pp 105–114, © 1988.

Exhibit 4–2 Categories of Coronary Heart Disease (Ischemic Heart Disease)

I20	Angina pectoris
I21	Acute myocardial infarction
I22	Subsequent myocardial infarction
I23	Certain current complications following acute myocardial infarction
I24	Other acute ischemic heart disease
I25	Chronic ischemic heart disease

such as coronary insufficiency or coronary thrombosis that did not develop into myocardial infarction. Chronic ischemic heart disease (I25) refers not only to healed or past myocardial infarction without current symptoms but also to coronary events with survival beyond 28 days and therefore not codable as acute.

Widespread use of the methods described here has greatly facilitated the collection and reporting of data from population studies that are more nearly comparable than would otherwise have been possible. Nevertheless, issues of comparability still require consideration in interpreting data from different populations or time periods, such as those reviewed in the following sections.

RATES OF OCCURRENCE IN POPULATIONS

The occurrence of coronary heart disease in populations is measured in several ways, each of which contributes some insight into the nature of the epidemic process. Mortality data, usually expressed as the number of coronary heart disease deaths per 100,000 population per year, are readily available in the vital statistics for many countries and other geopolitical units, often for population subgroups by age, race, and sex, and in some cases over periods of several decades. These data are based on the cause of death as stated by the party completing the death certificate and subsequently coded by a nosologist in accordance with the standard ICD procedures in effect at the time. Mortality is the measure of the rate of loss of life due to this disease and, by inference, an indicator of the social

and economic burden due to potential years of productive life lost.

Incidence data indicate the number of newly occurring cases usually expressed as per 1000 to 100,000 population per year (the smaller value of the denominator being used for groups with very high rates, such as those at older ages) and include both fatal and nonfatal cases. The special requirements for diagnosis and classification of these events, suggested above, result in much more limited availability of incidence data but also add importantly to their reliability when properly collected. The methods used are principally two. In one instance community surveillance, or long-term monitoring of defined populations, is undertaken to detect the occurrence of new coronary events, for example, through hospital admissions or death notices. The other is cohort studies, in which members of a population have been examined individually and those free of coronary disease at the starting point (baseline) are followed up by surveillance methods, periodic reexamination, or both, to detect new coronary events. Both methods can also provide mortality data, distinct from ordinary vital statistics in having the potential for diagnostic validation through methods specific to the individual study. It is especially difficult, except in a cohort study, to determine whether a particular event was in fact the first occurrence of coronary heart disease in that individual and therefore strictly an incident, not a recurrent, event. Incidence rates, so defined, are taken to reflect the operation of factors that are causally related to the occurrence of disease; inclusion of recurrent cases would cloud the interpretation due to factors influencing their survival from previous events.

Case-fatality is another useful measure. It indicates the proportion of all cases in the population that are fatal in outcome. Its determination requires knowledge of both the occurrence and the outcome of the incident event, obtained through surveillance or cohort studies. Case-fatality data are also therefore limited in their availability. As already noted, the arbitrary interval of 28 days or less from the onset of symptoms is the convention used to attribute death to a given coronary event. A special subset of case-fatality is sudden death, often defined as occurring within one hour. Case-fatality (ie, within 28 days) is often interpreted as a measure of the effectiveness (more properly, the ineffectiveness) of medical treatment of the acute coronary event. Sudden death, as defined, has been considered in some respects a distinct phenomenon that is less amenable to medical care and therefore less reflective of its impact, especially when death is essentially instantaneous. Sudden death is a particularly forceful indication of the need to prevent acute coronary events altogether.

Prevalence, or the proportion of the population surviving with recognized coronary heart disease, is typically expressed in cases per 1000 population, usually for specific age groups, by sex, and often by race. Estimates of prevalence depend on knowledge of individual histories obtained through interview and examination surveys, as described previously. Surveys typically provide for only a single contact with participants and are much more readily conducted than surveillance or cohort studies. They are commonly undertaken as a first step in study of the coronary heart disease situation of a population. Prevalence does not include those who have died and may reflect factors influencing survival, so its interpretation warrants some caution. Nevertheless, it indicates something of the magnitude of risk and is often useful in estimating health care needs in a population.

These several measures of disease occurrence in the population are interrelated in ways that bear on their interpretation. For example, incidence and case-fatality can be considered as components of mortality, because they indicate, respectively, the rate at which new cases occur and the proportion of cases with fatal outcomes. However, a death rate is usually calculated for the events in a 12-month interval, and case-fatality is restricted by definition to 28 days from the date of onset. Therefore the overall coronary death rate cannot be calculated from incidence and case-fatality alone, which does not account for all coronary deaths in 12 months among incident cases and in strict use excludes recurrent cases altogether. Also, prevalence is related to incidence and mortality, because it identifies previously incident cases that were nonfatal. But differences in prevalence between populations, or changes in prevalence over time, cannot be attributed simply to differences in incidence or to differences in mortality without additional information, because either or both of these measures could reflect the true explanation.

With this understanding of measures of disease occurrence, it is useful to examine data on coronary heart disease from these several perspectives, both in the United States and in other parts of the world.

Mortality

Statistical information on cardiovascular diseases in the United States is provided by the American Heart Association through annual publications and at www.amhrt.org on the Internet. As of August 1997, the most recent final US mortality data were for 1993 and indicated coronary heart disease mortality of 103.4/100,000, reflecting 490,063 deaths.[23] This rate was less than one-half that experienced in the United States in the mid-1960s, at the peak of the national epidemic of coronary heart disease mortality. At the time when the population studies described were initiated, coronary mortality in the United States had been increasing every year for several decades. Unexpectedly, and with no one predicting its occurrence, a decline in national coronary mortality began in the 1960s (although a sentinel report by Borhani and Hechter indicated a downturn in California in the late 1950s[24]). This major change was first doubted, then debated, and finally examined extensively in a conference of the National Heart, Lung and Blood Institute in 1978.[25] Two leading explanations were offered, either of which in principle could have reduced the death rate: first, that medical care, especially in coronary intensive care units, had reduced in-hospital mortality; second, that preventive efforts had reduced the incidence of coronary events. Data were lacking to substantiate either explanation—an unwelcome acknowledgment of igno-

rance in connection with the foremost cause of death in the United States.

One response to the decline was an effort to reconstruct the history of the epidemic throughout the 20th century by compiling mortality data from published vital statistics. Stallones undertook this analysis, beginning from the premise that "whatever comes down must have gone up" and seeking a unified explanation of the rise and fall of the epidemic.[26] The result is illustrated in Figure 4–3, in which each point represents the rate of death due to "diseases of the heart" in a given year from 1900 to 1978.

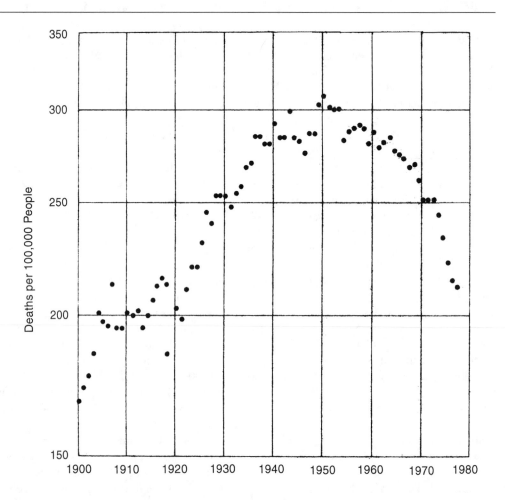

Figure 4–3 Heart Disease Mortality in the United States, 1900–1980. The vertical scale is logarithmic. *Source*: From *The Rise and Fall of Ischemic Heart Disease* by RA Stallones, copyright © 1980 by Scientific American, Inc. All rights reserved.

This category is broader than that described by *coronary heart disease*, because this term was not in use throughout the entire period, although it became the recognized term for the dominant cause of death in later decades. Each year's rate was adjusted to the age distribution of the US population in 1940, the midpoint of the period. This calculation removed any effect of increasing overall rates due to the shift in age composition of the population toward older ages. (This is in contrast to Figure 1–2, which shows the "crude" or absolute death rates for each category of disease each year, causing heart disease rates to appear to increase across the entire time period indicated.) The epidemic curve rises beginning in the 1920s, peaks at 1950, and

declines through the 1970s. (The apparent peak at 1950 in this representation rather than the mid-1960s as usually described is due to the choice of the 1940 age distribution for standardization, which has a smaller proportion of persons at older ages than in more recent standard populations.) Stallones found no compelling explanation for both the rise and the fall of the curve. However, the 20th-century epidemic in US mortality was clearly demonstrated.

The course of the epidemic in the United States has not been uniform in all population groups. Figure 4–4 updates to 1990 the secular trend, or long-term pattern over time, in coronary heart disease mortality for the United States beginning in 1950, based on the *Report*

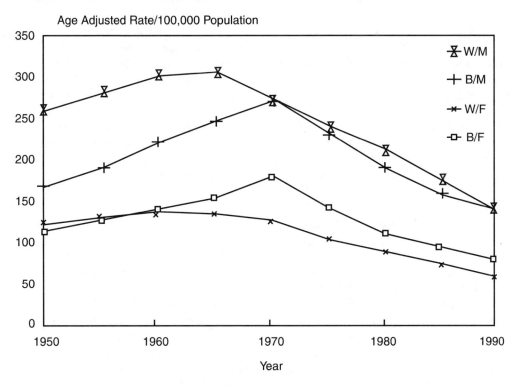

Note: W/M, White men; B/M, Black men; W/F, White women; B/F, Black women.

Figure 4–4 Coronary Heart Disease Mortality in the United States by Sex and Race (Black/White), 1950–1990. The ICD 9 to ICD 8 comparability ratio for the total population (0.8784) was applied to the rates for 1970 and 1975. *Source*: Reprinted from C Lenfant, *Epidemiology and Prevention of Cardiovascular Diseases*, p xii, National Heart, Lung and Blood Institute, National Institutes of Health.

of the Task Force on Research in Epidemiology and Prevention of Cardiovascular Diseases of the National Heart, Lung and Blood Institute.[27] Separately for Black and White males and females, the trends reversed from upward to downward, ending with rates as low or lower in 1990 than in 1950 for each group. From the year of peak mortality of each group—in 1960 for White females, 1965 for White males, and 1970 for Black males and females—rates declined continuously to 1990 for all groups. The net differences in rates in 1990 versus those in 1950 were greatest for White males. As of 1993, the sex-specific rates for males were nearly equal (133.0/100,000 for Whites and 139.3 for Blacks) but were higher for Black than for White females (85.7 for Blacks and 63.8 for Whites).[18] Recent variation in coronary heart disease mortality by state can be illustrated with data for Blacks and Whites aged 55–64 years, presented in the Task Force report.[27] A twofold range in rates was found between the highest- and lowest-rate states for both White and Black men, though rates for Blacks were one-third higher than for Whites in both low-rate and high-rate states. The corresponding ranges for both White and Black women were 2½-fold. For Black women, rates were twice those of White women in both low- and high-rate states.

It is useful to compare the situation of other countries with respect to coronary heart disease, both to put the US experience into perspective and to recognize the broad international basis for concern about this disease. Another sequel to the "decline conference" of 1978 was initiation of a major new international collaboration, the WHO MONICA Project, to obtain data on key aspects of the epidemic process, including incidence, case-fatality, and overall coronary mortality. Participating countries were primarily in Europe, but populations in Australia and New Zealand, China, and the United States (the Stanford Five-City Study) were also included. The basic design called for monitoring of coronary heart disease events, related personal characteristics of population samples, and medical care practices over the 10-year period from the mid-1980s to the mid-1990s.

At the start of the MONICA Project, coronary event registration under the Project protocol was reported in comparison with official coronary heart disease mortality for 38 populations in 21 countries, as shown in Figure 4–5.[21] The heavy horizontal bars represent the combined definite and possible coronary deaths according to MONICA registration, and the extended lines show the additional, nonclassifiable deaths. Official coronary heart disease mortality is represented by the short crossing vertical lines. A generally close correspondence between rates based on registered definite and possible coronary events and the official rates is apparent, although in some exceptional cases (eg, Canada-Halifax, for men) the differences were quite large. (The scale for mortality rates is logarithmic and not arithmetic; this means that equal distances along the scale are equal multiples of the rate.) For example, reading from the figure, the official rate for men in Finland-North Karelia (first entry in the left panel) was nearly 500/100,000, or about 10 times that of men in China-Beijing (last entry in the left panel) at 50/100,000. Similarly, a greater than 10-fold range characterized the difference in rates between women in United Kingdom-Glasgow (approximately 110/100,000) and in Spain-Catalonia (11/100,000). Clearly, the United States has not been unique in its 20th-century experience with coronary heart disease mortality and did not rank highest in rates in the mid-1980s; Finland, the United Kingdom, and the former Soviet Union were at or near the head of the list for both men and women.

Secular trends in coronary heart disease mortality over the past four decades have also shown striking national differences, as seen in Figure 4–6, compiled from data reported to the World Health Organization over this period.[28] This figure represents the average annual mortality for coronary heart disease at ages 45–64 years in each of eight time periods, from 1950–1954 to 1984–1987, for each of 27 countries. The countries are ordered from left to right in

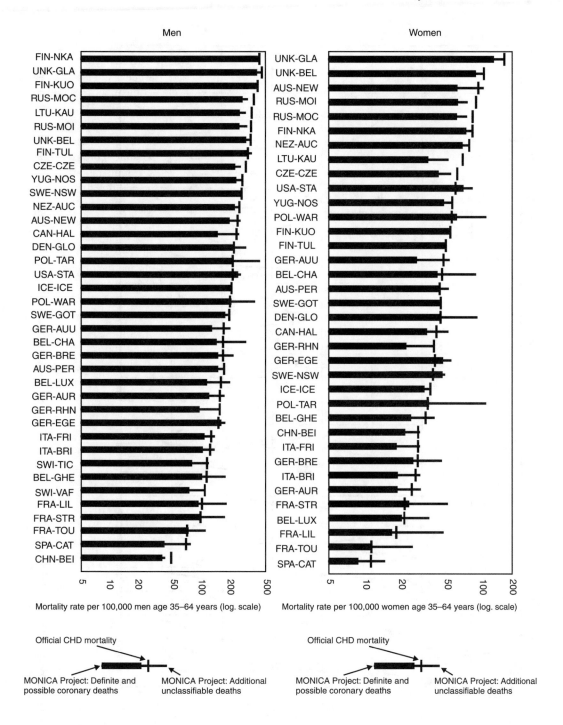

Figure 4–5 Coronary Heart Disease (CHD) Mortality in 38 Populations in 21 Countries, According to the WHO MONICA Project and Official Rates. See key for MONICA abbreviations in Appendix 4–A. *Source*: Reprinted with permission from *Circulation*, Special Report, Vol 90, No 1, p 599, © 1994, American Heart Association.

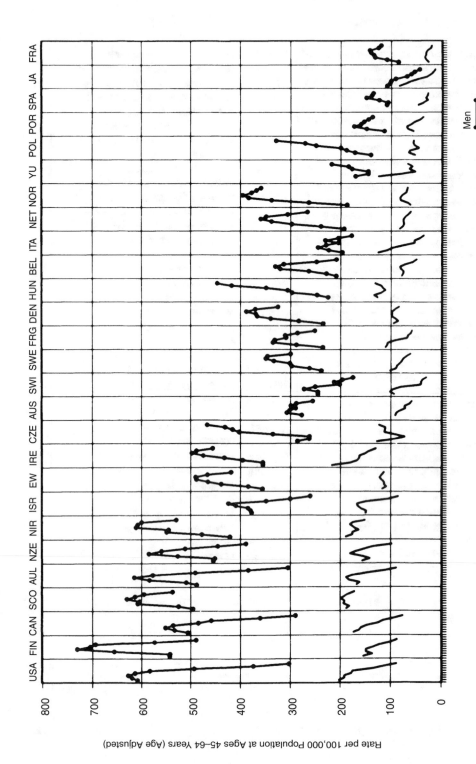

Figure 4–6 Coronary Heart Disease Mortality in 27 Countries, 1950–1987. *Source:* Reprinted from J Thom, FH Epstein, JJ Feldman, PE Leaverton, and M Wolz, 1992, National Institutes of Health, Pub No 92-3988.

descending rank for male coronary heart disease mortality in the first time period. The initial rates for males differed widely, about sixfold, among these populations, from about 600/100,000 per year in the United States to less than 100/100,000 in France, with the remaining 25 countries arrayed continuously between them. The rates for females in every country were typically half or less the rates for males, the only exception being Japan with its very low rates. The relative gradient in initial rates for females was similar to that for males, about sixfold from highest (Ireland) to lowest (France).

Over the eight time periods, dramatic changes in coronary heart disease mortality occurred in most of these countries for both males and females. Most striking for males are the marked decreases in countries such as the United States, Canada, and Australia and the increases in Czechoslovakia, Hungary, Norway, and Poland. Intermediate are several countries whose rates for males peaked near the midpoint and later declined toward the initial levels. Also notable is the consistently downward trend for Japan, whose clustering generally with Spain, Portugal, and France evokes imaginative geographical interpretation. By contrast, however, Japan attained the lowest coronary heart disease mortality rate of any of these countries by the early- to mid-1960s and has since remained in that rank. Trends for females were in general parallel to those for males, except in those countries where they changed little despite sharp increases in rates for males—Czechoslovakia, Hungary, Norway, and Poland. These data indicate that marked variation in coronary heart disease mortality can occur within populations over short historical intervals, which can only be explained by environmental factors, including social and behavioral changes. The diversity among these countries in degrees and directions of change offers some assurance that the WHO MONICA Project, even in its limited 10-year design, will have been able to provide meaningful insights into the determinants of such change.

Incidence

Understanding changes in mortality such as that for coronary heart disease in the United States and other countries would be aided greatly by availability of data on incidence, such as those being collected by the WHO MONICA Project. However, in the United States only a few localities can provide such data and none are available nationally, even 30 years after the peak of the mortality epidemic. This is due mainly to the special requirements noted above for ascertainment and standardized diagnostic validation of acute fatal and nonfatal coronary events in the conduct of both long-term surveillance and cohort studies. The few studies that have been carried out indicate the value of this approach.

Incidence of coronary heart disease can be estimated most reliably through studies of cohorts of persons judged to be free of coronary heart disease at the start of a common period of follow-up and determined, with virtually complete ascertainment, to have or not have coronary heart disease at a subsequent time. This approach is illustrated by the Seven Countries Study, whose incidence data at 10-year follow-up are shown in Table 4–1.[10] A familiar type of distinction is made in these data between "hard" and "any" coronary heart disease. The former category includes coronary heart disease death and definite myocardial infarction only, whereas the latter also includes angina pectoris and other conditions defined in a detailed protocol. The incidence of newly occurring hard coronary heart disease events over the full 10-year period ranged from 1074 per 10,000 in East Finland to 26 per 10,000 in Crete, a 40-fold difference. When all coronary heart disease events were included, the range was from 2868 per 10,000 in East Finland to 210 per 10,000 in Crete, more than a 10-fold difference. The proportions of events classified as hard coronary heart disease were compared in regional groupings of these cohorts and varied rather little, from 36.6% to 54.1%. This observation lends credence to the range of incidence rates reported, whereas wide

Table 4–1 Ten-Year Incidence of Coronary Heart Disease (CHD) among Men Free of Cardiovascular Disease at Entry (Age-Standardized Rate per 10,000), Seven Countries Study, 1958–1964 to 1968–1974

Cohort	Total N	Hard CHD			Any CHD		
		N	Rate	SE	N	Rate	SE
Dalmatia	662	13	185	52	40	629	94
Slavonia	680	18	253	60	40	561	88
Tanushimaru	504	8	148	54	20	354	82
East Finland	728	71	1,074	115	201	2,868	168
West Finland	806	45	539	80	129	1,582	129
Crevalcore	956	43	450	67	105	1,080	100
Montegiorgio	708	22	353	69	64	966	111
Zutphen	845	45	513	76	91	1,066	106
Ushibuka	496	11	204	63	23	458	94
Crete	655	2	26	20	13	210	56
Corfu	525	17	337	79	37	686	110
Rome railroad	736	25	357	68	57	786	99
Velika Krsna	487	6	132	52	21	452	94
Zrenjanin	476	12	239	70	37	715	118
Belgrade	516	13	317	77	35	794	119
Total	9,780	351	369.9[a]	19.1	913	943.8[a]	29.6

Note: SE, standard error.

a. Mean of the cohort rates weighted by the number at risk in each cohort.

Source: Reprinted by permission of the publisher from *Seven Countries* by A Keys, Cambridge, Mass; Harvard University Press, Copyright © 1980 by the President and Fellows of Harvard College.

---

variation in the proportion of hard coronary heart disease might suggest a systematic difference, or bias, in the identification or classification of cases between populations. Analysis of the relation of baseline measures of factors thought to affect the risk of coronary events (eg, diet, blood lipids, blood pressure, smoking) to event rates was conducted at the population level. That is, for each of the 16 cohorts, an average value was estimated for each characteristic (eg, baseline blood cholesterol concentration) and linked with the event rate for that population. By regression analysis, the question of whether differences in average cholesterol concentration were related to differences in event rates was evaluated. With this approach, the contribution of these and other factors to population differences in event rates was assessed. Results of these analyses are addressed in subsequent

chapters where the respective factors are discussed.

More recent data are provided by the WHO MONICA Project.[21] Tables 4–2 and 4–3 list study populations alphabetically by country and center and give age-standardized annual event rates for coronary heart disease for men and women, respectively. Events were enumerated for this tabulation in four classifications that included different combinations of the following subsets: F1 = definite fatal event; F2 = possible fatal event; F9 = unclassifiable fatal event; NF1 = definite nonfatal event; and NF2 = possible nonfatal event; 1st event = those cases meeting definition 1 for which there was a known negative history of prior myocardial infarction. The final column indicates the percentage of participants for whom history of myocardial infarction was unknown. Event rates were de-

Table 4–2 Age-Standardized Annual Event Rates per 100,000 Population, 28-Day Case-Fatality, and Confidence Intervals for Different Definitions of Events in Men Age 35 to 64

Population	Definition 1: F1+F2+F9+NF1 Event Rate, 95% CI	Case-Fatality, 95% CI	Definition 2: F1+F2+NF1 Event Rate, 95% CI	Case-Fatality, 95% CI	Definition 3: F1+F2+F9+NF1+NF2 Event Rate, 95% CI	Case-Fatality, 95% CI	1st Event[†]: Definition 1 No Previous MI Event Rate	Case-Fatality	Fatal Where History of MI Not Known, %
AUS-NEW	561 ± 32	43 ± 3	504 ± 31	36 ± 3	879 ± 41	28 ± 2	363	37	24
AUS-PER	422 ± 19	38 ± 2	405 ± 18	36 ± 2	474 ± 20	34 ± 2	259	25	28
BEL-CHA	514 ± 42	55 ± 4	369 ± 35	38 ± 4	549 ± 43	52 ± 4	270	32	49
BEL-GHE	360 ± 33	48 ± 4	295 ± 30	36 ± 5	393 ± 34	44 ± 4	243	34	29
BEL-LUX	433 ± 48	44 ± 5	352 ± 43	31 ± 6	526 ± 53	36 ± 5	317	35	18
CAN-HAL	605 ± 43	38 ± 3	519 ± 40	27 ± 3	809 ± 50	28 ± 3	175	14	66
CHN-BEI	76 ± 9	53 ± 6	73 ± 8	51 ± 6	80 ± 9	50 ± 5	58	51	3
CZE-CZE	495 ± 24	48 ± 2	470 ± 24	45 ± 2	553 ± 26	44 ± 2	288	32	36
DEN-GLO	529 ± 34	52 ± 3	468 ± 32	45 ± 3	591 ± 35	46 ± 3	328	42	14
FIN-KUO	824 ± 49	44 ± 3	819 ± 49	43 ± 3	1648 ± 69	22 ± 12	498	39	0
FIN-NKA	915 ± 62	48 ± 3	907 ± 62	47 ± 3	1300 ± 74	34 ± 3	586	44	1
FIN-TUL	593 ± 47	51 ± 4	592 ± 47	51 ± 4	844 ± 56	36 ± 3	387	48	2
FRA-LIL	314 ± 16	58 ± 3	227 ± 14	41 ± 3	407 ± 18	45 ± 2	197	46	35
FRA-STR	336 ± 17	51 ± 3	262 ± 15	37 ± 3	434 ± 20	40 ± 2	234	44	19
FRA-TOU	240 ± 15	45 ± 3	202 ± 13	34 ± 3	335 ± 17	33 ± 2	183	38	12
GER-AUR	295 ± 27	54 ± 5	249 ± 25	45 ± 5	343 ± 29	46 ± 4	208	45	12
GER-AUU	353 ± 32	52 ± 4	294 ± 29	42 ± 5	401 ± 34	46 ± 4	232	40	22
GER-BRE	404 ± 23	50 ± 3	342 ± 21	41 ± 3	429 ± 24	47 ± 3	238	31	31
GER-EGE	349 ± 21	47 ± 3	339 ± 21	45 ± 3	459 ± 24	36 ± 2	241	36	16
GER-RHN	326 ± 20	43 ± 3	279 ± 18	34 ± 3	359 ± 20	40 ± 3	209	32	33
ICE-ICE	540 ± 45	37 ± 4	530 ± 45	35 ± 4	590 ± 47	33 ± 4	395	33	4
ITA-BRI	305 ± 16	42 ± 3	277 ± 15	36 ± 3	421 ± 19	30 ± 2	219	36	5
ITA-FRI	270 ± 14	49 ± 2	246 ± 13	44 ± 3	385 ± 16	34 ± 2	197	43	11
LTU-KAU	492 ± 34	54 ± 3	467 ± 33	52 ± 4	600 ± 37	44 ± 3	311	45	17
NEZ-AUC	466 ± 22	49 ± 2	458 ± 21	48 ± 2	672 ± 26	34 ± 2	325	44	2
POL-TAR	465 ± 26	81 ± 2	311 ± 21	72 ± 3	845 ± 35	47 ± 2	45	12	93
POL-WAR	583 ± 30	60 ± 3	440 ± 26	48 ± 3	801 ± 35	45 ± 2	204	24	66
RUS-MOC	500 ± 42	56 ± 4	466 ± 40	53 ± 4	638 ± 47	43 ± 4	251	37	38
RUS-MOI	464 ± 26	57 ± 3	432 ± 25	54 ± 3	605 ± 30	44 ± 2	227	38	36
SPA-CAT	187 ± 12	41 ± 3	150 ± 10	27 ± 3	259 ± 14	30 ± 2	122	26	44
SWE-GOT	406 ± 26	42 ± 3	406 ± 26	42 ± 3	470 ± 28	36 ± 3	319	42	0
SWE-NSW	594 ± 35	40 ± 3	588 ± 34	40 ± 3	762 ± 39	32 ± 2	348	27	11
SWI-TIC	321 ± 28	38 ± 4	279 ± 26	28 ± 4	486 ± 35	25 ± 3	173	9	38
SWI-VAF	253 ± 16	42 ± 3	212 ± 14	32 ± 3	325 ± 18	33 ± 3	129	11	38
UNK-BEL	781 ± 36	40 ± 2	754 ± 36	38 ± 2	887 ± 39	35 ± 2	522	35	5
UNK-GLA	823 ± 39	49 ± 2	794 ± 39	47 ± 2	1264 ± 49	33 ± 2	557	47	3
USA-STA	508 ± 40	50 ± 4	496 ± 39	49 ± 4	814 ± 50	32 ± 3	299	41	18
YUG-NOS	423 ± 33	54 ± 4	415 ± 33	54 ± 4	451 ± 34	51 ± 4	277	44	6
Male 1*	456	48	413	42	608	38	275	35	23
Male 2*	465	49	422	43	619	39	281	37	22

Note: MI = myocardial infarction. For key to MONICA abbreviations, see Appendix 4–A.

*Male 1 is the average of all populations. Male 2 excludes SWI-TIC and SWI-VAF for better comparison with female results (see Table 4–3).

[†]First-event and case-fatality rates are biased by percentage of fatal cases where previous history of MI is not known (shown in last column of table).

Source: Reprinted with permission from *Circulation*, Special Report, Vol 90, No 1, p 599, © 1994, American Heart Association.

Table 4–3 Age-Standardized Annual Event Rates per 100,000 Population, 28-Day Case-Fatality, and Confidence Intervals for Different Definitions of Events in Women Age 35 to 64

Population	Definition 1: F1+F2+F9+NF1		Definition 2: F1+F2+NF1		Definition 3: F1+F2+F9+NF1+NF2		1st Event[†]: Definition 1 No Previous MI		Fatal Where History of MI Not Known, %
	Event Rate, 95% CI	Case-Fatality, 95% CI	Event Rate, 95% CI	Case-Fatality, 95% CI	Event Rate, 95% CI	Case-Fatality, 95% CI	Event Rate	Case-Fatality	
AUS-NEW	188 ± 18	45 ± 5	154 ± 17	33 ± 5	334 ± 25	26 ± 3	127	35	30
AUS-PER	95 ± 9	46 ± 5	89 ± 9	42 ± 5	111 ± 10	40 ± 4	55	39	22
BEL-CHA	118 ± 18	65 ± 7	80 ± 15	48 ± 10	128 ± 19	60 ± 7	59	46	49
BEL-GHE	70 ± 13	56 ± 9	57 ± 12	45 ± 9	81 ± 15	46 ± 10	47	39	18
BEL-LUX	75 ± 19	44 ± 12	62 ± 17	31 ± 12	101 ± 22	34 ± 10	52	29	22
CAN-HAL	138 ± 20	31 ± 6	123 ± 19	23 ± 6	188 ± 23	23 ± 5	46	9	69
CHN-BEI	37 ± 6	69 ± 8	33 ± 6	65 ± 9	41 ± 7	62 ± 8	30	66	4
CZE-CZE	89 ± 10	51 ± 5	82 ± 9	47 ± 6	109 ± 11	42 ± 5	54	32	43
DEN-GLO	141 ± 17	57 ± 6	106 ± 15	43 ± 7	155 ± 18	52 ± 6	90	50	20
FIN-KUO	129 ± 18	33 ± 6	129 ± 18	33 ± 6	461 ± 34	9 ± 2	95	30	1
FIN-NKA	165 ± 25	44 ± 8	162 ± 25	43 ± 8	320 ± 35	25 ± 6	115	38	1
FIN-TUL	86 ± 16	52 ± 10	86 ± 16	52 ± 10	197 ± 24	23 ± 6	63	54	0
FRA-LIL	67 ± 7	68 ± 5	38 ± 5	44 ± 7	97 ± 8	47 ± 4	46	58	31
FRA-STR	77 ± 8	62 ± 5	53 ± 6	45 ± 6	109 ± 9	44 ± 4	58	59	17
FRA-TOU	37 ± 5	65 ± 7	24 ± 4	44 ± 9	62 ± 7	39 ± 6	30	62	15
GER-AUR	43 ± 10	66 ± 11	33 ± 9	57 ± 13	50 ± 11	57 ± 11	37	63	9
GER-AUU	70 ± 13	66 ± 9	49 ± 10	52 ± 12	77 ± 13	59 ± 9	51	61	20
GER-BRE	79 ± 9	54 ± 6	60 ± 8	40 ± 7	83 ± 9	52 ± 6	50	38	36
GER-EGE	68 ± 8	68 ± 6	64 ± 8	66 ± 6	98 ± 10	47 ± 5	51	63	18
GER-RHN	72 ± 9	50 ± 6	57 ± 8	37 ± 7	78 ± 9	46 ± 6	50	39	27
ICE-ICE	94 ± 19	34 ± 11	91 ± 19	33 ± 11	112 ± 21	29 ± 10	67	33	6
ITA-BRI	48 ± 6	60 ± 6	38 ± 5	49 ± 7	78 ± 8	36 ± 5	41	58	5
ITA-FRI	50 ± 6	50 ± 6	43 ± 5	41 ± 6	95 ± 8	27 ± 4	38	46	14
LTU-KAU	84 ± 12	51 ± 8	72 ± 11	43 ± 8	120 ± 14	35 ± 6	57	36	34
NEZ-AUC	128 ± 11	50 ± 4	124 ± 11	48 ± 4	210 ± 14	30 ± 3	90	46	3
POL-TAR	110 ± 12	91 ± 3	44 ± 7	76 ± 7	276 ± 19	38 ± 3	7	4	97
POL-WAR	145 ± 14	63 ± 5	106 ± 12	49 ± 6	272 ± 19	35 ± 3	60	33	60
RUS-MOC	109 ± 15	57 ± 8	98 ± 14	52 ± 8	161 ± 19	38 ± 6	61	42	34
RUS-MOI	98 ± 10	63 ± 6	89 ± 9	58 ± 6	144 ± 12	42 ± 5	48	52	27
SPA-CAT	30 ± 4	46 ± 8	25 ± 4	35 ± 8	47 ± 6	29 ± 5	21	34	32
SWE-GOT	91 ± 12	42 ± 7	91 ± 12	42 ± 7	110 ± 13	35 ± 6	73	41	0
SWE-NSW	124 ± 16	34 ± 6	123 ± 16	33 ± 6	204 ± 20	21 ± 4	87	26	7
UNK-BEL	197 ± 17	44 ± 4	183 ± 16	40 ± 4	236 ± 18	37 ± 4	145	39	4
UNK-GLA	256 ± 20	49 ± 4	241 ± 20	46 ± 4	456 ± 28	29 ± 3	187	49	4
USA-STA	139 ± 19	52 ± 7	129 ± 18	49 ± 7	255 ± 26	29 ± 5	83	41	23
YUG-NOS	81 ± 14	58 ± 8	79 ± 13	57 ± 8	89 ± 14	52 ± 8	61	56	1
Females*	101	54	87	46	160	38	65	43	22

Note: MI, myocardial infarction. For key to MONICA abbreviations, see Appendix 4–A.

*Female should be compared with Male 2, as Male 1 includes more populations (see Table 4–2).

[†]First-event and case-fatality rates are biased by percentage of fatal cases where previous history of MI is not known (shown in last column of table).

Source: Reprinted with permission from *Circulation*, Special Report, Vol 90, No 1, p 599, © 1994, American Heart Association.

pendent, of course, on the inclusiveness of the definition. They ranged, for example, in men in Australia-Newcastle from a minimum value of 363/100,000 for true incidence (no previous myocardial infarction) to a maximum value of 879/100,000 for the combination of all definite and possible events, both fatal and nonfatal, plus unclassifiable deaths, without consideration of previous history of myocardial infarction. The last column indicates the frequency with which this history was unknown among fatal cases in each study population, a limiting factor in the reliability of the first-event definition. This striking demonstration of the dependence of rates on their definition underscores the need for explicit criteria when comparisons are made across studies.

Population differences are apparent. For example, in reference to definition 1, rates range for men from 915/100,000 in Finland-North Karelia to 76/100,000 in China-Beijing, and for women from 256/100,000 in United Kingdom-Glasgow to 30/100,000 in Spain-Catalonia. Summary rates are given for comparison of overall male and female rates by each definition; because two centers (Switzerland-Ticino and Switzerland-Vaud/Fribourg) did not include women, overall comparisons by reference to "Male 2" and "Female" at the foot of the tables are most appropriate. Event rates were four to five times as great among men as among women.

Case-Fatality

On a national basis, case-fatality for acute myocardial infarction in the United States is unknown, although some local data are available. Again, the MONICA experience provides a unique source of information on this aspect of coronary heart disease in many populations, as seen in Tables 4–2 and 4–3.[21] Case-fatality differs in accordance with definitions, as do event rates, for example, from 28% to 43% among men in Australia-Newcastle. The effects of inclusion or exclusion of categories of fatal or nonfatal events under different definitions are

obvious. Under definition 1, overall case-fatality was 48%–49% for men and 54% for women, with most centers reporting 40%–55% case-fatality for men and 45%–70% for women. Overall, regardless of definition, case fatality was about 1.1 times as great for women as for men.

The limitation of US data on incidence and case fatality of coronary heart disease to very few localities is a continuing problem, despite the 1979 recommendation of the Epidemiology Working Group of the National Heart, Lung and Blood Institute to establish community surveillance in a large network of centers throughout the country.[29] Nevertheless, data such as those from the Minnesota Heart Survey are valuable indicators for the local population and may have broader generality.[30] Even within the relatively brief period from 1985 to 1990, a decline in coronary heart disease mortality of 25% was observed, for both men and women, with evidence for both declining incidence and reduced case-fatality as contributing explanations. Supporting this interpretation was the observation, shown in Figure 4–7, that mortality decreased both in and out of hospital. In this context, in-hospital deaths excluded those occurring in the emergency department and those cases dead on arrival at the hospital. Thus the two categories of location distinguish crudely between cases with and without potential for receipt of hospital treatment. A decrease in out-of-hospital death tends to be interpreted as reflecting prevention, or reduced risk, of acute coronary events, while decreased in-hospital mortality reflects treatment, although this distinction is blurred by more frequent delivery of emergency care by mobile treatment units outside the hospital and by the probable effect of long-term preventive measures in reducing the risk of complications and death when acute coronary events do occur.

Prevalence

Survivors beyond 28 days from onset of an acute coronary event constitute the known non-

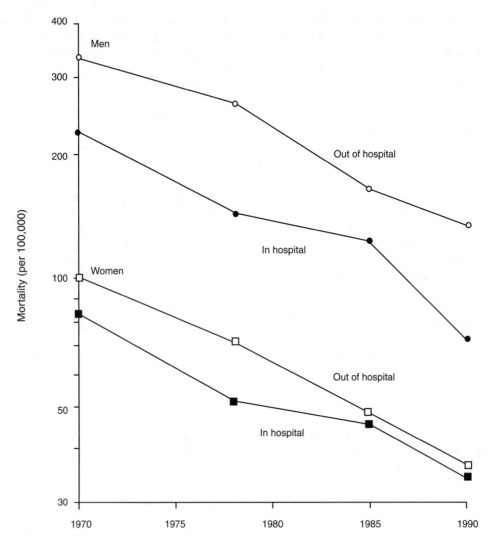

Figure 4–7 Coronary Heart Disease Mortality (among Those Aged 30–74 Years) by Location of Death, Twin Cities Area, 1970–1990. Mortality rates (shown on a logarithmic scale) have been adjusted by the direct method to the age distribution of the total US population in 1980. Deaths in the emergency room and on arrival at the hospital are included as out-of-hospital deaths. *Source*: Reprinted with permission from *The New England Journal of Medicine*, Vol 334, p 886, © 1986, The Massachusetts Medical Society.

fatal cases. Survivors together with persons with silent infarction (which is detectable only through screening for case detection by history or electrocardiography, as conducted in surveys of the general population) constitute the population alive with evidence of previous myocardial infarction. As a proportion of the total US population, they were estimated each year from 1991 to 1994 at approximately 2.5%, based on some 6 million cases living each year (Table 4–4) (based on *Heart and Stroke Facts/Statistical Supplement*, American Heart Association, Dallas, 1990, 1991, 1992, and 1993). In 1995–1996, the estimated prevalence of coronary

Table 4–4 Cases of Coronary Heart Disease in the US Population, 1991–1996

Year	Count	Population (Millions)	Prevalence (%)
1991	6,080,000	246	2.47
1992	6,160,000	248	2.48
1993	6,230,000	250	2.49
1994	6,300,000	252	2.50
1995	11,200,000	255	4.39
1996	13,490,000	258	5.23

Source: Data from *Heart and Stroke Facts/Statistical Supplement*, 1990–1995, American Heart Association, Dallas, Texas.

heart disease in the United States doubled due to the addition of persons with a positive history of angina pectoris, or chest pain indicative of ischemic heart disease (based on *Heart and Stroke Facts/Statistical Supplement*, American Heart Association, Dallas, 1994 and 1995). Currently it is estimated that more than 13 million Americans are affected.

The practicality of conducting field surveys to estimate the prevalence of coronary heart disease has led to their use in many populations since the 1950s. These surveys have often been altogether independent investigations with limited or no formal standardization, especially in circumstances of scant resources, as in many developing countries. One contrasting illustration of the application of standardized methods for such surveys is given in Table 4–5, which presents the electrocardiographic findings in surveys primarily of Pacific and Indian Ocean populations.[31] When classified according to the specific electrocardiographic findings (Q-wave codes 1.1–1.2) by Minnesota code, "probable coronary heart disease" was found in 0%–5.7% of men aged 35–59 years and in 0%–2.8% of women; "possible coronary heart disease" was several times more common in most populations for both sexes but especially for women, reflecting in part the lesser specificity of the less-stringent criterion for this classification. Taking both probable and possible coronary heart disease into account, the combined prevalence was estimated to range from 1.5% to

17.3% for men and from 4.1% to 34.1% for women. These estimates do not include self-reported angina pectoris, unlike the most recent data for the United States cited previously.

RISKS IN INDIVIDUALS

Variation in individual risks of coronary heart disease events within a population indicates the operation of factors at the individual level, within the context of determinants of the general population rate. A focus on individuals or groups (with characteristics of special interest), in relation to other members of the same population is the approach taken in several large cohort studies since the early 1950s. Though in design each such study is analogous to study of any one cohort in the Seven Countries Study, the objective was fundamentally different, that is, not to derive estimates of event rates and relevant exposures for comparison between whole cohorts but to compare individual subjects as the units of observation and analysis. The conceptualization and implementation of the Framingham Study in the United States at mid-century are addressed in detail by Dawber and coworkers.[14] Similar investigations in other community or employment settings were undertaken at about the same time in the United States. Although the Framingham Study has continued longest and is widely recognized on the basis of its exceptionally extensive collection and reporting of data, other studies of its

Table 4–5 Prevalence of Probable and Possible Coronary Heart Disease (CHD) in Developing Countries in Men and Women Aged 35 to 59 Years, by Ethnic Group, 1978–1987

Population Groups	Men			Women		
	Q[a]	ST-T[b]	Q and ST-T Together	Q	ST-T	Q and ST-T Together
Chinese						
Beijing—Chinese	0	1.5	1.5 (0–3.8)	0.2	4.1	3.6 (0.8–6.5)
Mauritius—Chinese	2.5	15.0	16.6 (10.6–22.6)	0	27.5	27.2 (21.2–33.2)
Polynesian						
Cook Islands—Rarotonga	3.5	3.1	6.3 (2.2–10.3)	0.7	18.2	19.3 (15.3–23.1)
Niue	0.9	2.6	3.3 (0–7.6)	0.7	9.9	10.8 (6.9–14.7)
Western Samoa	1.1	2.2	2.9 (0–6.9)	0.3	12.0	11.9 (8.3–15.5)
Asian Indian						
Fiji	3.5	13.7	17.3 (13.2–21.4)	0.9	23.6	24.4 (20.7–28.2)
Mauritius—Hindu	1.3	11.1	12.8 (10.2–15.3)	0.6	27.6	28.7 (26.1–31.2)
Mauritius—Muslim	1.8	8.4	10.9 (5.8–15.9)	0.6	28.5	29.6 (24.7–34.5)
Melanesian/Polynesian						
Fiji (Lakeba)	0	1.0	0.8 (0–7.2)	0	12.1	11.9 (5.3–18.4)
New Caledonia (Loyalty)	5.7	5.7	9.8 (0–20.9)	0	15.5	14.4 (5.8–23.0)
New Caledonia (areas of Touho, Oundjo, Noumea, and Wallis Island)	2.6	5.1	8.0 (4.7–11.4)	2.8	11.4	14.8 (11.1–18.4)
Melanesian—Fiji	2.5	6.4	8.7 (4.8–12.6)	1.0	17.5	18.7 (14.9–22.4)
Micronesian						
Kiribati	0	6.2	6.7 (4.0–9.3)	0.2	25.6	26.3 (23.6–28.9)
Nauru	1.8	5.9	7.3 (2.9–11.7)	0.8	5.1	5.5 (1.3–9.5)
Creole—Mauritius	1.4	14.5	15.5 (11.7–19.3)	0.5	34.1	34.3 (30.9–37.6)

a. Q: Probable CHD; Minnesota code 1.1, 1.2.

b. ST-T: Possible CHD; Minnesota code 1.3, 4.1, 5.1, 5.3, and 7.1.1.

Source: Reprinted by permission from *Journal of Clinical Epidemiology*, Vol 47, p 602. Copyright 1994 by Elsevier Science, Inc.

type have also contributed importantly to current knowledge of the epidemiology of coronary heart disease.

For example, it became apparent in the course of these US studies that more definitive analysis of individual differences in risks of coronary heart disease might be achieved by combining data from those studies most alike in design and examination methods. Under the aegis of the Committee on Epidemiological Studies (now the Scientific Council on Epidemiology and Prevention) of the American Heart Association, and its Subcommittee on Criteria and Methods, discussions began in 1961 that culminated in formation of the US National Cooperative Pooling Project. With support from the American Heart Association and both the Heart Disease Control Program and the (then) National Heart Institute of the US Public Health Service, this project was the major source of data for research planning and study design in the area of cardiovascular disease epidemiology and prevention for many years subsequent to its initiation in 1964. In 1978 its Final Report was published as a comprehensive presentation of the pooled analyses relating characteristics of

8422 men aged 40–64 years who were free of coronary heart disease at entry to the study to the subsequent occurrence of an initial coronary heart disease event.[13] The five participating studies (Albany Civil Servants, Chicago Gas Company, Chicago Western Electric Company, Framingham, and Tecumseh) provided information based on 72,011 person-years of experience and the occurrence of 658 first major coronary events prior to age 65.

Table 4–6 is taken from the Final Report and presents the results of multivariate analysis in which diastolic blood pressure, serum cholesterol concentration, smoking status, and age, all at the initial examination, were taken into account. The strategy of this analysis was to assess the contribution of each of these charac-

teristics to the probability of occurrence of a first major coronary event during the 8.6 years of observation for each man. The multivariate equation derived from the pooled experience yielded significant coefficients for all four factors. When the distribution of "expected risk" based on these results was categorized into quintile groups (each comprising one-fifth of the pooled study population), the expected and observed numbers of events and event rates could be examined in relation to the gradation of risk based on these four characteristics. The incidence of first major coronary events was 8.7 times as great in quintile V as in quintile I, and more than 40% of all events occurred in the group of men whose risk made up the highest 20% of the pooled population. This indicated

Table 4–6 Factors Related to the Incidence of Coronary Heart Disease, the US National Pooling Project, 1978

Parameters	Age	Diastolic Blood Pressure	Serum Cholesterol	Smoking
α		−10.328022		
β	0.068467*	0.030365*	0.006138*	0.304628*
SE β	0.008315	0.003584	0.000887	0.038270
t	6.234	8.473	6.920	10.050
Standard β	0.349599	0.361013	0.293662	0.428591

No. of Men: 6875

Quintile of Expected Risk	Risk/1,000 Men/ 8.6 Year	No. of Events		Rate/1,000 Men/8.6 Year	
		Expected	Observed	Expected	Observed
All		623.1	621	90.6	90.3
I	≤41.7	41.3	29	30.0	21.1
II	41.7–62.0	71.2	71	51.8	51.6
III	62.0–87.3	101.1	106	73.5	77.1
IV	87.3–129.0	145.5	164	105.8	119.3
V	≥129.0	264.0	251	192.0	182.5
Ratio: V/I		6.4	8.7	6.4	8.7
% of events in V		42.4	40.4		
% of events in VI +V		65.7	66.8		
Difference: V – I		222.7	222	162.0	161.4

*P≤.01

Source: Reprinted with permission from *Journal of Chronic Diseases*, Final Report of the Pooling Project, p 253, © 1978 Elsevier Science, Inc.

the strength of the predictive relation between these four factors and the individual risks of coronary heart disease. Notably, if the minimum risk in the pooled population were given by that of quintile I, the incidence of coronary heart disease was more than two times as great for the second quintile of risk (rate 51.6 versus 21.1), more than three times as great for the third quintile (rate 77.1 versus 21.1), nearly six times as great (119.3 versus 21.1) for the fourth quintile, and nearly nine times as great (182.5 versus 21.1) for the fifth quintile. These results for quintiles II–IV indicate that, within the population represented by these five pooled cohorts of middle-aged, predominantly White men in the United States during the 1950s and 1960s, substantial excess risk occurred well below the highest-risk category. This indicates further that preventive measures limited to the highest-risk group could not effectively address all of the increased risk in the population. This principle

is reinforced by data from other analyses and studies of other populations, but it was clearly demonstrated 20 years ago in this landmark report of the Pooling Project.

An example of the data available more recently to estimate the individual or relative risks of coronary events for individuals within a population is that of the exceptionally large cohort of men, also middle-aged Americans, who underwent risk factor screening in the mid-1970s as potential candidates for entry to the Multiple Risk Factor Intervention Trial (MRFIT).[32] Represented in Table 4–7 are the 342,815 men who were free of known prior heart attack or diabetes at the screening examination, which included measurements of blood pressure and serum cholesterol concentration and a questionnaire history of cigarette smoking. Death due to coronary heart disease over an average follow-up period of 11.6 years was ascertained through vital statistics sources.

Table 4–7 Factors Related to the Incidence of Coronary Heart Disease among Men Screened as Candidates for the Multiple Risk Factor Intervention Trial, 1992

Serum Total Cholesterol (mg/dl)	Systolic Pressure (mm Hg)					
	<118	118–124	125–131	132–141	142+	Q5/Q1
Nonsmokers						
<182	3.09	3.72	5.13	5.35	13.00	4.42
182–202	4.39	5.79	8.35	7.66	15.80	3.60
203–220	5.20	6.08	8.56	10.72	17.75	3.41
221–244	6.34	9.37	8.66	12.21	22.69	3.58
245+	12.36	12.68	16.31	20.68	33.40	2.70
Q5/Q1	4.00	3.41	3.18	3.87	2.45	—
Smokers						
<182	10.37	10.69	13.21	13.99	21.04	2.61
182–202	10.03	11.76	19.05	20.67	33.69	3.36
203–220	14.90	16.09	21.07	28.87	42.91	2.88
221–244	19.83	22.69	23.61	31.98	55.50	2.80
245+	25.24	30.50	35.26	41.47	62.11	2.46
Q5/Q1	2.43	2.85	2.67	2.96	2.30	—

Source: Reprinted from J Stamler, *Coronary Heart Disease Epidemiology from Aetiology to Public Health*, p 49, © 1992, by permission of Oxford University Press.

Because of the very large numbers of observations, it was possible to cross-classify the population according to quintile groups of systolic blood pressure (from <118 to 142+ mm Hg), quintile groups of serum cholesterol concentration (<182 to 245+ mg/dl), and two smoking categories (nonsmokers versus smokers). For each of the resulting 50 groups, the death rate from coronary heart disease is presented. This follow-up experience through the 1980s indicates the same general relation of risk to these factors as found in the Pooling Project and other reports. In addition it provides data indicating a much greater relative risk between categories than is possible in studies that are on the order of one-100th the size of this one: The highest risk, that of smokers in the top quintile of both systolic blood pressure and serum cholesterol concentration (62.11 deaths per 10,000 person-years) is more than 20 times that of the lowest-risk stratum, the nonsmokers in the lowest quintile groups of both systolic blood pressure and serum cholesterol concentration. The dependence of measures of relative risk, in small studies, on the limits of cross-classification is readily apparent: Demonstration of the continuous gradient of increasing risk beginning from the lowest levels of these characteristics is also important in considering preventive strategies. In this connection it is noteworthy that even among nonsmokers in the lowest quintile for systolic blood pressure, a marked gradient of increased risk is observed with increased cholesterol concentration; the same is true for those in the lowest quintile for cholesterol as systolic pressure increases. And in the lowest quintile class for both of these factors, smoking alone increases the risk more than threefold, that is, from 3.09 to 10.37 per 10,000 person-years.

IMPLICATIONS FOR PREVENTION AND TREATMENT: INDIVIDUALS AND POPULATIONS

Prevention of coronary heart disease is the topic of Part III. It is helpful here to indicate the broad outlines of current approaches. These were first presented by Rose in 1980 and continue to contribute importantly to concepts of cardiovascular disease prevention.[33] Two approaches were proposed, the high-risk strategy and the population strategy (originally termed the "mass strategy"). The aim of both strategies is to prevent the first occurrence of a coronary event, because these are so often fatal or disabling. The purpose of the high-risk strategy is to reduce the individual risks of persons identified as most likely to experience an event, in terms, for example, of blood cholesterol concentration, blood pressure, or smoking status. The population strategy, in contrast, is intended to reduce risk by measures directed not selectively to the individuals at highest risk but to the whole population. The two approaches are considered complementary, as each may confer benefit not attainable through the other alone. The potential effectiveness of each of the strategies and their adequacy to address the full potential for prevention depend on the epidemiology of factors accounting for the population rate and individual risks. These are examined in Chapters 7–20.

CURRENT ISSUES

Among the many important issues in the epidemiology and prevention of coronary heart disease, three issues are most central to its occurrence as a global public health problem from the perspectives of theory, practice, and research:

1. Can current and future changes in population rates of coronary heart disease occurrence—whether measured by mortality, incidence and case-fatality, prevalence of clinical or subclinical disease, or extent of coronary atherosclerosis at autopsy of young decedents—be predicted? An affirmative answer would imply that the nature and effects of determinants of coronary heart disease rates at the population level are sufficiently understood to permit

confident forecasts, subject to confirmation by planned observation.

2. Can the upward trends and existing population differentials in coronary heart disease occurrence be eliminated so that all populations share the most favorable disease experience? Can epidemic occurrence of coronary heart disease be prevented altogether? These are challenges for public health programs to apply current knowledge and to incorporate new insights as further experience is gained.

3. Can coronary heart disease surveillance be maintained and expanded to monitor future changes in disease rates effec-

tively? The WHO MONICA Project has established a substantial network of investigators and trained staff under a protocol that should be implemented—even if only selected components are feasible—in far more diverse settings in many countries, including the United States, and extending to regions of special concern, such as Eastern Europe and developing countries. This strategy of surveillance could, in some respects, offset limitations of resources for national death registration in areas where this remains impractical and could add greatly to the strength of the global effort to address this epidemic.

REFERENCES

1. Hutter AM. IX. Ischemic heart disease: angina pectoris. In: Rubenstein E, Federman DD, eds. *Scientific American Medicine*. New York: Scientific American Inc.; 1995:1–19.

2. Fuster V, Fallon JT, Nemerson Y. Coronary thrombosis. *Lancet*. 1996;348:S7–S10.

3. Antman EM, Braunwald E. Acute myocardial infarction. In: Braunwald E, ed. *Heart Disease. A Textbook of Cardiovascular Medicine*. 5th ed. Philadelphia, Pa: WB Saunders Co; 1997; 1184–1288.

4. Myerburg RJ, Castellanos A. Cardiac arrest and sudden death. In: Braunwald E, ed. *Heart Disease: A Textbook of Cardiovascular Medicine*. 5th ed. Philadelphia, Pa: WB Saunders Co; 1997; 742–779.

5. Willich SN, Muller JE. *Triggering of Acute Coronary Syndromes: Implications for Prevention*. Dutrecht, the Netherlands: Kluwer Academic Publishers; 1996.

6. Report of a WHO Scientific Group. *Sudden Cardiac Death*. Geneva, Switzerland: World Health Organization; 1985. Technical Report Series 726.

7. Liebowitz JO. *The History of Coronary Heart Disease*. Berkeley, Calif: University of California Press; 1970.

8. Frye WB. *William Osler's Collected Papers on the Cardiovascular System*. Birmingham, Ala: The Classics of Cardiology Library; 1985.

9. Keys A. From Naples to Seven Countries—a sentimental journey. *Prog Biochem Pharmacol*. 1983; 19:1–30.

10. Keys, A. *Seven Countries: A Multivariate Analysis of Death and Coronary Heart Disease*. Cambridge, Mass: Harvard University Press; 1980.

11. Gordon T. Mortality experience among the Japanese in the United States, Hawaii, and Japan. *Public Health Rep*. 1957;72:543–553.

12. Marmot M, Syme SL, Kagan A, Kato H, et al. Epidemiologic studies of coronary heart disease and stroke in Japanese men living in Japan, Hawaii and California: prevalence of coronary and hypertensive heart disease and associated risk factors. *Am J Epidemiol*. 1975; 102:514–525.

13. Pooling Project Research Group. Relationship of blood pressure, serum cholesterol, smoking habit, relative weight and ECG abnormalities to incidence of major coronary events: Final Report of the Pooling Project. *J Chronic Dis*. 1978;31:201–306.

14. Dawber TR, Meadors GF, Moore FE Jr. Epidemiological approaches to heart disease: the Framingham Study. *Am J Public Health*. 1951;41:279–286.

15. Blackburn H. *On the Trail of Heart Attacks in Seven Countries*. Middleborough, Ma: The Country Press, Inc; 1995.

16. Kromhout D, Menotti A, Blackburn H. *The Seven Countries Study: A Scientific Adventure in Cardiovascular Disease Epidemiology*. Utrecht, the Netherlands: Brouwer Offset bv; 1993.

17. Toshima H, Koga Y, Blackburn H, eds. Keys A, honorary ed. *Lessons for Science from the Seven Countries Study*. Tokyo, Japan: Springer; 1994.

18. Rose GA, Blackburn H. *Cardiovascular Survey Methods*. Geneva, Switzerland: World Health Organization; 1968.

19. Gillum RF, Fortmann SP, Prineas RJ, Kottke TE. International diagnostic criteria for acute myocardial infarction and stroke. *Am Heart J*. 1984;108:150–158.

20. World Health Organization MONICA Project Principal Investigators. The World Health Organization MONICA Project (Monitoring Trends and Determinants in Cardiovascular Disease): a major international collaboration. *J Clin Epidemiol*. 1988;41:105–114.

21. Tunstall-Pedoe H, Kuulasmaa K, Amouyel P, Arveiler D, et al. Myocardial infarction and coronary deaths in the World Health Organization MONICA Project. *Circ*. 1994;90:583–612.

22. World Health Organization. *International Statistical Classification of Diseases and Related Health Problems: Tenth Revision*. Geneva, Switzerland: World Health Organization; 1992; 1.

23. *1997 Heart and Stroke Statistical Update*. Dallas, Tex: American Heart Association; 1996.

24. Borhani NO, Hechter HH. Recent changes in CVR disease mortality in California. *Pub Health Rep*. 1964; 79:147–160.

25. Havlik RJ, Feinleib M, eds. *Proceedings of the Conference on the Decline in Coronary Heart Disease Mortality*. Bethesda, Md: National Heart, Lung and Blood Institute, National Institutes of Health; 1978. NIH publication 79-1610.

26. Stallones, RA. The rise and fall of ischemic heart disease. *Scientific American*. 1980; 243:53–59.

27. Task Force on Research in Epidemiology and Prevention of Cardiovascular Diseases. *Report of the Task Force on Research in Epidemiology and Prevention of Cardiovascular Diseases*. Bethesda, Md: National Heart, Lung and Blood Institute, National Institutes of Health; 1994.

28. Thom TJ, Epstein FH, Feldman JJ, Leaverton PE, et al. *Total Mortality and Mortality from Heart Disease, Cancer and Stroke from 1950 to 1987 in 27 Countries: Highlights of Trends and Their Interrelationships among Causes of Death*. Bethesda, Md: National Heart, Lung and Blood Institute, National Institutes of Health: September 1992. NIH publication 92-3088.

29. Working Group on Heart Disease Epidemiology. *Report of the National Heart, Lung and Blood Institute Working Group on Heart Disease Epidemiology*. Bethesda, Md: US Dept of Health, Education and Welfare, Public Health Service, National Institutes of Health: 1979. NIH publication 79-1667.

30. McGovern PG, Pankow JS, Shahar E, Doliszny KM, et al. Minnesota Heart Survey Investigators. Recent trends in acute coronary heart disease. *N Engl J Med*. 1996;334:884–890.

31. Li N, Tuomilehto J, Dowse G, Virtala E, et al. Prevalence of coronary heart disease indicated by electrocardiogram abnormalities and risk factors in developing countries. *J Clin Epidemiol*. 1994;47:599–611.

32. Stamler J. Established major coronary risk factors. In: Marmot M, Elliott P, eds. *Coronary Heart Disease Epidemiology: From Aetiology to Public Health*. Oxford, England: Oxford University Press: 1992; 35–66.

33. Rose GA. Strategy of prevention: lessons from cardiovascular disease. *Brit Med J*. 1981;282:1847–1851.

Key to Population Abbreviations Used by the WHO MONICA Project

Population Abbreviation	Country	Population	Population Abbreviation	Country	Population
AUS-NEW	Australia	Newcastle	GER-AUU		Augsburg
AUS-PER		Perth			Urban
BEL-CHA	Belgium	Charleroi	GER-BRE		Bremen
BEL-GHE		Ghent	GER-EGE		East Germany[b]
BEL-LUX		Luxembourg	GER-RHN		Rhein-Neckar Region[c]
CAN-HAL	Canada	Halifax County	HUN-BUD	Hungary	Budapest
			HUN-PEC		Pecs
CHN-BEI	China	Beijing	ICE-ICE	Iceland	Iceland
CZE-CZE	Czech Republic	Czech Republic[a]	ITA-BRI	Italy	Area Brianza
			ITA-FRI		Friuli
DEN-GLO	Denmark	Glostrup	LTU-KAU	Lithuania	Kaunas
FIN-KUO	Finland	Kuopio Province	NEZ-AUC	New Zeland	Auckland
FIN-NKA		North Karelia	POL-TAR	Poland	Tarnobrzeg Volvodship
			POL-WAR		Warsaw
FIN-TUL		Turku/Loimaa	RUS-MOC	Russia	Moscow Control
FRA-LIL	France	Lille			
FRA-STR		Strasbourg	RUS-MOI		Moscow Intervention
FRA-TOU		Toulouse	RUS-NOC		Novosibirsk Control
GER-AUR	Germany	Augsburg Rural			
			RUS-NOI		Novosibirsk Intervention

Population Abbreviation	Country	Population	Population Abbreviation	Country	Population
SPA-CAT	Spain	Catalonia	UNK-BEL	UK	Belfast
SWE-GOT	Sweden	Gothenburg	UNK-GLA		Glasgow
SWE-NSW		Northern Sweden	USA-STA	USA	Stanford
SWI-TIC	Switzerland	Ticino	YUG-NOS	Yugoslavia	Novi-Sad
SWI-VAF		Vaud/Fribourg			

a. Disagreement between local and national authorities on numbers of coronary deaths.
b. Data for this center were incomplete as of 1994.
c. This register no longer exists. Data queries were answered up to January 1992.

Source: Reprinted with permission from *Circulation*, Special Report, Vol 90, No 1, p 599, © 1994, American Heart Association.

CHAPTER 5

Stroke

SUMMARY

Stroke, or cerebrovascular accident (CVA)—also now termed "brain attack" by analogy to "heart attack"—is a second major class of "end-organ" outcomes of atherosclerotic and hypertensive disease. Just as the heart is damaged by disturbance of flow in the coronary circulation, the brain is damaged by disturbance of flow in the cerebral circulation. From brief, transient episodes to permanent brain dysfunction and disability or death, stroke has a wide range of clinical expressions and constitutes a large proportion of overall cardiovascular morbidity and mortality in many populations. In some, stroke predominates over coronary heart disease in its frequency. In the United States, it is about one-fourth to one-third as common as coronary disease in both death rate and prevalence of survivors. Stroke mortality ranges widely among different populations and has been observed to change markedly over a few decades, decreasing in most countries in which trends can be described. The role of environmental factors is implicit in this time-place variation and was recorded well in advance of any specific large-scale interventions, which have been introduced only in the most recent decades. Although particular factors contribute differently to different types of stroke, the most prominent potentially controllable factor common to all is high blood pressure. Population differences in the effectiveness of public health interventions for high blood pressure control contribute to but cannot wholly explain population differences in trends of stroke death rates. In the United States, racial differences in stroke deaths persist, with long-recognized excesses in Blacks. In addition, there are indications that the decades-long decline in stroke deaths has stalled or perhaps ended. Together, these considerations pose public health challenges for the United States that are shared with many other countries. There is a need for broad international collaboration in meeting this challenge if the greatest potential impact of stroke prevention is to be achieved for many diverse populations.

CLINICAL COURSE OF THE INDIVIDUAL CASE

The hallmark of a typical stroke is its abrupt onset, with sudden and dramatic loss of consciousness and motor and sensory function on one side of the body. These are the chief clinical manifestations of acute interruption of arterial blood supply to a focal area of the brain. The interruption is due either to hemorrhage or to obstruction of a major artery by thrombosis (formation of a blood clot locally) or embolism (lodging of a clot formed elsewhere, such as in the left side of the heart or in the carotid arteries of the neck). Figures 5–1 and 5–2 illustrate the

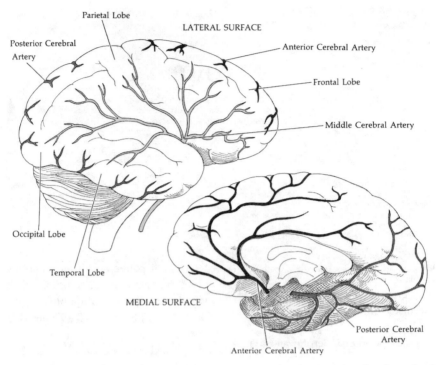

Figure 5–1 A Schematic View of the Posterior, Middle, and Anterior Cerebral Arteries, from the Outer (Lateral) and Inner (Medial) Aspects of the Right Hemisphere of the Brain. The middle cerebral artery (black), the posterior cerebral artery (light gray), and the anterior cerebral artery (dark gray) supply blood to the cerebral hemispheres. *Source*: Albers GP, Cutler RWP, "Cerebrovascular Diseases" from *Scientific American Medicine*, Dale DC, Ferderman DD, Eds. Copyright 1994. Scientific American, Inc. All rights reserved.

anatomical relations of the main intracranial arteries to the cerebral hemispheres[1] and the time course and potential outcomes of the typical acute cerebrovascular event.

Stroke occurs most often against a background of advanced atherosclerotic lesions in the cerebral arteries or long-established high blood pressure. Although it is plausible that precipitating factors may trigger plaque disruption and its consequences just as in the coronary arteries (see Chapter 4), this process has received less attention in connection with stroke. Whether due to occlusion or hemorrhage, suddenness of onset is a defining characteristic. Signs and symptoms of a stroke may diminish and disappear in minutes or hours without residual clinical abnormalities or may persist and progress, ending in permanent dis-

ability or death. Episodes that resolve completely within 24 hours (an arbitrary period) are designated *transient ischemic attacks* (TIAs), while those that persist longer than 24 hours are termed *completed strokes*. A completed stroke that is followed by death within a second arbitrary interval of 28 days from the onset of the episode is called a *fatal stroke* and is included in enumeration of case-fatality.

Although many variations occur in the time course, location, and clinical features of disturbances in cerebral circulation, including the cumulative effects of clinically inapparent events culminating in multi-infarct dementia, completed strokes, whether fatal or nonfatal, are the main topic of this chapter. These events currently constitute the third most frequent cause of death in the United States, with mortality of

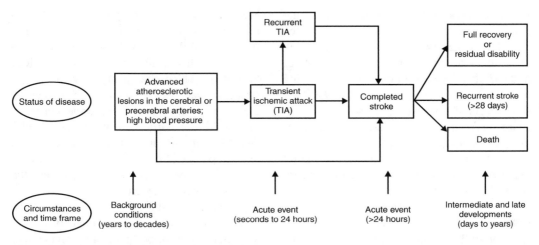

Figure 5–2 Common Features of the Course of Stroke

26.5 per 100,000 per year and an estimated 155,000 deaths in 1995 (personal communication, Nancy Hasse, American Heart Association, 1997). The estimated number of survivors of nonfatal events in 1997 was 3.8 million, of whom 1.9 million were men and 2.0 million were women.[2]

BACKGROUND OF EPIDEMIOLOGIC INVESTIGATION

Only in the late 1950s and early 1960s were geographic comparisons of stroke mortality first reported, and Stallones remarked in 1965 that little epidemiologic study of stroke had been undertaken, in contrast to studies of ischemic heart disease and hypertension.[3] His review noted several methodologic problems: In death certificate studies, it is difficult or impossible to distinguish between major types of stroke, and there is serious potential for variation in death certification practices in different countries. In early studies of incidence or prevalence of stroke, the study populations were often too young to generate substantial numbers of cases. Despite these limitations, it was possible to discern in studies based on death certificates an apparent threefold or greater range in mortality (from more than 150 to less than 50 per 100,000

population per year) from all classes of vascular lesions of the central nervous system, with Finland and Japan having the highest rates. The pioneering work of Gordon was noted, in which he described a sharp gradient of decreasing stroke mortality from Japan to Hawaii to California—opposite to the gradient for coronary heart disease—among men of Japanese ancestry.

On the presumption that atherosclerosis was a common underlying condition for both stroke and ischemic heart disease, Stallones expected to find a correlation in mortality rates for these two causes when rates for the two diseases were compared among the states. However, the result indicated no relation between the distributions of the causes of death in the United States, suggesting the operation of distinctive factors in the occurrence of stroke versus that of ischemic heart disease. A concentration of high stroke mortality rates in the Southeastern states was noted, a persistent distribution pattern first termed "the stroke belt" by Borhani (personal communication, George Howard, 1997). Striking secular trends, such as the decreasing mortality from 1900 in the United States, were also demonstrated (see below). Little information was available to address individual factors for their possible relation to differences in risk of stroke, other than a strong gradient of increasing risk with age and marked differences in sex ratio for Whites (with rates for males being higher than those for females) and non-Whites in the United States (with rates for males being lower than those for females). By the 1950s, US stroke death rates showed increased male dominance for Whites and decreased female dominance for Blacks.

Kurtzke, in a monograph appearing shortly after the Stallones review, was notably less confident that such analyses of the available mortality data offered meaningful evidence of population and group differences in the occurrence of stroke.[4] Since the 1960s, many of the features described by Stallones have been confirmed, and considerable progress has been made in the epidemiology of stroke. Some important issues remain unresolved, however, as will be seen below.

POPULATION STUDIES: DEFINITION AND CLASSIFICATION

As was the case for coronary heart disease, definitions and criteria for epidemiologic studies of stroke were developed by the Criteria and Methods Committee of the Council on Epidemiology and Prevention of the American Heart Association.[5] The methodologic report of the World Health Organization (WHO) MONICA Project, in which community surveillance for stroke was an optional addition to the central focus on coronary heart disease, demonstrates the resulting classification of strokes (Exhibit 5–1).[6] Because the acute stroke episode evolves through phases of differing severity, one useful convention for classification identifies the greatest degree of severity observed. It is also important to specify the type of stroke on the basis of either computed tomography (CT) scan in nonfatal cases or postmortem examination in the event of death. Thus whether the event was hemorrhagic or occlusive, whether occlusion arose by local thrombosis or by embolism, and in what location the pathology occurred can be classified in a standardized way.

The types of stroke are similarly distinguished in the classification system of the *International Classification of Diseases and Related Health Problems* (ICD), as summarized in Exhibit 5–2.[7] It is noted that transient ischemic attacks are not included with these classes of stroke in this revision of the ICD codes.

Exhibit 5–1 A Diagnostic Classification for Fatal and Nonfatal Strokes in Population Studies

Diagnostic categories (classification based on the most severe findings obtained within 28 days of onset):

- Definite stroke
- Not stroke
- Definite stroke associated with definite myocardial infarction
- Insufficient data

Subcategories of stroke (classification based on confirmatory findings from necropsy in fatal cases or computerized axial tomography [CT] scan in nonfatal cases; specific criteria are given for each subcategory):

- Subarachnoid hemorrhage
- Intracerebral hemorrhage
- Brain infarction due to occlusion of precerebral arteries
- Brain infarction due to cerebral thrombosis
- Embolic brain infarction

Source: Data from K Asplund, et al, Diagnostic Criteria and Quality Control of the Registration of Stroke Events in the MONICA Project, *Acta Med Scand* Suppl 728, pp 26–39, © 1988.

Exhibit 5–2 Categories of Cerebrovascular Diseases in ICD 10 (I60–I69)

I60	Subarachnoid hemorrhage
I61	Intracerebral hemorrhage
I62	Other nontraumatic intracranial hemorrhage
I63	Cerebral infarction
I64	Stroke, not specified as hemorrhage or infarction
I65	Occlusion and stenosis of precerebral arteries, not resulting in cerebral infarction
I66	Occlusion and stenosis of cerebral arteries, not resulting in cerebral infarction
I67	Other cerebrovascular diseases
I68	Cerebrovascular disorders in diseases classified elsewhere
I69	Sequelae of cerebrovascular disease

Note: Transient ischemic attacks are not included.

Because the inclusion or exclusion of transient ischemic attacks affects reported rates of nonfatal or total stroke (being excluded from fatal strokes by definition), comparisons among results of studies of stroke require caution in interpretation.

RATES OF OCCURRENCE IN POPULATIONS

Current Mortality

Mortality due to stroke by age, sex, and race in the United States for 1989 is tabulated in Table 5–1 from data reported by the US Centers for Disease Control and Prevention (CDC).[8] The very strong age gradient is apparent for the population as a whole and for each sex-race group for which data are shown. For ages 65–74 years, the overall stroke death rate was more than three times that at ages 55–64, and for ages 75–84 the rate was 10 times as high as at ages 55–64. Of the total number of stroke deaths (145,723 in 1989), nearly one-third occurred below age 75, and slightly more than two-thirds occurred at ages 75 and older. The basis for special concern about stroke among the older population is clear. The rates were substantially

Table 5–1 Stroke Mortality (Rates/100,000/yr) in the United States by Sex and Race (Black and White), Age Specific and Age Adjusted, 1989

Age Range	Black Male	Black Female	White Male	White Female	All Groups
0–34	2.0	2.4	0.9	0.8	1.0
35–44	25.1	17.0	5.1	4.4	6.5
45–54	67.3	44.6	15.0	13.3	18.6
55–64	136.5	100.2	47.9	35.8	49.3
65–74	303.6	249.7	153.4	118.6	145.8
75–84	720.1	705.5	558.3	482.9	523.4
85+	1343.2	1428.1	1578.0	1705.7	1640.8
Age adjusted	82.8	73.0	52.6	47.5	52.3
Age adjusted, 35+	193.2	169.5	123.3	111.2	122.3

Source: Data from Division of Chronic Disease Control and Community Intervention, Cardiovascular Disease Surveillance, *Stroke 1980–1989*, National Center for Chronic Disease Prevention and Health Promotion, Centers for Disease Control and Prevention, Atlanta, Georgia, 1994.

higher for Blacks than for Whites in every age group except those age 85 and older, and the overall age-adjusted rates were more than 50% higher among Blacks than Whites for both males (193.2 versus 123.3) and females (169.5 versus 111.2).

Population differences in stroke mortality are well documented in the recent report of the WHO MONICA Project, as shown in Figure 5–3 for the baseline period 1985 to 1987.[9] Stroke surveillance was reported for 18 populations in 10 countries located in Eastern and Western Europe and the People's Republic of China. Both men and women who died at ages 35–64 years were included. The figure indicates stroke mortality for each country and reporting area separately for men and women in descending order of the observed rates for definite stroke, within sex groups. Stroke mortality ranged about fourfold from lowest to highest for both men and women, although the rates were considerably lower for women than for men in this age range in every population.

Secular Trends

Stroke mortality has decreased in the United States throughout the 20th century. This was demonstrated clearly for the period from 1900 to 1960 in the epidemiologic review and analysis of stroke by Stallones published in 1965 (Figure 5–4).[3] This reconstruction of historical vital statistics for the United States was based on the nearest equivalent of the category, "vascular lesions of the central nervous system," in the first through sixth revisions of the International Classification of Diseases. Age-adjusted rates were presented to reflect a constant age structure of the population over this period and to remove the effect of the actual increased proportions of older persons, with the highest stroke rates, over time. The figure illustrates for these six decades a continuous decrease from more than 125 stroke deaths per 100,000 population per year to 75 or fewer, allowing for the noticeable effects of change in classification under the Sixth Revision, as shown.

Stroke mortality in the United States continued to decline through the late 1980s, as shown in the context of such changes in 26 other countries in Figure 5–5, which is analogous to that for secular trends in coronary heart disease in the preceding chapter.[10] Here, data for deaths at ages 65–74 years are presented. The US trend (the 16th in descending rank of stroke mortality in 1950–1954) reflects the decrease through the 1950s shown in Figure 5–4 and the sharp decline through 1984–1987. In this age group, stroke mortality for the United States declined for men from 600 to about 200 and for women from about 500 to 150 deaths per 100,000 population per year. In the other countries represented in Figure 5–5, far the dominant trend was declining stroke mortality as in the United States, with very close parallels for men and women. Striking for their exceptional patterns of increasing stroke mortality were Czechoslovakia and Hungary, which had higher rates at the end of this four-decade period than at the beginning, and Poland, where rates were also increasing over the most recent intervals.

Incidence and Survival

In addition to mortality data, the MONICA Project provides valuable data on incidence and survival from stroke.[9] The total stroke event rates presented in Table 5–2 take into account both initial and recurrent definite strokes of all types. These rates ranged threefold for men, from 121 per 100,000 population in Italy (Friuli) to 359 in Finland (Kuopio), and fivefold for women, from 58 per 100,000 in Germany (Rhein-Neckar Region) to 294 in Russia (Novosibirsk). (The countries and subunits are ordered alphabetically in Table 5–2.) These stroke events, all classified as definite stroke, constituted a very high proportion of all strokes reported in each population, typically well over 90%. The proportion of strokes that were recurrent rather than initial or truly incident events was below 10% in only one population for both men and women but above 25% in only two populations each for men and for women. Thus

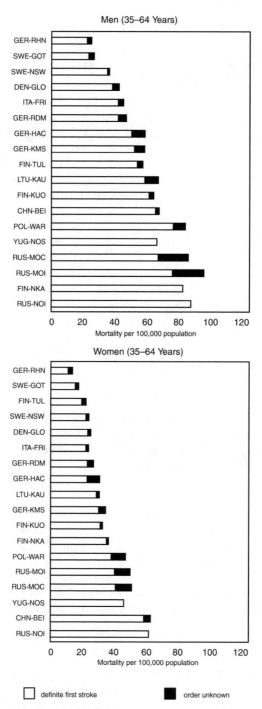

Figure 5–3 Annual Mortality from Stroke in 18 Populations in the WHO MONICA Project, by Sex, 1985–1987. For key to MONICA abbreviations, see Appendix 4–A. *Source*: Reprinted with permission from P Thorvaldsen, K Asplund, K Kuulasmas, AM Rajakangas, and M Schroll, *Stroke*, Vol 26, p 366, American Heart Association.

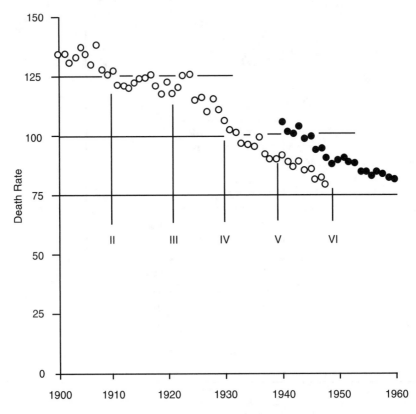

Figure 5–4 Secular Trend of Mortality from Stroke in the United States, 1900–1960. Roman numerals designate successive revisions of the International Statistical Classification of Diseases and Causes of Death. Black circles denote those rates computed using the Sixth Revision after 1948 and by applying the comparability ratio to the rates for the period 1940–1948. *Source:* Reprinted with permission from RA Stallones, *Journal of Chronic Diseases*, Vol 18, p 864, © 1965, Elsevier Science, Inc.

generally from 75% to 90% of these definite strokes were initial events. The frequency of death within the immediate 28 days after onset of the event, as case-fatality was defined for the MONICA Project, ranged for men from 15% to 49% and for women from 18% to 57%. For both men and women the highest case-fatality was observed in Poland. This threefold variation in case-fatality raises questions about possible differences among reporting areas in case severity, treatment, or other possibly influential factors.

Prevalence

The prevalence of stroke in the US population in both the first and second halves of the 1980s,

as reported by the CDC, is shown for White and Black men and women in Figures 5–6 and 5–7.[8] The basis for these estimates is a self-reported history of a nonfatal stroke by a household responding to the National Health Interview Survey. The sample results were extrapolated to the total noninstitutionalized US population by age, sex, and race. Because too few Blacks over age 75 were surveyed, the separate age categories above ages 65–74 are shown separately only for Whites. The results indicate a strong age gradient of increasing prevalence in each sex-race group. The increase was steeper at earlier ages for men than for women, for both Blacks and Whites. The prevalence was greater for Blacks than for Whites at each age from 35

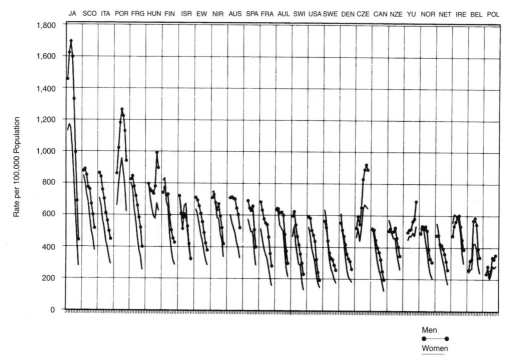

JA SCO ITA POR FRG HUN FIN ISR EW NIR AUS SPA FRA AUL SWI USA SWE DEN CZE CAN NZE YU NOR NET IRE BEL POL

Men

Women

Figure 5–5 Secular Trend of Mortality from Stroke in 27 Countries, Age 65–74 Years, by Sex, 1950–1987. *Source*: Reprinted from J Thom, FH Epstein, JJ Feldman, PE Leaverton, and M Wolz, 1992, National Institutes of Health, Pub No 92-3088.

to 44 and upward. Between the earlier and later 1980s, there was little difference in prevalence in any group; the exceptionally high prevalence for Black men aged 65 and older in 1980–1984 was described as not statistically significant and presumed to reflect sampling variation only.

RISKS IN INDIVIDUALS

Factors predictive of the occurrence of stroke have been investigated in many cohort studies, in which characteristics at entry (baseline) were evaluated for their relation to stroke incidence over several years of follow-up. Because of particular interest in the relation of blood cholesterol concentration and blood pressure to the individual risks of stroke, a group of investigators constituting the Prospective Studies Collaboration undertook to review cohort studies of stroke in which these two particular characteris-

tics were measured.[11] Altogether, 45 studies were included, with nearly 450,000 participants followed from 5 to 30 years (mean follow-up, 16 years) and a total of 13,397 persons with stroke in 7.3 million person-years of experience. The stroke events were predominantly deaths. By adjustment for variation in measurements of cholesterol and blood pressure (here, diastolic only) within individuals on repeated occasions of observation, the "usual total cholesterol" and "usual diastolic blood pressure" were estimated.

Results for total cholesterol, as shown in Figure 5–8, indicate no relation to stroke rates adjusted for study, age, sex, diastolic blood pressure, history of coronary heart disease, and ethnicity. It was noted that this result might reflect opposite effects of high and low cholesterol concentrations on different types of stroke, which could not be distinguished for this analysis. Usual diastolic blood pressure was exam-

Table 5–2 Stroke Attack Rates (per 100,000/yr), Recurrence, and 28-Day Case-Fatality in 18 Populations of the WHO MONICA Project, by Sex, 1985–1987

Location[a]	Males			Females		
	Stroke Rate	% Recurrent	% Case-Fatality	Stroke Rate	% Recurrent	% Case-Fatality
CHN-BEI	240	27	28	169	27	37
DEN-GLO	177	21	22	93	17	26
FIN-KUO	359	18	17	194	16	18
FIN-NKA	293	17	27	124	15	31
FIN-TUL	264	25	21	105	15	22
GER-HAC	150	17	36	84	17	36
GER-KMS	167	23	32	102	21	34
GER-RDM	136	17	30	74	19	36
GER-RHN	137	23	16	58	13	23
ITA-FRI	121	13	34	63	11	39
LTU-KAU	286	25	23	146	14	22
POL-WAR	152	13	49	76	12	57
RUS-MOC	251	21	32	136	24	38
RUS-MOI	229	25	38	123	26	39
RUS-NOI	344	27	25	294	23	22
SWE-GOT	128	9	18	67	6	25
SWE-NSW	216	20	15	115	18	21
YUG-NOS	235	20	28	110	15	44

a. For key to MONICA abbreviations, see Appendix 4–A.

Source: Reprinted with permission from P Thorvaldsen, K Asplund, K Kuulasmas, AM Rajakangas, and M Schroll, *Stroke*, Vol 26, © American Heart Association.

ined first in terms of proportional rates, or the ratio of the stroke rate in each successive stratum (category) of blood pressure to the rate in the lowest stratum. The analysis addressed the possibility that for younger persons these ratios at successively higher levels of pressure might increase more steeply than for older persons, as shown in Figure 5–9. For example, in the highest stratum (100 mm Hg or greater) versus the lowest (below 80 mm Hg), the rates were 10 times as high at ages below 45, five times as high at ages 45–64, and only two times as high at age 65 or more. Thus the relative importance of blood pressure was greatest for the younger adults and least for the oldest ones. However, the total or absolute impact on the rate of strokes was much greater for the oldest group,

because the stroke rate even in the lowest blood pressure category was many times greater for older than for younger adults. Figure 5–10 shows that the doubling of the reference rate for those 65 years and older at entry reflected an absolute increase in stroke rate of 8.4 per 1000 (18.4 – 10.0), while the 10-fold increase among the youngest group added less than 2 per 1000. Crude estimation of the numbers of years of life lost due to stroke death emphasized the relative cost of fatal strokes in younger adults. From one or another vantage point, then, the cost of stroke to both younger and older adults can be argued. No difference was reported in results for women and men.

The largest single follow-up study of stroke mortality was not included in the Prospective

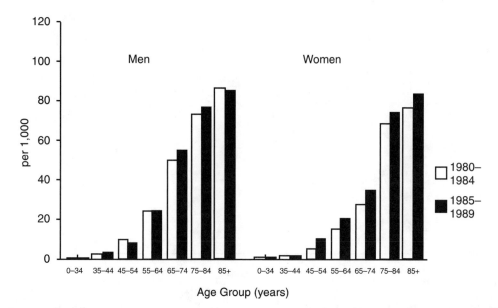

Figure 5–6 Prevalence of Nonfatal Stroke in the United States, by Age and Sex, for Whites, 1980–1989. *Source*: Reprinted from D Satcher, VS Bales, MA Speers, RF Anda, and RH Roegner, Cardiovascular Disease Surveillance, *Stroke 1980–1989*, p 60, © 1994, Centers for Disease Control and Prevention.

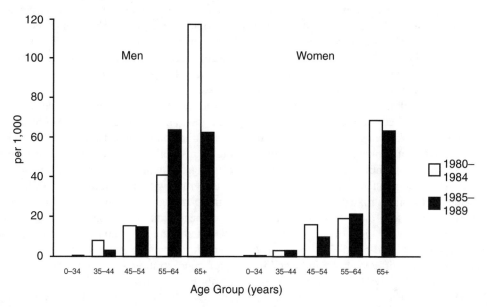

Figure 5–7 Prevalence of Nonfatal Stroke in the United States, by Age and Sex, for Blacks, 1980–1989. *Source*: Reprinted from D Satcher, VS Bales, MA Speers, RF Anda, and RH Roegner, Cardiovascular Disease Surveillance, *Stroke 1980–1989*, p 60, © 1994, Centers for Disease Control and Prevention.

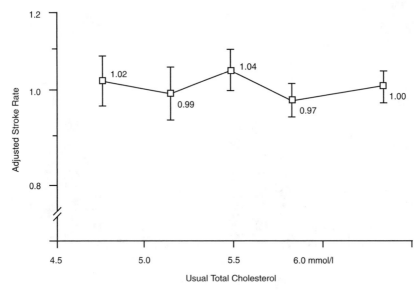

Figure 5–8 Stroke Risk by Usual Total Cholesterol. Floating absolute risk and 99% confidence interval, adjusted for study, age, sex, diastolic blood pressure, history of coronary heart disease, and ethnicity. *Source*: Reprinted with permission from Prospective Studies Collaboration, *The Lancet*, Vol 346, p 1650, © 1995, The Lancet, Ltd.

Studies Collaboration. In the six-year follow-up study, strokes were ascertained through the National Death Index for the decedents among 350,977 middle-aged US men screened for the Multiple Risk Factor Intervention Trial, or MRFIT.[12] As shown in Table 5–3, the relation of age, systolic and diastolic blood pressure, serum cholesterol concentration, cigarette smoking, and race (as reflected in the percentage of Blacks in each stroke category) was examined among three types of stroke: subarachnoid hemorrhage (55 deaths), intracranial hemorrhage (83 deaths), and nonhemorrhagic (that is, thrombotic or embolic) stroke (92 deaths).

In these comparisons of factors distinguishing between men who died of each type of stroke and those who did not die of stroke, statistically significant differences are indicated in Table 5–3 by the symbols *(*P*<0.01) or **(*P*<0.001). For each type of stroke death there were significantly higher mean values of systolic and diastolic blood pressure, a higher prevalence of diastolic pressure of 90 mm Hg or

greater, and a greater proportion of cigarette smokers than among men without stroke death. For intracranial hemorrhage and nonhemorrhagic stroke (but not subarachnoid hemorrhage) age was modestly, but in statistical terms significantly, greater than for men without stroke.

The mean values of serum cholesterol concentration among the groups with subarachnoid and intracranial hemorrhage (212.2 and 211.4 mg/dl, respectively) were slightly less than that of the group without stroke (214.4 mg/dl), but in the group with nonhemorrhagic stroke it was significantly greater. This observation indicates type-specific differences in the relation between cholesterol concentrations and stroke. There were not equal and opposite effects of cholesterol concentration on hemorrhagic and nonhemorrhagic stroke, as suggested by the Prospective Studies Collaboration. However, in further analysis (not shown), the lowest stratum of cholesterol concentration (below 160 mg/dl) was associated with a risk three times that of

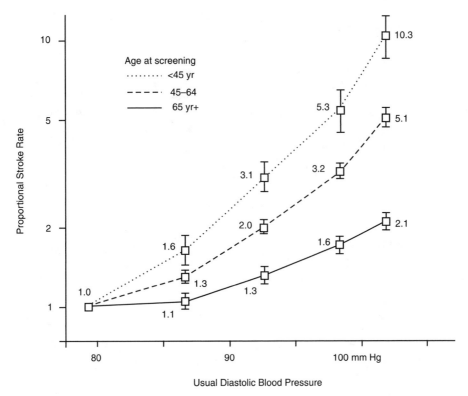

Figure 5–9 Proportional Stroke Risk, by Age and Usual Diastolic Blood Pressure. Floating absolute risk, adjusted for study, sex, total cholesterol, history of coronary heart disease, and ethnicity. *Source:* Reprinted with permission from Prospective Studies Collaboration, *The Lancet*, Vol 346, p 1651, © 1995, The Lancet, Ltd.

men with cholesterol concentrations of 160 mg/dl or more. Thus there were in fact opposite associations as discussed in the report of the collaborative review, but in this study the effect of the inverse relation with hemorrhagic stroke was dominated by the increased risk of nonhemorrhagic stroke with increased cholesterol concentration. The ability to investigate associations of blood lipids, and possibly other factors, on risk of stroke appears to depend crucially on identification of specific stroke types, as urged by Stallones 30 years ago.[3] The MRFIT data also show that cigarette smoking was significantly more frequent among subjects in each stroke group than among subjects without stroke. The percentages of Blacks among the stroke deaths were greater in all groups than in the group without strokes, significantly so for both intracranial hemorrhage and nonhemorrhagic stroke.

Other prominent predictors of stroke are prior cardiovascular conditions, such as coronary heart disease, cardiac failure, and atrial fibrillation (chronic irregularity of contraction of the upper chambers of the heart). These conditions, in addition to hypertension, were found in the Framingham Study to occur especially commonly among older persons with stroke (Table 5–4).[13] Even these conditions, however, with their direct pathological connections to risks of embolic stroke, contribute less than hypertension to the attributable risk (the proportion of events explained by the presence of that condition). Hypertension (high blood pressure) remains the dominant characteristic in the prediction of stroke.

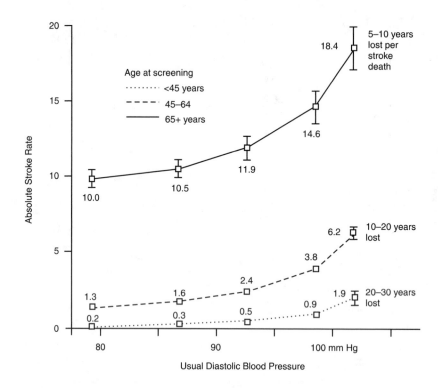

Figure 5–10 Absolute Stroke Risk, by Age and Usual Diastolic Blood Pressure. Estimates of years lost per stroke death are very approximate. *Source:* Reprinted with permission from Prospective Studies Collaboration, *The Lancet,* Vol 346, p 1651, © 1995, The Lancet, Ltd.

Still other factors were addressed briefly in a recent conference report on prevention and rehabilitation of stroke.[14] In addition to those already noted were diabetes and glucose metabolism, alcohol, illicit drug use, lifestyle factors (obesity, physical inactivity, diet, and "acute triggers"), oral contraceptives, migraine, hemostatic and inflammatory factors, homocysteine, subclinical disease, asymptomatic carotid stenosis, and transient ischemic attacks. Many of these factors are discussed in subsequent chapters of this book.

PREVENTION AND TREATMENT: INDIVIDUALS AND POPULATIONS

As discussed in reference to coronary heart disease (Chapter 4), strategies for prevention of stroke include both population-wide and high-risk components. Especially prominent elements of these strategies applied to stroke are interventions for prevention and control of high blood pressure. In addition, especially for non-hemorrhagic stroke, the list of related factors includes several in common with coronary heart disease. Measures to prevent or control these factors, such as high total cholesterol concentration and smoking, would be expected to enhance the effects of prevention and control of high blood pressure in reducing the rate of stroke, wherever nonhemorrhagic stroke is a substantial component of the stroke occurrence as a whole. The potential impact of these and other interventions to prevent stroke is addressed in subsequent chapters (see especially Chapter 12).

Table 5–3 Baseline Characteristics and Deaths from Stroke, by Type, among Men Screened for the Multiple Risk Factor Intervention Trial (*N* = 350,977, Age 35–57 Years)

Characteristic	No Stroke (N = 350,747)	Subarachnoid Hemorrhage (N = 55)	Intracranial Hemorrhage (N = 83)	Nonhemorrhagic Stroke (N = 92)
Age (yr)	45.8 ± 6.4	47.4 ± 5.6	49.9 ± 5.7**	50.5 ± 5.1**
Systolic blood pressure (mm Hg)[a]	129.9 ± 15.8	137.9 ± 15.5**	146.2 ± 23.6**	149.7 ± 26.1**
Diastolic blood pressure (mm Hg)	83.9 ± 10.6	89.2 ± 12.5**	93.9 ± 14.9**	94.0 ± 15.9**
Diastolic blood pressure ≥90 mm Hg (%)	27.9	50.9**	51.8**	62.0**
Serum cholesterol (mg/dl)	214.4 ± 39.3	212.2 ± 37.6	211.4 ± 43.9	232.4 ± 46.5**
Cigarette smokers (%)	36.8	63.6**	50.6*	60.9**
Black (%)	6.4	10.9	19.3**	13.0*

Note: Plus–minus values are means ±*SD*. Numbers in parentheses indicate the number of subjects for whom values were available. *P* values are for comparisons with men who did not die of stroke. To convert values for serum cholesterol to millimoles per liter, multiply by 0.02586.

a. The population whose systolic blood pressure was studied included 342,520 with no stroke, 49 with subarachnoid hemorrhage, 79 with intracranial hemorrhage, and 85 with nonhemorrhagic stroke.

*P<0.01.

**P<0.001.

CURRENT ISSUES

Among current issues in the epidemiology and prevention of stroke, the foremost question from the US perspective is whether the long-standing decline in mortality due to stroke has ceased. Starting at least from the beginning of this century, and thus long before the introduction of effective and widespread antihypertensive therapy, stroke rates declined until the rate for 1992 reached a low of 26.6 per 100,000 population (adjusted for comparison to the coding frequency for ICD 6).[2] This rate was less than one-third that in 1950. According to the American Heart Association, however, the preliminary data for 1995 indicate an increase in the stroke death rate, from an absolute (unadjusted) rate of 26.2 in 1992 to 26.5 currently; the number of stroke deaths also increased substantially, from 142,000 in 1992 to 155,000 in 1995 (personal communication, Nancy Hasse, American Heart Association, 1997).

Other questions remain to be answered: What is the role of secular trends in blood pressure in the declining rates of stroke death in recent decades? What is the contribution of treatment to these trends? What factors other than blood pressure levels and treatment of high blood pressure have contributed to declining stroke rates over the past century and may have continued until recently? Are the remaining differences in stroke mortality between US Blacks and Whites (nearly twofold for both men and women) indicative of failure to bring effective long-term antihypertensive therapy to this population, or are deeper social and economic factors accountable?

Discussion of the possibility that the decline in stroke mortality in the United States was ending appeared in the literature in the late 1980s.

Table 5–4 Contributions of Other Cardiovascular Conditions to Risk of Stroke, by Age, Framingham Study

Cardiovascular Condition	Age (Yr)			
	50–59	60–69	70–79	80–89
Number of stroke events	92	213	192	75
Hypertension				
Attributable risk (%)	48.8	53.2	48.6	33.4
% of events in persons with condition	72.8	80.3	83.9	84.0
Coronary heart disease				
Attributable risk (%)	11.1	12.4	12.6	0.0
% of events in persons with condition	25.0	32.9	38.0	28.0
Cardiac failure				
Attributable risk (%)	2.3	3.1	5.6	6.0
% of events in persons with condition	9.8	11.7	18.2	18.7
Atrial fibrillation				
Attributable risk (%)[a]	1.5	2.8	9.9	23.5
% of events in persons with condition	6.5	8.5	18.8	30.7

a. Significant increase with age ($P<0.01$).

Source: Reprinted with permission from PA Wolf, *Circulation*, Vol 88, p 2475, © 1993, American Heart Association.

Several more recent reports have analyzed secular trends locally or nationally, as well as racial differences in rates or trends, and their relation to potentially explanatory factors.[15-19] These reports illustrate the challenge of establishing conclusively the nature and determinants of immediate changes in such a broad epidemic process as that of the third-largest cause of death in the United States. For example, except in very few localities (eg, Rochester, Minnesota, or the Twin Cities of Minneapolis and St. Paul, Minnesota), data are lacking on incidence and case-fatality. This information is necessary to distinguish contributions of changing occurrence of initial stroke events and changing survival following a completed stroke and, correspondingly, prevention or treatment of the acute stroke event, either or both of which could underlie changes in mortality. Both the persistent Black-White differences in stroke deaths in the United States and the growing evidence of a stalling of the long-term decline add to the public health importance of resolving these questions.

It appears that currently available public health interventions need wider and more effective application, both to accelerate declines in blood pressure through antihypertensive therapy and to influence favorably the other factors contributing most importantly to the occurrence of stroke. Efforts to prevent the development of high blood pressure in the first place should be a central focus of the public health strategy against stroke. Gains in understanding secular trends and their determinants, as well as the ability through public health interventions to effect reductions in the occurrence of strokes of all types, may come from expanded studies in diverse populations, from which many populations could potentially benefit.

REFERENCES

1. Albers GP, Cutler RWP. Cerebrovascular diseases. In: Dale DC, Federman DD, eds. *Scientific American Medicine*. New York: Scientific American, Inc; 1994: 1–13.

2. *1997 Heart and Stroke Statistical Update*. Dallas, Tex: American Heart Association; 1996.

3. Stallones RA. Epidemiology of cerebrovascular disease: a review. *J Chronic Dis*. 1965;18:859–872.

4. Kurtzke JF. *Epidemiology of Cerebrovascular Disease*. Berlin, Germany: Springer-Verlag; 1969.

5. Gillum RF, Fortmann SP, Prineas RJ, Kottke TE. International diagnostic criteria for acute myocardial infarction and stroke. *Am Heart J*. 1984;108:150–158.

6. Asplund K, Tuomilehto J, Stegmayr B, Wester PO, et al. Diagnostic criteria and quality control of the registration of stroke events in the MONICA Project. *Acta Med Scand*. 1988;728(suppl):26–39.

7. World Health Organization. *International Statistical Classification of Diseases and Related Health Problems. Tenth Revision*. Geneva, Switzerland: World Health Organization; 1992;1.

8. Division of Chronic Disease Control and Community Intervention. *Cardiovascular Disease Surveillance. Stroke, 1980–1989*. Atlanta, Ga: National Center for Chronic Disease Prevention and Health Promotion, Centers for Disease Control and Prevention, Public Health Service, US Dept of Health and Human Services; 1994.

9. Thorvaldsen P, Asplund K, Kuulasmaa K, Rajakangas A-M, et al, for the WHO MONICA Project. Stroke incidence, case fatality, and mortality in the WHO MONICA Project. *Stroke*. 1995;26:361–367.

10. Thom TJ, Epstein FH, Feldman JJ, Leaverton PE, et al. *Total Mortality and Mortality from Heart Disease, Cancer, and Stroke from 1950 to 1987 in 27 Countries: Highlights of Trends and Their Interrelationships among Causes of Death*. Bethesda, Md: National Heart, Lung and Blood Institute, National Institutes of Health; September 1992. NIH publication 92-3088.

11. Prospective Studies Collaboration. Cholesterol, diastolic blood pressure, and stroke: 13,000 strokes in 450,000 people in 45 prospective cohorts. *Lancet*. 1995;346:1647–1653.

12. Iso H, Jacobs DR Jr, Wentworth D, Neaton JD, et al, for the MRFIT Research Group. Serum cholesterol levels and six-year mortality from stroke in 350,977 men screened for the Multiple Risk Factor Intervention Trial. *N Engl J Med*. 1989;320:904–910.

13. Wolf PA. Contributions of epidemiology to the prevention of stroke. Lewis A. Conner Lecture. *Circ*. 1993; 88:2471–2478.

14. Helgason CM, Wolf PA. American Heart Association Prevention Conference IV: Prevention and Rehabilitation of Stroke. Executive summary. *Circ*. 1997;96: 701–707.

15. Broderick JP, Phillips SJ, Whisnant JP, O Fallon WM, et al. Incidence rates of stroke in the eighties: the end of the decline in stroke? *Stroke*. 1989;20:577–582.

16. Cooper R, Sempos C, Hsieh S-C, Kovar MG. Slowdown in the decline of stroke mortality in the United States, 1978–1986. *Stroke*. 1990;21:1274–1279.

17. Casper M, Wing S, Strogatz D. Variation in the magnitude of Black-White differences in stroke mortality by community occupational structure. *Epidemiol Community Health*. 1991;45:302–306.

18. McGovern PG, Burke GL, Sprafka JM, Xue S, et al. Trends in mortality, morbidity, and risk factor levels for stroke from 1960 through 1990. The Minnesota Heart Survey. *JAMA*. 1992;268:753–759.

19. Jacobs DR Jr, McGovern PG, Blackburn H. The US decline in stroke mortality: what does ecological analysis tell us? *Am J Public Health*. 1992;82:1596–1599.

CHAPTER 6

Other Major Conditions

SUMMARY

In addition to coronary heart disease and stroke, other conditions related to atherosclerosis and hypertension contribute substantially to the overall burden of cardiovascular diseases in many populations. These conditions include, among many others, the effects of atherosclerosis in other regions of the circulation. Especially important are peripheral arterial disease, in which the lower extremities are affected, and aortic aneurysm, or distention and potential rupture of the major vessel between the heart and the peripheral arteries. Also included, though less clearly classifiable, is congestive heart failure, or loss of effective pumping action of the heart, especially from the left ventricle to the systemic circulation. Heart failure is most often a consequence of coronary heart disease or hypertension in populations where these are the dominant cardiovascular diseases; therefore it is appropriately addressed here. But in populations where, for example, rheumatic heart disease (Chapter 24) or Chagas' disease (Chapter 25) predominate over coronary or hypertensive heart disease, congestive heart failure is a reflection of the occurrence of these other conditions. This important qualification will be reemphasized below. For each of the three conditions—peripheral arterial disease, aortic aneurysms, and congestive heart failure—the main clinical and epidemiologic features are reviewed, along with comments on the implications of current knowledge for prevention and on the issues most immediately needing epidemiologic investigation. Finally, deep vein thrombosis and pulmonary embolism and the challenges to their epidemiologic investigation and public health intervention are addressed.

INTRODUCTION

The four major conditions discussed here are classified in the *International Classification of Diseases and Related Health Conditions, Tenth Revision* (ICD 10), as shown in Exhibit 6–1.[1] Peripheral arterial disease appears as a subclass of diseases of the arteries, arterioles, and capillaries (I70–I79) and is likely to be coded nearly always as I70.2, although some cases might be described only as "peripheral vascular disease" or "intermittent claudication" (a condition characterized by pain in the calf muscles during walking due to impaired blood supply) and require coding as I73.9. A single broad category, aortic aneurysm and dissection (I73), includes subclasses according to location of the aneurysm, whether in the abdominal or thoracic portion or both, and whether or not there is mention of rupture of the aneurysm. The abdominal aneurysms alone will be addressed here, as they are currently the predominant type in the United States. Congestive heart failure,

91

Exhibit 6–1 Classification of Peripheral Arterial Disease, Aortic Aneurysm, Congestive Heart Failure, and Deep Vein Thrombosis and Pulmonary Embolism

---

a. Peripheral arterial disease

  I70 Atherosclerosis
      I70.2 Atherosclerosis of arteries of extremities
  I73 Other peripheral vascular disease
      I73.9 Peripheral vascular disease, unspecified

b. Aortic aneurysm

  I71 Aortic aneurysm and dissection
      I71.3 Abdominal aortic aneurysm, ruptured
      I71.4 Abdominal aortic aneurysm, without mention of rupture

c. Congestive heart failure

  I50 Heart failure
      I50.0 Congestive heart failure
      I50.1 Left ventricular failure
      I50.9 Heart failure, unspecified
  I09 Other rheumatic heart diseases
      I09.9 Rheumatic heart disease, unspecified
  I11 Hypertensive heart disease
      I11.0 Hypertensive heart disease with (congestive) heart failure
  I13 Hypertensive renal disease
      I13.0 Hypertensive heart and renal disease with (congestive) heart failure
      I13.2 Hypertensive heart and renal disease with both (congestive) heart failure and renal failure

d. Deep vein thrombosis and pulmonary embolism

  I80 Phlebitis and thrombophlebitis
      I80.1 Phlebitis and thrombophlebitis of femoral vein
      I80.2 Phlebitis and thrombophlebitis of other deep vessels of lower extremities
      I80.3 Phlebitis and thrombophlebitis of lower extremities, unspecified
      I80.8 Phlebitis and thrombophlebitis of other sites
      I80.9 Phlebitis and thrombophlebitis of unspecified site
  I26 Pulmonary embolism
      I26.0 Pulmonary embolism with mention of acute cor pulmonale
      I26.9 Pulmonary embolism without mention of acute cor pulmonale

---

by contrast, is coded in any of several different categories, depending on the underlying condition. It includes left ventricular failure specifically, but also right ventricular failure if this is secondary to left ventricular failure. This occurs when long-standing congestion in the pulmonary circulation and resulting resistance to blood flow from the right heart to the lungs leads to failure of the right ventricle. Deep vein thrombosis (clotting of blood in the larger veins, especially in the lower extremities or pelvis) is especially common among hospitalized patients. It is often complicated by transport or embolization of a portion of the thrombus through the venous system and right side of the heart to reach the lung, causing acute respiratory compromise and sometimes death. ICD 10 provides for coding of the initial thrombosis by its venous location and of pulmonary embolism by the presence or absence of mention of acute failure of the right ventricle of the heart (cor pulmonale). The latter complication may occur due to increased resistance to blood flow through the obstructed pulmonary circulation.

As a measure of the importance of these four conditions, several indicators of their occurrence are presented in Table 6–1, based on US data for 1993.[2] The numbers of hospital discharges for which each condition was the first-listed diagnosis, the average length of hospital stay, the number of physician office visits, and the number of deaths attributed to each condition are shown. To provide some perspective on these numbers, the corresponding figures are given for coronary heart disease. Peripheral arterial disease (atherosclerosis) and aortic aneurysm (abdominal and thoracic together) are similar in all measures and represent only a small fraction of cardiovascular diseases relative to coronary heart disease. Hospitalizations are longer on average because surgery is often performed in treatment of these cases. In contrast, congestive heart failure is more than one-third as common as coronary heart disease as a

hospital discharge diagnosis and leads to nearly one-third as many physician office visits. The number of deaths coded as congestive heart failure in one year is less than one-tenth that due to coronary heart disease, perhaps reflecting diagnostic or coding practices when both conditions are present. Deep vein thrombosis probably is often not coded when pulmonary embolism occurs as a complication and therefore may be underreported. Its frequency as a reason for physician office visits is unknown, and deaths attributed to it are probable miscoding of deaths due to pulmonary embolism. Pulmonary embolism, on the other hand, is about as common as peripheral arterial atherosclerosis or aortic aneurysm as a first hospital discharge diagnosis, half as common as a cause of death, and rare as a basis for physician office visits, being principally associated with hospitalization. Cardiac arrhythmias, another group of cardiac conditions of interest, occur with frequencies similar to those for congestive heart failure according to these indicators. However, they are classified in six separate categories in the ICD 10 (I44–

Table 6–1 Some Indicators of the Occurrence of Peripheral Arterial Disease, Aortic Aneurysm, Congestive Heart Failure, and Deep Vein Thrombosis and Pulmonary Embolism in Relation to Coronary Heart Disease, United States, 1993

	Hospitalizations			
Condition (ICD 9 Codes)	*First-Listed Discharge*	*Length of Stay (Days)*	*Physician Office Visits*	*Deaths*
Diseases of arteries				
Atherosclerosis (440)	73,000	10.1	360,000	17,272
Aortic aneurysm (441)	51,000	10.3	246,000	16,475
Heart disease				
Congestive heart failure (428)	875,000	7.5	2,844,000	41,819
Venous thrombosis and pulmonary embolism				
Deep vein thrombosis	27,000	8.4	(?)	579
Pulmonary embolism	59,000	9.2	8,000	8,955
Coronary heart disease (410–414)	2,079,000	5.9	9,222,000	490,063

Source: Adapted from *Morbidity and Mortality: 1996 Chartbook on Cardiovascular, Lung, and Blood Diseases*, National Heart, Lung and Blood Institute, National Institutes of Health, Bethesda, Maryland.

I49) and constitute too heterogeneous a group to be addressed adequately here. Like congestive heart failure, their occurrence is very often a complication in the progression of coronary or hypertensive heart disease, whose prevention would do much to reduce their frequency of occurrence.

PERIPHERAL ARTERIAL DISEASE

Typical Course of the Individual Case

Typically, an older person with recognized peripheral arterial disease, or atherosclerotic impairment of arterial blood flow to the lower extremities, may experience intermittent claudication, or pain in the calf muscles after walking a short distance (eg, 100 yards or less) that is relieved temporarily by stopping. This condition may persist with little change for several years, as long as the affected person survives. But the presence of diagnosed peripheral arterial disease is often a marker for advanced coronary or cerebral atherosclerosis, which may lead to death within one to two years. The condition may also progress to the degree that vascular surgery is required to improve blood flow, or amputation may be required because adequate flow cannot be restored.[3]

Background of Epidemiologic Investigation

Until very recently, the epidemiology of peripheral arterial disease was the epidemiology of intermittent claudication, the symptomatic expression of impaired arterial blood flow in the lower extremities, described above. The subjective nature of perception and reports of pain by patients or study participants and of eliciting medical histories by physicians or other health personnel is compounded in such circumstances to make the diagnosis of peripheral arterial disease by history highly variable and of very uncertain comparability between observers or between studies.

For these reasons, and to support international comparative cardiovascular surveys,

Rose reported in 1962 on studies leading to the recommendation of a standard questionnaire to determine the presence or absence of intermittent claudication in addition to pain typical of myocardial infarction.[4] The "Rose (or London School of Hygiene) questionnaire" established a method by which use of the term *intermittent claudication* could become standardized, if necessary care were taken to ensure proper administration of the questionnaire. In many subsequent studies, this method was used, and intermittent claudication came to be incorporated often as a component in estimates of the prevalence of atherosclerosis in population surveys. Development of this questionnaire represented an important early advance in cardiovascular survey methods and is reflected in most of the knowledge of the epidemiology of peripheral arterial disease well into the 1980s. The limitations of this approach to detecting arterial pathology and estimating its prevalence could not be fully appreciated until newer, noninvasive diagnostic imaging techniques became available and were applied in population studies.

Population Studies: Definition and Classification, Diagnostic Algorithms, and Criteria

By the mid-1980s, application of noninvasive techniques for assessment of peripheral arterial blood flow had advanced to a level permitting detailed evaluation of this approach relative to the classic interview/questionnaire methods for ascertainment of intermittent claudication. These methods included calculation of the ratio of blood pressure measured at each of several selected points between the thigh and the toe to that measured in the brachial artery in the arm. These pressure measurements would be approximately equal in the absence of obstruction to blood flow in the artery to the lower extremity, and the expected ratio of pressures would therefore be 1. Obstruction of blood flow would reduce the measurement in the lower extremity, so the ratio would fall below 1. Several different values of this ratio have been proposed as criteria for peripheral arterial disease. Ultrasound techniques also permit measurement of blood flow through specific vessels, and still other indicators are available. On this basis, vascular disease can be detected before intermittent claudication is reported, and disease of the "large" (major) vessels to the lower extremity can be distinguished from that of "small" vessels. The impact of this methodologic development has been to shift the focus to large-vessel peripheral arterial disease (LV-PAD) as assessed, for example, by combined ankle-arm blood pressure ratio and ultrasound measurement of blood flow through one major artery, the posterior tibial artery in the calf.

These methods have been compared with the history of intermittent claudication as determined by the Rose questionnaire, with or without physical examination to check the presence and character of the pulse at several points in the extremities.[5] The results indicate a wide range of prevalence estimates, depending on the combination of indices included. Relative to the most-extensive set of measurements available, history of intermittent claudication detected only 9.2% of cases identified by other means, and only one-half of those positive by history had demonstrable disturbances of vascular flow. Accordingly, analyses of peripheral arterial disease with respect to causal factors and long-term outcomes based on history of intermittent claudication were limited by the inaccuracy of identification of true arterial disease. The newer approaches are more informative, in keeping with their greater reliability as indicators of true arterial disease.[6] For example, Table 6–2 presents results of an assessment of three classes of LV-PAD when the ankle-arm pressure ratio was taken to be diagnostic at values of 0.8 or less and forward blood flow through the posterior tibial artery was reduced to 3 cm/sec or less. When all evidence of disease was taken as the reference standard, this two-test combination detected 89% of limbs with LV-PAD; 99% of limbs classified as negative by these tests were judged so by the full battery of tests; positive classification by the two tests was associated with 90% confirmation from the full battery; and negative classification was confirmed in 99% of the limbs tested by the full battery. Accuracy, defined as the numbers of true posi-

Table 6–2 Evaluation of Measures of Large-Vessel Peripheral Arterial Disease (LV-PAD) among 484 Adults Originally Screened Between 1979 and 1981

Case Group	*Ankle-to-Arm Pressure Ratio ≤0.8 + Posterior Tibial Peak Forward Flow ≤3 cm/sec*									
	Sensitivity		Specificity		Positive Predictive Value		Negative Predictive Value		Accuracy	
	%	No. of limbs	%	No. of limbs	%	No. of limbs	%	No. of limbs	%	No. of limbs
All LV-PAD	89.0	81/91	99.0	867/876	90.0	81/90	99.0	867/876	98.0	948/967
LV-PAD with isolated posterior tibial cases excluded	82.4	42/51	99.0	864/876	82.4	42/51	99.0	867/876	98.1	909/927
Asymptomatic LV-PAD cases only	88.1	59/67	98.9	823/832	86.8	59/68	99.0	823/831	98.1	882/899

Source: Reprinted with permission from HS Feigelson, *American Journal of Epidemiology,* Vol 140, No 6, p 531, © 1994.

tives plus true negatives, divided by the total number of limbs, was 96%. These favorable findings for all LV-PAD were essentially the same after exclusion of cases with isolated posterior tibial artery disease and restriction to those with asymptomatic disease or those who had previous surgical treatment. Relative to the history of intermittent claudication, then, the combination of ankle-arm blood pressure ratio and posterior tibial artery flow provides a far superior index of true arterial disease. Interest focuses, then, on those studies evaluating peripheral arterial disease in relation to these measures, even though criteria have differed somewhat among studies.

Rates of Occurrence in Populations

The prevalence of large-vessel peripheral arterial disease, based on measured lower extremity–arm blood pressure ratios and blood flow in the lower extremity, was strongly related to age in both men and women participating in the Lipid Research Clinics study in southern California, as shown in Figure 6–1.[7] Prevalence in men increased consistently across five-year age groups, from about 2.5% below age 60 years to about 22.5% at age 75 years and above. For women the increase in prevalence lagged by about five years relative to that for men but was similar for the age group 75 years and older. Notably, for isolated small-vessel disease, which is much less reliably detected, the prevalence was between 10% and 20% at each age level with no age gradient for either men or women.

A further general observation about prevalent peripheral arterial disease is its contribution to the spectrum of subclinical atherosclerosis and cardiovascular disease, as discussed in Chapter 3. The report of the Cardiovascular Health Study on the prevalence of subclinical disease

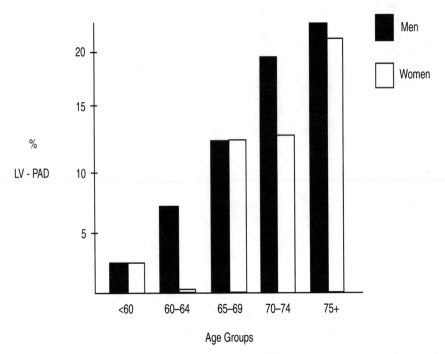

Figure 6–1 Prevalence of Large-Vessel Peripheral Arterial Disease (LV-PAD), by Age and Sex, Southern California. *Source:* Reprinted with permission from MH Criqui, *Circulation*, Vol 71, No 3, p 513, © 1985, American Heart Association.

indicated that undiagnosed peripheral arterial disease identified 16% of men and 19.9% of women who were free of known cardiovascular disease but were classified as having subclinical disease.[8] These cases were identified chiefly by ankle-arm blood pressure index without the addition of blood flow measurements and therefore represent an underestimate of the prevalence of subclinical disease. Rose questionnaire responses identified few additional cases not detected by ankle-arm index.

The prognostic importance of peripheral arterial disease is clear from the mortality experience of persons followed for up to 10 years from diagnosis, as summarized in Table 6–3.[9] Among 569 study participants available for analysis, 67 had been found to have large-vessel peripheral arterial disease. There were 32 deaths in the LV-PAD group, constituting 61.8% of the 34 men and 33.3% of the 33 women, whereas corresponding frequencies among those without peripheral arterial disease at baseline were 16.9% and 11.6%, respectively. Adjustment for differences between groups for age, sex, and

other cardiovascular risk factors resulted in relative risk estimates of 3.1 (95% confidence interval, 1.9–4.9) for death from all causes, 5.9 (3.0–11.4) for all cardiovascular deaths, and 6.6 (2.9–14.9) for coronary heart disease death. Detailed analysis shown in the table indicates greater relative risks for bilateral, symptomatic, and severe disease. A relative risk of 15 was reported for cardiovascular or coronary heart disease death among those with both severe and symptomatic disease versus those free of disease.

Risks in Individuals

The cross-sectional relation of peripheral arterial disease to the major risk factors for atherosclerosis and coronary heart disease can be compared between two methods of classification based on the Rose questionnaire and the ankle-brachial pressure index.[10] Table 6–4 presents the results of univariate and multivariate regression analysis of selected risk factors and peripheral arterial disease as detected by each of

Table 6–3 Relative Risk of Death among Subjects with Various Categories of Large-Vessel Peripheral Arterial Disease (LV-PAD)

	Relative Risk (95% Confidence Interval)							
Cause of Death	*Unilateral LV-PAD (N = 34)*	*Bilateral LV-PAD (N = 30)*	*Asymptomatic LV-PAD (N = 49)*	*Symptomatic LV-PAD (N = 18)*	*Moderate LV-PAD (N = 49)*	*Severe LV-PAD (N = 18)*	*Isolated Posterior Tibial LV-PAD (N = 31)*	*Other LV-PAD (N = 33)*
All causes	3.3 (1.9–5.9)	2.9 (1.5–5.5)	2.7 (1.6–4.5)	4.7 (2.3–9.6)	2.8 (1.6–4.8)	3.9 (1.9–8.0)	2.9 (1.6–5.4)	3.4 (1.9–6.0)
CVD	5.5 (2.5–12.1)	5.8 (2.5–13.3)	4.7 (2.3–9.8)	11.2 (4.5–27.9)	4.8 (2.3–10.3)	8.4 (3.4–20.8)	4.2 (1.7–10.4)	7.0 (3.2–14.9)
CHD	5.5 (2.0–15.2)	7.2 (2.6–19.7)	5.6 (2.3–13.5)	11.4 (3.6–35.8)	5.6 (2.2–14.2)	8.9 (3.0–26.8)	5.5 (1.8–16.7)	6.8 (2.7–17.5)

Note: CVD, cardiovascular disease; CHD, coronary heart disease. Relative risks have been adjusted for age, sex, number of cigarettes smoked per day, systolic blood pressure, HDL cholesterol level, LDL cholesterol level, logarithm of the triglyceride level, fasting plasma glucose level, body mass index, and selection criterion.

Source: Reprinted with permission from MH Criqui, *The New England Journal of Medicine*, Vol 326, No 6, p 384, © 1992, The Massachusetts Medical Society. All rights reserved.

Table 6–4 Univariate and Multivariate Regressions[a] of Risk Factors on Intermittent Claudication and Ankle-Brachial Pressure Index, Edinburgh, 1988

Change in Risk Factor	Odds Ratio of Intermittent Claudication		Ankle-Brachial Pressure Index Coefficient (Difference × 100)	
	Univariate	Multivariate	Univariate	Multivariate
Female (vs male)	1.0 (0.6–1.6)[b]	1.1 (0.4–3.0)	4.7 ± 0.9[****c]	1.5 ± 2.2
Age (+10 years)	2.0 (1.3–3.1)[***]	1.7 (1.0–2.8)[*]	−5.4 ± 0.8[****]	−5.1 ± 0.8[****]
Height (+10 cm)	0.8 (0.6–1.1)	0.8 (0.5–1.2)	3.3 ± 0.5[****]	1.4 ± 0.7[**]
Body mass index (+4 units)[d]	1.1 (0.9–1.4)	Not included	0.5 ± 0.5	Not included
Non-HDL[e] cholesterol (+1.3 mmol/l)[d]	1.7 (1.3–2.1)[****]	1.6 (1.2–2.1)[****]	−3.0 ± 0.5[****]	−2.0 ± 0.5[****]
HDL cholesterol (+0.4 mmol/l)[d]	0.6 (0.5–0.8)[****]	0.7 (0.5–1.0)[*]	0.8 ± 0.5[*]	1.2 ± 0.6[**]
Triglycerides (+58%)[d]	1.7 (1.3–2.1)[****]	1.0 (0.7–1.5)	−2.6 ± 0.5[****]	−0.6 ± 0.6
Diabetes mellitus				
Known	2.5 (0.7–8.4) ⎤	1.3 (0.3–5.2)	−12.4 ± 3.1 ⎤	−10.2 ± 2.9 ⎤
Diabetic GTT[e]	1.2 (0.4–4.0) ⎥[*]	0.8 (0.2–2.8)	−2.4 ± 2.3 ⎥[***]	−1.2 ± 2.2 ⎥[**]
Impaired GTT				
High ⎫	2.1 (1.1–3.9) ⎦	⎫1.7 (0.9–3.2)	−3.3 ± 2.6	2.0 ± 2.3
Low ⎭		⎭	−0.8 ± 1.7 ⎦	−0.6 ± 1.5 ⎦
Cigarette smoking				
Current smoker	1.2 (0.6–2.2) ⎤	1.3 (0.6–2.5) ⎤	−7.4 ± 1.3) ⎤	−6.0 ± 1.3 ⎤
Ex-smoker				
<5 years	1.8 (0.8–4.1) ⎥[****]	1.5 (0.6–3.7) ⎥[***]	−6.9 ± 2.0 ⎥[****]	−4.3 ± 1.9 ⎥[****]
Pack-years	1.1 (1.0–1.3) ⎦	1.2 (1.0–1.3) ⎦	−0.7 ± 0.2 ⎦	−1.2 ± 0.2 ⎦
Alcohol (weekly units)[f]				
Indulgers				
Female	0.8 (0.6–1.0)	0.9 (0.6–1.2)	−0.1 ± 0.5	−0.1 ± 0.5
Male	0.9 (0.8–1.0)	0.9 (0.8–1.1)	0.7 ± 0.3	0.7 ± 0.3
Abstainers				
Female	1.2 (0.5–2.8)	1.2 (0.4–3.3)	−3.1 ± 2.1	−2.6 ± 1.9
Male	0.7 (0.2–2.4)	0.5 (0.1–2.1)	0.4 ± 2.5	1.6 ± 2.3
Blood pressure (+10 mm Hg)				
Systolic	1.2 (1.1–1.3)[****]	1.1 (1.0–1.3)[**]	Not included	Not included
Diastolic	1.1 (0.9–1.3)	Not included	Not included	Not included

[*]$P<0.1$. [**]$P<0.05$. [***]$P<0.01$. [****]$P<0.001$.

a. Social class included in regressions; not significant on multivariate analysis.

b. Numbers in parentheses indicate 95% confidence interval.

c. Mean ± standard error.

d. Changes in body mass index and lipids were equivalent to approximately 1 standard deviation.

e. HDL, high-density lipoprotein; GTT, glucose tolerance test classified according to World Health Organization criteria (WHO Expert Committee on Diabetes Mellitus, 2nd report, Geneva: World Health Organization, 1980, WHO technical report series 646).

f. Change in risk factor is 1 unit on square root scale. One unit of alcohol is 8.5 g of pure alcohol, approximately the amount of alcohol contained in 285 ml of beer or 130 ml of wine.

these methods. The values shown are either odds ratios and their 95% confidence intervals or mean values and their standard errors. They represent the effect on the prevalence of claudication or extent of disease for a difference in level of the risk factor of the magnitude shown. For example, for age and intermittent claudication, a univariate odds ratio of 2.0 indicates a doubling of prevalence for each 10 years of age. The odds ratio is shown as negative for ankle-brachial index, because the value of the index decreases further below 1 as the extent of disease increases. With respect to the results for ankle-brachial index, significant findings included less disease among women, taller subjects, and those with greater HDL-cholesterol concentrations and more disease in relation to greater non-HDL cholesterol and triglyceride concentrations, combined measures of glucose intolerance or diabetes mellitus, and cigarette smoking. The results were not strikingly different between methods of classifying peripheral arterial disease, except that the ankle-brachial index appeared to be a more sensitive measure for evaluating cross-sectional associations with sex, height, and glucose tolerance and diabetes. The relation with systolic blood pressure recognized in other studies of intermittent claudication as well as in these data cannot be tested with the ankle-arm index because systolic blood pressure is itself part of the measure of ankle-arm index.

In a US study of risk factors in relation to location of peripheral arterial disease in the affected vessel or vessels, it was again observed that both smoking and elevated systolic blood pressure were related to the presence of stenosis of the aortoiliac or femoropopliteal arteries, but not of the tibioperoneal arteries.[11] In the latter region, diabetes was more clearly related, but only among men. Mortality 5 and 10 years after diagnosis was also greater for persons with aortoiliac or femoropopliteal lesions, being two to seven times that for persons free of disease, and there was no significant increase in mortality for those with tibioperoneal lesions alone.

In one small prospective study in Finland, asymptomatic femoral atherosclerosis was detected by ultrasonography eight years after baseline characteristics were assessed.[12] Of 118 subjects, all free of diabetes and in their mid-30s at baseline, 33 were found to have plaques in their femoral arteries at follow-up. Because this condition was not evaluated at baseline, it is unknown whether these were truly incident cases. The most strongly related predictors of femoral atherosclerosis in univariate analysis were age, systolic and diastolic blood pressure, and blood concentrations of total and LDL cholesterol, total and LDL-associated triglycerides, apolipoprotein B, and fasting glucose. Only age and LDL-cholesterol concentration were independently associated in multivariate analysis, however, by the criterion of a P-value of .05 or less. Current smoking was one-third more frequent at baseline among those found to have femoral plaques, but this difference was not significant. No other measure of smoking was used.

Implications for Prevention and Treatment: Individuals and Populations

The prognostic importance of peripheral arterial disease lies in both the high mortality due to associated coronary and cerebrovascular disease and in the progressive increase in severity of localized disease among those who survive. Although noninvasive techniques often permit identification of disease prior to the onset of symptoms, recognition of peripheral arterial disease generally still occurs late in the development of atherosclerosis. General preventive measures against atherosclerosis are therefore desirable, and such measures would be expected to confer benefit in reduced risk for peripheral arterial disease as for other aspects of atherosclerosis. Both population-wide and high-risk strategies are appropriate.

Current Issues

Detection of disease by noninvasive methods should continue to be investigated and further studies undertaken of the ability to retard or reverse the progression of disease and to reduce the attendant mortality from atherosclerosis in other regions of the circulation. A more detailed discussion of this cardiovascular disorder can be found in the proceedings of a 1991 conference, edited by Fowkes, that addresses issues of measurement, descriptive epidemiology, predictive factors, and natural history and prevention.[13]

AORTIC ANEURYSM

Aortic aneurysm contributes to cardiovascular morbidity and mortality to much the same degree as does peripheral arterial disease. Unlike the latter condition, however, aortic aneurysm may be directly fatal as a consequence of rupture or complications of reparative surgery. Opportunity thus exists to monitor the occurrence of this condition through trends in mortality. Until about 1950, aortic aneurysm in the United States was predominantly due to syphilis and was most often located in the thoracic aorta. A transition in factors causing aortic disease led to dominance of atherosclerosis as the underlying process and more common appearance of abdominal aneurysms, consistent with the anatomic distribution of this disease. Accordingly, discussion here focuses specifically on abdominal aortic aneurysm.

Typical Course of the Individual Case

An aneurysm may first be recognized when it causes pain in the abdomen or lower back in an adult aged 60 years or older and leads to physical examination and X-ray. More often, detection precedes any symptoms, a circumstance that must depend on routine palpation of the abdomen by an examiner sensitized to the possibility of finding such an asymptomatic abnormality. The typical course involves progressive enlargement of the aneurysmal mass, with continuing risk of rupture. This is due to increasing tension on the aortic wall, which results from increasing diameter of the aneurysm. The normal diameter of the abdominal aorta is 2.5 cm. Aneurysms of less than 6 cm in diameter have a 15–20% risk of rupture within 10 years. If the aneurysm is not surgically repaired when a diameter of about 6 cm has been attained, this being more than twice normal, the 10-year risk of rupture increases sharply, to 45–50%. Surgery carries significant risks even when done as an elective procedure, with 5–10% mortality. But rupture with emergency surgery may be fatal in half of the cases surviving long enough to reach this stage of treatment.[14] This estimate of emergency surgical risk, which assumes the availability of adequate facilities, naturally understates the actual risk of death if such resources are lacking or inaccessible.

Background of Epidemiologic Investigation

An early investigation of the epidemiology of aortic aneurysm was based on mortality statistics for the United States from 1951 to 1981. These early data included thoracic as well as abdominal aneurysms, and they also included dissecting aneurysms, which reflect a different disease process and are now separately classified.[15] The overall finding was increasing age-adjusted mortality due to aortic aneurysm from 1951 to a peak in about 1970, followed by a decline to 1981, for White and Black males and females separately. It appeared that over this period persons born in more recent years were more likely than those born earlier to die of aortic aneurysm on attaining any given age; that is, a cohort effect was evident, with increased risk among more recent cohorts. Abdominal aneurysm rates, analyzed separately from 1968 to 1981, were several times higher than thoracic aneurysm rates and changed little if at all. This was noted to contrast with the trend in mortality from another manifestation of atherosclerosis, coronary heart disease, which began its sharp decrease in the United States in the mid- or late 1960s. Typical of the race-sex differences in mortality from abdominal aneurysm over this period were the rates for the latest year studied, 1981: for White males, 4.97/100,000; for non-White males, 1.49/100,000; for White females, 0.91/100,000; and for non-White females, 0.64/100,000. However, deaths from unspecified types of aneurysms were relatively more frequent than those for abdominal aneurysm among females and non-Whites than among males and Whites. This indicates substantial unreliability of death rates for abdominal aneurysm and suggests the need for caution in interpreting comparisons among race-sex groups based on these data.

Population Studies: Definition and Classification, Diagnostic Algorithms, and Criteria

Beyond the statistical coding of deaths and hospital discharges, by use of the International Classification of Diseases, methods for ascertainment of cases of abdominal aneurysm depend on physical examination, noninvasive imaging techniques, and contrast aortography. Methods differ among studies and must therefore be considered specifically in evaluating each report.

On physical examination, a characteristically pulsating mass may be felt in the midabdomen,

and on X-ray the image of a calcified band may appear that marks a zone of advanced atherosclerosis in the wall of the aorta. More detailed evaluation is possible by ultrasound examination, computed tomography, or arteriography.

Rates of Occurrence in Populations

In the community setting of Rochester, Minnesota, which has an integrated medical records system for inpatient and outpatient experience of the total population, incidence of both abdominal and thoracic aortic aneurysm was studied over the period from 1951 to 1980.[16] For this study, the diagnosis was accepted on the basis of the medical record if made by physical examination and confirmed by a second physician; if the radiologist made a firm diagnosis by ordinary X-ray (KUB, or kidney-ureter-bladder X-ray); or if it was based on ultrasonography, aortography, surgery, or autopsy. In Figure 6–2, contrasting trends are apparent. Unlike the mor-

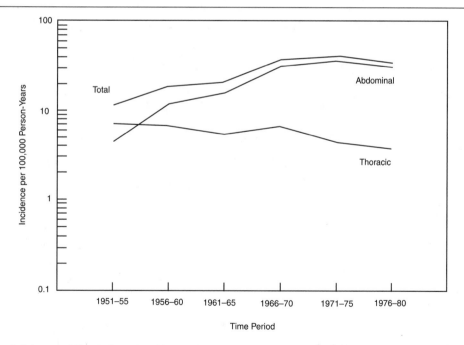

Figure 6–2 Age- and Sex-Adjusted Incidence of Abdominal, Thoracic, and Total Aortic Aneurysms, Rochester, Minnesota, Residents by Five-Year Time Periods, 1951–1980. *Source:* Reprinted with permission from JL Melton, *American Journal of Epidemiology*, Vol 120, No 3, p 381, © 1984, The Johns Hopkins University School of Hygiene and Public Health.

tality data seen nationally and discussed above, total incidence increased as a consequence of change in incidence of abdominal aneurysm, despite a continual decrease in incidence of thoracic aneurysm. To investigate the possibility that the increased incidence of abdominal aneurysm was due to greater frequency of smaller, previously less detectable lesions, the trends were examined for small, medium, and large aneurysms, as shown in Figure 6–3. The greatest increase was for small lesions, but both medium and large ones increased in incidence also. This issue was further evaluated by considering the basis for diagnosis, as described above and shown in Figure 6–4. Increased incidence was apparent from each of the methods from the 1950s to the 1960s, but during the 1960s and 1970s ultrasound became a major component of the diagnostic procedure and tended to displace physical examination and X-ray. Ultrasound contributed disproportionately more to detection of small lesions (less

than 5 cm diameter) in contrast to large ones. Overall, the smaller, asymptomatic, and uncomplicated lesions became more readily identifiable. These observations indicate that the occurrence of abdominal aneurysm should not be compared directly between studies in which different methods have been used.

Based on coded hospital discharges and deaths, investigators in England and Wales similarly observed increased incidence of abdominal aneurysms over the period from 1950 to 1984.[17] The increase in mortality was 20-fold for men and 11-fold, beginning a decade in age later, for women. By 1981–1983, the numbers of hospital admissions had increased to nearly three times the numbers in 1968–1971. Over this interval the percentage of admissions that were emergencies decreased only slightly (from 63% to 56%) and case-fatality also diminished slightly from 45% to 39%. Thus the marked rise in hospital admissions could not be explained by increased admission of cases milder than

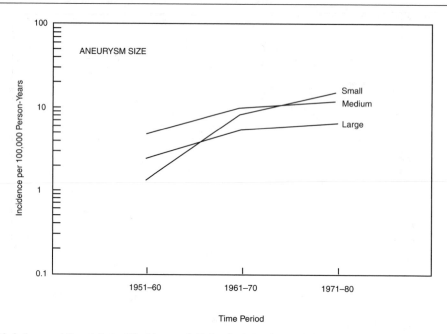

Figure 6–3 Age- and Sex-Adjusted Incidence of Abdominal Aortic Aneurysms by Size, Rochester, Minnesota, Residents by Decade of Study, 1951–1980. *Source:* Reprinted with permission from JL Melton, *American Journal of Epidemiology*, Vol 120, No 3, p 383, © 1984, The Johns Hopkins University School of Hygiene and Public Health.

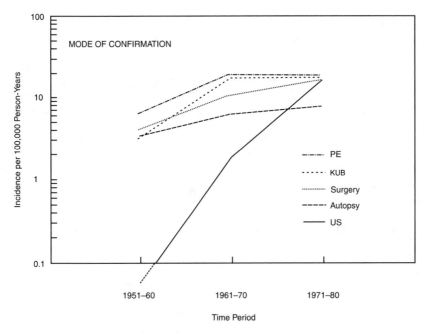

Figure 6–4 Age- and Sex-Adjusted Incidence of Abdominal Aortic Aneurysms by Mode of Confirmation, Rochester, Minnesota, Residents by Decade of Study, 1951–1980. *Source:* Reprinted with permission from JL Melton, *American Journal of Epidemiology,* Vol 120, No 3, p 383, © 1984, The Johns Hopkins University School of Hygiene and Public Health.

those admitted in the earlier period. It was noted that hospital data on deaths from abdominal aneurysm in the United Kingdom gave only limited insight, because one-half to two-thirds of such deaths occurred out of hospital.

Prevalence studies of abdominal aneurysm at autopsy have also shown increased occurrence of these lesions in recent decades, for example, in Sweden, Australia, and Japan. From 1965 to 1989, in Japan rates of unsuspected abdominal aneurysm at death in national autopsy surveys increased by 80% in men and by 50% in women.[18] Only abdominal aneurysm became more frequent over this period, while thoracic aneurysm became much less frequent and the occurrence of dissecting aneurysm fluctuated with no overall change. What changes have occurred in the population as a whole, beyond the hospitalized population alone, remains unknown.

Risks in Individuals

Based on a cross-sectional survey of more than 5000 adults aged 55 years and over, investigators in the Rotterdam Study in the Netherlands identified cases of abdominal aneurysm by ultrasound examination.[19] Aneurysm was diagnosed if the diameter of the most distant section of the abdominal aorta was 3.5 cm or greater, or if that diameter exceeded by 50% or more that of the most proximal section. Aneurysm was found in 91 of 2217 men and 21 of 3066 women examined. Prevalence increased sharply with age and was several times greater for men than women at every age, from 55–59 years to 80 years and over. Concurrent assessment (separately for men and women) of characteristics of the abdominal aneurysm cases relative to those without abdominal aneurysm indicated associations as shown in Table 6–5.

Table 6–5 Potential Risk Factors in Men and Women with and Without an Aneurysm of the Abdominal Aorta, Adjusted for Differences in Age, Rotterdam Study, 1989–1993

	Men			Women		
	Aneurysm of the Abdominal Aorta			Aneurysm of the Abdominal Aorta		
Risk Factor	Present (N = 91)	Absent (N = 2,126)	P Value	Present (N = 21)	Absent (N = 3,066)	P Value
Body mass index (kg/m²), mean	25.4	25.7	0.29	27.4	26.6	0.30
Systolic blood pressure (mm Hg), mean	142.0	138.6	0.14	142.8	139.5	0.48
Diastolic blood pressure (mm Hg), mean	76.5	74.7	0.14	75.5	73.5	0.41
Current smoking (%)	37.6	23.9	<0.01	56.0	19.1	<0.01
Serum cholesterol (mmol/l), mean	6.6	6.3	0.04	7.3	6.9	0.11
Serum HDL cholesterol[a] (mmol/l), mean	1.2	1.2	0.53	1.4	1.5	0.32
Hypertension (%)	29.2	26.5	0.59	42.1	32.9	0.37
Stroke (%)	1.8	3.9	0.31	9.0	2.3	0.05
Diabetes mellitus (%)	8.6	10.4	0.61	0.0	9.4	–
Intermittent claudication (%)	4.8	1.8	0.04	4.5	1.0	0.12
History of angina pectoris (%)	8.3	6.1	0.39	13.4	6.8	0.24
History of myocardial infarction (%)	15.7	11.0	0.17	8.7	3.3	0.37

a. HDL cholesterol, high-density lipoprotein cholesterol.

Source: Reprinted with permission from HJCM Pleumeekers, *American Journal of Epidemiology,* Vol 142, No 12, p 1297, © 1995, The Johns Hopkins University School of Hygiene and Public Health.

Current smoking was the most striking associated factor in both men and women, with serum cholesterol concentration in men and past stroke in women being additional statistically significant associated factors.

Aortic aneurysm has also been found to aggregate in families, as illustrated by a study of 91 first-degree relatives (parents and siblings but not, in this case, offspring) of cases identified in a regional hospital in Pittsburgh, Pennsylvania.[20] Compared with the corresponding relatives of persons without abdominal aortic aneurysm, the relative risks among fathers and mothers of cases were approximately 4, but with wide confidence limits that included 1. For siblings, however, the relative risks were large and the lower confidence bounds were greater

than 1, being 9.9 (4.3–19.5) for brothers and 22.9 (8.4–50.0) for sisters. This is strong evidence of a familial component, but further investigation is necessary to establish a meaningful pattern of inheritance. How much of this striking familial resemblance might reflect increased probability of detection due to diagnostic suspicion after the initial case is an unanswered question.

Implications for Prevention and Treatment: Individuals and Populations

Because emergency surgery may be unavailable and carries a high mortality risk in any case, reduction in case-fatality for abdominal aneurysm requires earlier intervention. This can be achieved only through systematic identification of subclinical or mildly symptomatic cases, which implies screening of selected population groups as a high-risk approach. The recent availability of noninvasive imaging techniques makes this approach possible in principle but, as discussed below, the topic is controversial.

From data so far available, prevention of abdominal aneurysms appears to require intervention on risk factors already identified for atherosclerosis and its other manifestations generally, especially blood lipids and smoking. It is paradoxical that, at least in the United States, the occurrence of this condition has increased markedly while coronary mortality has decreased dramatically over the same period. This suggests the need for much fuller investigation of abdominal aneurysm and caution against too simplistic an application of the same risk factor approaches to this disorder.

Current Issues

The question of whether population screening for abdominal aortic aneurysms should be recommended has been addressed in a number of reports. As with screening for any condition, considerations include the expected yield of cases, false positive and false negative rates from available screening methods, ability to confer benefit on identified cases, costs, and other aspects.

Favoring the adoption of a national screening program is a report from the Secretary of the Vascular Surgical Society of Great Britain and Ireland.[21] This report advocates use of portable ultrasound scanners for screening of men around their 65th birthday, their male siblings, and those with known chronic arterial disease, such as that manifested by intermittent claudication. Those found to have aneurysms of 5 cm diameter or greater would be selected for surgery, whereas those with lesser lesions would be monitored periodically. Economic analysis suggests that the costs would be minimal in relation to the "quality of life-adjusted years" (often called "QALYs") saved.

A contrary view is presented by the Canadian Task Force on the Periodic Health Examination, which concluded: "There is poor evidence to include screening through physical examination or ultrasonography for abdominal aortic aneurysms in or exclude it from the periodic health examination of asymptomatic people."[22(p 787)] The group recommended research related to several concerns, including the value of physical examination alone relative to ultrasonography as the standard, and of serial ultrasonography for small lesions; identification of predictors of development and enlargement of lesions; the role of ultrasound examination in high-risk persons; and effective strategies for education of physicians about the benefits of surgery for this condition.

CONGESTIVE HEART FAILURE

Congestive heart failure or, more simply, heart failure is a condition that reflects impairment of the pumping function of the left ventricle of the heart, as described earlier in this chapter. As a result, blood flow from the left ventricle into the aorta and to the peripheral arterial circulation is reduced. In addition, failure to eject the blood from the left ventricle leads to increased back-pressure in the pulmonary circulation, with reduced blood flow through the lungs and exudation (seepage of fluid) from the blood to the tissue spaces in the lung, producing the "congestive" component of the condition. Congestive heart failure may result from any of several underlying processes, such as myocardial infarction, which causes significant localized damage to the ventricular wall; cardiomyopathies such as Chagas' disease, which results in more-generalized loss of heart muscle cell function; or valvular heart disease, such as in chronic rheumatic heart disease, which causes valvular obstruction to outflow from and leakage or regurgitation of blood flow back into the left ventricle.

Typical Course of the Individual Case

As long as compensatory physiologic changes suffice to maintain adequate left ventricular function, the course of heart failure is the course of the underlying disease. Once heart failure develops, its main clinical manifestations are generally similar regardless of its origin. However, in the case of coronary heart disease, as in acute myocardial infarction, the onset of heart failure may be very sudden. The presence of heart failure in the acute phase of myocardial infarction is a poor prognostic sign, and its effective treatment is important for immediate survival. Recovery may be complete, however, with no recurring signs or symptoms of heart failure. Chronic congestive heart failure either reflects its persistence following an acute onset and partial recovery or indicates gradual ventricular decompensation occurring over weeks, months, or years. Fatigue and shortness of breath on minimal exertion are among the many clinical indications of heart failure. Treatment may improve function and prolong life for several years, but progressive decompensation or other complications result in death in a large proportion of cases.

Background of Epidemiologic Investigation

Epidemiologic investigation of heart failure has been limited due to some of the features just described. Its character as an end-stage development in the course of several distinct diseases has prevented its clear and consistent identification in mortality or hospital statistics. Gradual onset delays its recognition, so case incidence is difficult to define. Given its sometimes prolonged clinical course, death due to an intervening coronary event or stroke may overshadow the presence of heart failure and lead to its omission from the diagnoses entered or coded on the death certificate. Alternatively, a death may be attributed simply to heart failure when a more specific disease should have been indicated. Clinical definitions and classification have also been limited by the nonspecific nature of the symptoms of heart failure, in contrast, for example, to the distinctive pain of myocardial infarction or intermittent claudication.

Population Studies: Definition and Classification, Diagnostic Algorithms, and Criteria

Epidemiologic studies of heart failure have required criteria by which to identify cases. A prominent example is the Framingham Study, which has published several reports on heart failure with successively longer periods of follow-up, most recently for 40 years.[23] The Framingham criteria for heart failure are shown in Exhibit 6–2. They take the form of a list of symptoms, physical findings, and physiological measurements grouped as "major" and "minor" criteria. Classification as a case requires that two major or one major and two minor criteria be present, with no other medical explanation than heart failure for the presence of the minor criteria used in a given case.

As a cause of death or hospital admission or discharge, heart failure would be expected to appear under the ICD 10, as shown in Exhibit 6–1.[1] Uncertainty whether the presence of hypertensive heart or renal disease would be noted, leading to codes I11 or I13 would seem to require an attempt at comprehensive inclusion of these with I50 to identify all coded non-rheumatic cases of congestive heart failure. However, cases actually due to rheumatic heart disease or other nonhypertensive and nonatherosclerotic causes might be included erroneously under I50 due to incomplete specification. The extent of this misclassification and admixture of cases would be expected to vary with the relative frequencies of these diseases in different populations. Clearly, the comparison of mortality from congestive heart failure between populations or over periods of decades could be misleading if variations in underlying disease frequencies were not taken into account, and to do so is at best difficult.

Rates of Occurrence in Populations

With this understanding of case identification, available data can be illustrated from sev-

Exhibit 6–2 Criteria for Congestive Heart Failure, the Framingam Study

---

Major Criteria

Paroxysmal nocturnal dyspnea
Neck vein distention
Rales
Radiographic cardiomegaly (increasing heart size on chest X-ray film)
Acute pulmonary edema
Third sound gallop
Increased central venous pressure (>16 cm water at the right atrium)
Circulation time ≥25 seconds
Hepatojugular reflux
Pulmonary edema, visceral congestion, or cardiomegaly at autopsy
Weight loss ≥4.5 kg in 5 days in response to treatment of CHF

Minor Criteria

Bilateral ankle edema
Nocturnal cough
Dyspnea on ordinary exertion
Hepatomegaly
Pleural effusion
Decrease in vital capacity by 33% from maximal value recorded
Tachycardia (rate ≥120 beat/min)

Note: The diagnosis of congestive heart failure (CHF) required that two major or one major and two minor criteria be present concurrently. Minor criteria were acceptable only if they could not be attributed to another medical condition.

Source: Reprinted with permission from the American College of Cardiology, *Journal of the American College of Cardiology*, 1993, Vol 22, No 4, p 7A.

---

eral sources. Mortality and hospital discharge data for heart failure in the United States have been reviewed by Gillum, most recently for the period 1979 to 1990. These years were selected because coding for the whole period was under the Ninth Revision of the ICD; therefore trends would not be influenced by prescribed changes in coding procedures.[24] It was concluded from the mortality data that no decline in death rates from heart failure had occurred from 1979 through 1988 (while coronary heart disease deaths continued to decline sharply) and that changes in the standard death certificate itself could have accounted for an apparent decline in 1989 and 1990.

Mortality

Data compiled by the National Heart, Lung and Blood Institute for deaths due to heart failure from 1968 to 1993 are shown in Figure 6–5 for four sex-race groups.[25] They indicate the effect on trends of the change from ICD 8 to ICD 9 in 1978–1979 and the introduction of changes in the death certificate in 1989. For Whites in all time intervals, death rates increased. For Blacks they decreased overall in the first period, 1968–1978, increased overall in the second period, 1979–1988, and fluctuated in the third period, 1989–1993. In all periods rates were higher for Blacks, both men and women, than for either White men or White women.

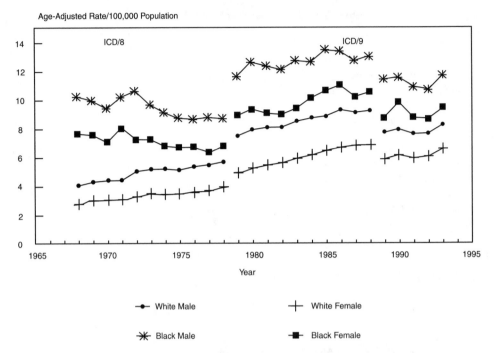

Figure 6–5 Death Rates for Heart Failure by Race and Sex, United States, 1968–1993. *Source:* Reprinted from National Heart, Lung and Blood Institute, National Institutes of Health, Bethesda, Maryland.

Another approach to estimation of mortality related to this condition was to exploit data from long-term follow-up of participants in the first US National Health and Nutrition Examination Survey (NHANES I) of noninstitutionalized persons aged 25–74.[26] Here the strategy was to identify cases of heart failure by criteria applied at the initial survey, conducted from 1971 to 1975, and to determine their subsequent mortality over a 15-year follow-up period. All deaths were included, irrespective of their cause according to the death certificate. Table 6–6 shows the results by age and sex in relation to two methods of case definition at baseline. The first method was self-report, based on survey responses to the medical history questionnaire that asked participants whether a physician had ever told them they had heart failure. The second method used a clinical score based on an adaptation of the Framingham criteria, above, which took into account the relevant observations available from the survey. For women

aged 55–64 and 65–74 years, respectively, the 15-year postsurvey mortality rates were approximately 40% and 60% for those identified by self-report and 25% and 50% for those identified by clinical score. For men, the corresponding frequencies were 50% and 75% (self-report) and 65% and 80% (clinical score) for age groups 55–64 and 65–74 years, respectively. Mortality was clearly very high in all age-sex groups, especially for men, by either method of case identification. Curiously, mortality was higher for self-reported than for clinically identified women, but the reverse was true for men.

A special aspect of death in the presence of heart failure is the high frequency of sudden death. It has been reported from the Framingham Study that 40%–50% of deaths in the presence of heart failure were sudden, defined as occurring within one hour in a previously stable patient.[27] Based on 30 years of follow-up in the Framingham Study population, the presence of previous heart failure increased the risk of sud-

Table 6–6 Estimated 15-Year Total Mortality for Persons with Congestive Heart Failure, United States, 1971–1986, NHANES-I Follow-Up

| | Total Mortality | | | |
| | Self-Report | | Clinical Score | |
Gender and Age (yr)	%	Estimated No. of Deaths	%	Estimated No. of Deaths
Women				
55 to 64	37.6	76,068	26.2	79,442
65 to 74	62.6	143,619	51.4	162,815
Total 55 to 74	50.8	219,687	39.1	242,257
Men				
55 to 64	52	101,897	66.8	271,963
65 to 74	73.2	149,060	79.3	216,940
Total 55 to 74	62.8	250,957	71.8	488,903
Women and Men				
55 to 64	44.7	177,965	49.5	351,405
65 to 74	67.6	292,679	64.3	379,755
Total 55 to 74	56.6	470,644	56.2	731,160

Source: Reprinted with permission from the American College of Cardiology, *Journal of the American College of Cardiology,* 1992, Vol 20, No 2, p 304.

den death sevenfold when coronary heart disease was absent and nearly ninefold in the presence of both coronary heart disease and heart failure.

Incidence and Hospitalization Rates

Incidence of heart failure can be studied only in cohort studies or in unusual settings for monitoring diagnoses in a community. For example, the Framingham Study used the criteria in Exhibit 6–2 to identify new cases of heart failure at each biennial examination after the baseline assessment, which began in 1948.[23] Annual incidence was nearly 0 through age 49 but increased sharply for men from 3/1000 at ages 50–59 to 27/1000 at ages 80–89. For women lower rates were observed at each age, but the increase with age was nearly as steep as for men and about one-half decade of age later. Notably, incidence decreased for both men and women over the 40 years of observation, by 11% per calendar decade for men and 17% for women.

Through use of community hospital and clinic records in Rochester, Minnesota, incidence of new diagnoses of congestive heart failure in one calendar year were determined.[28] From January 1 through December 31, 1981, a total of 46 new cases were diagnosed according to criteria published previously by the Framingham Study. The estimated incidence ranged from approximately 0.8 to 9.8 per 1000 from ages 55–59 to 70–74 for women, and from 2.75 to 16 per 1000 for men from ages 55–59 to 65–69 (the rate was somewhat lower but based on a small number of cases at ages 70–74). These rates were more or less consistent with those from Framingham, though this may be more coincidental than confirmatory because the calendar time of ascertainment was not comparable between studies.

Hospital discharge data presented by Gillum indicated the effect of choosing only the first-listed diagnosis or all diagnoses to identify cases.[24] On the basis of the first-listed discharge diagnosis alone, from 1986 to 1990 heart failure was responsible for 103,000 to 117,000 hospitalizations per year at ages 45–64 (corresponding to population rates of 227–249 per 100,000) and 461,000 to 560,000 per year at ages 65 and over (rates of 1582–1772 per 100,000). The estimated frequency of such discharges was about two and one-half to three times greater when all diagnoses were identified rather than when using the first diagnosis alone. For these two age groups, overall trends in hospital discharges attributed to heart failure (whether first-listed diagnosis or all diagnoses was not specified) increased steadily from 1971 to 1993 (Figure 6–6).[25] At ages over 65, congestive heart failure is reportedly the most frequent cause of hospitalization in the United States at this time.

Hospital case-fatality was also reported on the basis of hospital discharge data by the National Heart, Lung, and Blood Institute.[25] Figure 6–7 presents the trend in case-fatality for heart failure from 1981 to 1993 for persons aged under 65 and those aged 65 and over. For both groups, the trends were generally downward, and they were roughly parallel for the two age groups. Coupled with the increased hospitalization rates seen in Figure 6–6, these data suggest that either improved treatment or much-reduced severity of hospitalized cases must underlie these trends.

Prevalence

From the US National Health and Nutrition Examination Surveys I–III, conducted in 1971–1975, 1976–1980, and 1988–1991 (phase 1), estimates of the prevalence of heart failure can be compared over nearly two decades.[25] Figure 6–8 indicates the percentage prevalence of congestive heart failure for both men and women, by age from 35 to 75 years, based on self-report in health interviews, as in the report discussed above. Prevalence increased sharply by age for both men and women and was substantially greater in the most recent period than in the previous sur-

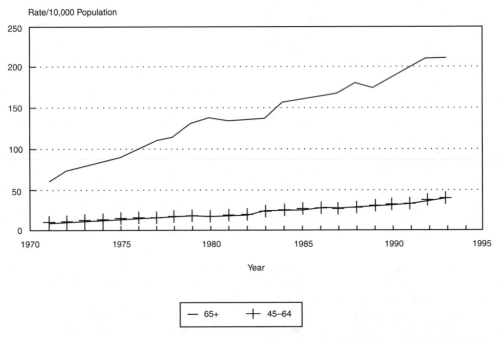

Figure 6–6 Hospitalization Rates for Congestive Heart Failure by Age, United States, 1971–1993. *Source:* Reprinted from National Heart, Lung and Blood Institute, National Institutes of Health, Bethesda, Maryland.

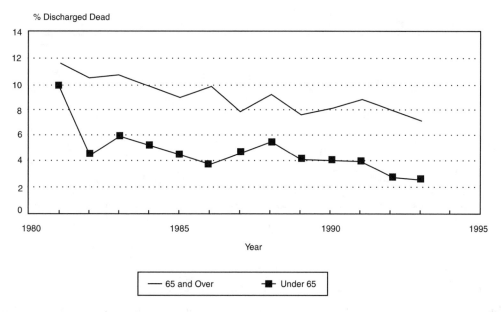

Figure 6–7 Hospital Case-Fatality Rate for Congestive Heart Failure by Age, United States, 1981–1993. *Source:* Reprinted from National Heart, Lung and Blood Institute, National Institutes of Health, Bethesda, Maryland.

veys. By extrapolation from the survey sample to the corresponding US population, the number of cases of heart failure increased from 1.5 million in the 1960s to 4.7 million by 1993.

Risks in Individuals

The factors predicting development of heart failure as observed in the Framingham Study are shown for men in Figure 6–9 and for women in Figure 6–10.[23] These figures show, separately by age groups 35–64 and 65–94 years, the relative risk of developing congestive heart failure in relation to cholesterol concentration, smoking, hypertension, diabetes, and presence of left ventricular hypertrophy (enlargement) as determined by electrocardiography (ECG-LVH). In addition, the age-adjusted incidence of heart failure in the presence or absence of each factor is shown. Inclusion of left ventricular hypertrophy as a risk factor is questionable, both because this finding is indicative of the disease process itself and because it appears to diminish the importance of the other predic-

tors. Among the other factors, those most strongly related to the risk of heart failure were hypertension and diabetes, for both men and women at both age levels.

Implications for Prevention and Treatment: Individuals and Populations

It is apparent from the high mortality associated with heart failure that its treatment, even though improving, remains limited in its impact on survival.[29] Increased survival to date means, in the United States, increasing numbers of hospital admissions for this condition each year. The potential benefit of further reducing the incidence of congestive heart failure is in reducing rates of disability, hospitalization, and death. Ideally, these goals would be attained by reduced incidence of the underlying cardiac disorders, including atherosclerotic and hypertensive heart disease and others discussed elsewhere in this book. Effective intervention to prevent the risks associated with smoking, hypertension, and diabetes would appear to be

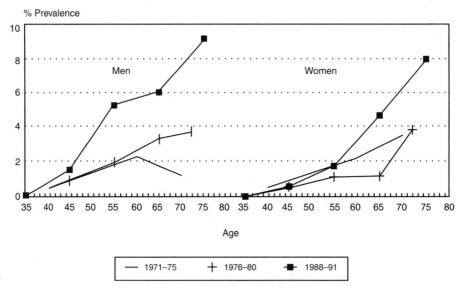

Figure 6–8 Prevalence of Congestive Heart Failure from Health Interviews, White Men and Women, United States, 1971–1975 to 1988–1991. *Source:* Reprinted from the US National Health and Nutrition Examination Survey.

especially likely to reduce the frequency of congestive heart failure based on coronary heart disease and hypertension. Any of these factors present in persons with rheumatic heart disease or cardiomyopathy also would seem to justify special control measures before overt cardiac failure has developed. As emphasized above, however, it is important to recognize the different contributions of specific cardiac disorders to the occurrence of congestive heart failure in different populations in which atherosclerotic and hypertensive diseases are not currently dominant.

Current Issues

The principal issues concerning congestive heart failure currently are the rising frequency of hospitalization for this condition, its continuing high disability and mortality, and the limited information about its occurrence due to difficulties in its epidemiologic investigation. Some of the problems in interpretation of mortality data have been discussed. Problems with hospital discharge data include their susceptibility to

influences on the use of discharge codes by their reimbursement value and their correspondence to episodes of hospitalization rather than individuals. Therefore these data are potentially unreliable as a measure of either incidence or prevalence of the condition. Community surveillance programs could, in principle, monitor indicators of the occurrence of congestive heart failure based on existing criteria, but the standardized recording of the requisite signs, symptoms, and physiologic measures for suspect cases is unlikely to be feasible, and new algorithms are required before practical and comparable methods of monitoring can be implemented.

Another issue not elsewhere addressed is that of right heart failure not consequent on primary left-sided failure but resulting from disease of the lungs and designated as *chronic cor pulmonale* (pulmonary heart disease). Among the terms used in connection with this condition is *chronic obstructive pulmonary disease*, which might arise from any of a number of underlying diseases, but especially chronic bronchitis or emphysema. A major contributor is cigarette

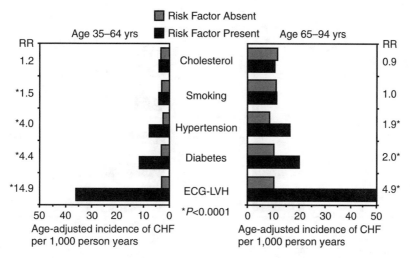

Figure 6–9 Risk Factors for Congestive Heart Failure (CHF) in Men, the Framingham Study, 1948–1988. Relative risks (RR) for the development of heart failure in the presence of the specified risk factor are displayed at the margins; values with asterisks are significant at *P*<0.0001. Cholesterol, serum cholesterol >6.2 mmol/l (240 mg/dl); ECG-LVH, electrocardiographic left ventricular hypertrophy. *Source:* Reprinted with permission from the American College of Cardiology, *Journal of the American College of Cardiology*, 1993, Vol 22, No 2, p 9A.

smoking, with air pollution, childhood respiratory tract infections, and occupational dust exposures among specific causes.[30] This condition, like congestive heart failure, is difficult to study epidemiologically because of lack of standardization in definition, diagnostic criteria, and classification. To the extent that the tobacco epidemic continues, the long-term future risks of right-sided heart failure will continue to increase. Better means are needed to monitor this condition also, and thereby to assess its natural history and potential responsiveness to preventive measures both for populations and for high-risk individuals.

DEEP VEIN THROMBOSIS AND PULMONARY EMBOLISM

Relative to the other conditions discussed here, less epidemiologic attention has been given to deep vein thrombosis and pulmonary embolism. For example, only very limited data on their frequency of occurrence are given in the annual chartbook of the National Heart, Lung and Blood Institute,[2] and none appears in

the annual statistical summaries from the American Heart Association (see citations in previous chapters). A recent review by Goldhaber[31] offers one epidemiologic citation, and the condition is not discussed in Fowkes' book on the epidemiology of peripheral vascular disease.[13] There is more extensive literature on prevention and treatment of these conditions, with a substantial basis of experience in randomized clinical trials[32,33]; the focus of this research is essentially on hospitalized patients, in whom these conditions are especially likely to be recognized. Therefore only a brief overview is presented here to call greater attention to the problems presented by these conditions and to support the view that wider epidemiologic investigation of them is warranted.

Typically, deep vein thrombosis is found in hospitalized patients who have been confined to bed, especially those who are immobilized to the greatest degree. The most apparent local complications include swelling and pain, often in the calf and below. The chief concern about deep vein thrombosis is the attendant risk of pulmonary embolism. This is a sometimes fatal

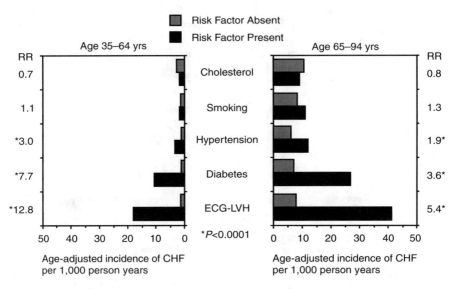

Figure 6–10 Risk Factors for Congestive Heart Failure (CHF) in Women, the Framingham Study, 1948–1988. Relative risks (RR) for the development of heart failure in the presence of the specified risk factor are displayed at the margins; values with asterisks are significant at P<0.0001. Definitions as in Figure 6–9. *Source:* Reprinted with permission from the American College of Cardiology, *Journal of the American College of Cardiology,* 1993, Vol 22, No 2, p 9A.

complication resulting from venous transport of a portion of a blood clot from the lower extremity through the right heart to the lung, where blood flow becomes obstructed, pulmonary function impaired, and acute right heart failure or cor pulmonale may be precipitated by increased resistance to outflow from the right ventricle. Although this progression is most readily observed in patients while in hospital, it has been reported that in surgical patients the occurrence of pulmonary embolism was frequently more than two weeks following surgery; the median onset was at the 18th postoperative day. Taking into account events within 30 days of surgery increased the estimated frequency by 30%.[31] The trend toward shorter periods of hospitalization after surgery, at least in the United States, raises the possibility that persons remaining relatively immobilized at home after discharge may be at risk of developing these complications without close observation and timely intervention if needed. Not only surgical patients but those in intensive care related to acute coronary events or stroke

share a relatively high risk of these complications. Anecdotal reports of cases occurring after air travel of several hours' duration add to concern about this problem.

Studies of hospital-based patient populations have included investigation of diagnostic approaches to both deep vein thrombosis and pulmonary embolism. Diagnosis of these conditions in many cases remains difficult, and diagnostic practices are likely to differ widely in different settings. Detection of thrombosis in deep calf veins is more reliable than detection in the more proximal veins of the lower extremity (a particular concern in patients undergoing hip surgery, for example).[32] Imaging techniques such as infusion of radioiodine (I-125) labeled fibrinogen followed by scanning of the leg are reportedly sensitive to the former type of thrombus but not the latter. Pulmonary embolism produces symptoms and signs of varying severity and may be difficult to detect clinically in mild cases.[31] Occurrence and recognition of these complications in hospital does not ensure their inclusion in reported hospital discharge statistics or in death certificate data, especially if only the first-listed diagnosis or underlying cause of death is coded and tabulated. This issue clouds interpretation and comparison of reported frequencies of these events over time or between populations.

For these reasons, the true rates of occurrence of deep vein thrombosis or pulmonary embolism are difficult to establish in any population. Goldhaber, for example, ascribed to these conditions "hundreds of thousands of hospitalizations annually in the U.S.,"[31(p 1582)] but this statement contrasts sharply with data in Table 6–1.[2] Further, Goldhaber and Sors attributed 50,000 deaths per year in the United States to pulmonary embolism,[33] a figure more than four times that shown in Table 6–1, based on reported deaths for 1993.[2] Frequencies of occurrence of fatal postoperative pulmonary embo-

lism in patients with general elective surgery, elective hip surgery, and emergency hip surgery have been reported to range from 0.1% to 0.8%, 0.3% to 1.7%, and 4% to 7%, respectively.[32] These figures are given for patient groups not receiving prophylaxis, however, so that in settings where standards of practice include currently recommended preventive measures, lower frequencies would be expected.

Factors that identify higher-risk individuals undergoing surgery are summarized in Table 6–7.[32] The relation between risk and the nature of the surgery may reflect aspects of the procedure that activate hemostatic mechanisms predisposing to thrombus formation, general health characteristics of the patients, association of the procedures with typical postoperative immobilization, or possibly other factors. Whatever the underlying mechanisms, the risk

Table 6–7 Risk Categories for Postoperative Venous Thromboembolism

Risk Category	Risk of Venous Thromboembolism (%)		
	Calf Vein Thrombosis[a]	Proximal Vein Thrombosis[a]	Fatal Pulmonary Embolism
High Risk	40–80	10–30	1–5
General surgery in patients >40 years with recent history of deep vein thrombosis or pulmonary embolism			
Extensive pelvic or abdominal surgery for malignant disease			
Major orthopaedic surgery of lower limbs			
Moderate Risk[b]	10–40	2–10	0.1–0.8
General surgery in patients >40 years lasting 30 minutes or more			
Low Risk	<10	<1	<0.01
Uncomplicated surgery in patients <40 years without additional risk factors			
Minor surgery (that is, <30 minutes) in patients >40 years without additional risk factors			

a. Venographically confirmed.

b. The risk is increased by advancing age, malignancy, prolonged immobility, and cardiac failure.

Source: Reprinted with permission from RD Hull, VV Kakkar, and GE Raskob, Prevention of Venous Thrombosis and Pulmonary Embolism, in *Thrombosis in Cardiovascular Disorders*, V Fuster and M Verstraete, eds, p 453, © 1992, WB Saunders Company.

profile helps to identify those most likely to benefit from intervention.

Prevention and treatment have been considered to date in reference to the individual patient. Population-wide measures applicable to these vascular conditions might include policies concerning counseling about risks of elective surgical procedures, prehospitalization risk assessment and early prophylaxis, standards of inpatient and posthospital diagnostic surveillance, and perhaps others, such as in-flight exercise. Individual interventions include both prophylaxis for prevention of deep vein thrombosis as well as treatment of deep vein thrombosis for prevention of pulmonary embolism.[31–33] Broadly, the main elements of prophylaxis are reduction of venous stasis (loss of normal venous blood flow) and of the propensity toward thrombosis in the peripheral venous circulation. The first depends on maintenance of venous flow by mechanical devices such as intermittent pneumatic leg compression or graduated compression stockings. The second depends on use of low-dose anticoagulants. In the presence of pulmonary embolism, intensive supportive care may be needed as well as more-aggressive anticoagulant therapy.

Current issues in the epidemiology and prevention of deep vein thrombosis and pulmonary embolism include the need for standardization of diagnostic procedures and the recording, coding, and tabulation of data in more consistent ways to provide better estimates of their frequency. Especially of concern is the increased period at risk after hospital discharge as a result of reduced hospital stays. Although much could be done to advance knowledge of these conditions within the hospital environment, it is apparent that posthospitalization follow-up is needed to document the incidence and prevalence of these conditions more fully. By implication, other settings in which persons at risk may be immobilized temporarily or long-term, such as in chronic care facilities, should be included in the interest of more complete case ascertainment. Whether factors predisposing to these complications can be more adequately defined to support further development of prevention strategies for high-risk cases is another question deserving epidemiologic investigation.

REFERENCES

1. World Health Organization. *International Statistical Classification of Diseases and Related Health Problems. Tenth Revision.* Geneva, Switzerland: World Health Organization; 1992;1.

2. *Morbidity and Mortality: 1996 Chartbook on Cardiovascular, Lung, and Blood Diseases.* Bethesda, Md: National Institutes of Health, National Heart, Lung and Blood Institute; 1996.

3. Criqui MH. Peripheral arterial disease. In: Pearson TA, Criqui MH, Luepker RV, Oberman A, Winston M, eds. *Primer in Preventive Cardiology.* Dallas, Texas: American Heart Association: 1994; 83–91.

4. Rose GA. The diagnosis of ischaemic heart pain and intermittent claudication in field surveys. *Bull World Health Organ.* 1962;27:645–658.

5. Criqui MH, Fronek A, Klauber MR, Barrett-Connor E, et al. The sensitivity, specificity, and predictive value of traditional clinical evaluation of peripheral arterial disease: results from noninvasive testing in a defined population. *Circ.* 1985;71:516–522.

6. Feigelson HS, Criqui MH, Fronek A, Langer RD, et al. Screening for peripheral arterial disease: the sensitivity, specificity, and predictive value of noninvasive tests in a defined population. *Am J Epidemiol.* 1994; 140:526–534.

7. Criqui MH, Fronek A, Barrett-Connor E, Klauber MR, et al. The prevalence of peripheral arterial disease in a defined population. *Circ.* 1985;71:510–515.

8. Kuller L, Borhani N, Furberg C, Gardin J, et al. Prevalence of subclinical atherosclerosis and cardiovascular disease and association with risk factors in the Cardiovascular Health Study. *Am J Epidemiol.* 1994;139: 1164–1179.

9. Criqui MH, Langer RD, Fronek A, Feigelson HS, et al. Mortality over a period of 10 years in patients with peripheral arterial disease. *N Eng J Med.* 1992;326: 381–386.

10. Fowkes FGR, Housley E, Riemersma RA, Macintyre CCA, et al. Smoking, lipids, glucose intolerance, and blood pressure as risk factors for peripheral atheroscle-

rosis compared with ischemic heart disease in the Edinburgh Artery Study. *Am J Epidemiol.* 1992;135: 331–340.

11. Vogt MT, Wolfson SK, Kuller LH. Segmental arterial disease in the lower extremities: correlates of disease and relationship to mortality. *J Clin Epidemiol.* 1993; 46:1267–1276.

12. Kekäläinen P, Sarlund H, Farin P, Kaukanen E, et al. Femoral atherosclerosis in middle-aged subjects: association with cardiovascular risk factors and insulin resistance. *Am J Epidemiol.* 1996;144:742–748.

13. Fowkes FGR, ed. *Epidemiology of Peripheral Vascular Disease.* London: Springer-Verlag; 1991.

14. Dalen JE. Diseases of the aorta. In: Braunwald E, Isselbacher KJ, Petersdorf RG, Wilson JD, Martin JB, Fauci AS, eds. *Harrison's Principles of Internal Medicine.* 11th ed. New York: McGraw-Hill Book Co; 1987.

15. Lilienfeld DE, Gunderson PD, Sprafka JM, Vargas C. Epidemiology of aortic aneurysms: I. mortality trends in the United States, 1951 to 1981. *Arteriosclerosis.* 1987;7:637–643.

16. Melton LJ III, Bickerstaff LK, Hollier LH, Van Peenen HJ, et al. Changing incidence of abdominal aortic aneurysms: a population-based study. *Am J Epidemiol.* 1984;120:379–386.

17. Fowkes FGR, Macintyre CCA, Ruckley CV. Increasing incidence of aortic aneurysms in England and Wales. *Br Med J.* 1989;298:33–35.

18. Hu Y, Shimizu H, Takatsuka N, Ido M, et al. Trends in prevalence rates of asymptomatic aortic aneurysms in Japan based on autopsy series. *Am J Epidemiol.* 1995; 5:159–163.

19. Pleumeekers HJCM, Hoes AW, van der Does E, van Urk H, et al. Aneurysms of the abdominal aorta in older adults. *Am J Epidemiol.* 1995;142:1291–1299.

20. Webster MW, St. Jean PL, Steed DL, Ferrell RE, et al. Abdominal aortic aneurysm: results of a family study. *J Vasc Surg.* 1991;13:366–372.

21. Harris PL. Reducing the mortality from abdominal aortic aneurysms: need for a national screening programme. *Br Med J.* 1992;305:697–699.

22. Canadian Task Force on the Periodic Health Examination. Periodic health examination, 1991 update: 5. Screening for abdominal aortic aneurysm. *Can Med Assoc J.* 1991;145:783–789.

23. Ho KKL, Pinsky JL, Kannel WB, Levy D. The epidemiology of heart failure: The Framingham Study. *J Amer Coll Cardiol.* 1993;22(suppl A):6A–13A.

24. Gillum RF. Epidemiology of heart failure in the United States. *Am Heart J.* 1993;126:1042–1047.

25. *Chartbook for the Special Emphasis Panel on Cardiovascular Disease Community Surveillance.* Bethesda, Md: US Dept of Health and Human Services, National Heart, Lung and Blood Institute; 1996.

26. Schocken DD, Arrieta MI, Leaverton PE, Ross EA. Prevalence and mortality rate of congestive heart failure in the United States. *J Am Coll Cardiol.* 1992; 20:301–306.

27. Kannel WB, Plehn JF, Cupples A. Cardiac failure and sudden death in the Framingham Study. *Am Heart J.* 1988;115:869–875.

28. Rodeheffer RJ, Jacobsen SJ, Gersh BJ, Kottke TE, et al. The incidence and prevalence of congestive heart failure in Rochester, Minnesota. *Mayo Clin Proc.* 1993;68:1143–1150.

29. Firth BG, Yancy CW. Jr. Survival in congestive heart failure: have we made a difference? *Am J Med.* 1990; 90:1-3N–1-7N.

30. Bumgarner JR, Speizer FE. Chronic obstructive pulmonary disease. In: Jamison DT, Mosley WH, Measham AR, Bobadilla JL, eds. *Disease Control Priorities in Developing Countries.* Oxford, England: Oxford University Press; 1993;595–608.

31. Goldhaber SZ. Pulmonary embolism. In: Braunwald E, ed. *Heart Disease: A Textbook of Cardiovascular Medicine,* 5th ed. Philadelphia, Pa: WB Saunders Co; 1997;1582–1603.

32. Hull RD, Kakkar VV, Raskob GE. Prevention of venous thrombosis and pulmonary embolism. In: Fuster V, Verstraete M, eds. *Thrombosis in Cardiovascular Disorders.* Philadelphia, Pa: WB Saunders Co; 1992: 451–464.

33. Goldhaber SZ, Sors H. Treatment of venous thrombosis and pulmonary embolism. In: Fuster V, Verstraete M, eds. *Thrombosis in Cardiovascular Disorders.* Philadelphia, Pa: WB Saunders Co; 1992:465–483.

CHAPTER 7

Age, Sex, Race, and Heredity

SUMMARY

Among the main determinants of the atherosclerotic and hypertensive diseases, and in principle all diseases, four are so fundamental as to require attention in connection with virtually every other specific factor. These are age, sex, race, and heredity. Although they are necessarily addressed throughout this book, each warrants brief discussion as background for its mention elsewhere. Each of these factors identifies one or more dimensions of diversity in populations. Each points to relative lack of health information about some important and identifiable populations or groups. Recognition of this circumstance has resulted in increased attention to the need for data specific for women and for minority populations in the United States. Increased sensitivity is also necessitated by the dilemma of prevention policies for which the efficacy or safety may not have been investigated sufficiently in diverse population groups. Balance between acquisition of further group-specific data and timely implementation of preventive policies that are reasonably expected to benefit the population as a whole should be maintained to ensure that these benefits are not denied to the groups who need them most. While the factors discussed here are often presumed to be unmodifiable, each serves in some respects as a marker for underlying behaviors, exposures, or other factors (cofactors) more directly related to disease risks and outcomes. Therefore, interpretation of associations of cofactors with, for example, race or ethnicity, as representing fixed genetic or cultural differences rather than modifiable aspects of living habits or environment, may be mistaken and misleading. Development of genetic epidemiology as a hybrid discipline is recent, yet a substantial body of research in this area has already contributed to understanding of genetic and environmental factors in coronary heart disease and its risk factors as well as in other areas. Deeper appreciation of the concepts of genetic determinants of disease by epidemiologists and new applications of these concepts in cardiovascular epidemiology are likely to yield significant research advances. These will progress most fruitfully if laboratory and population studies are pursued in concert.

INTRODUCTION

The characteristics of individuals addressed here—age, sex, race, and heredity—underlie the expression of each of the disease processes discussed in the preceding chapters as well as their determinants discussed in the chapters that follow. Their influence is ubiquitous. A separate book devoted to each of these characteristics would simply rearrange the same information along different axes of orientation. A separate chapter for each of them would not suffice, because each condition and each of the main determinants would require attention as it relates to each of these four characteristics. The present chapter, instead, offers a perspective on those aspects of age, sex, race, and heredity most useful for understanding the innumerable references to them throughout the book.

Age and sex, for example, are such fundamental characteristics of individuals that they are almost without exception considered in describing epidemiologic patterns in the occurrence of disease. Examples abound in the preceding chapters and demonstrate patterns by age and sex in the occurrence of atherosclerosis, coronary heart disease, stroke, and each of the other major conditions discussed. Variation by age and sex is as important for describing the main determinants of atherosclerotic and hypertensive diseases as it is in understanding the diseases themselves. Thus consideration of age and sex arises throughout this book.

The terms *race* and *ethnicity* are often used to designate other characteristics of individuals or groups when groups defined in these terms exhibit differences in rates, risks, or outcomes of disease. The fact that in current usage these terms have social or political, apart from scientific, meanings sometimes compromises objective discussion of this aspect of health and disease. Even the scientific concepts underlying these terms are less clearly or less consistently defined than in the past. The concept of race as connoting distinctive and more or less invariant genotypic or phenotypic characteristics, has become less applicable in many populations due to increased genetic admixture. The usage of *ethnicity* is also less specific now than in its original meaning in the context of cultural anthropology. This term has perhaps become in many instances a circumlocution for the term *race*. Still, to the extent that grouping of persons by race or ethnicity reveals meaningful patterns relevant to health, these terms remain useful and potentially important for understanding disease causation and targeting interventions. They do not necessarily correspond to either a cultural or a genetic basis for observed differences, however, as discussed further in this and subsequent chapters. Sources cited throughout the book have reported various data by classifications described as race, color, ethnicity, nationality, and the like, and the terms in the original sources are used in presentation of their data here.

The term *heredity* is usually understood to concern the transmission of genes from parents to offspring. Thus it potentially relates to certain familial patterns in the occurrence both of atherosclerotic and hypertensive diseases and of their determinants. Not all familial resemblance has a genetic basis, however, and "cultural heritability" is recognized by geneticists as a component of heredity to be taken into account in family studies. More generally, measures of health and disease on the whole reflect operation of the genetic material of individuals and populations, conditioned by the environments in which they live. Knowledge of genetic factors can therefore contribute usefully to understanding patterns of health and disease as they appear among persons or groups who are genetically related to different degrees. At quite another level, variations in the genetic material at a particular gene locus can also have very specific effects on risks related to a particular metabolic or physiologic trait. Examples include genes that determine the number or functional properties of receptors at cell surfaces for molecules of low density lipoprotein (LDL) cholesterol molecules. At different levels, from whole populations to individuals, genetic influences known or inferred from epidemiologic data are pertinent to several of the determinants of risk of atherosclerotic and hypertensive diseases addressed in later chapters.

Dimensions of Population Diversity

Together, these four characteristics have two aspects in common that warrant emphasis. The first aspect is that they are all dimensions of diversity among populations and individuals. Accordingly, their investigation in epidemiologic studies reveals health patterns—demonstrated variations in the distribution of disease or health-related conditions within or between populations—that may be of public health importance. Increasing recognition of population diversity has raised two issues in recent years. One issue is the need for more-extensive epidemiologic data on cardiovascular diseases for population groups underrepresented in earlier studies. The other issue concerns the validity of generalizing from observations in one group, such as White men, to other groups, such as women or non-Whites, for whom available information may be considered insufficient. While broader representation of women and non-Whites in future studies can address both issues in the long run, the latter concern may delay preventive or therapeutic measures when there is doubt of their efficacy or safety for groups not yet studied. Appropriate caution needs to be balanced against the risk that group or individual differences may dominate in prevention policy, perhaps to the degree that no general intervention policy is deemed safe or justifiable for the public at large as long as benefits and risks remain unclear for one or more major subgroups.

For both reasons, each of these aspects of population diversity has received increasing emphasis, in the United States and elsewhere, in connection with health research in general, including clinical and population studies of cardiovascular diseases. Specifically in cardiovascular epidemiology, many of the early population studies reviewed in preceding chapters focused on middle-aged White men. There are important counterexamples, such as the Framingham Heart Study of men and women, the Tecumseh Study of a whole community at all ages, and the Evans County Study in Black adults. But the major report of the US National Pooling Project presented data specifically for White men aged 40–59 years at entry to the respective studies.[1] This was the only population segment with sufficient numbers of events for detailed analysis, and the selective focus of that analysis was therefore necessary under the

circumstances. In addition to sex and race, consideration of age has also led to new research emphasis concerning mainly the elderly. But the general need for corresponding data for older and younger persons, for women, and for non-White groups has been much more fully appreciated in the past decade.

This recognition, reinforced by social and political influences, has led to explicit emphasis in policies of the US National Institutes of Health, for example, on inclusion of women and minorities in clinical and population research.[2] A Women's Pooling Project has been proposed to assemble the largest data sets on coronary heart disease in women, for joint analysis similar in principle to that of its predecessor (personal communications, Elizabeth Barrett-Connor and Lori Mosca, 1997). Finally, attention to genetic research in cardiovascular diseases has increased greatly as a result of recent advances in technology, analytic methods, and understanding.[3] Broadening research in all four of these respects represents a significant advance in research policy and it offers important new opportunities, insofar as resources become available to implement it.

Modifiability of These Factors

The second aspect common to these characteristics is the presumption that each of them is "unmodifiable," in contrast to such factors as dietary patterns, which are clearly responsive to intervention. However, association of any of these four characteristics with cardiovascular disease rates or risks may reflect underlying environmental factors related to social conditions, behavioral patterns, specific exposures, or other individual characteristics. To this extent health patterns by age, sex, race, or heredity may in fact point to modifiable characteristics. For example, increasing blood pressure in adulthood was long regarded as a natural or inevitable concomitant of aging. Epidemiologic studies have repeatedly shown that populations differ widely in the pattern of change in blood pressure with age, including the absence of any increase. Thus age, as it predicts blood pressure levels, is not in fact unmodifiable but is a marker for other factors whose modification eliminates the association with age, as addressed in Chapter 12. Similar relationships for the other three characteristics add to the value of identifying their operative cofactors and thereby understanding these pervasive characteristics more fully.

For several reasons, then, each of these four characteristics can identify, more or less specifically, subgroups of special interest or concern. Each characteristic is addressed below, and specific references to these factors occur at many points throughout the book. In addition, the roles of age, sex, race, and heredity—as well as roles of other factors—in identifying special populations in the context of preventive strategies are addressed further in Chapter 23.

AGE

For age, sex, and race, brief comments are included on definition and classification, ascertainment, and interpretation of health patterns in relation to the characteristic.

Definition and Classification

The range of ages relevant to cardiovascular diseases extends throughout the life span, from conception to the oldest attained ages: from determination of genetic makeup and the course of fetal development, which have a role in congenital heart disease and possibly are determinants of atherosclerosis and hypertension, to the ages of greatest risks of coronary events, strokes, and other major cardiovascular conditions. Quantitative measures of gestational age are usually expressed in weeks from the mother's last prepregnant menstrual period to a specified date; in the early postnatal period in days, weeks, or months since birth; and thereafter in completed years, that is, age in years at the most recent birthday. Categories of age are expressed either in class intervals of the quanti-

tative measures or in any of several qualitative terms, including the preadult categories of fetus, newborn, infant, child, adolescent, or youth (with some overlap) and young, middle-aged, older, or elderly adults. Often these terms are used without definition, so their age correspondence is unclear. Other terms related to physiological or social aspects of age include developmental age (as assessed by secondary sexual characteristics or skeletal age), age at menarche or menopause, age at majority or attainment of legal responsibility, reproductive age, retirement age, and others.

Ascertainment

Most simply, age is ascertained by determining from available records or by questionnaire the age of the subject or respondent, in years, as of the last birthday. A few special considerations sometimes arise, however. Ascertainment of gestational age, for example, is subject to uncertainty in the timing of the last menstrual period, based on information from the mother. Date of birth by day, month, and year is usually known and can often be confirmed from a birth certificate or other official record. Knowledge of the actual birth date is obviously more precise than age at last birthday, since exact age as of any given date can then be calculated and expressed in decimal years (eg, 10.3 years). This level of accuracy can be important in studies in childhood and adolescence, during which many characteristics change rapidly enough that an error of several months, based on age at last birthday, may seriously affect interpretation of the observations. For a victim of sudden death, knowledge of the decedent's age may depend on next of kin or another informant, which, in either case, may be of uncertain reliability. In general, however, reliability of classification by age is expected to be satisfactory in the absence of social or behavioral considerations that may lead to deliberate misrepresentation, except at the oldest ages where communication or recall may present special difficulties. In some populations, of course, birth records may be nonexistent or unavailable and ages known only approximately.

Age Adjustment

The biological significance of age for health and disease is so pervasive that most phenomena of interest are strongly age dependent. Therefore, groups with dissimilar age composition typically exhibit different patterns of health-related conditions. Accordingly, any differences in such patterns between populations might merely reflect underlying dissimilarities in age and offer little meaningful insight into association of disease with other possibly informative characteristics. In most populations, for example, blood pressure does increase with age in adulthood; if two populations were compared regarding the prevalence of high blood pressure, a finding of a higher prevalence in the population with the greater proportion of older adults would be uninformative. For this reason, age-specific comparisons are more informative than crude comparisons, which do not take age into account. Therefore, comparison of prevalence of high blood pressure between two populations is preferably based on rates for age strata of 10 years or less, such as ages 30–39, 40–49, and so on. Even so, a single value of the prevalence is useful to summarize this information and to compare the summary value between two or more populations. In that case, these age-specific data can be used to adjust for differences in the age distribution of each population, resulting in a single "age-adjusted" or "age-standardized" value for each population to be compared. This value is not the true prevalence in any of the populations but can be compared with others similarly standardized with the knowledge that the comparison is not distorted by differences in age composition of the populations. Ahlbom and Novell present a simple demonstration of this important principle, which can be applied to other characteristics as well as age.[4]

Interpretation of Health Patterns by Age

The Fetal and Neonatal Period

In addition to its obvious importance for congenital heart disease, the fetal and neonatal period has been the focus of an impressive body of research suggesting that conditions of life in this period may be critical for the determination of future risks of adult cardiovascular diseases.[5] For example, associations have been demonstrated between low birth weight, or limited weight gain to age 1 year, and adult cardiovascular mortality in a cohort of British men born in the early 1900s. This and many related observations have been interpreted as reflecting adverse social conditions that influence fetal and neonatal growth and development. In consequence, the developing metabolic and physiologic systems become "programmed" in response to these conditions in a manner that unfavorably affects risk factor development in later life. This provocative theory is addressed further in Chapter 19, Social Conditions.

Childhood and Youth

Next in sequence along the age spectrum are childhood, adolescence, and "youth" (defined by the World Health Organization as spanning the ages from birth to 24 years),[6] mutually overlapping categories denoting mainly preadult ages. Especially in this age range, chronologic age is only an approximate indicator of biological age because of wide variation between individuals in growth tempo, or rate of growth and maturation.[7]

Attention to cardiovascular risk factors in these age groups has also increased in the past two decades with the growing acceptance of the view that prevention of atherosclerotic and hypertensive cardiovascular diseases can be achieved by intervention before adulthood. The basis of this view includes several links between factors measured in youth and related observations in adults, as follows:

- "familial aggregation"—the greater similarity of risk factor levels of parents and offspring within families than between them

- "familial concordance"—the relatively adverse risk factor levels of offspring of parents with cardiovascular disease when compared with those of unaffected parents
- "tracking"—the tendency for risk factor levels in an individual at a given age in childhood or adolescence to be predictive of levels at later ages
- correlation between risk factor levels and the extent of atherosclerosis in the aorta and coronary arteries, in childhood, adolescence, and youth (discussed in Chapter 3).

The current view of the potential for preventive measures in this period of life is illustrated by extensive reviews and recommendations from the World Health Organization (WHO) and the American Heart Association, among others.[6,8] This broad, early age group is also discussed in Chapter 23.

Young and Middle Adulthood

Studies of the atherosclerotic and hypertensive diseases have tended to focus on middle adulthood. This emphasis was based primarily on the frequency of detectable disease, the feasibility of long-term follow-up, and other such considerations. Limitations of this emphasis have been recognized with respect to both older and younger age groups. Older people experience much higher event rates and constitute a growing proportion of most populations; younger people offer the greatest potential for prevention of advanced atherosclerosis altogether. The period of young and middle adulthood remains important for continued study, however, in part due to the need for continuity in preventive strategies throughout life. This includes the period of transition between childhood and later adult years.

The Elderly

The view that chronologic age is in some respects only a surrogate for modifiable underlying characteristics was suggested above. This view implies that many characteristics of older persons, while often predictable from chronologic age, are not inevitable concomitants of aging. Consistent with this view, current concepts of aging focus not on the inexorable progression of disease but on the potential for preservation of maximum functional capacity, independence of living, and quality of life.[9] As discussed in earlier chapters, greatly increasing numbers of persons in the United States and many other countries survive myocardial infarction or stroke only to then experience chronic ischemic heart disease, congestive heart failure, or central nervous system impairment, with significant disability and dependence. A major question is the extent to which these common occurrences can be prevented, resulting in greater freedom from morbidity in the later years of life. Better understanding of the conditions leading to good health in later years would be useful from this point of view.

Increases in life expectancy in many populations and the growing proportions of these populations attaining advanced ages have profound impacts on society and on health and disease. Recognizing this, the World Health Organization convened the Study Group on Epidemiology and Prevention of Cardiovascular Diseases in Elderly People.[10] The Study Group Report is a valuable resource for assessing the cardiovascular disease situation of the "elderly" (those aged 65 years and over) with respect to the occurrence of cardiovascular diseases and their prevention, rehabilitation, and related health policy, in the context of global demographic change affecting this age group. These matters are addressed further in Chapter 23, Groups of Special Concern.

It should also be noted that, in addition to usually higher rates, morbidity and mortality data in the elderly differ from those for younger adult age groups in two other respects. First, data on specific diagnoses and causes of death may be less reliable owing especially to the multiplicity of conditions affecting many older individuals. This is particularly at issue when data sources provide only the initial listed diagnosis for hospitalization or cause of death, since conditions of primary interest may not head the list. This difficulty was noted in connection with discrepant estimates of the frequency of deep vein thrombosis and pulmonary embolism in Chapter 6. Second, the high prevalence of many cardiovascular disease risk factors in older persons tends to result in reduced estimates of *relative* risk for cardiovascular events or conditions, because even those who remain clinically free of these conditions are, on average, at greater risk than younger persons. The *absolute* risks attributable to a given factor, on the other hand, are greater than in younger persons owing to the much higher disease rates at older ages. This was demonstrated in connection with the relation of blood pressure to risk of stroke in different age groups in Chapter 5. Interpretation of measures of risk among older adults therefore requires special caution.

SEX

Definition, Classification, and Ascertainment

In the cardiovascular field, there is little ambiguity about classification of males and females. The terms *sex* and *gender* are both used currently to denote this distinction. *Gender* is a grammatical term but may be preferred by some researchers. *Sex* is the biological term more frequently found in presentations of epidemiologic data and is therefore used here except when cited sources do otherwise.

Sex-Specific Observations

Patterns of health and disease, analogous to patterns by age, are commonly found in relation to sex, as illustrated in the preceding chapters. For this reason, epidemiologic observations are nearly always reported on a sex-specific basis. Less often, when the numbers of observations are insufficient for sex-specific analysis, combined rates may be presented instead. In such instances, comparisons between populations or groups whose proportionate composition by sex is dissimilar may, like those for age, be distorted unless adjustment is made for this difference.

Interpretation of Health Patterns by Sex

A widely recognized example of sex differences in the occurrence of cardiovascular disease is the lag of 10 to 15 years in coronary mortality by age in women relative to men. Such sex differences are interpreted variously as evidence of biological, social, cultural, or behavioral effects. Plausible bases for such effects include chromosomal, endocrinologic, or reproductive factors; sex-specific social roles leading to different patterns of activity, occupation, and interpersonal relationships with attendant differences in relevant exposures; or sex-related perceptions or practices that determine access to education, health information, or health services. Whether these factors are more fruitfully viewed as protective for women or hazardous for men in this particular context is unclear. Sex differences in distributions of blood lipids and blood pressure are apparent beginning in adolescence, and these and other risk factors progress differently between women and men throughout adulthood. The relative lack of information about several aspects of cardiovascular diseases in women—including evaluations of preventive strategies, diagnostic test performance, and responses to medical and surgical treatments—has been addressed in several recent publications. Reviews include the report of the National Heart, Lung, and Blood Institute conference, *Cardiovascular Health and Disease in Women*,[11] a text of the same title,[12] and the American Heart Association's *Report of the Special Writing Group on Cardiovascular Disease in Women*.[13]

A critical review of the underlying biologic interpretations of sex differences in the occurrence of coronary heart disease posed the question of what role sex hormones—either exogenous or endogenous—could actually be playing, especially at older ages where coronary heart disease incidence and mortality are greatest.[14] Data were cited to show that gradients in coronary mortality across countries are closely parallel for women and men, and rates are higher among women in the highest-rate countries than among men in the lowest-rate countries (see Chapter 4). Thus coronary mortality for women is not intrinsically low but varies widely in different environments. This view suggests that environmental factors are paramount determinants of these population differences and that hormonal differences between the sexes may have a lesser role than has often been assumed. Existing data were found inconclusive, however. The continuing uncertainties about the meaning of these and other sex differences in atherosclerotic and hypertensive diseases add to the importance of further study of women as a population of special concern, as addressed in Chapter 23.

RACE

Definition and Classification

As noted in the introduction to this chapter, definitions of *race* and *ethnicity* have become less clear in recent usage. Except in studies of particularly isolated populations with very limited genetic admixture and little contact with other cultures—of which few remain—the concept of genetically or culturally homogeneous groups may no longer be meaningful. It is nonetheless true that groups of persons who are either self-identified or classified by observers with respect to race or ethnicity often differ in disease rates or risk factor distributions. In the United States, where terminology changes rapidly, classifications of racial or ethnic minority populations are presently rather fluid. One system in current use includes Black Americans, Hispanics, Native Americans, and Asians/Pacific Islanders.[15] Other classifications include "color," which differentiates among non-Hispanic Blacks, non-Hispanic Whites, and Mexican-Americans, and "underprivileged minorities," intended to identify groups considered to represent lower socioeconomic status by measures of income, education, and occupation. In other countries, quite different group distinctions may be considered important and are approached differently.

Ascertainment

Ascertainment of individual race or ethnicity is usually by self-report in routine recording of health data or in population studies. Classification by simple observation may be unsatisfactory and unreliable, since subtle aspects of parental origins, language preference, and other considerations are difficult to take into account in this approach. Under some circumstances, skin reflectance has been used to measure relative intensity of pigmentation. In studies of children, the reported race or ethnicity of parents may be used to construct a classification for the offspring. Disparities between methods and classifications can introduce potential error or misinterpretation of vital statistics or other data sources where, for example, the numerator of a rate is based on death certificate information and the denominator on census information. This is because the methods of classification by race or ethnicity used in these systems do not necessarily correspond directly with one another.

Interpretation of Health Patterns by Race or Ethnicity

If such classifications identify groups at special risk, it is desirable from a public health perspective that this information be obtained and applied appropriately in targeted intervention strategies. This does not necessarily imply a genetic or specific cultural basis for the observed differences, however. Just as both age and sex may be markers for any of a variety of group differences, so may race or ethnicity have underlying bases that are known, such as typical income levels, or that remain to be discovered.

There is some risk of misinterpretation of group differences as being due to the classification imposed when potential confounding factors are not considered or are unknown. For example, if adolescent Black Americans on average experience an earlier skeletal growth spurt than White Americans, they should be expected to exhibit higher age-specific levels of systolic blood pressure, because blood pressure levels are strongly correlated with height in adolescence. Finding higher blood pressure levels in Black adolescents could be taken to suggest group differences in blood pressure regulation due to some genetically determined mechanism. Alternatively, the underlying difference in growth tempo suggests the explanation that, as in White adolescents, "growth" in blood pressure parallels skeletal growth. It is perhaps erroneous therefore to postulate mechanisms of blood pressure regulation based on genetic differences between these groups as the explanation. This kind of interpretive problem indicates the potential value of fuller understanding of cardiovascular diseases and their risk factors in the population as a whole so that important observations of group differences can be both interpreted and acted upon appropriately. In addition, the factors that underlie health patterns by race or ethnicity in one population may not do so in another, and so uniform interpretation of such associations may be invalid. Similarly, such relationships between health characteristics and race or ethnicity may change over time within a given population.

The Need for Health Data for Specific Population Groups

A relative lack of knowledge concerning cardiovascular diseases and other aspects of the health of Blacks and other minority groups in the United States has been recognized, especially in the past decade. This recognition has led to special reviews of available data, identification of priorities for acquiring needed health data, and adoption of policies for participation in research by certain minorities, in parallel with recent developments concerning women. Cardiovascular diseases have been a prominent part of this concern. These are addressed, for example, in the 1985 *Report of the Secretary's Task Force on Black and Minority Health* of the US Secretary of Health and Human Services,[15] and in a more recent special report from the American Heart Association, "Cardiovascular Diseases and Stroke in African-Americans and Other Racial Minorities in the United States, A Statement for Health Professionals."[16]

The first of these reports provided summary information on cardiovascular diseases for Black Americans, Hispanics, Native Americans, and Asian/Pacific Islanders. The paucity of information for all but Black Americans was emphasized. Figure 7–1 shows the average annual age-adjusted death rates, by sex, for three of these groups in comparison with White Americans, for the period 1979 to 1981.[15] Rates for Blacks, both males and females, substantially exceeded those for Whites. Data for other groups were of uncertain reliability, according to the authors, due to less frequent reporting of race on death certificates than in census data for these groups. This illustrates the problem cited above, in which ethnicity may not be ascertained similarly in the census and vital statistics systems. This results in distortion in the rates that combine these data sources. If non-White decedents with no entry for race were coded on death certificates as White, while in census data non-Whites are more completely enumerated, the mortality of non-Whites would be correspondingly underestimated. Another illustration concerns the absence of national data for Hispanics in the United States. State-level mortality statistics have therefore been relied upon and widely cited as indicating comparatively low coronary mortality among Mexican Americans (largest of the Hispanic subgroups). However, results of community surveillance for coronary heart disease in Corpus Christi/Nueces County, Texas, has shown higher rates of hospitalization, higher case-fatality, and higher long-term mortality for coronary disease among Mexican Americans than among non-Hispanic Whites in

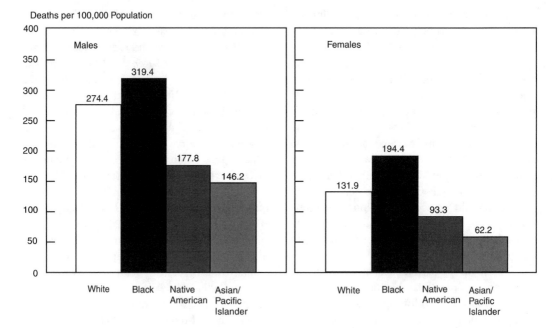

Note: Death rates for Hispanics are not available. Death rates for Native Americans and Asian/Pacific Islanders are probably underestimated due to less frequent reporting of these cases on death certificates as compared with the census.

Figure 7–1 Average Annual Age-Adjusted Death Rates for Heart Disease, 1979–1981. *Source:* Reprinted from *Report of the Secretary's Task Force on Black & Minority Health*, p. 108, 1985, National Center for the Health Statistics, Bureau of the Census and Task Force on Black and Minority Health.

the same community.[17] These particular mortality statistics may reflect similar problems of unequal ascertainment of ethnicity in death certification and census data or perhaps other limitations as well. Such observations underscore limitations of availability and interpretation of mortality statistics for US racial groups other than Whites and Blacks. Data on morbidity are even more limited. The resulting issues are addressed further in Chapter 23.

The committee report of the American Heart Association reviewed the data available by the late 1980s, which included information on hypertension, stroke, and coronary heart disease for Blacks and for Hispanics, Asians and Pacific Islanders, and Native Americans.[16] That review provided a point of departure for understanding variation in cardiovascular disease manifestations within the diverse population of the United States and suggested several questions

for research in these groups, which are addressed in Chapter 29.

HEREDITY

Discussion of heredity serves to introduce the broader topic of genetics in relation to atherosclerotic and hypertensive disease. Unlike the more specific characteristics of age, sex, and race, heredity or genetic factors encompass a wide array of concepts, methods, and levels of application, in short, a whole scientific discipline. Like the preceding three characteristics, heredity and genetics raise issues of diversity within and between populations. Similarly, aspects of genetics are receiving much-increased emphasis in current research priorities in cardiovascular diseases. The background provided here is limited to brief comments on family history and a review of several concepts of genetic epidemiology, to serve as an orientation to these topics as they arise throughout the book.

Family History

From the clinical perspective, and in earlier epidemiologic studies of coronary heart disease, attention to genetic aspects was largely limited to questions of family history. In connection with other cardiovascular diseases, family history refers, for example, to recurrence risk of congenital heart disease in successive offspring, secondary attack rates among siblings of children affected by Kawasaki disease, or social and environmental factors in the domestic setting of families at risk of Chagas' disease. For the atherosclerotic and hypertensive diseases, the main focus has been the degree of resemblance among differently related persons with respect to levels of particular risk factors, as an indication of possible inheritance of these traits. Studies of twins gave further insight into the role of the genotype in determining risk factor levels, through contrasts in the degree of resemblance between monozygotic (identical) versus dizygotic (fraternal) twins. Further studies have compared twins raised together and apart, and by natural or adoptive parents, to aid in assessment of environmental and genetic contributions to the observed phenotypes—specifically, in this context, risk factor levels. Based on such studies, estimates of the heritability of these traits have been derived, including partition into genetic and cultural components, the latter reflecting nongenetic or, broadly, environmental contributions.[18] Recently, the concept of family history has been tied more explicitly with intervention, especially under the stimulus of Williams and colleagues.[19] Concentrating on familial hypercholesterolemia (see Chapter 11), this group has advocated use of the family history to identify pedigrees or family trees with high risk of this condition. Such families are considered to be in special need of intervention. The program called "MED PED" (tracking *MEDical PEDigrees* to *Make Early Diagnoses* and *Prevent Early Death*), obtained "health

family trees" from nearly 90,000 Utah families. The results indicated that some 3000 families had a "strong history" of early coronary heart disease and 50,000 persons were sufficiently closely related to be considered as high-risk family members. This is an innovative approach to use of the family history concept to identify a population of special concern (see Chapter 23).

Genetic Epidemiology

In the recent past, genetic aspects of epidemiology have developed rapidly to incorporate a much broader range of genetic concepts and methods. This recent development and its historical context were addressed in a detailed review by Schull and Hanis.[20] According to their review, only gradually have epidemiologists and geneticists sought to join these disciplines in collaborative research, although at least 30 years ago the importance of genetic variation in the expression of disease was recognized in a conference on genetics and epidemiology of chronic diseases. They also noted the need for deeper insight into interactions between genes and environment, in view of abundant evidence of dependence of gene expression on environmental conditions. They added that many diseases may reflect the extremes of normal variation and not discrete gene effects, a viewpoint that had fueled a years-long debate in connection with hypertension. Incorporation of biochemical and molecular mechanisms in genetic, epidemiologic, and family studies was suggested by Schull and Hanis as an aid to distinguish between diseases representing discrete gene effects and others reflecting extremes of continuously distributed traits.

The emergence of genetic epidemiology as a hybrid discipline is illustrated by the publication of *Fundamentals of Genetic Epidemiology*, which reviews basic concepts and methods of both population-based and family studies.[21] The scope of genetic epidemiology is represented schematically in Figure 7–2. The phenotype, or observable characteristic (such as LDL-choles-

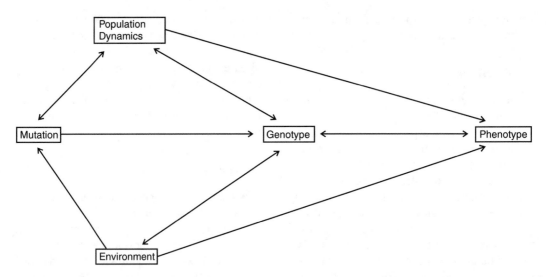

Figure 7–2 The Scope of Genetic Epidemiology. *Source:* From *Fundamentals of Genetic Epidemiology* by Muin J Khoury, Terri H Beatty, Bernice Cohen. Copyright © 1993 by Oxford University Press, Inc. Used by permission of Oxford University Press, Inc.

terol concentration), results from direct gene effects, direct and indirect environmental effects, and population dynamics, which determine parental mating patterns and hence the specific combination of genes in the individual. Under this scheme, the occurrence of gene mutation in a germ cell may or may not be expressed as a recognized change in phenotype, unless (1) it is immediately deleterious to the affected individual; (2) it is less deleterious but is eventually represented in an individual by two copies of the affected gene (which would occur only after the mutation became sufficiently common that it could, by chance, be received from both parents); or (3) it happens to arise in the particular environment required for its expression. It is clear that mutation alone is not equivalent to the occurrence of disease.

Concepts of Variability of Genetic Effects

Irrespective of the mechanism or type of mutation that occurs, several other properties of genetic effects must be considered in interpretation of studies in genetic epidemiology. Concepts of dominant and recessive genes are familiar and correspond to conditions (1) and (2) above, respectively. Among other aspects of gene expression, those especially relevant here are penetrance, expressivity, epistasis, and polygenic and multifactorial determination. Incomplete penetrance refers to the failure of the specific genotype to produce the predicted phenotype in all individuals. Variable expressivity reflects differences in the range of phenotypic expression of the particular genotype among individuals who carry that genotype. Epistasis is the property by which one gene locus affects the action of another and in which genes themselves interact to influence their phenotypic expression. Polygenic determination is the dependence of a phenotype on multiple genes to produce it, whereas multifactorial determination denotes effects produced by one or more genes only when certain environmental conditions obtain. These concepts illustrate further the point that mutation does not simply equate with disease. Thus, for example, identification of a link between a specific gene and a particular risk factor for atherosclerosis does not in itself establish the presence of a biologically important relationship.

The Candidate Gene Approach

Genetic Factors in Coronary Heart Disease is an extensive compilation of recent work in genetic epidemiology in this area.[22] Studies of coronary heart disease, its leading risk factors, monogenic traits related to coronary risk, and research and policy issues are addressed. This body of work illustrates the wide-ranging application of concepts in genetic epidemiology of coronary heart disease, from the molecular to the population level, with special emphasis on familial aspects. One example, elaborated more recently in a further report by Berg, illustrates the research strategy in genetic epidemiology termed the "functional candidate gene approach," in specific reference to lipoprotein (a), or Lp(a), a protein molecule involved in atherogenesis by its accumulation in atherosclerotic lesions.[23] A "candidate gene" is one whose protein product could be involved, in the present context, in any of the metabolic or physiologic mechanisms related to atherosclerosis or its clinical manifestations. "Functional" and "positional" candidate genes are those identified through such protein product effects or by gene mapping, respectively.

As a suspected marker of a functional candidate gene, the Lp(a) lipoprotein molecule has been studied by Berg[23] and by others since the early 1960s. Many of its chemical properties were described, and the gene controlling production of this lipoprotein was identified. Association between blood Lp(a) concentration and the occurrence of coronary heart disease was established, indicating an increased risk of coronary events, especially prior to age 60, among men in the top quartile of the distribution of Lp(a) concentration. It has been reported that this association is independent of other risk factors; its mechanism of action may relate to interference with hemostatic function. This one example serves to illustrate the potential progression from laboratory research to population studies in identifying and elucidating the possible role of a specific gene in atherogenesis.

A Genetic "Master Plan"

The potential for genetic studies in atherosclerosis and other heart, lung, and blood diseases was the focus of the Expert Panel Report, cited earlier.[3] The report presented a "master plan" to guide future research in this area. Formidable problems in progressing from recognition of a specific gene mutation to establishing causal linkages or new avenues of intervention were noted. But emphasis was placed on the opportunities presented by successes in molecular genetics of certain diseases, the context of the Human Genome Project, and the many questions arising for further investigation when suggestive genetic linkages are found. The implications of the opportunities identified in this report for the overall research agenda in the epidemiology and prevention of cardiovascular diseases are addressed in Chapter 29.

The complementary relation of laboratory and population studies of genetic aspects of disease was emphasized by Rao and Vogler: "Currently, genetic studies often favour molecular-based data over population-based statistics, such as heritabilities. Our perspective is that the genetic epidemiology of risk factors for coronary heart disease (CHD) is also central to public health issues. Coupling of the molecular basis of disease with population-based epidemiological data is required to effectively establish public health policy".[18(p 79)]

IMPLICATIONS FOR EPIDEMIOLOGY AND PREVENTION

This discussion of four ubiquitous factors in health and disease—age, sex, race, and heredity—introduced concepts, methods, and aspects of investigation helpful in understanding the place of these factors in epidemiologic studies. The factors are equally relevant to disease outcomes and the determinants of those outcomes. The frequent attention given to them in the following chapters reflects their importance both to understanding causation and to formulation of preventive policy.

REFERENCES

1. Pooling Project Research Group. Relationship of blood pressure, serum cholesterol, smoking habit, relative weight and ECG abnormalities to incidence of major coronary events: Final Report of the Pooling Project. *J Chronic Dis.* 1978;31:201–306.

2. Bennet JC, Board of Health Sciences Policy, Organization of the Institute of Medicine. Inclusion of women in clinical trials—policies for population subgroups. *N Engl J Med.* 1993;329:288–292.

3. National Heart, Lung and Blood Institute. *Report of the Expert Panel on Genetic Strategies for Heart, Lung and Blood Diseases.* Bethesda, Md: National Institutes of Health, Public Health Service, US Dept of Health and Human Services; 1993.

4. Ahlbom A, Novell S. *Introduction to Modern Epidemiology.* Chestnut Hill, Mass: Epidemiology Resources, Inc; 1990.

5. Barker DJP, Osmond C. The maternal and infant origins of cardiovascular disease. In: Marmot M, Elliott P, eds. *Coronary Heart Disease Epidemiology: From Aetiology to Public Health.* Oxford, England: Oxford University Press; 1992; 83–90.

6. World Health Organization Study Group. *Prevention in Childhood and Youth of Adult Cardiovascular Diseases: Time for Action.* Geneva, Switzerland: World Health Organization, 1990; Technical Report Series 792.

7. Tanner JM. *Foetus into Man. Physical Growth from Conception to Maturity.* Ware, England: Castlemead Publication; 1989.

8. Moller JH, Allen HD, Clark EB, Dajani AS, et al. Report of the Task Force on Children and Youth. *Circ.* 1993;188:2479–2486.

9. Harlan WR, Manolio TA. Coronary heart disease in the elderly. In: Marmot M, Elliott P, eds. *Coronary Heart Disease Epidemiology: From Aetiology to Public Health.* Oxford, England: Oxford University Press; 1992; 114–126.

10. World Health Organization Study Group. *Epidemiology and Prevention of Cardiovascular Diseases in Elderly People.* Geneva, Switzerland: World Health Organization; 1995. WHO Technical Report Series 853.

11. Wenger NK, Speroff L, Packard B. Cardiovascular health and disease in women. *N Eng J Med.* 1993;329: 247–256.

12. Douglas PS. *Cardiovascular Health and Disease in Women.* Philadelphia, Pa: WB Saunders Co; 1993.

13. Eaker ED, Chesebro JH, Sacks FM, Wenger NK, et al. Cardiovascular disease in women. *Circ.* 1993;88: 1999–2004.

14. Khaw K-T, Barrett-Connor E. Sex differences, hormones, and coronary heart disease. In: Marmot M, Elliott P, eds. *Coronary Heart Disease Epidemiology: From Aetiology to Public Health.* Oxford, England: Oxford University Press; 1992;- 274–286.

15. *Report of the Secretary's Task Force on Black and Minority Health.* Volume 1. Executive Summary. Bethesda, Md: US Dept of Health and Human Services; 1985.

16. Cardiovascular diseases and stroke in African-Americans and other racial minorities in the United States: a statement for health professionals. *Circ.* 1991;83: 1463–1480.

17. Goff DC Jr, Varas C, Ramsey DJ, Wear ML, et al. Mortality after hospitalization for myocardial infarction among Mexican-Americans and non-Hispanic Whites: the Corpus Christi Heart Project. *Ethnicity Dis.* 1993; 3:55–63.

18. Rao DC, Vogler GP. Assessing genetic and cultural heritabilities. In: Goldbourt U, de Faire U, Berg K, eds. *Genetic Factors in Coronary Heart Disease.* Dordrecht, the Netherlands: Kluwer Academic Publishers; 1994; 71–81.

19. Williams RR, Schumacher C, Hopkins PN, Hunt SC, et al. Practical approaches for finding and helping coronary-prone families with special reference to familial hypercholesterolemia. In: Goldbourt U, de Faire U, Berg K, eds. *Genetic Factors in Coronary Heart Disease.* Dordrecht, the Netherlands: Kluwer Academic Publishers; 1994;425–445.

20. Schull WJ, Hanis CL. Genetics and public health in the 1990s. *Annu Rev Public Health.* 1990;11:105–125.

21. Khoury MJ, Beaty TH, Cohen BH. *Fundamentals of Genetic Epidemiology.* Oxford, England: Oxford University Press, 1993; 22. Monographs in Epidemiology and Biostatistics.

22. Goldbourt U, de Faire U, Berg K, eds. *Genetic Factors in Coronary Heart Disease.* Dordrecht, the Netherlands: Kluwer Academic Publishers; 1994.

23. Berg K. Lp(a) genes, other genes, and coronary heart disease. In: Berg K, Boulyjenkov V, Christen Y, eds. *Genetic Approaches to Noncommunicable Diseases.* Berlin, Germany: Springer-Verlag; 1996; 27–33.

CHAPTER 8

Dietary Imbalance

SUMMARY

Dietary imbalance refers both to the relative excesses or deficiencies of particular nutrients in the dietary pattern of a population or an individual within the context of the diet alone and also to the relation between energy intake and expenditure. The consequences of dietary imbalance may thus extend from predominance of the effects of fat due to insufficient intake of complex carbohydrates and fiber or of caloric intake over expenditure through habitual physical inactivity. Various aspects of nutrient imbalance are addressed here, and energy intake/expenditure is discussed later, especially in Chapters 9 (Physical Inactivity) and 10 (Overweight, Fatness, and Central Adiposity). Evidence concerning evolution of human dietary patterns from conditions of primitive life suggests that modern diets differ drastically from those to which human beings were adapted over many millennia before the first and second agricultural revolutions of some 10,000 years and 150 years ago. The "rich" or "affluent" diet entails many adverse consequences, atherosclerosis and hypertension being most immediately relevant. Despite methodologic difficulties in population studies of diet, extensive observations documenting adverse effects of these dietary patterns exist. In the present context, dietary components of particular interest include total and saturated fats and specific fatty acids, cholesterol, fiber, and salt. Fish and coffee also have received recent attention and are addressed here. Alcohol and dietary antioxidants are discussed in Chapters 15 and 18, respectively. Efforts to modify dietary patterns through governmental regulation, public and professional education, and other means have been influential in some countries, including the United States. Current knowledge must be applied effectively if developing countries are to continue advancing in social and economic terms yet remain free of the affluent dietary pattern that has elsewhere brought about epidemic atherosclerotic and hypertensive diseases. The same is true if less-educated members of industrialized societies are to benefit from current knowledge as much as educated members, rather than experiencing a widening gap in rates of coronary heart disease and other outcomes of atherosclerosis and hypertension.

INTRODUCTION

Diet in Perspective

Considered in purely biological terms, consumption of food is an essential and universal human activity. Arrangements for its occurrence on a frequent, if not daily, basis from birth until death have always been a pervasive aspect of every culture, and diet shapes the daily habits of

133

every individual. Contemporary dietary behavior in modern societies is so much a matter of habit that, for most people, some of its most fundamental aspects—having access to food and arranging other activities around its consumption—are not ordinarily matters of conscious thought. Even the choice of foods, the timing, and the company of others, if any, for a given meal may be largely passive or automatic, on a day-to-day basis.

In examining human dietary behavior objectively, certain aspects surface. For example, how much food and drink does an individual consume in a lifetime? An average lifetime rate of only two pounds per day equates to 700+ pounds per year, or 3.5+ tons per decade, and at 70 years the cumulative total is about 25 tons of ingesta. Fortunately, the expression "You are what you eat" is only fractionally true, since the body rejects or uses only transiently all but a minute proportion of this alimentary glut.

How much cereal grain does a population require each year? An illustrative estimate of the supply for the United States would be approximately 800 kg per capita. However, only about 10% of this amount is used for direct human consumption, and most of the remainder is converted to animal products. By contrast, the corresponding estimates for India were a total cereal supply of about 125 kg per capita, or less than one-sixth the US quantity, of which more than 80% was consumed directly.[1] This contrast clearly reflects different national food production policies, resulting in very different dietary patterns in these two countries.

The Evolutionary Scale

The evolution of human eating patterns puts the habits of contemporary societies in perspective and demonstrates sharp contrasts between the dietary conditions characteristic of most of human existence and those of very recent times.[1,2] The dietary patterns of three human groups, hunter-gatherers, peasant agriculturalists, and modern affluent societies, are represented in terms of their major nutrient composition in Figure 8–1.[2] The hunter-gatherer pattern persisted throughout most of human existence until the first agricultural revolution some 10,000 years ago. The peasant agriculturalist pattern was characteristic until the second agricultural revolution of the mid-1800s in Europe. Already, however, dietary patterns of privileged classes of early Western civilization were much like those of modern affluent societies and appear to have produced atherosclerosis, as inferred from examination of mummified coronary arteries. The most striking differences in the figure are between the latter two patterns, in which the proportions of energy intake from fats and sugar became predominant over intake from starch. Relative to the low-fat, high-fiber diet of most of human existence, modern affluent societies consume 2 times the fat, half the starch and fiber, and 10 times the salt. Energy from sugar, which was absent from the historical diet, is one-fifth the total energy intake in the modern diet.

Recent Changes in National Dietary Patterns

The long-term history of dietary change can be traced broadly for each of the major geographic regions of the world, but, except in very recent years, data on specific dietary components have been available in few countries. Exceptions are the United Kingdom and Japan, for which dietary intakes of 200 and 100 years, respectively, can be estimated, as illustrated in Tables 8–1 and 8–2.[2] The ascendancy of fat and sugar and the decrease in flour and fiber in the United Kingdom, and the very recent sharp increase in animal protein and fat through an unprecedented pattern of meat and milk consumption in Japan, demonstrate marked rates of dietary change. Changes in food technology have brought about even more-accelerated dietary change in the most recent decades. Even in developing countries, food availability has resulted in large and rapid increases in energy consumption, as shown in Table 8–3.[2] The changes in diet composition that accompany economic development are clear from data

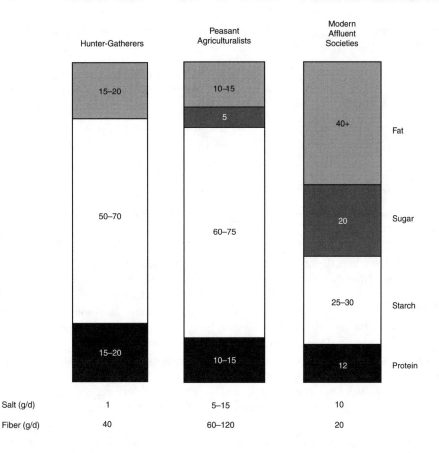

Figure 8–1 Percentage of Energy Intake Obtained from Different Food Components and Salt and Fiber Intakes of Different Human Groups. *Source:* Reprinted from Report of a WHO Study Group, *WHO TRS 797*, p 43, © 1990, by permission of Oxford University Press.

obtained from the Food and Agriculture Organization and the World Bank (summarized in Figure 8–2): Complex carbohydrates are replaced by animal fat.

Establishment of the relation between diet and atherosclerosis through animal experimental studies and laboratory, clinical, and epidemiologic observations in humans, and the especially prominent contributions of Keys, were reviewed in Chapter 3. Here the nature of the diet, its epidemiologic investigation, and its relation to atherosclerotic and hypertensive cardiovascular diseases are addressed. The most comprehensive review to date is *Diet and Health: Implications for Reducing Chronic Dis-*ease Risk*, a study undertaken by the National Research Council and published in 1989.[3] This encyclopedic report is cited at several points below.

CONCEPTS AND DEFINITIONS OF DIETARY PATTERNS

What is the diet? Definition of *diet* as the total oral intake of nutrient and nonnutritive material is comprehensive but uninformative. Diet can be described in various ways—in reference to specific nutrients, in terms of foods, and in terms of quality of dietary composition,

Table 8–1 Estimated per Capita Consumption in the United Kingdom of Various Foodstuffs, 1770, 1870, and 1970

	Grams per Person per Day		
Foodstuff	1770	1870	1970
Fat	25	75	145
Sugar	10	80	150
Potatoes	120	400	240
Wheat flour	500	375	200
Cereal crude fiber	5	1	0.2

Source: Reprinted with permission from Report of a WHO Study Group, *WHO TRS 797*, © 1990, Academic Press, Ltd.

such as regional or ethnic dietary characteristics or specific types of dietary prescriptions.

Nutrients

The categories of nutrients and other dietary components reviewed in *Diet and Health* are listed in Exhibit 8–1. Calories, or total macronutrients, account for the combined energy contribution of carbohydrates, protein, fat, and alcohol. The other lipids included with fats are fatty acids, phospholipids, and cholesterol. Fat-soluble and water-soluble vitamins are distinguished chiefly because of their associations with different food sources in the diet. Dietary supplements are noted because of their frequent use in some population groups and their often overriding contribution to intake of the vitamins and minerals they contain, though bioavailability may differ between these and food sources of the corresponding substances.

Table 8–2 Changes in Daily per Capita Intakes of Nutrients and Major Groups of Foods in Japan, 1850–1987

Nutrient/Food	1850[a]	1952[b]	1980[b]	1987[b]
Energy (kcal$_{th}$)	<1800	2109	2119	2075
Protein (g)	<50	70.0	78.7	78.9
Animal protein (g)	<20	22.6	39.2	40.1
Total fat (g)	<10	20.1	55.6	56.6
Animal fat (g)	<5	7.0	26.9	27.9
Carbohydrate (g)	<380	412	309	295
Rice (g)	<350	352	225	212
Meat (g)	<5	10.6	17.9	70.8
Milk (g)	0	10.8	115.2	117.9
Fish (g)	<60	82.3	92.5	90.5

a. From an old book referring to the Edo area.

b. Ministry of Health and Welfare of Japan, National Nutrition Survey.

Source: Reprinted with permission from Report of a WHO Study Group, *WHO TRS 797*, © 1990, Academic Press, Ltd.

Table 8–3 Trends in per Capita Dietary Energy Supplies, by Region and Economic Group

Region	Period A 1961–63 (kcal$_{th}$ per Capita per Day)	Period B 1981–83 (kcal$_{th}$ per Capita per Day)	% increase from A to B
Developed countries	3,110	3,390	9
Developing countries	1,980	2,400	21
Developing market economies	2,060	2,340	14
Africa	2,120	2,230	5
"Far East"[a]	1,940	2,190	13
Latin America	2,370	2,620	11
"Near East"[a]	2,230	2,900	30
Asian centrally planned economies	1,830	2,540	39
World	2,340	2,660	14

a. As defined by the Food and Agriculture Organization of the United Nations.

Source: Reprinted with permission from Report of a WHO Study Group, *WHO TRS 797*, p 18, © 1990, Food and Agriculture Organization of the United Nations.

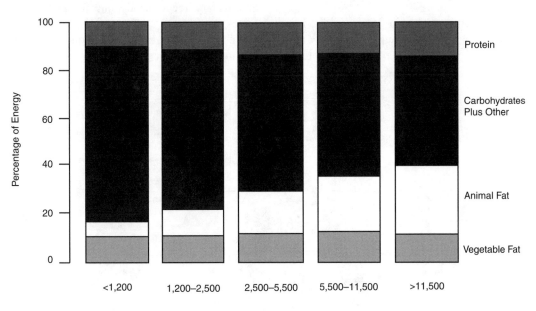

Note: This diagram is based on an analysis of diet components, GNP, and mortality rates. Fifty-two countries satisfied selection criteria for this analysis: information was available on per capita GNP and on energy and fat consumption, and the population numbered more than 1 million.

Figure 8–2 Components of Diet in Relation to per Capita Gross National Product (GNP). *Source:* Reprinted with permission from Report of a WHO Study Group, *WHO TRS 797*, p 35, © 1990, Food and Agriculture Organization of the United Nations.

Exhibit 8–1 Dietary Components Described as Categories of Nutrients and Reviewed in *Diet and Health*

- Calories: Total macronutrient intake
- Fats and other lipids
- Protein
- Carbohydrates
- Dietary fiber
- Fat-soluble vitamins
- Water-soluble vitamins
- Minerals
- Trace elements
- Electrolytes
- Alcohol
- Coffee, tea, and other nonnutritive dietary components
- Dietary supplements

Source: Data from Committee on Diet and Health, Food and Nutrition Board, Commission on Life Sciences, National Research Council, *Diet and Health: Implications for Reducing Chronic Disease Risk*, National Academy Press, © 1989.

Foods

Dietary composition in terms of foods is illustrated by the Food Guide Pyramid of the *Dietary Guidelines for Americans*, which represents the most recent stage in evolution of federal dietary recommendations for the United States (Figure 8–3).[4] The pyramid incorporates a quantitative dimension, in addition to itemizing the component food groups, and conveys

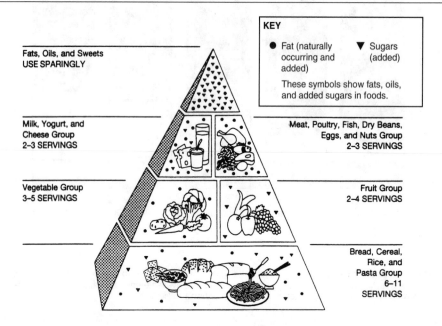

Figure 8–3 The Food Guide Pyramid. *Source:* Reprinted from US Department of Agriculture, US Department of Health and Human Services.

the relative amounts as well as types of foods in the recommended American diet: carbohydrates at the broad base; fruits and vegetables in the second tier; dairy products, animal protein, beans, and nuts in lesser quantities; and fats, oils and sweets at the narrow peak of the pyramid.

Dietary Composition

The rich or affluent diet, considered as the sine qua non of atherosclerosis, has been characterized by Stamler:

> "Rich" diet is a habitual fare high in animal products and processed animal products, high in total fat, hydrogenated fat, and separated (visible) fat, high in cholesterol and saturated fat, high in refined and processed sugars, high in salt, high in alcohol for many in the population, high in caloric density, in "empty" calories, and in ratio of calories to essential nutrients, low in potassium, fiber, and often other essential nutrients, and high in total calories for a low level of energy expenditure in the era of the automobile, television, and mechanized work.[5(p 36)]

A different characterization describes the "Mediterranean diet," long identified with low rates of coronary heart disease and widely publicized by Keys:

> What is the Mediterranean diet? One definition might be that it is what the Mediterranean native eats. But as we know and think of it now, it is a relatively new invention. Tomatoes, potatoes and beans, for example, came from America long after Christopher Columbus discovered the New World. . . . The heart of what we now consider the Mediterranean diet is mainly vegetarian: pasta in many forms, leaves sprinkled with olive oil, all kinds of vegetables in season, and often cheese, all finished off with fruit, and frequently washed down with wine.[6(p 1321S)]

Dietary Prescriptions

The prescriptive concept of diet is illustrated in the recommendations of the US National Cholesterol Education Program, which incorporate guidelines publicized by the American Heart Association (Table 8–4).[7] The Step One

---

Table 8–4 Dietary Therapy for High Blood Cholesterol Levels

Nutrient	Recommended Intake	
	Step-One Diet	*Step-Two Diet*
Total fat	Less than 30% of total calories	Less than 30% of total calories
Saturated fatty acids	Less than 10% of total calories	Less than 7% of total calories
Polyunsaturated fatty acids	Up to 10% of total calories	Up to 10% of total calories
Monounsaturated fatty acids	10% to 15% of total calories	10% to 15% of total calories
Carbohydrates	50% to 60% of total calories	50% to 60% of total calories
Protein	10% to 20% of total calories	10% to 20% of total calories
Cholesterol	Less than 300 mg/d	Less than 200 mg/d
Total calories	To achieve and maintain desirable weight	To achieve and maintain desirable weight

Source: Reprinted from Expert Panel, *Archives of Internal Medicine*, Vol 48, p 46, 1988, National Heart, Lung and Blood Institute.

approach to modification of diet to lower blood cholesterol concentrations is to establish goals for the pattern of diet that address the proportions of calories consumed as total fats and specific fat components and adjustment of caloric balance by increased intake of carbohydrates and protein. Limited cholesterol intake is also prescribed in relation to total caloric intake, which is set in relation to energy requirements of the individual to achieve and maintain desirable weight. At Step Two, this formula becomes more restrictive with respect to the intake of saturated fats and cholesterol if the desirable range of blood cholesterol concentration is not achieved with the Step-One plan. The Step One and Step Two diets are two formulations of the "prudent diet" advocated for the prevention of atherosclerosis and other chronic diseases.

Dietary Imbalance

Dietary imbalance is a term implicit in the characterization of the rich diet quoted from Stamler, above.[5] Especially because of its high ratio of total calories to essential nutrients, the rich diet is, in a sense, internally unbalanced, in that excess energy is consumed beyond that necessary to provide the required nutrients. The imbalance is also compounded externally by the high level of total calories in relation to the typical low level of energy expenditure. The term *dietary imbalance* thus directs attention both to the composition of the diet as a whole, beyond any single specific component, and to the relation between total energy intake and the other factors that determine energy balance, that is, physical activity, body size and composition, and metabolic efficiency.[3]

MEASUREMENT OF DIET

Dietary assessment of individuals or populations poses many difficulties. As indicated above, there are several concepts of diet, and one or more of these may be relevant to a particular question or investigation. Diet is complex, comprising countless specific nutrients, food sources, variations in preparation, and combinations of these. Within any population, there may be wide differences in typical dietary habits of individuals, and within individuals, diet may be highly variable from day to day or between periods of life. Clearly, a single inquiry on a given day may be a poor indicator of the usual current dietary behavior of an individual, much less a clue to a dietary pattern that may have been relevant to a process such as atherogenesis developing at ages some decades younger. Further, the importance of diet from a health perspective is not only the diet itself but the resulting nutritional status. For this reason interest in dietary assessment often extends to nutritional assessment. Some of the dimensions of this task, in contrast to dietary assessment alone, are suggested in Exhibit 8–2 (personal communication, Shiriki Kumanyika, 1997). The *level* of assessment influences the choice of methods, because very extensive data may be needed to characterize the range of dietary intakes of individuals, whereas many individuals providing more-limited information may be representative of the range of intakes across a population. Population data are often available for several indicators of food supply or food intake that may be useful for the purpose at hand. The *time* reference of interest may raise insurmountable obstacles, because some methods are applicable only to current diet and others are generally subject to greater error with increasing time intervals and thus of limited value in historical dietary assessment for individuals.

Anthropometric and *biochemical indicators* may be measured with greater reproducibility than dietary information, but these are influenced by factors other than diet alone, such as energy expenditure. Also, the biochemical indicators, especially in blood and urine, may be highly variable within individual subjects, requiring multiple occasions of sampling to obtain valid estimates.

Methods for dietary assessment itself are outlined and critically evaluated in both *Diet and Health*[3] and the Dietary Assessment Resource

Exhibit 8–2 Dimensions of Dietary and Nutritional Assessment

Level	*Anthropometric indicators*
Individuals	Relative weight
Groups within a population	Body mass index
Whole populations	Body fat distribution
	Body composition
Time	
	Biochemical indicators
Current intake	
Intake at a specified prior time or period	Blood concentrations of lipids and other sub-
Change in intake over time	stances
	Adipose tissue concentrations of fatty acids
	Urinary excretion of sodium, potassium, and
	other substances

Source: Data from personal communication, Shiriki Kumanyika, 1997.

Manual.[8] *Diet and Health* outlines several inherent problems in dietary assessment: sampling errors, nonresponse bias, reporting errors, errors related to day-to-day variability, interviewer bias, and errors due to use of food composition tables, which may not indicate the actual composition of the foods reported by respondents since they offer only "averages of representative samples." The Dietary Assessment Resource Manual addresses each of several methods—dietary records, the 24-hour recall, food frequency, brief dietary assessment methods, diet history, and observed intake with biochemical analysis—with comment on the strengths, weaknesses, and validity of each approach. In addition to the methods listed, the "gold standard" is the direct observation of food consumption of individual subjects, with duplicate servings obtained for biochemical analysis. This method is least likely to err in determining the composition of the foods as they are actually prepared, served, and consumed. However, this method is prohibitively costly for most epidemiologic studies and may in fact introduce error if food choices are influenced by presence of the observer. The Seven Countries Study is one of very few examples of population studies in which this method was used in subsamples of the cohorts.[9]

Further aspects of the collection, analysis, and interpretation of dietary data were ad-dressed by the Expert Panel on Guidelines for Use of Dietary Intake Data as advice to the Food and Drug Administration.[10] These guidelines are of value both in appreciating issues in interpretation of published reports and in planning studies in which dietary assessment is included. More recently, further issues in interpretation of dietary data and in dietary assessment in minority populations and in children and adolescents have been reviewed.[11–13] Finally, an extensive review of dietary issues, methods, and findings reported from the Multiple Risk Factor Intervention Trial (MRFIT) presents many aspects of the design, implementation, and evaluation of dietary assessment for intervention trials and programs.[14]

DETERMINANTS OF DIETARY PATTERNS

Especially when viewed from a population perspective, there are many determinants of dietary behavior that influence the ultimate nutritional status of individuals. Many of these are indicated in Exhibit 8–3.[15] It becomes readily apparent that the next meal is in only a limited sense a matter of choice. The diet of the individual is strongly, and in some circumstances completely, determined by external factors of which he or she is hardly conscious. It is useful to ask, as Zilversmit did some years ago,

Exhibit 8–3 Eating Pattern Determinants

The boxes depict the major elements in the food chain from the food science base to the outcomes of food consumption. Major influences on the food chain, each with an impact on several of the food chain steps, are listed.

Food Science Base	Food Manufacture	Food Distribution	Food Purchasing	Food Preparation	Food Consumption	Food Consumption Outcomes
Nutrition Biochemistry Preservation Genetics	Agriculture Synthesis Processing Additives Modifiers Hybridizers Mass preparation	Wholesale Retail Product-specific Route-specific	Cost Culture Advertising Knowledge Health	In-house Restaurants Institutions	Socialization Education Nutritive value Health Culture Taste Cost Mood	Pleasure Health Deficiencies Surpluses

Major influences on the food chain:

Agribusiness   Government agencies
Conglomerates   Health professionals
Grocery chains   General education
Advertising   Nutrition education
Profitability   Food science education
Special interest groups   Culinary education
Media

Source: Reprinted from Report of the Expert Panel on Population Strategies for Blood Cholesterol Reduction, NIH Publication No. 90-3046, National Institutes of Health, 1990.

whether the standard of scientific evidence demanded by some to justify the "prudent" diet could be met by the diet produced by these many influences, few of which are motivated by health concerns.[16]

In the larger perspective of governmental policies and practices affecting food production and supply, decisions seemingly remote from dietary patterns themselves can have pervasive effects on food availability. For example, national policies that allocate land use for cereal crops for human consumption or for production of animal protein and fats will determine the nature of the food supply in many countries. Demand for the affluent or rich diet may strongly influence land use policies and prevent uncoupling development of dietary imbalance from the attainment of economic affluence.

DIETARY PATTERNS AND CARDIOVASCULAR DISEASE

Diet and Cholesterol Concentration

Evidence that links dietary patterns—however they are determined—with the risks of chronic diseases, most specifically cardiovascular diseases, is reviewed in detail in relation to each of the components of diet considered in *Diet and Health* and listed in Exhibit 8–1.[3]

Most important in the present context is the understanding of the relation between dietary fat intake and the blood total cholesterol concentration, which was investigated extensively by Keys, by Hegsted, and by others. The question was whether the average change in total cholesterol concentration could be predicted from the average change in fat composition of the diet in groups of human subjects. The prediction equations that resulted from a series of dietary experiments in volunteers were similar in taking into account the intake of saturated fat, polyunsaturated fat, and dietary cholesterol. In the Keys formulation,

$$\Delta \text{Chol} = 1.35 \, (2S - P) + 1.5 \, Z$$

where Δ Chol or change in serum cholesterol concentration is determined by the relation

between change in saturated fat (S) and polyunsaturated fat (P), each as a percentage of calories, and a term (Z) is added for the difference in the square root of initial and final cholesterol intake in mg/1000 kcal. Approximately 90% of the effect of dietary change on serum cholesterol concentration was predicted from this equation, which expresses the direct relation between increase in cholesterol concentration and increase in saturated fat and dietary cholesterol and the inverse relation or decrease in cholesterol concentration with increased intake of polyunsaturates.

Dietary Patterns of Populations

The principal types of fat in the US diet over the current century are as shown in Figures 8–4 and 8–5.[3] Figure 8–4 indicates that the quantities

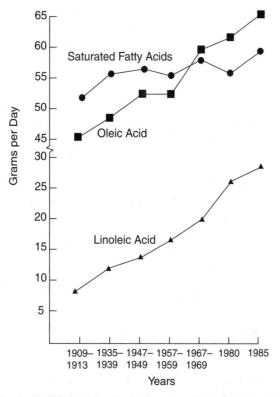

Figure 8–4 Principal Fats in the US Food Supply, in Grams per Day per Capita, 1909–1985. *Source:* Reprinted with permission from *Diet and Health: Implications for Reducing Chronic Disease Risk.* Copyright 1989 by the National Academy of Sciences. Courtesy of the National Academy Press, Washington, DC.

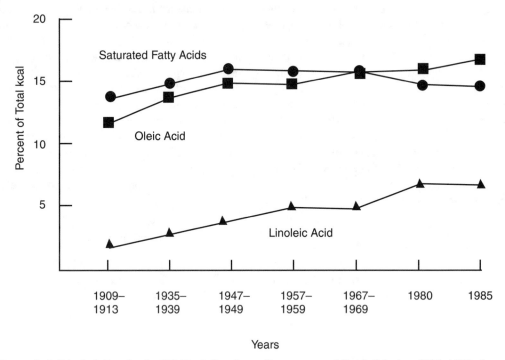

Figure 8–5 Principal Fats in the US Food Supply, as Percentages of Total Calories, 1909–1985. *Source:* Reprinted with permission from *Diet and Health: Implications for Reducing Chronic Disease Risk.* Copyright 1989 by the National Academy of Sciences. Courtesy of the National Academy Press, Washington, DC.

of three fat components, in grams per day—saturated fat, linoleic acid, and oleic acid—increased to 1985. This was especially true of linoleic and oleic acids, respectively the predominant polyunsaturated and monounsaturated fatty acids in the contemporary US food supply, provided mainly in salad and cooking oils and margarine. With respect to the composition of the diet, Figure 8–5 indicates that the increase in saturated fat intake over this same period was relatively less than the increase in total energy intake, so by 1985 it contributed a slightly smaller share of total energy as a percentage of calories. In the United States, the food sources of fats have changed during the 20th century, with a decrease in animal fat from 83% to 58% and an increase in vegetable fat from 17% to 42% of all fats. Especially striking are shifts from whole milk to low-fat and skim milk.[3] Trends in dietary change in the United Kingdom and Japan were noted earlier; Japan is exceptional in having annual

nutrition surveys by which to monitor the national diet closely, and the rate of change has been striking. In most of the world, much less information is available beyond food production data or broad qualitative observations.

Diet and Population Rates of Coronary Heart Disease

International Comparisons

Dietary Fats and Cholesterol. Among the classic epidemiologic observations suggesting a relation between dietary pattern and cardiovascular disease rates is the report of Malmros in 1950 on the Nordic experience during the Second World War, in contrast to that of the United States over the same period (Figure 8–6).[17] The substantial decline in coronary mortality in Sweden and Finland followed the beginning of sharp decreases in consumption of dietary fats by one to two years. Coronary mortality climbed

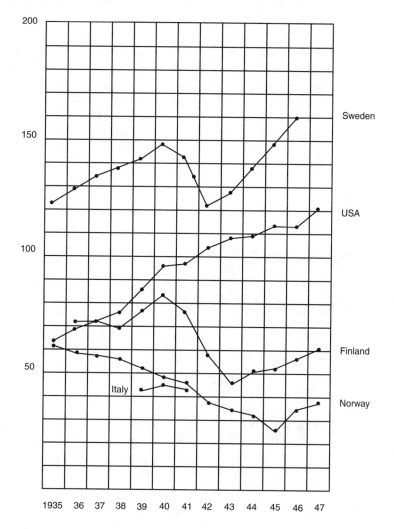

Figure 8–6 Death Rates from Arteriosclerosis (Including Diseases of the Coronary Arteries) per 100,000 Population, Sweden, United States, Finland, and Norway, 1935–1947. *Source:* Reprinted with permission from H Malmros, *Acta Med Scand*, Vol 246, p 142, © 1950, Journal of Internal Medicine.

beginning in 1942 or 1943, within a year of increased total fat consumption in Sweden, although fat consumption continued to decrease in Finland. In Norway, coronary mortality continued to decline while fat intake dropped and began to rise within a year of a marked upturn in fat consumption. In contrast, the US fat consumption continued to rise throughout this period, concurrently with coronary mortality. Referring to the wartime period as the "lean" years, Malmros drew the implication from these observations that the "luxury" consumption of dairy products should be avoided.

The Seven Countries Study has been described previously, including the detailed biochemical investigation of repeated weighted diet samples among men in 12 of the 16 cohorts (dietary assessment was by questionnaire and food composition tables in the other four cohorts).[9] For 12 of the 16 cohorts, the composition of the diet with respect to fats is shown in Figure 8–7. Saturated fat content was relatively high in East and West Finland, Zutphen (the Netherlands), and the United States at 17%–22%, and exceptionally low in Kyushu (Japan) at 3%. The Mediterranean populations varied little around sample means mostly of 7%–10% of calories from saturated fat. At the 10-year follow-up, the relation of dietary fats and cholesterol to coronary death and all incident coronary events was determined.[18] As shown in Figure 8–8, a strong correlation ($r = 0.73$) was found between dietary saturated fat intake, as a percentage of total calories, and incident coronary heart disease rates across the 16 study populations. East Finland, with the highest saturated fat intake (more than 20% of calories), exhibited especially high incidence of approximately 30% (over the 10-year period).

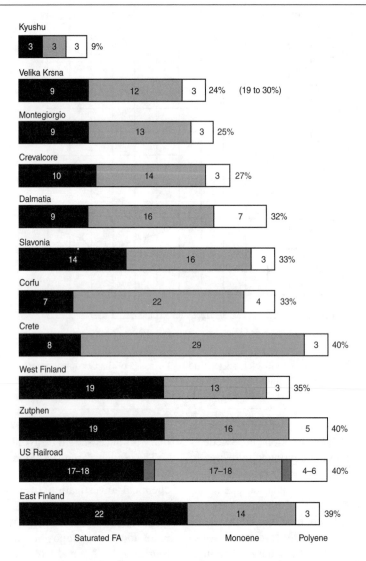

Figure 8–7 Average Percentage of Calories from Fats, Men, 40–59 Years. *Source:* Reproduced with permission from *American Heart Association Monograph*, No 29, p I-168, © 1970, American Heart Association.

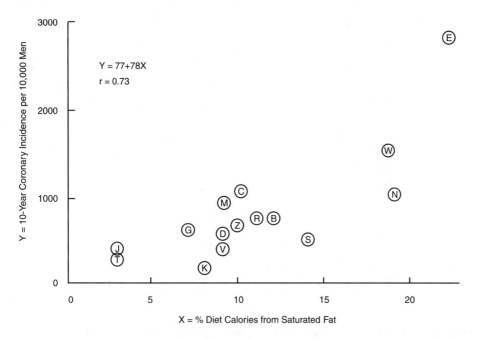

Note: B, Belgrade; C, Crevalcore; D, Dalmatia; E, East Finland; G, Corfu; J, Japan; K, Crete; M, Montegiorgio; N, Zutphen; R, Rome Railroad; S, Slavonia; T, Tanushimaru; V, Velika Krsna; W, West Finland; Z, Zrenjanin.

Figure 8–8 Ten-Year Incidence of Coronary Heart Disease in Relation to Percentage of Dietary Calories from Saturated Fat, Seven Countries Study. *Source:* Reprinted by permission of the publisher from *Seven Countries* by A Keys, Cambridge, Mass: Harvard University Press, Copyright © 1980 by the President and Fellows of Harvard College.

Another international comparison of variation in diet and coronary heart disease for countries with more than 1 million population used food disappearance data from the Food and Agriculture Organization and mortality data for coronary heart disease (ICD 8, codes 410–414) provided by the World Health Organization.[19] Average food disappearance data for the years 1975–1977 were used in conjunction with mortality data for 1977. Many foods were significantly correlated with differences in coronary heart disease mortality. Of particular interest was an index of cholesterol and saturated fat intake, or CSI, calculated as

$$CSI = (1.01 \times g \text{ saturated fat})$$
$$+ (0.05 \times mg \text{ cholesterol})$$

This index correlated very strongly ($r = 0.98$) with the Hegsted equation (similar to the Keys equation) in these data. The relation between CSI and coronary mortality in the 40 countries is shown in Figures 8–9 and 8–10, which indicate a sixfold range of CSI and a mortality range of from nearly 0 to more than 1000 per 100,000 population for men aged 55–64 years. The overall correlation coefficient was $r = 0.78$, a result consistent with the Seven Countries Study, although with altogether different methods. Emphasis was placed on the positions of Finland and France in the joint distribution of fat intake and coronary heart disease mortality because of the much-discussed "French paradox," whereby France enjoys one of the lowest national mortality rates for coronary heart disease in the presence of high saturated fat intake. This relationship is demonstrated by the contrasting disease rates for the two countries over the period from 1960 to 1987, during which

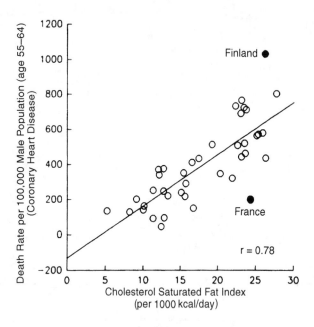

Figure 8–9 Coronary Heart Disease Mortality in 40 Countries in Relation to Cholesterol Saturated Fat Index, Men Aged 55–64 Years, 1977. *Source:* Reprinted with permission from SM Artaud, SL Connor, G Sexton, and WE Connor, *Circulation*, Vol 88, p 2774, © 1993, American Heart Association.

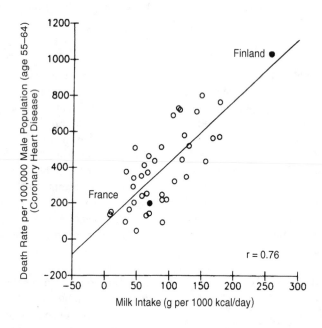

Figure 8–10 Coronary Heart Disease Mortality in 40 Countries in Relation to Milk Intake, Men Aged 55–64 Years, 1977. *Source:* Reprinted with permission from SM Artaud, SL Connor, G Sexton, and WE Connor, *Circulation*, Vol 88, p 2774, © 1993, American Heart Association.

both countries experienced increasing and then decreasing rates. Throughout the period, rates remained four to five times higher in Finland. Figure 8–10 supports the explanation of the paradox that milk intake, as an indicator of use of dairy products, is quite low in France but high in Finland, resulting in an overall correlation, $r = 0.76$, in which these two countries fit the overall international pattern much more closely. The investigators concluded that the paradox was explained by consumption of other food sources in France, especially plant foods, including vegetable oils and antioxidants (see Chapter 18), and greater intake in Finland of fats from milk and butter, which possibly affect thrombosis in addition to atherosclerosis.

The interpretation of these population differences as reflecting the overall dietary pattern, and not fat intake alone, is consistent with other data and reinforces the concept of dietary imbalance as the basis for strong predictive relations between diet and coronary heart disease. Nevertheless, interest in specific components of dietary fat and other nutrients has stimulated many further studies. For example, attention to particular fatty acids in the diet has resulted in numerous reports.

Specific Fatty Acids. Analysis of the food balance sheets of the Food and Agriculture Organization for 27 countries permitted correlation of overall national dietary patterns in 1964–1966 with their respective coronary heart disease mortality in 1975 for men aged 35–74 years.[20] The countries were predominantly European but included Japan, New Zealand, the United States, Canada, and Venezuela. For the 17 dietary components shown in Table 8–5, significant positive correlations were found for 9 ($r = 0.491$ to 0.736), including several specific fatty acids, and significant negative or inverse correlations were found for 5 ($r = -0.384$ to -0.590), including total carbohydrate (fiber), total α-tocopherol equivalent (vitamin E precursors), and vitamin C. Animal protein and plant protein were about equally, and oppositely, correlated with coronary heart disease mortality.

In the Seven Countries Study, special data collection in the course of follow-up permitted analysis of fat components not previously studied, especially *trans* fatty acids and the n-3 polyunsaturated fatty acids.[21] *Trans* fatty acids as they occur in the human diet are predominantly synthetic compounds formed in the partial hydrogenation of unsaturated fats for commercial products such as margarine. In 1987, new food samples to match the composition of those previously analyzed were obtained from markets in the area of each cohort in 1987, and new biochemical determinations were carried out to provide estimates of these fat components. The results were analyzed in relation to the 25-year mortality experience of the 16 cohorts.

These recent results from the Seven Countries Study are shown in Table 8–6. For dietary saturated fat intake (SFA) the strongest correlations were with the 12- to 18-carbon saturated fatty acids, the 18-carbon *trans* (monounsaturated) fatty acid, elaidic acid, and total fat intake. Each of these was also significantly correlated with coronary heart disease (CHD) mortality, as were total saturated fatty acids, total fat, and dietary cholesterol. Independence of these contributions of specific fat components could not be tested due to their close intercorrelations. The total variance in coronary mortality rates was most fully explained by saturated fatty acid intake (73% of the variance). Antioxidant flavonoids and cigarette smoking were the only other independently associated factors, and not physical activity or other antioxidants. The relation of saturated fatty acid intake to 25-year coronary heart disease mortality, shown in Figure 8–11, has a correlation coefficient of $r = 0.88$.

An international case-comparison study (EURAMIC) used another method to assess *trans* fatty acid intake—needle aspiration of tissue fat from the buttock—for both newly hospitalized cases with first myocardial infarction and comparison subjects sampled from the same geographic area.[22] Ten centers in nine countries collaborated in recruitment of 671 cases and 717 comparison subjects, all males. Overall comparisons by center indicated wide

Table 8–5 Simple Correlation Coefficients Between Average National Availability of Nutrients in 1964–1966 and Coronary Heart Disease (CHD) Mortality in 1975, for Men Aged 35–74 from 27 Countries

Nutrient	CHD Mortality (Men)
Total fat[a]	0.630[**]
Saturated fatty acids[a]	0.718[**]
Palmitic acid[a]	0.699[**]
Stearic acid[a]	0.690[**]
Monounsaturated fatty acids[a]	0.509[**]
Oleic acid[a]	0.491[**]
Polyunsaturated fatty acids[a]	−0.384[*]
Cholesterol[b]	0.716[**]
Keys score[c]	0.736[**]
Total protein[a]	0.228
Animal protein[a]	0.703[**]
Vegetable protein[a]	−0.649[**]
Total carbohydrate[a]	−0.569[**]
Total α-tocopherol equivalent[b]	−0.590[**]
Total vitamin A[d]	0.196
Vitamin C[b]	−0.552[**]
Energy	0.221

Note: Availability of nutrients based on food balance sheets from the Food and Agriculture Organization of the United Nations. CHD mortality rates, from the World Health Organization, are age averaged by 5-year age groups. The 27 countries are Australia, Austria, Belgium, Bulgaria, Canada, Czechoslovakia, Denmark, the Federal Republic of Germany, Finland, France, the German Democratic Republic, Hungary, Ireland, Israel, Italy, Japan, the Netherlands, New Zealand, Norway, Poland, Romania, Sweden, Switzerland, the United Kingdom, the United States, Venezuela, and Yugoslavia.

a. Percentage of total energy intake.

b. mg/4184 kJ (mg/1,000 kcal).

c. 1.35 (2SFA + PFA) + 1.5 $\sqrt{C}$, where SFA is percent energy from saturated fatty acids, PFA is percent energy from polyunsaturated fatty acids, and C is dietary cholesterol in mg/4,184 kJ (mg/1,000 kcal).

d. μg RE/4,184 kJ (μg RE/1,000 kcal).

* $P<0.05$.

** $P<0.01$.

Source: Reprinted with permission from J Stamler, *American Journal of Clinical Nutrition*, Vol 59, (Suppl), p 152S, © 1994, American Society for Clinical Nutrition.

variation in the proportion of tissue fatty acids of the *trans* type but no difference between case and comparison subjects when pooled across all centers (multivariate odds ratio, 0.97; 95% confidence limits, 0.56–1.67).

Some additional studies of *trans* fatty acids have suggested that the commercial process of making vegetable oils marketable by their par-tial hydrogenation into better-preserved and nonliquid products has increased the risk of coronary heart disease rather than reduced it, as substitution of vegetable fats for dairy and other animal fats was intended to do. However, clinical experiments have not supported an independent effect of *trans* fatty acids on blood cholesterol concentration, and doubt remains

Table 8–6 Correlations Between Average Intakes of Macronutrient and Specific Dietary Fats, as Percentage of Energy Intake, Average Intake of Saturated Fatty Acids, Serum Cholesterol, and 25-Year Coronary Heart Disease Mortality for 16 Cohorts, Seven Countries Study

	SFA	Serum CHOL	CHD
Serum CHOL	0.71**	***	0.73**
C12:0	0.83***	0.84***	0.84***
C14:0	0.88***	0.81***	0.86***
C16:0	0.97***	0.62*	0.81***
C18:0	0.97***	0.60*	0.84***
SFA	***	0.71**	0.88***
C18:1C	0.05	0.17	–0.08
C18:1T	0.84***	0.70**	0.78***
C18:2CC	0.30	–0.06	0.00
EPA + DHA (log)	–0.51*	–0.26	–0.36
Dietary CHOL	0.62*	0.46	0.55*
Total fat	0.80***	0.62*	0.60*
Energy	0.29	0.09	0.28

Note: SFA, saturated fatty acids; CHOL, cholesterol; CHD, coronary heart disease; C12:0, lauric acid; C14:0, myristic acid; C16:0, palmitic acid; C18:0, stearic acid; C18:1C, oleic acid; C18:1T, elaidic acid; C18:2CC, linoleic acid; EPA; eicosapentaenoic acid; DHA, docosahexaenoic acid.

*$P<0.05$

**$P<0.01$.

***$P<0.001$.

Source: Reprinted with permission from D Kromhout et al, *Preventive Medicine*, Vol 24, p 311, © 1995, Academic Press, Inc.

whether there is any adverse effect attributable to these substances.[3] In an extensive review of epidemiologic studies of dietary fat and fatty acids and their relation to both blood lipid concentrations and coronary artery disease risk, Caggiula and Mustad cited mixed results of studies on the relation of *trans* fatty acids and coronary heart disease and methodologic difficulties with each.[23] The issue appears to remain controversial.

Population-Specific Studies

Cholesterol. The Chicago Western Electric Study, one of the early cohort studies of cardiovascular disease organized in the United States and later pooled with others for collective analysis, has made exceptional contributions due to the unique quality of dietary data obtained from participants in that study, not only at baseline examinations but on a second occasion one year later. This dual-occasion assessment of diet by detailed interview methods has permitted adjustment of individual nutrient estimates by taking within-person variation into account, thereby improving precision of the estimates of diet–coronary heart disease relationships. Analysis of the experience of coronary heart disease events among 1824 middle-aged men over a 25-year period indicated significantly increased risks of coronary mortality. The relative hazard of the fifth versus the first quintile group of dietary cholesterol intake was 1.46 (95% confidence interval, 1.10–1.94), after adjustment for other cardiovascular risk factors,

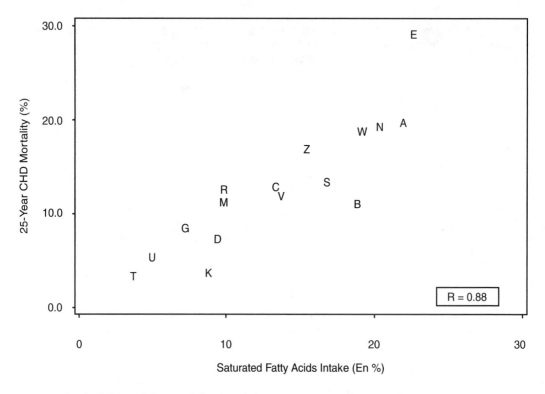

Note: A, US Railroad; B, Belgrade; C, Crevalcore; D, Dalmatia; E, East Finland; G, Corfu; K, Crete; M, Montegiorgio; N, Zutphen; R, Rome Railroad; S, Slavonia; T, Tanushimaru; U, Ushibuka; V, Velika Krsna; W, West Finland; Z, Zrenjanin.

Figure 8–11 Association Between Average Intake of Total Saturated Fatty Acids and 25-Year Coronary Heart Disease Mortality, Seven Countries Study. *Source:* Reprinted with permission from D Kromhout et al, *Preventive Medicine*, Vol 24, p 311, © 1995, Academic Press, Inc.

including total cholesterol concentration.[24] In a review of several studies of dietary cholesterol intake, Stamler and Shekelle noted an overall increase in risk of coronary heart disease of 30% (relative risk, 1.3; 95% confidence interval, 1.1–1.5), pooling results from the Chicago Western Electric Study, Honolulu Heart Program, Ireland-Boston Study, and Zutphen component of the Seven Countries Study.[25]

Dietary Fiber. Dietary fiber is complex carbohydrate material—nonstarch polysaccharides and lignins—that resists digestion in the alimentary tract. Food composition data for fiber have been available only recently, so population studies have been impractical. Cereals, fruits, and vegetables are the principal food sources of fiber, of which several types are distinguished by various properties. Many studies have addressed the effects of dietary fiber on risks of coronary heart disease, blood lipid concentrations, and other aspects of atherosclerosis. This work is reviewed extensively in *Diet and Health*, where no conclusion was reached on health effects of fiber, but recommendations for more rigorous epidemiologic studies were proposed.[3] The challenge was to undertake studies of larger sample size in populations with wider ranges of intake, using improved dietary assessment methods and enhanced nutrient databases for reference and conducting detailed analyses for the several components of fiber in the diet.

Two subsequent studies have more nearly met these criteria than did studies available to the authors of *Diet and Health*. First was the

Health Professionals Follow-up Study, in which a cohort of 43,757 men aged 40–75 years completed detailed dietary questionnaires in 1986 and were followed for six years to ascertain new coronary events.[26] Second was a cohort analysis of 21,930 Finnish men aged 50–69 years who were smokers at high risk of lung cancer at entry to a preventive trial of α-tocopherol and β-carotene supplements (the ATBC Study).[27]

In both studies, it was evident that characteristics of those consuming the greatest quantities of fiber (the highest quintile group of each study) differed in many respects from those consuming the least fiber. For example, in the ATBC study, the high-fiber group consumed less fat and cholesterol, more of vitamins C and E, two times the quantities of fruit and berries, and five times the quantity of rye products. They also exercised more. Adjustment for such factors led to results in both studies indicating significant inverse associations between maximum fiber intake and risk of coronary heart disease. In the Health Professionals Follow-Up Study, it was estimated that the average reduction in risk of coronary death per 10 g increase in fiber intake per day would be approximately 19%; the corresponding result in the ATBC was a reduction of 17% in risk. A 10 g increase in fiber intake would mean an average increase from about 15 to 25 g/day for women and from 18 to 28 g/day for men in the United States, conforming to current dietary recommendations.

Fish. The question of whether fish consumption is protective against coronary heart disease has been addressed in two recent reviews.[28,29] The hypothesis is traced to reports in 1971 and 1980 that Greenland Eskimos experienced a low frequency of coronary heart disease despite consumption of large quantities of marine meat and fat. The Eskimo diet contained less of both saturated fat and cholesterol than the Danish diet with which it was compared. Several specific fatty acids also appeared in different quantities in this diet than in that of the Danes. Particular attention focused on the relatively

increased content of omega-3 polyunsaturated fatty acids (usually denoted ω-3, or n-3, PUFAs), so called because the first of the multiple double bonds in each of the fatty acids of this class occurs at the third carbon atom in the chain. Specific compounds in this class are alphalinolenic acid (LNA), eicosapentaenoic acid (EPA), and docosahexaenoic acid (DHA). Their food sources differ, LNA being found in plant sources (tofu, soybean, and others) and EPA and DHA in marine sources.

The eicosanoid compounds include thromboxanes and prostacyclins, which are related to platelet and blood vessel wall function, and ω-3 PUFAs have anticoagulant effects in experimental studies. It is not clear from population studies in the Netherlands (Zutphen), Japan, and Norway that increased fish consumption, even though associated with measured differences in blood concentrations of ω-3 PUFAs, consistently affects hemostatic function. Other effects have been reported in clinical investigations. Increased dietary intake of ω-3 PUFAs from marine sources, but not from plants, reduces elevated blood triglyceride concentrations. Fish oil containing these compounds lowers elevated blood pressure for an uncertain duration.

The specific question of whether habitual consumption of fish as such is associated with reduced risk of coronary heart disease has been investigated in three large international comparative studies, in several cohort and case-comparison studies, and in one clinical trial. The assessment of this body of evidence identifies several issues common to evaluation of associations between specific components of diet and disease:

> Overall, the epidemiologic evidence is consistent with the idea that consuming fish once or twice a week may decrease risk of coronary heart disease in comparison to rarely or never eating fish, at least in populations with high mean serum cholesterol. However, many gaps remain in the body of evidence. Very little evi-

dence is available with respect to nonfatal coronary events and diseases other than coronary heart disease. Few data are available for women or for persons with ancestry other than European. Effects of other nutrients associated with fish have not been adequately studied. Further studies are needed to establish more clearly the dose-response relationship with total mortality and with nonfatal as well as fatal coronary events throughout a wide range of fish consumption, and the consistency of this association in a variety of populations. Further experimental studies are needed to establish firmly whether or not increasing the consumption of fish reduces risk of coronary heart disease.[28(p 50)]

Coffee. Coffee consumption has been found to be associated with risk of coronary heart disease in some studies but not in others. A recent review, a meta-analysis and a commentary together identify many of the relevant studies and summarize current knowledge.[3,30,31] Coffee has been in use for about 1000 years, and as of the mid-1980s was consumed by 52% of the US population. It is the major source of caffeine for those who drink it, delivering between 200 and 300 mg/day. Coffee is chemically complex, however, and may contain 100 or more active substances, depending on the manner of its preparation.

This consideration has led to identification of two specific components, kahweol and cafestol, which in human experiments have been found to increase blood cholesterol, particularly LDL-cholesterol, concentrations. Because these compounds are trapped by paper filtration in the brewing process, only coffee prepared by boiling and drunk without filtration would be expected to have this effect. Increased risk of coronary heart disease commensurate with this demonstrated blood lipid effect of unfiltered coffee would be expected if there were no opposing influences of other constituents of coffee. Review and meta-analysis of 8 case-control and 14 cohort studies concluded only that a relative risk from drinking five cups per day was unlikely to exceed 1.5 and that ambiguity of the evidence left doubt about the existence or size of a true effect. As in other contexts, the need for longer-term studies with more than baseline assessment of coffee intake was noted, including both regular and decaffeinated coffee drinking. Different preparation methods and the greatly increased variation in types of coffee consumed in some segments of society also require consideration.

Dietary Salt and Blood Pressure

The role of salt, or sodium ingested principally as sodium chloride, as a determinant of blood pressure levels and a cause of hypertensive diseases has been under study for many decades and has generated a vast body of evidence from laboratory, clinical, and population studies. A persisting aura of controversy about relationships between salt intake and blood pressure results in part from pursuit of several different questions whose answers are actually less contradictory than they are tangential to one another, for example:

- Does salt intake cause a rise in blood pressure in individuals, either within the desirable range or from desirable to undesirable levels?
- Does salt intake cause persistence or progression of high blood pressure following its initiation by other, unknown, causes?
- Are population differences in the increase of blood pressure with age (blood pressure "slope") associated with average salt intake of populations?
- Does reduction of salt intake result in lower blood pressure levels in persons with either high blood pressure or blood pressure within the desirable range?
- Will reduction in salt intake at the population level reduce the incidence of high blood pressure?

The last question is of greatest importance from the public health perspective, because judgment on this issue forms the basis of policy recommendations, including regulatory action on production and labeling of processed foods. Here lies a major reason for controversy, which has less to do with scientific than with policy conflict, as witnessed in mid-1996 in what might be termed the salt issue of the *British Medical Journal* (with an article by Godlee[32] and companion articles). That issue presents an unusual view of open conflict between scientific and commercial interests, as a series of articles and commentaries exchange allegations of withholding of data, improper secondary analysis of published data, and failure of government agencies to resist pressure from industry in setting health policies. Central to this conflict is the effort of the Salt Institute, the US-based agency of the commercial salt industry, to discredit the INTERSALT Study (discussed in Chapter 12) and the body of research cited in support of recommendations to reduce salt intake.

Recent reviews of the background and epidemiologic evidence include *Diet and Health* and a more extensive account by Stamler.[3,33] Salt intake is expressed in relation to sodium alone or as sodium chloride, other sodium-containing compounds being less often specified. Dietary intake of sodium is difficult to determine by interview methods because there are many sources, content in processed foods is determined by manufacturing techniques, and salt may or may not be added in preparation or at the table. Equilibrium in body content of sodium is maintained mainly through renal excretion, and thus, on the assumption of a steady physiologic state, urinary excretion of sodium serves as an estimate of intake. Overnight or, better, 24-hour urinary collections are conducted for this purpose in population studies, ideally on more than a single occasion to obtain an improved estimate of within-person values.

The estimated daily requirement for salt is no more than 8–10 mmol/day of sodium or 500 mg of sodium chloride, although unusual populations have been found with lower intakes. Intakes usually exceed this requirement by many times, with the median intake among 48 centers of the INTERSALT Study being 160 mmol/day. The major source of dietary sodium, perhaps 75% of the total intake, is in commercially processed foods. Therefore the potential for reduction in average population intakes of sodium depends on the availability and use of lower-sodium products. The food industry is said to resist reduction in salt content because of loss of flavor, and therefore marketability, of its products.[32] Salt taste is remarkably modifiable, however, and adaptation in only a matter of days can make many previously desirable foods seem unpalatable due to saltiness. In the United States, from 1972 to 1985, grocery store sales indicated reduction in purchases of food-grade salt from 2.2 to 1.4 lb/capita.

The INTERSALT Study estimated the public health benefit of reduced sodium intake by calculating the contribution of sodium intake to the cross-sectional slope of blood pressure increase with age in its many study populations, each of 200 men and women from 20 to 59 years of age.[33] If habitual sodium intake were reduced by 100 mmol/day, as from 170 to 70, the age-related increase in systolic blood pressure would be 10.2 mm Hg less and in diastolic pressure 6.3 mm Hg less, from age 25 to 55. The effect of these reductions in average later adult blood pressure levels would be a substantial reduction in incidence and prevalence of high blood pressure in the population. The further impact of a reduction in hypertension on mortality from cardiovascular diseases and all causes is shown in Table 8–7. For each of several degrees of reduction in systolic blood pressure—2, 5, or 9 mm Hg as population averages (all less than that projected above for a decrease of sodium consumption by 100 mmol/day)—the percentage reduction in mortality and number of deaths averted in the US male population aged 35–54 years are presented. The decrease of 9 mm Hg corresponds to mortality reductions of 18.0% in coronary heart disease, 26.2% in stroke, 19.4% in all cardiovascular disease, and

13.7% for all-cause mortality. These figures would underestimate substantially the impact at older ages, where rates are much higher.

Some health professionals consider the effects of sodium on blood pressure to require individual susceptibility based on genetic factors analogous to those studied extensively in specially bred strains of rats. However, review of population-wide data suggests a potential benefit of reduced sodium intake across whole populations without regard to the possibly greater salt sensitivity of some individuals.

Intervention studies on salt intake provide support for these projections and include clinical trials in adults and a community trial in Portugal, among others. The Trials of Hypertension Prevention sought to reduce sodium intake to 80 mmol/day in adults aged 30–54 years with diastolic blood pressure 80–89 mm Hg.[34] Sodium reductions in the 314 participants randomly allocated to active intervention were from 154.6 to 99.4 mmol/day at the 18-month follow-up visit, with significant reductions in both systolic

and diastolic blood pressure. In two Portuguese communities, education about the benefits of reducing salt in cooking and limiting consumption of particularly high-salt foods led to marked changes in salt intake and in prevalence of high blood pressure between the intervention and the control community.[35] Sodium consumption was reduced from 364 to 202 mmol/day in the intervention community, with corresponding net decreases of systolic and diastolic blood pressure of 13.3 and 6.1 mm Hg, respectively, relative to the control community. In the control community, sodium consumption increased from 352 to 371 mmol/day. Trials on salt intake and blood pressure are addressed further in Chapter 12. Notably, however, a recent review has considered the safety of dietary sodium reduction in view of concerns raised from time to time.[36] The authors concluded, "Overall, we identified extensive data supporting the safety of public health recommendations for moderate Na reduction and none suggesting cause for concern."[36 (p 192)]

Table 8–7 Reduction in Population Average Systolic Blood Pressure and Expected Reductions in Deaths in Six Years by Cause, US Men Aged 35–54

Reduction in Population Average Systolic Blood Pressure (mm Hg)	Expected Decreases in Death Rates[a] (and Number of Deaths) for 26,024,000[b] US Men Aged 35–54			
	Coronary Heart Disease	Stroke	Cardiovascular Disease	All Causes
2	4.3% (6,870)	6.5% (1,093)	4.7% (10,279)	3.2% (16,603)
5	10.5% (16,785)	15.5% (2,602)	11.3% (24,723)	7.9% (40,962)
9	18.0% (28,757)	26.2% (4,398)	19.4% (42,471)	13.7% (71,019)

a. Based on multiple logistic coefficient (with baseline systolic blood pressure, age, serum cholesterol, cigarettes per day, and diabetes in the model) for the cohort of 347,978 men screened for the Multiple Risk Factor Intervention Trial, from 6-year follow-up data.

b. US male population aged 35–54 in 1984.

Source: Reprinted with permission from J Stamler, Dietary Salt and Blood Pressure, *Annals of the New York Academy of Science*, Vol 676, p 145, © 1993, New York Academy of Science.

PREVENTION AND CONTROL OF DIETARY IMBALANCE

Population-Wide Measures

General Recommendations

Policy recommendations for prevention or reversal of dietary imbalance have been formulated and disseminated for many years by official international and national health agencies and by numerous voluntary health organizations such as the Nutrition Committee of the American Heart Association. The World Health Organization report of 1990, the US National Research Council report of 1989, the guidelines of the US Department of Agriculture/Department of Health and Human Services, and others have been cited above.[2,3,4,7,15] There is consistency in the general recommendations to limit intake of fats, saturated fats, and salt and to increase intake of fruits, vegetables, and legumes to maintain a balance between total energy intake and energy requirements.

Specific Nutrients

Provisions for specific nutrients and target levels of intake differ somewhat among national recommendations, as indicated in Table 8–8, on the basis of detailed recommendations from 20 countries representing most regions of the world except Africa. However, their common interest in these nutrients and similar quantitative goals indicate broad agreement. Some of the variation in suggested upper or lower limits of intake may reflect the intent for their use as individual goals rather than population mean values. The potential importance of this distinction was noted by the World Health Organization Study Group and is illustrated for saturated fatty acid intake as a percentage of energy intake in Figure 8–12.[2] Population goals, as indicated in the Study Group recommendations in Table 8–8, are intended to correspond to the dashed curve of Figure 8–12. In a population with a mean intake at the goal level of 10% of calories as saturated fatty acids, half the population will have greater intakes than 10%. If the goal for individuals is to consume less than 10% of calories as saturated fatty acids, then the resulting mean value would be well below 10% and few individuals would have intakes greater than this level. The Study Group termed this a "misinterpreted goal," but it is apparent in such high-risk or individual recommendations as those of the US National Cholesterol Education Program that the intent is for individuals to achieve the recommended levels of intake. In any case, the interpretation will clearly lead to different expectations of the distributions of nutrient intakes at the population level. Clarity is needed on this point in interpretation of published recommendations.

The evolution of these policies is discussed and the broader context of their place in food policy and national, regional, and global economics are noted in Chapter 22. They are also reviewed historically in the first US *Surgeon General's Report on Nutrition and Health*, which incorporates the specific *Dietary Guidelines for Americans* discussed above.[4,37] At the international level, corresponding recommendations on behalf of children and youth were addressed in a World Health Organization Expert Committee report,[38] and the primacy of population-level education on health and nutrition for children and adolescents was emphasized by the National Cholesterol Education Program in the United States.[39]

High-Risk or Individual Measures

At the individual level, high-risk strategies for dietary modification include screening to identify those in need of special intervention due to undesirable blood lipid concentration, blood pressure level, or, potentially, other risk factors or evidence of atherosclerosis. Among the most highly developed protocols for screening, evaluation, and management of cardiovascular risk factors based on dietary intervention are those of the National Cholesterol Education Program.[7,39] These are discussed in Chapter 11, in connection with adverse blood lipid profiles.

Table 8–8 Comparison of Dietary Recommendations of the WHO Study Group and National Recommendations

Nutrient	Study Group's Population Nutrient Goal		National Upper or Lower Limit Recommendation[a]		
	Lower Limit	Upper Limit	Lowest	Highest	Median
Total fat (% energy)	15	30	15	35	<30
SFA (% energy)	0	10	8	15	<10
PUFA (% energy)	3	7	10	13	10
P:S ratio[b]	—	—	0.45	1.2	1.0
Cholesterol (mg/d)	0	300	225	300	<300
Total CHO (% energy)[c]	55	75	40	70	55
Complex CHO (% energy)	50	70	—	—	—
Dietary fiber (g/d)					
As NSP	16	24	—	—	—
As total dietary fiber	27	40	20	35	30
Free sugars[d] (% energy)	0	10	9	25	<10
Salt (g/d)	—[e]	6	5	10	7

Note: SFA, saturated fatty acids; PUFA, polyunsaturated fatty acids; P:S, ratio of polyunsaturated to saturated fatty acids; CHO, carbohydrate; NSP, nonstarch polysaccharides.

a. Values for total fat, SFA, cholesterol, sugar, and salt are upper limits (the median value therefore implies that total fat intake, for example, should be less than 30% of energy); other nutrient values are lower limits (the median value therefore implies that PUFA intake, for example, should be greater than 10% of energy).

b. Earlier reports specified P:S ratios. Later reports offered recommendations on classes of fatty acids but not on ratios. In this report, care is taken not to specify a ratio, because the SFA value could in theory be reduced to 0%, but the Study Group recommends that PUFA intake should remain between 3% and 7%.

c. Most reports suggest that most of the carbohydrate should be complex carbohydrate without specifying a specific proportion.

d. These sugars include monosaccharides, disaccharides, and other short-chain sugars produced by refining carbohydrates.

e. Not defined.

Source: Reprinted with permission from Report of a WHO Study Group, *WHO TRS 797*, p 116, © 1990, World Health Organization.

They depend on individual, family, and group education and counseling to modify knowledge and behavior with respect to food choices and preparation as well as setting quantitative goals for evaluating the effect of dietary change. For adults with undesirable and inadequately responsive blood lipid levels (usually monitored by LDL-cholesterol levels), lipid-lowering drugs are recommended. Drugs are also proposed for use if necessary in older children and adolescents, but with greater reservation than in adults.

EXPERIENCE IN CHANGING DIETARY PATTERNS

At both population and individual levels, it is clear that dietary patterns can be modified. The

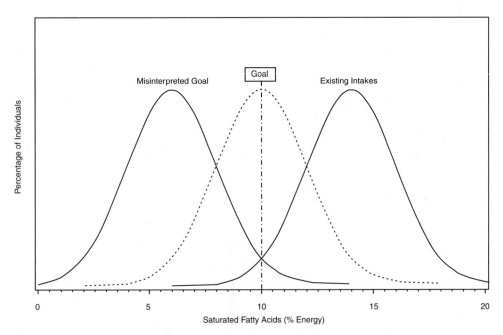

Figure 8–12 Distinction Between a Population Nutrient Goal and an Individual Nutrient Goal. This figure depicts the distribution of intakes of saturated fatty acids for three hypothetical populations, corresponding to an existing population whose intake is higher than recommended by the Study Group (right), a population that has achieved the *population goal* of a maximum intake of 10% of energy as saturated fatty acids (center), and a population in which nearly all individuals have an intake less than 10%, a situation that represents the result of misinterpretation of the population goal as an *individual goal* (left). *Source:* Reprinted with permission from Report of a WHO Study Group, *WHO TRS 797*, p 118, © 1990, World Health Organization.

World Health Organization Study Group Report reviews experience in Finland, the Netherlands, Norway, the United Kingdom, the United States, and Australia and New Zealand. These experiences reveal differences in governmental policies and actions, which reflect circumstances of each country. In the cases of Finland, Norway, the United Kingdom, and the United States, some components of diet have changed markedly, such as the adoption of low-fat dairy products in place of traditional ones. The extent of change in food availability in the United States in only the 20 years from 1965 to 1985 is striking in several respects, as shown in Table 8–9.[37] Substantial decreases in production occurred for eggs, fluid whole milk, butter, lard, and refined sugars, while marked increases occurred for poultry, low-fat dairy products, cheese, vegetable shortening and oils, fresh

fruits and vegetables, and corn sweeteners. It is reasonable to infer that the major factor leading to these changes has been changing demand in the marketplace. To the extent this is true, it reflects major favorable impacts of policy recommendations and public education, aided by such governmental intervention as adoption of more stringent food labeling regulations and other measures.

Intervention Studies

Dietary change can be achieved at both population and individual levels, as shown by a large number of intervention trials as well as by trends in national dietary data shown above. Trials of dietary intervention to prevent atherosclerotic and hypertensive diseases have been

Table 8-9 Annual per Capita Availability of Selected Commodities in the US Food Supply, 1965–1985, in Pounds

	Meat, Poultry, and Fish[a]					Dairy Products[b]			
Year	Meat	Poultry	Fish and Shellfish	Total	Eggs[d]	Fluid Whole Milk	Low-Fat Milk[c] and Milk Products (Fluid)	Cheese[e]	Total[f]
1965–67	123.6	30.6	10.8	165.0	40.0	240.3	41.7	9.8	343.9
1968–70	130.8	33.0	11.3	175.1	39.5	219.5	54.6	11.0	334.6
1971–73	129.5	35.1	12.3	176.9	38.2	199.2	69.3	12.9	327.7
1974–76	128.7	35.5	12.4	176.6	35.1	176.0	82.9	14.9	317.1
1977–79	126.2	40.1	13.0	179.3	34.6	155.9	95.3	16.8	310.2
1980–82	120.9	44.2	12.7	177.8	33.9	138.1	101.7	18.7	299.7
1983–85	120.9	47.6	13.8	182.3	32.8	125.3	111.4	21.5	301.7

Note: Totals may include more categories than the selected commodities.

a. Meat (beef, veal, pork, lamb), poultry, and fish, edible weight. Fish excludes game fish.

b. Dairy products are for civilian population, except fluid milk and cream data, which use US resident population.

c. Low-fat milk and milk products include low-fat, skim, buttermilk, flavored drinks, and yogurt.

d. Eggs, retail weight. Weight of a dozen eggs is assumed to be 1.57 lb.

e. Cheese is whole and part-whole milk cheese, excluding pot, baker's, and cottage cheese.

f. Total dairy products calculated as total retail product weight minus butter. Includes frozen dairy products, cottage cheese, and other products not indicated in table. The amount of calcium contributed by this food group has actually increased slightly during the 20-year period shown as a result of increase in products such as dry milk powder.

continues

Table 8–9 continued

		Fats and Oils[g]								*Fruits*[h]	
	Animal			*Vegetable*							
Year	*Butter*	*Lard*	*Total Animal*	*Margarine*	*Shortening*	*Salad and Cooking Oil*	*Total Vegetable*	*Total*	*Fresh*	*Processed*	*Total*
1965–67	5.9	5.7	16.9	10.3	15.4	12.6	35.2	52.1	79.0	35.3	114.3
1968–70	5.5	5.0	16.0	10.7	16.9	14.4	38.8	54.9	77.1	37.6	114.7
1971–73	4.9	3.7	14.1	11.0	17.2	16.7	41.9	56.0	75.5	39.4	114.9
1974–76	4.5	2.9	11.6	11.4	17.2	18.5	44.8	56.4	79.9	40.6	120.5
1977–79	4.4	2.3	11.6	11.3	17.9	20.0	46.3	57.9	80.4	39.8	120.2
1980–82	4.4	2.5	12.8	11.2	18.4	21.6	48.1	60.9	84.8	37.1	121.9
1983–85	4.9	2.0	13.5	10.5	20.9	22.3	50.6	64.1	87.9	34.8	122.7

g. Food fats and oils calculated on a total population basis except butter, which is based on civilian population. The animal and vegetable categories are not strictly distinct because some margarines and shortenings include animal fats.

h. Selected fruits, retail weights, include fruits for which data are available for the entire series: oranges, tangerines, tangelos, lemons and limes, grapefruit, apples, avocados, bananas, cherries, grapes, nectarines, peaches, pears, pineapples, plums and prunes, strawberries, minor fruits, and a variety of canned, frozen, and chilled fruit and juices.

continues

Table 8-9 continued

Year	Vegetables[i] Fresh	Processed	Total	Beans, Peas, and Nuts	Potatoes[k] and Sweet Potatoes	Flour and Cereal Products	Sugar and Sweeteners[j] Refined Cane and Beet	Corn Sweeteners	Total Caloric Sweeteners	Coffee, Tea, and Cocoa
1965–67	62.6	41.4	104.0	14.8	84.5	143.8	97.6	15.5	114.8	15.1
1968–70	65.2	45.4	110.6	14.8	85.1	141.9	100.6	18.2	120.4	14.5
1971–73	66.1	45.9	112.0	14.2	80.6	138.5	101.7	21.8	125.0	14.2
1974–76	68.9	46.1	115.0	15.1	81.5	143.6	92.7	27.3	121.4	13.1
1977–79	71.7	46.1	117.7	14.3	81.5	145.8	91.7	33.8	126.8	11.1
1980–82	74.3	44.2	118.6	14.0	76.3	150.2	78.9	44.4	124.6	11.3
1983–85	79.7	44.7	123.3	14.6	79.5	150.5	67.4	58.3	127.1	11.6

i. Selected vegetables: fresh vegetables for which data are available for entire series include broccoli, carrots, cauliflower, celery, corn, lettuce, onions and shallots, and tomatoes; 1985 data for processed vegetables are unavailable.

j. Potatoes and sweet potatoes: data not comparable to pre-1960 figures. Data revised to reflect conversion from processed weight to fresh-weight equivalent to dehydrated potatoes, frozen potatoes, chips, and shoestrings.

k. Sugars and sweeteners, dry weight basis.

Source: Reprinted from US Department of Health and Human Services.

designed chiefly to modify fat intake, and thereby reduce blood cholesterol concentrations, or to reduce salt intake, and thereby lower blood pressure or prevent its increase. Often dietary modification has been combined with other interventions. Therefore dietary intervention trials are discussed in the context of blood lipids (Chapter 11), blood pressure (Chapter 12), or of multifactor intervention trials (Chapter 21), as appropriate.

A proposal to conduct a major trial of dietary intervention alone for prevention of coronary heart disease led to the Diet-Heart Feasibility Study of the 1960s, which successfully implemented a double-blind trial in several test sites. However, despite this success, it was judged too costly to undertake the full-scale trial, and the desired evidence has never been obtained. Inference from all other available data and experience of many more-recent studies of diet modification have established that such change is feasible among high-risk individuals and can result in much of the expected health benefit.

CURRENT ISSUES

Chief among the issues in establishment and maintenance of a balanced diet is the government's role in adoption of policies concerning food production, food labeling, nutrition education, and other aspects to ensure availability and accessibility of foods constituting a healthy balance of nutrient components and to promote a healthy relationship between energy consumption and energy expenditure. The challenges of bringing about appropriate governmental action and public education have been addressed in many of the sources cited here. Especially informative from a global perspective is the World Health Organization Study Group Report.[2] In addition, recent insights into the difficulties of policy development and implementation are offered by editorial comments in both the United States and the United Kingdom, which are addressed further in Chapter 28.[40,41] Issues of public misperceptions or confusion, competing interests of health and the food industry, governmental inaction, and failure to provide sufficient support for research on diet and health are all at play. The challenges are many, as addressed further in subsequent chapters.

Further information to address the numerous questions about dietary effects on cardiovascular and other chronic diseases can be obtained only through substantial investment in the highest-quality population data on diet, which should consider major nutrients, micronutrients, vitamins, minerals, and supplements and should include long-term follow-up of large and diverse population groups. These data should be accompanied by appropriate assessment of biochemical or physiological indicators of dietary effects, as well as overt clinical disease.

REFERENCES

1. Stamler J. Population studies. In: Levy RI, Rifkind B, Dennis B, Ernst N, eds. *Nutrition, Lipids, and Coronary Heart Disease*. New York: Raven Press; 1979; 25–88.

2. World Health Organization Study Group. *Diet, Nutrition, and the Prevention of Chronic Diseases*. Geneva, Switzerland: World Health Organization; 1990. Technical Report Series 797.

3. Committee on Diet and Health, Food and Nutrition Board, Commission on Life Sciences, National Research Council. *Diet and Health: Implications for Reducing Chronic Disease Risk*. Washington, DC: National Academy Press; 1989.

4. *Nutrition and Your Health: Dietary Guidelines for Americans*. 4th ed. Washington, DC: US Dept of Health and Human Services; 1995.

5. Stamler J. Established major coronary risk factors. In: Marmot M, Elliott P, eds. *Coronary Heart Disease Epidemiology: From Aetiology to Public Health*. Oxford, England: Oxford University Publishers; 1992; 35–66.

6. Keys A. Mediterranean diet and public health: personal reflections. *Am J Clin Nutr.* 1995;61(suppl): 1321S–1323S.

7. Expert Panel National Cholesterol Education Program. Report of the National Cholesterol Education Program

Expert Panel on Detection, Evaluation, and Treatment of High Blood Cholesterol in Adults. *Arch Intern Med.* 1988;148:36–69.

8. Thompson FE, Byers T. Dietary assessment resource manual. *Am J Nutr.* 1994;124(suppl):2245S–2317S.

9. Keys A. *Coronary Heart Disease in Seven Countries.* Dallas, Tex: American Heart Association; 1970. Monograph 29.

10. Anderson SA. Guidelines for use of dietary intake data. *J Amer Diet Assoc.* 1988;88:1258.

11. Beaton GH, Burema J, Ritenbaugh C. Errors in the interpretation of dietary assessments. *Am J Clin Nutr.* 1997;65(suppl):1100S–1107S.

12. Coates RJ, Monteilh CP. Assessments of food-frequency questionnaires in minority populations. *Am J Clin Nutr.* 1997;65(suppl):1108S–1115S.

13. Rockett HRH, Colditz GA. Assessing diets of children and adolescents. *Am J Clin Nutr.* 1997;65(suppl):1116S–1122S.

14. Cutler JA, Stamler J. Introduction and summary of the dietary and nutritional methods and findings in the Multiple Risk Factor Intervention Trial. *Am J Clin Nutr.* 1997; 65(suppl):184S–190S.

15. *Report of the Expert Panel on Population Strategies for Blood Cholesterol Reduction.* Bethesda, Md: National Cholesterol Education Program, Public Health Service, National Institutes of Health; 1990. NIH publication 90-3046.

16. Zilversmit DB. Diet and heart disease: prudence, probability, and proof. *Arteriosclerosis.* 1982;2:83–84.

17. Malmros H. The relation of nutrition to health. *Acta Medica Scand.* 1950;246(suppl):137–153.

18. Keys A. *Seven Countries: A Multivariate Analysis of Death and Coronary Heart Disease.* Cambridge, Mass: Harvard University Press; 1980.

19. Artaud-Wild SM, Connor SL, Sexton G, Connor WE. Differences in coronary mortality can be explained by differences in cholesterol and saturated fat intakes in 40 countries but not in France and Finland. *Circ.* 1993; 88:2771–2779.

20. Stamler J. Assessing diets to improve world health: nutritional research on disease causation in populations. *Am J Clin Nutr.* 1994;59(suppl):146S–156S.

21. Kromhout D, Menotti A, Bloemberg B, Aravanis C, et al. Dietary saturated and *trans* fatty acids and cholesterol and 25-year mortality from coronary heart disease: the Seven Countries Study. *Prev Med.* 1995; 24:308–315.

22. Aro A, Kardinaal AFM, Saliminen I, Riemersma RA, et al. Adipose tissue isomeric trans fatty acids and risk of myocardial infarction in nine countries: the EURAMIC study. *Lancet.* 1995;345:273–278.

23. Caggiula AW, Mustad VA. Effects of dietary fat and fatty acids on coronary artery disease risk and total and lipoprotein cholesterol concentrations: epidemiologic studies. *Am J Clin Nutr.* 1997;65(suppl):1597S–1610S.

24. Shekelle RB, Stamler J. Dietary cholesterol and ischaemic heart disease. *Lancet.* 1989;i:1177–1179.

25. Stamler J, Shekelle RB. Dietary cholesterol and human coronary heart disease. *Arch Path Lab Med.* 1988; 112:1032–1040.

26. Rimm EB, Ascherio A, Giovannucci E, Spiegelman D, et al. Vegetable, fruit and cereal fiber intake and risk of coronary heart disease among men. *JAMA.* 1996; 275:447–451.

27. Pietinen P, Rimm EB, Korhonen P, Hartman AM, et al. Intake of dietary fiber and risk of coronary heart disease in a cohort of Finnish men: the Alpha-Tocopherol, Beta-Carotene Cancer Prevention Study. *Circ.* 1996; 94:2720–2727.

28. Shekelle RB, Stamler J. Fish and coronary heart disease: the epidemiologic evidence. *Nutr Metab Cardiovasc Dis.* 1993;3:46–51.

29. Stone NJ. Fish consumption, fish oil, lipids and coronary heart disease. *Circ.* 1996;94:2337–2340.

30. Greenland S. A meta-analysis of coffee, myocardial infarction, and coronary death. *Epidemiol.* 1993;4: 366–374.

31. Thelle DS. Coffee, tea and coronary heart disease. *Curr Opin Lipidology.* 1995;6:25–27.

32. Godlee F. The food industry fights for salt. *Br Med J.* 1996;312:1239–1240.

33. Stamler J. Dietary salt and blood pressure. *Ann NY Acad Sci.* 1993;676:122–156.

34. Kumanyika SK, Hebert PR, Cutler JA, Lasser VI, et al. Trials of Hypertension Prevention Collaborative Research Group: feasibility and efficacy of sodium reduction in the trials of hypertension prevention, phase I. *Hypertens.* 1993;22:502–511.

35. Forte JG, Pereira Miguel JM, Pereira Miguel MJ, de Pádua F, et al. Salt and blood pressure: a community trial. *J Hum Hypertens.* 1989;3:179–184.

36. Kumanyika S, Cutler JA. Dietary sodium restriction: is there cause for concern? *J Am Coll Nutr.* 1997; 16:192–203.

37. *The Surgeon General's Report on Nutrition and Health.* Bethesda, Md: National Cholesterol Education Program, Public Health Service, National Institutes of Health; 1988. NIH publication 88-50210.

38. World Health Organization Expert Committee. *Prevention in Childhood and Youth of Adult Cardiovascular Diseases: Time for Action.* Geneva, Switzerland: World Health Organization; 1990. WHO Technical Report Series 797.

39. National Cholesterol Education Program. Report of the Expert Panel on Blood Cholesterol Levels in Children and Adolescents. Bethesda, Md: National Cholesterol Program, National Heart, Lung and Blood Institute, National Institutes of Health, Public Health Service, US Dept of Health and Human Services; 1991. NIH publication 91-2732.

40. Nestle M. The politics of dietary guidance—a new opportunity. *Am J Public Health*. 1994;84:713–715.

41. Bingham S. Dietary aspects of a health strategy for England. *Br Med J*. 1991;303:353–355.

CHAPTER 9

Physical Inactivity

SUMMARY

Physical inactivity is a widely prevalent condition in all modern societies and represents, like contemporary dietary patterns, a radical change from the thousands of years of human development up until the most recent two centuries. Dietary change is recent, having shifted importantly with the first agricultural revolution some 10,000 years ago, but the change in physical activity associated with acquisition of food and other occupations is a still more recent and abrupt change. As an object of research, physical activity has many features in common with diet, and the methods of assessing usual habits of activity pose parallel difficulties. Still, many studies of the health effects of less than vigorous physical activity have been conducted using a wide variety of methods. Epidemiologic studies initiated decades ago by Morris, by Paffenbarger, and by others focused on occupational activity. Taylor and Rose contributed to the shift in focus to "leisure-time physical activity" because it seemed increasingly unlikely that work activity could contribute any longer to healthy activity levels, given mechanization and automation and the disappearance of personal locomotion to, at, and from the place of work. Major scientific conferences and reports in recent years have compiled an extensive body of research on physiology, epidemiology, and behavioral aspects of physical inactivity and have led to consensus statements and recommendations on physical activity from voluntary and official health organizations and agencies, including the office of the US Surgeon General. Based on the moderately strong but persuasive causal relation between physical inactivity and cardiovascular diseases (and others) and on the high prevalence of physical inactivity in the United States and the few other populations investigated, there is reason for belief that interventions from the personal to the governmental policy level could bring about changes favorable to the health of the public. The magnitude of change needed to restore natural biological function is immense, but from the current status of the population, even modest improvements are predicted to have significant health benefits.

INTRODUCTION

Physical inactivity as a prevailing characteristic of modern societies is, like dietary pattern, seen most clearly in relief against the human evolutionary background. As outlined by Blackburn, physical activity ranked for eons alongside food consumption as one of the two "primal human activities."[1] Each could be viewed as being necessary for the conduct of the other. Anthropological evidence on bone structure indicates smaller stature and heavier musculature in early *Homo sapiens*, who is also inferred to have had great capacity for meeting demands of strength and endurance as well as for surviving periods of food scarcity. Through several tens of thousands of years the conditions of life are thought to have changed little, until the first agricultural revolution, discussed in the previous chapter, which introduced plant and animal domestication. The contrast is offered between this long-standing human experience and the "relatively great height and mass and relatively less muscularity and bone strength of modern affluent humans who have been exposed to only a few generations of sedentariness in the presence of perpetual excess in calories and nutrients."[1(p 102)] Blackburn also noted: "The portrayal suggests that the recent magnitude of mass sedentation and caloric intake of modern man may act as a substantial adaptive stress that may result in mass metabolic maladaptations . . . [that] will surely persist in affluent societies unless there is a general cultural change."[1(p 102)]

Conscious attention to physical inactivity is not entirely a modern phenomenon, however.[2] Physical activity in various forms appears to have been prescribed, as well as being an integral part of cultural norms, in both East and West for several thousand years. Health benefits were attributed to exercise in ancient writings in China, India, and Greece. Through the Western Middle Ages and into the modern period, early Greek influences persisted, and by the 18th and 19th centuries several authoritative texts on physical activity had been produced. The view that lack of physical activity had its harmful effects was also explicit in the writing of prominent figures of the time.

Even the 19th-century introduction of the concept of physical education still claimed Greek antecedents. Scientific study of physical fitness in relation to anthropometry and cardiorespiratory physiology developed in the latter 19th and early 20th centuries, respectively. The practical importance of this science was stimulated by the perceptions in the United States at the time of both the First and Second World Wars that the physical condition of the population was suboptimal. National programs were instituted in the mid-1940s, and further reports of poor physical performance of US youth in relation to their European counterparts added further impetus and visibility to the issue.

Epidemiologic study of physical activity in relation to cardiovascular diseases—especially coronary heart disease—began in the 1950s, and Morris,[3] Taylor,[4] Paffenbarger,[5] and others were among the prominent contributors. On the basis of this and much other research, the American College of Sports Medicine developed extensive guidelines for evaluating individual fitness and prescribing remedial programs, which was already in its second edition by the 1990s.[6] National concern was given new prominence with issuance of the first report of the US Surgeon General on *Physical Activity and Health* coincident with the centennial Olympic Games in 1996.[2] The Surgeon General's report reviewed more than four decades of epidemiologic research on physical activity as well as laboratory and clinical investigations of the physiology of exercise. The report describes population patterns of physical activity in the United States and addresses the evolution of policies and recommendations (discussed in Chapter 22) and strategies for intervention in detail.

CONCEPTS AND DEFINITION

Many terms are encountered in connection with physical inactivity. Terms with proposed standard definitions include *physical activity* ("bodily movement produced by skeletal muscles that requires energy expenditure"); *exercise* ("a type of physical activity defined as a planned, structured, and repetitive bodily movement done to improve or maintain one or more components of physical fitness"); *physical fitness* ("a set of attributes that people have or achieve that relates to the ability to perform physical activity"); and *physical inactivity* ("a level of activity less than that needed to maintain good health").[2] Physical inactivity is thus unhealthy by definition, and it is this part of the activity spectrum that is most directly of concern, although many other aspects are addressed, in cardiovascular epidemiology.

Other dimensions of physical activity important for epidemiologic studies of physical inactivity and cardiovascular diseases include the distinction between occupational (work) activity and nonoccupational or leisure time physical activity. Early studies, through the 1970s, focused on occupational activity, while more recent ones have emphasized nonoccupational activity. Gradation of activity is commonly expressed in qualitative terms such as *light, moderate*, or *vigorous*. Alternatively, it may be measured in units of energy expenditure (kilocalories per minute [kcal/min] or kilojoules per minute [kjoule/min], in which 1 kcal = 4.184 kjoule) or expressed in effort required, as measured in terms of the ratio of work metabolic rate to resting metabolic rate, in units called METs. One MET is defined as the rate of oxygen consumption of an adult seated at rest, which is approximately 3.5 milliliters per minute per kilogram body weight (1 MET = 3.5 ml/min/kg). As an example, Table 9–1 shows several types of activities classified as light, moderate, or hard/vigorous, with corresponding measures of energy expenditure or oxygen consumption.[7]

ASSESSMENT

Procedures for assessment of physical activity (or inactivity) are evaluated for their potential research use in Table 9–2.[2] The process of eliciting information about individual activity

Table 9–1 Examples of Common Physical Activities for Healthy US Adults, by Intensity of Effort Required

Light *(<3.0 METs or <4 kcal/min)*	*Moderate* *(3.0–6.0 METs or 4–7 kcal/min)*	*Hard/Vigorous* *(>6.0 METs or >7 kcal/min)*
Walking, slowly (strolling) (1–2 mph)	Walking, briskly (3–4 mph)	Walking, briskly uphill or with a load
Cycling, stationary (<50 W)	Cycling for pleasure or transportation (≤10 mph)	Cycling, fast or racing (>10 mph)
Swimming, slow treading	Swimming, moderate effort	Swimming, fast treading or crawl
Conditioning exercise, light stretching	Conditioning exercise, general calisthenics	Conditioning exercise, stair ergometer, ski machine
. . .	Racket sports, table tennis	Racket sports, singles tennis, racquetball
Golf, power cart	Golf, pulling cart or carrying clubs	. . .
Bowling	. . .	. . .
Fishing, sitting	Fishing, standing/casting	Fishing in stream
Boating, power	Canoeing, leisurely (2.0–3.9 mph)	Canoeing, rapidly (≥4 mph)
Home care, carpet sweeping	Home care, general cleaning	Moving furniture
Mowing lawn, riding mower	Mowing lawn, power mower	Mowing lawn, hand mower
Home repair, carpentry	Home repair, painting	. . .

Note: The MET (work metabolic rate/resting metabolic rate) is a multiple of the resting rate of oxygen consumption during physical activity. One MET represents the approximate rate of oxygen consumption of a seated adult at rest, or about 3.5 ml/min/kg. The equivalent energy cost of 1 MET in kcal/min is about 1.2 for a 70-kg person or approximately 1 kcal/kg/hr. W = watts.

Source: Reprinted from *Journal of the American Medical Association*, Vol 273, p 404, 1995.

Table 9–2 Assessment Procedures and Their Potential Use in Epidemiologic Research

Measurement Tool	Applicable Age Groups	Use in Large-Scale Studies	Low $ Cost	Low Time Cost	Low Subject Time Cost	Low Subject Effort Cost	Likely To Influence Behavior	Acceptable to Persons	Socially Acceptable	Activity Specific
Surveying										
Task-specific diary	Adult, elderly	Yes	Yes	Yes	No	No	Yes	?	Yes	Yes
Recall questionnaire	Adult, elderly	Yes	Yes	Yes	Yes	Yes	No	Yes	Yes	Yes
Quantitative history	Adult, elderly	Yes	Yes	No	No	No	No	Yes	Yes	Yes
Global self-report	Adult, elderly	Yes	Yes	Yes	Yes	Yes	No	Yes	Yes	No
Monitoring										
Behavioral observation	Adult, elderly	No	No	No	No	Yes	Yes	?	?	Yes
Job classification	Adult	Yes	Yes	Yes	Yes	Yes	No	Yes	Yes	Yes
Heart rate monitor	All	No	No	No	Yes	Yes	No	Yes	Yes	No
Heart rate and motion sensor	All	No	No	No	Yes	Yes	No	Yes	Yes	No
Electronic motion sensor	Adult, elderly	Yes	No	Yes	Yes	Yes	No	Yes	Yes	No
Pedometer	Adult, elderly	Yes	Yes	Yes	Yes	Yes	No	Yes	Yes	No
Gait assessment	Child, adult, elderly	No	No	Yes	Yes	Yes	No	Yes	Yes	No
Accelerometers	All	Yes	Yes	Yes	Yes	Yes	No	Yes	Yes	No
Horizontal time monitor	Child, adult, elderly	No	No	Yes	Yes	Yes	No	Yes	Yes	No
Stabilometers	Infant	No	No	Yes	Yes	Yes	No	Yes	Yes	No
Direct calorimetry	All	No	No	No	No	No	Yes	No	No	Yes
Indirect calorimetry	Adult, elderly	No	No	No	No	No	Yes	No	No	Yes
Doubly labeled water	Child, adult, elderly	Yes	No	No	Yes	Yes	No	Yes	Yes	No

Note: Most tests that are applicable for adults can be used in adolescents as well. Few tests can be applied to the pediatric age groups. Among infants only, direct calorimetry, accelerometers, heart rate monitoring, and stabilometers can be used with accuracy.

Source: Reprinted from *Physical Activity and Health, A Report of the Surgeon General,* US Department of Health and Human Services, 1996.

has many parallels with describing dietary intakes. Four approaches to surveys for collection of individual accounts of activity are the task-specific diary, recall questionnaire, quantitative history, and global self-report. Important features of these methods are indicated in the table and have obvious implications for their practicality in various circumstances. The four approaches are all self-report methods with ranges of time reference from days to one year. The first three are limited in application by the need for understanding and ability to either record or recall details of activity in a specific time frame, and they are not feasible methods for characterizing activity of young children. The last survey method is a simpler self-rating of one's activity relative to that of others. Direct monitoring of activity can be accomplished by several means, also characterized in the table. Each technique has strengths and limitations, and applicability of a given method is generally dictated by the circumstances of investigation.

Assessing Physical Fitness and Physical Activity in Population-Based Surveys, published in 1989 by the National Center for Health Statistics, presented details of methods used for data collection in the United States.[8] It includes examples of survey instruments and methodologic studies of relations among many of the measures and strategies used to study activity and fitness and how they relate to health and disease. This comprehensive resource provides insight into the critical evaluation of studies in this area and valuable background information for planning new research. Similarly, a supplement to *Medicine and Science in Sports and Exercise*, "A Collection of Physical Activity Questionnaires for Health-Related Research,"[9] presents actual questionnaires used in the population at large, among the elderly, and in each of several major epidemiologic studies. A brief abstract introduces each questionnaire to identify the activity components assessed, time frame of recall, original mode of administration, and both contact information and a primary literature reference. This is a valuable resource for more-detailed information about methods of physical activity assessment.

DETERMINANTS

Factors of modern life that affect physical inactivity at the population level include disappearance of energy costs for obtaining food, substantial shift from heavy to light or nonphysical work in most daily occupations, reliance on motorized vehicles and elevators rather than personal locomotion for transport, and use of nonoccupational or leisure time for similarly passive pursuits exemplified most recently by the mass habit of viewing television. At the individual level, theories guiding behavioral research aimed at differentiating personal aspects of physical activity are reviewed in the Surgeon General's report.[2] This research has not established a clear understanding of why the majority of individuals in most modern societies are inactive while others are not. Studies of interventions to increase physical activity, based on many of the same behavioral theories, may indirectly shed light on determinants of individual behaviors in the first place. These are addressed in the section on prevention and control.

MECHANISMS

How physical inactivity affects cardiovascular function so as to increase population rates and individual risks of coronary heart disease may be inferred at one level from the expected benefits of a prescribed program of exercise.[10] Exhibit 9–1 outlines these benefits and ranks each on the likelihood of its occurrence for most people under the program indicated. Mechanisms that either increase myocardial oxygen supply or decrease myocardial work and oxygen demand are emphasized, suggesting that the principal effects of physical activity on the heart would tend to reduce the risk of myocardial ischemia or decrease its severity, especially under circumstances of increased workload or diminished blood flow. Physical inactivity also affects many other aspects of physiology, metabolism, and psychology, all of which are considered suboptimal in the absence of levels

Exhibit 9–1 Biological Mechanisms by Which Exercise May Contribute to the Primary or Secondary Prevention of Coronary Heart Disease

Maintain or increase myocardial oxygen supply
  Delay progression of coronary atherosclerosis (possible)
    Improve lipoprotein profile (increase HDL-C/LDL-C ratio) (probable)
    Improve carbohydrate metabolism (increase insulin sensitivity) (probable)
    Decrease platelet aggregation and increase fibrinolysis (probable)
    Decrease adiposity (usually)
  Increase coronary collateral vascularization (unlikely)
  Increase epicardial artery diameter (possible)
  Increase coronary blood flow (myocardial perfusion) or distribution (possible)
Decrease myocardial work and oxygen demand
  Decrease heart rate at rest and submaximal exercise (usually)
  Decrease systolic and mean systemic arterial pressure during submaximal exercise (usually) and at rest (possible)
  Decrease cardiac output during submaximal exercise (probable)
  Decrease circulating plasma catecholamine levels (decrease sympathetic tone) at rest (probable) and at submaximal exercise (usually)
Increase myocardial function
  Increase stroke volume at rest and in submaximal and maximal exercise (likely)
  Increase ejection fraction at rest and during exercise (likely)
  Increase intrinsic myocardial contractility (possible)
  Increase myocardial function by decreasing afterload (probable)
  Increase myocardial hypertrophy (although this might not reduce coronary heart disease risk) (probable)
Increase electrical stability of myocardium
  Decrease regional ischemia or at submaximal exercise (possible)
  Decrease catecholamines in myocardium at rest (possible) and at submaximal exercise (probable)
  Increase ventricular fibrillation threshold by reducing levels of cyclic AMP (possible)

Note: Likelihood that effect will occur for a person participating in endurance-type training program for 16 weeks or longer at 65% to 80% of functional capacity for 25 minutes or longer per session (300 kcal) for three or more sessions per week is expressed as "unlikely," "possible," "likely," "probable," or "usually." HDL-C, high-density lipoprotein cholesterol; LDL-C, low-density lipoprotein cholesterol; AMP, adenosine monophosphate.

Source: Reproduced with permission from WL Haskell, Sedentary Lifestyle as a Risk Factor for Coronary Heart Disease, in TA Pearson et al, eds, *Primer in Preventive Cardiology,* © 1994, American Heart Association.

of activity graded as at least moderate relative to currently typical behavior.

At another level, the mechanisms by which physical activity could influence measures of occurrence of cardiovascular diseases are through their effects on other risk factors. A substantial body of research concerning such effects is reviewed in the Surgeon General's report.[2] Briefly, physical activity is associated with reduced risks of obesity and undesirable body fat distribution, adverse blood lipid profile, high blood pressure, non–insulin-dependent diabetes mellitus, and propensity to thrombosis. An example of such studies is a survey among 412 male law enforcement officers on the basis of which physical activity, physical fitness, percentage of body fat, cigarettes smoked per day, Type A behavior score, high density lipoprotein (HDL) and total cholesterol concentration, and systolic and diastolic blood pressure were assessed.[11] Both physical fitness and physical activity were scaled as five categories of increasing levels, and group-specific mean values of each risk factor were examined by level of fitness or activity (Table 9–3). Details of the statistical tests are presented in the footnotes to

Table 9–3 Coronary Artery Disease (CAD) Risk Factors Associated with Physical Fitness and Physical Activity Levels

CAD Risk Factor	Physical Fitness Level					Physical Activity Level				
	1	2	3	4	5	1	2	3	4	5
% fat[a]	38.9*	34.9*	26.4*	23.3*	18.9	27.8	25.2	23.1	21.0	18.6
	(n = 11)	(n = 17)	(n = 129)	(n = 94)	(n = 136)	(n = 45)	(n = 130)	(n = 93)	(n = 83)	(n = 36)
Cigarettes/day[b]	10.0*	6.7*	3.0	3.1	0.0	5.1	3.2	1.2	0.8	1.3
	(n = 11)	(n = 17)	(n = 129)	(n = 94)	(n = 136)	(n = 45)	(n = 130)	(n = 93)	(n = 83)	(n = 36)
Type A score[b]	−9.4*	−8.3*	−1.8	−2.4	1.5	−6.2	−1.6	−1.1	−1.5	1.0
	(n = 10)	(n = 11)	(n = 107)	(n = 74)	(n = 111)	(n = 36)	(n = 109)	(n = 71)	(n = 66)	(n = 31)
HDL cholesterol[b]	37.7	41.2	40.1	40.9	45.5*	41.5	43.2	43.4	43.5	48.7
(mg/dl)	(n = 9)	(n = 11)	(n = 100)	(n = 71)	(n = 110)	(n = 34)	(n = 106)	(n = 67)	(n = 64)	(n = 31)
Total cholesterol[a]	210.5	226.8	212.6	206.5	200.0	207.9	210.0	211.9	195.6	202.6
(mg/dl)	(n = 11)	(n = 17)	(n = 129)	(n = 94)	(n = 136)	(n = 45)	(n = 130)	(n = 93)	(n = 83)	(n = 36)
Systolic BP[a]	128.0	131.1	123.7	122.7	119.9	121.0	122.5	122.3	121.8	123.4
(mm Hg)	(n = 11)	(n = 17)	(n = 129)	(n = 94)	(n = 136)	(n = 45)	(n = 130)	(n = 93)	(n = 83)	(n = 36)
Diastolic BP[a]	86.0	88.9	83.9	83.6	81.2	81.9	84.2	82.9	82.7	81.0
(mm Hg)	(n = 11)	(n = 17)	(n = 129)	(n = 94)	(n = 136)	(n = 45)	(n = 130)	(n = 93)	(n = 83)	(n = 36)

Note: BP, blood pressure; HDL, high-density lipoprotein.

a. adjusted for age

b. adjusted for age and previous variables.

*$P<0.05$:
  Percent fat: 1>2, 3, 4, 5; 2>3, 4, 5; 3>5; 4>5
  Cigarettes/day: 1>3, 4, 5; 2>3, 4, 5
  Type A score: 1<3, 4, 5; 2<5
  HDL cholesterol: 5>1

Source: Reprinted with permission from *Research Quarterly for Exercise and Sport*, Vol B4, pp 377–384, Copyright 1993 by the American Alliance for Health, Physical Education, Recreation and Dance, 1900 Association Drive, Reston, VA 20191.

the table. Generally, percentage of body fat, cigarettes per day, Type A behavior score, and total cholesterol concentration were less and HDL-cholesterol concentration was greater in the highest in contrast to the lowest levels of both fitness and activity. Blood pressure differences were present across fitness categories but not activity categories. Because these are cross-sectional observations, they do not necessarily indicate effects of fitness or physical activity but could instead reflect characteristics of persons who choose to be more physically active or more fit. In either case, they suggest that in some populations the study of cardiovascular rates or risks in relation to physical activity or physical fitness require data on other risk factors for sound interpretation of the results.

DISTRIBUTION

The frequencies of self-reported absence of any leisure-time physical activity among persons aged 18 years and older are presented by age, sex, race, education, income, and geographic region on the basis of three surveys in the United States: the 1991 National Health Interview Survey (NHIS), the 1988–1991 National Health and Nutrition Examination Survey (NHANES III), and the 1992 Behavioral Risk Factor Surveillance System Survey.[2] As shown in Table 9–4, the overall prevalence of no self-reported leisure-time physical activity ranged from 21.7% to 28.7%. The prevalence within demographic group categories was greater for women, Hispanics and non-Hispanic Blacks, older males and females, and less-educated and lower-income persons. Among geographic regions, absolute levels differed but the range of differences varied little.

Few comparisons of prevalence of physical inactivity or other activity levels are available. However, data from seven studies in Australia, Canada, England, Finland, and the United States reported in 1988–1991 are summarized in Table 9–5.[12] Leisure time was sedentary, variously defined, for 15%–43% of persons in these national samples, with little difference between men and women in most samples. The percentages of sedentary persons were greater in lower-income persons in each of the three surveys in which this was determined (in Australia, Canada, and the United States). In the seven studies, only 5%–15% of respondents were classified as aerobically active in their leisure time.

Two surveys provided data on nonparticipation in vigorous or moderate physical activity in the preceding seven days for US youths ranging in age from 12 to 21 years in the 1992 survey by the National Health Interview Survey–Youth Risk Behavior Survey (NHIS-YRBS) and in grades 9–12 in the 1995 YRBS (Table 9–6).[2] The overall frequency was from 10.4% to 13.7%. Nonparticipation was less common for Black males than other males and more common for Hispanics and non-Hispanic Blacks than for non-Hispanic Whites. It increased in prevalence from about 8% at age 12 to 20% at age 20 or 21 for both males and females in 1992 and tended to increase with decreasing annual family income. Separately, vigorous physical activity on three or more of the preceding seven days was reported by only about one-half of the 12- to 21-year-olds surveyed in 1992, although in a different survey nearly two-thirds of students in grades 9–12 indicated such activity in 1995. Such participation declined sharply with increasing age in both surveys. Finally, among 9th- to 12th-grade students, in 1995, only 60% were enrolled at all in physical education classes and only 25% attended such classes daily, but 70% of those enrolled reported at least 20 minutes of exercise or playing sports (Table 9–7). Each of these measures decreased abruptly for both males and females from grade 9 to grade 12.

Secular trends in physical inactivity have not been well documented in any country, except very recently, and the available data are limited in comparability by differences in methods between countries. However, the same countries represented in Table 9–5 are shown in Figure 9–1 to have had some decline in reported frequency of sedentary leisure-time activity over various intervals between 1981 and 1991.[12]

Table 9–4 Percentage of Adults Aged 18+ Years Reporting No Participation in Leisure-Time Physical Activity, United States

Demographic Group	1991 NHIS	1988–1991 NHANES III	1992 BRFSS[a]
Overall	24.3 (23.2, 25.3)[b]	21.7 (19.0, 24.5)	28.7 (28.3, 29.1)
Sex			
Males	21.4 (20.2, 22.6)	15.8 (12.4, 19.2)	26.5 (25.9, 27.1)
Females	26.9 (25.8, 28.0)	27.1 (23.0, 31.3)	30.7 (30.1, 31.3)
Race/ethnicity			
White, non-Hispanic	22.5 (21.4, 23.7)	18.2 (15.6, 20.8)	26.8 (26.4, 27.2)
Males	20.3 (19.0, 21.6)	12.9 (9.6, 16.1)	25.3 (24.7, 25.9)
Females	24.6 (23.4, 25.8)	23.1 (19.0, 27.1)	28.2 (27.6, 28.8)
Black, non-Hispanic	28.4 (26.4, 30.4)	30.4 (25.6, 35.3)	38.5 (36.9, 40.1)
Males	22.5 (20.0, 25.0)	20.6 (14.5, 26.8)	33.1 (30.9, 35.3)
Females	33.2 (30.8, 35.6)	38.1 (30.9, 45.2)	42.7 (40.7, 44.7)
Hispanic[c]	33.6 (31.0, 36.3)	36.0 (32.5, 39.5)	34.8 (32.8, 36.8)
Males	29.6 (26.0, 33.2)	29.1 (24.3, 33.9)	30.2 (27.3, 33.1)
Females	37.4 (34.1, 40.8)	43.8 (38.5, 49.1)	39.0 (36.5, 41.5)
Other	26.7 (23.4, 30.0)		31.4 (28.9, 33.9)
Males	22.8 (18.2, 27.3)	[d]	27.6 (24.1, 31.1)
Females	30.8 (27.0, 34.7)		35.8 (32.3, 39.3)
Age (years)			
Males			
18–29	17.6 (15.8, 19.4)	12.5 (9.0, 16.0)	18.9 (17.7, 20.1)
30–44	21.1 (19.8, 22.5)	14.5 (10.9, 18.1)	25.0 (24.0, 26.0)
45–64	23.9 (22.1, 25.7)	16.9 (13.0, 20.8)	32.0 (30.8, 33.2)
65–74	23.0 (20.4, 25.6)	17.5 (12.2, 22.8)	33.2 (31.2, 35.2)
75+	27.1 (23.8, 30.4)	34.5 (28.0, 41.1)	38.2 (35.3, 41.1)
Females			
18–29	25.0 (23.4, 26.6)	17.4 (13.4, 21.4)	25.4 (24.2, 26.6)
30–44	25.2 (23.8, 26.6)	24.9 (20.6, 29.3)	26.9 (25.9, 27.9)
45–64	27.4 (25.9, 28.9)	29.4 (24.6, 34.2)	32.1 (30.9, 33.3)
65–74	27.8 (25.7, 29.9)	32.5 (25.9, 39.2)	36.6 (34.8, 38.4)
75+	37.9 (35.3, 40.6)	54.3 (47.9, 60.6)	50.5 (48.5, 52.5)
Education			
<12 yrs	37.1 (35.3, 38.9)	34.5 (31.2, 37.8)	46.5 (45.3, 47.7)
12 yrs	25.9 (24.7, 27.1)	20.8 (17.4, 24.3)	32.8 (32.1, 33.6)
Some college (13–15 yr)	19.0 (17.8, 20.2)	15.7 (11.4, 19.9)	22.6 (21.9, 23.4)
College (16+ yr)	14.2 (13.1, 15.3)	11.1 (6.9, 15.4)	17.8 (17.0, 18.5)
Income[e]			
<$10,000	30.3 (28.4, 32.2)	34.5 (30.3, 38.7)	41.5 (40.1, 42.9)
$10,000–19,999	30.2 (28.5, 32.0)	28.5 (24.5, 32.6)	34.6 (33.6, 35.6)
$20,000–34,999	24.3 (22.9, 25.7)	18.7 (14.8, 22.6)	26.9 (26.1, 27.7)
$35,000–49,999	19.5 (18.1, 20.9)	15.9 (10.9, 20.9)	23.0 (22.0, 24.0)
$50,000+	14.4 (13.2, 15.6)	10.9 (6.7, 15.1)	17.7 (16.9, 18.5)

continues

Table 9–4 continued

Demographic Group	1991 NHIS	1988–1991 NHANES III	1992 BRFSS[a]
Geographic region			
Northeast	25.9 (24.5, 27.3)	21.6 (8.5, 34.6)	29.5 (28.5, 30.5)
North central	20.8 (18.7, 22.9)	16.7 (7.6, 25.8)	28.6 (27.8, 29.4)
South	27.0 (25.2, 28.8)	24.8 (18.4, 31.1)	32.4 (31.6, 33.2)
West	22.5 (19.5, 25.5)	22.6 (14.8, 30.5)	22.0 (21.0, 23.0)

Note: NHIS, National Health Interview Survey; NHANES III, Third National Health and Nutrition Examination Survey; BRFSS, Behavioral Risk Factor Surveillance System. NHIS asked about the prior 2 weeks; NHANES III and BRFSS asked about the prior month.

a. Based on data from 48 states and the District of Columbia.

b. 95% confidence intervals.

c. Hispanic reflects Mexican Americans in NHANES III.

d. Estimates unreliable.

e. Annual income per family (NHIS) or household (BRFSS); reference unit not described for NHANES III.

Source: Reprinted from *Physical Activity and Health, Report of the Surgeon General*, 1996, US Department of Health and Human Services.

Table 9–5 Percentages of National Populations That Are Sedentary in Their Leisure Time (Various Definitions), by Sex

Country, Year	Definition	Total	Male	Female
Australia, 1989	No exercise of any kind	27	27	27
Austria, 1990–1991	Less than 100 MET total over 2 weeks (~50 kcal/wk)	23	22	24
Canada, 1988	0–1.4 kcal/kg/day (~600 kcal/wk)	43	36	49
Canada, 1991	<500 kcal/wk	22	19	25
England, 1990	No 20-min occasions in 4 weeks of even moderate activity (5 kcal/min), *including occupational*	16	17	16
Finland, 1991	PA to produce light sweating a few times a year or less	15	17	14
USA, 1990	No PA reported for the last month	31	29	32

Note: PA, physical activity; MET, multiple of the resting metabolic rate.

Source: Reprinted by permission from Stephens T and Caspersen CJ, 1994, "The Demography of Physical Activity," in *Physical Activity, Fitness, and Health*, edited by C Bouchard, RJ Shepard, and T Stephens, Champaign, IL: Human Kinetics Publishers, p 206.

Table 9–6 Percentage of Young People Reporting No Participation in Vigorous or Moderate Physical Activity During Any of the 7 Days Preceding the Survey, United States

Demographic Group	1992 NHIS-YRBS[a]	1995 YRBS[b]
Overall	13.7 (12.9, 14.5)[c]	10.4 (9.0, 11.9)
Sex		
Males	12.1 (11.0, 13.2)	7.3 (6.5, 8.1)
Females	15.3 (14.1, 16.5)	13.8 (11.2, 16.3)
Race/Ethnicity		
White, non-Hispanic	13.4 (12.4, 14.5)	9.3 (7.9, 10.7)
Males	13.1 (11.7, 14.6)	7.3 (6.4, 8.1)
Females	13.7 (12.4, 15.1)	11.6 (8.7, 14.4)
Black, non-Hispanic	14.7 (12.7, 16.6)	15.3 (12.4, 18.2)
Males	9.2 (6.9, 11.5)	8.1 (5.4, 10.7)
Females	20.2 (17.0, 23.5)	21.4 (16.9, 25.8)
Hispanic	14.3 (12.4, 16.3)	11.3 (8.6, 14.1)
Males	11.1 (8.4, 13.8)	7.5 (5.1, 9.9)
Females	17.8 (14.9, 20.7)	15.0 (10.6, 19.5)

Age (years)		Grade in School	
Males		Males	
12	7.7 (5.1, 10.2)		
13	6.0 (3.6, 8.3)		
14	3.6 (2.1, 5.1)		
15	6.3 (3.7, 8.9)	9	6.0 (3.4, 8.7)
16	9.6 (6.8, 12.4)	10	5.2 (3.0, 7.4)
17	10.5 (7.2, 13.9)	11	7.9 (4.3, 11.4)
18	18.8 (14.4, 23.3)	12	10.0 (7.4, 12.5)
19	18.6 (14.7, 22.5)		
20	22.3 (17.9, 26.8)		
21	18.1 (14.3, 21.9)		
Females		Females	
12	8.4 (5.2, 11.5)		
13	6.8 (4.4, 9.2)		
14	8.3 (5.1, 11.5)		
15	9.8 (7.0, 12.6)	9	8.7 (6.1, 11.3)
16	14.4 (10.9, 17.9)	10	9.2 (7.3, 11.0)
17	16.8 (13.2, 20.3)	11	17.8 (13.6, 22.0)
18	18.7 (14.5, 22.8)	12	18.5 (13.3, 23.7)
19	22.3 (18.1, 26.5)		
20	25.0 (21.0, 28.9)		
21	19.6 (16.4, 22.9)		
Annual family income			
<$10,000	14.9 (12.6, 17.3)		
$10,000–19,999	16.0 (14.1, 17.9)		
$20,000–34,999	12.2 (10.6, 13.8)		
$35,000–49,999	13.8 (11.6, 15.9)		
$50,000+	11.2 (9.8, 12.7)		

a. 1992 National Health Interview Survey–Youth Risk Behavior Survey, a national household-based survey of youths aged 12–21 years.

b. 1995 Youth Risk Behavior Survey, a national school-based survey of students in grades 9–12.

c. 95% confidence intervals.

Source: Reprinted from *Physical Activity and Health, Report of the Surgeon General*, 1996, US Department of Health and Human Services.

Table 9–7 Percentage of Students in Grades 9–12 Reporting Enrollment in Physical Education Class, Daily Attendance in Physical Education Class, and Participation in Exercise or Sports for at Least 20 Minutes During an Average Physical Education Class, United States

Demographic Group	Enrolled in Physical Education	Attended Physical Education Daily	Exercised or Played Sports ≥20 Minutes per Class[a]
Overall	59.6 (48.6, 70.5)[b]	25.4 (15.8, 34.9)	69.7 (66.4, 72.9)
Sex			
Males	62.2 (52.5, 71.8)	27.0 (16.8, 37.2)	74.8 (71.8, 77.8)
Females	56.8 (44.1, 69.6)	23.5 (14.5, 32.4)	63.7 (59.3, 68.1)
Race/Ethnicity			
White, non-Hispanic	62.9 (49.8, 76.1)	21.7 (9.9, 33.5)	71.3 (67.0, 75.6)
Males	64.2 (52.6, 75.8)	23.3 (11.2, 35.3)	74.8 (71.1, 78.5)
Females	61.7 (46.4, 77.0)	19.9 (8.0, 31.8)	67.1 (60.5, 73.8)
Black, non-Hispanic	50.2 (45.1, 55.3)	33.8 (29.9, 37.8)	59.0 (54.6, 63.3)
Males	56.8 (50.6, 62.9)	37.7 (32.3, 43.0)	71.8 (65.9, 77.8)
Females	44.4 (37.3, 51.5)	30.1 (25.8, 34.5)	46.6 (39.3, 53.8)
Hispanic	51.0 (40.9, 61.2)	33.1 (24.5, 41.8)	68.5 (62.8, 74.1)
Males	57.6 (48.6, 66.6)	36.2 (28.8, 43.6)	76.0 (67.0, 85.0)
Females	44.6 (31.2, 58.0)	30.1 (18.7, 41.5)	59.0 (52.5, 65.6)
Grade in School			
Males			
9	80.5 (75.1, 85.9)	42.1 (23.3, 60.8)	76.5 (72.2, 80.9)
10	72.6 (62.3, 82.8)	34.8 (18.9, 50.8)	73.1 (67.9, 78.3)
11	51.5 (32.8, 70.1)	17.4 (9.3, 25.6)	75.8 (70.3, 81.2)
12	45.4 (29.0, 61.9)	14.8 (9.2, 20.4)	73.7 (68.1, 79.3)
Females			
9	80.8 (73.8, 87.8)	39.7 (21.5, 58.0)	65.6 (57.2, 74.1)
10	71.4 (59.3, 83.5)	33.8 (17.4, 50.3)	63.9 (58.8, 68.9)
11	41.2 (22.8, 59.6)	12.3 (7.6, 17.1)	57.2 (48.4, 66.0)
12	39.1 (20.9, 57.2)	11.1 (6.5, 15.7)	66.0 (59.7, 72.4)

a. Among students enrolled in physical education.

b. 95% confidence intervals.

Source: Reprinted from *Physical Activity and Health, Report of the Surgeon General,* 1996, US Department of Health and Human Services.

POPULATION RATES

The contribution of physical activity to prediction of differences in coronary heart disease or total mortality between populations was one focus of the Seven Countries Study of 16 cohorts of men aged 40–59 years at entry between 1958 and 1964.[13] Keys described the physical activity of the men in most cohorts in that study as primarily occupational, with little significant activity at leisure. "Except for the Finnish and American cohorts, the idea of exercise for its own sake was considered a little mad by men beyond the age of 40; that view prevails today in many rural areas."[13(p 197)] Based mainly on occupation, but adjusted for substantial outside activity, physical activity was categorized into levels: 1 (sedentary), 2 (moderate), and 3

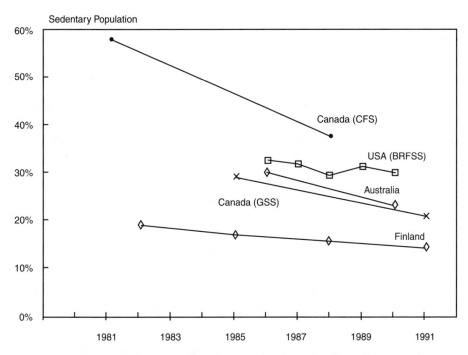

Note: Definitions vary between countries but are consistent within countries. BRFSS, Behavioral Risk Factor Surveillance System; CFS, Canada Fitness Survey; GSS, General Social Survey.

Figure 9–1 Temporal Trends in Sedentary Leisure-Time Activity. *Source:* Reprinted by permission from Stephens T, Caspersen CJ, 1994, "The Demography of Physical Activity" in *Physical Activity, Fitness, and Health*, edited by C Bouchard, RJ Shepard, and T Stephens, Champaign, IL: Human Kinetics Publishers, p 208.

(heavy work, very active). The frequency distributions of activity levels for the cohorts, excluding men with any evidence of cardiovascular disease, are shown in Table 9–8. The variation in proportions of men who were sedentary is striking, even excluding the Belgrade professors, ranging from 3.9% to 49.7% sedentary (Tanushimaru, Japan, and US railroad workers, respectively). Heavy work was absent in two cohorts but accounted for 60%–80% of men in most other cohorts.

Baseline differences in characteristics of sedentary versus the most active men in some cohorts were older age, higher blood pressure, higher resting pulse rate, higher serum cholesterol concentration, and lower income, although some of these relations were found in only a

few cohorts. The relation of baseline physical activity level to death from all causes and from coronary heart disease was examined as was the relation of baseline activity to incidence of "hard" coronary heart disease (acute myocardial infarction or coronary death) and incidence of all coronary heart disease. For all coronary heart disease, the relation was as shown in Figure 9–2 (legend: B = Belgrade; F = Finland; G = Greece; I = rural Italy; J = Japan; R = Rome railroad; U = US railroad; Y = Yugoslavia except Belgrade; Z = Zutphen). The overall regression coefficient, $r = -0.13$, indicates that incidence of coronary disease tended to decrease as the proportion of men in a population who were sedentary increased. It is apparent that this result is heavily influenced by the

Table 9–8 Distribution by Physical Activity Class at Entry in Men Free of Cardiovascular Disease, Seven Countries Study

Cohort	Activity Class (%)			Cohort	Activity Class (%)		
	1	2	3		1	2	3
US railroad[a]	49.7	35.3	0.0	Montegiorgio	5.8	25.8	68.4
Dalmatia	7.9	11.6	80.5	Zutphen	23.7	65.7	10.6
Slavonia	17.1	9.2	73.7	Crete	6.6	30.9	62.5
Tanushimaru	3.9	36.6	59.5	Corfu	31.0	37.8	31.2
East Finland	9.6	12.6	73.8	Rome railroad	22.0	40.4	37.6
West Finland	7.5	12.5	80.0	Velika Krsna	8.5	24.5	67.0
Ushibuka	7.6	17.1	75.3	Zrenjanin	35.2	35.2	29.6
Crevalcore	10.5	18.8	70.7	Belgrade	99.4	0.6	0.0

Note: Activity class 1 = sedentary; 2 = moderate activity; 3 = heavy work, very active.

a. 15.1% not readily classifiable between activity classes 1 and 2.

Source: Reprinted by permission of the publisher from *Seven Countries* by A Keys, Cambridge, Mass: Harvard University Press, Copyright © 1980 by the President and Fellows of Harvard College.

extreme positions of both Finland and Belgrade, with high and low incidence of coronary heart disease and low and high prevalence of sedentary living, respectively. In the remaining subset of countries, higher mortality appears to be related to higher prevalence of sedentary living, but such post hoc selection of the data can offer only very frail inferences and fails to account for the exceptions. Within some cohorts, but not others, there was a tendency for sedentary men to exhibit higher mortality than men whose physical activity was level 2 or 3. This occurred in rural Italy, among Rome railroad workers, and in Greece. Overall the results did not demonstrate an important contribution of average levels of physical activity to the wide differences in population rates of death or incident coronary heart disease.

INDIVIDUAL RISKS

Within populations, variation in risks of cardiovascular diseases in relation to physical inactivity, other levels of activity, and physical fitness has been reported from numerous studies, albeit with diverse methods of assessment of activity and fitness. The Surgeon General's report summarizes 36 studies of physical activity and 7 studies of physical fitness in relation to coronary heart disease, 14 studies of physical activity and stroke, and 6 studies of physical activity and hypertension.[2] For each report the study population, definitions of physical activity or fitness and the cardiovascular outcome, main findings, evidence for a dose response, adjustment for confounders, and other comments are presented in table form. The Surgeon General's report concludes that the epidemiologic literature supports the presence of an inverse association between physical activity or physical fitness and coronary heart disease and hypertension but is unclear with respect to stroke.

A more-detailed evaluation of studies of physical activity and incidence of coronary heart disease was reported by Powell in 1987, including systematic evaluation of the quality of each study with respect to measures of physical activity and coronary heart disease and epidemiologic methods in general.[14] Occupational or nonoccupational cohort studies constituted 36 of the total of 43 studies. Most studies were con-

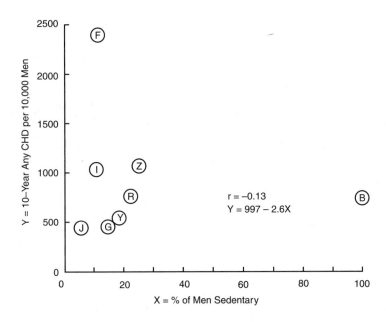

Note: B, Belgrade; F, Finland; G, Greece; I, Rural Italy; J, Japan; R, Rome railroad; Y, Yugoslavia except Belgrade; Z, Zutphen.

Figure 9–2 Ten-Year Age-Standardized Incidence of Any CHD (Any Diagnosis of Coronary Heart Disease) in Population Samples Versus Percentage of Sedentary Men in Those Samples, Seven Countries Study. All men aged 40–59 and free of cardiovascular disease at entry. *Source:* Reprinted by permission of the publisher from *Seven Countries* by A Keys, Cambridge, Mass: Harvard University Press, Copyright © 1980 by the President and Fellows of Harvard College.

ducted in the United States, with several in the United Kingdom and others mainly in Europe, all chiefly among men under 65 years of age. Results were available for women from only five of these studies. The preponderance of studies that could be scored, in men, indicated an inverse relation between physical activity and incidence of coronary heart disease. This finding was most frequent among the studies rated as best in quality. It was concluded that an inverse, causal relation was supported by these studies. Further, the magnitude of the relative risk of inactivity was judged to be similar to that for hypertension, elevated blood cholesterol concentration, and smoking. High prevalence of inactivity in the US population suggested that this widespread risk factor makes a large contribution to the incidence of coronary heart disease

and therefore warrants public policy to support increased physical activity in the population.

Berlin and Colditz used Powell's ratings and selected additional studies to include those published through the end of the 1980s as the basis for a meta-analysis, or formal statistical derivation of summary estimates, of the relative risk of coronary heart disease from specified groups of studies.[15] Table 9–9 illustrates the results for the group of nonoccupational studies, all of which were included in Powell's review. Several types of coronary events were considered when represented in the reports, which were further categorized based on the comparisons they presented—high versus moderate activity, high versus moderate and sedentary activity, and high versus sedentary activity. (The actual comparisons were made in the inverse manner, with the

Table 9–9 Pooled Relative Risks from Studies of Nonoccupational Activity and Risk of Heart Disease

	Outcome[a]	No. of Studies	Relative Risk (95% CI)[b]	χ^2 for Heterogeneity[c]
For high activity compared with moderate activity groups from studies that reported both moderate and sedentary comparison groups	CHD		No studies	
	CHD death	1	1.3 (1.0–1.7)	–
	MI	2	1.4 (1.1–1.7)	0.77
	MI + SD		No studies	
	AP		No studies	
For high activity compared with low activity groups from studies that did not separate moderate and sedentary comparison groups	CHD	5	1.6 (1.3–1.8)	4.47
	CHD death	2	1.9 (1.0–3.4)	2.87
	MI	1	1.3 (1.0–1.7)	–
	MI + SD	2	2.3 (1.5–3.6)	0.01
	AP	2	1.1 (0.4–3.0)	11.90
For high activity compared with sedentary groups from studies that reported both moderate and sedentary comparison groups	CHD		No studies	
	CHD death	1	1.6 (1.2–2.2)	–
	MI	2	2.9 (1.9–4.5)	1.51
	MI + SD		No studies	
	AP		No studies	

a. AP, angina pectoris; CHD, coronary heart disease; MI, myocardial infarction; SD, sudden death.

b. CI, confidence interval.

c. Degrees of freedom from χ^2 are one less than the number of studies.

Source: Reprinted with permission from JA Berlin, *American Journal of Epidemiology,* Vol 132, No 4, p 621, © 1990, The Johns Hopkins University School of Hygiene and Public Health.

result that the higher risks in moderately active or sedentary persons, as compared with risks in highly active ones, give a relative risk greater than 1.) The number of studies, relative risk (RR) and 95% confidence interval (CI), and χ^2 test for heterogeneity or diversity of results within the subset of studies, are all shown. The comparison with the greatest number of contributing studies is that between combined moderate and sedentary versus high activity, with relative risks from 1.1 to 2.3 for different coronary disease outcomes, most strongly indicative of an effect for all coronary disease (RR 1.6, CI 1.3–1.8) and for myocardial infarction plus sudden death (RR 2.3, CI 1.5–3.6). These events were then about 1½–2½ times as frequent in the moderate and sedentary activity group as in the high activity group. Results for these particular outcomes could not be evaluated in the other comparisons because no such results were reported in the original studies. Addition of more recent studies modified some estimates and not others, but as they were not evaluated in accordance with Powell's method their contribution is unclear. A similar array of results was found for occupational as for nonoccupational studies. Relative risk estimates were higher in the better-evaluated studies, as was suggested by Powell. The authors concluded that physical activity protects against coronary heart disease but added that this effect has not been shown to be independent of other risk factors.

A more recent study is the second follow-up report from the Multiple Risk Factor Intervention Trial (MRFIT), which addressed the question of the independence of the contribution of physical activity to lower coronary disease risks in men with more than sedentary activity.[16] More than 12,000 high-risk men were enrolled in this long-term trial of risk factor reduction. They received no intervention on physical activity but completed the Minnesota Leisure Time Physical Activity questionnaire. Scores were recorded in minutes per day of mostly light- or moderate-intensity activity, less than 25 kjoule/min. Mortality over 10.5 years of follow-up (including 3.5 posttrial years) was compared among groups defined by tertiles of physical activity score, from low (1) to high (3). Figure 9–3 indicates that for cardiovascular death and coronary heart disease death, but not

for cancer death, mortality was highest for men with least activity and did not differ appreciably between intermediate and higher activity groups. Table 9–10 further demonstrates that levels 2 and 3 did not differ in mortality reduction relative to level 1. The lower portion of the table reports results by proportional hazards regression, which adjusts for baseline risk factors (age, diastolic blood pressure, total cholesterol concentration, and number of cigarettes smoked per day). The mortality reduction associated with leisure-time physical activity was essentially independent of these other factors, since the adjustment resulted in little change in the risk ratios. To relate these results to those

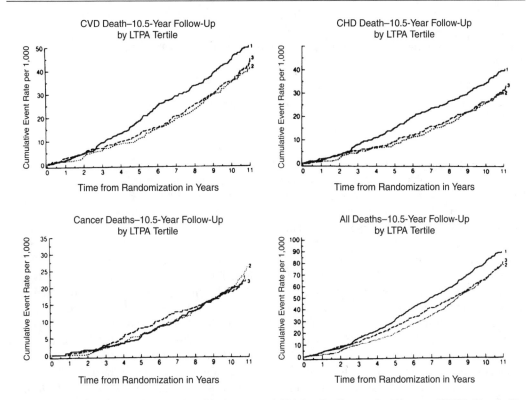

Figure 9–3 Cumulative 10.5-Year Mortality Rates per 1,000 for Cardiovascular Diseases (CVD) (Top Left), Coronary Heart Diseases (CHD) (Top Right), Cancer (Bottom Left), and All Causes (Bottom Right) by Tertile of Leisure-Time Physical Activity (LTPA), Multiple Risk Factor Intervention Trial. The solid line represents men with the lowest third of leisure-time physical activity (tertile 1); the dotted line; the middle third (tertile 2); and the broken line, the upper third (tertile 3). *Source:* Reprinted with permission from AS Leon and J Connett, MRFIT Research Group, *American Journal of Epidemiology*, Vol 20, p 692, © 1991, The Johns Hopkins University School of Hygiene and Public Health.

Table 9–10 Risk Ratios and Major Endpoints (and 95% Confidence Limits) by Tertile of Leisure-Time Physical Activity in Men in the Multiple Risk Factor Intervention Trial

Fatal Endpoints	Tertile 1	Tertile 2	Tertile 3
		Age-Adjusted Risk Ratios	
Cardiovascular disease	1.00	0.78* (0.63, 0.96)	0.79* (0.68, 1.04)
Coronary heart disease	1.00	0.73* (0.57, 0.92)	0.84 (0.62, 1.00)
Cancer	1.00	1.15 (0.85, 1.52)	1.00 (0.66, 1.21)
All causes	1.00	0.85* (0.73, 0.99)	0.87* (0.74, 1.01)
		Proportional Hazards Regression	
Cardiovascular disease	1.00	0.81* (0.66, 1.01)	0.89 (0.72, 1.09)
Coronary heart disease	1.00	0.75* (0.59, 0.96)	0.82 (0.65, 1.04)
Cancer	1.00	1.22 (0.91, 1.63)	1.06 (0.78, 1.44)
All causes	1.00	0.89 (0.77, 1.04)	0.92 (0.79, 1.07)

Note: Regression of endpoints by age (years), level of diastolic blood pressure (mm Hg), total cholesterol (mmol/l), number of cigarettes per day, treatment group (Special Intervention or Usual Care), and tertile of physical activity.

* $P<0.05$.

Source: Reprinted from AS Leon and J Connett (for MRFIT Research Group), Vol 20, p 693, © 1991, by permission of Oxford University Press.

---

calculated in the foregoing meta-analysis, results for level 3 in Table 9–10 can be inverted to compare level 1 with level 3; for example, the result for coronary heart disease mortality adjusted for age alone (upper portion of Table 9–10), shown as a risk ratio of 0.84, would correspond with an increased risk of lowest versus highest activity of 1/0.84, or 1.19, about a 20% increase. This is notably less than the relative risks found in the meta-analysis, perhaps due to a narrower range of activity between strata in MRFIT compared with that in the meta-analysis.

Studies including women are fewer, but a study of cardiorespiratory fitness—by maximal exercise treadmill test—in women and men in the Aerobics Center Longitudinal Study provides an example.[17] Among women there were fewer participants (7080 women and 25,431 men) and fewer deaths (21 cardiovascular and 89 total in women and 226 and 601 deaths, respectively, in men). Tables 9–11 and 9–12

compare observations on predictors of death between women and men. "Low fitness" characterized the 20% of each age-sex group with the poorest cardiorespiratory fitness. The risk of cardiovascular death for low versus high-fitness categories was 2.42 (CI 0.99–5.92) for women and 1.70 (CI 1.28–2.25) for men, after adjustment for all other factors shown in the tables. This adjustment would be expected to underestimate the total effect of fitness, to the extent that it modifies these other factors adversely. For both cardiovascular and all-cause mortality, the adjusted relative risk for low fitness was greater for women than for men.

The question of adverse effects of physical activity has also been addressed. Studies have focused on precipitation of sudden death and other fatal and nonfatal coronary events as well as musculoskeletal injuries as potential hazards. Many reports concerning sudden death were reviewed by Kohl and colleagues, who noted that the overall risk of sudden death is less

Table 9–11 Cardiovascular Disease Mortality and All-Cause Mortality Risk Analyses for Selected Mortality Predictors, Women, Aerobics Center Longitudinal Study, 1970–1989

Mortality Predictor	No. of Subjects	Person-Years of Follow-Up (% of Person-Years)	Cardiovascular Disease				All Causes			
			No. of Deaths	Death Rate/10,000 Person-Years[a]	Relative Risk		No. of Deaths	Death Rate/10,000 Person-Years[a]	Relative Risk	
					Adjusted[a]	Adjusted[b] (95% Confidence Interval)			Adjusted[a]	Adjusted[b] (95% Confidence Interval)
Low fitness (20% least fit)	1,352	13,086 (25)	11	7.7	2.79	2.42 (0.99–5.92)	40	28.8	2.32	2.10 (1.36–3.26)
Current or recent smoker	1,321	10,811 (20)	5	6.0	1.73	1.70 (0.58–4.97)	27	29.0	2.12	1.99 (1.25–3.17)
Systolic blood pressure ≥140 mm Hg	416	3,959 (7)	8	7.6	2.06	1.47 (0.55–3.93)	15	15.1	0.89	0.76 (0.41–1.40)
Cholesterol ≥6.2 mmol/l (≥240 mg/dl)	1,223	9,034 (17)	8	3.9	0.99	0.74 (0.28–1.95)	31	18.9	1.16	1.09 (0.68–1.74)
Either parent dead of coronary heart disease	1,788	13,474 (25)	6	3.2	0.76	0.58 (0.20–1.72)	24	12.9	0.71	0.70 (0.43–1.16)
Body mass index ≥27 kg/m²	777	5,486 (10)	2	2.0	0.48	0.28 (0.06–1.26)	15	19.5	1.18	0.94 (0.52–1.69)
Fasting glucose ≥6.7 mmol/l (≥120 mg/dl)	148	1,202 (2)	3	14.2	3.80	4.10 (1.11–15.2)	7	33.3	2.03	1.79 (0.80–4.00)
Abnormal electrocardiogram	350	2,816 (5)	10	17.3	5.38	5.02 (1.90–13.3)	16	26.2	1.61	1.55 (0.87–2.77)
Chronic illness	958	7,085 (13)	7	6.9	1.98	1.66 (0.59–4.64)	18	18.1	1.09	1.05 (0.61–1.82)
Totals	7,080	52,982 (100)	21	4.0[c]	...	...	89	16.8[c]	...	...

Note: All comparisons are dichotomies, with the referent category being the low-risk group (relative risk = 1) and the high-risk group data shown in the table. Data for the reference categories are not included but can be estimated for each predictor by subtracting the values in the table for the high-risk group from the totals (25,341 men, 211,996 man-years. 601 deaths from all causes, 226 deaths from cardiovascular disease; 7,080 women, 52,982 woman-years, 89 deaths from all causes, 21 from cardiovascular disease). Ellipses indicate "not applicable."

a. Adjusted for age and examination year.

b. Adjusted for age, examination year, and each of the other variables in the table.

c. Crude rate.

Source: Reprinted with permission from *Journal of the American Medical Association*, Vol 276, No 3, p 207, Copyright 1996, American Medical Association.

Table 9–12 Cardiovascular Disease Mortality and All-Cause Mortality Risk Analyses for Selected Mortality Predictors, Men, Aerobics Center Longitudinal Study, 1970–1989

Mortality Predictor	No. of Subjects	Person-Years of Follow-Up (% of Person-Years)	Cardiovascular Disease				All Causes			
			No. of Deaths	Death Rate/ 10,000 Person-Years [a]	Relative Risk Adjusted [a]	Adjusted [b] (95% Confidence Interval)	No. of Deaths	Death Rate/ 10,000 Person-Years [a]	Relative Risk Adjusted [a]	Adjusted [b] (95% Confidence Interval)
Low fitness (20% least fit)	5,223	54,729 (26)	111	20.0	2.69	1.70 (1.28–2.25)	250	45.5	2.03	1.52 (1.28–1.82)
Current or recent smoker	6,730	60,829 (29)	82	16.6	2.01	1.57 (1.18–2.10)	222	42.7	1.89	1.65 (1.39–1.97)
Systolic blood pressure ≥140 mm Hg	2,759	26,398 (12)	87	19.5	2.07	1.34 (1.00–1.80)	184	43.6	1.67	1.30 (1.08–1.58)
Cholesterol ≥6.2 mmol/l (≥240 mg/dl)	6,025	51,262 (24)	106	16.5	1.86	1.65 (1.26–2.15)	229	37.0	1.45	1.34 (1.13–1.59)
Either parent dead of coronary heart disease	6,499	53,440 (25)	84	14.3	1.51	1.18 (0.89–1.57)	203	33.1	1.24	1.07 (0.90–1.29)
Body mass index ≥27 kg/m²	8,198	65,534 (31)	96	14.9	1.70	1.20 (0.91–1.58)	223	34.3	1.33	1.02 (0.86–1.22)
Fasting glucose ≥6.7 mmol/l (≥120 mg/dl)	1,396	13,229 (6)	36	15.4	1.49	0.95 (0.66–1.37)	92	44.3	1.63	1.24 (0.98–1.56)
Abnormal electrocardiogram	1,866	15,680 (7)	99	36.7	4.28	3.01 (2.24–4.04)	158	54.0	2.05	1.64 (1.34–2.01)
Chronic illness	4,802	41,016 (19)	124	26.3	3.80	2.52 (1.89–3.36)	242	49.8	2.15	1.63 (1.37–1.95)
Totals	25,341	211,996 (100)	226	10.7 [c]	...	...	601	28.3 [c]	...	...

Note: All comparisons are dichotomies, with the referent category being the low-risk group (relative risk = 1) and the high-risk group data shown in the table. Data for the reference categories are not included but can be estimated for each predictor by subtracting the values in the table for the high-risk group from the totals (25,341 men, 211,996 man-years, 601 deaths from all causes, 226 deaths from cardiovascular disease; 7,080 women, 52,982 woman-years, 89 deaths from all causes, 21 from cardiovascular disease). Ellipses indicate "not applicable."

a. Adjusted for age and examination year.

b. Adjusted for age, examination year, and each of the other variables in the table.

c. Crude rate.

Source: Reprinted with permission from Journal of the American Medical Association, Vol 276, No 3, p 207, Copyright 1996, American Medical Association.

among habitually active than among sedentary persons even though an excess risk obtains specifically during periods of vigorous activity.[18] Evidence on "triggering" of acute coronary events has been reviewed recently by Mittleman, who addressed physical activity in general and sexual activity in particular, in addition to emotional stress.[19] With respect to physical activity, use of an imaginative "case-crossover" design revealed that risk of acute myocardial infarction was greater in the first hour following heavy physical exertion than at other times. However, risk of myocardial infarction associated with heavy exertion was least for those whose habitual frequency of such exertion was five or more times per week. The increased risk in the first hour following exertion appeared to be largely mitigated by better habits of exercise. For the effect of sexual activity, also, any excess risk of precipitating an acute coronary event appeared to be reduced to a negligible degree by regular physical activity. These and other reports emphasize the overall benefit of habitual exercise, the hazards of rapid change from sedentary to active status, and the appropriate caution in making this change, especially for adults. Due caution and, if necessary, initial supervision are expected to minimize risks of both acute coronary events and musculoskeletal injury.

Figure 9–4, from the consensus conference report,[7] summarizes several studies examining the activity level necessary for cardiovascular benefit. Only men were studied in five of the six reports represented in the figure, but women were included in the study of Blair and colleagues,[17] with comparable results for women and men. The pattern shown here and in several analogous figures published elsewhere has been interpreted as evidence of a continuous gradient of benefit over a wide range of activity levels. The implications of this view are discussed in the following section.

PREVENTION AND CONTROL

As observed by Morris, because physical inactivity is so highly prevalent, the distinction between population-wide and individual strategies may not be appropriate in this instance. That is, those at high risk encompass so large a proportion of the population that the distinction becomes artificial.[3] Nonetheless, intervention studies whose focus is at population and individual levels exist, and they were reviewed in the Surgeon General's report. These were nearly all studies in which change in activity status was the test outcome, and, except in the special case of exercise rehabilitation following acute myocardial infarction, none of the studies investigated effects of physical activity intervention on morbidity or mortality. This limitation of research in this area has been at issue for many years, as discussed by Taylor and colleagues, for example, as early as 1973.[20] They reviewed their experience with marked loss of participation in a feasibility study—50% in six months—and noted that both the Task Force on Arteriosclerosis of the National Heart and Lung Institute and the Inter-Society Commission for Heart Disease Resources had recommended against a trial of exercise in primary prevention of coronary heart disease. Policy development, therefore, remains dependent on observational studies of disease outcome, and intervention studies have been essentially limited to behavioral responses alone. The available evidence is summarized below.

On the basis of available evidence, recommendations have now been advanced by the Centers for Disease Control and Prevention jointly with the American College of Sports Medicine,[7] the National Institutes of Health,[21] and the American Heart Association[22] to support increased habitual physical activity for prevention of cardiovascular diseases.

Population-Wide Measures

Interventions to influence physical activity in populations can potentially affect both the incidence and the prevalence of physical inactivity. In the short term, its prevalence could be reduced only by measures bringing about change to a physically active state for a substan-

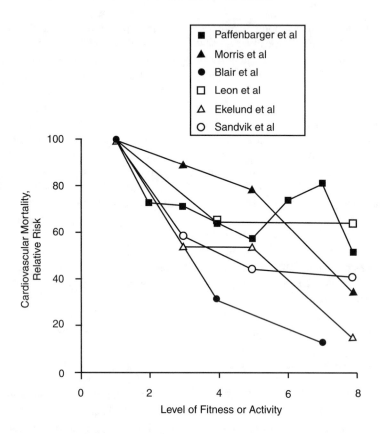

Figure 9–4 Relationship Between Level of Physical Activity or Exercise Capacity and Cardiovascular Disease Mortality. *Source:* Reprinted with permission from *Journal of the American Medical Association*, Vol 273, No 5, p 405, Copyright 1995, American Medical Association.

---

tial proportion of the population who are currently physically inactive. Reducing incidence of physical inactivity requires measures to establish nonsedentary habits early in life and maintain them. As a long-term result, prevalence of inactivity in adulthood would thereby be reduced also.

In reviewing studies aimed at population-wide intervention in adults, the Surgeon General's report summarized five studies in targeted communities, three in worksites, and two in health care settings, as well as four broad communications campaigns.[2] Some studies in special populations focused on minorities or older persons. These studies were typically quasi-experimental in design, without random assignment of communities to intervention or compar-

ison status, and were several years in duration. A variety of theoretical approaches were used. In each case the study population, intervention, and findings were briefly characterized.

Population studies in children were also aimed at increasing physical activity and were either school programs or school and community programs. They ranged from a few weeks to four years in duration and targeted age groups from as early as grade 3 to as late as grade 12. The interventions included classroom health education, modification of physical education classes, or both. The largest and most recent of these studies was the Children's Activity Trial for Cardiovascular Health (CATCH), whose results are shown in Figure 9–5. Involving more than 3000 students in 96 schools, the

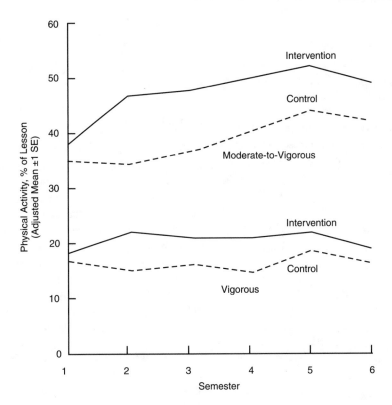

Note: Observed at six time points, 1991 through 1994. The CATCH intervention was introduced during semester 2, increased the percentage of time spent in moderate-to-vigorous and vigorous activity as measured by the System for Observing Fitness Instruction Time classroom observation system. Intervention and control curves diverged significantly according to repeated-measures analysis of variance with the class session as the unit of analysis: for moderate-to-vigorous activity, $F = 2.17$, $df = 5$, 1979, $P = .02$; for vigorous activity, $F = 2.95$, $df = 5$, 1979, $P = .04$. Analysis controlled for CATCH site, the location of the lesson, the specialty of the teacher, and random variation among the schools and weeks of observation. SE, standard error.

Figure 9–5 Moderate-to-Vigorous and Vigorous Physical Activity Observed During the Child and Adolescent Trial for Cardiovascular Health (CATCH) Physical Education Classes. *Source:* Reprinted with permission from RV Luepker et al, Outcomes of a Field Trial to Improve Children's Dietary Patterns and Physical Activity: The Child and Adolescent Trial for Cardiovascular Health (CATCH), *Journal of the American Medical Association,* Vol 275, p 772, Copyright 1996, American Medical Association.

CATCH interventions resulted in change in physical education classes with the percentage of class time occupied by moderate to vigorous activity increasing from less than 40% to more than 50% in the intervention schools but remaining less than 40% in the control schools. Vigorous activity constituted about 20% of time in intervention schools and 18% in control schools.

International public policy development in the area of physical activity has been reviewed recently by Blair and colleagues.[23] Nearly 20 excerpts from conference or workshop reports of the late 1980s and early- to mid-1990s indicate widening attention to the need for public policy concerning physical activity if any perceptible impact on this factor in health is to be achieved.

Individual Measures

The 13 reviewed studies of individual approaches among adults were typically much smaller, with about 50 to 350 participants, and included women in several instances, and often employee groups.[2] The duration of study was from 10 weeks to two years. The interventions principally involved group exercise activities. No individual-level intervention studies in children were described. The Surgeon General's report concluded this review of intervention studies as follows:

> The review of adult intervention research literature provides limited evidence that interventions to promote physical activity can be effective in a variety of settings using a variety of strategies. . . . Intervention studies with adults were often conducted over a brief period of time, had little or no follow-up, and focused on the endpoint of specified vigorous physical activity rather than on moderate-intensity physical activity or total amount of activity. Studies used different endpoints . . . making them difficult to compare. . . . Few if any studies compared their results to a standard of effectiveness, such as recommended frequency or duration of moderate or vigorous physical activity.[2(p 234)]

The special case of rehabilitation following myocardial infarction requires mention because it is the one area in which clinical trials of physical activity have been conducted with evaluation of intervention in relation to disease outcomes. Review of 22 randomized trials of rehabilitation with exercise indicates benefit for up to three years in reduced total and cardiovascular mortality, fatal reinfarction and, at one year, sudden death.[24] Nonfatal reinfarction was not reduced in frequency. Interpretation of these results is limited by the concurrent interventions in some studies, so the indicated effect may not be attributable to exercise alone. Principles of exercise programs designed for rehabilitation of those surviving an acute coronary event have been presented by the American Heart Association.[25]

CURRENT ISSUES

Several major steps have been taken in recent years to consolidate current knowledge about physical activity, physical fitness, and health. These efforts include the extensive reports from the Surgeon General, the National Center for Health Statistics, and the Second International Consensus Symposium.[2,4,26] A related report was previously prepared as a World Health Organization (WHO) Regional Publication, European Series, addressing in detail both technical aspects and practical tools for physical activity assessment.[27] The International Consensus Conference on Physical Activity Guidelines for Adolescents recommended intervention guidelines for the adolescent population at large and addressed the need for their implementation through primary health care providers.[28] The US Preventive Services Task Force offers recommendations for promoting physical activity by physicians.[29] The policy developments represented by these and other sources are addressed in Chapter 22.

The leading issue in the area of prevention policy concerning physical activity is less its development than its implementation. One obstacle is current debate over recommendations for moderate, cumulative activity in contrast to prior prescriptions for more intensive, time-concentrated activity. In "How Much Pain for Cardiac Gain?" the journal *Science* highlighted the disagreement between those who interpret the data (eg, Figure 9–4) as supporting cumulative exercise of moderate degree and those who reject this view.[30] As the *Science* reporter noted, the reception to the recommendation in the consensus report[7] was: "For a nation of couch potatoes, the news seemed too good to be true."[30(p 1324)] At issue in part is a broader debate about public health recommendations that are moderate by intent, with the aim of wider and perhaps more gradual public adoption than may be expected for more extreme measures, which could be easily ignored as impracticable or too drastic for individual adoption. An argument in support of moderate amounts and intensities of physical activity is presented by Blair and Connelly, who note that the optimum prescription cannot be written on current evidence but that a major public health objective must be to mobilize the most sedentary 20%–30% of the adult population, "perhaps with a strategy of making gradual changes over time.[31(p 203)]

In any case, a large scientific constituency supports the recently formulated recommendations. Available knowledge has been assembled and documented in several reports, which makes the evidence readily accessible to those interested and concerned. Further steps will depend on social and political responses to this scientific information. Put simply by Morris, "Exercise is today's best buy in public health,

not only because of the need and potential, but because it is positive and acceptable, has insignificant side-effects, and can be inexpensive."[3(p 252)] At the same time he noted, "The return of physical activity as the norm in everyone's everyday life—the 'restoration of biological normality' in Rose's words—will require cultural change on a scale similar to that which has occurred with smoking."[3(p 253)]

In addition, an extensive research agenda has been identified in each of the major reports cited here, including information needed from the most elementary prevalence surveys of physical activity in diverse population groups to demonstrations of effective means of mass change in physical activity behavior among both children and adults. Evaluation is needed of long-term effectiveness of such interventions in terms of maintenance of desirable patterns of activity and benefit, as measured by changes in incidence and prevalence of sedentary behavior and concurrent changes in risks and population rates of cardiovascular and other chronic disease.

REFERENCES

1. Blackburn H. Physical activity and coronary heart disease: a brief update and population view (Part I). *J Card Rehabil.* 1983;3:101–111.

2. The President's Council on Physical Fitness and Sports. *Physical Activity and Health: A Report of the Surgeon General.* Atlanta, Ga: National Center for Chronic Disease Prevention and Health Promotion, Centers for Disease Control and Prevention, US Dept of Health and Human Services; 1996.

3. Morris JN. Exercise versus heart attack: history of a hypothesis. In: Marmot M, Elliott P, eds. *Coronary Heart Disease Epidemiology: From Aetiology to Public Health.* Oxford, England: Oxford Medical Publications; 1992: 242–255.

4. Taylor HL, Jacobs DR Jr, Shucker B, Knudsen J, et al. A questionnaire for the assessment of leisure-time physical activities. *J Chronic Dis.* 1978;31:741–755.

5. Paffenbarger RS, Hyde RT. Exercise in the prevention of coronary heart disease. *Prev Med.* 1984; 13:3–22.

6. Durstine JL, King AC, Painter PL, Roitman JL, et al, eds. *ACSM's Resource Manual for Guidelines for Exercise Testing and Prescription.* 2nd ed. Philadel-

phia, Pa: American College of Sports Medicine; Lea & Febiger; 1993.

7. Pate RR, Pratt M, Blair SN, Haskell WL, et al. Physical activity and public health. *JAMA.* 1995;273:402–407.

8. National Center for Health Statistics. *Assessing Physical Fitness and Physical Activity in Population-Based Surveys.* Hyattsville, Md: National Center for Health Statistics, Centers for Disease Control, Public Health Service, US Dept of Health and Human Services; 1989. DHHS publication no. (PHS) 89-1253.

9. Pereira MA, FitzGerald SJ, Gregg EW, Joswiak ML, et al, eds. A collection of physical activity questionnaires for health-related research. *Med Sci Sports Exercise.* 1997;29(suppl):S1–S205.

10. Haskell WL. Sedentary lifestyle as a risk factor for coronary heart disease. In: Pearson TA, Criqui MH, Luepker RV, Oberman A, Winston M, eds. *Primer in Preventive Cardiology.* Dallas, Tex: American Heart Association; 1994:173–187.

11. Young DR, Steinhardt MA. The importance of physical fitness versus physical activity for coronary artery

disease risk factors: a cross-sectional analysis. *Res Q Exercise Sport*. 1993;B4:377–384.

12. Stephens T, Caspersen CJ. The demography of physical activity. In: Bouchard C, Shepard RJ, Stephens T, eds. *Human Physical Activity, Fitness, and Health: International Proceedings and Consensus Statement*. Champaign, Ill: Human Kinetics; 1994: 204–213.

13. Keys A. *Seven Countries: A Multivariate Analysis of Death and Coronary Heart Disease*. Cambridge, Mass: Harvard University Press; 1980.

14. Powell KE, Thompson PD, Caspersen CJ, Kendrik JS. Physical activity and the incidence of coronary heart disease. *Annu Rev Public Health*. 1987;8:253–287.

15. Berlin JA, Colditz GA. A meta-analysis of physical activity in the prevention of coronary heart disease. *Am J Epidemiol*. 1990;132:612–628.

16. Leon AS, Connett J, MRFIT Research Group. Physical activity and 10.5 year mortality in the Multiple Risk Factor Intervention Trial (MRFIT). *Int J Epidemiol*. 1991;20:690–697.

17. Blair SN, Kampert JB, Kohl HW, Barlow CE, et al. Influences of cardiorespiratory fitness and other precursors on cardiovascular disease and all-cause mortality in men and women. *JAMA*. 1996;276:205–210.

18. Kohl HW, Powell KE, Gordon NF, Blair SN, et al. Physical activity, physical fitness, and sudden cardiac death. *Epidemiol Rev*. 1992;14:37–58.

19. Mittleman MA. Triggering of myocardial infarction by physical activity, emotional stress and sexual activity. In: Willich SN, Muller JE, eds. *Triggering of Acute Coronary Syndromes*. Dordrecht, the Netherlands: Kluwer Academic Publishers; 1996: 71–80.

20. Taylor HL, Buskirk ER, Remington RD. Exercise in controlled trials of the prevention of coronary heart disease. *Fed Proc*. 1973;32:1623–1627.

21. NIH Consensus Development Panel on Physical Activity and Cardiovascular Health. Physical activity and cardiovascular health. *JAMA*. 1996;276:241–246.

22. Fletcher GF, Balady G, Blair SN, Blumenthal J, et al. Statement on exercise: benefits and recommendations for physical activity programs for all Americans: a statement for health professionals by the Committee on Exercise and Cardiac Rehabilitation of the Council on Clinical Cardiology, American Heart Association. *Circ*. 1996;94:857–862.

23. Blair SN, Booth M, Gyarfas I, Iwane H, et al. Development of public policy and physical activity initiatives internationally. *Sports Med*. 1996;21:157–163.

24. Fletcher GF. How to implement physical activity in primary and secondary prevention. A statement for healthcare professionals from the Task Force on Risk Reduction, American Heart Association. *Circ*. 1997; 96:355–357.

25. O'Connor GT, Buring JE, Yusuf S, Goldhaber SZ, et al. An overview of randomized trials of rehabilitation with exercise after myocardial infarction. *Circ*. 1989; 80:234–244.

26. Bouchard C, Shephard RJ, Stephen T, eds. *Physical Activity, Fitness and Health: International Proceedings and Consensus Statement*. Champaign, Ill: Human Kinetics; 1994.

27. Anderson KL, Rutenfranz J, Masironi R, Seliger V. *Habitual Physical Activity and Health*. Copenhagen, Denmark: World Health Organization Regional Publication; 1978. European Series No. 6.

28. Sallis JF, Patrick K. Physical activity guidelines for adolescents: consensus statement. *Pediatr Exercise Sci*. 1994;6:302–314.

29. US Preventive Services Task Force. *Guide to Clinical Preventive Services*. 2nd ed. Alexandria, Va: International Medical Publishers; 1996.

30. Barinaga M. How much pain for cardiac gain? *Science*. 1997;276:1324–1327.

31. Blair SN, Connelly JC. How much physical activity should we do? The case for moderate amounts and intensities of physical activity. *Res Q Exercise Sport*. 1996;67:193–205.

CHAPTER 10

Fatness, Overweight, and Central Adiposity

SUMMARY

Obesity represents several distinct concepts pertinent to body composition, relative body weight, and fat distribution. Measures of some aspects of obesity are limited to highly technical laboratory facilities, while others can be approximated or precisely estimated with field methods in epidemiologic studies. Studies of determinants of obesity and of potential mechanisms by which obesity could have adverse cardiovascular effects have provided extensive but sometimes conflicting results. The general conclusion is that obesity, variously measured, is related to high blood pressure, adverse blood lipid profile, and insulin resistance, among other factors. Review of experimental studies supports the view that the relation of obesity to these conditions is causal and can be reversed by weight loss. It appears that in some populations, such as those providing much of the US experience, smoking and obesity are strongly confounded; that is, smokers are especially often found in the lowest category of obesity. There is disagreement about the role of this confounding in the weakness or absence of association between obesity and coronary heart disease incidence and mortality, or all-cause mortality, in some studies. Regardless of these reservations, a US consensus panel report has concluded that persons whose relative weight is 20% or more above the "desired weight" for sex and height are at increased risk of chronic diseases and require treatment and that, as of the mid-1980s, there were 34 million such adults in the United States. More-recent estimates are higher still. By this criterion virtually the whole of some populations, such as some Pacific Islanders, would require treatment. The prospects for increasing obesity with economic and social development in many areas of the world raise serious concern, for even the extreme categories of obesity may become many times more common than in the past. Individual measures for reduction of obesity are available but have had little lasting success and raise some questions of safety as well. Population approaches are preferred as the strategy for prevention of obesity in the first place, but the secular trends toward increasing obesity in populations such as the United States pose major challenges to these approaches.

INTRODUCTION

When in 1985 the National Institutes of Health convened an expert panel to develop a consensus report on the health implications of obesity, the first question addressed was, "What is obesity?"[1] The panel defined it as "an excess of body fat frequently resulting in a significant impairment of health."[1(p 1073)] Noting the impracticality of actually determining the quantity of fat in the body except by techniques limited to research laboratories, the panel recommended use of anthropometric methods based on measurement of height, weight, and skinfold thickness. The measurement of height and weight could be compared with reference values (the Metropolitan Life Insurance Company tables of "desirable weight") or expressed as the "body mass index," calculated as the ratio of weight (in kilograms) to the square of height (in meters). The location of body fat was also emphasized, as assessed by the ratio of body circumferences measured at the waist and hip. Higher values of the waist-hip ratio represent increased abdominal or central, in contrast to peripheral, fat accumulation.

The term *obesity* thus represented several concepts: fatness, in terms of tissue composition of the body; overweight, relative to either reference standards or individual body height; and central adiposity, or fat distribution with a relative excess of abdominal girth. The panel concluded that weight at 20% or more above desirable levels was a degree of obesity constituting "an established health hazard" and that 34 million Americans had body mass index values indicative of this degree of overweight and were in need of treatment.

Obesity, like patterns of diet and physical activity, can be viewed in the perspective of human evolution.[2] Like the diet, in which animal fat has displaced fiber, and like the adoption of nonphysical pursuits in place of physical work, obesity is mainly a modern phenomenon considered not to have been possible in ordinary circumstances throughout most of human history. Success in reproduction and survival depended on adaptation to the nutritional demands of pregnancy and lactation, seasonal variation in food availability, and periodic famine sometimes in cycles as short as only two or three years. These are considered to be determinants of both genetic and cultural evolution through which humans adapted to have the capacity to store fat, an efficient and readily mobilized energy reserve. Mechanisms that once ensured an essential capacity now produce the adverse effect of excess fat accumulation under the highly prevalent conditions of modern dietary imbalance and physical inactivity. Thus obesity, variously defined (and often, surprisingly undefined), enters into the consideration of atherosclerotic and hypertensive diseases.

CONCEPTS AND DEFINITIONS

Obesity

Obesity has become a nonspecific term that may represent any of several distinct concepts. At the individual level, the term may refer to the appearance of extreme physical bulk characteristic of sumo wrestlers or ancient Polynesian royalty or to the status of having a body weight of 174 pounds for a height of 5'10", corresponding to a body mass index of 25 kg/m². At the population level, *obesity* may refer to the prevalence of an arbitrarily specified level of body mass index, waist-hip ratio, sum of skinfold thickness as measured at selected body sites, or some other measure. It is helpful to make explicit the aspect of obesity addressed in any particular context and to begin by clarifying the principal concepts of obesity found relevant to health: fatness, overweight, and central adiposity.

Fatness

If *fatness* means the quantity of adipose tissue in the body, this may be expressed either in absolute units (fat mass, in kg) or as the corresponding percentage of the total body mass that is adipose tissue (percent body fat, without units). Several methods for determination of body composition permit estimation of fatness and are reviewed in *Human Body Composition*.[3] Field methods applicable in population studies depend on anthropometry, alone or in combination with determination of bioelectrical impedance. Prediction equations relate these measurements to fat mass as estimated from laboratory investigation by other techniques. No single method is considered as a "gold standard," nor can the validity of published prediction equations be assumed for all populations.

Percent body fat changes markedly during infancy and childhood. For both boys and girls, the change is from about 14% at birth to 26% at age 6 months. Percent body fat decreases to age 5, when it reaches 15% for boys and 17% for girls.[4] From ages 10 to 18 years, percent body fat changes little in girls but decreases by about 1% per year for boys, due to sex differences in patterns of growth in tissue mass, girls adding proportionately equal amounts of fat and fat-free mass, while fat-free mass dominates growth in boys. During adulthood, percent body fat appears to increase slowly in both men and women, perhaps stabilizing at about age 50 at 25% for men and 35% for women. Neither ethnic differences nor longitudinal changes in body composition have been extensively described.

Overweight

Overweight connotes a relative excess of weight. A major reference standard for overweight has been the actuarial tables on the relation between weight, height, and longevity among insured persons published by the Metropolitan Life Insurance Company.[5] For many years the desirable weight tables based on the 1959 Society of Actuaries data were used, as shown in Tables 10–1 and 10–2. Weights corresponding to the Metropolitan relative weight, or MRW, of 120 are 20% above the observed optimum for longevity in the actuarial analyses, the

Table 10–1 Desirable Weight Ranges for Men Aged 25 and Over

Height (ft, in)	Weight Range (lb)	Weight[a] MRW = 100	Weight[b] MRW = 110	Weight MRW = 120
5'1"	105–134	117	129	140
5'2"	108–137	120	132	144
5'3"	111–141	123	135	148
5'4"	114–145	126	139	151
5'5"	117–149	129	142	155
5'6"	121–154	133	146	160
5'7"	125–159	138	152	166
5'8"	129–163	142	156	170
5'9"	133–167	146	161	175
5'10"	137–172	150	165	180
5'11"	141–177	155	170	186
6'0"	145–182	159	175	191
6'1"	149–187	164	180	197
6'2"	153–192	169	186	203
6'3"	157–197	174	191	209
BMI (all heights):		21.66	23.83	26.00

Note: Weight is given in pounds, without clothing; height without shoes. MRW = Metropolitan relative weight, BMI = body mass index.

a. Midpoint of medium frame range, used to compute MRW: MRW = (Actual weight)/(Midpoint of medium frame range) $\times$ 100.

b. In the US adult population over 40 years of age, 80% of men and 70% of women have weights that exceed MRW = 110 and consequently are at increased risk for cardiovascular disease. The average weight of the adult US population is above MRW = 120; an individual with a weight over MRW = 120 is "obese."

Source: Reprinted with permission from AP Simopoulos, *Obesity,* p 311, © 1992, Lippincott-Raven Publishers.

Table 10–2 Desirable Weight Ranges for Women Aged 25 and Over

Height (ft, in)	Weight Range (lb)	Weight[a] MRW = 100	Weight[b] MRW = 110	Weight MRW = 120
4'9"	90–118	100	110	120
4'10"	92–121	103	113	124
4'11"	95–124	106	117	127
5'0"	98–127	109	120	131
5'1"	101–130	112	124	134
5'2"	104–134	116	128	139
5'3"	107–138	120	132	144
5'4"	110–142	124	136	149
5'5"	114–146	128	141	154
5'6"	118–150	132	145	158
5'7"	122–154	136	150	163
5'8"	126–159	140	154	168
5'9"	130–164	144	158	173
5'10"	134–169	148	163	177
BMI (all heights):		21.32	23.47	25.58

Note: Weight is measured in pounds, without clothing; height without shoes. MRW = Metropolitan relative weight, BMI = body mass index. For women between the ages of 18 and 25 years, subtract 1 pound for each year under 25.

a. Midpoint of medium frame range, used to compute MRW: MRW = (Actual weight)/(Midpoint of medium frame range) × 100.

b. In the US adult population over 40 years of age, 80% of men and 70% of women have weights that exceed MRW = 110 and consequently are at increased risk for cardiovascular disease. The average weight of the adult US population is above MRW = 120; an individual with a weight over MRW = 120 is "obese."

Source: Reprinted with permission from AP Simopoulos, *Obesity,* p 312, © 1992, Lippincott-Raven Publishers.

level specified by the consensus panel cited above as "obese." Recent updating of these tables poses an issue currently under debate, which is addressed below.

Body Mass Index

The second approach to the concept of overweight is use of one or another of several indices relating weight to height of the individual in the form of a ratio. Most common among these is the body mass index (BMI), also known as Quetelet's index after its originator in the mid-19th century. The continuum of body mass index values in a population has been classified by a World Health Organization Study Group as

shown in Figure 10–1.[6] The "normal" range of body mass index for individuals was indicated as from 18.5 to 25 kg/m^2, and obesity of three grades was defined corresponding to values of 25–30, 30–40, and 40 or greater kg/m^2. It was noted that for populations to achieve a distribution of body mass index such that values of 25 kg/m^2 or greater occurred only rarely would require that a mean value of 22 kg/m^2 be attained. In an extensive review of methods of body measurement (anthropometry) and its public health applications, a recent report from the World Health Organization rates these categories of body mass index as normal and grade 1, grade 2, and grade 3 overweight.[7] Recommendations for preventive measures specific to

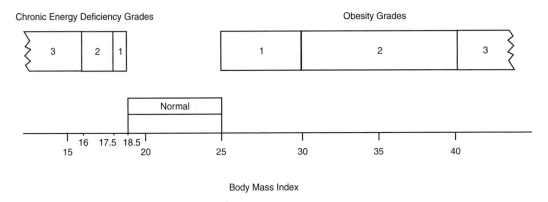

Note: Grades 1 and 2 require that energy expenditure be also below 1.4 times the estimated basal metabolic rate, based on the weight of the individuals. Body mass index = mass in kg/(height in meters)^2.

Figure 10–1 Degrees of Chronic Energy Deficiency and Obesity in Relation to Body Mass Index. *Source:* Reprinted with permission from Report of a WHO Study Group, *WHO TRS 797*, p 71, © 1990, World Health Organization.

each category are given in the report and are discussed in this chapter. Terms corresponding to the grades of obesity and an algorithm for classification of risk were presented by Bray (Figure 10–2).[8] *Risk* in this instance refers to any of the adverse health outcomes associated with overweight. The determination of risk level incorporates consideration of the following complicating factors: waist-hip ratio greater than 0.95 for males and 0.85 for females; diabetes mellitus, hypertension or hyperlipidemia; male sex; and age below 40 years.

Fat Distribution

The third concept of obesity concerns the anatomic distribution of body fat. This is only one aspect of the more fundamental phenomenon of body composition considered specifically for different anatomic regions. Some of the laboratory techniques alluded to previously provide direct measures of tissue composition in sites such as the abdomen. Field methods are limited to anthropometry, with various derived indices based on anatomic diameters, circumferences, and skinfold thicknesses. Waist-hip ratio, for example, has been of interest in many recent epidemiologic studies. It is taken as an

indirect measure of visceral adipose tissue. This includes the mesenteric and omental fat depots, which differ in metabolic characteristics from peripheral fat stores.[9] Roughly equivalent terms in reference to concentration of fat in this region are *central adiposity, abdominal obesity*, and *truncal obesity*.

Periods of Life

One further aspect of definition concerns the contrast between adulthood and earlier periods of life. Attainment of adult stature, which remains essentially constant throughout the remainder of life, simplifies the interpretation of subsequent changes in weight, body mass index, and related measures for adults. But during infancy, childhood, and adolescence, major changes occur concomitantly in body mass, body composition, stature, and sexual maturity. As a result, correspondence among various indirect measures of obesity, however defined, is dynamic rather than fixed during this period. More detailed age- and sex-specific observations are needed in the preadult years, beginning from early ages. Available data on measures of obesity in infancy, childhood, and adolescence may then be interpreted more confidently.

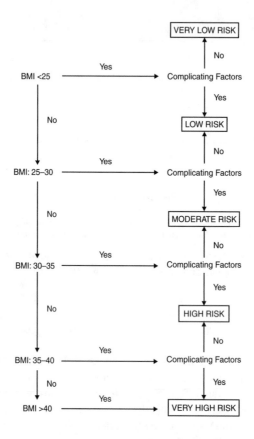

Note: Complicating factors include elevated abdominal-gluteal ratio (male, >0.95, female, >0.85), diabetes mellitus, hypertension, hyperlipidemia, male sex, and age less than 40 years.

Figure 10–2 Risk Classification Algorithm for Body Mass Index. *Source:* Reprinted with permission from GA Bray, An Approach to the Classification and Evaluation of Obesity, in *Obesity*, P Björntorp and BN Brodoff, eds, p 306, © 1992, Lippincott-Raven Publishers.

MEASUREMENT

General methods of anthropometry have become well standardized, and reference works for these procedures are readily available, some well illustrated to demonstrate the techniques (eg, Lohman et al[10]). Measurements specifically related to fatness, overweight, and body composition are reviewed here in detail.

Body Composition

Methods for assessing body composition include densitometry, hydrometry, whole-body counting, neutron activation analysis, dual energy X-ray absorptiometry, electrical impedance and total body electrical conductivity, multicomponent molecular level methods, and several imaging techniques. Several of these techniques incorporate anthropometry. Brown reviewed both the methods and the findings from their application, including their determinants and relation of various measures of body composition to health.[3] Estimation of percent body fat by anthropometry, alone or with bioelectrical impedance, is the most widely applied approach to assessment of body composition in epidemiologic research. These specific methods are reviewed by Roche and by Baumgartner, respectively.[11,12] Potentially, several kinds of anthropometric variables may be combined for this purpose, including lengths, breadths, circumferences, skinfold thicknesses, and others. With or without bioelectrical impedance, estimation of fat mass depends on application of prediction equations in which the selected measurements have been evaluated statistically against laboratory-based procedures. Attention to several aspects of the measurement situation, including instruments, subject, standardized protocols, and validity of the prediction equation for the population studied are all required for appropriate results to be obtained.

Relative Weight

Relative indices of obesity depend more simply on measurement of height and weight. These measures are not without sources of error, however, and also require standardization of technique, especially for longitudinal studies or population comparisons. Relative weight tables from a standard population, described above, provide the basis in the United States for evaluating weight for height. The Metropolitan Tables in use since 1959 were updated in 1983 on the basis of more-recent actuarial experience, with the result that "desirable weights" increased for every height category but the tallest, for both men and women. For the lower height categories, several pounds were added. Some controversy ensued about the desirability, from a public health perspective, of a change in desirable weights, but the revised recommendations stand.[13]

The body mass index, weight (kg)/height $(m)^2$, has also received extensive comment. It is also simply determined from measured weight and height, which are reliable under appropriate field conditions. This is only one of a family of potential weight-for-height indices in which the power for height (here, 2) may take different values. Mathematical properties of such indices were addressed by Benn over 25 years ago, leading to the conclusion that, for adults, the body mass index is likely to be preferable but

that ideally this should be verified by testing for independence of the index from height in the population for which it is to be used.[14] More recently, attention has been recalled to problems in the interpretation of results from multivariate regression analysis based on ratios, of which the body mass index is an example; it is argued that the component variables are better included as individual terms in a linear model.[15] The use of the body mass index as a descriptor for relative weight is unlikely to be discarded on this basis. However, it may be that analysis by the suggested approach would be more informative—especially in studies including children and adolescents, in which the interpretation of height and of weight differs through the course of growth and development.

Body Fat Distribution

Reliability of measures for characterizing body fat distribution, such as waist-hip ratio, depend on measurement procedures as do other anthropometric data. Values of waist-hip ratio suggested as indicative of increased risk of chronic diseases are shown in Figures 10–3 and 10–4.[8] In this scheme, waist measurements associated with low risk are less than corresponding hip measurements, especially for women, and for both men and women the threshold at the 70th percentile increases slightly with age. Interpretation of the waist-hip ratio may require consideration of the potential meaning of excess abdominal fat on the one hand and deficient gluteal muscle mass at the hip level, on the other.[9] The principle of avoidance of ratio measures in statistical analysis, raised above in connection with body mass index, would also apply to the waist-hip ratio.

DETERMINANTS

The determinants of obesity and its various manifestations can be viewed very broadly, in evolutionary terms, or in a narrower and more immediate perspective. The list in Exhibit 10–1 of factors related to obesity reflects the latter

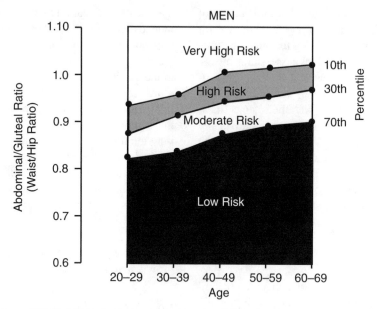

Figure 10–3 Values of Waist-Hip Ratio Equated with Levels of Risk, for Men, by Age. *Source:* Reprinted with permission from GA Bray and DS Gray, Obesity PAI-Pathogenesis, *Western Journal of Medicine*, Vol 149, pp 429–441, © 1989, George Bray.

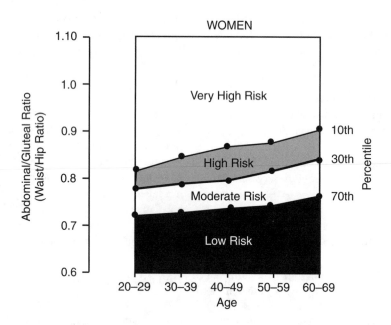

Figure 10–4 Values of Waist-Hip Ratio Equated with Levels of Risk, for Women, by Age. *Source:* Reprinted with permission from GA Bray and DS Gray, Obesity PAI-Pathogenesis, *Western Journal of Medicine*, Vol 149, pp 429–441, © 1989, George Bray.

Exhibit 10–1 Obesity: Determinants and Risk Factors

Demographic Factors

Age
Sex
Race
Socioeconomic circumstances
Geography: country of residence, urbanization,
    industrialization, migration

Familial Factors

Heredity: polygenes; single gene(s) with major
    effect
Shared environments (cultural inheritance)
Interaction between genetic susceptibility and
    environmental exposure

Personal Factors

Fetal growth and birth weight
Past or current overweight
Age at adiposity rebound
Eating habits
Physical inactivity/sedentary lifestyle
Metabolic characteristics, including diabetes
    mellitus
Neural controls
Cigarette smoking
Psychological factors, including body image
Pregnancy, including age at first pregnancy
Concurrent illness or disability

Source: Reprinted with permission from FH Epstein and M Higgins, Epidemiology of Obesity, in *Obesity*, P Björn-torp and BN Brodoff, eds, p 340, © 1992, Lippincott-Raven Publishers.

viewpoint and, while not exhaustive, is expanded from the original to indicate additional factors of recent interest.[16] Demographic, familial, and personal factors are suggested, with emphasis on the complexity of their relations, including different effects of a given factor in different periods of life.

Genetic influences have been studied in relation to different aspects of obesity, such as body mass index and body composition, as summarized from family studies by Bouchard in Figure 10–5.[17] Body mass index appeared to have a large heritable component, only a small part of which was genetic, whereas body composition,

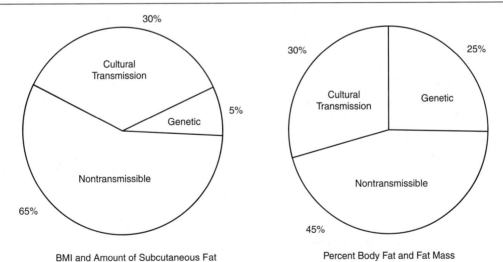

BMI and Amount of Subcutaneous Fat

Percent Body Fat and Fat Mass

Figure 10–5 Total Transmissible Variance and Its Genetic Component for BMI, Subcutaneous Fat (Sum of Six Skinfolds), and Total Body Fat from Underwater Weighing. *Source:* Reprinted from Goldbourt, *Genetic Factors in Coronary Heart Disease*, p 191, © 1994, with kind permission from Kluwer Academic Publishers.

measured as percent body fat or fat mass, had similar cultural heritability but substantially greater genetic heritability. How genetic effects might influence obesity was suggested in a model (also proposed by Bouchard) illustrated in Figure 10–6. High levels of energy intake and low levels of energy expenditure might each have several metabolic or physiologic bases. Several types of interactions are indicated, some of which are viewed as affecting nutrient partitioning, or "the proneness to store the ingested energy in the form of fat (triglycerides) or lean tissue."[17(p 196)] The elements of the model are taken to suggest numerous candidate genes for further investigation.

MECHANISMS

Obesity, in its various manifestations, contributes to the occurrence of atherosclerotic and hypertensive diseases, and many studies have demonstrated associations between obesity and other risk factors.

Linkages in Childhood and Adolescence

The Bogalusa Heart Study of more than 3000 Black and White 5- to 18-year-old males and females included estimation of percent body fat from the sum of subscapular and triceps skinfold thicknesses. The relation of this measure to total cholesterol concentration (TCHOL), low-density lipoprotein (LDL) to high-density lipoprotein (HDL) cholesterol ratio (LR-1), [very–low-density lipoprotein + LDL] to HDL cholesterol ratio (LR-2), and systolic and diastolic blood pressure (SBP, DBP) is shown in Figures 10–7 and 10–8, for males and females, respectively.[18] The range of values of quintile groups by percent body fat

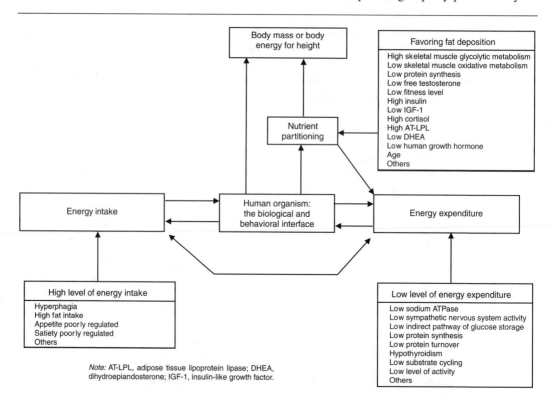

Figure 10–6 Major Factors Affecting Body Mass Index and Body Composition. *Source:* Reprinted from Goldbourt, *Genetic Factors in Coronary Heart Disease*, p 193, © 1994, with kind permission from Kluwer Academic Publishers.

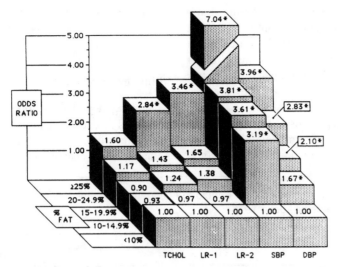

Figure 10–7 Adjusted Estimates of Relative Odds for Ranking in the Age- and Race-Specific Highest Quintile of Selected Risk Factors, for Males, Bogalusa Heart Study. *Source:* Reprinted with permission from DP Williams, *American Journal of Public Health*, Vol 82, No 3, p 361, © 1992, American Public Health Association.

was from less than 10% to 25% or greater for males and from less than 20% to 35% or greater for females. The odds ratio shown for each intersection in the figures represents the odds of being in the highest quintile category of the risk factor given the position in the first through fifth quintiles of the distribution of percent body fat.

The odds for each analysis are set at 1.00 for the lowest quintile group by percent body fat. Most striking for males is the sharply increasing odds for systolic blood pressure from the first to the middle three quintiles and again to the fifth quintile of percent body fat. The gradient is more regular but less steep for diastolic blood

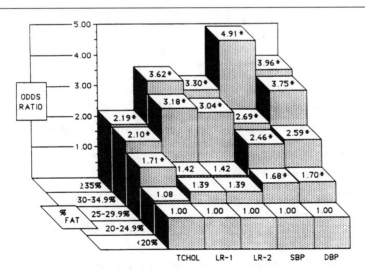

Figure 10–8 Adjusted Estimates of Relative Odds for Ranking in the Age- and Race-Specific Highest Quintile of Selected Risk Factors, for Females, Bogalusa Heart Study. *Source:* Reprinted with permission from DP Williams, *American Journal of Public Health*, Vol 82, No 3, p 361, © 1992, American Public Health Association.

pressure and for the two blood lipid ratios is significant only for the highest quintile of percent body fat. The patterns for females differ in that the odds ratios are lower than for males at the one level of percent body fat where the results can be compared, 20%–24.9%. They are also significant for every risk factor among those in the fourth and fifth quintiles of percent body fat (30%–34.9% fat), together accounting for 40% of the female study population. The fatness lev-

els of 25% for males and 30% for females were proposed as standards to define high-risk groups of children and adolescents.

Linkages in Women

Among more than 115,000 women aged 30 to 55 years at entry to the Nurses' Health Study, body mass index was investigated in relation to other personal characteristics (Table 10–3).[19] In

Table 10–3 Distribution of Potential Risk Factors, According to Quetelet Index Category in a Cohort of US Women 30–55 Years of Age in 1976

Characteristic	Quetelet Index				
	<21	21–<23	23–<25	25–<29	≥29
No. of women[a]	30,164	30,512	22,709	20,107	12,394
Mean age (yr)	40.1±7.1	41.7±7.1	43.1±7.1	43.8±7.0	43.8± 6.9
Mean weight (kg)	53.7±4.7	59.3±4.8	64.0±4.8	71.7±6.3	87.3±11.9
Mean height (cm)	164.4±6.2	163.9±6.1	163.3±5.9	163.8±6.4	163.1± 6.2
Cigarette smoking status (%)[b]					
Current smokers	39.9	33.0	31.0	29.2	25.1
Former smokers	21.5	23.7	23.8	23.1	24.5
Never smoked	38.0	42.4	44.6	46.6	49.9
Mean alcohol intake (g/d)[c]	7.9	7.6	6.8	5.7	4.0
Hypertension (%)	6.4	7.9	9.4	13.8	26.5
Diabetes mellitus (%)	1.0	1.0	1.2	1.7	5.1
High cholesterol (%)	2.3	2.5	3.1	3.5	4.8
Premenopausal (%)	71.0	72.4	71.9	71.9	72.6
Parent with infarction (%)[d]	13.6	14.2	15.4	15.0	16.0
Mean fat intake (g/d)[c]					
Total	75.5	75.6	75.8	75.8	75.9
Saturated	30.0	30.0	30.1	30.2	30.2
Polyunsaturated	11.4	11.4	11.4	11.4	11.5
Monounsaturated	31.2	31.3	31.4	31.4	31.4
Mean cholesterol intake (mg/d)[c]	314.2	323.8	323.3	322.4	322.6

Note: Percentages and means shown (except for ages, weights, and heights) are adjusted to the age distribution of the entire cohort according to 5-year categories. Plus-minus values are means ± standard deviation. The Quetelet index is the weight in kilograms divided by the square of the height in meters.

a. Numbers shown are the numbers of women in each category at the beginning of follow-up in 1976.

b. Totals for each category are less than 100% because of rounding and missing values for smoking in 0.3% of participants.

c. Data are from a 1980 food-frequency questionnaire. Values are adjusted for age and total caloric intake, except those for alcohol, which are adjusted only for age.

d. Denotes a parent with a myocardial infarction that occurred ≤60 years of age.

Source: Reprinted with permission from JE Manson et al, A Prospective Study of Obesity and Risk of Coronary Heart Disease in Women, *The New England Journal of Medicine*, Vol 332, p 884, Massachusetts Medical Society. All rights reserved.

relation to quintile group of body mass index, mean values or percentage frequencies of the following factors increased with body mass index: age, weight, hypertension, diabetes mellitus, elevated total cholesterol concentration, and parental history of myocardial infarction. Dietary intakes of fats were remarkably similar across quintile groups, and cholesterol intake varied only in being exceptionally low in the lowest quintile group of body mass index. Smoking history was essentially opposite, in that current smokers were successively less prevalent and those who never smoked were more prevalent in higher quintile groups by body mass index. Mean daily intake of alcohol decreased by about 50% from lowest to highest quintile group of body mass index. These relations indicated the importance of adjustment for smoking status in analysis of risks where obesity, at least as represented by body mass index, is included.

Linkages in Men

The extent to which body mass index and factors predictive of cardiovascular events may be correlated in men is illustrated by data from the Seven Countries Study, shown in Table 10–4.[20] All correlations of 0.09 or greater were statistically significant, due to the large sample size in each study cohort, although such small correlations contribute little to understanding the relations among these characteristics. Modest correlates of body mass index with blood pressure and serum cholesterol concentration, as well as pulse rate, were noted, and the correlation with cigarette smoking was consistently negative, as was true for age. The mixed pattern of associations of body mass index at baseline with these other factors predictive of coronary events would make difficult the identification of a meaningful relation of this measure of obesity to outcomes of interest.

Relations of Obesity with Other Factors

A summary of cardiovascular risk factor associations identified for body mass index and waist-hip ratio is presented in Exhibit 10–2.[21] In addition to altered concentrations of several biochemical components of blood, other factors related to obesity include blood pressure, cardiac function, blood viscosity, and sleep disturbances. For blood lipids, blood pressure, and insulin resistance, there is some experimental evidence of improvement in risk status with weight reduction. This is consistent with results of studies in adolescence and early adulthood indicating that change in body mass index is one of the few strong predictors of change in blood lipid concentrations and blood pressure. The relationships of obesity and blood pressure in adolescence are complex, however, and necessitate cautious interpretation in specific age-sex groups.[22]

A hypothetical scheme by which to link obesity and its determinants with other cardiovascular risk factors and disease events was proposed by Björntorp (Figure 10–9).[9] In this scheme, primary risk factors (pathogenetic factors) or "inducers" lead through obesity to secondary risk factors—early symptoms and "disease triggers." Positive energy balance operates through general obesity to affect blood pressure, certain blood lipids (but not LDL cholesterol), and insulin and glucose, leading to diabetes. Additional factors operate independently or through neuroendocrine mechanisms and portal adipose tissue—the mesenteric and omental fat depots—to affect LDL cholesterol and Apo-B100 as well as the other secondary factors. With the added adverse effects of smoking as a secondary factor, these conditions produce clinical disease. It is suggested that this model may stimulate research focusing on the central role of abdominal adiposity.

DISTRIBUTION

Prevalence in US Adults

In the United States, prevalence of obesity in adults has been estimated in part on the basis of body mass index at or above the values of 27.8

Table 10–4 Correlations Between Body Mass Index and Other Characteristics at Entry, Seven Countries Study, 1958–1964

Cohort	Age	Skinfold	Lat/lin	SBP	DBP	Chol	Pulse	Smoking
US railroad	−0.02	0.75	0.43	0.23	0.27	0.09	0.05	−0.10
Dalmatia	−0.08	0.82	—	0.38	0.30	0.24	0.05	−0.20
Slavonia	−0.07	0.83	0.35	0.34	0.39	0.26	0.10	−0.38
Tanushimaru	−0.09	0.54	—	0.05	0.04	0.03	0.08	−0.04
East Finland	−0.04	0.77	0.32	0.11	0.21	0.10	0.16	−0.21
West Finland	0.00	0.80	0.40	0.21	0.28	0.13	0.20	−0.26
Ushibuka	−0.03	—	—	0.17	0.19	0.09	−0.07	−0.08
Crevalcore	−0.01	0.71	0.47	0.20	0.22	0.21	0.12	−0.21
Montegiorgio	0.01	0.80	0.39	0.21	0.27	0.33	0.17	−0.23
Zutphen	−0.08	0.70	0.61	0.32	0.36	0.21	0.08	−0.09
Crete	−0.05	0.79	0.40	0.27	0.33	0.28	0.09	−0.20
Corfu	0.01	0.84	0.44	0.29	0.35	0.28	0.23	−0.25
Rome railroad	−0.08	0.77	0.49	0.26	0.34	0.09	0.10	−0.25
Velika Krsna	0.06	0.76	0.29	0.06	0.10	0.21	0.05	−0.15
Zrenjanin	−0.06	0.87	—	0.23	0.32	0.26	—	−0.27
Belgrade	−0.06	0.77	—	0.12	0.21	0.13	—	−0.16
Mean	−0.04	0.77	0.42	0.21	0.26	0.19	0.10	−0.19
Standard error	0.01	0.02	0.02	0.02	0.02	0.02	0.02	0.02

Note: Lat/lin, standing height divided by the sum of the biacromial and bicristal diameters; SBP, systolic blood pressure; DBP, diastolic blood pressure; Chol, serum total cholesterol concentration.

Source: Reprinted by permission of the publisher from *Seven Countries* by A Keys, Cambridge, Mass: Harvard University Press, Copyright © 1980 by the President and Fellows of Harvard College.

kg/m² for men and 27.3 kg/m² for women.[16] These values were chosen to correspond to the 85th percentile values of body mass index for men and women in the Second National Health and Nutrition Examination Survey (NHANES II), conducted from 1976 to 1980. They also correspond, approximately, to the relative weight value of 120% in the 1983 Metropolitan Life Insurance Company tables. Prevalence for Black and White men and women, by age from 25 to 74 years, is shown for three successive surveys among probability samples of the US population in Figure 10–10. Prevalence was especially high in Black women and younger Black men but also increased sharply with age in White women. Differences between surveys indicated no change or slight decreases in prevalence for Whites and increases or no differences for Blacks. The category of overweight included 26% or 34 million of the US adult population in the latest of those surveys, and 9% or 13 million were classified as severely overweight. By the time of the next survey, however (NHANES III, Phase 1, 1988–1991), a major increase in prevalence of overweight had occurred, reaching 33.4% of the US population aged 20 and older.[23] Clearly, national goals for reduction in prevalence of obesity were becoming more distant.

US Minorities

Additional data on US minority populations, based on the same criteria, indicate the very high prevalence of overweight and severe overweight, especially in native Hawaiians and Samoans (Figure 10–11).[24] The relatively adverse situation of these population groups,

Exhibit 10–2 Cardiovascular Risk Factors Associated with Body Mass Index and Waist-Hip Ratio

---

Elevated Concentrations
- very–low-density lipoproteins, triglycerides
- glucose and insulin (glucose intolerance and insulin resistance)
- uric acid

Normal Concentrations
- total and LDL cholesterol, but the particles are smaller and more dense (richer in apolipoprotein B and cholesterol)

Reduced Concentrations
- high-density lipoprotein (especially HDL_2)

Other Risk Factors
- increased blood pressure (hypertension)
- alteration in cardiac structure (eg, eccentric left ventricular hypertrophy)
- sleeping disturbances (snoring, sleep apnea)
- electrophysiological abnormalities (eg, prolonged QT interval on electrocardiogram)
- increased blood viscosity and decreased fibrinolytic capacity

Source: Reprinted by permission from JC Seidell, 1996, Relationships of Total and Regional Body Composition to Morbidity and Mortality, in *Human Body Composition*, edited by AF Roche, SB Heymsfield, and TG Lohman, Champaign, IL: Human Kinetics Publishers, p 347.

---

especially women, is readily apparent. Comparisons among countries show very wide ranges of indicators, as in Table 10–5.[16] The age gradient of obesity is especially marked in the high-prevalence populations; the lack of standardization of age classification in published reports

therefore limits such comparisons. Still, the US range from 7% to 14% of men and from 7% to 21% of women with body mass index ≥30 kg/m² contrasts strikingly with the United Kingdom range, where prevalences were reported to be 3% to 8% of men and 5% to 14% of women

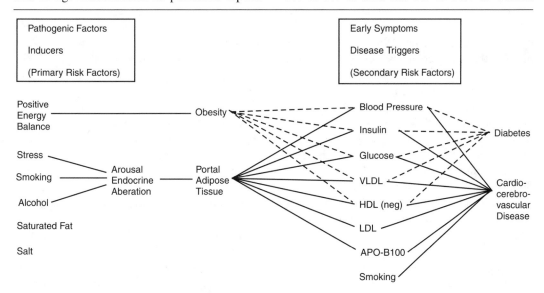

Note: HDL, high-density lipoprotein; LDL, low-density lipoprotein; VLDL, very–low-density lipoprotein.

Figure 10–9 The Role of "Primary" and "Secondary" Risk Factors in the Pathogenesis of Cardiovascular Disease, Stroke, and Diabetes. *Source:* Reprinted with permission from P Björntorp, "Portal" Adipose Tissue as a Generator of Risk Factors for Cardiovascular Disease and Diabetes, *Arteriosclerosis*, Vol 10, pp 493–496, © 1990, American Heart Association.

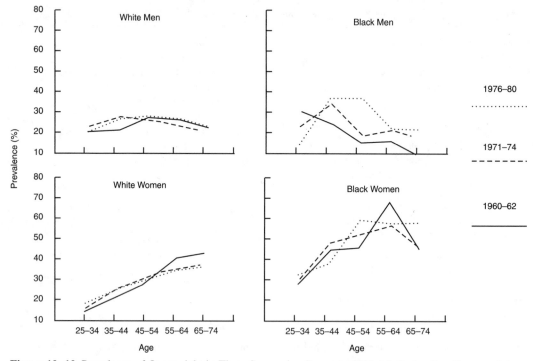

Figure 10–10 Prevalence of Overweight in Three Successive Surveys of US Adults, by Sex, Race, and Age. Overweight is defined as BMI ≥27.8 kg/m^2 for men and ≥27.3 kg/m^2 for women. *Source:* Reprinted from Division of Health Examination Statistics, National Center for Health Statistics, Washington, DC.

over the same age range. Where prevalence is highest, the age gradient is steepest and most distinct for women in comparison with men. The rarity or virtual absence of obesity of this degree in some populations, such as El Salvador, is consistent with low mean values of body mass index in other populations, such as 22 kg/m^2 or less in surveys from the INTERSALT project (some samples in Brazil, India, Japan, South Korea, People's Republic of China, and Kenya). This underscores the observation that overweight is not an inevitable concomitant of aging.

Longitudinal Studies in Individuals

Change in body mass index over time within individuals was reported from the First National Health and Nutrition Examination Epidemiologic Survey Follow-Up Study, as shown in Figures 10–12 and 10–13.[25] Gain in body mass

index was the dominant pattern for both men and women age 25–44 years. At ages 45–64, gains and losses were about equally represented, while losses outweighed gains among those 65–74 years of age at baseline. The younger adults who gained most were overweight at baseline. Women age 25–34 at baseline gained more than women age 35–44. Major weight gain (5 kg or more) was more common among Black than among White women. This major analysis of incidence of significant weight gain in early through late adult years calls special attention to the changes beginning in the 20s. However, the observation that those already overweight at baseline experienced the greatest increases in weight indicates that preventive measures even in the 20s are late in the process for some.

An extreme example of rapid weight change among individuals is especially germane to the circumstances of many developing countries.

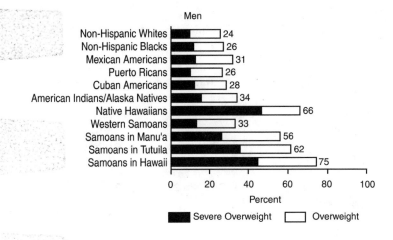

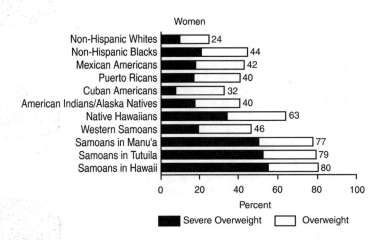

Figure 10–11 Prevalence of Overweight in Adult US Minority Populations, by Sex. Overweight is defined as a BMI ≥ 27.8 kg/m^2 for men and ≥ 27.3 kg/m^2 for women. *Source:* Reprinted with permission from S Kumanyika, Special Issues Regarding Obesity in Minority Populations, *Annals of Internal Medicine*, Vol 119, pp 650–654, © 1993, American College of Physicians.

This is the experience of the Nauruans, a small Western Pacific island population undergoing very rapid economic development in consequence of phosphate mining.[26] This circumstance has left a highly sedentary native Micronesian population with extremely high energy intakes—more than 7000 kcal/day for men and more than 5000 for women. Nauruans were found to have experienced a marked increase in population mean body mass index, from 32.3 to 37.1 kg/m^2 for men and from 34.4 to 38.3 for women at ages 20–29 years. This change occurred between the mid-1970s and early 1980s, only a 6½-year period.

Secular Trends

In the United States, secular trends toward increasing prevalence of obesity have been occurring also in childhood, at least by the measure of triceps skinfold thickness.[27] Analysis of data in successive national health surveys

Table 10–5 International Comparisons of Indicators of Obesity

| Area | Country | Mean BMI[b] | BMI at 90th Percentile Point[a] | |
			Men	Women
Northern Europe	Denmark	24.5	30.3	30.0
	Sweden		29.1, 30.4	29.6, 32.0
	Finland	25.4, 25.3	31.6, 31.6, 31.7	32.7, 31.4, 33.0
	Iceland	24.5	30.3	30.5
Western and Central Europe	United Kingdom	25.7, 24.8, 25.2	30.1, 30.2	32.4, 31.4
	Netherlands	24.4		
	Belgium	25.9, 24.9	30.4, 31.5	32.5, 33.6
	France		29.8, 32.5	30.2, 34.2
	Federal Republic of Germany	24.5, 24.5	30.8, 30.9, 31.3, 31.9	31.5, 32.7, 33.2, 32.1
	Switzerland		30.3, 31.8	30.8, 31.2
	Luxemburg		30.8	32.1
Southern Europe	Italy	28.0, 25.4, 25.4, 25.4	30.3, 31.3	31.5, 32.6
	Malta	26.9	32.7	36.5
	Portugal	25.8		
	Spain	25.4, 26.7	30.3	33.4
Eastern Europe	German Democratic Republic	24.9	30.9, 30.6, 31.2	32.0, 33.6, 34.2
	Hungary	26.2	30.8, 31.6	32.4, 33.8
	Poland	26.4, 26.5	31.7	34.3
	Yugoslavia		31.2	34.9
	Czechoslovakia		32.4	34.9
	[Former] USSR	25.7	30.6, 30.8, 30.4, 31.1, 30.7	34.5, 36.0, 34.3, 36.1, 36.2
North America	USA	26.4, 30.3, 28.2, 28.0, 25.1	29.9	31.8
	Canada	25.1, 25.2		
South and Central America	Argentina	25.0		
	Brazil	23.4, 21.2		
	Colombia	23.0		
	Mexico	24.4		
	Trinidad	28.2		
Asian-Pacific	India	20.1, 23.7		
	Japan	21.6, 22.5, 23.1		
	Hawaii	31.2		
	Taiwan	23.1		

continues

Table 10–5 continued

Area	Country	Mean BMI[b]	BMI at 90th Percentile Point[a]	
			Men	Women
	South Korea	22.2		
	Papua, New Guinea	21.7		
	People's Republic of China	22.8, 21.3, 23.8	27.6	29.5
	New Zealand		29.5	29.9
	Australia		29.8, 30.8	30.0, 31.5
Africa	Kenya	20.8		
	Zimbabwe	26.1		

Note: Multiple values within a country refer to different cities.

a. The 90th percentile points refer to men and women aged 35–64 years (MONICA data).

b. Mean BMI refers to age-adjusted values of men and women aged 30–59 years (INTERSALT data).

Source: Reprinted with permission from FH Epstein, *Obesity,* p 334, © 1992, Lippincott-Raven Publishers.

shows increases in the proportions of 6- to 11-year-olds and of 12- to 17-year-olds with triceps skinfold thicknesses at or above the 85th percentile level of the first of these surveys, conducted in 1960–1962. While other investigators found no change in mean body mass index and argued against any increase in the prevalence of childhood or adolescent obesity on this ground, increasing obesity in young women was observed by this criterion.[28] There is little disagreement that childhood obesity is a significant health concern in the United States, with or without an increasing trend within this age range. The evidence of increasing mean values of body mass index in the adult population suggests the importance of preventive measures at earlier ages, as discussed later under Prevention and Control.

POPULATION RATES

The question of whether population differences in rates of atherosclerotic and hypertensive diseases or of all-cause mortality are attributable to obesity has been addressed in few studies. Among them, the Seven Countries Study provides the most extensive results to date. Additional information from the World Health Organization MONICA Project will be forthcoming soon.

The Seven Countries Study

In the Seven Countries Study, coronary heart disease events and death from all causes in 10 years' follow-up experience provided the basis for analysis.[20] Both body mass index and the sum of the triceps and subscapular skinfold thicknesses were used as measures of obesity in relation to the experience of men 40–59 years of age at entry and initially free of detectable coronary heart disease. Over wide ranges of both measures across the 16 cohorts studied, the trends of both coronary and all-cause mortality were negative, that is, increasing measures of obesity were associated with decreasing mortality. Correlations standardized for age between each measure of obesity and incident coronary

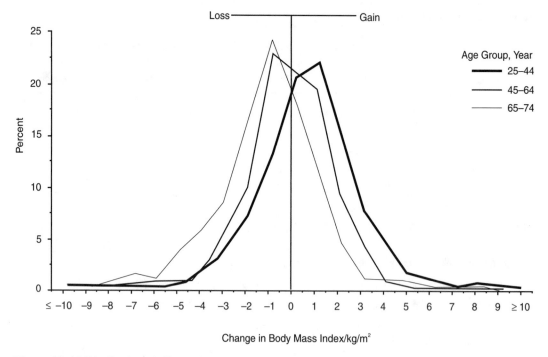

Figure 10–12 Distribution of Change in Body Mass Index over 10 Years for Men, United States. *Source:* Reprinted from DF Williamson, HS Kahn, PL Remington, and RF Anda, *Archives of Internal Medicine*, Vol 150, p 668, 1990.

heart disease were not statistically significant. However, body mass index was correlated weakly (with *r*, the measure of correlation, from 0.19–0.26) with values at entry of systolic and diastolic blood pressure and serum cholesterol concentration, and equally but negatively correlated with smoking history. Within each of the several populations, the lowest coronary heart disease incidence tended to occur at the lowest or an intermediate level of either body mass index or skinfold thickness. Keys concluded, "In none of the areas of this study was overweight or obesity a major risk factor for death or the incidence of coronary heart disease. In most of the areas the probability of death in ten years appeared to be least for the men somewhat over the average in relative weight or fatness."[20(pp 194–195)] In short, in men aged 40–59 years and free of detectable coronary heart disease at entry, differences in event rates among

16 European, North American, and Japanese populations over the following 10 years were not explained by differences in body mass index or the sum of the triceps and subscapular skinfold thicknesses.

Pacific Island Populations

The review by Dowse and others of the experience of Pacific Island populations included mortality follow-up of both men and women, Nauruans, and indigenous and Asian Indian residents of Fiji, in the early to mid-1980s.[26] The numbers of deaths were not large, and none of the relative risks was inconsistent with absence of effect of body mass index on mortality, in that all confidence intervals included 1. Cross-sectional data on the prevalence of body mass index of 30 kg/m² or greater in relation to electrocardiographic evidence of coronary heart dis-

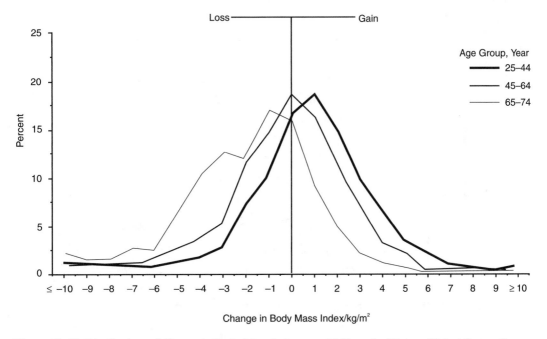

Figure 10–13 Distributions of Change in Body Mass Index over 10 Years for Women, United States. *Source:* Reprinted from DF Williamson, HS Kahn, PL Remington, and RF Anda, *Archives of Internal Medicine*, Vol 150, p 668, 1990.

ease in 10 Pacific Island populations indicated an inverse relation, with or without inclusion of Nauru with its exceptionally high prevalence of obesity (Figure 10–14).

INDIVIDUAL RISKS

The US Pooling Project

In the US Pooling Project,[29] analysis centered on the five cohorts of men aged 40–64 years at entry who were free of detectable coronary heart disease, as in the Seven Countries Study. The data were combined into a single pool for analysis, although cohort-specific results were also presented. As a measure of obesity, relative weight was determined from measured weight and height, with the ratio of measured height to desirable weight for that height multiplied by 100. Thus the mean values of relative weight by age group ranged from 115.8–118.6 across the four 5-year age subgroups. Analysis was based

on 8.6 years of follow-up. Among men age 40–44 or 45–49 years at entry, men experiencing first coronary events had higher baseline relative weights, by four to five units, whereas for older men 50–54 and 55–59 years of age at entry, the baseline relative weights were only slightly greater or even less among those experiencing first coronary events. Therefore only a modest association was present and was limited to men in their 40s at the beginning of follow-up.

The Framingham Heart Study

In subsequent analysis of 26-year follow-up within the Framingham Heart Study, one component of the Pooling Project, the relation between "desirable weight" or Metropolitan Relative Weight and mortality was further investigated to take smoking history into account.[30] At the beginning of the study in 1949, baseline data showed that men whose relative

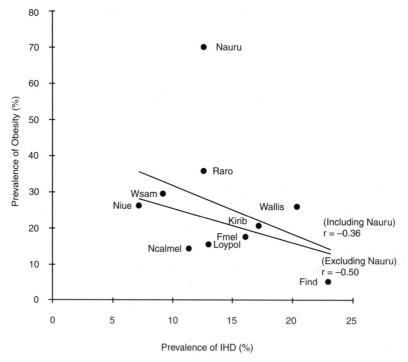

Note: Find, Fiji Indians; Fmel, Fiji Melanesians; Kirib, Kiribati; Loypol, Loyalty Islands Polynesians; Ncalmel, New Caledonia Melanesians; Niue, Niue Island; Raro, Rarotonga; Wallis, Wallis Island; Wsam, Western Samoa.

Figure 10–14 Ecological Comparison of Age-Standardized Prevalence of Obesity (BMI ≥ 30 kg/m^2) and Prevalence of Electrocardiographic Abnormalities Suggesting Coronary Heart Disease in 10 Pacific Island Populations. *Source:* Reprinted with permission from G Dowse, *Obesity*, p 631, © 1992, Lippincott-Raven Publishers.

weight was below 100 were predominantly (80%) smokers, while in the highest strata of relative weight, smoking was less common (55%). Further, former smokers were also more common among nonsmokers in the lowest relative weight men when compared with the highest relative weight category. When separately classified for mortality analysis, smokers and nonsmokers were found to differ as shown in Figure 10–15. Except for the lowest relative weight class, below 100, mortality tended to increase with increasing relative weight, though not in a consistent pattern for each age group. Mortality among smokers was substantially higher in both 30- and 40-year-old men at entry irrespective of relative weight, and mortality

among the lowest relative weight group of smokers was greater than among the highest relative weight group of nonsmokers, with about equal numbers of men in these two extreme categories for all age groups together. The report concluded that the concept of desirable weight is supported by this analysis and that the strong confounding between smoking and low relative weight requires adjustment for smoking for meaningful evaluation of the relation of relative weight and mortality.

Further data from the Framingham Heart Study indicated that relative weight was especially predictive of incident cardiovascular disease, at 26-year follow-up, in men and women less than age 50 years at entry in contrast to

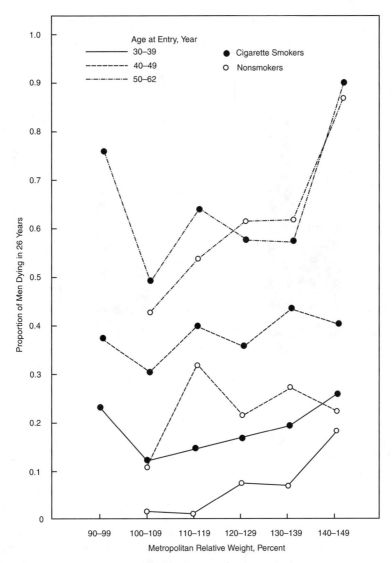

Figure 10–15 Proportion of Men Free of Cardiovascular Disease at Baseline Dying in 26 Years for Each Metropolitan Relative Weight Class by 10-Year Age Group and Smoking Status at Entry, Framingham Heart Study. *Source:* Reprinted from RJ Garrison, *Journal of the American Medical Association,* Vol 249, p 2201, 1983.

those age 50 years and older (Figure 10–16).[31] In the absence of elevated blood pressure or blood cholesterol, smoking, glucose intolerance, or electrocardiographic evidence of left ventricular hypertrophy, tertile of relative weight predicted coronary events, coronary death, and congestive heart failure in men and fatal and nonfatal coronary heart disease, stroke, and congestive heart failure in women.

The Nurses' Health Study

The Nurses' Health Study, addressed above, provides data for a large cohort of women in the

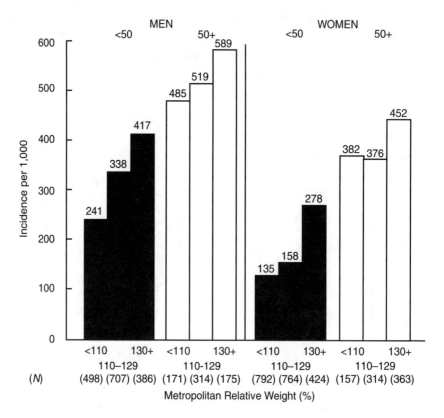

Note: N = the number at risk for an event. Numbers above the bars give the actual incidence rates per 1,000.

Figure 10–16 Incidence of Cardiovascular Disease in 26 Years' Follow-Up in Relation to Metropolitan Relative Weight among Men and Women above and below Age 50 at Entry, Framingham Heart Study. *Source:* Reprinted with permission from HB Hubert, M Feinleib, PM McNamara, and WP Castelli, *Circulation,* Vol 67, No 5, p 970, © 1983, American Heart Association.

United States and showed that baseline smoking prevalence was strongly related to body mass index in that population, entering follow-up beginning in 1976.[19] Table 10–3 indicates that smoking was about 60% (39.9%/25.1%) more common in the lowest (<21 kg/m²) than in the highest (29+ kg/m²) quintile group by body mass index, similar to the ratio in Framingham men in the lowest and highest categories of relative weight (80%/55%, ie, 45% more common). When relative risks for coronary events were estimated with and without adjustment for smoking history, the adjusted relative risks were higher at every level of body mass index and were higher in the top quintile by 20%–30%.

Thus for women, also, the relation between at least this one measure of obesity and risk of coronary heart disease is considerably stronger in analyses that take smoking history into account.

The PDAY Study

Studies of atherosclerosis in childhood and adolescence add very few observations about associations with obesity. The Pathobiological Determinants of Atherosclerosis in Youth (PDAY) Study, however, does report that in postmortem examination at ages from 15 through 34 years there is a significant relation between the weight of the panniculus adiposus (abdominal fat pad) and the extent of atherosclerotic involvement of the coronary circulation.[32]

INTERPRETATION

The differences in results among studies raise many questions about interpretation of these data as noted by Barrett-Connor and by Stallones.[33,34] If obesity were equivalently measured by the several indices cited above, and if it had a direct causal relation to atherosclerotic and hypertensive diseases independent of other major factors, the varied findings would be unexpected. The strongest evidence of concern is in the relation of obesity to other risk factors, with associations in cross-sectional and longitudinal studies and demonstration of beneficial effects on these factors by reduction of weight. The focus on control of obesity in youth and young adulthood, aimed at prevention of further weight gain and increase in risk due to other factors—especially blood pressure, blood lipids, and glucose and insulin regulation—appears sound but would be intensified if further clarification of obesity and its role were achieved.

PREVENTION AND CONTROL

Population-Wide Measures

Because of the predictive relations between obesity in adolescence or early adulthood and obesity in later life and the observation that weight loss is difficult to achieve and maintain once obesity has become established, control of the incidence of obesity in the first place is the logical priority. This implies early intervention by establishment of environmental conditions favoring optimum growth and development without lasting excess weight gain. The population-wide measures advocated for improvement of dietary patterns and reduction of physical inactivity are the principal means proposed for prevention of obesity at the population level. In many countries, the United States being prominent among them, the secular trend toward increasing prevalence of obesity is evidence of failure of population-wide strategies against this disorder. Understanding why this is the case is a high priority for the epidemiology and prevention of cardiovascular diseases.

Individual Measures

Individual measures for control of obesity are addressed in many official recommendations and are linked with those specific to management of adverse blood lipid profiles, high blood pressure, glucose intolerance, and other cardiovascular risk factors. In these latter circumstances, it is expected that most high-risk individuals are overweight to a sufficient degree that weight reduction will contribute to risk factor control. In the absence of other risk factors, the criteria for identification of the high-risk individual are less clear. Indications for individual intervention would depend on the measure of obesity used and the age and sex of the individual, as well as other considerations.

The World Health Organization Expert Committee report on anthropometry offered specific recommendations for individuals in each category, from normal to grade 3 overweight, by body mass criteria.[7]

The recommendations indicate much about the current concept of overweight as it relates to other factors predisposing to cardiovascular and other chronic conditions. Therefore, they are quoted here in full:

> For individuals with BMI 18.50–24.99: avoid becoming overweight. There are no recommendations for weight loss.
>
> For individuals with BMI 25.00–29.99: avoid weight gain. Before recommending any type of intervention, assess other risk factors. If there are additional risk factors (high abdomen:hip ratio, hypertension, hyperlipidaemia, glucose intolerance or

[non–insulin-dependent diabetes mellitus] NIDDM, strong family history of diabetes mellitus or premature coronary heart disease), recommend a healthy lifestyle that will contribute to improvement of the risk profile: cessation of smoking, increased physical activity, reduced intake of (saturated) fat. Moderate weight loss is recommended but weight loss *per se* should not be the primary target of intervention. A large proportion of the adult population will usually fall into this category, and most will receive advice on healthy nutrition and physical activity appropriate for the general population. Regular (yearly) weight measurement will be helpful in monitoring weight development, and weight histories should be noted. Individuals who have continued to gain weight (e.g. > 5 kg during the previous 2 years) should be identified for weight maintenance programs designed to halt the weight gain.

For individuals with BMI 30.00–39.99: the same recommendations as for grade 1 overweight, although the prevalence of risk factors and of overweight-associated disorders that require medical attention is usually markedly higher and moderate weight loss is therefore more urgently recommended. In many populations, the proportion of adults falling into this category is still considerable, and treatment priorities will have to be set on the basis of, among other things, the prevalence of health problems in the community concerned. The higher the prevalence of chronic diseases such as diabetes and [cardiovascular disease] CVD, the greater is the need for individuals with BMI 30.00–39.99 to lose weight. In other words, the potential impact of weight modification in preventing these problems is likely to be influenced by the disease rates in the population. The risks related to grade 2 overweight in adults depend on other, coexisting, risk factors for chronic noncommunicable diseases. Obese individuals with no additional risk factors or conditions that require medical supervision may be referred to self-help organizations. Such organizations are effective if their leaders have sufficient training in the principles of healthy weight loss (a maximum of about 0.5 kg/week) and of balanced nutrition. For individuals with conditions that do require medical supervision, the focus should be on normalizing the risk factors or alleviating health problems (e.g., improving respiratory function or arthritis in weight-bearing joints) rather than on achieving weight loss *per se*.

For individuals with BMI ≥ 40: intensive action to reduce weight. The proportion of adults with grade 3 overweight is small; for these individuals, weight loss *per se* may be the primary target and options such as surgical treatment for obesity should be considered.[7(pp 329–330)]

Methods for attempting to bring about weight change in individuals include weight loss prescriptions, weight loss plans based on considerations of general nutrition, reduction of calorie and fat intake, avoidance of situations leading to undesirable eating patterns, increased physical activity, motivational aspects, and monitoring of progress. It appears that weight reduction can significantly delay or prevent progression of blood pressure to levels requiring treatment.[35] A similar benefit has been shown in a meta-analysis of 70 studies of blood lipid modification by weight reduction, with decrease in total and low-density and very–low-density lipoprotein cholesterol and triglyceride concentrations and increased high-density lipoprotein cholesterol concentration.[36] With detailed techniques and effective counseling approaches, success can be achieved in some individuals. How long such intervention effects on weight can be maintained remains uncertain.[37]

CURRENT ISSUES

The range of health disorders related to obesity or overweight includes problems in most organ systems, with those of the heart and vascular system being among the most prominent: premature coronary heart disease, left ventricular hypertrophy, angina pectoris, sudden death, congestive heart failure, hypertension, stroke, and venous stasis including pulmonary embolism.[38] Emphasis here on coronary heart disease as an example is not intended to understate the importance of these other conditions.

Evidence of continuing increase in age- and sex-specific mean values of body mass index in the United States is of concern even though the concurrent trends in blood pressure levels and total cholesterol concentrations have been downward. As average body mass index increases, the proportion of the population at higher extremes increases sharply and may contribute to slowing of the decline in coronary heart disease and stroke incidence and mortality of past years, and other chronic conditions associated with obesity would be expected to increase in frequency of occurrence. An understanding of the trend in body mass index is therefore important, especially regarding what groups in the population are contributing most to this trend, who is most at risk, and what interventions may be effective in halting or reversing the trend.

Also of current importance are issues such as self-treatment to modify body weight, for example, self-imposed dietary restriction or bulimia in young women; widespread use of toxic medications to induce weight loss; and weight cycling, with alternating phases of marked weight loss and return to pretreatment levels.

More broadly, the risks of cardiovascular and other chronic diseases that may be increased directly or indirectly through obesity, at least at its upper extreme, are prominent health concerns. This is especially true for societies expected to experience increased affluence and to progress toward the common contemporary patterns of dietary imbalance and physical inactivity that promote the development of obesity. Those individuals and groups who modernize most rapidly and, eventually, whole populations, are at risk.

Further insight into components of obesity that are especially significant for health risks and the means and ability to modify their development would add importantly to formulation of appropriate and effective prevention policies at both individual and population levels.

REFERENCES

1. National Institutes of Health Consensus Development Panel on the Health Implications of Obesity. Health implications of obesity. *Ann Intern Med*. 1985;103 (suppl 6):1073–1077.

2. Brown PJ. The biocultural evolution of obesity: an anthropological view. In: Björntorp P, Brodoff BN, eds. *Obesity*. Philadelphia, Pa: JB Lippincott Co; 1992: 320–329.

3. Roche AF, Heymsfield SB, Lohman TG, eds. *Human Body Composition*. Champaign, Ill: Human Kinetics; 1996.

4. Van Loan MD. Total body composition: birth to old age. In: Roche AF, Heymsfield SB, Lohman TG, eds. *Human Body Composition*. Champaign, Ill: Human Kinetics; 1996: 205–215.

5. Simopoulos AP. Characteristics of obesity. In: Björntorp P, Brodoff BN, eds. *Obesity*. Philadelphia, Pa: JB Lippincott Co; 1992: 309–329.

6. World Health Organization Study Group. *Diet, Nutrition, and the Prevention of Chronic Diseases*. Geneva, Switzerland: World Health Organization; 1990. Technical Report Series 797.

7. World Health Organization Expert Committee. *Physical Status: The Use and Interpretation of Anthropometry*. Geneva, Switzerland: World Health Organization; 1995. Technical Report Series 854.

8. Bray GA. An approach to the classification and evaluation of obesity. In: Björntorp P, Brodoff BN, eds. *Obesity*. Philadelphia, Pa: JB Lippincott Co; 1992: 294–308.

9. Björntorp P. Regional obesity. In: Björntorp P, Brodoff BN, eds. *Obesity*. Philadelphia, Pa: JB Lippincott Co; 1992: 579–586.

10. Lohman TG, Roche AF, Martorell R. *Anthropometric Standardization Reference Manual*. Champaign, Ill: Human Kinetics; 1988.

11. Roche AF. Anthropometry and ultrasound. In: Roche AF, Heymsfield SB, Lohman TG, eds. *Human Body Composition*. Champaign, Ill: Human Kinetics; 1996: 167–189.

12. Baumgartner RN. Electrical impedance and total body electrical conductivity. In: Roche AF, Heymsfield SB, Lohman TG, eds. *Human Body Composition*. Champaign, Ill: Human Kinetics; 1996: 79–107.

13. Manson JE, Stampfer MJ, Hennekens CH, Willett WC. Body weight and longevity. *JAMA*. 1987;257:353–358.

14. Benn RT. Some mathematical properties of weight-for-height indices used as measures of adiposity. *Br J Prev Social Med*. 1971;25:42–50.

15. Kronmal RA. Spurious correlation and the fallacy of the ratio standard revisited. *J Royal Stat Soc*. 1993; 156(pt 3):379–392.

16. Epstein FH, Higgins M. Epidemiology of obesity. In: Björntorp P, Brodoff BN, eds. *Obesity*. Philadelphia, Pa: JB Lippincott Co; 1992: 330–342.

17. Bouchard C. Human obesities. In: Goldbourt U, de Faire U, Berg K, eds. *Genetic Factors in Coronary Heart Disease*. Dordrecht, the Netherlands: Kluwer Academic Publishers; 1994: 189–202.

18. Williams DP, Going SB, Lohman TG, Harsha DW, et al. Body fatness and risk for elevated blood pressure, total cholesterol, and serum lipoprotein ratios in children and adolescents. *Am J Public Health*. 1992; 82:358–363.

19. Manson JE, Colditz GA, Stampfer MJ, Willett WC, et al. A prospective study of obesity and risk of coronary heart disease in women. *N Engl J Med*. 1990;322: 882–889.

20. Keys A. *Seven Countries. A Multivariate Analysis of Death and Coronary Heart Disease*. Cambridge, Mass: Harvard University Press; 1980.

21. Seidell JC. Relationships of total and regional body composition to morbidity and mortality. In: Roche AF, Heymsfield SB, Lohman TG, eds. *Human Body Composition*. Champaign, Ill: Human Kinetics; 1996: 345–353.

22. Labarthe DR, Mueller WH, Eissa M. Blood pressure and obesity in childhood and adolescence. Epidemiologic aspects. *Ann Epidemiol*. 1991;1:337–345.

23. Kuczmarski RJ, Flegal KM, Campbell SM, Johnson CL. Increasing prevalence of overweight among US adults: the National Health and Nutrition Examination Surveys, 1960 to 1991. *JAMA*. 1994;272:205–211.

24. Kumanyika SK. Special issues regarding obesity in minority populations. *Ann Intern Med*. 1993;119 (suppl 7 pt 2):650–654.

25. Williamson DF, Kahn HS, Remington PL, Anda RF. The 10-year incidence of overweight and major weight gain in US adults. *Arch Intern Med*. 1990;150:665–672.

26. Dowse G, Zimmet P, Collins V, Finch C. Obesity in Pacific populations. In: Björntorp P, Brodoff BN, eds. *Obesity*. Philadelphia, Pa: JB Lippincott Co; 1992: 619–639.

27. Gortmaker SL, Dietz WH Jr, Sobol AM, Wehler CA. Increasing pediatric obesity in the United States. *Am J Dis Child*. 1987;141:535–540.

28. Harlan WR. Epidemiology of childhood obesity: a national perspective. *Ann NY Acad Sci*. 1993;699:1–5.

29. The Pooling Project Research Group. Relationship of blood pressure, serum cholesterol, smoking habit, relative weight and ECG abnormalities to incidence of major coronary events: Final Report of the Pooling Project. *J Chronic Dis*. 1978;31:201–306.

30. Garrison RJ, Feinleib M, Castelli WP, McNamara PM. Cigarette smoking as a confounder of the relationship between relative weight and long-term mortality: the Framingham Heart Study. *JAMA*. 1983;249:2199–2203.

31. Hubert HB, Feinleib M, McNamara PM, Castelli WP. Obesity as an independent risk factor for cardiovascular disease: a 26-year follow-up of participants in the Framingham Heart Study. *Circ*. 1982;67:968–977.

32. Strong JP, Oalmann MC, Malcom GT, Pathobiological Determinants of Atherosclerosis in Youth (PDAY) Research Group. Atherosclerosis in youth: relationship of risk factors to arterial lesions. In: Filer LJ Jr, Lauer RM, Luepker RV, eds. *Prevention of Atherosclerosis and Hypertension Beginning in Youth*. Philadelphia, Pa; Lea & Febiger; 1994: 13–18.

33. Barrett-Connor EL. Obesity, atherosclerosis, and coronary artery disease. *Ann Intern Med*. 1985;103:1010–1019.

34. Stallones RA. Epidemiologic studies of obesity. *Ann Intern Med*. 1985;103(suppl 6 pt 2):1003–1005.

35. Cutler JA. Randomized clinical trials of weight reduction in nonhypertensive persons. *Ann Epidemiol.* 1991; 1:363–370.

36. Dattilo AM, Kris-Etherton PM. Effects of weight reduction on blood lipids and lipoproteins: a meta-analysis. *Am J Clin Nutr.* 1992;56:320–328.

37. Elmer PJ. Obesity and cardiovascular disease: practical approaches for weight loss in clinical practice. In: Pearson TA, Criqui MH, Luepker RV, Oberman A, Winston M, eds. *Primer in Preventive Cardiology.* Dallas, Tex: American Heart Association; 1994: 189–204.

38. Vanitallie TB. Body weight, morbidity, and longevity. In: Björntorp P, Brodoff BN, eds. *Obesity.* Philadelphia, Pa: JB Lippincott Co; 1992: 361–369.

CHAPTER 11

Adverse Blood Lipid Profile

SUMMARY

Adverse blood lipid profile comprises the variations in absolute and relative blood concentrations of several types of lipid (fat) molecules and the protein molecules with which they are associated in the blood and body tissues. Due to the longer history of interest and the feasibility for epidemiologic field research, total cholesterol has been most widely studied in populations, but there is now a substantial body of information on distributions and predictive importance of other blood lipids as well. This evidence complements laboratory and clinical research on the metabolism and transport of blood lipids and lipoproteins, together establishing the basis for preventive strategies at both the population and the high-risk individual levels. Issues remain that in part reflect different views on policies for screening and treatment of adverse blood lipid profiles and in part concern areas in need of further epidemiologic and related research, such as the applicability to women of lipid research in men, the ability to prevent the development of adverse blood lipid profiles in the first place, and associations between low cholesterol concentration and mortality.

INTRODUCTION

The term *adverse blood lipid profile* denotes the multiplicity of lipid substances in blood now implicated in the pathogenesis of atherosclerosis and its manifestations. *Hypercholesterolemia* (the term used for many years) refers simply to elevated total cholesterol concentrations, even though laboratory research as early as the 1950s had already demonstrated component cholesterol fractions carried in the blood by linkage to proteins (lipoproteins) distinct in size and other properties. Determination of total cholesterol concentration remains important as a predictor of population rates of atherosclerotic diseases and in estimation of individual risks. However, it is often supplemented by measurement of other lipid components and proteins involved in lipid transport and metabolism. Interest in these other aspects of the blood lipid profile has increased greatly with advances in laboratory techniques; laboratory, clinical, and epidemiologic investigations of their several roles in atherogenesis; and their applicability to clinical practice and public health policy.

HISTORY OF RESEARCH ON BLOOD LIPIDS

The progression from early animal experimental research on diet and atherosclerosis to contemporary understanding of the roles of blood lipids at both population and individual levels is documented in reviews by Stamler,[1] Keys,[2] the National Research Council,[3] and others. Very briefly, in the early 1900s, it was discovered that cholesterol was the necessary dietary constituent in production of experimental atherosclerosis in rabbits and other species. Recognition of the significance of this knowledge for human atherosclerosis came much later, although as early as 1916 plasma cholesterol concentrations were observed in Indonesia to be lower in the native population than in Dutch immigrants, a difference inferred to relate to the much lower rate of occurrence of coronary heart disease in the indigenous population. This report, in conjunction with other observations cited by Keys "seemed to fit into one picture."[2(p 1)] That picture suggested the importance of differences in population distributions of blood cholesterol concentration and led to surveys in several populations as background to development of the Seven Countries Study in the mid- to late 1950s. Thereafter, on the basis of this and several cohort studies in the United States and elsewhere, the predictive relation of blood cholesterol concentration for the occurrence of coronary heart disease became established.

The relation between dietary fat and cholesterol intake and blood cholesterol concentration was quantified, as described in Chapter 8, during the 1950s and 1960s. The composition of blood lipids and their transporting proteins (lipoproteins) was investigated further through the 1970s and 1980s, while mechanisms of lipid transport and metabolism were also being described at a new level of detail. Epidemiologic studies over this period established the inverse relation of the concentration of high-density lipoprotein (HDL) cholesterol (popularly, the "good" cholesterol) to risk of coronary heart disease. This fact requires use of the term *adverse blood lipid profile* and not only *hypercholesterolemia,* since it is low, not high, HDL-cholesterol concentration that is associated with increased risk of atherosclerosis and its complications.

At the same time, clinical trials of dietary or drug interventions to modify blood lipid composition, principally by reducing total cholesterol concentrations, were undertaken. Evidence that incidence of coronary heart disease could thereby be reduced was a major stimulus to public health action with respect to blood lipid concentrations. Thus a significant outcome of this progression of research on blood lipids has been the application of this knowledge to clinical practice and public health policies, as illustrated in the United States by the reports of the National Cholesterol Education Program, discussed below.

Currently, laboratory research on blood lipids continues to expand and now includes molecular genetics, findings that relate to particular types of lipid molecules and their roles in atherogenesis. One result may be more specific biochemical characterization of individual risks in relation to blood lipids. This could eventually lead to development of interventions tailored to those risks, which would have important potential for enhancement of high-risk intervention strategies, also addressed below. Caution is needed in implementing this approach, however, as noted in Chapter 28.

DEFINITIONS AND CLASSIFICATION

Lipoprotein Molecules

Table 11–1 presents a current, broad classification of plasma lipoproteins and indicates several of their properties, which include, in the second column, the major lipids associated with each.[4] The metabolism of lipoproteins and their relation to atherosclerosis have been reviewed recently.[5] One or more apolipoproteins occupy the surface of the lipoprotein molecule, giving it surface properties that determine its potential interactions with specific enzymes and cell-surface receptors. Electrophoretic mobility refers to the extent of migration of each lipoprotein class from the point of origin when a processed blood sample is subjected to an electrical potential across a suitable transport medium. This technique of lipid separation, used for many years, was the basis for an earlier classification

Table 11–1 Classification and Properties of Plasma Lipoproteins

Lipoprotein Class	Major Lipids	Apolipoproteins	Density (g/ml)	Diameter (Å)	Electrophoretic Mobility
Chylomicrons	Dietary triglycerides, cholesteryl esters	A-I, A-II, A-IV, B-48, C-I, C-II, C-III, E	<0.95	800–5000	Origin
Remnants	Dietary cholesteryl esters	B-48, E	<1.006	>300	Origin
VLDL	Endogenous triglycerides	B-100, C-I, C-II, C-III, E	<1.006	300–800	Pre-β
IDL	Cholesteryl esters, triglycerides	B-100, E	1.006–1.019	250–350	Pre-β/β
LDL	Cholesteryl esters	B-100	1.019–1.063	180–280	β
HDL$_2$	Cholesteryl esters	A-I, A-II	1.063–1.125	90–120	α
HDL$_3$	Cholesteryl esters	A-I, A-II	1.125–1.210	50–90	α

Note: VLDL, very–low-density lipoprotein; IDL, intermediate-density lipoprotein; LDL, low-density lipoprotein; HDL, high-density lipoprotein.

Source: Reprinted with permission from PH Jones, J Patsch, and AM Gotto, Jr, The Biochemistry of Blood Lipid Regulation and the Assessment of Lipid Abnormalities, in *The Heart: Arteries and Veins*, RC Schlant and RW Alexander, p 975, © 1994, The McGraw-Hill Companies.

under the terms indicated in the right-hand column of the table. For example, the concentration of cholesterol found in low-density lipoprotein (LDL) cholesterol was denoted as β cholesterol.

The listed lipoprotein classes are arrayed in descending order of molecular size and density. Chylomicrons carry dietary (exogenous) triglycerides and cholesterol from the intestine into the circulation, and 80%–95% of their lipid content is triglycerides. Remnants are portions of cholesterol-laden lipoprotein remaining after breakdown of chylomicrons. Very–low-density and intermediate-density lipoproteins (VLDL and IDL) both carry endogenous triglycerides as about 55%–80% and 20%–50% of their lipid content, respectively, and IDL carries endogenous cholesterol as about 20%–40% of its lipid content. LDL and HDL both carry endogenous cholesterol—40%–50% and 15%–25% of their lipid content, respectively—but they are associated with different apolipoproteins and have different metabolic pathways, which contribute to their reciprocal roles in atherogenesis. A number of epidemiologic investigations are currently addressing the relations between these various molecular classes, and in some instances subcomponents within these classes, and measures of atherosclerosis.

Examples of other molecular components of the blood lipid profile that have been investigated both in the laboratory and in population studies are lipoprotein(a) (Lp(a), read: "L P little a") and apolipoprotein E (apoE, read: "apo E"). Lp(a) is a circulating protein whose blood concentration appears to be primarily genetically controlled. Its metabolism and mechanisms of action are little understood but may include effects on blood coagulation, binding of materials within the atherosclerotic plaque, and others. It is linked with triglyceride metabolism and with the risk of cardiovascular conditions (see below).[6] ApoE is also genetically determined, and three alleles (designated ε2–ε4) account for most of the observed genotypes. Their association with severe lipid disorders led to studies that revealed their role in relation to blood lipid profiles within the usual range of variation as well as to risk of coronary artery disease.[7]

Blood Lipid Phenotypes

A second approach to classification of blood lipids, the so-called Frederickson classification, addresses a series of phenotypes, or clinical patterns that represent specific profiles of lipoprotein, total cholesterol, and triglyceride concentrations; different degrees of atherogenicity; and associations with particular genetic disorders (Table 11–2).[4] The Frederickson types I–V and their equivalent terms, such as *familial hypercholesterolemia* for type II a or b, are encountered in much of the clinical and some of the epidemiologic literature of the past. This classification does not take HDL-cholesterol concen-

tration into account and has, in this respect, been superseded by more recent approaches that recognize epidemiologic observations in several populations, discussed under Individual Risks, below. Attention to HDL cholesterol as well as triglycerides, for example, was emphasized in the report of a National Institutes of Health (NIH) consensus panel addressing these lipid components and their relation to coronary heart disease.[8] They have subsequently been incorporated in updated screening recommendations for the US adult population (see below).

Classification in Screening and Treatment

Classification by blood lipid concentrations to identify high-risk adults in accordance with the reports of the National Cholesterol Educa-

Table 11–2 Fredrickson Classification of the Hyperlipidemias

Phenotype	Lipoprotein(s) Elevated	Serum Cholesterol Level	Serum Triglyceride Level	Atherogenicity	Associated with Genetic Disorders
I	Chylomicrons	Normal to ↑	↑↑↑↑	None seen	Familial lipoprotein lipase deficiency Apolipoprotein C-II deficiency
IIa	LDL	↑↑	Normal	+++	Familial hypercholesterolemia LDL receptor abnormal Familial combined hyperlipidemia Polygenic hypercholesterolemia
IIb	LDL and VLDL	↑↑	↑↑	+++	Familial hypercholesterolemia Familial combined hyperlipidemia
III	IDL	↑↑	↑↑↑	+++	Familial dysbetalipoproteinemia
IV	VLDL	Normal to ↑	↑↑	+	Familial hypertriglyceridemia Familial combined hyperlipidemia
V	VLDL and chylomicrons	Normal to ↑	↑↑↑↑	+	Familial hypertriglyceridemia Familial multiple-lipoprotein–type hyperlipidemia

Note: LDL, low-density lipoprotein; VLDL, very–low-density lipoprotein; IDL, intermediate-density lipoprotein. Relative degrees of atherogenicity are indicated by plus signs. High-density lipoprotein (HDL) cholesterol levels are not considered in the Fredrickson classification.

Source: Reprinted with permission from AM Gotto, Jr, Lipid and Lipoprotein Disorders, in TA Pearson et al, *Primer in Preventive Cardiology,* © 1994, American Heart Association, and by permission from *Southern Medical Journal,* Vol 88, No 4, pp 379–391, 1995.

tion Program requires distinctions between "desirable," "borderline-high," and "high" total cholesterol concentration and also, in the most recent report, between "low" and other levels of HDL-cholesterol concentration.[9] The corresponding criteria for total cholesterol categories are below 200 mg/dl, 200–239 mg/dl, and 240 mg/dl or greater; for LDL cholesterol the criteria are below 130 mg/dl, 130–159 mg/dl, and 160 mg/dl or greater; and for HDL cholesterol criteria are below 35 mg/dl versus higher values. For children (age 2–19 years), the National Cholesterol Education Program currently recommends as criteria for "acceptable," "borderline," and "high" categories values for total cholesterol concentration below 170 mg/dl, 170–199 mg/dl, and 200 mg/dl or greater; and corresponding values for LDL cholesterol are recommended at below 110 mg/dl, 110–129 mg/dl, and 130 mg/dl or greater. No HDL-cholesterol criteria are indicated for this age group.[10] The appropriateness of fixed screening criteria for all ages from 2 to 19 years, and both males and females, has been questioned (see Population Differences in Blood Lipid Distributions below). For both adults and children, determination of LDL-cholesterol concentration requires a fasting blood sample, unlike total or HDL-cholesterol determination.

MEASUREMENT

Laboratory Aspects

Public health concerns about measurement of blood lipids center on accuracy of methods for determination of total cholesterol concentration and limited reliability of a single determination for characterizing an individual due to within-person variation. Recent addition of LDL and HDL cholesterol and possibly triglycerides to recommendations for classifying persons as being at high risk broadens these concerns. This is especially so because LDL cholesterol is usually not directly measured but is calculated according to the equation

$$\text{LDL-C} = (\text{Total cholesterol}) - (\text{HDL-C}) - (\text{triglycerides}/5)$$

This poses difficulties because triglyceride determination carries substantial laboratory error, it requires a fasting sample, and the assumption that one-fifth of the triglyceride value represents LDL cholesterol is only approximate. In fact it is recommended that, if the triglyceride concentration exceeds 400 mg/dl, this estimation of LDL cholesterol not be performed due to departure from that assumption.

Issues about between-laboratory variation in methods and reliability of cholesterol determination led to establishment in the United States of a laboratory standardization program, the National Reference System for Cholesterol Measurements, by the Centers for Disease Control and Prevention and the National Bureau of Standards. Through this program, a reference method (the Abell-Kendall method) and a detailed quality control program are maintained, and other laboratories in the United States and elsewhere may be certified as meeting published standards.

A more recent concern about cholesterol determination arose with the introduction of desktop analyzers, of which 37 models were listed in a broad assessment of cholesterol measurement methods by the US General Accounting Office.[11] It was noted that measurement performance is generally good under controlled laboratory conditions, but that the desktop analyzers had not yet been evaluated sufficiently to judge their reliability.

Variability Within Individuals

In addition, the General Accounting Office report emphasized the need for multiple measurements in order to classify an individual as requiring treatment or not, due to variability associated with single measurements. The ranges of actual values represented by single test results, as estimated by the General Accounting Office, are shown in Table 11–3. Both analytical variability, based on current goals for measurement performance, and biological variability,

Table 11–3 The Effect of Analytical and Biological Variability on Total Cholesterol Test Results

Test Result	Potential Range		
	Based on Analytical Variability Alone[a]	Based on Biological Variability Alone[b]	Based on Total Variability[c]
180	164–196	158–202	151–209
200	182–218	176–224	167–233
220	200–240	193–247	184–256
240	219–261	211–269	201–279
260	237–283	228–292	218–302

Note: Values are mg/dl.

a. Calculated using the NCEP Laboratory Standardization Panel goal of ± 8.9% (0.05 level, 2-tailed test). The total analytic error of 8.9% is derived by summing the precision and bias components in the following manner:

$$3 + 1.96 \sqrt{3^2}$$

b. Calculated using an estimate of intraindividual biological variability (6.1% coefficient of variation) derived from a meta-analysis of 30 studies.

c. Total percentage error calculated from the following expression: $3 + 1.96 \sqrt{3^2 + 6.1^2}$

Source: Reprinted from *Cholesterol Measurement, Test Accuracy and Factors That Influence Cholesterol Levels*, GAO/PEMD-95-8, General Accounting Office, 1994.

due to true individual variability from dietary and other factors, were considered, first separately and then jointly. For example, a test result of 200 mg/dl, which for an adult would represent a borderline-high value, was taken to represent a range from 182–218 mg/dl, 176–224 mg/dl, or 167–233 mg/dl, depending on which components of variability were considered. The implications for use of single measurements of cholesterol concentration typical of epidemiologic studies are readily apparent.

Further support for the use of multiple measurements comes from epidemiologic studies in which more than a single measurement was recorded, whether in the recruitment phase of a trial or in the early follow-up experience of a long-term cohort study. The strength of association between cholesterol concentration and outcomes has been demonstrated to increase importantly when values from two occasions of measurement could be included in the analysis.

More-general considerations about cholesterol measurement in public screening situations, including technician training, participant education and follow-up, and other aspects, are addressed in a recent report from the National Cholesterol Education Program and the American Heart Association.[12] This is a helpful resource for planners of screening projects or other field studies in which cholesterol determinations will be performed. Policy recommendations about cholesterol screening continue to stimulate debate, as noted in the Current Issues section below.

DETERMINANTS AND MECHANISMS

Diet

The role of dietary fat and cholesterol intake in determining the blood total cholesterol concentration has been expressed in the prediction equations of Keys and of Hegsted, as described in Chapter 8. As recently summarized by Hegsted and colleagues:

1) Saturated fatty acids increase and are the primary determinants of serum cholesterol, 2) polyunsaturated fatty acids actively lower serum cholesterol, 3) monounsaturated fatty acids have no independent effect on serum cholesterol and, 4) dietary cholesterol increases serum cholesterol and must be considered when the effects of fatty acids are evaluated. More limited data on low-density-lipoprotein cholesterol (LDL-C) show that changes in LDL-C roughly parallel the changes in serum cholesterol but that changes in high-density-lipoprotein cholesterol cannot be satisfactorily predicted from available data.[13(p 875)]

Other dietary influences on blood lipids, such as fiber intake, are addressed in Chapter 8.

Lipid Metabolism and Transport

Interacting with dietary fats in the digestive tract, endogenous production of lipids, and measurable concentrations of the lipids in the blood, are mechanisms of metabolism and transport including those alluded to above. These mechanisms suggest something of the regulatory processes that balance the normal and pathophysiological phenomena involving blood lipids that operate throughout the individual life span. Three sets of such regulatory processes have been proposed.[5] First are those involved in transport of exogenous lipids, via the chylomicron system, from the intestine to the liver and peripheral tissues. Second is the transport of lipids synthesized in the liver to peripheral tissues, to circulating free fatty acids, or back to the liver. Third, the reverse cholesterol transport, which is thought to depend on HDL metabolism, removes cholesterol from tissues such as blood vessels. Each of these and the other processes currently described comprise multiple enzymatic reactions and changes in molecular composition, which can readily be imagined to involve many elements not yet identified.

Beyond the immediate regulatory mechanisms, a number of conditions or disease states are associated with increased blood lipid concentrations and are therefore termed *secondary hyperlipidemia*. These are subclassified as to whether cholesterol or triglyceride concentrations are affected. Exhibit 11–1 lists many of

Exhibit 11–1 Selected Causes of Secondary Hyperlipidemia

Related to hypercholesterolemia	Cushing's syndrome
Hypothyroidism	Glucocorticoid use
Nephrotic syndrome	Beta-blocker use
Chronic liver disease (mainly primary biliary cirrhosis)	Diuretic use
	Hypopituitarism
Dysglobulinemia	Hypothyroidism
Cushing's syndrome	Pancreatitis
Hyperparathyroidism	Dysglobulinemia
Acute intermittent porphyria	Glycogen storage disease
Related to hypertriglyceridemia	Lipodystrophy
Alcoholism	Acute intermittent porphyria
Diabetes mellitus	Pregnancy
Obesity	Stress
Estrogen use	Uremia
Chronic renal failure	

Source: Reprinted with permission from AM Gotto, Jr, Lipid and Lipoprotein Disorders, in TA Pearson et al, *Primer in Preventive Cardiology*, p 123, © 1994, American Heart Association.

these factors, indicating the broad variety of endocrinologic and other conditions that can influence blood lipids.[4] Genetic influences on some aspects of blood lipid regulation are well described, such as homozygous familial hypercholesterolemia, in which receptors for LDL cholesterol are absent and LDL cholesterol concentration in the blood increases greatly. This results from a specific mutation in the gene for LDL receptors, which occurs in 1 out of 300 to 500 persons, with accelerated atherosclerosis as a result.

Blood Lipids and Atherogenesis

The process by which adverse blood lipid profiles lead to atherosclerosis was addressed briefly in Chapter 3. A more detailed representation is shown in Figure 11–1, based on the recent review by St. Clair, who noted: "any hypothetical scheme of the pathogenesis of atherosclerosis will be revised as new information becomes available . . . the pathogenic scheme will also be complex, because it must account for the fact that atherosclerosis is a disease of multiple etiologies and is influenced by a variety of environmental and genetic factors."[14(p 16)] This view is thus analogous to a composite police sketch of a suspected villain, with elements from many different reports pieced together to form a coherent, although tentative, picture.

As indicated in Figure 11–1, the early stages of the process are at the left, and later ones are at the right. The row of elongated cells represents the single-layer endothelium (inner lining) of an arterial wall; above is the lumen and circu-

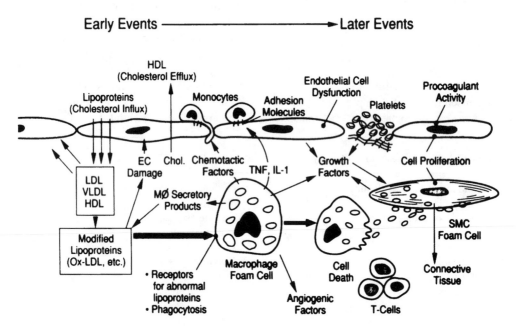

Early Events ————————————▶ Later Events

Note: HDL, high-density lipoprotein; LDL, low-density lipoprotein; VLDL, very–low-density lipoprotein; EC, endothelial cell; TNF, tumor necrosis factor; IL-1, interleukin-1; MØ, macrophage; SMC, smooth muscle cell; Ox-LDL, oxidized low-density lipoprotein.

Figure 11–1 Schematic of Cellular and Molecular Events in Pathogenesis of Atherosclerosis. Proposed early events (typical of fatty streaks) are depicted toward the left, and later events (typical of fatty plaques, fibrous plaques, and complicated plaques) toward the right. *Source:* Reproduced with permission from RW St Clair, Biology of Atherosclerosis, in TA Pearson et al, *Primer in Preventive Cardioology,* © 1994, American Heart Association.

lating blood, and below is the intimal layer of the arterial wall, with both cellular and extracellular components. The earliest steps shown involve the influx of cholesterol-laden lipoproteins through the endothelial cells and into the intima. This flow is counterbalanced by cholesterol efflux, mediated by HDL. Within the intima, biochemical modifications such as oxidation of LDL may occur to produce molecular forms that damage endothelial cells. These products also convert macrophages (scavenger blood cells) that have migrated from the circulating blood into the intima, into macrophage-derived "foam" cells (so named from their microscopic appearance, since they are filled with cholesterol esters). These foam cells in turn release several substances that affect endothelial cell function and stimulate growth of arterial smooth muscle cells. Late in the process, smooth muscle cells also may become foam cells with high cholesterol ester content. Disruption of the connections between endothelial cells and changes in endothelial cell function promote the adhesion of blood platelets, leading to localized thrombosis or clot formation. Small thrombi may only add to the size of the growing atherosclerotic plaque, but large ones likely result in occlusion of the vessel with the attendant clinical manifestations of myocardial ischemia.

From the earlier discussion of blood lipid metabolism and transport, coupled with this scheme of pathogenesis of atherosclerosis, it would be expected that high total cholesterol concentrations, which usually reflect high LDL cholesterol and a high ratio of LDL to HDL cholesterol, would contribute to atherogenesis. If a favorable balance is maintained under conditions of optimum levels of the respective blood lipids—perhaps in both absolute and relative terms—the major and possibly decisive component of atherogenesis is lacking. It appears that in the absence of hypercholesterolemia, the other identified risk factors have only weak atherogenic effects.

That atherosclerosis progresses at all under this circumstance may be due to the complexity already noted, which indicates that factors other than blood concentrations of lipids may sometimes be crucial. For example, even with only usual quantities of LDL cholesterol in the intima, if factors were present that increased the probabilities of oxidation or other adverse molecular changes, atherogenesis might still be stimulated. There are also several other mechanisms of action of HDL that could, alternatively or in addition to its role in reverse cholesterol transport, explain the antiatherogenic effect of high HDL-cholesterol concentration, including removal of LDL from atherosclerotic lesions, protection of LDL from oxidation, and other metabolic effects.[5] As noted by St. Clair, "Although a great deal about the cellular and molecular changes that occur in the developing atherosclerotic lesion is known, it is unclear whether there is a single rate-limiting step on which all risk factors must act or if risk factors can act at different steps in the pathogenic scheme. The latter possibility seems more likely."[14(p 20)]

DISTRIBUTION

Prevalence in US Adults

The percentage frequencies of several categories of total cholesterol concentration for US adults, in accordance with screening criteria outlined above, are shown in Table 11–4.[15] These data, from the Third National Health and Nutrition Examination Survey (NHANES III), collected from 1988 to 1991, are from a representative national sample of 7775 persons aged 20 and over. They are classified as in the National Cholesterol Education Program recommendations from the second Adult Treatment Panel report. The first-level distinction is between those who would and those who would not require a second fasting blood lipid analysis. Not requiring blood lipid analysis are those with either desirable or borderline-high total cholesterol concentration and HDL-cholesterol concentration of 35 mg/dl or greater and fewer than two other risk factors. Requiring fasting

Table 11–4 Prevalence of Categories of Blood Total Cholesterol Concentration in US Adults, by Ethnicity, Race, and Sex/Age, in Accordance with Screening Recommendations of the Adult Treatment Panel II, National Cholesterol Education Program

Population Group	Do Not Require Fasting Analysis		Require Fasting Analysis					
	Desirable (<200 mg/dl [<5.17 mmol/l]; HDL ≥35 mg/dl [≥0.91 mmol/l])	Borderline-High (200–239 mg/dl [5.17–6.20 mmol/l]; HDL ≥35 mg/dl [≥0.91 mmol/l] <2 RFs)	Borderline-High			High (≥240 mg/dl [≥6.21 mmol/l])	CHD	Total[a]
			Desirable (<200 mg/dl [<5.17 mmol/l]; HDL <35 mg/dl [<0.91 mmol/l])	(200–239 mg/dl [5.17–6.20 mmol/l]; HDL ≥35 mg/dl [≥0.91 mmol/l] ≥2 RFs)	(200–239 mg/dl [5.17–6.20 mmol/l]; HDL <35 mg/dl [<0.91 mmol/l])			
All persons	41	19	4	7	3	18	7	40
Ethnicity								
Mexican American	46	20	5	5	3	15	6	34
Non-Hispanic Black[b]	45	20	3	7	2	16	7	35
Non-Hispanic White[b]	40	19	5	7	4	19	8	42
Races[c]								
Black	46	20	3	7	2	16	7	34
White	40	19	4	7	4	19	7	41
Sex/age; yr								
Men								
≥20	39	18	6	7	5	17	8	44
20–34	58	20	7	2	3	9	2	23
35–44	37	25	6	2	7	18	3	38
45–54	25	14	5	14	7	25	9	61
55–64	19	13	3	15	7	25	17	68
65–74	22	9	7	16	6	22	17	69
≥75	31	11	6	11	3	14	23	58

continues

Table 11–4 continued

Population Group	Do Not Require Fasting Analysis		Require Fasting Analysis					
			Borderline-High					
	Desirable (<200 mg/dl [<5.17 mmol/l]; HDL ≥35 mg/dl [≥0.91 mmol/l])	Borderline-High (200–239 mg/dl [5.17–6.20 mmol/l]; HDL ≥35 mg/dl [≥0.91 mmol/l]; <2 RFs)	Desirable (<200 mg/dl [<5.17 mmol/l]; HDL <35 mg/dl [<0.91 mmol/l])	(200–239 mg/dl [5.17–6.20 mmol/l]; HDL ≥35 mg/dl [≥0.91 mmol/l]; ≥2 RFs)	(200–239 mg/dl [5.17–6.20 mmol/l]; HDL <35 mg/dl [<0.91 mmol/l])	High (≥240 mg/dl [≥6.21 mmol/l])	CHD	Total[a]
Women								
≥20	43	20	2	6	1	20	7	36
20–34	65	17	4	2	1	8	3	18
35–44	53	24	3	3	3	11	4	24
45–54	36	30	0	5	1	23	6	34
55–64	17	19	1	13	2	37	12	64
65–74	17	18	2	14	0	39	11	65
≥75	22	12	2	13	1	32	16	65

Note: This is the initial classification, based on total and high-density lipoprotein (HDL) cholesterol levels, presence of coronary heart disease (CHD), and risk factors (RFs) for CHD (unpublished data from the third National Health and Nutrition Examination Survey).

a. Rows may not sum to the total due to rounding.

b. All Hispanic persons were excluded.

c. Includes Hispanic persons.

Source: Reprinted from CT Sempos et al, Journal of the American Medical Association, Vol 269, p 3011, 1993.

analysis are those with desirable total cholesterol but low HDL cholesterol; borderline-high
total cholesterol and either sufficient HDL cholesterol but two or more other risk factors or
insufficient HDL cholesterol; high total cholesterol; or known coronary heart disease. Data are
shown for all persons, for three ethnic groups
(as self-identified in the course of the survey),
for two race groups, and for the combined
groups classified by sex and age. The former
categories were age-adjusted for comparison.

Of the 45% of the population with desirable
cholesterol concentration, 4% had low HDL
cholesterol. Borderline-high cholesterol was
found in 29% of adults, but 10% of them had
low HDL cholesterol or two or more other risk
factors. High cholesterol was found in 18% of
the population and known coronary heart disease in 7%. Altogether, 40% of adults were projected to require second-stage screening by
fasting blood lipid analysis. Differences in prevalence by ethnicity and race indicated that
Whites generally had less favorable blood lipid
profiles and would require rescreening in
greater proportions than other groups. Women
of most age groups had desirable total cholesterol in combination with favorable HDL cholesterol more frequently than did men, for
whom desirable total cholesterol levels were
more often accompanied by low HDL cholesterol. Desirable total cholesterol concentrations
were less prevalent in older age groups, for
whom high cholesterol increased, especially for
women (as did the prevalence of coronary heart
disease).

Distribution in US Children

For US children age 8–10 years, data on distributions of the major lipid components,
including the total cholesterol/HDL-cholesterol
ratio, are given for White, Black, and Hispanic
males and females enrolled in the Children's
Activity Trial for Cardiovascular Health
(CATCH), as shown in Table 11–5.[16] The mean,
standard deviation, and 10th and 90th percentile
values are given for each lipid measure. Statisti-

cally significant differences in mean values by
ethnicity or sex are those with P values of .05 or
less. The principal differences are in HDL-cholesterol and total cholesterol/HDL-cholesterol
ratio, for which Blacks had respectively higher
and lower values than did other groups. Sex differences were also mainly related to HDL cholesterol, with higher values in males for both
Whites and Blacks. However, the changes in
these lipid components by age in childhood and
adolescence and differential changes among
blood lipid components by sex are substantial,
and such cross-sectional comparisons for a single age stratum do not give a full picture of the
overall comparability between sex and race
groups.[17]

Secular Trends in Prevalence, US Adults

Secular trends in cholesterol concentration in
US adults can be evaluated through the series of
national health surveys conducted in 1960–1962,
1971–1974, 1976–1980, and 1988–1991, as
shown in Table 11–6.[18] Results were adjusted
for differences in laboratory methods across
surveys. For the total population sampled in
1960–1962, the mean serum total cholesterol
concentration was 220 mg/dl, well above the
current criterion to distinguish borderline-high
from desirable levels. By 1988–1991 this value
had decreased to 205, an overall decrease of
15mg/dl, of which about one-half occurred in
the decade between the late 1970s and late
1980s. Decreases occurred in all race-sex and
sex-age groups but were most striking for men
at ages 35–44 and for women at ages 55–74.

Population Differences in Blood Lipid Distributions

Differences between populations in distributions of total cholesterol concentration were
recognized several decades ago and were
emphasized especially by Keys, as illustrated
for clinically healthy men in Figure 11–2.[19] The
contrast between age patterns of cholesterol
concentration between the two lower curves
from Japan and the others from Berlin, New

Table 11–5 Blood Lipid Concentrations in Children at Age 8–10, by Sex and Ethnicity, Children's Activity Trial for Cardiovascular Health (CATCH)

Measure [a]	Gender	Ethnicity [b]	N	Mean (mg/dl)	SD	Percentile		P values, Ethnicity			P values, Gender
						10th	90th	W-B	B-H	W-H	
TC	M	W	131	167.4	28.2	131.5	207.3	0.01			0.55
		B	40	180.2	29.8	149.6	218.5		0.15		0.25
		H	31	170.1	24.7	136.1	203.8			0.61	0.83
	F	W	121	165.1	28.6	132.6	202.2	0.14			
		B	41	172.8	25.9	148.1	203.4		0.53		
		H	37	168.6	37.9	127.2	220.8			0.51	
LDL-C	M	W	131	97.8	21.7	70.8	125.7	0.49			0.44
		B	40	100.5	22.4	75.0	129.1		0.48		0.63
		H	31	104.8	21.7	70.8	133.8			0.14	0.92
	F	W	121	100.1	22.8	74.6	127.6	0.46			
		B	41	103.2	22.8	80.4	129.5		0.86		
		H	37	104.0	31.3	68.1	148.5			0.36	
VLDL-C	M	W	131	17.8	7.0	8.9	25.9	0.50			0.51
		B	40	18.6	8.9	9.3	28.2		0.07		0.12
		H	31	15.9	6.6	7.7	25.9			0.13	0.34
	F	W	121	17.4	6.2	10.1	26.7	0.44			
		B	41	16.2	6.6	9.3	27.5		0.51		
		H	37	17.4	8.9	7.3	29.0			0.95	
HDL-C	M	W	131	51.8	14.7	34.8	70.0	0.0003			0.03
		B	40	60.7	18.2	44.1	85.8		0.001		0.02
		H	31	49.9	12.4	35.2	61.9			0.51	0.53
	F	W	121	47.9	11.6	34.0	63.0	0.03			
		B	41	53.4	15.1	35.2	73.9		0.07		
		H	37	47.9	14.3	28.6	69.6			0.95	
TC/ HDL-C	M	W	131	3.43	0.93	2.38	4.75	0.10			0.20
		B	40	3.13	0.75	2.31	4.09		0.03		0.15
		H	31	3.67	1.37	2.45	4.51			0.23	0.46
	F	W	121	3.59	0.85	2.53	4.78	0.46			
		B	41	3.46	1.04	2.23	5.02		0.08		
		H	37	3.86	1.61	2.54	6.56			0.17	

a. TC, total cholesterol; LDL-C, low-density lipoprotein cholesterol; VLDL-C, very–low-density lipoprotein cholesterol; HDL-C, high-density lipoprotein cholesterol.

b. W, White; B, Black; H, Hispanic.

c. *P* values for ethnicity are specific for comparison between White and Black, Black and Hispanic, and White and Hispanic, separately by gender. *P* values for gender are specific for ethnic groups.

Source: Reprinted by JD Belcher et al, *Preventive Medicine*, Vol 22, p 148, © 1993, Academic Press, Inc.

Table 11-6 Trends in Mean Serum Cholesterol Concentration in US Adults

Serum Total Cholesterol, mg/dl (mmol/l)

Population Group	Mean				Change in Mean	
	1960–1962	1971–1974	1976–1980	1988–1991	1960–1962 to 1988–1991	1976–1980 to 1988–1991
Age 20–74 yr[a]	220 (5.69)	214 (5.53)	213 (5.51)	205 (5.30)	−15 (−0.39)	−8 (−0.21)
Race/sex[b]						
Black men	210 (5.43)	212 (5.48)	208 (5.38)	200 (5.17)	−10 (−0.26)	−8 (−0.21)
Black women	216 (5.59)	217 (5.61)	213 (5.51)	205 (5.30)	−11 (−0.28)	−8 (−0.21)
White men	218 (5.64)	213 (5.51)	211 (5.46)	205 (5.30)	−13 (−0.34)	−6 (−0.16)
White women	223 (5.77)	215 (5.56)	214 (5.53)	205 (5.30)	−18 (−0.47)	−9 (−0.23)
Sex/age, yr[a]						
Men						
20–74	217 (5.61)	213 (5.51)	211 (5.46)	205 (5.30)	−12 (−0.31)	−6 (−0.16)
20–34	198 (5.12)	194 (5.02)	192 (4.97)	189 (4.89)	−9 (−0.23)	−3 (−0.08)
35–44	227 (5.87)	221 (5.72)	217 (5.61)	207 (5.35)	−20 (−0.52)	−10 (−0.26)
45–54	231 (5.97)	229 (5.92)	227 (5.87)	218 (5.64)	−13 (−0.34)	−9 (−0.23)
55–64	233 (6.03)	229 (5.92)	229 (5.92)	221 (5.72)	12 (0.31)	−8 (−0.21)
65–74	230 (5.95)	226 (5.84)	221 (5.72)	218 (5.64)	−12 (−0.31)	−3 (−0.08)
≥75	NA[c]	NA	NA	205 (5.30)	NA	NA
Women						
20–74	222 (5.74)	215 (5.56)	214 (5.53)	205 (5.30)	−17 (−0.44)	−9 (−0.23)
20–34	194 (5.02)	191 (4.94)	189 (4.89)	185 (4.78)	−9 (−0.23)	−4 (−0.10)
35–44	214 (5.53)	207 (5.53)	207 (5.35)	195 (5.04)	−19 (−0.49)	−12 (−0.31)
45–54	237 (6.13)	232 (6.00)	232 (6.00)	217 (5.61)	−20 (−0.52)	−15 (−0.39)
55–64	262 (6.78)	245 (6.34)	249 (6.44)	237 (6.13)	−25 (−0.65)	−12 (−0.31)
65–74	266 (6.88)	250 (6.46)	246 (6.36)	234 (6.05)	−32 (−0.83)	−12 (−0.31)
≥75	NA	NA	NA	230 (5.95)	NA	NA

a. Includes race/ethnic groups not shown separately.

b. Includes Hispanic persons.

c. Data not available.

Source: Reprinted from CL Johnson et al, *Journal of the American Medical Association*, Vol 269, No 23, p 3005, 1993.

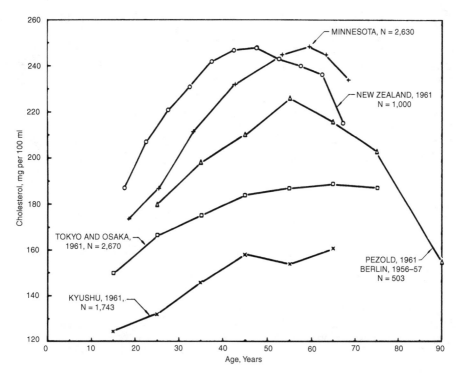

Figure 11–2 Mean Values of Serum Cholesterol Concentration by Age in Clinically Healthy Men in Selected Populations. *Source:* Reprinted with permission from A Keys, Serum Cholesterol and the Question of Normal, in *Multiple Laboratory Screening*, ES Benson and PE Strandjord, eds, p 169, © 1969, Academic Press, Inc.

Zealand, and Minnesota is striking. In each population, regardless of the absolute mean values at any age, increases with age are apparent from the 20s to the 40s or beyond. Decreasing values at older ages in the higher-level populations are also notable and could, in these cross-sectional data, reflect differences in lifetime history of the different age groups represented (cohort effects), selective mortality of older persons with the highest cholesterol concentrations, or possibly other factors. For women, comparable data were obtained from the Minnesota population. Their age curve for total cholesterol concentration also fell at the oldest ages, like that for men, but with a peak in the curve at ages about 15 years older.

In a wider range of populations studied in 1980, including Ghana, Ivory Coast, and Nigeria in Africa; Surinam in South America; Paki-

stan and the Philippines in the Pacific and Asia; and three groups in Europe (East and West Finland, and Hungary), Knuimann and colleagues found total cholesterol concentrations to vary widely among adults age 33–38 and 43–48 years (Table 11–7).[20] For example, total cholesterol concentration ranged from about 116 mg/dl (3.0 mmol/l divided by 0.02586) in Nigerian men to 247 mg/dl in East Finnish men. A twofold range in HDL-cholesterol concentrations was also found, and HDL cholesterol as a proportion of the total varied from 15%–18% in Pakistani men to 29%–32% in Ghanaians. Body mass index was positively associated with total cholesterol concentration and inversely related to HDL-cholesterol concentration across these populations.

In childhood and adolescence, too, international comparisons have been made by various

Table 11-7 Serum Lipid Concentrations and Anthropometric Data for Adult Men in 13 Countries, 1980

Country and Age Category (Years)	Sample Size	Weight (kg)	Height (cm)	Body Mass Index (kg/m^2)	Total Cholesterol (mmol/liter)	HDL Cholesterol (mmol/liter)	HDL Cholesterol/ Total Cholesterol
Africa							
Ghana							
33–38	40	60 ± 8	167 ± 6	21.5 ± 2.1	4.3 ± 1.0	1.31 ± 0.30	0.32 ± 0.08
43–48	36	61 ± 8	170 ± 7	21.3 ± 2.8	3.9 ± 1.0	1.13 ± 0.42	0.29 ± 0.08
Ivory Coast							
33–38	80	66 ± 7	169 ± 6	23.1 ± 2.3	4.0 ± 0.8	1.14 ± 0.32	0.30 ± 0.09
43–48	80	65 ± 8	167 ± 7	23.5 ± 2.8	4.2 ± 0.8	1.20 ± 0.33	0.29 ± 0.09
Nigeria							
33–38	40	60 ± 6	169 ± 5	20.8 ± 1.8	3.1 ± 0.6	0.81 ± 0.22	0.26 ± 0.07
43–48	40	62 ± 7	169 ± 5	21.9 ± 1.9	3.0 ± 0.6	0.84 ± 0.22	0.29 ± 0.08
America							
Surinam							
33–38	40	67 ± 9	169 ± 6	23.5 ± 3.7	5.3 ± 1.0	1.06 ± 0.28	0.21 ± 0.06
43–48	39	66 ± 10	169 ± 6	23.2 ± 3.0	5.3 ± 1.1	1.08 ± 0.30	0.21 ± 0.08
Asia							
Pakistan							
33–38	39	70 ± 9	166 ± 5	25.5 ± 3.4	4.4 ± 1.0	0.76 ± 0.22	0.18 ± 0.03
43–48	39	75 ± 7	165 ± 5	27.5 ± 2.6	5.1 ± 1.0	0.71 ± 0.19	0.15 ± 0.05
Philippines							
33–38	39	61 ± 9	164 ± 6	22.7 ± 3.2	4.6 ± 1.0	0.98 ± 0.22	0.22 ± 0.07
43–48	40	57 ± 8	162 ± 5	21.8 ± 3.0	5.0 ± 1.1	1.06 ± 0.30	0.22 ± 0.07
Europe							
E. Finland							
33–38	41	78 ± 9	174 ± 6	25.9 ± 2.8	6.3 ± 1.1	1.32 ± 0.42	0.22 ± 0.09
43–48	40	77 ± 12	170 ± 7	26.6 ± 4.0	6.4 ± 1.2	1.50 ± 0.36	0.24 ± 0.07
W. Finland							
33–38	38	78 ± 9	177 ± 6	25.0 ± 2.5	5.9 ± 1.2	1.39 ± 0.36	0.25 ± 0.10
43–48	38	80 ± 9	175 ± 8	26.2 ± 2.5	6.2 ± 1.0	1.38 ± 0.38	0.23 ± 0.07

continues

Table 11-7 continued

Country and Age Category (Years)	Sample Size	Weight (kg)	Height (cm)	Body Mass Index (kg/m^2)	Total Cholesterol (mmol/liter)	HDL Cholesterol (mmol/liter)	HDL Cholesterol/ Total Cholesterol
Hungary							
33–38	33	74 ± 9	177 ± 5	24.6 ± 2.8	5.2 ± 1.0	1.41 ± 0.31	0.28 ± 0.08
43–48	18	75 ± 7	175 ± 8	24.6 ± 2.4	5.3 ± 0.8	1.43 ± 0.26	0.28 ± 0.07
Italy							
33–38	38	74 ± 9	168 ± 6	26.1 ± 2.6	5.1 ± 0.8	1.22 ± 0.38	0.24 ± 0.08
43–48	26	73 ± 11	167 ± 6	26.2 ± 4.2	5.3 ± 1.0	1.15 ± 0.28	0.23 ± 0.08
Netherlands							
33–38	41	77 ± 8	178 ± 5	24.5 ± 2.4	5.6 ± 1.0	1.18 ± 0.27	0.22 ± 0.08
43–48	42	80 ± 9	176 ± 7	25.7 ± 2.6	5.8 ± 1.1	1.10 ± 0.31	0.20 ± 0.07
Poland							
33–38	40	74 ± 9	170 ± 5	25.7 ± 2.6	4.8 ± 0.9	1.27 ± 0.30	0.28 ± 0.09
43–48	40	77 ± 9	170 ± 6	26.6 ± 3.1	5.1 ± 0.9	1.13 ± 0.34	0.23 ± 0.08
Portugal							
33–38	40	68 ± 9	166 ± 7	24.7 ± 2.9	5.4 ± 1.1	1.27 ± 0.40	0.24 ± 0.07
43–48	37	69 ± 11	165 ± 6	25.3 ± 3.6	5.1 ± 0.9	1.41 ± 0.52	0.28 ± 0.09
Spain							
33–38	39	75 ± 11	169 ± 6	26.1 ± 3.7	5.3 ± 1.0	1.19 ± 0.24	0.23 ± 0.08
43–48	39	73 ± 8	167 ± 7	26.1 ± 2.4	5.5 ± 0.9	1.21 ± 0.29	0.23 ± 0.06

Note: All results are expressed as mean ± SD (standard deviation). 1 mmol/liter = 38.7 mg/dl.

Source: Reprinted with permission from JT Knuiman, CE West, and J Burema, *American Journal of Epidemiology,* Vol 116, No 4, p 636, © 1982, The Johns Hopkins University School of Hygiene and Public Health.

researchers, as recently reviewed.[21] Age patterns are shown in Figure 11–3 for four populations in which data were reported for specific age groups, most informatively by single year of age. Clearly, very sharp increases occur from birth to age 1, as also found in other data, and mean values by age appear rather stable within each population across the school-age years. However, closer evaluation reveals a systematic pattern of a decrease and subsequent increase in total cholesterol concentration in adolescence in each population, though with some population differences in ages at the inflection points in the curve. This pattern of variation in total cholesterol concentration with age, and its difference by about one year in timing between sexes, is sufficient to raise concern about screening criteria in youth, as noted above.[22]

POPULATION RATES

The question of how the blood lipid profile relates to population differences in risk of coronary heart disease or other complications of atherosclerosis can be addressed almost exclusively by reference to total cholesterol concentration. This is because at the inception of the long-term follow-up studies contributing such information only total cholesterol determination was both practical and widely regarded as important. This is the case, for example, in the Seven Countries Study, which is uniquely valuable for such population comparisons.[23] The 10-year mortality experience in that study shows the relation between coronary heart disease death rates and median serum total cholesterol concentration for each population across the 16

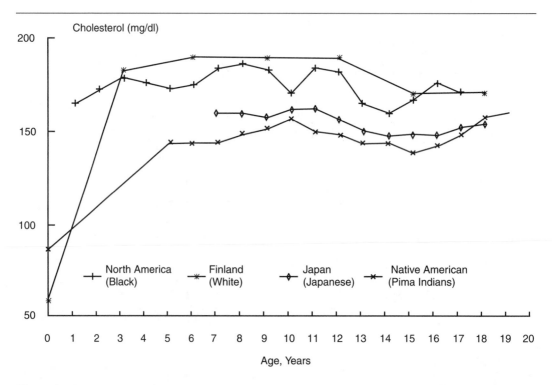

Figure 11–3 Mean Values of Serum Total Cholesterol Concentration among US Black, White, Japanese, and Native American Male Children and Adolescents, Aged 0–19 Years. *Source:* Reprinted with permission from D Labarthe, B O'Brien, and K Dunn, International Comparisons of Plasma Cholesterol and Lipoproteins, in *Hyperlipidemia in Childhood and the Development of Artherosclerosis*, CL Williams and EL Wynder, eds, Vol 623, p 117, © 1991, Annals of the New York Academy of Sciences.

cohorts of men age 40–59 years at entry, in the late 1950s to mid-1960s (Figure 11–4). Chol-e2sterol values ranged from about 160 mg/dl to 265 mg/dl, and coronary mortality varied from 1/1000 or less in Crete (K) to about 70/1000 in East Finland (E). The resulting regression equation indicates the positive coefficient for the relation between cholesterol concentration and coronary mortality. A correlation coefficient calculated with adjustment for age, systolic blood pressure, and smoking history was 0.82; the square of this value indicates the proportion of variation in rates among populations accounted for by median cholesterol concentration, approximately 67%. As is evident in this figure and as noted by Keys, there was little relation with population differences in mortality

when cholesterol concentrations were below 200 mg/dl or 220 mg/dl. In general, however, within-population relationships were strong at levels above 200 mg/dl, except in the lowest-rate populations.

Further follow-up of the Seven Countries Study cohorts to 25 years permitted more-detailed analysis, given greater numbers of events, especially when cohorts were grouped on the basis of geography, culture, and patterns of interim change in cholesterol concentration.[24] Figure 11–5 illustrates the results of analysis by quartiles of baseline serum total cholesterol concentration. Coronary mortality increased with baseline cholesterol concentration in every group of populations except Japan, especially steeply for the higher observed cholesterol val-

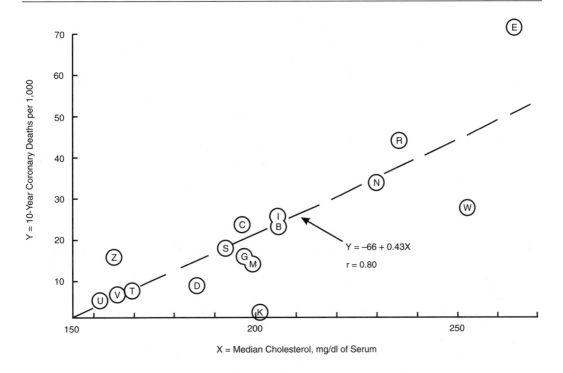

Note: B, Belgrade; C, Crevalcore; D, Dalmatia; E, East Finland; G, Corfu; I, Italian Railroad; K, Crete; M, Montegiorgio; N, Zutphen; R, American Railroad; S, Slavonia; T, Tanushimaru; U, Ushibuka; V, Velika Krsna; W, West Finland; Z, Zrenjanin.

Figure 11–4 Ten-Year Coronary Death Rates and Median Serum Cholesterol Concentration. *Source:* Reprinted by permission of the publisher from *Seven Countries* by A Keys, Cambridge, Mass: Harvard University Press, Copyright © 1980 by the President and Fellows of Harvard College.

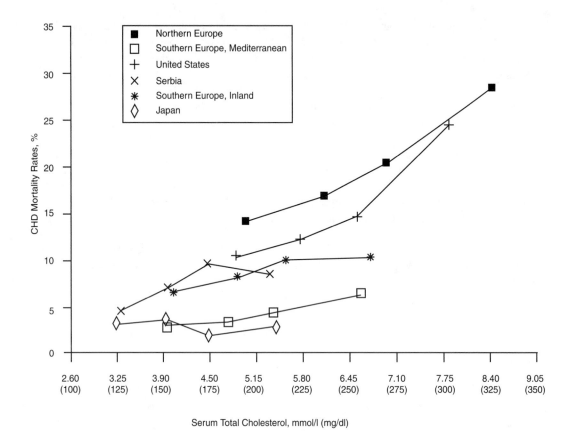

Figure 11–5 Twenty-Five–Year Coronary Death and Quartiles of Serum Cholesterol Concentration, Adjusted for Age, Cigarette Smoking, and Systolic Blood Pressure. *Source:* Reprinted with permission from WMM Verschuren et al, *Journal of the American Medical Association*, Vol 274, p 131, © 1995.

ues. Further analysis took advantage of the repeated cholesterol determinations in most of the cohorts, at a five-year follow-up examination, to estimate and adjust for misclassification due to measurement variability. This latter analysis showed, for all cohorts taken together, an overall average increase of 17% in coronary mortality for an increment of 20 mg/dl in median cholesterol concentration (relative risk 1.12, 95% confidence interval 1.09–1.16; risk estimate after adjustment, 1.17). The figure also shows wide population differences in mortality at fixed levels of cholesterol concentration, which overlap across regions at levels from between 175 mg/dl and 200 mg/dl to between

250 mg/dl and 275 mg/dl. The range in mortality for a fixed cholesterol concentration was threefold or greater and indicates the collective influence of factors other than age, smoking, and systolic blood pressure, for which adjustment was made in the analysis.

INDIVIDUAL RISKS

Total cholesterol concentration was also measured in each of the cohort studies included in the US Pooling Project, with results as shown in Table 11–8.[25] Among 8274 men age 40–59 years at entry, 647 events were recorded over 8.6 years of follow-up. The data are presented

Table 11–8 Serum Cholesterol: Parameters of the Bivariate Model for First Major Coronary Events, Pooling Project

Quintile and Level (mg/dl)		Pool 5	ALB	CH-GAS	CH-WE	FRAM	TECUM	LA	MI-EX	MI-RR
		Study Group								
		Standardized Incidence Ratio								
All		100	100	100	100	100	100	100	100	100
I + II	≤218	66	70	79	60	62	49	(42)	70	49
I	≤194	72	72	100	62	74	(10)	(37)	(64)	(47)
II	194–218	61	67	61	57	50	(83)	(46)	(78)	50
III	218–240	78	72	89	70	88	(56)	116	(117)	77
IV	240–268	129	129	124	99	160	145	73	(117)	96
V	>268	158	177	118	159	167	242	143	(189)	194
Risk ratio: V/(I+II)		2.4	2.5	1.5	2.7	2.7	4.9	( )	( )	4.0
95% confidence interval:	low	1.9	1.7	0.9	1.7	1.7	2.0	( )	( )	3.4
	high	2.9	3.8	2.4	4.6	4.0	13.1	( )	( )	7.6
Number of men at risk		8,274	1,765	1,264	1,980	2,130	1,135	1,104	283	2,551
Person-years of experience		70,781	16,878	11,064	16,505	19,480	6,854	10,137	4,008	12,484
Number of first events		647	156	123	142	177	49	72	28	112

Note: ( ), Based on fewer than 10 first events; ALB, Albany Civil Servants; CH-GAS, Chicago Gas Company; CH-WE, Chicago Western Electric Company; FRAM, Framingham; TECUM, Tecumseh, Michigan; LA, Los Angeles Civil Servants; MI-EX, Minnesota Businessmen; MI-RR, Minnesota Railroad Workers.

Source: Reprinted with permission from *Journal of Chronic Diseases*, The Pooling Project Research Group, Vol 31, p 230, © 1978, Elsevier Science, Inc.

first for the standard pool of the five most comparable studies, together and separately (Albany, Chicago Gas, Chicago Western Electric, Framingham, Tecumseh), and then for the three remaining studies (Los Angeles, Minnesota executives, Minnesota Railroad workers). For each quintile category of baseline serum total cholesterol concentration, the incidence of first major coronary events is expressed as the ratio (times 100) of that rate to the overall rate in the total group. Thus, incidence less than the population average results in a standardized incidence ratio below 100, and conversely for greater than average incidence. For example, the standardized incidence ratio for the lowest quintile of total cholesterol concentration (below 195 mg/dl) was 72, whereas that for the highest quintile (greater than 268 mg/dl) was 158. It was noted that for several of the cohorts, and all of those in Pool 5, the lowest incidence ratio was in the second, not the first, quintile of cholesterol concentration. Therefore the overall risk ratios were defined arbitrarily by relating incidence for quintile group V to that for quintile groups I and II combined. This risk ratio was 2.4 for Pool 5 and varied from 1.5 to 4.9 among studies. The 95% confidence intervals, having lower limits greater than 1 in all but one study, indicated that the results were not consistent with absence of association.

Based on the follow-up of men screened for the Multiple Risk Factor Intervention Trial, more-detailed analysis of this relation was possible.[26] This very large study population of 361,662 men with, on average, six years of follow-up could be grouped in 20 units of 5 percentile levels, in contrast to the 5 units of 20 percentiles in the Pooling Project example. This offers much greater resolution in examination of risk gradients, as shown in Figure 11–6. From the extreme values of 150 to nearly 300 mg/dl in cholesterol concentration, an exponential pattern of increasing risk was observed. Minimum risk was at the lowest levels, in contrast to the Pooling Project findings. The risk ratio between the highest and lowest of the 20 strata would be greater than 4 on the basis of this analysis.

A study of the longer-term prediction of cardiovascular disease occurrence from much earlier in adulthood (ie, baseline median age 22) was reported from the 27- to 42-year follow-up of medical students in Johns Hopkins University.[27] The predictive value of cholesterol concentration was again demonstrated, though event rates increased sharply only after 20 years of follow-up. As shown in Figure 11–7, the lowest quartile group of baseline cholesterol concentration (118–172 mg/dl) was found to have the lowest cardiovascular disease incidence rates, still reaching 10%, whereas rates for the highest quartile group (209–315 mg/dl) reached nearly 40%.

The data cited above pertain only to total cholesterol concentration in men, chiefly White men of middle age. Additional information, though much less extensive, addresses the situation of women with respect to the relation of adverse blood lipid profiles to atherosclerosis. In women, age-specific mean values of LDL cholesterol have been described as lower than those in men until ages in the 50s, after which cholesterol levels of males are exceeded. This reflects rising concentrations in women from the mid-30s and their attainment, on average, of a plateau in levels in the late 50s that is higher than the average levels reached by men at any age. Throughout the age span from the 20s through the 70s, women have slightly higher HDL-cholesterol concentrations on average than do men. It has been suggested that, while in general both LDL and HDL cholesterol relate to coronary risk in women as in men, the inverse risk gradient for HDL cholesterol is stronger for women and that LDL cholesterol of a given level may be less atherogenic for women.[28]

As noted previously, the implication of HDL cholesterol as having an independent and inverse relation to risk of coronary heart disease has long antecedents, as early as 1951, as reviewed in a 1977 report on coronary heart disease in five diverse populations.[29] This report,

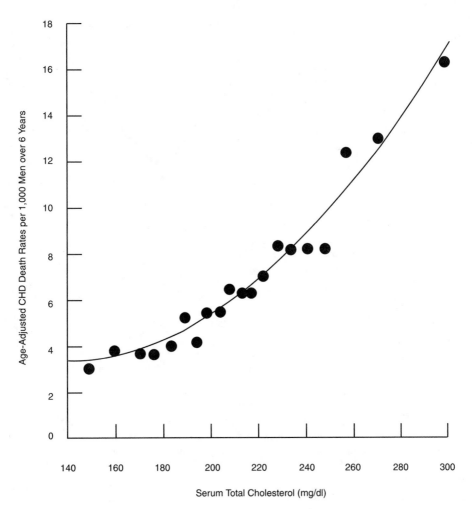

Figure 11–6 Serum Cholesterol Concentration and 6-Year Mortality from Coronary Heart Disease (CHD), Multiple Risk Factor Intervention Trial Screenees Aged 35–57 Years. Each point represents the median value for 5% of the population. *Source:* Reprinted with permission from MJ Martin et al, Serum Cholesterol, Blood Pressure, and Mortality: Implications from a Cohort of 361,662 Men, *Lancet*, Vol 2, pp 933–936, © 1986, The Lancet, Ltd.

from the Cooperative Lipoprotein Phenotyping Study, compared blood lipid concentrations, including total, HDL and LDL cholesterol, and triglycerides, between cases of coronary heart disease and control subjects age 40 years and older in men from cohort studies in Albany, New York; Framingham, Massachusetts; Honolulu, Hawaii; San Francisco, California; and Evans County, Georgia, and in women from Framingham and Evans County. The men stud- ied in Honolulu were of Japanese ancestry, and the men and women in Evans County included both Blacks and Whites. Comparing mean val- ues of the blood concentration for each lipid component between cases and controls for each population, the investigators reported signifi- cant inverse relations for the combined age groups in four of six study populations for men and two of three populations for women. Pool- ing all data, they also found an inverse relation

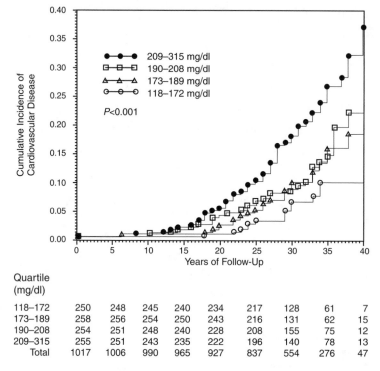

Quartile (mg/dl)								
118–172	250	248	245	240	234	217	128	61	7
173–189	258	256	254	250	243	216	131	62	15
190–208	254	251	248	240	228	208	155	75	12
209–315	255	251	243	235	222	196	140	78	13
Total	1017	1006	990	965	927	837	554	276	47

Note: To convert values for cholesterol to mmol/l, multiply by 0.02586. The numbers below the figure are the numbers of men included in the analysis at each point.

Figure 11–7 Forty-Year Cumulative Incidence of Cardiovascular Disease in 1,017 White Men Following Baseline Serum Cholesterol Determination at Median Age 22. *Source:* Reprinted with permission from MJ Klag et al, Serum Cholesterol in Young Men and Subsequent Cardiovascular Disease, *The New England Journal of Medicine*, Vol 328, No 5, pp 313–318, Copyright 1993 Massachusetts Medical Society. All rights reserved.

between HDL-cholesterol concentration and prevalence of coronary heart disease in the several populations. The authors noted that the case-control comparisons were more nearly consistent for the inverse relation of HDL cholesterol than for the positive associations with total and LDL cholesterol and triglyceride concentrations.

Additional data on coronary heart disease in relation to blood lipids in women, older age groups, and Blacks variously include reports from such studies as the Framingham Heart Study, the Tecumseh Community Health Study, and the Evans County Heart Study. The Framingham Study reported an analysis of trends in decreasing incidence and mortality

from coronary heart disease in three cohorts of men and women each followed for 20 years from a baseline examination at ages 50–59 years.[30] For both women and men, mortality declined significantly, but only for women did incidence rates do so. Parallel trends in total cholesterol concentration were significant for women, based on lower values at baseline and at the 10-year follow-up for those examined in 1970 versus 1960 or 1950. For men, only those in the 1970 cohort, and only at the 10-year follow-up, had cholesterol concentrations significantly lower than in the earlier observations. The Tecumseh Study of men and women followed since baseline examination between 1959 and 1965 found that cholesterol concentration related inconsistently to coronary heart disease and total mortality when examined separately by sex and age (45–64 and 65+ years).[31] Relative risks for both outcomes were irregular with increasing cholesterol concentration in women in both age groups. The gradient in classes of cholesterol concentration was significantly related to coronary death in men alone and not related to total mortality. The Evans County Study included Black and White men and women first examined between 1960 and 1962.[32] Among participants age 65 years or older at entry, coronary heart disease mortality was related to total cholesterol concentration in White men (relative risk 1.54 for each increment of 40 mg/dl, *P* <0.05) but not in women or Black men. These observations illustrate the absence of association between coronary risk and cholesterol concentration within some populations. As discussed in Chapter 8, Dietary Imbalance, analysis of the exceptionally detailed data from the Chicago Western Electric Study demonstrated the limitation of single-occasion measurement of cholesterol concentration, due to intraindividual variability, and the presence of within-population associations when repeated measures permit adjustment for this source of error. This may explain the lack of association in the Tecumseh and Evans County data.

The relation of blood lipids to risk of cardiovascular diseases is not limited to cholesterol concentrations with coronary heart disease, although such associations have been investigated much more extensively than others. Total cholesterol concentration was related to risk of stroke, for example, in the analysis of data specific for thromboembolic stroke from the Multiple Risk Factor Intervention Trial screenees presented in Chapter 5. Lp(a) concentration has been found to predict coronary heart disease in men and women, as illustrated in a cohort study from Rochester, Minnesota.[33] When nearly 10,000 men and women were followed for 15 years, strong gradients of risk of both coronary heart disease and stroke with increasing Lp(a) concentration at baseline were found for women

(nearly threefold) and weaker gradients for men (1.5- to 1.7-fold), though all were statistically significant trends. As summarized by Sullivan, several other cardiovascular conditions have been found to be associated with Lp(a) concentration: carotid atherosclerosis, peripheral arterial disease, coronary artery bypass graft occlusion, and others.[6] ApoE genotype predicts coronary artery disease in men and women, according to a recent meta-analysis of 14 clinical and angiographic studies.[7] Among the six possible genotypes by paired combination of the three alleles ($\epsilon2$, $\epsilon3$, $\epsilon4$), the presence of the $\epsilon4$ allele, compared with the $\epsilon3/\epsilon3$ genotype, resulted in an overall relative risk of coronary heart disease of 1.38 (confidence interval [CI] 1.22–1.57) for men and 1.82 (CI 1.30–2.54) for women.

PREVENTION AND CONTROL

Population-Wide Strategy

Population-wide measures for prevention and control of blood lipids have been included in recommendations from national and regional organizations as well as the World Health Organization. The evolution of these recommendations is reviewed in Chapter 22. The World Health Assembly in 1976 adopted a resolution calling for development of a comprehensive research program and for coordination of international activities in prevention of coronary heart disease. In keeping with that charge, an Expert Committee, convened in late 1981, addressed this topic by reviewing concepts of prevention at the population and individual levels, outlining elements of the population-wide strategy in particular—including reference to the problem in developing countries—and offering recommendations for program implementation.[34] Directly relevant here are the conclusions and recommendations concerning blood lipids:

1. attainment of a population mean value of total cholesterol concentration less than 200 mg/dl by reduction of saturated fat intake to less than 10% of energy intake and of dietary cholesterol intake to less than 300 mg/day and by avoidance of obesity
2. increase in habitual physical activity for several purposes, including reduction of cholesterol concentration
3. beginning intervention in youth to avert the development of elevated blood cholesterol concentrations in the first place

Special emphasis on prevention beginning in youth was reflected in a subsequent Expert Committee report that addressed other major cardiovascular diseases as well as atherosclerotic and hypertensive diseases.[35] Again the population-wide approach was emphasized, and recommendations included modifying dietary patterns to reduce intake of saturated fat and cholesterol, increasing the intake of complex carbohydrates, and avoiding or correcting overweight, all for the purpose of reducing undesirable cholesterol concentrations or averting them in the first place.

Similarly, in the United States detailed recommendations have been developed by the National Cholesterol Education Program for control of blood lipids in order to prevent atherosclerosis and its complications, both in adults and in children and adolescents. The *Report of the Expert Panel on Population Strategies for Blood Cholesterol Reduction* presents recommendations in 11 areas, as follows[36]:

1. nutrient intake—quantitative goals for fats and cholesterol
2. eating patterns—food choices to promote the desired nutrient intake, along with attention to other risk factors
3. healthy children and adolescents—adoption of similar eating patterns from age two
4. special groups—general application of the above recommendations to all (women, elderly, diverse ethnic groups, low-income groups) with special considerations when appropriate
5. health professionals—their role in communicating these recommendations
6. the food industry—support to make foods lower in saturated and total fats and cholesterol more readily available and better labeled and advertised
7. mass media—publicity for the desired eating pattern
8. government—adoption of appropriate policies
9. educational systems—enhanced dissemination of information supporting the desired eating patterns in a consistent way between official education agencies and health organizations
10. measurement of blood cholesterol—assurance of high-quality standards for cholesterol screening
11. research and surveillance—continuing investigation of relations between food and health and revision of guidelines accordingly

Effectively implemented, these recommendations would be expected to reduce the prevalence of adverse blood lipid profiles among older and younger adults and prevent their initial development in youth and young adults.

High-Risk Strategy

Individual approaches to blood lipid control are addressed in the *Second Report of the National Cholesterol Education Program (NCEP) Expert Panel on Detection, Evaluation, and Treatment of High Blood Cholesterol in Adults (Adult Treatment Panel II)*, and in the *Report of the Expert Panel on Blood Cholesterol Levels in Children and Adolescents*.[9,10] The classification of blood lipid levels proposed in these reports was discussed above. The scheme for adult screening, confirmation, and treatment is summarized in Figures 11–8 and 11–9 and Table 11–9.[9] Initial screening in the nonfasting state includes measurement of total and HDL-

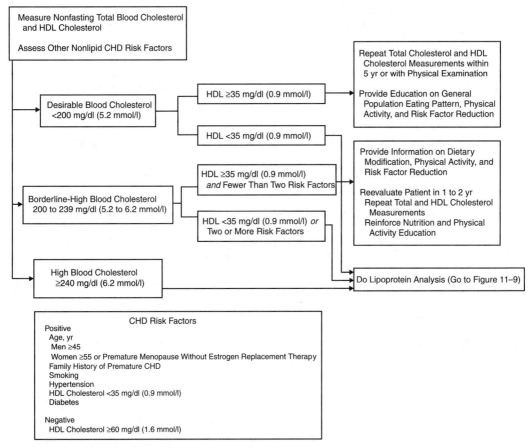

Note: HDL, high-density lipoprotein; CHD, coronary heart disease.

Figure 11–8 Blood Lipid Levels (Total and HDL Cholesterol) and Risk Factors in Initial Classification of Adults for Blood Lipid Evaluation, Adult Treatment Panel II. *Source:* Reprinted from Expert Panel on Detection, Evaluation and Treatment of High Blood Cholesterol in Adults, *Journal of the American Medical Association*, Vol 274, p 3018, 1993.

cholesterol concentrations and assessment of additional risk factors. Several actions may follow, as dictated by the specific combination of findings. The process may begin with lipoprotein analysis or continue, if indicated, from primary nonfasting screening. The focus at this stage is on LDL-cholesterol concentration, which becomes the basis for goals and evaluation if treatment is needed. As shown in the table, dietary and, if necessary, drug treatment are initiated and targeted for either persons without existing coronary heart disease (with or without two or more other risk factors) and for

persons with coronary heart disease (details of classification procedure not shown).

For children and adolescents, analogous assessment is performed, but selectively on the basis of family history, as shown in Figures 11–10 and 11–11.[10] Persons to be screened are only those who have a positive history of coronary atherosclerosis by arteriography; evidence of coronary, cerebral, or peripheral vascular disease or sudden cardiac death, all before age 55 years in a parent or grandparent; or a parental history of total cholesterol concentration of 240 mg/dl or higher. Advancing across the classifi-

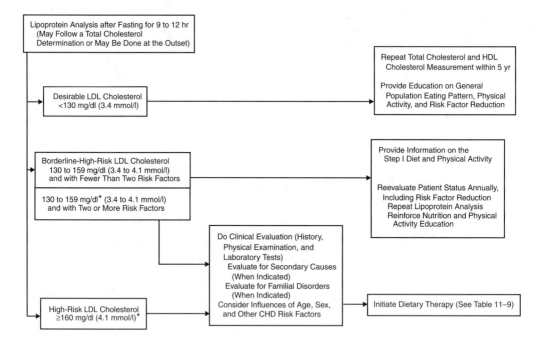

Note: HDL, high-density lipoprotein; LDL, low-density lipoprotein; CHD, coronary heart disease.

* On the basis of the average of two determinations. If the first two LDL-cholesterol test results differ by more than 30 mg/dl (0.7 mmol/l), a third test result should be obtained within 1 to 8 weeks, and the average value of the three tests should be used.

Figure 11–9 Blood Lipid Levels (LDL Cholesterol) in Classification of Adults for Treatment of Blood Lipids, Adult Lipid Panel II. *Source:* Reprinted from Expert Panel on Detection, Evaluation and Treatment of High Blood Cholesterol in Adults, *Journal of the American Medical Association*, Vol 274, p 3019, 1993.

Table 11–9 Treatment Decisions for Lowering LDL Cholesterol, Adult Treatment Panel

Patient Category	Initiation Level	LDL Goal
Dietary Therapy		
Without CHD and with fewer than two risk factors	≥160 mg/dl (4.1 mmol/l)	<160 mg/dl (4.1 mmol/l)
Without CHD and with two or more risk factors	≥130 mg/dl (3.4 mmol/l)	<130 mg/dl (3.4 mmol/l)
With CHD	>100 mg/dl (2.6 mmol/l)	≤100 mg/dl (2.6 mmol/l)
Drug Treatment		
Without CHD and with fewer than two risk factors	≥190 mg/dl (4.9 mmol/l)	<160 mg/dl (4.1 mmol/l)
Without CHD and with two or more risk factors	≥160 mg/dl (4.1 mmol/l)	<130 mg/dl (3.4 mmol/l)
With CHD	≥130 mg/dl (3.4 mmol/l)	≤100 mg/dl (2.6 mmol/l)

Note: LDL, low-density lipoprotein; CHD, coronary heart disease.

Source: Reprinted with permission from *Journal of the American Medical Association*, Vol 269, No 23, p 3020, 1993.

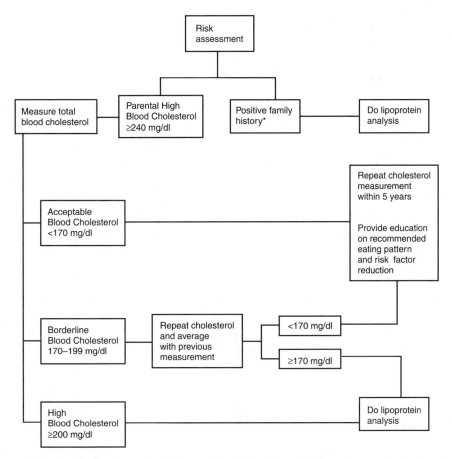

*Defined as a history of premature (before age 55 years) cardiovascular disease in a parent or grandparent.

Figure 11–10 Blood Lipid Levels (Total Cholesterol) in Initial Classification of Children and Adolescents for Blood Lipid Evaluation. *Source:* Reprinted from National Cholesterol Education Program, NIH Publication No. 91-2732, National Heart, Lung and Blood Institute, National Institutes of Health, 1991.

cation scheme to the stage of treatment, those with borderline or high LDL cholesterol are to be treated with diet (Step-One Diet initially, or Step Two if the response is inadequate and further reduction of saturated fat and cholesterol intake is advised); later, only as a last resort, drugs are used for those unresponsive to diet and aged 10 or older. These measures may be considered as potentially reducing the risk of those with borderline or high cholesterol concentrations, whether measured as total or LDL cholesterol, and with some evidence for a familial blood lipid disorder, since all must have a positive family history as a prerequisite for screening. The Expert Panel emphasized that the primary strategy for blood lipid control in childhood and adolescence is the population strategy and that the high-risk approach is intended only for those with the strongest presumption of future risk.

EFFECTS OF INTERVENTION ON RATES AND RISKS OF EVENTS

Population Changes in Mortality

At the population level in the United States, it is clear that age-specific death rates from coro-

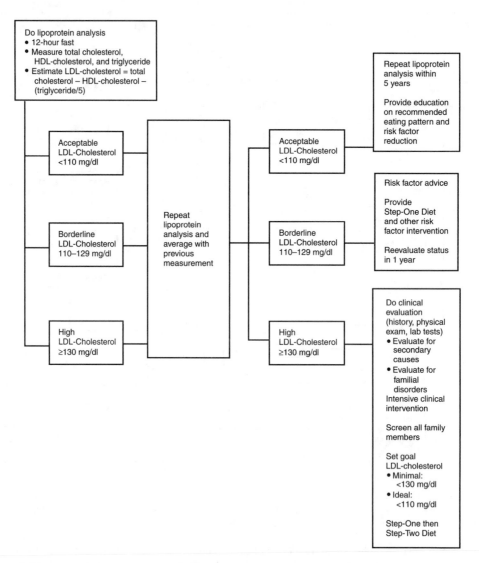

Figure 11–11 Blood Lipid Levels (LDL Cholesterol) in Classification for Treatment in Children and Adolescents. *Source:* Reprinted from National Cholesterol Education Program, NIH Publication No. 91-2732, National Heart, Lung and Blood Institute, National Institutes of Health, 1991.

nary heart disease have declined while decreases have occurred in mean total cholesterol concentration. Mortality has declined continuously from the mid-1960s to the early 1990s, and national surveys beginning from the period 1960–1962 have shown declining mean total cholesterol concentrations in all intervals for Whites and the recent ones for Blacks. Whether coronary mortality has ceased its decline and

whether the second phase of the Third National Health and Nutrition Examination Survey and future surveys will show a similar change in trend in cholesterol values remain to be seen. Trend analyses from the World Health Organization MONICA Study, which was designed specifically to test hypotheses concerning such relationships, will appear soon and are awaited with interest.

Secondary Prevention Trials

At the individual level, the effect of cholesterol reduction on risks of coronary heart disease has been investigated in many trials. The earliest of these were drug trials conducted among groups at very high risk: men with previous myocardial infarction. Recurrent infarction and death were the outcomes against which treatment was evaluated. The Coronary Drug Project was a prototype for subsequent treatment trials in the United States and the most extensive undertaken up to the time of its initiation in 1965.[37] It involved 53 clinical centers and recruitment of 8341 participants for random allocation to one of its five active treatment arms or the placebo control group. High- and low-dose conjugated estrogens, clofibrate, dextrothyroxine, and niacin were known to have cholesterol-lowering effects, but their efficacy and safety for coronary heart disease prevention were still in very early stages of investigation. The high- and (later) low-dose estrogen treatments were discontinued in the course of the trial due to excess adverse events or lack of benefit. At the scheduled completion of the trial, neither clofibrate nor niacin was found to confer benefit in reducing mortality. However, after extended posttrial follow-up, there was a significantly lower mortality among niacin-treated patients than placebo controls. Despite this finding, Borhani concluded in a 1985 review that secondary prevention by means of lipid-lowering regimens was ineffective in reducing mortality.[38]

With more recent pharmaceutical developments, the picture has changed, to the extent that Brown and Goldstein, Nobel laureates for their work on lipid transport, forecast the disappearance of coronary heart disease as a public health problem early in the next century.[39] While this view appears overly optimistic in the face of the large forces underlying epidemic coronary heart disease, it does convey the enthusiasm with which the "statins," or inhibitors of an enzyme involved in cholesterol synthesis, have been greeted on the basis of favorable trial results.

Two of these trials, the Scandinavian Simvastatin Survival Study (4S)[40] and the Cholesterol and Recurrent Events (CARE) trial,[41] were in men and women survivors of previous myocardial infarction, with mean baseline cholesterol concentrations of approximately 260 mg/dl (reported as 6.74–6.75 mmol/l) in 4S and 209 mg/dl in CARE. In 4S, all-cause mortality was 8% in the active treatment group and 12% in the placebo control group, a difference of 30% or relative risk of 0.70 (CI 0.58–0.85). Coronary events were significantly less frequent in the simvastatin group, and strokes were fewer (2.7% versus 4.3%) but not tested statistically. Women experienced significantly fewer coronary events with treatment (14.5% versus 21.7%) but a similar frequency of deaths. In CARE, the combined fatal and nonfatal myocardial infarction rate was 10.2% in the treatment group and 13.2% in controls, a difference of 24% (CI 9–36%). Other end points, including stroke, were significantly less frequent in the pravastatin group, and benefit was significant in both women and men and in those aged 60 or above as well as younger participants. No significant difference in all-cause mortality was observed, although deaths were 9% fewer in the active treatment group. It is important to note that, despite the importance of these findings, in neither trial was mortality reduced by as much as one-half. Recalling that survival of the initial coronary event was necessary to be eligible for either study, one must recognize that the majority of deaths from acute coronary events and related causes were not preventable by even this major advance in treatment.

Primary Prevention Trials

Primary prevention trials have also been conducted and were reviewed for the National Research Council report, *Diet and Health*, as shown in Tables 11–10 and 11–11.[3] Conducted over an interval of nearly 15 years, until the mid-1980s, these studies differed widely in

Table 11–10 Trials on Primary Prevention of Coronary Heart Disease (CHD), Including Cholesterol Lowering by Diet or Drugs: Design

Study	Study Population	Double Blind	Interventions and Targets of Interventions
Göteborg Multifactor Trial	20,015 men ages 47 to 55	No	Diet, cigarette smoking, high blood pressure
WHO Multifactor Trial	66 employed groups totaling 49,781 men ages 40 to 59	No	Diet, cigarette smoking, high blood pressure
Multiple Risk Factor Intervention Trial	12,886 high-risk men ages 35 to 57	No	Diet, cigarette smoking, high blood pressure
Lipid Research Clinics Coronary Primary Prevention Trial	3,806 hypercholesterolemic men ages 35 to 59	Yes	Cholestyramine
WHO Clofibrate Trial	11,627 hypercholesterolemic men ages 30 to 59	Yes	Clofibrate
Helsinki Heart Study	4,081 hypercholesterolemic men ages 40 to 55	Yes	Gemfibrozil
Los Angeles Veterans Administration Domiciliary Study	846 men ages 55 to 89	Yes	Diet only
Oslo Study	1,232 hypercholesterolemic normotensive men ages 40 to 49	No	Diet, cigarette smoking
Finnish Mental Hospital Study	2 mental hospitals totaling 4,178 male patients and 6,434 female patients ages 15 and older	No	Diet only

Source: Reprinted with permission from *Diet and Health: Implications for Reducing Chronic Disease Risk.* Copyright 1989 by the National Academy of Sciences. Courtesy of the National Academy Press, Washington, DC.

design, including the entry levels of cholesterol concentration, based on their respective eligibility criteria. In Table 11–11, the corresponding differences in relative reduction of cholesterol concentration between treatment and control groups are shown, and the studies are ranked according to the accompanying differences in coronary heart disease events. It is notable that the percentage decrease in coronary events closely paralleled the degree of relative cholesterol reduction. This observation has suggested that failure to observe benefit in some trials reflects only their limited effectiveness in lowering cholesterol or their short duration of follow-up.

The results of the Lipid Research Clinics Coronary Primary Prevention Trial, included in these tables, were the major stimulus to the National Heart, Lung and Blood Institute in implementing the National Cholesterol Education Program. This was despite the fact that overall mortality was not reduced in this trial, an issue noted previously.[38] A more encouraging result was observed in the only statin trial that enrolled men essentially free of coronary heart disease at entry, in contrast to survivors of myocardial infarction, that is, the West of Scotland Coronary Prevention Study (WOSCOP).[42] This primary prevention trial used pravastatin (like the CARE trial) for lipid modification among men without history of myocardial infarction but with a mean cholesterol concentration at entry of 272 mg/dl. The reduction in risk of fatal or nonfatal coronary events was 31% (CI 17%–43%). All-cause mortality was reduced by 22% (CI 0%–40%), just short of the criterion of statistical significance ($P = 0.051$). These studies necessarily leave open the question of

Table 11–11 Randomized Trials on Primary Prevention of Coronary Heart Disease (CHD) Including Cholesterol Lowering by Diet or Drugs: Results

Study	Serum Cholesterol at Entry (mg/dl)	% Differences Between Treated and Control Groups[a]	
		Serum Cholesterol	CHD[b]
Göteborg Multifactor Trial	250	0	0
WHO Multifactor Trial	216	−1	−7
Multiple Risk Factor Intervention Trial	254	−2	−7
Lipid Research Clinics Coronary Primary Prevention Trial	292	−8	−19*
WHO Clofibrate Trial	242	−9	−20*
Helsinki Heart Study	270	−9	−34*
Finnish Mental Hospital Study (women)	275	−12	−34
Los Angeles Veterans Administration Domiciliary Study	233	−13	−24
Oslo Study	329	−13	−47*
Finnish Mental Hospital Study (men)	267	−15	−53*

a. At the end of the trial.

b. CHD death was the endpoint in the WHO Multifactor Trial, the Multiple Risk Factor Intervention Trial, and the Finnish Mental Hospital Study. CHD death and nonfatal myocardial infarction were endpoints in the other studies. The studies varied in their technical definitions of these events.

*$P<0.05$.

Source: Reprinted with permission from *Diet and Health: Implications for Reducing Chronic Disease Risk.* Copyright 1989 by the National Academy of Sciences. Courtesy of the National Academy Press, Washington, DC.

whether longer-term experience will reveal important adverse effects of drug therapy to lower cholesterol concentrations, a liability that would not be expected of dietary intervention.

Regression of Coronary Atherosclerotic Lesions

Additional recent studies have exploited the technological developments permitting serial angiographic examination of the coronary arteries to evaluate cholesterol-lowering interventions. These studies were reviewed by Gotto and are summarized in Table 11–12.[43] They were mainly of relatively small size, included diet plus drug intervention, and had two to five years of follow-up, with apparent benefit in change in coronary lesions (less progression or greater regression with treatment) but mixed results when evaluated by event rates. An exception in several respects was the Program on Surgical Control of Hyperlipidemia (POSCH), which was several times larger, included 10 years of follow-up, and had a substantially favorable difference in event rates between treated and control groups. The intervention was partial ileal bypass surgery to remove a segment of small intestine in which much of dietary fat is absorbed. This one-time intervention produced cholesterol reductions similar to the most effective drugs and, with the longer follow-up period, led to a highly significant difference. These results add importantly to the evidence for benefit from cholesterol reduction among persons at high risk due to existing elevation of cholesterol concentration.

Table 11–12 Major Angiographically Monitored Lipid-Lowering Trials

| Trial | | | | Lipid Response, % (Treatment/Control) | | | Patients with Coronary Lesion, % | | Events |
| | | | | | | | | | |
Trial	Subjects	Period, yr	Intervention[a]	TC	LDL-C	Assessment[b]	Progression (Treatment/Control)	Regression (Treatment/Control)	(Treatment/Control)[c]
NHLBI	143 M+F	5	Ch	-17/-1	-26/-5	P	32/49	7/7	8/12
CLAS I	162 M	2	C+N	-26/-4	-43/-5	P	39/61	16/4	25/25
CLAS II	103 M	4	C+N	-25/-6	-40/-6	P	48/85	18/6	15/14
FATS	146 M	2.5	C+N	-23/-3	-32/-7	Q	25/46	39/11	2/10
			C+L	-34/-3	-46/-7	Q	21/46	32/11	3/10
UCSF-SCOR	72 M+F	2	C/N/L[d]	-31/-9	-39/-12	Q	20/41	32/13	0/1
STARS	90 M	3	Ch	-25/-2	-36/-3	Q	12/46	33/4	1/10
			Diet alone	-14/-2	-16/-3	Q	15/46	38/4	3/10
POSCH	838 M+F	5[e]	PIB	-28/-5	-42/-7	P	37/65	13/5	82/125
		10[e]		-22/-4	-39/-6	P	55/85	6/4	

Note: CLAS, Cholesterol Lowering Atherosclerosis Study; FATS, Familial Atherosclerosis Treatment Study; LDL-C, low-density lipoprotein cholesterol; NHLBI, National Heart, Lung, and Blood Institute; POSCH, Program on Surgical Control of Hyperlipidemia; STARS, St. Thomas' Atherosclerosis Regression Study; TC, total cholesterol; UCSF-SCOR, University of California—San Francisco Arteriosclerosis Specialized Center of Research.

a. All interventions included diet. Ch, cholestyramine; C, colestipol; N, nicotinic acid; L, lovastatin; PIB, partial ileal bypass.

b. P, panel assessment of lesion change (viewer estimation); Q, assessment by quantitative coronary angiography.

c. Events variably defined among trials; generally, coronary death, myocardial infarction, and unstable ischemia requiring revascularization.

d. Various binary and ternary drug combinations.

e. Follow-up rather than trial period (intervention was surgery).

Source: Reprinted with permission from *Circulation,* Vol 92, No 3, p 648, © 1995, American Heart Association.

Intervention Trials in Children and Adolescents

Cholesterol-lowering interventions have also been tested in children and adolescents. To date, no systematic review has been reported, although an unpublished review indicates marked heterogeneity among these studies in subject selection, sample size, type of intervention, duration of follow-up, and outcome—necessarily limited to postintervention cholesterol concentration and possible side effects (personal communication, Elizabeth Cocanougher-Short, 1996). One high-risk intervention trial recently reported is the Dietary Intervention Study in Children (DISC).[44] LDL-cholesterol concentration was the criterion for entry and ranged from 129 mg/dl to 133 mg/dl among treatment groups by sex at randomization. Results showed significant reduction in LDL-cholesterol concentration and no detection of adverse effects in the treated relative to the control group. In the population at large, children age 8–10 years at entry were studied in the CATCH trial described previously.[15,16,45] Favorable changes were observed in relation to reported dietary behavior, choices provided by school food services, and other behavioral characteristics, but no relative decrease in cholesterol concentrations in this general population of children could be demonstrated, perhaps due to design limitations of the study.

CURRENT ISSUES

Differences of Opinion

Several public health issues are of present concern in the area of adverse blood lipid profiles. In some instances divergent views of the evidence are at issue. Resolution of these differences may depend less on further research than on reasoned argument based on current knowledge. Briefly, questions of this type concern broad policy views with respect to programs for cholesterol screening and control in the population at large. This topic fosters debate about actual or potential practices of physicians with respect to currently recommended guidelines and intervention costs, especially for widespread use of the most recently reported drugs for cholesterol reduction, the statins. The argument in the United States over cholesterol screening in adults is illustrated by four items appearing together in early 1996. A commentary and an editorial preceded two Clinical Guidelines from the American College of Physicians.[46–49] Screening is not recommended in these Clinical Guidelines for most men 20–35 years of age or women 20–44 years of age, nor for men or women age 65 years or older.[48] The context of these recommendations is that of medical care and the prospect of drug treatment in the event of positive screening; consideration of screening as a basis for advice on dietary approaches to cholesterol reduction seems an inappropriate omission. There are serious cost implications for long-term use of cholesterol-lowering drugs, a topic addressed in several recent reports such as the review by Cohen and colleagues.[50] It is important to appreciate both the assumptions and the methods of cost analyses in order to evaluate their contribution to policy debate, and in the US context their importance appears likely to increase.

Applicability to Women of Observations in Men

This second issue is addressed in several of the sources cited in Chapter 7, as well as in a review by LaRosa.[28] That review suggested that the available evidence, though quite limited relative to that for men, indicates similar benefit in risk reduction for women with cholesterol-lowering interventions. It is noted, further, that the guidelines of the National Cholesterol Education Program have the effect of limiting intervention for women relative to the criteria for men in that they require two or more risk factors for women before the fasting blood lipid profile or drug treatment is considered. For men, by contrast, male sex is itself considered a risk factor and therefore leads to intervention for men at a lesser cholesterol concentration than is true for women. The appropriateness of this difference in policy may be reevaluated when further evidence on women becomes available. The role of estrogen replacement therapy as a preventive measure against coronary heart disease in women is a related issue for which directly relevant trial data are currently being acquired. Further issues specific to women and atherosclerotic and hypertensive diseases are addressed in Chapter 23, Groups of Special Concern.

Ability To Modify the Course of Cholesterol Change in Youth and Early Adulthood

A high priority in seeking to prevent atherosclerosis from the earliest stage is to modify the course of change in the blood lipid profile that in many populations leads to treatable levels in a high proportion of adults by middle age, and in many individuals much earlier. The high-risk approach to cholesterol reduction or, more broadly, blood lipid modification might more feasibly be concentrated in a smaller segment of the population if the prevalence of treatable levels were much reduced. While experimental evidence indicates in some studies that cholesterol concentrations in youth have been reduced by intervention, it remains to be determined

whether lasting change in the typical progression toward adverse blood lipid profiles can be achieved. This may be especially important for populations undergoing change in dietary patterns likely to accelerate development of undesirable blood lipid levels.

Low Cholesterol Concentration and Increased Mortality

The relation of low total cholesterol concentrations to morbidity and mortality was reviewed in a conference report based on collaborative analysis of data from 19 cohort studies from the United States, Europe, Israel, and Japan to determine whether low cholesterol concentrations are associated with mortality, either overall or for specific causes.[51] While it was concluded that mortality was often greater at the lowest levels of cholesterol concentration observed in a population than at somewhat higher values, this was judged likely to reflect confounding not controlled for by the data available. Most clearly related to low cholesterol concentrations is increased risk of hemorrhagic stroke, as investigated especially in Japan. Several questions for epidemiologic and other areas of research in this connection have been proposed.

REFERENCES

1. Stamler J. Established major coronary risk factors. In: Marmot M, Elliott P, eds. *Coronary Heart Disease Epidemiology: From Aetiology to Public Health.* Oxford, England: Oxford University Press; 1992: 35–66.

2. Keys A. From Naples to Seven Countries—a sentimental journey. *Prog Biochem Pharmacol.* 1983;19: 1–30.

3. National Research Council (US) Food and Nutrition Board. *Diet and Health Implications for Reducing Chronic Disease Risk.* Washington, DC: Committee on Diet and Health, Food and Nutrition Board, Commission on Life Sciences, National Research Council, National Academy Press; 1989.

4. Gotto AM Jr. Lipid and lipoprotein disorders. In: Pearson TA, Criqui MH, Luepker RV, Oberman A, Winston

M, eds. *Primer in Preventive Cardiology.* Dallas, Tex: American Heart Association; 1994:107–129.

5. Ginsberg HN. Lipoprotein metabolism and its relationship to atherosclerosis. *Med Clin North Am.* 1994; 78:1–20.

6. Sullivan DR. Lipoprotein (a). *J Cardiovasc Risk.* 1994; 1:212–216.

7. Wilson PWF, Schaefer EJ, Larson MG, Ordovas JM. Apolipoprotein E alleles and risk of coronary disease. A meta-analysis. *Arterioscler, Thromb Vasc Biol.* 1996; 16:1250–1255.

8. NIH Consensus Development Panel on Triglyceride, High-Density Lipoprotein and Coronary Heart Disease. Triglyceride, high-density lipoprotein, and coronary heart disease. *JAMA.* 1993;269:505–510.

9. Expert Panel on Detection, Evaluation and Treatment of High Blood Cholesterol in Adults. Summary of the Second Report of the National Cholesterol Education Program (NCEP) Expert Panel on Detection, Evaluation, and Treatment of High Blood Cholesterol in Adults (Adult Treatment Panel II). *JAMA.* 1993; 269:3015–3023.

10. National Cholesterol Education Program. *Report of the Expert Panel on Blood Cholesterol Levels in Children and Adolescents.* Bethesda, Md: National Cholesterol Program, National Heart, Lung and Blood Institute, National Institutes of Health, Public Health Service, US Dept of Health and Human Services; 1991. NIH publication 91-2732.

11. United States General Accounting Office. Report to the Chairman, Subcommittee on Investigations and Oversight, Committee on Science, Space, and Technology, House of Representatives. *Cholesterol Measurement, Test Accuracy and Factors That Influence Cholesterol Levels.* Washington, DC: General Accounting Office; 1994. GAO/PEMD-95-8.

12. *Guidelines for Cholesterol Screening Programs.* Dallas, Tex: American Heart Association; 1989.

13. Hegsted DM, Ausman LM, Johnson JA, Dallal GE. Dietary fat and serum lipids: an evaluation of the experimental data. *Am J Clin Nutr.* 1993;57:875–883.

14. St. Clair RW. Biology of atherosclerosis. In: Pearson TA, Criqui MH, Luepker RV, Oberman A, Winston M, eds. *Primer in Preventive Cardiology.* Dallas, Tex: American Heart Association; 1994: 11–24.

15. Sempos CT, Cleeman JI, Carroll MD, Johnson CL, et al. Prevalence of high blood cholesterol among US adults. *JAMA.* 1993;269:3009–3014.

16. Belcher JD, Ellison RC, Shepard WE, Bigelow C, et al. Lipid and lipoprotein distributions in children by ethnic group, gender, and geographic location—preliminary findings of the Child and Adolescent Trial for Cardiovascular Health (CATCH). *Prev Med.* 1993; 22:143–153.

17. Labarthe DR, Nichaman MZ, Harrist RB, Grunbaum JA, et al. Change in blood lipid components during adolescence differs importantly by sex and is not consistently related to change in body fat: Project HeartBeat! *Can J Cardiol.* 1997;13(suppl B):162B. Abstract.

18. Johnson CL, Rifkind BM, Sempos CT, Carroll MD, et al. Declining serum total cholesterol levels among US adults: the National Health and Nutrition Examination Surveys. *JAMA.* 1993;269:3002–3008.

19. Keys A. Serum cholesterol and the question of "normal." In: Benson ES, Strandjord PE, eds. *Multiple Laboratory Screening.* New York: Academic Press; 1969: 147–170.

20. Knuiman JT, West CE, Burema J. Serum total and high density lipoprotein cholesterol concentrations and body mass index in adult men from 13 countries. *Am J Epidemiol.* 1982;116:631–642.

21. Labarthe DR, O'Brien B, Dunn K. International comparisons of plasma cholesterol and lipoproteins. In: Williams CL, Wynder EL, eds. *Hyperlipidemia in Childhood and the Development of Atherosclerosis: Annals of the New York Academy of Sciences.* New York; New York Academy of Sciences; 1991; 623:108–119.

22. Labarthe DR, Nichaman MZ, Harrist RB, Grunbaum JA, et al, for the Project HeartBeat! Investigators. Development of cardiovascular risk factors from ages 8 to 18 in Project HeartBeat! Study design and patterns of change in plasma total cholesterol concentration. *Circ.* 1997;95:2636–2642.

23. Keys A. *Seven Countries. A Multivariate Analysis of Death and Coronary Heart Disease.* Cambridge, Mass: Harvard University Press; 1980.

24. Verschuren WMM, Jocobs DR, Bloemberg BPM, Kromhout D, et al. Serum total cholesterol and long-term coronary heart disease mortality in different cultures: twenty-five year follow-up of the Seven Countries Study. *JAMA.* 1995;274:131–136.

25. The Pooling Project Research Group. Relationship of blood pressure, serum cholesterol, smoking habit, relative weight and ECG abnormalities to incidence of major coronary events: Final Report of the Pooling Project. *J Chronic Dis.* 1978;31:201–306.

26. Martin MJ, Hulley SB, Browner WS, Kuller LH, et al. Serum cholesterol, blood pressure, and mortality: implications from a cohort of 361,622 men. *Lancet.* 1986;2:933–936.

27. Klag MJ, Ford DE, Mead LA, He J, et al. Serum cholesterol in young men and subsequent cardiovascular disease. *N Engl J Med.* 1993;328:313–318.

28. LaRosa JC. Lipoproteins and lipid disorders. In: Douglas PS, ed. *Cardiovascular Health and Disease in Women.* Philadelphia, Pa: WB Saunders Co; 1993: 175–189.

29. Castelli WP, Doyle JT, Gordon T, Hanes CG, et al. HDL cholesterol and other lipids in coronary heart disease: the Cooperative Lipoprotein Phenotyping Study. *Circ.* 1977;55:767–772.

30. Sytkowski PA, D'Agostino RB, Belanger A, Kannel WB. Sex and time trends in cardiovascular disease incidence and mortality: the Framingham Heart Study, 1950–1989. *Am J Epidemiol.* 1996;143:338–350.

31. Higgins M, Keller JB. Cholesterol, coronary heart disease, and total mortality in middle-aged and elderly men and women in Tecumseh. *Ann Epidemiol.* 1992; 2:69–76.

32. White AD, Hames CG, Tyroler HA. Serum cholesterol and 20-year mortality in Black and White men and women aged 65 and older in the Evans County Heart Study. *Ann Epidemiol.* 1992;2:85–91.

33. Nguyen TT, Ellefson RD, Hodge DO, Bailey KR, et al. Predictive value of electrophoretically detected lipoprotein(a) for coronary heart disease and cerebrovascular disease in a community-based cohort of 9936 men and women. *Circ.* 1997;96:1390–1397.

34. World Health Organization. Report of a WHO Expert Committee. *Prevention of Coronary Heart Disease.* Geneva, Switzerland: World Health Organization; 1982. Technical Report Series 678.

35. World Health Organization. Report of a WHO Expert Committee. *Prevention in Childhood and Youth of Adult Cardiovascular Diseases: Time for Action.* Geneva, Switzerland: World Health Organization; 1990. Technical Report Series 792.

36. National Cholesterol Education Program. *Report of the Expert Panel on Population Strategies for Blood Cholesterol Reduction.* Bethesda, Md: National Heart, Lung and Blood Institute, National Institutes of Health, Public Health Service, US Dept of Health and Human Services; 1990. NIH publication 90-3046.

37. The Coronary Drug Project Research Group. Clofibrate and niacin in coronary heart disease. *JAMA.* 1975;231:360–381.

38. Borhani NO. Prevention of coronary heart disease in practice. *JAMA.* 1985;254:257–262.

39. Brown MS, Goldstein JL. Heart attacks: gone with the century? *Science.* 1996;272:629.

40. Scandinavian Simvastatin Survival Study Group. Randomised trial of cholesterol lowering in 4444 patients with coronary heart disease: the Scandinavian Simvastatin Survival Study (4S). *Lancet.* 1994;344:1383–1389.

41. Sacks FM, Pfeffer MA, Moye LA. Rouleau JL, et al, for the Cholesterol and Recurrent Events Trial Investigators. The effect of pravastatin on coronary events after myocardial infarction in patients with average cholesterol levels. *N Engl J Med.* 1996;335:1001–1009.

42. Shepherd J, Cobbe SM, Ford I, Isles CG, et al, for the West of Scotland Coronary Prevention Study Group. Prevention of coronary heart disease with pravastatin in men with hypercholesterolemia. *N Engl J Med.* 1995;333:1301–1307.

43. Gotto AM Jr. Lipid lowering, regression, and coronary events. *Circ.* 1995;92:646–656.

44. Writing Group for the DISC Collaborative Research Group. Efficacy and safety of lowering dietary intake of fat and cholesterol in children with elevated low-density lipoprotein cholesterol: the Dietary Study in Children (DISC). *JAMA.* 1995;273:1429–1435.

45. Luepker RV, Perry CL, McKinlay SM, Nader PR, et al, for the CATCH Collaborative Group. Outcomes of a field trial to improve children's dietary patterns and physical activity: the Child and Adolescent Trial for Cardiovascular Health. *JAMA.* 1996;275:768–776.

46. LaRosa JC. Cholesterol agonistics. *Ann Intern Med.* 1996;124:505–508.

47. Davidoff F. Evangelists and snails redux: the case of cholesterol screening. *Ann Intern Med.* 1996;124:513–514.

48. American College of Physicians. Clinical guideline, I: guidelines for using serum cholesterol, high-density lipoprotein cholesterol, and triglyceride levels as screening tests for preventing coronary heart disease in adults. *Ann Intern Med.* 1996;124:515–517.

49. Garber AM, Browner WS, Hulley SB. Clinical guideline, II: cholesterol screening in asymptomatic adults, revisited. *Ann Intern Med.* 1996;124:518–531.

50. Cohen DJ, Goldman L, Weinstein MC. The cost-effectiveness of programs to lower serum cholesterol. In: Rifkind BM, ed. *Lowering Cholesterol in High Risk Individuals and Populations.* New York: Marcel Dekker Inc; 1995: 311–336.

51. Jacobs D, Blackburn H, Higgins M, Reed D, et al, participants in the Conference on Low Cholesterol: Mortality Associations. Report of the Conference on Low Blood Cholesterol: Mortality Associations. *Circ.* 1992; 86:1046–1060.

CHAPTER 12

High Blood Pressure

SUMMARY

Blood pressure is a continuously distributed characteristic in populations, as are the related risks of atherosclerotic and hypertensive diseases. High blood pressure represents an upper extreme of such distributions and is one of several categories arbitrarily defined for purposes of clinical and public health decision making for individuals. The most informative observations on blood pressure are based on standardized and documented measurement procedures. The great majority of cases of high blood pressure are not attributable to any specific underlying cause and have conventionally been termed *essential hypertension*. The pathological effects of high blood pressure relate primarily to its physical properties. Populations exist in which low average blood pressure levels persist across the age range, but more commonly a substantial upward shift with age occurs in the blood pressure distribution, resulting in a high proportion of the population—especially those at older ages—having values classified as high blood pressure. The distribution of blood pressure may vary over time within a population, and such secular trends in the United States indicate reduced frequencies of extreme high values, and lower median values, from the 1960s through the 1980s. Population differences in rates of coronary heart disease and stroke are explained to a significant degree by differences in the prevalence of high blood pressure. Blood pressure is also a substantial factor in differential risks of these events, especially stroke, within populations. Interventions to control high blood pressure in whole communities or to treat individuals to reduce or prevent high blood pressure have been shown to be effective. Contemporary public health therefore faces the challenge of realizing the potential for community-wide blood pressure control, especially in populations that have yet to benefit from available knowledge. It is even more important to determine how to prevent the development of high blood pressure in the first place, a task that belongs high on the research agenda.

INTRODUCTION

Blood pressure is a critical measure of the adequacy of circulatory function. At a given moment it reflects the balance between the blood volume ejected from the left ventricle of the heart with each cardiac cycle and the resistance to blood flow, which is controlled especially by the distal vasculature. A great many mechanisms operate continuously to maintain blood pressure at a level sufficient for the perfusion of body tissues.

Blood pressure varies from moment to moment throughout each cardiac cycle, is altered rapidly in response to acute physical and

261

psychological influences, and changes in predictable ways throughout the life span of the healthy individual. Blood pressure too low to sustain tissue perfusion constitutes a medical emergency and is part of the clinical syndrome of circulatory shock. Blood pressure that is too high is related to pathological changes in several organ systems, thus contributing to the progression of atherosclerosis as well as vascular changes characteristic of hypertension alone.

High blood pressure is of public health concern because of the frequency with which it occurs in many populations; the severity of the pathological changes it causes with consequent burdens of illness, disability, and death; and the great potential for its prevention or control. Correspondingly, this chapter addresses blood pressure as measured in the ordinary outpatient setting or similar circumstances and not in emergency situations or with invasive techniques.

DEFINITION AND CLASSIFICATION

Dichotomies Versus Continuity

Terminology in relation to blood pressure has changed over the years. Until well into the latter half of this century, the levels of blood pressure recognized as abnormally high were thought to characterize a distinct disease. The terms *hypertension* and, in the especially severe case, *malignant hypertension* were applied to this disease, whose specific cause was identifiable in only a small proportion of cases. The first task of the physician concerned about a patient's blood pressure was to determine whether the patient was "hypertensive" or "normal." To make this diagnosis required measurement of the blood pressure and application of some fixed numerical cutpoint or dividing line thought to discriminate correctly between these two classes.

In the 1950s, Pickering argued especially effectively that the absolute distinction between hypertensive and normal was a false dichotomy.[1] Instead, he advanced the concept of blood pressure as a continuous or graded characteristic: The higher the usual blood pressure level, the greater was the risk of progressive pathological change and cardiovascular complications, and no clear dividing line separated diseased from normal persons.

While this concept has long been accepted, decisions are still needed in practice about which patients' blood pressure is high enough to receive clinical attention. Therefore some elements of the earlier terminology persist, and numerical blood pressure criteria, however arbitrary, remain in use in making individual decisions about diagnosis and treatment.

Current terminology and criteria are not uniform throughout the world, but standard usages have been recommended. The example shown here is that of the (US) Joint National Committee on Detection, Evaluation, and Treatment of High Blood Pressure (notably, the term is not *hypertension*) in its Fifth Report (JNC V), published in 1993.[2] Blood pressure is usually measured at two points in its continuous cycle—the higher reading representing the pressure peak after ventricular contraction or systole (hence systolic pressure) and the lower reading representing a lower point in the pressure cycle, closer to the maximum ventricular relaxation or diastole (hence diastolic pressure)—and current definitions and criteria usually refer to both measurements, as will be seen.

Figure 12–1 illustrates the fact that the frequencies of blood pressure levels (here, diastolic) in a large screened population show no distinct separation between normal and high but indicate a single continuous distribution, though for both systolic and diastolic pressure the distributions are typically skewed to the right, especially for older age groups.[3] Also, the answer to the question of how large a proportion of the population has hypertension—an important public health question—is shown to depend simply on the level of pressure chosen to make the distinction. This is not a trivial point, because for every downward change of 5 units in the criterion, for example, from 115 to

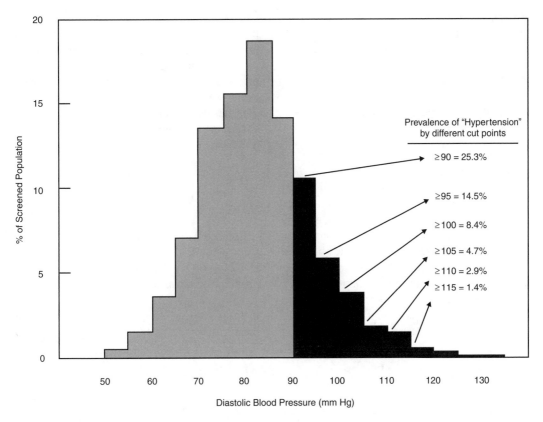

Figure 12–1 Frequency Distribution of Diastolic Blood Pressure at Home Screen of 158,906 Persons, 30–69 Years of Age. *Source*: Reprinted with permission from Hypertension Detection and Follow-Up Cooperative Group, The Hypertension Detection and Follow-Up Program: A Progress Report, *Circulation Research*, Supplement 40, p I-107, © 1977, American Heart Association.

110 mm Hg (millimeters of mercury), the estimated proportion of the population with hypertension doubles.

Systolic or Diastolic?

Much attention has been given over the years to whether systolic or diastolic pressure is the better measure. Each of these measures has been shown to predict outcomes such as coronary events, stroke, and death; each is correlated with most of the same factors; and each responds to treatment to reduce risks. A recent contribution to the debate is based on data from follow-up of the men screened for the Multiple Risk Factor Intervention Trial because so many

individuals could be observed and the baseline blood pressures could be stratified by quintiles of both systolic and diastolic pressure for cross-tabulation of risks.[4] The data clearly show that within each of five categories of diastolic pressure, increasing levels of systolic pressure were associated with increases in risk of coronary heart disease death, the risks being three to four times that of the lowest risk group by both measures. Conversely, within each stratum of systolic blood pressure at baseline, risk tended to increase with increasing diastolic pressure; however, the increases were not so great nor were they quite so consistent as in the reverse comparison. Whether the apparent difference is true and important is less clear, as it may be an artifact due to less-precise measurement of diastolic pressure (if this is the case), and regardless of this evidence both systolic and diastolic pressure are incorporated in the definition and classification of blood pressure.

Currently Recommended Classification for the United States

Table 12–1 presents the classification of blood pressure for adults age 18 years and older.[2] Three categories, "normal," "high normal," and "hypertension" are used, and four stages are identified within the latter category, with both numerical and verbal equivalents. For each category and stage, both systolic and diastolic criteria are indicated. Detailed notes to the table, as originally published, point to a number of considerations for appropriate use of the table as intended. This classification and the terms employed to describe it reflect current

concepts about blood pressure with respect to the levels at which treatment to reduce blood pressure is warranted, levels at which the risk of progression to hypertension is high, and levels that may be considered normal or optimal. Either systolic or diastolic pressure, whichever indicates the higher category, is decisive in classification of an individual.

MEASUREMENT

The Technique of Indirect Auscultatory Determination

Blood pressure measurement became widely applicable as a diagnostic procedure when Korotkov, in 1905, described the auscultatory phenomena (changes in sounds) heard through a stethoscope applied over the brachial artery (the major artery to the forearm) as constricting pressure is released from a cuff encircling the

Table 12–1 Classification of Blood Pressure for Adults Age 18 Years and Older

Category	Systolic (mm Hg)	Diastolic (mm Hg)
Normal[a]	<130	<85
High normal	130–139	85–89
Hypertension[b]		
STAGE 1 (mild)	140–159	90–99
STAGE 2 (moderate)	160–179	100–109
STAGE 3 (severe)	180–209	110–119
STAGE 4 (very severe)	≥210	≥120

Note: Classification is for those not taking antihypertensive drugs and not acutely ill. When systolic and diastolic pressures fall into different categories, the higher category should be selected to classify the individual's blood pressure status. For instance, 160/92 mm Hg should be classified as stage 2, and 180/120 mm Hg should be classified as stage 4. Isolated systolic hypertension (ISH) is defined as systolic blood pressure (SBP) ≥140 mm Hg and diastolic blood pressure (DBP) <90 mm Hg and staged appropriately (eg, 170/85 mm Hg is defined as stage 2 ISH). In addition to classifying stages of hypertension based on average blood pressure levels, the clinician should specify presence or absence of target-organ disease and additional risk factors. For example, a patient with diabetes and a blood pressure of 142/94 mm Hg plus left ventricular hypertrophy should be classified as "stage 1 hypertension with target-organ disease (left ventricular hypertrophy) and with another major risk factor (diabetes)." This specificity is important for risk classification and management.

a. Optimal blood pressure with respect to cardiovascular risk is SBP <120 mm Hg and DBP <80 mm Hg. However, unusually low readings should be evaluated for clinical significance.

b. Based on the average of two or more readings taken at each of two or more visits following an initial screening.

Source: Reprinted from the National Institutes of Health, Public Health Service, National High Blood Pressure Education Program, NIH Publication No. 93-1088, 1993.

upper arm.[5] His apparatus combined the stethoscope of von Recklinghausen, the cuff of Riva-Rocci, and the mercury manometer of Poiseuille. His method linked the changes in sounds with the successive pressure levels read from the scale on the manometer, and unlike prior laboratory methods it required no insertion of a needle directly into the artery to make the measurement. This noninvasive method of blood pressure measurement, the indirect auscultatory method, was simple, could be performed easily in routine examinations, and quickly became the standard technique.

The so-called Korotkov sounds identify systolic pressure, at the first "phase" and two levels of diastolic pressure, related to his fourth and fifth phases. The American Heart Association has published guidelines for blood pressure measurement from time to time since 1939 and has variously recommended use of the fourth or the fifth phase Korotkov sound as the basis for reading the diastolic pressure. In adults, fifth-phase pressure has been favored most recently.[2] Special concerns about its interpretation in some readings in children led to use of fourth-phase diastolic pressure below age 14, until appearance of a 1996 update on recommendations for blood pressure measurement in children and adolescents.[6] Because there is typically a difference of several millimeters of mercury in these two results, knowledge of the method that was used is needed to interpret or compare data on diastolic blood pressure.

Alternative Techniques

Other techniques and devices have been introduced since the time of Korotkov. Aneroid manometers are less reliable but are in common use as an alternative to the mercury type, which remains the standard for calibration. Electronic devices of several types are used where they have advantages due to special measurement requirements, such as in intensive-care settings, measurements in newborns and infants, and ambulatory monitoring for clinical or research purposes, in which blood pressure measurements may be recorded very frequently throughout a period of usual activity for 24 hours or longer. For reasons of practicality and consistency with long-established methods, Korotkov's indirect auscultatory method with a mercury manometer is generally preferred for epidemiologic research. A variant on this approach is a device that blinds the observer to the true zero-pressure level of mercury in the manometer column until the reading has been completed. This is the "zero-muddler" or "random-zero" device. It has been used in many studies in which observer bias may be a particular concern, such as in trials of blood pressure treatment or prevention.

Standardization of Procedures

The most significant advances in blood pressure measurement for epidemiologic research and public health practice have been those in training of blood pressure observers and in control of the circumstances of measurement.[7,8] These approaches are aimed at eliminating the sources of incidental variation in measurements that may limit the reliability and comparability of data within and among individuals or for entire research projects and add importantly to confidence in the quality of such data. Therefore study protocols often address in some detail the provisions for training and certification of blood pressure observers (such as by use of quantitative testing by videotape methods), the conditions of measurement (such as a resting period, quiet, proper relative positions of the subject and equipment, voiding in advance, and others), and the numbers of readings to be obtained (such as a fixed number to be averaged on each occasion and possibly multiple occasions of examination), with the goal of attaining the highest standards of data collection. Some issues remain despite these efforts at standardization, such as the awkward possibility that an individual may respond psychologically to the blood pressure measurement situation and therefore show higher than typical blood pressure. This phenomenon has been associated with the physician as observer and is thus designated "white coat hypertension," presuming the physician's professional uniform is symbolic of the problem. One stimulus to ambulatory monitoring of blood pressure has been to overcome this possibly misleading effect of measurement limited to the medical setting.

DETERMINANTS

Secondary and Essential Hypertension

The occurrence specifically of *high* blood pressure, which is most relevant here, is in some cases clearly attributable to a particular structural or functional abnormality of the regulatory mechanisms controlling blood pressure, such as diseases affecting the kidney. High blood pressure in the presence of any of these recognized causes is termed *secondary hypertension*. The remainder, and the great majority, of instances of high blood pressure occur in the absence of these conditions and constitute *primary* or *essential hypertension*. Secondary hypertension is generally rare. The potential for discovery of a specific cause is greatest in cases of severe hypertension, especially in childhood, or among persons whose blood pressure levels increase suddenly or do not respond to treatment. Evaluation of each case of hypertension for possible causes is recommended by the Joint National Committee, but extensive laboratory investigation is considered justified only when suggestive clinical findings are present.[2]

Epidemiologic pursuit of the determinants of high blood pressure is documented in extensive literature. Many factors have been investigated regarding the possibility of their association with high blood pressure or, more broadly, with blood pressure levels or distributions in the population, including the prevalence of high blood pressure. As might be expected from the numerous regulatory mechanisms involved in maintenance of physiologically required blood pressure levels, many of these factors have been associated with blood pressure. In addition to variation by age, sex, and race or ethnicity, these include genetic predisposition, diet, physical activity, obesity or weight change, psychological and sociocultural characteristics, and others.

Rise of Blood Pressure with Age

Populations have long been known to differ markedly in the tendency of blood pressure to increase with age in adulthood, such that high blood pressure is virtually absent among adults in some populations and very common in others.[9] Factors associated with population differences in the increase of blood pressure with age were investigated in the INTERSALT Study of 200 men and women age 20–59 years in each of 52 populations from 32 countries around the world.[10] The selected populations were found to represent the same wide range of slopes of increasing systolic blood pressure by age previously described,[9] and the slopes were related to several characteristics of the populations, as shown in Table 12–2.[11] The range of slopes coded from 0 to 4 corresponds to increases in systolic pressure from 0 to 0.67 mm Hg per year of age as a population average; slope 4 thus represents an average increase of nearly 7 mm Hg over a 10-year age interval, such as from age 30 to age 40. From 24-hour urine collections, concentrations of sodium and potassium were determined as estimates of their dietary intake; body mass index (BMI) is a ratio that increases as weight increases for any given height; and alcohol intake was assessed by interview. Sodium and potassium excretion were oppositely related to blood pressure slope; body mass index was related to the contrast between slopes 0–1 and slopes 2–4; and blood pressure slope was successively greater in populations with greater average alcohol intake.

Incidence of High Blood Pressure

The incidence of high blood pressure, or progression from blood pressure levels below a specified criterion value to those above, has

Table 12–2 Mean Values of Urinary Sodium and Other Factors in Relation to Slope of Systolic Blood Pressure Increase with Age

Slope	N	Na, mmol/24 h	K, mmol/24 h	Na-K Ratio	BMI, kg/m²	Alcohol, ml/wk
0	393	6.6	75.3	0.1	22.3	0.0
1	929	133.7	53.6	2.8	22.2	74.0
2	2,695	154.1	56.4	3.0	25.1	115.1[a]
3	3,300	159.3	57.2	3.1	25.8	126.0
4	2,762	182.7	49.2	4.2	25.0	130.0

Note: BMI, body mass index.

a. Mexico was excluded from the alcohol analysis because of an unusual high consumption during data collection because of a holiday.

Source: Reprinted with permission from BL Rodriguez et al, *Hypertension*, Vol 24, p 784, © 1994, American Heart Association.

been investigated less often than prevalence, due to the necessity for years-long observation and the difficulty of classifying individuals reliably at any given occasion due to the moment-to-moment variability of each person's blood pressure. Langford characterized this problem as like that of "counting fireflies" (personal communication, Herbert Langford, 1973). An early opportunity for a study of prevalence presented itself to several investigators of health outcomes in 22,741 US military officers over an average of 9.8 years of follow-up.[12] The sixth in a series of reports appearing between 1944 and 1947 described predictors of "sustained hypertension," or persistent readings of greater than 150 mm Hg systolic or 90 mm Hg diastolic pressure within an examination and without lower values on subsequent examinations. So defined, sustained hypertension was predicted by transient elevations of either blood pressure or heart rate (over, then below 100 beats per min), or overweight (20 pounds or more above the Army standard by age and height for each man). The frequency of sustained hypertension during follow-up was shown to multiply in the presence of more than one or two of these three factors, reaching 12 times the frequency observed in the absence of all three.

A more recent example of such an investigation is that conducted among more than 7000 participants age 25–74 years at first observation in the National Health and Nutrition Examination Survey Epidemiologic Follow-Up Study (1971–1984).[13] The criterion for the new appearance of high blood pressure was an increase from below 160 mm Hg systolic and 95 mm Hg diastolic to above one or both of these values or from a negative to a positive history of using blood pressure–lowering medications. The factors most strongly predictive of this change were the initial body mass index in Black and White men and women, and low educational attainment, especially in White women. No relation was found with dietary factors, perhaps because of the limitations of these data for this type of analysis. In childhood and adolescence also, body mass index and its change with age has been found to be a strong predictor for having the highest relative blood pressure levels in early adulthood.[14]

Since the 1960s or earlier, interest in high blood pressure from a social science viewpoint has led to studies of migrant populations, or the process of migration, as a factor in the development of high blood pressure. This literature is discussed only briefly in Chapter 19, Social Conditions, but has been of particular interest in connection with blood pressure. In general, the surveys of cross-sectional design in which migrant groups have been surveyed, often in comparison with nonmigrant groups of the same origin, suffer the limitation that factors of self-selection to migrate cannot be taken adequately into account. Therefore longitudinal studies are much preferred in which persons may be examined before and after migration, perhaps in comparison with nonmigrants at both ends of the process. This approach has been applied, for example, in studies of Tokelau Island groups in the southwestern Pacific and the Luo tribes of Kenya. Studies of both types are reviewed in the recent report of the Yi migrant population in Sichuan, China.[15] A consistent impression from such studies is that the personal, social, and broader environmental changes associated with migration often result in higher blood pressure among migrants than among nonmigrants, sometimes developing within weeks to months. Dietary aspects are implicated, including changes in salt intake and in energy balance with resulting weight gain.

The recent detailed review, *Diet and Health*, concluded that obesity and alcohol intake are related to increased risk of high blood pressure and that dietary sodium is a major factor but requires individual susceptibility for its effect.[16] The role of genetic determination of such susceptibility is well established in selectively bred strains of rats, although corresponding predictors of salt sensitivity in humans have not been identified. A more extensive review of salt intake and its role in high blood pressure has been presented by the INTERSALT investigators,[17] and this issue is addressed in Chapter 8 (Dietary Imbalance) and below. Further evidence from clinical trials adds weight to the role of energy balance (studied as caloric intake, physical activity, or both) and specific dietary elements, especially sodium, potassium, and alcohol.[18] (See Chapter 15, Alcohol Consumption.)

MECHANISMS OF TARGET ORGAN DAMAGE

How does the presence of successively higher blood pressure levels or, in the extreme,

high blood pressure, lead to serious complications such as myocardial infarction, stroke, congestive heart failure, and other outcomes? The *Hypertension Primer* is a recent compendium of short essays on laboratory, clinical, and epidemiologic aspects of blood pressure, including several contributions on mechanisms that collectively produce these results.[19] Prominent among these are the mechanical effects of sustained high pressure in the arterial and capillary circulation, with the direct consequence of damaging blood vessels particularly in the major "target organs": heart, brain, kidneys, and eyes.

A regulatory dysfunction that results in high blood pressure may itself have other effects that consequently appear to be associated with high blood pressure. In this way, for example, catecholamines (epinephrine and norepinephrine) act to increase arterial resistance, contributing to high blood pressure, and may also have a direct deleterious effect on heart muscle cells.[20] Or blood pressure damage to the heart may produce both structural and functional changes that reduce its ability to respond to increased demand, increasing the risk of muscle injury due to a relative decrease in oxygen supply.[21] Regardless of the mechanism, it appears that prevention of high blood pressure in the first place, or effective intervention to restore desirable blood pressure levels in those with high blood pressure, is necessary to avoid the adverse consequences of sustained and progressive blood pressure elevations.

DISTRIBUTION IN THE POPULATION

Childhood and Adolescence

Based on pooled results of eight surveys conducted in the United States and one in the United Kingdom, a task force on blood pressure control in children published reference values for blood pressure from ages 1 to 18, which have now been presented according to percentiles of height, as illustrated by data for girls in Table 12–3.[6] The current report has incorporated more fully the concept that during child-

Table 12-3 Blood Pressure Levels for the 90th and 95th Percentiles of Blood Pressure for Girls Aged 1 to 17 Years, by Percentiles of Height

Age, yr	Blood Pressure Percentile[a]	Systolic Blood Pressure by Percentile of Height,[b] mm Hg							Diastolic Blood Pressure by Percentile of Height,[b] mm Hg						
		5%	10%	25%	50%	75%	90%	95%	5%	10%	25%	50%	75%	90%	95%
1	90th	97	98	99	100	102	103	104	53	53	53	54	55	56	56
	95th	101	102	103	104	105	107	107	57	57	57	58	59	60	60
2	90th	99	99	100	102	103	104	105	57	57	58	58	59	60	61
	95th	102	103	104	105	107	108	109	61	61	62	62	63	64	65
3	90th	100	100	102	103	104	105	106	61	61	61	62	63	63	64
	95th	104	104	105	107	108	109	110	65	65	65	66	67	67	68
4	90th	101	102	103	104	106	107	108	63	63	64	65	65	66	67
	95th	105	106	107	108	109	111	111	67	67	68	69	69	70	71
5	90th	103	103	104	106	107	108	109	65	66	66	67	68	68	69
	95th	107	107	108	110	111	112	113	69	70	70	71	72	72	73
6	90th	104	105	106	107	109	110	111	67	67	68	69	69	70	71
	95th	108	109	110	111	112	114	114	71	71	72	73	73	74	75
7	90th	106	107	108	109	110	112	112	69	69	69	70	71	72	72
	95th	110	110	112	113	114	115	116	73	73	73	74	75	76	76
8	90th	108	109	110	111	112	113	114	70	70	71	71	72	73	74
	95th	112	112	113	115	116	117	118	74	74	75	75	76	77	78
9	90th	110	110	112	113	114	115	116	71	72	72	73	74	74	75
	95th	114	114	115	117	118	119	120	75	76	76	77	78	78	79
10	90th	112	112	114	115	116	117	118	73	73	73	74	75	76	76
	95th	116	116	117	119	120	121	122	77	77	77	78	79	80	80
11	90th	114	114	116	117	118	119	120	74	74	75	75	76	77	77
	95th	118	118	119	121	122	123	124	78	78	79	79	80	81	81
12	90th	116	116	118	119	120	121	122	75	75	76	76	77	78	78
	95th	120	120	121	123	124	125	126	79	79	80	80	81	82	82
13	90th	118	118	119	121	122	123	124	76	76	77	78	78	79	80
	95th	121	122	123	125	126	127	128	80	80	81	82	82	83	84

continues

Table 12-3 continued

Age, yr	Blood Pressure Percentile[a]	Systolic Blood Pressure by Percentile of Height,[b] mm Hg							Diastolic Blood Pressure by Percentile of Height,[b] mm Hg						
		5%	10%	25%	50%	75%	90%	95%	5%	10%	25%	50%	75%	90%	95%
14	90th	119	120	121	122	124	125	126	77	77	78	79	79	80	81
	95th	123	124	125	126	128	129	130	81	81	82	83	83	84	85
15	90th	121	121	122	124	125	126	127	78	78	79	79	80	81	82
	95th	124	125	126	128	129	130	131	82	82	83	83	84	85	86
16	90th	122	122	123	125	126	127	128	79	79	79	80	81	82	82
	95th	125	126	127	128	130	131	132	83	83	83	84	85	86	86
17	90th	122	123	124	125	126	128	128	79	79	79	80	81	82	82
	95th	126	126	127	129	130	131	132	83	83	83	84	85	86	86

a. Blood pressure percentile was determined by a single reading.

b. Height percentile was determined by standard growth curves.

Source: Adapted by permission of *Pediatrics*, Vol 98, 1996.

hood and adolescence blood pressure levels should be interpreted in conjunction with the relative rank of the individual in growth and development, for which height percentile is used as the marker. In this report, only fifth-phase diastolic pressure is reported, fourth-phase readings having been set aside. The increasing values for both systolic and diastolic pressure, for example, those at the median or 50th percentile, are typical of those observed in this age range, in which two periods—infancy and early adolescence—are characterized by accelerated increases in blood pressure accompanying these periods of rapid growth. A detailed algorithm provided by the prior report indicated actions to be taken in the event of blood pressure readings meeting the age-specific values proposed as criteria for hypertension in this period of life.[22]

US Adults

In a classic epidemiologic study originally published in 1957 and republished in 1995, Comstock described many basic aspects of the population distribution of blood pressure by age, sex, and race in the southern United States.[23] The report portrays the early development of the epidemiology of hypertension and points to Black-White differences that are as important today as when Comstock first described them.

For the current adult population of the United States, Figures 12–2 and 12–3 present the mean values of systolic and diastolic pressure for men and women for three ethnic groups: non-Hispanic Black, non-Hispanic White, and Mexican American.[24] From ages 18 to 80 and above, these patterns of difference in blood pressure by age are broadly similar among ethnic groups in showing successively higher systolic pressures across the age range (except above 60 years for women other than non-Hispanic Whites) and successively higher diastolic pressures up to about age 50 with lower values at greater ages. Though the scale of the figure fails to emphasize it, the higher curves for non-Hispanic Blacks are reflected in substantially higher prevalence of high blood pressure, as seen in

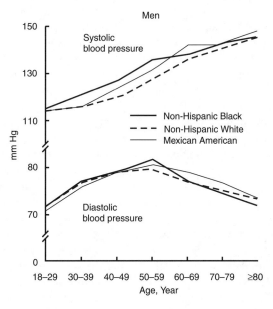

Figure 12–2 Mean Systolic and Diastolic Blood Pressure by Age and Race/Ethnicity, US Men 18 Years of Age and Older. *Source:* Reprinted with permission from VL Burt et al, *Hypertension*, Vol 25, p 309, © 1995, American Heart Association.

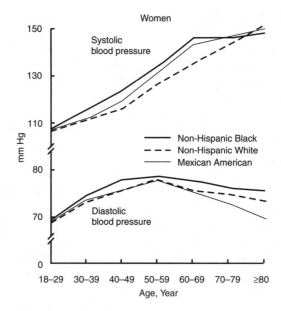

Figure 12–3 Mean Systolic and Diastolic Blood Pressure by Age and Race/Ethnicity, US Women 18 Years of Age and Older. *Source:* Reproduced with permission from VL Burt et al, *Hypertension*, Vol 25, p 309, © 1995, American Heart Association.

Table 12–4. This observation is reminiscent of Comstock's work 30 years earlier. The divergence of patterns between systolic and diastolic pressure for all groups suggests both a progressive rise in systolic pressure, which is common among the older population, and a fall in average diastolic pressure, which may be an artifact of loss from the population of those whose high diastolic pressures were associated with early mortality. This pattern also indicates the basis for the marked increase in prevalence of isolated systolic hypertension (see definition in Table 12–1) with age.

International Variation

Large population differences in the pattern of systolic blood pressure by age were addressed above in connection with the review by Epstein and Eckoff[9] and the INTERSALT Study and contrast sharply with these general similarities within the three main ethnic groups in the United States. The magnitude of between-population differences in the prevalence of high blood pressure is apparent in data from the World Health Organization MONICA Project, in which 40 reporting population units are represented.[25] Figures 12–4 and 12–5 show for men and women, respectively, the distribution of each population among four categories, from the highest as the left segment of the bar (systolic pressure greater than 160 mm Hg, diastolic pressure greater than 95 mm Hg, and on treatment for hypertension) to the lowest as the right segment (systolic pressure below 160, diastolic pressure below 95, and not on treatment). The proportion of each population in each class and the number of participants are indicated. The proportions of the populations in the lowest category (which would include the JNC V classes of both stage I or mild hypertension and high normal) ranged for men from 91.6% in the study sample in Catalonia, Spain, to only 54.7% in Kuopio Province, Finland. The corresponding range for women was similar.

For developing countries, the principal sources of data are surveys conducted independently and without intersurvey coordination to

Table 12–4 Age-Adjusted and Age-Specific Prevalence of Hypertension, US Population Aged 18–74 Years, 1960–1991

	160/95 mm Hg				140/90 mm Hg			
Population Group	NHES I (1960–1962)	NHANES I (1971–1974)	NHANES II (1976–1980)	NHANES III Phase 1 (1988–1991)	NHES I (1960–1962)	NHANES I (1971–1974)	NHANES II (1976–1980)	NHANES III Phase 1 (1988–1991)
Aged 18–74 years[a]	16.9	20.7	19.8	14.2	29.7	36.3	31.8	20.4
Men	15.1	21.5	20.9	14.7	31.5	40.7	36.8	22.8
Women	18.5	19.8	18.6	13.6	28.1	32.1	27.2	18.0
Black	31.0	34.0	29.4	23.1	42.5	48.2	42.6	30.2
Men	27.8	33.7	25.2	22.8	42.7	49.0	42.3	32.6
Women	34.2	34.3	32.7	23.4	43.1	47.5	42.8	28.1
White	15.4	19.3	18.8	13.2	28.3	35.0	30.6	19.2
Men	13.8	20.3	20.6	13.8	30.4	40.1	36.3	21.6
Women	16.7	18.1	17.1	12.5	26.4	30.2	25.2	16.7

Note: NHES, National Health Examination Survey; NHANES, National Health and Nutrition Examination Survey.

a. Includes racial groups not shown separately.

Source: Reproduced with permission from VL Burt et al, *Hypertension*, Vol 26, p 63, Copyright 1995, American Heart Association.

enhance comparability of results. Whether apparent differences in absolute values of blood pressure are real is therefore less clear in such comparisons. Surveys in developing countries or in rural areas of industrial countries can thus be grouped with other studies with greater than usual comparability of methods but no formal standardization to permit examination of population mean values of systolic and diastolic pressure and the prevalence of hypertension from a large number of populations, as in Table 12–5.[26]

Populations in diverse regions of the world are represented, by surveys conducted in the period from 1972 to 1984; age groups of men and women in the 30s, 40s, and 50s were included, in numbers ranging from tens to thousands per age-sex subgroup. Different criteria defining hypertension are indicated, but the mean values for systolic and diastolic pressure are more directly comparable. The mean blood pressure values were generally higher for the older age group within each population surveyed, and the prevalence of high blood pres-

sure at older ages was correspondingly greater also. For any given definition, there was striking variation among populations in the prevalence of high blood pressure, but by any definition more than 10% of the population surveyed was classified as having high blood pressure in these surveys.

US Secular Trends

The distribution of blood pressure values in a population would be expected to change if extrinsic determinants of blood pressure changed. Analysis of trends in blood pressure distributions among US adults indicates substantial downward shifts in systolic pressures across the series of representative sample surveys of the national population, most recently designated the National Health and Nutrition Examination Surveys (NHANES), as shown in Figure 12–6.[27]

These surveys were conducted in the early 1960s, early and late 1970s, and late 1980s. At both the youngest and oldest age levels, both

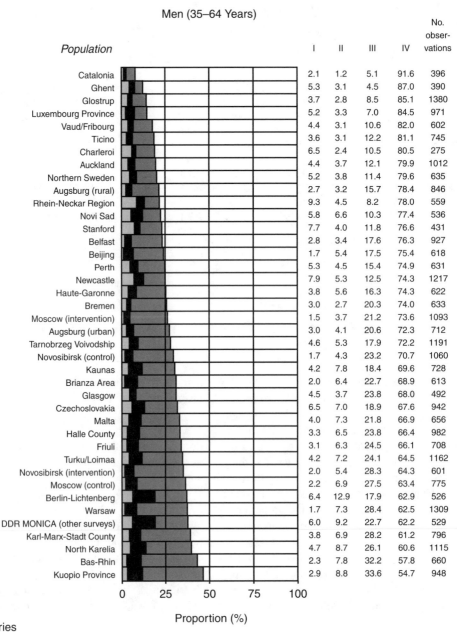

Men (35–64 Years)

Population	I	II	III	IV	No. observations
Catalonia	2.1	1.2	5.1	91.6	396
Ghent	5.3	3.1	4.5	87.0	390
Glostrup	3.7	2.8	8.5	85.1	1380
Luxembourg Province	5.2	3.3	7.0	84.5	971
Vaud/Fribourg	4.4	3.1	10.6	82.0	602
Ticino	3.6	3.1	12.2	81.1	745
Charleroi	6.5	2.4	10.5	80.5	275
Auckland	4.4	3.7	12.1	79.9	1012
Northern Sweden	5.2	3.8	11.4	79.6	635
Augsburg (rural)	2.7	3.2	15.7	78.4	846
Rhein-Neckar Region	9.3	4.5	8.2	78.0	559
Novi Sad	5.8	6.6	10.3	77.4	536
Stanford	7.7	4.0	11.8	76.6	431
Belfast	2.8	3.4	17.6	76.3	927
Beijing	1.7	5.4	17.5	75.4	618
Perth	5.3	4.5	15.4	74.9	631
Newcastle	7.9	5.3	12.5	74.3	1217
Haute-Garonne	3.8	5.6	16.3	74.3	622
Bremen	3.0	2.7	20.3	74.0	633
Moscow (intervention)	1.5	3.7	21.2	73.6	1093
Augsburg (urban)	3.0	4.1	20.6	72.3	712
Tarnobrzeg Voivodship	4.6	5.3	17.9	72.2	1191
Novosibirsk (control)	1.7	4.3	23.2	70.7	1060
Kaunas	4.2	7.8	18.4	69.6	728
Brianza Area	2.0	6.4	22.7	68.9	613
Glasgow	4.5	3.7	23.8	68.0	492
Czechoslovakia	6.5	7.0	18.9	67.6	942
Malta	4.0	7.3	21.8	66.9	656
Halle County	3.3	6.5	23.8	66.4	982
Friuli	3.1	6.3	24.5	66.1	708
Turku/Loimaa	4.2	7.2	24.1	64.5	1162
Novosibirsk (intervention)	2.0	5.4	28.3	64.3	601
Moscow (control)	2.2	6.9	27.5	63.4	775
Berlin-Lichtenberg	6.4	12.9	17.9	62.9	526
Warsaw	1.7	7.3	28.4	62.5	1309
DDR MONICA (other surveys)	6.0	9.2	22.7	62.2	529
Karl-Marx-Stadt County	3.8	6.9	28.2	61.2	796
North Karelia	4.7	8.7	26.1	60.6	1115
Bas-Rhin	2.3	7.8	32.2	57.8	660
Kuopio Province	2.9	8.8	33.6	54.7	948

0   25   50   75   100

Proportion (%)

Categories

I. Systolic blood pressure <160 and diastolic blood pressure <95; on treatment for hypertension.
II. Systolic blood pressure >159 and/or diastolic blood pressure >94; on treatment for hypertension.
III. Systolic blood pressure >159 and/or diastolic blood pressure >94; not on treatment for hypertension.
IV. Systolic blood pressure <160 and diastolic blood pressure <95; not on treatment for hypertension.

Figure 12–4 Age-Standardized Proportions of Categories of Blood Pressure Index, Men, WHO MONICA Project. *Source*: Reprinted with permission from The WHO MONICA Project, *World Health Statistics Quarterly*, Vol 41, p 128, © 1988, World Health Organization.

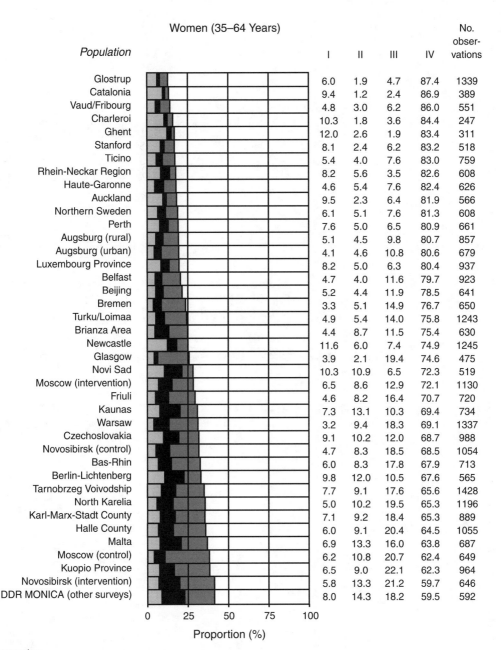

Population	Women (35–64 Years)	I	II	III	IV	No. obser-vations
Glostrup		6.0	1.9	4.7	87.4	1339
Catalonia		9.4	1.2	2.4	86.9	389
Vaud/Fribourg		4.8	3.0	6.2	86.0	551
Charleroi		10.3	1.8	3.6	84.4	247
Ghent		12.0	2.6	1.9	83.4	311
Stanford		8.1	2.4	6.2	83.2	518
Ticino		5.4	4.0	7.6	83.0	759
Rhein-Neckar Region		8.2	5.6	3.5	82.6	608
Haute-Garonne		4.6	5.4	7.6	82.4	626
Auckland		9.5	2.3	6.4	81.9	566
Northern Sweden		6.1	5.1	7.6	81.3	608
Perth		7.6	5.0	6.5	80.9	661
Augsburg (rural)		5.1	4.5	9.8	80.7	857
Augsburg (urban)		4.1	4.6	10.8	80.6	679
Luxembourg Province		8.2	5.0	6.3	80.4	937
Belfast		4.7	4.0	11.6	79.7	923
Beijing		5.2	4.4	11.9	78.5	641
Bremen		3.3	5.1	14.9	76.7	650
Turku/Loimaa		4.9	5.4	14.0	75.8	1243
Brianza Area		4.4	8.7	11.5	75.4	630
Newcastle		11.6	6.0	7.4	74.9	1245
Glasgow		3.9	2.1	19.4	74.6	475
Novi Sad		10.3	10.9	6.5	72.3	519
Moscow (intervention)		6.5	8.6	12.9	72.1	1130
Friuli		4.6	8.2	16.4	70.7	720
Kaunas		7.3	13.1	10.3	69.4	734
Warsaw		3.2	9.4	18.3	69.1	1337
Czechoslovakia		9.1	10.2	12.0	68.7	988
Novosibirsk (control)		4.7	8.3	18.5	68.5	1054
Bas-Rhin		6.0	8.3	17.8	67.9	713
Berlin-Lichtenberg		9.8	12.0	10.5	67.6	565
Tarnobrzeg Voivodship		7.7	9.1	17.6	65.6	1428
North Karelia		5.0	10.2	19.5	65.3	1196
Karl-Marx-Stadt County		7.1	9.2	18.4	65.3	889
Halle County		6.0	9.1	20.4	64.5	1055
Malta		6.9	13.3	16.0	63.8	687
Moscow (control)		6.2	10.8	20.7	62.4	649
Kuopio Province		6.5	9.0	22.1	62.3	964
Novosibirsk (intervention)		5.8	13.3	21.2	59.7	646
DDR MONICA (other surveys)		8.0	14.3	18.2	59.5	592

Proportion (%)

Categories

I. Systolic blood pressure <160 and diastolic blood pressure <95; on treatment for hypertension.
II. Systolic blood pressure >159 and/or diastolic blood pressure >94; on treatment for hypertension.
III. Systolic blood pressure >159 and/or diastolic blood pressure >94; not on treatment for hypertension.
IV. Systolic blood pressure <160 and diastolic blood pressure <95; not on treatment for hypertension.

Figure 12–5 Age-Standardized Proportions of Categories of Blood Pressure Index, Women, WHO MONICA PROJECT. *Source*: Reprinted with permission from VL Burt et al, *Hypertension*, Vol 26, p 66, © 1995, American Heart Association.

Table 12–5 Blood Pressure and Prevalence of Hypertension (%) in Subjects Aged Approximately 40–55 Years, Selected Surveys in Developing Countries

WHO Region and Country/Area	Population Basis	Year of Survey	Definition of Hypertension[a]	Age	Males N	BP	Prevalence	Females N	BP	Prevalence
Africa										
Ethiopia	Rural	1983	X	30–39	(60)	110/69	3	(51)	107/65	2
				40–49	(42)	119/72	11	(31)	113/71	3
Kenya	Rural	1980–1981	—	35–44	(280)	117/66	—	—	—	—
			—	45–54	(35)	121/71	—	—	—	—
Malawi	Rural	1983	—	35–44	(39)	120/74	—	(57)	112/68	—
				45–54	(22)	116/67	—	(43)	121/70	—
	Urban	1983	—	35–44	(64)	130/84	—	(36)	123/75	—
				45–54	(20)	141/87	—	—	—	—
Nigeria										
Bendal State	Civil servants	1977	—	35–39	(120)	130/83	—	(23)	124/80	—
				40–49	(110)	134/87	—	(10)	133/83	—
Bendal State	Civil servants	1983	—	35–39	(42)	131/78	10	—	—	—
				40–49	(49)	132/77	12	—	—	—
	Police	1983	—	35–39	(69)	126/74	13	—	—	—
				40–49	(38)	133/76	11	—	—	—
South Africa										
Zulu	Urban	1976	XX	31–40	(109)	122/79	17	(106)	124/81	25
				41–50	(80)	124/83	20	(83)	136/89	41
	Rural	1976	XX	31–40	(80)	119/72	1	(163)	122/74	10
				41–50	(86)	126/77	14	(132)	130/79	19
Tanzania	Rural	?	XX	35–44	(88)	125/77	2	(94)	119/75	2
				45–54	(75)	123/76	3	(58)	124/76	—
Zaire										
Bantu	Urban	1983–1984	XX	40–49	(21)	137/88	33	(34)	133/79	15
Zambia	Rural	1979	X	35–44	(20)	120/73	5	(61)	119/72	11
				45–54	(27)	122/75	11	(32)	123/74	9
Americas										
Brazil										
São Paulo	City workers	1976	X	35–44	(796)	–/84	30	(179)	–/80	18
				45–54	(405)	–/86	34	(54)	–/84	24
South-East Asia										
India										
Haryana	Urban/rural	?	XX	35–44	(470)	—	5	(395)	—	4
				45–54	(316)	—	8	(220)	—	13

continues

Table 12-5 continued

WHO Region and Country/Area	Population Basis	Year of Survey	Definition of Hypertension[a]	Males				Females		
				Age	N	BP	Prevalence	N	BP	Prevalence
Ludhiana	Industrial workers	?	XX	40–45	(339)	129/84	6	—	—	—
				50–59	(170)	136/91	7	—	—	—
Sundergrarh	Rural	1980–1982	XXX	41–50	(642)	124/82	5	(440)	112/80	2
				51–60	(468)	130/84	9	(217)	123/85	9
Nepal	Rural	?	XX	41–50	(109)	—	7	(155)	—	3
				51–60	(91)	—	9	(86)	—	12
Europe										
Finland	Rural	1972	XXX	40–44 ⎫	(699)	146/91	23 ⎫	(716)	148/91	27
				45–49 ⎭		148/92	32 ⎭		156/94	37
		1977	XXX	40–44 ⎫	(607)	140/89	19 ⎫	(616)	137/86	14
				45–49 ⎭		146/91	27 ⎭		145/89	24
		1982	XXX	40–44 ⎫	(366)	141/86	24 ⎫	(412)	136/84	14
				45–49 ⎭		141/88	28 ⎭		146/87	29
Western Pacific										
China										
Beijing	Urban	1975	XX	35–44	(791)	—	4	(1,237)	—	5
				45–54	(880)	—	9	(995)	—	10
Tibet	Rural	1979	XX	35–44	(2,652)	—	7	(3,392)	—	9
				45–54	(2,381)	—	18	(3,241)	—	20
Shanghai	Petrochemical industry	1979–1982	XX	40–49	(3,490)	—	5	(952)	—	4
				50–59	(1,754)	—	16	(217)	—	12
Japan										
Tsumagoi	Rural	?	XX	40–49	(171)	133/79	17	(221)	128/75	10
				50–59	(186)	139/81	21	(257)	137/79	19
Republic of Korea										
Kang Wha	Rural	?	XX	40–49	(266)	123/82	14	(425)	122/79	10
				50–59	(116)	131/85	24	(227)	128/82	18
Philippines										
Quezon	Urban	1976	XX	40–49	(82)	122/82	15	(147)	116/76	8
				50–59	(82)	128/84	22	(98)	126/80	13

a. Definition of hypertension: X = diastolic blood pressure ≥90 mm Hg; XX = blood pressure ≥160 and/or ≥95 mm Hg; XXX = blood pressure ≥175 and/or ≥100 mm Hg or under antihypertensive drug treatment.

Source: Reprinted with permission from K Uemura and Z Pisa, *World Health Statistics Quarterly,* Vol 41, pp 149–150, © 1988, World Health Organization.

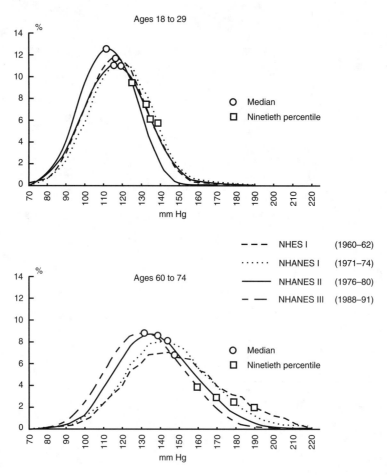

Figure 12–6 Systolic Blood Pressure Distributions at Successive Surveys, US National Center for Health Statistics. *Source:* Reproduced with permission from VL Burt et al, *Hypertension*, Vol 26, p 66, Copyright 1995, American Heart Association.

the median or 50th percentile and the 90th percentile values decreased from the earliest to the latest survey, with clear incremental decreases in successive surveys for those aged 60 to 74. The decreases were greater for the 90th percentile than for the median values and indicate a selective influence on the highest pressures, probably the increased frequency of treatment of high blood pressure in the US population beginning in the early to mid-1970s. The fact that the median values also decreased suggests that factors other than treatment must also have changed, because treatment would not affect the blood pressure values of persons at the midpoint

of these distributions. The corresponding secular trends in blood pressure treatment status are shown in Table 12–4.[27]

For the US population in the age range from 18 to 74, for men and women, Blacks and Whites, the percentages of each group classified as having high blood pressure are presented for each survey. These frequencies are shown for two sets of blood pressure criteria, 160/95 mm Hg or greater and 140/90 mm Hg or greater. In either case, persons reporting current treatment with blood pressure–lowering medication are included regardless of their actual blood pressure levels. This methodologic approach has become important in population studies in areas where treatment is common, as it avoids under-estimation of the prevalence of high blood pressure by omission of those under treatment. The overall trend for all persons age 18–74 years was an increase from the early 1960s to the early 1970s with decreases thereafter and a net decrease from 16.9% to 14.2% (at 160/95 mm Hg) or from 29.7% to 20.4% (at 140/90 mm Hg). From the peak values in the early 1970s, the decreases in prevalence of high blood pressure ranged from about one-third to nearly one-half across subgroups of the population. These observations support the suggested interpretation of Figure 12–6 that the marked decrease in the 90th percentile values of the population distributions of blood pressure in the United States are consistent with effects of blood pressure

treatment. Data are more limited for Mexican Americans, who were not represented in sufficient numbers for analysis except in the special survey among US Hispanics conducted in 1982–1984 and in Phase 1 of the NHANES III in 1988–1991. For all ages 18–74, the age-adjusted prevalence of hypertension decreased from 21.0% to 19.9%; the greater part of that decrease occurred among women, from 19.2% to 17.4%.

RATES AND RISKS

Population Differences in Mortality

The death rate of a population is determined in part by its blood pressure distribution. This is demonstrated by the Seven Countries Study, described in previous chapters.[28] Figure 12–7

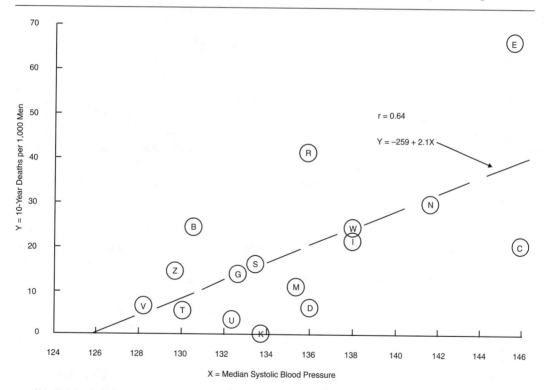

$$r = 0.64$$

$$Y = -259 + 2.1X$$

Note: B, Belgrade; C, Crevalcore; D, Dalmatia; E, East Finland; G, Corfu; I, Italian Railroad; K, Crete; M, Montegiorgio; N, Zutphen; R, American Railroad; S, Slavonia; T, Tanushimaru; U, Ushibuka; V, Velika Krsna; W, West Finland; Z, Zvenjanin.

Figure 12–7 Ten-Year Mortality in Relation to Median Levels of Systolic Blood Pressure, Seven Countries Study. *Source:* Reprinted by permission of the publisher from *Seven Countries* by A Keys, Cambridge, Mass: Harvard University Press, Copyright © 1980 by the President and Fellows of Harvard College.

illustrates the relation of the median values of systolic blood pressure in the 16 study cohorts to their 10-year death rates for coronary heart disease. The coronary death rates were generally higher for cohorts with higher blood median pressure values. The regression coefficient of 2.1 shown in the figure represents slightly more than a doubling of the coronary death rate for every upward change of 10 mm Hg of the population median systolic pressure. Very similar results were reported for median diastolic pressure.

Risks Within a Population

Among the earliest investigations of risks related to blood pressure were those of the life insurance industry, which in the United States conducted studies of mortality among policyholders beginning with its first report in 1925, and in 1979 the Society of Actuaries and Association of Life Insurance Medical Directors of America published the *Blood Pressure Study.*[29] The report was based on some 4 million policies (not accounting for individuals as holders of multiple policies) and an average of 6.6 years of follow-up from the date of issuance. As in earlier reports, death was strongly related to blood pressure. For men it increased from less than average (0.84 times the overall rate) at pressures below 128 mm Hg systolic and 83 mm Hg diastolic to 2.69 times the overall rate at pressures over 167 mm Hg systolic and 97 mm Hg diastolic. Overweight compounded the risk, such that overweight of only 15%–25% was associated with elimination of the benefit of the lowest blood pressure category and increased relative risk in the highest category from 2.69 to 3.19 times the overall risk. For women the same general pattern was reported: Risk in the lowest blood pressure category and standard weight was 0.90 times the overall risk, and this rose to 2.16 times the overall risk for the highest category; 15%–25% overweight increased these relative risks to 0.95 and 2.94, respectively. As in previous insurance industry reports, the data indicated increased risks of death from the low-

est to the second category of blood pressure, still within the range even now considered normal or high normal. At pressures from 128 to 137 mm Hg systolic and 78 to 87 mm Hg diastolic, relative risks were 1.11 for men and 1.08 for women. There are, of course, questions about the interpretation of the absolute blood pressure values identified with insurance examination, but the consistency of findings from these and other studies lends them credence as an indication of overall patterns of risk. For example, the report of Levy and colleagues[12] also concluded that death or retirement due to cardiovascular-renal conditions among US Army officers was related to transient hypertension or tachycardia or to overweight at entry to military service and also to sustained hypertension as it developed later.

The risks specifically for coronary heart disease and stroke are also related to blood pressure levels, as shown in Figures 12–8 and 12–9.[30] Separately for coronary heart disease and for stroke, these figures summarize, on the basis of a meta-analysis, the relation between individual levels of diastolic pressure at the start of follow-up and the relative risks of these events. A relative risk of 1.0 represents the average risk for the pooled populations included in the analyses (nine for coronary heart disease and seven for stroke), while lower or higher risks are shown for strata of these two pooled populations with lower or higher mean values of usual diastolic pressure. In each case, a clear gradient of risk with higher baseline diastolic pressure is apparent. Not even the lowest increments in blood pressure, from category 1 to category 2 in each figure, were free of an increase in the risk of an event. The risk gradient was less steep for coronary heart disease than for stroke. For both categories of events, the numbers of events were greater (as shown by the relative sizes of the darkened squares) at intermediate than at either the lowest or the highest levels of blood pressure. This indicates that a major proportion of events attributed to elevated blood pressure come from categories of modest rather than extreme elevation.

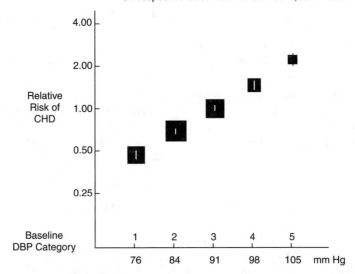

9 Prospective Observational Studies: 4,856 Events

Note: Squares represent disease risks in each category relative to risk in the whole study population. Sizes of squares are proportional to number of events in each DBP category. A 95% confidence interval for estimates of relative risk is denoted by vertical lines.

Figure 12–8 Coronary Heart Disease (CHD) and Usual Level of Diastolic Blood Pressure (DBP). *Source*: Reprinted with permission from S MacMahon et al, *Lancet*, Vol 335, pp 765–774, © 1990, The Lancet, Ltd.

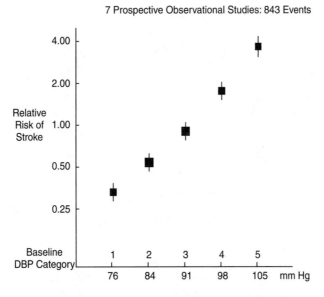

7 Prospective Observational Studies: 843 Events

Note: Squares represent disease risks in each category relative to risk in the whole study population. Sizes of squares are proportional to number of events in each DBP category. A 95% confidence interval for estimates of relative risk is denoted by vertical lines.

Figure 12–9 Stroke and Usual Level of Diastolic Blood Pressure (DBP). *Source*: Reprinted with permission from S MacMahon et al, *Lancet*, Vol 335, pp 765–774, © 1990, The Lancet, Ltd.

PREVENTION AND CONTROL

Population-Wide Strategy

In most populations blood pressure distributions of successive age groups shift to higher values, at both the center and the upper extreme, at later ages for systolic than for diastolic pressure. The underlying determinants of blood pressure levels in the population therefore result in a continuous progression with increasing age from relatively lower-risk to higher-risk blood pressure levels (systolic, diastolic, or both), including those levels considered to warrant individual detection and long-term treatment.

Treatment of those with high blood pressure can reduce the prevalence of the highest levels of risk (see below). But only intervention for the population as a whole, especially at young adult or earlier ages, can reduce the otherwise expected incidence of the highest-risk status, thereby reducing the public health burden of both high risk and the need for treatment.

The goal of population interventions is both to control the incidence of new cases of high blood pressure, resulting in fewer new cases, and to reduce its prevalence. Success therefore depends both on influencing modifiable causes of progression in blood pressure levels and on reinforcing behavior by health professionals and affected individuals to ensure detection and control of already-established high blood pressure. Interventions for these purposes have been advocated and implemented at least since the early 1970s. For example, beginning in 1973, the National High Blood Pressure Education Program (NHBPEP) has emphasized public and professional education as a means to promote the detection, evaluation, and management of high blood pressure.[31] The World Health Organization has also recommended national policies for prevention of high blood pressure.[32,33]

A model community organization to implement effective population-level and individual-level measures for prevention and control of high blood pressure is addressed by McClellan and Wilber, who derived from the experience of numerous programs in the United States the prototype presented in Figure 12–10.[34] The

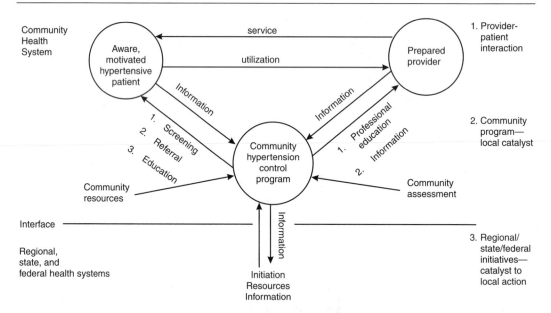

Figure 12–10 Schematic View of a Model Community Hypertension Control Program. *Source*: From *Chronic Disease Epidemiology and Control*. Copyright 1993 by the American Public Health Association. Reprinted with permission.

message is that an effective community-oriented agency must have linkages of several kinds with affected individuals, providers, and political units and their agencies concerned with the problem.

High-Risk Strategy

Individual measures for the prevention and control of high blood pressure address both the progression of blood pressure in individuals, especially those most likely to develop sustained high blood pressure, and management of established high blood pressure to reduce the pressure to desirable levels and thereby to reduce the attendant risks. With respect to prevention, the NHBPEP's Working Group Report on Primary Prevention of Hypertension is an important recent advance in the arena of practice-level interventions for prevention of high blood pressure.[18] Interventions judged effective on the basis of published studies include weight loss, reduced sodium intake, reduced alcohol consumption, and exercise. Interventions considered to have only limited or unproved efficacy were stress management; dietary supplementation with fiber, potassium, fish oil, magnesium, or calcium; and other dietary modification.

For treatment of individuals with documented sustained high blood pressure, the recommendations of the Joint National Committee (a committee of the NHBPEP) included the algorithm presented in Figure 12–11.[2] The recommended strategy is to initiate treatment by lifestyle or nonpharmacological interventions to modify weight, alcohol intake, physical activity, sodium intake, and smoking habits. Only if the response to these measures is inadequate, that is, little progress toward the goal blood pressure level is attained, is the first step of drug treatment to be introduced. Successive steps in drug therapy are similarly deferred unless the response to intermediate steps is inadequate. The intent is to achieve the target blood pressure level without medication or with the least medication necessary.

EFFECTS OF INTERVENTION

The changes in populations described above appear, at least in part, to reflect the impact of preventive measures. Interventions aimed at treatment of individuals with high blood pressure seem reasonably credited with downward shifts in the 90th percentile values of distributions of systolic blood pressure in periodic surveys in the United States. Explanation of decreasing values of the median, perhaps reflecting behavioral or broader environmental changes affecting the population at large, is less secure.

Impact on Morbidity and Mortality

The question of whether blood pressure could be reduced effectively and rates of outcomes such as coronary events, stroke, all-cause mortality, or others could be diminished as a result has been investigated in many experimental studies over several decades. Random-allocation designs, most often with placebo controls, have become standard since the adoption of this approach by the Veterans Administration Cooperative Group trials beginning in the 1960s, a critical period in this area of research recently recounted by Freis, the director of that group.[35] Earlier studies are documented and unanswered questions posed by Collins and Peto in a recent update of their review of the effects of blood pressure–lowering treatment.[36] Table 12–6 and Figure 12–12 summarize the experience of 17 trials of drug treatment of individuals with high blood pressure. Table 12–6 describes the trials and indicates the blood pressure reductions attained in each trial and overall. Largest among these were the Hypertension Detection and Follow-Up Program (HDFP), the Medical Research Council (MRC) trials in younger and older adults, and the Systolic Hypertension in the Elderly Program (SHEP). Their aggregate participant population was 47,653, of whom about equal proportions were women and men. The mean follow-up duration was 4.9 years.

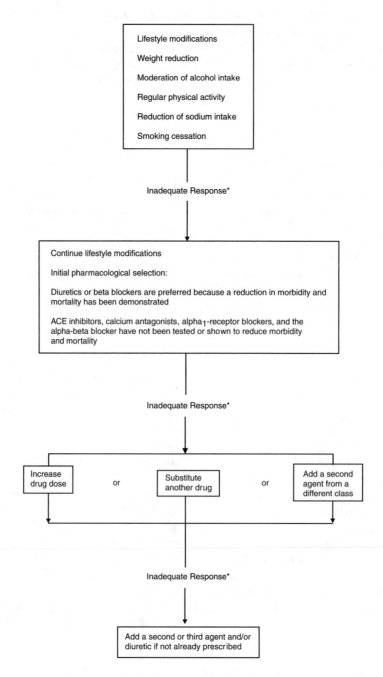

Figure 12–11 Treatment Algorithm for High Blood Pressure. *Source:* Reprinted from *The Fifth Report of the Joint National Committee on Detection, Evaluation, and Treatment of High Blood Pressure*, National Heart, Lung and Blood Institute, National Institutes of Health, 1993.

Table 12–6 Population and Trial Design in Recent and Previous Unconfounded Randomized Trials of at Least 1 Year of Antihypertensive Drug Treatment

Trial[a]	No. of Patients	Entry DBP and/or SBP[b]	Mean Age (yr)	Male (%)	Mean Follow-Up (yr)	Blinding	Main Drugs[c]	Mean DBP Difference (mm Hg) in Attenders[d]
HDFP	10,940	DBP ≥90	51	55	5.0	None	CD	5
MRC younger adults	17,354	DBP of 90–109	52	52	5.0	Single	BF or PR	4
SHEP	4,736	DBP <90 with SBP of 160–219	72	43	4.5	Double	CD + AT (or RE)	4
MRC older adults	4,396	DBP <115 and SBP of 160–209	70	42	5.8	Single	AT or HZ	8
STOP-H	1,627	DBP of 105–120, or DBP of 90–104 with SBP of 180–230	76	37	2.1	Double	AT or ME or PI or HZ + AM	10
12 smaller trials	8,614	DBP ≥85	53	63	5.0	Various	DI or BB	6
Total: all trials	47,653	—	56	52	4.9	—	—	6[d]

a. HDFP, Hypertension Detection and Follow-Up Program; MRC, Medical Research Council (Britain); SHEP, Systolic Hypertension in the Elderly Program; STOP-H, Swedish Trial in Old Patients with Hypertension.

b. DBP, diastolic blood pressure; SBP, systolic blood pressure.

c. AM, amiloride; AT, atenolol; BB, β-blocker-based regimens; BF, bendrofluazide; CD, chlorthalidone; DI, diuretic-based regimens; HZ, hydrochlorothiazide; ME, metoprolol; PI, pindolol; PR, propranolol; RE, reserpine.

d. The difference in mean DBP per person-year of follow-up, based on data from those who attended follow-up for blood pressure measurement, was 6 mm Hg. The difference between all those allocated treatment (irrespective of compliance) and all those allocated control is likely to have been somewhat smaller—eg, 5–6 mm Hg.

Source: Reprinted with permission from R Collins et al, *Lancet*, Vol 335, pp 827–838, © 1990, The Lancet, Ltd.

The mean decrease in diastolic pressure observed among active treated participants in each trial ranged widely, in part reflecting the different starting levels selected for the respective trials, but overall averaged about 6 mm Hg. Typically from hundreds to thousands of participants are represented in each trial, and an average reduction of this magnitude is substantial.

The effects of treatment on stroke and coronary heart disease event rates are shown in Figure 12–12. Variation in point estimates of effect and in their confidence limits is apparent in the figure, but the overall estimates of effect were of clear-cut benefit in both instances: 38% (CI 31–45) reduction for stroke and 16% (CI 18–23) for coronary events, both highly significant. Total mortality was also significantly reduced, by 21% (CI 13–28). Collins and Peto remarked that the reduction in stroke events by treatment matches the prediction from the attributable risk of stroke due to blood pressure in observational epidemiologic studies. For coronary events, however, only about two-thirds of the predicted treatment effect was found, as in previous analyses addressing this question. While possible offsetting harm of blood pressure treatment has been raised as a possible explanation of this finding, they argue that the difference in stroke and coronary heart disease responses to treatment may reflect differences in the relation of blood pressure to these two outcomes. Stroke may reflect more immediate blood pressure effects that respond to treatment rapidly, whereas coronary atherosclerosis, accelerated in its development by high blood pressure, may require longer to exhibit the full benefit of blood pressure reduction. If so, longer-term follow-up may reveal the expected outcome. This explanation would predict a difference in time to benefit between hemorrhagic and thromboembolic stroke, the latter being expected to parallel the time course for coronary events. This could be tested in a trial where stroke types are differentiated and occurred in sufficient numbers for separate analysis.

Other trials of blood pressure treatment have addressed additional questions. SHEP, already described in the foregoing analysis, specifically tested the effects of treatment in isolated systolic hypertension, a condition especially prevalent in the elderly.[37] This and other trials in similar age ranges thus contribute to the evidence that older persons can be treated effectively and safely with blood pressure–lowering medications.

Impact on Blood Pressure

Use of interventions other than drugs has been investigated also, both for treatment of established high blood pressure and for its prevention. Dietary approaches have been most extensively studied, and reports of the effects of weight loss and sodium restriction have been prominent examples of such trials. Most recently reported is the Trials of Hypertension Prevention (TOHP), Phase II, a study of 2382 men and women age 30 to 54 years who had high normal blood pressure and body mass index in the range representing 110%–165% of desirable weight at entry.[38] Both systolic and diastolic pressure were lowered by intervention, with the maximum effect at six months. The effect declined over the remaining 30 months of follow-up, but significant reduction in incidence of high blood pressure was achieved.

Studies specifically of reduced-salt dietary interventions have received great interest and have been reviewed on several occasions. For example, Cutler and colleagues recently conducted an overview of 32 trials of blood pressure reduction with such interventions.[39] The studies were mixed in design and selection criteria but showed significant reductions in systolic and diastolic pressure in the several subgroups of studies examined. Their overall estimate of effects per 100 mmol of sodium intake per day were reductions (systolic/diastolic) of −5.8/−2.5 mm Hg among hypertensive subjects and −2.3/−1.4 mm Hg among normotensives. They noted no evidence of safety hazards in the context of these trials and projected

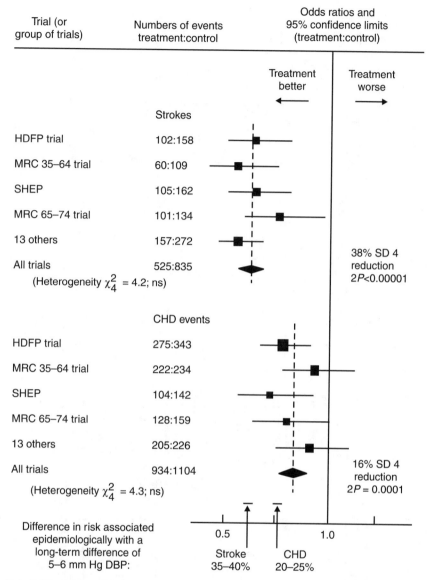

Trial (or group of trials)	Numbers of events treatment:control	Odds ratios and 95% confidence limits (treatment:control)

Strokes

HDFP trial	102:158	
MRC 35–64 trial	60:109	
SHEP	105:162	
MRC 65–74 trial	101:134	
13 others	157:272	
All trials	525:835	38% SD 4 reduction 2P<0.00001
(Heterogeneity χ_4^2 = 4.2; ns)		

CHD events

HDFP trial	275:343	
MRC 35–64 trial	222:234	
SHEP	104:142	
MRC 65–74 trial	128:159	
13 others	205:226	
All trials	934:1104	16% SD 4 reduction 2P = 0.0001
(Heterogeneity χ_4^2 = 4.3; ns)		

Difference in risk associated epidemiologically with a long-term difference of 5–6 mm Hg DBP:
Stroke 35–40%   CHD 20–25%

Note: Solid squares represent the odds ratios (treatment:control) for the 4 larger trials and the properly stratified odds ratio for the combination of the 13 smaller trials. The sizes of the squares are proportional to the amount of "information" contributed by that study, and 95% confidence intervals are denoted by horizontal lines (for individual large trials or the combined small trials) and by diamonds (for overviews of all trials). HDFP, Hypertension Detection and Follow-Up Program; MRC, Medical Research Council (Britain); SHEP, Systolic Hypertension in the Elderly Program.

Figure 12–12 Reduction in the Odds of Stroke and Coronary Heart Disease (CHD) in 17 Trials of Antihypertensive Drug Treatment. *Source:* Reprinted with permission from R Collins and R Peto, Antihypertensive Drug Therapy: Effects on Stroke and Coronary Heart Disease, in *Textbook of Hypertension*, JD Swales, ed, p 1159, © 1994, Blackwell Scientific Publications.

Table 12–7 Trials of Prevention of Progressive Rise in Blood Pressure (BP) to Treatable Levels

Study	Demographic Characteristics				Intervention	Duration of Follow-Up	Average Initial BP, mm Hg		Average Net (Active-Control) Effect		
	Sample Size	Mean Age, yr	% Male	% White			Systolic	Diastolic	Change in BP, mm Hg		Relative Risk of Hypertension[b] (95% Confidence Interval)
									Systolic[a]	Diastolic[a]	
Primary Prevention of Hypertension (PPH)	201	38	87	82	Multifactorial (reduced calorie, sodium, and alcohol intake, and increased physical activity)	5 yr	122.6	82.5	-1.3	-1.2	0.46
Hypertension Prevention Trial (HPT)	252	38	68	80	Reduced calorie intake	3 yr	125.0	83.2	-2.4	-1.8	0.77
	392	39	62	84	Reduced sodium intake	3 yr	123.9	82.8	0.2	0.1	0.79
	255	39	62	82	Reduced calorie and sodium intake	3 yr	124.5	82.9	-1.0	-1.3	0.95
	391	38	63	85	Reduced sodium and increased potassium intake	3 yr	124.0	82.6	-1.2	-0.7	0.77
Trials of Hypertension Prevention (TOHP), phase I	564	43	72	79	Weight loss (reduced calorie intake and increased physical activity)	18 mo	124.4	83.8	-2.9	-2.3	0.49 (0.29–0.83)
	744	43	72	77	Reduced sodium intake	18 mo	125.0	83.8	-1.7	-0.9	0.76 (0.49–1.18)
	562	43	71	84	Stress management	18 mo	124.6	83.7	-0.5	-0.8	1.07 (0.65–1.76)
	471	43	68	85	Calcium supplementation	6 mo	125.7	84.0	-0.5	0.2	0.91 (0.43–1.96)
	461	43	68	85	Magnesium supplementation	6 mo	125.1	83.9	-0.2	-0.1	0.63 (0.27–1.50)
	351	43	72	87	Potassium supplementation	6 mo	121.6	80.9	0.1	-0.4	0.87 (0.34–2.21)
	350	43	70	86	Fish oil supplementation	6 mo	122.7	81.1	-0.2	-0.6	1.11 (0.46–2.67)

a. Trial average for PPH; point estimates at 18 and 36 months for TOHP and HPT, respectively.

b. Defined as diastolic BP of 90 mm Hg or more, or antihypertensive drug therapy during follow-up.

Source: Reprinted from National High Blood Pressure Program Working Group, *Archives of Internal Medicine*, Vol 153, No 154, p 192, 1993.

that substantial lowering of sodium intake in the US population at large could reduce cardiovascular morbidity and mortality. However, published reviews on a given topic at the same time can come to different conclusions, as reflected in two examples of conflicting views on a contentious topic.[40,41]

Prevention of high blood pressure itself by interventions tested to date, including only the first phase of TOHP, was summarized on the basis of several trials by the Working Group on Primary Prevention of Hypertension, as shown in Table 12–7.[18] In three trials, two of them having multiple treatment strata, persons with pre-intervention diastolic pressure levels below 90 mm Hg and not on treatment experienced reduced incidence of high blood pressure. The net blood pressure differences between treated and control groups were small, but the estimated reductions in incidence of high blood pressure ranged from none in some of the short-term (six-month) trials to more than 50% in the five-year trial. This area continues to receive attention, and behavioral and psychological interventions are still being evaluated.

Studies of interventions to control increasing blood pressure in childhood and adolescence have had very mixed results, in part reflecting differences in selection of participants and interventions and in study designs. Most trials have been of nonpharmacologic interventions. One drug trial was conducted in 8- to 18-year-olds with greater than 90th percentile values of blood pressure repeatedly over a four-month period.[42] Low-dose medication and education on diet and physical activity were combined. With evaluation at the close of the treatment period of 30 months, significant reductions in systolic (−3.59 mm Hg) and diastolic (−1.73 mm Hg) pressure were reported. Overall it is not yet established, however, that long-term change in blood pressure is influenced by the interventions applied to date in childhood and adolescence. This is an important area for research if prevention of high blood pressure in the first place is to be achieved.

CURRENT ISSUES

Prevention of High Blood Pressure in the First Place

The greatest public health challenge in relation to blood pressure is the prevention of this risk factor in the first place, so that both the population risks and the societal costs of high blood pressure could be greatly reduced. Evidence from studies of both the natural history of blood pressure change with age and the blood pressure response to behavioral interventions greatly strengthens the view that more effective population-wide measures may be devised and implemented toward this goal. The basic question of causation of the unwanted rise in blood pressure through middle adulthood or beyond remains only partially answered, however, and there may be potentially identifiable subpopulations for whom more specific interventions or strategies for their delivery could be developed. Genetic studies and other areas of research may lead to the discovery of such groups, which could have an impact on this problem at the population level if the groups are sufficiently large.

Control of Established High Blood Pressure in the Whole Population

The effective control of already-established high blood pressure is not equally attained in all population groups within the United States, and for many countries the effort to achieve control of existing high blood pressure is at a very early stage. How to reach those population groups benefiting least from current knowledge about treatment will remain an important question as long as the current high incidence persists.

Optimum Choices in Long-Term Drug Therapy

Questions remain about the relative efficacy and safety of the various classes of blood pressure–lowering agents, and new agents will doubtless continue to become available. These questions require continued investigation if choices of treatment are to be based on sound evidence of relative efficacy and safety as well as cost. A major trial in this area now in progress is the Antihypertensive and Lipid-Lowering Heart Attack Trial (ALLHAT), whose results among some 40,000 randomized participants are anticipated with great interest.

REFERENCES

1. Pickering GW. *The Nature of Essential Hypertension.* New York: Grune & Stratton; 1961.

2. National High Blood Pressure Education Program. *The Fifth Report of the Joint National Committee on Detection, Evaluation, and Treatment of High Blood Pressure.* Bethesda, Md: National Heart, Lung and Blood Institute, National Institutes of Health; 1993. NIH publication 93-1088.

3. Hypertension Detection and Follow-Up Cooperative Group. The Hypertension Detection and Follow-Up Program. A progress report. *Circ Res.* 1977;40(suppl I):I-107–I-109.

4. Stamler J, Stamler R, Neaton JD. Blood pressure, systolic and diastolic, and cardiovascular risks. *Arch Intern Med.* 1993;153:598–615.

5. Korotkov NS. A contribution to the problem of methods for the determination of the blood pressure. (English translation). In: Ruskin A, ed. *Classics in Arterial Hypertension.* Springfield, Ill: Charles C Thomas; 1956: 127–133.

6. National High Blood Pressure Education Working Group on Hypertension Control in Children and Adolescents. Update on the 1987 Task Force Report on High Blood Pressure in Children and Adolescents: a Working Group report from the National High Blood Pressure Education Program. *Pediatr.* 1996;98:649–658.

7. Rose G. Standardization of observers in blood pressure measurement. *Lancet.* 1965;1:673–674.

8. Curb JD, Labarthe DR, Cooper SP, Cutter GR, et al. Training and certification of blood pressure observers. *Hypertens.* 1983;5:610–614.

9. Epstein FH, Eckoff RD. The epidemiology of high blood pressure—geographic distributions and etiological factors. In: Stamler J, Stamler R, Pullman TN, eds. *The Epidemiology of Hypertension.* New York: Grune & Stratton; 1967: 155–166.

10. The INTERSALT Co-operative Research Group. INTERSALT Study. An international co-operative study on the relation of blood pressure to electrolyte excretion in populations, I: design and methods. *Hypertens.* 1986;4:781–787.

11. Rodriguez BL, Labarthe DR, Huang B, Lopez-Gomez J. Rise of blood pressure with age: new evidence of population differences. *Hypertens.* 1994;24:779–785.

12. Levy RL, White PD, Stroud WD, Hillman CC. Sustained hypertension: predisposing factors and causes of disability and death. *JAMA.* 1947;135:77–80.

13. Ford ES, Cooper RS. Risk factors for hypertension in a national cohort study. *Hypertens.* 1991;18:598–606.

14. Mahoney LT, Lauer RM, Lee J, Clarke WR. Factors affecting tracking of coronary heart disease risk factors in children: the Muscatine Study. In: Williams CL, Wynder EL, eds. *Hyperlipidemia in Childhood and the Development of Atherosclerosis: Annals of the New York Academy of Sciences.* New York: New York Academy of Sciences; 1991;623:120–132.

15. He J, Klag MJ, Whelton PK, Chen J-Y, et al. Migration, blood pressure pattern, and hypertension: the Yi Migrant Study. *Am J Epidemiol.* 1991;134:1085–1101.

16. Committee on Diet and Health. *Diet and Health: Implications for Reducing Chronic Disease Risk.* Washington, DC: Food and Nutrition Board, Commission on Life Sciences, National Research Council, National Academy of Sciences; 1989.

17. The INTERSALT Study: background, methods, findings, and implications. *Am J Clin Nutr.* 1997;65 (suppl):626S–642S.

18. National High Blood Pressure Education Program. Working group report on primary prevention of hypertension. *Arch Int Med.* 1993;153:186–208.

19. Izzo JL Jr, Black HR, eds. *Hypertension Primer.* Dallas, Tex: American Heart Association; 1993.

20. Keiser HR. Catecholamines and target organ damage. In: Izzo JL Jr, Black HR, eds. *Hypertension Primer.* Dallas, Tex: American Heart Association; 1993: 123–124.

21. Sullivan JM. Coronary artery disease: pathophysiology. In: Izzo JL Jr, Black HR, eds. *Hypertension Primer.* Dallas, Tex: American Heart Association; 1993: 133–134.

22. Task Force on Blood Pressure Control in Children. Report of the Second Task Force on Blood Pressure Control in Children—1987. *Pediat.* 1987;79:1–25.

23. Comstock GW. An epidemiologic study of blood pressure levels in a biracial community in the southern United States. *Am J Epidemiol.* 1995;141:584–628. [Reprinted from *Am J Hyg.* 1957;65:271–315].

24. Burt VL, Whelton P, Rocella EJ, Brown C, et al. Prevalence of hypertension in the US adult population:

results from the Third National Health and Nutrition Examination Survey, 1988–1991. *Hypertens.* 1995;25: 305–313.

25. The WHO MONICA Project. Geographical variation in the major risk factors of coronary heart disease in men and women aged 35–64 years. *World Health Stat Q.* 1988;41:115–140.

26. Nissinen A, Böthig S, Granroth H, Lopez AD. Hypertension in developing countries. *World Health Stat Q.* 1988;41:141–154.

27. Burt VL, Cutler JA, Higgins M, Horan MJ, et al. Trends in the prevalence, awareness, treatment, and control of hypertension in the adult US population: data from the Health Examination Surveys, 1960 to 1991. *Hypertens.* 1995;26:60–69.

28. Keys A. *Seven Countries: A Multivariate Analysis of Death and Coronary Heart Disease.* Cambridge, Mass: Harvard University Press; 1980.

29. Society of Actuaries and Association of Life Insurance Medical Directors of America. *Blood Pressure Study 1979.* Chicago: Society of Actuaries and Association of Life Insurance Medical Directors of America; 1980.

30. MacMahon S, Peto R, Cutler J, Collins R, et al. Blood pressure, stroke, and coronary heart disease, I: prolonged differences in blood pressure: prospective observational studies corrected for the regression dilution bias. *Lancet.* 1990;335:765–774.

31. Roccella EJ, Horan MJ. The National High Blood Pressure Education Program: measuring progress and assessing its impact. *Health Psychol.* 1988;7(suppl): 297–303.

32. World Health Organization. *Primary Prevention of Essential Hypertension: Report of a WHO Scientific Group.* Geneva, Switzerland: World Health Organization; 1983. Technical Report Series 686.

33. World Health Organization. *Hypertension Control: Report of a WHO Expert Committee.* Geneva, Switzerland: World Health Organization; 1996. Technical Report Series 862.

34. McClellan W, Wilber JA. A decade's experience with hypertension control programs in the United States: the empirical basis for a model of community control programs. In: Rosenfeld JB, Silverberg DS, Viskiper R, eds. *Hypertension Control in the Community.* London: John Libbey; 1985: 1–16.

35. Freis ED. Reminiscences of the Veterans Administration Trial of the Treatment of Hypertension. *Hypertens.* 1990;16:472–475.

36. Collins R, Peto R. Antihypertensive drug therapy: effects on stroke and coronary heart disease. In: Swales JD, ed. *Textbook of Hypertension.* Oxford, England: Blackwell Scientific Publications; 1994: 1156–1164.

37. SHEP Cooperative Research Group. Prevention of stroke by antihypertensive drug treatment in older persons with isolated systolic hypertension: final results of the Systolic Hypertension in the Elderly Program (SHEP). *JAMA.* 1991;265:3255–3264.

38. The Trials of Hypertension Prevention Collaborative Research Group. Effects of weight loss and sodium reduction intervention on blood pressure and hypertension incidence in overweight people with high-normal blood pressure: the Trials of Hypertension Prevention, Phase II. *Arch Intern Med.* 1997;157:657–667.

39. Cutler JA, Follman D, Allender PS. Randomized trials of sodium reduction: an overview. *Am J Clin Nutr.* 1997;65(suppl):643S–651S.

40. Midgley JP, Matthew AG, Greenwood CMT, Logan AG. Effect of reduced dietary sodium on blood pressure: a meta-analysis of randomized controlled trials. *JAMA.* 1996;275:1590–1597.

41. Staessen JA, Lijnen P, Thijs L, Fagard R. Salt and blood pressure in community-based intervention trials. *Am J Clin Nutr.* 1997;65(suppl):661S–670S.

42. Berenson GS, Shear CL, Chiang YK, Webber LS, et al. Combined low-dose medication and primary intervention over a 30-month period for sustained high blood pressure in childhood. *Am J Med Sci.* 1990;299:79–86.

Glucose Intolerance, Insulin Resistance, and Diabetes

SUMMARY

A spectrum of conditions from transiently elevated blood glucose concentration to severe disturbance of insulin-glucose regulation is represented by terms such as *hyperglycemia, impaired glucose tolerance, insulin resistance,* and *non–insulin-dependent* or *insulin-dependent diabetes mellitus.* Together these terms refer to disorders that are closely related to risks of atherosclerotic and hypertensive cardiovascular diseases, both because of recurring, but inconsistent, associations between high blood concentrations of glucose or insulin and these conditions and because of their common clustering with other risk factors such as adverse blood lipid profiles, high blood pressure, obesity, and others. Recent advances in the epidemiology of diabetes and related disorders stem from adoption of standard criteria for diagnosis and classification in population-based and clinical studies. Major impetus to international collaboration in study of diabetes has come from the World Health Organization (WHO) and from efforts to assemble comprehensive reviews of the epidemiologic and other literature concerning diabetes, making this extensive literature more accessible than previously to those interested in public health and other applications. Broad outlines of preventive measures have been formulated, along with accompanying protocols for implementation at the community level. At the same time, many questions remain for epidemiologic investigation.

INTRODUCTION

Diabetes mellitus may be characterized as a disorder of glucose transport or metabolism due to reduced production or effectiveness of insulin, a hormone produced by specialized cells in the pancreas and having multiple regulatory functions. The terms *insulin resistance* and *diabetes* require explanation, as provided below, in the context of current definition and classification of these conditions. In its classic form, marked by passage of large quantities of sugar-containing urine, diabetes mellitus is said to have been recognized for more than 2000 years. Current concepts of diabetes are much broader and include, among others, its vascular manifestations, which together constitute the leading cause of death among persons with diabetes.

Because the presence of diabetes increases the risk of coronary heart disease and other consequences of atherosclerosis, emphasis has increased in recent years on the prevention of these cardiovascular conditions as an important component of care in diabetes. More broadly still, lesser disturbances of insulin production or function and attendant impairment of glucose utilization, including "insulin resistance," have also been recognized. These disorders also are related to increased cardiovascular risks. Public health concern has therefore expanded to include a wider spectrum of disturbances of this regulatory complex. In addition, these disorders may offer further insights into mechanisms of atherogenesis in diabetes.

In *Epidemiology of Diabetes and Its Vascular Lesions*, published in 1978, West presented an extensive review of work in this field, which he dated from the earliest collection of death certificate information on diabetes in Europe and the United States in 1850.[1] Other early epidemiologic observations included geographic differences and secular changes in the prevalence of diabetes that were reported well before the 20th century. He noted at the same time, however, that until the 1960s very little systematic epidemiologic investigation of diabetes had been accomplished. This fact was attributed to lack of epidemiologic training and experience on the part of those studying diabetes in the earlier years. Another factor in the recent dramatic change in this field was the adoption of methods and criteria for population studies, without which the progress of the past three decades would not have been possible.

Recent epidemiologic studies have contributed importantly to understanding the relation between insulin resistance and diabetes and the relation between insulin resistance and atherosclerosis and its manifestations, including the view that obesity, or central adiposity, and physical inactivity are prominent among the factors common to both disorders. The emerging concept that the cardiovascular conditions found in diabetes are better thought of as an inherent part of that disorder and not as more adventitious complications suggests that the epidemiology of cardiovascular diseases and of diabetes and insulin resistance may become still more closely integrated in the future.

DEFINITION AND CLASSIFICATION

Terminology

In the major 1992 compendium, *International Textbook of Diabetes Mellitus*, Harris and Zimmet presented the extensively annotated "Classification of Diabetes Mellitus and Other Categories of Glucose Intolerance" (Table 13–1).[2] This classification represents the deliberations of an international working group convened in the United States, a WHO Expert Committee, several national diabetes societies, and other organizations. It reflects the view that diabetes mellitus is a heterogeneous group of disorders both in causation and in clinical manifestations, with elevated blood glucose concentration as the major unifying characteristic. Of particular value is the inclusion in the table of older terms encountered often in the literature. Especially relevant here are the distinction of non–insulin-dependent diabetes mellitus (NIDDM) from insulin-dependent diabetes mellitus (IDDM) and the identification of impaired glucose tolerance (IGT) as a separate class. As shown in the table, several terms have been used synonymously with NIDDM (*type 2 diabetes, adult onset diabetes*, etc) and IDDM (*type 1 diabetes, juvenile onset diabetes*, etc). Because NIDDM is far more prevalent than IDDM, it contributes more to the relation between diabetes and cardiovascular diseases than does IDDM; reference hereafter to "diabetes" is therefore to NIDDM unless otherwise noted. IGT represents a range of blood glucose responses to diagnostic testing, defined below, which is analogous to the "borderline" categories of blood cholesterol concentration or blood pressure.

Natural History

The natural history of NIDDM is depicted in Figure 13–1, from the 1994 WHO Study Group report, *Prevention of Diabetes Mellitus*.[3] It indicates the broad time course, usually over many years, of progression from onset to development of complications, disability, and death. Prior to the onset of clinical signs, genetic susceptibility and environmental factors, especially unfavorable nutrition, obesity, and physical inactivity, are thought to result in progressive IGT. This is detectable by measures of insulin resistance (impairment of glucose uptake in tissues despite

Table 13–1 Classification of Diabetes Mellitus and Other Categories of Glucose Intolerance

Class	Former Terminology	Associated Factors	Characteristics
Insulin-dependent diabetes mellitus (IDDM, type 1)	Juvenile diabetes, juvenile onset diabetes, juvenile onset type diabetes, JOD, ketosis-prone diabetes, brittle diabetes	Evidence regarding etiology suggests genetic and environmental or acquired factors, association with certain human leukocyte antigen (HLA) types, and abnormal immune responses, including autoimmune reactions	Persons in this subclass are dependent on injected insulin to prevent ketosis and to preserve life, although there may be preketotic, non–insulin-dependent phases in the natural history of the disease. In the preponderance of cases, onset is in youth, but IDDM may occur at any age. Characterized by insulinopenia. Islet cell antibodies are frequently present at diagnosis in this type
Non–insulin-dependent diabetes mellitus (NIDDM, type 2) (a) Nonobese (b) Obese	Adult onset diabetes, maturity-onset diabetes, maturity-onset type diabetes, MOD, ketosis-resistant diabetes, stable diabetes	There are probably multiple etiologies for this class, the common outcome being derangement of carbohydrate metabolism. Evidence on familial aggregation of diabetes implies genetic factors, and this class includes diabetes presenting in children and adults in which autosomal dominant inheritance has been clearly established (formerly termed the MODY type, maturity onset diabetes in the young). Environmental factors superimposed on genetic susceptibility are probably involved in the onset of the NIDDM types. Obesity is suspected as an etiologic factor and is recommended as a criterion for dividing NIDDM into two subclasses, according to the presence or absence of obesity	Persons in this subclass are not insulin-dependent or ketosis-prone, although they may use insulin for correction of symptomatic or persistent hyperglycemia and they can develop ketosis under special circumstances, such as episodes of infection or stress. Serum insulin levels may be normal, elevated, or depressed. In the preponderance of cases, onset is after age 40, but NIDDM is known to occur at all ages. About 60%–90% of NIDDM subjects are obese and constitute a subtype of NIDDM; in these patients, glucose tolerance is often improved by weight loss. Hyperinsulinemia and insulin resistance characterize some patients in this subtype
Malnutrition-related diabetes mellitus (MRDM)	Tropical diabetes, pancreatic diabetes, ketosis-resistant diabetes of the young	Occurs in tropical developing countries, in which young diabetics often present with a history of nutritional deficiency and a constellation of symptoms, signs, and metabolic characteristics that fail to meet the criteria used to classify IDDM and NIDDM. Distinctive clinical features and course, uncertain etiology and pathophysiology	

continues

Table 13–1 continued

Class	Former Terminology	Associated Factors	Characteristics
(a) Fibrocalculous pancreatic diabetes			Characterized by stone formation in the main pancreatic duct and its branches, together with extensive fibrosis of the pancreas
(b) Protein-deficient pancreatic diabetes			Characterized by ketosis resistance, insulin resistance, extreme degrees of wasting and emaciation, onset of symptoms before age 35; pancreatic calcification and fibrosis are absent
Gestational diabetes (GDM)	Gestational diabetes	Glucose tolerance with onset during pregnancy is thought to be due to the complex metabolic and hormonal changes that are incompletely understood. Insulin resistance may be responsible in part for gestational diabetes	Glucose intolerance that has its onset or recognition during pregnancy. Thus, diabetics who become pregnant are not included in this class. Associated with increased perinatal complications and with increased risk for progression to diabetes within 5–10 yr after parturition. Requires reclassification after pregnancy terminates into PrevAGT, DM, or IGT
Other types of diabetes, including diabetes associated with certain conditions and syndromes: (a) Pancreatic disease (b) Hormonal (c) Drug or chemical induced (d) Insulin receptor abnormalities (e) Certain genetic syndromes	Secondary diabetes	This subclass contains a variety of types of diabetes, in some of which the etiological relationship is known (eg, diabetes secondary to the pancreatic disease, endocrine disease, or administration of certain drugs). In others, an etiologic relationship is suspected because of a higher frequency of association of diabetes with a syndrome or condition (eg, a number of the genetic syndromes)	In addition to the presence of the specific condition or syndrome, diabetes mellitus is also present

continues

Table 13–1 continued

Class	Former Terminology	Associated Factors	Characteristics
Impaired glucose tolerance (IGT) (a) Nonobese IGT (b) Obese IGT (c) IGT associated with pancreatic disease, hormonal conditions, drug- or chemical-induced insulin receptor abnormalities, certain genetic syndromes	Asymptomatic diabetes, chemical diabetes, subclinical diabetes, borderline diabetes, latent diabetes	Mild glucose intolerance in subjects in this class may be attributable to normal variation of glucose tolerance within a population. In some subjects, IGT may represent a stage in the development of NIDDM or IDDM although the majority of persons with IGT remain in this class for many years or return to normal glucose tolerance	Nondiagnostic fasting glucose levels and glucose intolerance of a degree between normal and diabetic. Some studies have shown increased prevalence of arterial disease symptoms and electrocardiographic abnormalities and increased susceptibility to atherosclerotic disease associated with known risk factors including hypertension, hyperlipidemia, adiposity, and age. Clinically significant renal and retinal complications of diabetes are absent

Source: MI Harris and P Zimmet, Classification of Diabetes Mellitus and Other Categories of Glucose Intolerance, in *International Textbook of Diabetes Mellitus*, KGMM Alberti et al, Vol 1, eds, pp 4–5, Copyright © 1992, John Wiley & Sons Limited. Reproduced with permission.

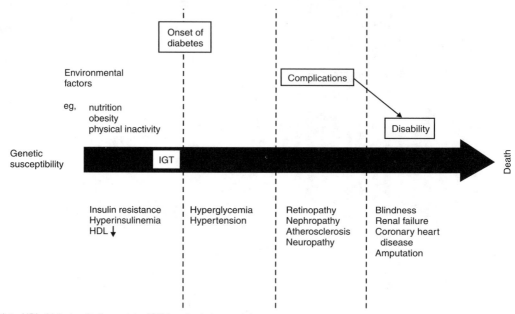

Note: HDL, high-density lipoprotein; IGT, impaired glucose tolerance.

Figure 13–1 The Natural History of Non–Insulin-Dependent Diabetes Mellitus. *Source:* Reprinted with permission from Report of a WHO Study Group, *WHO TRS 844*, p 25, © 1994, World Health Organization.

insulin loading), hyperinsulinemia (increased blood concentration of insulin), and decrease in concentration of high-density lipoprotein (HDL) cholesterol. Both hyperglycemia and hypertension are characteristic of the clinical phase of NIDDM, with eventual development of manifestations (complications) affecting the eyes, kidneys, and peripheral nerves and promoting atherosclerosis. Progression of these conditions may result in disability and death. IDDM differs especially in the absence of obesity and physical inactivity, presence of certain immunologic markers as risk factors in the pre-onset phase, absence of an IGT phase, and post-onset dependency on exogenous insulin. Although hypertension is not typical of IDDM, the later phases are otherwise similar to NIDDM in clinical features but accelerated in their development and progression.

International Statistical Classification

Another approach to classification is that of the *International Statistical Classification of Diseases and Related Health Problems, Tenth Revision*, which specifies five main categories for diabetes: IDDM is coded as E10, NIDDM as E11, malnutrition-related diabetes mellitus as E12, and other specified or unspecified diabetes mellitus as E13 or E14, respectively.[4] Subcategories for each code identify the absence, or the presence and type, of complications present.

The Insulin Resistance Syndrome

Insulin resistance is one dimension of the insulin-glucose relationship that has received increased attention in the past decade. It was recognized decades ago that hyperglycemia could occur in the presence of normal or even increased blood concentrations of insulin, a circumstance considered to be due to some aberration of the insulin molecule itself or its site of action. Therefore diabetes is not necessarily a consequence of failure of the pancreas to secrete insulin. This understanding formed part of the basis for distinguishing both NIDDM and

IGT from IDDM. However, the broader concept of insulin resistance, or decreased insulin sensitivity, as constituting part of a syndrome of physiologic and metabolic disorders has received wide attention only recently. What has been variously termed the *insulin resistance syndrome* or the *metabolic syndrome* was dubbed "syndrome X" in the 1988 Banting Lecture by Reaven, a designation that became popular.[5] Its components, according to Reaven, are resistance to insulin-stimulated glucose uptake, glucose intolerance, hyperinsulinemia, increased very–low-intensity lipoprotein (VLDL)-triglyceride and decreased HDL-cholesterol concentrations, and hypertension. The meaning of this syndrome for risks of atherosclerotic and hypertensive diseases is vigorously debated, as discussed below. It has been suggested that a still broader interpretation applies. In this view, expressed by Keen, the part of the spectrum of NIDDM and IGT that is characterized by insulin resistance represents a form of glucose intolerance resulting from "some much more general disturbance of adaptation to the conditions of modern life."[6 (p xxviii)]

MEASUREMENT

The WHO Criteria

The unifying element of all diagnostic categories in diabetes mellitus is elevated blood glucose concentration or hyperglycemia. Measurement of blood glucose concentration and the criteria for classification on this basis are the foundation of population studies and of comparability of case identification in clinical research as well. Because blood glucose concentration varies in relation to the timing of food intake, values based on casual samples uncontrolled for food intake are of little use. Standardization by assurance of fasting for a fixed minimum period or by feeding a known quantity of glucose is required for reliable screening or diagnostic testing. On this basis, blood samples can be obtained in the fasting state and at one or more fixed intervals, such as two hours, after ingestion of a glucose load. This approach is indicated in the diagnostic values for the oral glucose tolerance test as recommended by the WHO Study Group on Prevention of Diabetes, shown in Table 13–2.[3] Values in mmol/l and mg/dl are given for classification of diabetes mellitus or IGT in either fasting or postload status and whether obtained as venous or capillary (finger stick) samples of whole blood or plasma. Even under these standardized conditions, classification for clinical purposes requires confirmatory testing due to intraindividual and laboratory variation and the prognostic importance of the diagnosis.

Screening Tests for NIDDM and IDDM

Additional measures are available for classifying individuals with respect to NIDDM and IDDM, as shown in Table 13–3.[3] Specificity indicates the proportion of individuals who truly lack the condition who will be identified as negative by the test; sensitivity indicates the proportion of those truly positive who will be identified as positive by the test. For example, the oral glucose tolerance test is equal or superior in performance to other tests for NIDDM, though at intermediate cost, whereas most tests to distinguish IDDM are higher in cost. These considerations enter into the design of population studies to estimate prevalence of diabetes as well as other epidemiologic investigations, but population screening for purposes of case detection is currently considered unjustified due to lack of overall benefit of early detection and treatment.

DETERMINANTS

Pathways of Insulin Action

NIDDM and insulin resistance together are the most relevant aspects of diabetes for risks of atherosclerosis and hypertension in the population at large. It is therefore especially important to appreciate the current understanding of the determinants of these conditions and the mechanisms by which they may contribute to these risks. The

Table 13–2 Diagnostic Values for the Oral Glucose Tolerance Test

	Glucose Concentration, mmol/l(mg/dl)			
	Whole Blood		Plasma	
	Venous	Capillary	Venous	Capillary
Diabetes mellitus				
Fasting value	>6.7	>6.7	>7.8	>7.8
	(<120)	(<120)	(<140)	(<140)
2 hours after glucose load[a]	≥10.0	≥11.1	≥11.1	≥12.2
	(≥180)	(≥200)	(≥200)	(≥220)
Impaired glucose tolerance				
Fasting value	<6.7	<6.7	<7.8	<7.8
	(<120)	(<120)	(<140)	(<140)
2 hours after glucose load[a]	6.7–10.0	7.8–11.1	7.8–11.1	8.9–12.2
	(120–180)	(140–200)	(140–200)	(160–220)

a. For epidemiological or population screening purposes, the 2-hour value determined by a specific enzymic assay after an oral glucose load (75 g in 250–300 ml of water for adults and 1.75 g/kg of body weight, up to a maximum of 75 g for children) may be used alone or with the fasting value. The fasting value alone is considered less reliable, because true fasting cannot be ensured and spurious diagnosis of diabetes may more readily occur.

Source: Reprinted with permission from Report of a WHO Study Group, *WHO TRS 844*, p 17, © 1994, World Health Organization.

Table 13–3 Summary of Screening Methods for Diabetes

Diabetes Type	Method	Specificity	Sensitivity	Cost
NIDDM[a]	Glycated hemoglobin A_{1c} or proteins	+ + +	+/–	+ + +
	Urine glucose	+/–	+/–	+
	Causal blood glucose	+ +	+	+
	Fasting blood glucose	+ + +	+	+
	Oral glucose tolerance test	+ + +	+ +	+ +
IDDM[b]	HLA type	+/–	–	+ + +
	ICA	+	+	+ + +
	Anti-GAD	+	+	+ + +
	Early insulin secretion	+/–	+	+ +

Note: Key: – none; +/– none or minimal; + low; ++ intermediate; + + + high. NIDDM, non–insulin-dependent diabetes mellitus; IDDM, insulin-dependent diabetes mellitus.

a. At present, screening can be recommended only for high-risk individuals or for epidemiological studies.

b. HLA, human leukocyte antigen; ICA, islet-cell cytoplasmic antibodies; anti-GAD, antibodies to glutamate decarboxylase.

Source: Reprinted with permission from Report of a WHO Study Group, *WHO TRS 844*, p 36, © 1994, World Health Organization.

pathogenesis of insulin resistance is outlined schematically in Figure 13–2.[7] Decrease in either glucose-induced insulin secretion from the pancreas or in tissue response to insulin or uptake of glucose from the circulation lead to a chain of events that results in or intensifies insulin resistance. This is true, according to this scheme, even if the initiating process is impairment of beta-cell function in the pancreas, where insulin is produced, although this is considered the less common sequence.

The Thrifty Gene Hypothesis

Viewed from other perspectives, different mechanisms come into consideration. Neel, for example, introduced a genetic concept to explain the paradoxical observation that diabetes is

detrimental to reproduction, yet is also a common condition in human populations and appears to have been so over a great many generations.[8] He postulated that, to counterbalance the evident selective disadvantage of diabetes itself, a genetic mechanism conferred a selective advantage under conditions of most of human evolution by facilitating energy conservation against periods of acute starvation. This advantage was attributed to what he termed a "thrifty" genotype, which became detrimental under the living conditions of modern societies. This theory has support from archeological, historical, and ethnographic observations. It is also reminiscent of discussions in previous chapters concerning sweeping changes in human history with respect to patterns of diet and physical activity. An extensive review of current knowledge con-

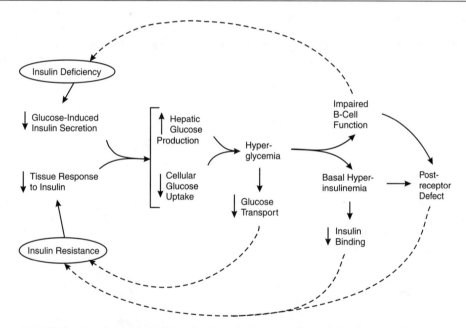

Note: Whether the primary defect initiating the glucose intolerance resides in the B cell or in peripheral tissues, development of insulin resistance will eventually ensue or become aggravated, respectively. By the time that overt fasting hyperglycemia (>140 mg/dl) develops, both impaired insulin secretion and severe insulin resistance are present. Broken arrows represent positive feedback loops, which result in self-perpetuation of primary defect.

Figure 13–2 Pathogenesis of Insulin Resistance in Non–Insulin-Dependent Diabetes Mellitus (NIDDM). *Source:* RA DeFronzo, RC Bonadonna, and E Ferrannini, Pathogenesis of NIDDM: A Precarious Balance between Insulin Action and Insulin Secretion, in International Textbook of Diabetes Mellitus, KGMM Alberti et al, eds, Vol 1, p 617, Copyright © 1992, John Wiley & Sons Limited. Reproduced with permission.

cerning specific genetic mechanisms in IDDM and NIDDM is given by Vadheim and Rotter, who indicated that major gene loci contributing to susceptibility to the immunologically mediated process of IDDM are well established but that in NIDDM candidate genes are still under investigation.[9] (More recently, the gene NIDDM1 has been identified, but to establish its correspondence to the population-level phenomena of diabetes will require extensive investigation.) They note, however, that congruence of NIDDM between identical twins is nearly 100%, indicating strong genetic determination of susceptibility. Such genetic susceptibility poses significant hazards of NIDDM for those who experience the adverse changes in physical and social environment that accompany Westernization and its characteristic habits of living.

Predisposing Factors

Population studies have suggested a number of predisposing factors for diabetes, such as those recently reported for men in the British Regional Heart Study (Table 13–4).[10] Men age 40–59 years were followed for more than 12 years on average, and 178 of 7097 participants developed NIDDM. Each characteristic was evaluated with adjustment for all others in the table so that jointly contributed effects were removed, and the total effect of a particular characteristic may therefore be underestimated. Body mass index was clearly the strongest positive predictor of later NIDDM, whereas physical activity was strongly inverse or negative as a predictor. In a further analysis, serum triglyceride concentration was included and showed a positive relative risk of 2.8 (95% confidence interval 1.4–5.8), reducing somewhat the adjusted relative risk for body mass index. Other studies of NIDDM, IGT, or insulin resistance in diverse populations and including women support the finding of body mass index, central adiposity, and other anthropometric indices of obesity as consistent predictors. There are conflicting observations on whether fetal or

Table 13–4 Predictors of Non–Insulin-Dependent Diabetes

Variable[a]	Adjusted Relative Risk (95% Confidence Interval)	P Value[b]
Body mass index[c]	7.3 (3.4 to 15.6)	0.0001
Prevalent coronary heart disease (yes/no)	1.4 (1.0 to 1.9)	0.04
Physical activity (moderate versus inactive)	0.4 (0.2 to 0.8)	0.003
Alcohol intake (moderate versus occasional)	0.6 (0.4 to 1.0)	0.04
Current smoker (yes versus never smoked)	1.2 (0.8 to 1.8)	
Systolic blood pressure[c]	1.3 (0.8 to 1.7)	
High-density lipoprotein cholesterol[c]	0.7 (0.5 to 1.2)	0.03
Heart rate[c]	2.2 (1.1 to 4.2)	0.01
Uric acid[c]	1.5 (0.9 to 2.5)	0.01

Note: Analysis includes 7097 men, 178 cases with data on all covariables in table.

a. Each variable has been adjusted for age and for each of the other variables in the model.

b. Test for linear trend.

c. Upper fifth versus lower fifth.

Source: Reprinted with permission from J Perry, SG Wannamethee, et al, *British Medical Journal*, Vol 310, pp 560–564, © 1995, BMJ Publishing Group.

neonatal influences bear on risk of NIDDM. This question is addressed further in Chapter 19, Social Conditions.

MECHANISMS OF EXACERBATION OF ATHEROGENESIS

Effects of Insulin

How diabetes and states now recognized as insulin resistance contribute to exacerbation of atherogenesis has been discussed for more than 75 years.[1] Stout advanced the proposition, now incorporated in the concept of the insulin resistance syndrome, that insulin has a direct atherogenic effect in addition to potential secondary effects on other risk factors.[11] Schematically, his concept is as shown in Figure 13–3. Insulin resistance, resulting from a combination of factors, leads to hyperinsulinemia, with or without overt diabetes. Hyperinsulinemia leads to increased atherogenesis both directly and through effects of insulin on blood lipids and blood pressure. Direct effects are attributable to five actions of insulin on arterial tissue, including its effects on growth and persistence of lipid lesions, on synthesis of lipids and connective tissue, on smooth muscle cells, and on sterol and low-density lipoprotein (LDL)-cholesterol activity in smooth muscle cells and macrophages.

Isolation of the postulated effects of insulin from those of concomitant factors has been a

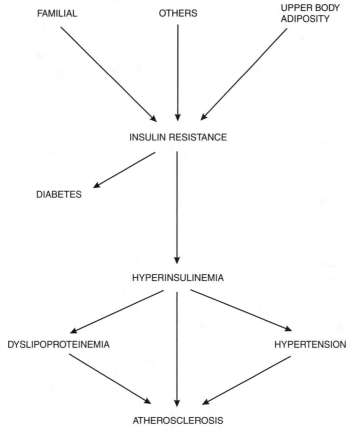

Figure 13–3 Schematic Representation of the Relation of Hyperinsulinemia with Atherosclerosis and Some of Its Major Risk Factors. *Source*: Reprinted with permission from RW Stout, Insulin and Atheroma, *Diabetes Care*, Vol 13, p 647, © 1990, American Diabetes Association.

major challenge, addressed most recently by the Insulin Resistance Atherosclerosis Study (IRAS).[12] In this study, insulin *sensitivity*, rather than insulin resistance, was assessed in relation to internal and common carotid arterial thickness, as an index of atherosclerosis, measured by B-mode ultrasound examination. In a cross-sectional analysis of these measurements in several hundred Hispanic and non-Hispanic White men and women with an average age of about 55 years, an inverse relation was found between insulin sensitivity and arterial wall thickness, especially of the internal carotid artery. This association was attenuated by adjustment for other risk factors. No such association was found for Blacks. With this latter exception, and with the limitation of the cross-sectional design, the results supported the concept of a direct role of insulin in atherogenesis. Its additional, indirect roles through dyslipidemia and hypertension are supported by evidence of several mechanisms linking diabetes with these effects.[13]

Effects of Other Factors

Other factors may participate in the increased atherogenesis of insulin resistance and diabetes, including elevated blood concentrations of glucose, triglyceride, and fibrinogen, among others. Association of risk factors such as obesity, hypertension, and adverse blood lipid profiles with elevated insulin concentrations also is evident in early adulthood and even in childhood.[14,15] Already at ages 9–10 years, Hispanic (Mexican American) children were found to have, in comparison with non-Hispanic White children, significantly greater clustering of elevated blood sugar and insulin concentrations with high triglyceride and low HDL-cholesterol concentrations, high systolic blood pressure, and high body mass index, suggesting early appearance of features of the insulin resistance syndrome in this group, whose risk of diabetes in adulthood is especially high. Thus factors by which diabetes and hyperinsulinemia accelerate atherosclerosis are clearly present and may

already have pathological effects well before adulthood.

DISTRIBUTION IN THE POPULATION

Prevalence

The United States

The frequency of occurrence of diabetes in the US population for NIDDM and IDDM combined has been estimated from results of the Second National Health and Nutrition Examination Survey (NHANES II), conducted from 1976 to 1980.[16] Table 13–5 indicates the combined prevalence of a positive history of medically diagnosed diabetes plus newly detected diabetes according to the criteria of either the National Diabetes Data Group (NDDG) or WHO. These criteria differ in that, in contrast to the WHO criteria shown in Table 13–1, the NDDG criteria include specific requirements for the fasting blood glucose concentration and for a midtest value in addition to the two-hour postload value. These prevalence estimates were generally either identical or slightly greater under the WHO criteria. Prevalence increased about ninefold from the youngest to oldest age groups in every race-sex category, rates were consistently higher for women than for men except in the oldest age group, and rates for Blacks were about 50% greater than for Whites in all age-sex groups.

The additional component of prevalence contributed by IGT is indicated in Table 13–6.[16] Here the effect of the choice of criteria is striking, for there is consistently much higher prevalence in accordance with the WHO than the NDDG criteria. Prevalence of IGT increased with age for Whites but was less among the older than the younger age groups. This suggests either cohort differences between these racial groups or greater selective mortality for Blacks than Whites with IGT at older ages.

International Variation

Figure 13–4 indicates the prevalence of diabetes (IDDM and NIDDM) and glucose intoler-

Table 13–5 Total Prevalence of Diabetes in the US Population Aged 20–74 Years, NHANES II, 1976–1980

	% of Population				
	20–74 yr	20–44 yr	45–54 yr	55–64 yr	65–74 yr
NDDG criteria					
All races	6.6	2.0	8.5	12.8	17.7
Men	5.7	1.4	7.9	9.6	19.2
Women	7.4	2.5	9.0	15.5	16.5
White	6.2	1.7	8.2	11.9	16.9
Men	5.3	1.0	7.7	9.1	18.1
Women	7.0	2.2	8.5	14.5	16.1
Black	9.6	3.1	12.9	20.8	25.9
Men	8.5	2.8	11.1	14.4	29.4
Women	10.5	3.5	14.5	25.4	23.1
WHO criteria					
All races	6.8	2.0	8.5	13.4	18.7
Men	5.9	1.4	7.9	9.9	20.1
Women	7.7	2.5	9.1	16.4	17.4
White	6.4	1.7	8.2	12.5	17.9
Men	5.5	1.0	7.8	9.4	19.1
Women	7.3	2.2	8.7	15.2	17.0
Black	9.9	3.2	12.9	22.5	26.4
Men	8.6	2.8	11.1	14.6	29.4
Women	11.0	3.5	14.6	27.9	24.1

Note: Sum of percentage of people with physician-diagnosed medical history of diabetes and of undiagnosed diabetes by NDDG or WHO criteria. Standard errors cannot be calculated because rates of undiagnosed diabetes are based on subsample of people from which rates of diagnosed diabetes are derived. NDDG, National Diabetes Data Group.

Source: Reprinted with permission from MI Harris et al, *Diabetes*, Vol 34, p 531, © 1987, American Diabetes Association.

ance according to WHO criteria in 33 population groups.[17] The range is from less than 5% to more than 60% of affected persons in the group aged 30–64. These results combine sex groups and are age standardized to the world population. In most populations the combined frequency was below 25% but in two it exceeded 50%. With the exception of Nauru and the Pima Indian population of the United States, prevalence varied along a continuous gradient. This suggests that common influences varying only in degree may account for differences in prevalence in most populations, whereas determinants of prevalence in the two extreme cases may be qualitatively distinct. The impression from the figure is that the prevalence of diabetes contributed more than did IGT to these population differences. More-detailed information from several populations demonstrates ethnic differences in prevalence of NIDDM within the same country.[18] In some instances, ethnic variation was marked, with a fourfold or greater difference among groups such as White and Aborigine groups in Australia. The gradient in the United States was from 6.1% to 9.9%, 12.6%, and 34.1% prevalence among Whites, Blacks, Mexican Americans, and Pima Indians, respectively. Similarly,

Table 13–6 Prevalence of Impaired Glucose Tolerance in the US Population Aged 20–74 Years, NHANES II, 1976–1980

Race and Sex	% of Population				
	20–74 yr	*20–44 yr*	*45–54 yr*	*55–64 yr*	*65–74 yr*
NDDG criteria					
All races					
Both sexes	4.6 (0.39)	2.1 (0.39)	7.0 (0.93)	7.4 (0.91)	9.2 (0.85)
Men	4.6 (0.58)	1.2 (0.39)	7.3 (1.65)	9.8 (1.44)	8.9 (1.50)
Women	4.7 (0.67)	2.8 (0.70)	6.7 (1.48)	5.2 (1.24)	9.4 (1.15)
White					
Both sexes	4.6 (0.42)	2.0 (0.38)	6.3 (1.04)	7.7 (0.98)	9.5 (0.87)
Men	4.4 (0.61)	1.0 (0.34)	6.3 (1.79)	10.1 (1.48)	9.0 (1.55)
Women	4.7 (0.68)	2.8 (0.73)	6.2 (1.15)	5.5 (1.43)	9.9 (1.20)
Black					
Both sexes	3.8 (0.82)	1.2 (0.84)	10.7 (3.23)	4.5 (2.19)	3.4 (2.09)
Men	5.9 (1.18)	1.4 (1.30)	18.3 (3.90)	7.0 (4.78)	5.4 (3.80)
Women	2.3 (1.24)	1.1 (1.11)	5.1 (4.86)	3.1 (2.07)	1.9 (2.22)
WHO criteria					
All races					
Both sexes	11.2 (0.52)	6.4 (0.59)	14.8 (1.48)	15.1 (1.23)	22.8 (1.70)
Men	10.3 (0.72)	4.7 (0.69)	13.1 (2.09)	17.2 (1.67)	22.8 (2.05)
Women	12.0 (0.97)	7.8 (0.98)	16.3 (2.52)	13.4 (1.89)	22.7 (2.59)
White					
Both sexes	10.7 (0.57)	5.6 (0.64)	13.6 (1.50)	15.3 (1.28)	23.0 (1.65)
Men	10.2 (0.76)	4.6 (0.72)	12.6 (2.25)	17.2 (1.79)	22.8 (2.04)
Women	11.1 (1.03)	6.5 (1.05)	14.5 (2.38)	13.7 (2.04)	23.0 (2.55)
Black					
Both sexes	12.7 (2.15)	10.3 (1.97)	17.0 (5.35)	14.4 (2.24)	14.5 (4.93)
Men	11.3 (2.02)	4.7 (1.80)	18.8 (3.90)	18.6 (6.02)	22.6 (8.62)
Women	13.6 (2.70)	14.2 (2.98)	15.8 (8.05)	12.2 (1.94)	8.2 (4.94)

Note: Based on results of 75-g oral glucose tolerance test conducted in morning after overnight 10- to 16-hour fast in people with no medical history of diabetes. Standard error is given in parentheses. NDDG, National Diabetes Data Group.

Source: Reprinted with permission from MI Harris et al, *Diabetes*, Vol 34, p 532, © 1987, American Diabetes Association.

the contrasting situation of Asians and Europeans in the United Kingdom has been of special interest, the former having prevalence of diagnosed diabetes 3.8 times or more that of Europeans in the same geographic area.[19] Evidence suggests strongly that diabetes is a significant problem in developing countries and especially in their urban components. It appears that South Asians need not emigrate to experience a high risk of diabetes.

Blood Glucose Distributions and Bimodality

Analyses of the distributions of blood glucose concentrations in populations have raised the question of whether bimodality is present. Bimodality occurs when the frequencies of values above the first, and main, peak in the distribution do not decrease consistently to zero but show a second peak, or mode, above the primary one. Whether an apparent hump in the

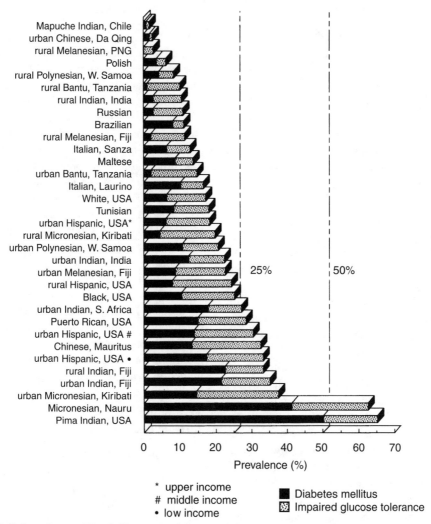

Figure 13–4 Prevalence of Total Glucose Intolerance (Diabetes and Impaired Glucose Tolerance) in Selected Populations Aged 30–64 Years, Age Standardized to the World Population of Segi, Sexes Combined. *Source*: Reprinted with permission from H King and M Rewers, WHO Ad Hoc Diabetes Reporting Group, *Diabetes Care*, Vol 16, p 170, © 1993, American Diabetes Association.

upper part of the frequency distribution is a true second mode or is only an artifact or a chance variation is often difficult to resolve convincingly. However, in the actual presence of such a distribution, there may be an underlying factor that causes a subgroup of the population to exhibit, as a group, higher values than the remainder of the population. Such a pattern may be taken as evidence of a genetic basis for the most extreme values in the population, although arguably any other factor selectively operating in one subgroup could have a similar effect. In any case, such findings have been reported for several populations in which especially high prevalence of NIDDM has been observed, such as the Pima Indians and the indigenous population of Nauru.[20] This finding is consistent with the interpretation of variation in prevalence of diabetes among populations discussed above.

Incidence

Few studies have estimated the incidence of diabetes in previously undiagnosed persons or those with "normal" blood glucose concentrations in a baseline examination. Conversion from IGT to NIDDM categories has been reported from several populations, however, as summarized in Table 13–7.[21] These studies were conducted between the mid-1960s and mid-1980s and were typically of 5–10 years' duration. From 1.5% to 6.8% per year of those initially having IGT were found at the end of follow-up to be classified as NIDDM. The risk was several times greater for those with IGT than for those with lower baseline blood glucose concentrations, from twofold to ninefold, as would be expected. The analogy between blood glucose levels and blood pressure, with a continuous progression from lower values to borderline levels to the range in which treatment is warranted, is readily apparent.

In the United States, the 16-year follow-up of participants in the First National Health and Nutrition Examination Survey identified 880 incident cases of diabetes among 11,097 White and Black participants age 25–70 years at baseline.[22] Age-adjusted incidence rates by race and sex over the 16 years were 15.0% for Black women, 10.9% for Black men, 7.0% for White women, and 6.9% for White men. Results of analysis of predictors of incident diabetes are shown in Table 13–8. Obesity, when measured by either body mass index or the ratio of subscapular:triceps skinfold thickness, was the major predictor after age and race. For women, physical inactivity, blood pressure, and lower educational attainment were also significantly related. The pattern of obesity suggested by the skinfold ratio is that of the abdominal (central) fat pattern identified with the insulin resistance syndrome. Among Blacks, incidence of diabetes exceeded that for Whites in most strata of obesity, by both measures, indicating that additional factors must account for their greater incidence of diabetes.

RATES AND RISKS

Unlike factors considered in previous chapters, the complex of blood glucose, insulin, and diabetes has not been examined for its possible role in explaining variation in coronary or all-cause death rates among different populations. The view that reliable assessment of blood glucose required fasting and postglucose-load blood samples discouraged investigators from this procedure in baseline examinations, for example, in the Seven Countries Study (cited elsewhere), a prominent source of international comparisons of this kind. International collaborations have been undertaken, however, to address other questions. In addition, data are available to examine the relation between different aspects of this complex and occurrence of coronary heart disease and other cardiovascular conditions from hospital discharge records, population surveys, case-comparison studies, cohort studies, and community surveillance programs. Some of these sources will be addressed in the following summary.

Asymptomatic Hyperglycemia and Coronary Heart Disease

A landmark international collaboration reported in 1979 led to assembly of data from 14 population studies in Australia, Europe, Japan, and the United States to analyze whether elevated blood glucose concentration, in the absence of diabetes, was associated with coronary heart disease (eg, "Glycemia and Prevalence of ECG Abnormalities"[23] and companion reports). The focus was on the relation between blood glucose concentration and coronary disease as assessed within each of the studies rather than cross-study comparisons, because methods of glucose determination differed among studies. Prevalent coronary heart disease qualifying as definite past myocardial infarction at baseline was associated with baseline glucose concentration in four of the seven studies with postload glucose determinations as the basis for measurement. Other criteria for coronary heart

Table 13-7 Estimated Conversion Rate from Impaired Glucose Tolerance (IGT) to Non–Insulin-Dependent Diabetes Mellitus (NIDDM) in Various Populations

Population	Period[a]	Baseline			Conversion Rate (%/yr)	Relative Risk[b]	Diagnostic Criteria and Notes	Study
		Age (yr)	NIDDM (%)	IGT (%)				
British men (Whitehall)	1968–1970 (5 yr)	>40	NA	NA	3.0	NA	Screening test + 50-g OGTT with 2-h capillary glucose 6.7–11.0 mm	Jarrett et al
British (Bedford)	1962 (10 yr)	Adult	NA	NA	1.5	NA	Glycosuria + 50-g OGTT with 2-h capillary glucose 6.7–11.1 mm	Keen et al
Japanese	1964–1965 (7 yr)	All ages (bias to older)	15.9	6.3	5.5	9.0	Glycosuria + 50-g OGGT; baseline = 13 IGT only	Sasaki et al
Pima Indians	1972–1985 (mean 3.3 yr)	≥5	24.8	NA	6.1	6.3	Estimated 10-yr cumulative incidence	Saad et al
Maltese	1981 (6 yr)	≥29	6.8	5.3	5.1	7.2		Schranz
Mexican Americans	1979–1982 (8 yr)	25–64	10.2	11.6	2.7	6.2	Numbers calculated indirectly from paper	Haffner et al
Japanese American men	1983–1985 (mean 2.5 yr)	44–73	34.1	32.3	6.8	4.2		Bergstrom et al
Nauruans	1975–1976 (6.2 yr)	≥20	27.9	21.1	3.5	2.1	Age standardized for comparison	Dowse et al
Nauruans	1982 (5 yr)	≥20	24.7	17.4	5.6	7.6	Age standardized for comparison	Dowse et al

Note: NA, not available; OGGT, oral glucose tolerance test.

a. Baseline investigations + duration of follow-up.

b. Relative risk of conversion to NIDDM: IGT relative to normal.

Source: Reprinted with permission from GK Cowse, PZ Zimmet, and H King, *Diabetes Care*, Vol 14, p 970, © 1991, American Diabetes Association.

Table 13–8 Logistic Regression Coefficients of Baseline Risk Variables and Incident Diabetes Mellitus in Entire Study Group and by Sex. First National Health and Nutrition Examination Survey Epidemiologic Follow-Up Study, 1971–1987

Group Variable	Contrast	β	SE (β)	Odds Ratio
Entire Study Group (N = 11,097)				
Race	Black vs white	1.7174***	0.4316	9.57
Sex	Women vs men	0.2989**	0.0951	1.35
Baseline age	Per 10 years	0.0186***	0.0032	1.20
Body mass index	Per unit (kg/m²)	0.1444***	0.0081	1.16
Subscapular:triceps	Per unit	0.5866***	0.0778	1.80
Systolic blood pressure	Per 2 mm Hg	0.0048**	0.0017	1.01
Education	≤12 years vs >12 years	0.1683	0.1103	1.18
	<9 years vs >12 years	0.5082***	0.1195	1.66
Activity level	Moderate vs high	0.1475	0.0957	1.16
	Low vs high	0.2507*	0.0991	1.28
Race-BMI interaction		−0.0505***	0.0145	
Constant		−9.2407	0.3122	
Men (N = 4,454)				
Race	Black vs white	2.3785**	0.8268	10.79
Baseline age	Per 10 years	0.0318***	0.0051	3.95
Body mass index	Per unit (kg/m²)	0.1782***	0.0156	1.20
Subscapular:triceps	Per unit	0.4481***	0.0928	1.57
Systolic blood pressure	per 2 mm Hg	0.0009	0.0027	1.00
Education	≤12 years vs >12 years	0.1177	0.1592	1.12
	<9 years vs >12 years	0.2075	0.1733	1.23
Activity level	Moderate vs high	0.1248	0.1363	1.13
	Low vs high	0.1869	0.1493	1.21
Race-BMI interaction		−0.0780**	0.0295	
Constant		−9.9260	0.5575	
Women (N = 6,643)				
Race	Black vs white	1.5711**	0.5267	1.69
Baseline age	Per 10 years	0.0104*	0.0042	1.11
Body mass index	Per unit (kg/m²)	0.1264***	0.0097	1.13
Subscapular:triceps	Per unit	0.9421***	0.1460	2.57
Systolic blood pressure	Per 2 mm Hg	0.0075***	0.0021	2.76
Education	≤12 years vs >12 years	0.2115	0.1558	1.24
	<9 years vs >12 years	0.7442***	0.1679	2.10
Activity level	Moderate vs high	0.1529	0.1357	1.17
	Low vs high	0.2727*	0.1358	1.31
Race-BMI interaction		−0.0446**	0.0171	
Constant		−8.8635	0.3788	

Note: SE, standard error; BMI, body mass index.

*P<0.05; **P<0.01; ***P<0.001.

Source: Reprinted with permission from RB Lipton et al, Determinants of Incident Non-Insulin-Dependent Diabetes Mellitus Among Blacks and Whites in a National Sample: The NHANESI Epidemiologic Follow-Up Study, *American Journal of Epidemiology*, Vol 138, No 10, p 836, © 1993, The Johns Hopkins University School of Hygiene and Public Health.

disease identified classes of disease that were significantly more frequent in the highest quintile group of the blood glucose distribution in most of the studies.

Coronary heart disease mortality at five years was examined in 11 of the studies, as shown in Table 13–9 (Finland-HP = Helsinki Policemen; Finland-SI = Social Insurance Study; US-PG = Peoples Gas Company; US-CHA = Chicago Heart Association; US-WE = Chicago Western Electric Company). The *t* statistic derived from multiple logistic analysis is presented for the relation of baseline blood glucose concentration to death from all causes, cardiovascular causes, and coronary heart disease separately for each study. Adjustment for age, body mass index,

systolic blood pressure, serum cholesterol, and cigarette smoking was included so that only the remaining independent relation with blood glucose would be reflected in this analysis. The level of significance of each result is shown and indicates that no significant relation was found for each end point in most studies. Most striking was the highly significant association for each cause of death category in the Chicago Peoples Gas Study when restricted to postload glucose determinations. The few other significant values showed no consistent pattern. Although these results may be viewed as minimizing the measure of association with blood glucose by adjustment for other factors with which it is associated—especially body mass index and

Table 13–9 Relationship of Baseline Glucose Level and Subsequent Mortality; *t* Value in Multiple Logistic Analysis; 11 Studies, Middle-Aged Men, International Collaborative Group

Study	Total Number of Deaths	t Value All Causes	t Value Cardiovascular	CHD
Australia	56	0.35	−1.06	0.78
Denmark: 50	43	−0.25	−1.11[a]	0.21[a]
England	414	−0.45	0.60	1.01
Finland: Helsinki Policemen Study	70	0.72	0.38	0.87
Finland: Social Insurance Institution	121	1.01	−0.51	−0.21
France	141	3.39***	0.81	0.40
Scotland				
Excluding hypertensives on Rx	60	1.47	1.94	−0.95
Including hypertensives on Rx	100	1.87	2.19*	−0.05
Switzerland	34	1.67	0.84	[b]
US: Peoples Gas Company[c]				
post-load	116	3.67***	3.42***	3.23**
casual	190	−1.42	−2.10*	−1.63
US: Chicago Heart Association	169	2.34*	0.45	0.31
US: Western Electric Company[c]	271	−0.91	−0.83	−0.95

Note: In most studies, the variables in the multiple logistic analysis included glucose, age, body mass index, systolic blood pressure, serum cholesterol, and cigarette smoking.

a. Combined fatal and nonfatal events.

b. Less than 10 deaths.

c. Hypertensives on treatment included.

*P<0.05; **P<0.01; ***P≤0.001

Source: Reprinted with permission from R Stamler et al, *Journal of Chronic Diseases*, Vol 32, p 834, © 1979, Elsevier Science, Inc.

systolic blood pressure—the univariate analysis, free of any such adjustment, also indicated mixed relationships with coronary mortality: In the same 11 studies, the ratio of mortality in the highest quintile of baseline blood glucose concentration to that in the lowest quintile range from 0.34 to 6.07; five results were below 1.00. Overall, the conclusion was reached that "At this juncture, therefore, asymptomatic hyperglycemia cannot be designated an established risk factor for coronary heart disease and the major adult cardiovascular diseases."[23(p 837)]

Diabetes and Coronary Heart Disease

Further investigation of the relation of diabetes or categories of baseline blood glucose levels and risk of coronary heart disease is illustrated by studies of the Pima Indians of central Arizona,[24] previously noted as a population with exceptionally high prevalence of diabetes, and the Bedford Survey in the United Kingdom.[25] In the Pima Indians, higher prevalence of coronary heart disease (though not statistically significant) was found among diabetics than nondiabetics, but the overall prevalence was about one-half that of the adult population of Tecumseh, Michigan, with which formal comparison was made. Regardless of the limitations of the cross-sectional survey approach, these results were notably counter to expectation and were not explained by consideration of other risk factors. In a longitudinal approach analogous to the studies reviewed above, but not excluding diabetics, the Bedford Survey in the United Kingdom reported 10-year mortality rates for coronary heart disease and all causes among men and women classified at baseline as newly diagnosed diabetics, borderline diabetics, or persons with normal glucose tolerance.[25] The relative odds (none of which was significant) of coronary death for borderline diabetics compared with normal controls were 5.16 for women and 1.42 for men, and for diabetics compared with borderline diabetics the odds were 2.12 for women and 1.31 for men after multivariate adjustment for age, systolic blood pressure, obesity, and cigarette smoking. Only for all-cause mortality for women were the relative odds (2.76 versus 1.10 for men) statistically significant. The effect of borderline or newly diagnosed diabetes was to raise the overall rates of coronary and all-cause mortality to those observed in men, that is, to remove the differential in risk usually seen to favor women. Hypertension was a prominent covariate in this analysis, leading to the interpretation that blood pressure control could be an important factor in prevention of cardiovascular disease outcomes in persons with impaired glucose tolerance.

Wingard and Barrett-Connor, in *Diabetes in America* (1995), summarized the extensive literature on coronary heart disease and diabetes.[26] The National Hospital Discharge Surveys between 1989 and 1991 reported the frequencies of cardiovascular diagnoses, including several categories of coronary heart disease among persons whose discharge diagnoses did or did not include diabetes. In every category, the diagnosis of diabetes was associated with a higher percentage of cardiovascular diagnoses, for both women and men. Studies of prevalence of coronary heart disease in relation to concurrent findings of NIDDM, impaired glucose tolerance, or normal blood glucose indicated higher frequency of coronary heart disease among women in each of four comparisons and among men in three of four comparisons. The gradients of difference in prevalence were greater for women than for men, suggesting again that diabetes may overshadow the usually observed advantage of women over men in age-specific coronary heart disease rates. Incident coronary heart disease was compared between categories of diabetes in four cohort studies, summarized in Table 13–10. In the three studies that included women, the estimated risk ratio for new coronary events was greater in women than in men, whether adjusted for age alone (2.9 versus 2.3 and 12.2 versus 6.7) or for multiple (unspecified) factors (3.2 versus 1.8). Similarly, risks of reinfarction after acute myocardial infarction were reviewed, and risk ratios, many of

Table 13–10 Risk of Incident Coronary Heart Disease in Diabetic Versus Nondiabetic Adults, US Occupation/Population-Based Studies

Population	Type of Diabetes	Years Follow-Up	Sex	Number Diabetic	Number Nondiabetic	Adjusted Risk Ratio[a] Age	Adjusted Risk Ratio[a] Multiple
Framingham Study (population-based, 1969–79, age 45–84 years)	Unspecified; history or causal glucose	2	M F	1,382 2,094		2.3 2.9	
Honolulu Heart Study (Japanese Americans, 1970–72, age 51–72 years)	NIDDM and IGT; history or non-fasting glucose challenge	18	M	376	2,042	1.7	
Nurses' Health Study (registered nurses, 1976, age 30–55 years)	NIDDM; self-report IDDM; self-report	8 8	F F	1,483 226	114,694 114,694	6.7* 12.2*	3.1*
New Haven, CT (population-based, 1982, age 65+ years)	Unspecified; self-report	6	M F	156 230	994 1,388		1.8 3.2**

Note: NIDDM, non–insulin-dependent diabetes mellitus; IDDM, insulin-dependent diabetes mellitus; IGT, impaired glucose tolerance.

a. Framingham, Honolulu, Nurses' Health studies—risk of nonfatal myocardial infarction and fatal coronary heart disease; New Haven—nonfatal and fatal myocardial infarction; prevalent heart disease at baseline was excluded in all four studies.

*95% confidence interval does not contain 1.0.

**$P \leq 0.01$.

Source: Reprinted from National Institutes of Health, Bethesda, Maryland.

which were significant, were found to range from 1.0 to 3.8 for diabetics, variously defined.

Mortality from ischemic heart disease in four US sex-race groups, at ages 45–64 years, is shown in Figure 13–5.[27] Data from national death certificate data, the National Health Interview Survey, and the 1986 National Mortality Follow-Back Survey were used to improve estimates of the true frequency of diabetes among coronary heart disease decedents and to estimate corrected mortality for only those without diabetes after those with diabetes were taken into account. The results indicate for both women and men, and for both Blacks and Whites, a marked excess in ischemic heart disease mortality among those with diabetes, especially after adjustment for underreporting of diabetes. This report emphasized limitations of death certificate data as a basis for ascertaining the presence of diabetes: The follow-back data showed diabetes was present in from two to three times as many decedents as was indicated on their death certificates. The relation of diabetes to cardiovascular death has therefore been

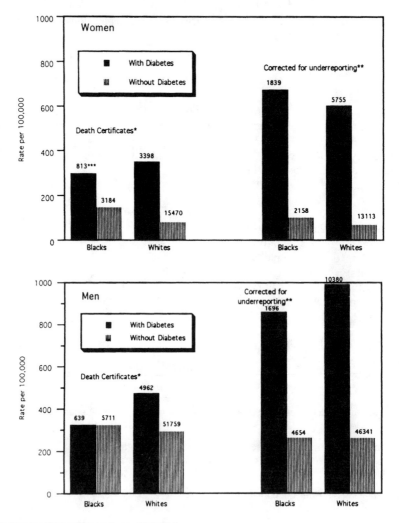

*Data from the National Center for Health Statistics.
**Using informants' reports of decedents' diabetes mellitus status, 1986 National Mortality Follow-Back Survey.
***Numbers above bars indicate the number of deaths.

Figure 13–5 Death Rates for Ischemic Heart Disease among Persons Aged 45–64 Years, by Gender, Diabetic Status, and Race, United States, 1986. *Source*: Reprinted with permission from JC Will and M Casper, *American Journal of Public Health*, Vol 86, p 577, © 1996, American Public Health Association.

subject to substantial underestimation in many previous studies.

Mexican Americans, once thought to experience less mortality from coronary heart disease on the basis of state-level statistical reports, have been found in direct community surveillance to have greater hospitalization rates and less survival following acute myocardial infarction than their non-Hispanic White counterparts in the same community, Corpus Christi, Texas. Because diabetes is more prevalent in the Mexican-American population, analysis of the relation of a self-reported history of diabetes to coronary events was undertaken (Figure 13–6).[28] The pattern of survival following myocardial infarction indicates that diabetes conferred similar losses in

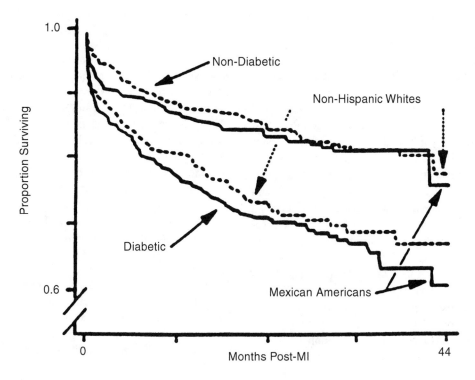

Note: Log-rank $\chi^2_{3df} = 32.84$; $P<0.001$.

Figure 13–6 Proportion of Patients Hospitalized with Acute Myocardial Infarction (MI) Surviving 0–44 Months, by Diabetic Status and Ethnicity, Corpus Christi Heart Project, 1988–1990. *Source*: Reprinted with permission from PR Orlander et al, The Relation of Diabetes to the Severity of Acute Myocardial Infarction and Post-Myocardial Infarction Survival in Mexican-Americans and Non-Hispanic Whites: The Corpus Christi Heart Project, *Diabetes*, Vol 43, p 900, © 1994, American Diabetes Association.

survival for both Mexican Americans and non-Hispanic Whites and that much, though not all, of the mortality differential between ethnic groups can be accounted for by the more frequent presence of diabetes among Mexican Americans.

Insulin and Coronary Heart Disease

Whether blood insulin concentration is itself a risk factor for coronary heart disease has been studied with respect to both endogenous insulin (hyperinsulinemia or insulin resistance) and exogenous insulin (insulin therapy). The studies of both aspects can be described as inconsistent.

Possible reasons for differences in findings were discussed in the review by Wingard and Barrett-Connor of epidemiologic work on this question, which concluded that "the role of insulin as a heart disease risk factor remains controversial."[26(p 444)] McKeigue and Keen, evaluating the evidence available in 1991, expressed doubt that the insulin in the insulin resistance syndrome was the cause of its relation to coronary risk and pointed to the possibility that pro-insulin or split pro-insulins, which are separately identifiable insulin-like molecules, may be more directly involved.[29] Further population studies, they noted, may help to resolve this question.

Stroke

Association between diabetes and stroke has been demonstrated in many studies, including autopsy examination of cerebral circulation and carotid arteries, clinical series of diabetics, and population studies in several countries. A review by Pyörälä and colleagues demonstrates increased risk of stroke by a factor of 2 to 4 times in diabetics when compared with nondiabetics.[30] The 20-year follow-up of women and men in the Framingham Heart Study reported that fatal and nonfatal occlusive stroke, together, occurred 2.6 times more frequently in diabetic men and 3.8 times more frequently in diabetic women than in their nondiabetic counterparts. Again, as for coronary heart disease, diabetes had a greater impact on risk for women than for men. The American Heart Association report on risk factors for stroke emphasized diabetes among the "potentially modifiable" factors in relation to occlusive stroke, implicating impaired glucose tolerance, hyperinsulinemia, and insulin resistance syndrome in the increased risk.[31] The diabetes surveillance program of the Centers for Disease Control and Prevention reported that hospital discharges in which stroke was associated with diagnoses of diabetes increased from 77,000 in 1980 to 128,000 in 1987.[32] The increase occurred in each age stratum and not only the oldest age groups, although the rates were much higher for those above than below age 74. Deaths with stroke as the underlying cause and diabetes as a contributing cause declined over this time interval, especially in persons age 75 years or older. (However, the limitation of such estimates was noted above.)

Wingard and Barrett-Connor have reviewed data linking diabetes with congestive heart failure and cardiomyopathy,[26] and Pyörälä and colleagues have addressed associations of diabetes with atherosclerosis of the aorta and peripheral arteries as well as stroke and coronary heart disease.[30]

Large- and Small-Vessel Disease

A leading source of information on factors associated with development of vascular disease among diabetics is the WHO Multinational Study of Vascular Disease in Diabetics.[33] In this study, the prevalence of large-vessel disease (affecting the coronary, cerebral, and peripheral arteries) and small-vessel disease of the eyes and kidneys was determined among 6695 diabetic men and women in three age groups from 35 to 54 years in local centers in 14 countries. The results shown in Table 13–11 indicate an overall prevalence of large-vessel disease in nearly 30% of males and 40% of females. For all ages together, prevalence of this condition ranged from 21.9% to 52.9% for women and from 19.1% to 38.4% for men across the distribution of rates by country. Cultural differences in interpretation of questionnaire items for chest pain and other symptoms limit the interpretation of these population differences, however. In multivariate regression analysis, significant correlates of large-vessel disease varied in relation to different components. Overall, age, duration of diabetes, systolic blood pressure, body mass index, and total cholesterol were related in men, whereas only age, blood pressure, and body mass index were related in women. In both men and women, small-vessel disease of the eye was associated in men and women with duration of diabetes, systolic blood pressure, body mass index, and treatment of diabetes, whereas kidney involvement was associated with duration of diabetes and cholesterol concentration.

Microalbuminuria, another manifestation of renal involvement with diabetes, has been studied in recent years and found to be significantly associated with all-cause mortality in several European studies and often, though not always, correlated with manifestations of coronary heart disease in cross-sectional surveys.[26] It is unclear from these studies to what extent these associations are independent of other risk factors or whether this condition may itself be a marker for heart disease as a joint expression of the

Table 13–11 Large Vessel Disease Prevalence (%) by Age Group, Sex, and Center

| Center | Sex | Age Group | | | |
		35–41 Years	42–48 Years	49–54 Years	All Ages
London	Male	19.7	31.6	33.6	29.1
	Female	9.4	26.4	40.8	28.8
Switzerland	Male	13.3	31.6	38.9	28.1
	Female	20.7	25.8	41.3	28.9
Brussels	Male	8.3	11.3	30.5	19.1
	Female	13.8	26.8	36.1	26.3
Moscow	Male	21.2	32.1	39.6	32.7
	Female	40.0	48.1	46.7	45.4
Warsaw	Male	28.8	23.8	49.5	36.5
	Female	29.3	45.2	45.6	41.6
Berlin	Male	13.3	31.1	56.3	35.8
	Female	32.4	50.0	61.3	49.8
Zagreb	Male	15.4	25.0	35.3	26.1
	Female	21.1	27.1	43.1	32.2
New Delhi	Male	22.5	36.3	37.8	32.5
	Female	22.1	40.6	43.3	36.8
Hong Kong	Male	3.6	8.7	32.7	20.2
	Female	22.0	33.3	27.6	27.7
Tokyo	Male	8.0	17.1	15.5	14.5
	Female	23.1	28.1	18.1	21.9
Havana	Male	32.9	39.1	42.5	38.4
	Female	47.7	61.4	49.4	52.9
Oklahoma	Male	20.1	40.4	38.7	34.8
	Female	30.2	40.3	53.6	43.3
Arizona	Male	33.3	24.1	35.3	31.0
	Female	32.3	27.3	40.3	34.0
Bulgaria	Male	17.6	26.2	38.7	30.2
	Female	23.8	46.3	41.7	38.6
Total	Male	18.5	28.1	37.7	29.5
	Female	27.3	39.0	42.5	37.4

Source: Reprinted with permission from Diabetes Drafting Group, *Diabetologia*, Vol 28, p 625, © 1985, Springer-Verlag.

underlying disease process rather than a predictor or risk factor in the usual sense.

PREVENTION AND CONTROL

Prevention and control of diabetes mellitus were first addressed by the World Health Assembly of WHO in 1989 in a resolution calling on member states to assess the problem, implement population-based measures for prevention and control, share training opportunities, and establish model community programs. The Director-General was requested to support these activities, develop collaborative arrangements with the International Diabetes Federation and other agencies, and engage the WHO collaborating centers on diabetes in these efforts.[34] The Study Group convened in 1992 was a part of the response to this resolution.[3] The concepts of prevention outlined in the Study Group report addressed both population-wide and high-risk strategies. On the basis that risks of morbid events in diabetes are low except for those with blood glucose values near the upper extreme, it was judged that the population strategy may be inappropriate in many populations and that high-risk approaches for those with familial risks or clusters of other risk characteristics may be more cost-effective. Assessment of the distribution of diabetes and its determinants in each target population was recommended in establishing the best approach or combination of approaches for that population.

Against this background, the Study Group report noted the importance of IGT as a target for intervention, given its intermediate position in the distribution between normal and diabetic categories. This is analogous, as noted earlier, to the identification of borderline high blood pressure or cholesterol concentration as especially warranting preventive measures, although the language of the report suggests the interpretation that IGT is in some sense an entity in itself and not only part of the continuum of the blood glucose distribution. A focus on the "putative risk factors"—physical inactivity, nutritional factors, and obesity (shown in Figure 13–1)—was proposed, with the conclusion that "there is general agreement that dietary modification and exercise should serve as the cornerstones in the prevention of diabetes and the treatment of people with the disease."[3(p 29)] It was noted that malnutrition in utero leading to low birth weight may also predispose to diabetes in adult life, suggesting very early preventive measures if these findings are confirmed.

High-risk individuals were characterized as those with strong family history of NIDDM; persons changing to Westernized, urban, or sedentary lifestyles; women with histories of gestational diabetes or IGT; and persons with other components of the chronic metabolic (or insulin resistance) syndrome. The measures to be sought for such high-risk persons are control of obesity; maintenance of low-fat, high-fiber dietary habits; increased physical activity; and avoidance of specific drugs that may impair glucose metabolism.

Guidelines and programs to implement these recommendations have also been addressed in recent publications from WHO.[34,35] These reports provide references to a number of detailed manuals and materials valuable in the support of such programs. It is noteworthy that recommendations generally disfavor screening for purposes of case detection, even among family members of known cases, except in high-risk populations.[36]

An increasingly recognized principle of prevention in diabetes is attention to other risk factors for major cardiovascular complications.[30] Inability presently to demonstrate successful prevention of diabetes itself lends great importance to control of the factors, including high blood pressure, adverse lipid profile, overweight, physical inactivity, and others, that are associated with the progressive development of cardiovascular manifestations.

EFFECTS OF INTERVENTION ON RATES AND RISKS OF EVENTS: RECENT TRIALS

The effects of intervention on cardiovascular rates and risks have been evaluated in some recent controlled trials, which are described here briefly. The Diabetes Intervention Study investigated the impact of intensified health education on the metabolic control of NIDDM, reduction of cardiovascular risk factors, and incidence of coronary heart disease.[37] Nested in the design was a drug trial of clofibrate to reduce blood glucose and improve the blood lipid profile. Treatment in this trial improved risk factors other than blood lipids but did not reduce the rate of coronary events. The Diabetes Control and Complications Trial, among patients with IDDM, tested the benefits of closely monitored blood glucose levels controlled by frequent injections of insulin each day.[38] There was substantial benefit in reduced incidence or progression of small-vessel disease of the retina and kidney and of neuropathy, although the frequency of severe hypoglycemia resulting from such tight control of blood glucose was increased two- to threefold. Large-vessel disease was reduced by 40% but occurred infrequently in the young age group studied, and this result was not statistically significant. These and other trials, such as the University Group Diabetes Project reported in the late 1970s, have yet to demonstrate that treatment of established diabetes will reduce the frequency of its cardiovascular consequences.[26]

CURRENT ISSUES

From the foregoing discussion it is apparent that many issues concerning the place of diabetes in the epidemiology and prevention of cardiovascular disease remain unresolved. Major efforts of recent years have increased the accessibility of an extensive body of literature on the epidemiology of diabetes and especially its relation to cardiovascular diseases. This has been accompanied by adoption of standard criteria for definition and classification across the spectrum of blood glucose concentrations and their application in population studies. In part, the resulting evidence has pointed to new questions or perhaps refocused attention on older ones. Among the issues now prominent in the epidemiology of diabetes as it relates to cardiovascular diseases are the following.

Natural History

There are some methodologic issues at the basic level of determining prevalence of diabetes, principally NIDDM and IGT, in diverse populations. Alternatives to the WHO criteria for classification in prevalence surveys have been advocated,[39] as have sampling strategies for such surveys, based on "capture-recapture" methods used in field studies of animal populations.[40] Detailed protocols have been proposed for community assessment of diabetes preva-

lence,[3,34,35] but population screening as a means of case detection is generally considered unwarranted on the basis of expected yield and benefit to those identified.

How early the risk of cardiovascular diseases begins in the background of diabetes is also at issue. The development of cardiovascular risk factors long in advance of the diagnosis of diabetes was reported in a study of Mexican Americans in San Antonio, Texas[41]; the clustering of risk factors in children by age 9–10 in Mexican American versus non-Hispanic White children was noted above[15]; and detection of a genetic marker for insulin regulation and its relation to risk factors in 5-year-old children was reported from the Bogalusa Heart Study.[42] These observations indicate the importance of investigations of early precursors of frank diabetes or IGT and their relation to cardiovascular risk in populations with differing prevalence of diabetes.

Better information is needed in many populations about the distribution of blood glucose concentrations, related risk factors for cardiovascular diseases, and needs for intervention at both population and high-risk levels.

How the distinguishing characteristics of diabetes and its related conditions—hyperglycemia and insulin resistance—contribute to risks of atherosclerosis and its component vascular conditions remains unclear despite decades of investigation. Inconsistency of findings leaves these questions open to resolution through future studies.

Prevention and Control

Policies for prevention and control of diabetes in the United States and worldwide, especially in developing countries, depend on oftententative assumptions about the true prevalence of the condition, its true frequency among persons hospitalized or dying from conditions coded as other than diabetes, and its actual contribution to the disability and early mortality with which it is associated in available statistics. These and other considerations affect the interpretation of projections of costs and the cost-benefit balances among policy options.[43,44] Model projects as suggested by the World Health Assembly may contribute importantly to strengthening these projections in future years if the needed resources are allocated for this research.

REFERENCES

1. West KM. Epidemiologic approaches in the study and control of diabetes. In: West KM, ed. *Epidemiology of Diabetes and Its Vascular Lesions.* New York: Elsevier North-Holland Inc; 1978;1:1–13.

2. Harris MI, Zimmet P. Classification of diabetes mellitus and other categories of glucose intolerance. In: Alberti KGMM, Defronzo RA, Keen H, Zimmet P, eds. *International Textbook of Diabetes Mellitus.* Chichester, England: John Wiley & Sons; 1992: 3–18.

3. Report of a WHO Study Group. *Prevention of Diabetes Mellitus.* Geneva, Switzerland: World Health Organization; 1994. WHO Technical Report Series 844.

4. World Health Organization. *International Statistical Classification of Diseases and Related Health Problems, Tenth Revision.* Geneva, Switzerland: World Health Organization; 1992; l.

5. Reaven GM. Banting Lecture 1988. Role of insulin resistance in human disease. *Diabetes.* 1988;37:1595–1607.

6. Keen H. Introduction. In: Alberti KGMM, DeFronzo RA, Keen H, Zimmet P, eds. *International Textbook of Diabetes Mellitus.* Chichester, England: John Wiley & Sons; 1992;1:xxvii–xxix.

7. DeFronzo RA, Bonadonna RC, Ferrannini E. Pathogenesis of NIDDM: a precarious balance between insulin action and insulin secretion. In: Alberti KGMM, DeFronzo RA, Keen H, Zimmet P, eds. *International Textbook of Diabetes Mellitus.* Chichester, England: John Wiley & Sons; 1992;1:569–633.

8. Neel JV. Diabetes mellitus: a "thrifty" genotype rendered detrimental by "progress"? *Am J Hum Genet.* 1962;14:353–362.

9. Vadheim CM, Rotter JI. Genetics of diabetes mellitus. In: Alberti KGMM, DeFronzo RA, Keen H, Zimmet P, eds. *International Textbook of Diabetes Mellitus.* Chichester, England: John Wiley & Sons; 1992;1:31–98.

10. Perry IJ, Wannamethee SG, Walker MK, Thomson AG, et al. Prospective study of risk factors for development of non-insulin dependent diabetes in middle-aged British men. *Br Med J.* 1995;310:560–564.

11. Stout RW. Insulin and atheroma: 20-yr perspective. *Diabetes Care.* 1990;13:631–654.

12. Howard G, O'Leary DH, Zaccaro D, Haffner S, et al for the IRAS Investigators. Insulin sensitivity and atherosclerosis. *Circ.* 1996;93:1809–1817.

13. Orchard TJ. Diabetes. In: Pearson TA, Criqui MH, Luepker RV, Oberman A, Winston M, eds. *Primer in Preventive Cardiology.* Dallas, Tex: American Heart Association; 1994: 159–171.

14. Bao W, Srinivasan SR, Berenson GS. Persistent elevation of plasma insulin levels is associated with increased cardiovascular risk in children and young adults: the Bogalusa Heart Study. *Circ.* 1996;93:54–59.

15. Steffen-Batey L, Goff D, Chan M, Chan W, et al. Greater insulin resistance among Mexican-American children than among non-Hispanic White children: the Corpus Christi Heart Study. *Circ.* In press.

16. Harris MI, Hadden WC, Knowler WC, Bennett PH. Prevalence of diabetes and impaired glucose tolerance and plasma glucose levels in US population aged 20–74 years. *Diabetes.* 1987;36:523–534.

17. King H. Global estimates for prevalence of diabetes mellitus and impaired glucose tolerance in adults. *Diabetes Care.* 1993;16:157–177.

18. Bennett PH, Bogardus C, Tuomilehto J, Zimmet P. Epidemiology and natural history of NIDDM: non-obese and obese. In: Alberti KGMM, DeFronzo RA, Keen H, Zimmet P, eds. *International Textbook of Diabetes Mellitus.* Chichester, England: John Wiley & Sons; 1992;1:147–176.

19. Mather HM, Keen H. The Southall Diabetes Survey: prevalence of known diabetes in Asians and Europeans. *Br Med J.* 1985;291:1081–1084.

20. Zimmet MB, Whitehouse S. Bimodality of fasting and two-hour glucose tolerance distributions in a Micronesian population. *Diabetes.* 1978;27:793–800.

21. Dowse GK, Zimmet PZ, King H. Relationship between prevalence of impaired glucose tolerance and NIDDM in a population. *Diabetes Care.* 1991;14:968–974.

22. Lipton RB, Liao Y, Cao G, Cooper RS, et al. Determinants of incident non–insulin-dependent diabetes mellitus among Blacks and Whites in a national sample: the NHANES I Epidemiologic Follow-Up Study. *Am J Epidemiol.* 1993;138:826–839.

23. The International Collaborative Group. Joint Discussion. Glycemia and prevalence of ECG abnormalities. *J Chronic Dis.* 1979;32:829–837.

24. Ingelfinger JA, Bennett PH, Liebow IM, Miller M. Coronary heart disease in the Pima Indians: electrocar-

diographic findings and postmortem evidence of myocardial infarction in a population with a high prevalence of diabetes mellitus. *Diabetes.* 1976;25:561–565.

25. Jarrett RJ, McCartney P, Keen H. The Bedford Survey: ten year mortality rates in newly diagnosed diabetics, borderline diabetics and normoglycemic controls and risk indices for coronary heart disease in borderline diabetics. *Diabetologia.* 1982;22:79–84.

26. Wingard DL, Barrett-Connor E. Heart disease and diabetes. In: National Diabetes Data Group. *Diabetes in America.* 2nd ed. Bethesda, Md: National Institute of Diabetes and Digestive and Kidney Diseases, National Institutes of Health; 1995: 429–448. NIH publication 95-1468.

27. Will JC, Casper M. The contribution of diabetes to early deaths from ischemic heart disease: US gender and racial comparisons. *Am J Public Health.* 1996; 86:576–579.

28. Orlander PR, Goff DC, Morrissey M, Ramsey DJ, et al. The relation of diabetes to the severity of acute myocardial infarction and post-myocardial infarction survival in Mexican-Americans and non-Hispanic Whites: the Corpus Christi Heart Project. *Diabetes.* 1994;43:897–902.

29. McKeigue PM, Keen H. Diabetes, insulin, ethnicity, and coronary heart disease. In: Marmot M, Elliott P, eds. *Coronary Heart Disease Epidemiology: From Aetiology to Public Health.* Oxford, England: Oxford University Press; 1992: 217–232.

30. Pyörälä K, Laakso M, Uusitupa M. Diabetes and atherosclerosis: an epidemiologic view. *Diabetes Meta Rev.* 1987;3:463–524.

31. Sacco RL, Benjamin EJ, Broderick JP, Dyken M, et al. Risk factors. *Stroke.* 1997;28:1507–1517.

32. The Division of Diabetes Translation. *Diabetes Surveillance, 1991.* Atlanta, Ga: National Center for Chronic Disease Prevention and Health Promotion, Centers for Disease Control, US Dept of Health and Human Services, Public Health Service; 1991.

33. Diabetes Drafting Group. Prevalence of small vessel and large vessel disease in diabetic patients from 14 centres: the World Health Organization Multinational Study of Vascular Disease in Diabetics. *Diabetologia.* 1985;28:615–640.

34. Reiber GE, King H. *Guidelines for the Development of a National Programme for Diabetes Mellitus.* Geneva, Switzerland: Division of Noncommunicable Diseases and Health Technology, World Health Organization; 1991.

35. King H, Gruber W, Lander T, eds. *Implementing National Diabetes Programmes: Report of a WHO Meeting.* Geneva Switzerland: Division of Noncommunicable Diseases, World Health Organization; 1995.

36. Tuomilehto J, Tuomilehto-Wolf E, Zimmet P, Alberti KGMM, et al. Primary prevention of diabetes mellitus. In: Alberti KGMM, DeFronzo RA, Keen H, Zimmet P, eds. *International Textbook of Diabetes Mellitus.* Chichester, England: John Wiley & Sons; 1992; 2:1655–1673.

37. Hanefeld M, Fischer S, Schmechel H, Rothe G, et al. Diabetes Intervention Study: multi-intervention trial in newly diagnosed NIDDM. *Diabetes Care.* 1991; 14:308–317.

38. The Diabetes Control and Complications Trial Research Group. The effect of intensive treatment of diabetes on the development and progression of long-term complications in insulin-dependent diabetes mellitus. *N Eng J Med.* 1993;329:977–986.

39. Finch CF, Zimmet PZ, Alberti KGMM. Determining diabetes prevalence: a rational basis for the use of fasting plasma glucose concentrations? *Diabetic Med.* 1990;7:603–610.

40. LaPorte RE, McCarty D, Bruno G. Counting diabetes in the next millennium. *Diabetes Care.* 1993;16:528–534.

41. Haffner ST, Stern MP, Hazuda HP, Mitchell BD, et al. Cardiovascular risk factors in confirmed prediabetic individuals: does the clock for coronary heart disease start ticking before the onset of clinical diabetes? *JAMA.* 1990;263:2893–2898.

42. Amos CI, Cohen JC, Srinivasan SR, Freedman DS, et al. Polymorphism in the 5′-flanking region of the insulin gene and its potential relation to cardiovascular disease risk: observations in a biracial community: the Bogalusa Heart Study. *Atherosclerosis.* 1989;79:51–57.

43. Huse DM, Oster G, Killen AR, Lacey MJ, et al. The economic costs of non–insulin-dependent diabetes mellitus. *JAMA.* 1989;262:2708–2713.

44. Vaughan JP, Gilson L, Mills A. In: Jamison DT, Mosley WH, Measham AR, Bobadilla JL, eds. *Disease Control Priorities in Developing Countries.* Oxford, England: Oxford University Press; 1993: 561–576.

CHAPTER 14

Smoking and Other Tobacco Use

SUMMARY

The habits of smoking and other tobacco use have in common an underlying addiction to nicotine. The process of addiction begins with the recruitment of the school-age population through marketing and distribution of tobacco products, which in many countries reach youth in violation of existing laws or regulations. The cigarette as a source of nicotine carries with it all the combustion products of tobacco and cigarette additives that together cause cardiovascular and other diseases. Epidemiologic studies of smoking habits include population surveys to determine patterns of use and trends, cohort studies to measure the effects of smoking on population rates and individual risks of cardiovascular and other diseases, and trials of strategies for prevention or cessation of the smoking habit. Called "the risk factor of the century" as of the mid-1990s, smoking has become an increasingly common target not only of health professionals but of legislative and regulatory bodies. The public health goal is to promote those social changes, considered broadly, that will bring about the disappearance of tobacco use as a common habit. Aggressive measures are needed to achieve this goal, especially in developing countries where the tobacco industry openly strives to expand the market for its products.

INTRODUCTION

Cigarette smoking is regarded justifiably as "the risk factor of the century." Mortality, morbidity, and consumption of health care resources on a vast scale are attributable to the rising epidemic of cigarette smoking during the 20th century. Projections into the next century portend a still-mounting public health burden as a result of expanded marketing and use of tobacco products in much of the developing world.[1] Unless the epidemic of cigarette smoking is controlled, this may constitute the risk factor of the next century as well. The hazards of cigarette smoking for increased risks of lung cancer and other respiratory conditions are widely recognized. In fact, however, a greater public health burden of cigarette smoking is represented by vascular diseases. For this reason, cigarette smoking is a prominent topic for the theme of this book. In addition, because cigarette smoking is an expression of nicotine addiction, which may develop from using other forms of tobacco, this chapter includes reference to the use of such products in addition to discussion of cigarette smoking.

DEFINITION AND CLASSIFICATION

Aspects of the definition and classification of smoking and tobacco use include types of tobacco exposure, categories of smoking status, quantitation of smoking, and the processes of starting and stopping tobacco use. These aspects have been addressed in different degrees and by various methods in epidemiologic investigations of smoking and tobacco use.

Types of Tobacco Exposure

The personal habit of cigarette smoking is most important for the occurrence of cardiovascular diseases due to its very high prevalence in many populations and its attendant risks. Detailed information is sometimes sought about the particular brand or type of cigarette smoked, extent of smoke inhalation, or portion of the cigarette usually smoked. Pipe and cigar smoking are often ascertained but are generally much less prevalent. Exposure to smoked tobacco occurs passively when nonsmoking persons share the environment of smokers. This form of exposure underlies studies of the effects of environmental tobacco smoke (ETS). In such studies, mainstream smoke (drawn through the cigarette and exhaled into the environment) may be distinguished from sidestream smoke (entering the air directly from the burning cigarette, whether or not it is actively being smoked).

Smokeless tobacco is commonly used in the forms of a plug, dipping or chewing tobacco, or snuff. These forms of smokeless tobacco exposure cause local pathology, including cancer in the mouth and upper airway, but their immediate relevance is due to their yield of nicotine by solution into the saliva. This results in their potential for causing nicotine addiction, which may lead to cigarette smoking.

Smoking Status and Quantitation of Smoking

With respect to personal smoking behavior, a common classification system is never smoked, former smoker, and current smoker. Definitions and criteria must be specified for each class. For both former and current smokers, quantitation of exposure may be approximated by determining the age at the start of smoking, present age

(or the age at stopping if not a current smoker), and the average number of cigarettes smoked per day over the smoking lifetime in units of cigarettes, packs, or portions of packs. This approach provides an estimate of exposure in units of pack-years (eg, 36 years of smoking $\times$ ½ pack of cigarettes per day = 18 pack-years of exposure) for either former or current smokers.

With recognition of the importance of exposure to ETS, the complexity of accurate quantitation becomes apparent. For smokers, there is often additional exposure to smoke generated by others, and for nonsmokers this is the only source. Beyond the determination whether a nonsmoker shares a residence or workplace with a smoker, and if so over what interval of time, it is difficult to estimate ETS exposure and, therefore, total exposure for smokers.

Starting and Stopping Smoking

Intervention studies and other investigations of the dynamics of smoking behavior address in greater detail the processes of starting and stopping smoking. In these contexts, several stages of change have been suggested by which to classify individuals. For example, stages in starting to smoke are identified as preparatory, trying, experimental, regular, and addicted or dependent.[2] In smoking cessation, stages of contemplation or of actually attempting to quit are identified, and the duration of periods of cessation may be determined.

Issues in Observation and Measurement

In collecting data on smoking and tobacco use, reliance is often placed on indirect measures or self-report. For the population of a geopolitical area, data on tobacco sales or tax revenues may be available. Potential error in such data may result from the use of tobacco products legally or illegally imported from lower-tax areas or acquired through untaxed, black-market sources. Changes in tax rates over time must be taken into account if changes in tax revenues are used to estimate trends in tobacco consumption.

For individuals, self-reports of smoking and tobacco use are commonly elicited by interview or questionnaire methods designed to permit the classification and quantitation discussed above. Where cultural factors make these behaviors undesirable or even illegal, response bias in the direction of underreporting is to be expected. Similarly, participants in smoking prevention or cessation programs might be expected to exaggerate their success and thereby to minimize their reported tobacco use.

Biochemical markers of tobacco products or tobacco smoke can be used in place of or as a supplement to self-report methods.[3] Nicotine, cotinine, thiocyanate, and carbon monoxide can be tested for this purpose. Depending on the choice of marker, samples of saliva, urine, blood, or expired air may be used. In a strategy designed to improve the reliability of self-reported smoking behavior in school populations (the "bogus pipeline" method), such samples are obtained from all participants but are processed for only a small proportion of them. All participants are informed that the samples can be tested, and evidence suggests that more reliable reporting occurs as a result.

Different issues arise when the respondent is a relative or an acquaintance of the index subject (a surrogate respondent) or when existing records are searched for data on the smoking history. A recent study evaluated the use of smoking history data that was introduced to the state of Washington's standard death certificate.[4] Depending on the reliability of the knowledge of the informant, this is a potentially valuable addition to data sources on smoking and causes of death.

DETERMINANTS OF SMOKING BEHAVIOR AND MECHANISMS OF RISK

Why Do Smokers Smoke?

The initiation of smoking and other forms of tobacco use most often occurs in childhood and adolescence. This period of life was therefore the special focus of the 1994 report of the US Surgeon General, *Preventing Tobacco Use Among Young People*.[2] Figure 14–1 outlines the stages of smoking initiation. Factors that influence the progression from each stage to the next are described on the left, and particular patterns of behavior that define each stage are described on the right. These determinants of smoking behavior provide the points of intervention in programs aimed at preventing progression from the preparatory stage to addiction or dependency.

The same report presents a summary of studies indicating that several additional categories of conditions are predictive of progression in smoking behavior. These include socioeconomic, environmental, behavioral, and personal factors as well as the role and tactics of the tobacco industry.

Toxicity

The toxicity of tobacco smoke results from some of the thousands of organic and inorganic compounds it contains as components of tobacco or products of the combustion of tobacco and cigarette additives. These compounds include nicotine, carbon monoxide, hydrogen cyanide, acrolein, and mutagens and carcinogens (eg, polycyclic aromatic hydrocarbons).

Exposure to tobacco smoke is associated with several factors specifically relevant to cardiovascular diseases, including lipid abnormalities such as increased low-density lipoprotein cholesterol, very low-density lipoprotein cholesterol, and triglycerides and decreased high-density lipoprotein cholesterol; increased carboxyhemoglobin and other abnormalities of red blood cell chemistry; increased platelet aggregation; chronic reduction of fibrinolysis; increased blood pressure and vasoconstriction; and cardiac arrhythmias.

Smokeless tobacco is toxic due to constituents of tobacco juices, even without tobacco's combustion products. Its use may result in higher nicotine absorption than from smoked tobacco due to the acidity of saliva and its prolonged contact with the tobacco.

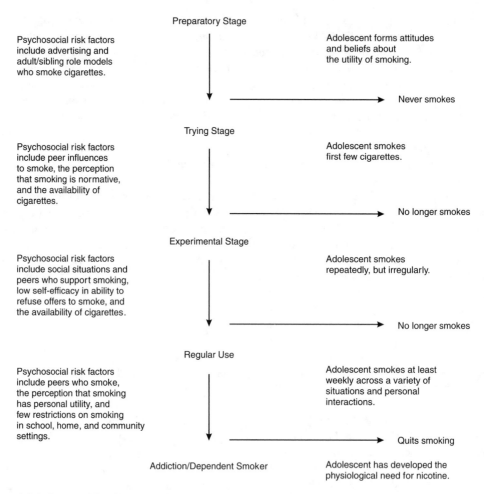

Figure 14–1 Stages of Smoking Initiation among Children and Adolescents. *Source*: Reprinted from Preventing Tobacco Use Among Young People, A Report of the Surgeon General, p 126, 1994, National Center for Chronic Disease Prevention and Health Promotion, Office on Smoking and Health.

DISTRIBUTION OF EXPOSURE

Prevalence of Smoking in the United States

The prevalence of cigarette smoking in the US adult population age 18 years and older in 1990 is shown in Table 14–1 for men, women, and the total population by age, race, origin, and education.[5] Smoking was defined as an affirmative response to the question, "Do you smoke now?" The overall frequency of smoking was 25.5%, slightly greater for men and less for women. The prevalence was notably less for Asians/Pacific Islanders (16.4%) and greater for American Indians/Alaska Natives (38.1%). The lower prevalence among the older age groups, 65–74 years and 75 or over, is also noteworthy and could reflect reduced survival of smokers to these ages, greater frequency of smoking cessation, or less incidence of smoking at earlier ages among these groups born in 1925 or earlier. The strong gradient of less frequent smoking among successively more highly educated groups is also striking. An update of overall prevalence of cigarette smoking in the United States to 1994 indicated frequencies of 28.0% and 24.7% for White men and women, 33.9% and 21.8% for

Table 14–1 Percentage of Adults Who Smoke Cigarettes, by Sex, Age, Race, Origin, and Level of Education, United States, 1990

	Men		Women		Total	
	%	*(95% CI)* [a]	%	*(95% CI)*	%	*(95% CI)*
Age (yr)						
18–24	26.6	(24.3–28.9)	22.5	(20.6–24.4)	24.9	(23.0–26.0)
25–44	32.9	(31.7–34.1)	26.6	(25.6–27.6)	29.7	(28.9–30.5)
45–64	29.3	(27.8–30.8)	24.8	(23.5–26.1)	27.0	(26.0–28.0)
65–74	18.3	(16.2–20.5)	15.6	(14.2–17.0)	16.8	(15.5–18.1)
>75	7.6	(5.8–9.4)	5.8	(4.7–6.9)	6.5	(5.6–7.5)
Race						
White	27.9	(27.1–28.9)	23.5	(22.7–24.2)	25.6	(25.0–26.2)
Black	32.5	(30.2–34.8)	21.2	(19.6–22.8)	26.2	(24.8–27.6)
Asian/Pacific Islander	24.8	(20.4–29.2)	6.2	(4.1–8.3)	16.4	(13.5–19.3)
American Indian/Alaska Native	40.1	(29.4–50.8)	36.2	(24.4–48.0)	38.1	(28.3–47.9)
Origin						
Hispanic	30.9	(27.8–34.0)	16.3	(14.1–18.5)	23.0	(21.1–24.9)
Non-Hispanic	28.2	(27.4–29.1)	23.4	(22.7–24.1)	25.7	(25.1–26.3)
Education						
Less than high school diploma	37.3	(35.4–39.2)	27.1	(25.7–28.5)	31.1	(30.6–33.0)
High school diploma	33.5	(32.1–34.9)	26.5	(25.5–27.5)	29.6	(28.7–30.5)
Some college	26.2	(24.5–27.9)	20.2	(19.0–21.4)	23.0	(22.0–24.0)
College degree	14.5	(13.3–15.7)	12.3	(11.2–13.4)	13.5	(12.7–14.3)
Total	28.4	(27.6–29.2)	22.8	(22.1–23.5)	25.5	(25.0–26.1)

a. 95% confidence interval (CI).

Source: Reprinted with permission from TE Novotney, *Chronic Disease Epidemiology and Control*, p 204, © 1993, American Public Health Association.

Black men and women, and 24.3% and 15.2% for Hispanic men and women.[6]

For younger persons, the Youth Risk Behavior Survey of 1991 defined current smoking as smoking within the past 30 days.[2] This survey showed that the adult prevalence of smoking already had been reached among US high school students by the level of the 10th grade (25.2%). Among 11th and 12th graders, more than 30% of respondents were current smokers. Smoking was one-half as frequent or less among Black boys and girls than among other groups; it was especially frequent in the North Central region of the United States (36.5%).

The progression during youth from the first experience with smoking to becoming a daily smoker is demonstrated in Table 14–2.[2] Persons aged 30–39 were asked to recall the ages at which they had first tried a cigarette and at which they began smoking daily. The prevalence of both experimentation and daily smoking increased from below age 12 to each successively older age category, most sharply over the groups from below age 12 years to below age 18. By the latter age, more than one-third of all persons had begun smoking daily, and more than 70% of those who became daily smokers had done so by this age.

Table 14-2 Cumulative Percentages of Recalled Age at Which a Respondent First Tried a Cigarette and Began Smoking Daily, among Persons Aged 30–39, National Household Surveys on Drug Abuse, United States, 1991

Age (yrs)	All Persons[a]		Persons Who Had Ever Tried a Cigarette	Persons Who Had Ever Smoked Daily	
	First Tried a Cigarette	Began Smoking Daily	First Tried a Cigarette	First Tried a Cigarette	Began Smoking Daily
<12	14.1	0.9	18.0	15.6	1.9
<14	29.7	3.9	38.0	36.7	8.0
<16	48.2	12.2	61.9	62.2	24.9
<18	63.7	26.0	81.6	81.9	53.0
≤18	68.8	34.9	88.2	89.0	71.2
<20	71.0	37.8	91.0	91.3	77.0
<25	76.6	46.5	98.2	98.4	94.8
<30	77.4	48.1	99.3	99.4	98.1
≤39	78.0	49.0	100.0	100.0	100.0
Never smoked	100.0	100.0	NA	NA	NA
Mean age	NA	NA	14.5	14.6	17.7

Note: NA, not applicable.

a. All persons (*N* = 6,388).

Source: Reprinted from Preventing Tobacco Use Among Young People, A Report of the Surgeon General, p 65, 1994, National Center for Chronic Disease Prevention and Health Promotion, Office on Smoking and Health.

Limitations of International Comparisons

These data indicate the magnitude of the problem of smoking among youth in the United States alone in the early 1990s. Surveys from many areas of the world suggest that the prevalence differs widely, from nearly 0% to more than 50%.[7] However, lack of standardization of survey questions and the potential for variation in reliability of responses suggest caution in interpreting such comparisons.

Trends in US Smoking Patterns

Trends in the prevalence of smoking have indicated a reduction among adults aged 20 and older in the United States from 1965 to 1990.[5] The reduction for men was from 50% to 28%; for women it was from 32% to 23%. Among high school students, those reporting smoking one or more cigarettes per day decreased from

1976 to 1984 from 28% to about 18%, with no further decrease through 1991.[2] The rate of decrease in smoking prevalence among US adolescents slowed especially for Whites. In fact, an increase in prevalence of smoking has been observed among 8th, 10th, and 12th graders in the United States from 1992 to 1994, as shown in Figure 14–2.[8] Smoking prevalence is currently much higher in White than in Black adolescents.[9]

At the population level, these trends imply large changes in the frequency of exposure to tobacco smoke. In addition, especially among youth, smokeless tobacco use has become increasingly common.[2] The Youth Risk Behavior Study of 1991 showed that 10% of high school students used smokeless tobacco on one or more of the preceding 30 days. This was almost entirely a male behavior pattern, with positive responses for 19% of males and 1% of

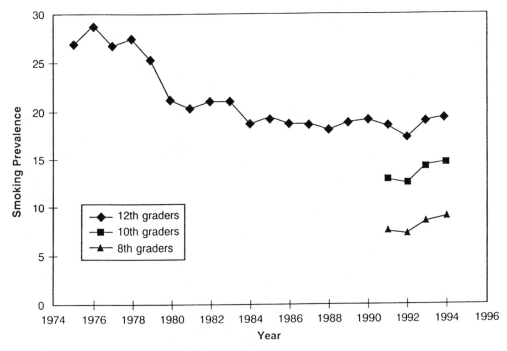

Figure 14–2 Prevalence of Daily Cigarette Smoking among 8th-, 10th-, and 12th-Grade Students, 1975 to 1994. *Source*: Reprinted from National Cancer Institute, National Institutes of Health, Bethesda, Maryland.

females. Although some survey respondents reported use of both smokeless tobacco and cigarettes, it is clear that cigarette smoking alone does not indicate the full extent of tobacco exposure in the population, especially among youth.

RATES AND RISKS

Population Differences in Incidence of Coronary Heart Disease and Total Mortality

The relation of cigarette smoking to the occurrence of coronary heart disease can be illustrated by comparisons both between populations and among individuals within a population. The Seven Countries Study, described in Chapter 4, investigated the relation between cigarette smoking behavior and population rates of coronary heart disease events in 13 of the 16 cohorts in the study. The use of cigarettes as

reported at the baseline examination was examined in relation to the incidence of coronary heart disease over the next 10 years in these study cohorts, grouped by geographic area, as shown in Figure 14–3.[10] Cigarette smoking was classified "never," "stopped," or as intervals of current smoking of less than 10, 10 to 19, or 20 or more cigarettes per day. Among nonsmokers, the number of "hard" coronary events per 100 men ranged from less than two for the Yugoslavian cohorts to four for the Northern European cohorts. With successively greater exposure, from those who had already stopped smoking to those smoking 20 or more cigarettes per day, this difference was amplified. The relation between smoking and coronary heart disease event rates was strongest for the populations with the highest rates (Northern Europe) and notably less strong for the populations with lower rates (Yugoslavia, Italy, and Greece). Parallel differences were observed in the relation between smoking and death from all causes, and

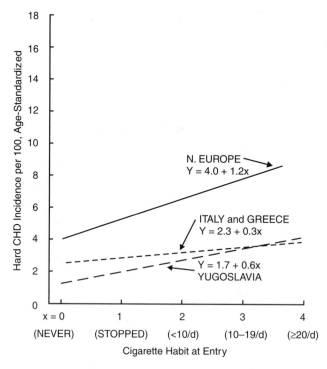

Figure 14–3 Regression of Age-Standardized 10-Year Incidence Rate of Hard Coronary Heart Disease (CHD) on Smoking Class of 8,717 Men Free of Cardiovascular Disease at Entry in Northern Europe (East and West Finland, Zutphen), in Yugoslavia (Dalmatia, Slavonia, Velika Krsna, Zrenjanin, and Belgrade), and in Italy and Greece (Crevalcore, Montegiorgio, Rome Railroad, Crete, and Corfu). *Source*: Reprinted by permission of the publisher from *Seven Countries* by A Keys, Cambridge, Mass: Harvard University Press, © 1980 by the President and Fellows of Harvard College.

the corresponding regression coefficients were each greater than those for coronary heart disease events by a factor of two or more.

Smoking and Individual Risks

The effect of smoking on the risk of coronary heart disease risk within a population has been assessed in many studies. Among the forerunners of these was the US National Pooling Project, described in Chapter 4.[11] By combining the data from five independent cohort studies, the Pooling Project obtained improved estimates of the risks due to smoking and other factors. Men age 40–64 years and free of coronary heart disease at baseline examination were classified as nonsmokers (never, past, or less than

one-half pack per day); smokers of cigars or pipes only; or cigarette smokers who smoked about one-half pack per day, about one pack per day, or more than one pack per day. After 8.6 years of follow-up, the rate of first coronary events was 143.1 per 1000 men among nonsmokers and 343.3 per 1000 men among smokers of more than one pack of cigarettes per day. The corresponding risk ratio was 2.4, and a consistent gradient in rates was found in relation to the amount smoked. (The risk ratio for smokers of cigars and pipes only, relative to nonsmokers, was 1.2.)

More recently, results were reported from 40-year follow-up of the landmark study of the mortality of British doctors in relation to their smoking habits.[12] Table 14–3 presents data from

Table 14–3 Mortality from Respiratory and Vascular Diseases, by Smoking Habits

Type of Disease (No. of Deaths, 1951–1991)	Non-smokers (Never Smoked Regularly)	Cigarette Smokers		Current No. of Cigarettes			Other Smokers		Standardized Test for Trend	
		Former	Current	1–14	15–24	≥25	Former	Current	N/X/S[a]	0/1–14/ 15–24/ ≥25[b]
Pulmonary tuberculosis (66)	4	8	11	7	9	20	8	4	1.1	3.7
Chronic obstructive lung disease (542)	10	57	127	86	112	225	40	51	9.9	14.2
Pneumonia (864)	71	90	138	113	154	169	94	85	3.3	5.6
Asthma (70)	4	11	7	6	8	6	9	7	0.4	1.4
Other respiratory disease (216)	19	28	30	26	31	33	24	18	0.1	2.1
All respiratory disease	107	192	313	237	310	471	176	164	8.2	14.2
(No. of deaths—1,758)	(131)	(455)	(490)	(161)	(170)	(159)	(290)	(392)		
Pulmonary heart disease (64)	0	7	10	5	10	21	3	10	3.7	4.2
Ischemic heart disease (6,438)	572	678	892	802	892	1,025	676	653	7.5	10.8
Myocardial degeneration (841)	61	88	125	122	109	173	96	85	3.5	5.4
Aortic aneurysm (331)	15	33	62	38	74	81	22	43	6.9	7.0
Arteriosclerosis (232)	22	18	40	31	38	72	28	23	1.9	3.8
Hypertension (330)	32	33	44	28	51	60	37	33	1.1	3.0
Cerebral thrombosis (956)	93	95	122	93	150	143	100	106	2.4	3.9
Cerebral hemorrhage (607)	59	63	81	74	81	92	69	58	1.0	2.6
Subarachnoid hemorrhage (82)	7	10	15	10	12	24	4	6	1.4	3.4
Other cerebrovascular disease (1,025)	94	110	164	167	145	188	101	103	3.2	5.0
Venous thrombosis (103)	9	11	14	17	11	14	13	9	0.5	0.6
Rheumatic heart disease (125)	15	10	15	15	20	8	17	13	-0.1	-0.5
Other cardiovascular disease (575)	58	63	71	60	82	74	62	59	0.7	1.5
All vascular deaths	1,037	1,221	1,643	1,447	1,671	1,938	1,226	1,201	10.5	15.7
(No. of deaths—11,709)	(1,304)	(2,761)	(2,870)	(1,026)	(1,045)	(799)	(1,878)	(2,986)		

Note: If smoking is unrelated to mortality from a particular disease, the standardized trend test has expectation 0 and a standard deviation of unity, so values above 1.96, 2.57, and 3.29 correspond to *P* values (two-tailed) of 0.05, 0.01, and 0.001.

a. N, nonsmokers; X, former smokers of any type of tobacco; S, current smokers of any type.

b. 0/1–14/15–24/≥25 = nonsmokers, smokers of 1–14, 15–24, and 25 or more cigarettes only.

Source: Reprinted with permission from R Doll et al, Mortality in Relation to Smoking: 40 Years' Observations on Male British Doctors, *British Medical Journal*, Vol 309, pp 904–905, © 1994, BMJ Publishing Group.

that report, including 13 categories of vascular deaths. For each category of death, the annual mortality rate is given for nonsmokers, former smokers, and current smokers overall and by current number of cigarettes smoked (at baseline). Other smokers (users of cigars or pipes) are also represented. The columns under "Standardized test for trend" present the value of the t-statistic for each calculated trend in mortality both among nonsmokers, former smokers, and current smokers (N/X/S) and by quantity smoked among current smokers. Values of t greater than 1.96 indicate a statistically significant trend (see legend). For all vascular deaths, for example, annual mortality rates were 1037 per 100,000 men per year among nonsmokers, 1221 among former smokers, and 1643 among current smokers, giving a t-value of 10.5, which was highly significant. Other significant trends with respect to smoking status or amount smoked were found for every vascular disease category except venous thrombosis, rheumatic heart disease, and the residual category, "Other."

Extensive data on the relation between smoking history and occurrence of coronary heart disease and stroke, as well as cancer, in both men and women, are provided by the American Cancer Society Cancer Prevention Study II, reported in detail in a recent National Cancer Institute monograph.[13] Additional data on these conditions among women were reported from the Nurses' Health Study in the same publication.[14] Together, these sources offer important new information on the relation of smoking to these conditions. The Cancer Prevention Study II entailed mortality follow-up of 1,185,106 men and women residing in all 50 states and the District of Columbia, Puerto Rico, and Guam when surveyed in 1982.[13] In six years of follow-up, 70,802 deaths were identified. The basis for the present analyses was the subset of the total cohort for whom complete smoking information was available at baseline and who were classified as lifelong nonsmokers (482,681) and current smokers of cigarettes only (228,682).

In Figures 14–4 and 14–5, coronary heart disease death rates are shown by age at death for men and women, respectively, contrasting current smokers (at baseline) and those who had never smoked. Coronary deaths occurred at appreciable rates after age 35–39 in men and 50–54 in women, consistent with earlier observations of the difference in age at coronary

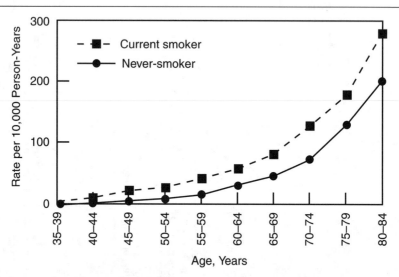

Figure 14–4 Coronary Heart Disease Death Rates in Current Cigarette Smokers and Lifelong Nonsmokers, by Age, Men. *Source*: Reprinted from National Cancer Institute, National Institutes of Health, Bethesda, Maryland.

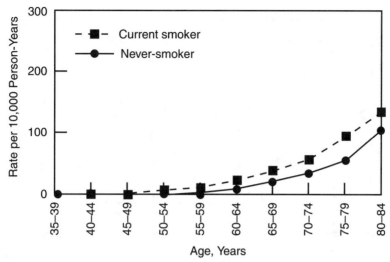

Figure 14–5 Coronary Heart Disease Death Rates in Current Cigarette Smokers and Lifelong Nonsmokers, by Age, Women. *Source*: Reprinted from National Cancer Institute, National Institutes of Health, Bethesda, Maryland.

death by sex. The curve of increasing coronary mortality, though beginning later for women, rose more steeply with age for women than for men, and in both women and men the rate of increasing mortality with age was greater in smokers. This observation underlies the pattern in Figures 14–6 and 14–7, in which the rate differences (death rate in smokers minus death rate in nonsmokers) increase continuously with age, as mortality continues to exceed by greater and greater amounts than among nonsmokers. The effect is greater in men, with higher mortality in both groups at all midadult and later ages. The rate ratio, by contrast, expresses the relative excess in mortality between groups, a measure that is greatest at younger ages when coronary death is less frequent and that decreases as coronary mortality increases in the population as a whole, smokers and nonsmokers alike. The patterns are essentially the same for women as for men. The age-specific data represented in the figures are given in Tables 14–4 and 14–5 for men and women, respectively. Also shown there are the overall death rates, rate ratios, and rate differences for men and women.

The Nurses' Health Study provided more-detailed information on exposure to cigarettes, for 121,700 female registered nurses first evaluated by mailed questionnaire in 1976, analogous to the data for British doctors.[14] Smoking status was updated by questionnaire every two years, and incident cases of coronary heart disease and stroke were identified by standardized procedures through mid-1988. Over this period, 970 cases of definite or probable coronary heart disease and 448 cases of stroke were identified. Table 14–6 indicates the smoking category and degree of exposure among smokers for fatal coronary heart disease, nonfatal myocardial infarction, and all coronary heart disease. Relative risks (RRs) were calculated first with adjustment for age alone and then for multivariate adjustment, as described in the legend. All relative risks were greater than 1, and their confidence limits did not include 1. The risks were closely parallel for fatal and nonfatal events, increased consistently with increasing exposure, and also increased by adjustment for other risk factors in most of the dose-specific analyses. Numbers of cases in the extreme exposure groups were few.

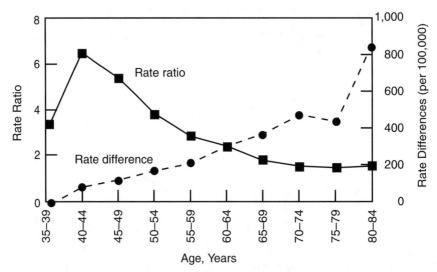

Figure 14–6 Coronary Heart Disease Rate Ratios and Rate Differences in Current Cigarette Smokers and Lifelong Nonsmokers, by Age, Men. *Source*: Reprinted from National Cancer Institute, National Institutes of Health, Bethesda, Maryland.

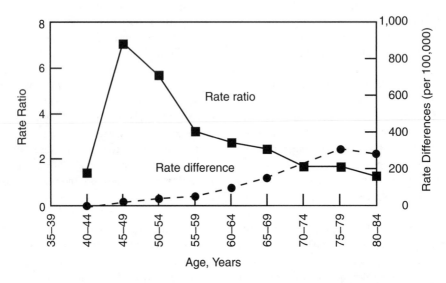

Figure 14–7 Coronary Heart Disease Rate Ratios and Rate Differences in Current Cigarette Smokers and Lifelong Nonsmokers, by Age, Women. *Source*: Reprinted from National Cancer Institute, National Institutes of Health, Bethesda, Maryland.

Tables 14–7 and 14–8 show mortality from stroke for men and women, respectively, as presented in the report on Cancer Prevention Study II.[13] The picture was much the same as for coronary heart disease, except that rate differences were smaller due to the less frequent occurrence of stroke death than coronary death in both smokers and nonsmokers. Rate ratios were similar for stroke as for coronary death. In addition, the onset of rising death rates with age were essentially the same for women as for men, with no lag as is seen in coronary event rates. The rates for women did not reach the same high values as did those for men after age 74. The relation of smoking to stroke incidence among women also was examined in the Nurses' Health Study, as shown in Table 14–9.[14] For total stroke, as well as subtypes (subarachnoid hemorrhage, ischemic stroke, and cerebral hemorrhage), relative risks were calculated as for coronary heart disease, above. Risks were increased for former smokers (not beyond chance variation in all comparisons), for current smokers, and generally across successively higher degrees of exposure among current smokers, although some irregularity in the pattern was apparent. Numbers of cases were small in some categories of stroke type and exposure level, especially for cerebral hemorrhage.

Table 14–4 Mortality from Coronary Heart Disease as Underlying Cause of Death among Lifelong Nonsmokers and Current Cigarette Smokers: Men, Cancer Prevention Study II

Age Specific

	Nonsmokers		Current Cigarette Smokers			
Age	Deaths	Rate[a]	Deaths	Rate[a]	Rate Ratio	Rate Difference[a]
35–39	2	9.1	5	29.6	3.3	20.5
40–44	3	13.4	18	84.1	6.3	70.7
45–49	18	26.8	92	146.6	5.5	119.8
50–54	72	56.3	251	212.9	3.8	156.6
55–59	157	118.6	407	322.7	2.7	204.1
60–64	277	228.6	576	545.9	2.4	317.3
65–69	414	405.4	531	772.1	1.9	366.7
70–74	490	685.0	437	1,158.2	1.7	473.2
75–79	497	1,231.3	254	1,670.9	1.4	439.6
80+	340	1,894.6	113	2,720.3	1.4	825.7
Total	2,270		2,684			

Age Standardized to 1980 US Population

	Nonsmokers	Current Cigarette Smokers
Death rate[a]	240.9	408.0
Rate ratio	1.0	1.7
(95% confidence interval)	–	(1.6–1.8)
Rate difference[a]	–	167.1
(95% confidence interval)	–	(138.3–195.8)

a. Death rate and rate difference per 100,000 person-years.

Source: Reprinted from National Cancer Institute, National Institutes of Health, Bethesda, Maryland.

Table 14–5 Mortality from Coronary Heart Disease as Underlying Cause of Death among Lifelong Nonsmokers and Current Cigarette Smokers: Women, Cancer Prevention Study II

			Age Specific			
	Nonsmokers		Current Cigarette Smokers			
Age	Deaths	Rate[a]	Deaths	Rate[a]	Rate Ratio	Rate Difference[a]
35–39	1	2.0	0	–	–	(2.0)
40–44	5	5.9	4	8.9	1.5	3.0
45–49	8	3.8	28	27.6	7.2	23.8
50–54	25	8.1	66	45.9	5.7	37.8
55–59	84	24.3	112	76.7	3.2	52.4
60–64	211	62.0	198	162.6	2.6	100.6
65–69	353	125.7	249	307.2	2.4	181.5
70–74	523	253.5	219	478.2	1.9	224.7
75–79	717	530.1	163	846.7	1.6	316.6
80+	694	975.1	73	1,270.2	1.3	295.1
Total	2,621		1,112			

Age Standardized to 1980 US Population		
	Nonsmokers	Current Cigarette Smokers
Death rate[a]	115.4	181.9
Rate ratio	1.0	1.6
(95% confidence interval)	–	(1.4–1.7)
Rate difference[a]	–	66.5
(95% confidence interval)	–	(48.7–84.3)

a. Death rate and rate difference per 100,000 person-years.

Source: Reprinted from National Cancer Institute, National Institutes of Health, Bethesda, Maryland.

Smoking is also strongly related to risk of peripheral arterial disease, and Powell designated smoking as the primary risk factor for this cardiovascular condition.[15] The view is suggested that this aspect of advanced atherosclerosis is perhaps least dependent on other risk factors and most specifically related to smoking. When peripheral arterial disease in smokers has progressed to the point of surgical treatment with vein grafts to bypass occluded arterial segments, continued smoking is associated with the rate of graft occlusion. This sequence of events is not unlike that for patients following acute myocardial infarction or coronary artery bypass procedures, in which failure to stop smoking is associated with reinfarction. Because of these further risks—even beyond occurrence of serious, nonfatal cardiovascular events—attention to smoking cessation is urged upon physicians caring for those with recognized coronary heart disease.[16]

Smoking in Relation to Other Risk Factors

The relation between smoking and two other major risk factors for coronary heart disease mortality is indicated by the experience of men screened as potential candidates for the Multi-

Table 14–6 Daily Number of Cigarettes Smoked and Age-Adjusted and Multivariate Relative Risks of Fatal Coronary Heart Disease and Nonfatal Myocardial Infarction, Compared with Never-Smokers

Event	Never-Smoker	Former Smoker	Cigarettes Smoked/Day among Current Smokers[a]					
			1–4	5–14	15–24	25–34	35–44	≥45
Fatal Coronary Heart Disease								
Cases	49	53	4	18	53	28	14	4
Relative Risk[b]	1.00	1.63	1.87	2.78	4.29	5.36	5.56	10.00
		(1.11–2.40)	(0.69–5.09)	(1.66–4.67)	(3.00–6.15)	(3.53–8.14)	(3.26–9.50)	(4.35–22.97)
Relative Risk[c]	1.00	1.62	←2.85→		4.85	6.96	←7.84→	
		(1.09–2.40)	(1.53–5.32)		(3.01–7.81)	(3.90–12.43)	(3.71–16.57)	
Nonfatal Myocardial Infarction								
Cases	166	161	15	56	189	95	54	7
Relative Risk[b]	1.00	1.47	1.97	2.46	4.21	4.87	5.58	4.64
		(1.19–1.83)	(1.17–3.30)	(1.83–3.29)	(3.48–5.11)	(3.87–6.13)	(4.24–7.35)	(2.34–9.21)
Relative Risk[c]	1.00	1.44	←2.45→		4.77	5.21	←5.32→	
		(1.16–1.79)	(1.69–3.56)		(3.64–6.26)	(3.73–7.28)	(3.61–7.86)	
Total Coronary Heart Disease								
Cases	215	214	19	74	242	123	68	11
Relative Risk[b]	1.00	1.51	1.94	2.53	4.22	4.97	5.57	5.74
		(1.25–1.82)	(1.23–3.08)	(1.96–3.26)	(3.56–5.00)	(4.06–6.08)	(4.36–7.11)	(3.36–9.81)
Relative Risk[c]	1.00	1.48	←2.53→		4.79	5.49	←5.49→	
		(1.22–1.79)	(1.84–3.50)		(3.78–6.08)	(4.10–7.35)	(3.87–7.77)	

a. Daily number smoked was missing for four cases, including two cases of fatal coronary heart disease and two of nonfatal myocardial infarction.

b. Age-adjusted relative risk.

c. Adjusted for age in five-year intervals, follow-up period (1976–1978, 1978–1980, 1980–1982, 1982–1984, 1984–1986, or 1986–1988), history of hypertension, diabetes, high cholesterol levels, body mass index, past use of oral contraceptives, menopausal status, postmenopausal estrogen therapy, and age at starting smoking.

Source: Reprinted from National Cancer Institute, National Institutes of Health, Bethesda, Maryland.

Table 14–7 Mortality from Stroke as Underlying Cause of Death among Lifelong Nonsmokers and Current Cigarette Smokers: Men, Cancer Prevention Study II

Age Specific

	Nonsmokers		Current Cigarette Smokers			
Age	Deaths	Rate[a]	Deaths	Rate[a]	Rate Ratio	Rate Difference[a]
35–39	0	0.0	2	11.9	–	11.9
40–44	1	4.5	1	4.7	–	0.2
45–49	4	6.0	14	22.3	3.8	16.3
50–54	6	4.7	28	23.7	5.1	19.0
55–59	13	9.8	49	38.8	4.0	29.0
60–64	35	28.9	83	78.7	2.7	49.8
65–69	52	50.9	91	132.3	2.6	81.4
70–74	80	111.8	83	220.0	2.0	108.2
75–79	113	280.0	81	532.8	1.9	252.8
80+	108	601.8	36	866.6	1.4	264.8
Total	412		468			

Age Standardized to 1980 US Population

	Nonsmokers	Current Cigarette Smokers
Death rate[a]	55.5	87.2
Rate ratio	1.0	1.6
(95% confidence interval)	–	(1.3–1.9)
Rate difference[a]	–	31.7
(95% confidence interval)	–	(17.8–45.6)

a. Death rate and rate difference per 100,000 person-years.

Source: Reprinted from National Cancer Institute, National Institutes of Health, Bethesda, Maryland.

ple Risk Factor Intervention Study (MRFIT), described in Chapter 4.[17] This exceptionally large population of more than 360,000 men permitted more-detailed examination of these relations than was previously possible. The data were cross-classified by quintile groups for systolic blood pressure, serum total cholesterol concentration, and smoking status at the screening examination, as was shown in Table 4–7. Relative to nonsmokers, smokers experienced from more than three times the rate of coronary heart disease death at the lowest levels of systolic blood pressure and serum total cholesterol concentration (10.37 versus 3.09 deaths per 10,000 person-years, risk ratio 3.4) to nearly two times the rate at the highest levels of these other factors (62.11 versus 33.40 deaths per 10,000 person-years, risk ratio 1.9). The multiplication of risks by smoking, at all levels of these two other risk factors, is striking. As addressed elsewhere, the major cardiovascular disease risk factors are closely interrelated and it is important that they be considered together and not in isolation.

It is notable also that smoking has been shown to interact with these same risk factors and others in the development of atherosclerosis during adolescence and young adulthood. One

Table 14–8 Mortality from Stroke as Underlying Cause of Death among Lifelong Nonsmokers and Current Cigarette Smokers: Women, Cancer Prevention Study II

	Age Specific					
	Nonsmokers		Current Cigarette Smokers			
Age	Deaths	Rate[a]	Deaths	Rate[a]	Rate Ratio	Rate Difference[a]
35–39	1	2.0	1	4.0	2.0	2.0
40–44	1	1.2	3	6.7	5.7	5.5
45–49	6	2.9	22	21.7	7.5	18.8
50–54	16	5.2	36	25.0	4.9	19.8
55–59	23	6.7	58	39.7	6.0	33.0
60–64	55	16.1	50	41.1	2.5	25.0
65–69	104	37.0	78	96.2	2.6	59.2
70–74	135	65.4	81	176.9	2.7	111.5
75–79	215	159.0	61	316.9	2.0	157.9
80+	273	383.6	19	330.6	0.9	(53.0)
Total	829		409			

	Age Standardized to 1980 US Population	
	Nonsmokers	Current Cigarette Smokers
Death rate[a]	44.1	61.1
Rate ratio	1.0	1.5
(95% confidence interval)	–	(1.2–1.7)
Rate difference[a]	–	17.1
(95% confidence interval)	–	(6.9–27.2)

a. Death rate and rate difference per 100,000 person-years.

Source: Reprinted from National Cancer Institute, National Institutes of Health, Bethesda, Maryland.

demonstration of this relationship is found in the results of the Pathobiological Determinants of Atherosclerosis in Youth (PDAY) study.[18] Serum thiocyanate concentrations determined just following death were correlated with the extent of the endothelial surface of the aorta and coronary arteries that was affected by atherosclerosis.

In addition, a recent review of studies of environmental tobacco smoke suggests that passive smoke exposure by itself is associated with increased mortality from coronary heart disease.[19] Of 12 studies represented, relative risks or odds ratios in the range from about 1.1 to 2.0 were shown for 9 studies, while higher values (2.6–5.8) were observed in 3 studies and a value of less than 1 (about 0.5) was found in 1 study.

PREVENTION AND CONTROL

The Population-Wide Strategy

Population-wide measures for the prevention and control of smoking and tobacco use are intended, in principle, to reduce or eliminate both the incidence and the prevalence of these practices. Because their incidence occurs predominantly in childhood and adolescence, strategies to prevent smoking and tobacco use specifically target youth. Strategies to reduce prevalence, in contrast, must also address cessa-

Table 14–9 Age-Adjusted Relative Risks (RRs) of Stroke (Fatal and Nonfatal Combined), by Daily Number of Cigarettes Consumed among Current Smokers

Event	Never-Smoker	Former Smoker	Current Smoker	Cigarettes Smoked per Day among Current Smokers[a]			
				1–14	15–24	25–34	≥35
Total stroke							
Cases	126	114	208	40	92	38	34
RR[b]	1.00	1.34	2.58	1.79	2.84	2.70	4.23
		(1.04–1.73)	(2.08–3.19)	(1.26–2.54)	(2.19–3.67)	(1.91–3.84)	(2.99–6.00)
RR[c]	1.00	1.35	2.73	2.02	3.34	3.08	4.48
		(0.98–1.85)	(2.18–3.41)	(1.29–3.14)	(2.38–4.70)	(1.94–4.87)	(2.78–7.23)
Subarachnoid hemorrhage							
Cases	19	25	64	13	21	17	11
RR[b]	1.00	2.01	4.96	3.68	4.05	7.31	8.28
		(1.12–3.61)	(3.13–7.87)	(1.91–7.11)	(2.30–7.14)	(4.15–12.85)	(4.45–15.42)
RR[c]	1.00	2.26	4.85	4.28	4.02	7.95	10.22
		(1.16–4.42)	(2.90–8.11)	(1.88–9.77)	(1.90–8.54)	(3.50–18.07)	(4.03–25.94)
Ischemic stroke							
Cases	85	70	120	23	58	19	18
RR[b]	1.00	1.20	2.25	1.54	2.69	2.06	3.43
		(0.88–1.65)	(1.72–2.95)	(0.98–2.44)	(1.95–3.72)	(1.27–3.36)	(2.13–5.51)
RR[c]	1.00	1.27	2.53	1.83	3.57	2.73	3.97
		(0.85–1.89)	(1.91–3.35)	(1.04–3.23)	(2.36–5.42)	(1.49–5.03)	(2.09–7.53)
Cerebral hemorrhage							
Cases	19	16	18	4	10	←4[d]→	
RR[b]	1.00	1.27	1.46	1.18	2.01	1.18	
		(0.66–2.44)	(0.77–2.78)	(0.40–3.46)	(0.94–4.28)	(0.41–3.46)	
RR[c]	1.00	1.24	1.24	1.68	2.53	1.41	
		(0.64–2.42)	(0.64–2.42)	(0.34–5.28)	(0.71–6.05)	(0.39–5.05)	

a. Cigarettes smoked per day were unknown for four cases, including two cases of subarachnoid hemorrhage and two cases of ischemic stroke.

b. Age-adjusted RR.

c. Adjusted for age in five-year intervals, follow-up period (1976–1978, 1978–1980, 1980–1982, 1982–1984, 1984–1986, or 1986–1988), history of hypertension, diabetes, high cholesterol levels, body mass index, past use of oral contraceptives, postmenopausal estrogen therapy, and age at starting smoking.

d. These two categories were combined due to small numbers.

Source: Reprinted from National Cancer Institute, National Institutes of Health, Bethesda, Maryland.

tion of smoking by current smokers. Therefore these strategies include the adult population because of the age distribution of current smokers.

Policies for prevention have been articulated by many organizations and agencies. An example at the international level in the context of cardiovascular disease prevention is provided by a scientific advisory group report prepared under the auspices of the World Health Organization, *Prevention in Childhood and Youth of Adult Cardiovascular Diseases*, which recommended that the overall goal of national policies should be "the elimination of smoking and other forms of tobacco use."[7(p 83)] Specific recommended strategies address school-based prevention and control activities, prohibition of the sale of cigarettes to minors, prohibition of the advertising and promotion of tobacco products, disallowing tobacco industry sponsorship of sporting events, discouraging passive smoke exposure of children by their parents who smoke, legislation to prohibit the promotion of smokeless tobacco, and encouragement of parents to become nonsmoking role models.

At the national level, the focus on prevention of tobacco use and addiction is illustrated by the guidelines for school health programs developed by the US Centers for Disease Control and Prevention (CDC) that appeared in 1994.[20] It is recommended that all schools develop and enforce tobacco policies; instruct students on tobacco effects, social influences and peer pressure, and refusal skills; provide education at all grade levels from kindergarten through high school; provide teacher training and parental involvement; support cessation efforts by teachers and students; and assess these programs regularly.

The High-Risk Strategy

To the extent that these population-level measures are effective, they will tend to reduce both the incidence and the prevalence of smoking and tobacco use. At the individual level, emphasis is placed on smoking cessation, which directly affects the prevalence of tobacco use. Policies and approaches for reduction of the prevalence of smoking through cessation by current smokers are addressed in a report from the American Heart Association, "Statement on Smoking and Cardiovascular Disease for Health Care Professionals."[21] The report observes that smoking cessation has been achieved by nearly half of all those who were ever smokers in the United States, and that this has occurred in 90% of instances through self-initiated efforts rather than formal programs. As experience with smoking cessation has grown, the frequent problem of relapse has been addressed. In addition to social and psychological approaches to support the cessation of smoking, pharmacological intervention for replacement of the nicotine previously obtained from tobacco has been investigated. To the extent that smoking and other forms of tobacco use are maintained by nicotine addiction, this latter approach would seem to have only short-term utility, though it may be valuable at a critical point in the cessation process for some individuals.

EFFECTIVENESS OF INTERVENTION OR CESSATION

Community-level effects of intervention on smoking prevalence have been evaluated in several studies. Recent examples include the Community Intervention Trial for Smoking Cessation (COMMIT), the Minnesota Heart Health Program (MHHP), and a state-wide tobacco education media campaign in California. In COMMIT, one community out of each of 11 community pairs was randomly allocated to receive interventions aimed at media and community events, health professionals, worksites, and other organizations in the community and to facilitate (except through payment for services) the awareness and use of existing resources for assistance in smoking cessation.[22] Community residents identified through survey methods as heavy or as light-to-moderate smokers constituted cohorts followed for five years, 1988–1993, for their responses to these community-wide interventions. A modest effect was found for the light-to-moderate smokers, with an estimate of 30.6% quitting in the intervention communities and 27.5% quitting in the control communities. For heavy smokers, however, the quit rate was actually slightly higher in the control than in the intervention communities (18.7% versus 18.0%). These results are presented in Figure 14–8.

The Minnesota Heart Health Program studied three matched pairs of communities and in a series of reports summarized and evaluated sev-

eral of its component programs.[23] Some favorable indications were observed, but except for the experience of women when evaluated by cross-sectional surveys, the intervention effect did not exceed the secular trends toward decreased smoking in these communities.

The media campaign in California included several waves of data collection by survey methods among both students and adults.[24] It appeared that measures among students of campaign awareness, smoking prevalence, thoughts about smoking (about quitting by smokers and

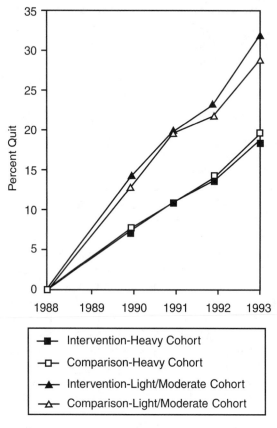

Note: Different numbers of subjects contribute at each time point. MCAR = missing completely at random.

Figure 14–8 Observed Quit Rates (MCAR) over Time for Heavy and Light-to-Moderate Smoker Cohorts. *Source*: Reprinted with permission from The COMMIT Research Group (Sylvan B Green), p 187, *American Journal of Public Health*, Vol 85, No 2, © 1995, American Public Health Association.

not thinking about starting among nonsmokers), and attitudes toward smoking tended to change in favorable directions over the course of the intervention. For adults the results were less clearly positive except for media awareness.

These experiences illustrate the force of secular trends, which may be difficult to exceed by these population-wide interventions, as well as the problem of reversing already-established smoking habits, especially among heavy smokers. It may be that the initiative of many individuals to quit smoking has already removed many of the more easily reached smokers from the target population. Effective strategies for prevention of smoking in the first place are needed to the extent that reversal of this remaining addictive behavior cannot be attained by the means presently available.

As for evidence that smoking cessation does reduce substantially—though not completely—the risks examined earlier in this chapter, both the experience of the Seven Countries investigators and that of the British doctors can be cited. At the population level, a recent symposium to update the Seven Countries experience included reports on long-term trends in the occurrence of coronary heart disease in conjunction with trends in the major risk factors, including smoking, in those countries.[25] Though the data were subject to many sources of confounding by extraneous influences, it is of interest that in the four countries with decreasing coronary heart disease mortality (Italy, the Netherlands, the United States, and Finland) the national prevalence of smoking had also decreased in recent decades. In Japan, despite increasing population values for both mean total serum cholesterol concentration and the prevalence of high blood pressure, there had been no reported increase in coronary heart disease mortality, and the prevalence of smoking had declined. In the two countries with increasing coronary heart disease mortality, smoking prevalence had increased in one (Greece) and had changed inconsistently in the other (Yugoslavia).

It has already been noted in reference to the studies of British doctors and US nurses that former smokers had mortality from vascular and other causes intermediate between those who were never smokers and those who were current smokers.[12,14] Thus, much of the excess risk can be reduced, but it does not appear that the risks of outcomes that result from smoking are eliminated entirely even over an interval of many years. The extent to which this occurs can be seen in data from the latter study, in which the risk of those classified as current smokers is taken as the reference value and the risks for those quitting for successively longer time intervals are then calculated (Table 14–10). Risks for total mortality and cardiovascular disease mortality, especially when adjusted for other cardiovascular risk factors, decreased sharply and continuously with smoking cessation. Only for cancer deaths that included cancer of the lung was this benefit not observed. Cardiovascular mortality was reduced to an age-adjusted risk of 0.76 times that of current smokers within 2 years, or a 24% reduction, and an eventual reduction of 60%–70% was observed after 15 years or more.

Changes in risk through individual-level intervention were tested in the Whitehall Study of London civil servants.[26] Among men who were smokers and also at the highest risks for coronary heart disease or chronic bronchitis on the basis of a multivariate risk score, 714 men were randomly allocated to a smoking cessation intervention group and 731 men served as controls with no systematic advice concerning their smoking. Overall, after 10 years in the trial, the occurrence of coronary heart disease was reduced in the intervention group by 18%, based on cumulative event rates of 7.3% versus 8.9%. At the first reported point in follow-up, at 2 years, there was already a reduction of nearly 50% in the observed rates, based on event rates of 1.1% and 0.6%. Although these were quite low rates in both groups, it is notable that the benefit of smoking cessation was suggested at the first available comparison, after only two years in the trial. (Overall mortality was not

Table 14–10 Total and Cause-Specific Mortality by Time since Quitting: Comparison of Analyses with and Without 2-Year Exclusion of Disease at the Start of Each Follow-Up Period: Multivariate Relative Risks (RRs)

Event	Never-Smoker	Current Smoker	Years Since Quitting among Former Smokers				
			<2	2–4	5–9	10–14	≥15
Total Mortality							
Cases[a]	933	1,115	127	106	131	66	231
RR	0.56	1.00	1.19	1.00	0.79	0.53	0.61
Cases[b]	632	884	51	58	84	46	137
RR	0.49	1.00	0.76	0.73	0.70	0.47	0.49
	(0.44–0.54)		(0.53–1.08)	(0.53–1.01)	(0.53–0.92)	(0.33–0.67)	(0.39–0.62)
Cardiovascular Disease							
Cases[a]	131	284	20	24	32	9	39
RR	0.30	1.00	0.76	0.90	0.75	0.29	0.42
Cases[b]	111	254	11	11	23	7	33
RR	0.29	1.00	0.63	0.53	0.67	0.27	0.46
	(0.23–0.37)		(0.28–1.45)	(0.25–1.13)	(0.40–1.15)	(0.11–0.65)	(0.29–0.74)
Total Cancer, Including Lung							
Cases[a]	516	502	75	48	69	37	134
RR	0.99	1.00	1.37	0.97	1.12	0.91	1.10
Cases[b]	562	339	13	19	33	20	53
RR	0.54	1.00	0.42	0.66	0.75	0.56	0.51
	(0.46–0.64)		(0.20–0.89)	(0.38–1.16)	(0.49–1.16)	(0.33–0.96)	(0.35–0.74)
Total Cancer, Excluding Lung							
Cases[a]	492	351	49	33	57	34	127
RR	0.60	1.00	1.22	0.99	0.63	0.70	0.72
Cases[b]	244	201	9	11	25	18	50
RR	0.85	1.00	0.44	0.71	1.03	0.85	0.81
	(0.71–1.03)		(0.18–1.08)	(0.34–1.48)	(0.63–1.69)	(0.48–1.51)	(0.54–1.20)

a. Cases and multivariate RRs after baseline exclusion of coronary heart disease, stroke, and cancer except nonmelanoma skin cancer. Multivariate RRs were adjusted for age in five-year intervals, follow-up period (1976–1978, 1978–1980, 1980–1982, 1982–1984, 1984–1986, or 1986–1988), body mass index, history of hypertension, diabetes, high cholesterol levels, postmenopausal estrogen therapy, menopausal status, past use of oral contraceptives, parental history of myocardial infarction before age 60, and daily number of cigarettes smoked during the period before stopping smoking (95% confidence intervals in parentheses).

b. Cases and multivariate RRs after exclusion of coronary heart disease, stroke, and cancer (except nonmelanoma skin cancer) at the beginning of each two-year follow-up interval.

Source: Reprinted from National Cancer Institute, National Institutes of Health, Bethesda, Maryland.

reduced in the intervention group despite reductions in both coronary heart disease and lung cancer, for reasons discussed in that report.)

CURRENT ISSUES

Can the tobacco epidemic be controlled? This is the global question of greatest importance concerning smoking and other tobacco use because of the projected increases in smoking prevalence and its adverse health consequences in the decades ahead. Pressures to reduce tobacco consumption in the United States and several other industrialized countries have had the negative effect of intensified marketing of tobacco products elsewhere, especially in developing countries. In many of these developing countries, efforts are in progress to adopt legal controls of tobacco sales and imports, but the countervailing influences are powerful and may be difficult to overcome. This issue is expected to remain a major challenge for some years to come.

Can effective regulatory authority regarding tobacco products be established despite the powerful opposition of the tobacco industry? In the United States, disclosures of tobacco industry documents and Congressional testimony by industry leaders have stimulated renewed efforts to regulate tobacco products under the same authority as for pharmaceuticals, the Food and Drug Administration. In July 1995 the *Journal of the American Medical Association* devoted its primary attention to this issue through a series of articles introduced by Glantz and colleagues.[27] A central aspect of the discussion is the industry's alleged knowledge of the addictive properties of nicotine and use of these properties to formulate tobacco products specifically intended to bring about addiction of the users. At the same time, President Clinton proposed intensified enforcement of existing regulations concerning access to cigarettes by minors. Such action could reinforce many of the policy recommendations discussed above. However, the use of smokeless tobacco products as substitutes for cigarettes early in the process of nicotine addiction could allow the tobacco industry to circumvent the intended effect of restricted access to cigarettes. If so, the epidemiologic pattern of adolescent onset of smoking could change to early adult onset, if restriction on access to cigarettes applies only to persons under age 18. Much remains to be accomplished in the prevention of cigarette smoking in the first place.

Can health professionals be persuaded to discontinue smoking, and can students in health professional schools be persuaded to quit or not to begin? Smoking by physicians and other health professionals constitutes a particularly negative behavioral model. But in many countries smoking by these groups is highly prevalent. Efforts are now in progress to mount preventive strategies for reduction of the incidence and prevalence of smoking by health professionals. Perhaps if better informed of the need to achieve control of the tobacco epidemic, health professionals will more commonly take the strong exemplary roles that may be needed to bring this about.

REFERENCES

1. Peto R. Smoking and death: the past 40 years and the next 40. *Br Med J.* 1994;209:937–939.

2. US Dept of Health and Human Services. *Preventing Tobacco Use among Young People: A Report of the Surgeon General.* Atlanta, Ga: Office on Smoking and Health, National Center for Chronic Disease Prevention and Health Promotion, Centers for Disease Control and Prevention, Public Health Service, US Dept of Health and Human Services; 1994.

3. Wagenknecht LE, Burke GL, Perkins LL, Haley NJ, et al. Misclassification of smoking status in the CARDIA Study: a comparison of self-report with serum cotinine levels. *Am J Public Health.* 1992;82:33–36.

4. Frost F, Tollestrup K, Starzyk P. History of smoking from the Washington state death certificate. *Am J Prev Med.* 1994;10:335–339.

5. Novotny TE. Tobacco use. In: Brownson RC, Remington PL, David JR, eds. *Chronic Disease Epidemiology*

and Control. Washington, DC: American Public Health Association; 1993: 199–220.

6. *1997 Heart and Stroke Statistical Update.* Dallas, Tex: American Heart Association; 1996.

7. WHO Expert Committee on Prevention in Childhood and Youth of Adult Cardiovascular Diseases. *Prevention in Childhood and Youth of Adult Cardiovascular Diseases: Time for Action.* Geneva, Switzerland: World Health Organization; 1990. Technical Report Series 792.

8. Burns DM, Garfinkel L, Samet JM. Introduction, summary, and conclusions. In: Burns DM, Garfinkel L, Samet JM, eds. *Changes in Cigarette-Related Disease Risks and Their Implication for Prevention and Control.* Bethesda, Md: National Cancer Institute, National Institutes of Health; 1997, Smoking and Tobacco Control, Monograph 8. NIH publication 97-4213.

9. Nelson DE, Giovino GA, Shopland DR, Mowery PD, et al. Trends in cigarette smoking among US adolescents, 1974 through 1991. *Am J Public Health.* 1995; 85:34–40.

10. Keys A. *Seven Countries: A Multivariate Analysis of Death and Coronary Heart Disease.* Cambridge, Mass: Harvard University Press; 1980.

11. Pooling Project Research Group. Relationship of blood pressure, serum cholesterol, smoking habit, relative weight and ECG abnormalities to incidence of major coronary events: final report of the Pooling Project. *J Chronic Dis.* 1978;31:201–306.

12. Doll R, Peto R, Wheatley K, Gray R, et al. Mortality in relation to smoking: 40 years' observations on male British doctors. *Br Med J.* 1994;309:901–911.

13. Thun MJ, Myers DG, Day-Lally C, Namboodiri MM, et al. Age and the exposure-response relationships between cigarette smoking and premature death in Cancer Prevention Study II. In: Burns DM, Garfinkel L, Samet JM, eds. *Changes in Cigarette-Related Disease Risks and Their Implication for Prevention and Control.* Bethesda, Md: National Cancer Institute, National Institutes of Health; 1997:383–413. Smoking and Tobacco Control, Monograph 8. NIH publication 97-4213.

14. Kawachi I, Colditz GA, Stampfer MJ, Willett WC, et al. Smoking cessation and decreased risks of total mortality, stroke, and coronary heart disease incidence among women: a prospective cohort study. In: Burns DM, Garfinkel L, Samet JM, eds. *Changes in Cigarette-Related Disease Risks and Their Implication for Prevention and Control.* Bethesda, Md: National Cancer Institute, National Institutes of Health; 1997, Smo-

king and Tobacco Control, Monograph 8. NIH publication 97-4213.

15. Powell JT. Smoking. In: Fowkes FGR, ed. *Epidemiology of Peripheral Vascular Disease.* London: Springer-Verlag; 1991: 141–153.

16. Pasternak RC, Grundy SM, Levy D, Thompson PD. Task Force 3. Spectrum of risk factors for coronary heart disease. *J Am Coll Cardiol.* 1996;27:978–990.

17. Stamler J. Established major coronary risk factors. In: Marmot M, Elliott P, eds. *Coronary Heart Disease Epidemiology: From Aetiology to Public Health.* Oxford, England: Oxford University Press; 1992:35–66.

18. Pathobiological Determinants of Atherosclerosis in Youth (PDAY) Research Group. Relationship of atherosclerosis in young men to serum lipoprotein cholesterol concentrations and smoking. *JAMA.* 1990; 264: 3018–3024.

19. Wells AJ. Passive smoking as a cause of heart disease. *J Am Coll Cardiol.* 1994; 24:546–554.

20. Centers for Disease Control and Prevention. Guidelines for school health programs to prevent tobacco use and addiction. *J School Health.* 1994;64:353–360.

21. Jonas MA, Oates JA, Ockene JK, Hennekens CH. Statement on smoking and cardiovascular disease for health care professionals. *Circ.* 1992;86:1664–1669.

22. The COMMIT Research Group. Community intervention trial for smoking cessation (COMMIT), I: cohort results from a four-year community intervention. *Am J Public Health.* 1995;85:183–192.

23. Lando HA, Pechacek TF, Pirie PL, Murray DM, et al. Changes in adult cigarette smoking in the Minnesota Heart Health Program. *Am J Public Health.* 1995; 85:201–208.

24. Popham WJ, Potter LD, Hetrick MA, Muthen LK, et al. Effectiveness of the California 1990–1991 tobacco education media campaign. *Am J Prev Med.* 1994; 10:319–326.

25. Toshima H, Koga Y, Blackburn H, eds, Keys A, honorary ed. *Lessons for Science from the Seven Countries Study.* Tokyo: Springer-Verlag; 1994.

26. Rose G, Hamilton PJS, Colwell L, Shipley MJ. A randomized controlled trial of anti-smoking advice: 10-year results. *J Epidemiol Community Health.* 1982; 36:102–108.

27. Glantz SA, Barnes DE, Bero L, Hanauer P, et al. Looking through a keyhole at the tobacco industry: the Brown and Williamson Documents: Special Communications. *JAMA.* 1995;274:219–224.

CHAPTER 15

Alcohol Consumption

SUMMARY

Although alcohol consumption may be considered a component of diet, it is addressed separately owing to special interest in the association of some levels of intake, in comparison with others, with lower risks of coronary heart disease and ischemic stroke. Because of many known adverse effects of alcohol from health and social perspectives, this association poses a policy dilemma. Although much, if not all, of the epidemiologic evidence supports such an association, and although mechanisms of action such as increased concentration of high-density lipoprotein cholesterol and others make a causal relation plausible, no clinical trials provide the kind of information usually sought as a basis for recommendations for a preventive measure. There is controversy, therefore, as to appropriate policy but perhaps less prominent concern than is warranted in view of apparent underlying social influences toward increased alcohol consumption and the recognized hazards for individuals and populations.

INTRODUCTION

Alcohol consumption has received considerable attention in the past 10–20 years as a factor that has, in addition to its many known adverse health effects, properties that tend to reduce the risk of coronary heart disease. In some respects alcohol-containing beverages simply constitute one of several potentially major dietary constituents. In this sense, assessment of alcohol consumption poses difficulties similar to those encountered in other aspects of dietary data collection. But special social and cultural considerations surrounding the use of alcohol compound these difficulties, add to problems in interpretation of data, and complicate establishment and implementation of policy concerning its use. Alcohol consumption therefore warrants separate discussion from dietary imbalance, addressed in a previous chapter, even though its relation with other aspects of diet is also important.

DEFINITION

Qualitative Categories

Alcohol consumption refers to individual practices with respect to use of alcoholic beverages of all types, including beer, wine, fortified wine, and distilled spirits. Absence of alcohol use as a lifelong practice characterizes persons or groups identified as *abstainers* or *teetotalers* (from "T-total" to emphasize total abstinence), both terms carrying judgmental, if not moralistic, overtones. Use of alcohol may be classified as past, for persons reporting previous but not current use, or current for persons who are then

347

further classifiable as to type, time pattern, and quantity of use. Quantities of alcohol are variously described in epidemiologic reports. Each type of beverage has its own unit of measure and conversion factor for ethanol content, as indicated in Table 15–1.[1,2]

Quantitative Units

Other dimensions of alcohol intake include numbers of drinks per unit of time (usually daily or weekly), semiquantitative units of intake (usually categorized as light, moderate, or heavy), and categories of user versus abuser or alcoholic. Time patterns of consumption may be distinguished as number of drinks per occasion of drinking. Finally, blood alcohol level (BAL) may be referred to, in units of parts alcohol/10,000 parts blood, with a ratio of 5/10,000 (BAL = 0.05 ml ethanol/100 ml blood) associated with sensory and psychological symptoms and 10/10,000 (BAL = 0.10) often legally defined as alcohol intoxication.[1]

MEASUREMENT

General Reliability

In a report on the relation of alcohol consumption and mortality among British physicians, Doll and others summarized succinctly the problem of assessment of this characteristic:

Reliable quantitative evidence is, however, difficult to obtain. Information about drinking habits has to be obtained not from direct measurement but from answers provided by individual people about themselves or their close relatives and friends. Unless the amount usually drunk is close to zero it is intrinsically difficult to describe, and the description is peculiarly liable to bias. For many people, the consumption of alcohol has emotional and moral overtones, and respondents may underestimate the amount drunk from feelings of guilt or, perhaps less often, exaggerate it out of bravado. Moreover, the amount that a person normally drinks may vary substantially from one period to another, affecting the relevance of answers at one time to subsequent mortality.[3(pp 911–912)]

The susceptibility to error in such self-reports is reminiscent of that confronting dietary assessment generally. The advantage of study of persons of middle or older age, whose habits may be rather stable, was noted in support of the use of such data in studies among adult physicians. It may be difficult to judge the applicability of current information to past habits,

Table 15–1 Quantities of Alcohol (Ethanol) Consumption

Type of Beverage	Ethanol Content (%)	Unit of Measure	Ethanol Amount in oz (ml)	Conversion from oz of Beverage to oz of Ethanol[a]
Beer (US)	3.5	12-oz bottle, 355 ml	0.42 (12.43)	0.045
Wine	12.1	3.5-oz glass, 104 ml	0.42 (12.58)	0.129
Distilled spirits, 80 proof	40.0	1-oz shot, 30 ml	0.40 (12.00)	0.411[b]

a. Ethanol in grams = 23 × (ethanol in oz).

b. Ethanol in spirits = 0.411 × (oz of spirits), not × (volume of mixed drink).

Source: Data from Committee on Diet and Health, National Academy of Sciences, Washington, DC, 1989; Kuller LH, Alcohol and Cardiovascular Disease, In: Pearson TA, Criqui MH, Luepker RV, Oberman A, Winston M, eds, *Primer in Preventive Cardiology,* American Heart Association, Dallas, 1994.

however. In one investigation, consistency of reported alcohol consumption on two occasions 10 years apart was tested, and those whose current drinking on the second occasion was in the upper extreme recalled less drinking 10 years earlier than they had reported at that time.[4] This suggested that long-term history of alcohol intake might be distorted by being systematically less reliable among those with the highest alcohol intake than among those with less intake.

The Special Problem of Ex-Drinkers

A particular concern about interpretation of reported alcohol intake centers on those classified as ex-drinkers. This arises because of the frequent finding that ex-drinkers exhibit greater cardiovascular morbidity or mortality than those reported as consuming relatively low quantities of alcohol. Does this give a valid impression that no alcohol intake is less than optimum for the risk of cardiovascular diseases? Or does the U-shaped curve of cardiovascular disease risk with increasing alcohol intake reflect admixture of the nondrinking category with persons who stopped drinking for health reasons and who were therefore already at increased risk? A review of this issue by Criqui points to four counterarguments[5]: First, any substantial degree of "migration" from high to low or no intake would have to occur before classification (eg, at baseline in cohort studies), because later migration would weaken the association of higher intake with cardiovascular diseases. Second, the postulated shift would have to be specific to persons with cardiovascular diseases and not others, because the excess risk at the lowest levels of alcohol intake is mainly related to these diseases. However, this seems implausible. (This premise is not always true. See the section on Within-Population Comparisons.) Third, some studies have been able to exclude from analysis persons with known cardiovascular diseases at baseline, and the U-shape of the risk curve has remained. Fourth, when those who report never having consumed alcohol are compared with current drinkers,

their risk is higher, and this cannot be explained by change in status among past drinkers. Notwithstanding these arguments, the issue continues to be debated.

Other aspects of the collection of data on habits of alcohol consumption were reviewed by Cahalan, including insights especially into concerns about survey methods for eliciting valid responses to questions, considering the sensitivity sometimes accorded to drinking habits.[6]

DETERMINANTS OF ALCOHOL CONSUMPTION

In principle, both population-wide or cultural determinants and individual or personal determinants of alcohol consumption can be considered. Both sets of factors are reviewed in *Diet and Health*, which notes a long history of traditional use of alcoholic beverages in many societies without record of alcohol intake as a social problem until the advent of distillation, reportedly near AD 1100.[1] It is chiefly problem drinking or alcoholism that has been investigated as to its causes. Beyond the cultural factors promoting the use of alcohol, those that give rise to problems in connection with alcohol consumption are seen as partly intrinsic to Western societies, in which particular mores and values condition the expression of effects of alcohol. At the individual level, again relating to alcoholism and not alcohol consumption in general, studies indicate genetic contributions to familial recurrence of alcoholism, which is perhaps four times as common among sons of alcoholic than of nonalcoholic fathers, even if rearing is not by the biologic parents. It seems reasonable to believe that more general patterns of alcohol intake at the individual level may reflect beliefs about the benefits or risks involved, peer influences, and the marketing of alcoholic beverages.

MECHANISMS OF ACTION OF ALCOHOL

High-Density Lipoprotein Cholesterol

Mechanisms of action by which alcohol intake could affect risks of atherosclerotic and hypertensive diseases are several.[1] The most frequently reported apparently favorable effect of alcohol consumption with respect to factors in the occurrence of coronary heart disease is an increase in blood concentrations of high-density lipoprotein (HDL) cholesterol. This mediating mechanism has been observed directly in several prospective studies and in small clinical experiments. For example, in the Honolulu Heart Program, which studied more than 8000 Japanese-American men, mean values of HDL cholesterol increased from 42.2 mg/dl in nondrinkers to 56.7 mg/dl in those reporting drinking 20 or more oz of alcohol weekly.[7] These and similar findings in other US centers participating in the Collaborative Lipoprotein Phenotyping Study are shown in Figure 15–1.[8] In analyses designed to test the hypothesis that the role of alcohol in modifying coronary risk was mediated through its effect on HDL cholesterol,

Criqui observed that approximately one-half the influence of alcohol was through this pathway, based on reduction of the regression coefficient for alcohol when HDL-cholesterol concentration was included in the statistical model.[5]

In the Honolulu Heart Program, low-density lipoprotein (LDL)–cholesterol concentration decreased from 147.0 to 97.7 mg/dl over the same range of alcohol intake as described for HDL cholesterol.[7] In addition, however, other studies have shown that triglyceride concentration increases with alcohol intake, as does the degree of increase in blood fats following fatty meals.[1]

Blood Pressure

Also on the adverse side, blood pressure appears to be increased among drinkers of alcohol, perhaps to a greater extent during the with-

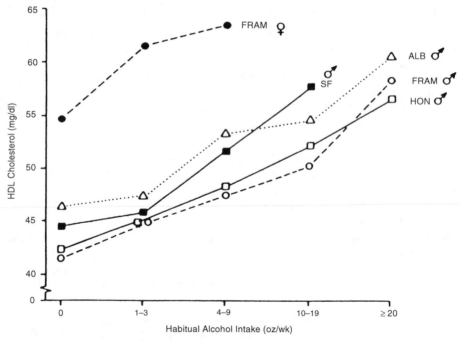

Note: ALB, Albany; FRAM, Framingham; HON, Honolulu; SF, San Francisco.

Figure 15–1 Mean High-Density Lipoprotein (HDL) Cholesterol Levels, According to Reported Habitual Alcohol Intake in the Cooperative Lipoprotein Phenotyping Study. Data omitted from categories with fewer than 10 persons. *Source:* Reprinted with permission from SB Hulley and S Gordon, *Circulation*, Vol 64 (Supp III), p III-59, © 1981, American Heart Association.

drawal phase following intake than during drinking or immediately following drinking. This could explain the reported pattern of high blood pressure on hospital admission with gradual return to lower values during hospital confinement, by persons known to be drinking heavily beforehand.[9] In any case, both blood pressure distributions and the prevalence of high blood pressure have been found related to reported alcohol intake in numerous epidemiologic studies, usually indicating a gradient of risk between categories of intake. For example, the study of male workers in the Chicago Western Electric Company showed increases in mean values of systolic and diastolic blood pressure from 132.9 to 146.5 mm Hg and from 85.8 to 94.3 mm Hg, respectively, from occasional drinks or none per day to six or more equivalents of one beer each per day, without adjustment for other factors.[10] The proportion of men with high blood pressure also increased over this range of alcohol intake, as would be expected from these findings, from 20.0% to 47.4%. Similar results were reported for men in the Honolulu Heart Program[7] and, in the Kaiser-Permanente experience, for both Black and White men and women.[11] These latter observations on increased triglyceride concentration and blood pressure at greater levels of alcohol consumption suggest that not all effects of alcohol on cardiovascular disease may be beneficial, despite the increases in HDL-cholesterol concentration.

Genetic Influences

Even the beneficial effect may be restricted to a subset of the population with a specific genotype, according to a recent case-comparison study of myocardial infarction in the setting of the World Health Organization MONICA Project centers in Ireland and France (Etude Cas-Temoin de l'Infarctus du Myocarde, or ECTIM).[12] A gene that controls activity of the cholesteryl ester transfer protein (CETP) gene, prominently involved in HDL-cholesterol metabolism, has two alleles, B1 and B2. The B2

allele was found to interact with alcohol consumption in determining blood concentrations of both CETP and HDL cholesterol, as apparently independent effects, in that among men who drank less than 25 g/day of alcohol there was no effect on the blood levels of HDL cholesterol and a weaker effect of CETP concentrations than at higher levels of intake, as shown in Table 15–2. Among men drinking 75 g/day or more, the HDL-cholesterol concentration was greater by 13% among those with both B1 and B2 alleles, or heterozygotes, and by 30% in the B2B2 homozygotes. The odds ratio for the B2B2 genotype versus B1B1 or B1B2 was 0.34 (95% confidence limits 0.14–0.83) for those drinking 75 g/day of alcohol or more; it was 0.56 (0.22–1.47) at 50–74 g/day intake and not reduced at lower levels of alcohol intake. (The level of 75 g/day corresponds to more than 3 oz ethanol or nearly eight drinks per day, calculating from Table 15–1.) Although not wholly consistent with other studies of this genotype, it appears to confirm findings among heavy drinkers in a Finnish study and to support the concept of a gene-environment interaction involving HDL-cholesterol metabolism and alcohol consumption.

Hemostasis

Finally, it has been suggested from studies, such as that in a random sample of men free of coronary heart disease at baseline and throughout follow-up in the Physicians' Health Study, that alcohol consumption relates to hemostasis.[13] This relates to the finding that level of alcohol intake was directly associated with concentration of tissue-type plasminogen activator (t-PA), an enzyme involved in reversal of blood clot formation (fibrinolysis). Among persons classified as drinking alcohol daily, weekly, monthly, and rarely or never, t-PA concentrations decreased from 10.9 to 9.7, 9.1, and 8.1 nanograms/ml (P for trend 0.0002). This effect was independent of HDL-cholesterol concentration and offers a distinct mechanism by which alcohol intake could reduce the risk of coronary

Table 15–2 Mean (SD) Levels of Plasma High-Density Lipoprotein (HDL) Cholesterol and Cholesteryl Ester Transfer Protein (CETP) According to CETP Genotypes and Alcohol Consumption in Controls

Alcohol Consumption g/d	CETP/Taq1B Genotypes			Test of Linear Trend[a]
	11	12	22	
HDL cholesterol (mg/dl)[b]				
0	$n = 36$	$n = 52$	$n = 15$	
	48.3 (12.7)	48.7 (13.5)	46.3 (10.0)	NS
>0 and <25	$n = 83$	$n = 110$	$n = 36$	
	49.9 (13.9)	48.4 (12.8)	51.9 (14.1)	NS
≥25 and <50	$n = 56$	$n = 78$	$n = 27$	
	48.5 (11.3)	50.1 (12.2)	57.1 (13.8)	$P<0.01$
≥50 and <75	$n = 43$	$n = 46$	$n = 17$	
	49.3 (9.0)	52.6 (17.8)	60.9 (22.1)	$P<0.02$
≥75	$n = 40$	$n = 60$	$n = 25$	
	51.6 (14.1)	58.5 (17.3)	67.0 (19.6)	$P<0.001$
CETP (mg/dl)[b]				
0	$n = 31$	$n = 43$	$n = 10$	
	0.234 (0.132)	0.236 (0.098)	0.171 (0.059)	NS
>0 and <25	$n = 64$	$n = 91$	$n = 23$	
	0.207 (0.089)	0.200 (0.074)	0.168 (0.060)	$P<0.05$
≥25 and <50	$n = 40$	$n = 62$	$n = 20$	
	0.226 (0.103)	0.207 (0.121)	0.177 (0.065)	$P<0.05$
≥50 and <75	$n = 35$	$n = 35$	$n = 11$	
	0.260 (0.130)	0.201 (0.090)	0.143 (0.064)	$P<0.001$
≥75	$n = 33$	$n = 46$	$n = 21$	
	0.241 (0.101)	0.225 (0.132)	0.165 (0.083)	$P<0.03$

a. The number of alleles 2 (coded 0, 1, 2) is used as a continuous variable and tested in a regression model with HDL cholesterol (CETP) as the dependent variable. The tests of linear trend within each class of alcohol consumption are adjusted on population. Global statistical analysis: regression analysis adjusted on population, the number of alleles 2 (coded 0, 1, 2), and classes of alcohol consumption (coded 0, 1, 2, 3, 4 for consumption of 0, >0 and <25, ≥25 and <50, ≥50 and <75, and ≥75, respectively) are used as continuous independent variables. HDL cholesterol:alcohol (NS), CETP/Taq1B (NS), interaction ($P<0.0001$); CETP:alcohol (NS), CETP/Taq1B ($P<0.0001$) interaction (NS).

b. The means are unadjusted.

Source: Reproduced from *The Journal of Clinical Investigation*, 1995, Vol 96, p 1667, by copyright permission of The American Society for Clinical Investigation.

heart disease. The quantity of intake was not determined except that those classified as daily drinkers included persons reporting consumption of two or more drinks every day and possibly others with lesser consumption. Also, studies in US middle-aged and young adults, among others, have shown fibrinogen concentrations to be inversely related to alcohol intake.[14,15] In the Atherosclerosis Risk in Communities Study, a 100 ml/week increment of ethanol intake was equivalent to a decrement of 2.2 mg/dl (+/− standard error of 0.8) in the concentration of fibrinogen ($P< 0.01$), but in a second multivariate model that included biochemical factors (lipids, insulin, and leukocyte count) the predicted change in fibrinogen was reduced to 0.9 mg/dl, no longer statistically significant. In the Coronary Artery Risk Development in Young Adults Study, a model similar to the first gave approximately the same result.

DISTRIBUTION

US Adults

Alcohol intake of the US adult population aged 25–74 has been estimated from the probability samples of the National Health and Nutrition Examination Surveys. Data from the survey of 1971–1975 provide the baseline data for a cohort of 2907 adults reinterviewed in 1982–1984 to determine current and recalled alcohol intake.[4] As shown in Table 15–3, respondents were classified as reporting fewer than 12 alcoholic drinks per year, fewer than 1 drink per week, 1–9 drinks per week, and 10 or more drinks per week. In 1982–1984, 37% of men and 59% of women reported drinking fewer than 12 drinks per year, while 22% and 6%, respectively, reported 10 or more drinks per week. These frequencies of lowest and highest categories of intake both increased in this cohort relative to the reports a decade earlier, especially for least-frequent drinking, whereas intermediate levels of intake became less prevalent. This general trend toward more polarized responses appeared for each subgroup, whether classified by age, race, education, smoking status, or presence of chronic health conditions. Overall, the results indicate that approximately one-half of men and one-quarter of women reported weekly to daily intake of alcohol in the early 1980s, versus 60% and 33% in the early 1970s. Drinking daily or weekly was more frequent among younger age groups, Whites, those with more than high school education, and former and current smokers.

Also referring to adults, data reviewed in *Diet and Health* indicate that in the United States 18 million persons aged 18 or older were estimated to have alcohol-related problems as of the mid-1980s.[1] Of these, 41% were classified as alcohol abusers and 59% as alcoholics, the distinction being made on the basis of attributed social or health problems, including job loss, arrest, illness, loss of behavioral control, symptoms of alcohol withdrawal, and others. The high prevalence of drinking especially among some groups of Native American adults was noted.

US Youths

Among youth aged 12–19 participating in the Collaborative Lipid Research Clinics Prevalence Study, the reported frequency of alcohol use was as shown in Figure 15–2.[16] Overall, nearly one-fourth of all youth in this age range reported drinking alcohol, with a sharp increase in prevalence from less than 10% at ages 12–13 to 52.5% and 54.6% for males and females, respectively, at ages 18–19. (The age pattern for smoking was closely parallel, with 70% of participants reporting neither smoking nor drinking, about 10% reporting both, and 20% reporting one or the other behavior.) Age differences in drinking behavior complicate interpretation of relations between alcohol intake and other characteristics that also change markedly with age in adolescence, such as HDL cholesterol, and thus conclusions about the early effects of alcohol intake on such factors require more-detailed analysis than provided in this report.

Variation in Prevalence among Populations

The INTERSALT Study included 52 cross-sectional sample surveys in men and women who were classified according to both weekly alcohol intake (in ml) and categories of heavy versus lesser degrees of drinking.[17] The relation between population mean values for alcohol intake and the proportions of persons who were heavy drinkers is shown by the scatterplot in Figure 15–3 in which each point represents one of the 52 populations. The correlation coefficient for this joint distribution was 0.97, which, though influenced by the one population at the highest extreme of both scales, appears strongly

Table 15-3 Prevalence (%) of Alcohol Drinking Categories in a Sample of US Adults in 1971–1975 and Repeated in 1982–1984

Characteristics/Drinking Category	Baseline (1971–1975)				Follow-Up (1982–1984)			
	<12 Drinks per Year	<1 Drink per Week	1–9 Drinks per Week	≥10 Drinks per Week	<12 Drinks per Year	<1 Drink per Week	1–9 Drinks per Week	≥10 Drinks per Week
Sex								
Men ($n = 1,106$)	29	12	42	18	37	14	27	22
Women ($n = 1,801$)	54	14	29	4	59	15	21	6
Age (years)								
24–26 ($n = 543$)	33	14	45	8	38	18	32	13
34–36 ($n = 683$)	39	14	38	9	44	15	28	13
44–46 ($n = 549$)	40	13	36	11	47	15	25	13
54–56 ($n = 483$)	47	12	32	9	54	15	19	12
64–66 ($n = 649$)	60	11	21	8	70	8	13	9
Race								
White ($n = 2,517$)	43	13	35	10	49	15	24	12
Nonwhite ($n = 390$)	51	14	31	4	61	11	20	9
Education								
Less than high school ($n = 1,081$)	55	12	25	8	64	10	17	10
High school ($n = 1,100$)	42	14	36	8	47	19	23	11
More than high school ($n = 726$)	31	13	44	13	37	15	33	16
Smoking status								
Never ($n = 1,357$)	59	14	23	4	66	13	17	4
Former ($n = 462$)	35	14	40	11	41	14	30	14
Current ($n = 1,088$)	29	11	45	15	36	16	28	20
Disease status[a]								
Yes ($n = 1,374$)	49	13	29	9	59	12	18	11
No ($n = 1,533$)	39	13	39	9	44	16	28	12

a. Disease status during the follow-up was based on newly diagnosed chronic conditions reported at the follow-up interview, including diabetes, hypertension, thyroid problem, heart diseases, cancer, chronic lung disease, and colitis.

Source: Reprinted with permission from S Liu et al, *American Journal of Epidemiology,* Vol 143, p 179, © 1996, The Johns Hopkins University School of Hygiene and Public Health.

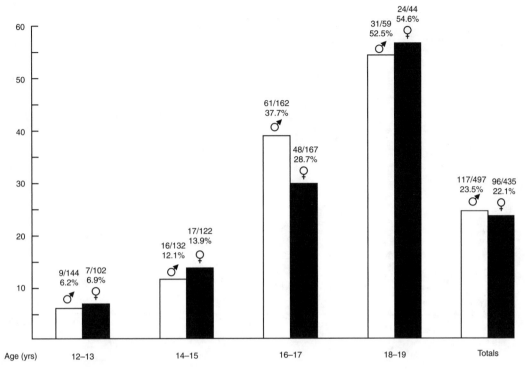

Figure 15–2 Reported Prevalence of Alcoholic Beverage Use by White 12- to 19-Year-Olds from a Random Recall Group by Sex and 2-Year Age Intervals, and for All Ages. *Source*: Reprinted with permission from CJ Glueck et al, *Circulation*, Vol 64 (Supp III), p III-51, © 1981, American Heart Association.

positive for the remaining 51 populations as well.

RATES AND RISKS

Between-Population Differences

Whether population differences in rates of coronary heart disease are attributable to differences in alcohol intake has been a fashionable topic, especially in view of the perception that France may experience low mortality because of high consumption of wine—hence the question, "Does diet or alcohol explain the French paradox?"[18] To address this question, Criqui and Ringel analyzed published statistics on mortality from all causes and from coronary heart disease at ages 35–74 years for 1965, 1970, 1980, and 1988; food disappearance data centering on

the same years; and corresponding data on alcohol use by type of beverage among 21 economically developed countries. Gross measures of population use of ethanol in wine, beer, and spirits and of animal fat, vegetables, and fruits were presented for each country (Table 15–4). Wine ethanol was exceptionally high for France and Italy, at 14.3 and 11.1 liters ethanol per capita. A much narrower range without such marked variation was found for ethanol in beer and spirits. Animal fat intake was exceptionally low in Japan, although it increased to nearly twice the initial level by 1988. Figure 15–4 indicates the relation between coronary heart disease death rates and use of wine ethanol, total ethanol, and the three food components, each separately, for the 1988 data. A positive correlation with animal fat and negative correlations with vegetable and fruit consumption were accompanied by negative correlations with total

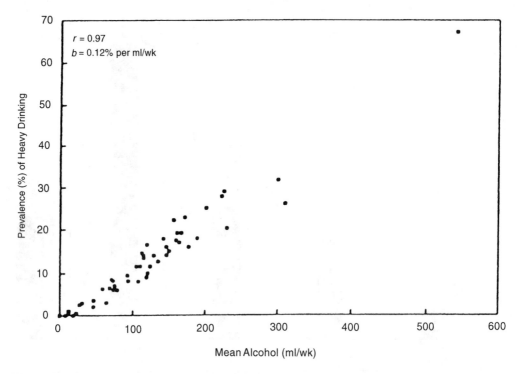

Figure 15–3 Scatterplot Showing Association Between Mean Alcohol Intake and Prevalence of Heavy Drinking (More Than 300 ml/wk) in 52 Populations Surveyed by Standard Methods. *Source*: Reprinted with permission from G Rose, *Circulation*, Vol 84, p 1409, © 1981, American Heart Association.

and wine ethanol, the latter being the strongest negative relation with a correlation coefficient, *R*, of −0.66. Because wine volume itself was not more strongly correlated than wine ethanol, it was concluded that wine ingredients other than ethanol were not the basis for the correlation. Examination of the multivariate relations of these dietary components with age-adjusted mortality from coronary heart disease gave the results shown in Table 15–5. These data varied most strikingly in a reversal of the regression coefficients for fruit, from nearly significant positive to negative values for coronary mortality, and the decreased strength of the wine ethanol association by 1988. This and other changes in multivariate relations of diet and mortality reflect the complexity and interdependence of dietary components as they vary within and between countries over 5- to 10-year intervals.

The impression from this analysis that ethanol from wine is specifically related to reduced coronary mortality was explained as reflecting the dominance in the analysis of data for France, which had exceptionally high wine intake and low coronary mortality, whereas in most countries wine was not the main ethanol source. This probably accounts for the variation in reports from within-population studies regarding the ethanol source that relates to coronary heart disease risk. Especially important was the further observation that for all-cause mortality ethanol from beer was significantly positively associated in both 1980 and 1988. Fruit availability was strongly negatively correlated with all-cause mortality in the same years, but there was no overall indication of lower total mortality in relation to ethanol. France, with the highest per capita ethanol intake

Table 15–4 Nutrient and Ethanol Intake in 21 Countries in Years 1965, 1970, 1980, and 1988

Country	Wine Ethanol[a] 1965	1970	1980	1988	Beer Ethanol[a] 1965	1970	1980	1988	Spirits Ethanol[a] 1965	1970	1980	1988	Animal Fat[b] 1965	1970	1980	1988	Vegetables[b] 1965	1970	1980	1988	Fruit[b] 1965	1970	1980	1988
Australia	0.7	1.1	2.2	2.5	5.4	6.1	6.7	5.5	0.9	1.0	1.1	1.2	30.8	29.6	22.7	23.7	1.5	1.5	2.9	2.8	3.3	3.5	4.1	3.9
Austria	4.5	4.9	4.1	3.9	4.6	4.9	5.2	5.9	1.9	2.2	1.5	1.5	23.7	24.3	25.6	27.1	1.3	1.3	1.3	1.4	4.2	4.1	3.9	4.7
Belgium/ Luxembourg	1.4	1.8	2.5	2.9	5.0	5.8	5.5	4.4	1.1	1.3	2.2	2.2	28.9	30.3	31.5	35.0	1.8	2.0	1.6	2.2	2.6	3.1	2.7	3.0
Canada	1.1	1.3	2.2	2.4	3.2	3.7	4.3	4.2	1.9	2.2	3.3	2.5	27.6	26.5	28.1	22.5	1.9	1.9	1.0	1.6	3.2	3.1	2.9	3.6
Denmark	0.6	0.8	2.3	2.9	3.5	4.8	5.7	5.1	1.0	1.3	1.5	1.5	32.0	32.8	34.5	36.4	0.8	0.9	1.0	1.7	2.6	2.5	2.1	2.6
Finland	0.4	0.5	0.9	0.8	0.8	2.1	2.5	2.9	1.4	1.8	2.8	3.2	30.5	29.6	30.9	29.2	0.4	0.4	0.6	1.1	1.9	2.2	2.9	3.4
France	14.3	12.8	10.8	9.1	1.6	1.7	1.8	1.6	2.5	2.3	2.5	2.4	20.5	21.7	28.1	25.7	2.6	2.6	2.1	2.4	3.6	3.6	2.2	2.6
Iceland	0.0	0.2	0.8	0.8	0.2	0.3	0.3	0.3	1.8	2.2	2.2	2.4	29.3	26.9	28.1	26.8	0.3	0.3	0.6	0.8	2.3	2.1	2.1	2.4
Ireland	0.4	0.6	0.5	0.7	3.1	3.4	5.8	4.7	1.1	1.5	1.9	1.7	30.4	30.1	25.7	27.3	0.8	1.0	1.9	1.5	1.8	2.0	2.0	2.1
Israel	0.6	0.5	0.8	0.6	0.5	0.5	0.6	0.6	1.0	0.7	2.0	3.1	11.9	11.9	13.2	11.8	2.6	2.6	1.0	1.3	6.7	6.1	2.8	3.5
Italy	11.1	11.4	7.4	7.9	0.4	0.6	0.9	1.3	1.4	1.8	1.9	1.0	11.7	12.4	17.6	18.2	2.9	2.8	2.6	2.7	5.0	4.9	3.8	4.3
Japan	2.7	2.7	1.5	1.5	1.0	1.4	2.0	2.2	1.0	1.1	3.2	2.3	6.6	8.9	12.3	11.9	2.7	2.7	1.4	1.6	1.8	2.2	4.3	4.5
Netherlands	0.4	0.6	1.6	1.8	1.9	2.9	4.5	4.2	1.9	2.0	2.6	2.1	26.0	26.3	32.0	27.8	1.6	1.6	1.0	1.6	3.1	3.5	2.9	3.6
New Zealand	0.3	0.7	1.7	1.9	5.2	5.8	5.9	6.1	1.3	1.0	1.8	1.6	32.1	33.2	32.8	29.7	1.7	1.7	1.6	1.9	3.2	2.8	1.9	2.4
Norway	0.2	0.3	0.6	0.8	1.3	1.7	2.0	2.3	1.3	1.6	1.6	1.3	26.7	26.2	25.1	23.8	0.9	1.0	0.9	1.1	3.1	3.2	2.8	3.5
Spain	7.2	6.4	7.2	6.5	0.9	1.5	2.2	2.7	2.6	2.8	3.0	3.0	12.0	14.7	17.2	21.1	3.2	3.1	2.9	2.8	3.4	3.7	4.1	3.9
Sweden	0.6	0.8	1.3	1.6	1.1	2.2	1.9	2.0	2.7	2.6	2.8	2.0	26.5	25.2	30.8	26.2	0.9	0.9	1.0	1.3	3.3	3.3	2.8	3.5
Switzerland	4.8	5.1	5.7	5.8	3.6	3.8	3.4	3.3	1.9	1.7	2.1	2.0	23.6	25.2	29.3	29.1	1.4	1.4	1.4	1.6	4.7	4.8	4.3	4.5
UK	0.3	0.4	1.0	1.3	4.6	5.1	5.6	5.5	0.8	0.9	1.7	1.7	30.8	29.9	27.4	27.0	1.4	1.6	1.6	1.9	2.3	2.3	1.9	2.4
US	0.5	0.6	1.1	1.2	2.4	2.8	3.7	3.6	2.4	2.8	3.0	2.4	26.7	26.0	25.2	22.8	1.8	1.9	0.9	1.1	2.9	2.8	2.8	3.5
West Germany	1.8	1.8	2.1	2.7	4.9	5.6	5.9	5.8	2.7	3.0	2.9	2.2	25.4	26.5	26.2	27.5	1.1	1.2	1.5	1.7	4.3	4.7	3.9	4.3

a. Annual liters per capita.

b. % of kilocalories.

Source: Reprinted with permission from MH Criqui and BL Ringel, *Lancet,* Vol 344, p 1720, © 1994, The Lancet, Ltd.

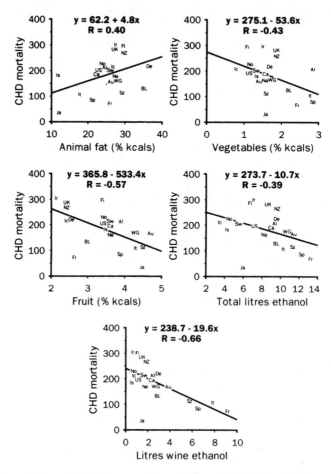

Figure 15–4 Correlations of Age-Adjusted Coronary Heart Disease (CHD) Mortality Rates per 100,000 Population with Dietary Items in 1988. *Source*: Reprinted with permission from MH Criqui and BL Ringel, *Lancet*, Vol 344, p 1721, © 1994, The Lancet, Ltd.

among the 21 countries, did not rank lowest in total mortality, due to association of noncardiovascular deaths with ethanol consumption, which offset any national benefit from reduced coronary mortality.

Within-Population Comparisons

Within-population analysis of alcohol consumption and coronary mortality has been reported in a number of cohort and case-comparison studies. Results from the study of British doctors, cited above, show for ischemic heart disease (ICD 9 codes 410–414) a decrease

in rates from 12.3 to 7.1/1000 per year across intake categories from none to 15–21 units per week and an increase with further increments of alcohol intake to 9.2 and 8.9/1000 per year at 29–42 and 43 or more units per week, respectively (Table 15–6).[3] The data are evaluated first by categorical comparison of the combined groups from 1–14 units per week versus none and, second, by testing the significance of the trend over paired categories of drinkers with intakes of 1–14, 15–28, or 29 or more units per week. The results of the first comparison were significant for all causes of death (last row of the table) and for both ischemic heart disease

Table 15–5 Multiple Linear Regression of Dietary Items on Age-Adjusted Coronary Heart Disease Mortality Rates, Ages 35–74

	1965		1970		1980		1988	
Dietary Item	*Coeff (SE)*	*P Value*	*Coeff (SE)*	*P Value*	*Coeff (SE)*	*P Value*	*Coeff (SE)*	*P Value*
Wine ethanol	−11.5 (5.9)	0.07	−23.3 (7.5)	<0.01	−25.0 (7.1)	<0.01	−13.1 (7.9)	0.12
Beer ethanol	−14.4 (12.9)	NS	−32.8 (17.8)	0.09	−4.3 (9.4)	NS	8.7 (9.5)	NS
Spirits ethanol	−47.5 (28.7)	0.12	−40.0 (31.9)	NS	−20.9 (20.6)	NS	−14.3 (19.7)	NS
Animal fat, % kcal	12.7 (4.9)	0.02	16.5 (7.0)	0.03	5.3 (3.3)	0.14	0.9 (2.8)	NS
Vegetables, % kcal	38.6 (39.6)	NS	60.7 (47.3)	NS	43.6 (32.8)	NS	−16.4 (31.7)	NS
Fruit, % kcal	33.4 (16.1)	0.06	40.8 (22.9)	0.10	−34.8 (18.5)	0.08	−36.5 (18.1)	0.06

Note: Beta coefficients reflect differences in total death rate per 100,000, and for ethanol are per liter per capita per annum, and for nutrients per 1% kcal.

Source: Reprinted with permission from MH Criqui and BL Ringel, *Lancet*, Vol 344, p 1721, © 1994, The Lancet, Ltd.

and other known causes of death. The minimum risk was at the level of 8–14 or 15–21 units of alcohol per week (1–3 drinks per day, as defined in this study). For each of these categories of cause of death, rates were somewhat higher with lower intake; only for ischemic heart disease was this a strong enough effect to make the linear trend nonsignificant. For "alcohol-augmented causes," only the linear trend was significant, indicating a generally continuous increase in risk from lowest to highest categories of intake. Also noteworthy was the significant trend of risk for cerebrovascular disease, attributable to the highest intake group, a finding reported elsewhere as well. As the authors concluded, ischemic heart disease mortality was reduced among alcohol users in contrast to nonusers, and they judged the effect to be "largely irrespective of amount."[3(p 911)]

A review of reports on moderate alcohol use (5 or fewer units per day) compared with the experiences of nondrinkers was conducted by Marmot and Brunner and is summarized in Figures 15–5 and 15–6.[19] The odds ratios or relative risks presented are largely below 1.0, as are the upper bounds of 4 of the 11 available confidence intervals. Several of the studies show little or no relation between moderate alcohol intake and coronary heart disease, but none indicates an unequivocal excess at this level of consumption.

Meta-Analysis of Observational Studies

Another approach to synthesis of the epidemiologic studies of alcohol intake and coronary heart disease is a meta-analysis that included 30 groups, in some instances more than one group in a given study (Table 15–7).[20] Extensive analysis led the author to conclude that alternative hypotheses to explain the apparent association were apparently weakened and that the "preventive hypothesis" was thereby strengthened.

PREVENTION AND CONTROL

Canada, 1993

The dilemma posed by the foregoing evidence is whether policies and practices regarding alcohol use, or their implementation, should be modified on this basis. The issue has been addressed differently in various settings. An International Symposium on Moderate Drinking and Health met in 1993 under sponsorship of several Canadian organizations and identified both policy implications and "best advice" for individuals.[21] Policy implications were that alcohol control policies should not be relaxed, that substitution of lower-risk drinking for higher-risk drinking should be encouraged, and that educational messages should not suggest adoption of regular drinking by those who cur-

Table 15–6 Annual Mortality (per 1,000 Men) by Alcohol Consumption Reported in 1978 Questionnaire

| Cause of Death | Total No. of Deaths | Units of Alcohol Consumed a Week | | | | | | | χ^2_1 Test of Alcohol Effect | |
		None	1–7 (Mean 4.6)	8–14 (Mean 11.3)	15–21 (Mean 18.0)	22–28 (Mean 25.5)	29–42 (Mean 35.0)	≥43 (Mean 61.3)	None vs 1–14 Units a Week	Trend of 1–14 vs 15–28 vs ≥29 Units a Week
Alcohol-augmented causes[a]	208	1.6 (0.4)	1.3 (0.2)	1.3 (0.2)	1.6 (0.3)	1.8 (0.4)	2.9 (0.6)	4.0 (0.9)	0.7	20.9***
Ischemic heart disease	1,061	12.3 (1.2)	10.0 (0.8)	8.5 (0.6)	7.1 (0.6)	7.8 (0.7)	9.2 (0.9)	8.9 (1.0)	6.8**	0.5
Other known causes:	1,988	19.8 (1.4)	16.4 (0.9)	14.0 (0.7)	15.4 (0.9)	16.9 (1.2)	17.9 (1.2)	23.3 (1.9)	10.4**	17.9***
Cerebrovascular disease	380	3.6 (0.5)	3.0 (0.4)	2.6 (0.3)	3.0 (0.4)	3.0 (0.5)	3.3 (0.5)	6.0 (1.1)	1.9	8.3**
Residual vascular disease	242	2.8 (0.5)	1.9 (0.3)	1.6 (0.2)	1.6 (0.3)	1.8 (0.4)	2.6 (0.5)	3.5 (0.8)	3.7	5.8*
Respiratory disease	234	2.0 (0.4)	1.5 (0.3)	1.7 (0.2)	1.3 (0.2)	3.0 (0.6)	2.5 (0.5)	3.5 (0.8)	0.6	9.9**
Lung cancer	163	1.1 (0.3)	1.8 (0.4)	1.5 (0.3)	1.0 (0.2)	1.0 (0.2)	1.4 (0.3)	2.3 (0.6)	0.9	0
Cancer of large bowel	127	0.9 (0.3)	1.3 (0.3)	0.7 (0.1)	1.7 (0.4)	1.5 (0.4)	0.7 (0.2)	1.8 (0.6)	0	0.5
Other cancers	508	5.7 (0.8)	4.2 (0.5)	3.6 (0.3)	4.5 (0.5)	4.2 (0.6)	4.9 (0.7)	3.7 (0.6)	5.5*	0.9
Residual known causes	334	3.9 (0.7)	2.9 (0.4)	2.4 (0.3)	2.6 (0.4)	2.7 (0.5)	3.0 (0.5)	3.2 (0.7)	2.9	0.9
All causes (including unknown)	3,328	34.4 (1.8)	28.1 (1.2)	24.5 (0.9)	24.7 (1.1)	26.9 (1.4)	30.4 (1.6)	36.2 (2.3)	17.9***	16.7***

Note: Those with undefined consumption were excluded. Values are death rates (SE) standardized for age, smoking, year of death, and history of previous disease unless stated otherwise. Values of χ^2 more extreme than 3.84, 6.64, and 10.83 correspond to P values of *<0.05, **<0.01, and ***<0.001, respectively.

a. Injury, poisoning, liver disease, upper aerodigestive cancer, alcoholic psychosis.

Source: Reprinted with permission from R Doll et al, Mortality in Relation to Consumption of Alcohol: 13 Years' Observations on Male British Doctors, *British Medical Journal*, Vol 309, pp 911–918, © 1994, BMJ Publishing Group.

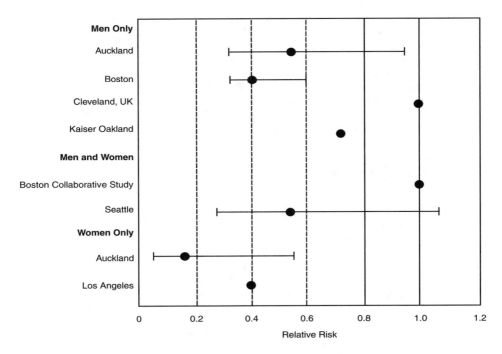

Figure 15–5 Relative Risk of Coronary Heart Disease in Moderate Drinkers Compared with Nondrinkers in Case-Control Studies. Bars show 95% confidence interval where available. (Moderate drinking, <5 units of alcohol daily; if >1, drinking category rate ratio was calculated for highest consumption category.) *Source*: Reprinted with permission from M Marmot and E Brunner, Alcohol and Cardiovascular Disease: The Status of the U Shaped Curve, *British Medical Journal*, Vol 303, pp 565–568, © 1991, BMJ Publishing Group.

rently drink only irregularly or not at all. At the individual level, 10 points of advice were suggested, indicating that two standard drinks per day, omitting one day per week, should be the maximum intake and should not be adopted for health reasons by those who currently drink less; that intoxication should be avoided; that special circumstances have separate requirements, such as abstention during pregnancy; and that those planning to increase alcohol intake for health reasons should first consult their physicians, who may identify contraindications or alternative means of risk reduction.

US Youths to 1994

Long-standing policies of 18 US health organizations and agencies with respect to prevention of substance abuse in adolescence were compiled by the American Medical Association

and published in 1994, but these do not address the question of the possible beneficial effect of alcohol on atherosclerosis or its risk factors.[22]

The United Kingdom to 1995 and Six Other Countries to 1993

A report in the United Kingdom titled *Sensible Drinking* reviewed the basis for official alcohol policy.[23] It traced the development of this policy from its inception in 1976 through the report date of 1995. Current policy was to recommend that drinking less than 21 units weekly by men and 14 units by women was unlikely to damage health (one unit in United Kingdom usage = 8 g ethanol, equivalent to one-half pint of beer or lager, a small glass of wine, or a standard measure of spirits). The report included a detailed review of studies on

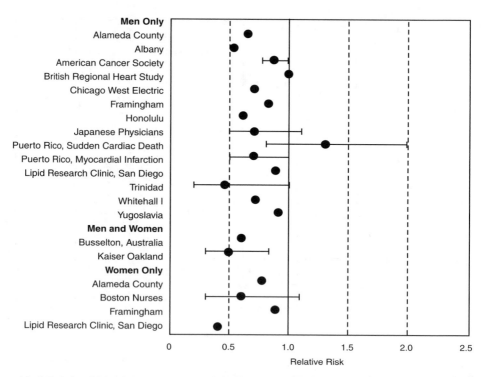

Figure 15–6 Relative Risk of Coronary Heart Disease in Moderate Drinkers Compared with Nondrinkers in Cohort Studies. Bars show 95% confidence interval where available. (Moderate drinking, ≤5 units of alcohol daily.) *Source*: Reprinted with permission from M Marmot and E Brunner, Alcohol and Cardiovascular Disease: The Status of the U Shaped Curve, *British Medical Journal*, Vol 303, pp 565–568, © 1991, BMJ Publishing Group.

beneficial and adverse health effects of alcohol, as well as its own recommendations. Another valuable inclusion was a chart comparing drinking messages in various countries (Table 15–8). The seven countries listed, including the United States, recommended drinking levels to minimize risk, identified here as "low risk." The right-hand column notes gram-equivalents of ethanol for each country's definition of drinks or units, and the resulting low-risk recommendations range from as low as 7 g/day for both men and women in Sweden to less than 32–40 g/day for men and 16–20 g/day for women in Australia. The US standard advocated by the Department of Health and Human Services is no more than 24 g/day for men and 12 g/day for women. Higher risk levels are specified by five of the seven countries. The lower levels for women reflect the evidence that metabolism of alcohol and tissue compartments differ by sex

so as to generate substantially greater blood levels of alcohol in women at the same level of intake as for men.

The new report changed the advice on "sensible drinking" for the United Kingdom to indicate that for men at all ages regular drinking of between three and four units (between 24 and 32 g ethanol) daily and for women drinking between two and three units (between 16 and 24 g ethanol) daily will not accrue significant health risk. It was indicated that the "maximum health advantage" would be attained for both men and women at a level between one and two units (between 8 and 16 g ethanol) daily. These values compare with the provisions shown in Table 15–8 of low risk at less than 21 standard drinks (210 g ethanol per week or 30 g daily) for men and less than 14 standard drinks (140 g ethanol per week or 20 g daily) for women in the United Kingdom.

Table 15–7 Characteristics of Cohort Studies (1968–1993) of Ethanol Intake and Fatal or Nonfatal Coronary Heart Disease Included in a Meta-Analysis Suggesting an L-Shaped Dose-Response Relation

Cohort Study (in Chronologic Order)	Exposure Assessment			Outcomes			
	Instrument[a]	Time[b]	No of Levels[c]	Years of Follow-Up	Types[d]	No. of Cases	RR[e]
Honolulu Heart Study	I	Ever	4	6	NF	278	0.61
Chicago Western Electric Company Study	E	Current	5	17	F	149	1.8
Yugoslavia Cardiovascular Disease Study	I	<40 g/mo	4	7	NF	166	0.40
Kaiser Permanente Matched-Cohorts Study	E	1 year	4	10	F	8.060	0.70
Whitehall Study	I	3 days	3	10	M	63	0.59
Puerto Rico Heart Health Program	I	24 hours	4	8	NM	170	0.58
North Karelia Project (Eastern Finland)	E	1 year	3	7	F	95	1.16
Framingham Study	E	Current	8	22	M	532	0.72
Study of Massachusetts Elderly	I	Current	3	4.8	F	42	0.58
Study of Japanese Physicians	Q	20 years	4	19	F	123	0.64
Lipid Research Clinics Follow-Up Study	E	1 week	4	8.5	F	89	0.82
British Regional Heart Study	I	Ever	7	7.5	M	265	1.02
Albany Study	E	Current	6	18	M	348	0.84
Albany Study	E	Current	6	10	M	159	0.77
Finnish Mobile Clinic Health Survey	I	Current	2	5	F	140	1.5
Nurses' Health Study	Q	1 year	5	4	NF	200	0.55
American Cancer Society Prospective Study (Women)	Q	Current	8	12	F	19.661	0.94
Kaiser Permanente Cohort Study	E	Ever	7	2.5	N	355	0.66
Nutrition Canada Survey Cohort Study	I	Current	2	10	M	155	0.90
Finnish Rural Cohorts of the Seven Countries Study	E	30 days	2	10	F	119	1.1
St. James Survey (Trinidad) Follow-Up	I	1 week	4	10	M	49	0.46
NHANES I[f] Epidemiologic Follow-Up Study	E	Current	>9	10	F	287	1.0
American Cancer Society Prospective Study (Men)	Q	Current	8	12	F	18.771	0.83
Health Professionals Follow-Up Study	Q	1 year	6	1.5	NFM	350	0.64
MRFIT[g]	I	Current	4	10	F	427	0.88
Alameda County Study	Q	Current	2	10	F	135	0.65
Normative Aging Study	Q	1 year	3	12	F	74	0.63
Established Populations for Epidemiologic Study of the Elderly	I	1 year	3	5	M	677	0.73
Busselton Population Study	Q	Current	3	13	F	325	0.66
Copenhagen Male Study	Q	Current	5	4	M	100	0.73

a. Instrument used to measure ethanol intake: Q, questionnaire; I, interview; E, either Q or I in connection with a physical examination.

b. Time period defining "nondrinker": ie, the period to which questions on alcohol intake referred.

c. Number of levels into which alcohol drinkers were categorized.

d. Types of outcome: N, nonfatal myocardial infarction; F, fatal coronary heart disease; M, a mixture of nonfatal and fatal coronary outcomes.

e. RR, relative risk of coronary disease, a weighted average of all relative risks for ethanol doses of $\geq$10 g/d.

f. NHANES I, First National Health and Nutrition Examination Survey.

g. MRFIT, Multiple Risk Factor Intervention Trial.

Source: Reprinted with permission from M Maclure, *Epidemiologic Reviews*, Vol 19, p 332, © 1993, The Johns Hopkins University School of Hygiene and Public Health.

Table 15–8 Sensible Drinking Messages in Seven Countries, up to 1993

Risk Level	Low Risk[a]	Intermediate Risk	High Risk	Notes
Australia (National Health & Medical Research Council)	Men: less than 4 standard drinks per day[b] Women: less than 2 standard drinks per day	Men: 4–6 standard drinks per day Women: 2–4 standard drinks per day	Men: 6 plus standard drinks per day Women: 4 plus standard drinks per day	One standard drink equates to 8–10 g of absolute alcohol
United Kingdom	Men: less than 21 standard drinks per week Women: less than 14 standard drinks per week		Men: 8 plus standard drinks per day Women: 5 plus standard drinks per day	One standard drink equates to 10 g of absolute alcohol
New Zealand (Alcohol Advisory Council)	Men: 3–4 standard drinks per day Women: 2–3 standard drinks per day		Men: 6 plus standard drinks per day Women: 4 plus standard drinks per day	No equivalent in terms of grams of absolute alcohol is specified
Canada (Addiction Research Foundation)	Men: up to 2 standard drinks per day Women: are advised to not exceed one-third of the limit set for men	Men: 3–6 standard drinks per day	Men: 7 plus standard drinks per day	One standard drink equates to 13.6 g of absolute alcohol
Sweden (State Alcohol Monopoly)	Men and women not to exceed more than 50 g of absolute alcohol per week	Men and women drinking 51–250 g of absolute alcohol per week	Men and women drinking in excess of 251 g of absolute alcohol per week	
Denmark (National Board of Health)	Men: less than 21 units per week Women: less than 14 units per week			While no absolute alcohol equivalence is provided, the note is made that Danish units contain more absolute alcohol than British units.
USA (Department of Health and Human Resources)	Men: no more than 2 drinks per day Women: no more than 1 drink per day			A drink equates to 12 g of absolute alcohol

a. Different terms used by different authorities to describe drinking of varying risk.

b. While limits are expressed here in terms of the number of standard drinks per day or per week, most authorities recommend at least two alcohol-free days per week.

Source: Reprinted with permission from Report of an Inter-Departmental Working Group, *Sensible Drinking*, p 54, © 1995, Department of Health.

EFFECTS OF INTERVENTION ON RATES AND RISKS OF EVENTS

As pointed out by Kuller, "It is important to note that no experimental clinical trials have shown that either increasing or decreasing alcohol consumption changes the risk of heart attack."[2(p 230)]

CURRENT ISSUES

Conflicting Attitudes and Judgments

The dilemma addressed above concerning policy and practice is the most immediate issue with respect to alcohol consumption. Strongly held opinions are discordant with respect to whether alcohol use should be positively recommended, whether potential risks outweigh potential benefits, and whether one form of alcoholic beverage may convey still greater or lesser benefit than others, for example:

> The Group concludes . . . that light to moderate consumption of alcohol confers a protective effect against a number of serious diseases, in particular CHD and ischemic stroke, and also against cholesterol gallstones.[23(p 28)]

> This report [*Sensible Drinking*, 1995] comes less than 6 months after the Royal Colleges of Physicians, Psychiatrists, and General Practitioners jointly concluded that low to moderate alcohol consumption protected against coronary heart disease but confirmed that the sensible limits of 21 and 14 units should continue because to increase them would do more harm than good.[24(p 1643)]

> The potential reduction in risk of CHD from drinking modest amounts of alcohol must be balanced against the fact that there is no level of drinking which is without risk of adverse consequences.[21(p 13)]

> [W]ell-intentioned information about moderate alcohol consumption and CHD could be used as an excuse to abuse alcohol. . . . [M]oderate alcohol consumption for the prevention of CHD as a public health policy would be irresponsible. . . . However, in selected patients at elevated CHD risk, responsible use of alcohol may offer some benefit. Advice beyond this limited arena could well do more harm than good, particularly given the evidence that average alcohol consumption in a given population faithfully predicts the extent of alcohol abuse, with a correlation coefficient of 0.97.[5(p 138)]

> [P]rudence suggests a lowering of or abstention from alcohol consumption.[1(p 451)]

It has been remarkable to participate in social-scientific gatherings of cardiovascular epidemiologists and other health professionals in recent years and to observe the now commonplace toast to HDL cholesterol raised by successive clusters of attendees (the present author, perhaps, among them). The contrast to objectivity, or skepticism, which greets virtually every other proposed intervention to reduce population rates and individual risks of cardiovascular diseases, requiring not one but multiple experimental tests of efficacy and safety, is extraordinary. The seeming obstacles to feasibility of such experiments are not unique to alcohol, but the dismissal of concern for the lack of such evidence is so. In view of the apparently narrow "window of benefit"[5] in relation to known adverse effects of exposure, the readiness in many quarters to embrace as public health policy the recommendation to take up or increase one's alcohol use for prophylactic purposes will likely continue to be controversial.

A Question of Substance

In the further debate, it may be useful to ask, "Is atherosclerosis an alcohol-deficiency disease?" If the answer is no, then the admonition of Rose perhaps should be recalled:

> In mass prevention each individual has usually only a small expectation of benefit, and this benefit can easily be outweighed by a small risk. . . . This makes it important to distinguish two approaches. The first is the restoration of biological normality by the removal of an abnormal exposure. . . ; here there can be some presumption of safety. This is not true for the other kind of preventive approach, which leaves intact the underlying causes of incidence and seeks instead to interpose some new, supposedly protective intervention. . . . Here the onus is on the activists to produce adequate evidence of safety.[25(p 38)]

REFERENCES

1. Committee on Diet and Health, Food and Nutrition Board, Commission on Life Sciences, National Research Council. *Diet and Health*. Washington, DC: National Academy of Sciences; 1989.

2. Kuller LH. Alcohol and cardiovascular disease. In: Pearson TA, Criqui MH, Luepker RV, Oberman A, Winston M, eds. *Primer in Preventive Cardiology*. Dallas, Tex: American Heart Association; 1994: 227–233.

3. Doll R, Peto R, Hall E, Wheatley K, et al. Mortality in relation to consumption of alcohol: 13 years' observations on male British doctors. *Br Med J*. 1994; 309:911–918.

4. Liu S, Serdula MK, Byers T, Willamson DF, et al. Reliability of alcohol intake as recalled from 10 years in the past. *Am J Epidemiol*. 1996;143:177–186.

5. Criqui MH. Alcohol and the heart: implications of present epidemiologic knowledge. *Contemp Drug Prob*. Spring 1994:125–142.

6. Cahalan D. Quantifying alcohol consumption: patterns and problems. *Circ*. 1981;64(suppl III):III-7–III-13.

7. Kagan A, Yano K, Rhoads GG, McGee DL. Alcohol and cardiovascular disease: the Hawaiian experience. *Circ*. 1981;64(suppl III):III-27–III-31.

8. Hulley SB, Gordon S. Alcohol and high-density lipoprotein cholesterol. *Circ* 1981;64(suppl III):III-57–III-67.

9. Wallace RB, Lynch CF, Pomrehn PR, Criqui MH, et al. Alcohol and hypertension: epidemiologic and experimental considerations. *Circ*. 1981;64(suppl III):III-41–III-47.

10. Dyer AR, Stamler J, Paul O, Berkson DM, et al. Alcohol, cardiovascular risk factors and mortality: the Chicago experience. *Circ*. 1981;64(suppl III):III-20–III-27.

11. Klatsky AL, Friedman GD, Siegelaub AB. Alcohol use and cardiovascular disease: the Kaiser-Permanente experience. *Circ*. 1981;64(suppl III):III-32–III-41.

12. Fumeron F, Betoulle D, Luc G, Behague I, et al. Alcohol intake modulates the effect of a polymorphism of the cholesterol ester transfer protein gene on plasma high density lipoprotein and the risk of myocardial infarction. *J Clin Invest*. 1995;96:1664–1671.

13. Ridker PM, Vaughan DE, Stampfer MJ, Glynn RJ, et al. Association of moderate alcohol consumption and plasma concentration of endogenous tissue-type plasminogen activator. *JAMA*. 1994;272:929–933.

14. Folsom AR, Wu KK, Davis CE, Conlan MG, et al. Population correlates of plasma fibrinogen and factor VII, putative cardiovascular risk factors. *Atherosclerosis*. 1991;91:191–205.

15. Folsom AR, Qamhieh HT, Flack JM, Hilner JE, et al for the investigators of the Coronary Artery Risk Development in Young Adults (CARDIA) Study. *Am J Epidemiol*. 1993;138:1023–1026.

16. Glueck CJ, Heiss G, Morrison JA, Khoury P, et al. Alcohol intake, cigarette smoking and plasma lipids and lipoproteins in 12–19-year-old children. *Circ*. 1981;64(suppl III):III-48–III-56.

17. Rose G. Ancel Keys lecture. *Circ*. 1991;84:1405–1409.

18. Criqui MH, Ringel BL. Does diet or alcohol explain the French paradox? *Lancet*. 1994;344:1719–1723.

19. Marmot M, Brunner E. Alcohol and cardiovascular disease: the status of the U-shaped curve. *Br Med J*. 1991;303:565–568.

20. Maclure M. Demonstration of deductive meta-analysis: ethanol intake and risk of myocardial infarction. *Epidemiol Rev*. 1993;15:328–351.

21. Addiction Research Foundation of Ontario and the Canadian Centre on Substance Abuse. Appendix 1—Moderate drinking and health. *Can Med Assoc J*. 1994; 151:13–16.

22. Gans JE, Shook KL, eds. *Policy Compendium on Tobacco, Alcohol, and Other Harmful Substances Affecting Adolescents: Alcohol and Other Harmful Substances*. Chicago: American Medical Association; 1994.

23. *Sensible Drinking: The Report of an Inter-Departmental Working Group*. London: Department of Health; 1995.

24. Marmot M. A not-so-sensible drinks policy. *Lancet*. 1995;346:1643–1644.

25. Rose G. Sick individuals and sick populations. *Int J Epidemiol*. 1985;14:32–38.

CHAPTER 16

Hemostatic Dysfunction

SUMMARY

Blood coagulation is a protective process when blood loss is threatened and an adverse one when thrombosis occurs within a coronary artery or elsewhere and obstructs the circulation. Thrombosis has been known for more than 80 years to be linked with coronary heart disease and other manifestations of advanced atherosclerosis. Only recently, however, have epidemiologic studies of elements of the hemostatic process been conducted. Blood vessel, blood platelet, and coagulation phases contribute jointly to this process. Epidemiologic studies relate mainly to the last of these. Fibrinogen, factor VII, and other hemostatic factors have been found to be associated with many other established risk factors as well as with risks of coronary heart disease, stroke, and peripheral arterial disease. Genetic epidemiology has demonstrated gene-environment interactions involving some coagulation factors, indicating that associations found in some populations or groups may depend on specific allelic forms of genes affecting production or function of that factor. Trials of drugs to modify platelet function or promote resolution of thrombi have shown benefit in high-risk persons, such as those with acute myocardial infarction or stroke or prior events. Less clear-cut is whether antiplatelet drugs, principally aspirin, confer greater benefit or risk when applied in primary prevention. Much remains to be learned about the extent of an independent causal role for any of the coagulation factors, although the case for fibrinogen is fairly strong. Meanwhile, application of knowledge about antiplatelet and thrombolytic therapy in acute cardiovascular episodes requires changes in physician practice and in timeliness of the victim's response if the potential benefit of these interventions is to be realized.

INTRODUCTION

The term *hemostatic dysfunction* encompasses the three phases of hemostasis, the spontaneous process by which the flow of blood in a vessel can be arrested: the vascular phase, the platelet phase, and the coagulation phase.[1] Hemostasis is highly regulated, involving a complex and delicate balance of biochemical and physiological interactions that maintain blood flow under normal conditions but have the capacity to interrupt blood loss rapidly, under conditions such as gross injury to a vessel. The relation of thrombosis (formation of a blood clot within a vessel) to the occlusive events of advanced atherosclerosis has long been recognized, at least in its general properties. The dynamics of the atherosclerotic plaque and the intricacies of the biochemical and hemostatic response to plaque disruption, noted in Chapter 3, are very recent advances. Thrombosis is a pathological occurrence, which could be considered to reflect either normal hemostasis in response to adverse stimuli or a disorder of hemostasis itself that compounds the underlying vascular pathology of atherosclerosis. The term *dysfunction* is used here, without commitment to one or the other interpretation, to denote the potentially negative outcome of the hemostatic process when a thrombus is formed in conjunction with an atherosclerotic plaque.

Of the three phases of hemostasis, the coagulation phase has received much more extensive epidemiologic investigation than have the vascular and platelet phases, and this has mainly been a development within the past 20 years. *Coagulation* as used here is intended to encompass thrombogenesis (clot formation) and thrombolysis (clot dissolution). The following

discussion therefore focuses on coagulation as recently studied in populations in this dual sense, except that aspects of hemostasis relevant to prevention and control require attention to platelet-oriented interventions also.

DEFINITION AND CLASSIFICATION

Coagulation Factors

The coagulation factors have been designated variously over the many years of their study and description, as illustrated in Table 16–1.[2] In some cases (eg, factor VII), reference is commonly to the Roman numeral, whereas in others (eg, fibrinogen) the functional descriptive term is used more often. Each factor can be characterized in some detail with respect to its molecular type and size, site of biosynthesis, biolog-

Table 16–1 Nomenclature and Synonyms for Coagulation Factors

Roman Numeral	Preferred Descriptive Name	Synonyms
I	Fibrinogen	
II	Prothrombin	
III	Tissue factor	Thromboplastin
IV	Calcium ions	
V	Proaccelerin	Labile factor, accelerator globulin (AcG), thrombogen
VII	Proconvertin	Stable factor, serum prothrombin conversion accelerator (SPCA)
VIII	Antihemophilic factor (AHF)	Antihemophilic globulin (AHG), antihemophilic factor A, platelet cofactor 1, thromboplastinogen
IX	Plasma thromboplastin component (PTC)	Christmas factor, antihemophilic factor B, autoprothrombin II, platelet cofactor 2
X	Stuart factor	Prower factor, autoprothrombin III, thrombokinase
XI	Plasma thromboplastin antecedent (PTA)	Antihemophilic factor C
XII	Hageman factor	Glass factor, contact factor
XIII	Fibrin stabilizing factor (FSF)	Laki-Lorand factor (LLF), fibrinase, plasma transglutaminase, fibrinoligase
—	Prekallikrein	Fletcher factor
—	HMW kininogen	High molecular weight kininogen, contact activation cofactor, Fitzgerald factor, Williams factor, Flaujeac factor, Reid factor, Washington factor

Source: Reprinted with permission from TC Bithell, Blood Coagulation, in *Wintrobe's Clinical Hematology*, 9th ed, Vol 1, GR Lee et al, eds, p 567, © 1993, Lea & Febiger.

ically effective half-life in the circulation, and function, according to current understanding of the coagulation process. Although several of these factors and additional related enzymes or intermediate products have been addressed in some epidemiologic studies, the greatest attention to date has been directed to fibrinogen, which therefore warrants fuller description here.

Fibrinogen

Fibrinogen is the precursor of fibrin in the coagulation process and thus provides the material that becomes the physical framework of a thrombus when the process is fully developed. Fibrinogen is synthesized in the liver and is mainly found circulating in the blood, its concentration in plasma ranging typically from 160 to 415 mg/dl. When an antihemostatic process is taking place, fibrinogen is catabolized into smaller units that can be identified in plasma, and their concentrations are measured as indicators of this process. This substance is one of many characterized as "acute phase reactants," which are found in greatly increased plasma concentration in the course of inflammation or certain other processes. Thus high plasma fibrinogen concentration may reflect an active but subclinical process, including actively progressive atherosclerosis itself. This fact requires caution in interpreting values of fibrinogen concentration in individuals when determined on a single occasion or, especially for present interest, in the acute course or immediate aftermath of myocardial infarction or stroke.

MEASUREMENT

For all of the coagulation factors, between-laboratory standardization is limited or lacking altogether. But the best laboratory procedure may be overshadowed by the influence of blood-drawing technique on the results, because disturbances of hemostasis caused by this procedure may include activation of some of the component substances.[3] Frozen storage may fail to preserve full biological activity of some fac-

tors, and therefore specimens held long term may not provide valid results. Fibrinogen, in particular, can be assayed by allowing its conversion to fibrin, which can then be determined quantitatively by any of several techniques that are potentially practical for use in most clinical laboratories. In studies of the many hemostatic factors, bioassays are commonly used to evaluate the relative functional activity of a component, for which results are expressed as a percentage of normal functional activity.

Contributions of within-person variability, processing and assay variability, and between-person variability to total variance in determinations of seven hemostatic factors—including fibrinogen, factors VII and VIII, and von Willebrand factor—were reported from a sample of participants in the Atherosclerosis Risk in Communities (ARIC) Study.[4] Reliability coefficients were high for factor VIII and intermediate for the other three among the seven factors studied.

DETERMINANTS AND MECHANISMS

Theoretical Schemes of Hemostasis

Concentrations of fibrinogen or other coagulation factors are presumed to influence the regulatory balance of hemostasis in the direction of their dominant mode of action. It is therefore necessary to consider the context in which these factors operate. Figure 16–1 indicates the relationships among coagulation, platelet function, and endothelial function.[5] Above the horizontal lines are the prohemostatic components, involving fibrin, proteolytic enzymes, and activated (a) factors V and VII. Independently, substances called thromboxanes and PAF (platelet activating factor) are released by blood platelets and function in the same direction. All of these factors and their attendant processes are balanced by opposing influences of the vascular endothelium. Here, heparin and thrombomodulin contribute to the function of plasminogen activators and fibrinolysis, AT-III (antithrombin III), HCF-II (heparin cofactor II), and proteins C and S. Thus

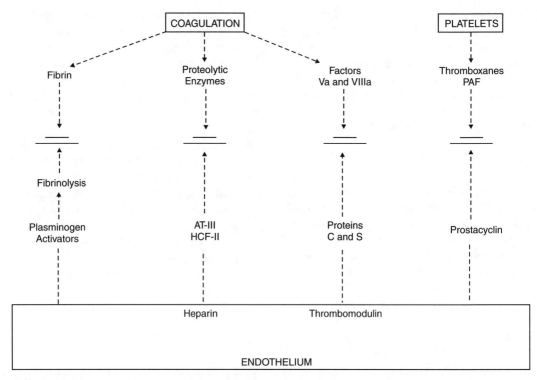

Figure 16–1 Interactions of Prohemostatic and Antihemostatic Mechanisms. Thrombosis may result when an imbalance of these phenomena occurs. The interactions indicated mainly occur in the microvasculature, which, because of the relatively large endothelial surface in proportion to the small volume of flow, may act to clear the circulation of prothrombotic debris. *Source*: Reprinted with permission from TC Bithell, Thrombosis and Antithrombotic Therapy, in *Wintrobe's Clinical Hematology*, 9th ed, Vol 2, GR Lee et al, eds, p 1516, © 1993, Lea & Febiger.

the coagulation phase is only one aspect of a complex set of regulatory interactions. Loss of balance in these interactions may result in either failure or excess of hemostatic function. Of concern in the present context is any dysfunctional state or condition that fosters thrombogenesis or inhibits thrombolysis.

Coagulation Pathways

To appreciate the roles of various components investigated in population studies, it is helpful to examine their pathways of action in somewhat greater detail. The pathways of coagulation and of fibrinolysis are illustrated in Figures 16–2 and 16–3, respectively.[2] The pathway of coagulation represents the two distinct processes by which

coagulation is considered to be initiated and promoted. The intrinsic pathway of "contact activation" involves one set of factors that sequentially act upon one another to convert inactive protein molecules into activated enzymes, beginning with factor XII and proceeding through factor X to the ultimate production of fibrin. Separately, the extrinsic pathway originates with tissue factor and factor VII to activate factor X and proceed thereafter as does the intrinsic pathway. Thus the shared portion of the process is considered to be a common pathway that either process alone may activate.

The process of fibrinolysis, by which a clot is dissolved, is outlined in Figure 16–3. The figure notes the location of several inhibitors that have the potential role of limiting the anticoagulation

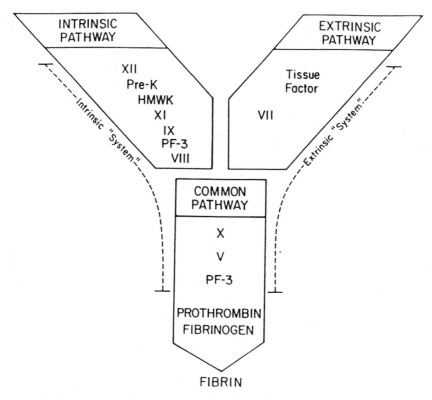

Note: PF-3, platelet factor 3; Pre-K, prekallikrein; HMWK, high molecular weight kininogen.

Figure 16–2 Pathways of Coagulation. *Source:* Reprinted with permission from TC Bithell, Blood Coagulation, in *Wintrobe's Clinical Hematology*, 9th ed, Vol 1, GR Lee et al, eds, p 580, © 1993, Lea & Febiger.

process. For example, the inhibitors of plasminogen activators, or plasminogen activator inhibitor (PAI), counter fibrinolysis. PAI-1, for example, has been investigated in several epidemiologic studies to determine whether relatively high concentrations are associated with arterial thrombosis or other manifestations of atherosclerosis. Thus a high concentration of PAI-1 is interpreted as reflecting a high level of opposition to clot lysis or, in effect, of promotion of progressive thrombus formation. Once activated, plasminogen becomes plasmin in either bound or free form and acts to break down either fibrin in "physiologic" proteolysis if bound, or fibrinogen in "pathologic" proteolysis if free.

There appear to be many redundancies in the mechanisms of coagulation. Thus, although there are multiple points at which rate-limiting processes might occur, these redundancies may serve to overdetermine some of the critical steps in the process. Further, a high concentration of one component may down-regulate production or activation of other components so that the net effect may be opposite to its independent mode of action in pro- or antihemostasis. For these reasons it is difficult to select with confidence among factors available for study. Timing of their measurement, in relation to the course of the atherosclerotic process or to other conditions that may distort the picture, poses problems of study design. Interpretation of observations on one or more factors when others of importance are unmeasured may be erroneous. Finally, choosing avenues for potential inter-

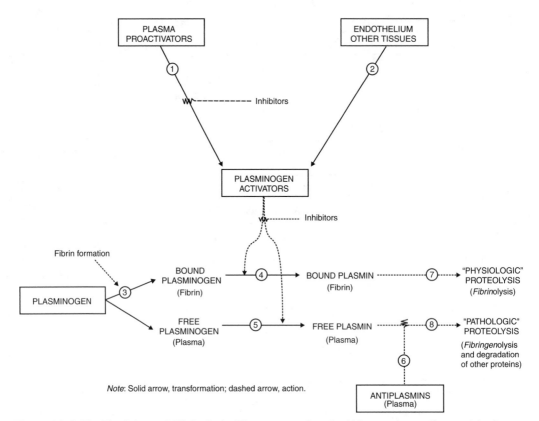

Figure 16–3 The Physiology of Fibrinolysis. The steps numbered within arrows are discussed in the text. "Fluid phase" activation of plasminogen is produced by the conversion of several plasma proenzymes ("proactivators") into proteolytic enzymes that act as plasminogen activators (step 1). Activators derived from endothelium are probably more important physiologically (step 2). *Source*: Reprinted with permission from TC Bithell, Blood Coagulation, in *Wintrobe's Clinical Hematology*, 9th ed, Vol 1, GR Lee et al, eds, p 593, © 1993, Lea & Febiger.

vention in the hemostatic process poses a challenge to balance potential efficacy and safety, because blood coagulation is a necessary physiologic function.

Associations with Established Risk Factors

At another level of consideration, epidemiologic studies have shown fibrinogen concentrations to be associated with many other factors related to atherosclerosis and its manifestations. A summary of the findings by Folsom is presented in Table 16–2.[6] The factors studied included age, sex, and race; diet and physical activity or fitness; obesity; blood lipids; blood

pressure; diabetes, serum insulin, and microalbuminuria; smoking; and several others, including social class and seasonal variation. The direction and relative strength of association with each factor is indicated, from strongly or moderately positive to moderately or strongly negative, with two factors lacking association also included. The conclusion was offered that such a nonspecific pattern of association with these diverse factors hinders the determination of whether fibrinogen has an independent causal role in cardiovascular diseases. A related question is which of these associations indicate pathways through which fibrinogen or other factors may be influenced. This direction of

Table 16–2 Factors Associated with Plasma Fibrinogen Concentration

Positive Association		*No Association*	*Negative Association*	
Strong	*Modest*		*Modest*	*Strong*
Age	Winter season	Dietary fat	Alcohol intake	Social class Education level
Female gender	African-American ethnicity	Nicotine gum	Physical activity, fitness	Japanese ethnicity
Cigarette smoking	Blood pressure		Fish oil	Estrogen replacement
Inflammatory conditions	LDL cholesterol		HDL cholesterol	Birth weight
Stress	Triglycerides			
Obesity	Lipoprotein(a)			
Diabetes	Homocysteine			
Menopause	Serum insulin			
Oral contraceptives	Microalbuminuria			
Leucocyte count				

Note: LDL, low density lipoprotein; HDL, high density lipoprotein.

Source: Reprinted from *European Heart Journal*, Vol 6A, AR Folsom, Epidemiology of Fibrinogen, p 22, © 1995, by permission of the publisher WB Saunders Company Limited London.

inquiry may help to elucidate further mechanisms by which previously recognized risk factors promote atherogenesis or precipitate acute thrombotic events. Similar questions would apply to the other associated hemostatic factors.

The link between hemostatic and social factors represents one of the more challenging observations for interpretation. Results of a cross-sectional analysis of fibrinogen concentration with other risk factors were reported from the Kuopio Ischemic Heart Disease Risk Factor Study, as shown in Table 16–3.[7] Both age-adjusted and covariate-adjusted mean values of fibrinogen concentration were presented for each stratum of the five indices. In age-adjusted analyses, significantly higher fibrinogen concentrations were observed for blue-collar workers and farmers, in contrast to white-collar workers; for the lowest versus the highest income strata of the population; for those with education of less than high school level versus high school or more; and for those with the lowest score for material possessions. It is interesting in view of the previous summary that extensive covariate adjustment changed very few of these results.

Genetic Factors

Genetic variations in fibrinogen and factor VII loci have also been studied and indicate that the manner in which specific alleles control concentrations of hemostatic factors depends on additional factors, such as smoking status or triglyceride concentrations. These are potentially important demonstrations of gene-environment interactions—the phenomena interpreted as conditioning of genetic influences by the environment (broadly understood) in which they operate. An implication of such findings is that comparison of risks of atherosclerosis and its complications between some populations or subgroups may be misleading unless both the genotypes and the other relevant personal or environmental characteristics are taken into account. Much remains to be learned in order to identify pertinent genetic variants and determine the population distributions of these genotypes

Table 16–3 Relation of Fibrinogen Concentration (g/l) to Five Socioeconomic Indices, Kuopio, Finland

Sample Characteristics			Age-Adjusted Means			Covariate[a]-Adjusted Means		
Variable	No.	%	Mean	95% Confidence Interval	P Value[b]	Mean	95% Confidence Interval	P Value[b]
Occupation								
Farmer	841	42.4	3.06	3.00–3.12	0.004	3.07	3.01–3.13	0.008
Blue-collar	307	15.5	3.06	3.02–3.10	<0.001	3.03	3.00–3.07	0.022
White-collar	837	42.2	2.95	2.91–2.99	Reference	2.98	2.94–3.01	Reference
Income (quintiles)								
1 (low)	349	17.6	3.19	3.14–3.25	<0.001	3.13	3.06–3.17	<0.001
2	380	19.1	3.03	2.98–3.09	<0.001	3.02	2.96–3.07	0.050
3	427	21.5	2.99	2.94–3.05	0.004	2.98	2.94–3.04	0.201
4	416	20.9	3.01	2.96–3.06	0.001	3.04	3.00–3.09	0.004
5 (high)	415	20.9	2.89	2.83–2.94	Reference	2.94	2.90–2.99	Reference
Education								
Less than elementary	181	9.0	3.06	2.98–3.15	<0.001	3.00	2.91–3.06	0.054
Elementary	948	47.2	3.05	3.02–3.09	<0.001	3.03	3.01–3.07	<0.001
Middle school	735	36.6	2.99	2.95–3.03	0.003	3.02	2.98–3.06	0.002
High school or greater	145	7.2	2.84	2.75–2.93	Reference	2.87	2.79–2.96	Reference
Material possessions (quartiles)								
1 (low)	292	14.5	3.12	3.06–3.19	<0.001	3.05	2.97–3.14	0.455
2	816	40.6	3.02	2.98–3.05	0.121	3.01	2.98–3.05	0.715
3	480	23.9	2.99	2.94–3.04	0.423	3.01	2.97–3.07	0.547
4 (high)	420	20.9	2.96	2.91–3.02	Reference	3.00	2.95–3.05	Reference
Childhood socioeconomic status (tertiles)								
1 (low)	686	34.1	3.04	3.00–3.08	0.132	3.03	3.00–3.07	0.400
2	897	44.6	3.01	2.97–3.05	0.470	3.01	2.97–3.04	0.786
3 (high)	428	21.3	2.99	2.93–3.04	Reference	3.00	2.96–3.06	Reference

a. Alcohol consumption, body mass index, physical fitness, smoking, coffee consumption, high-density lipoprotein cholesterol, low-density lipoprotein cholesterol, blood leukocyte count, and prevalent disease (at least one sign of ischemic heart disease, hypertension, diabetes, or previous stroke).

b. P value for comparison between reference level and other levels of the socioeconomic index.

Source: Reprinted with permission from TW Wilson et al, *American Journal of Epidemiology*, Vol 137, p 296, © 1993, The Johns Hopkins University School of Hygiene and Public Health.

so that their contribution to population differences in atherosclerosis can be appreciated.

DISTRIBUTION

General Frequency Distributions

Substantial contributions to the epidemiology of hemostatic factors have come from the Northwick Park (England) Heart Study, in which several factors have been investigated.[8] Figure 16–4 shows the population distribution, including the mean value and standard deviation, for each of eight hemostatic factors and platelet characteristics in some 2000 men and women, aged from 18 to the late 50s or mid-60s. In general, there was little sex difference in

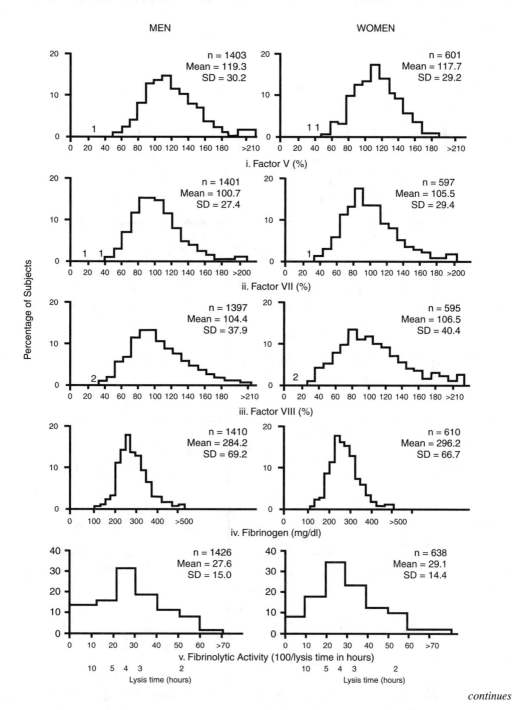

Figure 16–4 Distributions of Hemostatic Variables in Men and Women in the Northwick Park Heart Study. Figures at extremes of some distributions indicate numbers (not percentages) of individuals having values within the intervals specified. *Source*: Reprinted with permission from TW Meade et al, *British Medical Bulletin*, Vol 33, p 284, © 1977, The British Council.

continues

Figure 16–4 continued

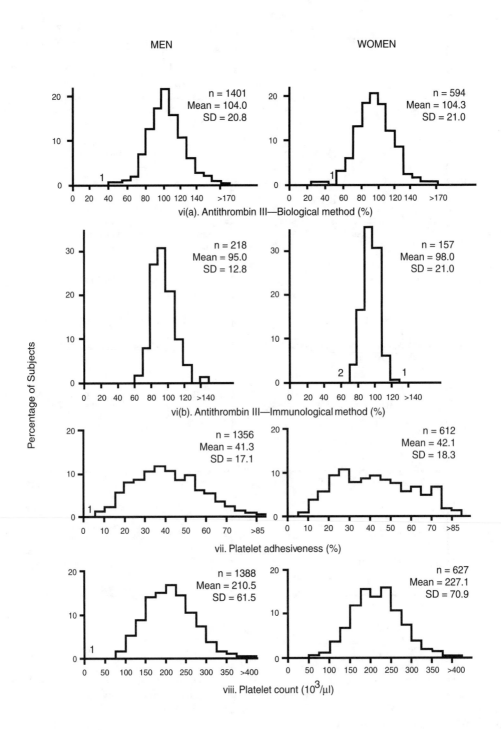

MEN

WOMEN

vi(a). Antithrombin III—Biological method (%)

vi(b). Antithrombin III—Immunological method (%)

vii. Platelet adhesiveness (%)

viii. Platelet count ($10^3/\mu l$)

these measures, although these differences were not tested statistically. Several issues in the performance and interpretation of these measures were addressed in the report, as in the discussion above,[5] including laboratory error, within- versus between-individual variation on repeated testing, and others. Relations of these characteristics with several other cardiovascular risk factors were also addressed.

Population Differences: Japan and the United States

Population differences in hemostatic variables were compared among small samples of Japanese men in rural and urban Japan and the United States, and White men in the United States. The aim was to test the hypothesis that these factors would indicate lower risk of coronary heart disease for Japanese men in Japan than the other men, consistent with previous knowledge of marked differences in coronary heart disease rates among these populations.[9] Fibrinogen concentration was highest in Whites in contrast to the other three groups (290 mg/dl versus a range from 223 to 250 mg/dl). Factors VII and VIII were measured as coagulation activities and were greater for US Japanese and Whites than for Japanese in Japan (only Factor VII was significantly higher). Von Willebrand factor did not differ among the four groups. In all samples, in addition, fibrinogen concentration was significantly greater in smokers than in nonsmokers, consistent with discussion of chronic effects of smoking in Chapter 14.

Variation at Menopause and with Estrogen Replacement

A study of hemostatic factors in 207 eligible US women around the age of menopause (mean age 52 years) indicated a generally lower prohemostatic profile, or thrombogenic predisposition, before menopause than after. For women using hormone replacement therapy after menopause (predominantly conjugated estrogen plus progesterone), there was less tendency in this direction.[10] However, while fibrinogen concentrations were increased only for women without hormonal treatment, factor VII activity was increased even more for those women with hormonal treatment than for those without, as shown in Figure 16–5. This seemingly discrepant finding can be explained by the effect of hormone replacement therapy to increase triglyceride concentration, which in turn causes an increase in concentration of factor VII.[11]

Correlates of Impaired Fibrinolysis

Discussion of the role of thrombosis in acute coronary heart disease syndromes includes the impairment of fibrinolysis. The state constitutes an imbalance of hemostasis predisposing to more extensive or prolonged thrombogenesis, the process thought to underlie the progression from plaque disruption to arterial occlusion. Both fibrinogen and factor VII levels are increased, and fibrinolysis decreased, in the presence of obesity, hyperlipidemia, diabetes, smoking, and emotional stress.[12]

RATES AND RISKS

The Northwick Park Heart Study

Several cohort studies of hemostatic factors and coronary heart disease have been conducted, perhaps earliest among them the Northwick Park Heart Study cited above. By 1986 that group found that both factor VII coagulant activity and fibrinogen concentration were important predictors of coronary events, based on the occurrence of 109 first major events among 1511 White men age 40–64 years at entry.[13] Independent relations were examined for factor VII, fibrinogen, cholesterol concentration, and systolic blood pressure with fatal, nonfatal, and total coronary events, both within 5 years of measurement and over the total mean follow-up period of 10 years. The strongest predictive relations were found for fatal events

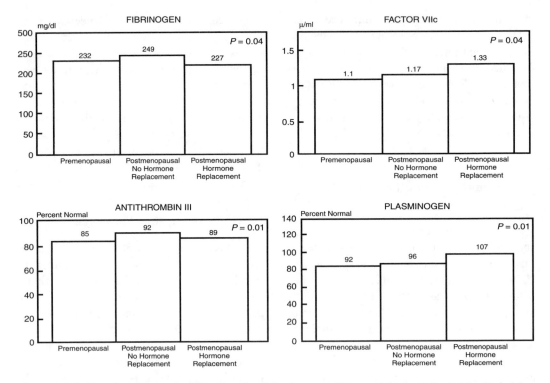

Figure 16–5 Hemostatic Factors by Menopausal and Replacement Hormonal Status, Adjusted for Body Mass Index. *Source*: Reprinted with permission from *Annals of Epidemiology*, Vol 2, LH Kuller et al, p 449, © 1992, Elsevier Science, Inc.

within 5 years. Based on standard deviation units for each variable, each unit increase in age, factor VII, fibrinogen, cholesterol, and systolic blood pressure increased the risk by 92%, 55%, 67%, 36%, and 21%, respectively, with corresponding *P*-values reported as 0.006, 0.04, 0.02, and (for cholesterol and blood pressure) not significant. Other observations led the authors to suggest that fibrinogen concentration may be an important mechanism underlying the relation between smoking and coronary heart disease. Overall, Meade and colleagues concluded, "There is increasing reason to consider the prevention of thrombosis as an effective approach to the prevention of IHD. The case for doing so is strengthened by the possibility that the biochemical disturbance in IHD may lie at least as much in the coagulation system as in the metabolism of cholesterol."[13(p 537)]

Meta-Analysis of Six Cohort Studies

In addition to the Northwick Park Heart Study, six others were included in a review and five of these in a meta-analysis of cohort studies of fibrinogen and coronary heart disease reported in 1993.[14] Methods and results of these studies are presented in Tables 16–4 and 16–5 and in Figure 16–6. The studies were conducted in the United Kingdom (NPHS, Leigh, CSCHDS), Sweden (Gothenburg), the United States (Framingham), and Germany (PROCAM, GRIPS). From 300 to 5000 men were included in these studies and followed for 2–13 years, with coronary disease or stroke end points, or both. Fibrinogen determination was by several different methods among the studies. (See the report for references to specific methods.[3]) The baseline fibrinogen concentration, in

Table 16–4 Prospective Epidemiologic Studies of Fibrinogen—Methods

Study	Sample Size and Composition	Length of Follow-Up (yr)	End Point	Fibrinogen Method
NPHS	1,511 men	10	1. Death from ischemic heart disease 2. Nonfatal ischemic heart disease event	Gravimetry
Gothenburg	792 men	13.5	1. Myocardial infarction 2. Stroke	Thrombin clotting
Leigh	297 men	7.3	Myocardial infarction	Nephelometry
Framingham	554 men, 761 women	12	1. Ischemic heart disease 2. Stroke	Ratnoff, Menzie
CSCHDS	4,860 men	5.1/3.2	Ischemic heart disease	Nephelometry and gravimetry
PROCAM	1,674 men	2	Major ischemic heart disease	Thrombin clotting
GRIPS	5,239 men	5	Myocardial infarction	Nephelometry

Note: CSCHDS, Caerphilly and Speedwell Collaborative Heart Disease Studies; GRIPS, Göttingen Risk, Incidence and Prevalence Study; NPHS, Northwick Park Heart Health Study; PROCAM, Prospective Cardiovascular Münster Study.

Source: Reprinted with permission from Ernst and Resch, Fibrinogen as a Cardiovascular Risk Factor: A Meta-Analysis and Review of the Literature, *Annals of Internal Medicine*, Vol 118, pp 956–963, © 1993, American College of Physicians.

grams per liter, for categories of participants as classified by disease status at the end of follow-up is shown for each study in Table 16–5, though without statistical evaluation.

Among the studies included in the meta-analysis (the Leigh study having been excluded on methodologic grounds), the individual odds ratios for end-point events and highest versus lowest one-third of the distribution of fibrinogen concentration ranged from 1.8 (95% confidence interval 1.2–2.5) to 4.1 (2.3–6.9), with an overall summary odds ratio of 2.3 (1.9–2.8) (Figure 16–6). Other risk factors were not addressed in this analysis, but the original reports were cited as indicating significant independent associations of fibrinogen concentration with coronary heart disease events, as seen above for the Northwick Park Heart Study. Many factors influence fibrinogen concentrations, however, as discussed above. The difficulty of accounting

completely for even these known relationships is considerable. Nonetheless, the authors described fibrinogen as a major cardiovascular risk factor that should be included in future studies of risk factor modification.

The ARIC Study

A subsequent report of another cohort study, the ARIC Study, also reported that fibrinogen concentration was significantly related to risk of incident coronary heart disease events among men and women followed for 5.2 years (Table 16–6).[15] White blood cell count was also a significant predictor of coronary events for both non-Black men and for Black and non-Black women. As shown in Table 16–7, multivariate adjustment for other risk factors (see Table 16–7 notes) reduced the relative risks for coronary events to nonsignificant levels except for fibrin-

Table 16–5 Prospective Epidemiologic Studies of Fibrinogen—Results

Study	Number of Events	Person-Years	Fibrinogen Level According to End Point (g/l)	Comment
Northwick Park Heart Study	68 deaths from ischemic heart disease, 60 nonfatal heart disease events	15,110	No end point, 2.9; ischemic heart disease deaths, 3.1; nonfatal, 3.2; all ischemic heart disease end points, 3.2; other deaths, 3.0	Association with fibrinogen stronger than that for cholesterol; effect particularly strong for events occurring within 5 years of recruitment
Gothenburg Study	92 myocardial infarctions; 38 strokes	10,692	No end point, 3.3; myocardial infarction, 3.6; stroke, 3.7; other deaths, 3.3	Fibrinogen risk factor for both end points in univariate analysis but only for stroke in multivariate analysis (no confounding by the risk factor age)
Leigh Study	40	2,168	No end point, 3.0 (subgroup of participants aged 40–54 years); myocardial infarction, 4.0	Fibrinogen was strongest predictor, with an excessively high odds ratio (study withdrawn from meta-analysis because of methodologic flaws)
Framingham Study	312 ischemic heart diseases, 92 strokes	15,780	Event rate/1,000 per year: 16 (<2.7 g/l), 18 (2.7 to 3.1 g/l), 26 (>3.1 g/l)	Fibrinogen independent risk factor for both end points (only study including both sexes)
Caerphilly and Speedwell Collaborative Heart Disease Studies	251	20,325	No end point, 3.7; ischemic heart disease, 4.1	Fibrinogen independent risk factor comparable in strength to conventional risk factors (two independent measurement techniques of fibrinogen)
Prospective Cardiovascular Münster Study	15	4,045	No end point, 2.6; events, 3.3	Fibrinogen independent risk factor (only preliminary publication available as yet)
Göttingen Risk, Incidence, and Prevalence Study	107	26,195	No end point, 3.7; myocardial infarction, 4.0	Fibrinogen independent risk factor (detailed consideration of lipid variables)

Source: Reprinted with permission from Ernst and Resch, Fibrinogen as a Cardiovascular Risk Factor: A Meta-Analysis and Review of the Literature, *Annals of Internal Medicine*, Vol 118, pp 956–963, © 1993, American College of Physicians.

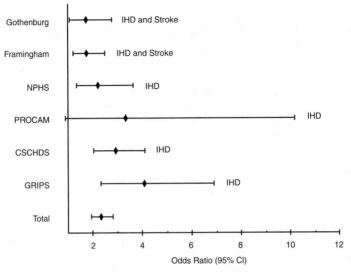

Figure 16–6 Cardiovascular Events by Fibrinogen Levels in the Upper Tertile Compared to the Lower Tertile in Six Prospective Studies. *Source*: Reprinted with permission from Ernst and Resch, Fibrinogen as a Cardiovascular Risk Factor: A Meta-Analysis and Review of the Literature, *Annals of Internal Medicine*, Vol 118, pp 956–963, © 1993, American College of Physicians.

ogen in both men and women and white blood cell count in women alone. Notably, all four hemostatic factors were significant predictors of all-cause mortality: fibrinogen, factor VIII, von Willebrand factor, and white blood cell count. These investigators concluded:

> From a preventive-medicine point of view, only measurement of fibrinogen (and not the other hemostatic factors) contributed anything beyond traditional risk factors in the prediction of CHD. A fibrinogen measurement costs approximately the same as a lipid profile, so it could be considered for risk factor screening. However, there is no universal standardization system for the fibrinogen assay, and the independent contribution of fibrinogen to prediction of risk appears to be modest. There also has been no clinical trial yet to dem-

onstrate that lowering fibrinogen will prevent CHD. These facts suggest that routine screening for elevated fibrinogen in healthy adults is currently not warranted.[15(p 1107)]

Other Factors and Outcomes

Other observations in relation to hemostatic dysfunction and cardiovascular disease include studies of fibrin breakdown products and both coronary and peripheral arterial disease, suggesting prognostic importance of the level of fibrin turnover in the progression of disease. Endogenous tissue-type plasminogen activator (tPA) has also been studied in connection with both myocardial infarction and stroke. For myocardial infarction, for example, baseline concentrations of tPA antigen were greater in 231 men free of evident coronary heart disease at entry who developed myocardial infarction during follow-up than in 231 control subjects,

Table 16–6 Age-, Race-, and Field Center–Adjusted[a] Relative Risk and 95% Confidence Interval of Incident Coronary Heart Disease for the Highest Versus Lowest Third of the Distribution of Hemostatic Factors According to Levels of Other Factors in the Atherosclerosis Risk in Communities (ARIC) Study

Sex/Factor Level	CHD Events, n	Fibrinogen		Factor VIII		Von Willebrand		WBC	
		RR	95% CI	RR	95% CI	RR	95% CI	RR	95% CI
Men									
Race (age adjusted)									
Black	59	1.87	0.97–3.6	1.59	0.8–3.2	1.73	0.8–3.7	1.49	0.79–2.8
Other	178	3.11	2.1–4.6	1.13	0.8–1.6	1.28	0.9–1.8	3.33	2.1–5.3
Age (race adjusted)									
<55 yr	76	3.11	1.8–5.3	1.30	0.8–2.2	1.34	0.8–2.4	2.87	1.6–5.1
≥55 yr	153	2.64	1.7–4.0	1.28	0.9–1.9	1.39	0.9–2.1	2.47	1.6–3.8
Current smoker									
Yes	102	2.34	1.5–3.5	1.38	0.9–2.1	1.49	0.97–2.3	2.65	1.7–4.1
No	135	2.17	1.2–4.0	1.21	0.7–2.0	1.11	0.7–1.8	1.18	0.6–2.3
Carotid intima-media thickness									
Above median	173	2.20	1.5–3.2	1.08	0.8–1.5	1.19	0.8–1.7	2.45	1.6–3.7
Below median	42	6.94	2.8–17.4	1.22	0.6–2.6	1.36	0.6–3.1	3.46	1.6–7.6
Women									
Race (age adjusted)									
Black	44	2.85	1.00–8.1	5.15	1.2–21.6	2.00	0.8–4.8	4.38	2.0–9.6
Other	65	2.48	1.3–4.8	1.04	0.6–1.9	1.05	0.6–1.9	4.10	2.0–8.5
Age (race adjusted)									
<55 yr	33	1.61	0.70–3.7	2.12	0.9–5.1	1.33	0.6–3.0	6.20	2.1–18.2
≥55 yr	84	3.83	1.7–8.5	1.36	0.7–2.5	1.42	0.8–2.6	3.58	1.9–6.6
Current smoker									
Yes	54	2.46	1.2–5.2	1.79	0.8–3.8	1.26	0.7–2.4	2.93	1.5–5.8
No	55	1.74	0.76–4.0	1.58	0.8–3.2	1.23	0.6–2.4	3.30	1.1–9.5
Carotid intima-media thickness									
Above median	73	2.18	1.1–4.3	1.33	0.7–2.4	1.41	0.8–2.5	4.25	2.1–8.6
Below median	27	4.03	1.2–14.0	1.83	0.6–5.9	1.51	0.6–3.8	3.92	1.5–10.3

Note: RR, relative risk; CI, confidence interval; CHD, coronary heart disease; WBC, white blood cell.

a. Derived from sex-specific proportional hazards regression models.

Source: Reproduced with permission from AR Folsom et al, Prospective Study of Hemostatic Factors and Incidence of Coronary Heart Disease, *Circulation*, Vol 96, p 1105, © 1997, American Heart Association.

drawn from the (United States) Physicians' Health Study.[16] This direction of association is explained by high concentrations of tPA reflecting elevated PAI-1 concentrations and therefore impaired fibrinolysis. The estimated relative risks by quintile group of baseline tPA concentration were 1.00, 1.27, 1.75, 1.88, and 2.81, with a 95% confidence interval for the ratio of the fifth to the first quintile risk of 1.47–5.37 and *P*-value for the trend reported as 0.0008. However, after analysis controlling for other risk factors, mainly high-density lipoprotein (HDL) cholesterol, the relation of tPA was no longer significant. In relation to stroke inci-

Table 16–7 Multivariate Relative Risk and 95% Confidence Interval of Incident Events in Relation to 1-*SD*-Higher Level of Hemostatic Factors in the Atherosclerosis Risk in Communities (ARIC) Study

Event/Factor	Men RR[a]	Men 95% CI	Women RR[a]	Women 95% CI
CHD				
Fibrinogen	1.48[*][b]	1.19–1.84	1.21[*]	1.02–1.44
Factor VIII	1.01	0.86–1.18	0.99	0.81–1.23
von Willebrand factor	1.05	0.91–1.20	1.02	0.84–1.25
WBC	1.13	0.98–1.31	1.45[b]	0.86–2.44
Total mortality				
Fibrinogen	1.30[*]	1.18–1.44	1.37[*]	1.22–1.54
Factor VIII	1.28[*]	1.14–1.44	1.37[*]	1.21–1.55
von Willebrand factor	1.13[*]	1.02–1.27	1.27[*]	1.12–1.44
WBC	1.15[*]	1.01–1.31	1.29[*]	1.13–1.48

Note: RR, relative risk; CI, confidence interval; CHD, coronary heart disease; WBC, white blood cell.

a. Relative risks were computed for each factor separately and adjusted by sex-specific proportional hazards regression for age, race, ARIC field center, low-density lipoprotein cholesterol, high-density lipoprotein cholesterol, systolic blood pressure, use of antihypertensives, diabetes, cigarette smoking (status and pack-years), waist-to-hip ratio, and sport index. Number of events: CHD, 200 men and 89 women; total mortality, 237 men and 174 women.

b. Because of significant quadratic associations, these two relative risks were per 1-*SD* increment centered at the mean.

*P<0.05.

Source: Reproduced with permission from AR Folsom et al, Prospective Study of Hemostatic Factors and Incidence of Coronary Heart Disease, *Circulation*, Vol 96, p 1106, © 1997, American Heart Association.

dence, also investigated in the setting of the Physicians' Health Study, estimated relative risks of 3.51 (95% CI 1.72–7.17) and 3.89 (95% CI 1.83–8.26) were reported for total and thromboembolic stroke, respectively.[17] However, these relative risks pertain to the highest 5% of values in the distribution among controls, unlike the more commonly encountered estimates such as those for the highest 20%, as in the analysis described above for myocardial infarction. Unlike the latter association, this one remained significant after adjustment for several established risk factors.

PREVENTION AND CONTROL

Antiplatelet Therapy

Although evidence on the possible association of measurable factors in hemostasis has continued to accumulate in recent years, intervention has progressed especially in two related areas, platelet function and coagulation. In the first area, antiplatelet therapy has been evaluated for both its role in acute myocardial infarction and stroke and its potential value in primary prevention.[18] The trials addressing these issues are summarized in a recent series of publications from the Antiplatelet Trialists' Collaboration, an international cooperative group, and the results are illustrated in Figure 16–7.

Altogether 174 trials were reviewed, comprising some 70,000 high-risk and 30,000 low-risk participants, the latter in primary prevention trials, and an additional 10,000 participants in trials in which multiple treatments were compared. The intervention most commonly tested was aspirin, in doses ranging from 75 to 325

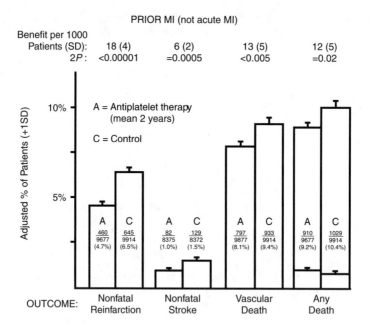

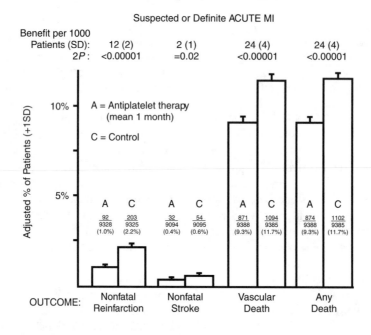

continues

Figure 16–7 Effects of Antiplatelet Therapy in High- and Low-Risk Persons, the Antiplatelet Trialists' Collaboration. *Source*: Reprinted with permission from *British Medical Journal*, Vol 308, pp 81–106, © 1994, BMJ Publishing Group.

Figure 16–7 continued

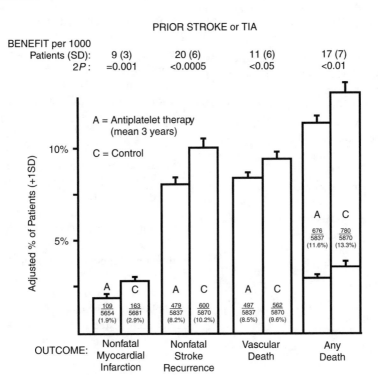

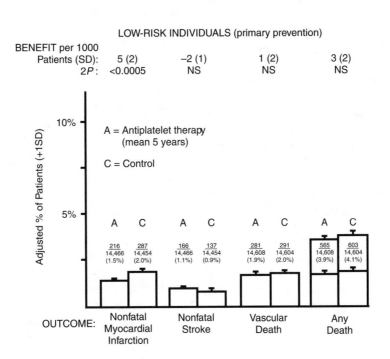

mg/day. Figure 16–7 presents combined results of trials of at least one month of therapy in accordance with several features:

- clinical status of eligible participants: prior, but not acute, myocardial infarction; suspected or definite acute myocardial infarction; prior stroke or transient ischemic attack (TIA); and low-risk individuals with none of the preceding conditions
- type of therapy: antiplatelet therapy (A) or control (C)
- end point for outcome evaluation: nonfatal myocardial infarction or reinfarction, non-fatal stroke or stroke recurrence, vascular death, and any death

The adjusted percentage of patients experiencing each outcome is the vertical axis and is indicated by the height of each bar, and the number of events prevented per 1000 persons treated is shown at the top of each panel in the figure. Actual numbers and percentages of participants in each category of eligibility and outcome are shown within each bar.

Benefits of antiplatelet therapy were statistically significant for all outcomes in all high-risk groups and for nonfatal myocardial infarction but not the other outcomes in the low-risk or primary prevention stratum of treated persons. The reduction in vascular events in the high-risk groups was approximately 25% and was reported to be statistically significant in men and women, middle and old age, hypertensive and normotensive patients, and patients with or without diabetes. It was noted that treatment in low-risk persons was accompanied by an apparent increase in risk of stroke, which was not statistically significant, and that the benefit was only about four events prevented per 1000 persons treated for five years. The authors concluded that benefit was clear for high-risk patient groups and that wider use of antiplatelet therapy was warranted but that use for primary prevention could not be recommended in view of current uncertainty about risks and benefits.

Thrombolytic Therapy

The second broad area of intervention is thrombolytic therapy, use of which has been evaluated in the acute stage of myocardial infarction or stroke. The larger trials are characterized in Table 16–8.[19] Among 58,600 patients with acute myocardial infarction studied in these trials, mortality in 35 days from onset was reduced by 18% among those treated (from 11.4% in controls to 9.6% in those treated). Of particular practical importance has been the observation that treatment must be administered very early in the episode if it is to be effective. Table 16–9 indicates the projected benefit of therapy in relation to the hours elapsed from onset of the event to initiation of therapy. The contrast between the effectiveness of treatment within 1–3 hours versus 4–12 hours, or more than 12 hours, is striking. The implications for medical practice are complex and include the needs for more rapid determination of indications for therapy, earlier discrimination between those with acute myocardial infarction in progress and other patients, and reduction in cost of this form of treatment. This avenue of prevention, afforded only in the context of long-standing atherosclerosis, clearly offers no benefit to those with silent infarction or those who die suddenly and cannot reach medical care.

Thrombolytic therapy has subsequently been shown to be effective in treatment of acute stroke as well as coronary events if received within three hours of symptom onset.[20]

CURRENT ISSUES

Further Investigation

Many of the observational studies to date were reviewed recently by Pearson and colleagues, who concluded that, with the exception of fibrinogen, strong evidence of a causal relation to risk of cardiovascular disease is thus far lacking for hemostatic factors.[21] Even here, however, the limited data for women and non-

Table 16–8 Design Characteristics of Trials of Fibrinolytic Therapy

Design Feature	GISSI-1	ISAM	AIMS	ISIS-2	ASSET	USIM	ISIS-3[a]	EM-ERAS	LATE
Fibrinolytic regimen	SK	SK	APSAC	SK	t-PA	UK	SK; t-PA APSAC	SK	t-PA
Number of patients	11,802	1,741	1,254	17,187	5,012	2,201	9,158	4,534	5,711
Control allocation	Open	Placebo	Placebo	Placebo	Placebo	Open	Open	Placebo	Placebo
Routine antiplatelet	No	Aspirin (single IV bolus)	No	Aspirin (50%)	No	No	Aspirin	Aspirin	Aspirin
Routine heparin	No	Yes: IV	Yes: IV	No	Yes: IV	Yes: IV	50%: SC	No	64%: IV

Note: AIMS, APSAC Intervention Mortality Study; APSAC, anistreplase; ASSET, Anglo-Scandinavian Study of Early Thrombosis; EMERAS, Estudio Multicentrico Estreptoquinasa Republicas de America del Sur; GISSI-1, Gruppo Italiano per lo Studio della Streptochnasi nell'infarto miocardico; ISAM, Intravenous Streptokinase in Acute Myocardial Infarction; ISIS-2, Second International Study of Infarct Survival; ISIS-3, Third International Study of Infarct Survival; IV, intravenous; LATE, Late Assessment of Thrombolytic Effect; SC, subcutaneous; SK, streptokinase; t-PA, tissue-plasminogen activator; UK, urokinase; USIM, Urochnasi per via Sistemica nell'Infarto Miocardico.

a. In ISIS-3, 37,000 patients considered to have a "certain" indication for fibrinolysis therapy were randomized between SK, t-PA, and APSAC and are not part of the present report, which is restricted to those in whom the indication was considered "uncertain." The latter were allocated half to fibrinolysis (1/3 SK, 1/3 t-PA, 1/3 APSAC; all taken together in this report) and half to open control (ie, no fibrinolysis).

Source: Reprinted with permission from J Herlitz, Workshop, *Thrombolytic Therapy in Myocardial Infarction*, p 50, © 1994, The Norwegian Medicines Control Authority.

Whites, inability to control for several potential confounding factors in studies to date, and other concerns warrant continued reservation even on the nature of the association of fibrinogen with cardiovascular disease. Although many interesting observations have appeared with respect to other hemostatic factors, the data were judged less compelling than those for fibrinogen. Further work may advance this area considerably but faces methodologic and analytic challenges, several of which have been alluded to above. At the same time, the opportunity to deepen under-

Table 16–9 Benefit of Fibrinolytic Therapy in Relation to Interval Between Onset of Symptoms and Start of Treatment

	Treatment Allocation				No. of Saved Lives per 1,000 Treated Patients
	Fibrinolytic		Control		
Hours from Onset	n	%	n	%	
0–1	1,678	9.5	1,670	13.0	35
2–3	8,297	8.2	8,315	10.7	25
4–6	8,294	9.7	8,195	11.5	19
7–12	6,478	11.1	6,404	12.7	16
13–24	4,568	10.0	4,701	10.5	5

Source: Reprinted with permission from J Herlitz, Workshop, *Thrombolytic Therapy in Myocardial Infarction*, p 53, © 1994, The Norwegian Medicines Control Authority.

standing of the "thrombotic side" of the athero-thrombotic process is important, at least for its potential for prevention in high-risk persons close to the time of clinical events. Whether long-term preventive strategies will also be found practical and whether population interventions may be shown to be beneficial in bringing about favorable change in the delicate balance of hemostatic factors will be important revelations. Both optimistic and cautionary views have been expressed.[13,21]

Application of Current Knowledge

With respect to intervention, the indication that antiplatelet therapy may be used less widely than is appropriate and that its potential for risk reduction is not being fully realized due to physician practices is a clear message from the Antiplatelet Trialists and appears well supported.[18] Others may be more optimistic about the benefits of aspirin use as a routine preventive measure, but the admonitions concerning prescription of alcohol in the preceding chapter may be germane here also, though with fewer concerns—not to say none—about potential adverse effects.

The present use of thrombolytic therapy is also lacking relative to its potential for improving short- and long-term survival in myocardial infarction, as shown in a recent community-based survey in the United States.[22] Figure 16–8 indicates the survival curves for those who did and did not receive thrombolytic therapy in the course of treatment for acute myocardial infarction in Corpus Christi, Texas, in the years 1988–1990. The results in part reflect selection of patients for treatment by community physicians and do not represent the outcome of a randomized trial. However, they suggest that actual benefit is realized in whole communities, and not only in the special settings of clinical trials, when thrombolytic therapy is used. Figure 16–9, on the other hand, shows that only 159 of 1199 patients (13.3%) received this intervention. The decline in proportion treated by time since onset meant that very few of the large proportion of persons with 4–24 hours of delay time

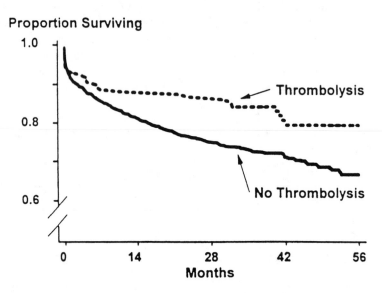

Figure 16–8 Probability of Survival over 56 Months Following Hospitalization for Acute Myocardial Infarction, According to Use of Thrombolytic Therapy. *Source*: Reprinted with permission from *Annals of Epidemiology*, Vol 5, DC Goff, Jr et al, p 176, © 1995, Elsevier Science, Inc.

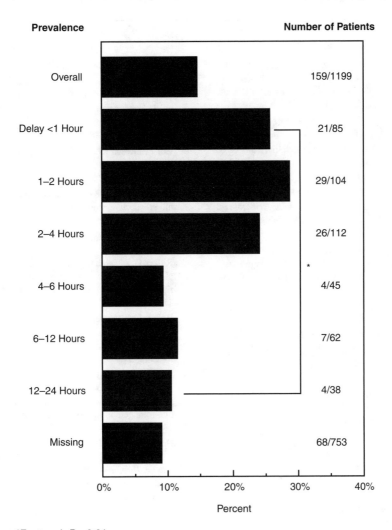

Figure 16–9 Prevalence of Receipt of Thrombolytic Therapy by Delay from Onset of Symptoms to Arrival at Hospital. *Source*: Reprinted with permission from *Annals of Epidemiology*, Vol 5, DC Goff, Jr et al, p 175, © 1995, Elsevier Science, Inc.

were evidently considered eligible to benefit, consistent with the trial results shown in Table 16–9. This combination of observations, consistent with others,[23] indicates that greater application of the demonstrated benefit of this form of therapy may require substantial reduction in the delay between onset of symptoms and presenta-tion for treatment in the acute phase of myocar-dial infarction. In the United States, a multi-center trial of community intervention to reduce delay time in treatment of acute myocardial in-farction is now in progress and a corresponding trial for early treatment of acute stroke is con-templated.

REFERENCES

1. Bithell TC. Platelets, hemostasis, and coagulation. In: Lee RG, Bithell TC, Foerster J, Athens JW, Lukens JN, eds. *Wintrobe's Clinical Hematology*. 9th ed. Philadelphia, Pa: Lea & Febiger; 1993;1:509.

2. Bithell TC. Blood coagulation. In: Lee RG, Bithell TC, Foerster J, Athens JW, Lukens JN, eds. *Wintrobe's Clinical Hematology*. 9th ed. Philadelphia, Pa: Lea & Febiger; 1993;1:566–615.

3. Bithell TC. The diagnostic approach to the bleeding disorders. In: Lee RG, Bithell TC, Foerster J, Athens JW, Lukens JN, eds. *Wintrobe's Clinical Hematology*. 9th ed. Philadelphia, Pa: Lea & Febiger; 1993; 2:1301–1324.

4. Chambless LE, McMahon R, Wu K, Folsom A, et al. Short-term intraindividual variability in hemostasis factors: the ARIC Study. *Ann Epidemiol*. 1992;2:723–733.

5. Bithell TC. Thrombosis and antithrombotic therapy. In: Lee RG, Bithell TC, Foerster J, Athens JW, Lukens JN, eds. *Wintrobe's Clinical Hematology*. 9th ed. Philadelphia, Pa: Lea & Febiger; 1993;2:1515–1551.

6. Folsom AR. Epidemiology of fibrinogen. *Eur Heart J*. 1995;16(suppl A):21–24.

7. Wilson TW, Kaplan GA, Kauhanen J, Cohen RD, et al. Association between plasma fibrinogen concentration and five socioeconomic indices in the Kuopio Ischemic Heart Disease Risk Factor Study. *Am J Epidemiol*. 1993;137:292–300.

8. Meade TW, North WRS. Population-based distributions of haemostatic variables. *Br Med Bull*. 1977; 33:283–288.

9. Iso H, Folsom AR, Wu KK, Finch A, et al. Hemostatic variables in Japanese and Caucasian men. *Am J Epidemiol*. 1989;130:925–934.

10. Meilahn EN, Kuller HL, Matthews KA, Kiss JE. Hemostatic factors according to menopausal status and use of hormone replacement therapy. *Ann Epidemiol*. 1992;2:445–455.

11. Nabulsi AA, Folsom AR, White A, Patsch W, et al, for the Atherosclerosis Risk in Communities Study Investigators. Association of hormone-replacement therapy with various cardiovascular risk factors in postmenopausal women. *N Engl J Med*. 1993;328:1069–1075.

12. Fernandez-Ortiz A, Fuster V. The role of thrombosis in acute coronary heart disease. In: Willich SN, Muller JE, eds. *Triggering of Acute Coronary Syndromes*. Dordrecht, the Netherlands: Kluwer Academic Publishers; 1996: 201–218.

13. Meade TW, Brozovic M, Chakrabarti RR, Haines AP, et al. Haemostatic function and ischaemic heart disease: principal results of the Northwick Park Heart Study. *Lancet*. 1986;2:533–537.

14. Ernst E, Resch KL. Fibrinogen as a cardiovascular risk factor: a meta-analysis and review of the literature. *Ann Intern Med*. 1993;118:956–963.

15. Folsom AR, Wu KK, Rosamond WD, Sharrett AR, et al. Prospective study of hemostatic factors and incidence of coronary heart disease: the Atherosclerosis Risk in Communities (ARIC) Study. *Circ*. 1997;96: 1102–1108.

16. Ridker PM, Vaughan DE, Stampfer MJ, Manson JE, et al. Endogenous tissue-type plasminogen activator and risk of myocardial infarction. *Lancet*. 1993;341:1165–1168.

17. Ridker PM, Hennekens CH, Stampfer MJ, Manson JE, et al. Prospective study of endogenous tissue plasminogen activator and risk of stroke. *Lancet*. 1994; 343:940–943.

18. Antiplatelet Trialists' Collaboration. Collaborative overview of randomised trials of antiplatelet therapy I: prevention of death, myocardial infarction, and stroke by prolonged antiplatelet therapy in various categories of patients. *Br Med J*. 1994;308:81–106.

19. Herlitz J. Fibrinolytic treatment in acute myocardial infarction: benefits and risks. In: *Workshop: Thrombolytic Therapy in Myocardial Infarction*. Oslo, Norway: Medical Products Agency, The Norwegian Medicines Control Authority; 1994: 49–59.

20. The National Institute of Neurological Disorders and Stroke rt-PA Stroke Study Group. Tissue plasminogen activator for acute ischemic stroke. *N Engl J Med*. 1995;333:1581–1587.

21. Pearson TA, LaCava J, Weil HC. Epidemiology of thrombotic/hemostatic factors and their associations with cardiovascular disease. *Am J Clin Nutr*. In press.

22. Goff DC, Nichaman MZ, Ramsey DJ, Meyer PS, et al. A population-based assessment of the use and effectiveness of thrombolytic therapy: the Corpus Christi Heart Project. *Ann Epidemiol*. 1995;5:171–178.

23. European Secondary Prevention Study Group. Translation of clinical trials into practice: a European population-based study of the use of thrombolysis for acute myocardial infarction. *Lancet*. 1996;347:1203–1207.

CHAPTER 17

Adverse Psychosocial Patterns

SUMMARY

Like metabolic or physiologic factors, psychosocial factors pose their particular challenges for research. For population studies, standardization of definitions, classification, and methods of observation and measurement is essential for comparability across studies and for consistent interpretation of results. These qualities have been difficult to achieve in connection with many of the concepts investigated in the area of psychosocial factors. Nonetheless, much of the work to date in this area supports the general theoretical view that socially conditioned stimuli have psychological effects and, through these, neurohumoral effects that may increase (or decrease) susceptibility to disease, both generally and specifically. Three areas most extensively or recently investigated are Type A behavior pattern, occupational stress, and social support. The concepts underlying these areas of research and some of the results of particular studies are discussed as illustrations of this area of research as a whole. Many observations support the general theory as it applies to cardiovascular diseases, but others do not, and their synthesis is difficult owing to the wide diversity of concepts and methods employed. Recent literature lacks the far-reaching and integrative character of some provocative papers of two decades or more ago and tends to reflect a greater concentration on methodologic issues or branching into new concepts. Reconsideration of earlier work and development of new approaches to investigation may result in new advances in an area that is at least as important currently as when an upsurgence of such research occurred in the 1970s.

INTRODUCTION

Distinctions among Types of Personal Characteristics

A qualitative distinction between the topic of this chapter and the preceding chapters is its focus on those personal characteristics that are primarily psychological rather than metabolic or physiological in nature. Consequently the phenomena addressed here pose distinct—not to imply greater—issues of conceptualization, definition, measurement, and interpretation as they have been investigated in epidemiology. At the same time, these psychosocial patterns share with factors discussed earlier the property of the personal, or individual, level of correspondence. For this reason a further distinction is made between this topic and "social conditions" (Chapter 19), such as socioeconomic status and socially determined conditions of early life, which may be considered primarily population-level phenomena. Although these distinctions are useful to emphasize the uniqueness of each of these groups of factors, they are not absolute. In fact it is the many established or hypothetical connections among the factors addressed throughout Part II that underlie the importance of these factors for understanding the causation of atherosclerotic and hypertensive diseases and implementing strategies for their prevention.

The term *adverse psychosocial patterns* is intended to encompass the broad array of psychological factors, stress, behavior patterns, and other like phenomena that may, under specific conditions, affect adversely the risks of atherosclerotic and hypertensive diseases. Specifically addressed here are the Type A behavior pattern, occupational stress, and lack of social support, whereas other conditions are noted only briefly. The concepts of these and related factors, including social conditions, were reviewed recently by Theorell, who noted the multidisciplinary character of research in this area, which involves epidemiology and social science, psychology and behavioral science, and medicine.[1]

The Theoretical Background of the Recent Past

Much of the literature from a period of especially active development in this area, the 1960s and 1970s, addresses the difficulties of conceptualization of ideas, formulation of hypotheses, and operationalization of research in this area, in part due to the necessity of communication across these several disciplines. For example, in 1974 Cassel presented a theoretical formulation for research on psychosocial processes and stress, noting common misinterpretation by epidemiologists and others of the original medical concept of stress expressed by Selye and Wolff—that of a bodily state and not a component of the environment.[2] A consequence of this misunderstanding was to misconceive of stress by analogy to a microorganism as an external agent of disease, resulting in inappropriate expectations of both specificity and dose-response relations between exposure to stress and occurrence of disease.

The argument was advanced, to the contrary, that psychosocial processes or stressors should be expected to modify susceptibility to disease risks more generally, through the well-supported mechanism of their effects on neuroendocrine balance. The cultural dependence of these effects was also emphasized to indicate that not only individuals but different social groups might differ in their characteristic responses to particular external psychological stimuli. Finally, it was proposed that both potentially beneficial and adverse effects of psychosocial processes should be recognized. Interventions to prevent disease might thus focus on strengthening the beneficial psychosocial influences, thereby reducing the influence of other adverse factors. This view contributes to the idea that attention to the whole pattern of psychosocial influences, rather than to isolated components, may be necessary for the most fruitful observations and conclusions in this area of research. The analogies with dietary patterns, addressed previously, are readily apparent.

Application of these concepts to coronary heart disease led one observer in the late 1970s to consider those aspects of social stress that might contribute to the marked differences in disease rates between the United States and Japan.[3] The many features of Japanese life that seemed clearly to imply stress appeared to be balanced by many other institutionalized provisions for relief of stress, suggesting the hypothesis that stress actually contributes less to coronary heart disease risks in Japan than in the United States and offering a partial explanation of the population differences in coronary mortality.

A Conceptual Scheme for Stress Research

The concept of competing or balancing influences was incorporated more explicitly by House in the schematic representation of stress research shown in Figure 17–1.[4] Stress is understood here as a subjective phenomenon, perhaps less clearly a "bodily state" than in the view of

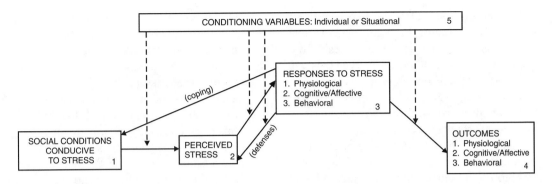

Figure 17–1 A Paradigm of Stress Research. Solid arrows between boxes indicate presumed causal relationships among variables. Dotted arrows from the box labeled "Conditioning Variables" intersect solid arrows, indicating an interaction between the conditioning variables and the variables in the box at the beginning of the solid arrow in predicting variables in the box at the head of the solid arrow. *Source*: Reprinted with permission from J House, A Paradigm of Stress Research, *Journal of Health and Social Behavior*, p 13, © American Sociological Association.

Selye, Wolff, and Cassel. Although House's context was occupational stress, the figure is applicable more broadly to encompass each of the psychosocial patterns addressed here. Outcomes such as coronary events are determined by responses to stress at physiological, cognitive, and behavioral levels, as influenced by unspecified conditioning variables, which might include diet, physical activity, and all other relevant factors. Response to stress requires that stress be perceived as such; this perception then leads to potentially counterbalancing defenses; and this interaction between stress and defenses is then in turn subject to the effects of conditioning variables. The qualification that the latter may be either individual or situational points to important sources of variability in response to perceived stress. The perception of stress arises from the interaction of "particular objective social conditions and particular personal characteristics"[4(p 14)] in a process influenced by both extrinsic conditioning variables and by coping responses once stress has been perceived. Significant elements of this scheme are the concept of counterbalancing mechanisms within the pathway from conducive social situations to disease outcomes and the dependence of steps in the pathway and overall outcome on

the role of other, conditioning variables, both individual and situational.

Jenkins, in a concluding essay for the National Workshop Conference on Socioenvironmental Stress and Cardiovascular Disease, included health-related behaviors such as diet, physical activity, and smoking among the consequences of socioenvironmental stresses, together with "those [stimuli] that repeatedly arouse the autonomic nervous system."[5(p 149)] He noted the importance of interpretation of these stresses, which interposes individual variation between these stresses and their potential effects. He also implied that such stresses need not be conscious, as they may operate even if psychological defenses prevent their conscious perception. These considerations would broaden the scheme in Figure 17–1 and offer a more comprehensive view of the potential pathways of adverse psychosocial patterns.

Favorable Behavioral Patterns

In the area of health-promoting behavior and adherence to preventive or therapeutic programs, adverse psychosocial patterns may be considered influential for causation of atherosclerotic and hypertensive diseases or for limiting the effectiveness of preventive measures.[6] Conversely, favorable behavior patterns that occur spontaneously or as a result of health education, counseling, or other interventions are expected to reduce risks and to reinforce preventive strategies by favorable effects on patterns of diet, physical activity, medication adherence, and other such behaviors.

Against this background, three of the more prominently investigated aspects of psychosocial profile and related conditions are reviewed here: Type A behavior pattern, occupational stress, and social support.

TYPE A BEHAVIOR PATTERN AND RELATED CHARACTERISTICS

Development of the Type A Behavior Pattern Concept

In 1959, Friedman and Rosenman reported that they had identified an "overt behavior pattern" that their results suggested was largely responsible for the marked increase in frequency of coronary heart disease found in one of three groups of men studied.[7] In a preliminary study, they surveyed more than 200 business executives and physicians and asked them their opinions about major causes of coronary heart disease. They found "chronic exposure to emotional trauma" to be a dominant theme in the responses, the trauma being attributed to conditions such as competitiveness, consciousness of deadlines, and related characteristics. The concept that this set of conditions might cause coronary heart disease led to a further study in which they examined a group of accountants before, during, and after occasions of such trauma, and they found them to exhibit acute increases in blood cholesterol concentration and blood coagulability during the exposure period.

On the basis of these two studies, the investigators then defined three categories of overt behavior pattern, designated patterns A, B, and C, in which pattern A incorporated the following characteristics:

(1) an intense, sustained drive to achieve self-selected but usually poorly defined goals, (2) profound inclination and eagerness to compete, (3) persistent desire for recognition and advancement, (4) continuous involvement in multiple and diverse functions constantly subject to time restrictions (deadlines), (5) habitual propensity to accelerate the rate of execution of many physical and mental functions, and (6) extraordinary mental and physical alertness.[7(p 1286)]

Pattern B was defined as lacking all features of pattern A, and pattern C differed from pattern B only in being accompanied by chronic anxiety.

Initial Results

To test the prediction that men exhibiting pattern A would have a greater tendency to manifest coronary heart disease and some of its risks, Friedman and Rosenman used nonmedical volunteers to recruit groups of men who conformed to these respective patterns.[7] They interviewed the men to document the degree to which they exhibited the patterns and examined them with respect to clinical evidence of coronary heart disease (by history and electrocardiography) and other characteristics. Men in groups A and B were categorized as exhibiting a "completely" or "incompletely" developed pattern on the basis of the interviews. The frequencies of clinical coronary heart disease in the five groups were as follows: A (complete), 34%; A (incomplete), 28%; B (complete), 0%; B (incomplete), 4%; and C, 4%. Although the study had many limitations, what came to be termed *Type A* was not long in becoming a household expression.

The Western Collaborative Group Study

Of the many studies of Type A behavior that followed, the most direct follow-up to the initial investigation was the Western Collaborative Group Study (WCGS), organized by Rosenman and Friedman with participation of 10 California companies.[8] From 1960 to 1961 the WCGS enrolled 3154 healthy men age 39–59 years at entry. In this study, a structured interview was used for classification of each participant as Type A or B, each completely or incompletely developed, or neither Type A nor B. The few "indeterminate" individuals were grouped separately.

The main results were reported after 8.5 years of follow-up. The overall frequencies of new events by age at entry were, for the age group 39–49 years, 95/1067 (8.9%) in Type A and 50/1182 (4.2%) in Type B and, for the age group 50–59 years, 83/522 (15.9%) in Type A and 29/383 (7.6%) in Type B (no confidence limits were reported). The relation of behavior pattern and other risk factors to the incidence of coronary heart disease in multivariate analysis indicated significant associations with age, smoking, systolic blood pressure, total cholesterol concentration, and behavior pattern for men in the age group 39–49 years and for the same factors except age and systolic blood pressure for the older group. The estimated relative risks for Type A behavior pattern after adjustment for other factors were 1.87 and 2.16 in the two age groups, calculated from the logistic coefficients in Table 17–1, or an increase of 1.37 and 1.46 per standard deviation unit of the two-point score from B = 0 to A = 1. The investigators interpreted the results as indicating direct effects of Type A behavior pattern, perhaps through neurohumoral pathways, in addition to any effect through the other risk factors.

Modification of Type A Behavior Pattern

In subsequent studies, intervention to alter Type A behavior was undertaken among 862 men who previously experienced myocardial infarction.[9] One group of 592 patients received group counseling concerning Type A behavior in addition to cardiology counseling, while 270 patients received only cardiology counseling.

Intervention for Type A behavior included muscle relaxation techniques, behavioral training to recognize and modify Type A manifestations, environmental changes, and changes in values and goals. After three years of study, Friedman and colleagues reported net reduction in scores for Type A behavior that were greater in the intervention than in the control group by each of several measures used, thus supporting the view that Type A behavior could be modified. Survival analysis indicated greater duration of follow-up time free of recurrent myocardial infarction or death in the intervention group, as shown in Figure 17–2. Analysis of the groups as randomly allocated, irrespective of treatment adherence, indicated recurrence rates of 7.2% versus 13.2% in treated versus control men ($P<0.005$).

Extended Follow-Up of Cases in the WCGS

However, subsequent study of the relation of Type A behavior to recurrent coronary heart disease added to some of the inconsistencies in the accumulating observations. Prospective assessment of the association of Type A behavior with risk of coronary heart disease was undertaken in the setting of the Multiple Risk Factor Intervention Trial, and no increase in risk was found in men classified as Type A.[10] In a study designed to investigate further the experience of the WCGS, 257 men who had experienced coronary events in the initial 8.5 years of follow-up were evaluated in greater detail to determine the relation of Type A behavior to mortality from coronary events.[11] Of the 257 men, 135 had symptomatic acute myocardial infarction or sudden death as the initial manifestation. Of these, 18 of 93 Type A men (19.4%) and 8 of 42 Type B men (19.0%) died within 24 hours, indicating no relation between Type A and 24-hour mortality. Of 231 men who survived the first 24 hours, subsequent mortality was 19.1% for Type A men and 31.7% for Type B men ($P=0.04$). Figure 17–3 demonstrates this result as the cumulative proportion dying of coronary heart disease through a total of 22 years of fol-

Table 17–1 Multiple Logistic Coefficients for Reduced Set of Risk Factors for Coronary Heart Disease in 8.5 Years

	Logistic Coefficient	Standard Deviation of Risk Factor	Standardized Relative Risk[a]	Significance Probability (P=)
Men Aged 39–49 Years				
Intercept	−11.747	...	...	...
Cholesterol	0.010	43.123	1.57	<0.001
Behavior pattern	0.628	0.497	1.37	<0.001
Cigarette smoking	0.223	1.244	1.32	0.001
Age	0.079	3.079	1.28	0.006
Systolic blood pressure	0.017	14.155	1.27	0.003
Corneal arcus	0.458	0.434	1.22	0.014
Parental coronary heart disease	0.356	0.386	1.15	0.084
Schooling	−0.146	0.930	0.87 (1.15)[b]	0.142
Beta/alpha lipoprotein ratio	0.112	1.046	1.12	0.157
Men Aged 50–59 Years				
Intercept	−11.790	...	...	...
Behavior pattern	0.774	0.491	1.46	0.001
Cigarette smoking	0.285	1.222	1.42	<0.001
Systolic BP	0.020	16.544	1.40	<0.001
Cholesterol	0.008	41.429	1.40	0.001
Schooling	−0.214	0.907	0.82 (1.22)	0.085
Body mass index	0.071	2.515	1.20	0.082
Exercise habits	−0.348	0.450	0.86 (1.16)	0.182
Age	0.053	2.721	1.16	0.169

a. The approximate relative risk (odds ratio) for a change in the risk factor by an amount equal to its standard deviation.

b. Reciprocals of standardized relative risks less than 1 are provided for comparison with relative risks greater than 1.

Source: Reprinted by permission of the publisher from RH Rosenman et al, *American Journal of Cardiology*, Vol 37, pp 903–910. Copyright 1976 by Excerpta Medica, Inc.

low-up. This result indicated that men with coronary heart disease and Type A behavior experienced a *decreased* risk of death from coronary heart disease.

Hostility and Anger

Because some doubt has remained about whether the Type A behavior pattern correctly identified those at increased risk in diverse populations, attention has focused on aspects of behavior thought to be subsumed within this pattern but not detected with sufficient specificity by the overall Type A construct. Other psychological profiles also suggested that the element of hostility or anger was associated with coronary heart disease risk and could be the specific component of interest. Accordingly, increasing emphasis has been placed on this aspect. For example, a group of 255 physicians was followed for 25 years after questionnaire assessment of health characteristics through the Minnesota Multiphasic Personality Inventory (MMPI), which includes items on hostility.[12]

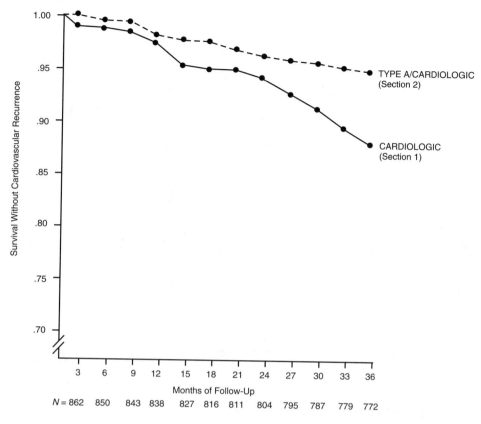

Figure 17–2 Cumulative Recurrence-Free Survival Curves for Trial of Reduction of Type A Behavior Score Employing the "Intention-to-Treat" Principle. *N* indicates the total number of participants followed at the beginning of each time point. A participant is censored (ie, removed from further calculations) upon cardiovascular recurrence or inability to trace. The section 2 curve is significantly different from that of section 1 (chi-square = 7.8, *P*<0.01). *Source*: Reprinted with permission from M Friedman et al, *American Heart Journal*, Vol 108, p 244, © 1984, Mosby-Year Book, Inc.

When the group was divided at the median score, it was found that respondents in the upper half for hostility experienced coronary events at the rate of 4.5/1000 person-years, whereas those in the lower half had a rate of 0.9/1000 (*P*<0.0005). The timeline of differential incidence is shown in Figure 17–4.

Still more recently, a study to investigate precipitating factors for acute coronary events has demonstrated a triggering effect of episodes of anger within two hours of onset of myocardial infarction.[13] The study design for evaluating triggering events was innovative and depended on comparison, within the experience of each case, of such events during the time period immediately preceding the event with the circumstances of the corresponding time period on the preceding day and also with the usual frequency of the events or conditions of interest over the year prior to the event. The estimated relative risk of myocardial infarction within two hours of an episode of anger among 39 patients, according to a scale devised for this study, was 2.3 (confidence interval [CI] 1.7–3.2). There are sufficient reports in the literature concerning anger and its physiological effects to make this finding plausible, and its replication will likely be pursued in future studies.

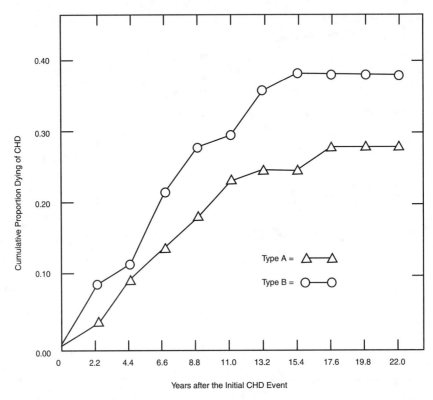

Figure 17–3 Cumulative Case Fatality Rates among 231 Patients with Coronary Heart Disease (CHD) Who Survived for 24 Hours, by Behavior Pattern. *Source*: Reprinted with permission from DR Ragland and RJ Brand, Type A Behavior and Mortality from Coronary Heart Disease, *The New England Journal of Medicine*, Vol 318, pp 65–69, © 1988, The Massachusetts Medical Society. All rights reserved.

Studies in Adolescents

All the foregoing observations were based on coronary events among adults. However, relations between Type A behavior pattern, hostility, and anger and their suppression or expression have been studied in children and adolescents as well for their possible relation to known risk factors for atherosclerosis. Much of this literature was reviewed recently, indicating inconsistent results.[14] This reflects in part the different instruments used and lack of ancillary data needed to compare and interpret studies adequately.

The experience through the middle to late 1970s with the Type A behavior pattern, the self-administered Jenkins Activity Survey (JAS) devised to identify some key components

of Type A, and other studies in this area were reviewed extensively by Jenkins and in the report of a Forum on Coronary-Prone Behavior.[15–17] These reviews identified many of the issues in this area of research prior to its more recent focus on component factors such as hostility and anger and methodologic aspects of these studies.

OCCUPATIONAL STRESS

Concepts of Occupational Stress and Job Strain

Conditions of work affect employed persons during a significant portion of their lives and could, if they influence health adversely, be

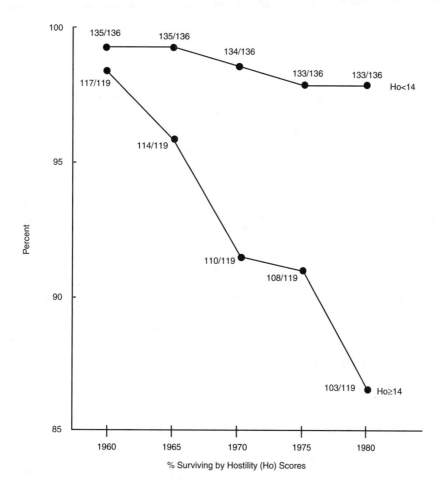

Figure 17–4 Differential Survival Rates at Five-Year Intervals by Hostility (Ho) Scores Above and Below the Median. *Source*: Reprinted with permission from *Physchosomatic Medicine*, Vol 45, pp 59–63, © 1983, Williams & Wilkins.

expected to be associated with coronary heart disease risks or other commonly occurring health problems. This area has received attention for several decades and was reviewed recently by Theorell, a major contributor to the field.[1] Concepts now common to discussions in this area include demand, control, decision latitude, and others. These aspects of the work situation are traceable in part to the work of Alfredsson and colleagues, whose conceptual scheme representing these phenomena is shown in Figure 17–5.[18]

Studies of Job Strain and Iso-Strain

The two dimensions underlying the concept of occupational stress are demand and control, with the potential for occupational and personal advancement as an additional feature. Attention focuses chiefly on the conjunction of high demand and low control, identified as "strain." In this case-comparison study of Swedish men under age 65, occupational data for 334 cases of fatal and nonfatal myocardial infarction and 882 controls were analyzed.[18] The occupations of

Control and possibility for growth and
development high

Relaxed	Active
Passive	Strain

Demands low   Demands high

Control and possibility for growth and
development low

Figure 17–5 Conceptual Scheme for "Job Strain." *Source*: Reprinted from *Social Science & Medicine*, Vol 16, L Alfredsson, R Karasek, and T Theorell, p 465. Copyright 1982, with kind permission from Elsevier Science, Ltd, The Boulevard, Lanford Lane, Kidlington 0X5 1GB, UK.

the men were classified by their psychological characteristics on the basis of a national survey among workers in those occupations. For young men, below age 50, the dual characteristic of "hectic" work and lack of control over the tempo of work (ie, strain) resulted in approximately a twofold risk of myocardial infarction, though details of the analysis were not provided.

The relation of job strain to prevalence of indicators of previous myocardial infarction was studied in data from two US national health surveys conducted in 1960–1962 and 1971–1975.[19] In this study, jobs characterized as having job strain were associated with substantially greater prevalence of myocardial infarction, as shown in Figure 17–6. Relative risk estimates for job strain as assigned to the reported occupations were 3.8 and 4.8 in the highest versus the lowest decile of the scale in the two respective surveys, similar to the relative risks found for smoking and cholesterol concentrations. Despite the limitations of cross-sectional investigation for interpretation of these results, implications were raised for the organization of the work environment and decision-making powers of workers. There has been some speculation about the potential impact on the long-term health of workers in many occupations were these issues to be addressed from perspectives of both health and productivity.

Prospective data are also available, as illustrated by a Swedish study of 7219 working men with nine years' follow-up.[20] Cardiovascular diseases, including coronary heart disease, stroke, and peripheral vascular disease, accounted for 193 deaths over this period. Workers were classified according to an index of job demands and control and also social support. This composite index was termed *iso-strain* to reflect both social isolation at work and job strain, as previously defined. Figure 17–7 indicates, for blue-collar workers, the probability of cardiovascular death in nine years for three strata of the population, those with high, intermediate, and low iso-strain. The lowest probability, for all age groups according to the model, was for those with least isolation and job strain, whereas the intermediate and highest groups were similar in their high probabilities of cardiovascular death. For white-collar workers, similar curves were presented, though at lower probabilities of mortality at all ages. Future studies were proposed in which social class would be taken more fully into account to investigate the different contributions to iso-strain at different social and occupational levels.

Additional information on established risk factors is needed for adequate interpretation of these relationships between group characteristics of circumstances of work and disease. The

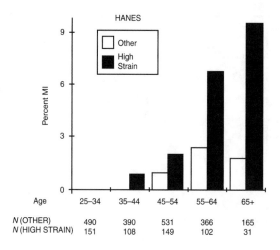

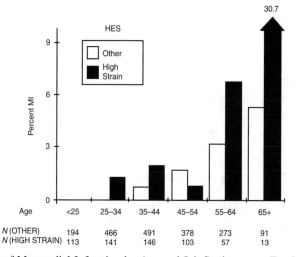

Figure 17–6 Prevalence of Myocardial Infarction by Age and Job Strain among Employed Males, US Health and Nutrition Examination Survey and Health Examination Survey. *Source*: From *Chronic Disease Epidemiology and Control*. Copyright 1993 by the American Public Health Association. Reprinted with permission.

extent to which conditions other than cardiovascular disease are related to occupational stress and related characteristics of the work environment would also be of interest.

SOCIAL SUPPORT

Concepts and Definitions

Several concepts of interpersonal relationships and their effects on health are linked with the term *social support*. A decade ago, Berkman emphasized the distinction between social networks and social support, with the admonition that an individual's identification with a social network should not be presumed to constitute social support.[21] It was therefore considered important to recognize and assess several dimensions of both.

Social networks were defined as "the web of social ties that surrounds an individual,"[21(p 414)] which had the following structural dimensions: density and complexity, that is, measures of interaction within the group; group size; sym-

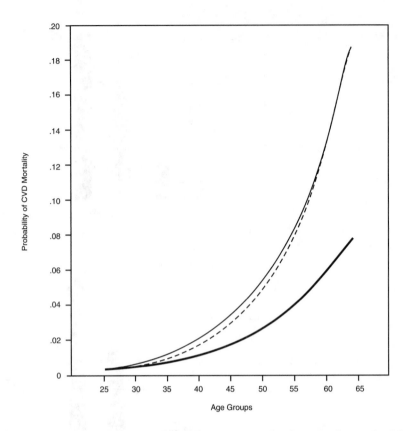

Figure 17–7 Logistic Estimates of Age Trends in Nine-Year Mortality from Cardiovascular Disease (CVD) Within a Random Sample of Blue-Collar Working Men in Sweden (N = 4,235) by Low (———), Medium (---), and High (———) Levels of Iso-Strain (ie, Combination of Social Isolation and Job Strain). *Source*: Reprinted with permission from JV Johnson, EM Hall, and T Theorell, *Scandinavian Journal of Work and Environmental Health*, Vol 15, p 276, © 1989, University of Massachusetts, Lowell.

metry or reciprocity, defined as equality of supports and obligations among members; geographic proximity or dispersion; homogeneity, assessed with respect to age, social class, and religion; and accessibility.

Social support, in turn, was defined as "the emotional, instrumental, and financial aid that is obtained from one's social network."[21(p 415)] The difficulty of separating objective, external measures of support from the subjective, psychological states of emotion makes this definition problematic. A more detached concept of social support, attributed to House, involves "a transaction of (a) emotional concern, (b) instrumental aid (goods and services), (c) information, or

(d) appraisal (information relevant to self-evaluation)."[21(p 415)]

Methodologic aspects of research in this area were discussed in Berkman's review, including matters of definition and measurement. Several studies of social networks, social support, and physical health were also summarized, with the general criticism that measurement of either social networks or social support was inadequate in most or all of them.

Results of Recent Studies

House and colleagues reviewed social support under a perhaps broader concept, "social relationships," using a scale of "level of social integration" (both undefined).[22] The review cited the seminal contributions of Cassel and of Cobb, who separately had assembled prior work on stress and psychosocial factors as studied both in human and in animal experiments up to the mid-1970s, leading them to formulate theoretical frameworks for future research. Several studies published after the Berkman review were summarized (Figures 17–8 and 17–9). All were prospective studies of mortality, and populations in Finland and Sweden, as well as both Blacks and Whites in the United States, were represented. In each study population, though at different levels of mortality, higher mortality was associated with low levels of social integration. Relative risks of lowest versus highest categories ranged, for men, from 1.08 in Evans County, Georgia, Blacks to 4.00 in Gothenburg, Sweden, and, for women, from 1.07 in Evans County Whites to 2.81 in Alameda County, California (confidence limits were not reported).

Also, the report briefly discussed conclusions from animal experiments and human clinical studies that suggested potential neuroendocrine pathways to link psychosocial phenomena with physiologic responses having adverse health effects.

In the view of House and colleagues, "The evidence on social relationships is probably stronger, especially in terms of prospective studies, than the evidence which led to the certification of the Type A behavior pattern as a risk factor for coronary heart disease. The evidence regarding social relationships and health increasingly approximates the evidence in the 1964 Surgeon General's report that established cigarette smoking as a cause or risk factor for morbidity and mortality from a range of diseases."[22(p 543)] The report noted the need for research in three areas: determinants of "exposure" to social relationships, mechanisms linking such exposures with health, and means of intervention against "relative social isolation."

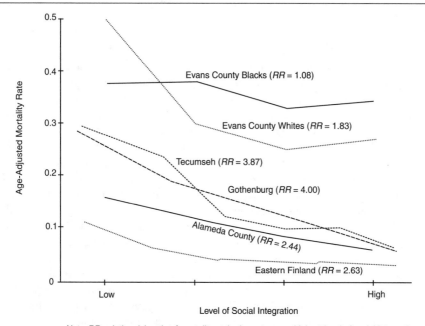

Note: *RR*, relative risk ratio of mortality at the lowest versus highest level of social integration.

Figure 17–8 Level of Social Integration and Age-Adjusted Mortality for Males in Five Prospective Studies. *Source*: Reprinted with permission from JS House, KR Lands, and D Umberson, Social Relationships and Health, *Science*, Vol 241, p 540, copyright 1988, American Association for the Advancement of Science.

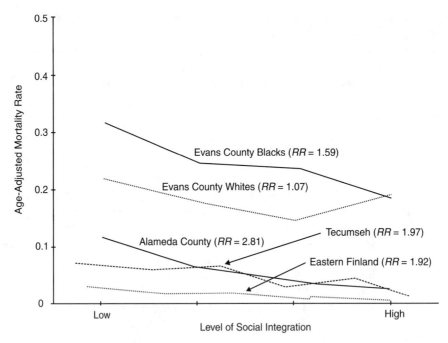

Note: RR, relative risk ratio of mortality at the lowest versus highest level of social integration.

Figure 17–9 Level of Social Integration and Age-Adjusted Mortality for Females in Five Prospective Studies. *Source*: Reprinted with permission from JS House, KR Lands, and D Umberson, Social Relationships and Health, *Science*, Vol 241, p 543, copyright 1988, American Association for the Advancement of Science.

House and colleagues presented prospective studies only, because these provided direct evidence of time sequence between social circumstances and the health outcomes assessed. However, work by Reed and colleagues in the Honolulu Heart Program, also prospective, resulted in different conclusions.[23] Among 4251 men of Japanese ancestry classified according to a variety of psychosocial characteristics in 1971, seven-year incidence of all diseases combined was unrelated to social networks, and persons in the highest categories of mobility and status inconsistency evidenced no lesser health outcomes in the presence of social networks. Only coronary heart disease incidence, interestingly, was associated with the social network scale, the rates ranging in a consistent gradient from 45/1000 men over the seven years in the lowest to 30/1000 in the highest category ($P<0.05$). After multivariate analysis to take known risk factors into account, this association was no longer significant, except marginally so for nonfatal myocardial infarction alone. Whether this suggests confounding of the association by other risk factors or operation of social network effects through those risk factors is unresolved. Reed and colleagues concluded that their measures of social networks did not indicate an effect on general susceptibility to illness. They noted, however, that cultural differences among particular groups should perhaps be expected to yield inconsistent findings and offered several suggestions for strengthening epidemiologic research in this area.

Such cultural specificity as may differentiate Japanese men in Hawaii from other groups studied previously was investigated within a single, bi-ethnic community, Corpus Christi, Texas, as reported more recently.[24] Farmer and colleagues devised a social support scale based on data previously collected in hospital interviews of persons admitted with acute myocar-

Table 17–2 Low Social Support and Other Factors and Relative Risk of Death in 55 Months after Initial Survival of Hospitalized Myocardial Infarction in Mexican Americans

Variable	RR	95% CI
Low social support	3.38	1.73–6.62
>60 years of age	1.73	1.19–2.51
Employed vs unemployed	0.38	0.15–0.92
Smoker vs nonsmoker	1.50	0.86–2.61
Diagnosed		
Diabetes mellitus	1.98	1.10–3.25
Hypertension	0.40	0.23–0.70

Note: The relative risk and 95% confidence interval were calculated after excluding from the regression model the variables that were not statistically significant. RR, relative risk; CI, confidence interval.

Source: *Behavioral Medicine*, Vol 22, pp 59–66, 1996. Reprinted with permission of the Helen Dwight Reid Educational Foundation. Published by Heldref Publications, 1319 Eighteenth St, NW, Washington, DC 20036-1802. Copyright © 1996.

dial infarction. The available items were related to marital status, solitary living conditions, and history of advice from others to seek help in the course of the immediate illness. A scale was constructed with five levels, from low to high social support. Survival time by social support category was determined over 55 months of follow-up for 596 Mexican-American and non–Hispanic-White survivors of acute myocardial infarction, beginning after initial survival for the first 28 days from onset of symptoms. In the total study population, low social support was associated with lesser survival over most of the follow-up period, though by 55 months the groups had experienced similar mortality. Of particular interest was the finding of an ethnic group difference in the association between low social support and mortality, as shown in Tables 17–2 and 17–3. For Mexican Americans the relative risk of death in 55 months for those with low versus high social support was 3.38 (CI 1.73–6.62), whereas for non-Hispanic Whites

Table 17–3 Low Social Support and Other Factors and Relative Risk of Death in 55 Months after Initial Survival of Hospitalized Myocardial Infarction in Non-Hispanic Whites

Variable	RR	95% CI
Low social support	1.21	0.64–2.30
>60 years of age	2.30	1.43–3.70
Employed vs unemployed	0.59	0.29–1.23
Smoker vs nonsmoker	1.45	0.80–2.61
Diagnosed		
Diabetes mellitus	1.86	1.07–3.24
Hypertension	0.89	0.51–1.55

Note: The relative risk and 95% confidence interval were calculated after excluding from the regression model the variables that were not statistically significant. RR, relative risk; CI, confidence interval.

Source: *Behavioral Medicine*, Vol 22, pp 59–66, 1996. Reprinted with permission of the Helen Dwight Reid Educational Foundation. Published by Heldref Publications, 1319 Eighteenth St, NW, Washington, DC 20036-1802. Copyright © 1996.

the corresponding relative risk was 1.21 (CI 0.64–2.30). Thus the same measure of social support appeared to have quite different health implications between two ethnic groups in the same community, a finding that underscores the comments of Reed and colleagues.

Future Studies

Many of the issues in this area of research were addressed in detail in *Social Support and Health*, published in 1985.[25] More recent studies of coronary heart disease were reviewed in the mid-1990s.[26] The perspectives offered by these reviews support continued investigation in this area.

OTHER CHARACTERISTICS

A number of other psychosocial characteristics have been addressed in epidemiologic studies of cardiovascular diseases. Each contributes to the persisting view that health in general or cardiovascular health in particular reflects the influence of interpersonal relations and other psychosocial processes and the mechanisms that may link them with human physiology and pathology. These factors include stressful life events, depression, perception of illness, disparities in social status with one's spouse or other associates, discontinuities between current life situation and upbringing, marital and employment status, John Henryism (hard work and determination to overcome psychosocial stressors), and the stress of experiencing natural disasters, among others. The methodologic issues in research on these topics have much in common with those addressed in connection with Type A behavior pattern, occupational stress, and social support. Some of these are addressed in the review by Theorell cited earlier.[1]

CURRENT ISSUES

Challenges to Evaluation of Research to Date

The upsurgence of interest in psychosocial factors and cardiovascular diseases that characterized the 1960s and 1970s has been followed by a large number of studies on diverse yet often interrelated aspects of social interaction, psychology, and behavior. It is difficult to evaluate the status of this area of research, or even subtopics within it, in part because of the seeming elusiveness of standard definitions, classifications, and methods of observation and measurement. Perhaps the greatest success in these respects was with Type A behavior pattern, especially as formulated in the Jenkins Activity Survey, which was a self-administered questionnaire applicable in many studies of diverse populations. However, in this case as in many other instances, investigators have extracted differing subsets of items to address what may be more useful components, but comparability across studies is thereby lost. The current situation thus appears fragmented, suggesting that a higher value has been accorded to innovation than to integration.

Importance of Integration and Planning for Future Studies

It remains instructive to read such thoughtful essays as those of Cassel[2] and of others cited in Chapter 19. These provocative theoretical writings continue to reinforce the view that psychosocial factors must be relevant to human health and particularly to the chronic diseases long experienced by contemporary industrialized societies and now becoming established in many developing countries. If this is true generally, then it is presumably true for one of the major component chronic conditions, atherosclerotic and hypertensive diseases. And if this is true in turn, it is necessary to take this aspect into account to understand the causation and formulate the most effective strategies for the prevention of these diseases. It remains to be demonstrated whether anger and hostility, occupational strain, social isolation, or other aspects constitute the key adverse psychosocial patterns that answer the theoretical questions posed two decades or more ago. These questions may be at least as important currently as they were perceived to be at that time.

REFERENCES

1. Theorell T. The psycho-social environment, stress, and coronary heart disease. In: Marmot M, Elliott P, eds. *Coronary Heart Disease Epidemiology: From Aetiology to Public Health.* Oxford, England: Oxford University Press; 1992:256–273.

2. Cassel J. Psychosocial process and "stress": theoretical formulation. *Int J Health Serv.* 1974;4:471–482.

3. Matsumoto YS. Social stress and coronary heart disease in Japan. *Milbank Memorial Fund Quar Bull.* 1979;48:9–36.

4. House JS. Occupational stress and coronary heart disease: a review and theoretical integration. *J Health Soc Behav.* 1974;15:12–26.

5. Jenkins CD. Appraisal and implications for theoretical development. *Milbank Memorial Fund Quar Bull.* 1967;45:141–150.

6. Levine DM. Behavioral and psychosocial factors, processes, and strategies. In: Pearson TA, Criqui MH, Luepker RV, Oberman A, Winston M, eds. *Primer in Preventive Cardiology.* Dallas, Tex: American Heart Association; 1994: 217–226.

7. Friedman M, Rosenman RH. Association of specific overt behavior pattern with blood and cardiovascular findings. *JAMA.* 1959;169:1286–1296.

8. Rosenman RH, Brand RJ, Sholtz RI, Friedman M. Multivariate prediction of coronary heart disease during 8.5 year follow-up in the Western Collaborative Group Study. *Am J Cardiol.* 1976;37:903–910.

9. Friedman M, Thoresen CE, Powell LH, Ulmer D, et al. Alteration of Type A behavior and reduction in cardiac recurrences in postmyocardial infarction patients. *Am Heart J.* 1984;108:237–248.

10. Shekelle RB, Hulley SB, Neaton JD, Billings JH, et al, Multiple Risk Factor Intervention Trial Research Group. The MRFIT behavior pattern study, II: type A behavior and incidence of coronary heart disease. *Am J Epidemiol.* 1985;122:559–570.

11. Ragland DR, Brand RJ. Type A behavior and mortality from coronary heart disease. *N Engl J Med.* 1988;318:65–69.

12. Barefoot JC, Dahlstrom G, Williams RB Jr. Hostility, CHD incidence, and total mortality: a 25-year follow-up study of 255 physicians. *Psychosom Med.* 1983;45:59–63.

13. Mittleman MA, Maclure M, Sherwood JB, Mulry RP, et al. Triggering of acute myocadial infarction onset by episodes of anger. *Circ.* 1995;92:1720–1725.

14. Grunbaum J, Vernon SW, Clasen CM. The association between anger and hostility and risk factors for coronary heart disease in children and adolescents: a review. *Ann Behav Med.* In press.

15. Jenkins CD. Recent evidence supporting psychologic and social risk factors for coronary disease. (First of two parts.) *N Engl J Med.* 1976;294:987–994.

16. Jenkins CD. Recent evidence supporting psychological and social risk factors for coronary disease. (Second of two parts.) *N Engl J Med.* 1976;294:1033–1038.

17. Dembroski TM, Weiss SM, Shields JL, Haynes SG, Feinleib M, eds. *Coronary-Prone Behavior.* New York: Springer-Verlag; 1978.

18. Alfredsson L, Karasek R, Theorell T. Myocardial infarction risk and psychosocial work environment: an analysis of the male Swedish working force. *Soc Sci Med.* 1982;16:463–467.

19. Karasek RA, Theorell T, Schwartz JE, Schnall PL, et al. Job characteristics in relation to the prevalence of myocardial infarction in the US Health Examination Survey (HES) and the Health and Nutrition Examination Survey (HANES). *Am J Public Health.* 1988;78:910–918.

20. Johnson JV, Hall EM, Theorell T. Combined effects of job strain and social isolation on cardiovascular disease morbidity and mortality in a random sample of the Swedish male working population. *Scand J Work Environ Health.* 1989;15:271–279.

21. Berkman LF. Assessing the physical health effects of social networks and social support. *Ann Rev Public Health.* 1984;5:413–432.

22. House JS, Landis KR, Umberson D. Social relationships and health. *Science.* 1988;241:540–545.

23. Reed D, McGee D, Yano K. Psychosocial processes and general susceptibility to chronic disease. *Am J Epidemiol.* 1984;119:356–370.

24. Farmer IP, Meyer PS, Ramsey DJ, Goff DC, et al. Higher levels of social support predict greater survival following acute myocardial infarction: the Corpus Christi Heart Project. *Behav Med.* 1996;22:59–66.

25. Cohen S, Syme SL, eds. *Social Support and Health.* Orlando, Fla: Academic Press, Inc; 1985.

26. Eriksen W. The role of social support in the pathogenesis of coronary heart disease: a literature review. *Fam Prac.* 1994;11:201–209.

Other Personal Characteristics

SUMMARY

As early as 1981 a very methodical compilation listed 246 factors suggested by published reports to affect the risk of coronary heart disease. Many additional ones are of interest and are being investigated actively. Not all of these factors have been addressed in the preceding chapters. Several are identified here as "social conditions," meaning factors more or less clearly external to the individual, and these are reviewed as a distinct class in Chapter 19. There remain several personal factors or characteristics that warrant brief review based on current interest. Those selected among numerous candidates are the antioxidants and their countervailing pro-oxidants; homocysteine and its dietary antagonists; and factors identified with vascular biology and endothelial function. Each of these topics bears some similarity, at least potentially, to hemostatic dysfunction: In each case, deeper appreciation of possible cellular and molecular mechanisms, based on laboratory investigation, leads to new epidemiologic investigations such as describing relevant population distributions, measuring risks, and evaluating the potential for intervention or its impact if intervention is found to be feasible.

INTRODUCTION

Chapters 7 through 17 have not exhausted the list of personal characteristics investigated for their association with atherosclerotic and hypertensive diseases. Similarly, this chapter presents only selected factors and aspects of their investigation that can point to future directions in research and application of current knowledge. However, these additional factors, like those previously addressed, warrant attention because of the especially active interest they are currently receiving. Discussion of these other factors ensures inclusion of all the new and candidate risk factors for coronary heart disease identified in a recent review under auspices of the International Society and Federation of Cardiology.[1] These include pro- and antioxidants, homocysteinemia, and vascular and endothelial factors. Each is reviewed briefly with citations to the recent literature.

PRO- AND ANTIOXIDANTS

Background

Based on Steinberg and colleagues' review of laboratory investigations conducted over a 20-year period[2] and a workshop of the National Heart, Lung, and Blood Institute in 1991,[3] a metabolic mechanism has been proposed that strongly influences the behavior of the low-density lipoprotein (LDL) molecule and potentiates its role in atherogenesis. This process results in oxidatively modified (oxidized) LDL (O-LDL), which functions in four ways to promote athero-genesis, as shown schematically in Figure 18–1.[2] Arrow I indicates the effect of facilitating migration of monocytes from the circulation into the intima of the arterial wall, and arrow II points to inhibition of motility of these cells, limiting their out-migration. The joint effect is increased accumulation of monocytes and con-version of these to macrophages (scavenger cells) in the intima. Arrow III shows a greatly increased rate of production of "foam cells," due to both the increased number of macro-phages and the greatly increased propensity of O-LDL, over that of nonoxidized LDL, to enter these cells. A direct action of O-LDL, at arrow IV, is damage to endothelial cells, which results in loss of integrity of the endothelial layer and initiates a succession of adverse consequences, including localized platelet adhesion and pro-motion of thrombosis.

Antioxidants

The natural defenses against this process comprise a variety of biochemical competitors for free oxygen radicals and related forms of oxygen, shown at the far right side of the figure. They effectively prevent oxidation of LDL, as well as DNA and other molecules, thus protect-ing against atherosclerosis, cancer, and other disorders. These competitors are the antioxi-dants, described in Exhibit 18–1.[4] Several of them are familiar as vitamins or vitamin precur-sors and include substances related to both fat-

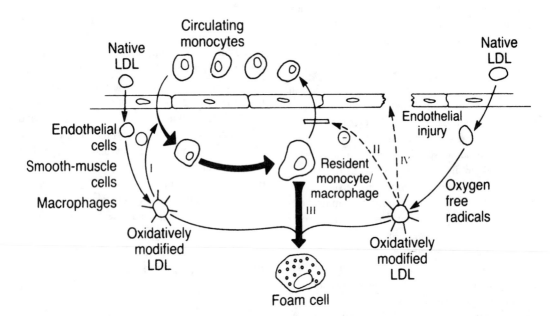

Figure 18–1 Four Mechanisms by Which the Oxidation of Low-Density Lipoprotein (LDL) May Contribute to Atherogenesis. Mechanisms are (I) the recruitment of circulating monocytes by means of the chemotactic factor present in oxidized LDL, but absent in native LDL; (II) inhibition by oxidized LDL of the motility of resident macrophages and therefore of their ability to leave the intima; (III) enhanced rate of uptake of oxidized LDL by resident macrophages, leading to the generation of foam cells; and (IV) cytotoxity of oxidized LDL, leading to loss of endothelial integrity. *Source*: Reprinted with permission from MT Quinn, S Parthasarathy, and D Stein-berg, Endothelial Cell-Derived Chemotactic Activity for Mouse Peritoneal Macrophages and the Effects of Modified Forms of Low Density Lipoprotein, *Proceedings of the National Academy of Sciences, USA*, Vol 82, pp 5949–5953, © 1985, National Academy Press.

Exhibit 18–1 The Nature of Selected Antioxidants

Type and Location of Antioxidants in Blood

Antioxidant	Tocopherols, β-carotene, lycopenes, coenzyme Q-10	Ascorbic acid, protein thiols, bilirubin, urate
Type	Fat-soluble	Water-soluble
Location	LDL particle, cell membrane	Blood plasma (extracellular fluid)

Proposed Mechanisms for Relationship of Antioxidants to Risk Factors for Heart Disease

	Vitamin Antioxidant	
	Tocopherols (Vitamin E), β-Carotene (Vitamin A)	*Ascorbic Acid (Vitamin C)*
Relationship to risk factors (epidemiological)	Smokers found to have lower carotene levels	Inverse relationship to blood pressure
	Smokers found to have more oxidized E in lungs	Direct relationship to HDL levels
		Lower levels in smokers
Hypothesized mechanism of action	Inhibits LDL oxidation[a]	Protects and restores parent vitamin E
	Suppresses LDL uptake by macrophages[a]	Inhibits LDL oxidation in vitro
	Reduces incidence of major coronary events[a,b]	Suppresses LDL uptake by macrophages
	Protects against oxidative damage during reperfusion[a]	Inhibits lipid peroxide formation

Note: HDL, high-density lipoprotein; LDL, low-density lipoprotein.

a. Vitamin E.

b. β-carotene.

Source: Reprinted with permission from *Nutrition Today*, Vol 27, pp 30–33, ©1992, Williams & Wilkins.

soluble vitamins (A and E) and the water-soluble vitamin C. These antioxidants have been the most closely studied epidemiologically. Various mechanisms of action are indicated by which one or another prevents production of O-LDL. As either vitamins or their precursors, these antioxidants are dietary constituents and as such might have been considered in Chapter 8, Dietary Imbalance. However, because they are available and commonly consumed as supplements to the diet, often in quantities many times greater than those provided in the usual diet, they are considered separately here. The distinction between dietary and supplementary intake

of the antioxidants is important to interpretation of evidence in both observational studies and trials, as noted below.

Population Comparisons

Population differences in plasma concentrations of vitamin E were investigated in relation to coronary heart disease mortality in a case-comparison study organized within the framework of the World Health Organization MONICA Project.[5] Men aged 40–49 were selected in 16 European centers of the Project, and plasma samples were processed to determine concentrations of vitamins A, C, and E; precursors of vitamin A (carotene and other carotenoids); and selenium. The population rates of ischemic heart disease were calculated as the mean value of the death rate over at least the three preceding years. Univariate correlations of vitamin concentrations with coronary mortality were substantially stronger for vitamin E than others ($r^2 = 0.62$, $P = 0.0003$), although inverse correlations were observed for α-tocopherol (precursor of vitamin E), retinol (precursor of vitamin A), and vitamin C. Significant regression coefficients for vitamin E were those in which the concentration of vitamin E was standardized for cholesterol and triglyceride concentrations. This observation was consistent with the view that the effect of vitamin E is dependent on its rela-

tion to the quantity of lipid in the circulation. The strongest predictive relation between plasma antioxidant levels and coronary mortality was found in a model that included vitamins E and A, cholesterol, and diastolic blood pressure. The mortality predicted from this model and actual mortality were closely related, as shown in Figure 18–2. This study thus suggested association between plasma concentration of vitamin E and coronary mortality as these varied across 16 European populations with an approximate fivefold range of mortality.

Cohort Studies

Cohort studies in large numbers of US health professionals indicated, for both women and

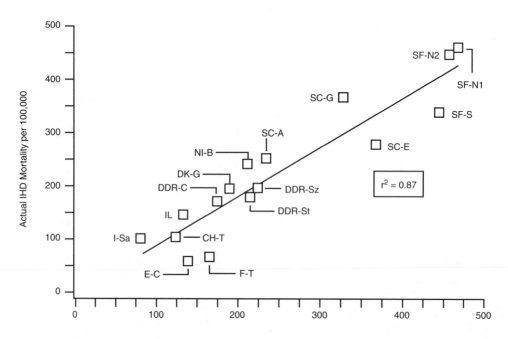

Note: CH-T, Switzerland, Thun; DDR-C, -St, and -Sz, German Democratic Republic, Cottbus, Schwedt, and Schleiz, respectively; DK-G, Denmark, Glostrup/Copenhagen; E-C, Spain, Catalonia; F, France, F-T, Toulouse/Haute Garonne; IL, Israel, Tel Aviv; I-Sa, Italy, Sapri; NI-B, Northern Ireland, semiurban Belfast; SC-A, -E, and -G, Scotland, Aberdeen, Edinburgh, and Glasgow, respectively; SF-N1, -N2, and -S, Finland rural North Karelia 1 (1983), rural/semiurban North Karelia 2 (1987), and rural Southwest Finland (1983), respectively.

Figure 18–2 Correlation Between Actual Age-Specific IHD Mortality in Middle-Aged Males of 16 Study Populations and the IHD Mortality as Predicted by Multiple-Regression Analysis with Four Variables. The variables are lipid-standardized vitamins E and A, total cholesterol, and diastolic blood pressure. *Source*: Reprinted with permission from KF Gey et al, *American Journal of Clinical Nutrition*, Vol 53 (Supp I), p 332S, 1991 © *Amer J Clin Nutr*, American Society for Clinical Nutrition.

men, association between use of vitamin E supplements and risk of coronary events, with relative risks of 0.59 (confidence interval [CI] 0.38–0.91) for women and 0.63 (CI 0.47–0.84) for men.[6,7] In neither group was dietary intake alone significantly related to coronary event rates. The analysis for men indicates the results separately for dietary and supplemental intake of vitamin E, as shown in Table 18–1.[7] Notable findings include the striking differences in intake between groups—ranging 1.6–6.9 to 11.1 or more International Units (IU) per day by diet and from 0 to 250 or more IU per day by supplements—and a weaker trend for supplements than for dietary intake, with the relative

risks of the highest quintile group very similar to those of the lowest group despite a 25-fold apparent difference in intake. The impression is inescapable that qualitative differences exist between dietary patterns associated with maximal intake and behaviors associated with maximal supplementation, and thus interpretation of the results is uncertain. A more recent cohort study report among more than 34,000 postmenopausal women indicated that reported dietary intake of vitamin E, but not of vitamin A, retinol, carotenoids, or vitamin C, was associated with lower coronary mortality (multivariate-adjusted relative risk, 0.38, CI 0.18–.080).[8] The dietary intakes appeared to be only slightly

Table 18–1 Relative Risks of Coronary Heart Disease by Category of Dietary or Supplemental Intake of Vitamin E

Variable	Quintile Group for Dietary Intake[a]					P Value for Trend
	1	2	3	4	5	
Dietary vitamin E (IU/d)	1.6–6.9	7.0–8.1	8.2–9.3	9.4–11.0	11.1	
Coronary disease— no. of cases	79	89	90	79	56	
No. of person-years	17,617	16,560	15,605	14,569	12,591	0.11
Relative risk[b]	1.0	1.10	1.17	0.97	0.79	
95% CI	—	0.80–1.51	0.84–1.62	0.69–1.37	0.54–1.15	
Supplemental vitamin E (IU/d)	0	<25	25–99	100–249	≥250	
Coronary disease— no. of cases	406	120	40	17	84	
No. of person-years	79,699	26,197	9,607	5,677	18,700	0.22[c]
Relative risk[b]	1.0	0.85	0.78	0.54	0.70	
95% CI	—	0.69–1.05	0.59–1.08	0.33–0.88	0.55–0.89	

Note: Relative risks for dietary vitamin E intake were calculated among nonusers of vitamin E supplements. There was a total of 393 cases of coronary heart disease after the exclusion of 17,916 men who reported current use of either multivitamins or vitamin E supplements in 1986. CI, confidence interval.

a. Quintiles of dietary vitamin E intake were derived from the entire cohort.

b. Relative risks were derived by multivariate logistic regression analysis.

c. Calculated after the exclusion of nonusers of supplements.

Source: Reprinted with permission from Rimm, Vitamin E Consumption and the Risk of Coronary Heart Disease in Men, *The New England Journal of Medicine*, Vol 328, pp 1450–1456, © 1993, The Massachusetts Medical Society. All rights reserved.

greater than in the health professional women described above.

According to other reports, vitamin C, flavonoids (another type of antioxidants found principally in tea), and metabolic products of sun-induced vitamin D all add to the menu of antioxidants apparently associated with reduced risk of coronary heart disease.

Clinical and Preventive Trials

Trials of antioxidant administration to prevent coronary events have been conducted with vitamin E (α-tocopherol) or with β-carotene, with or without vitamin A. The vitamin E trial among 2002 persons with angiographically confirmed coronary artery disease found significant reduction in nonfatal, but not fatal, coronary events over an average period of 510 days' follow-up.[9] The two trials in healthy participants showed no benefit, and one showed possible harm, with respect to coronary events.[10,11]

A summary of evidence from available studies, both observational and experimental, was reported by Jha and colleagues in 1995[12] and has been updated by Folsom (Aaron Folsom, personal communication, 1997). Studies of β-carotene, vitamin E, and vitamin C were reviewed as well as a newer series of three reports on dietary flavonoids, antioxidants identified in food sources such as tea, red wine, apples, beans, onions, and soy products. For β-carotene, vitamin E, and vitamin C, the observational study results were mixed but, on balance, favorable for lower coronary heart disease risk, whereas the trials showed no benefit of intervention. Stroke incidence was not generally affected in the results of the one study (in Zutphen, the Netherlands) in which this was an evaluated end point. For flavonoids, the observational studies were again mixed, and no trial results were available. Folsom has offered explanations for the partial discrepancy between results of observational and experimental studies by which the former could overestimate and the latter underestimate antioxidant effects (eg, low dose or short duration of vitamin E trials). Without further trials, and without separate data for natural food source and supplemental antioxidant intakes, the questions surrounding these substances are unlikely to be answered.

Thus the evidence remains unclear about appropriate recommendations. It is apparent from laboratory investigation that the various antioxidants differ in important respects in their relative potency and behavior as protective agents against LDL oxidation. From this perspective vitamin E might be expected to have greatest potential benefit, but further evidence is required. Results of β-carotene trials show need for concern about safety as well.

Pro-Oxidants

If the action of antioxidants protects against transformation of LDL to an especially virulent promoter of atherosclerosis, antioxidants would be opposed by any factor whose action favors production of O-LDL. Certain metals or their compounds may be candidates. In the laboratory, iron and copper may be used to amplify oxidation of LDL, and hemin (an iron-containing compound) renders endothelial cells in culture highly vulnerable to damage by oxidants.[13] LDL that has been oxidized by hemin is also reported to be extremely toxic to endothelial cells in culture. An epidemiologic observation adds to the plausibility of such a process in human atherosclerosis, based on a cohort study of 1931 Finnish men at selected ages in their 40s, 50s, or 60s at the beginning of a five-year follow-up period.[14] Serum ferritin concentration was measured as an index of excess iron storage in the body and ranged from 10 to 2270 µg/l (mean value, 166 µg/l). When the men with ferritin concentrations of 200 µg/l or greater were compared with those with lower values, after adjustment for several correlated risk factors, the relative risk was 2.2 (CI 1.2–4.0). In the group of men with LDL-cholesterol concentration of 5 mmol/l or greater, the corresponding relative risk was 4.7 (CI 1.4–16.3). These results were interpreted as evidence for a role of excess dietary iron in increasing the risk of acute myocardial infarction in men and possibly postmenopausal women, explaining variation in the relation of LDL cholesterol to risk of coronary heart disease in some populations (by implication, those with low levels of stored iron) and suggesting that dietary guidelines should caution against excessive iron intake.

Subsequent reports include the 13-year follow-up of 4237 participants aged 40–74 in the First National Health and Nutrition Examination Survey, in which serum iron concentration was found inversely related to risk of myocardial infarction in women (relative risk 0.82, CI 0.70–0.95).[15] There was no association in men. Both serum iron and transferrin concentrations were studied, and no support for an increase in risk was found for either of them. Complexities in interpretation of differences between the US and Finnish studies include differences in iron components measured (iron and transferrin versus ferritin), variability in the measures used in the US study, and less frequent excess iron stores in the US population, among others. Further studies can be expected, with possible policy recommendations to follow in relation to antioxidants, pro-oxidants, or both.

HOMOCYSTEINEMIA

Background

Biochemical, animal experimental, and clinical observations from the 1930s to the 1970s identified several metabolic products of methionine (a sulfur-containing essential amino acid), linked them with a rare human disease that included atherosclerosis and thrombotic complications at very early ages, and established their potential role in atherogenesis.[16] The central focus is on three closely related compounds: homocysteine, a single-chain four-carbon molecule with one amino and one sulfhydryl group; homocystine, with a disulfide bond joining two such molecules; and cystine-homocysteine disulfide, in which homocysteine and a three-carbon sulfhydryl-containing amine are joined. The total plasma concentration of the homocysteine derived from the three compounds together is conventionally denoted by *homocyst(e)ine*, *tHcy*, *H(e)*, or simply *homocysteine*, the present usage.

Aspects of metabolism, laboratory determination, and nutritional and genetic influences were reviewed recently.[17] There is a close link between homocysteine metabolism and the B vitamins in that either a pyridoxal phosphate-dependent enzymatic reaction or a transfer of methyl groups from vitamin B_{12} or folic acid is required to convert homocysteine to its immediate metabolic products. This suggests strongly that adverse levels of homocysteine may reflect relative deficiency of one or more components of the B vitamins, a potential point of intervention should elevated homocysteine concentration be considered causally related to cardiovascular disease.

Risks Within Populations

A quantitative assessment reviewed epidemiologic studies, conducted chiefly in the 1980s and 1990s, that had been published and indexed through June 1994.[18] Studies of homocysteine concentrations in relation to coronary heart disease, stroke, and peripheral arterial disease were described in reference to sample size, age range, design (cross-sectional or case-comparison), laboratory methods for homocysteine determination, mean value of homocysteine concentration, and percentage of persons with elevated homocysteine per group. For each disease category, studies are illustrated separately in Figure 18–3 and grouped in accordance with the condition of measurement, whether in a postmethionine load test (P) or fasting (F). Studies limited to males are so designated (M). For each disease category a summary odds ratio and confidence interval are shown separately for studies of fasting homocysteine determination and for all studies. Within each disease category, the range of odds ratios is notable, even within groups by method of homocysteine determination. There is an apparent tendency for stronger

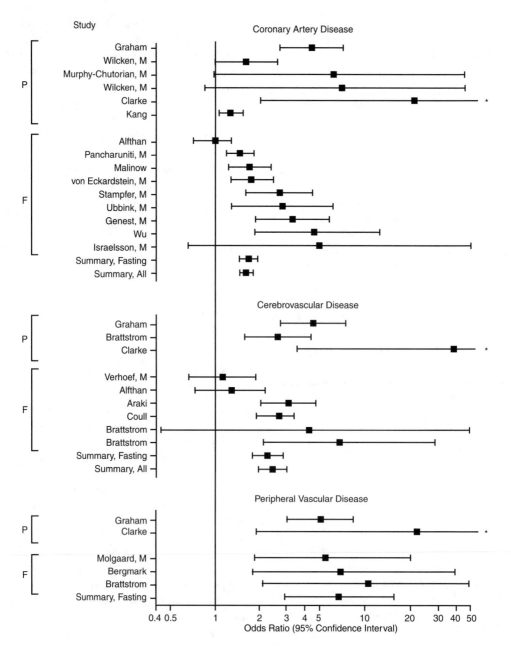

Note: Unless indicated, ORs are for both males (M) and females. Asterisks indicate that the upper bound of the risk estimate was infinity. The "Summary, All" includes all studies in each figure (except Graham because separate risk estimates for coronary artery disease, cerebrovascular disease, and peripheral vascular disease were not provided), and the "Summary, Fasting" includes only studies that measured fasting levels of total homocysteine (tHcy). P, homocysteine measured by postmethionine load test; F, fasting tHcy.

Figure 18–3 Quantitative Analysis of Studies of Homocysteine Levels and Vascular Disease. Presented as odds ratios (ORs) with 95% confidence intervals on a log scale. An OR greater than 1.0 indicates that elevated homocysteine levels increase the risk for vascular disease. *Source:* Reprinted with permission from *Journal of the American Medical Association*, Vol 274, p 1052, Copyright 1995, American Medical Association.

measures of association when postload determinations were done.

The summary odds ratios were in any case significantly greater than 1 for coronary heart disease, stroke, and peripheral arterial disease, increasing in magnitude respectively. Further analysis to assess the average increase in odds ratio for each 0.5 μmol/L increment in homocysteine concentration indicated similar significant increases in risk of coronary heart disease for both men and women. Based on the estimated frequency of increased homocysteine concentration in the general population, it was concluded that 10% of the population risk of coronary heart disease was attributable to this factor.

Dietary Relationships

Further analysis addressed the potential reduction in coronary heart disease rates by increased folic acid intake, under the assumption that the reduction of homocysteine concentration known to result from folate administration would, in fact, reduce disease rates. Among three alternatives of increased dietary intake—natural food sources, supplementation by tablets, and fortification of grains to increase folate content—the study concluded that the latter would be the most effective and could prevent from 13,500 to 50,000 coronary deaths annually in the United States.

A more recent study examined in greater detail than others the relation of vitamins B_6, B_{12}, and folate to the association between homocysteine concentration and coronary heart disease.[19] In a case-comparison study of newly hospitalized cases of first myocardial infarction in the Boston area, dietary interviews and blood samples were obtained approximately two months following hospital discharge. A positive association between homocysteine concentration and case or control status was found that was weakened but still statistically significant after adjustment for other risk factors. Significant inverse associations were also found for dietary levels and plasma concentrations of vitamin B_6 and folate. Analysis of the relations of each vitamin component and the respective levels of several homocysteine metabolites to case and control status led to the interpretation that the vitamin B_6 and folate levels were more closely related than vitamin B_{12} to homocysteine concentration. This result strengthens the argument for consideration of increased folate intake as a potential intervention to reduce this component of risk for coronary heart disease and other vascular diseases.

Other Observations

Several other recent observations in this connection warrant mention. One case series of 482 patients referred for treatment of hyperlipidemia was found to include 18 patients (3.7%) with homocysteine concentrations of 16.2 μmol/L or greater, considered high.[20] In 14 of these patients (77.8%), one or more first-degree relatives had experienced atherosclerotic cardiovascular disease before age 65, according to the family history, versus 50.0% of those without elevated homocysteine concentration. In a health survey among 16,000 Norwegian men and women free of known cardiovascular disease, homocysteine concentration increased with age in adulthood, was greater for men than women at each age, and was found strongly associated with number of cigarettes smoked per day, especially in women.[21] Correlations were found with several other risk factors, as in previous studies, leading the authors to question how much of the apparent homocysteine effect is attributable to those other factors. A case-comparison study of coronary heart disease including women and older subjects (mean age 62 years) found significant associations with homocysteine concentration for both women and older persons.[22] Also, low concentrations of pyridoxal-5'-phosphate were independently associated with coronary heart disease in addition to the metabolic link between this vitamin precursor and homocysteine. Interest has also been drawn to genetic variation in an enzyme that facilitates the transfer of a methyl group from a folate derivative to homocysteine, converting it to methionine.[23] A common mutation in this enzyme, methylenetetrahydrofolate reductase (MTHFR) renders it unstable and may lead to elevated homocysteine concentration, possibly requiring even greater folate supplementation than has generally been proposed.

Implications for Research and Policy

Among the issues raised by these studies, and addressed in several of them, is the question of policy concerning folate intake by the population at large. Although the desirability of formal evaluation in preventive trials has been emphasized, several reports have advocated policy change on the basis of current evidence alone. An intermediate position has also been expressed:

> [B]ecause the weight of the evidence is substantial and the intervention appears to be benign, it may be possible to make broad preliminary recommendations based on trials of secondary prevention or disease progression (eg, thickening of the carotid-artery wall) rather than wait for large, expensive, and prolonged trials of primary prevention. In the meantime, it will be prudent to ensure adequate dietary intake of folate.[24(p 329)]

It has been recommended recently in the United States that all women of reproductive age increase their folate intake for the prevention of neural tube defects in their offspring. The effect of this policy may introduce difficulties in later evaluation of folate supplementation for prevention of cardiovascular diseases and introduce another sex difference in exposures to be considered in future studies.

VASCULAR AND ENDOTHELIAL FACTORS

Insights from Vascular Biology

Laboratory and, to a lesser extent, clinical research have expanded greatly in the past decade or more in the study of vascular biology, including study of the endothelium and its role in vascular function.[25,26] Changes in the field of cardiology implied by this new emphasis in research have been characterized as shifting attention from the vessel lumen, revealed through technology of the past 30 years, to the vessel wall and a new appreciation of its complexity—or, as expressed in one review, a shift to focus on the "donut," and not on the "hole."[25] Dzau and colleagues described some of the complexity:

> It is now recognized that the vasculature is a complex organ capable of sensing its environment, transducing signals to the cells within the vasculature or to the surrounding tissue, and synthesizing local mediators that promote functional or structural responses. A constant feature of these interactions is the delicate balance between countervailing mechanisms. Vascular cells produce vasoconstrictors as well as vasodilators, procoagulants as well as anticoagulants, proinflammatory mediators as well as anti-inflammatory agents, and growth stimulators as well as inhibitors. Disturbances in this delicate balance may play a role in the development of vascular pathology.[26(p 705)]

Implications for Epidemiology

To date there has been little involvement of epidemiology in these developments, and little public health application has yet emerged. But the characterization above is strongly reminiscent of the intricate balances in hemostasis that have led to extensive epidemiologic study to take such new measurements as become feasible into the field, to determine the correspondence at the population level of the phenomena described, to link newly described phenomena to known predictors of risk, to estimate contributions to risk (whether independent or mediated through known factors), and to evaluate proposed interventions based on new knowledge from the laboratory.

The forecast for the 1990s and beyond in vascular biology portends advances in noninvasive techniques for imaging studies within and around vascular walls, new avenues of therapy based on deeper insights to vascular metabolism and physiology, and further development of methods of genetic engineering to deliver innovative "corrections" to cellular control mechanisms. Continued application of new imaging techniques may expand epidemiologic study of atherosclerosis to a much greater extent than has carotid ultrasound examination. Definition of appropriate target groups to receive new therapies and in whom to evaluate those therapies will also present continuing opportunities for epidemiology. Thus, whereas vascular biology has yet to present a clear set of new or candidate factors for epidemiologic investigation, such an agenda may develop soon.

OTHER FACTORS

Infection has long been considered a potential explanation of the origin of atherosclerotic lesions, as noted briefly in Chapter 3, and interest in this area continues. Agents suggested most often or most recently have included especially cytomegaloviruses, *Helicobacter pylori*, and *Chlamydia pneumoniae*. Many other factors, some of continuing and others of more sporadic interest, were documented by Hopkins and Williams in the extensive 1981 review of 246 factors addressed in the literature to that date.[27] Some of those (see Chapter 20) were aspects of physical environment that were not included in this and the preceding chapters as personal factors, but the great majority would still be of interest, and a reinvestigation with more current epidemiologic designs and methods might be useful.

It remains in the following two chapters to address aspects of social conditions that are more clearly external to the individual (Chapter 19, Social Conditions) and to consider the framework (Chapter 20, The Causal Complex) in which the factors discussed in Chapters 7–19 can be viewed as offering an intelligible picture of the causation of atherosclerotic and hypertensive diseases.

REFERENCES

1. Postiglione A, Panico S, Lewis B, Eisenberg S, et al, for the Council on Arteriosclerosis of the International Society and Federation of Cardiology (ISFC). New and candidate risk factors for coronary heart disease. *Nutr Metab Cardiovas Dis.* 1994;4:233–256.

2. Steinberg D, Parthasarathy S, Carew TE, Khoo JC, et al. Beyond cholesterol: modifications of low-density lipoprotein that increase its atherogenicity. *N Engl J Med.* 1989;320:915–924.

3. Steinberg D, National Heart, Lung, and Blood Institute Workshop Participants. Antioxidants in the prevention of human atherosclerosis, Summary of the proceedings of a National Heart, Lung, and Blood Institute Workshop: September 5–6, 1991, Bethesda, Maryland. *Circ.* 1992;85:2338–2344.

4. Kritchevsky D. Antioxidant vitamins in the prevention of cardiovascular disease. *Nutr Today.* 1992;27:30–33.

5. Gey FK, Puska P, Jordan P, Moser UK. Inverse correlation between plasma vitamin E and mortality from ischemic heart disease in cross-cultural epidemiology. *Am J Clin Nutr.* 1991;53(suppl):326S–334S.

6. Stampfer MJ, Hennekens CH, Manson JE, Colditz GA, et al. Vitamin E consumption and the risk of coronary disease in women. *N Engl J Med.* 1993;328:1444–1449.

7. Rimm EB, Stampfer MJ, Ascherio A, Giovannucci E, et al. Vitamin E consumption and the risk of coronary heart disease in men. *N Engl J Med.* 1993;328:1450–1456.

8. Kushi LH, Folsom AR, Prineas RJ, Mink PJ, et al. Dietary antioxidant vitamins and death from coronary heart disease in postmenopausal women. *N Engl J Med.* 1996;334:1156–1162.

9. Stephens NG, Parsons A, Schofield PM, Kelly F, et al. Randomised controlled trial of vitamin E in patients with coronary disease: Cambridge Heart Antioxidant Study (CHAOS). *Lancet.* 1996;347:781–786.

10. Omenn GS, Goodman GE, Thornquist MD, Balmes J, et al. Effects of a combination of beta carotene and vitamin A on lung cancer and cardiovascular disease. *N Engl J Med.* 1996;334:1150–1155.

11. Hennekens CH, Buring JE, Manson JE, Stampfer M, et al. Lack of effect of long-term supplementation with beta carotene on the incidence of malignant neoplasms and cardiovascular disease. *N Eng J Med.* 1996; 334:1145–1149.

12. Jha P, Flather M, Lonn E, Farkouh M, et al. The antioxidant vitamins and cardiovascular disease: a critical review of epidemiologic and clinical trial data. *Ann Intern Med.* 1995;123:860–872.

13. Balla G, Jacob HS, Eaton JW, Belcher JD, et al. Hemin: a possible physiological mediator of low density lipoprotein oxidation and endothelial injury. *Arteriosclerosis Thromb.* 1991;11:1700–1711.

14. Salonen JT, Nyyssönen K, Korpela H, Tuomilehto J, et al. High stored iron levels are associated with excess risk of myocardial infarction in Eastern Finnish men. *Circ.* 1992;86:803–811.

15. Liao Y, Cooper RS, McGee DL. Iron status and coronary heart disease: negative findings from the NHANES I Epidemiologic Follow-Up Study. *Am J Epidemiol.* 1994;139:704–712.

16. Malinow MR. Homocyst(e)ine and arterial occlusive diseases. *J Intern Med.* 1994;236:603–617.

17. Fortin LJ, Genest J Jr. Measurement of homocyst(e)ine in the prediction of arteriosclerosis. *Clin Biochem.* 1995;28:155–162.

18. Boushey CJ, Beresford SAA, Omenn GS, Motulsky AG. A quantitative assessment of plasma homocysteine as a risk factor for vascular disease. *JAMA.* 1995; 274:1049–1057.

19. Verhoef P, Stampfer MJ, Buring JE, Gaziano JM, et al. Homocysteine metabolism and risk of myocardial infarction: relation with vitamins B_6, B_{12}, and folate. *Am J Epidemiol.* 1996;143:845–859.

20. Glueck CJ, Shaw P, Lang JE, Tracy T, et al. Evidence that homocysteine is an independent risk factor for atherosclerosis in hyperlipidemic patients. *Am J Cardiol.* 1995;75:132–136.

21. Nygård O, Vollset SE, Rafsum H, Stensvold I, et al. Total plasma homocysteine and cardiovascular risk profile: the Hordaland Homocysteine Study. *JAMA.* 1995;274:1526–1533.

22. Robinson K, Mayer EL, Miller DP, Green R, et al. Hyperhomocysteinemia and low pyridoxal phosphate. *Circ.* 1995;92:2825–2830.

23. Jacques PF, Bostom AG, Williams RR, Ellison RC, et al. Relation between folate status, a common mutation in methylenetetrahydrofolate reductase, and plasma homocysteine concentrations. *Circ.* 1996;93:7–9.

24. Stampfer MJ, Malinow MR. Can lowering homocysteine levels reduce cardiovascular risk? *N Engl J Med.* 1995;332:328–329.

25. Meredith IT, Yeung AC, Weidinger FF, Anderson TJ, et al. Role of impaired endothelium-dependent vasodilation in ischemic manifestations of coronary artery disease. *Circ.* 1993;87(suppl V):V-56–V-66.

26. Dzau VJ, Gibbons GH, Cooke JP, Omoigui N. Vascular biology and medicine in the 1990s: scope, concepts, potentials, and perspectives. *Circ.* 1993;87:705–719.

27. Hopkins PN, Williams RR. A survey of 246 suggested coronary risk factors. *Atherosclerosis.* 1981;40:1–52.

CHAPTER 19

Social Conditions

SUMMARY

Social conditions, as properties of societies or populations rather than of individuals, have been subjects of theory and research in connection with cardiovascular epidemiology for several decades. Work in this area was stimulated especially by several writers around the early 1960s. Culture change or cultural mobility, occupational status and social class, and measures of education, income, and income distribution within societies have all been studied. Until recently, this research has focused on adults. Especially in the past decade, however, increased attention had focused on aspects of fetal and early postnatal development and their relation to risks of cardiovascular diseases in adulthood, with the implication that social conditions affecting this critical period may have lifelong health effects. A further development is the concept of "fundamental causes" of disease, which is the idea that social conditions affect health in ways that transcend specific risk factors. In this view poverty, for example, is always associated with adverse health effects irrespective of the particular concomitants of poverty present in a given society at any given time. At a practical level, several of these ideas could potentially be merged in future thinking about prevention of cardiovascular diseases and their risk factors. This may be especially relevant for developing countries undergoing culture change or "Westernization," a process recognized as leading to transformation of disease-related conditions in many societies. From a theoretical viewpoint, consideration of social conditions also gives rise to interesting issues including the meaning of *causation* of disease, a topic addressed in the chapter that follows.

INTRODUCTION

Culture Change and Epidemic Diseases

As often quoted by Stamler, Virchow expressed the view a century and a half ago that human culture is a decisive determinant of epidemic diseases:

> Epidemics of a character unknown so far appear, and often disappear without traces when a new culture period has started. . . . The history of artificial epidemics is therefore the history of disturbances of human culture. Their changes announce to us in gigantic signs the turning points of culture into new directions.[1(p 35)]

This view directs attention to broad features of social conditions and their changes over time. Many reflections of this perspective are found in the epidemiology of the past 40 years as it has addressed coronary heart disease and hypertension in particular. For example, the concepts of the epidemiologic transition and the evolution of culture leading to habitual patterns of dietary imbalance and physical inactivity have been addressed in earlier chapters.

This chapter addresses the early conceptualization of culture change and other social conditions in epidemiology, studies of economic conditions in adulthood and in fetal and postnatal development, and "Westernization" as a form of culture change that is increasingly relevant as many populations experience economic development.

The Population Level

Some measures of social conditions are attributable only to geopolitical units, such as the median income levels of US states, for which there is no corresponding value at the individual level. Many other measures of social conditions are applicable at both population and individual levels, such as indicators of social status, household income, or migrational history. For example, a more or a less formally defined social class hierarchy is a property of a population, not of an individual. However, a classification in one or another specific rank is an attribute of an individual. Even though health effects associated with social conditions are presumably mediated in some way at the individual level, in this chapter social conditions are considered in relation to their broadest implications—at the population level. This is distinct from the "social" aspect of the psychosocial patterns addressed in Chapter 17. The reintegration of these complementary levels of interest is discussed in the next chapter.

Conceptual Background

The Social Milieu

Among the early epidemiologic writers on health aspects of the social environment was Hinkle, who in 1961 wrote:

One cannot doubt the need for studies of health and the social milieu. Questions of the relations between illness and social class, economic conditions, migration, social mobility, status change, acculturation, and similar social phenomena are pressing, and the methods of the social scientist readily lend themselves to their investigation. Nevertheless, it may be predicted that the answers that are obtained will be complex and that it will be much easier to see the application of these to the sample and to the circumstances under study than to extrapolate them to any large segment of mankind, or to any general class of social phenomena.[2(p 290)]

Hinkle's statement added impetus to epidemiologic study of social conditions. But it also expressed reservations about whether general inferences could be reached from such research, which might be limited to only isolated observations in particular populations under momentary circumstances.

Culture Change

Cassel and colleagues viewed the usefulness of epidemiology for study of a broad variety of health phenomena as depending on generation and testing of specific hypotheses to understand the significance of social and cultural processes for health.[3] This view indicated confidence in the potential for deriving valid general inferences from studies of multiple populations or groups.

Contemporary sociology and anthropology offered many concepts for potential investigation but without sufficient evidence to establish the relevance of any of them to health. Cassel and Tyroler chose to focus on culture change, specifically on changes in way of life from rural agricultural to industrial settings.[4,5] They adopted an "open" model of chronic disease causation, which meant that social factors might have very diverse health effects and that any particular health effect might occur in consequence of a variety of social factors. Specific associations would be highly conditional on immediate circumstances. Health status should therefore be studied, in their view, by reference to several dimensions of health: specific diseases; growth, nutritional status, and selected physiological functions; psychological attributes; and social adjustment. Hypotheses proposed and later tested were as follows: (1) Among workers in industrialized areas of the Appalachian Mountain region, recent migrants from rural areas would exhibit poorer health status than either those who had not migrated or those who had migrated a generation earlier; and (2) those recent migrants with the least family solidarity or experiencing upward social mobility would manifest the greatest adverse effects of culture change. Their results from this line of investigation, in relation to both general health and coronary heart disease, were generally consistent with these hypotheses.[4,5]

Cultural Mobility

Syme and colleagues considered culture change to have four aspects: "generational, career, residential, and situational mobility."[6(p 178)] They investigated several social factors in relation to coronary heart disease occurrence in a case-comparison study in the early 1960s. Factors such as urban residence, white-collar occupation, and geographic and occupational mobility were present in newly occurring cases of coronary heart disease significantly more frequently than in comparison subjects. These associations were independent of diet, relative body weight, blood pressure, smoking, and parental longevity.

Occupation

The occupational situation was the primary focus of work by Reeder[7] and Hinkle and colleagues,[8] but from different perspectives. Reeder reviewed studies in which the status aspect of occupation or socioeconomic level was emphasized. He found no coherent theoretical framework guiding these studies, but their findings were generally consistent in that higher occupational or socioeconomic status was associated with increased frequency of coronary heart disease. Hinkle and colleagues studied health records based on the experience of 270,000 men in the Bell System Operating Companies in the early 1960s and investigated the relation between educational background (with or without college degree), occupational level (from executives to skilled workers, on a seven-point scale), and incidence of coronary heart disease. They found prior education to be more strongly related to risk than job classification. Higher educational level was interpreted as reflecting more favorable opportunities and conditions of life through the school years, rather than education itself, as the operative influence on risk. The observation that factors determining risk in later adult years were better explained by differences in level of education than by occupational level led Hinkle and colleagues to conclude that "some aspects of the origin of coronary heart disease must be sought for in childhood or adolescence, if not earlier."[8(p 244)] This study was perhaps more productive of valid general inferences than they had anticipated.

Social Class

Occupation has been studied extensively in England and Wales, where the Registrar General's "social class" is based on this characteristic. Classes range from professionals and certain others (Class I) to unskilled occupations (Class V). The review by Marmot and colleagues of social class and health emphasized the importance of social forces, such as those represented by social class, as they operate through variation in lifestyles and specific exposures to produce differences in health.[9] The basis for associations between social class and health status is unlikely to be understood completely. Therefore, to intervene on particular aspects of risk or risk factors identified with a given class is necessarily incomplete and may overlook factors that are inherent in social class and are no less important in causing disease.

These considerations may be particularly relevant for coronary heart disease, whose relation to social class in England and Wales was shown to have changed from 1951 to 1971. For the category of nonvalvular heart disease, thought to be consistent in meaning across several revisions of the ICD code, rates increased sharply for social classes IV and V over the 20 years and surpassed the modest continuing increase for social classes I and II. Thus, although this cause of death was more frequent among the higher social classes in 1951, the relative frequencies were reversed within 10 years, and this trend was amplified further over the next 10 years. Notably, these changes were observed for men only, and no change in relative frequencies was observed for women, for whom the rates were consistently higher for the lower classes. Analysis by social class has thus revealed interesting changes in the natural history of coronary heart disease or in social class itself as a determinant of lifestyles and exposures, as well as inconsistencies in these changes between men and women.

The following sections focus on applications of these concepts of social conditions or socioeconomic status, first in adulthood and then in early life, and then return to discussion of migration and culture change.

SOCIOECONOMIC STATUS

Change in Social Class Distribution of Coronary Heart Disease

The change in the relationship between social class and coronary mortality noted in Marmot and colleagues' review[9] was examined in greater detail in an earlier report.[10] Some intermediate factors between social class and coronary mortality—specifically, dietary intakes of fat, refined sugar and fiber, and smoking behavior—were investigated within the limitations of data available at the national level over the 40-year period of interest, 1931 to 1971. The shift to relative dominance of the lower social classes (IV and V) over the higher classes (I and II) in

coronary mortality in the more recent years could not be explained by differential changes between the classes. Fat intake changed similarly in the upper and lower classes with no net difference in change over time. There were relative changes in intake of both fiber and refined sugars, and both were correlated with changing mortality, but because they were strongly correlated with each other (inversely) no separate effects could be evaluated. A relative decrease in smoking in the higher classes did explain a part of the relative difference in coronary mortality trends over this period. It was observed that a pattern of decreasing coronary mortality, experienced earlier in the United States and Australia, had begun in Great Britain with greater benefit for the upper classes.

As suggested earlier by Hinkle, by Cassel, and by others, social conditions may relate to disease occurrence in a complex manner, depending on circumstances that may not be completely identified or understood.

A Recent Review

Kaplan and Keil presented an extensive review of relationships between socioeconomic factors and cardiovascular diseases.[11] They addressed methodologic aspects, including assessment of education, income, occupation, employment status, social class, and living conditions, as well as several area-based measurements. Special problems of assessing socioeconomic status over the lifespan and opportunities for study of income inequalities were also discussed. Numerous studies of socioeconomic status and coronary heart disease were reviewed, from work by Lilienfeld in the 1950s to the report of the Scottish Heart Study in 1992. Occupational studies and studies of psychosocial factors as mediators between social class and coronary heart disease were included. The decline of coronary mortality in the United States was found to be associated with socioeconomic status for males but not for females, with more highly educated males experiencing more rapid decline in coronary mortality. Widening disparities in coronary mortality between higher and lower socioeconomic strata, even while absolute rates fell in all strata, were observed in both the United States and Great Britain.

They concluded that (1) socioeconomic status has been found to be associated with coronary heart disease in many studies over a 40-year period; (2) patterns of association between socioeconomic status and coronary heart disease have changed, among men, over this period; (3) declines in coronary mortality have not affected all socioeconomic groups equally; and (4) several cardiovascular risk factors are inversely associated with socioeconomic status, such that higher risk is found in lower socioeconomic categories, yet some residual association between socioeconomic status and coronary heart disease remains when these factors are taken into account, suggesting a possible independent contribution of socioeconomic status to risk.

A Current Assessment

In a 1995 conference on socioeconomic status and cardiovascular health and disease, sev-

eral presentations addressed background data (principally for the United States), possible mechanisms linking socioeconomic status and cardiovascular disease, and experience in educational and preventive programs among different socioeconomic groups.[12] An extensive chartbook of data on socioeconomic indicators and cardiovascular disease for the United States was compiled for the conference and was the basis for several presentations cited below.

Income, Education, and Cardiovascular Mortality

In the United States, a major data source for analysis of demographic factors and mortality is the National Longitudinal Mortality Study, which links data from household surveys of the Bureau of the Census with National Death Index information and death certificates. Data for some 600,000 people aged 25–64 were investigated for the conference.[13] Figures 19–1 and 19–2 indicate, for men and women from 1979 through 1989, the relation between cardiovascular mortality, plotted on a logarithmic

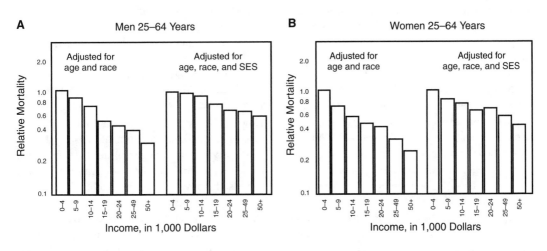

Figure 19–1 Relative Cardiovascular Mortality by Income for (A) Men and (B) Women. Estimates were obtained from the proportional hazards model, using indicator variables for each income category, with the lowest income as the reference point. The *y* axis displays the relative risk on a logarithmic scale. *Source*: Reprinted from PD Sorlie, NJ Johnson, and E Backlund, Report of the Conference on Socioeconomic Status and Cardiovascular Health and Disease, p 24, 1995, National Institutes of Health.

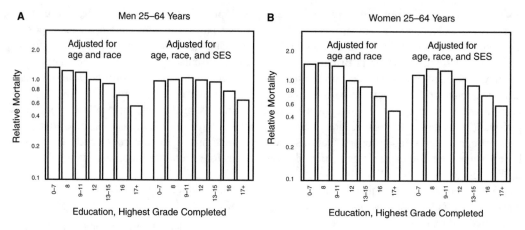

Figure 19–2 Relative Cardiovascular Mortality by Education for (A) Men and (B) Women. High school graduate is used as the reference group. *Source:* Reprinted from PD Sorlie, NJ Johnson, and E Backlund, Report of the Conference on Socioeconomic Status and Cardiovascular Health and Disease, p 24, 1995, National Institutes of Health.

scale, and income or education. For the analysis by income shown in Figure 19–1, the lowest stratum of $0–4000 was the reference category, and relative mortality for that group was set at 1.0. All analyses were adjusted for age and race (on the left in each panel of the figures) and, in addition, for socioeconomic status (SES) (on the right). For mortality by income, the socioeconomic adjustment included education, marital status, employment status, and household size; for mortality by education, income was substituted for education among the adjusting variables.

Analyses by income (Figure 19–1) showed consistent trends of decreasing relative cardiovascular mortality with increasing categories of income for both men and women. After adjustment these gradients were attenuated but remained substantial, with decrements of 40% for men and 50% for women from lowest to highest income. Analysis by years of education (Figure 19–2) was based on 12 years, or completion of high school, as the reference category. In general, fewer years of school completed meant higher mortality and more years of school lesser mortality from cardiovascular diseases. Peak mortality was generally not in the lowest category. Figure 19–3 indicates

similar patterns by race (African American, Hispanic White, and non-Hispanic White) and shows consistent trends of lesser mortality with higher educational status in every group of both men and women.

Educational Inequality and Total Mortality

Further insight into the strength of socioeconomic status as a predictor of total mortality is given in Figure 19–4, which shows the slope index of inequality in 1980, contrasted with 1960, for White men aged 25–64 in six strata of increasing educational attainment. Total mortality, on a logarithmic scale, averaged 5.1/1000 in 1980, a substantially lower rate than 8.0/1000 in 1960. However, the differential across categories of educational attainment increased over this interval. Thus the gap in mortality between the lowest and highest educational strata increased from 3.9/1000 in 1960 to 4.1/1000 in 1980, and the ratio of this difference to the overall average mortality increased from 49% to 80%. Expressed in various terms, the highest educational stratum gained most in reduced mortality, the lowest stratum gained least, or the gap widened. Graphically, the slope of differential mortality by education increased despite the overall decrease in mortality.

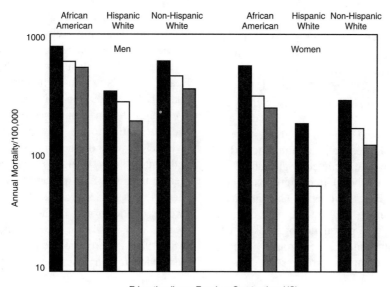

Figure 19–3 Cardiovascular Mortality by Education, Sex, and Race for Those Aged 45–64 Years. *Source*: Reprinted from PD Sorlie, NJ Johnson, and E Backlund, Report of the Conference on Socioeconomic Status and Cardiovascular Health and Disease, p 25, 1995, National Institutes of Health.

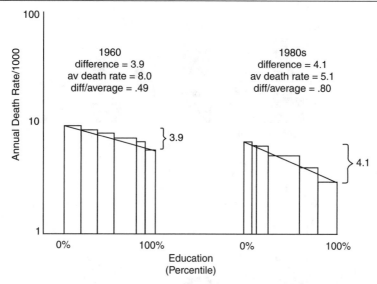

Figure 19–4 Estimation of Slope Index of Inequality for White Men Aged 25–64 Years. The slope index of inequality represents the decrease in the death rate from the lowest education to the highest education, with education scaled as a percentile. The bars indicate the death rates for each level of education. The width of each bar represents the percent of population at each education category. The line shows the slope of a regression of the death rates on education scaled as cumulative percentiles of the actual education levels. "Difference" is the difference in the death rate from the lowest to the highest education level. "Average death rate" is the death rate for the group as a whole. *Source:* SH Preston and IT Elo, *Journal of Aging and Health*, Vol 7, p 486, copyright © 1995 by Sage Publications, Inc. Reprinted by permission of Sage Publications, Inc.

Socioeconomic Measures and Risk Factors

Data on risk factor distributions by socioeconomic status for the Untied States are illustrated by smoking and overweight, which have different patterns (Figures 19–5 and 19–6).[14] From the National Health Interview Survey for 1993, current cigarette smoking by race or ethnicity for men and women aged 45–64 was strongly related to educational attainment (less than high school, completed high school, or more than high school) in all groups except non-Hispanic Black women. The gradients were strong among all three groups of men, even though overall prevalence of smoking differed markedly among the groups. Among women, the gradient was strongest, and smoking among the least educated was most prevalent for non-Hispanic Whites.

The picture for overweight was quite different (Figure 19–6). Data from the Third National Health and Nutrition Examination Survey, Phase 1, 1988–1991, indicate the prevalence of overweight for men and women aged 20 and over, in relation to the "poverty income ratio." Overweight was defined for this analysis as body mass index (weight in kg/height^2 in m) greater than the 85th percentile value among persons ages 20–29 years, of the same sex and race or ethnic group, in the Second National Health and Nutrition Examination Survey, 1980–1984. Poverty income ratio is a standardized index relating total household income to

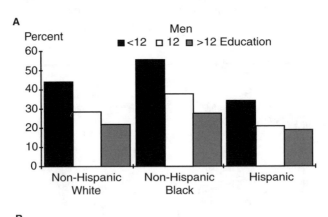

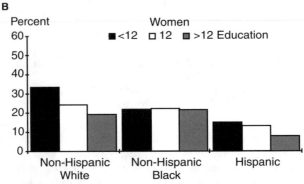

Figure 19–5 Current Cigarette Smoking by Race/Ethnicity and Education for (A) Men and (B) Women Aged 45–64 Years. *Source*: Reprinted from CL Johnson and CT Sempos, Report of the Conference on Socioeconomic Status and Cardiovascular Health and Disease, p 37, 1995, National Institutes of Health.

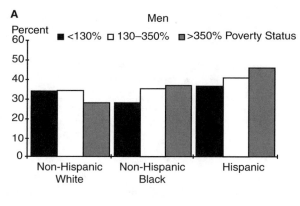

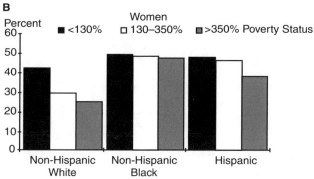

Figure 19–6 Age-Adjusted Prevalence of Overweight by Poverty Status and Race/Ethnicity for (A) Men and (B) Women Aged 20 and Over. *Source*: Reprinted from CL Johnson and CT Sempos, Report of the Conference on Socioeconomic Status and Cardiovascular Health and Disease, p 38, 1995, National Institutes of Health.

family size and composition. The lowest one-third of the distribution of this index defines eligibility for certain public assistance programs in the United States and corresponds to values of the index of 1.30 or less. The upper one-third of the population corresponds to values of 3.50 or greater. For non-Hispanic Black and Hispanic men, there were clear positive gradients of overweight with increasing socioeconomic status. The gradient was opposite in non-Hispanic White men. For women, there were clear gradients of lower prevalence of overweight with increasing poverty income ratio except for non-Hispanic Blacks, for whom no gradient was observed. These mixed findings by race or ethnicity and sex preclude simple interpretation of the role of socioeconomic status in the causa-

tion of cardiovascular diseases across these diverse groups.

Social (Occupational) Class in Europe

Data for several European countries permit comparison of the relation of occupational class to mortality from both ischemic heart disease and cerebrovascular disease (Table 19–1).[15] The data were obtained from longitudinal studies in some countries and cross-sectional studies in others and reflect experience of the early or later 1980s. Classification of occupations was condensed to three categories applicable to all of the countries, including the combined class, "manual and nonmanual workers." Men who were not economically active were excluded from analysis. The risk ratios shown express the ratio of the

Table 19–1 Ischemic Heart Disease and Cerebrovascular Disease Mortality Rate Ratios for Manual and Nonmanual Workers

| Country[a] | Rate Ratio (95% Confidence Interval)[b] | |
	Ischemic Heart Disease	Cerebrovascular Disease
England/Wales	1.51 (1.33–1.73)	1.74 (1.21–2.49)
Finland	1.44 (1.37–1.52)	1.52 (1.35–1.70)
Sweden	1.36 (1.31–1.42)	1.30 (1.16–1.46)
Norway	1.36 (1.28–1.43)	1.22 (1.02–1.44)
Denmark	1.28 (1.21–1.34)	1.26 (1.11–1.42)
Ireland	1.23 (1.11–1.35)	1.49 (1.10–2.02)
Spain	1.00 (0.95–1.05)	1.20 (1.11–1.29)
France	1.00 (0.95–1.03)	1.33 (1.24–1.41)
Switzerland	0.97 (0.90–1.05)	1.42 (1.17–1.73)
Portugal	0.78 (0.70–0.86)	1.42 (1.25–1.60)

a. No data are available for Italy for specific cardiovascular diseases.

b. Adjusted for the exclusion of economically inactive men.

Source: Reprinted from the National Institutes of Health, Bethesda, Maryland.

cause-specific death rate for men in the category of manual and nonmanual workers to the overall national rate for each respective country, adjusted for age. The rates for ischemic heart disease were significantly in excess among these workers for most of the northern countries of Europe, were unrelated in Spain and France, and were significantly less than the national average in Portugal. The relative excesses in rates for cerebrovascular disease were as great or greater than those for ischemic heart disease in the northern European countries and, unlike the findings for ischemic heart disease, were also in excess in the remaining countries. Several cautions are noted in the interpretation of such data, however, and evaluation of the data sources, country by country, is advised. Again, the implication is clear that generalization of findings concerning socioeconomic status remains very tentative on the basis of currently available data.

Psychosocial Correlates

Relationships between socioeconomic status and psychosocial characteristics, as potentially intervening factors, were described on the basis of data obtained from national samples of US adults aged 45–64 in the mid-1980s.[16] As shown in Figure 19–7, each of seven characteristics indicative of adverse psychosocial patterns is related to both education and income and is most prevalent in the lowest stratum: high hostility, unmarried, never attending meetings, talking with others less than once per week, low self-efficacy, high depressive symptoms, and two or more recent negative events. Education and income are not equally strong correlates of these variables, however. A comparison of the two panels in the figure indicates that educational status identifies a stronger gradient in hostility than does income, for example, and income identifies a stronger gradient for marital status and occurrence of negative life events.

Income Inequalities: The "Robin Hood Index"

The recognition of widening differentials in income and related indicators within the United

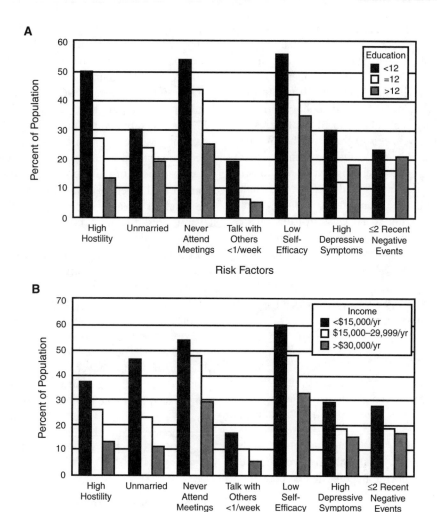

Figure 19–7 Psychosocial Risk Factor Status in US Residents, Aged 45–64, by (A) Education and (B) Income. *Source*: Reprinted from JS House and DR Williams, Report of the Conference on Socioeconomic Status and Cardiovascular Health and Disease, p 122, 1995, National Institutes of Health.

States has brought attention to the possible relation of this phenomenon to health. The example in Figure 19–4 illustrates that, although total mortality declined from 1960 to the 1980s, the disparity in mortality between strata by educational attainment increased. To investigate such relationships further, the "Robin Hood index"—the proportion of income to be redistributed from higher to lower income strata to eliminate

disproportionate income distribution—was calculated for each US state for 1990.[17] Analyses of mortality for the same year showed that even after adjustment for absolute differences in income level by state, the wider the income disparity as measured by the Robin Hood index, the higher the heart disease ($P<0.004$) and cerebrovascular disease ($P<0.058$) mortality, as well as total mortality, infant mortality, deaths from malignant neoplasms, and homicide. It was projected that proportionate redistribution of incomes in the United States to resemble those in the United Kingdom would correspond to a decrease in the Robin Hood index from 30% to 25% and a 25% reduction in coronary heart disease mortality. It should be noted that this result would not have been expected earlier in the course of the US epidemic of coronary heart disease, when rates were highest in the higher socioeconomic strata. The dependence of such relations on other circumstances is also evident from the changing social class distribution of coronary heart disease in the United Kingdom, shown above in the analysis by Marmot and colleagues.[9]

CONDITIONS OF FETAL AND INFANT DEVELOPMENT

Forsdahl on Norway

The foregoing discussion was limited to the relation of social conditions to cardiovascular diseases and other health problems in adults. This section addresses whether social conditions much earlier in life are associated with later-appearing atherosclerotic and hypertensive diseases. The specific hypothesis that poor living conditions in childhood and adolescence portend increased mortality from atherosclerotic heart disease in adulthood (in contrast to more-general theories of social conditions and health) appears to have originated in the writing of Forsdahl, whose first-cited Norwegian-language papers on the topic appeared in the early 1970s.[18] He noted the principle of a generally inverse relation between standard of living and mortality, which was in contrast with the contemporary situation among adults in Norway, where there was little variation in living conditions but considerable variation in mortality by county. He reasoned that current differences in mortality might reflect former differences in living conditions earlier in life, when these conditions did vary greatly by county. His specific hypothesis was that "poverty during adolescence is positively correlated with the risk of dying from arteriosclerotic heart disease."[18(p 91)]

Forsdahl used as a measure of historical social conditions infant mortality by county in Norway for the years 1896–1925. Mortality from arteriosclerotic heart disease in 1964–1967 (as coded under the International Classification of Diseases, Eighth Revision) was analyzed for men and women in the age group 40–69, whose years of childhood and youth corresponded to the period of infant mortality data. The results shown in Figures 19–8 and 19–9 illustrate his findings. For both males and females, death rates for arteriosclerotic heart disease and previous infant mortality by county were strongly and significantly associated, whether measured by product-moment (r) or Spearman (r_s) correlation coefficients. These and other results led Forsdahl to speculate that the association was not explained by early poverty alone but depended on later affluence, which perhaps had adverse effects in consequence of an early nutritional deficiency, such as a reduced tolerance to some types of dietary fats. He concluded, "it seems justified to consider a poor standard of living in early years followed by prosperity as a potential risk factor."[18(p 95)]

The Southampton Group

In a prodigious program of research over the decade beginning in the mid-1980s, Barker and colleagues at Southampton, England, have pursued the concept of early origins of coronary heart disease and have stimulated related studies and several reviews of work in this area by others. Recently summarizing the results to date, Barker wrote:

> A new model for the causation of coronary heart disease is emerging [citation to Barker DJP. *Mothers, Babies and Disease in Later Life.* London, England: British Medical Journal Publications, 1994]. Under the old model an inappropriate life-

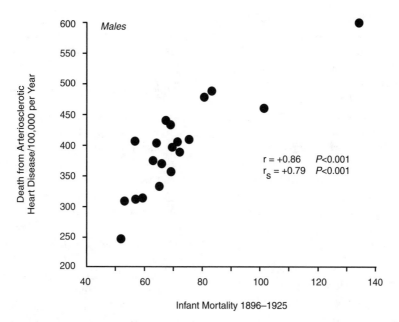

Figure 19–8 Correlation Between Mortality from Arteriosclerotic Heart Disease, 1964–1967, in Men Aged 40–69 Years and Infant Mortality Rates, 1896–1925. *Source*: Reprinted with permission from A Forsdahl, *British Journal of Preventive & Social Medicine*, Vol 31, p 92, © 1977, BMJ Publishing Group.

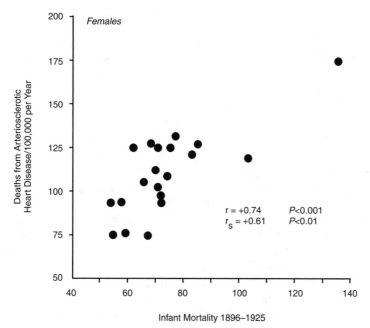

Figure 19–9 Correlation Between Mortality from Arteriosclerotic Heart Disease, 1964–1967, in Women Aged 40–69 Years and Infant Mortality Rates, 1896–1925. *Source*: Reprinted with permission from A Forsdahl, *British Journal of Preventive & Social Medicine*, Vol 31, p 92, © 1977, BMJ Publishing Group.

style, including cigarette smoking and lack of exercise, leads to accelerated destruction of the body in middle and late life, including the more rapid development of insulin resistance. Under the new model, coronary heart disease results not primarily from external forces but from the body's internal environment, homeostatic settings of enzyme activity, cell receptors, and hormone feedback, which are established in response to undernutrition *in utero* and lead eventually to premature death.[19(p 162)]

The background of this conclusion includes numerous reports by this group of investigators and others, many of which were collected in *Mothers, Babies and Disease* or in *Fetal and Infant Origins of Adult Disease*.[20]

Infant Death Rates and Cardiovascular Mortality

Among the earliest studies by the Southampton group was an historical-ecological investigation of mortality in infancy and adulthood, similar to that of Forsdahl. Adult mortality at ages 35–74 years in 1968–1978 was analyzed in relation to the corresponding infant mortality in 1921–1925 in each of the 212 local authority areas of England and Wales. The results for ischemic heart disease (ICD, Eighth Revision, codes 410–414) and other selected causes of death (bronchitis, stomach cancer, and rheumatic heart disease) indicated strong correlations ($r = 0.72$–0.82).[20] Stroke and lung cancer, though they had weaker correlations, were included in the analysis because they might serve as surrogates for hypertension and smoking history. Correlations of mortality from ischemic heart disease with these other causes of death and with infant mortality in 1921–1925 are presented in Table 19–2. Ischemic heart disease was more strongly related to stroke and infant mortality than to other causes for both men and women, except for women in urban areas. This overall result suggested that the relation of infant to adult mortality was to some degree specific for cardiovascular causes.

Weight at Birth and Age One Year

A further stage of investigation was to link individual data from birth and early postnatal records with mortality in adult years in a historical cohort approach. This was done through identification of 5654 men born in Hertfordshire, England, in the period 1911–1930, whose vital status was ascertained at ages 20–74 years from 1951 through 1987.[21] Early records for each man included weight at birth and age one year, as well as feeding practices (breast, bottle, or both) and other information. For men who had been breast fed, who constituted all but 7.6% of the cohort, the relation of ischemic heart disease mortality to weight at birth and one year is shown in Table 19–3. Standardized mortality ratios (SMRs) represent the relation of the death rate for each category to that for the national population of the same age and calendar period. The lowest ratios occurred in the categories of above average weights both at birth and at age one. By Cox proportional hazards regression, the investigators addressed the joint dependency of ischemic heart disease mortality on these two factors, as shown in Figure 19–10. The SMRs increased from 45 at the highest one-year weight level and midrange birth weight to 155 for those with lowest weights at birth and one year.

A similar analysis was subsequently reported for women and showed a similar pattern for weight at birth but not at age one year. For a sample of women, as for men, who were still residing in Hertfordshire, risk factors were assessed by direct physical and laboratory examination.[22] For risk factors, as for mortality, associations in women were present for birth weight but not for weight at age one year. However, like men, women who were smaller at birth, and especially those who became obese as adults, exhibited higher blood pressure and triglyceride concentrations and lower concentra-

Table 19–2 Correlation of Death from Ischemic Heart Disease and from Other Causes of Death (Standardized Mortality Ratios) in Three Geographical Groups in Men and Women

	Geographical Group			
Cause of Death	County and London Boroughs	Urban Areas	Rural Areas	All Areas
Men				
Bronchitis	0.49	0.49	0.67	0.58
Stomach cancer	0.48	0.72	0.53	0.62
Rheumatic heart disease	0.27	0.48	0.58	0.45
Stroke	0.73	0.68	0.78	0.72
Lung cancer	0.18	−0.09	−0.03	0.30
Infant mortality 1921–25	0.65	0.70	0.75	0.69
Women				
Bronchitis	0.59	0.64	0.50	0.60
Stomach cancer	0.64	0.36	0.43	0.57
Rheumatic heart disease	0.50	0.46	0.52	0.55
Stroke	0.73	0.44	0.70	0.59
Lung cancer	−0.16	−0.09	−0.40	−0.03
Infant mortality 1921–25	0.73	0.68	0.72	0.73

Source: Reprinted with permission from DJP Barker and C Osmond, Infant Mortality, Childhood Nutrition, and Ischaemic Heart Disease in England and Wales, in *Fetal and Infant Origins of Adult Disease*, DJP Barker, ed, p 29, © 1992, BMJ Publishing Group.

tions of high-density lipoprotein cholesterol—prominent features of insulin resistance.

A Mechanism: "Programming"

A plethora of relationships has been identified in this area of research, implicating multiple risk factors or disease outcomes, at various ages, in associations with different aspects of fetal and early infant development. These, in turn, have been measured by weight at birth or age one, placental weight, abdominal girth at birth, and other indices. The fundamental mechanism that Barker proposes to account for these relationships is deficiency of nutrient or oxygen

Table 19–3 Standardized Mortality Ratios for Ischemic Heart Disease According to Birth Weight and Weight at One Year in Men Who Had Been Breast Fed (Numbers of Deaths in Parentheses)

	Weight at Birth (lb)			
Weight (lb) at 1 Year	Below Average (≤7)	Average (7.5–8.5)	Above Average (≥9)	Total
Below average (≤21)	100 (80)	100 (77)	58 (17)	93 (174)
Average (22–23)	86 (34)	87 (67)	80 (29)	85 (130)
Above average (≥24)	53 (14)	65 (42)	59 (32)	60 (88)
Total	88 (128)	85 (186)	65 (78)	81 (392)

Source: Reprinted with permission from DJP Barker et al, Weight in Infancy and Death from Ischaemic Heart Disease, in *Fetal and Infant Origins of Adult Disease*, DJP Barker, ed, p 145, © 1992, BMJ Publishing Group.

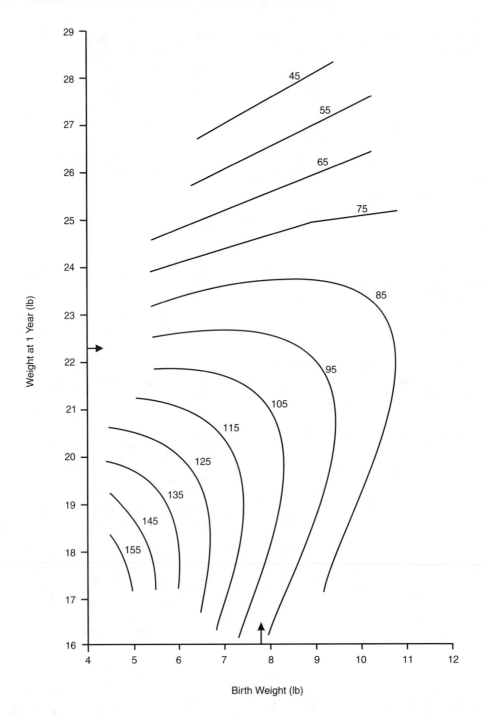

Figure 19–10 Relative Risks for Ischemic Heart Disease in Men Who Had Been Breast Fed, According to Birth Weight and Weight at One Year. Lines join points with equal risk. Arrows indicate mean weights. *Source*: Reprinted with permission from DJP Barker et al, Weight in Infancy and Death from Ischaemic Heart Disease, in *Fetal and Infant Origins of Adult Disease*, DJP Barker, ed, p 146, © 1992, BMJ Publishing Group.

supply to the fetus or infant, to which the body responds with particular physiologic or metabolic adaptations. When these adaptations occur at critical points in early development they constitute "programming," which determines the subsequent expression of genetic controls over growth, physiology, and metabolism throughout later life, a phenomenon recognized in animal experimental research.[19]

The link between programming and social conditions derives from the expectation that an adverse fetal or infant environment is especially likely to occur under circumstances of maternal poverty. Clearly, if major determinants of adult cardiovascular diseases operate in this period of life, intervention strategies for modification of behavior and social environment in adulthood may be too little, and too late, relative to the potential for true "early" intervention.

Counterargument

The theory that risks of coronary heart disease are determined during fetal development and infancy has received much comment and has met with some skepticism. Two reports have reviewed related work, one on 10 ecological studies[23] and the other on 15 longitudinal and 4 case-comparison studies.[24] Their findings led Elford and colleagues to conclude in 1992 that the hypothesis was insufficiently clear; that biological mechanisms specific to the hypothesis remained to be formulated; and that tests of the hypothesis in relation to geographic and temporal variations in coronary heart disease occurrence were required for rigorous testing of the hypothesis. In summary, they found the evidence insufficient to support a claim of causality as the basis for the reported associations. A more recent editorial expressed concurrence with these reservations: "The Southampton group has provided an intriguing but very general hypothesis, often ingeniously pursued, that has served to provoke the somewhat complacent world of cardiac epidemiology. As a hypothesis with substantial implications for public policy it deserves rigorous testing."[25(p 412)]

The charge of excessive claims for what has been dubbed by some "the Barker hypothesis" (by others than Barker himself) points to issues in evaluation of competing theories of disease causation that are addressed in Chapter 20, The Causal Complex. The potential immediate importance of Barker's "new model for the causation of coronary heart disease"[19(p 162)] will be addressed further at the close of this chapter.

WESTERNIZATION AND MIGRATION

Among the commoner changes in social conditions taking place in recent decades, and presumably to continue, are changes in culture, lifestyle, and environment attendant on economic development, migration, or both. Studies of these processes and their relation to cardiovascular disease and other health conditions have drawn on the concepts reviewed above and the works of Hinkle, Cassel, Tyroler, Syme, and others. This area of work is illustrated by an investigation of the Palauan people of the Western Caroline Islands, a post–World War II protectorate of the United States.[26]

In the late 1960s and early 1970s a study compared inhabitants of one traditional area of Palau not greatly changed from prewar village life (Ngerchelong), those of another area undergoing major social and environmental change as the administrative center for this district of the US Trust Territory (Koror), and those of an area intermediate in exposure to such change (Peleliu). Interview questionnaires and health examinations documented differences in culture, behaviors, and risk factors for cardiovascular diseases. Risk factors and prevalence of electrocardiographic abnormalities were, overall, least favorable in Koror, the most modern of the three settings, and most favorable in Ngerchelong, the most traditional area (Table 19–4). The age patterns of change in systolic blood pressure also favored the most traditional area, which exhibited similar slopes of increase in blood pressure with age, but lower levels at all ages for both males and females (Figure 19–11). Other examples of the impact of change from traditional to

Western culture include the local island population of Nauru, discussed in Chapter 13, whose epidemic obesity and diabetes of recent decades are clearly linked to this change.

Western Diseases

Trowell and Burkitt, in *Western Diseases: Their Emergence and Prevention*, justified the designation of the "man-made" diseases as Western in the sense that they are typical of affluent Western technologies, are less common in other countries and especially in lower socioeconomic groups, and are linked to the greater longevity and consequently increased opportunity for their expression in Western society.[27] They identified several conditions as Western diseases by these criteria and indicated their increased frequency in the course of Westernization in many population groups, as shown in Table 19–5. Prominent among them are coronary heart disease (CHD), hypertension, obesity, and diabetes.

Culture Change in Japanese Americans

The effect of migration on coronary heart disease in Japanese men residing in Hawaii or California, relative to the situation of those remaining in Japan, and the role of culture change in this process were studied in detail in the Ni-Hon-San Study, especially in a cross-sectional analysis of the three study groups.[28] Analysis of differences in prevalence of coronary heart disease in baseline surveys in the three areas indicated only partial explanation by differences in distributions of dietary pattern, blood cholesterol concentration, blood pressure, smoking, or other specific risk factors. Indices of culture change from traditional Japanese orientations to the conditions of Hawaii and California were also studied. These measured both the degree of acculturation versus adherence to traditional patterns of behavior and the extent of access to and reliance upon other members of the Japanese community. Further analyses incorporating these measures indicated that those who changed least and had the strongest support for adherence to aspects of traditional culture had the lowest prevalence of coronary heart disease. Thus, for the men age 45–54 years, the highest prevalence of coronary heart disease was 7.3% in those who were most acculturated and had least reliance on the Japanese community. This was about 2.5 times the lowest prevalence,

Table 19–4 Age-Adjusted Mean Values for Selected Characteristics, by Sex and Area, Palau, 1968/1970

Characteristic	Males			Females		
	Koror	Peleliu	Ngerchelong	Koror	Peleliu	Ngerchelong
Blood pressure, systolic (mm Hg)	136	135	121	133	137	124
Blood pressure, diastolic (mm Hg)	88	83	81	84	82	77
ECG abnormality[a]	43.0	46.4	37.2	36.4	29.1	29.3
Cholesterol (mg/100 ml)	171	163	147	177	175	165
Triglycerides (mEq/l)	4.7	3.6	3.1	4.0	3.5	3.0
Glucose (mg/100 ml)	134	111	112	121	107	118
Uric acid (mg/100 ml)	6.8	6.2	6.7	5.2	5.5	4.8

a. Percentage of persons with electrocardiographic examinations who manifested one or more items classifiable under the Minnesota Code, except for subclasses 9–4 and 9–8.

Source: Reprinted with permission from *American Journal of Epidemiology*, Vol 98, p 167, © 1973, The Johns Hopkins University School of Hygiene and Public Health.

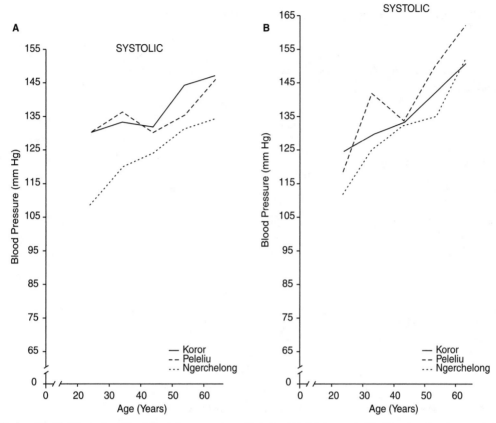

Figure 19–11 Mean Systolic Blood Pressure (mm Hg) for (A) Males and (B) Females, by Age and Area, Palau, 1968/1970. *Source*: Reprinted with permission from D Labarthe et al, *American Journal of Epidemiology*, Vol 98, p 166, © 1973, The Johns Hopkins University School of Hygiene and Public Health.

which was in those who were more traditional and reliant on the Japanese community. Corresponding frequencies for the age group below 45 years ranged from 5.1% to 1.0%, a fivefold difference.

Rural India: A Paradox?

In a rural population of Rajhastan, India, a survey of 3182 men and women villagers above age 20 permitted comparison of risk factors and prevalence of coronary heart disease by level of education.[29] Educational levels were graded as nil (group 1), 1–5 years (group 2), 6–10 years (group 3), and more than 10 years (group 4). Proportions of men and women who had ele-

vated blood pressure, cholesterol concentration (based on a subsample of 300 participants), and body mass index; who smoked; and who had a sedentary lifestyle were determined (Table 19–6). Except for sedentary living, all factors tended to be most adverse for the group with no education, for both men and women. High proportions of persons in all groups were reported as having a sedentary lifestyle. Coronary heart disease prevalence by specified criteria in each group is shown in Table 19–7 and was greatest among those without education, for both men and women. This report is contrary to the preconception that higher socioeconomic status will necessarily be associated with the early phases of epidemic coronary heart disease in

Table 19–5 Increased Incidence of Medical Diseases During Westernization

Group	Hypertension	Obesity	Diabetes[a]	Gall Stones[b]	Renal Stones	CHD[c]
Hunter-gatherers						
Eskimos	+	+	+	+		+
Australian Aborigines	+	+	+		+	+
North American Indians		+	+	+		+
Agriculturalists in:						
West Nile, Uganda	+	+	+	+d	+d	+d
Zimbabwe	O		+	+	+d	+
South Africa (Bantu)	+	+	+	+	+	+
Papua New Guinea	+	+	+d			+
Pacific Islands	+	+	+			+
Sub-Saharal Africa	+	+	+			+
Polynesia	+	+	+			
Migrants						
Maoris	+	+	+	+		+
South African Indians	+	+	+	+	+	+
Israelis	±		±	+		+
Far East						
Japan			+	+		+
Taiwan	+	+	+	+		+
Hawaiian groups		+		O		+

Note: Increase, +; doubtful increase, ±; no change, O; no report, blank space.

a. Type 2 non–insulin-dependent variety, formerly called *maturity-onset type*.

b. Cholesterol-rich variety.

c. Coronary heart disease and angina.

d. Very rare in rural areas; no data concerning increased incidence.

Source: Reprinted with permission from H Trowell, D Burkitt, Joint Enquiry into *Western Disease, in Western Diseases: Their Emergence and Prevention*, HC Trowell and D Burkitt, eds, © 1981, Edward Arnold/Hodder & Stoughton Educational.

developing countries. This observation suggests the importance of further studies in more diverse community settings and the need to understand the situation in a particular locality more clearly before planning targeted intervention toward one or another presumed high-risk stratum of the population.

CURRENT ISSUES

Material Conditions

A World Health Organization Study Group meeting in 1992 considered new areas for research in connection with cardiovascular disease risk factors.[30] It is of interest that several aspects of social conditions addressed above were included among research needs, as either "material conditions" or factors operating at different stages of life, specifically, the postulated childhood origins of adult cardiovascular disease. In connection with material conditions, the issue of inequality of income distribution was discussed. Emphasis was placed on the failure in some countries to meet even subsistence needs, so that health problems result from specific material deprivation.

Table 19-6 Prevalence of Major Coronary Risk Factors and Level of Education, as Numbers (Percentages) of Men and Women

Educational Status	No. of Subjects	Major Coronary Risk Factors				
		Blood Pressure ≥140/90 mm Hg	Cholesterol ≥5.18 mmol/l[a]	Body Mass Index ≥27	Smoking	Sedentary Lifestyle
Men						
Group 1 (nil)	765	207 (27)	23/87 (26)	38 (5)	458 (60)	534 (70)
Group 2 (1–5 years)	350	78 (22)	2/22 (9)	29 (8)	180 (51)	281 (80)
Group 3 (6–10 years)	591	126 (21)	12/52 (23)	26 (4)	270 (46)	519 (88)
Group 4 (>10 years)	276	59 (21)	7/41 (17)	10 (4)	98 (36)	262 (95)
Mantel-Haenszel χ^2		6.41	3.63	0.43	56.61	111.75
P value		0.011	0.060	0.51	<0.001	<0.001
Women						
Group 1 (nil)	608	141 (23)	14/62 (22)	44 (7)	35 (6)	528 (87)
Group 2 (1–5 years)	304	29 (10)	7/29 (24)	21 (7)	13 (4)	294 (97)
Group 3 (>5 years)[b]	254	27 (11)	1/7 (14)	9 (4)	6 (2)	253 (100)
Mantel-Haenszel χ^2		27.70	0.31	3.50	4.76	48.57
P value		<0.001	0.58	0.061	0.029	<0.001

a. Cholesterol concentrations were available in 202 men and women.

b. Some women in group 3 had education of more than 10 years.

Source: Reprinted with permission from R Gupta and VP Gupta, Education Status, Coronary Heart Disease, and Coronary Risk Factor Prevalence in Rural Population of India, *British Medical Journal*, Vol 309, p 1335, © 1994, BMJ Publishing Group.

Table 19–7 Educational Level and Prevalence of Coronary Heart Disease, as Numbers (Percentages) of Men and Women

	Men			Women		
Educational Status	Clinical and Electrocardiographic Findings	ST-T and Q Wave Changes	Q Waves Only	Clinical and Electrocardiographic Findings	ST-T and Q Wave Changes	Q Waves Only
Group 1 (nil)	36 (4.7)	31 (4.1)	27 (2.0)	32 (5.3)	30 (4.9)	10 (1.6)
Group 2 (1–5 years)	8 (2.3)	8 (2.3)	2 (0.6)	6 (2.0)	4 (1.3)	—
Group 3 (6–10 years)[a]	14 (2.4)	9 (1.5)	6 (1.0)	5 (2.0)	4 (1.6)	1 (0.4)
Group 4 (>10 years)	10 (3.6)	7 (2.5)	3 (1.1)	—	—	—
Mantel-Haenszel χ^2	2.83	5.30	6.01	7.25	8.79	4.54
P value	0.093	0.021	0.014	0.007	0.003	0.033

Coronary Heart Disease Prevalence

a. Some women in group 3 had education of more than 10 years.

Source: Reprinted with permission from R Gupta and VP Gupta, *British Medical Journal*, Vol 309, p 1335, © 1994, BMJ Publishing Group.

It was also recognized that where wide income differentials remain even when minimum subsistence needs are met for the whole of a society, gradients in cardiovascular disease rates may persist that seem attributable to relative rather than absolute deprivation. The correct explanation of these latter associations may be in psychosocial terms. Alternatively they may reflect failure to invest sufficiently in meeting further needs of the lowest-income strata, such as access to preventive services or less obviously relevant resources, with resulting adverse impacts on health. The contributions of these and other potential explanations remain to be determined. The potential impact of such results on social and economic policy could be substantial. It remains to be seen, however, whether sufficiently compelling arguments can be put forward on the basis of health and other considerations, as they are presently understood, to reverse the trend toward widening disparities in measures of socioeconomic status and increasing prevalence of poverty in the United States and elsewhere. The time required to establish more clearly the causal pathways between social conditions and health, including cardiovascular diseases, could be compressed greatly if comparable studies of multiple, diverse populations were undertaken soon and in a coordinated manner. Some difficulties in interpretation and generalization across cultures and political systems will likely remain, as noted by Hinkle more than 30 years ago.[2] However, systematic investigation under well-standardized protocols permitting comparative evaluation and synthesis of results would seem the most promising approach for progress in this area.

Stages of Life

With respect to stages of life, the Working Group noted the importance of distinguishing between a true effect of childhood (fetal and neonatal) factors and factors in adulthood in determining risks of adult cardiovascular diseases. They attached considerable importance to this question: "[I]t is important to attempt to distinguish between these two sets of influences since their relative importance is crucial to determining the appropriate locus for interventions which may not improve overall adult health and reduce socioeconomic differentials. This is a vital area for further research."[30(p 41)] Not surprisingly, this theme is found also in the reflections of Barker on the implications of the theory of fetal and early postnatal origins of coronary heart disease:

> The search for causes of "Western" diseases has concentrated on the adult environment. The importance of the childhood environment in determining responses throughout life may have been underestimated. . . . Where differences in individuals' susceptibility to disease cannot be explained by differences in the adult environment, as is the case for coronary heart disease, they have often been attributed to genetic causes—especially if the disease has a familial tendency. Part of what is now regarded as the genetic contribution to ischemic heart disease may turn out to be the effect of the intrauterine or early postnatal environment. . . . If more was known about the processes by which the environment in early life influences adult health, the hygienic and nutritional benefits which will accompany industrial development might be maximised, and the risk in incidence of "Western" disease minimised.[31(pp 334–335)]

Contrary to Barker's statement, it is widely recognized that origins of atherosclerosis and its later complications precede adulthood. It is true, however, that the pursuit of these origins from adolescence or childhood into the period of fetal development is very recent. To date, scant attention has been given to the potentially very important connection between the concept of exposures in the fetal and postnatal period and the concept of change in social conditions with economic development, or to their joint effects on future cardiovascular disease rates.

Fundamental Causes

A final note concerns the concept that social conditions constitute "fundamental causes" of disease, not merely markers of true causes or pointers toward risk factors that operate more proximally in relation to disease.[32] Social conditions are claimed to be fundamental causes on grounds that they lack dependence on specific, biologically plausible mechanisms and persist in producing disease even if one or another particular associated mechanism is successfully countered by intervention. For example, the relation of poverty with excess morbidity and mortality persists despite the removal of successive hazards to which the poor are known to be differentially exposed. The argument is advanced that intervention against specific risk factors is inherently less promising than intervention that addresses fundamental causes, that is, the social conditions under which the occurrence of diseases aggregates. One corollary of this argument is that broad social policies may have far-reaching effects on health through their influence on these fundamental causes, and that medical sociologists and social epidemiologists should become capable of preparing a "health impact statement" as part of the development of social and economic policy.

This is a provocative proposal that warrants scrutiny. It is considered further, in the context of concepts of causation and their application to the atherosclerotic and hypertensive diseases, in the chapter that follows.

REFERENCES

1. Stamler J. Established major coronary risk factors. In: Marmot M, Elliott P, eds. *Coronary Heart Disease Epidemiology: From Aetiology to Public Health.* Oxford, England: Oxford University Press; 1992:35–66.

2. Hinkle LE. Ecological observations of the relation of physical illness, mental illness, and the social environment. *Psychosom Med.* 1961;23:289–296.

3. Cassel J, Patrick R, Jenkins D. Epidemiological analysis of the health implications of culture change: a conceptual model. *Ann NY Acad Sci.* 1960;84:938–949.

4. Cassel J, Tyroler HA. Epidemiological studies of cultural change. *Arch Environ Health.* 1961;13:31–39.

5. Tyroler HA, Cassel J. Health consequences of cultural change—II. *J Chronic Dis.* 1964;17:167–177.

6. Syme SL, Hyman MM, Enterline PE. Cultural mobility and the occurrence of coronary heart disease. *J Health Hum Behav.* 1965;6:178–189.

7. Reeder LG. Occupation and socioeconomic status as variables in heart disease research: a critique. *Am J Med Sci.* 1959;238:297–307.

8. Hinkle LE, Whitney H, Lehman EW, Dunn J, et al. Occupation, education, and coronary heart disease. *Science.* 1968;161:238–246.

9. Marmot MG, Kogevinas M, Elston MA. Social/economic status and disease. *Ann Rev Public Health.* 1987;8:111–135.

10. Marmot MG, Adelstein AM, Robinson N, Rose GA. Changing social-class distribution of heart disease. *Br Med J.* 1978;2:1109–1112.

11. Kaplan GA, Keil JE. Socioeconomic factors and cardiovascular disease: a review of the literature. *Circ.* 1993;88:1973–1998.

12. Lenfant C. Conference on Socioeconomic Status and Cardiovascular Health and Disease. *Circ.* 1996;94:2041–2044.

13. Sorlie PD, Johnson NJ, Backlund E. Socioeconomic status and cardiovascular disease mortality: National Longitudinal Mortality Study. In: *Report of the Conference on Socioeconomic Status and Cardiovascular Health and Disease, November 6–7, 1995.* Bethesda, Md: National Heart, Lung and Blood Institute, National Institutes of Health; 1995: 23–26.

14. Johnson CL, Sempos CT. Socioeconomic status and biomedical, lifestyle, and psychosocial risk factors for CVD: selected U.S. national data and trends. In: *Report of the Conference on Socioeconomic Status and Cardiovascular Health and Disease, November 6–7, 1995.* Bethesda, Md: National Heart, Lung and Blood Institute, National Institutes of Health; 1995: 35–39.

15. Kunst AE, Groenhof F, Mackenbach J, European Union Working Group on Socioeconomic Inequalities in Health. Differences between occupational classes in cardiovascular disease mortality: a comparison of 11 European countries. In: *Report of the Conference on*

Socioeconomic Status and Cardiovascular Health and Disease, November 6–7, 1995. Bethesda, Md: National Heart, Lung and Blood Institute, National Institutes of Health; 1995: 49–56.

16. House JS, Williams DR. Psychosocial pathways linking SES and CVD. In: *Report of the Conference on Socioeconomic Status and Cardiovascular Health and Disease, November 6–7, 1995.* Bethesda, Md: National Heart, Lung and Blood Institute, National Institutes of Health; 1995: 119–124.

17. Kennedy BP, Kawachi I, Prothrow-Stith D. Income distribution and mortality: cross sectional ecological study of the Robin Hood index in the United States. *Br Med J.* 1996;312:1004–1007.

18. Forsdahl A. Are poor living conditions in childhood and adolescence an important risk factor for arteriosclerotic heart disease? *Br J Prev Soc Med.* 1977; 31:91–95.

19. Barker DJP. The origins of coronary heart disease in early life. In: Henry CJK, Ulijaszek SJ, eds. *Long-Term Consequences of Early Environment.* Cambridge, England: Cambridge University Press; 1996: 155–162.

20. Barker DJP, Osmond C. 1: Infant mortality, childhood nutrition, and ischaemic heart disease in England and Wales. In: Barker DJP, ed. *Fetal and Infant Origins of Adult Disease.* London: British Medical Journal; 1992: 23–37.

21. Barker DJP, Winter PD, Osmond C, Margetts BM, et al. 13: Weight in infancy from ischaemic heart disease. In: Barker DJP, ed. *Fetal and Infant Origins of Adult Disease.* London: British Medical Journal; 1992:141–149.

22. Fall CHD, Osmond C, Barker DJP, Clark PMS, et al. Fetal and infant growth and cardiovascular risk factors in women. *Br Med J.* 1995;310:428–432.

23. Elford J, Shaper AG, Whincup P. Early life experience and cardiovascular disease—ecological studies. *J Epidemiol Community Health.* 1992;46:1–11.

24. Elford J, Whincup P, Shaper AG. Early life experience and adult cardiovascular disease: longitudinal and case-control studies. *Int J Epidemiol.* 1991;20:833–844.

25. Paneth N, Susser M. Early origin of coronary heart disease (the "Barker hypothesis"). *Br Med J.* 1995; 310:411–412. Editorial.

26. Labarthe D, Reed D, Brody J, Stallones R. Health effects of modernization in Palau. *Am J Epidemiol.* 1973;98:161–174.

27. Trowell H, Burkitt D. Joint enquiry into Western diseases. In: Trowell HC, Burkitt DP, eds. *Western Diseases: Their Emergence and Prevention.* Cambridge, Mass: Harvard University Press; 1981: 427–435.

28. Marmot MG, Syme SL. Acculturation and coronary heart disease in Japanese-Americans. *J Epidemiol.* 1976;104:225–247.

29. Gupta R, Gupta VP, Ahluwalia NS. Educational status, coronary heart disease, and coronary risk factor prevalence in a rural population of India. *Br Med J.* 1994; 309:1332–1336.

30. Report of a WHO Scientific Group. Cardiovascular disease risk factors: new areas for research. Geneva, Switzerland: World Health Organization; 1994. WHO Technical Report Series 841.

31. Barker DJP. Review: rise and fall of Western diseases. In: Barker DJP, ed. *Fetal and Infant Origins of Adult Disease.* London, England: British Medical Journal; 1992:330–335.

32. Link BG, Phelan J. Social conditions as fundamental causes of disease. *J Health Soc Behav.* 1995; 36:80–94.

CHAPTER 20

The Causal Complex

SUMMARY

The preceding chapters have presented the natural history of atherosclerosis and hypertension and their major outcomes, coronary heart disease, stroke, peripheral arterial disease, aortic aneurysm, and congestive heart failure. The main determinants of the onset and progression of these conditions have also been reviewed. They include personal characteristics, patterns of behavior, metabolic and physiologic conditions, psychosocial aspects, and social conditions. No single answer to the question of what causes atherosclerotic and hypertensive diseases can be both complete and simple. Different bases for inclusion of factors in a given causal scheme and different approaches to recognizing causation itself foster some misunderstanding and can impede scientific communication as well as development and implementation of preventive policies. Therefore this chapter addresses concepts of causation both in general and in relation specifically to atherosclerotic and hypertension diseases. It is suggested that a twofold approach serves best to advance understanding of the "n-dimensional causal complex" and at the same time to exercise judicious selection of those factors most important for prevention. These complementary concepts of an open framework to accommodate still-expanding knowledge of causal relations and of a selective emphasis on several established major risk factors appear to offer the best opportunity for both broader scientific understanding and more-effective public health action.

INTRODUCTION

The *British Medical Journal* for December 29, 1909, reported: "Professor Osler delivered an address on arterio-sclerosis. Though there were sixty-two theories of its causation, he thought the three main factors were time, tension, and toxins."[1(p 1800)] *Time* denoted the concept of atheromata as a manifestation of senility, at age 70, although for Osler heredity might explain the appearance of these lesions at much earlier ages, and he recognized "fatty degeneration" in the aorta even in childhood. *Tension* comprised both "the tension of life," exemplified by a man working in the New York Stock Exchange, and "muscular tension, due to overexertion." *Toxins* were both "exogenous" (excess of food, alcohol, tobacco, tea, and coffee) and "endogenous" ("waste products which irritated the endothelium and kept up a high tension"). Osler's recommendation for prevention was summarized as follows: "For those with tendencies towards arterio-sclerosis the guiding motto was: 'Nothing too much'—the life of the tortoise, not that of the hare." His concluding remarks were paraphrased, somewhat enigmatically, "Success was largely a matter of survivorship."

Nearly a century after Osler's assessment, the number of factors implicated in the causation of atherosclerotic and hypertensive diseases has multiplied several-fold, and, for practical purposes, it is no less necessary today to select for emphasis those thought to be "main factors." The magnitude, complexity, and continuing growth of this body of evidence provide opportunity for confusion or misinterpretation, sometimes leading to controversy about both current understanding and the scientific basis for intervention. It is therefore important to address several questions:

- What is the nature of the process to be explained?
- What factors need to be taken into account?
- What would constitute a satisfactory explanation?

The first two questions have been addressed extensively in Chapters 3 through 19. They are considered in a brief overview below to provide the context for the present discussion. The third question concerns concepts of causation in general and cardiovascular disease epidemiology in particular. This question is the main focus of the present chapter. It is emphasized for two reasons: first, to reinforce the concept of established major risk factors, discussed below, which is essential for development and implementation of preventive policies and practices; second, to provide a framework for inclusion of the remaining factors in a comprehensive, if necessarily incomplete, array of causal relations that represents current understanding of this disease process and serves to identify goals for future research.

OVERVIEW OF ATHEROSCLEROTIC AND HYPERTENSIVE DISEASES AND THEIR DETERMINANTS

The Disease Process

Parts II and III of this book address the atherosclerotic and hypertensive diseases, a cate-gorization based on the extensively, though not completely, overlapping processes leading to coronary heart disease, cerebrovascular disease, peripheral arterial disease, aortic aneurysm, and, at least in Western industrialized countries, much of congestive heart failure. What is to be explained, therefore, is a multifaceted disease process that has been investigated extensively at several distinct levels: In different populations and communities, it exhibits marked variation in mortality with sharply divergent trends; within families, from extended pedigrees to parents and offspring to twin pairs, it clusters and occurs more often among relatives than would be expected from the population at large; within individuals, it progresses predictably from early indicators of risk to fully developed disease; it affects specific regions of the circulation, especially the heart, brain, lower extremities, and aorta, with characteristic derangements and lesions in the arterial wall; structural and functional variation at cell surfaces are implicated; and genes, regulatory proteins, lipid transport molecules, and many other molecular phenomena are involved.

The Main Determinants

Similarly, the potential explanatory factors extend across many levels—for example, from the determinants of national policies for land use and food production to genetic variation and factors that influence gene expression. These factors include intrinsic personal characteristics such as age, sex, race or ethnicity, and heredity; individual patterns of behavior, such as diet, physical activity, and use of tobacco and alcohol; physiologic and metabolic processes, such as regulation of lipid metabolism, blood pressure, blood coagulation, and glucose concentration and insulin activity; psychosocial factors; and extrinsic social conditions. In addition, many interactions occur among these factors, and for each one of the factors a network of determinants is established or proposed in varying degrees of detail.

It is reasonable to ask whether, in principle, an intelligible understanding of the causation of the atherosclerotic and hypertensive diseases should be expected to accommodate all aspects of the disease process, each of the explanatory factors, and the determinants of these factors, in turn. Would such an all-inclusive formulation, if attainable, be meaningful or useful? Or might it be too broad to be of interest to an investigator working within only one level or area? Alternatively, would a narrow, selective model of causation lack credibility in failing to include important aspects of the evidence?

The need to consider these questions stems in part from frequently encountered skepticism or confusion about the current state of knowledge of causation of these diseases. For some persons concerned about preventive policies and practices, the evidence that many factors are related to this process and that none alone is a sufficient explanation seriously weakens the rationale for intervention. Well-founded skepticism can be of value in stimulating due rigor in scientific thinking and caution in development of public policy and practice guidelines, but skepticism based on misunderstanding can be a costly impediment to action and a disservice to the health of the public. Clarity about the nature of causal explanations may therefore help to direct constructive skepticism toward identification of crucial questions for research whose resolution will advance both understanding and the potential for prevention.

The discussion that follows addresses general concepts of causation, causal concepts applied to atherosclerosis and hypertension, and an approach to answering the question, What causes atherosclerotic and hypertensive diseases?

GENERAL CONCEPTS OF CAUSATION

Causation is a fundamental concept in science and is central to epidemiology and public health. Acceptance of the results of epidemiologic studies as reflecting causation, when appropriate to do so, is a necessary step in translating research into policy and practice. Differences in understanding and interpretation of causation, not surprisingly, can foster confusion and controversy. Where controversy is found concerning cardiovascular disease prevention, it often appears to stem from such differences.

Difficulties in understanding issues of causation are not confined within the scientific community, however, as many examples from the news media show—such as Figure 20–1, a particularly expressive recent cartoon from the *Cincinnati Enquirer*.[2] Lack of confidence in health messages from prominent scientific journals is the overt theme, but a major part of the underlying problem is failure of epidemiologists and others to convey adequately the difference in meaning between two types of evidence. One type concerns the typical newly reported finding, often with limited confirmation, which is primarily of theoretical interest to the scientific community; the other concerns well-established causal relations with implications for policy and practice, perhaps implying recommendations for individual behavior. Promotion of research results as being of the latter kind when they are in fact the former is a common error that is perhaps avoidable if concepts of causation are understood clearly and applied consistently.

In *Causal Thinking in the Health Sciences: Concepts and Strategies in Epidemiology,* Susser in 1973 traced the background of causal thinking and elaborated conceptual models applicable in epidemiology, including aspects of judgment that finally enter into most, if not all, questions of causation in the health sciences.[3] His continuing reflections on this topic were published nearly 20 years later, in 1991, with the apt title, "What Is a Cause and How Do We Know One? A Grammar for Pragmatic Epidemiology."[4] The value of this essay derives especially from its refinement of considerations raised in coming to judgments about causation and its differentiation among types of epidemiologic studies regarding their distinctive contributions to these judgments. Formal application

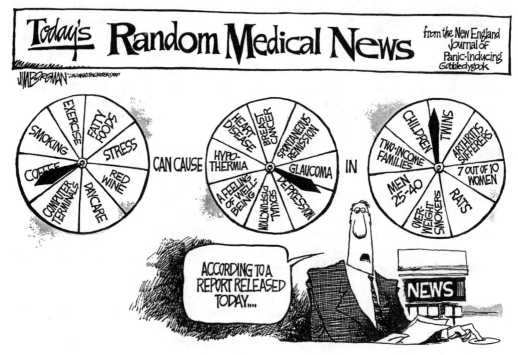

Figure 20–1 "Today's Random Medical News": A Reflection of Differences in Understanding of Causation. *Source*: Copyright © The Hearst Corporation.

of Susser's "grammar" to the causation of the atherosclerotic and hypertensive diseases could be a rewarding, though monumental, task. For the present, only a less ambitious and more conjectural approach is feasible.

A second, very accessible, general approach to concepts of causation is that of MacMahon and Pugh, whose 1970 text posed the following question:

> What, then, leads one to think of certain relationships as causal? The word *cause* is an abstract noun and, like *beauty*, will have different meanings in different contexts. No definition will be equally appropriate in all branches of science. Epidemiology has the practical purpose of discovering relations which offer possibilities of disease prevention and for this

purpose a causal association may usefully be defined as an association between categories of events or characteristics in which an alteration in the frequency or quality of one category is followed by a change in the other. . . . [T]he idea of changeability is a basic component of epidemiologic concepts of causation.[5(pp 18–19)]

The implications of this view of causation are considered in the conclusion of this chapter. At this point, it offers an appropriately broad perspective in which to open the discussion.

From Single Agent to "N-Dimensional Complex"

The view that diseases other than specific infections are caused by single agents has long been superseded by recognition that multiple factors are required to produce most noninfectious chronic diseases, which are often therefore considered "multifactorial" in causation. The limited utility of the single-agent concept even for infectious diseases is obvious on consideration that such agents produce disease only when other factors lead to exposure of susceptible individuals. Further, the agent of the disease does not explain the occurrence of epidemics or the rate of occurrence of the disease but only the infection in the individual case. Nonetheless, writers such as Stehbens continue to hold that the causation of atherosclerosis remains unknown, "cause" in his view being "the essential antecedent or sole prerequisite determinant by which the disease is brought about and without which the disease cannot occur."[6(pp 99–100)]

The idea that a number of preconditions are required for relevant exposures to occur and produce disease led to the metaphor of the "chain of causation." Links in the chain can be discovered through appropriate investigation and potentially broken through targeted intervention. It is unnecessary to identify every link if one or more critical ones can be identified and their connections interrupted, as in immunization to prevent infection when an otherwise effective exposure occurs. Notably, the discovery of each new link requires further research to connect it—at both ends—with links already known.

MacMahon and Pugh, in their text cited above, found the chain analogy insufficient to account for interactions among many antecedent factors in the causation of disease.[5] According to MacMahon (personal communication, 1996), Pugh deserves the credit for proposing the "web of causation" to fill this need, having in MacMahon's words "invented it out of whole cloth." With this more accommodating metaphor, they could construct a two-dimensional graphic scheme of the causation of icterus (jaundice) as a sign of serum hepatitis resulting from use of contaminated syringes in treatment of persons with syphilis. Their observations

about this web are instructive for the present discussion:

> When it is considered that only a few of the major components are shown, that these are indicated as broad classes of events rather than as the multiple minor events which make up each class, that each component shown is itself the result of a complex genealogy of antecedents, and that the myriad effects of these components other than those contributing to the development of icterus are not shown, then it becomes evident that the chains of causation represent only a fraction of the reality, and the whole genealogy may be thought of more appropriately as a web, which in its complexity and origins lies quite beyond our understanding.
>
> Fortunately it is not necessary to understand causal mechanisms in their entirety to effect preventive measures. Knowledge of even one small component may allow significant degrees of prevention.[5(pp 23–24)]

Stallones expanded the framework still further by suggesting a view of causality that extends beyond the two-dimensional web and encompasses the possibility of multiple interrelated outcomes, such as coronary heart disease and stroke, rather than only one as in the previous example:

> Whatever constructs we may devise must be understood to represent our biased views of what a representation of reality should be. Because it is not the reality, the value of the model depends upon its utility, and utility depends upon the purpose for which the model is used. Rothman has spoken of a constellation of component causes [Rothman KJ. Causes. *Am J Epidemiol.* 1976;104:587–592.], but I think his concept is closely akin to

the web of causation model, in which the causes converge upon an effect. If the purpose is more global than studying one disease at a time, then the multiple regression/web of causation model is inadequate. An approach that holds promise is to consider the interdependence of a number of diseases, characteristics of individuals, and environmental and social variables as elements in a constellation which is n-dimensional, and within which directed pathways are incidental to the complex as a whole.[7(p 76)]

The potential suitability of this approach is apparent in the present context, where both outcomes and levels and dimensions of related factors are multiple and diverse. Further, the same inherent incompleteness applies as was suggested by MacMahon and Pugh, where extensive detail could be specified—now or in the future—at many points. If the full ramifications of the web were beyond understanding, those of the "n-dimensional complex" would be more so.

These views of causality indicate progressive concern for comprehensiveness, and increasingly they risk loss of direct practical utility as a result. Encyclopedic inclusiveness is of value for intellectual purposes aimed at complete scientific understanding, but applicability to policy and practice implies identification of "directed pathways," in Stallone's terms. Selection of particular pathways or specific factors for attention within such a framework requires justification in terms of their relative importance, perhaps in terms of utility for development of preventive strategies, as indicated by MacMahon and Pugh. This adds to the likelihood that, as they suggested, the meaning of causation may differ in different branches of science. To accept this view, however, is to threaten communication and understanding among scientists working at different levels or in different zones of the complex, a direction counter to that needed if

knowledge is to be integrated across disciplines and areas of investigation. How far such integration must reach can be illustrated by two major contributors, one beginning from the gene, the other from population differences in rates of disease occurrence.

From Molecules to Populations

Sing and colleagues addressed the problem of linking DNA variations with interindividual variation in risk of coronary artery disease.[8] Three levels of analysis were represented schematically as in Figure 20–2. First is the genotype, second is the network of intermediate traits, and third is the probability of developing coronary artery disease. Multiple genes contribute to each of the intermediate traits, which are regulatory phenomena illustrated by hemostasis, lipid and carbohydrate metabolism, and blood pressure regulation. (Each "trait," of course, is itself a complex regulatory system, the number of whose recognized component processes and determinants expands continuously with advancing knowledge.) The resultant of these four traits leads to varying probabilities of expressing coronary artery disease, conditional on environment and age. This figure contrasts with several figures in previous chapters, as those figures are specific to one or another single factor and equal or greater detail was presented for that factor alone. As a grand summary, then, this scheme goes considerably further in linking genes, through intermediate phenotypes, to individual probabilities of disease, though omitting the voluminous detail already established at each level.

Even so, this scheme goes only part way toward the full range of considerations important for public health. It omits the level of population differences, which for Rose was the cardinal point of concern.[9] In "Sick Individuals and Sick Populations," he emphasized causes of two kinds whose distinction was critical: causes of incidence and causes of cases. The distinction is analogous to that between the factors required to cause an epidemic of a disease and

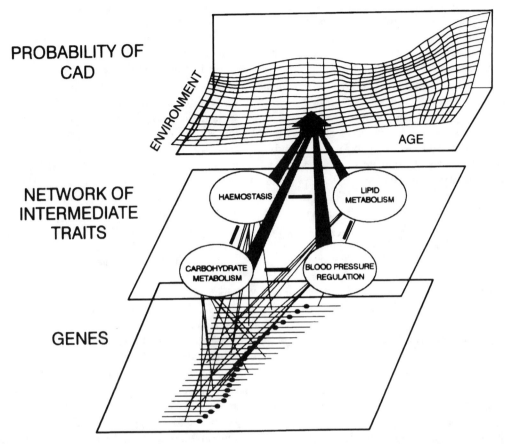

PROBABILITY OF
CAD

NETWORK OF
INTERMEDIATE
TRAITS

GENES

Figure 20–2 Biological Complexity of Coronary Artery Disease (CAD): Genes, Intermediate Traits, and Probability of CAD. *Source*: Reprinted with permission from CF Sing et al, *Annals of Medicine*, Vol 24, p 541, © 1992, The Finnish Medical Society Duodecim.

the specific agent established as causing individual cases of that disease. For example, epidemics of an infectious disease known to occur sporadically, that is, in seemingly isolated, infrequent cases, require additional explanatory factors beyond the infecting organism itself. Thus, causes of incidence operate to produce differences in disease rates between populations or within a population over time, whereas causes of cases account only for differences in risk among individuals within a population at a particular time.

From the public health viewpoint, Rose argued, the primary question is why a disease is common in one population and rare in another; to focus only, or primarily, on differences in individual risks may fail to identify the most potent, population-wide influences on the occurrence of disease and the furthest-reaching preventive measures. To give primary consideration to utility of particular factors for public health intervention offers a rational approach for their selection, out of the extensive complex of causes, to receive particular attention. This approach reflects a common view that narrowly construed causal pathways are most useful in epidemiology; that is, they have the greatest practical applicability to disease prevention and control.

The value of the more comprehensive frameworks must also be fully appreciated, however. From the perspective of interdisciplinary research, the most inclusive array of causal factors may be the most likely to foster innovative collaborations and stimulate studies across levels of understanding. For example, a potential link between the scheme of Sing and others and the population perspective of Rose would be to investigate especially those genetic factors thought to differ in distribution among populations that differ in rates of coronary artery disease. The potential role for genetic epidemiology in this aspect of research on cardiovascular diseases seems clear from this perspective.

CAUSAL JUDGMENT

Inclusion as a factor in any particular version of a causal framework may or may not be based on an established causal association with disease, depending on its author's intent. Thus, published causal schemes related to atherosclerotic and hypertensive diseases are sometimes simplistic and lack formal attention to issues of causation in the relations they display. By contrast, explicit justification of causal interpretation of several associations has been presented on many occasions, as illustrated by Stamler's review, "Established Coronary Risk Factors."[10] In such discussions, the argument typically invokes several conventional considerations about the evidence for causation.

The considerations applied are variously attributed to the first report of the US Surgeon General on smoking and health,[11] a paper by Hill,[12] the book by Susser cited earlier,[3] or other sources. In fact, the bases for these widely employed considerations are traceable to earlier thinking in 20th-century epidemiology.[13] Variously formulated, the considerations are essentially as described in the following.

Once an association has met standards of statistical significance, independence from other factors, and absence of explanation by spurious relationships, the following properties are considered: "strength" of the relationship as measured by magnitude of the measure of association (eg, the relative risk or odds ratio); variation in strength with variation in degree or intensity of exposure (dose-response gradient); "consistency" of the association, whether found in studies of different populations and under different methods and circumstances of investigation; "temporal sequence," or unequivocal evidence concerning presence of the factor prior to onset of the disease; "specificity," or the degree to which other associations involving either the factor or the disease are uncommon; and "biological plausibility" (coherence), by which the epidemiologic association has corresponding support from other kinds of evidence, such as research in other disciplines. In addition, experimental evidence of change in disease outcome following change in exposure may be considered separately from results of other epidemiologic methods. This is because of the special weight often, though not necessarily, given to experimental evidence. This consideration invokes again the concept of changeability discussed above.

The frequent characterization of these considerations as "criteria" is erroneous, because none of them can be regarded as decisive in the differential diagnosis between causal and noncausal associations.[12] Rather, to the extent that each is supportive of a causal interpretation, it contributes to confidence that such an interpretation is more reasonable than attribution to chance, bias, or confounding. This attitude applies equally to biological plausibility, because preventive action need not always await such evidence. For example, the classic epidemiologic gesture by John Snow in removing the handle of the Broad Street pump in the London cholera outbreak of 1853 antedated by decades the microbiologic understanding of this waterborne disease. In this case, intervention based on inference from observations within the population level alone was at least symbolically effective in prevention of the disease.

Causes and Mechanisms, Etiology and Pathogenesis

The n-dimensional complex and web of causation are both intended to include all phenomena related to the production of disease, from all levels of observation. The array of relevant levels is represented in Figure 20–3, adapted from Stallones' original figure to suggest an appropriate connection for contemporary epidemiology, beyond that of traditional epidemiology, across the full spectrum. Accordingly, for example, details of the intrinsic and extrinsic pathways of blood coagulation are incorporated in the same framework as differential trends in coronary heart disease mortality between countries during the 20th century. The sharpness of the distinction often made between research on outcomes and research on mechanisms, the latter being construed as exclusively "fundamental," is greatly diminished in this perspective. All observations, whether in laboratory, clinical, or population settings, gain plausibility from demonstration of linkages with the remainder of the complex. Those most firmly linked in a number of directed pathways would contribute most importantly to understanding of the process as a whole.

Etiology refers literally to the study of causation but is often equated with causation itself. Distinction between *etiology* and *pathogenesis* is also often blurred, the latter referring strictly to the development or progression of a disease once it has been caused. Whether the relation of a factor associated with occurrence of the atherosclerotic and hypertensive diseases is thought to concern etiology or pathogenesis is rarely made explicit. The multiple outcomes at issue invite inconsistency. For example, the etiology of coronary heart disease may be considered as operating at the onset of atherosclerosis in childhood or at the moment of precipitation of an acute myocardial infarction as the first clinical manifestation of the disease. What is meant by causation in the present context, then, should be understood as the complex of factors that operate at any point from prior to the first manifestation of atherosclerosis or hypertension to the last, perhaps fatal, step in the course of disease.

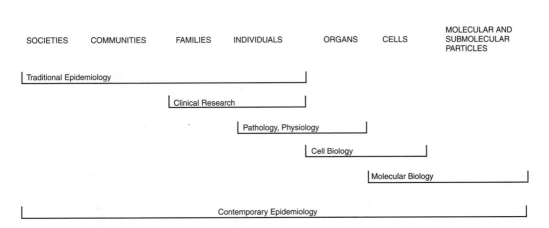

Figure 20–3 The Biomedical and Community Health Sciences Arrayed on a Scale of Biological Organization. *Source*: Adapted with permission, from the *Annual Review of Public Health*, Vol 1, © 1980, by Annual Reviews, Inc.

CAUSAL CONCEPTS APPLIED TO ATHEROSCLEROTIC AND HYPERTENSIVE DISEASES

The earliest known statement on prevention of coronary heart disease and stroke was that of the National Health Education Committee, Inc, published in 1959: *A Statement on Arteriosclerosis, Main Cause of "Heart Attacks" and "Strokes."*[14] The conditions addressed in that report as contributing or predisposing factors are discussed further in Chapter 22, as well as in several preceding chapters: overweight, elevated blood cholesterol level, elevated blood pressure, excessive cigarette smoking, and heredity. The Statement also noted that moderate physical activity appeared to reduce the hazards of arteriosclerosis. The connection of each factor with the disease was supported by reference to studies published in the 1940s and 1950s.

Risk Factors

The now commonplace term *risk factor* was introduced in 1961 in a report by Kannel, Dawber, Kagan, Revotskie, and Stokes on the first six years of experience in the Framingham Study.[15] (Authority for this claim rests with the late Frederick Epstein, whose diligent and thoroughly reliable scholarship revealed no prior use of the term, according to informed sources [Kannel WB, Higgins I, Higgins M, personal communication, 1996].) Referring to serum cholesterol concentration, blood pressure, and electrocardiographic evidence of left ventricular hypertrophy, Kannel and colleagues wrote:

> Combinations of the three risk factors under consideration appear to augment further the risk of subsequent development of coronary heart disease. It has been demonstrated . . . that the incidence of coronary heart disease rises progressively as these factors are combined. . . . Whether or not the correction of these abnormalities once they are discovered will

favorably alter the risk of development of disease, while reasonable to contemplate and perhaps attempt, remains to be demonstrated. . . . As additional longitudinal observations are made, it is hoped that additional risk factors will be determined. This will allow further identification of susceptible individuals and hopefully suggest methods of control.[15(pp 47–48)]

Emphasis was placed on the evidence in the Framingham Study that these conditions preceded the appearance of coronary heart disease, in contrast to prior clinical studies among existing cases of the disease. However, demonstration of change in outcome with change in exposure (MacMahon and Pugh's later "changeability") was clearly not a requirement. Further, no distinction was made between left ventricular hypertrophy, a sign of existing cardiac disease commonly associated with long-standing high blood pressure, and elevated blood pressure itself, notwithstanding the presumed sequential relation between these two factors.

The authors' hope that additional risk factors might be identified was amply fulfilled and documented by Hopkins and Williams, who reported 20 years later on a survey of coronary risk factors.[16] The 246 diverse factors reviewed and referenced in detail are categorized in Table 20–1. The criterion for inclusion of each factor was at least one publication that suggested either its direct or inverse association with occurrence of coronary heart disease. The value of this heroic exercise was lost on two especially vocal critics of the risk factor concept, McCormick and Skrbanek,[17] who took the number of 246 factors as sufficient evidence of the fallacy of this approach to understanding causation, a view shared by some others. The further elaboration of many of these factors and the numerous determinants of these factors in the ensuing 15 years has doubtless multiplied the count of candidates by many times, thereby greatly expanding the n-dimensional complex of causation.

Models of Causation

Synthesis of the plethora of suggested or identified risk factors into a coherent picture has been undertaken on several occasions. The linkage of genes, intermediate phenotypes, and coronary artery disease as in Figure 20–1 is one example. Greater detail at the intermediate level, and multiple possible outcomes anticipating the n-dimensional concept, was presented by Stallones in the 1960s (Figure 20–4).[18] Outcomes affecting the heart, brain, and arterial circulation were distinguished, as were subtypes of coronary and cerebral vascular diseases. Contributions of hemostatic function, atherosclerosis, and hypertension were placed closest to these outcomes as "immediate precursors," and a network of associated factors was arrayed more distant from the outcomes. (This figure is said to have prompted Stallones to claim the "St. Sebastian award" in view of the numerous arrows it features [Reed DM, personal communication, 1996].)

Hopkins and Williams, in turn, attempted to organize selected factors among those reviewed into a causal framework for heart attack (Figure 20–5).[16] Their approach was based on a concept of pathogenesis of atherosclerosis progressing from the earliest endothelial abnormalities to cholesterol deposition in the arterial wall, increased likelihood or risk of thrombosis, and precipitation of acute ischemia or arrhythmia. Factors especially linked with these successive phases of atherosclerosis were termed, respectively, *initiators*, *promoters*, *potentiators*, and *precipitators*. In stating that "the major CHD risk factor tends to have multiple roles in atherogenesis,"[16(p 18)] the authors reflected the view that importance of a given factor was dependent on its recurrent appearance in multiple causal pathways. For example, from Figure 20–5, this approach would especially implicate high-fat diet and cigarette smoking.

Another approach to synthesis of current understanding into a coherent picture of causation was taken by Pearson and colleagues (Figure 20–6).[19] Their review was presented in the context of the projected cardiovascular disease experience of developing countries in the decades ahead. Multiple end points were recognized, as in the scheme shown previously in Figure 20–4, with segregation of primarily hypertensive from primarily atherosclerotic outcomes in the heart and brain and the addition of

Table 20–1 Coronary Heart Disease Risk Factors and Suggested Associations

Category	No.	%
Constitutional and demographic factors	16	6.5
Environmental exposure	5	2.0
Habits, lifestyle, and psychosocial factors	54	22.0
Physical and biochemical measurements	16	6.5
Serum or blood measurements	44	17.9
Platelet and coagulation tests	16	6.5
Medical conditions	45	18.3
Dietary excesses and positive associations	21	8.5
Dietary deficiencies and inverse associations or possible protective factors	23	9.3
Drug liabilities	6	2.4
Total	246	100.0

Source: Data from PN Hopkins and RR Williams, A Survey of 246 Suggested Coronary Risk Factors, *Atherosclerosis*, Vol 40, pp 1–52, © 1981.

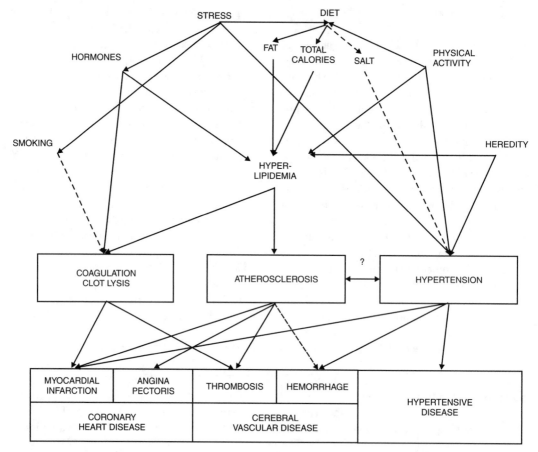

Figure 20–4 Relations Between Major Clinical Components of the Cardiovascular Diseases, Their Immediate Precursors, and Selected Associated Factors of Epidemiologic Concern. *Source*: Reprinted from National Heart, Lung and Blood Institute, National Institutes of Health, Bethesda, Maryland.

peripheral vascular disease. These conditions were not differentiated in their relation to the risk factors, however, because the three broad categories—nonmodifiable, behavioral, and physiological risk factors—all bear on the end points jointly in this scheme. Partition of the risk factors in this way was intended to suggest different aspects for policy development. For example, the behavioral risk factors could be addressed through health education and the physiological ones through medical interventions. Interactions among these factors, especially the most important factors, were acknowledged, however, and the multifactorial

nature of cardiovascular diseases was seen as providing "a rich and complex range of possibilities in the development of preventive strategies."[19(p 580)]

CONCLUSION: WHAT CAUSES ATHEROSCLEROTIC AND HYPERTENSIVE DISEASES?

The concept that many factors relate to the occurrence of atherosclerotic and hypertensive diseases and their several outcomes is supported by decades of laboratory, clinical, and population research. Because the disease process is

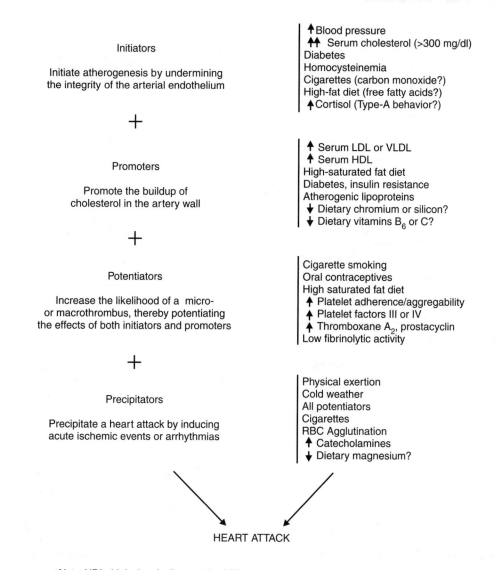

Initiators

Initiate atherogenesis by undermining
the integrity of the arterial endothelium

↑ Blood pressure
↑↑ Serum cholesterol (>300 mg/dl)
Diabetes
Homocysteinemia
Cigarettes (carbon monoxide?)
High-fat diet (free fatty acids?)
↑ Cortisol (Type-A behavior?)

+

Promoters

Promote the buildup of
cholesterol in the artery wall

↑ Serum LDL or VLDL
↑ Serum HDL
High-saturated fat diet
Diabetes, insulin resistance
Atherogenic lipoproteins
↓ Dietary chromium or silicon?
↓ Dietary vitamins B_6 or C?

+

Potentiators

Increase the likelihood of a micro-
or macrothrombus, thereby potentiating
the effects of both initiators and promoters

Cigarette smoking
Oral contraceptives
High saturated fat diet
↑ Platelet adherence/aggregability
↑ Platelet factors III or IV
↑ Thromboxane A_2, prostacyclin
Low fibrinolytic activity

+

Precipitators

Precipitate a heart attack by inducing
acute ischemic events or arrhythmias

Physical exertion
Cold weather
All potentiators
Cigarettes
RBC Agglutination
↑ Catecholamines
↓ Dietary magnesium?

HEART ATTACK

Note: HDL, high-density lipoprotein; LDL, low-density lipoprotein; RBC, red blood cell;
VLDL, very–low-density lipoprotein.

Figure 20–5 What Causes Heart Attacks? A Synthesis by Hopkins and Williams, 1981. *Source*: Reprinted from *Atherosclerosis*, Vol 40, PN Hopkins and RR Williams, p 18, Copyright 1981, with kind permission from Elsevier Science Ireland Ltd, Bay 15K, Shannon Industrial Estate, Co, Clare, Ireland.

protracted and multifaceted, even the discovery of one factor, such as a viral infection that was critical in triggering the onset of atherosclerosis, would be insufficient to explain its varied rates of progression and frequencies of outcomes in different populations and over time. Nor would it seem that programming in fetal or early neonatal life (see Chapter 19) would suffice to dispose of all subsequent influences as being unimportant to progression and outcomes.

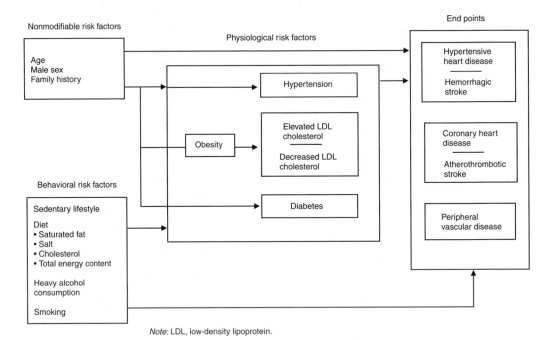

Note: LDL, low-density lipoprotein.

Figure 20–6 Relationships among Risk Factors for Cardiovascular Disease. *Source*: Reprinted from *Disease Control Priorities in Developing Countries*, edited by DT Jamison et al. Copyright © 1993, The International Bank for Reconstruction and Development/The World Bank. Used with permission of Oxford University Press, Inc.

The number of factors and determinants accepted as causally related to this disease process can be expected to increase rather than to diminish as presently suspected factors are investigated in more intricate detail. Identified candidate genes will likely proliferate in number and may lead to recognition of a great many genetic variants and intermediate environmental factors interacting to affect individuals who have the genotype in question. The concept of the n-dimensional complex seems logically necessary to accommodate current and anticipated knowledge of causal factors. In addition, it can have a salutary effect in bringing into a common framework research findings from multiple levels and scientific disciplines, thereby facilitating communication among workers in different specific areas. For advancement of understanding, the richer the multifactorial array, the

better. Thus, for the scientific and intellectual purpose of epidemiology, this is an essential view of causation.

Still, against the criterion of utility noted by MacMahon and Pugh, Stallones, and others, a causal scheme that accommodates all valid observations fails as a direct consequence of its comprehensiveness. To formulate practical implications from such extensive knowledge of causation requires a process of judicious selection. Assembly of the selected elements that lead to well-founded and coherent prevention policies requires emphasis on factors considered most fundamental to the disease process, amenable to intervention, beneficial to public health, and free of undue risks. In the view of Rose, the interventions best justified on these grounds are those tending to restore "biological normality."[9] From the discussions of preceding chapters, two cardinal examples would be reestablishment of patterns of diet and physical activity that are associated with low rates of atherosclerotic and hypertensive diseases and are also characteristic of the human species throughout most of its existence. Elimination of toxic exposures, principally tobacco smoke, is a third such example. The ramifications of preventive strategies based on these three areas of intervention alone would clearly affect many of the intermediate factors and mechanisms recognized as being associated with disease progression and outcomes. Additional selected factors are reasonably included in intervention strategies for specific populations or groups or in circumstances that offer special promise of benefit from other approaches.

In what sense are the "main factors" or "established major risk factors" distinct from the rest of the myriad factors now identified? Evidence for their causal role and their actual or potential changeability is strong; practical means for intervention to modify them have been devised and extensively investigated; and they offer the potential for major impact on the occurrence of atherosclerotic and hypertensive diseases in populations. An understanding of causation that includes a selective emphasis on preventive utility and therefore on the established major risk factors is no less essential to fulfilling the purposes of epidemiology than is the comprehensive causal complex from which it derives. Epidemiology and public health have the luxury as well as the necessity of entertaining both views of causation in pursuit of the complementary purposes of advancing knowledge and serving the health of the public.

REFERENCES

1. Arterio-sclerosis. *Br Med J*. December 29, 1909: 1800. Editorial.

2. Borgman J. Today's random medical news from the New England Journal of Panic-Inducing Gobbledygook (cartoon). *Cincinnati Enquirer*. 1997.

3. Susser M. *Causal Thinking in the Health Sciences: Concepts and Strategies in Epidemiology*. New York: Oxford University Press; 1973.

4. Susser M. What is a cause and how do we know one? A grammar for pragmatic epidemiology. *Am J Epidemiol*. 1991;133:635–648.

5. MacMahon B, Pugh TF. *Epidemiology: Principles and Methods*. Boston, Mass: Little, Brown & Co; 1970.

6. Stehbens WE. Causality in medical science with particular reference to heart disease and atherosclerosis. *Perspect Biol Med*. 1992;36:97–119.

7. Stallones RA. To advance epidemiology. *Ann Rev Public Health*. 1980;1:69–82.

8. Sing CF, Haviland MB, Templeton AR, Zerba KE, et al. Biological complexity and strategies for finding DNA variations responsible for inter-individual variation in risk of a common chronic disease, coronary artery disease. *Ann Med*. 1992;24:539–547.

9. Rose G. Sick individuals and sick populations. *Int J Epidemiol*. 1985;14:32–38.

10. Stamler J. Established major coronary risk factors. In: Marmot M, Elliott P, eds. *Coronary Heart Disease: From Aetiology to Pubic Health*. Oxford, England: Oxford University Press; 1992: 35–66.

11. Advisory Committee to the Surgeon General of the Public Health Service. *Smoking and Health: Report of the Advisory Committee to the Surgeon General*. Atlanta, Ga: Public Health Service, US Dept of Health, Education and Welfare; 1964.

12. Hill AB. The environment and disease: association or causation? *Proc Soc Med*. 1965;58:295–300.

13. Labarthe DR, Stallones RA. Epidemiologic inference. In: Rothman KJ, ed. *Causal Inference*. Chestnut Hill, Mass: Epidemiology Resources, Inc; 1988: 119–129.

14. White PD, Wright IS, Sprague HB, Katz LN, et al. *A Statement on Arteriosclerosis: Main Cause of "Heart Attacks" and "Strokes."* New York: National Health Education Committee, Inc; 1959.

15. Kannel WB, Dawber TR, Kagan A, Revotskie N, et al. Factors of risk in the development of coronary heart disease—six-year follow-up experience: the Framingham Study. *Ann Intern Med*. 1961;55:33–50.

16. Hopkins PN, Williams RR: A survey of 246 suggested coronary risk factors. *Atherosclerosis*. 1981; 40:1–52.

17. McCormick J, Skrbanek P. Coronary heart disease is not preventable by population interventions. *Lancet.* 1988;ii:839–841.

18. Stallones RA. Prospective epidemiologic studies of cerebrovascular disease. *Public Health Monogr.* 1966; 76:51–55.

19. Pearson TA, Jamison DT, Trejo-Gutierrez J. Cardiovascular disease. In: Jamison DT, Mosely WH, Measham AR, Bobadilla JL, eds. *Disease Control Priorities in Developing Countries.* Oxford, England: Oxford University Press; 1993: 577–594.

PART III

Atherosclerotic and Hypertensive Diseases: Prevention and Control

CHAPTER 21

Multifactor Primary Prevention Trials in Individuals and Communities

SUMMARY

Because many influences determine rates of coronary heart disease in populations and risks in individuals, a correspondingly multifaceted approach to intervention promises greater benefit than an approach that targets any one factor alone. A public health perspective suggests that, rather than highly particular interventions, comprehensive interventions applicable to whole communities are preferred, especially those of low or modest cost that can be disseminated widely through existing channels of organization and communication. After a large number of trials of treatment or prevention of single risk factors, multifactor intervention trials began in the 1970s. With the goal of reduced frequency of coronary heart disease and other cardiovascular events, or of reduced risk of these events as measured by several factors taken jointly, these trials were implemented at two levels: high-risk groups and whole communities. Examples of major studies of these kinds conducted over the past 25 years indicate a range of outcomes, from favorable to unfavorable. Difficulties, especially at the community level, of epidemiologic investigation are more fully appreciated as a result, including limitations of intensity and duration of intervention; follow-up time to detect intervention effects; dilution of intervention by secular trends in behaviors, risk factors, and event rates; and several aspects of design and analysis. Together, the completed studies provide a very large body of experience on which to build future research, and there remains optimism that such studies can contribute importantly to further the prevention of cardiovascular diseases.

MULTIFACTOR INTERVENTION: GOALS AND CONCEPTS

Studies of intervention on a single risk factor in affected persons, such as adverse blood lipid profile, high blood pressure, or smoking, have contributed to understanding the relation between these risk factors and coronary heart disease and other cardiovascular conditions. Such studies, many of which are reviewed in preceding chapters, have established the possibility of effective treatment of these risk factors once detected in the individual. They have also stimulated community programs for their treatment in the population as a whole, such as the Hypertension Detection and Follow-Up Program (Chapter 12), which tested the applicability at the community level of the results of the Veterans Administration trials in highly selected hypertensive patients. National and international policy recommendations for risk factor control have been established largely on the basis of studies addressing one or another single risk factor.

It is well recognized, however, in view of the nature of the disease process and the optimum public health policy, that the dominant factors in the causal complex producing epidemic atherosclerosis and its outward manifestations such as coronary heart disease are more appropriately addressed together and not separately. Therefore, concurrent intervention on multiple factors—multifactor intervention—became a focus of attention by the early 1970s. One early proposal in the United States would have assessed through a factorial design the independent contributions as well as the joint effect of changes in diet, physical activity, and smoking habits on coronary heart disease risk in a single trial, aptly titled "Jumbo." The projected size and cost of the trial were considered prohibitive by contemporary standards, and the proposal was never implemented. Instead, the single-factor trials cited in previous chapters were undertaken.

The collective impact of well-founded measures for risk factor change would remain unknown until multifactor trials could be accomplished, however, and the need for this knowledge became compelling. Studies were initiated reflecting the concept of dual strategies for risk factor change, later articulated by Rose as the "high-risk strategy" and the "mass strategy" (later, the "population strategy").[1] The high-risk strategy led to clinical trials in groups selected for having already-established risk factors, for whom intervention would be applied individually, with spouses, or in groups. The population strategy led to community intervention trials with population-wide intervention through various means, especially involving education and community organization and sometimes including risk factor screening with targeted intervention for those identified at high risk. Multifactor intervention was also tested among persons with recognized coronary heart disease with evidence of benefit, but the present focus is on primary prevention.

The ultimate goal of these studies was to test the degree to which multifactor intervention could reduce the frequency of coronary heart disease, the dominant manifestation of atherosclerotic and hypertensive diseases in the populations studied. The clinical trials were therefore conducted among adults, and the community intervention trials were also assessed chiefly in relation to outcomes among adults. Studies in school-age populations were also initiated, usually separately, with change in risk factor levels as the primary outcome. Most of these studies included as intermediate objectives the assessment of success in delivery of their interventions and the ability to bring about the behavior changes thought to be essential for improvement in the risk factors. The lessons learned were expected to guide the further development of policies and practices for cardiovascular disease prevention and to strengthen the scientific basis for their application by the public and by health professionals.

Several examples will serve to illustrate the methods and results of such multifactor intervention trials. Recent commentaries on the experience of these and other completed trials, especially in community settings, provide further background for discussion in this and subsequent chapters. Sources of information on other community prevention studies are also identified.

INTERVENTION IN HIGH-RISK GROUPS

The Multiple Risk Factor Intervention Trial

It was recommended in 1971 that a trial be undertaken of the combined effects of intervention to reduce high concentrations of total cholesterol, high blood pressure, and smoking among men found on screening examination to have one or more of these risk factors.[2] Independent effects of the interventions could not be evaluated statistically, as Jumbo would have allowed, but study size and cost would be acceptable with the proposed design. High risk was defined in relation to a three-variable risk score from the Framingham Study based on the targeted risk factors.[3] Initially the scores at or above the 85th percentile defined eligibility, but to increase the average risk level of participants this was raised to the 90th percentile after one-third of the screening had been completed. Men aged 35–57 were invited to participate. Screenees still qualifying after the third visit were randomly allocated to intervention (special intervention, SI) or control (usual care, UC). The UC group members were expected to receive risk factor intervention as customarily delivered by their own sources of medical care. The SI group members received interventions for their respective risk factors, beginning with intensive group counseling and reinforced with individual counseling and therapy by a multidisciplinary team throughout the course of the trial. The primary end point of the trial was mortality from coronary heart disease. As a result of screening 361,662 men in 22 clinical centers, 12,866 men were randomized into the trial.

Results reported at the close of the intervention period were based on an average follow-up of 7.0 years. As shown in Table 21–1, cumulative coronary mortality was 17.9/1000 in SI and 19.3/1000 in UC, a difference of 7.1% with a 90% confidence interval of −15% to +25%, and nonsignificant. A difference of 26.6% had been projected in the design. Total mortality was slightly greater in SI than UC (41.2 versus 40.4/1000). Failure of intervention to bring about the expected relative reduction in coronary heart disease mortality was due, in part, to unexpected improvement in risk factors in UC and occurrence of only about two-thirds of the expected coronary mortality in this group. The consequence was to make the difference between groups more difficult to detect.

In addition, it was considered likely that adverse effects of antihypertensive drug therapy in some participants may have offset the benefits of reductions in cholesterol concentration and smoking in others without hypertension. One

Table 21–1 Number of Deaths and Cumulative Mortality (per 1,000) by Year of Follow-Up for Men in the Multiple Risk Factor Intervention Trial, Special Intervention (SI) and Usual Care (UC) Groups

	No. of Deaths						Cumulative Mortality, Deaths per 1,000 Men					
	CHD		CVD		All Causes		CHD		CVD		All Causes	
Year	SI	UC	SI	UC	SI	UC	SI	UC	SI	UC	SI	UC
1	11	9	14	10	19	17	1.7	1.4	2.2	1.6	3.0	2.6
2	11	20	14	23	22	31	3.4	4.5	4.4	5.1	6.4	7.5
3	16	18	17	20	29	37	5.9	7.3	7.0	8.2	10.9	13.2
4	16	16	18	18	34	39	8.4	9.8	9.8	11.1	16.2	19.3
5	21	15	25	19	52	41	11.7	12.2	13.8	14.0	24.3	25.6
6	17	26	24	33	55	54	14.4	16.3	17.5	19.2	32.8	34.0
6-yr Total	92	104	112	123	211	219	—	—	—	—	—	—
As of 2/28/82[a]	115	124	138	145	265	260	17.9	19.3	21.5	22.5	41.2	40.4

Note: CHD, coronary heart disease; CVD, cardiovascular disease. All men had at least six years of follow-up.

a. Mortality rates as of Feb 28, 1982, the last day of follow-up for all men, are simple proportions; for years 1 through 6, life table rates are given.

Source: Reprinted from *Journal of the American Medical Association*, Vol 248, p 1470, 1982.

reading of the data was that SI participants who had high blood pressure at baseline along with abnormalities of the resting electrocardiogram experienced excess mortality. This interpretation of the results stimulated much controversy, and concern has persisted about the safety of certain antihypertensive drugs except at lower doses than were initially used in the Multiple Risk Factor Intervention Trial (MRFIT). Alternatively, the same data pointed to an unexpected deficiency of deaths in the corresponding UC subgroup, since mortality in UC hypertensives actually decreased in the presence of electrocardiographic abnormalities, a paradoxical finding. Perhaps the apparent failure of SI to produce an overall mortality benefit was simply a chance occurrence, a fluke. Whatever the explanation, despite its contributions to methods of risk factor change in high-risk individuals and its pioneering partnerships among behavioral scientists, nutritionists, nurses, physicians, and health counselors in the delivery of risk factor interventions, the results of this major research effort appeared be nil, counter to expectations and hopes.

Through continuing mortality follow-up of study participants after the close of the intervention period, MRFIT extended the analysis of intervention effects through 10.5 years in a subsequent report, based on nearly twice the number of deaths as in the initial period.[4] At this point coronary mortality in SI was 10.6% lower than in UC. Total mortality was also lower, by 7.7%. Neither result was significant by one-sided statistical tests. During the period following intervention and the first reported results, acute myocardial infarction was 24% less frequent in SI than in UC, indicating a marked change in relative outcomes during this latter period. Subgroup analysis for hypertensive participants revealed a reversal in the relative mortality between SI and UC between the initial 7-year period and the more recent 3.8 years: The coronary death rate was greater in SI than UC by 78.0% in the first period; it was greater in UC than SI by 43.1% in the second period.[5] The aberrant observation of the first period was thus reversed. The overall results suggested the interpretation that trends in outcome were now favorable, but the benefits of cholesterol reduction and smoking cessation might not become fully apparent for 10–20 years after the start of intervention.

A still further follow-up for mortality in MRFIT participants was reported after 16 years.[6] Total deaths had reached three times the number in the initial analysis, with coronary deaths 11.4% lower in SI than in UC and total mortality 5.7% less. For fatal acute myocardial infarction the SI-UC difference, 20.4%, was statistically significant, as shown in Table 21–2. Because risk factor status was not being monitored in most centers in the post-trial period, interpretation of this result is limited. However, during the intervention period fewer nonfatal coronary events had occurred in SI. This was taken as a basis to predict reduced mortality in SI subsequently, and the 16-year findings confirmed this prediction. These later results were taken as evidence that all three interventions conferred benefit that might continue to favor SI over still-longer follow-up.

Other Trials: Oslo, Göteborg, and Helsinki

Other clinical trials of multifactor intervention were reviewed in the 16-year MRFIT report and include studies in Oslo (Norway), Göteborg (Sweden), and Helsinki (Finland), whose results appeared from 1980 through 1995. The Oslo Study included 1232 men aged 40–49 at entry and free of cardiovascular symptoms and diabetes. Cholesterol concentrations were quite high, from 290 to 379 mg/dl, or the coronary risk score was in the upper 25% without high blood pressure.[7] Eighty percent of the men were smokers. Aggressive advice on smoking cessation and dietary change to reduce fat and cholesterol and increase polyunsaturated fats in the diet was provided to men randomized to intervention. At five years, several coronary heart disease end points were significantly less frequent in the intervention group. After an additional 2.5 years of follow-up, without inter-

Table 21-2 Cause of Death for Men in the Multiple Risk Factor Intervention Trial, Special Intervention (SI) and Usual Care (UC) Groups, Through December 1990

Cause of Death	ICD-9 Code No.	SI, n	UC, n	Relative Difference, %[a]
All cardiovascular	390–459	507	550	−7.9
Acute myocardial infarction	410	185	232	−20.4[b]
Other ischemic (coronary) heart disease	411–414, 429.2[c]	185	185	−0.1
Cardiac dysrhythmias	427	15	21	−29.0
Hypertensive heart disease	402	10	12	−17.2
Other hypertensive	401, 403–405	6	2	—
Cerebrovascular	430–438	46	44	+5.2
Other cardiovascular disease	—	60	54	+11.0
All noncardiovascular		483	499	−3.3
Neoplastic	140–239	316	321	−1.8
Lip, oral cavity, and pharynx	140–149	5	12	—
Digestive organs and peritoneum	150–159	73	88	−17.2
Colorectal	153–154	28	33	−15.2
Other gastrointestinal	150–152, 155–159	45	55	−18.5
Respiratory and intrathoracic organs	160–165	141	122	+15.2
Lung	162	135	117	+15.0
Other neoplasms	—	97	99	−2.3
Respiratory	460–519	25	31	−19.2
Digestive system	520–579	40	33	+21.0
Accidents, suicides, and homicides	800–999	55	58	−5.1
Other noncardiovascular disease	—	47	56	−15.9
Cause unknown (death certificate not found)	—	1	1	—
Total	—	991	1,050	−5.7

a. (RR − 1) × 100%, where the RR (relative risk) is estimated from the proportional hazards regression model.

b. P=.02; P>.05 for all other relative differences. Relative difference is not given if there were <10 deaths in either the SI or UC.

c. In ICD-9, No. 429.2 is cardiovascular disease, unspecified; in ICD-8, this is coded to coronary heart disease, No. 412.4.

Source: Reprinted with permission from MO Kjelsberg, MRFIT Trial, *Circulation*, Vol 94, p 948, © 1996, American Heart Association.

vention, risk factor levels converged between groups: Prior smokers in the intervention group relapsed, but prior controls reduced their cholesterol levels. Reported mortality differences remained significant.

The Swedish multifactor intervention trial sampled men aged 47–55 years in Göteborg, with approximately 10,000 participants in intervention and in each of two control groups.[8] In the intervention group, all men were screened to identify those at high risk, for whom intervention was directly implemented. Criteria for high-risk status included quite high levels of blood pressure or cholesterol concentration and smoking of at least 15 cigarettes per day. One of the two control groups was sampled (2% at baseline, 11% at 4 years, and 20% at 10 years) for risk factor assessment without intervention, and the second control group was not screened at all but only monitored to ascertain occurrence of end-point events. Reductions in risk factors were closely parallel between intervention and control groups, and mortality after 11.8 years follow-up was not appreciably different between groups. Within the intervention group, there were nonparticipants whose mortality was notably higher than that for participants. Partial explanation of the apparent lack of mortality benefit of intervention was the residual high mortality among those not participating. In addition, since only the highest-risk individuals were targeted for intervention and since many events arise from more moderate levels of risk in the population, intervention may not have reached a sufficiently broad segment of the population to attain the intended effect.

The fourth study, again with distinctive design features, was the Helsinki Multifactorial Primary Prevention Trial.[9] More than 1200 business executives, about 40–55 years of age at randomization in 1974, were enrolled in a trial of dietary and hygienic measures and drugs to lower cholesterol concentrations or blood pressure. The control group participants were untreated by the investigators. After five years of initial follow-up, total risk showed a net reduction of 46% in the intervention group. Strokes were significantly less frequent but coronary events were more frequent in the intervention group. The first post-trial follow-up was completed five years later, in 1985, and the second after another five years, or 15 years after randomization. The intervention group experienced significantly higher mortality for cardiac events and accidents and for all causes together. The use of multiple and changing drugs for therapy throughout the trial period complicated attempts to explain the findings, although particular drugs were implicated by the authors. Regardless, the mortality outcome remained clearly negative.

INTERVENTION IN COMMUNITIES

In contrast to the foregoing examples, in which intervention was directed to individually identified persons at high risk of coronary and other cardiovascular events, other multifactor intervention studies were designed primarily to modify knowledge, attitudes, and behavior related to the major risk factors through community-wide action. In some instances risk factor detection was included, with reinforcement of local health services to improve risk factor treatment and control, but educational and other community strategies remained the central aspect of the program.

The North Karelia Project

Among the earliest community intervention trials was the North Karelia Project, undertaken in 1972 in view of the exceptionally high mortality from coronary heart disease in Eastern Finland in the late 1960s.[10] Recognition of the magnitude of the problem had led to recruitment of two cohorts, in East and West Finland, into the Seven Countries Study more than a decade earlier. A recently published account offers a comprehensive view of the extraordinary 20-year North Karelia Project and its local, national, and international impact.[11]

One intervention area, North Karelia (population 210,000), was compared with one reference area, Kuopio (population 250,000). Multiple programs were implemented in North Karelia with the aim of reducing blood cholesterol concentration, controlling high blood pressure, and achieving smoking cessation for as many persons as possible in this target population. Risk factor distributions in both communities were assessed by cross-sectional surveys in independently drawn random samples, including men and women aged 30–59 in each population. The surveys were conducted every five years from 1972 to 1992. In 1982 a third area, southwestern Finland, was added for further comparison of data from the last three surveys. Mortality was monitored from 1969 through 1992.

Evaluation of the impact of intervention in North Karelia has been complicated by large concurrent changes in risk factors and coronary mortality (Table 21–3).[12] Risk factor changes from 1972 to 1992 were substantial in North Karelia, with cholesterol concentration decreasing by 13% for men and 18% for women, diastolic blood pressure decreasing by 9% for men and 13% for women, and smoking decreasing

Table 21–3 Mean (and Standard Error) Level of Coronary Risk Factors in Subjects in Finland, by Year and Sex

Risk Factors	1972	1977	1982	1987	1992
Men					
Cholesterol (mmol/l)	6.78 (0.02)	6.55 (0.02)	6.28 (0.02)	6.23 (0.03)	5.90 (0.03)
Diastolic blood pressure (mm Hg)	92.8 (0.18)	91.0 (0.18)	87.8 (0.26)	88.4 (0.28)	84.2 (0.37)
Smoking (% of study population who were smokers)	53 (0.8)	47 (0.8)	42 (1.0)	39 (1.2)	37 (1.5)
Women					
Cholesterol (mmol/l)	6.72 (0.02)	6.36 (0.02)	6.10 (0.03)	5.94 (0.03)	5.54 (0.03)
Diastolic blood pressure (mm Hg)	91.8 (0.19)	87.6 (0.17)	84.6 (0.25)	83.5 (0.26)	79.6 (0.33)
Smoking (% of study population who were smokers)	11 (0.5)	12 (0.5)	16 (0.8)	16 (0.9)	20 (1.1)

Source: Reprinted with permission from E Vartiainen et al, Changes in Risk Factors Explain Changes in Mortality from Ischaemic Heart Disease in Finland, *British Medical Journal*, Vol 309, pp 23–27, © 1994, BMJ Publishing Group.

from 53% to 37% for men but increasing from 11% to 20% for women. But changes in these risk factors were greater in North Karelia than in Kuopio only during the first five years of the program. They were similar thereafter, and coronary mortality decreased 50% in Finland as a whole from 1970 to 1992. These circumstances, in addition to the sample size of only one intervention unit and one reference or control unit (despite the later addition of a second control area), seriously limited the ability to evaluate program effects.

One approach to analysis of risk factor and mortality change was to derive estimates of the relation between each risk factor and coronary mortality within the Kuopio population and then to predict the mortality that would be observed at each survey year based on the risk factor levels in the population at that time. The predicted mortality with smoking, blood pressure, and cholesterol concentration taken into account was then compared with the observed mortality trends from 1972 to 1992 for men and women aged 35–64 in Finland. These results are shown in Figure 21–1 for men and Figure 21–2 for women. The results indicate a marked predicted decline in coronary mortality throughout the period, which was close to that observed until 1985 for men, when the actual decline began to exceed the prediction. For women the decline exceeded the prediction throughout the period. Further analysis demonstrated that from 1972 through 1987, for both men and women, the observed and predicted trends were consistent, and it was concluded that the decline in mortality could be explained by the risk factor changes over the same period.

The interventions are not the only plausible explanation of these mortality changes, since there were risk factor changes in the reference area. The implementation of a number of prevention activities nationally during the course of intervention in North Karelia may have affected this target area as well as other regions, independent of the planned local programs. Nonetheless, this program contributed importantly to the development and implementation of community intervention strategies widely regarded as pioneering work in the field that have provided tested models for programs applied nationally throughout Finland and elsewhere.

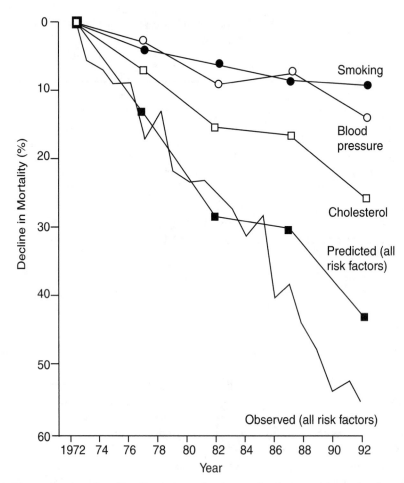

Figure 21–1 Observed and Predicted Decline in Mortality from Ischemic Heart Disease in Men Aged 35–64 in Finland. *Source*: Reprinted with permission from E Vartiainen et al, Changes in Risk Factors Explain Changes in Mortality from Ischaemic Heart Disease in Finland, *British Medical Journal*, Vol 309, p 25, © 1994, BMJ Publishing Group.

The Major US Community Trials: Stanford, Minnesota, and Pawtucket

The Stanford Three-City Study and Five-City Projects

Concurrent with initiation of the North Karelia Project, and with close collaboration between the two responsible research groups, the Stanford Three-City Study began in northern California.[13] The strategy was to implement community-wide health education in two communities, with supplemental individual counseling for a sample of high-risk individuals iden-

tified in one of them; the third community would serve as the control. The initial results after two years of intervention suggested that community-wide health education had substantial impact, with an overall reduction in a multivariate risk score of 23–28% in treatment compared with control communities.

This favorable early experience led to a second study, the Stanford Five-City Project, based on newly selected communities. Stroke and coronary heart disease were the primary end points, and change in blood cholesterol concentration, blood pressure, smoking prevalence, body

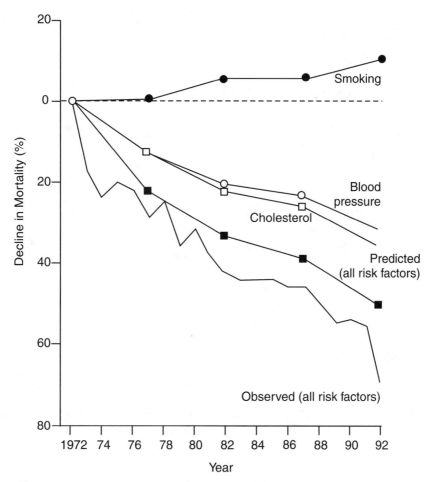

Figure 21–2 Observed and Predicted Decline in Mortality from Ischemic Heart Disease in Women Aged 35–64 in Finland. *Source*: Reprinted with permission from E Vartiainen et al, Changes in Risk Factors Explain Changes in Mortality from Ischaemic Heart Disease in Finland, *British Medical Journal*, Vol 309, p 25, © 1994, BMJ Publishing Group.

weight, resting pulse rate, and knowledge of risk factors were intermediate end points.[14] The program used several approaches to bring about risk factor change. Two communities received a five-year intervention program based on social learning theory, a communication-behavior change model, community organization principles, and social marketing methods. In addition to continuous education programs, several short-term campaigns were also conducted in the two intervention communities. Two of the remaining communities served as observed controls and

the third was subject only to monitoring of event rates as an unobserved control.

Evaluation of risk factor change was conducted both in cohorts and in independent cross-sectional samples in four of the study communities. Changes over time in risk factor knowledge and each of the intermediate risk factor variables are indicated in Table 21–4. Members of the first survey were reexamined as cohorts at 17, 39, and 60 months from baseline. New population samples were surveyed in a serial cross-sectional design at 25, 51, and 73

Table 21–4 Knowledge and Risk Factor Change from Baseline During 5⅓ Years of Education for Persons Aged 25–74 Years, Stanford Five-City Project

	Cohort Samples			Independent Samples		
	Treatment	Control	P^a	Treatment	Control	P^a
Knowledge of coronary heart disease risk factors points						
Baseline	6.59 ± 0.14	7.09 ± 0.15	≤.01	5.59 ± 0.10	5.91 ± 0.12	≤.025
C-2, I-2	1.28 ± 0.12	0.89 ± 0.12	≤.02	1.31 ± 0.15	0.67 ± 0.16	≤.005
C-3, I-3	2.04 ± 0.12	1.36 ± 0.12	≤.001	0.92 ± 0.15	0.29 ± 0.16	≤.005
C-4, I-4	2.31 ± 0.12	1.72 ± 0.12	≤.001	1.61 ± 0.16	0.97 ± 0.17	≤.005
Total cholesterol level, mmol/l						
Baseline	5.45 ± 0.06	5.30 ± 0.05	≤.025	5.36 ± 0.04	5.22 ± 0.04	≤.01
C-2, I-2	-0.13 ± 0.04	-0.04 ± 0.04	≤.06	-0.08 ± 0.05	-0.03 ± 0.05	
C-3, I-3	-0.08 ± 0.04	0.05 ± 0.04	≤.01	-0.04 ± 0.06	0.01 ± 0.05	
C-4, I-4	0.04 ± 0.04	0.07 ± 0.05	...	-0.13 ± 0.06	-0.04 ± 0.06	≤.12
Mean systolic blood pressure, mm Hg						
Baseline	129.65 ± 0.91	126.00 ± 0.92	≤.005	130.54 ± 0.60	127.40 ± 0.67	≤.001
C-2, I-2	-2.36 ± 0.72	-3.19 ± 0.83	...	-3.15 ± 0.60	-1.50 ± 0.90	≤.10
C-3, I-3	-6.45 ± 0.88	-3.80 ± 0.87	≤.02	-8.65 ± 0.87	-2.07 ± 0.88	≤.001
C-4, I-4	-8.88 ± 0.96	-3.71 ± 0.89	≤.001	-5.04 ± 0.86	-3.61 ± 0.85	≤.12
Mean diastolic blood pressure, mm Hg						
Baseline	80.43 ± 0.54	76.99 ± 0.51	≤.001	81.70 ± 0.38	77.97 ± 0.39	≤.001
C-2, I-2	-0.94 ± 0.53	-0.45 ± 0.50	...	-4.01 ± 0.53	-2.04 ± 0.57	≤.01
C-3, I-3	-6.80 ± 0.56	-2.52 ± 0.56	≤.001	-7.49 ± 0.55	-0.15 ± 0.55	≤.001
C-4, I-4	-5.13 ± 0.66	-1.41 ± 0.54	≤.001	-3.22 ± 0.54	-2.04 ± 0.56	≤.07
Smokers, %						
Baseline	28.35 ± 2.28	26.98 ± 2.39	...	38.22 ± 1.71	37.62 ± 1.79	
C-2, I-2	-2.87 ± 1.26	0.00 ± 1.07	≤.05	-1.62 ± 2.39	-3.42 ± 2.44	
C-3, I-3	-5.26 ± 1.60	-1.00 ± 1.28	≤.02	-5.17 ± 2.33	-3.88 ± 2.34	
C-4, I-4	-7.66 ± 1.69	-3.76 ± 1.28	≤.04	-9.02 ± 2.26	-10.24 ± 2.39	

continues

Table 21–4 continued

	Cohort Samples			Independent Samples		
	Treatment	Control	P^a	Treatment	Control	P^a
Body mass index, kg/m²						
Baseline	24.63 ± 0.20	24.20 ± 0.19	≤.06	24.79 ± 0.14	24.38 ± 0.14	≤.025
C-2, I-2	0.19 ± 0.06	0.02 ± 0.06	...	0.36 ± 0.20	0.55 ± 0.22	
C-3, I-3	0.35 ± 0.07	0.44 ± 0.08	≤.20	0.69 ± 0.22	0.88 ± 0.22	
C-4, I-4	0.51 ± 0.09	0.42 ± 0.08		0.49 ± 0.21	1.12 ± 0.22	≤.02
Resting pulse rate, beats per minute						
Baseline	68.01 ± 0.52	67.00 ± 0.57	≤.10	69.07 ± 0.38	68.29 ± 0.43	≤.09
C-2, I-2	0.76 ± 0.47	2.42 ± 0.59	≤.02	0.85 ± 0.54	2.11 ± 0.58	≤.06
C-3, I-3	−0.87 ± 0.45	2.13 ± 0.65	≤.001	2.19 ± 0.55	4.12 ± 0.57	≤.01
C-4, I-4	−0.64 ± 0.53	0.44 ± 0.60	≤.09	0.51 ± 0.54	2.08 ± 0.60	≤.03

Note: Values are mean ± *SEM* at baseline and mean change ± *SE* of the change from baseline at the second (C-2, I-2), third (C-3, I-3), and fourth (C-4, I-4) surveys adjusted for age, sex, education, and household size.

a. One-tailed *P* values less than .20 are listed.

Source: Reprinted with permission from JW Farquhar, Effects of Community-Wide Education, *Journal of the American Medical Association,* Vol 264, p 361, Copyright 1990, American Medical Association.

months from baseline. For each variable, the baseline mean value (or for smoking, the percentage positive) and standard error of the mean are shown in the first row of the table. Changes relative to baseline are reported for successive cohort examinations (C-2, C-3, C-4) and successive independent surveys (I-2, I-3, I-4), with the standard error of each change, after adjustment for age, sex, education, and household size. P values are given for one-sided tests of significance, except where the value was greater than .20. By this analysis, most risk factors improved from baseline, to a greater extent in the treatment communities, either in cohort or cross-sectional evaluation or in both. Favorable change in total cholesterol concentration at the third cohort examination was not maintained at the final evaluation.

The overall multivariate risk score, based on a model for 12-year coronary event rates in the Framingham Study, was predicted to show a net reduction of 20% in treatment communities; the results are shown in Table 21–5. For all-cause mortality, significant decreases in risk score of 16% and 14% were observed at the third and fourth cohort examinations, respectively; coronary event risks were correspondingly reduced 17% and 16% in the cohort evaluation. Independent samples showed a significant decline in total mortality risk only at the third evaluation.

The result for total mortality based on cohort evaluation is further detailed in a regression analysis shown in Figure 21–3. The upper panel indicates the treatment versus control result for the combined pairs of communities, and the lower panel gives the result for

Table 21–5 Changes from Baseline in Estimated All-Cause Mortality Risk and Coronary Heart Disease Risk During 5⅓ Years of Education for Persons Aged 25–74 Years, Stanford Five-City Project

	Cohort Samples			Independent Samples		
	Treatment	Control	P^a	Treatment	Control	P^a
Estimated all-cause mortality risk, deaths per 1,000 persons in 10 years						
Baseline	51.97 ± 2.98	48.18 ± 2.85	≤.18	55.69 ± 2.43	50.80 ± 2.24	≤.08
C-2, I-2	−2.17 ± 2.10	−0.72 ± 1.32	—	−5.52 ± 3.29	−4.05 ± 3.11	
C-3, I-3	−12.88 ± 2.20	−4.20 ± 1.54	≤.001	−11.82 ± 3.15	−0.26 ± 3.00	≤.005
C-4, I-4	−11.16 ± 2.47	−3.54 ± 1.57	≤.005	−10.57 ± 3.09	−10.39 ± 2.80	b
Estimated coronary heart disease risk, morbidity and mortality events per 1,000 persons in 12 years						
Baseline	83.57 ± 4.98	71.28 ± 4.97	≤.05	87.46 ± 3.95	76.90 ± 4.00	≤.03
C-2, I-2	−10.75 ± 3.47	−10.52 ± 2.81	—	−2.99 ± 5.70	−6.64 ± 5.57	
C-3, I-3	−17.57 ± 3.59	−3.05 ± 3.31	≤.005	−14.88 ± 5.56	−4.52 ± 5.17	≤.09
C-4, I-4	−16.38 ± 4.35	−2.81 ± 3.90	≤.02	−15.97 ± 5.40	−13.62 ± 5.15	c

Note: Values are mean ± *SEM* at baseline and mean change ± *SE* of the change from baseline at the second (C-2, I-2), third (C-3, I-3), and fourth (C-4, I-4) cohort (C) and independent (I) sample surveys, adjusted for age, sex, education, and household size.

a. One-tailed *P* values less than .20 are listed.

b. This estimated difference has a large 95% confidence interval: (−10.57) − (−10.39) = −0.18 ± 8.25.

c. This estimated difference has a large 95% confidence interval: (−15.97) − (−13.62) = −2.35 ± 14.62.

Source: Reprinted with permission from JW Farquhar, Effects of Community-Wide Education, *Journal of the American Medical Association,* Vol 264, p 363, Copyright 1990, American Medical Association.

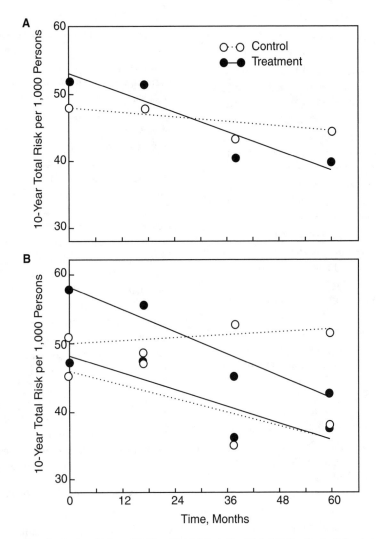

Figure 21–3 Regression Analysis of Mean 10-Year Total Mortality Risk (A) for Pooled Treatment and Pooled Control Cities and (B) for Each City, for Persons Aged 25–74 Years, Stanford Five-City Project. *Source*: Reprinted with permission from JW Farquhar, Effects of Community-Wide Education, *Journal of the American Medical Association*, Vol 264, p 363, © 1990, American Medical Association.

each community. While treatment was consistently favorable, one control community also exhibited a favorable trend in risk, although it was insufficient to outweigh the adverse trend in the other control community. The evaluation concluded that the results supported the effectiveness of this type of low-cost program and that the study should serve as a model for risk factor intervention programs, in addition to those already in place for smoking, on a national basis: "The cost of such national programs is moderate, but the cost of *not* launching such programs is to accept the notion that the energies of communities cannot be harnessed for planned social change for health benefit."[14(p 365)]

The Minnesota Heart Health Program

In 1980, a six-community intervention trial began in the upper Midwest of the United States, the Minnesota Heart Health Program.[15] Three pairs of communities were matched on population size, type (from small to urban), and distance from metropolitan Minneapolis-St. Paul. One community of each pair was to receive a multi-component education program and the other to serve as a control. The program was described as a high-intensity campaign that included risk factor screening, education and intervention programs, involvement of most primary care physicians and many other health professionals in training activities, changes in community organization and environment conducive to heart health, and participation by youth in school-based health promotion programs. An intervention program of five or six years' duration was projected to reduce population mean values for blood cholesterol concentration by 7 mg/dl, blood pressure by 2 mmHg, and cigarette smoking by 3% and to increase energy expenditure in physical activity by 50 kcal/day.

Both cohort and cross-sectional examinations were conducted, beginning prior to intervention in most communities. Table 21–6 indicates the results of the cross-sectional comparisons in the pooled education and comparison communities for media exposure score; risk factor determinations; and a coronary heart disease risk score based on age, systolic blood pressure, total cholesterol concentration, and cigarette smoking status. Changes from preintervention to final assessment were in several instances as great in the comparison communities as were originally projected for intervention. In the education communities the corresponding changes were greater than in the comparison communities for reduction in smoking for males, increase in percentage physically active, and reduction in coronary risk score. However, further analysis did not reveal consistent evidence of intervention effect in the cohort evaluation or in regression models over the full study period, separately for cross-sectional and cohort data.

Figure 21–4 indicates the results of the Minnesota Heart Health Program for the coronary risk score. In the cross-sectional analysis, the score decreased in both the education and comparison communities, showing no evidence of intervention effect. The cohort analysis showed the expected increase in risk score due to increasing risk components with age, but the changes in score were overall no less in the education than in the comparison communities. The final analysis of event rates for stroke and coronary heart disease has been reported recently.[16] For neither coronary heart disease nor stroke was there a significant difference in rates between intervention and control communities. Secular trends of decreasing rates for coronary disease for both men and women and of stroke for men were not clearly distinguishable between study communities. For women stroke rates appeared to increase similarly across communities. The change in risk factors in all communities was much greater than expected and appeared to have precluded a meaningful test of the original hypothesis. At the same time, the Minnesota Heart Health Program contributed a large body of experience in development and implementation of intervention programs with substantial community impact as measured for several components of the program.

The Pawtucket Heart Health Program

The third major multifactor community intervention trial of cardiovascular disease prevention in the United States was the Pawtucket (Rhode Island) Heart Health Program, in which one intervention and one control community were enrolled.[17] The aim was to evaluate the impact on single risk factors and projected cardiovascular disease rates based on composite risk score for persons aged 35–64 years in the Framingham Study. Low-cost approaches to community behavior change and environmental changes conducive to the desired behaviors were implemented from 1984 to 1991. Heart health curricula in schools from grades one to high school were included. As in the Stanford and Minnesota programs, both cross-sectional

Table 21–6 Pooled Mean Values for Program Exposure, Risk Factors, and Coronary Heart Disease Risk in Education and Comparison Cities, by Study Year, from Cross-Sectional Surveys, Minnesota Heart Health Program

	Cities	-3[b]	-2[b]	-1	0	1	3	5	6
						Education Year[a]			
Exposure score (range, 1–10)	Education				1.3	2.3	2.9	2.4	2.5
	Comparison				1.2	1.6	1.8	1.9	2.1
Blood cholesterol, mg/dl	Education	213.5	207.2	206.5	207.3	199.8	199.0	204.1	203.8
	Comparison	212.3	208.2	209.3	208.3	208.8	199.4	199.9	203.8
Smoking, males (% smokers)	Education	38.7	45.2	34.5	37.9	34.0	33.7	30.4	29.4
	Comparison	34.5	43.8	36.3	39.5	32.3	31.6	27.2	31.1
Smoking, females (% smokers)	Education	25.3	31.6	33.3	28.0	30.5	23.8	22.8	22.8
	Comparison	22.1	31.0	29.3	27.8	26.7	23.4	28.3	26.0
Systolic blood pressure, mm Hg	Education	120.8	120.7	121.5	121.7	121.6	118.2	119.4	118.6
	Comparison	124.5	122.6	124.3	125.7	124.4	121.7	120.5	121.6
Diastolic blood pressure, mm Hg	Education	74.6	73.8	75.2	76.2	75.4	71.6	73.4	73.3
	Comparison	76.5	74.0	76.6	76.8	75.1	74.5	74.1	74.1
Body mass index, kg/m²	Education	25.3	25.6	25.8	25.6	25.7	26.0	26.3	26.0
	Comparison	25.5	25.7	25.8	25.8	26.3	26.2	26.4	26.5
Physical activity (% active)	Education	50.9	49.5	45.5	48.4	54.2	54.3	55.2	57.1
	Comparison	52.1	49.0	50.3	47.3	48.4	51.3	53.9	52.8
Coronary heart disease risk (deaths/1,000 persons)	Education	28.7	26.9	26.5	25.5	26.3	22.6	23.8	24.4
	Comparison	32.2	35.3	33.7	33.6	34.3	29.7	28.1	31.2

a. Negative values refer to observations made before the intervention program; a value of 0 refers to observations made immediately before the intervention program; positive values refer to observations made after the intervention program began.

b. Data were not collected from Mankato, Winona, in E-3 or E-2, nor in Fargo/Moorhead, Sioux Falls, in E-3. Pooled means for E-3 and E-2 were calculated after imputing values for the missing components based on the differences in the city levels as estimated in the regressions.

Source: Reprinted with permission from RV Luepker, *American Journal of Public Health,* Vol 84, No 9, p 1385, © 1994, American Public Health Association.

and cohort examinations were conducted for evaluation, beginning with preintervention assessment in 1981.

Table 21–7 indicates the cross-sectional survey results, which include the first two surveys as baseline, the fourth and fifth as coincident with the peak of the intervention effort, and the sixth as a postintervention evaluation. Each of the latter results is compared with baseline risk factor and projected cardiovascular disease rates, in the last columns of the table. By the statistical criterion of a *P* value less than .05 in two-sided tests, the only significant difference in single risk factor change between Pawtucket

and the comparison city was the lesser increase in body mass index with intervention, a difference that was greater at postintervention follow-up than at the peak of intervention. The composite measure of projected risk was decreased with intervention at the peak of activity, at which time it was increased in the comparison city. But in the postintervention period, projected risk decreased in the comparison city to nearly the value for Pawtucket, where this measure had not changed after the peak of intervention.

Table 21–8 presents the cohort data, which indicate progressive upward change in total

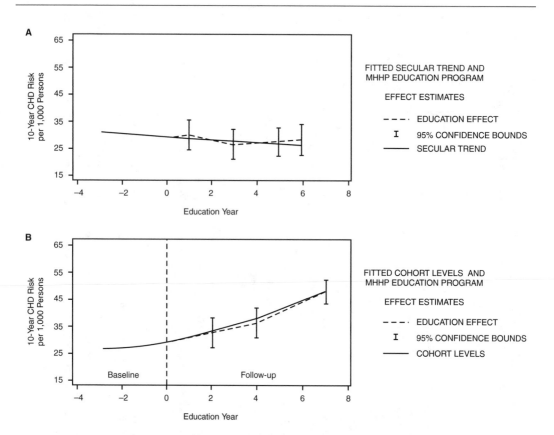

Note: CHD, coronary heart disease; MHHP, Minnesota Heart Health Program.

Figure 21–4 Coronary Heart Disease Risk Score in Education and Control Cities, from (A) Cross-Sectional and (B) Cohort Analysis, Minnesota Heart Health Program. *Source*: Reprinted with permission from RV Luepker, *American Journal of Public Health*, Vol 84, No 9, p 1390, © 1994, American Public Health Association.

Table 21–7 Mean Values (Percentages) of Risk Factors and Estimated Cardiovascular Disease Risks from Cross-Sectional Surveys at Baseline (Surveys 1 and 2), and Postintervention (Survey 6), Pawtucket Heart Health Program

Risk Factor	City and City Differences	Study Stage (Surveys)				
		Baseline (1 and 2)	Peak Intervention (4 and 5)	Postintervention (6)	Peak Intervention to Baseline Difference[a] (4 and 5 vs 1 and 2)	Postintervention to Baseline Difference[a] (6 vs 1 and 2)
Total cholesterol, mg/dl	Pawtucket (SEM)	204.2 (1.03)	202.2 (1.08)	199.1 (1.76)	−2.00 (1.50)	−5.06 (2.04)
	Comparison city (SEM)	205.5 (1.02)	203.2 (1.02)	200.8 (1.72)	−2.29 (1.44)	−4.73 (2.00)
	City difference (SE)	−1.35 (1.45)	−1.07 (1.49)	−1.69 (2.46)	0.29 (2.08)	−0.33 (2.85)
	P	.350	.474	.493	.890	.907
Systolic blood pressure, mm Hg	Pawtucket (SEM)	124.6 (0.67)	125.0 (0.42)	122.8 (0.62)	0.42 (0.79)	−1.81 (0.91)
	Comparison city (SEM)	123.9 (0.66)	124.9 (0.41)	123.5 (0.64)	0.96 (0.78)	−0.42 (0.92)
	City difference (SE)	0.66 (0.94)	0.12 (0.59)	−0.74 (0.89)	−0.54 (1.11)	−1.39 (1.29)
	P	.482	.840	.410	.627	.281
Diastolic blood pressure, mm Hg	Pawtucket (SEM)	76.2 (0.49)	76.3 (0.30)	76.4 (0.44)	0.19 (0.58)	0.28 (0.66)
	Comparison city (SEM)	75.6 (0.49)	76.9 (0.29)	76.7 (0.46)	1.27 (0.57)	1.12 (0.67)
	City difference (SE)	0.58 (0.69)	−0.51 (0.42)	−0.26 (0.63)	−1.08 (0.81)	−0.84 (0.94)
	P	.405	.224	.682	.180	.373
Currently smoking, %	Pawtucket (SEM)	40.0 (0.97)	35.1 (1.08)	35.5 (1.58)	−4.89 (1.45)	−4.45 (1.85)
	Comparison city (SEM)	39.6 (0.94)	34.4 (1.00)	32.5 (1.53)	−5.22 (1.37)	−7.05 (1.80)
	City difference (SE)	0.4 (1.35)	0.7 (1.47)	3.01 (2.20)	0.34 (2.00)	2.60 (2.58)
	P	.762	.613	.172	.867	.315
Body mass index, kg/m²	Pawtucket (SEM)	26.1 (0.12)	26.2 (0.12)	26.3 (0.18)	0.14 (0.17)	0.25 (0.22)
	Comparison city (SEM)	26.4 (0.12)	26.7 (0.11)	27.3 (0.18)	0.25 (0.17)	0.88 (0.21)
	City difference (SE)	−0.35 (0.17)	−0.46 (0.17)	−0.97 (0.25)	−0.11 (0.24)	−0.62 (0.31)
	P	.043	.006	.000	.645	.042

continues

Table 21-7 continued

Risk Factor	City and City Differences	Study Stage (Surveys)			Peak Intervention to Baseline Difference[a] (4 and 5 vs 1 and 2)	Postintervention to Baseline Difference[a] (6 vs 1 and 2)
		Baseline (1 and 2)	Peak Intervention (4 and 5)	Postintervention (6)		
Projected CVD (rates/ 10,000 people within 10 yr)[b]	Pawtucket (95% CI)	215 (189, 244)	180 (162, 201)	180 (153, 213)	0.84 (0.71, 0.99)	0.84 (0.68, 1.03)
	Comparison city (95% CI)	203 (180, 230)	214 (194, 236)	186 (158, 220)	1.05 (0.90, 1.23)	0.92 (0.74, 1.13)
	Risk ratio (95% CI)	1.06 (089, 1.26)	0.84 (0.73, 0.97)	0.97 (0.77, 1.22)	0.80 (0.63, 1.00)	0.92 (0.68, 1.23)
	P	.542	.021	.789	.052	.562

Note: Mean survey values are weighted for the number of eligible adults in the household and controlled for the proportions by sex, age, educational attainment, and being foreign or US born. CVD, cardiovascular disease.

a. Absolute differences between cities for risk factors are given; for CVD, the ratios of rates are presented.

b. CVD risk projections and Pawtucket/Comparison city risk ratios are for people aged 35–64 years.

Source: Reprinted with permission from RA Carleton, *American Journal of Public Health*, Vol 85, No 6, p 781, © 1995, American Public Health Association.

Table 21–8 Mean Values (Percentages) of Risk Factors at Baseline, Follow-Up, and Change over 8–9 Years from Cohort Analysis of Persons Aged 18–64 Years at First Examination, Pawtucket Heart Health Program

Cohort and Factors[a,b]	Pawtucket	Comparison City
Respondents at baseline, no.	2,523	2,718
Completed follow-up, no.	1,260	1,665
Moved, no.	943	699
Deceased, no.	115	110
Declined, no.	205	246
Total cholesterol, mg/dl[c] (*SD*)		
Baseline	214.4 (47.1)	212.0 (46.9)
Follow-up	220.8 (41.3)	219.8 (43.9)
Change	7.4 (1.2)	8.1 (1.0)
Systolic blood pressure, mm Hg (*SD*)		
Baseline	125.4 (16.9)	124.7 (16.9)
Follow-up	130.9 (18.6)	129.6 (19.0)
Change	6.0 (0.4)	5.2 (0.4)
Diastolic blood pressure, mm Hg (*SD*)		
Baseline	77.2 (10.8)	76.3 (11.3)
Follow-up	78.5 (10.7)	78.3 (10.6)
Change	2.1 (0.3)	1.9 (0.3)
Currently smoking, %		
Baseline	36.1	36.5
Follow-up	27.1	28.9
Change	−8.9 (1.2)	−8.2 (1.1)
Body mass index, kg/m^2 (*SD*)		
Baseline	26.5 (5.0)	26.9 (5.2)
Follow-up	27.3 (5.5)	27.7 (5.5)
Change	0.7 (0.2)	0.8 (0.2)
Projected CVD[d] (95% CI)		
Baseline	174 (20, 1538)	155 (17, 1459)
Follow-up	455 (103, 2003)	445 (94, 2110)
Change	2.79 (2.53, 3.07)	2.83 (2.57, 311)

Note: CVD, cardiovascular disease. CI, confidence interval.

a. Baseline and follow-up values under each factor are unadjusted means ±*SD*. For smoking, values are simple percentages. For CVD risk, the values are geometric means with 1 = *SD* limits on a logarithmic scale.

b. Change under each factor is mean ± *SE* of the follow-up value, expressed as the excess over the baseline value, weighted by eligible adults in each household and adjusted for baseline value, place of birth, study cycle, sex, baseline age, and education. For CVD risk, change is risk ratio with 1 = *SE* limits on logarithmic scale.

c. Cholesterol in mg/dl ÷ 38.7 = cholesterol in mmol/l.

d. Rate/10,000 people within 10 years.

Source: Reprinted with permission from RA Carleton, *American Journal of Public Health*, Vol 85, No 6, p 783, © 1995, American Public Health Association.

cholesterol concentration, systolic and diastolic blood pressure, body mass index, and projected cardiovascular risk. Smoking was reduced in the cohorts in both communities, to similar degrees. Overall, the changes observed were generally favorable but modest, and they were similar between intervention and comparison communities. This outcome was attributed to the relatively small proportion of total messages affecting health-related behavior represented by the program, in contrast with the total environment of advertising, marketplace displays, and countless inputs from other sources. Integration of community-level efforts with those at state and national levels was proposed as a more effective means of altering prevention policies and practices and thereby altering individual risk-related behaviors.

Bringing together the results of these three US community intervention studies, Winkelby and colleagues conducted a joint analysis with respect to their effects on cardiovascular disease risk.[18] For women and for men in the age range from age 25 to 64 years, results of change in single risk factors (cigarette smoking, blood pressure, total cholesterol concentration, and body mass index) and in the composite coronary heart disease mortality risk score were presented for each study and the three studies combined. Overall, 9 of 12 comparisons were favorable in direction, showing greater change in the intervention communities (five for women and four for men), but none of these results was statistically significant. The authors concluded that sample size limitations had not contributed importantly to the outcomes of the several trials. Further implications of these studies are discussed below and in succeeding chapters.

The European Collaborative Group Study

Communities are definable in other than geographic terms, and employment communities or worksites have also been used for multifactorial cardiovascular risk reduction programs. A major example of this approach is the European Collaborative Trial of Multifactorial Prevention of Coronary Heart Disease, conducted in 80 factories in Belgium, Italy, Poland, and the United Kingdom.[19,20] The intent was to assess the degree to which educational efforts, undertaken at modest cost, could bring about risk factor change and thereby reduce incidence and mortality from coronary heart disease. Within each country, factories or other large occupational units were matched as pairs and randomly allocated to intervention or control. In intervention factories, all men aged 50–69 underwent risk factor screening. This was followed for the higher-risk men, those in the upper 10–20% of risk in accordance with a simple risk function, by treatment or advice for lowering cholesterol, discontinuation of smoking, daily physical exercise, weight reduction, and blood pressure–lowering drug therapy. Less intensive education was provided to the remaining men. In the control factories, only a 10% random sample of men were examined for risk factor status, leaving 90% unaffected or even unaware of the trial. Follow-up for risk factor change occurred in independent samples of men in the intervention factories, while the 10% sample in control factories underwent a repeat examination. Morbidity and mortality data were obtained through continuous monitoring of the study sites.

Recruitment into the trial in the four countries took place in the early 1970s, and 60,881 men were entered. Results were presented in 1986, with extension of the analysis and some corrections appearing in 1987.[21] After adjustment for baseline differences in risk factors within each pair of intervention and control factories, risk factor change in intervention factories relative to control factories was found to be significantly associated with reduction in six-year incidence of fatal coronary heart disease, total coronary heart disease, and total mortality. The actual reduction in coronary disease incidence was 62% of the amount predicted from the observed risk factor changes. Pooled results for the whole trial were not significant by two-tailed statistical tests, an outcome attributed to limited achievement of risk factor control, specifically in the United Kingdom factories.

In the Belgian component of this study, which included 15 pairs of factories and 19,409 men, exceptionally large reductions in risk factors were observed early in the trial during the most intensive intervention. The net difference in risk factor change was attenuated thereafter, and mortality follow-up was extended to 10 years from baseline to assess the effects of this loss of relative risk factor control.[22] Figure 21–5 shows the early net difference in cumulative incidence of coronary events, all cardiovascular events, and total mortality, as well as the convergence of all three outcomes toward no difference at 10 years.

The intensity of intervention was diminished after three years of the trial, and the net difference in risk factors was greatest, 26%, after two years and narrowed thereafter; the cardiovascular mortality difference narrowed in parallel with a lag time of one to two years (Figure 21–6). The indication that more sustained and integrated prevention efforts are needed for lasting public health effect was emphasized in discussion of these results.

Other Trials

Among other community intervention trials reported recently, the German Cardiovascular Prevention Study illustrates a different approach to design, in that outcomes in selected intervention regions were compared against samples of the total national population as the control.[23] In six regions of former West Germany, a seven-year program was implemented to achieve reductions in blood pressure and

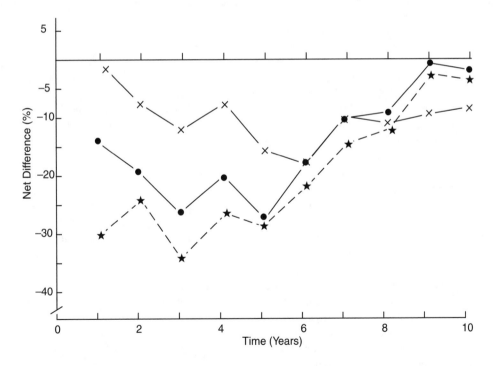

Figure 21–5 Net Difference in Cumulative Incidence of Coronary (★), Cardiovascular (λ), and Total Mortality (×) Between Intervention and Control Groups, Belgian Heart Disease Prevention Project. *Source*: Reprinted with permission from G DeBacker et al, The Belgian Heart Disease Prevention Project: 10-Year Mortality Follow-Up, *European Heart Journal*, Vol 9, p 240, © 1988, WB Saunders Company, Ltd, London.

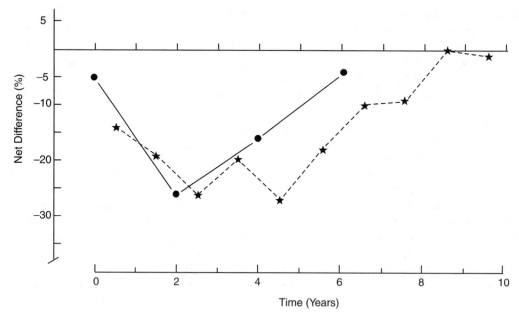

Figure 21–6 Net Difference in Coronary Risk Estimate (λ) and in Cumulative Incidence of Cardiovascular Mortality (★), Belgian Heart Disease Prevention Project. *Source*: Reprinted with permission from G DeBacker et al, The Belgian Heart Disease Prevention Project: 10-Year Mortality Follow-Up, *European Heart Journal*, Vol 9, p 241, © 1988, WB Saunders Company, Ltd, London.

prevalence of hypertension, total cholesterol concentration, smoking prevalence, and body mass index. From 1985 to 1991, significant net reductions were found between intervention communities and control samples for systolic and diastolic blood pressure and total cholesterol concentration. Concentration of high-density lipoprotein cholesterol increased initially and then declined, and the overall net decrease was not significant. Overall, body mass index showed no net difference in change. Results over the full intervention period were similar for women and men, with somewhat greater net decreases in blood pressure for women.

A much wider representation of experience in community intervention can be found in the report of the Second International Heart Health Conference, *The Catalonia Declaration. Investing in Heart Health.*[24] Some of the report's brief synopses of programs throughout the world address single-factor interventions, but others are multifactor projects with some features similar to those reviewed here, and references are

provided for each of them. Citing this body of work as well as the US community intervention studies and others in particular, Farquhar has concluded in a synthesis of this experience that behavior can be influenced by community intervention, research is needed on options in the mix and sequencing of components in an intervention program, and environmental change (in the sense of the policy setting in which intervention occurs) must be incorporated for effective community change. Further, "The greatest unmet need is now for dissemination research and concurrent international technology transfer of the vast number of lessons learned and the many widely accepted practice principles of community-based interventions" (J Farquhar, personal communication, 1997).

INTERVENTION IN YOUTH

A fundamental distinction between prevention trials in children or youths and those in adults is the necessity, in practical terms, for circumscribed evaluation of effects. Since the events of concern in adulthood are not expected to occur in youth, the outcomes amenable to assessment are limited to changes in the risk factors themselves or in the behaviors, attitudes, or knowledge regarded as conditions underlying risk factor development. Many studies have been conducted in which children with high blood cholesterol concentration or high blood pressure have been selected for treatment with drugs or with nonpharmacologic means. These studies correspond to the high-risk strategy of intervention in adults, except that the determination of risk may be only in terms of the relative rank of values in the age- and sex-specific distribution and not in absolute terms. They are heterogeneous in sample size (often small), age and sex of participants (sometimes unspecified), nature and duration of intervention (usually brief), and approaches to evaluation (usually as intervention ends and not later, and sometimes with only pre- and postintervention measurement comparisons but no control group). Their interpretation and systematic review are very difficult for these reasons. Less so are the community-based or population-wide intervention studies in which, for example, whole school populations are randomized to intervention or control status and evaluation extends over several years.

The Know Your Body Study

An early example of such a study is the evaluation of the Know Your Body Program, a school-based health education program for children at several grade levels. In addition to its descriptive epidemiologic component based on school examinations conducted in several countries, this program was evaluated in two settings at one, three, and five years from initiation.[25-27] Initially, children in six school districts in Westchester County, New York, participated. By random assignment of school districts, children in fourth grade (approximately nine years old) in 11 schools were to receive a curriculum beginning in grade four and continuing through grade nine, addressing nutrition, physical fitness, and cigarette smoking prevention. Those in 11 other schools were to serve as controls. Implementation of the intervention required two class periods per week throughout the entire school year. Curriculum materials were provided by the program, but only for intervention schools. First-year evaluation was by measurement of systolic and diastolic blood pressure, plasma total and high-density lipoprotein cholesterol concentration, serum thiocyanate, ponderosity index, triceps skinfold thickness, and postexercise recovery rate (recovery index).

At one year, 25% of the initial participants could not be reexamined due to loss to follow-up. After adjustment for baseline risk factor differences, mean values for all students in intervention versus control showed significant differences only in decreased diastolic blood pressure and serum thiocyanate (a marker of smoking) and increased ponderosity index. The possibilities were addressed that screening of controls may have stimulated risk factor change on their part and that intervention may have lacked sufficient intensity or duration to confer the expected benefit.[25]

At three years, or average age about 12 years, further evaluation was restricted to four of the six districts, as two had withdrawn from participation on grounds of logistical difficulties chiefly concerning the time required for the curriculum.[26] At this stage, with about 20% loss to follow-up, adjusted net differences from baseline were favorable on average for intervention relative to control participants for diastolic blood pressure and plasma total cholesterol concentration, with desirable trends for dietary practices and cigarette smoking. The small observed effects were taken as encouraging that such a program could have benefit in lowering coronary risk.

At the five-year evaluation, students in 22 elementary schools in Bronx, New York, who were in the fourth grade in 1980, were added.[27] The Westchester population had reached the ninth grade at this evaluation and those in the Bronx the eighth grade. Follow-up was limited in completeness, with 80% of the baseline participants reexamined in Westchester and 66% in the Bronx. Analysis was based on regression of each individual participant's change in a risk factor over time, as measured at baseline and at least two subsequent occasions. The average slopes of the regression lines for all individuals in each intervention school were compared with those for all individuals in each control school. The net effect of intervention was the difference in risk factor change between groups of schools. Reduction of cholesterol concentrations was significantly greater in intervention than control schools in Westchester but not in the Bronx. In Westchester, this result was significant only for girls, though the trend for boys was similar. Trends were favorable for dietary intake of fat and knowledge of the risk factors in both study areas. It was concluded that educational programs could have favorable, though small, effects on cholesterol concentration in children and that there were no effects on blood pressure, body mass, or physical fitness. Difficulties encountered were losses to participation, low power due to the limited number of schools, contamination of control experience by repeated risk factor examinations just as in the intervention group, and uncertainty about appropriateness of linear modeling of the patterns of risk factor change. Cautious interpretation of the results and replication of the study were recommended.

The Child and Adolescent Trial for Cardiovascular Health

Based on the Know Your Body experience and others through the 1980s, a major new school-based intervention program was undertaken in the United States with prerandomization assessment in 1991 and postintervention assessment in 1994.[28] Participants were 5,106 students in third grade at entry who attended one of 56 intervention or 40 control schools in California, Louisiana, Minnesota, and Texas. Half of the intervention schools received school food service and physical education changes and classroom health curricula, and the other half received family education in addition. After extensive debate in the design phase, outcomes for evaluation were specified at two levels: at the school level, change in fat content of school lunches and the amount of moderate-to-vigorous physical activity in physical education programs; and at the individual level, change in serum cholesterol concentration. Additional outcomes at the individual level included dietary and activity patterns.

The results at the school level were significantly favorable. The relative decrease in fat content of lunch menus and increase in moderate-to-vigorous physical activity were both greater in intervention schools, as shown in Table 21–9 and Figure 21–7. Changes in self-reported dietary and activity behaviors were also significantly more favorable among intervention than control children (Tables 21–10 and 21–11). However, changes in cholesterol concentration and other physiologic characteristics did not differ between groups of children. It was judged that the dietary changes were insufficient to produce a detectable change in cholesterol concentration, especially in view of the pubertal influences on total cholesterol concentration, which may be overriding at the ages studied. The longer-term impact of the observed changes in diet and activity and the effects of more intensive, longer-lasting intervention remain to be investigated. The ability to modify the school environment and curriculum in favorable ways appears to be well established.

A collection of reports from the Child and Adolescent Trial for Cardiovascular Health project is introduced with an overview that contrasts the individual-level and school-level results, a distinction important to the analysis and interpretation of community intervention trials in which the number of available units is large.[29] The point is emphasized that the school-level intervention goals were largely achieved and that the lesson of lesser success at the individual level is the need for newer strategies to compete with other influences on individual behavior.

Table 21–9 School Lunch Menu Analysis at Three Time Points, 1991 Through 1994, Child and Adolescent Trial for Cardiovascular Health Intervention (I) and Control (C) Groups

Value Measured	Group	Baseline	Interim	Follow-Up
Total energy content, MJ	C	2.97 (0.04)	3.04 (0.04)	3.12 (0.04)
	I	3.01 (0.04)	2.93 (0.04)	2.86 (0.04)
			$P=.05$	$P<.001$
Energy from total fat, %	C	38.9 (0.5)	36.2 (0.5)	36.2 (0.5)
	I	38.7 (0.4)	32.5 (0.4)	31.9 (0.4)
			$P<.001$	$P<.001$
Energy from saturated fat, %	C	15.1 (0.3)	13.6 (0.3)	13.7 (0.3)
	I	14.8 (0.2)	12.1 (0.2)	12.0 (0.2)
			$P=.02$	$P=.007$
Cholesterol content, mg	C	80.3 (2.4)	75.2 (2.4)	83.2 (2.4)
	I	77.7 (2.0)	72.3 (2.0)	74.9 (2.0)
			$P=.95$	$P=.17$
Sodium content, mg/MJ	C	386 (7)	415 (7)	421 (7)
	I	377(6)	401 (6)	423 (6)
			$P=.64$	$P=.34$
Potassium content, mg/MJ	C	325 (5)	333 (5)	327 (5)
	I	331 (4)	350 (4)	357 (4)
			$P=.18$	$P=.004$

Note: Data for baseline, interim, and follow-up are adjusted means (*SE*) from repeated-measures analysis of variance, adjusted for site and school random effect. *P* values compare C with I, adjusting for baseline difference. The school + family intervention group did not differ from the school-only group for any endpoint (*P*>.20). 1 MJ = 239 kcal. 1 mg/MJ = 4.184 mg/1,000 kcal.

Source: Reprinted with permission from RV Luepker et al, *Journal of the American Medical Association*, Vol 275, No 10, p 772, Copyright 1996, American Medical Association.

OTHER TRIALS OF MULTIFACTOR INTERVENTION IN COMMUNITIES AND WORKSITES AND AMONG YOUTHS

Still other trials have been conducted in communities or worksites and among youth (usually in schools), which were reviewed in a Conference on Multifactor Community Trials for Cardiopulmonary Health convened in September, 1996, by the National Heart, Lung and Blood Institute. The reviews and discussion in that conference reflected mixed results of intervention to prevent coronary heart disease in all intervention settings (geographic communities, worksites, schools, religious organizations, and medical care organizations), although in many studies components were identified that had appeared to contribute importantly to changes in risk. The morbidity and mortality outcomes that were positive were taken as reinforcing the possibility of benefit from intervention, but all studies were regarded as presenting challenges in design, conduct, and analysis that have not yet been fully resolved. Overriding concerns were the inherent limitations of power to detect small but important effects when only a small number of units (such as communities) can be allocated randomly to intervention or control status and the frequent problem of strong, perhaps overwhelming, influence on risks reflected in secular trends in risk factors and event rates in the planned control units. These and other concerns are relevant background for consider-

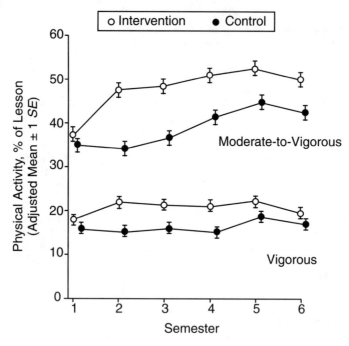

Figure 21–7 Moderate-to-Vigorous and Vigorous Physical Activity Observed During Physical Education Classes at Six Time Points, 1991–1994, Child and Adolescent Trial for Cardiovascular Health (CATCH). The CATCH intervention, introduced during semester 2, increased the percentage of time spent in moderate-to-vigorous activity as measured by the System for Observing Fitness Instruction Time classroom observation system. Intervention and control curves diverged significantly according to repeated-measures analysis of variance with the class session as the unit of analysis: for moderate-to-vigorous activity, $F = 2.17$, $df = 5$, 1979, $P = .02$; for vigorous activity, $F = 2.35$, $df = 5$, 1979, $P = .04$. Analysis was controlled for CATCH site, the location of the lesson, the specialty of the teacher, and random variation among schools and weeks of observation. *Source*: Reprinted from RV Luepker et al, *Journal of the American Medical Association*, Vol 275, p 772, © 1996, American Medical Association.

---

ing implications of this research to the present time.

SOME IMPLICATIONS OF EXPERIENCE WITH MULTIFACTOR INTERVENTION

The lessons of multifactor intervention trials are many, at both the high-risk or clinical level and the population-wide level in whole communities, whether among adults or youth. Investigators, funding agencies, and participating individuals or communities involved in these trials surely required that the studies be thought of as demonstrations, albeit with extensive formal evaluation, rather than strictly as tests of only hypothetical effects. The expectations of favorable outcomes were high, and disappointment at lesser outcomes has been correspondingly deep. For those who have been most skeptical about cardiovascular disease prevention, the mixed or negative results have reinforced the counterarguments. For those who have been most optimistic about the potential for effective prevention, the positive results stand out regarding both disease outcomes and intermediate effects, and the negative or borderline results are taken as cause for reflection and reevaluation of expectations.

Table 21–10 Results of the Health Behavior Questionnaire at Four Time Points, 1991–1994, Child and Adolescent Trial for Cardiovascular Health

Scale[a]	Group	Baseline	Semester 2	Semester 4	Semester 6
Dietary knowledge	C	4.0 (0.3)	5.5 (0.3)	6.9 (0.3)	7.6 (0.3)
(± 14, α = 78)	I	4.8 (0.2)	9.4 (0.2)	10.0 (0.2)	10.0 (0.2)
	P	—	<.001	<.001	<.001
	S	4.7 (0.3)	9.1 (0.3)	9.5 (0.3)	9.7 (0.3)
	SF	4.8 (0.3)	9.7 (0.3)	10.5 (0.3)	10.3 (0.3)
	P	>.10	.05	.002	.06
Dietary intention	C	1.4 (0.3)	−2.1 (0.3)	−1.2 (0.3)	−0.8 (0.3)
(± 13, α = 76)	I	1.8 (0.2)	6.2 (0.2)	4.8 (0.2)	1.1 (0.2)
	P	—	<.001	<.001	<.001
Usual food choice	C	0.8 (0.3)	0.7 (0.3)	0.0 (0.3)	−1.1 (0.3)
(± 14, α = 76)	I	0.8 (0.2)	4.2 (0.2)	2.9 (0.2)	0.2 (0.2)
	P	—	<.001	<.001	<.001
Food choice, social reinforcement	C	−1.0 (0.4)	0.6 (0.4)	0.0 (0.4)	−2.0 (0.4)
(± 21, α = 89)	I	−0.4 (0.3)	6.8 (0.3)	6.7 (0.3)	3.3 (0.3)
	P	—	<.001	<.001	<.001
Food choice, friend reinforcement	C	−1.5 (0.1)	−1.5 (0.1)	−1.9 (0.1)	−2.8 (0.1)
(± 7, α = 83)	I	−1.3 (0.1)	−0.0 (0.1)	−0.4 (0.1)	−2.2 (0.1)
	P	—	<.001	<.001	.04
Food choice, parent reinforcement	C	0.8 (0.01)	1.4 (0.1)	1.2 (0.1)	−0.9 (0.1)
(± 7, α = 74)	I	1.0 (0.1)	2.9 (0.1)	2.8 (0.1)	2.0 (0.1)
	P	—	<.001	<.001	<.001
Food choice, teacher reinforcement	C	−0.2 (0.2)	0.7 (0.2)	0.8 (0.2)	0.0 (0.2)
(± 7, α = 87)	I	0.0 (0.1)	3.9 (0.1)	4.2 (0.1)	3.4 (0.1)
	P	—	<.001	<.001	<.001
Diet self-efficacy	C	5.5 (0.2)	6.2 (0.2)	6.3 (0.2)	5.8 (0.2)
(± 15, α = 87)	I	5.9 (0.2)	7.6 (0.2)	6.7 (0.2)	5.6 (0.2)
	P	—	<.001	.89	.09
Physical activity, positive support	C	5.2 (0.1)	5.6 (0.1)	−6.0 (0.1)	−5.7 (0.1)
(± 11, α = 67)	I	5.3 (0.1)	6.4 (0.1)	6.4 (0.1)	5.7 (0.1)
	P	—	<.001	.11	72
Physical activity, negative support	C	3.1 (0.1)	3.9 (0.1)	−4.3 (0.1)	−4.7 (0.1)
(± 7, α = 56)	I	3.5 (0.1)	4.3 (0.1)	4.7 (0.1)	4.9 (0.1)
	P	—	.59	.81	.43
Physical activity, self-efficacy	C	2.1 (0.1)	2.5 (0.1)	2.7 (0.1)	2.8 (0.1)
(± 5, α = 69)	I	2.2 (0.1)	2.9 (0.1)	3.0 (0.1)	2.7 (0.1)
	P	—	.006	.04	.07

Note: C, control; I, intervention; S, school intervention alone; SF, school + family intervention.

a. With numerical range and Cronbach reliability coefficient α. Scales are based on a series of questions, scored +1 for correct or healthy response, and −1 for incorrect or less healthy response. Data for baseline and semesters 2, 4, and 6 are adjusted means (*SE*) from repeated-measures analysis of variance on school-aggregated data, adjusted for site and school random effect. *P* values compare C with I (all scales) or S with SF (dietary knowledge only), adjusting for baseline difference.

Source: Reprinted with permission from RV Luepker et al, *Journal of the American Medical Association*, Vol 275, No 10, p 773, Copyright 1996, American Medical Association.

Table 21–11 Total Daily Intakes (24-Hour Recall) at Baseline and Follow-Up, Child and Adolescent Trial for Cardiovascular Health

Value Measured	Group	Baseline	Follow-Up	Change[a]	P
Total energy intake, MJ	C	8.49 (0.13)	9.08 (0.15)	0.60 (0.15)	.01
	I	8.55 (0.10)	8.68 (0.12)	0.14 (0.12)	
Energy intake, % total fat	C	32.6 (0.3)	32.2 (0.3)	−0.5 (0.4)	.001
	I	32.7 (0.3)	30.3 (0.3)	−2.3 (0.3)	
Saturated fat	C	12.5 (0.1)	12.1 (0.2)	−0.4 (0.2)	.005
	I	12.7 (0.1)	11.4 (0.1)	−1.1 (0.1)	
Polyunsaturated fat	C	5.9 (0.1)	6.1 (0.1)	0.3 (0.1)	.01
	I	5.7 (0.1)	5.6 (0.1)	−0.1 (0.1)	
Monounsaturated fat	C	11.9 (0.1)	11.6 (0.1)	−0.3 (0.2)	.02
	I	11.9 (0.1)	11.1 (0.1)	−0.8 (0.1)	
Carbohydrate	C	53.7 (0.4)	54.7 (0.4)	1.0 (0.5)	.06
	I	53.9 (0.3)	56.1 (0.3)	2.2 (0.4)	
Protein	C	14.9 (0.2)	14.3 (0.2)	−0.5 (0.2)	.07
	I	14.6 (0.1)	14.8 (0.1)	0.1 (0.2)	
Cholesterol intake, mg	C	218 (7)	225 (8)	5 (8)	.05
	I	223 (6)	206 (6)	−15 (6)	
Sodium intake, mg	C	3,042 (62)	3,168 (65)	184 (69)	.61
	I	2,929 (46)	3,107 (48)	138 (57)	
Sodium intake, mg/MJ	C	362 (5)	354 (5)	−2 (5)	.06
	I	347 (4)	364 (4)	12 (4)	

Note: Restricted to cohort substudy students with paired data. C, control (40 schools, 473 students); I, intervention (56 schools, 709 students).

a. Data for baseline and follow-up are unadjusted means (*SE*). Change estimate (*SE*) is the excess of the group's follow-up mean over the pooled baseline mean, after adjustment by analysis of variance for baseline value, site, sex, race, and school random effect. *P* value compares C with I. The school + family intervention group did not differ from the school-only group for any endpoint (*P*>30). 1 MJ = 239 kcal, 1 mg/MJ = 4.184 mg/1,000 kcal.

Source: Reprinted with permission from RV Luepker et al, *Journal of the American Medical Association*, Vol 275, No 10, p 774, Copyright 1996, American Medical Association.

In retrospect, some negative assessments have been too hasty. Noting the initial MRFIT results and the interpretation that, but for adverse effects of treatment in some hypertensives, a true overall benefit of intervention would have been evident, the editor of the *Lancet* stated: "Maybe it would: one will never know."[30(p 803)] This conclusion failed to anticipate the potential for longer-term follow-up and evaluation in MRFIT, which demonstrated a reversal of the outcome in the critical stratum of hypertensive participants and increasingly favorable overall trends for major end points,

which became significant for reduction of acute myocardial infarction after 16 years. This and other findings after extended follow-up in some of the other trials support the view suggested in many reports that appropriate evaluation requires longer than usual observation and perhaps much longer periods of intervention than have been planned at the outset of these studies.

One recent commentary on "great expectations" contrasts the world of community interventions with that of advertising.[31] The implication is that, at least for the relative investment made, the likely impact of some public health interventions may be important but too small, under the conditions of study, to meet conventional criteria for statistical significance. But in a nonscientific context such as advertising, small effects (even if achieved through sometimes very large investments) are considered highly successful. The admonition is not, however, to abandon conventional statistical standards. Instead, it is to ensure that more realistic, and therefore conservative, design assumptions are made, such as those about effect sizes. Consideration of the many practical limitations of implementing studies in the community at large should be reflected in truly adequate (ie, much larger) sample sizes.

These and other issues in design and interpretation of community intervention trials have been reviewed recently to update a symposium on community trials in coronary heart disease published in 1978 by the *American Journal of Epidemiology* (see volume 108).[32] This review was based in part on the experience of the Stanford and Minnesota studies and on the COMMIT study of smoking cessation (see Chapter 14). Random allocation of communities, matching, estimation of variation among communities, use of cohorts versus cross-sectional samples for evaluation, and aspects of intervention, measurement, and analysis are addressed. The theme was that the preceding 15 years or more of experience provide a greatly strengthened foundation for future community trials, although much remains to be learned.

Several approaches for future community-based cardiovascular disease intervention studies were suggested in another recent review based on the Stanford, Minnesota, and Pawtucket studies.[33] Broader approaches would be taken within a context of public policy initiatives as part of the intervention. Complementary small-scale studies would target especially low-income groups and others not yet reached effectively by preventive measures. Broader concepts of evaluation were also suggested, including not only biomedical but other responses such as behaviors and attitudes influential on the risk factors of interest. Qualitative as well as quantitative measures of program impact should also be incorporated.

In his essay on the "tribulations of trials," Susser placed community trials in the context of social movements and policy change.[34] His conclusions suggested that the scope of experimental evaluation is unlikely ever to match the breadth of the larger forces operating on the phenomena of interest due to practical limitations. This view would lead to consideration by investigators of the social and policy milieu when interventions are to be evaluated at the community level. For example, the choice of time, place, and characteristics of the target population; the intervention strategies; and the most relevant outcomes for evaluation might all be influenced decisively by explicit analysis of the context in these respects. Success requires both correct current insight and an accurate forecast of changes over the course of what may be well over a decade of study.

To date, the lessons taken as positive include many aspects of methods for community-level intervention and some supportive evidence for desired community impact. Where such evidence is weaker or absent, explanations based on circumstance or limitations of study design are often plausible, though they have unfortunately been offered only in hindsight. As these reflections and the recent National Heart, Lung and Blood Institute conference on community trials indicate, confidence remains high that such studies will continue and that the lessons of the completed studies will lead to further improvement in methods and add to the strength of future results.

REFERENCES

1. Rose GA. Strategy of prevention: lessons from cardiovascular disease. *Br Med J*. 1981;282:1847–1851.

2. The Multiple Risk Factor Intervention Trial (MRFIT). A national study of primary prevention of coronary heart disease. *JAMA*. 1976;235:825–827.

3. The Multiple Risk Factor Intervention Trial Research Group. The Multiple Risk Factor Intervention Trial (MRFIT). Risk factor changes and mortality results. *JAMA*. 1982;248:1465–1477.

4. The Multiple Risk Factor Intervention Trial Research Group. Mortality rates after 10.5 years for participants in the Multiple Risk Factor Intervention Trial: findings related to a priori hypothesis of the trial. *JAMA*. 1990; 263:1795–1801.

5. The Multiple Risk Factor Intervention Trial Research Group. Mortality after 10½ years for hypertensive participants in the Multiple Risk Factor Intervention trial. *Circ*. 1990;82:1616–1628.

6. The Multiple Risk Factor Intervention Trial Research Group. Mortality after 16 years for participants randomized to the Multiple Risk Factor Intervention Trial. *Circ*. 1996;94:946–951.

7. Holme I, Hjermann I, Helgelland A, Leren P. The Oslo Study: diet and antismoking advice. *Prev Med*. 1985; 14:279–292.

8. Wilhelmsen L, Berglund D, Elmfeldt D, Tibblin G, et al. The multifactor primary prevention trial in Göteborg, Sweden. *Eur Heart J*. 1986;7:279–288.

9. Strandberg TE, Salomaa VV, Naukkarinen VA, Vanhanen HT, et al. Long-term mortality after 5-year multifactorial primary prevention of cardiovascular diseases in middle-aged men. *JAMA*. 1991;266:1225–1229.

10. Vartiainen E, Puska P, Jousilahti P, Korhonen HJ, et al. Twenty-year trends in coronary risk factors in North Karelia and in other areas of Finland. *Int J Epidemiol*. 1994;23:495–504.

11. Puska P, Tuomilehto J, Nissinen A, Vartiainen E, eds. The North Karelia Project. *20 Year Results and Experiences*. Helsinki, Finland: National Public Health Institute, KTL; 1995.

12. Vartiainen E, Puska P, Pekkanen J, Tuomilehto J, et al. Changes in risk factors explain changes in mortality from ischaemic heart disease in Finland. *Br Med J*. 1994;309:23–27.

13. Farquhar JW, Maccoby N, Wood PD, Alexander JK, et al. Community education for cardiovascular health. *Lancet*. 1977;i:1192–1195.

14. Farquhar JW, Fortmann SP, Flora JA, Taylor B, et al. Effects of community wide education on cardiovascular disease risk factors: the Stanford Five-City Project. *JAMA*. 1990;264:359–365.

15. Luepker RV, Murray DM, Jacobs DR Jr, Mittlemark MB, et al. Community education for cardiovascular disease prevention: risk factor changes in the Minnesota Heart Health Program. *Am J Public Health*. 1994; 84:1383–1393.

16. Luepker R, Rastam L, Hannan PJ, Murray DM, et al. Community education for cardiovascular disease prevention: morbidity and mortality results from the Minnesota Heart Health Program. *Am J Epidemiol*. 1996; 144:351–362.

17. Carleton RA, Lasater TM, Assaf AR, Feldman HA, et al, Pawtucket Heart Health Program Writing Group. The Pawtucket Heart Health Program: community changes in cardiovascular risk factors and projected disease risk. *Am J Public Health*. 1995;85:777–785.

18. Winkelby MA, Feldman HA, Murray DM. Joint analysis of three US community intervention trials for reduction of cardiovascular disease risk. *J Clin Epidemiol*. 1997;50:645–658.

19. World Health Organization European Collaborative Group. An international controlled trial in the multifactorial prevention of coronary heart disease. *Int J Epidemiol*. 1974;3:219–224.

20. World Health Organization European Collaborative Group. European Collaborative Trial of Multifactorial Prevention of Coronary Heart Disease: final report on the 6-year results. *Lancet*. 1986;i:869–872.

21. World Health Organization Collaborative Group. European collaborative trial of multifactorial prevention of coronary heart disease. *Lancet*. 1987;i:685.

22. De Backer G, Kornitzer M, Dramaix M, Kittel F, et al. The Belgian Heart Disease Prevention Project: 10-year mortality follow-up. *Eur Heart J*. 1988;9:238–242.

23. Hoffmeister H, Mensink GBM, Stolzenberg H, Hoeltz J, et al. Reduction of coronary heart disease risk factors in the German Cardiovascular Prevention Study. *Prev Med*. 1996;25:135–145.

24. Advisory Board of the Second International Heart Health Conference. *The Catalonia Declaration: Investing in Heart Health*. Barcelona, Spain: Department of Health and Social Security, Autonomous Government of Catalonia; 1996.

25. Walter HJ, Hofman A, Connelly PA, Barrett LT, et al. Coronary heart disease prevention in childhood: one-year results of a randomized intervention study. *Am J Prev Med*. 1986;2:239–451.

26. Walter HJ, Hofman A, Barrett LT, Connelly PA, et al. Primary prevention of cardiovascular disease among children: three year results of a randomized interven-

tion trial. In: Hetzel B, Berenson GS, eds. *Cardiovascular Risk Factors in Childhood: Epidemiology and Prevention*. New York: Elsevier Science Publishers; 1987:161–181.

27. Walter HJ, Hofman A, Vaughan RD, Wynder EL. Modification of risk factors for coronary heart disease: five-year results of a school-based intervention trial. *N Engl J Med*. 1988;318:1093–1100.

28. Luepker RV, Perry CL, McKinlay SM, Nader PR, et al. Outcomes of a field trial to improve children's dietary patterns and physical activity: the Child and Adolescent Trial for Cardiovascular Health (CATCH). *JAMA*. 1996;275:768–776.

29. Resnicow K, Robinson TN, Frank E. Advances and future directions for school-based health promotion research: commentary on the CATCH intervention trial. *Prev Med*. 1996;25:378–383.

30. Trials of coronary heart disease prevention. *Lancet*. 1982;ii:803–840. Editorial.

31. Fishbein M. Great expectations, or do we ask too much from community-level interventions? *Am J Public Health*. 1996;86:1075–1076.

32. Koepsell TD, Diehr PH, Cheadle A, Kristal A. Invited commentary: Symposium on Community Intervention Trials. *Am J Epidemiol*. 1995;142:594–599.

33. Winkleby M. The future of community-based cardiovascular disease intervention studies. *Am J Public Health*. 1994;84:1369–1372.

34. Susser M. The tribulations of trials-intervention in communities. *Am J Public Health*. 1995;85:156–158.

CHAPTER 22

The Evolution of Prevention Policies

SUMMARY

The evolution of prevention policies for atherosclerotic and hypertensive diseases from their apparent beginning in 1959 to the present reflects advancing knowledge over the same period. In addition to results from epidemiologic as well as laboratory and clinical research, policy development has been influenced by two especially prominent conceptual contributions. From Rose came the clear articulation of the duality of prevention strategies and their underlying epidemiologic rationale: the population-wide and the high-risk strategy. From Strasser came the radical idea of "primordial prevention"—that is, intervention to prevent epidemics of the major risk factors themselves and not only of their late consequences, overt cardiovascular events. Most discussion of prevention policy in recent years has been presented within the framework of the complementary strategies described by Rose. Primordial prevention has served to call greater attention to the potential for effective intervention in populations where major risk factor epidemics may be believed to be early in their progress or in young people regarded similarly, by analogy, on an individual basis; however, there is less evidence to date of application of this concept as Strasser intended it. This chapter reviews the development of prevention policy especially for the population-wide strategy with respect to diet, physical activity, and tobacco. Discussions in preceding chapters with respect to both levels of intervention for several of the risk factors are put into the perspective of policy development. The concept of highest-risk strategies applicable to persons with known cardiovascular disease is also reviewed, for it illustrates a distinct aspect of the high-risk concept. Current prevention policy in its full detail is complex, yet it retains the same essential components as were proposed in 1959. The central issue with respect to prevention policy for cardiovascular diseases today is to ensure its implementation.

THE BEGINNING—1959

The first report to address prevention of atherosclerosis and related conditions is believed to be *A Statement on Arteriosclerosis. Main Cause of "Heart Attacks" and "Strokes,"* a 21-page booklet published in 1959 by the National Health Education Committee, Inc.[1] Chaired by Mrs. Albert D. (Mary) Lasker, the Committee requested a report from an eight-author panel that included five past presidents of the American Heart Association and Paul Dudley White, then President of the International Society of Cardiology, at the head of the list (see reference). The report was endorsed by 106 members of the American Society for the Study of Arteriosclerosis, the organization that was to become the Council on Arteriosclerosis of the American Heart Association. The document was intended to provide "a simple guide which would give the average man and woman something he or she could do in cooperation with the physician to minimize the hazards of arteriosclerosis, main cause of 'heart attacks' and 'strokes.'"[1(p 1)]

The factors identified as predisposing an individual to these events were overweight, elevated blood cholesterol level, elevated blood pressure, excessive cigarette smoking, and heredity. A family history of cardiovascular disease was acknowledged as unchangeable but was an indication for special concern in the presence of any of the other factors. A further observation was that "regular, moderate, physical activity appears to lessen the hazards of arteriosclerosis."[1(p 1)] Scientific support was cited for inclusion of each "contributing factor" from publications appearing in the 1950s.

It is instructive to recognize that this report antedated the entire 35 years of research of the 1960s through the mid-1990s, from whose perspective we can regard its recommendations today. It is also worth considering what this further experience has added and in what respects current policy recommendations have advanced from this "simple guide."

SUBSEQUENT DEVELOPMENTS AFFECTING POLICY

The intervening years have provided an immense wealth of additional knowledge about and insight to atherosclerosis and hypertension and their contributing factors. These results from population studies and clinical and laboratory research together offer previously unrecognized strategies and techniques of intervention. Epidemiologic aspects of this and subsequent knowledge are indicated in the preceding chapters on the distributions and determinants of these diseases and the trials of multifactor intervention toward their prevention. From a public health perspective, the epidemiologic aspects of developing knowledge are especially relevant,

and these aspects have therefore been emphasized in the foregoing chapters. This background provides for a fuller appreciation of the evolution of prevention policy, which would be expected in general to mirror advancing knowledge.

The High-Risk and Population-Wide Strategies

In addition, certain conceptual developments alluded to in previous chapters might be thought to have influenced the evolution of prevention policy. Two of these stand out prominently in historical perspective. Foremost is the articulation by Rose in 1980 of the distinction between two broad strategies of intervention.[2] The epidemiologic roots of this distinction are deep and there may be precedent for its expression in earlier discussions about cardiovascular disease prevention, but it was formulated and proposed most effectively by Rose. According to his concept of prevention, one approach targets those members of the population who are at highest risk by virtue of having extreme values of one or more of the major risk factors. This is termed the *high-risk* strategy. The other approach targets the whole population because, for example, most coronary heart disease events or strokes in a population with high incidence of atherosclerosis and hypertensive diseases arise from levels of risk factors that are not extreme, and such cases are therefore not preventable by the high-risk approach. This approach was initially termed the *mass* strategy but soon came to be known as the *population* or *population-wide* strategy. Potential risks and benefits of intervention through each of these strategies—which are seen as complementary, not competing, alternatives—were discussed in Rose's initial report.

Rose subsequently elaborated on this concept in his commentary, "Sick Individuals and Sick Populations," in which the higher public health priority was clearly inherent in the population strategy.[3] This strategy has the greater relative importance because it alone addresses the "causes of incidence" (the determinants of the rate of disease in the whole population). Its ultimate cumulative impact for the benefit of the population as a whole must therefore be greater than that limited to the individuals reached through the high-risk strategy. Notably, although Rose wrote largely in the context of cardiovascular disease prevention, broader applicability of this concept was demonstrated both in the commentary and, with much fuller elaboration, in his later book, *The Strategy of Preventive Medicine*.[4]

Primordial Prevention

The second conceptual development that may in the long term prove equally influential on cardiovascular prevention policy was presented by Strasser, who was then in the Cardiovascular Diseases Unit of the World Health Organization.[5] Speculating on the future of cardiovascular disease prevention, he noted first the familiar roles of tertiary prevention, such as rehabilitation following myocardial infarction; secondary prevention, for example, treatment to avert recurrent coronary events; and primary prevention, to prevent the occurrence of clinical events such as myocardial infarction or stroke. Importantly, he contemplated a further, more radical approach:

> From the viewpoint of world health for tomorrow, however, one has to go one step further. While the epidemic of risk factors has pervaded the consumer societies, it still has not reached the majority of the developing world. Real grassroot prevention should start by preserving entire risk-factor-free societies from the penetration of risk factor epidemics. Here lies the possibility of averting one of tomorrow's world health problems. For expressing this important concept, I wish to propose the term of *proto-prophylaxis* or *primordial prevention*.[5(p 228)]

The concept of primordial prevention as originally described is not encountered as often as that of the high-risk and population strategies. This could be a consequence of its specific reference to the developing world and the delay until recently in wide recognition of the importance of epidemic atherosclerosis and its complications for developing countries. It has been cited often in discussion of cardiovascular disease prevention in children and youth, in part through misappropriation of the term to denote simply early intervention to prevent risk factor development in children. However, the broad implications of primordial prevention, as intended by Strasser, for strategies of prevention in developing countries have begun to be more widely appreciated. The additional possibility that societal conditions favoring risk factor development could be controlled or reversed, even once established, adds further importance to the concept of primordial prevention.

An Abundance of Reports and Recommendations

In addition to advances both in knowledge and in concepts of cardiovascular disease prevention since 1959, the third critical ingredient has been the broadening of interest, concern, and attention to prevention on the part of official and voluntary health agencies, the health professions, and the public. As a result of this increased emphasis on prevention, hundreds of formal recommendations on various aspects of cardiovascular disease prevention have been published. An exhaustive collection of such reports would permit an interesting analysis of policy development in this area, but none is known to exist.

One difficulty in attempting such a collection is the breadth of the subject area that has evolved since the National Health Education Committee report of 1959. The scope of recommendations now includes not only the risk factors themselves and their relation to primary prevention, as in the 1959 report, but also the underlying behaviors, other stages of prevention, population-wide and high-risk strategies, the circumstances of special population groups, information for health professionals and the general public, and materials for use in specific settings—schools, worksites, health care facilities, and others. The wide range of health-related behaviors addressed in these recommendations also broadens their scope. For this reason, major reports on diet, for example, have health implications not only for cardiovascular diseases but for cancer and other chronic conditions or health and well-being more generally. Thus, many relevant recommendations are no longer restricted to cardiovascular diseases.

Stamler, tracing this policy development through the 1960s and 1970s, cited several prominent landmarks that indicate the growing involvement in the United States of multiple governmental and nongovernmental agencies. Those reports addressed prevention of cardiovascular diseases either very broadly or in terms specific to nutrition, smoking, or general health improvement.[6] Additional policy reports were published in this period in several places— Scandinavia, Germany, Australia, New Zealand, and the United Kingdom—and by the World Health Organization (WHO) and the International Society and Federation of Cardiology. Clearly, wider recognition of the problem was emerging.

Among the many prevention policy statements appearing in the 1980s were three from WHO Expert Committees that addressed prevention of coronary heart disease alone or jointly with other cardiovascular diseases. The 29th World Health Assembly adopted a resolution in 1976 calling for the preparation of a long-term WHO program that would include promotion of research on cardiovascular disease prevention and coordination of international cooperative activities in the cardiovascular area. WHO Member States were also urged to implement prevention programs as necessary and feasible. That resolution stimulated the appointment, somewhat tardily, of the first of these three Expert Committees in late 1981.

The resulting report, *Prevention of Coronary Heart Disease*, appeared in 1982.[7] Its content paralleled the dual population and high-risk strategies and incorporated primordial prevention as the foundation of the strategy for developing countries. The report suggested implementation of a close linkage between primordial prevention and primary health care resources, whose strengthening was already advocated by WHO. The next of these Expert Committee reports, *Community Prevention and Control of Cardiovascular Diseases*, was published in 1986.[8] The Committee adopted the recommendations of the prior report and addressed means of implementation at the community level, including the outline of a model regional plan for cardiovascular disease prevention. The third report, *Prevention in Childhood and Youth of Adult Cardiovascular Diseases: Time for Action*, resulted from an Expert Committee meeting in 1988 and appeared in 1990.[9] Here the emphasis was on youth (to age 24) and the need for early intervention to avert the risk factors themselves as well as later complications of advanced atherosclerosis, hypertension, or other major cardiovascular conditions. Again, the population and high-risk strategies were taken as organizing concepts for the recommendations, with the following emphasis on Strasser's concept of primordial prevention (though his term was not used):

> It is therefore recommended that countries develop and pursue a comprehensive population strategy for the primary prevention of these diseases as part of their long-term national health development plan. This strategy should emphasize primary prevention beginning in early childhood and youth, in order to avoid the emergence of the established major risk factors for adult CVD and prevent their persistence on a mass scale in the community.[9(p 83)]

The 1990s

Prevention policies in the 1990s identify essentially the same factors for intervention as did the 1959 *Statement on Arteriosclerosis*. Specially emphasized as the "major" factors are blood lipids, blood pressure, and smoking. Blood lipids now commonly include components in addition to total cholesterol concentration, and blood pressure is categorized in greater detail than was conventional in 1959. Tobacco use in any degree, not just "excessive smoking," is considered to convey risk, owing to the known addictive properties of nicotine and the manipulation of its concentration in the manufacture of tobacco products. Obesity or overweight is considered important for cardiovascular risk chiefly as an intermediate in the pathway leading to adverse lipid profiles, high blood pressure, and other risk factors. Heredity, in the sense of a positive family history of arteriosclerosis, continues to serve principally as a marker to increase concern and reinforce measures taken against the other factors. Physical inactivity is increasingly recognized as a widespread problem throughout the US population and many others. While the 1959 *Statement* was cautious about exercise due to concern that heavy exertion carried increased risks, it now appears that habitual exercise and desirable fitness nullify any such excess risk of precipitating acute cardiovascular events. Incremental improvement in activity levels through even moderate daily exercise is regarded as offering substantial benefit in reduced cardiovascular risks. Prevention policies remain dependent for their full implementation on participation of physicians and other health care professionals on behalf of their patients. This clinically oriented approach is inherent in the high-risk strategy of intervention and was also reflected in the admonition of the 1959 report to address the contributing factors "in cooperation with the physician to minimize the hazards of arteriosclerosis."[1(p 1)]

With respect to the main targets of intervention, the development outlined broadly here indicates refinements more than substantial changes in prevention policy for cardiovascular diseases from the 1950s to the 1990s. However, profound change has taken place in the following respects:

- incorporation of the population strategy
- introduction of the concept of primordial prevention
- emphasis on diet and physical activity, together with prevention or cessation of tobacco use, as the first-line approach to risk factor prevention and control even in high-risk individuals
- development of highly detailed algorithms and protocols for detection and management of high-risk blood lipid profiles and/or blood pressure, which include attention to other factors as needed and postponement of drug therapy until behavioral change has been tried and found insufficient to attain intervention goals

Current policies can now be reviewed against this background of their development. Highlighted first, in keeping with the public health perspective, are recommendations aimed primarily at the population level. These principally address diet, physical activity, and tobacco use. Aspects of prevention policies and guidelines applicable to clinical settings or the high-risk strategy are reviewed later in this chapter.

POLICIES APPLICABLE IN THE POPULATION-WIDE STRATEGY OF PREVENTION

Diet

Among the sources of recommendations concerning diet in the prevention of heart disease and stroke, the American Heart Association has played a prominent role. Its first report, published by the Central Committee for Medical and Community Program in 1961, discussed the development of atherosclerosis, research relating diet to atherosclerosis, and recommendations to reduce blood cholesterol by decreasing intake of calories and saturated fat and adoption of a habit of regular, moderate exercise.[10] Advice for dietary change was especially directed at those with a family history of cardiovascular disease; with other risk factors such as elevated blood pressure, overweight, or "sedentary lives of relentless frustration"[10(p 134)]; and with a prior heart attack or stroke. The recommended goal of a dietary pattern with 25%–35% of total calories from fat and substitution of polyunsaturated for saturated fats was to be pursued under medical supervision.

Since 1961, seven further statements on diet have been provided by the American Heart Association. The most recent report, "Dietary Guidelines for Healthy American Adults," was prepared by its Nutrition Committee.[11] This report incorporates more comprehensive dietary principles that have evolved over the intervening years, in part under the aegis of the US Dietary Guideline Committee of the US Department of Agriculture, discussed below. It was addressed to the general population and referred to cigarette smoking, physical activity, and obesity as well as specific, quantitative goals for dietary composition with respect to types of fat and amounts of cholesterol, sodium, complex carbohydrates, and alcohol. Incorporation of the *Dietary Guidelines for Americans* within these recommendations recognized the potential value for the population as a whole of a dietary pattern thought to contribute to prevention of not only cardiovascular diseases but also some cancers, renal disease, osteoporosis, and diabetes. Contrary to the title, its recommendations were not limited to adults but were intended as goals for children over two years of age, in the expectation that this dietary pattern would be adopted gradually, by age five, in conformity with the family's dietary pattern.

The national guidelines referred to above are themselves an outgrowth of developments over 15 years. *Nutrition and Your Health: Dietary Guidelines for Americans* appeared in its fourth edition in 1995. It was organized around seven aspects of diet, each presented with a nontechnical explanation and indicating types of food choices consistent with each recommendation.[12] This edition continued a schedule of five-yearly updates that began in 1980, building on principles of nutrition traceable to the origins of the Department of Agriculture before 1900.[13] Table 22–1 outlines the evolution of the essential elements of the guidelines over this period. The traditional concepts of variety, proportionality, and moderation are explicit in each version. The fourth edition introduced the concept of balance between food intake and physical activity. The change in style from "avoidance" to "choice" and "moderation" was intended both to establish positive attitudes toward dietary change and to avert exaggerated reductions in one or another dietary constituent. Reduction in intake of fats and cholesterol became explicit for the first time in the 1995 edition, consistent with guidelines published by the American Heart Association since 1961, with quantitative recommendations now included.

One of the major resources for preparation of the current *Guidelines* was an extensive report by the Committee on Diet and Health conducted for the National Research Council of the National Academy of Sciences, *Diet and Health: Implications for Reducing Chronic Disease Risk*.[14] The encyclopedic and extensively referenced report was a landmark in assessment of research in nutrition, epidemiology, and related fields as they bear on relations between diet and chronic diseases. It has been cited extensively in preceding chapters, especially Chapter 8.

In its recommendations, the Committee considered both the individual-based or high-risk approach and the public health or population-based approach. The intended application of these recommendations was for the whole population of healthy North American adults and children. Although specific provisions for individuals or special groups at high risk of chronic diseases were judged by the Committee to be premature on the basis of current knowledge, the overall recommendations were expressed in terms of dietary goals for individuals. This

Table 22–1 Dietary Guidelines for Americans, 1980–1995

1980	1985	1990	1995
Eat a variety of foods	Eat a variety of foods	Eat a variety of foods	Eat a variety of foods
Maintain ideal weight	Maintain desirable weight	Maintain healthy weight	Balance the food you eat with physical activity—maintain or improve your weight
Avoid too much fat, saturated fat, and cholesterol	Avoid too much fat, saturated fat, and cholesterol	Choose a diet low in fat, saturated fat, and cholesterol	Choose a diet with plenty of grain products, vegetables, and fruits[a]
Eat foods with adequate starch and fiber	Eat foods with adequate starch and fiber	Choose a diet with plenty of vegetables, fruits, and grain products	Choose a diet low in fat, saturated fat, and cholesterol[a]
Avoid too much sugar	Avoid too much sugar	Use sugars only in moderation	Choose a diet moderate in sugars
Avoid too much sodium	Avoid too much sodium	Use salt and sodium only in moderation	Choose a diet moderate in salt and sodium
If you drink alcohol, do so in moderation	If you drink alcoholic beverages, do so in moderation	If you drink alcoholic beverages, do so in moderation	If you drink alcoholic beverages, do so in moderation

a. In the 1995 edition, the order of the third and fourth guidelines has been reversed.

Source: Data from CA Davis and EA Saltos, The Dietary Guidelines for Americans—Past, Present, Future, *Family Economics and Nutrition Review*, Vol 9, pp 4–13, © 1996.

aspect of dietary recommendations calls attention to an important distinction between the anticipated effects of intervention goals for populations and those for individuals: If the goal were, for example, to reduce the *population mean* serum cholesterol concentration to 200 mg/dl, the expected between-individual variation about this level, within ± 2 standard deviations, would be from about 140 to 260 mg/dl. If the goal were to reduce *each individual's average* cholesterol concentration to 200 mg/dl level or below, then individual mean values as great as 200 mg/dl should become rare; the corresponding population mean value in this circumstance would be well below 200 mg/dl. Accordingly, the Committee anticipated that successful achievement of its dietary recommendations, expressed as daily goals for individuals, would result in population averages well below the target levels for individuals.

Recommended intakes were the following: total fat, 30% or less of calories; saturated fat, 10% or less of calories; cholesterol, less than 300 mg daily; vegetables and fruits, five or more servings daily; starches and other complex carbohydrates, six or more servings daily; protein, moderate levels; salt, 6 g/day or less; calcium, "adequate"; and fluoride, "optimal." A balance between food intake and physical activity was recommended in order to maintain appropriate body weight. The committee does not recommend alcohol consumption and advised only limited intake (less than 1 ounce pure alcohol per day) for those who do use it. Use of dietary supplements in excess of the Recommended Daily Allowance (RDA) was discouraged. The recommendations closed with the following statement:

> With regard to the risk of chronic diseases, maximum benefit can be attained and any unknown, potentially harmful effects of dietary constituents minimized by selecting a variety of foods from each food group, avoiding excessive caloric intake (especially excessive intake of any one item or food group), and engaging regularly in moderate physical exercise.[14(p 675)]

Finally, the report compared these recommendations with others intended to reduce the risk of coronary heart disease published in 1968–1988 in North America, Europe, Australia, New Zealand, and Japan and by WHO (Table 22–2). The recommendations were broadly similar in reference to particular dietary components and the direction of recommended change. They differed or their intent was unclear regarding whether the goals were for the individual or population level. Notably, an apparently small difference in goals—such as that between saturated fat intake of 35% of calories for the United Kingdom versus less than 30% in the United States—implies a much higher frequency of high saturated fat intakes in the United Kingdom. Finally, no such recommendations were identified for developing countries.

A subsequent WHO Study Group report, *Diet, Nutrition, and the Prevention of Chronic Diseases*, addressed this topic from a global and historical perspective, tracing developments in nutrition and food policies from the 1940s.[15] The report acknowledged the coexistence of nutritional deficiencies and the "affluent" diet in many countries, both developed and developing, but its emphasis was on the latter dietary problem. Published dietary recommendations for both industrialized and developing countries were summarized. Developing countries were represented only by India and Latin America and these by only two recent reports (Table 22–3). For India, it is remarkable that for the high-risk, affluent segment of the population it was still considered feasible to target total fat intake at 20% of calories or less, and mention of cholesterol intake was apparently considered unnecessary. For Latin America, the suggested intake of total fats was also low in comparison with those in Table 22–2, and the saturated fat intake was especially so, perhaps as a target for population and not individual mean values. Generally similar components of the diet were addressed here and in the industrialized countries, but goals reflected intervention much earlier in the course of population trends toward increased average fat intake.

Dietary recommendations have clearly evolved toward more explicit goals for intake of fats and sodium, inclusion of physical activity for caloric balance, and presentation in terms of specific food choices. This evolution is in keeping with advances in knowledge of dietary imbalance and its central role in cardiovascular disease risk, as reviewed in Chapter 8. The relative dearth of such recommendations from developing countries—or knowledge of those that may exist—points to an area of urgent need in public health policy in much of the world.

Physical Activity

Coincident with the Centennial Olympic Games in the United States in 1996, the National Center for Chronic Disease Prevention and Health Promotion of the Centers for Disease Control and Prevention issued *Physical Activity and Health: A Report of the Surgeon General*.[16] This report provided a historical background of physical activity in Western and other cultures, reviewed the evolution of recommendations for physical activity, addressed scientific knowledge about its physiological and health effects, described trends in activity behavior in the United States, and presented issues in the promotion of physical activity in both youth and adulthood.

Recommendations concerning physical activity in the United States are traceable to the 1950s, if not earlier. The *Statement on Arterio-*

Table 22-2 Dietary Recommendations To Lower Coronary Heart Disease Risk in the United States and Abroad

Country	Target Population	Body Weight/ Exercise	Total Fat (% kcal)	SFA (% kcal)	PUFA (% kcal)	Cholesterol (mg/day)	Complex Carbohydrates and Fiber	Simple Sugars	Sodium Chloride	Alcohol Intake	Other Recommendations
Sweden, Finland, Norway (1968)	GP	Reduce calories to avoid obesity; exercise	Reduce to 25–35	Reduce	Increase	NC	Increase vegetables, fruits, potatoes	Decrease	NC	NC	10–12% of calories from protein, of which 30–50% should be of animal origin
United States (1972)	GP	Avoid obesity	Reduce to 35	Isocaloric amounts of SFA, PUFA, and MUFA		300	Increase	NC	NC	NC	NC
Netherlands (1973)	GP	Maintain appropriate body weight	33	Restrict	10–13	250–300	Increase to make up caloric needs	Use little	NC	NC	NC
Federal Republic of Germany (1975)	GP	NC	Reduce	Reduce	Increase	Reduce	NC	NC	NC	NC	NC
New Zealand (1976)	GP HR	Maintain appropriate body weight	35	Reduce, especially for HR	HR should substitute for SFA	Reduce	NC	Restrict to reduce weight	NC	Restrict to reduce weight	NC
Canada (1977)	GP	Maintain appropriate body weight	Reduce to 35	10	10	NC	Increase	NC	Restrict	NC	Variety of foods
Australia (1979)	HR	Avoid obesity	Reduce to 30–35	P:S = 1:0	P:S = 1:0	Restrict	Eat enough	Use less	Restrict	Moderation	Focus on HR groups, food labeling
United Kingdom (1982)	GP	Avoid obesity; increase exercise	30	<10	NC	NC	Increase	NC	NC	NC	Special attention to children

continues

Table 22-2 continued

Country	Target Population	Body Weight/ Exercise	Total Fat (% kcal)	SFA (% kcal)	PUFA (% kcal)	Cholesterol (mg/day)	Complex Carbohydrates and Fiber	Simple Sugars	Sodium Chloride	Alcohol Intake	Other Recommendations
World Health Organization (1982)	GP	Avoid obesity	Reduce to 20–30	<10	Up to 10	<300	Increase	NC	<5 g/day	Drink less	Emphasis on plant foods, fish, poultry, lean meats, low-fat dairy products, and fewer whole eggs
Japan (1983)	GP	NC	20–25	NC	Cook with vegetable oil	NC	Increase	Reduce	Limit to <10 g/ day	Avoid too much	Variety; eat enough protein, half from vegetables and half from animal sources; eat enough potassium, especially from green vegetables. Eat lean meat and fish; eat fewer confections
United Kingdom (1984)	GP	Avoid obesity; exercise	Reduce to 35	Reduce to 15	NS; PUFA/ SFA ~0.45	NS	Increase breads, cereals, fruits, vegetables	NC	Decrease	<90 ml/day for males; <65 ml/day for females	Special recommendations to government, professionals, industry
United States (1984)	GP	Control obesity	<30	8	10	<250	Increase to make up caloric loss	NC	5 g/day	NC	NS
United States (1985)	GP HR	Maintain appropriate body weight	<30	<10	Up to 10	250–300	Endorsed earlier recommendations of AHA (1982) and the Inter-Society Commission for Heart Disease Resources (1984)	NC	NC	NC	Special recommendations for high-risk groups; guidelines for health professionals, industry, and public

continues

Table 22–2 continued

Country	Target Population	Body Weight/ Exercise	Total Fat (% kcal)	SFA (% kcal)	PUFA (% kcal)	Cholesterol (mg/day)	Complex Carbohydrates and Fiber	Simple Sugars	Sodium Chloride	Alcohol Intake	Other Recommendations
Finland (1987)	GP HR	Avoid excess weight; exercise	<30	Reduce	PUFA/ SFA >0.5	Reduce	NC	NC	Reduce for HR <5 g/ day	Moderation	Avoid trace element deficiencies; food labeling; focus on HR groups
Canada (1988)	GP HR	Adjust caloric intake and expenditure	<30	<10	<10	Restrict through less organ meats and egg yolks; for HR <300 mg	Increase	NC	Limit	Limit	Focus on HR groups; limit protein
United States (1988)	GP	Maintain appropriate body weight	<30	<10	Up to 10	<300	Increase to derive ≥50% kcal from total carbohydrates	NS	≤3 g/day of sodium	1–2 oz ethanol/day	Protein to make up remainder of calories; wide variety of foods

Note: GP, general population; HR, high-risk population; MUFA, monounsaturated fatty acids; NC, no comment; NS, not specified; P:S, ratio of polyunsaturated to saturated fatty acids; PUFA, polyunsaturated fatty acids; SFA, saturated fatty acids.

Source: Reprinted with permission from *Diet and Health: Implications for Reducing Chronic Disease Risk.* Copyright 1989 by the National Academy of Sciences. Courtesy of the National Academy Press, Washington, DC.

Table 22–3 Dietary Recommendations in Developing Countries: India and Latin America, 1988

Country/Region	India[a]	Latin America[b]
Target group	HR (affluent people)	GP
Body weight/exercise (maintain appropriate levels)	Yes	Yes
Total fat (% energy)	15–20	20–25
SFA (% energy)	NC	≤8
PUFA (% energy)	Balance (n-3/n-6) ratio	P:S ≈ 1.0
Cholesterol (mg/day)	NC	<100 mg/1,000 kcal (max 300)
Complex carbohydrates (increase)	Yes; avoid refined and polished grains	Yes
Dietary fiber (g/day)	Include grains, leafy veg., whole grains	>8g/1,000 kcal
Sodium chloride (g/day) (restrict)	Yes	≤5
Alcohol (% energy) (moderate intake)	NC	NC

Note: GP, general population; HR, high-risk population; NC, no comment; P:S, ratio of polyunsaturated to saturated fatty acids; PUFA, polyunsaturated fatty acids; SFA, saturated fatty acids.

a. Other recommendations: variety; focus on cooking methods; consume milk and cheese as skimmed-milk products; four or even five meals daily; food labeling.

b. Other recommendations: protein 10%–12% energy; dietary interactions; vitamin C with iron-containing foods; calcium intake.

Source: Adapted with permission from *Report of a WHO Study Group*, WHO TRS 797, pp 180–181, © 1990, World Health Organization.

sclerosis approached physical inactivity not as one of the five contributing factors to heart attacks and strokes but as one to be mentioned and supported by citations to recent studies.[1] The emphasis of the *Statement* was on refuting the concept that heart attacks and strokes resulted from heavy work and advocating, in conjunction with the other factors discussed, the desirability of moderate, regular exercise.

Recommendations on physical activity have addressed a variety of health outcomes. Of 33 such documents listed in the Surgeon General's report and appearing between 1965 and 1996, 17 had cardiovascular disease prevention or health promotion as their objectives, while the others concerned fitness, weight control, rehabilitation, or prevention of osteoporosis.[16] These 17 recommendations are summarized in Table 22–4. The mode of physical activity common to most was endurance training. The recommended intensity and methods and criteria for

monitoring it have varied from time to time. The most recent approach refers to "moderate" or "hard" intensity only qualitatively, requiring no measurement as before. In a similar conversion of form, the recommended frequency has changed from a specific number or range of days per week to "most" or "all or most" days, and duration is simply a cumulative 30 minutes or more per day. This most recent formulation reflects an increasing tendency to express desirable exercise patterns less as a prescription than as a normal habit. The controversy surrounding this approach was discussed in Chapter 9.

The intended application of this recommendation to the whole population is clear in the conclusions of the *NIH Consensus Development Conference Statement on Physical Activity and Cardiovascular Health*, cited in the report:

All Americans should engage in regular physical activity at a level appro-

Table 22–4 Selected Physical Activity Recommendations in the United States, 1965–1996

Source	Objective	Type/Mode
AHA Recommendations (1972)	CHD prevention	Endurance
AHA Recommendations (1975)	Secondary prevention in patients with heart disease	Endurance
USDHEW-Healthy People (1979)	Disease prevention/health promotion	Endurance
USPSTF (1989)	Primary prevention in clinical practice	Not specified, implied endurance
USHHS/USDA Dietary Guidelines (1990)	Health promotion/disease prevention, weight maintenance	Not specified
DHHS-Healthy People 2000 (1991)	Disease prevention/health promotion	Endurance, strength, flexibility
AHA Position Statement (1992)	CVD prevention and rehabilitation	Endurance
AHA Standards (1992 and 1995)	CHD prevention and rehabilitation	Endurance, strength
ACSM Position Statement (1993)	Prevention and treatment of hypertension	Endurance, strength
AHA Position Statement (1993)	CVD prevention and rehabilitation	Moderate intensity (ie, brisk walking) integrated into daily routine
ACSM Position Stand (1994)	Secondary prevention in patients with coronary heart disease	Endurance, strength
Physical Activity Guidelines for Adolescents (1994)	Lifetime health promotion for adolescents	Endurance
AMA Guidelines for Adolescent Preventive Services (1994)	Health promotion/physical fitness	Endurance
CDC/ACSM (1995)	Health promotion	Endurance
USHHS/USDA Dietary Guidelines (1995)	Health promotion/disease prevention, weight maintenance	Endurance
NHLBI Consensus Conference (1996)	CVD prevention for adults and children and cardiac rehabilitation	Endurance
CSPSTF (1996)	Primary prevention in clinical practice	Endurance, strength, flexibility

Source: Data from *Physical Activity and Health: A Report of the Surgeon General*, US Department of Health and Human Services, 1996.

priate to their capacities, needs, and interests. All children and adults should set and reach a goal of accumulating at least 30 minutes of moderate-intensity physical activity on most, and preferably all, days of the week. Those who currently meet these standards may derive additional health and fitness benefits by becoming more physically active or including more vigorous activity.[16(p 47)]

In addition to the endurance-type activity addressed in the reports summarized in Table 22–4, strength-developing activities were included in the Surgeon General's report, which recommended at least twice-weekly sessions of one to two sets of 8–10 repetitions of strength-developing exercises of the major muscle groups. For high-risk individuals or groups, no different standards were proposed but medical evaluation was considered necessary in the presence of chronic conditions, high risk of cardiovascular diseases, or age—40 or over for men and 50 or over for women. The whole population, beginning at age two years, was intended to adopt these recommendations.

In the international arena, the Surgeon General's report cited the 1993 International Consensus Conference on Physical Activity Guidelines for Adolescents. In the report of that conference, daily moderate to vigorous activity for three or more sessions of 20 minutes each was recommended for all adolescents. Similarly, the American Academy of Pediatrics has recommended active play in preschool children, assessment of children's activity levels, and evaluation of their fitness. The underlying concept of activity for health and not skills training is evident in these most recent recommendations.

In the area of physical activity, as in dietary patterns, policy development has reflected advancing knowledge. Here a major influence on recent policy has been the evidence for reduction in cardiovascular risk from even moderate levels of activity. However, as discussed in

Chapter 9, the focus on youth continues and should be strengthened at the level of school-based health promotion in view of the success of the Child and Adolescent Trial for Cardiovascular Health (Chapter 21) in demonstrating improvement in activity levels with intervention.

Tobacco

In 1956, the American Heart Association's Committee on Smoking and Cardiovascular Disease issued the organization's first report on tobacco.[17] The Committee recognized the relations of smoking both with peripheral arterial disease and with the precipitation of angina pectoris among persons with coronary artery disease. However, reservations were expressed about a role of smoking in the causation of coronary heart disease. The report emphasized the need for further studies of this question. In 1960, still four years before the landmark Surgeon General's report, the second commentary by the American Heart Association appeared, amending the 1956 statement, which was included among several supporting appendixes. The new statement conveyed a different assessment, that a role of heavy cigarette smoking in coronary heart disease was strongly suggested. The recommendation was that the related data "should be called to the attention of the medical profession, allied health professions, health educators, and the general public."[17(p 160)] As already seen, a role for "excessive" smoking had already been incorporated in the *Statement on Arteriosclerosis* of 1959.

The 1964 Report of the Advisory Committee to the Surgeon General of the Public Health Service, *Smoking and Health*, marked the official designation by a US governmental agency of cigarette smoking as a cause of lung cancer.[18] With respect to cardiovascular diseases, it was concluded that it would be "more prudent from the public health viewpoint to assume that the established association has causative meaning than to suspend judgment until no uncertainty remains."[18(p 327)] However, no specific recommendation was proposed with respect to cardio-vascular disease prevention.

In 1994, with tobacco use still epidemic in the United States, the most recent of many reports of the Surgeon General concerning tobacco was published, *Preventing Tobacco Use among Young People*.[19] The focus on youth and young adults has been a feature of smoking prevention efforts since the mid-1960s on the bases that the smoking habit begins in youth and smoking cessation by habituated adults is at best difficult and often unsuccessful or only temporary. Therefore control of tobacco use depends upon preventive efforts before the habit begins. This same premise underlies the policy endorsed by President Clinton in 1996 to prohibit tobacco advertising that targets youth and to strengthen controls on tobacco access by youth.

The 1994 report reviewed programs to prevent tobacco use initiated over the past three decades, including school-based programs, clinical and community programs, and the role of mass media in reducing tobacco use. Many specific studies were discussed. Policies were also reviewed relating to smoking restrictions for the general public, restriction on minors' access to tobacco, warning labels on tobacco products, and tobacco taxation. Given the strong emphasis on prevention programs targeting youth, with the goal of averting the onset of tobacco use in the first place, school-based programs were identified as having a central role.

The links between these preventive strategies and the stages of adoption of tobacco use discussed in Chapter 14 are indicated in Figure 22–1. At the stage of "never smoker," mass media programming, counteradvertising, and community-wide programs are applicable. Once "trying" tobacco products has begun, programs to instill skills at resisting negative social influences, counterincentives through price increases, and restrictions on access become important. At the further stage of "experimentation," broader social influences are considered to have added benefit along with continued pricing counterincentives. Once "regular use" has become established, further restrictive poli-cies such as prohibition of smoking in the school setting and offering tobacco cessation programs have been attempted.

The report concluded a review of programs to prevent tobacco use by noting the diversity of studies, complexity of design issues, and variable degrees of program implementation that have resulted in great heterogeneity in the available data. Overall, however, the programs to inoculate against adverse social influences such as peer pressure have had a favorable impact, resulting in reductions in prevalence of smoking by some 25%–60% in groups receiving these programs relative to control groups, with differences lasting from one to four years. The duration of effect of programs targeting school-age groups appears to be longer when periodic "booster" programs are offered, prevention of tobacco use is incorporated in broader health curricula, and community-wide programs provide a reinforcing context for school-based programs.

Guidelines for school health programs to prevent tobacco use were formulated by the Centers for Disease Control and Prevention in collaboration with representatives of a large number of organizations and agencies concerned with prevention of tobacco use.[20] The recommendations are listed in Exhibit 22–1. The report concluded that such programs "could become one of the most effective national strategies to reduce the burden of physical, emotional, and monetary expense incurred by tobacco use."[20(p 359)] It closed with the caveat that effectiveness of this strategy is conditional on commitment of school and community leaders both to implement and to sustain such programs. The need for long-term support was emphasized.

From an international perspective, WHO has issued several reports on the tobacco problem worldwide and specifically in relation to developing countries. The history of this activity through the early 1980s was reviewed by Roemer.[21] She cited national findings in the United Kingdom and Sweden that antedated the US Surgeon General's Advisory Committee report

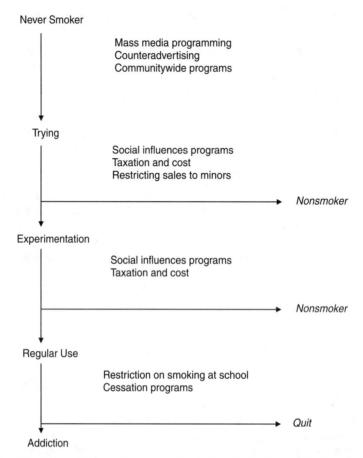

Figure 22–1 Efforts To Prevent Tobacco Use among Young People, by Stage of Initiation. *Source*: Reprinted from *Preventing Tobacco Use among Young People: A Report of the Surgeon General*, US Department of Health and Human Services, 1994.

of 1964, reviewed actions by WHO, and chronicled and analyzed legislative actions against tobacco throughout the world. In 1970, the World Health Assembly first adopted a resolution on this issue as the basis for the antismoking policy of WHO.

The first WHO Expert Committee to consider this topic was convened in 1974.[22] Its report recommended that governments should assess the presence or potential for smoking-related health problems and, if findings were affirmative, institute programs for control and prevention of tobacco smoking. Programs should be planned as long-term activities. They should include recommended elements of educational efforts and target special programs to two groups in particular: women and health workers. The groups were selected because of the risks of smoking during pregnancy and the specific role models that nonsmoking women and health care workers could become. Legislative action should be taken to address advertising and promotion, labeling and warnings, taxation, protection of minors from distribution of or access to tobacco products, and securing the rights of nonsmokers. Measures to support smoking cessation should be adopted. Finally, research should be pursued addressing a range of topics from mechanisms of toxicity to determination of the country-specific economic burden of smoking.

Exhibit 22–1 Recommendations for School Health Programs To Prevent Tobacco Use and Addiction

- Recommendation 1: Develop and enforce a school policy on tobacco use.
- Recommendation 2: Provide instruction about the short-term and long-term negative physiologic and social consequences of tobacco use, social influences on tobacco use, peer norms regarding tobacco use, and refusal skills. Some tobacco-use prevention.
- Recommendation 3: Provide K–12 tobacco-use prevention education.
- Recommendation 4: Provide program-specific training for teachers.
- Recommendation 5: Involve parents or families in support of school-based tobacco-use prevention programs.
- Recommendation 6: Support cessation efforts among students and all school staff who use tobacco.
- Recommendation 7: Assess the tobacco-use prevention program at regular intervals.

Source: Data from Recommendations for School Health Programs To Prevent Tobacco Use and Addiction, *Journal of School Health*, Vol 64, No 9, © 1994.

The Expert Committee Report of 1979 reflected intensified concern both in its title, *Controlling the Smoking Epidemic*, and in its strengthened recommendations.[23] These included the recommendation to all countries that tobacco-growing and manufacturing industries should be progressively but rapidly reduced in size. Developed countries should cease export of tobacco products more toxic than those allowed domestically and should label export products correspondingly. Developing countries should bring the existing problem under control where it was present and prevent the establishment of tobacco growing or manufacture wherever it remained absent.

The latter recommendations were amplified in a subsequent Expert Committee Report devoted to the tobacco problem in developing countries.[24] The urgency of the problem was conveyed in these terms:

> The Committee stressed that while its recommendations are again directed to WHO and, through WHO, to governments (and not only health ministries), and to official organizations, they are also intended for a wider public. The Committee hopes that this report will succeed in drawing attention, internationally and nationally, to the urgency of the need for action to control smoking in develop-

ing countries, if a preventable human disaster of proportions unprecedented in the modern world in time of peace is to be avoided. It is hoped that, for the sake of the developing countries, the recommendations will be implemented while there is still time to prevent the problem reaching in those countries the levels it has already assumed in developed countries.[24(p 68)]

The recommendations against tobacco use from three decades ago remain to be fully implemented, and while some notable progress has been made the tobacco epidemic looms larger now than in the past. As a result, the challenges to implementation of policy and practices in regard to tobacco remain urgent.

Impact on Other Risk Factors

The broad areas of intervention through the population-wide strategy reviewed above—diet, physical activity, and tobacco—have been regarded as the cornerstone of cardiovascular disease prevention at the population level because of their several anticipated benefits in reducing risk. These are the keys to prevention and control of adverse blood lipid profiles; high blood pressure; glucose intolerance, insulin resistance, and diabetes; and, to some degree, adverse psychosocial patterns. In most cases, the several preceding chapters devoted to these specific risk factors indicate the potential for population-wide measures to reduce their incidence and prevalence and thus their contribution to risks of atherosclerotic and hypertensive diseases. Policies for prevention of high blood pressure, for example, are based principally on modification of dietary patterns and habits of physical activity. Thus the primary prevention of high blood pressure depends on the population-wide policies reviewed above. There are, of course, many policy statements specific to high blood pressure that refer to population-level aspects, such as the more recent reports of the (US) Joint National Committee and the Working Group on Primary Prevention of Hypertension. These are cited and discussed in Chapter 12, High Blood Pressure. Corresponding comments apply to most of the other risk factors.

In considering the components of population-wide strategies for cardiovascular disease prevention identified in even the most current recommendations, there is a noticeable omission, however. The social conditions discussed in Chapter 19 have not been referred to along with diet, physical activity, and tobacco use in the context of cardiovascular disease prevention. The relation of social conditions to health encompasses more than cardiovascular diseases alone, of course, but the same is true of the aspects that are commonly addressed. There is a need for closer examination of the connection between social conditions, which are intrinsically population-level phenomena, and the occurrence of at least the major risk factors. Recommendations for population-wide interventions to minimize the adverse impact of these conditions on cardiovascular risk is a valuable potential outcome.

POLICIES APPLICABLE IN THE HIGH-RISK STRATEGY OF PREVENTION

The foregoing discussion indicates the development of recommendations for population-wide implementation to prevent atherosclerotic and hypertensive diseases. The following is a review of the complementary development of clinical interventions, viewed here as representing the high-risk strategy.

Risk Factor–Specific Policies

Policies and guidelines that address single risk factors, multiple risk factors, or composite risk scores in the high-risk approach have been alluded to at many points in previous chapters. In each case the concept of high risk presumes a distribution of risk levels throughout the population such that some individuals are identifiable as having relatively higher risk than others. For characteristics such as blood lipids, blood pressure, and blood glucose concentration, criteria have been adopted by which to define high risk within the continuous distribution of the relevant biochemical or physiologic measure. For others, such as physical inactivity, semi-quantitative scales are used to discriminate higher from lower risk. Corresponding to the definitions of high risk with respect to each of these factors, interventions have been developed that are intended to reduce the risk for those in the extreme category or categories of that distribution. It has become typical for policy statements or guidelines for high-risk approaches regarding these factors to refer to the same population-wide interventions already reviewed. These "hygienic measures" are often advocated as the preferred approach for initial case management and as a component of comprehensive long-term management for any specific risk factor or combination of factors.

From these observations, two points are perhaps self-evident. First, the population-wide and high-risk strategies are closely complementary. Second, and especially relevant here, is that the concept of high risk has been, since its articulation by Rose, an epidemiologic concept in that it is related to the distributions throughout the population of relevant characteristics influencing rates and risks of cardiovascular diseases or other health problems. From this view, the high-risk strategies for case identification have been presented in earlier chapters, as have some aspects of their treatment or management to reduce individual risk. But another concept of high risk is a more recent focus of attention: the patient with known coronary heart disease, peripheral vascular disease, or prior stroke. In addition to those with multiple risk factors or extreme values of one risk factor, those with recognized disease constitute a subgroup of the population who are clearly at highest risk. Discussion of the high-risk strategy requires separate consideration of this aspect, which has become more widely recognized in the very recent past.

Highest Risk: Patients with Known Cardiovascular Disease

The simple five-point message of the *Statement on Arteriosclerosis* of 1959, which is the forerunner of clinical recommendations for high-risk patients and their physicians, can be compared with the contemporary view expressed in the report of a recent conference of the American College of Cardiology, the "27th Bethesda Conference: Matching the Intensity of Risk Factor Management with the Hazard for Coronary Disease Events."[25] The objective of this conference was to address a gap between policy and practice at the high-risk level, specifically in the sense of "highest risk" noted above: "Despite the currently available evidence in support of risk factor management, the proportion of high risk patients receiving appropriate care is alarmingly low."[25(p 962)]

Exhibit 22–2 summarizes the conference recommendations for high-risk intervention, adopted from a previous report. The recommended risk interventions for smoking, lipids, blood pressure, and physical activity have many features similar to those reviewed in the respective previous chapters. Diet was addressed separately under each of several topics—lipids, weight management, and blood pressure. Reference to anticoagulants, ACE (acetyl-cholinesterase) inhibitors, beta-blockers, and estrogens reflects the orientation of these recommenda-

tions to persons with advanced coronary heart disease, especially survivors of myocardial infarction. At this level of risk, procedures for diagnosis, risk stratification, and management require intensive individual attention and entail costs and potential for adverse effects not acceptable in the absence of very high risk. However, population interventions could have little if any impact on this very high-risk stratum, so the effort to narrow the gap between policy and practice for those at extremely high risk, through intensive clinical interventions, is quite appropriate. Resource issues arise, of course, because costs are high and the potential gains in years of life or quality of those years may be much less than the same investment to preserve lower risk in the first place. Some of the implications for implementation of prevention policies are addressed further in Chapter 28.

COMPREHENSIVE PREVENTION STRATEGIES

The United States: *Healthy People 2000*

Discussion of population strategies for prevention of cardiovascular diseases in the United States would be incomplete without emphasis on the report, *Healthy People 2000: National Health Promotion and Disease Prevention Objectives.*[26] This report builds on its antecedents, in reports of 1979 and 1980, concerning the health of the nation and national objectives in health promotion and disease prevention. Its recommendations are both general, for the population as a whole, and specific to children, adolescents and young adults, adults, older adults, people with low income, minorities, and people with disabilities. Its leading topics in health promotion concern physical activity and fitness, nutrition, and tobacco. For heart disease and stroke mortality, goals for the year 2000 were no more than 100/100,000 and 20/100,000 deaths per year, respectively, which in each case would be a one-third reduction from the base rate in 1987. Improvements were also targeted

Exhibit 22–2 Guide to Comprehensive Risk Reduction for Patients with Coronary and Other Vascular Disease

Risk Intervention	Recommendations
Smoking: *Goal* complete cessation	Strongly encourage patient and family to stop smoking. Provide counseling, nicotine replacement, and formal cessation programs as appropriate.
Lipid management: *Primary goal* LDL <100 mg/dl *Secondary goals* HDL >35 mg/dl; TG <200 mg/dl	Start AHA Step II Diet in all patients: ≤30% fat, <7% saturated fat, <200 mg/dl cholesterol Assess fasting lipid profile. In post-MI patients, lipid profile may take 4 to 6 weeks to stabilize. Add drug therapy according to the following guide:

LDL <100 mg/dl	LDL 100 to 130 mg/dl	LDL >130 mg/dl	HDL <30 mg/dl
No drug therapy	Consider adding drug therapy to diet, as follows:	Add drug therapy to diet, as follows:	Emphasize weight management and physical activity. Advise smoking cessation. If needed to achieve LDL goals, consider niacin, statin, fibrate.

Suggested drug therapy

TG <200 mg/dl	TG 200–400 mg/dl	TG >400 mg/dl
Statin Resin Niacin	Statin Niacin	Consider combined drug therapy (niacin, fibrate, statin)

If LDL goal not achieved, consider combination therapy

Physical activity: *Minimum goal* 30 minutes 3 to 4 times per week	Assess risk, preferably with exercise test, to guide prescription. Encourage minimum of 30 to 60 minutes of moderate-intensity activity 3 or 4 times weekly (walking, jogging, cycling, or other aerobic activity) supplemented by an increase in daily lifestyle activities (eg, walking breaks at work, using stairs, gardening, household work). Maximum benefit 5 to 6 hours a week. Advise medically supervised programs for moderate- to high-risk patients.
Weight management:	Start intensive diet and appropriate physical activity intervention, as outlined above, in patients >120% of ideal weight for height. Particularly emphasize need for weight loss in patients with hypertension, elevated triglycerides, or elevated glucose levels.
Antiplatelet agents/ anticoagulants:	Start aspirin 80 to 325 mg/day if not contraindicated. Manage warfarin to international normalized ratio = 2 to 3.5 for post-MI patients not able to take aspirin.
ACE inhibitors post-MI:	Start early post-MI in stable high-risk patients (anterior MI, previous MI, Killip class II [S_3 gallop, rales, radiographic CHF]). Continue indefinitely for all with LV dysfunction (ejection fraction ≤40) or symptoms of failure. Use as needed to manage blood pressure or symptoms in all other patients.

continues

Exhibit 22–2 continued

Risk Intervention	Recommendations
Beta blockers:	Start in high-risk post-MI patients (arrhythmia, LV dysfunction, inducible ischemia) at 5 to 28 days. Continue 6 months minimum. Observe usual contraindications.
	Use as needed to manage angina rhythm or blood pressure in all other patients.
Estrogens:	Consider estrogen replacement in all postmenopausal women.
	Individualize recommendation consistent with other health risks.
Blood pressure control:	Initiate lifestyle modification—weight control, physical activity, alcohol moderation, and moderate sodium restriction—in all patients with blood pressure >140 mm Hg systolic or 90 mm Hg diastolic.
Goal	
≤140/90 mm Hg	Add blood pressure medication, individualized to other patient requirements and characteristics (ie, age, race, need for drugs with specific benefits) if blood pressure is not less than 140 mm Hg systolic or 90 mm Hg diastolic in 3 months or if initial blood pressure >160 mm Hg systolic or 100 mm Hg diastolic.

Note: ACE, angiotensin-converting enzyme; AHA, American Heart Association; CHF, congestive heart failure; HDL, high-density lipoprotein; LDL, low-density lipoprotein; LV, left ventricular; MI, myocardial infarction; TG, triglycerides.

Source: Reprinted with permission from *Circulation*, Vol 92, pp 2–4, © 1995, American Heart Association.

in the prevalence and control of high blood pressure, elevated cholesterol concentration, high dietary fat intake, overweight, physical inactivity, and smoking. The following services were to be made more widely available: blood pressure and cholesterol measurement, intervention to control high cholesterol concentrations, worksite activities for blood pressure and cholesterol control, and accurate laboratory determination of cholesterol concentrations. This one-volume report, which presents a comprehensive outline of health objectives for the nation for the year 2000, illustrates the evolution of both population-wide and high-risk strategies for prevention of heart attack and stroke in the United States to the present time.

Developing Countries: Disease Control Priorities

Finally, in the global perspective, the analysis of the World Bank report, *Disease Control Priorities in Developing Countries*, portrays an assessment of efficacy and cost of preventive strategies for major cardiovascular disease from both community-based and clinic-based—or population-wide and high-risk—approaches.[27] (See Table 22–5.) Separately for coronary heart disease, stroke, and hypertension, the effectiveness of each of several interventions was rated in relation to compliance (practical adherence by the recipient of that intervention) and clinical efficacy (the impact of that intervention as observed under the special circumstances of evaluation in the clinical research setting). Costs were partitioned into components for manpower, technology, and drugs. Compliance was considered poor for obesity control, and clinical efficacy was judged to be unknown for diabetic drugs. A wide range of clinical efficacy characterized the remaining interventions, some of which were notably favorable. Costs were consistently higher for clinic-based than for community-based interventions. The potential for greater long-term preventive benefit from less economically demanding population-wide programs than from more costly and restrictive high-risk approaches is an important consideration in prevention policy not just for developing countries but worldwide.

Table 22–5 Efficacy and Cost of Preventive Strategies for Major Cardiovascular Diseases

Preventive Strategy	Effectiveness		Costs		
	Compliance	Clinical Efficacy	Manpower	Technology	Drugs
Coronary heart disease					
Community-based					
Smoking cessation	+	++++	+/–	0	0
Low-salt diet	+	?	+/–	0	0
Modified fat diet	+	+++	+/–	0	0
Exercise	+	+++	+/–	0	0
Diabetic diet	+	—	+/–	0	0
Obesity control	–	?	+/–	0	0
Clinic-based					
Antihypertensive drugs	+	++	++	+	++
Lipid-lowering drugs	+/-	++++	++	++	++
Diabetic drugs	+	—	++++	++	++++
Antiplatelet drugs	++	++	+	+	+
Stroke					
Community-based					
Smoking cessation	+	+++	+/–	0	0
Low-salt diet	+	+	+/–	0	0
Obesity control	–	+	+/–	0	0
Clinic-based					
Antihypertensive drugs	+	++++	++	+	++
Antiplatelet drugs	++	++++	+	+	+
Hypertension					
Community-based					
Low-salt diet	+	+	+/–	0	0
Exercise	++	++	+	0	0
Obesity control	–	+++	+/–	0	0
Alcohol restriction	?	+	0	0	0
Clinic-based					
Antihypertensive drugs	+/++	++++	++	+	++

Note: ++++, highly favorable; +++ , moderately favorable; ++, favorable; +, minimal; +/–, variable; – poor; —, not effective; 0, not required; ?, unknown.

Source: Disease Control Priorities in Developing Countries, edited by DT Jamison et al. Copyright © 1993 The International Bank for Reconstruction and Development/The World Bank. Used by permission of Oxford University Press, Inc.

CURRENT ISSUES

The many aspects of policy for prevention of cardiovascular diseases addressed here engender two impressions that may seem at the surface to be mutually contradictory but perhaps reflect complementary aspects of the same circumstances. One impression is that the multifactor concept of causation and prevention of atherosclerotic and hypertensive cardiovascular diseases has resulted in a proliferation of policy recommendations that are quite complex in their details and require action at levels ranging from the individual to the international organization and agency level. Incorporation of newly identified factors in the array of recommended interventions will likely add to their complexity. Considerable effort may be required to maintain the coherent, relatively long-term programs necessary to bring about substantial change in the epidemic process in many populations.

The second impression is that of remarkable simplicity and consistency over the past 35 years in the primacy of a very few major factors and their determinants, which have changed little in priority over this period. Much

has been learned about methods for applying this knowledge in both population-wide and high-risk strategies, and it is from this viewpoint reassuring that the central issues in prevention are generally familiar and not new and strange.

It appears that the outstanding issue concerning prevention policy at the present time concerns the implementation of already-formulated strategies, both population-wide and high risk. Approaches to this public health challenge will be discussed in Chapter 28.

REFERENCES

1. White PD, Wright IS, Sprague HB, Katz LN, et al. *A Statement on Arteriosclerosis: Main Cause of "Heart Attacks" and "Strokes."* New York: National Health Education Committee, Inc; 1959.

2. Rose G. Strategy of prevention: lessons from cardiovascular disease. *Br Med J.* 1981;282:1847–1851.

3. Rose G. Sick individuals and sick populations. *Int J Epidemiol.* 1985;14:32–38.

4. Rose G. *The Strategy of Preventive Medicine.* Oxford, England: Oxford University Press; 1992.

5. Strasser T. Reflections on cardiovascular diseases. *Interdisc Sci Rev.* 1978;3:225–230.

6. Stamler J. Primary prevention of coronary heart disease: the last 20 years. *Am J Cardiol.* 1981;47:722–735.

7. World Health Organization Expert Committee. *Prevention of Coronary Heart Disease.* Geneva, Switzerland: World Health Organization; 1982. WHO Technical Report Series 679.

8. World Health Organization Expert Committee. *Community Prevention and Control of Cardiovascular Diseases.* Geneva, Switzerland: World Health Organization; 1986. WHO Technical Report Series 732.

9. World Health Organization Expert Committee. *Prevention in Childhood and Youth of Adult Cardiovascular Diseases: Time for Action.* Geneva, Switzerland: World Health Organization; 1990. WHO Technical Report Series 792.

10. Central Committee for Medical and Community Program of the American Heart Association. Dietary fat and its relation to heart attacks and strokes. *Circ.* 1961; 23:133–136.

11. Krauss RM, Deckelbaum RJ, Ernst N, Fisher E, et al. Dietary guidelines for healthy American adults: a statement for health professionals from the Nutrition

Committee, American Heart Association. *Circ.* 1996; 94:1795–1800.

12. *Nutrition and Your Health: Dietary Guidelines for Americans.* 4th ed. Washington, DC: US Dept of Agriculture, US Dept of Health and Human Services; 1995.

13. Davis CA, Saltos EA. The dietary guidelines for Americans—past, present, future. *Fam Econ Nutr Rev.* 1996;9:4–13.

14. Committee on Diet and Health. *Diet and Health: Implications for Reducing Chronic Disease Risk.* Washington, DC: Food and Nutrition Board, National Research Council, National Academy Press; 1989.

15. World Health Organization Study Group. *Diet, Nutrition, and the Prevention of Chronic Diseases.* Geneva, Switzerland: World Health Organization; 1990. WHO Technical Report Series 797.

16. US Dept of Health and Human Services. *Physical Activity and Health: A Report of the Surgeon General.* Atlanta, Ga: National Center for Chronic Disease Prevention and Health Promotion, Centers for Disease Control and Prevention, US Dept of Health and Human Services; 1996.

17. Katz LN, Allen EV, Cherkasky M, Davis FW, et al. Cigarette smoking and cardiovascular diseases: report by the American Heart Association. *Circ.* 1960;22: 160–166.

18. Advisory Committee to the Surgeon General of the Public Health Service. *Smoking and Health. Report of the Advisory Committee to the Surgeon General of the Public Health Service.* Atlanta, Ga: Public Health Service, US Dept of Health, Education, and Welfare; 1964.

19. US Department of Health and Human Services. *Preventing Tobacco Use among Young People: A Report of the Surgeon General.* Atlanta, Ga: Office on Smok-

ing and Health, National Center for Chronic Disease Prevention and Health Promotion, Centers for Disease Control and Prevention, Public Health Service, US Dept of Health and Human Services; 1994.

20. Guidelines for school health programs to prevent tobacco use and addiction. *J School Health*. 1994;64: 353–360.

21. Roemer R. *Legislative Action To Combat the World Smoking Epidemic*. Geneva, Switzerland: World Health Organization; 1982.

22. World Health Organization Expert Committee. *Smoking and Its Effects on Health*. Geneva, Switzerland: World Health Organization; 1975. WHO Technical Report Series 568.

23. World Health Organization Expert Committee. *Controlling the Smoking Epidemic*. Geneva, Switzerland: World Health Organization; 1979. WHO Technical Report Series 636.

24. World Health Organization Expert Committee. *Smoking Control Strategies in Developing Countries*. Geneva, Switzerland: World Health Organization; 1983. WHO Technical Report Series 695.

25. 27th Bethesda Conference: Matching the intensity of risk factor management with the hazard for coronary disease events; September 14–15, 1995. *J Am Coll Cardiol*. 1996;27:957–1047.

26. US Dept of Health and Human Services. *Healthy People 2000: National Health Promotion and Disease Prevention Objectives: Full Report with Commentary*. Washington, DC: Public Health Service, US Dept of Health and Human Services; 1991. DHHS publication no. (PHS) 91-50212.

27. Pearson TA, Jamison DT, Trejo-Gutierrez J. Cardiovascular disease. In: Jamison DT, Mosely WH, Measham AR, Bobadilla JL, eds. *Disease Control Priorities in Developing Countries*. Oxford, England: Oxford University Press; 1993:577–594.

CHAPTER 23

Groups of Special Concern

SUMMARY

Middle-aged White men have been the principal, though not exclusive, focus of epidemiologic studies concerning prevention of atherosclerotic and hypertensive diseases. How broadly this experience should be applied beyond this segment of the population is a matter of judgment. In many respects there are special opportunities or obstacles to intervention that affect particular subgroups of the population, whether distinguished by age, sex, race or ethnicity, genetic factors, or socioeconomic status. This chapter highlights some groups of special interest or concern from this point of view. Intervention guidelines from the American Heart Association and the National Heart, Lung and Blood Institute are cited, since they reflect a variety of assumptions about groups defined by age or sex and therefore serve for illustration. In other populations and with other guidelines in view, analogous concerns would doubtless arise. Data are likely to be needed for multiple subgroups of any population to permit proper planning for intervention. The findings may reveal differences important for intervention strategies or may, alternatively, demonstrate intergroup similarities that justify broader rather than more-limited application of proposed interventions.

INTRODUCTION

With respect to prevention and control of atherosclerotic and hypertensive diseases or their risk factors, special attention should be given to certain groups that have exceptional requirements or pose particular challenges to effective intervention. These groups are identified mainly by age, sex, and race or ethnicity. Therefore these comments extend consideration of fundamental personal characteristics introduced in Chapter 7 but now in the context of intervention. The purpose is to note aspects—for example, of the age spectrum—that present particular obstacles or offer special opportunities for intervention. Particular age groups are identified in *Healthy People 2000*, for example, with separate health objectives for infants (to 1 year of age), children (1–14 years of age), adolescents and young adults (15–24 years of age), adults (25–64 years of age), and older adults (65 years and over).[1] Similarly, the *Guide to Clinical Preventive Services* of the US Preventive Services Task Force specifies recommended periodic screening and counseling activities for defined age categories—birth to 10 years, 11 to 24 years, 25 to 64 years, and 65 years and older.[2] Implicitly, such recommendations acknowledge differences in health risks, intervention opportunities, or both at different ages. Also in *Healthy People 2000*, "special population objectives" are presented for groups of three other kinds: people with low income (less than $20,000 per year); minorities (Blacks, Hispanics, Asians and Pacific Islanders, and American Indians and Native Americans); and people with disabilities (those reporting any limitation in activity due to chronic conditions). Thus minority groups are specially recognized, as are groups identified by socioeconomic and functional status. Neither of these reports distinguishes broad areas of preventive recommendations by sex, but both identify women or men within categories such as age, minority status, or others where special considerations apply.

This chapter therefore addresses age, sex, race or ethnicity, heredity or genotype, and socioeconomic groups as they warrant special consideration in prevention policy and practice. As background, aspects of the natural history of atherosclerotic and hypertensive diseases and their main determinants are briefly reviewed in relation to each of these group characteristics. As a result, a number of issues concerning cardiovascular disease prevention and control are noted that might otherwise be overlooked.

AGE

The Life Span from a Cardiovascular Perspective

The life span can be considered to range, from conception to death, over a maximum period (to date) of 122 years (C Truehart, "Champion of Longevity Ends Her Reign at 122," Washington Post Foreign Service, Paris, August 4, 1997, via washingtonpost.com). Various designations identify periods within the life span, as discussed in Chapter 7. From the perspective of disease development and opportunities for intervention, certain time relations generally apply:

- Genetic and environmental factors operate from conception onward.
- Predisposition to development of risk factors and vascular pathology in adulthood may be initiated by conditions of fetal life.
- Preatherosclerotic changes in the arterial intima may be detectable in the first year

of life and progress to raised lesions commonly within the second decade.

- Changes in blood lipids and blood pressure that are especially predictive of high-risk status in adulthood emerge and tobacco use becomes highly prevalent during adolescence.
- Risk factor levels tend to progress toward established high-risk thresholds; subclinical atherosclerosis becomes more often detectable; and early occurrence of overt clinical coronary heart disease, cerebrovascular disease, and peripheral arterial disease are not unusual from the attainment of physical maturity through middle adulthood.
- The burden of established risk factors and mounting rates of occurrence of coronary events, strokes, peripheral arterial disease, congestive heart failure, aortic aneurysm, and venous thromboembolism all become increasingly common throughout older adulthood.

Given these relationships, what interventions are especially appropriate in different periods of life and against what obstacles associated with particular periods?

Natural History and Opportunities for Intervention

A "cardiovascular health schedule" has been proposed by the American Heart Association Subcommittee on Atherosclerosis and Hypertension in Childhood of the Council on Cardiovascular Disease in the Young in "Integrated Cardiovascular Health Promotion in Childhood."[3] This report incorporates guidelines for action by health care for children from birth to ages over 10 years, presumably to age 17 or 18 (Exhibit 23–1). On reflection, there are implicit assumptions that the child both has caring and involved parents and experiences continuity of health care throughout this period of life. Although it would be desirable for these conditions to exist for most children, one or both

Exhibit 23–1 Cardiovascular Health Schedule

Birth
- Family history for early coronary heart disease, hyperlipidemia → if positive, introduce risk factors; parental referral
- Start growth chart
- Parental smoking history → smoking cessation referral

0–2 years
- Update family history, growth chart
- With introduction of solids, begin teaching about healthy diet (nutritionally adequate, low in salt, low in saturated fats)
- Recommend healthy snacks as finger foods
- Change to whole milk from formula or breast feeding at approximately 1 year of age

2–6 years
- Update family history, growth chart → review growth chart[a] with family (concept of weight for height)
- Introduce prudent diet (<30% of calories from fat)
- Change to low-fat milk
- Start blood pressure chart at approximately 3 years of age[b]; review for concept of lower salt intake
- Encourage active parent-child play

- Lipid determination in children with positive family history or with parental cholesterol >240 mg/dl (obtain parental lipid levels if necessary) → if abnormal, initiate nutrition counseling

6–10 years
- Update family history, blood pressure and growth charts
- Complete cardiovascular health profile with child; determine family history, smoking history, blood pressure percentile, weight for height, fingerstick cholesterol, and level of activity and fitness
- Reinforce prudent diet
- Begin active antismoking counseling
- Introduce fitness for health → life sport activities for child and family
- Discuss role of watching television in sedentary lifestyle and obesity

>10 years
- Update family history, blood pressure and growth charts annually
- Review prudent diet, risks of smoking, fitness benefits whenever possible
- Consider lipid profile in all patients
- Final review of personal cardiovascular health status

a. If weight >120% of normal for height, diagnosis of obesity should be considered and the subject addressed with child and family.

b. If three consecutive interval blood pressure measurements exceed the 90th percentile and blood pressure is not explained by height or weight, diagnosis of hypertension should be made and appropriate evaluation considered.

Source: Reprinted with permission from *Circulation*, Vol 85, p 1648, Copyright 1992, American Heart Association.

assumptions are false for many children in contemporary American society and doubtless elsewhere. How to provide the early attention to prevention of cardiovascular risk factors conveyed in these guidelines for children under unfavorable circumstances is an issue in need of attention. For those who are fortunate, the schedule outlined by the Subcommittee would apply for intervals from birth to about age 18, as will be described. For earlier and later periods of life, arbitrary intervals will be used. The age categories defined by the *Guide to Clinical Preventive Services*, like those found in *Healthy People 2000*, are too broad for present purposes.[1,2]

Gestation

The possibility that "programming" of regulatory mechanisms during fetal and early neonatal life contributes importantly to cardiovascular risk suggests that intervention in the course of pregnancy or before (eg, premarital or preconception counseling) may be necessary to minimize that risk. This is the clear implication of the work of Barker and colleagues discussed in

Chapter 19. Hygienic measures to ensure good maternal and infant health are fully justified on other grounds but too often receive inadequate attention. The added potential for prevention of the major cause of death in industrialized countries, and possibly for primordial prevention in many other countries, could stimulate greater investment in this area of health policy and practice. Greater conviction about the underlying theory may follow from further studies now in progress; it was evidently not sufficient for inclusion of this period in the American Heart Association Subcommittee's schedule.

Birth

The foregoing comments about programming carry over to birth and the neonatal period with implications for infant nutrition and possibly other aspects of nurture throughout early development. The work of Barker and colleagues (see Chapter 19) again suggests several potentially available measurements at birth that could be used for risk classification of newborns, including not only birth weight but also placental weight and several anthropometric indicators. At birth, the American Heart Association schedule calls for ascertainment of the family history of early coronary heart disease or hyperlipidemia. (Because it is a dynamic characteristic of the family, it is to be updated throughout childhood.) The child's growth chart is to be initiated at birth and updated periodically thereafter. The parental smoking history is also to be ascertained at this time, with referral for smoking cessation if it is positive for either parent. Because this item is not included in the schedule at later ages, it was evidently assumed that a nonsmoking parent would remain a nonsmoker. This may be incorrect if a mother discontinued smoking only during pregnancy and later resumed smoking or if there were a change in parents. It would be prudent to repeat this history at subsequent visits.

Early Childhood

From birth to two years of age, dietary recommendations are the focus of intervention. Foods are to be introduced toward establishment of a dietary pattern free of high fat and salt content, and whole milk is to be substituted for breast milk beginning at age one year. The potential role of persons other than parents in establishment of dietary patterns should be recognized. For example, day care involves feeding the child away from parental supervision and raises the possibility of introducing different nutritional patterns than intended. This suggests the need for education of child-care personnel also. This general concern for nonparental influences on diet extends throughout the years of the child's dependency on others for food choices, preparation, and portion sizes.

Midchildhood

At ages two to six years, the growth chart is reviewed to include introduction to the parents of the concept of the child's weight in relation to height. The "prudent diet" is to be introduced, with the goal of less than 30% of calories from fat and replacement of whole milk by low-fat milk. Active parent-child play is encouraged to involve mutual participation in physical activity. Monitoring of blood pressure is undertaken from age three years, with intervention if readings are persistently high and advice to maintain low salt intake for all children. Blood lipids are to be evaluated for those children whose family history includes early coronary heart disease or hypercholesterolemia, followed by dietary advice if indicated.

The concept of weight for height indicates adoption of the body mass index or analogous weight/height ratio as the standard for evaluation of overweight in the growing child. Use of skinfold thickness or other indicators of body composition are recommended adjuncts to the weight/height index. While there is disagreement over the most appropriate measurements for these purposes, practicality of measurement in the usual office setting and availability of reference standards are essential to the choice. The schedule refers to a "blood pressure chart," implying a monitoring process analogous to that underlying use of the growth chart, although the corresponding longitudinal reference values for blood pressure are not yet available. Again, in the preschool setting, influences outside the family may contribute importantly to establishment of dietary patterns.

Late Childhood

At ages 6–10 years, in addition to updating the assessments of family history and the blood pressure and growth charts, the cardiovascular profile is to be completed. This includes the child's smoking history, weight for height, fingerstick cholesterol determination, and level of physical fitness and activity. Counseling is to be provided on diet, physical activity, tobacco, and the role of television watching in leading to sedentary habits and obesity.

Throughout this and later periods, influences outside the family setting become increasingly prominent in the life of the child, for example, peer pressure; commercial advertising; school curricula; and the school environment, which includes health education, physical activity, and food service. The content of these influences can obviously reinforce or undermine favorable influences on health from parents and health professionals.

Adolescence

Continuing from age 10, annual updates of family history, growth charts, and blood pressure are recommended. Counseling on the prudent diet, risks of smoking, and benefits of fitness is to occur "whenever possible." This statement acknowledges the decreasing likelihood of contact with health professionals outside specific illness episodes except for such examinations as may be required for sports participation or summer camp. Laboratory determination of the lipid profile is to be considered in all patients. The "final review" of cardiovascular health status contemplates a valedictory physician visit for a precollege or preemployment final examination as a pediatric patient.

In this period, reliance on reference charts for blood pressure measurements continues. The recognition that opportunities for the recom-

mended counseling may be unpredictable and infrequent raises concern about the continuity of the proposed communication and monitoring of progress. Interpretation of the blood lipid profile, if obtained, also depends on reference data that have been quite limited to date, and interpretation may need to take expected age and sex differences into account.[4] In keeping with the purpose of the American Heart Association guidelines, the importance of the "final review" deserves emphasis for those who may take advantage of it. For those who do not, the question remains how to assess the risk factor status and convey the intended health messages at this critical point.

With respect to the period of the school years, reinforcement of many elements of these guidelines through school health education is widely discussed and advocated, as noted in several preceding chapters. Again, however, it is necessary to recognize that adolescents who are in alternative schools at the junior or senior high school level, or out of school altogether, are at increased risk of many health problems related to their patterns of behavior and are also inaccessible to school health education. Those who have remained in school but are neither continuing nor about to be employed would also be unlikely to experience the "final" pediatric visit. How to reach these groups of special concern remains to be addressed adequately.

Early Adulthood

Early adulthood can be defined arbitrarily to include the 20s and 30s or from age 18 to 39. Most people in this age group, even in a high-risk population such as that of the United States, remain at levels of blood pressure or cholesterol concentration below those considered to require individual, high-risk intervention. Both the Joint National Committee on Detection, Evaluation, and Treatment of High Blood Pressure[5] and the Adult Treatment Panel of the National Cholesterol Education Program[6] in the United States recommend regular risk factor measurements beginning in this period: at age 18 and every two years thereafter for blood pressure and at age 20 and every five years thereafter for cholesterol concentration. Over this period, average blood pressure levels and blood lipid concentrations in the population continue to advance toward treatable levels of these major risk factors, and these levels are attained by successively larger proportions of the population.[5] Therefore prevention of the risk factors themselves remains possible, and their monitoring is important for a large majority of the population throughout this period. The opportunity may also continue, especially at the start of this period, to prevent use of tobacco. For those who smoke, support of smoking cessation should be a major focus of preventive practice in this period.

But because the pediatrician has said farewell and contact with health professionals in this period tends to be limited to episodes of illness or pregnancy, the continuity of care assumed under most guidelines is likely to be lost. Behavior patterns with potential adverse consequences for cardiovascular and general health are now documented among US college students.[7] If college students are expected to exhibit the best-informed health behavior, the remaining 75% of persons 18–24 years of age in the United States who are not in college are presumably at still greater risk. They represent a largely unappreciated and unmet area of need for preventive measures.

Attention has been focused on worksites as a partial solution to this problem in early and middle adulthood. For example, *Healthy People 2000* includes among its objectives an increase from 16%–17% at the 1985 baseline to at least 50% in the year 2000 of worksites offering high blood pressure or cholesterol education and control activities.[1] The benefit of such programs, if available, obviously reaches only those who are employed, and the targets apply only to places of employment with 50 workers or more. The comprehensive approach of the American Heart Association guidelines, desirable for all young adults, would reach those who become parents but would be missed by others. The goal of prevention of the risk factors

in the first place requires continuity of information and education beyond the pediatric age group and points to a serious gap in health education and preventive health care in early adulthood at the present time in the United States.

Middle Adulthood

The range from 40 to 64 years fills the interval between early and older adulthood. This constitutes the period in which the epidemiology and prevention of atherosclerotic and hypertensive diseases have been studied most extensively, primarily in men. Most of the resulting guidelines for detection and management of risk factors and knowledge about the potential benefits of intervention therefore apply directly to this age group. From this point of view, the groups of special concern addressed in this chapter are those for whom the general recommendations for middle-aged men require some qualification or more cautious generalization.

Older Adulthood

For many years, the stated mission of the American Heart Association was to prevent "premature" heart disease and stroke. This mission was consistent with the idea that it was the occurrence of these events in young and middle-aged adults that was the primary, if not exclusive, target of prevention. The word *premature* has disappeared from the mission statement. This reflects growing recognition of the burden of disability due to cardiovascular conditions among older persons, as well as the fact that incidence and mortality from these conditions can be reduced in older persons, resulting in improved quality of life and increased independence. It has been noted in previous chapters that the risks of cardiovascular events in older adulthood are much increased over earlier ages and that while relative risks tend to diminish, risk differences or attributable risks increase. If risks can be reduced without unacceptable side effects of intervention, much is potentially to be gained in well-being in the latest years of life.

In relation to blood pressure, specific reference to persons age 60 years and older in the Joint National Committee's fifth report emphasized the results of several treatment trials among persons in their 60s to 80s indicating substantial decreases in risks of stroke, coronary heart disease, congestive heart failure, and total cardiovascular conditions.[5] That report also addressed the need for particular caution to avoid overtreatment in initiating drug treatment and setting treatment goals. With respect to blood lipids, neither the National Cholesterol Education Program guidelines[6] nor those of the World Health Organization Study Group on Cardiovascular Disease Prevention in the Elderly[8] offered special recommendations for older persons. It was noted in the latter report, as in Chapter 7, that the high absolute risk of cardiovascular events in this age group lent continued importance to prevention among those with established elevations of cholesterol concentration. However, the lack of clinical trials of lipid modification in the elderly, unlike the case for blood pressure, still requires extrapolation from studies in middle-aged adults to estimate the potential impact among older persons.[9]

SEX

Discussion of differences by sex in the natural history of atherosclerotic and hypertensive diseases has focused on women and the disparities between their experience and that of men. A recent essay by Barrett-Connor is a particularly illuminating example.[10] This emphasis reflects in large part a sense of relative neglect of the problem of coronary heart disease in women, for whom its cumulative lifelong burden is actually no less than that for men in the United States and several other populations. The differences by sex in age-specific rates of coronary events, such that there is a lag of 10–15 years in rates for women versus those for men, have been addressed at several points in previous chapters and explain the failure to recognize the similarity in overall experience when comparisons have been limited to age-specific rates.

Whether women are considered advantaged or men disadvantaged by the relative disparity in their coronary event rates at a given age is perhaps less important than the realization that sex differences in the natural history of these diseases exist. Recognition of the differences that occur in periods throughout the life span may contribute to understanding their causes and devising more effective strategies for prevention through more-detailed investigation of the course of risk factor and disease development in both groups.

Risks and Rates in Successive Periods of Life

Observations made in previous chapters will be highlighted briefly as background for discussion of issues specific to women with respect to prevention and control of atherosclerotic and hypertensive diseases. Sex differences in risk factors are recognized in the first months of life but become clearer with adolescence and the many changes associated with puberty. Age-specific mean values for systolic and diastolic blood pressure and for multiple components of the blood lipid profile differ by sex from various ages in puberty onward, depending on their distinct time patterns of development. Smoking behavior progresses rapidly in this period and tends to remain somewhat less prevalent among females than among males at successive ages. In the age interval from 15–34 years, atherosclerosis of the coronary arteries is about equally frequent between females and males, but raised lesions constitute a lesser proportion of the total among females.[11] Through early and middle adulthood, women tend to have lower age-specific mean values for blood pressure and total cholesterol concentration but greater prevalence of physical inactivity and overweight.[12] In middle age, as rates for coronary heart disease events increase for women more gradually than for men, the rates of stroke for women parallel those for men closely. In later adulthood, both total cholesterol concentration and blood pressure (especially systolic pressure) increase to values greater than those for men of the same age. Rates of coronary heart disease and stroke both increase sharply among women and men with further increase in age, as do rates of other complications of advanced atherosclerosis and hypertension.

Sex-Specific Recommendations for Risk Factor Screening and Management

Reference blood pressure percentiles have been presented separately by sex from birth to age 18 since the first report of the Task Force on Blood Pressure Control in Children and Adolescents and they remain so in the most recent update.[13] Currently, sex-specific percentile values for systolic and fifth-phase diastolic blood pressure and for height are considered together to determine the classification of a child or adolescent of a given age with respect to hypertension. No difference by sex is proposed for management of hypertension in this age group. However, oral contraceptive use is associated with elevated blood pressure, and its discontinuation is recommended for women with high blood pressure, potentially including those in their teens. High blood pressure is not uncommonly a complication of pregnancy, and careful management is required to prevent fully developed toxemia. High blood pressure in a woman using estrogen replacement therapy may be related to this treatment, which requires blood pressure monitoring under recommendations of the National High Blood Pressure Education Program.

In detection and management of adverse blood lipid profiles, no sex differences are recognized in current recommendations for children and adolescents, although consideration of sex-specific reference values has been proposed on the basis of differences in blood lipid patterns by sex throughout adolescence.[4] Sex differences in evaluation and management of elevated blood cholesterol are included in the Adult Treatment Panel recommendations of the National Cholesterol Education Program.[6] The decision of whether a fasting blood lipid profile should be determined following initial screening is to be based in part on the presence of other risk factors. One such factor is male sex; lacking this factor, women are less often than men considered to require further evaluation. Another risk factor to be considered is age. For men, age 45 or greater is taken as a "positive risk factor," while for women the corresponding age is 55. Ordinarily, then, women under 55 will be still less likely to require further evaluation. An exception to this provision is that women under 55 who have experienced premature menopause without estrogen replacement therapy are assigned the risk factor for age regardless of their chronologic age. For postmenopausal women with elevated cholesterol concentration, estrogen replacement therapy is suggested due to its effects of lowering low-density lipoprotein (LDL) and raising high-density lipoprotein (HDL) cholesterol concentrations (see below). No other provision specific to women or men is presented in these cholesterol screening guidelines.

Interventions to prevent tobacco use or to support smoking cessation are differentiated by sex mainly, or perhaps exclusively, in connection with pregnancy and the special need and opportunity to bring about smoking cessation under this circumstance. Programs have been developed both to accomplish smoking cessation in pregnancy and to maintain successful discontinuation after pregnancy. All women of reproductive age are regarded in the recommendations of *Healthy People 2000* as a special population for smoking prevention, as are women using oral contraceptives.[1] Also in the recommendations of *Healthy People 2000*, women aged 20 years and above are identified as a priority group for interventions to reduce overweight and increase physical activity.

Sex Differences in Diagnosis and Treatment

Access to long-term programs supporting risk factor assessment and management may present different opportunities for women and men. Worksite programs, especially if limited to places employing 50 or more persons, are likely to be less frequently available to women than to men. However, occasional or even regular medical contacts are more likely to occur for women than men during the reproductive years. The opportunity for incorporation of preventive guidelines into family and gynecological practice is therefore important specifically for the benefit of women.

Whether women are as likely to receive available diagnostic or therapeutic interventions for acute coronary events has begun to be investigated. For example, women in the Corpus Christi Heart Project hospitalized for acute coronary heart disease received coronary angiography less often than men.[14] However, the extent and severity of coronary lesions were similar among women and men with angiograms, suggesting that men might be overevaluated rather than women being underevaluated by use of this procedure. In addition, however, women received fewer prescriptions for posthospital treatment than did men.[15] Further assessment is needed of such apparent differences by sex in procedures and practices in cardiovascular care and their implications for the relative effectiveness of prevention policies for highest-risk women and men.

The Question of Hormone Replacement Therapy in Women

Whether sex differences in development of risk factors or clinical coronary heart disease are attributable to sex hormones, or specifically to estrogen levels in premenopausal women, has been discussed widely and is addressed in numerous reviews.[10,16] Several mechanisms of action of estrogen suggest a beneficial role, consistent with epidemiologic studies showing increased risk of coronary events in women following early menopause and reduced risks of fatal and nonfatal cardiovascular events among women using estrogen, among others.[16] A clinical trial (the Postmenopausal Estrogen/Progestin Interventions [PEPI] Trial) was conducted to evaluate the effect over three years of exogenous estrogen, either unopposed or with one of three estrogen/progestin regimens, on four risk factors: HDL-cholesterol concentration, systolic blood pressure, serum insulin concentration, and fibrinogen concentration.[17] Participants were 875 postmenopausal women age 45 to 64 years and in good health. The effects on HDL-cholesterol and fibrinogen were favorable without adverse effects on blood pressure or insulin, with some variation in effects among the several regimens tested. This evidence further supports the role of estrogen in favorably influencing risk of coronary and other cardiovascular events. Whether these outcomes themselves are prevented by estrogen use in postmenopausal women continues to be investigated in various studies, including the major trial of the Women's Health Initiative.

An extensive review of laboratory, clinical, and epidemiologic studies was compiled as the proceedings of the conference on Hormonal, Metabolic, and Cellular Influences on Cardiovascular Disease in Women, with a concluding commentary by LaRosa.[18] Several unresolved issues were identified that will require considerable further investigation. The questions of benefit versus risks of estrogen replacement in postmenopausal women are complicated in part by the need for progestins to counter the increased risk of endometrial cancer in the woman with an intact uterus, as well as by the side effects of the progestins. Over what period of life hormone replacement therapy is needed for maximum benefit, what the optimum route of administration is, how to improve compliance with its prescribed administration, and other questions remain. Clearest among current opinion appears to be the contraindication of estrogen use by women with a family history of breast cancer in first-degree relatives, although even in this area the evidence is judged inconclusive on whether the estrogen–breast cancer association is causal.

RACE OR ETHNICITY

US Minority Groups

Blacks in the United States have been recognized longest as having particular cardiovascular risks as a group. The *Report of the Secretary's Task Force on Black and Minority Health* from the US Department of Health and Human Services was noted in Chapter 7 as emphasizing the lack of needed data for most minority groups, although for Blacks the deficiencies were less extreme.[19] The special concern about particular racial or ethnic groups in the United States was also addressed in a report from the American Heart Association.[20] Most notable have been the greater frequencies of high blood pressure and stroke among Blacks. But, as noted in the American Heart Association report, review of this topic revealed broader issues than those affecting Blacks or the occurrence of high blood pressure and stroke alone, especially the dearth of data for other groups in the population.

Representation of minorities in national data sources has been quite limited and remains a serious shortcoming. Even for Blacks, sample sizes in specific age-sex groups within the National Health and Nutrition Examination Surveys have been small—too small, for example, to derive reliable estimates of risk factor levels in adolescence.

Heterogeneity within groups further compounds this limitation. "Hispanic," for example, includes Mexican Americans, Puerto Ricans, Cuban Hispanics, and Central American immigrants to the United States. Further data limitations were addressed in Chapter 7, illustrated by the potential for disparities between ethnic identification in census and death certificate data, which may result in underestimation of mortality for some racial or ethnic groups. This type of error appears to contribute to the persisting view that Mexican Americans experience lower mortality from coronary heart disease than do non-Hispanic Whites, although direct observation through community surveillance has shown this to be untrue.

These considerations emphasize the importance both socially and scientifically of increased representation of diverse components of the US population in both official health surveillance activities and in health research projects aimed at documenting and clarifying group differences—or similarities—in cardiovascular disease risks, morbidity, and mortality. Whether such expanded information will reveal new insights into causation or point to distinct requirements for intervention remains to be seen. To the extent that knowledge and practices continue to be based on quite limited data, appropriate and effective measures may be less extensively applied than is justified, due to reservations about their applicability to specific groups. General recommendations to tailor interventions in "culturally sensitive" ways acknowledge that intervention methods that are effective in one group may not be so in another. But whether the actual content of the interventions should also be tailored to specific groups is thus far largely unknown.

Other Populations

As noted in Chapter 7, the examples of racial or ethnic groups in the United States and the attendant issues for cardiovascular disease prevention can be assumed to apply to populations in other countries in analogous ways. That is, it is presumably possible to identify in every country subgroups of the population that experience differences in rates of cardiovascular events, distributions of risk factors, and accessibility to preventive measures. Many reports document such differences within and between countries. The functions of public health are intended to ensure that the health problems of all groups are assessed, appropriate policies for intervention are formulated and adopted, and assurance of optimum health is sought for all segments of the population. The situation of the United States in this respect serves not as a model of the solution but as an illustration of the problems and challenges posed by this dimension of diversity in the population. It is important that this aspect of cardiovascular disease prevention be investigated as a matter of policy in all countries insofar as this is feasible.

HEREDITY AND GENETICS

Family History

Family history of cardiovascular disease events or of risk factors, principally high blood pressure and elevated cholesterol concentration, figures prominently in intervention strategies recommended for identifying high-risk individuals. Already noted above in connection with blood pressure and blood lipid screening and management, family history has been championed as a key to identification of the coronary heart disease–prone family. Williams and colleagues, for example, have developed the application of the "health family tree" to identify families and close relatives at greater than average risk of coronary heart disease.[21] Their "medical pedigree" (MED PED) approach succeeded in finding, from 100 index cases, 500 others with heterozygous familial hypercholesterolemia, two-thirds of whom had not been diagnosed or were not effectively treated to reduce LDL-cholesterol levels.

More broadly, the family unit is important for prevention of the risk factors in the first place, in keeping with the cardiovascular prevention schedule outlined by the American Heart Association and discussed above. The possibility of favorable "cultural inheritance" through well-informed families offers promise for effective preventive measures where circumstances support such intervention.

Specific Genotypes

Although genetic testing for certain of the lipid disorders is potentially applicable at birth for those with known family histories of such conditions, few if any recommendations for neonatal testing are proposed currently. Rather, as in the American Heart Association scheme, family history is emphasized as a means of predicting increased risk for individual children and adolescents. Because parents and even grandparents of young children may not yet have reached the peak ages at risk of the risk factors themselves or for major cardiovascular events, updating the family history is needed and could then lead to more specific investigation if warranted.

Specific genetic determinants of risk could potentially be evaluated once an individual was found, for example, to have an elevated cholesterol concentration. The possibility that many such determinants may be increasingly recognized as mapping of the human genome proceeds raises both opportunities and concerns. The opportunity stems from the scientific insight that could follow into causal pathways underlying common lipid disorders or other risk factors. A concern is that genetic heterogeneity of populations may be emphasized to such a degree that general recommendations lose acceptance in favor of individualization of all interventions, perhaps requiring genotyping before action is taken on behalf of any individual.[22] In this circumstance the concept of the population as a whole could be lost in an atomized view in which no intervention is justified except on a highly individualized basis. Unless such strategies became feasible on a very broad scale, great caution would be indicated in considering the implications for public health of dismantling population-wide recommendations.

SOCIOECONOMIC GROUPS

Low socioeconomic status is marked by higher risks of many diseases and adverse health conditions, among them atherosclerotic and hypertensive diseases, at least late in the epidemic process. The observations of Osler (see Chapter 20) that acute angina pectoris was an affliction of the fast-paced, overindulgent businessman have yielded in most industrialized societies to predominance of disease among those with lowest income, least education, and least skilled occupations. Concentration of cardiovascular risk factors in conjunction with lower socioeconomic status overlaps to a large degree with minority status by race and ethnicity in the United States currently. Therefore issues about data availability and targeting of intervention strategies for these groups are compounded by lower levels of literacy or education; less likelihood of employ-

ment, especially in worksites offering risk factor management programs; and more limited access to health care sources. These considerations doubtless explain in part the widening gap in health status and in specific cardiovascular risks between higher and lower socioeconomic levels in the United States. They are noted here as background for discussion of challenges to implementation of cardiovascular prevention programs, addressed more fully in Chapter 28.

REFERENCES

1. US Dept of Health and Human Services. *Healthy People 2000: National Health Promotion and Disease Prevention Objectives: Full Report with Commentary.* Washington, DC: Public Health Service, US Dept of Health and Human Services: 1991. DHHS publication (PHS) 91-50212.

2. Report of the US Preventive Services Task Force. *Guide to Clinical Preventive Services.* 2nd ed. Alexandria, Va: International Medical Publishing, Inc; 1989.

3. Strong WB, Deckelbaum RJ, Gidding SS, Kavey RW, et al. Special report: integrated cardiovascular health promotion in childhood: a statement for health professionals from the Subcommittee on Atherosclerosis and Hypertension in Childhood of the Council on Cardiovascular Disease in the Young, American Heart Association. *Circ.* 1992;85:1638–1644.

4. Labarthe DR, Nichaman MZ, Harrist RB, Grunbaum JA, et al, for the Project HeartBeat! Investigators. Development of cardiovascular risk factors from ages 8 to 18 in Project HeartBeat! Study design and patterns of change in plasma total cholesterol concentration. *Circ.* 1997;95:2636–2642.

5. National High Blood Pressure Education Program. *The Fifth Report of the Joint National Committee on Detection, Evaluation, and Treatment of High Blood Pressure.* Bethesda, Md: National Heart, Lung and Blood Institute, National Institutes of Health, US Dept of Health and Human Services; 1993. NIH publication 93-1088.

6. Expert Panel on Detection, Evaluation, and Treatment of High Blood Cholesterol in Adults. Summary of the second report of the National Cholesterol Education Program (NCEP) Expert Panel on Detection, Evaluation, and Treatment of High Blood Cholesterol in Adults (adult treatment panel II). *JAMA.* 1993; 269:3015–3023.

7. Douglas KA, Collins JL, Warren C, Kann L, et al. Results from the 1995 National College Health Risk Behavior Survey. *J Am Coll Health Assoc.* 1997; 46:55–66.

8. Report of a WHO Study Group. *Epidemiology and Prevention of Cardiovascular Diseases in Elderly People.* Geneva, Switzerland: World Health Organization; 1995. WHO Technical Report Series 853.

9. Kannel WB, Vokonas PS. Preventive cardiology in the elderly: the Framingham Study. In: Pearson TA, Criqui MH, Luepker RV, Oberman A, Winston M, eds. *Primer in Preventive Cardiology.* Dallas, Tex: American Heart Association; 1994:261–272.

10. Barrett-Connor E. Sex differences in coronary heart disease: why are women so superior? The 1995 Ancel Keys Lecture. *Circ.* 1997;95:252–264.

11. Strong JP, Oalmann MC, Malcolm GT. Pathobiological Determinants of Atherosclerosis in Youth (PDAY) Research Group. Atherosclerosis in youth: relationships of risk factors to arterial lesions. In: Filer LJ Jr, Lauer RM, Luepker RV, eds. *Prevention of Atherosclerosis and Hypertension Beginning in Youth.* Philadelphia, Pa: Lea & Febiger; 1994: 13–20.

12. American Heart Association. *1997 Heart and Stroke Statistical Update.* Dallas, Tex: American Heart Association; 1996.

13. National High Blood Pressure Education Working Group on Hypertension Control in Children and Adolescents. Update on the 1987 Task Force Report on High Blood Pressure in Children and Adolescents: a working group report from the National High Blood Pressure Education Program. *Pediatr.* 1996;98:649–658.

14. Ramsey DJ, Goff DC, Wear ML, Labarthe DR, et al. Sex and ethnic differences in use of myocardial revascularization procedures in Mexican Americans and non-Hispanic Whites: the Corpus Christi Heart Project. *J Clin Epidemiol.* 1997;50:603–609.

15. Herholz H, Goff DC, Ramsey DJ, Chan FA, et al. Women and Mexican Americans receive fewer cardiovascular drugs following myocardial infarction than men and non-Hispanic Whites: the Corpus Christi Heart Project, 1988–1990. *J Clin Epidemiol.* 1996; 49:279–287.

16. Barrett-Connor E, Bush TL. Estrogen and coronary heart disease in women. *JAMA.* 1991;265:1861–1867.

17. The Writing Group for the PEPI Trial. Effects of estrogen or estrogen/progestin regimens on heart disease risk factors in postmenopausal women. *JAMA.* 1995; 273:199–208.

18. LaRosa JC. Hormone replacement therapy: outlook for the future. In: Forte TM, ed. *Hormonal, Metabolic, and Cellular Influences on Cardiovascular Disease in Women.* Armonk, NY: Futura Publishing Co; 1997: 339–347.

19. US Dept of Health and Human Services. *Report of the Secretary's Task Force on Black and Minority Health, 1: Executive Summary.* Bethesda, Md: US Dept of Health and Human Services; 1985.

20. Cardiovascular diseases and stroke in African-Americans and other racial minorities in the United States: a statement for health professionals. *Circ.* 1991;83: 1463–1480.

21. Williams RR, Schumacher C, Hopkins PN, Hunt SC, et al. Practical approaches for finding and helping coronary-prone families with special reference to familial hypercholesterolaemia. In: Goldbourt U, de Faire U, Berg K, eds. *Genetic Factors in Coronary Heart Disease.* Dordrecht, the Netherlands: Kluwer Academic Publishers; 1994: 425–445.

22. Omenn GS. Comment: genetics and public health. *Am J Public Health.* 1996;86:1701–1704.

PART IV

Other Major Cardiovascular Diseases

Chapter 24

Rheumatic Fever and Rheumatic Heart Disease

SUMMARY

Rheumatic fever and rheumatic heart disease are sequential outcomes of streptococcal pharyngitis, a throat infection, that occur only in a small proportion of cases. Nonetheless, rheumatic heart disease constitutes the dominant component of cardiovascular morbidity and mortality in many populations around the world. Rheumatic fever follows either symptomatic or subclinical pharyngeal infection with certain strains of streptococci and may include carditis (inflammatory disease of the heart), which can vary in severity from a mild to a fatal complication. Rheumatic fever may recur on reinfection with "rheumatogenic" streptococci. But with or without such recurrences, cases with carditis can progress to a disabling or fatal disease of the heart, chronic rheumatic heart disease, which affects especially the heart valves, disrupting both their structure and function. Subject to clinical and laboratory investigation over at least four centuries, this disease complex is often referred to as enigmatic, in that the mechanisms of progression from infection to heart disease remain obscure. Irrespective of this lack of understanding of mechanisms, the essential role of the streptococcus and the demonstrated effectiveness of penicillin therapy in preventing infection, progression to rheumatic fever, or development of rheumatic heart disease have become well established. On
this basis global prevention programs have been devised, demonstrated, and evaluated by the World Health Organization (WHO) and collaborating agencies. Although it virtually disappeared from the United States between the 1940s and the 1970s, recent resurgence of rheumatic fever in some localities has stirred new awareness of the disease in this country. The global problem has remained one of broad public health concern. Especially valuable sources for review of current concepts of this disease and for access to the rich literature on the subject are recent reports of WHO and the World Bank.[1,2]

CLINICAL COURSE OF THE INDIVIDUAL CASE

Rheumatic fever results in cardiovascular disease in two fundamental ways: first, by production of fatal or nonfatal carditis (inflammatory disease of the heart) during either the first acute episode or an acute recurrence; and second, by structural damage, especially to the heart valves, potentially causing long-term disability or death due to valvular dysfunction and heart failure or to severe systemic infection arising from bacterial colonization on the damaged valves. The first process is almost exclusively one of childhood or very early adulthood, whereas the second typically progresses from the time of onset through early, middle, or sometimes even late adulthood.

As outlined schematically in Figure 24–1, the precursors to these cardiovascular outcomes are the following: First is exposure to a human host with active infection by one of several particular strains of bacteria known as Group A beta-hemolytic streptococci. (The name of this type of organism is based on its microscopic appearance, its effect on red blood cells in growth media for bacterial culture, and one level of its immunologic characteristics.) Second is the development of actual infection by this organism, specifically in the pharynx, so as to stimulate a potentially measurable immune response (indicating that true infection has occurred). Third is the progression from this acute pharyngitis to rheumatic fever, a syndrome (combination of clinical manifestations) that may include carditis. Fourth is the possibility of recurrence of rheumatic fever within several months or after a longer interval following the initial episode. Fifth is the clinical appearance of chronic rheumatic heart disease, indicated by the foregoing history and the presence of characteristic changes, especially in the structure and function of the heart valves.

As the figure indicates, this is not the only sequence of events that may follow exposure to Group A beta-hemolytic streptococci. Exposure may also lead to either a long-term carrier state, without true infection, or to no identifiable acquisition of the agent at all. Even in the event of true infection, only a few cases of recognized rheumatic fever (by conventional wisdom, perhaps 3%) typically result. Not all cases of rheumatic fever are preceded by a clinical illness. By current definition, however, antibody evidence of prior infection is ordinarily required for the diagnosis of acute rheumatic fever in the absence of a previous positive throat culture. This kind of "silent infection" poses special difficulties for prevention. The initial episode of acute rheumatic fever is often followed by recurrences in which the risk of carditis is increased. Mild carditis may appear to resolve completely, whereas moderate or severe carditis leads to permanent cardiac dysfunction and disability or death. These varied sequential pathways in the natural history of rheumatic fever and rheumatic heart disease are fundamental to strategies for prevention, as discussed below.

The time course of appearance of each of the various manifestations of rheumatic fever is indicated in Figure 24–2.[3] The figure represents for a hypothetical group of cases the frequency distributions of the day of appearance, relative to the date of infection, for carditis (whether by electrocardiographic or clinical examination),

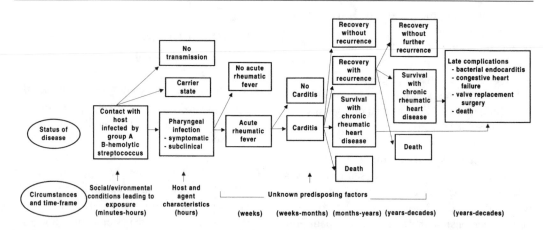

Figure 24–1 Common Features of the Course of Acute Rheumatic Fever and Acute and Chronic Rheumatic Heart Disease

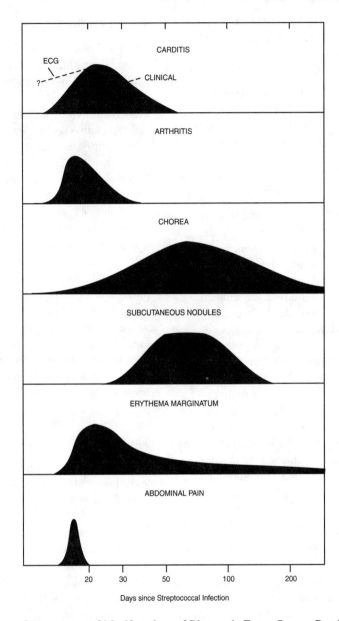

Figure 24–2 Sequence of Appearance of Manifestations of Rheumatic Fever. *Source:* Reprinted with permission from G DiSciascio and A Taranta, Rheumatic Fever in Children, *American Heart Journal,* Vol 99, p 641, © 1980, Mosby-Year Book, Inc.

arthritis (especially inflammation of the large joints of the lower extremities), chorea (central nervous system involvement, with distinctive abnormal movements called "St. Vitus' dance"), subcutaneous nodules, erythema marginatum (a characteristic type of skin rash), and abdominal pain. The early occurrence of carditis offers little opportunity for prevention if the preceding streptococcal infection was subclinical or for other reasons was undetected.

BACKGROUND OF EPIDEMIOLOGIC AND RELATED INVESTIGATIONS

Through the 19th Century

The history of investigations leading to the current understanding of rheumatic fever and rheumatic heart disease has been recounted in several scholarly reviews. A monograph by Stollerman is especially informative about the premodern era and opens by setting the stage for a detailed review of the disease:

> The riddle of acute rheumatic fever is characterized in many ways by the inappropriate name by which the syndrome is known—for it may be neither acute, rheumatic, nor febrile! . . . The unification of the clinical syndrome as a single disease entity has required the combined wisdom of the clinicians, pathologists, microbiologists, immunologists, and epidemiologists of the modern era of medicine spanning the past four centuries. And to date, despite the illuminating microbiologic and immunologic advances of the twentieth century, the precise pathogenetic mechanism by which the streptococcus causes rheumatic fever remains tantalizingly elusive.[4(p 1)]

Milestones in clinical understanding of the disease included the first distinctions made among different forms of arthritis (17th century); recognition through pathologic anatomy of the forms of valvular heart disease and linkage of these forms with what was later termed *acute rheumatic fever* (18th century); and, finally, development of the concept of rheumatic heart disease. Following the introduction of the stethoscope, which permitted auscultation and description of the heart sounds characteristic of rheumatic valvular disease, these advances led further to synthesis of the components of the disease into a unified concept by Cheadle (19th century).

The Early 20th Century

Around the end of the 19th century, and essentially within the past 100 years, the first epidemiologic investigations of rheumatic fever were conducted. Already in 1895, according to Stollerman, epidemiologic studies in Britain and Scandinavia by Sir Arthur Newsholme were reported as indicating that acute rheumatic fever was the result of a specific infection occurring in particularly predisposed or susceptible persons, with seasonal and geographic variation in its occurrence.

The next major steps were to deepen the understanding of the role of infection, specifically by Group A beta-hemolytic streptococci, and to apply the newly discovered penicillin for prevention of acute rheumatic fever and rheumatic heart disease for whole populations as well as in individual clinical practice. Microbiologic and immunologic developments over the next several decades set the stage for much broader epidemiologic investigation based on bacteriologic and serologic surveys of many populations.

The Second World War and After

A particularly strong impetus to epidemiologic investigation was the recognition of the importance of streptococcal infection and acute rheumatic fever as a military medical problem in the Second World War. The US Armed Forces Epidemiological Board (AFEB) established the Commission on Hemolytic Streptococcal Infections in early 1941. This inaugurated an era of research on rheumatic fever that made fundamental contributions to understanding the natural history of streptococcal transmission, the natural history of progression to rheumatic fever, and means of intervention with penicillin to prevent both infection and primary and recurrent episodes of acute rheumatic fever and its later consequences. This history is documented extensively in a recent compendium of accounts of the several AFEB commissions and conveys a sense of both the concern about the problem and the determination to pursue the investigations needed to resolve it.[5]

The more recent history as summarized by Markowitz continues a military metaphor ("Thirty Years' War against the Streptococcus").[6] He outlined progress in the 1950s in establishing the scientific basis for preventive strategies against both primary and recurrent attacks of rheumatic fever and progression of heart disease among those affected. Through the 1960s the actual practices following from this scientific base began to be implemented in the United States, in part through campaigns for public and professional education undertaken by the American Heart Association. Use of throat cultures became a widespread practice to identify the 15%–20% of cases of acute pharyngitis that might be expected to be due to Group A beta-hemolytic streptococci. This was the specific target population for treatment with penicillin.

In the 1970s, concern was mounting over the common occurrence of persons who were carriers of the organism but not truly infected. Carriers might constitute up to one-half of those with positive throat cultures, and the carrier state tends to persist despite treatment. Further, carriers are considered to be neither infective nor at risk of rheumatic fever. Because the physician could not distinguish between the carrier state and true infection in the case of a positive culture, unnecessary and ineffective treatment was being administered to perhaps one-half of the positives. Persistent positive cultures left uncertainty about whether treatment was inadequate or the carrier state was present. Both patients and their parents therefore remained anxious when a post-treatment throat culture was found still positive. The use of other antibiotics, with attendant costs and risks, might then follow. With epidemiologic evidence that the incidence of rheumatic fever was steeply declining in the United States (discussed below), serious questions arose about the benefit of these interventions relative to their costs and other implications of prevailing prevention policy.

Over the postwar years, the incidence of rheumatic fever appeared generally to decline in industrialized countries other than the United States. But there was growing recognition of rheumatic fever and rheumatic heart disease as a major health problem in developing countries. Under the auspices of WHO, the first expert committee on rheumatic diseases—not limited to rheumatic fever—was convened in 1953 to review current information and recommend research and preventive measures. Soon thereafter a second WHO committee met in 1956 specifically to address prevention of rheumatic fever. Successive WHO committees met in 1966 and 1987 (the latter reporting in 1988), and an intervening committee on community prevention and control of cardiovascular diseases, including rheumatic fever and rheumatic heart disease, convened in 1984. The reports of all of these meetings are cited in the 1988 report.[1]

Over this recent period of some 35 years, recommendations have been formulated by successive WHO expert committees. In the past 15 years these recommendations have been implemented in model programs on an international collaborative basis. The background data and intervention strategies underlying these programs have been cited extensively in the 1994 report of the Joint WHO/International Society and Federation of Cardiology (ISFC) Meeting on Rheumatic Fever/Rheumatic Heart Disease Control, with Emphasis on Primary Prevention.[7] As will be discussed below, the global picture of rheumatic fever and rheumatic heart disease differs strikingly from the contemporary situation of the industrialized countries alone, and issues of prevention and control are accordingly different in these distinct situations.

POPULATION STUDIES: CRITERIA AND CLASSIFICATION

The Jones Criteria

Considering the rich history of investigation of rheumatic fever and rheumatic heart disease, one might be surprised by the recency of its emergence as a major public health concern. Writing in the *Journal of the American Medical*

Association in 1944, T Duckett Jones noted "acceptance by an increasing number of physicians of the public health or community aspects" of rheumatic fever and that "small public programs of care have been developed in some states by the Children's Bureau of the US Department of Labor."[8(p 481)] He also cited outbreaks of rheumatic fever in the US military as a stimulus to increasing attention to the problem. Jones emphasized the lack of any specific diagnostic test for this condition as an impediment to progress: "From the study of the medical literature it is obvious that each observer has his own diagnostic criteria and that these may differ widely."[8(p 481)]

Jones proposed in this report an approach to diagnosis based on the detection of what he termed "major manifestations," thought least likely to reflect some other medical condition, and "minor manifestations," which occur more frequently in a variety of other conditions. He proposed restricting the diagnosis of rheumatic fever to those cases in which any one major manifestation was accompanied by at least two minor ones; strong additional support for the diagnosis would be a history of respiratory infection or exposure to hemolytic streptococcal infection in an epidemic situation or detection of elevated antistreptococcal antibodies. The chance of misdiagnosis was recognized, but it was thought unlikely either that a large proportion of true cases would be missed or that overdiagnosis of noncases would be common with close adherence to these criteria.

This proposition is, of course, untestable in terms of the sensitivity, specificity, and predictive value of the criteria in the absence of an agreed-upon standard of a "true" case. However, the continued reliance on essentially these criteria, more than 50 years later, attests to their serviceability as well as to the persistent elusiveness of the definitive diagnostic test. The most recent expert committee report of the WHO reaffirms the use of the Jones criteria, as revised, as of 1988 (Exhibit 24–1).[1] Either two major criteria or one major and two minor criteria suffice for the diagnosis of acute rheumatic

fever if additional evidence of prior streptococcal infection is available. The WHO committee accepted these criteria as adopted by the American Heart Association only with the qualification that three conditions be accepted without fulfillment of the criteria: "pure" chorea, late-onset carditis, and recurrent rheumatic attacks. In the first two instances evidence of prior streptococcal infection is sometimes unobtainable in practice, and in the third instance only one major criterion may suffice.

Modifications of the criteria from their introduction in 1944 until 1984 have been compiled

---

Exhibit 24–1 Jones Criteria (Revised) for Guidance in the Diagnosis of Acute Rheumatic Fever

Major Manifestations
   Carditis
   Polyarthritis
   Chorea
   Erythema marginatum
   Subcutaneous nodules

Minor Manifestations
   Clinical
   Fever
   Arthralgia
   Previous rheumatic fever or rheumatic
      heart disease
   Laboratory
   Acute-phase reactions:
      abnormal erythrocyte sedimentation
      rate, C-reactive protein, leukocytosis
   Prolonged P-R interval

Note: The presence of two major, or one major and two minor, manifestations *plus* evidence of a preceding streptococcal infection indicates a high probability of rheumatic fever. Previous infection is indicated by increased antistreptolysin 0 or other streptococcal antibody; positive throat culture for group A streptococcus; or recent scarlet fever. Manifestations with a long latent period, such as chorea and late-onset carditis, are exempted from this last requirement.

Source: Reprinted with permission from *Rheumatic Fever and Rheumatic Heart Disease: Report of a WHO Study Group*, WHO TRS 764, p 20, © 1988, World Health Organization.

(see Table 24–1).[2] They are classified as follows: *M* indicates manifestations classified as major, *m* those classified as minor, and *R* the requirement (only in the most recent modifications) for diagnostic confirmation of beta-hemolytic streptococcal infection by antibody tests or, alternatively, a positive throat culture or overt scarlet fever. This recent requirement is now considered feasible and therefore applicable in most countries due to wider availability of diagnostic laboratory support. The Jones criteria, while thus undergoing some modification over these decades, are more remarkable for their durability.

International Statistical Classification

In the *International Statistical Classification of Diseases and Related Health Problems, Tenth Revision*, these conditions are classified as shown in Exhibit 24–2.[9] Subcategories are provided under I01 to identify the type of heart involvement, such as peri-, endo-, or myocarditis (affecting the outer or inner tissue lining of the heart or the heart muscle itself, respectively). For chronic rheumatic heart disease

affecting a particular heart valve (I05–I08), subcategories denote particular structural or functional defects associated with the disease, such as stenosis (pathologic resistance or obstruction to blood flow through the valve) or regurgitation (reflux of blood flow). This classification has remained essentially the same over recent decades except for change in the actual numeric codes assigned to the several categories.

On the basis of these standardized diagnostic criteria and nosologic classifications, a tendency toward uniformity of case identification has become potentially attainable despite the continuing absence of a specific diagnostic test. This circumstance permits the interpretation and comparison of reports of cases of rheumatic fever and rheumatic heart disease among observers and between reporting areas, greatly facilitating their epidemiologic study.

RATES OF OCCURRENCE IN POPULATIONS

The Early Post-War Decades: US Experience

The rising recognition of acute rheumatic fever and rheumatic heart disease as a public

Table 24–1 Changes in the Original Jones Criteria for the Diagnosis of Acute Rheumatic Fever

Manifestation	Year			
	1944	1951	1956	1965/1984
Carditis	M	M	M	M
Polyarthritis	—	M	M	M
Chorea	M	M	M	M
Subcutaneous nodules	M	M	M	M
Erythema marginatum	m	—	m	m
Arthralgia	M	—	m	m
Fever	m	m	m	m
Erythrocyte sedimentation rate	m	m	m	m
History of acute rheumatic fever or rheumatic heart disease	M	m	m	m
Evidence of prior streptococcal infection	—	m	m	R

Note: M, major manifestation; m, minor manifestation; R, required manifestation; — not available.

Source: From *Disease Control Priorities in Developing Countries*, edited by DT Jamison et al. Copyright © 1993 The International Bank for Reconstruction and Development/The World Bank. Used by permission of Oxford University Press, Inc.

Exhibit 24–2 Classification of Acute Rheumatic Fever and Chronic Rheumatic Heart Disease

Acute rheumatic fever
I00–I02

    I00   Rheumatic fever without mention of heart involvement
    I01   Rheumatic fever with heart involvement
    I02   Rheumatic chorea

Chronic rheumatic heart disease
I05–I09

    I05   Rheumatic mitral valve diseases
    I06   Rheumatic aortic valve diseases
    I07   Rheumatic tricuspid valve diseases
    I08   Multiple valve diseases
    I09   Other rheumatic heart diseases

health problem in the United States was noted in the mid-1940s by Jones. In 1965 Acheson was able to demonstrate that already in the 1940s, mortality from these conditions was declining in the United States and had continued to do so throughout the 25-year period from 1940 to 1964.[10] This trend is seen in Figure 24–3, which shows mortality from acute rheumatic fever and chronic rheumatic heart disease, combined, of 20 per 100,000 population for Whites and 30 per 100,000 for Blacks in 1940. By 1960 these rates had decreased by about 50% for White males and females and 65% for non-White males and females, and thus rates for the

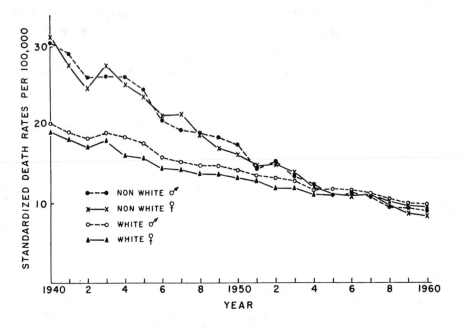

Figure 24–3 Age-Adjusted Secular Trends in Rheumatic Fever/Rheumatic Heart Disease Mortality, ISC 400–416, United States, 1940–1960. *Source:* Reprinted with permission from *Journal of Chronic Diseases*, Vol 18, RM Acheson, The Epidemiology of Acute Rheumatic Fever 1950–1964, p 724, © 1965, Elsevier Science, Inc.

four sex-race groups converged at about 8–10 deaths per 100,000 population.

Separate analysis for specific age groups was revealing and showed, as in Figure 24–4 (on a logarithmic scale for death rates), that the decreases were especially striking among the younger age groups, under 5 years old and from 5 to 14 years of age. This suggested that deaths from acute rheumatic fever (especially concentrated in the younger age groups) were declining more rapidly than those from chronic

rheumatic heart disease (occurring especially in the older age groups). As Acheson noted, mortality declined despite the frequent epidemic occurrence of streptococcal pharyngitis. The decline also predated the introduction of antibiotic treatment of such infections. (A commonly reproduced figure—for example, in the Joint WHO/ISFC Meeting report[7]—shows a similar trend for the incidence of rheumatic fever in Denmark over an entire century, 1860–1960, which even more forcefully points to broad

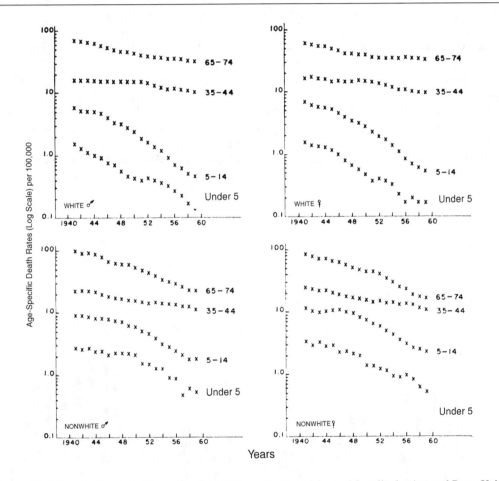

Figure 24–4 Secular Trends in Rheumatic Fever/Rheumatic Heart Disease Mortality by Age and Race, United States, 1940–1960. Especially among the White races, the rate of fall is much greater among the children, who presumably died of acute rheumatic fever, than among adults, whose cause of death is more likely to have been chronic rheumatic heart disease (two-point moving averages). *Source:* Reprinted with permission from *Journal of Chronic Diseases*, Vol 18, RM Acheson, The Epidemiology of Acute Rheumatic Fever 1950–1964, p 725, © 1965, Elsevier Science, Inc.

environmental determinants of the natural history of this disease.) This phenomenon was interpreted as reflecting chiefly improved housing conditions and school environments, which resulted in decreased crowding and reduced frequency of person-to-person transmission of the agent.

Current Morbidity and Mortality in the United States

As of 1993, mortality from rheumatic fever and rheumatic heart disease in the United States had reached the low rate of 1.0 per 100,000 for White males and 1.6 for White females, with approximately equal rates for Blacks and Whites within each sex group.[11] Mortality had thus decreased further over the subsequent 30 years to about one-10th that shown by Acheson for 1960. Nonetheless, 5,540 deaths and 17,000 hospitalizations were due to rheumatic fever and rheumatic heart disease in the United States in 1994. Chronic rheumatic heart disease was

reported to account for many of the 60,000 valve replacement procedures performed annually in the United States. The American Heart Association estimated that 1.38 million Americans currently have rheumatic heart disease.

One of several exceptions to the general trend of decreasing occurrence of acute rheumatic fever in the United States is its persistently high incidence in the intermountain area surrounding Salt Lake City, Utah, following a resurgence of cases there in the mid-1980s.[12] Figure 24–5 illustrates the yearly reports of cases of acute rheumatic fever in this area, showing a general decline from 1960 to 1983 or 1984 and an abrupt six- to ten-fold increase (depending on the choice of reference point) in 1985. The frequency of reported cases had remained higher through 1992 than for any year since the mid-1970s. A notable feature of the resurgence of acute rheumatic fever in this area has been the demographic characteristics of the affected population—not ethnic minorities in low socioeconomic areas but middle-class Whites described

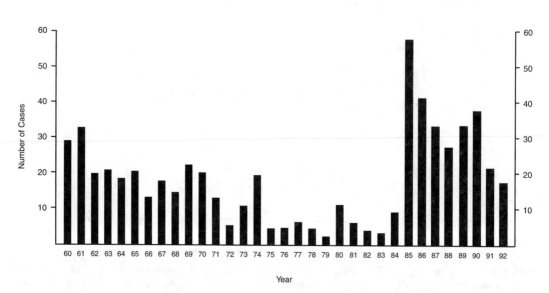

Figure 24–5 Salt Lake City, Utah, Area Outbreak and Endemicity of Acute Rheumatic Fever. *Source:* Reprinted with permission from LG Veasy, LY Tani, and HR Hill, Persistence of Acute Rheumatic Fever in the Intermountain Area of the United States, *Journal of Pediatrics*, Vol 124, No 1, p 11, © 1994, Mosby-Year Book, Inc.

as having ready access to medical care. Determinants of natural history such as decreased crowding and reduced opportunities for transmission of appropriate streptococcal strains appear not to offer protection against the disease under these apparently changed, but not yet understood, circumstances in this region.

This has not been the only geographic area of the United States to experience increased incidence in recent years, but one further exception, Hawaii, deserves comment.[13] There, the first officially recorded case occurred in 1941. Incidence of acute rheumatic fever has been consistently higher in Hawaii than on the US Mainland, where it is said to have declined to fewer than 2 cases per 100,000 population per year by the late 1970s. By contrast, it has remained at 12 or more per 100,000 per year in Hawaii through the 1980s. Within the multiethnic population of Hawaii, the Samoan community has been especially affected. Constituting about one-fourth of the population, the Samoan community accounts for nearly one-half of all cases and more than one-half of the cases of rheumatic carditis in the state.

A Global View of Morbidity from Rheumatic Fever and Rheumatic Heart Disease

Elsewhere in the world, data compiled by the WHO indicate something of the frequency of rheumatic fever in schoolchildren in the several WHO Regions (Table 24–2).[7] Whether the population differences suggested by these data are real or instead reflect sampling and other methodologic differences among studies cannot be answered without detailed review of each report. With this qualification borne in mind, there appear to be some very large and presumably real contrasts, such as that between Europe or the Americas and the other WHO Regions.

The data further permit some comparisons, even if tentative, within the same population over time or within different population groups in the same geographic area. The typical secular trend toward lower incidence is illustrated for Rochester, Minnesota, and Havana, Cuba, in the

Americas; in Sweden; and even for India, though incidence remained very high, based on data available at the time of this 1990 report. Certain population groups, such as the Maori in New Zealand and the Samoans in Hawaii, are at exceptional risk relative to other local groups. The rates that have stimulated concern in the intermountain area of the United States are greatly exceeded by those most recently reported in every other region but Europe. It is clear that the experience of the United States and other industrialized countries gives no hint of the problem of acute rheumatic fever as it exists today throughout much of the developing world.

This point is further underscored by reference to the prevalence of rheumatic heart disease in school-age children around the world. Estimates of the prevalence of rheumatic heart disease based on screening of school-age populations have been compiled by WHO on a regional basis in the same manner as for the incidence of acute rheumatic fever (Table 24–3).[7] These estimates also require caution against overinterpretation because of possible methodologic differences but seem clearly to distinguish high-prevalence from low-prevalence areas. The available data as of 1994 were in many instances from the 1970s or even earlier and thus long out of date.

As was observed for the incidence of acute rheumatic fever, apparent decreases in the childhood prevalence of rheumatic heart disease over time were reported for some areas, for example, in Bolivia, from 17.1 per 1,000 in 1973 to 7.9 in 1986–1990; in Missouri, from 8.7 in 1961 to 0.2 in 1982; in Pakistan, from 1.8–11.0 in the 1970s to 0.9 in 1986–1990; in Egypt, from 10.0 in 1973 to 5.1 in 1986–1990; and in the Philippines, from 2.0 in 1974–1977 to 0.6 in 1986–1990. Still, the most recent prevalence estimates reported in many areas were typically on the order of 1–10 per 1,000, with few below 1 per 1,000. As noted in the WHO report, approximately one to two cases of inactive rheumatic fever are expected for each case of detectable rheumatic heart disease, so the

Table 24–2 Incidence of Acute Rheumatic Fever in Schoolchildren

Source	WHO Region (City and Country)	Year	Rate per 100,000
Africa			
WHO Chronicle	Algeria	1971	300.0
Americas			
Anneger	Rochester, USA	1935–44	65.1
	Rochester, USA	1965–78	9.0
	Memphis, USA	1977–81	1.8
Markowitz & Kaplan	Baltimore	1977–81	0.5
	Rhode Island	1976–80	0.2
Mohs	San Jose, Costa Rica	1990	0.9
Nordet	Havana, Cuba	1972	32.2
	Havana, Cuba	1982	10.5
Nordet	Cuba	1982	10.5–50.5
Europe			
Quinn	Sweden	1930–34	2.5
		1950–54	0.7
East Mediterranean			
WHO Chronicle	Sudan	1970s	100.0
	Abadan, Iran	1971	100.0
WHO Chronicle	Iran	1972–74	51.0–80.0
Southeast Asia			
WHO Chronicle	India	1970s	54.0
Grover	India	1990	30.0
Western Pacific			
WHO Chronicle	Guang-Dong, China	1971	150.0
Light	Northland, New Zealand[a]	1980–81	115.1 (Maoris)
			15.9 (non-Maoris)
Talbot	Hamilton, New Zealand	1973–83	88.0 (Maoris)
			9.3 (non-Maoris)
Alto	FE Micronesia	1986–88	25.0
	French Polynesia	1980–84	72.2
Chun	Oahu, Hawaii	1976–80	14.4 (all)
			96.5 (Samoan)

a. 34.5% experienced a recurrent attack.

Source: Reprinted with permission from *WHO/CVD/94.1*, p 24, © World Health Organization.

Table 24–3 Prevalence of Rheumatic Heart Disease (RHD) in Schoolchildren

Source	WHO Region (City and Country)	Year	Rate per 1,000
	Africa		
WHO/TRS 764	Nigeria	1970	0.3–3.0
	Algeria	1971	15.0
	Soweto (South Africa)	1975	6.9
	Cote d'Ivoire	1985	1.9
Agboton	Benin	1983–85	1.4–10.4
Anabwani	Kenya	1985	1.7
WHO/Bull	Mali	1986–90	3.4
	Zambia	1986–90	12.5
	Zimbabwe	1986–90	3.4
Din-Dzietham	Cameroon	1989	3.0
Oli	Ethiopia	1991	4.6
Touré	Conakry (R Guinée)	1992	3.9
	Americas		
WHO/TRS 764	Brazil	1968–70	1.0–6.8
	Uruguay	1970	1.0
	Bolivia	1973	17.1
	Venezuela	1976	1.5
	Mexico	1977	8.5
	Puerto Rico	1980	1.6
Hassel	Barbados	1970	1.1
WHO Chronicle	Peru	1976	2.0–8.0
Nordet	Cuba	1987	0.2–2.9
WHO/Bull	Bolivia	1986–90	7.9
	El Salvador	1986–90	0.3
	Jamaica	1986–90	2.9
Quinn	Missouri, USA	1961	8.7
		1982	0.2
	East Mediterranean		
WHO/TRS 764	Pakistan	1970s	1.8–11.0
	Egypt	1973	10.0
	Morocco	1973	9.9
WHO Chronicle	Iran	1970s	2.5–22.0
L'Objectif médical	Tunisla	1977	1.6
Maroc	Morocco	1989	3.3–10.5
WHO/Bull	Egypt	1986–90	5.1
	Iraq	1986–90	2.0
	Pakistan	1986–90	0.9
	Sudan	1986–90	10.2
Al-Sekait	Saudi Arabia	1990	2.4

continues

Table 24-3 continued

Source	WHO Region (City and Country)	Year	Rate per 1,000
	Southeast Asia		
WHO/TRS 764	India	1970s	6.0–11.0
	Myanmar	1970	2.0
WHO Chronicle	Indonesia	1977–78	0.7–2.9
	Mongolia	1972–78	3.0–5.0
	Thailand	1974–77	1.2–2.5
ICMR	New Delhi, India	1990	1.2
	Vellore, India	1990	2.0
	Varanasi, India	1990	4.0
Shrestha	Nepal	1990	1.3
Haque	Bangladesh	1990	0.8
	Western Pacific		
WHO/TRS 764	China	1979	0.4–2.7
	Cook Islands	1982	18.6
	French Polynesia	1985	8.0
Talbot	Hamilton (New Zealand)	1983	6.5 (Maoris)
			0.9 (non-Maoris)
WHO Chronicle	Philippines	1974–77	2.0
Tran	Viet Nam	1980s	3.2–9.3
Hallali	Japan	1958	4.6
		1971	0.1
WHO Bull	China	1986–90	0.7
	Philippines	1986–90	0.6
	Tonga	1986–90	1.4

Note: The prevalence of RHD in young adults (20–40 years) is 50% lower than in schoolchildren. There are one to two cases of inactive rheumatic fever for each RHD case. In most developing countries, more than 50% of the cases are unaware of their disease and without secondary prophylaxis. One-third of RHD patients will require heart valve surgery within the next 5 to 20 years.

Source: Reprinted with permission from *WHO/CVD/94.1*, p 23, © World Health Organization.

true prevalence may be two to three times that reported. A serious consequence of such undetected cases is that secondary prophylaxis cannot reach them and they remain unprotected from further progression and complications of the disease. It is estimated that surgical replacement of affected heart valves is needed by one-third of cases over the 5- to 20-year period following detection.

To provide regional estimates of the prevalence of rheumatic fever or rheumatic heart disease in schoolchildren within the period 1986–1990, WHO undertook, in 1984, its Global Programme for the Prevention of Rheumatic Fever/Rheumatic Heart Disease in 16 Developing Countries.[14] This program was conducted through collaboration with the ISFC and with support from the Arab Gulf Program for United Nations Development Organizations (AGFUND).

In Phase I of this project, involving the AGFUND-supported centers, 1,433,710 school children were screened, under a common protocol, leading to the identification of 3,135 newly detected cases and registration of an additional 33,651 known cases of rheumatic fever or rheumatic heart disease. As shown in Table 24–4, 58 surveys were conducted in the six WHO Regions. Prevalence estimates of cases newly detected by school-based screening were derived from the pooled results of the several surveys within each region. The highest prevalence estimates were found in Africa and in the Eastern Mediterranean—4.7 and 4.4 per 1,000, respectively, reaching 10 cases per 1,000 or higher in some individual surveys. These estimates were three times as high as that for the Americas, six times that for the Western Pacific, and 36 times that for Southeast Asia.

Newly detected cases constitute only a part of the total prevalence, however, as the numbers of cases identified through other sources and those already known to the case register must be included for a comprehensive enumeration. Some additional data on this aspect of the WHO program are shown in Table 24–5. For all WHO Regions together, the total number of registered cases at the conclusion of Phase I of the program was 33,651; 3,135 cases or 9.3% of the total were newly detected by school surveys, and 5,754 cases or 17.1% were "discovered" (from the viewpoint of the central register) from other sources, such as hospital or other patient records. The differences by WHO Region in the proportionate yield of new cases by screening (range 0.4%–26.1%) or record searches (range 0.1%–54.8%) reveal marked differences in the background experience in each area with respect to case detection, case registration, and availability of relevant case records. Clearly, prevalence estimates based on these varied sources require different interpretations, and comparisons between populations or over time must take possible differences in data sources into account. (No estimates were provided for the total school population of each survey area, so overall prevalence could not be estimated on the basis of this report.)

Limited data on the medical care requirements for managing rheumatic fever and rheumatic heart disease were provided by the 1994 WHO report.[7] Hospitalization for rheumatic heart disease constitutes from one-fourth to more than half of all cardiovascular disease admissions for the population as a whole, according to surveys in parts of Africa, the Eastern Mediterranean, Southeast Asia, and the Western Pacific WHO Regions.

These measures of the magnitude of the problem of acute rheumatic fever and its progression to rheumatic heart disease emphasize that for much of the world this constitutes a very burdensome and costly health problem. Its persistence at high frequency, despite a common

Table 24–4 Prevalence of Rheumatic Fever (RF)/Rheumatic Heart Disease (RHD) by World Health Organization (WHO) Region

WHO Region	No. of Surveys	No. of Schoolchildren Screened	No. of RF/RHD Cases Detected	Prevalence per 1,000 (Range)
Africa	11	173,408	818	4.7 (3.4–12.6)
Americas	5	23,328	35	1.5 (0.1–7.9)
Eastern Mediterranean	19	409,933	1,807	4.4 (0.9–10.2)
Southeast Asia	6	195,142	26	0.12 (0.1–1.3)
Western Pacific	17	631,899	449	0.7 (0.6–1.4)
All regions	58	1,433,710	3,135	2.2 (0.7–4.7)

Source: Reprinted with permission from WHO Programme for the Prevention of Rheumatic Fever/Rheumatic Heart Disease in 16 Developing Countries: Report from Phase I (1986–1990), *Bulletin of the World Health Organization 70*, p 215, © 1992, World Health Organization.

Table 24–5 Screening Yields of Rheumatic Heart Disease, by World Health Organization (WHO) Region

| | Newly Discovered Cases | | | | | | Known Cases | | Total Cases | |
| | Screening | | Other Sources | | Subtotal | | | | | |
WHO Region	No.	%	No.	%	No.	%	No.	%	No.	%
Africa	818	11.2	91	1.3	909	12.5	6,390	87.5	7,299	100.0
Americas	35	0.4	881	9.1	916	9.5	8,729	90.5	9,645	100.0
Eastern Mediterranean	1,807	26.1	3,790	54.8	5,597	80.9	1,323	19.1	6,920	100.0
Southeast Asia	26	0.4	685	9.9	711	10.3	6,167	89.7	6,878	100.0
Western Pacific	449	15.4	307	10.6	756	26.0	2,153	74.0	2,909	100.0
All regions	3,135	9.3	5,754	17.1	8,889	26.4	24,762	73.6	33,651	100.0

Source: Reprinted with permission from WHO Programme for the Prevention of Rheumatic Fever/Rheumatic Heart Disease in 16 Developing Countries: Report from Phase I (1986–1990), *Bulletin of the World Health Organization 70,* p 216, © 1992, World Health Organization.

pattern of decreasing incidence over time in other geographic areas, may offer clues to causation of this problem on an epidemic scale and, potentially, may offer new insights into its prevention.

Projection of Outcomes among Cases of Acute Rheumatic Fever

To project the expected outcomes following the occurrence of acute rheumatic fever in the absence of treatment, frequencies have been estimated as shown in Table 24–6.[2] For a total of 100 such hypothetical cases, 75 cases would be expected to have one or more recurrent episodes of rheumatic fever, while 25 would not. The outcomes for those two groups, shown in the corresponding columns of the table, are quite different. For those experiencing no recurrence, 15 would recover uneventfully and 10 would develop carditis following this solitary attack. Among the 75 cases with recurrence of rheumatic fever, carditis would be a much more common outcome, affecting 60 cases. The carditis occurring among those with a solitary episode of rheumatic fever is less severe, with the majority having mild or moderate carditis (four

cases each) and only two progressing to death. By contrast, for those developing carditis after multiple episodes of rheumatic fever, the majority (32) would be fatal. The fact that outcomes are very much more favorable in the presence of penicillin prophylaxis provides the rationale for intervention strategies, as discussed below.

RISKS IN INDIVIDUALS

Age

The factors affecting risk of acute rheumatic fever and its consequences remain little understood. Age differences in risk are sharply defined for the initial attack of acute rheumatic fever, but age at death is much more broadly distributed. Table 24–7 illustrates these patterns for a hypothetical population in which no prophylaxis is received.[2] The age distribution at initial attacks peaks in late childhood, with 36% of all cases occurring within the three-year age span from 9 to 11 years and 90% of cases occurring by age 15. Deaths through age 15, by contrast, constitute only about 16% of all deaths, the majority (57%) occurring between ages 15 and 44 years.

Table 24–6 Projected Outcomes per 100 Initial Attacks of Acute Rheumatic Fever Without Treatment

Outcome	Initial Attack Without Recurrence No.	Initial Attack with Recurrence No.	Total No.
Total cases	25	75	100
Recover	15	15	30
Carditis	10	60	70
Mild	4	8	12
Moderate/severe cardiomegaly	4	20	24
Congestive heart failure leading to death	2	32	34

Source: From *Disease Control Priorities in Developing Countries*, edited by DT Jamison et al. Copyright © 1993 The International Bank for Reconstruction and Development/The World Bank. Used by permission of Oxford University Press, Inc.

Sex and Race

One example of the reports on risk by sex and race (see Figure 24–4) indicated no difference in the mid-1960s in mortality from rheumatic heart disease in the United States by sex or between Whites and non-Whites.[10] However, as of 1993, mortality was at much lower rates but was 60% higher for females than for males, while it was approximately equal between Blacks and Whites of the same sex.[11] Other ethnic differences in risk, affecting especially the Samoans in Hawaii or the Maori in New Zealand, have already been noted and are unexplained.

Table 24–7 Age Distributions at First Attack of Rheumatic Fever and at Death

Ages (Years)	No.	%
At first attack		
<5	800	8
6–8	2,000	20
9–11	3,600	36
12–15	2,600	26
>15	1,000	10
Total	10,000	100
At death		
<5	87	2.5
5–14	485	14
15–44	1,975	57
45–64	814	23.5
>65	104	3
Total	3,465	100

Source: From Disease Control Priorities in Developing Countries, edited by DT Jamison et al. Copyright © 1993 The International Bank for Reconstruction and Development/The World Bank. Used by permission of Oxford University Press, Inc.

Other Factors

Investigation continues into factors related to the disease agent, the human host, and the environment that account for variation in population rates and individual risks of rheumatic fever and rheumatic heart disease; the "rheumatogenicity" of particular strains of the Group A beta-hemolytic streptococcus; the susceptibility of the small proportion of cases whose infections lead to rheumatic fever and the very few that progress to serious cardiovascular outcomes; and the factors in the physical and social environment that affect the probability of exposure or offer possibilities for effective public health interventions.

The recent appearance and persistence of higher than usual frequencies of acute rheumatic fever in the intermountain region and other areas of the mainland United States, the continued high incidence among several ethnic groups in Hawaii, and the general long-term secular trend toward lower frequencies of rheumatic fever and rheumatic heart disease in many countries all remain to be explained. The major emphasis of public health programs, meanwhile, is to apply as effectively as possible the well-established knowledge of means of prevention.

PREVENTION AND CONTROL

The US Context

Studies in the 1940s, such as those conducted in the US military,[5] established that intervention by antibiotic prophylaxis (protection) can prevent both infection with Group A beta-hemolytic streptococcal pharyngitis and development of acute rheumatic fever in infected persons. Prophylaxis against infection in the first place is practical only in situations where exposure to potential epidemic spread of the organism is likely, such as in military recruit camps. The second-stage, postinfection intervention, depends for its individual and public health effectiveness on the detection and treatment of true infections. The practical problems of obtaining throat cultures and the inability to distinguish the carrier state from true infection, with resultant doubts by US physicians in the 1970s about the cost-effectiveness of this widespread practice, were reviewed by Markowitz and noted above.[6]

A subsequent report from the American Heart Association outlined recommendations for prevention of rheumatic fever in the United States and emphasized that the context for these recommendations was one of "current rarity of acute rheumatic fever in most areas of the United States."[15] The strategies consisted principally of selective use of throat cultures to discriminate between Group A beta-hemolytic streptococcal infection and other causes, treatment with penicillin if the culture were positive, and continuous long-term prophylaxis for those who developed rheumatic fever or rheumatic heart disease. Circumstances in which household contacts should be cultured or treated were also described.

The Global Context

Current policies and practices for control of rheumatic fever and rheumatic heart disease for the majority of the world's population are products of both national and international efforts, the latter best exemplified by work of WHO over several decades and recently by that of the World Bank.[2,7] Summarizing three studies reported since 1965, Majeed and colleagues demonstrated recurrence rates for acute rheumatic fever that approached zero in groups with prevalence of rheumatic heart disease from 20% to 29% (Tables 24–8 and 24–9).[16] In addition, in six studies reported since 1961, maintenance of regular secondary prophylaxis in patients who did not develop initial carditis appeared to provide nearly complete protection against rheumatic heart disease, based on 0 cases occurring out of 22–180 patients in 4 studies and in 3 out of 40 and 5 out of 80 patients in 2 others. These were observational data, however, and not results of controlled trials. With this limitation in mind, the contrast between these observations and the expected outcomes in the absence of treatment, shown in Table 24–6, is nonetheless striking.

In the face of often formidable obstacles to immediate postinfection prophylaxis in many localities, recommendations for developing countries have emphasized secondary prophylaxis. The two critical components of this strategy are (1) aggressive efforts to identify cases of acute rheumatic fever or rheumatic heart disease and (2) initiation and long-term maintenance of penicillin treatment to prevent recurrences and the onset or progression of rheumatic heart disease. Public health programs to implement this strategy have been devised and evaluated extensively, especially by WHO.

The WHO undertook, in 1984, its Global Programme for the Prevention of Rheumatic

Table 24–8 Evolution of Rheumatic Heart Disease (RHD) in Patients with Regular Secondary Prophylaxis

Study (Follow-Up)	Patients		Recurrences		RHD	
	N	P/yr[a]	N	RR[b]	N	PR[c]
UK-US report (10 yr)	266	2,660		NA[d]	77	29%
Tompkins (9.3 yr)	115	565	1	0.001	30	26%
Present study (12.3 yr)	64	775	2	0.003	13	20%

a. P/yr, patient-years.

b. RR, recurrence rate per patient per year.

c. PR, prevalence rate.

d. NA, not available.

Source: From *Disease Control Priorities in Developing Countries*, edited by DT Jamison et al. Copyright © 1993 The International Bank for Reconstruction and Development/The World Bank. Used by permission of Oxford University Press, Inc.

Fever/Rheumatic Heart Disease in Sixteen Developing Countries, noted above in connection with the rates of detection of new cases through school-based screening in the WHO Regions.[7] The participating countries by WHO Region and their sources of support are listed in Table 24–10. The AGFUND and the ISFC together have sponsored participation by countries in all six of the WHO Regions.

Data were collected on the extent to which secondary prophylaxis was being delivered in selected areas in the participating countries, as shown in Table 24–11.[7] This indicated a wide margin for improvement in the application of this key strategy for prevention of rheumatic heart disease. Coverage was as low as 24.8%, and the overall rate was 63.2% but reached as high as 96.9% under the best conditions.

Table 24–9 Evolution of Rheumatic Heart Disease (RHD) in Patients Who Escaped Carditis in the Initial Attack and Maintained Regular Secondary Prophylaxis

Study	No. of Patients	(Follow-Up)		RHD
		Years	Patient-Years	N (%)
Thomas	22	5	110	0 (0)
Feinstein	180	7.8	1,404	0 (0)
UK-US study	80	10	800	5 (6)
Tompkins	35	9.3	326	0 (0)
Sanyal	40	5	200	3 (8)
Present study	35	12.3	430	0 (0)

Source: From *Disease Control Priorities in Developing Countries*, edited by DT Jamison et al. Copyright © 1993 The International Bank for Reconstruction and Development/The World Bank. Used by permission of Oxford University Press, Inc.

Reports of adverse reactions to penicillin were very rare (0.3%), and recurrent episodes were equally rare (0.4%). Both of these observations served to encourage the further application of the proposed prevention strategies.

The current concept of community control of rheumatic fever and rheumatic heart disease as outlined by WHO begins with the national program components shown in Figure 24–6.[7] Primary prevention is identified as a component to be included whenever feasible, but the mainstay is comprehensive and permanent medical care for those with rheumatic fever or rheumatic heart disease. Several supporting functions are required, involving personnel training; information, education, and community participation;

and statistical reporting to monitor disease occurrence and program effectiveness.

Primary prevention activities, wherever feasible, are to follow the scheme indicated in Figure 24–7. Health personnel from the full spectrum of settings are to be informed about detection of Group A beta-hemolytic streptococcal infection, targeting children age 5 to 15 years. Standard procedures are offered as a guide to diagnosis. Treatment to eradicate the organism is indicated, by the use of long- or short-acting penicillin or an alternative antibiotic in the presence of penicillin sensitivity.

This approach would greatly reduce the incidence of acute rheumatic fever but not eliminate it, as many infections leading to acute rheu-

Table 24–10 World Health Organization Global Programme for the Prevention of Rheumatic Fever/Rheumatic Heart Disease: Participants by Region, with Sources of Support

Region	Participating Countries	
	AGFUND Supported	ISFC Supported
Africa		
	Mali	Benin
	Zambia	Cameroon
	Zimbabwe	
Americas		
	Bolivia	Brazil
	El Salvador	Cuba
	Jamaica	
East Mediterranean		
	Egypt	
	Iraq	
	Pakistan	
	Sudan	
Europe		
		Romania
Southeast Asia		
	India	Indonesia
	Sri Lanka	
	Thailand	
Western Pacific		
	PR China	Vietnam
	Philippines	
	Tonga	

Source: Reprinted with permission from *WHO/CVD/94.1*, p 25, © World Health Organization.

Table 24–11 World Health Organization (WHO) Global Programme for the Prevention of Rheumatic Fever/Rheumatic Heart Disease: Coverage by Secondary Prophylaxis, by Regions

WHO Regions	Average Coverage Rate (%)	Range
Africa	74.1	31.8–88.1
Americas	47.2	23.8–75.6
East Mediterranean	51.5	39.4–83.9
Southeast Asia	58.8	56.6–82.9
Western Pacific	90.2	80.2–96.9
All regions	63.2	23.8–96.9

Note: 95.7% used benzathine penicillin; 2.1% used oral penicillin; 0.1% used sulfadiazine; and 2.1% used erythromycin. In 0.3% of patient-years, there was an adverse reaction to B. penicillin. In 0.4% of patient-years, there was recurrence of attack. 1,433,710 schoolchildren were screened, and 33,651 cases were registered.

Source: Reprinted with permission from *WHO/CVD/94.1*, pp 213–218, © World Health Organization.

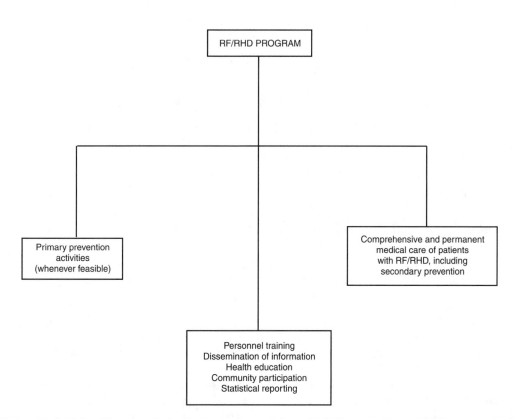

Figure 24–6 National Programme for the Prevention and Control of Rheumatic Fever (RF)/Rheumatic Heart Disease (RHD). *Source:* Reprinted with permission from *WHO/CVD/94.1*, p 49, © World Health Organization.

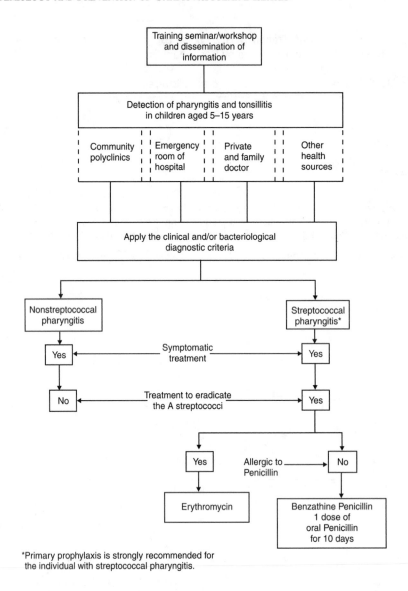

Figure 24–7 Primary Prevention of Rheumatic Fever/Rheumatic Heart Disease, World Health Organization. *Source*: Reprinted with permission from *WHO/CVD/94.1*, p 50, © World Health Organization.

matic fever are silent (subclinical), being detectable only by elevated streptococcal antibody titers once acute rheumatic fever is suspected. For this reason, even when primary prevention is feasible this does not eliminate the need for secondary prophylaxis against recurrences or progression to rheumatic heart disease.

The outline of "comprehensive and permanent medical care"—a term that underscores the requirement of long-term, sustained follow-up and management—begins with case finding, in either the stage of acute rheumatic fever or rheumatic heart disease (Figure 24–8).[7] Acute or severe chronic cases require hospital care

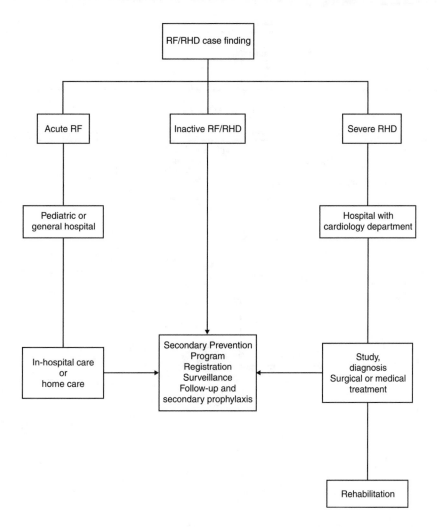

Figure 24–8 Case Finding in Rheumatic Fever (RF)/Rheumatic Heart Disease (RHD), World Health Organization. *Source:* Reprinted with permission from *WHO/CVD/94.1*, p 51, © World Health Organization.

with appropriate treatment of the existing complications. Posthospitalization, these cases as well as those inactive at first detection require secondary prevention, which includes program registration, secondary prophylaxis, and surveillance and follow-up.

Detailed procedures are also outlined for secondary prevention (Figure 24–9). Settings for case detection are indicated, and the centrality of the program register is emphasized. Multifaceted follow-up to ensure secondary prophylaxis is needed and involves the several potential

sources of care and program reinforcement. Monitoring of compliance with prophylaxis is to be ensured as feedback to the case register.

The Economic Perspective

The economics of preventive strategies for acute rheumatic fever and rheumatic heart disease favor secondary prophylaxis.[2,17,18] Pharyngitis or sore throat is among the commonest of human ailments, and the great majority of those caused by infection are viral, not bacterial, ill-

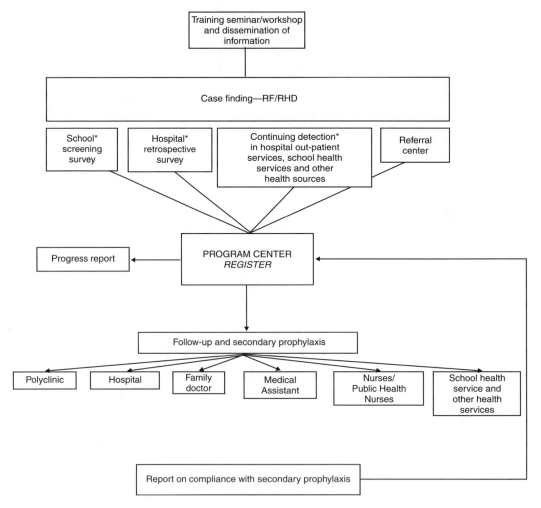

Figure 24–9 Secondary Prevention in Rheumatic Fever (RF)/Rheumatic Heart Disease (RHD), World Health Organization. *Source:* Reprinted with permission from *WHO/CVD/94.1*, pp 52, © World Health Organization.

nesses. Therefore treatment with penicillin should be restricted to those found to have Group A beta-hemolytic streptococcal pharyngitis. Even with such appropriate etiologic selection, in the absence of treatment only some 3% of these cases of pharyngitis would be expected to develop acute rheumatic fever and 1% or 2% would develop rheumatic heart disease (while perhaps an equal number will occur without antecedent clinical pharyngitis). It has

been estimated that in countries such as the United States, 200,000 or more cases of acute pharyngitis must be managed correctly—antibiotics being reserved for the appropriate cases only—to prevent 100 cases of rheumatic heart disease.[18] This circumstance was implicit in the concerns of US physicians addressed earlier by Markowitz.[6]

In another approach to evaluating costs, three alternative strategies were compared: (1) prevention of pharyngitis in the first place, (2) prevention of rheumatic fever given infection, and (3) prevention of rheumatic heart disease after rheumatic fever has developed. For each strategy, Table 24–12 shows the assumed treatment costs per case, the number of cases treated to prevent one death, and the costs per death averted.[2] Disability and duration of survival are considered in further estimates expressed in terms of disability-adjusted life-years (DALYs). (For example, 10% disability over a 10-year period would be equivalent to .10 × 10 = 1 DALY.)

If the cost of treatment for one case of Group A streptococcal pharyngitis (once identified and confirmed, although laboratory tests are not included in these costs) were $60 (US), and if 682 cases must be treated to prevent one death, then the cost of averting one death would be nearly $41,000. Reduction in disability in this example is 39 DALYs under the assumptions used, for a cost of more than $1000 for each DALY gained. The most cost-effective strategy from this point of view is the second, in which each case of rheumatic fever is once hospitalized and then treated with penicillin for 10 years, at a cost of $1380, for four cases resulting in a cost of $5520 per death averted. DALYs gained would be the same as in the first strategy, but the cost per DALY would now be reduced to $142. Prophylaxis of rheumatic heart disease refers here to surgical correction of valvular disease of the heart. This strategy would entail much higher unit cost.

Table 24–12 Cost-Effectiveness of Different Prophylactic Strategies

Treatment	Unit Cost ($)	Cases Treated To Prevent One Death[a]	Cost per Death Averted ($)	DALYs gained[b]	Cost per DALY ($)
Prevention of pharyngitis[c]	60	682	40,920	39	1,049
Prevention of RF[d]	1,380	4	5,520	39	142
Prophylaxis of RHD[e]	8,500	1.5	12,750	30	425

Note: RF, rheumatic fever; RHD, rheumatic heart disease; GASP, group A streptococcal pharyngitis; DALY, disability-adjusted life-year.

a. Assuming 100% efficacy of each treatment, approximately 500 pharyngitis cases, 100 GASP, three RF, or one severe RHD case would have to be treated to prevent one death.

b. Twenty DALYs per death averted. DALYs per disability reduction: 3 for mild carditis (10% for 30 years); 6 for moderate carditis (20% for 30 years); 10 for severe carditis (50% for 20 years). The first two prevention strategies provide a gain of 39 DALYs because these interventions reduce the disability from mild and moderate carditis in addition to reducing disability and death from severe carditis; the last strategy does not reduce disability from mild or moderate carditis.

c. Primary prevention entails one benzathine-penicillin injection each year for 10 years. Efficacy of intervention is 70%.

d. Secondary prevention entails one benzathine-penicillin injection per month for five years and assumes one hospitalization of 24 days. Efficacy of intervention is 80%.

e. Tertiary prophylaxis entails valvuloplasty or valve replacement and includes hospitalization. Efficacy of intervention is 70%. Unit costs range from $5,000 to $12,000; costs per death averted, from $7,500 to $18,000; and costs per DALY, from $250 to $600.

Source: From *Disease Control Priorities in Developing Countries*, edited by DT Jamison et al. Copyright © 1993 The International Bank for Reconstruction and Development/The World Bank. Used by permission of Oxford University Press, Inc.

Fewer cases need treatment at this advanced stage of disease to avert each death, but fewer DALYs would be gained because the disability of each case persists until effective surgical correction is achieved.[2]

A significant concern in lifelong protection of the person with rheumatic heart disease is the risk of bacterial endocarditis localized to the damaged heart valves. This condition may arise whenever bacterial infection of even a minor degree is to be anticipated, as in connection with dental procedures. Recommendations for these and related circumstances are given, for example, in a Special Report from the American Heart Association.[19]

CURRENT ISSUES

Issues for epidemiologic and public health attention now and in the near (and possibly distant) future are suggested by the foregoing review and are more or less explicit in two recent perspectives on rheumatic fever and rheumatic heart disease: "The Future of Rheumatic Fever" concludes a 1989 text by Taranta and Markowitz.[20] "Global Assessment of Rheumatic Fever and Rheumatic Heart Disease at the Close of the Century" is Kaplan's 30th Anniversary T Duckett Jones Memorial Lecture, presented in 1992[21] (see below).

Agent

To use the commonly invoked triad of agent, host, and environment in the epidemiology of infectious diseases, agent factors require attention in at least two respects: continued pursuit of the possibility of an effective vaccine against the Group A beta-hemolytic streptococcus and increased efforts to monitor the movement of relevant streptococcal strains through human populations around the world. A major obstacle to vaccine development is the evidence that streptococcal outbreaks, and perhaps local endemic isolates, differ importantly in antigenic properties, so an effective vaccine against one or more strains may confer no protection against others. These two issues are therefore interrelated. The concept of a "dynamic epidemiology of virulent Group A streptococcal infections"[21(p 1967)] proposed by Kaplan implies the need for monitoring the movement of these agents through human populations, including their routes of spread, rates of dissemination through newly exposed populations, and possible strain differences in virulence and in rheumatogenicity.

Host

Still to be firmly established are host factors that could differentiate between individuals at different risks of streptococcal pharyngitis, rheumatic fever, carditis, or progressive rheumatic heart disease. The ability to narrow the risk groups, and thereby to increase selectivity for treatment of the initial or recurrent infection or for lifelong prophylaxis, would clearly offer great potential for increasing efficiency and reducing costs for prevention programs such as those demonstrated by the WHO studies. Issues of individual susceptibility or risk and of the pathogenesis from infection to rheumatic disease are seen as continuing enigmas despite decades of investigation. From his inaugural T Duckett Jones Memorial Lecture of 1962, Paul Dudley White is quoted by Kaplan as stating: "the chain of events, biochemical and immunological, between the original streptococcal infection and the beginning of the rheumatic process is still unknown."[21(p 1971)] In Kaplan's view, the discovery of this process remains "a challenge still to be met."[21(p 1971)]

Environment

From the environmental perspective, lessons of recent years in the United States and some other countries indicate that the historical association of rheumatic fever with poverty, crowding, and ethnic minorities is an incomplete picture of the disease and that resurgence can occur under much more favorable social and economic conditions. This does not diminish concern, however, about the more traditional epidemiologic settings of rheumatic fever, which may become increasingly prominent as urban crowding progresses in many developing countries. The social, political, and organizational environment is most clearly at issue if the well-established programs for control of rheumatic fever and rheumatic heart disease are to be implemented with maximum effectiveness. As noted by Taranta and Markowitz, regardless of the longstanding questions about agent and host, "the means of control . . . are at hand."[20(p 95)]

REFERENCES

1. World Health Organization. *Rheumatic Fever and Rheumatic Heart Disease: Report of a WHO Study Group.* Geneva, Switzerland: World Health Organization; 1988. WHO Technical Report Series 764.

2. Michaud C, Trejo-Gutierrez J, Cruz C, Pearson TA. Rheumatic heart disease. In: Jamison DT, Mosley WH, Measham AR, Babadilla JL, eds. *Disease Control Priorities in Developing Countries.* Oxford, England: Oxford University Press; 1993:221–232.

3. DiSciascio G, Taranta A. Rheumatic fever in children. *Am Heart J.* 1980;99:635–658.

4. Stollerman GH. *Rheumatic Fever and Streptococcal Infection.* New York: Grune & Stratton; 1975.

5. Denny FW Jr, Houser HB. History of the Commission on Streptococcal and Staphylococcal diseases. In: Woodward TE, ed. *The Armed Forces Epidemiological Board: The Histories of the Commissions.* Washington, DC: Borden Institute, Office of the Surgeon General, Department of the Army, United States; 1994: 263–382.

6. Markowitz M. Thirty years' war against the streptococcus: a historic prospective. In: *Management of Pharyngitis in an Era of Declining Rheumatic Fever. Report of the Eighty-Sixth Ross Conference on Pediatric Research.* Columbus, Oh: Ross Laboratories; 1983: 2–7.

7. World Health Organization. *Joint WHO/ISFC Meeting on Rheumatic Fever/Rheumatic Heart Disease Control, with Emphasis on Primary Prevention.* Geneva, 7–9 September 1994. Geneva, Switzerland: World Health Organization; 1994. WHO/CVD/94.1.

8. Jones TD. The diagnosis of rheumatic fever. *JAMA.* 1944;126:481–484.

9. World Health Organization. *International Statistical Classification of Diseases and Related Health Problems: Tenth Revision.* Geneva, Switzerland: World Health Organization; 1992: 1.

10. Acheson RM. The epidemiology of acute rheumatic fever 1950–1964. *J Chronic Dis.* 1965;18:723–734.

11. American Heart Association. *1997 Heart and Stroke Statistical Update.* Dallas, Tex: American Heart Association; 1996.

12. Veasy LG, Tani LY, Hill HR. Persistence of acute rheumatic fever in the intermountain area of the United States. *J Pediatr.* 1994;124:9–16.

13. Chun LT, Reddy DV, Yim GK, Yamamoto LG. Acute rheumatic fever in Hawaii: 1966 to 1988. *Hawaii Med J.* 1992;51:206–211.

14. WHO Cardiovascular Diseases Unit and Principal Investigators. WHO programme for the prevention of rheumatic fever/rheumatic heart disease in 16 developing countries: report from Phase I (1986–1990). *Bull World Health Organ.* 1992;70:213–218.

15. Shulman ST, Amren DP, Bisno AL, Dajani AS, et al. Prevention of rheumatic fever: a statement for health professionals by the Committee on Rheumatic Fever and Infective Endocarditis of the Council on Cardiovascular Disease in the Young. *Circ.* 1984;70:1118A–1122A.

16. Majeed HA, Batnager S, Yousof AM, Khuffash F, et al. Acute rheumatic fever and the evolution of rheumatic heart disease: a prospective 12 year follow-up report. *J Clin Epidemiol.* 1992;45:871–875.

17. Strasser T, Dondog N, El Kholy A, Gharagozloo R, et al. The community control of rheumatic fever and rheumatic heart disease: report of a WHO international cooperative project. *Bull World Health Organ.* 1981; 59:285–294.

18. Strasser T. Cost-effective control of rheumatic fever in the community. *Health Policy.* 1985;5:159–164.

19. Shulman ST, Amren DP, Bisno AL, Dajani AS, et al. Prevention of bacterial endocarditis: a statement for health professionals by the Committee on Rheumatic Fever and Infective Endocarditis of the Council on Cardiovascular Disease in the Young. *Circ.* 1984; 70:1123A–1127A.

20. Taranta A, Markowitz M. *Rheumatic Fever.* 2nd ed. Dordrecht, the Netherlands: Kluwer Academic Publishers; 1989.

21. Kaplan EL. Global assessment of rheumatic fever and rheumatic heart disease at the close of the century. Influences and dynamics of populations and pathogens: a failure to realize prevention? T. Duckett Jones Memorial Lecture. *Circ.* 1993;88:1964–1972.

Chagas' Disease and Other Cardiomyopathies

SUMMARY

The cardiomyopathies are a diverse and in some instances little-understood group of often disabling or fatal conditions of the heart muscle that are likely to occur in all populations. Some cardiomyopathies are quite specific in their causation and geographic distribution; however, a leading example is Chagas' disease, a major form of cardiovascular disease throughout Central and South America. Its natural history is well established on the basis of investigations over several decades. The agent of the disease is known (*Trypanosoma cruzi*), as are the life cycles through which this agent is perpetuated either in sylvatic (wild) environments or in peridomestic human domiciliary environments. The disease is a zoonosis, that is, an infection communicable to man but involving other host species in nature. The proximity of domestic animals in the simple rural living conditions common in much of the region intensifies transmission. The insect vectors, the direct transmitters to humans, are various species of triatomine bugs, that feed on blood from humans or from a number of mammalian hosts. This disease constitutes a sign of ecologic change and destruction in many of the endemic or high-prevalence areas, since human encroachment on the environment places individuals in close contact with the natural animal reservoir and vectors of the organism. Urban migration adds to the complexity of the occurrence and control of the disease. The cardiomyopathies of unknown cause are also briefly reviewed to indicate the very limited epidemiologic and other investigation of these conditions to date and thus the inability at present to prevent them.

INTRODUCTION

Cardiomyopathies (disorders of heart muscle) comprise a diverse set of conditions of which some have been classified as idiopathic (of unknown cause) and others as specific, that is, having known causes or being associated with recognized disorders of other body systems than the cardiovascular system alone (Exhibit 25–1).[1] The heterogeneity among these conditions suggests there is no meaningful epidemiology of cardiomyopathies taken as a whole. Yet some specific diseases within this category do represent widespread public health problems with a history of epidemiologic study and for which control programs have been undertaken. And epidemiologic investigation of the idiopathic cardiomyopathies may lead to discovery of causes for subsets of this category also. Therefore what little is known about their occurrence is of potential epidemiologic interest.

One example of the specific cardiomyopathies, Chagas' disease, is classified among the

Exhibit 25–1 Classification of the Cardiomyopathies, World Health Organization/International Society and Federation of Cardiology

Idiopathic cardiomyopathies
    Dilated cardiomyopathy
    Hypertrophic cardiomyopathy
    Restrictive cardiomyopathy
    Arrhythmogenic right ventricular cardiomyopathy
    Unclassified cardiomyopathy
Specific cardiomyopathies
    Ischemic cardiomyopathy
    Valvular cardiomyopathy
    Hypertensive cardiomyopathy
    Inflammatory cardiomyopathy
    Metabolic cardiomyopathy
    General system disease
    Muscular dystrophies
    Neuromuscular disorders
    Sensitivity and toxic reactions
    Peripartal cardiomyopathy

Source: Data from Report of the 1995 World Health Organization International Society and Federation of Cardiology: Task Force on the Definition and Classification of Cardiomyopathies, *Circulation*, Vol 93, pp 841–842, © 1996.

inflammatory cardiomyopathies and provides an illustration that contrasts in many respects with the other cardiovascular diseases addressed in this book. The primary focus of this chapter is on this disease. The idiopathic cardiomyopathies are highlighted briefly thereafter.

CHAGAS' DISEASE

Clinical Course of the Individual Case

Chagas' disease may begin at any age but occurs predominantly in childhood, especially between ages one and five years.[2,3] The variations in clinical course of individual cases are illustrated schematically in Figure 25–1. It begins with an acute illness in which typically edema or swelling around one or both eyes is accompanied by skin rashes; fever; enlargement of lymph nodes, liver, and spleen; and increased heart rate. Nonspecific electrocardiographic abnormalities may be present. The gastrointestinal and central nervous systems may be involved. The acute phase can be fatal in a minority of cases, reportedly about 10% in one series.

After recovery over a period of months to years, a latent phase of 10 to 20 years follows that is termed the *asymptomatic period* or the *chronic indeterminate form* of the disease. A gradual and often unrecognized transition into the chronic phase progresses to a first stage that either continues without symptoms or is characterized by cardiac arrhythmias, dizziness, and fainting episodes. The second stage of chronic Chagas' disease is marked by the beginning of cardiomegaly (heart enlargement). In the third stage, congestive heart failure and thromboembolism occur. It appears that the onset of cardiac involvement in chronic Chagas' disease occurs most often between ages 20 and 40. There may be rapid progression to death. Though this process is usually more gradual, the majority of deaths occur at age 40 or earlier.

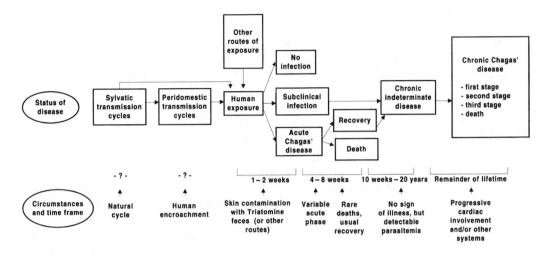

Figure 25–1 Common Features of the Course of Cardiomyopathy Due to Chagas' Disease

Background of Epidemiologic Investigation

Carlos Chagas is reported to have begun work as a malaria control officer in the interior of Minas Gerais State, Brazil, in 1907.[4] He found houses there to be heavily infested with a large blood-sucking insect, a triatomid bug, and presumed this to be a potential vector of a human pathogen, especially since contamination of the skin with its feces was common when it fed on the human host. Finding microorganisms in the triatomid feces, he sent infected bugs for laboratory examination in Rio de Janeiro, where marmosets exposed to their bites developed a new parasite. The subsequent observation of this same parasite in a blood sample from a sick child led Chagas to his first case description of this disease, published in 1909. Thus the biological agent, *Trypanosoma cruzi* (*T. cruzi*), was identified even before the disease it causes.[3] Describing the acute and chronic forms of the disease and especially its cardiac aspects in reports over the next 12 years, Chagas alternately termed it *American trypanosomiasis* and *Chagas' disease*.

The association of *T. cruzi*, transmitted primarily through triatomid bites, and the acute disease was apparently accepted more readily than its link with the chronic disease Chagas described.[3] Case reports of the acute disease arose from several countries in the Americas through the mid-1940s, but few chronic cases were reported. By the mid-1950s, however, the understanding of the disease as a potentially significant public health problem had begun to emerge, and knowledge about the disease had expanded as follows:

- More than 30 species of triatomids had been found infected with *T. cruzi* over a geographic range extending from Argentina to the southwestern United States.
- Those species adapted to conditions of human habitation readily transmitted the organism from infected domestic animals to humans.
- A developmental cycle of *T. cruzi* was found to occur in the digestive tract of the triatomid without apparent adverse effect on this vector.
- Conditions of housing in rural areas, such as use of thatch in roofing, provide a suitable niche for such species of triatomids.
- Clinical characterization of the disease was advanced by analysis of a large series of several hundred cases that included

Exhibit 25–2 Classification of Chagas' Disease, Protozoal Diseases (B50–B64)

B57 Chagas' disease

    B57.0   Acute Chagas' disease with heart involvement
    B57.1   Acute Chagas' disease without heart involvement
    B57.2   Chagas' disease (chronic) with heart involvement
    B57.3   Chagas' disease (chronic) with digestive system involvement
    B57.4   Chagas' disease (chronic) with nervous system involvement
    B57.5   Chagas' disease (chronic) with other organ involvement

---

acute Chagas' disease, chronic asymptomatic infection, and chronic Chagas' heart disease.

What remained to be investigated included the prevalence of infection in human populations in different parts of the Americas, the distribution of disease in relation to infection, and potential means of control of transmission of *T. cruzi* to humans.

By the mid-1980s the identified mammalian hosts and vector species for *T. cruzi* each numbered more than 100. Especially important among domestic animal hosts were cats, that might become infected through ingestion of either infected mice or the triatomines themselves.[4]

Population Studies: Definition and Classification

Exhibit 25–1 shows the classification of Chagas' disease among the specific, inflammatory cardiomyopathies in the scheme of the World Health Organization/International Society and Federation of Cardiology (WHO/ISFC) Task Force on the Definition and Classification of the Cardiomyopathies. In the *International Statistical Classification of Diseases and Related Health Problems, Tenth Revision* (ICD 10), Chagas' disease is classified among the infectious and parasitic diseases, as summarized in Exhibit 25–2.[5]

Clinical classification of the phases and forms of the disease as in Exhibit 25–3 indicates the wide variability of expression of *T.*

cruzi infection as currently recognized.[6] The occurrence of asymptomatic infection in the acute phase makes diagnosis in the chronic phase more difficult and also accounts for the much higher prevalence of positive serological

Exhibit 25–3 Chagas' Disease Phases and Clinical Forms

Acute phase
  Inapparent form
  Apparent form
    Cardiac
    Meningoencephalic
Chronic phase
  Indeterminate form
  Cardiac form
    Asymptomatic
    Symptomatic
      With predominance of arrhythmias
      With predominance of cardiac failure:
        compensated and decompensated
  Digestive form
    Esophagopathy
      Anectasic
      Ectasic
    Colonopathy
      Anectasic
      Ectasic
    Other organs
  Nervous form
  Form with acute exacerbations
  Others

Source: Reprinted with permission from A Prata, *Infectious Disease Clinics of North America*, Vol 8, No 1, p 65, © 1994, WB Saunders.

---

tests than of positive histories of infection in population studies of Chagas' disease.

Specific diagnosis of Chagas' disease is made by parasitological or serological means.[7] Direct parasitological examination of the blood detects circulating organisms and can be performed by microscopic examination based on several techniques: stained thin or thick smears of whole blood; fresh blood with or without centrifugation to concentrate the parasites; or special procedures to facilitate concentration and preparation of the material for examination (Strout method and buffy coat method) (Table 25–1). Indirect parasitological methods require either xenodiagnosis—that is, infection of laboratory-bred triatomines that are allowed to feed on the patient—or blood culture in laboratory media. The direct procedures can be carried out in qualified health center laboratories or specialized laboratories for parasitological diagnosis (A and B in Table 25–1). In the acute stage, direct methods can be compared for their sensitivity (ability to detect the true positive cases) against xenodiagnosis as the standard. Fewer than 60% of cases are detected by thin smear, but 90%–100% are detected by the Strout or buffy coat methods of concentration of blood samples or by blood culture. In the chronic stage, organisms may not be detectable and diagnosis depends on serologic tests. Taking serologic tests as the standard for diagnosis of chronic cases, the direct methods identify fewer than 10% of cases, and indirect methods only up to 50%. Several such tests are available, but their performance can vary widely between laboratories. For this reason, in endemic countries, laboratory networks are desirable for purposes of training, supply, and quality control. Such laboratory support is necessary for reliable monitoring of the incidence and prevalence of *T. cruzi* infection and to ensure comparability over time and between locations.

Rates of Occurrence in Populations

Because the occurrence of infection with *T. cruzi* is primarily dependent on transmission by triatomine bites, a fundamental determinant of

Table 25–1 Parasitological Methods for the Diagnosis of Chagas' Disease

		% Sensitivity[b]	
Methods	*Type of Laboratory*[a]	*Acute Stage*	*Chronic Stage*
Direct			
Thin smear	A/B	<60	<10
Thick blood smear	A/B	<70	<10
Fresh blood examination	A/B	80–90	<10
Strout	A/B	90–100	<10
Buffy coat on slide	A/B	90–100	<10
Indirect			
Xenodiagnosis	B	100	20–50
Blood culture	B	100	40–50

a. A, Health center laboratories located in areas at risk of vectorial and nonvectorial transmission (the infrastructure is that from the first level of medical care upward); B, specialized laboratories for parasitological diagnosis.

b. As compared to xenodiagnosis for the acute stage of the infection and to serological diagnosis for the chronic stage.

Source: Reprinted with permission from WHO Expert Committee, *WHO Technical Report 811*, p 38, © 1991, World Health Organization.

the occurrence of Chagas' disease is the geographic distribution of these vectors. Through Central and South America, the six most important species of triatomine vectors are distributed as shown in Figure 25–2.[7] Those species found in the United States are not adapted to the household environment and are therefore not effective vectors. Animal reservoirs of *T. cruzi* are also widespread, in both wild and domestic environments. Among many known hosts in the wild (sylvatic) setting, opossums and armadillos are most important, whereas dogs, cats, and rodents contribute most as host species in the peridomestic setting. The frequencies of *T. cruzi* infection in samples from these animal populations have been studied in several countries but are difficult to compare due to differences in laboratory methods.

Data on the occurrence of Chagas' disease are essentially limited to cross-sectional surveys. Human infection was thought to be distributed as shown in Figure 25–3 as of the mid-1980s.[7] Although data were limited, it was estimated that one-fourth of the population of the endemic countries, or 90 of 360 million persons, were at risk of infection and some 16–18 million were infected. If 30% of human infections are clinically apparent, then some 5 million persons are overtly affected and more than 10 million have subclinical disease.

Country-specific data are presented for the endemic countries, with persistent *T. cruzi*

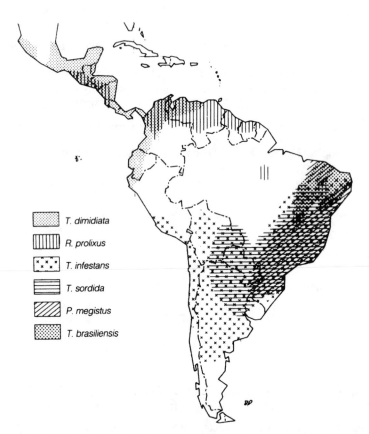

T. dimidiata

R. prolixus

T. infestans

T. sordida

P. megistus

T. brasiliensis

Figure 25–2 Geographical Distribution of the Six Major Triatomine Vectors of Chagas' Disease. *Source:* Adapted with permission from Z Brener and Z Andrade, eds, Trypanosoma cruzie doenca de Chagas (*T. cruzi* and Chagas' disease). Rio de Janeiro, Guanabara Koogan, p 83, © 1979, Zigman Brener.

Figure 25–3 Geographical Distribution of Human *T. cruzi* Infection in the Americas. *Source:* Reprinted with permission from WHO Expert Committee, *WHO Technical Report 811*, p 29, © 1991, World Health Organization.

infections in Table 25–2, in which populations are grouped as follows: Group I countries have high prevalence of *T. cruzi* infections and high infestation rates of houses with triatomines. Group II countries have evidence of transmission within the household and clear association between *T. cruzi* infection and indications of Chagas' disease, but they lack control programs. Group III countries have evidence of transmission within the household but no clear link with disease, though acute-phase Chagas' disease is common. Group IV countries have *T. cruzi* infections that are enzootic (persistent in host animal species) but only infrequent human infections (data not shown).[8] By country, the exposed population ranges from 10% to 68% of the total. Even wider variation in infection rates is apparent, from 1% to 81%, although in all countries of groups I–III the more typical prevalence is between 10% and 30%. Comparison of the exposure and infection rates indicates large differences between countries. For example, in Venezuela, 68% of the population is exposed but only 11% of those exposed are infected, whereas in Chile, 15% of the population is exposed but 81% of those are infected. Data from Mexico and Nicaragua were insufficient for inclusion in the table.

Table 25–2 Prevalence of Human *T. cruzi* Infection in Latin America, 1980–1985

	Population at Risk		Population Infected	
Endemic Countries	No. (000s)	As % of Total Population	No. (000s)	As % of Population at Risk
Group I (High *T. cruzi* prevalence and triatomine infestation; control)				
Argentina	6,900	33%	2,640	38%
Brazil	41,054	32%	6,340	26%
Chile	1,800	15%	1,460	81%
Ecuador	3,823	41%	30	1%
Honduras	1,824	42%	300	16%
Paraguay	1,475	45%	397	27%
Peru	6,676	34%	643	10%
Uruguay	975	33%	37	4%
Venezuela	11,392	68%	1,200	11%
Group II (Intradomiciliary transmission; clear clinical correlations)				
Bolivia	1,800	30%	500	28%
Columbia	3,000	10%	900	30%
Costa Rica	1,112	45%	130	12%
Mexico[a]	—	—	—	
Group III (Intradomiciliary transmission; unclear clinical correlations)				
El Salvador	146	43%	322	15%
Guatemala	4,022	52%	730	18%
Nicaragua	—	—	—	—
Panama	898	42%	220	24%
Total	86,897	25%	15,849	18%

Note: A small number of cases has been reported from the following countries: Belize, Trinidad and Tobago, and the United States.

a. No data available.

Source: Reprinted with permission from *Weekly Epidemiological Record*, p 259, © 1990, World Health Organization.

Risks in Individuals

Social and Environmental Conditions

Factors associated with high prevalence of *T. cruzi* infections were summarized in the WHO Expert Committee report, *Control of Chagas Disease* (see Table 25–3).[7] The "social risk factors" mix environmental and personal characteristics that increase the risk of infection and contribute to both differences in rates among populations and risks of infection for particular individuals. The implications of these factors for control measures are addressed below.

An aspect of transmission of *T. cruzi* noted above that constitutes a specific risk factor for exposed humans is the presence in the living area of domestic dogs and cats.[9] At least one triatomine vector species (*Triatoma infestans*)

Table 25–3 Social Risk Factors for *T. cruzi* Infection

Social Risk Factors	Variables To Be Defined
Lack of stability; temporary nature of settlement	Modes of crop culture Agricultural practices and crop cycles Housing/land ownership
Lack of land ownership	Legal/cultural and economic aspects
High degree of human movement/migration	Domestic objects and clothing of migrants: organization, storage, and disposal Kind of occupation: seasonal workers, day laborers Distance between home and workplace
Low or subsistence income	Patterns of production; occupation; temporary income Future aspirations
Low level of hygienic practices	Future aspirations Knowledge of disease transmission Supply of and demand for public health services Adequacy of furniture and fitments
Low education level; inappropriate practices and beliefs related to modes of transmission	Supply of and demand for public educational services Knowledge, attitudes, and practices concerning health protection Future aspirations
Housing propitious for colonization	Housing technology Motivation for settlement Family composition
Lack of insecticide use	Regularity of house spraying Household use of domestic insecticide High cost or difficulty of delivery of chemical products
Presence of infected domestic animals	Cultural habits, beliefs, and knowledge of hygiene
Animal/storage shelters in the peridomestic area and inside houses	Knowledge of construction technology Cultural/traditional habits
Lack of low-price housing and construction materials	Industrial production Retailers in the area Autochthonous construction techniques
Isolation or difficult accessibility of houses	Existence of roads Public transportation

Source: Reprinted with permission from WHO Expert Committee, *WHO Technical Report 811*, p 29, © 1991, World Health Organization.

feeds preferentially on canine hosts, and infected animals therefore increase the probability that triatomines in the dwelling area will become infected. Cats are also highly attractive to triatomines, and it appears that infected dogs and cats together have an additive effect on the prevalence of infection among triatomines in the household. Presumably the risk to humans is thereby increased also.

Blood Transfusion as a Mode of Transmission

In addition to the social-environmental characteristics identified above, additional factors increase the risk of infection under specific circumstances. Blood transfusion is a major example, as shown in Table 25–4 for Group I and II countries.[10] Because poor rural-to-urban migrants—a group with high probability of being infected—often live in conditions that favor sale of their blood, blood supplies are also a source of infection in endemic countries. Such population movements in Central and South America occurring in the 1970s and 1980s are considered the basis for transformation of Chagas' disease from an almost exclusively rural to an urban health problem. The data shown indicate that blood bank samples were not uncommonly positive, with frequencies as high as 20.5% in some localities even in the 1960s and

Table 25–4 Prevalence of *T. Cruzi*-Infected Blood Banks in Selected Countries

Country Group	No. of Samples Tested	% Positive
Group I		
Argentina:		
Buenos Aires (1970)	97,308	6.0
Santiago del Estero (1966)	1,700	20.5
Córdoba (1982)	2,441	8.4
Brazil:		
Brasilia (1984)	2,413	14.6
Rio (1979)	3,501	3.9
Sáo Paulo (1982)	56,902	2.9
Chile:		
Santiago (1983)	214	3.7
Vicuna (1983)	62	14.5
Ecuador:		
Guayaquil (1961)	1,054	3.2
Honduras:		
Tegucigalpa	50	28.0
Paraguay:		
Asunción (1972)	562	11.3
Peru:		
Tacna (1972)	329	12.9
Uruguay:		
Endemic areas (1972)	329	5.5
Venezuela:		
Valencia (1973)	733	10.3
Caracas (1973)	98,620	5.1
Group II		
Bolivia:		
Santacruz (1983)	268	63.0
Colombia	—	—
Costa Rica:		
San José	221	7.6
Mexico:		
Queretaro (1984)	200	16.5

Source: Reprinted with permission from A Moncayo, Chagas' Disease: Epidemiology and Prospects for Interruption of Transmission in the Americas, *World Health Statistics Quarterly*, Vol 45, p 278, © 1992, World Health Organization.

early 1970s. The need for protection of blood supplies is clear from these data.

Possible Oral Transmission

A second route of infection other than triatomine bites has been suggested by at least one outbreak of acute Chagas' disease.[11] In that outbreak, 26 persons became ill 7 to 22 days following a meeting on a farm in rural Brazil. Xenodiagnosis of *T. cruzi* infection was positive in 9 of 14 patients tested; blood examination demonstrated the *T. cruzi* in two cases; and acute Chagas' cardiomyopathy was demonstrated in the one fatal case, at autopsy. Triatomines were not found in the two farmhouses to which participants were exposed. The fact that most participants took meals in common during the meeting had suggested contamination of food prior to serving. However, exceptions to this pattern of exposure pointed elsewhere, to sugar cane juice that could have become contaminated by the secretions of infected opossums in the area after crushing of the cane or by crushed triatomines carrying *T. cruzi* acquired from the opossums. This epidemiologic investigation provided strong circumstantial evidence for oral transmission of the agent, and supporting evidence has been reported in previous field and laboratory research.

Congenital Transmission

Another series of factors increasing the risk of *T. cruzi* infection relates specifically to women. For example, in Santa Cruz, Bolivia, where 54% of pregnant women are seropositive, epidemiologic investigation has demonstrated the occurrence of congenital transmission of the agent to the offspring and perhaps second-generation transmission from infected daughters to their offspring, in turn.[12] Previous reports suggested that 5% of newborns were congenitally infected in some series. Detection and treatment of the infected woman before pregnancy could in principle prevent such transmission, but many obstacles tend to prevent this, especially among less educated women.

Susceptibility of Immune-Compromised Persons

Finally, immunosuppression increases the risk of *T. cruzi* infections, as it does susceptibility to infection in general.[13] In Central and South America, immune-compromised patients are especially at risk if blood products are used to treat their underlying condition, such as in renal transplantation or leukemia.

Implications for Prevention and Treatment: Individuals and Populations

Rationale for Control Programs

The rationale for prevention of Chagas' disease includes several elements: the sometimes fatal outcome of the acute case; the inaccessibility of treatment for a large proportion of infected persons; the frequent occurrence of subclinical infections that remain undetected and untreated, thus contributing to maintenance of the transmission cycle; and the large and increasing numbers of persons exposed to the risk of infection. This latter factor is due to population growth, migration into periurban and urban areas by infected persons from rural settings, and the likely continued incursion of human settlement into areas initially free of human disease but harboring active sylvatic transmission cycles based on the existing animal reservoirs.

Theoretical Approaches

To achieve control of this disease requires effective measures to control the insect vector through residual or long-acting insecticide spraying and other chemical means; improving housing construction to prevent vector colonization; interrupting transmission through contaminated blood and blood products; early diagnosis of congenital infections; and protection against other less common routes of infection, such as laboratory accidents and organ transplantation.[7] Detailed consideration of the elements of control programs for this disease is presented in the WHO Expert Committee report, *Control of Chagas Disease.* Beginning with a local situation and resources analysis, the planning process requires taking account of existing data, obtaining supplemental current and site-specific information, and identifying needed and available resources. Strategies differ among urban centers, rural concentrations of population, and scattered populations, since modes of transmission, conditions of housing, logistics of area coverage, and approaches for follow-up surveillance differ in each setting. Operational phases are distinguished as an "attack phase," such as mass house spraying, and a "surveillance phase," which depends heavily on community participation to monitor the presence of vectors. Cost-effectiveness evaluation is recommended also, and a budget framework is available for planning. Ideally, programs are integrated with local community workers in primary health care, in keeping with a health planning strategy widely advocated for developing countries. Health and other public sector activities relevant to the program should be linked with those in private sectors. Responsibility should be allocated appropriately to each level of organizational structure. Community participation is a prominent aspect of program planning and implementation.

Case Examples

Against this theoretical view of program planning for control of Chagas' disease, examples have been reported by several investigators. For example, García-Zapata and Marsden presented in 1993 a detailed account of the implementation of a control program in Mambaí, Goiás, Brazil, beginning in 1974.[14] Preliminary studies led to mass application of insecticides in households in 1980, and post-treatment surveillance began in 1981. Stations for submitting captured triatomine specimens multiplied and became more convenient to places of residence by 1984, and in 1988 a simplified surveillance kit, the "minimal surveillance unit," was put in use for subsequent household monitoring of reinfestation. As described by the authors:

This latter unit . . . consists of an attractive educational calendar 42 cm × 30.5 cm. . . . The calendar, containing a warning about triatomines and a request for their collection, was hung on the wall of each participant's home above the home's most important blood source (the conjugal bed), so that triatomine bugs could defecate on its front and back surfaces after feeding on the largest available blood mass. Attached to the calendar was a self-sealing plastic bag labeled with the name and address of the head of the household. . . . Each home's residents were asked to put all the triatomine bugs they captured in the bag and take them to a collection post . . . so that workers could respond with appropriate fumigation.[14(p 266)]

Other collecting devices designed to trap bugs outside the dwelling were also used. Factors in the operational success of the program were discussed in detail and indicate the practical complexities of such a program.

A second program was reported in 1994 from the area of Minas Gerais, Brazil, where Chagas first identified the disease.[15] In this case epidemiologic surveillance had included serological surveys in 1978 and 1987 that indicated a marked reduction in prevalence of *T. cruzi* infections as well as reduced frequency of capture of vector species. Figure 25–4 illustrates the lower prevalence of infection in each of seven municipalities monitored over this period. Data collected over the course of this program indicated marked shifts in the household infestation rates with specific triatomine species. The initially predominant species, *Triatoma infestans*, was in effect replaced by *T. sordida* in the exterior environs of dwellings but not in the interior. Accordingly, transmission of *T. cruzi* was substantially reduced by the program. The increase in *T. sordida* captures around dwellings was attributed to deforestation in the vicinity. In

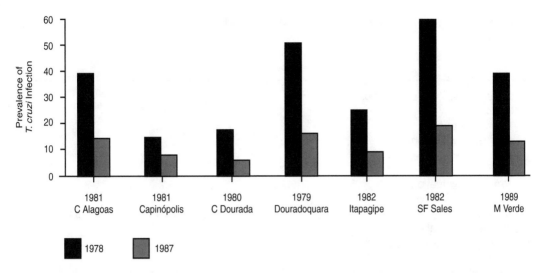

Figure 25–4 Human Prevalences of *T. cruzi* Infection in Seven Study Municipalities in Minas Gerais, Brazil, in 1978 and 1987, as Indicated by Serologic Surveys. The most recent year of *T. infestans* capture in each municipality is shown below the bars. *Source:* Reprinted with permission from L Diotaiuti, *Bulletin of the Pan American Health Organization*, Vol 28, No 3, p 215, © 1994, Pan American Health Organization.

many endemic areas, deforestation is a problem that continues to bring the human population into close proximity to the disease vectors.

A leading success story in control programs for Chagas' disease was reported in 1994 in connection with the Southern Cone Countries Initiative, in which Argentina, Bolivia, Brazil, Chile, Paraguay, and Uruguay participate.[16] The goal is to eliminate transmission of *T. cruzi* through both vectorial and transfusion routes. From the program beginning in mid-1991 to late 1992, marked declines in infection rates were observed in Uruguay, which was scheduled to be declared free of these transmission routes by 1995. At the same time, issues in the evaluation of Chagas' disease control programs were addressed in a report on a quasi-experimental evaluation model with data from both cross-sectional and cohort monitoring of three communities in Brazil.[17] The advantage of the cohort approach in reaching sound conclusions was demonstrated. Table 25–5 illustrates the cohort analysis of the comparison of national with local survey results. The effect appeared substantial on a cross-sectional basis for those

age two to six years, with decreases from 6.9% to 2.4% (a 65% decrease) in the control area, from 15.5% to 5.7% (a 63.2% decrease) in the five-year intervention area, and from 19.0% to 1.0% (a 94.7% decrease) in the 10-year intervention area. Viewed from a cohort perspective, persons in the 10-year intervention community alone experienced a marked decrease in infection rates, whereas the other intervention community had insufficient time to exhibit any benefit. It was emphasized that the evaluation of such programs requires extensive investment of time for data collection and analysis concerning the appropriate health indicators. This experience is in some respects reminiscent of the community trials in coronary heart disease risk factor reductions addressed in Chapter 21.

OTHER CARDIOMYOPATHIES

As noted at the beginning of this chapter, cardiomyopathies are classified in relation to current views of their causation (specific or idiopathic) and, for those of unknown cause, simply by their anatomic form. The ICD 10

Table 25–5 Relative Reduction in *T. cruzi* Infection Rates in the Study Areas, Minas Gerais, Brazil, 1987

	Age Group (Years)	% Positive	δ (%)
Cross-sectional, for 2–6-year-olds:			
Control area			
National survey	2–6	6.9	65.2↓
Program evaluation	2–6	2.4	
Intervention-5 area			
National survey	2–6	15.5	63.2↓
Program evaluation	2–6	5.7	
Intervention-10 area			
National survey	2–6	19.0	94.7↓
Program evaluation	2–6	1.0	
Relative to 2–6-year-olds' cohort:			
Control area			
National survey[a]	2–6	6.9	89.9↑
Program evaluation[b]	7–14	13.1	
Intervention-5 area			
National survey[a]	2–6	15.5	248.4↑
Program evaluation[b]	7–14	54.0	
Intervention-10 area			
National survey[a]	2–6	19.0	52.6↓
Program evaluation[b]	7–14	9.0	

a. For 1975–1980.

b. For 1987.

Source: Reprinted with permission from *WHO Bulletin,* Vol 72, No 5, p 726, © 1994, World Health Organization.

classifies the cardiomyopathies as shown in Exhibit 25–4.[5] Correspondence with the classification in Exhibit 25–1 is limited, but the system of ICD 10 represents an advance in detail over previous editions and may help to differentiate the various classes of cardiomyopathies in future data. For the present, the paucity of information on the cardiomyopathies generally is indicated by the current Chartbook of the National Heart, Lung and Blood Institute, which presents overall mortality data (for 1992) by sex and race (Black/White) and by age, sex, and race (Figures 25–5 and 25–6).[18] For both males and females, death rates from cardiomyopathy were approximately twice as great for Blacks as for Whites at every age from 35–39 to 80–84. Little further detail was provided by the

Chartbook except to note 33,000 hospital discharges, 484,000 physician office visits, and 26,214 deaths attributed to this group of conditions in the United States in 1993. When reviewed in the mid-1980s, US data from 1970–1982 indicated an upward trend in frequency of idiopathic cardiomyopathy, but the possible effects of changes in diagnostic criteria and related factors could not be assessed.[19] Issues in the validity of death certificate diagnosis of cardiomyopathy, relative frequency of hospitalization for this condition, and other factors critical to assessing frequency of occurrence in different populations or over time are all unresolved. Few epidemiologic studies have been reported, but some information is available concerning occurrence of idiopathic cardiomyopathy in

Exhibit 25–4 Classification of Cardiomyopathies

142 Cardiomyopathy	142.8 Other cardiomyopathies
142.0 Dilated cardiomyopathy	142.9 Cardiomyopathy, unspecified
142.1 Obstructive hypertrophic cardiomyopathy	143 Cardiomyopathy in diseases classified elsewhere
142.2 Other hypertrophic cardiomyopathy	
142.3 Endomyocardial (eosinophilic) disease	143.0 Cardiomyopathy in infectious and parasitic diseases classified elsewhere
142.4 Endocardial fibroelastosis	
142.5 Other restrictive cardiomyopathy	143.1 Cardiomyopathy in metabolic diseases
142.6 Alcoholic cardiomyopathy	143.2 Cardiomyopathy in nutritional diseases
142.7 Cardiomyopathy due to drugs and other external agents	143.8 Cardiomyopathy in other diseases classified elsewhere

infants, youth, and the elderly. Other than hypertension in older persons, no predisposing factors to idiopathic cardiomyopathy have been identified. The importance of this condition, especially the dilated form, reflects its poor prognosis; for example, among young persons there is 40% to 50% mortality within two years of diagnosis.[20] For this reason, this condition has become the basis for a significant proportion, perhaps one-half, of all heart transplants.

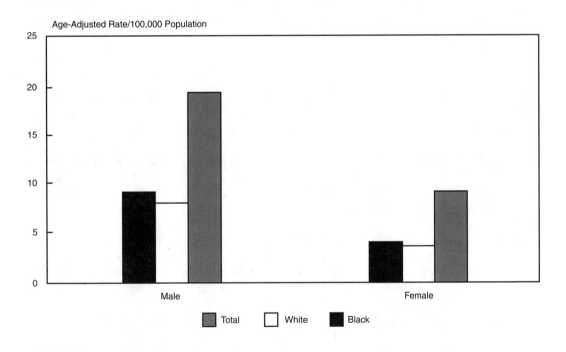

Figure 25–5 Death Rates for Cardiomyopathy by Race and Sex, United States, 1992. *Source:* Reprinted from *Morbidity & Mortality: 1996 Chartbook on Cardiovascular, Lung and Blood Disease*, p 35, 1996 National Heart, Lung and Blood Institute, National Institutes of Health.

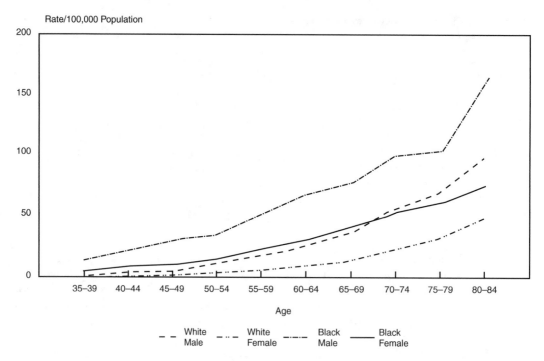

Figure 25–6 Death Rates for Cardiomyopathy by Age, Race, and Sex, United States, 1992. *Source:* Reprinted from *Morbidity & Mortality: 1996 Chartbook on Cardiovascular, Lung and Blood Disease,* p 35, © 1996 National Heart, Lung and Blood Institute, National Institutes of Health.

CURRENT ISSUES

Chagas' Disease

Control of Transmission of T. cruzi in Endemic Areas

The foremost issue concerning Chagas' disease, the leading cause of cardiomyopathy in the Western hemisphere, is whether its control can be achieved on a large scale. The potential certification of Uruguay as a disease-free area seems promising, yet the obstacles to reaching that objective and maintaining control are formidable. A review of the public health problem of the trypanosomiases on a worldwide basis that appeared in 1979 noted the complexities: "Thus Chagas' disease presents, not a stable pattern of infection and pathogenicity, but a dynamic situation in which vectors, infection rates, and pathogenicity appear to be in a state

of flux."[21(p 11)] Of particular concern was the potential impact of commercial deforestation and continued soil degradation in many areas of Latin America. Consequences of these ecological changes are population movement, entry to new areas of exposure to triatomines with their existing sylvatic cycles of *T. cruzi* transmission, and transport of infected triatomines along with population movement to other rural areas and increasingly into cities. Thus even those areas in which effective control has been achieved may be subject to reinfestation and reestablishment of human transmission.

Prevention of Transfusion-Acquired Cases

The second issue is the continuing need for protection of the blood supply to minimize the risk of transfusion-related cases of Chagas' disease.[22] Because lack of treatment early in the infection leads to persistent circulation of the parasite in the blood in 50% of those infected, the risk of transmission through contaminated blood can be high when infected persons are donors, depending on the infectivity of the organism under these circumstances. Perhaps between 15% and 50% of transfusion-exposed persons become infected. It is estimated that 10,000 to 20,000 cases of transfusion-acquired *T. cruzi* infections occur each year in Brazil alone. Serologic screening of blood is proposed to reduce the risk of this mode of transmission in endemic countries. Because false-negative tests would still allow some contaminated blood to be used, use of two tests is therefore recommended. Blood samples can also be treated with crystal violet as an anti-trypanosomal agent so that the blood supply need not be seriously compromised even if a high proportion of donors are seropositive, as in many endemic areas. The extent to which these procedures are actually used is in some doubt, however. Donors themselves may be screened by serologic testing. Problems with this approach include the false-positive rate of screening, which could require discarding an unacceptably high proportion of blood units. In nonendemic areas, the expected frequency of infected donors is very much less than in endemic areas, and screening becomes impractical because of the very low yield. Truly positive cases are a smaller proportion of those with positive tests when the prevalence of the condition in the population at large is very low. Instead, screening by residential and illness histories among persons known to have lived or traveled in endemic areas may suffice. Such a method in the United States, for example, might be adequate to identify and exclude suspect blood donors.

The Question of Chagas' Disease in the United States

Finally, because the United States is the destination of many immigrants from Central and South America, the question has been raised whether Chagas' disease exists in the United States as an undiagnosed form of cardiomyopathy.[23] It has been concluded that virtually the only cases of Chagas' disease in the United States occur among immigrants from Latin America infected before migration. Still, the number of such infected persons may be on the order of 75,000 or more, most of them unrecognized or misdiagnosed as idiopathic dilated cardiomyopathy or coronary heart disease. Although triatomine vectors of *T. cruzi* are found in the United States, they exhibit behaviors different from those to the south. Further, because of different housing conditions, vector transmission of the agent is considered very unlikely in most settings. Transfusion of contaminated blood is a more likely mode of transmission. According to a 1993 account, three vector-transmitted cases, two transfusion-related cases, and six laboratory-acquired infections with *T. cruzi* had been reported in the United States.[24] The fact that the transfusion-associated cases occurred in immunosuppressed patients suggests both the special risk to such patients and the likelihood that their cases of acute Chagas' disease were much more carefully investigated than usual, and therefore many more undetected infections may be presumed to have taken place.

Other Cardiomyopathies

The natural history of the cardiomyopathies remains largely unknown, as indicated by the WHO/ISFC Task Force in proposing its classification scheme outlined in Exhibit 25–1.[1] The classification was offered as a means "to bridge the gap between the known and the unknown."[1(p 841)] The WHO Expert Committee report indicated that prevention of neither dilated nor hypertrophic cardiomyopathies is currently possible. Further, case detection for eosinophilic or restrictive cardiomyopathy requires recognition of an abnormal appearance of blood cells during routine school examinations, not a highly likely occurrence.[2] The current priority is for case identification over large geographic areas and support for epidemiologic, clinical, and laboratory investigations of cases toward better understanding of their natural history. To the present, investigation has been impeded by inadequacies of terminology and limited methods for study. A standard classification, such as those of the WHO/ISFC Task Force and the ICD 10, should permit progress to be made. As suggested in the mid-1980s,[19] validation studies of death certificates and hospital discharge diagnoses should be undertaken, and the recent classification schemes will make such studies more fruitful than they could have been previously.

REFERENCES

1. Report of the 1995 World Health Organization/International Society and Federation of Cardiology Task Force on the Definition and Classification of Cardiomyopathies. *Circ.* 1996;93:841–842.

2. World Health Organization. *Report of a WHO Expert Committee: Cardiomyopathies.* Geneva, Switzerland: World Health Organization; 1984. WHO Technical Report Series 697.

3. Laranja FS, Dias E, Nobrega G, Miranda A. Chagas disease: a clinical, epidemiologic, and pathologic study. *Circ.* 1956;14:1035–1060.

4. Miles MA. The epidemiology of South American trypanosomiasis—biochemical and immunological approaches and their relevance to control. *Trans Royal Soc Trop Med Hyg.* 1983;77:5–23.

5. World Health Organization. *International Statistical Classification of Diseases and Related Health Problems. Tenth Revision.* Geneva, Switzerland: World Health Organization; 1992: 1.

6. Prata A. Chagas disease. *Infect Dis Clin North Am.* 1994;8:61–76.

7. World Health Organization. *Report of a WHO Expert Committee: Control of Chagas Disease.* Geneva, Switzerland: World Health Organization; 1991. WHO Technical Report Series 811.

8. Chagas disease. *Weekly Epidemiol Rec.* 1990;65:257–264.

9. Gürtler RE, Cécere MC, Petersen RM, Rubel DN, et al. Chagas disease in north-west Argentina: association between *Trypanosoma cruzi* parasitemia in dogs and cats and infection rates in domestic *Triatoma infestans*. *Trans Royal Soc Trop Med Hyg.* 1993;87:12–15.

10. Moncayo A. Chagas disease: epidemiology and prospects for interruption of transmission in the Americas. *World Health Stat Q.* 1992;45:276–279.

11. Shikanai-Yasuda MA, Marcondes CB, Guedes A, Siqueira CS, et al. Possible oral transmission of acute Chagas disease in Brazil. *Revista Instituto de Medicina Tropical de São Paulo.* 1991;3:351–357.

12. Azogue E. Women and congenital Chagas disease in Santa Cruz, Bolivia: epidemiological and sociocultural aspects. *Soc Sci Med.* 1993;37:503–511.

13. Leiguarda R, Taratuto AL, Roncoroni A, Berthier M, et al. Acute CNS infection by *Trypanosoma cruzi* (Chagas disease) in immunosuppressed patients. *Neurol.* 1988;38(suppl 1):65.

14. García-Zapata MTA, Marsden PD. Chagas disease: control and surveillance through use of insecticides and community participation in Mambaí, Goiás, Brazil. *Bull Pan Am Health Organ.* 1993;27:265–279.

15. Diotaiuti L, Ribeiro de Paula O, Falcão PL, Pinto Dias JC. Evaluation of the Chagas disease vector control program in Minas Gerais, Brazil, with special reference to *Triatoma sordida. Bull Pan Am Health Organ.* 1994;28:211–219.

16. Elimination of transmission of Chagas disease in southernmost Latin America. WHO notes and news. *World Health Forum.* 1994;15:299–300.

17. Carneiro M, Antunes CMF. A quasi-experimental epidemiological model for evaluating public health programmes: efficacy of a Chagas disease control programme in Brazil. *Bull World Health Organ.* 1994;72:721–728.

18. US Dept of Health and Human Services. *Morbidity & Mortality: 1996 Chartbook on Cardiovascular, Lung and Blood Diseases.* Bethesda, Md: National Heart, Lung and Blood Institute, National Institutes of Health; 1996.

19. Gillum RF. Idiopathic cardiomyopathy in the United States, 1970–1982. *Am Heart J.* 1996;111:752–754.

20. Caforio ALP. Idiopathic dilated cardiomyopathy. *Br Med J.* 1990;300:890–891.

21. Ormerod WE. Human and animal trypanosomiases and world public health problems. *Pharmacol Ther.* 1979;6:1–40.

22. Schmuñis GA. *Trypanosoma cruzi*, the etiologic agent of Chagas disease: status in the blood supply in endemic and nonendemic countries. *Transfus.* 1991; 31:547–557.

23. Milei J, Mautner B, Storino R, Sanchez JA, et al. Does Chagas disease exist as an undiagnosed form of cardiomyopathy in the United States? *Am Heart J.* 1992; 123:1732–1735.

24. Kirchhoff LV. American trypanosomiasis (Chagas disease)—a tropical disease now in the United States. *N Eng J Med.* 1993;329:639–644.

Congenital Heart Disease

SUMMARY

The congenital heart diseases comprise numerous specific malformations of the heart and great vessels communicating with the respiratory and systemic circulation. These arise principally through disorders of organogenesis during the earliest weeks of gestation. A wide spectrum of severity, from undetectable to rapidly fatal conditions are included, some of which cause intrauterine death and others that are fully compatible with life. For the liveborn affected infant, surgical intervention to correct anatomic derangements has become a highly effective mode of treatment where it is accessible. As a result of this success, increasing numbers of persons with corrected defects now survive into the adult years. Issues therefore arise about potential risks of affected offspring as well as personal risks of the affected mother in pregnancy. Both men and women with the residual effects of congenital heart disease or its surgical repair are at increased risk of vascular and other complications in adulthood and therefore represent a population in special need of medical recognition. Interest in causation of congenital heart disease has focused largely on familial and genetic factors, although increasing attention is given to environmental factors also. Potential value of innovative approaches to classification of these defects based not on their anatomic location but on their embryogenesis may offer new opportunities for fruitful investigation. Collaboration between epidemiologists and molecular geneticists may be especially opportune in this field.

INTRODUCTION

A broad outline of the time course of congenital heart disease—really, diseases—in the individual case is presented first. This provides a useful background for discussion of four aspects of congenital heart diseases that are basic to their epidemiologic investigation: (1) the diversity of specific defects of the heart and great vessels, which raises issues of heterogeneity of causation; (2) their low rates of occurrence, which necessitates large population bases for their study; (3) temporal aspects of development and detection of these "birth defects," not limited in their investigation to the perinatal period but beginning in the early weeks of gestation and extending throughout adult life; and (4) differences in definition of source populations for study and methods of case ascertainment that limit comparability of studies between populations or over time. Reference to a number of major epidemiologic studies in this area, selective illustration of results of these and other investigations, and discussion of aspects of congenital heart defects bearing on both intervention and future research are included to

585

provide a useful introduction to this complex and challenging component of cardiovascular diseases.

Clinical Course of the Individual Case

In Figure 26–1, common features of the course of congenital heart disease are shown schematically from conception through adult life. While no one condition among the many in this mixed category can be taken as typical, the broad aspects may be characterized as shown. Some defects are determined at conception, based on potent genetic factors from single genes to chromosomal abnormalities. Under the combined genetic and environmental influences on the fetus, development of the heart and great vessels proceeds early and is especially vulnerable to disturbance between the 18th and the 30th to 60th day of gestation.[1] Some defects are already detectable by fetal echocardiography by the 12th to 14th weeks. Anomalous fetal cardiac development represents a wealth of research on structural and functional development of the heart at levels of genetics, molecular and cell biology, and embryology.[2] Major malformations are commonly found in products of conception lost before term birth. Some conditions not incompatible with intrauterine life lead to severe dysfunction at birth with rapidly ensuing death. At the opposite extreme are cases of such a mild degree that they are not recognized and

may be undetectable at birth and for several years subsequently. In between are recognized cases in which judgment is required about whether to intervene surgically in the hope of effective repair. Advances in such surgery have led to establishment of adequate circulatory function in large numbers of cases. Whether through surgical correction, through spontaneous resolution (as with some septal defects), or despite continued functional limitation, a great many cases of congenital heart disease now continue through childhood, adolescence, and into adult life. Reproductive potential then becomes an issue due to concern about the effects of pregnancy on an affected female and, in the case of any affected parent, about the risk of the same or another congenital defect in the offspring. Several personal and social issues such as employability and insurability often require assistance. Finally, late-occurring health complications of several kinds may also arise, and these warrant some vigilance throughout life.

Diversity of Specific Defects

Congenital heart diseases comprise a number of specific conditions. These are primarily structural defects of the heart and great vessels. Their identification and classification depends on the performance and interpretation of diagnostic procedures, which may differ from one setting to another but have advanced markedly

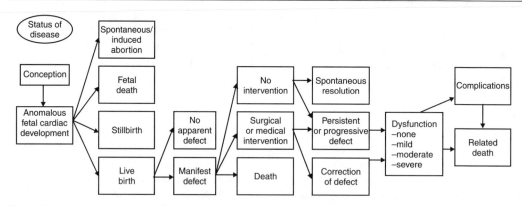

Figure 26–1 Common Features of the Course of Congenital Heart Disease

in recent decades. The extent of diversity among particular malformations is indicated in Table 26–1, a list of several diagnoses with their relative frequencies as observed in a classic series of cases studied by the New England Regional Infant Cardiac Program and reported in 1980.[3] Of the 19 specific anomalies listed, none except ventricular septal defect constituted more than 10% of the total. However, the first five conditions on the list constituted one-half the total. Clearly, the study of congenital heart diseases is complicated by the multiple condi-

tions as they are conventionally identified and distinguished.

Low Rates of Occurrence

The "diagnostic frequencies" in Table 26–1 call attention to measures of frequency of congenital defects, which pose some particular problems. The frequency of occurrence of congenital conditions is typically indexed to the total number of live births in the source population during the birth interval of the cases. The

Table 26–1 Diagnostic Frequencies of Infants, by Specific Diagnosis of Congenital Heart Defects, 1969–1977

Diagnosis	Infants No.	%	1969–1974, N = 2,381 No./1,000 Live Births	1975–1977, N = 1,236 No./1,000 Live Births
Ventricular septal defect	374	(15.7)	0.345	*0.462*
D-Transposition of great arteries	236	(9.9)	0.218	*0.206*
Tetralogy of Fallot	212	(8.9)	0.196	*0.258*
Coarctation of aorta	179	(7.5)	0.165	*0.233*
Hypoplastic left heart syndrome	177	(7.4)	0.163	*0.166*
Patent ductus arteriosus	146	(6.1)	0.135	*0.141*
Endocardial cushion defect	119	(5.0)	0.110	*0.137*
Heterotaxias (dextro-, meso-, levo-, asplenia)	95	(4.0)	0.088	*0.103*
Pulmonary stenosis	79	(3.3)	0.073	*0.074*
Pulmonary atresia with intact ventricular septum	75	(3.1)	0.069	*0.074*
Atrial septal defect secundum	70	(2.9)	0.065	*0.092*
Total anomalous pulmonary venous return	63	(2.6)	0.058	*0.056*
Myocardial disease	61	(2.6)	0.056	*0.045*
Tricuspid atresia	61	(2.6)	0.056	*0.058*
Single ventricle	58	(2.4)	0.054	*0.103*
Aortic stenosis	45	(1.9)	0.041	*0.040*
Double-outlet right ventricle	35	(1.5)	0.032	*0.034*
Truncus arteriosus	33	(1.4)	0.030	*0.043*
L-Transposition of great arteries	16	(0.7)	0.015	*0.022*
Other heart disease	117	(4.9)	0.108	*0.132*
No significant heart disease	24	(1.0)	0.022	*0.017*
Primary pulmonary disease	106	(4.5)	0.097	*0.274*
Total	2,381	(100)		

Note: Statistics after 1974 are shown in *italic type.*

Source: Reproduced by permission of *Pediatrics*, Vol 65, 1980.

resulting index is usually expressed as the number of cases per 1,000 live births. This measure differs from conventional epidemiologic estimates of frequency such as prevalence or incidence, both of which refer to an estimate of the total population as well as to the total number of cases at a specific point or over a specific interval in calendar time.

A constant ratio of cases to live births would obviously add different numbers of cases to a population as the birth rate changed. Accordingly, especially for long-term projections, the birth rate must be taken into account if the usually cited frequencies are to be used for estimating the number of cases entering the population. Strictly, if all defects were recognized, including those in stillbirths, a preferred index would relate to the total number of conceptions, but in practice this quantity is unknown. Use of the term *prevalence* to refer to the usual index of frequency remains a special usage but one much preferred to use of *incidence*, which is clearly incorrect.

In the New England Regional Infant Cardiac Program (Table 26–1), 2,381 cases of confirmed malformations were reported within the first 12 months of life.[3] For the conditions listed, the frequencies ranged from 0.462 per 1,000 live births for ventricular septal defects, the most common condition, to one-30th as many (0.015 per 1,000 or 1.5 per 100,000) for L-transposition of the great arteries. The need for accrual of very large numbers of pregnancy outcomes is evident if these conditions are to be studied epidemiologically. It is not surprising, therefore, to find that the most extensive contributions to this field have been made from a few long-term studies in large, defined geographic areas. Surveillance methods have been used both in local or regional studies and in national ones, as at the Centers for Disease Control and Prevention (CDC), to permit case ascertainment in numbers sufficient to permit case-comparison studies, analysis of secular trends in the occurrence of specific defects, and many other investigations.

Temporal Aspects

As noted earlier, the appearance and disappearance rates of specific congenital defects from birth to later school-age years pose difficulties in estimating the frequency of these defects as a whole in any one population or in comparing frequencies found in different reports. While late-appearing defects, such as mitral prolapse, are presumed to be congenital in nature, postnatal influences seem as plausible as causes of their appearance as do those that cause spontaneous closure of ventricular septal defects. Regardless, the time course of certain of these conditions, extending for years following birth, adds complexity to their study.

A further temporal aspect is the potential for changes in technology that may bear on case detection. Diagnostic criteria are dependent on the available methods of investigation. As these methods change, concepts and classifications of disease, and therefore the enumeration of cases, also change. Where interventions alter the population base from which cases come, as with the increased salvage of impaired fetuses to the point of live birth, the apparent frequencies of various congenital defects would be expected to increase as well, even in the absence of any change in causal factors. Further, with increased survival of cases due to corrective surgery, the numbers of patients with certain defects reaching adulthood increase greatly. The prevalence of these defects at adult ages may thus rise sharply over time in regions where such treatment is available. The epidemiology of congenital heart diseases therefore includes the residual defects, the stigmata of surgery, and the risks of late complications, together constituting a new health problem to be understood and, as far as possible, controlled.

Early observations also have become essential to ascertainment of cases of congenital cardiac defects as a result of the increasingly widespread use of fetal echocardiography for screening. Case detection may lead to early termination of pregnancy, and there is a possibility that such cases would be missed unless specially notified. In addition, surgical intervention may become feasible in the fetal period, allowing correction of defects prior to birth. The early detection of cases and monitoring of their course through the remainder of fetal life, together with advances in understanding of cardiac morphogenesis, may dramatically change the temporal perspective on congenital heart disease in the future.

Differences in Definition of Source Populations

Epidemiologic study of congenital heart diseases is complicated by potential differences in source populations for the ascertainment of cases, as is true for other congenital conditions. If only live births are included, the greater frequency of cases among stillbirths will be missed and the overall frequency and distribution of types of cases will be distorted accordingly. This problem is clearest when autopsy series, including stillbirths, are compared with series derived from live births alone. Other selections from special populations, such as patients referred for cardiologic evaluation or catheterized patients, pose similar problems of interpretation and comparison. Still other types of source populations may be identified to pursue certain questions concerning relative frequencies of occurrence, as in offspring of parents with cleft lip or cleft palate, offspring of parents with epilepsy, or offspring who are twins. Finally, populations selected by age, as in school-based screening programs, or populations followed from birth to several years of age, will reflect both the loss of cases owing to early mortality or to spontaneous resolution and the addition of cases owing to conditions detectable only long after birth. These aspects of population selection need to be borne in mind when evaluating reports on studies of congenital heart diseases.

BACKGROUND OF EPIDEMIOLOGIC AND RELATED INVESTIGATION

In the history of congenital heart disease over recent decades, two of the prominent landmarks are the identification of maternal rubella infection and maternal thalidomide use as causes of such defects. The connection between trisomy 21, which causes Down syndrome, and cardiac defects is a third. In each instance, understanding of aspects of congenital cardiac defects was advanced. From rubella and thalidomide, it became clear that narrow windows of exposure time during gestation were critical to the risk of defects.[4,5] The experience with Down syndrome established that a given genetic abnormality could produce variable phenotypic expressions, since cardiac defects are absent in perhaps 60% of cases, but when present they often include endocardial cushion defects, which make up only about 5% of defects in the population at large.[1]

The earliest US population studies to detect heart disease in children were school surveys conducted within the period from 1915–1930.[6] Both mass screening and selective examinations were carried out over this period in eastern and western US communities. Early impressions from these projects included the insight that offspring of older mothers were more likely to be found with cardiac abnormalities. By the mid-1940s more formal surveys were conducted, now constituting part of a succession of studies over a 50-year period that represent several mainly North American and European investigations. Over these decades technological developments have introduced significant changes in both research and practice approaches to congenital heart disease. Case detection and case management have been transformed, and with them the epidemiology of these conditions has changed importantly also. Still, the requirements to identify cases in a consistent manner, in sufficient numbers for meaningful analysis, and with additional information on possible relevant exposures remain fundamental. Most important for new investigations may be the formulation of new questions based on innovative concepts of classification of the cardiac defects and new leads from genetic research into these conditions.

POPULATION STUDIES: DEFINITIONS, CRITERIA, AND CLASSIFICATION

Traditionally, the congenital cardiac defects have been classified according to anatomical and functional features important from a clinical point of view. Such recognition of specific congenital heart diseases is crucial from the view of medical and surgical treatment but, as with many other health problems, etiologic and preventive approaches may be guided better by a different type of classification. Criteria for diagnosis have evolved with technology and now depend especially on echocardiographic confirmation in living cases, as well as autopsy in those who have died. Inconsistency in the application of these criteria introduces substantial variation in the reported overall frequencies of these defects, as discussed below.

The most appropriate concepts of causation and the potential for prevention may derive from other groupings of these conditions, based, for example, on the characteristics of the parents whose offspring are affected or on the period of gestation when insults must occur to produce the observed anomalies. The latter approach has been explored in recent work by Gensburg.[7] This has revealed, among other findings, that the later-occurring defects are more often isolated ones, whereas those occur-

ring earlier in gestation are more often associated with other defects, suggesting a time gradient of vulnerability of multiple organ systems to teratogenic influences. Another conceptual approach based on cardiac morphogenesis has been proposed by Clark, who groups defects by their common timing in fetal development as understood from embryological and related studies of organogenesis.[2] The epidemiologist should be open to applying various classifications in the hope that one or another may offer an improved basis for causal inferences or recommended intervention strategies.

The detection of a congenital cardiac anomaly before delivery was a reportable event in the 1930s,[8] but fetal diagnosis now has become common.[9] This has raised both opportunities for early intervention and issues in interpretation of trends in reported cardiovascular malformations. The general trend toward increasing salvage of newborns with very low birthweight has also affected the frequency of cardiac and other congenital defects, which occur more frequently in such offspring.

The newest classification of congenital malformations affecting the circulatory system under the *International Statistical Classification of Diseases and Related Health Problems, Tenth Revision* (ICD 10) is summarized in Exhibit 26–1.[10] The basis of the classification is

---

Exhibit 26–1 Categories of Congenital Heart Disease

Congenital malformations of the circulatory system (Q20–Q28)

Q20   Congenital malformations of cardiac chambers and connections
Q21   Congenital malformations of cardiac septa
Q22   Congenital malformations of pulmonary and tricuspid valves
Q23   Congenital malformations of aortic and mitral valves
Q24   Other congenital malformations of heart
Q25   Congenital malformations of great arteries
Q26   Congenital malformations of great veins
Q27   Other congenital malformations of peripheral vascular system
Q28   Other congenital malformations of circulatory system[a]

a. Malformations of precerebral and cerebral vessels are included here.

the anatomic location of the defect. Each two-digit code is subclassified into several categories to identify specific anomalies, including those referring to the cerebral circulation. The coding structure represents a number of changes from recent versions and requires careful study to assess conversion rates between ICD 9 and ICD 10.

RATES OF OCCURRENCE IN POPULATIONS

Current Frequency in the United States

National Data

Data from national vital statistics and surveys of hospital discharges and physician office visits provide estimates of the frequency of congenital heart disease in the United States for 1993.[11] There were approximately 44,000 hospitalizations, 131,000 physician office visits, and 5,400 deaths attributed to congenital anomalies of the cardiovascular system in that year. Approximately 32,000 newborns were affected, and the most recent estimate of persons alive in the United States with congenital heart

defects projected there would be 960,000 in 1997.[12] In a recent review of the epidemiology of congenital heart disease in the United States based on national mortality data for the years 1979–1988, Gillum presented mortality by type of malformation and all malformations together for infants, that is, within the first 12 months of age (Table 26–2).[13] Pooled data for the entire 10-year period included 26,319 deaths and gave an overall rate of 66.0 deaths/100,000 live births, of which more than one-third (26.6/100,000) were due to unspecified anomalies. The leading specified condition was hypoplastic left heart syndrome (15.3/100,000). Notably, ventricular septal defect, most common as a condition at birth or within the first year of life, was a small contributor to mortality in the first year, being about one-15th of the total rate. The age distribution at death among those surviving the first 12 months is shown in Figure 26–2 and Table 26–3. For both males and females the average annual death rate from congenital heart disease beginning from one year of age was greatest in the age range one to four years and about one-fourth that rate by age five to nine years and thereafter, until after age 65. Rates

Table 26–2 Deaths from Congenital Heart Disease under Age One Year, United States, 1979–1988

Diagnosis	Deaths	Rate[a]
All[b]	26,319	66.0
Unspecified anomalies (ICD-9 746.9)	9,827	26.6
Hypoplastic left heart syndrome (ICD-9 746.7)	5,673	15.3
Other specified anomalies (ICD-9 746.8)	2,142	5.8
Transposition of great vessels (ICD-9 745.1)	1,787	4.8
Ventricular septal defect (ICD-9 745.4)	1,378	3.7
Endocardial cushion defects (ICD-9 745.6)	1,102	3.0
Common truncus (ICD-9 745.0)	977	2.6
Tetralogy of Fallot (ICD-9 745.2)	960	2.6
Other diagnoses	2,473	6.4

a. Deaths per 100,000 live births.

b. *International Classification of Diseases, 9th Revision* (ICD-9) codes 745–746.

Source: Reprinted with permission from RF Gillum, Epidemiology of Congenital Heart Disease in the United States, *American Heart Journal*, Vol 127, p 919, © 1994, Mosby-Year Book, Inc.

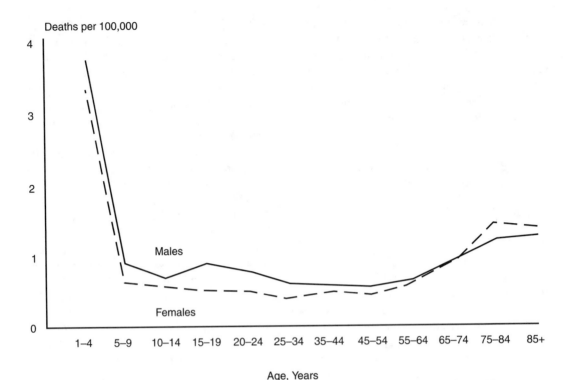

Figure 26–2 Average Annual Death Rate per 100,000 for Congenital Heart Disease by Age and Sex in Persons Aged ≥1 Year, United States, 1979–1988. *Source:* Reprinted with permission from RF Gillum, Epidemiology of Congenital Heart Disease in the United States, *American Heart Journal*, Vol 127, p 923, © 1994, Mosby-Year Book, Inc.

were generally somewhat higher for males than for females.

Gillum also presented age-race comparisons for mothers of affected and nonaffected offspring (Table 26–4). These national data for the United States demonstrate the well-recognized pattern of increased risk of cardiac malformations in the offspring of older mothers, specifically those in the 35–39 age group or older. This pattern was found for both White and Black mothers for cardiac anomalies in contrast to other circulatory and respiratory defects. At every age level, and for both categories of defects, the rates were higher for offspring of White than of Black mothers. Whether case ascertainment was equivalent in the two groups is questionable, but from other data where this has been investigated a similar pattern was found to be independent of case detection procedures (see below).

Regional and Local Data

Major sources of data on the regional or local occurrence of congenital heart diseases in the United States include the Collaborative Perinatal Project,[14] the Child Health and Development Studies,[15] the New England Regional Infant Cardiac Program,[3] the Baltimore-Washington Infant Study,[16] and the Metropolitan Atlanta Congenital Defects Program and Birth Defects Monitoring Program.[17] Additional data on natural history of three specific conditions (pulmonary stenosis, aortic stenosis, and ventricular septal defect) were reported by the Joint Study of the Natural History of Congenital Heart Defects.[18] The difficulty of comparing frequen-

Table 26-3 Deaths and Average Annual Death Rates per 100,000 for Congenital Heart Disease[a] in Persons Aged ≥1 Year, United States, 1979-1988

Age (yr)	Deaths	Rate	Deaths	Rate
	Males		Females	
1–4	2,690	3.79	2,288	3.38
5–9	788	0.91	543	0.66
10–14	642	0.71	517	0.60
15–19	915	0.92	533	0.55
20–24	841	0.80	564	0.54
25–34	1,296	0.64	893	0.43
35–44	902	0.61	793	0.52
45–54	675	0.60	584	0.49
55–64	718	0.69	745	0.63
65–74	725	0.99	916	0.98
75–84	403	1.26	790	1.47
85+	98	1.31	259	1.42

a. *International Classification of Diseases, 9th Revision* (ICD-9) codes 745–746.

Source: Reprinted with permission from RF Gillum, Epidemiology of Congenital Heart Disease in the United States, *American Heart Journal,* Vol 127, p 924, © 1994, Mosby-Year Book, Inc.

cies of congenital heart diseases among such studies is demonstrated by the review by Ferencz and colleagues.[16] They characterized eight studies in addition to their own and included, where applicable, two overall estimates of frequency, one based on the total number of cases and the other based on confirmed cases. The latter subset required diagnosis by catheterization, surgery, autopsy, or (in the case of their own study) echocardiography. In seven of the nine studies, approximately 30% to 50% of the total cases were identified by clinical diagnosis alone without confirmation as defined by the authors. (In the remaining two studies, all cases were confirmed.) For the total of cases, the range of frequencies and median value were 2.03 to 8.56 per 1,000 and 5.93 per 1,000 live births, respectively; for confirmed cases, 2.03 to 4.30 per 1,000 and 3.99 per 1,000, respectively. When the restriction to confirmed cases was introduced, a greatly reduced variation in the population frequencies was observed, with a very narrow range about the median value, even

though the studies differed markedly in the upper age limit at follow-up, from one year to 16 years.

Population Comparisons

The most commonly cited figure for the frequency of congenital heart diseases even in international comparisons is a ratio of 8 per 1,000 births.[19] Though not always specified, the reference is most often to live births; the frequency of such malformations among stillbirths is generally recognized to be substantially greater, perhaps by as much as 10 times according to material reviewed by Campbell. A detailed review of population studies conducted between 1945 and 1994 identified 27 studies in the United States, Europe, Australia, and the West Indies that gave widely divergent estimates of birth prevalence of cardiovascular malformations. The results considered most consistent were the most recent studies, which also included objective diagnosis and ascer-

Table 26–4 Rate[a] of Live Births with Selected Congenital Anomalies, by Age and Race of Mother, 45 Reporting States and District of Columbia, 1989

| | Race of Mother | | | | | |
| | All | | White | | Black | |
Age of Mother (yr)	Heart	Other Circ/Resp	Heart	Other Circ/Resp	Heart	Other Circ/Resp
<20	133.4	156.7	140.5	180.1	112.6	97.7
20–24	132.9	160.5	138.1	172.3	112.0	114.4
25–29	135.2	156.9	137.9	162.7	123.5	124.3
30–34	140.9	155.2	143.1	156.7	130.0	152.3
35–39	169.2	175.9	177.4	182.4	152.6	136.1
40–49	229.2	191.0	231.7	184.7	b	b

Note: Heart, heart malformations; Other Circ/Resp, other circulatory respiratory anomalies.

a. Number of live births with specified anomaly reported per 100,000 live births in specified group.

b. <20 births.

Source: Reprinted with permission from RF Gillum, Epidemiology of Congenital Heart Disease in the United States, American Heart Journal, Vol 127, p 925, © 1994, Mosby-Year Book, Inc.

tained cases appearing beyond one year of age.[6] The results of those studies were in a range similar to that described in the report by Ferencz and colleagues cited above.

A collaborative investigation of congenital anomalies among nine European centers (EUROCAT) includes follow-up of a combined cohort of 2,293 liveborn children with significant cardiac impairments.[20] Limited data specific to cardiac malformations were presented in the 1994 report, but joint epidemiologic analysis of the study experience was anticipated. However, this study contributed to a comparison among several reports cited by Nora and colleagues in their recent review, *Cardiovascular Diseases, Genetics, Epidemiology and Prevention* (see Table 26–5).[1] The range of frequencies shown is remarkable in that it was more than five-fold within the EUROCAT centers (from 1.89 to 10.75 cases/1,000) and altogether six-fold among the reports (from the lowest EUROCAT center to the highest rate in the California-Kaiser data). Discussion does not suggest these differences are given credence as

reflecting true variation among populations in the natural history of congenital heart disease, and the impression remains that methodologic differences are the leading interpretation of such data. If true population differences exist, this has not yet been widely acknowledged.

The difficulties often found in attempting to compare such reports are inconsistency in the range of conditions included, variation in ages at ascertainment, irregular inclusion of stillbirths, and lack of standardization in diagnostic procedures and criteria. When results between two or more studies are consistent, their apparent agreement may be only accidental.

Secular Trends

Comparisons of population data over time also pose difficulties, as illustrated by a report from the Birth Defects Monitoring Program on trends in the occurrence of birth defects.[21] Among other conditions, congenital heart diseases were classified as exhibiting increased, decreased, or stable rates of occurrence between

Table 26–5 Frequency Rates of Congenital Heart Diseases in Defined Populations

Population	Cases/1,000	Time Frame
Sweden, Gothenburg	6.35	1941–1950
USA, NIH Collaborative	7.67	1956–1965
USA, California-Kaiser	11.7	1960–1966
Denmark	6.14	1963–1973
USA, New England	2.08	1969–1974
USA, Baltimore-Washington	3.70	1981–1982
EUROCAT	1.89–10.75	1979–1982
European Collaborative	6.04 ± 2.53	1986
Switzerland	4.01	1986
Japan	10.6	1985

Source: Reprinted with permission from JJ Nora, NK Berg, and AH Nora, *Cardiovascular Diseases: Genetics, Epidemiology, and Prevention*. Copyright © 1991 by JJ Nora, NK Berg, and AH Nora. Used by permission of Oxford University Press, Inc.

two reporting periods, 1970–1971 and 1979–1980. Marked increases were apparent for ventricular septal defect and patent ductus arteriosus. No explanation for these changes (annual increases of 11% and 18%, respectively) was offered, though it was noted that chance, diagnostic practices, or reporting procedures could be contributing factors. The fact that the eight specific conditions that were listed as increasing, decreasing, or stable in frequency when taken together constituted 1.36 per 1,000 total births in the earlier period and 3.30 per 1,000 total births in the latter period, with ventricular septal defects nearly constant in proportion to the total at approximately 33% in both periods, suggests a general increase from initial underreporting to a frequency well within the usual range rather than a true increase in the rate of occurrence. Insufficient detail is provided to support this interpretation strongly, however.

Further illustration of the problem of interpretation also relates to ventricular septal defects. For example, the Heritage Pediatric Cardiology Program in Alberta, Canada, found upward trends in birth prevalence of congenital heart disease from 1981 through 1984, including a doubling of the rate for ventricular septal defects, from 1.2 to 2.5 cases per 1,000 live births.[22] While no methodologic explanation was

identified, it was acknowledged that possible ethnic differences could not be evaluated because ethnic classification of the total liveborn population was unavailable. The Baltimore-Washington Infant Study, on the other hand, experienced over the same calendar period an increased frequency of ventricular septal defects, though at lower rates (from 0.67 to 1.17 per 1,000 live births), but attributed the increase to improved detection by echocardiography of small, isolated defects.[23] Others (eg, Spooner et al[24]) have similarly concluded that methodologic changes, not true change in event rates, underlie these apparent secular trends. The study of congenital heart disease in Dallas County, Texas, similarly demonstrated increased frequency of these defects but in a period antedating the widespread use of echocardiography.[25] A plausible interpretation in this instance was that milder cases were being referred over the early part of the period from 1971 to 1984, since severe cases were no more common than previously but the overall rate increased.

For the United States as a whole, mortality before age one due to congenital heart disease declined from 1979 through 1988, as shown in Figure 26–3.[13] Generally similar trends were found for Black and White males and females. Rates in most years tended to be highest for

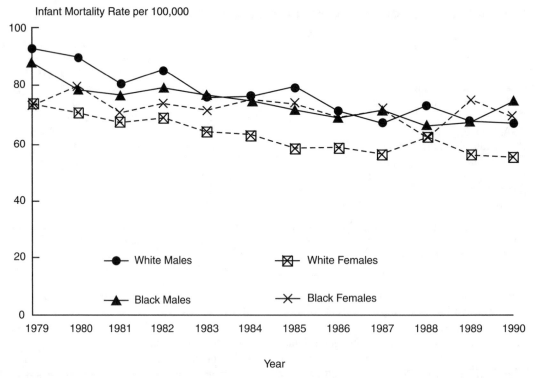

Figure 26–3 Infant Mortality Rates per 100,000 for Congenital Heart Disease by Race and Sex, United States, 1979–1990. *Source:* Reprinted with permission from RF Gillum, Epidemiology of Congenital Heart Disease in the United States, *American Heart Journal*, Vol 127, p 920, © 1994, Mosby-Year Book, Inc.

White males and lowest for White females. As these data were collected from death certificates with no apparent basis for change in methods over the time period studied, they may be reliable indicators of trends. They are modest in degree, however, and do not result in a major proportionate change in death rate from these conditions from year to year.

Projections of Survival into Adulthood

What are expectations of the natural course of disease in the population at large in future years? How many cases, and of what kinds, can be anticipated on the basis of current frequencies, the continuing operation of causal factors, and the influences of intervention? Partial answers to these questions have been offered in several reports. Engle and colleagues, present-

ing the report of the Inter-Society Commission on Heart Disease Resources, estimated that effective application of preventive measures available at that time could reduce premature mortality owing to congenital heart diseases by 7,000–10,000 deaths per year in the United States.[26] More recently, McNamara and Latson estimated the annual number of live births with congenital heart diseases at approximately 25,900 in the United States.[27] They suggested that for the five most common types of defects, which together account for 15,300 (59%) of these births, some 8,500 cases each year would reach adult life having experienced surgical repair of the defect. This result underscores the potential importance of long-term follow-up of such cases.

More formal attempts have been made to estimate the future number of persons surviving through age 20 with residua of congenital cardiac defects or corrective surgery in California,[28] the United States as a whole,[29] and Florida.[30] These estimates reflect different assumptions concerning rates of occurrence, operation, and survival, which limits confidence in the results. The projection for the United States as a whole for the year 1995 was for 296,141 surviving cases below age 21, with 37.6% having had prior surgery, and 10,413 cardiac surgical procedures for congenital heart diseases in patients between birth and age 20, with 2,193 surgical deaths. The authors emphasized the dependence of these results on a series of assumptions, the validity of which are not easily verified. A similar report from Liverpool and applied to England and Wales appears to suggest rather higher estimates of operations needed below age one.[31] The results of these and other reports are difficult to reconcile. Nevertheless, this work does illustrate attempts to apply existing evidence to the question of the future population of patients with congenital defects. Further, despite their inconsistencies, the reports all convey the expectation that postoperative cases will continue to be increasingly common in the adult population and therefore in the practice of adult medicine and cardiology: Congenital heart diseases are not a matter of pediatric practice alone.

The key to success of patients who reach adult ages with congenital heart disease is to monitor and limit the continued risks, however.[32] A recent report on state-wide cases in Oregon with follow-up to age 25, after surgical repair taking place between birth and age 18, has shown high risk of death from each of several conditions, for example, aortic stenosis, 17%; coarctation of the aorta, 10%; tetralogy of Fallot or ventricular septal defect, 5%. The concern about late mortality underscores the observation made elsewhere that the problem of congenital heart disease is increasingly an adult as well as a pediatric problem, and available preventive strategies require application through a longer age span than previously recognized. The causes of death in the categories

of corrected defects above, which ranged from 3 to 12 times expected mortality, were arrhythmias, congestive heart failure, and pulmonary hypertension. The opportunity to limit the progression of these conditions through treatment represents an element of high-risk intervention for these patients, but it may be possible to prolong life and reduce disability to some degree through these available means.

RISKS IN INDIVIDUALS

Commentaries on the causation of congenital heart diseases reflect general agreement that the causes are largely unknown. Conventional estimates place some 90% of cases in this category. However, many areas of investigation are being pursued. The literature reflects a strong emphasis on studies of genetic or familial characteristics, and recently reports on potential environmental factors have appeared more frequently. The emphasis on familial and genetic aspects presumably reflects an expectation that the congenital heart diseases will ultimately be explained largely by genetic mechanisms. New opportunities for investigation of genetic hypotheses may develop in the future, and the balance of research efforts between primarily genetic and primarily environmental factors—neither set of conditions operates independent of the other—may then be better assessed.

Age

Age is at issue in congenital heart disease in several respects, as noted previously. First, the age of the fetus at which critical developments occur in cardiogenesis is considered to be early in the first trimester. Second, age at diagnosis may range widely, from an early, preterm developmental age (whether through fetal diagnosis, premature delivery, or stillbirth) to several years of age. Therefore the potential for diagnosis is not limited to the newborn period but extends both earlier and later as well. Further, some defects detectable at birth can be expected to resolve spontaneously over months or years after birth. The term *birth defects* has perhaps become an anachronism for these reasons. Third, attained ages of affected individuals now commonly extend through childhood and adolescence into adulthood, with associated risks of complications and issues concerning reproduction. Thus several aspects of age bear on relevant exposure time, times of occurrence of a defect and its detection and treatment, and long-term management of the surviving case. Finally, age arises in the sense of parental age as a predictor of malformations in the offspring. Table 26–4 shows US mortality data at ages one year and over, and the marked increase in mortality of offspring of mothers age 35–39 years or older.[13] Paternal age may also be related to risk, as illustrated for some but not all cardiac anomalies in a U-shaped distribution with endpoint paternal ages, both highest and lowest (below age 20), associated with higher frequencies of affected offspring.[33]

Sex

The sex ratio of mortality from congenital heart disease, with the commonly observed excess risk in males, is shown for death rates at age one year and older in Figure 26–2 and Table 26–3.[13] Not all studies have shown male preponderance in the prevalence of cardiac defects at birth, nor are the findings consistent for all specific malformations. For example, the US data on infant mortality (at ages below one year only) from congenital heart disease in Figure 26–3 show a male excess in rates for Whites only and not for Blacks. A recent large, population-based study of more than 650,000 live births with 4,409 having congenital heart defects found male predominance among live births of 1.06:1 and among cases of defects 1.09:1.[34] Sex ratios varied widely from a maximum male predominance of 2.68:1 for double-outlet right ventricle to female predominance of 1.66:1 for persistent ductus arteriosus. As with other aspects of the field of congenital cardiac malformations, the multiplicity of conditions studied adds to difficulty in finding consistent patterns, yet the variation found does not appear to lead to new hypotheses to explain the differences.

Race or Ethnicity

Within US ethnic groups, national data show two patterns for Blacks and Whites. For birth prevalence in 1989 (Table 26–4), at all maternal ages, rates for offspring of White women exceeded those for offspring of Black women. However, the secular trends in infant mortality (Figure 26–3) indicated generally somewhat higher death rates for White than for Black male infants and lower rates for White than for Black female infants.[13] One of the higher frequencies reported in a particular ethnic group was claimed by Harvald and Hels in reference to 14 affected births in the Eskimo population of Godthåb, Greenland, between 1957 and 1964.[35] The reported frequency was 12.9 per 1,000 total births if four "doubtful" cases were excluded, but the 10 remaining cases all occurred among the 757 live births; therefore, the frequency among live births (more nearly comparable with Campbell's figure[19]) was 13.2 per 1,000. Inclusion of the doubtful cases would increase this value to 18.5 per 1,000 live births. This series had an unusual preponderance of cases of ventricular septal defects. The authors postulated the apparently high frequency of congenital heart diseases in this population to be due to high maternal age, high birth order of the affected offspring, and poor socioeconomic conditions. It should be noted that the number of cases was quite small and the apparent rate could reflect chance variation or detection bias for some inapparent reason during this calendar period.

Ethnicity was found to be related differently to different anomalies in a recent report among Blacks, Whites, and Mexican Americans in Dallas County, Texas, where nearly 380,000 live births were recorded.[36] No differences in frequency by ethnicity were found for the more severe lesions, but Whites predominated among the less severe cases. Potential explanations in reference to practices of referral and diagnosis among the three groups were excluded by the reported analyses. No overall conclusion about ethnic differences in the frequency of congenital heart defects seems warranted from the data available.

Heredity and Genetics

Familial Recurrence Rates

It is important to recognize the distinction between studies of strictly genetic characteristics and those of familial characteristics. The latter require consideration of common environmental, social, and behavioral factors in their interpretation and do not necessarily indicate genetic factors. The studies of familial characteristics in relation to occurrence of congenital heart diseases have been most consistent in showing that first-degree relatives of a known case are more often affected than would be expected from the rates in the general population.[37–41] This information provides a basis for genetic counseling of parents when one of them is affected or when a prior offspring is affected by a congenital heart defect. The approach has been criticized on grounds of the limited predictive value of the recurrence rates used, their prediction of other types of defect and not only the same type, and the uncertainty of underlying assumptions about the population distribution of risk.[42,43] That is, the average recurrence risks rarely exceed 5%, a low proportion in contrast to the theoretical 50% expectation for Mendelian dominant inheritance and 25% for recessive traits. While presence of a particular defect is associated with increased probability of the same type in siblings or offspring, other defects are also found to occur in increased frequency, though more weakly predicted than the same type. It has been suggested that the focus on specific anatomical defects as the basis for prediction may be less informative than an approach such as that cited earlier in which defects are grouped in accordance with their developmental origins.

The observed "recurrence risks" have varied among studies such that the conformity to predictions from genetic models is much less consistent than the fact of the excess frequency itself. In one recent report, Ferencz failed to find in offspring of a small number of affected fathers any excess frequency of congenital heart diseases, while the general population frequency was observed for other malformations.[44] Shortly thereafter, Nora and Nora showed that recurrence risks for offspring differed according to the sex of the affected parent.[45] If the mother was affected rather than the father, the recurrence risk was substantially greater. The report of Nora and Meyer points to the problem of differential ascertainment when family members of probands are examined for possible cardiac abnormalities.[40] Further, Nora and colleagues observed a much lower frequency of marriage among affected men and women than in the general population, so the contribution of affected parents to new cases in the next generation may be substantially less than expected.[39] These latter considerations suggest the need for caution in the interpretation of the recurrence rates reported to date.

Examples of recurrence risks for siblings and for offspring, respectively, are summarized in Tables 26–6 and 26–7.[1] Overall estimates of risk of each listed defect for siblings are pooled from multiple studies, as shown. The risks ranged from 1% to 4% if one sibling were affected and from 3% to 12% if two siblings were affected. For offspring, the difference in recurrence risk between that for affected mothers and affected fathers is striking. Especially when the mother is affected, relative to the overall population frequencies of specific anomalies shown in Table 26–1, recurrence risks are greatly increased over the average risk.

Other results of familial studies have shown an increased frequency of congenital heart diseases with increasing birth order but only an inconsistent relation to maternal or paternal age.[37,46,47] Several reports have noted an association of these malformations with maternal diabetes, as illustrated by the report from Mitchell and colleagues, which showed the frequency of congenital heart diseases to be one in three

Table 26–6 Recurrence Risks in Sibs for Any Congenital Heart Defect: Combined Data Published During Two Decades from European and North American Populations

Defect	1968–1990 Risk (%)	Suggested Risk (%)	
		If 1 Sib Affected	If 2 Sibs Affected
Ventricular septal defect	3.2	3	10
Hypoplastic left heart	3.2	3	10
Patent ductus	3.1	3	10
Atrial septal defect	2.7	2.5	8
Endocardial cushion	2.5	2.5	10
Tetralogy of Fallot	2.4	2.5	8
Pulmonary stenosis	2.2	2	6
Coarctation of aorta	2.1	2	6
Aortic stenosis	2.0	2	6
Transposition	1.4	1.5	5
Truncus	4.1	1–4	3–12
Pulmonary atresia	1.2	1	3
Tricuspid atresia	1.0	1	3
Ebstein anomaly	0.9	1	3
Interrupted aortic arch	2.0	1–2	3–6

Note: Suggested risk rounded to nearest 0.5%.

Source: Reprinted with permission from JJ Nora, NK Berg, and AH Nora, *Cardiovascular Diseases: Genetics, Epidemiology, and Prevention*. Copyright © 1991 by JJ Nora, NK Berg, and AH Nora. Used by permission of Oxford University Press, Inc.

among offspring with Down syndrome, one in 20 in the presence of a maternal cardiac defect, and one in 39 if the mother was diabetic during the pregnancy.[38]

Studies of special groups of cases or of the frequencies of cases arising from special populations, provide some insights into natural history beyond those that can be inferred from general or unselected populations. Of greatest interest among studies of this type are those of twins[48] and of offspring of parents with specific disorders, such as congenital defects (eg, cleft lip and palate)[49] or conditions that may directly or indirectly place the offspring at risk (eg, parental epilepsy).[50] The much greater concordance of congenital heart disease between twins (especially monozygotic versus dizygotic twins) than between nontwin siblings provides strongly suggestive evidence of a genetic contribution to the causation of these conditions. The limited prediction of the specific anomaly from one twin to another, however, clouds the picture.

Genetic Disorders

With respect to genetic disorders, it appears that a few single-gene defects of certain types may be found regularly to manifest characteristic cardiac abnormalities, although they do so as part of complex conditions that include other structural and functional abnormalities as well. These conditions were summarized by McKusick in his Lewis A Conner Memorial Lecture of 1963, a point now seeming remote in the modern history of medical genetics (Exhibit 26–2).[51] In a more current assessment, Nora and colleagues have attributed 3% to 5% of congenital heart diseases to single gene mutations, 8% to 10% to chromosomal anomalies, and the balance of 85% or more to "multifactorial inheritance," which includes environmental interactions (see

Table 26–7 Suggested Offspring Recurrence Risk for Congenital Heart Defects Given One Affected Parent, Based on Combined Data and Rounded to the Nearest 0.5%

Defect	Mother Affected	Father Affected
Aortic stenosis	18	5
Atrial septal defect	6	1.5
Coarctation of aorta	4	2.5
Endocardial cushion defect	14	1
Patent ductus arteriosus	4	2
Pulmonary stenosis	6.5	2
Tetralogy of Fallot	2.5	1.5
Ventricular septal defect	9.5	2.5

Source: Reprinted with permission from JJ Nora, NK Berg, and AH Nora, *Cardiovascular Diseases: Genetics, Epidemiology, and Prevention.* Copyright © 1991 by JJ Nora, NK Berg, and AH Nora. Used by permission of Oxford University Press, Inc.

Exhibit 26–2 Single-Gene Mutants with Cardiovascular Involvement (a Partial List)

I. Heritable disorders of connective tissue
   Marfan syndrome
   Pseudoxanthoma elasticum
   Hurler syndrome
   Two other mucopolysaccharidoses
   Ehlers-Danlos syndrome
   Osteogenesis imperfecta
II. Neurologic and muscular disorders
   Friedreich's ataxia
   Riley-Day familial dysautonomia
   Duchenne muscular dystrophy
   Myotonic dystrophy
   Refsum's disease
III. Phacomatoses
   Neurofibromatosis
   von Hippel-Lindau syndrome
   Tuberous sclerosis
IV. Inborn errors of metabolism
   Glycogen-storage disease, especially Type III
   Adrenal hyperplasia

V. Vascular malformations
   Osler-Rendu-Weber hereditary hemorrhagic telangiectasia
   Hereditary lymphedema (Milroy type; Meige type)
VI. Complex syndromes with malformations of heart
   Kartagener's syndrome
   Holt-Oram syndrome
   Ellis-van Creveld syndrome
   Fanconi's anemia
VII. Miscellaneous
   Werner syndrome
   Hemochromatosis
   Congenital deafness, electrocardiographic changes, sudden death
   Pheochromocytoma, apparently isolated
   Pheochromocytoma in multiple endocrine adenomatosis
   Disturbances of rhythm or conduction
   Pulmonary hypertension
   Familial amyloidosis

Source: Reprinted with permission from V McKusick, A Genetical View of Cardiovascular Disease. The Lewis A Conner Memorial Lecture, *Circulation*, Vol 30, p 331, © 1964, American Heart Association.

below).[1] A discussion of each type of defect, defined in its conventional gross anatomic classification, is given by these authors. The example of ventricular septal defect indicates the approach. The condition is described as occurring equally frequently as an isolated finding and as part of a complex of cardiac abnormalities. Subtle degrees of the defect (such that 3/1000 subjects were found in the control group for a study of congenital heart disease) and spontaneous closure of some of them raise questions about the ascertainment of this condition. Recurrence risks are given, as shown in Tables 26–6 and 26–7, and environmental factors associated with this type of defect are presented. Illustrative pedigrees are given for some of these conditions, but in few instances is there reference to a specific genetic defect.

In the presence of chromosomal aberrations, varied frequencies of congenital heart diseases may be observed (perhaps from 1% to 100%) and, with multiple family members exhibiting the same chromosomal pattern, it is sometimes observed that no two members have the same cardiac malformation.[52] Thus, the relationship between these genetic disorders and congenital heart diseases has limited consistency and specificity.

Teratogens

Teratogens may be defined as agents capable of inducing congenital anomalies.[5] A recent systematic review of studies of several categories of possible teratogens included agents (as listed in Exhibit 26–3) for which one or more reports had indicated an odds ratio or relative risk estimate of 2 or greater (confidence limits were not considered). For each item within a category, the array of studies was summarized. In some instances, the overall conclusion was not supportive of a teratogenic role of the exposure. Maternal use of drugs was of particular interest, as were maternal rubella infection and diabetes. Chemical and physical factors appeared to have received much less investigation.

Given the established relation between early maternal rubella infection and cardiovascular

and other defects of the fetus, attention has been devoted to intrauterine exposures to viruses and, less often, to other infectious agents. Numerous agents have been discussed as possibly related to congenital heart diseases and other defects, but none (including the Coxsackie B viruses, mumps virus, cytomegalovirus, and others) has been widely considered to be an established causal agent.[53-55] In his review, Wagner called attention to an issue important in the investigation and interpretation of such relationships, the distinction between the early insults producing congenital structural defects and the damage to already developed fetal tissues that may occur from later in utero infection.[55] He thus distinguished between congenital infections that may occur throughout gestation and congenital heart disease whose onset in most cases occurs before the eighth week of gestation. Interest in the potential role of infection continues, as illustrated by the speculation of Paneth and colleagues that a striking cluster of cases of mixed cardiac defects, which occurred within a two-month period in New England, might be due to exposure to influenza B virus.[56]

Exhibit 26–3 Possible Teratogens in Congenital Heart Disease Recently Reviewed

- Thalidomide
- Bendectin
- Anticonvulsants
- Exogenous hormone exposure
- Other drug exposure during pregnancy
- Alcohol intake during pregnancy
- Smoking
- Maternal diabetes
- Maternal rubella infection
- Other maternal infections
- Parental epilepsy
- Other parental diseases
- Chemicals
- Physical factors

Source: Data from T Pexeider, Teratogens, in *The Genetics of Cardiovascular Disease*, MAM Pierpont and JH Moller, eds, Martinus Nijhoff Publishing, 1986.

Certain drug exposures have also been investigated and several are cited in a review by Nora and colleagues:[57] alcohol, amphetamines, anticonvulsants, lithium, propranolol, sex hormones, thalidomide, and warfarin. Supporting evidence is not provided, however, and published reports are conflicting. Therefore, the estimated frequencies of drug-induced cardiovascular disorders must be viewed cautiously. The authors also proposed a biochemical mechanism by which they considered exogenous agents to have potential teratogenic effects. It is important to note both the potential impact of truly teratogenic exposures that may be common in pregnancy and the limited investigation to date of specific agents to establish clearly the presence of such risk. The implications of this circumstance are discussed in the context of intervention later in this chapter. The evidence relating a maternal smoking history to congenital heart diseases is conflicting, although other adverse fetal effects of smoking are well established.[14,58,59] Abnormalities of pregnancy have sometimes been found to be associated with the occurrence of congenital heart diseases, as described by Lamy and colleagues.[37] Specifically, threatened abortion, in women under 35 years of age, occurred twice as frequently in mothers of cases as in mothers of a comparison group of noncases.

The investigation of general environmental characteristics has, as noted, been limited. Some studies have found season, altitude, and population density to be related to the occurrence of specific congenital heart diseases. Paneth and colleagues analyzed a seasonal cluster of hypoplastic left heart cases.[56,60] Rothman and Fyler investigated seasonal patterns in data from the New England Regional Infant Cardiac Program and found such patterns for complex ventricular septal defects, malposition defects, and transposition of the great arteries.[61] They also found ventricular septal defects, pulmonary atresia, and tricuspid atresia to be associated with population density, that is, residence in areas classified as urban in contrast to rural. Lequime and colleagues reviewed evidence that persistent patent ductus arteriosus is several times more common at high altitude, as in Mexico City or the mountains of Peru, than at sea level.[53]

The difficulty of acquiring sufficient numbers of cases for effective epidemiologic study of congenital heart disease was noted in the introduction to this chapter. This limits attempts to clarify associations suggested from occasional studies of a particular potentially teratogenic exposure. The review of teratogens cited above presented examples of databases that may provide new opportunities for such studies.[5] One is the International Clearinghouse for Birth Defects Monitoring Systems, in San Francisco, California, which has operated since 1974. It currently receives reports of national birth defects data from 19 countries in North and South America, Europe, New Zealand, and Japan based on more than 2.5 million births per year. The EUROCAT program was described above. Local and national data systems are also available, and many may be reached through contact with the Cardiology Data Centre, Hospital for Sick Children, Toronto, Ontario.

THEORIES OF CAUSATION OF CONGENITAL HEART DISEASE

The association of the congenital heart diseases with a wide variety of genetic, familial, intrauterine, and environmental factors suggests a diverse set of causal conditions as determinants of these abnormalities. Since the specific anatomic forms of the defects are varied and their occurrence is commonly associated with defects in other organ systems, the expectation is that no satisfactory single causal theory will be found. A single theory would need to be so broad and inclusive regarding both causes and effects that it might offer no specific predictions for rigorous testing through research and no direct application to prevention. It would also have to account for many features of the occurrence of the conditions from a genetic and familial point of view that are difficult to reconcile.[51]

These reservations seem wholly applicable to Nora's commonly cited "multifactorial inheritance hypothesis."[62] The term implies that the theory is chiefly concerned with the heritability of congenital heart diseases but is countered by the author's explicit assimilation into the theory of whatever environmental influences or "triggers" may operate. As Nora and Nora state, "Should not all teratogens be recorded in the category of multifactorial inheritance? After all, genetic predisposition interacting with a teratogen is likely."[63(p 96)] The authors also acknowledge the requirement for "frequent modification" of the theory on the basis of changing views of the relative contributions of heredity and environment to the conditions under consideration. These aspects of the theory, as presented, appear in part to beg the question of whether hereditary factors are operating, since environmental ones are subsumed under the category of inheritance. They further undermine the status of the theory by indicating its adaptability, a property that is inversely related to its testability. Newman discusses further limitations of this theory in the context of the epidemiology of ventricular septal defects.[64]

Another theory to account for the occurrence of congenital heart diseases was proposed by Taussig.[65] In essence, she argued that the variations in cardiac structure regarded as "malformations," or development errors, are in fact simply genetic variants that reflect evolutionary history in other species, for whom these variants were normal. This is an interesting, but not immediately compelling, idea.

Newman's alternative formulation to "multifactorial inheritance," his "chance + genes + environmental hypothesis," is most remarkable in being even more comprehensive (and thereby absolutely secure against refutation) than Nora's.[64] The most difficult observation to explain under Nora's theory, that of discordance between identical twins whose environments are virtually identical, is disposed of by Newman with the observation that "most individuals are lucky enough to escape a VSD [ventricular septal defect]."[64(p 747)]

The point was raised in the introduction that classification of these conditions should be considered openly with the possibility of new insights from alternative approaches. In this connection, the view of Clark has been noted above as offering such an alternative. The classification of defects he proposes based on morphogenetic grounds is shown in Exhibit 26–4.[2] The categories are based on embryological processes and conditions, including migration of formative tissues, intracardiac hemodynamics, cell death, extracellular matrix, and abnormal targeted growth. It is instructive to observe how ventricular septal defects, for example, are distributed in this scheme in comparison with conventional classification. They are found in categories IA2 and IA5, IIA, III, and IVA2. The implication is that the clinically derived classification that combines all ventricular septal defects into a single category obscures fundamental differences in their mechanisms of development that may be critical for etiological insights. It is of interest that at least one epidemiologic study has already been reported in which such an approach to classification was adopted.[66] Among the results was the observation that familial aggregation was found for flow-related lesions but not for "nonflow" lesions, contrasting Clark's group II with all other categories. New theories of causation and their many implications may follow from such work, which appears to open new possibilities for the field.

PREVENTION AND CONTROL

The potential for intervention in congenital heart disease extends beyond treatment alone. The issues addressed include both prevention (measures that may prevent the occurrence of congenital heart diseases) and treatment (measures intended to ameliorate the course of disease relative to expectation). As commonly discussed in other aspects of cardiovascular disease prevention, the complementarity of the population approach (measures that may impact the risk of the congenital heart diseases in the population as a whole) and the high-risk approach (measures that prevent conceptions that are at high risk because of identifiable factors in the parents or other family members)

Exhibit 26–4 Pathogenic Mechanism for Some Congenital Cardiac Malformations, Classification Based on Mechanism Rather Than Anatomic Anomaly

I. Ectomesenchymal tissue migration abnormalities
  A. Conotruncal septation defects
    1. Increased mitral aortic separation (a clinically silent forme fruste)
    2. Subarterial, type I ventricular septal defect
    3. Double-outlet right ventricle
    4. Tetralogy of Fallot
    5. Pulmonary atresia with ventricular septal defect
    6. Aorticopulmonary window
    7. Truncus arteriosus communis
  B. Abnormal conotruncal cushion position
    1. D-transposition of the great arteries
  C. Branchial arch defects
    1. Interrupted aortic arch, type B
    2. Double aortic arch
    3. Right aortic arch with mirror-image branching

II. Abnormal intracardiac blood flow
  A. Perimembranous ventricular septal defect
  B. Left-sided cardiac anomalies
    1. Bicuspid aortic valve
    2. Aortic valve stenosis
    3. Coarctation of the aorta
    4. Interrupted aortic arch, type A
    5. Hypoplastic left heart, aortic atresia, and/or mitral atresia
  C. Right-sided cardiac anomalies
    1. Bicuspid pulmonary valve
    2. Secundum atrial septal defect
    3. Pulmonary valvar stenosis
    4. Pulmonary valvar atresia with intact ventricular septum

III. Cell death
  A. Muscular ventricular septal defect
  B. Ebstein's anomaly of the tricuspid valve

IV. Extracellular matrix
  A. Endocardial cushion defects
    1. Ostium primum atrial septal defect
    2. Type III inflow ventricular septal defect
    3. Atrioventricular canal
  B. Dysplastic pulmonary or aortic valve

V. Abnormal targeted growth
  A. Anomalous pulmonary venous return
    1. Partial anomalous pulmonary venous return
    2. Total anomalous pulmonary venous return
    3. Cor triatriatum

Source: Reprinted with permission from EB Clark, Growth, Morphogenesis, and Function, in *Fetal, Neonatal, and Infant Cardiac Disease*, JH Moller and WA Neal, eds, p 21, © 1989, Appleton & Lange.

deserves recognition. The measures currently considered applicable are discussed briefly here.

The Population-Wide Level

The population approach today depends on protection of the mother against rubella infection and exposure to other agents that may be harmful to the fetus, such as drugs and alcohol.[67,68] Few specific agents have been established as teratogenic in humans in the manner of thalidomide, so this approach must be general. Accordingly, physicians providing prenatal care are often admonished to avoid prescribing agents not judged to be free of teratogenic potential, and pregnant women are advised against use of any drug without prior consultation with a physician.[26,68] The dilemma may result in both insufficient protection where teratogenic potential is unrecognized and unnecessary restriction or concern about the use of medications that may in fact pose no risk of congenital disorders. In addition, the period of greatest risk falls in the early weeks of gestation when pregnancy may be unrecognized and when many women have yet to seek prenatal care.

The Individual, High-Risk Level

The high-risk approach depends on the identification of potential conceptions in which the risk of congenital defects is substantially greater than in the general population. Presently, such identification rests almost entirely on the history of affected family members—one or both parents, a sibling, or in some instances other relatives. The objective of prevention in this somewhat restricted circumstance is to reduce the likelihood of a recurrence of an affected birth within the same family. The approach requires recognition of a genetic or phenotypic abnormality in a family member, counseling of the prospective parents, and their decision on whether to have further offspring. In the event of conception, amniocentesis with fetal cell culture has been suggested as a means of detecting abnormalities that could lead to elective termination of pregnancy.[68]

It should be noted that none of these preventive measures is specific to the congenital heart diseases as distinct from other congenital defects. Thus, their effective application should serve to reduce the overall population risk of congenital defects. Whether such an impact has been realized cannot be judged from available evidence. Werko noted that in neither Holland nor Sweden was there a decrease in reported new cases of congenital heart diseases over the decades of the 1940s, 1950s, and 1960s, despite institution of rubella vaccination as well as genetic counseling over the same period.[69] Complete evaluation, however, would require standardization of methods of case detection over time and accounting for any factors whose introduction or increased influence might increase the frequency of occurrence of these conditions over the period of study. No such evaluation of preventive measures against the congenital heart diseases has been reported to date.

With respect to treatment, once a conception with an identifiable abnormality has occurred, early termination of the affected pregnancy is the first possible intervention.[26] (Although it prevents the live birth of an affected infant, such intervention is better viewed as treatment of the established condition, whose presence reflects the failure of the preventive measures addressed above.)

Among the several aspects of treatment, clearly the most dramatic has been the development in recent decades of advanced surgical techniques, including supportive measures. For some time these procedures have permitted early correction as well as palliation of the anatomical and functional abnormalities associated with many specific defects of the heart and major vessels. In general, these measures have so greatly improved the survival of cases, especially those treated in the first year of life, that there has been little doubt of their effectiveness. No formal experimental evaluation of alternative strategies—such as specific procedures, their timing, or the selection of cases—appears to have been conducted to date, however. Strict comparison of treatment results among published reports is difficult owing to differences in case selection and other aspects central to their interpretation.[68] Because longterm sequelae, as well as early operative or postoperative mortality, may well differ in accordance with these aspects of treatment, cooperative clinical trials may become recognized as useful in the pursuit of further improvements in treatment, both surgical and medical.

Given the greatly increased number of cases surviving into adulthood, there follows a corresponding need for long-term care in three particular respects: clinical monitoring; prophylaxis against bacterial endocarditis; and counseling in relation to physical capacity and limitations, social and psychological development, and issues such as employability, insurability, and parenthood.[26,27,68,70] These aspects of treatment have in common the objective of reducing the potential disability in physical, psychological, and social terms that may persist into adulthood. McNamara and Latson reviewed the long-term follow-up of patients with early surgery for correction of congenital heart defects to determine the variations in relative importance of these and other aspects of long-term management, specific to each of the more common conditions.[27] Ferencz and colleagues pointed out the lack of knowledge by patients themselves, as adults, of their own condition and its medical and surgical history and emphasized the need for much-improved patient awareness through counseling and education.[70] Their representation of the needs for intervention is shown in Table 26–8.[71] It perhaps errs only in omission of the fetal period, on which so much activity is now centered for diagnosis and early intervention.

A FRAMEWORK FOR INTERVENTION

The spectrum of interventions outlined above depends for its effectiveness on timely detection of cases, which in turn depends on professional education chiefly for the obstetrician, pediatrician, and family practitioner. Through appropriate clinical observation, then, the suspect case becomes subject to referral, definitive diagnosis, and classification. These activities may also apply in adolescent or adult medicine and general cardiology, for those conditions or late sequelae detectable beyond childhood. The pathologist's examination of the stillborn or other fatal case is also important if parents are to be fully aware of the condition of their offspring and the high-risk approach is to be implemented where appropriate.

Further professional education is necessary in the highly specialized skills of diagnosis and treatment of congenital heart diseases. As noted above, the long-term survival of increasing proportions of cases increases the additional professional resources that are needed. Skills in professional counseling must be complemented by a system of follow-up that ensures that the necessary communication with patients and their parents can occur.

Numerous reports have given attention to the importance of regionalization of facilities and services for this highly technical and special-

Table 26–8 Congenital Heart Disease: A Cycle of Lifetime Concerns

Life Period	Concerns
Infant	Diagnosis
	Medical/surgical care
	Impact on family
	Costs
Child	Ongoing medical/surgical care
	Educational plans
	Peer activities
Adolescent	Old and new medical problems
	Antibiotic prophylaxis
	Lifestyle hazards
	Safe contraception
	Assessment of reproductive risks
Adult Reproduction	Assessment of genetic risks
	Assessment of maternal and fetal risks
	Prenatal diagnostic procedures
	Pregnancy management
Growing older	Unrecognized lesions
	Complications of defect
	Complications of surgery
	Bacterial endocarditis
	Employment and insurance
	Healthful and productive life course

Source: Reprinted with permission from C Ferencz, Congenital Heart Disease: An Epidemiologic and Teratologic Challenge, in *Perspectives in Pediatric Cardiology: Volume 4, Epidemiology of Congenital Heart Disease*, C Ferencz, JD Rubin, CA Loffredo, and CA Magee, eds, p 2, © 1993, Futura Publishing Company, Inc.

ized field. In the United States, the outstanding example is the New England Regional Infant Cardiac Program.[3] Several related issues have been addressed in the United Kingdom as well.[72] Most relevant to the present context is the presumption, with supporting observations, that apart from considerations of cost, the most satisfactory performance of the intervention required depends on a concentration of resources accessible by referral rather than diffuse distribution of these resources over a large geographic area or widely dispersed population.

Finally, the financing of services, for prevention and treatment remains a major limitation in many settings, especially in countries with scarce resources. This is particularly unfortunate since, as suggested by others, the cost of definitive surgery and long-term follow-up is small in relation to the years of healthy and productive life that can be attained for many. Not only is the application of available treatment limited, but limited diagnostic facilities lead to incomplete knowledge about the nature and extent of the congenital heart diseases as well.

CURRENT ISSUES

From the view of epidemiology and prevention, the current issues in connection with congenital heart disease concern the continued search for understanding of causes so that prevention can be achieved for a much broader spectrum of these conditions. Many of the inherent difficulties in epidemiologic research discussed in the introduction remain. New approaches to classification of cardiac defects offer promise of new insight into their epidemiologic associations. The exceptional degree to which familial and genetic factors have been pursued in this field offers the possibility that in study of congenital heart disease epidemiologists may have correspondingly exceptional opportunities for collaboration with colleagues in laboratory and population genetics in working on this problem.

The challenges of practical prevention expand as the relevant time course of congenital heart disease reaches back to conception and ahead to adult reproductive and later life. Issues of fetal diagnosis and intervention arise as do those of lifelong awareness of risk of complications that may often be preventable with adequate medical attention. Prevention may be improved in consequence of better prediction of recurrence risks based on genetic theories of causation, but better identification of environmental factors that increase the probability of affected offspring may be of equal or greater importance.

REFERENCES

1. Nora JJ, Berg K, Nora AH. *Cardiovascular Diseases: Genetics, Epidemiology and Prevention.* Oxford, England: Oxford University Press; 1991. Oxford Monographs on Medical Genetics, no. 22.

2. Clark EB. Growth, morphogenesis, and function: the dynamics of cardiac development. In: Moller JH, Neal WA, eds. *Fetal, Neonatal, and Infant Cardiac Disease.* Norwalk, Conn: Appleton & Lange; 1989: 3–23.

3. Fyler DC. Report of the New England Regional Infant Cardiac Program. *Pediatr.* 1980;65:375–461.

4. Gregg N. Congenital cataract following German measles in the mother. *Trans Opthalmol Soc of Aust.* 1941; 3:35–46.

5. Pexeider T. Teratogens. In: Pierpont MAM, Moller JH, eds. *The Genetics of Cardiovascular Disease.* Boston, Mass: Martinus Nijhoff Publishing; 1986: 25–68.

6. Rosenthal GL. Prevalence and risk factors: public health scope. In: Garson A Jr, Bricker JT, Fisher EJ, Neish SR, eds. *The Science and Practice of Pediatric Cardiology.* 2nd ed. Baltimore, Md: Williams & Wilkins; 1997.

7. Gensburg LJ, Marshall EG, Druschel CM. Examining potential demographic risk factors for congenital cardiovascular malformations on a time-developmental model. *Paediatr Perinat Epidemiol.* 1993;7:434–449.

8. Dippel AL. Two cases of congenital heart disease in which the diagnosis was made before birth. *Am J Obstet Gynecol.* 1934;27:120–123.

9. Allan LD, Sharland GK, Milburn A, Lockhart SM, et al. Prospective diagnosis of 1,006 consecutive cases of congenital heart disease in the fetus. *J Am Coll Cardiol.* 1994;23:1452–1458.

10. World Health Organization. *International Statistical Classification of Diseases and Related Health Problems: Tenth Revision.* Geneva, Switzerland: World Health Organization; 1992: 1.

11. US Dept of Health and Human Services. *Morbidity & Mortality: 1996 Chartbook on Cardiovascular, Lung, and Blood Diseases.* Bethesda, Md: National Heart, Lung and Blood Institute, National Institutes of Health, Public Health Service, US Dept of Health and Human Services; 1996.

12. American Heart Association. *1997 Heart and Stroke Statistical Update.* Dallas, Tex: American Heart Association; 1996.

13. Gillum RF. Epidemiology of congenital heart disease in the United States. *Am Heart J.* 1994;127:919–927.

14. Heinonen OP. Risk factors for congenital heart disease: a prospective study. In: Kelly S, ed. *Birth Defects, Risks and Consequences: Proceeding of a Symposium on Birth Defects, Risks and Consequences.* Sponsored by the Birth Defects Institute of the New York State Department of Health. New York: Academic Press; 1976: 221–264.

15. Hoffman J, Christianson R. Congenital heart disease in a cohort of 19,502 births: long-term follow-up. *Am J Cardiol.* 1978;42:641–647.

16. Ferencz C, Rubin JD, McCarter RJ, Brenner JI, et al. Congenital heart disease: prevalence at livebirth: the Baltimore-Washington infant study. *Am J Epidemiol.* 1985;121:31–36.

17. Edmonds L, Layde PM, James LM, Flynt JW, et al. Congenital malformations surveillance: two American systems. *Int J Epidemiol.* 1981;10:247–252.

18. Nadas AS, Ellison RC, Weidman WH, eds. Report from the Joint Study of the Natural History of Congenital Heart Defects: pulmonary stenosis, aortic stenosis, ventricular septal defect: clinical course and indirect assessment. *Circ.* 1977;56(suppl):1–87.

19. Campbell M. Incidence of cardiac malformations at birth and later, and neonatal mortality. *Br Heart J.* 1973;35:189–200.

20. Lechat MF. European registration of congenital anomalies (EUROCAT). Vuylsteek K, Hallen M, eds. *Epidemiology.* Amsterdam, the Netherlands: IOS Press; 1994: 57–72.

21. Oakley GP, Levy MJ, Edmonds LD. Temporal trends in reported malformation incidents for the United States Birth Defects Monitoring Program. *Clin Pediatr.* 1984;23:246–247.

22. Grabits RG, Joffres MR, Collins-Nakai RL. Congenital heart disease: incidence in the first year of life. The Alberta Heritage Pediatric Cardiology Program. *Am J Epidemiol.* 1988;128:381–388.

23. Martin GR, Perry LW, Ferencz C. Increased prevalence of ventricular septal defect: epidemic or improved diagnosis. *Pediatr.* 1989;83:200–203.

24. Spooner EW, Hook EB, Farina MA, Shaher RM. Evaluation of a temporal increase in ventricular septal defects: estimated prevalence and severity in northeastern New York, 1970–1983. *Teratol.* 1988;37:21–28.

25. Fixler DE, Pastor P, Chamberlin M, Sigman E, et al. Trends in congenital heart disease in Dallas County births 1971–1984. *Circ.* 1990;81:137–142.

26. Engle M, Adams FH, Betson C, DuShane J, et al. Primary prevention of congenital heart disease. *J Am Osteopath Assoc.* 1970;69:1147–1151.

27. McNamara D, Latson LA. Long-term follow-up of patients with malformations for which definitive surgical repair has been available for 25 years or more. *Am J Cardiol.* 1982;50:560–568.

28. Roberts N. A predictive study of congenital heart disease and need for care. *West J Med.* 1978;129:19–25.

29. Roberts NK, Cretin S. The changing face of congenital heart disease: a method for predicting the influence of cardiac surgery upon the prevalence and spectrum of congenital heart disease. *Med Care.* 1980;18:930–939.

30. Levine R, Roberts N, Cretin S, Gelband H. Congenital heart disease in Florida: a predictive study. *J Fl Med Assoc.* 1980;67:563–565.

31. Dickinson D, Arnold R, Wilkinson JL. Congenital heart disease among 160,480 liveborn children in Liverpool 1960 to 1969: implications for surgical treatment. *Br Heart J.* 1981;46:55–62.

32. Morris CD, Menashe VD. 25-year mortality after surgical repair of congenital heart defect in childhood. *JAMA.* 1991;266:3447–3452.

33. Olshan AF, Schnitzer PG, Baird PA. Paternal age and the risk of congenital heart defects. *Teratol.* 1994;50: 80–84.

34. Šamánek M. Boy:girl ratio in children born with different forms of cardiac malformation: a population-based study. *Pediatr Cardiol.* 1994;15:53–57.

35. Harvald B, Hels J. Incidence of cardiac malformations in Greenlandic Eskimos. *Humangenetik.* 1972;15:257–260.

36. Fixler DE, Pastor P, Sigman E, Eifler CW. Ethnicity and socioeconomic status: impact on the diagnosis of congenital heart disease. *J Am Coll Cardiol.* 1993;21: 1722–1726.

37. Lamy M, De Grouchy J, Schweisguth O. Genetic and non-genetic factors in the etiology of congenital heart disease: a study of 1188 cases. *Am J Hum Genet.* 1957; 9:17–41.

38. Mitchell SC, Sellmann AH, Westphal MC, Park J. Etiologic correlates in a study of congenital heart disease in 56,109 births. *Am J Cardiol.* 1971;28:653–657.

39. Nora JJ, Dodd PF, McNamara DG, Hattwick MAW, et al. Risk to offspring of parents with congenital heart defects. *JAMA.* 1969;209:2052–2053.

40. Nora JJ, Meyer TC. Familial nature of congenital heart diseases. *Pediatr.* 1966;37:329–334.

41. Rose V, Gold RJM, Lindsay G, Allen M. A possible increase in the incidence of congenital heart defects

among the offspring of affected parents. *J Am Coll Cardiol*. 1985;6:376–382.

42. Murphy EA, Pyeritz RE. Assessment of genetic risk in congenital heart disease. *J Am Coll Cardiol*. 1991;18: 338–340.

43. Pierpont MAM, Moller JH. Congenital cardiac malformations. In: Pierpont MAM, Moller JH, eds. *The Genetics of Cardiovascular Disease*. Boston, Mass: Martinus Nijhoff Publishing; 1986: 13–24.

44. Ferencz C. Offspring of fathers with cardiovascular malformations. *Am Heart J*. 1986;111:1212–1213.

45. Nora JJ, Nora AH. Maternal transmission of congenital heart diseases: new recurrence risk figures and the questions of cytoplasmic inheritance and vulnerability to teratogens. *Am J Cardiol*. 1987;59:459–463.

46. Hay S, Barbano H. Independent effects of maternal age and birth order on the incidence of selected congenital malformations. *Teratol*. 1972;6:271–280.

47. Tay JSH, Yip WCL, Joseph R. Parental age and birth order in Chinese children with congenital heart disease. *J Med Genet*. 1982;19:441–443.

48. Nora JJ, Gillihand JC, Sommerville RJ, McNamara DG. Congenital heart disease in twins. *N Engl J Med*. 1967;277:568–571.

49. Geis N, Seto B, Bartoshesky L, Lewis MB, et al. The prevalence of congenital heart disease among the population of a metropolitan cleft lip and palate clinic. *Cleft Palate J*. 1981;18:19–23.

50. Friis M, Hauge M. Congenital heart defects in liveborn children of epileptic parents. *Arch Neurol*. 1985; 42:374–376.

51. McKusick VA. A genetical view of cardiovascular disease. The Lewis A. Conner Memorial Lecture. *Circ*. 1964;30:326–357.

52. Schinzel AA. Cardiac defects in chromosome aberrations in general. *Prog Med Genet*. 1983;5:307–379.

53. Lequime J, Doumit J, Polis O. The role of environment in the aetiology of congenital heart diseases. *Z Kreislauffuksen*. 1970;59:559–565.

54. Overall JC. Intrauterine virus infections and congenital heart disease. *Am Heart J*. 1972;84:823–833.

55. Wagner HR. Cardiac disease in congenital infections. *Clin Perinatol*. 1981;8:481–497.

56. Paneth N, Kiely M, Hegyi T, Hiatt IM. Investigation of a temporal cluster of left sided congenital heart disease. *J Epidemiol Community Health*. 1984;38:340–344.

57. Nora JJ, Nora AH, Wexler P. Hereditary and environmental aspects as they affect the fetus and newborn. *Clin Obstet Gynecol*. 1981;24:851–861.

58. Fedrick J, Alberman ED, Goldstein H. Possible teratogenic effect of cigarette smoking. *Nature*. 1971;231: 529–530.

59. Yerushalmy J. Congenital heart disease and maternal smoking habits. *Nature*. 1973;242:262–263.

60. Paneth N, Lansky M, Hiatt IM, Hegyi T. Congenital malformation clusters in eastern United States. *Lancet*. 1980;2:808–809.

61. Rothman KJ, Fyler DC. Association of congenital heart defects with season and population density. *Teratol*. 1975;13:29–34.

62. Nora JJ. Multifactorial inheritance hypothesis for the etiology of congenital heart diseases: the genetic-environmental interaction. *Circ*. 1968;38:604–617.

63. Nora JJ, Nora AH. Genetic epidemiology of congenital heart diseases. *Prog Med Genet*. 1983;5:91–137.

64. Newman TB. Etiology of ventricular septal defects: an epidemiologic approach. *Pediatr*. 1985;76:741–749.

65. Taussig HB. World survey of the common cardiac malformations: developmental error or genetic variant? *Am J Cardiol*. 1982;50:544–559.

66. Maestri NE, Beaty TH, Liang K-Y, Boughman JA, et al. Assessing familial aggregation of congenital cardiovascular malformations in case-control studies. *Genet Epidemiol*. 1988;5:343–354.

67. Rao PS. Preventive aspects of heart disease in infants and children. *South Med J*. 1977;70:728–740.

68. Rao PS. Prevention of heart disease in infants and children. *Curr Probl Pediatr*. 1977;7:1–48.

69. Werko L. Can we prevent heart disease? *Ann Intern Med*. 1971;74:278–288.

70. Ferencz C, Wiegmann FL, Dunning RE. Medical knowledge of young persons with heart disease. *J School Health*. 1980;50:133–136.

71. Ferencz C. Congenital heart disease: an epidemiologic and teratologic challenge. In: Ferencz C, Rubin JD, Loffredo CA, Magee CA, eds. *Perspectives in Pediatric Cardiology, IV: Epidemiology of Congenital Heart Disease. The Baltimore-Washington Infant Study 1981–1989*. Mount Kisco, NY: Futura Publishing Co, Inc; 1993: 1–15.

72. Macartney F. A better deal for newborns with congenital heart disease. *Arch Dis Children*. 1979;54:268–270.

CHAPTER 27

Kawasaki Disease

SUMMARY

Kawasaki disease, also termed mucocutaneous lymph node syndrome (MLNS, or MCLS) was first described by Kawasaki in the early 1960s in Japan, where this has become a major disease of early childhood with both endemic occurrence and epidemic outbreaks involving several thousand cases annually. Children from several months to very few years of age are the most frequently affected age group both in Japan and in the many other parts of the world where occurrence of this disease has now been reported. Kawasaki disease in the United States has overtaken acute rheumatic fever and rheumatic heart disease in annual frequency of new cases. The importance of this disease is based largely on its effects on the coronary arteries, where in some 10%–15% of cases it produces aneurysms or dilatations that may rupture or become a site of thrombosis and occlusion, leading to myocardial infarction. Current approaches to prevention are limited to treatment of the acute case to counter inflammation, coagulation, and adverse immune responses. Case fatality has become 1% or less, possibly reflecting the effectiveness of treatment. However, the cause of this recently discovered disease remains unknown, and control of neither incidence rates in populations nor risks in individual cases is yet possible. Its long-term implication for the risk of accelerated atherosclerosis in early adulthood is just beginning to be described, now that the earliest-known cases are in their 30s. Further understanding of this disease is needed from new epidemiologic and other research.

CLINICAL COURSE OF THE INDIVIDUAL CASE

In its clinical aspects, Kawasaki disease typically progresses over a period of several weeks from an acute phase of about 10 days' duration, beginning with high fever and other characteristic features. A subacute phase lasts from about 10 days to 5 weeks, during which cardiac disease most often develops in the affected cases. A convalescent phase lasts a further week or more (Figure 27–1).[1] Manifestations especially characteristic of the acute phase include an unusual-appearing conjunctivitis; red, cracked and bleeding lips and a "strawberry"-like appearance of the tongue; swelling and discoloration of the hands and feet and loss of the epithelium, the surface layer of the skin, at first from under the tips of the fingernails and then from the palms and soles; and exceptional irritability. Throughout this clinical course, laboratory investigation shows an elevated erythrocyte sedimentation rate and other indicators of an underlying inflammatory process. Very high blood platelet counts may also occur, contributing to the risks of coronary thrombosis.

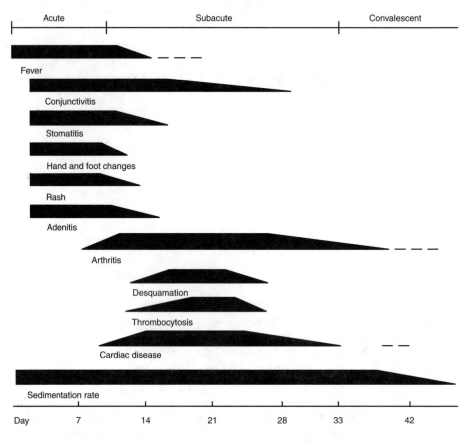

Figure 27–1 Chronology of Clinical Manifestations of Kawasaki Disease. *Source:* Copyrighted and reprinted with the permission of Clinical Cardiology Publishing Company, Inc, and/or the Foundation for Advances in Medicine and Science, Inc, Mahwah, NJ 07430-0832, USA.

The pathologic picture with respect to the coronary arteries and the heart can be described as a progression through three stages roughly concurrent with the three clinical phases just described, as well as a fourth stage extending beyond seven weeks (Exhibit 27–1).[2] The rapid development from inflammation to aneurysmal dilatations to thrombosis and obstruction of the coronary arteries, with subsequent scarring and calcification of the healed lesions, underlies the major concern about both the immediate and long-term prognosis. Serious, even fatal, complications may occur in the acute and subacute phases of the disease. The long-term effects of the arterial pathology on the rate of progression

of atherosclerosis may be considerable but have yet to be clearly determined.

BACKGROUND OF EPIDEMIOLOGIC INVESTIGATION

The disease was first reported in the Japanese medical literature in 1967 when Kawasaki described 50 cases of a condition he termed *mucocutaneous lymph node syndrome* (MLNS). He believed this to be a new disease that he had first observed in January 1961. Outside Japan, Kawasaki and colleagues' first report of this disease was published in 1974.[3] Several cases of the same condition had been recognized in Hawaii since early 1971 by Melish and, accord-

Exhibit 27–1 Stages of Pathologic Change in Kawasaki Syndrome

Stage I—Disease duration <10 days
Acute perivasculitis of coronary arteries
Microvascular angiitis of coronary arteries and aorta
Pancarditis with pericardial, myocardial, endocardial inflammation
Inflammation with atrioventricular conduction system

Stage II—Disease duration 12–28 days
Acute panvasculitis of coronary arteries
Coronary artery aneurysms present
Coronary obstruction and thrombosis
Myocardial and endocardial inflammation less intense

Stage III—Disease duration 28–45 days
Subacute inflammation in coronary arteries
Coronary artery aneurysms present
Myocardial, endocardial inflammation much depressed

Stage IV—Disease duration >50 days
Scar formation, calcification in coronary arteries
Stenosis and recanalization coronary vessel lumen
Myocardial fibrosis without acute inflammation

Source: Reprinted with permission from the *Annual Review of Medicine,* Vol 33, © 1982, by Annual Reviews, Inc.

ing to a later account, were also first reported in the United States in 1974.[4]

Stimulated by Kawasaki's initial report, the Research Committee of MLNS (hereafter termed "the Research Committee," although it is designated variously in different reports) was established in 1970 by the Japanese Ministry of Health and Welfare to investigate all major aspects of this disease. The Research Committee undertook large-scale surveys of hospitals throughout Japan to enumerate cases of this disease and obtained more detailed information for cases sampled from the total pool of those identified. Nine such surveys from 1970 through 1985–1986 had found 83,857 cases in Japan. In the interim, the Centers for Disease Control and Prevention (CDC) had established a passive surveillance system that, though presumed to be far from complete, had identified more than 2,000 cases by the end of 1985.[5] More localized surveillance in several US communities had by 1991 provided more detailed information about the US experience of this disease that included,

in addition to Hawaii, centers in New York City, Chicago, and Los Angeles. Reports had also appeared from investigations elsewhere in North and South America, Europe, Africa, Asia, and Australia.

The literature by now includes numerous epidemiologic reports of systematic surveys and long-term surveillance, especially in Japan; investigations of outbreaks or case clusters in the United States and elsewhere; occasional case-comparison studies; and extensive laboratory and clinical research, including trials of therapy in the acute and subacute phases of the disease. Highlights of the global epidemiology based on recently published reports from 22 countries are summarized by Yanagawa and Nakamura.[6] More extensive still are the proceedings of the 1995 symposium on Kawasaki disease, which addresses epidemiologic, clinical, and laboratory investigations of this disease.[7] On the basis of these numerous studies, a partial account of Kawasaki disease can be presented, although major questions about its causation and prevention and even its long-term natural course remain to be answered.

POPULATION STUDIES: DEFINITION AND CLASSIFICATION, DIAGNOSTIC ALGORITHMS, AND CRITERIA

An early task for Japan's Research Committee was to establish a working definition of the disease to standardize reporting in response to its national surveys of hospitals. The Research Committee's 1991 report published in English included a diagnostic guideline for Kawasaki disease that reflects the designation of clinical features generally maintained since the investigation of the disease began (Exhibit 27–2).[8] The presence of any five of the six principal symptoms is sufficient for the diagnosis, but four are

---

Exhibit 27–2 Diagnostic Guidelines for Kawasaki Disease, Japan, Mucocutaneous Lymph Node Syndrome Research Committee

---

This is a disease of unknown etiology affecting most frequently infants and young children under five years of age. The symptoms can be classified into two categories, principal symptoms and other significant symptoms or findings.

A. PRINCIPAL SYMPTOMS
1. Fever persisting for five days or more
2. Changes in peripheral extremities:
   [Initial stage]: reddening of palms and soles, indurative edema
   [Convalescent stage]: membranous desquamation from fingertips
3. Polymorphous exanthema
4. Bilateral conjunctival congestion
5. Changes in lips and oral cavity: reddening of lips, strawberry tongue, diffuse injection of oral and pharyngeal mucosa
6. Acute nonpurulent cervical lymphadenopathy

At least five of items 1–6 should be satisfied for diagnosis of Kawasaki disease. However, patients with four of the principal symptoms can be diagnosed as having Kawasaki disease when coronary aneurysm is recognized by two-dimensional echocardiography or coronary angiography.

B. OTHER SIGNIFICANT SYMPTOMS OR FINDINGS
   The following symptoms and findings should be clinically considered:

1. Cardiovascular: auscultation (heart murmur, gallop rhythm, distant heart sounds), ECG changes (prolonged PR-QT intervals, abnormal Q wave, low voltage, ST-T changes, arrhythmias), chest X-ray findings (cardiomegaly), 2-D echo findings (pericardial effusion, coronary aneurysms), aneurysm of peripheral arteries other than coronary (axillary, etc.), angina pectoris or myocardial infarction
2. GI tract: diarrhea, vomiting, abdominal pain, hydrops of gallbladder, paralytic ileus, mild jaundice, slight increase of serum transaminase
3. Blood: leukocytosis with shift to the left, thrombocytosis, increased ESR, positive CRP, hypoalbuminemia, increased α_2-globulin, slight decrease in erythrocyte and hemoglobin levels
4. Urine: proteinuria, increase of leukocytes in urine sediment
5. Skin: redness and crust at the site of BCG inoculation, small pustules, transverse furrows of the fingernails
6. Respiratory: cough, rhinorrhea, abnormal shadow on chest X-ray
7. Joint: pain, swelling
8. Neurological: pleocytosis of mononuclear cells in CSF, convulsions, unconsciousness, facial palsy, paralysis of the extremities

Note: CSF, cerebrospinal fluid; CRP, C-reactive protein; ESR, erythrocyte sedimentation rate; ECG, electrocardiogram; GI, gastrointestinal. For item 2 under "Principal Symptoms," the convalescent stage is considered important. Male: Female ratio, 1.3–1.5:1. Patients under 5 years of age: 80%–85%. Fatality rate: 0.3%–0.5%. Recurrence rate: 2%–3%. Proportion of sibling cases: 1%–2%.

Source: Reprinted with permission from S Naoe, *Acta Pathologica Japonica*, Vol 41, No 11, p 793, © 1991, Japanese Society of Pathology, University of Tokyo Press.

diagnostic in conjunction with echocardiographic or angiographic evidence of coronary aneurysm. Other features are noted that may also be present but do not contribute to confirmation of the diagnosis. With some variations, similar criteria are used in the United States. For example, the presence of fever is sometimes considered an absolute requirement, with the other characteristics constituting the additional criteria. Fever may be accepted as a basis for diagnosis even prior to the fifth day of illness.[9] For purposes of coding in the *International Statistical Classification of Diseases and Related Health Problems, Tenth Revision,* the category is M30.3, mucocutaneous lymph node syndrome.[10]

It has been suggested that additional illnesses should be classified with Kawasaki disease, under the designation of atypical[11] or incomplete[12] Kawasaki disease. The arguments favoring these broader definitions concern the appearance of coronary abnormalities similar to those of Kawasaki disease in all (atypical) or some (incomplete) cases not fulfilling the clinical criteria as promulgated. Perhaps such cases may closely resemble Kawasaki disease and actually represent variant forms of the disease, including prognosis and potential benefit from treatment. If so, the argument for inclusion of such cases has merit.

As with other conditions, the data on Kawasaki disease must be interpreted with recognition of variation in disease definitions and criteria, especially in comparisons over time or between data sources, in which differences in diagnostic criteria may have been introduced. However, the numbers of cases meeting only the broader definition are thought to be large, so their impact on disease statistics may be small.

RATES OF OCCURRENCE IN POPULATIONS

Japan

As of 1995, the most current data on the occurrence of Kawasaki disease in Japan were based on the 12th nationwide survey of hospitals for case enumeration.[13] Several observations can be made from these data. Nearly 70% of hospitals with 100 or more beds responded to the 1991–1992 survey, and altogether 11,221 new cases were reported, in about equal proportions for each year. The incidence estimate for Japan derived from these reports was 90 cases per 100,000 children below age five per year. This rate was described as 10 times higher than in Western countries. There was no indication of recent change in the incidence rate in Japan. Some geographic variation by prefecture was observed, with no clear pattern in the incidence rates by area but with a tendency for higher-rate areas to center around Tokyo. Cardiac manifestations were reported for about 15% of males and 10% of females with the disease. This frequency is difficult to compare with estimates in the earliest reports because neither classification of these manifestations nor diagnostic procedures were standardized over time. Deaths occurred in only 9 cases, or 0.08% of the total, in contrast to the early reports of case fatality about 20 times greater—as high as 1.7% in Kawasaki and colleagues' 1974 report of the experience in Japan through 1972.[3] This marked difference can be presumed to reflect mainly the selective identification of the severest cases initially, in contrast to the broad nationwide ascertainment of qualifying cases under the officially published guidelines in the more recent period. In addition, evidence suggests that treatment in the acute and subacute phase reduces the frequency of serious complications. Finally, the natural history of the disease may have changed over the three decades since its recognition, such that true case-fatality has decreased.

In winter of 1985–1986, Japan experienced the third in a series of epidemics that had occurred at three-year intervals since 1979 (Figure 27–2).[14] At the peak of this epidemic, the number of cases reported during a 10-day period was four to five times the number in the corresponding period during the preceding year. A space-time map charts the progression of the epidemic through the 47 prefectures by month

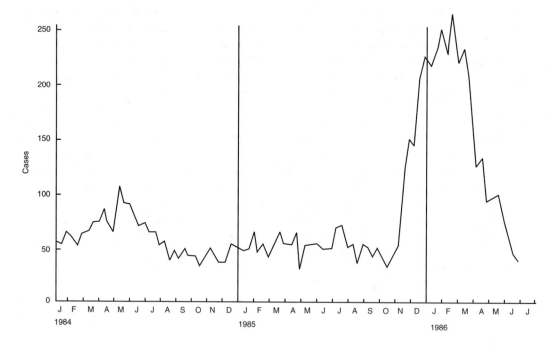

Figure 27–2 Epidemic Curve of the 1985–1986 Outbreak of Kawasaki Disease in Japan (Reported Cases per 10-Day Interval). *Source:* Reprinted with permission from JH Yanagawa et al, *Lancet,* p 1138, © 1986, The Lancet, Ltd.

from January 1985 through December 1986 (Figure 27–3).[15] The contrast of the epidemic period with the earlier and later endemic background is striking, as is the variation in peak reporting frequencies among prefectures. Characteristics of the geographic areas underlying these different slopes and peaks would be of interest.

The United States

In the United States, the voluntary reporting system for Kawasaki disease used by the CDC has continued to compile cases. Another strategy of surveillance has been a medical record department survey in selected hospitals throughout the United States—all children's hospitals and all general hospitals with 400 or more beds containing a pediatric ward—for the period 1984–1993.[16] Based on a 58% response rate, the data presented in Figure 27–4 were obtained. In

general, the number of hospital discharges coded as Kawasaki disease increased yearly over this period, reaching nearly 1,400 from all reporting hospitals by 1990, with no indication of a decrease in recent years.

A population-based survey in the Chicago area included all echocardiographic laboratories and other sources of information on pediatric patients undergoing this examination from 1979 through 1983. The survey identified 190 cases, which corresponded to an estimated mean annual incidence rate of 5.95 per 100,000 population less than 5 years of age.[17] The yield of this survey was 10 times that of the CDC surveillance program and lower than several more comparable estimates from other regional studies in the United States, generally between 5 and 10 cases per 100,000 population below age five per year. The frequency of coronary artery abnormalities among the 190 cases was 16%, and there were no deaths in this small series.

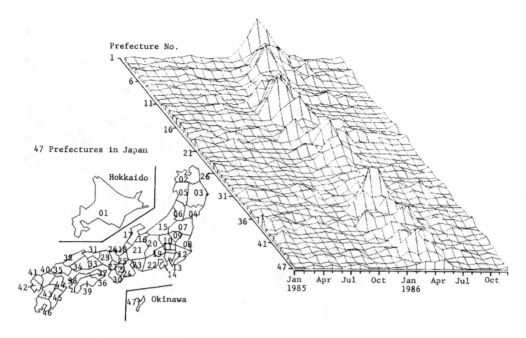

Prefecture No.

47 Prefectures in Japan

Hokkaido

Okinawa

Jan Apr Jul Oct Jan Apr Jul Oct
1985 1986

Figure 27–3 Spatiotemporal Pattern of Reported Cases in the 1985–1986 Outbreak of Kawasaki Disease in Japan. For graphic convenience, Hokkaido and Okinawa are not correctly located on the map. *Source:* Reprinted with permission from JH Yanagawa et al, A Nationwide Survey of Kawasaki Disease in 1985–1986 in Japan, *Journal of Infectious Diseases*, Vol 158, p 1299, © 1988, University of Chicago Press.

Other Countries

Reports from Finland concern both an outbreak—the first reported in Europe—occurring in 1981–1982 and the endemic situation from 1982–1992.[18,19] Evaluation of the outbreak involved contact with all 34 pediatric hospitals in the country. Of 129 suspected cases, 83 met the diagnostic criteria and had occurred from 1981 through 1984. The peak incidence was from June 1981 through March 1982, corresponding to an annual rate of 26 cases per 100,000 children under age five, in contrast to about 4 cases per 100,000 during the pre- and postoutbreak periods. A south-to-north progression in dates of peak incidence was observed. Cardiac findings included clinical symptoms in 43% of cases, electrocardiographic abnormalities in 59%, and both of these manifestations in 20%. These proportions were similar to those reported elsewhere. One death occurred due to rupture of a coronary aneurysm. In subsequent years, no epidemic has been reported from Finland, and the incidence has varied from 3 to 7 per 100,000 children under age five per year.[19]

Reports from many other localities have been noted above and document the worldwide occurrence of this disease, though nowhere have the incidence rates been known to equal those in Japan.

RISKS IN INDIVIDUALS

Consideration of factors related to individual risks begins with age, sex, race, and heredity. The age distribution of cases typical of Japan's experience over the years is illustrated in Figure 27–5.[3] The peak age at onset in Japan has remained below one year of age, perhaps younger than elsewhere, with only occasional cases occurring at age 10 or older. The ratio of male to female cases is generally between 1.0

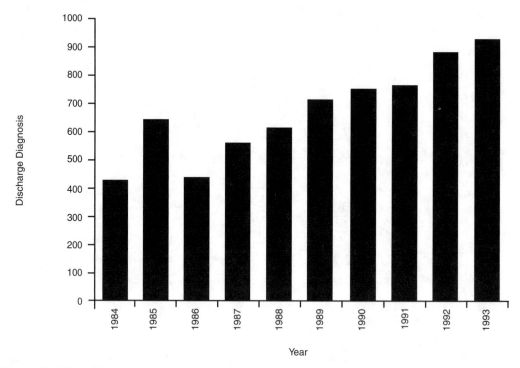

Figure 27–4 Surveillance of Discharge Diagnoses of Kawasaki Disease in Selected US Hospitals, 1984–1993. *Source:* Reprinted from KA Taubert, International Congress Series, No 1093, p 36, Copyright 1995, with kind permission of Elsevier Science-NL, Sara Burgerhartstraat 25, 1055 KV Amsterdam, The Netherlands.

and 2.0. Children of Asian background exhibit higher incidence rates than others in the same localities (eg, as in Hawaii), though Japanese outside Japan do not exhibit the same high rate as those in Japan.

Recurrent episodes of disease in the same individual have been reported from several months up to two years or more from the first episode, the incidence being about 5 per 1,000 person-years in one follow-up study in Japan.[20] Second cases in the same family occur only rarely (overall, about 2% of siblings being affected) but are many times more frequent than in the population at large (Table 27–1).[21] This relation is age-dependent, decreasing from 8% to 9% for siblings under age two to less than 1% among siblings four to five years old. No clear genetic relationships have been identified to explain either this limited concordance within families nor the general excess risk among chil-

dren of Japanese and perhaps other Asian ancestry relative to other racial groups.

From the many studies in search of possible etiologic associations, no well-established risk factor has emerged. Retroviruses and many other infectious agents have been proposed, environmental exposures to house dusts or waterborne substances have been suggested, and countless other potential exposures have been addressed in one study or another. Possible immune mechanisms and other factors in the progression from the initial (still unknown) event to the progressive arteritis, vascular damage, and thrombosis characteristic of the most severe cases have been studied in many centers around the world. The proceedings of international conferences on Kawasaki disease include reports on much of this work and references to their findings to date (eg, Kato[7]; Shulman[22]). Despite this extensive body of material, the cau-

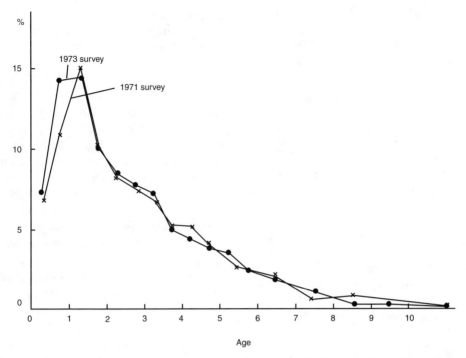

Figure 27–5 Distribution of Age at Onset among Cases of Kawasaki Disease in Japan, 1971–1973. *Source:* Reproduced by permission of *Pediatrics,* Vol 54, p 275, 1974.

sation of Kawasaki disease remains unknown at present.

Only very limited information is available concerning the long-term survival and health status of nonfatal cases of Kawasaki disease.[7] In some cases, apparently complete regression of the coronary lesions occurs. The extent of scarring and calcification of healed coronary artery lesions among some other cases raises serious concern about the risk of unusually rapid pro-

Table 27–1 Secondary Attack Rate for Kawasaki Disease among Siblings of Index Cases

Age at Onset of First Cases	No. of Siblings	No. of Secondary Attacks	Secondary Attack Rate (%)
Birth–≤1 yr	143	12	8.4
>1 yr–≤2 yr	107	10	9.3
>2 yr–≤3 yr	184	8	4.3
>3 yr–≤4 yr	232	3	1.3
>4 yr–≤5 yr	230	2	0.9
>5 yr	723	0	
1–5 mo[a]	85	2	2.4
6–11 mo[a]	84	0	

a. Siblings born after 0–5 months or 6–11 months of the onset of first case.

Source: Reproduced by permission of *Pediatrics,* Vol 84, p 667, 1989.

gression of atherosclerosis to complicated lesions and acute coronary events, yet few observations to address this issue have been identified.

PREVENTION AND TREATMENT

From the foregoing review it is apparent that control of Kawasaki disease at the population level is presently unattainable in either its endemic or its epidemic occurrence. At the individual level, intervention in the acute phase of the disease is now widely practiced with anti-inflammatory/anticoagulant and immunologic therapy, by use of aspirin and intravenous immune globulin. One formulation of longer-term intervention strategies for individual patients is shown in Table 27–2.[23] In this approach, risk is first assessed in reference to the status of the coronary arteries. Then anticoagulant therapy, limitation of physical activity, diagnostic follow-up, and possibly invasive testing are recommended in accordance with the severity of residual coronary disease.

Effectiveness of various treatment regimens in the acute phase of the disease is addressed in several reports from the 1995 symposium. In a small number of cases, cardiac transplantation has been performed.[7] Whether longer-term intervention would reduce the risk of accelerated atherosclerosis and other late consequences of Kawasaki disease after childhood does not appear to have received extensive investigation. The importance of this question is underscored by reports of long-term follow-up of cases into early adulthood, with detection of subclinical (inapparent) coronary abnormalities by coronary arteriography or ultrafast computed tomographic scanning of the heart.[24]

CURRENT ISSUES

Clearly, the leading issue at present is to explain the differences among populations in their incidence rates of Kawasaki disease, which is by definition quite uniform in its clinical appearance and laboratory findings throughout the world but occurs many times more frequently among Japanese in Japan than in any other reported population, including, for example, children of Japanese ancestry living in Hawaii.

Second in importance is to understand the factors that place some children individually at greater risk than others. The strongest predictor of individual risk appears to be having an affected sibling, especially one of age two years or younger. Causal explanation of the disease will need to be consistent with this striking observation.

In addition, interventions are needed to prevent destructive coronary artery and other cardiac complications so as to further reduce case fatality and improve long-term prognosis. In the latter connection, follow-up of cases who are now young adults (many are now in their 20s or 30s) to evaluate their cardiovascular status would be revealing as to long-term prognosis and the need for high-risk interventions to prevent very early complications of atherosclerosis.

Table 27–2 Risk Stratification and Recommended Case Management

Risk Level	Pharmacologic Therapy	Physical Activity	Follow-Up and Diagnostic Testing	Invasive Testing
I (no coronary artery changes at any stage of illness)	None beyond initial 6 to 8 weeks	No restrictions beyond initial 6 to 8 weeks	None beyond first year unless cardiac disease suspected	None recommended
II (transient coronary artery ectasia that disappears during acute illness)	None beyond initial 6 to 8 weeks	No restrictions beyond initial 6 to 8 weeks	None beyond first year unless cardiac disease suspected. Physician may choose to see patient at 3- to 5-year intervals.	None recommended
III (small to medium solitary coronary artery aneurysm)	3 to 5 mg/kg of aspirin per day, at least until abnormalities resolve	For patients in first decade of life, no restriction beyond initial 6 to 8 weeks. For patients in second decade, physical activity guided by stress testing every other year. Competitive contact athletics with endurance training discouraged.	Annual follow-up with echocardiogram ± electrocardiogram in first decade of life	Angiography, if stress testing or echocardiography suggests stenosis
IV (one or more giant coronary artery aneurysms, or multiple small to medium aneurysms, without obstruction)	Long-term aspirin (3 to 5 mg/kg per day) ± warfarin	For patients in first decade of life, no restriction beyond initial 6 to 8 weeks. For patients in second decade, annual stress testing guides recommendations. Strenuous athletics are strongly discouraged. If stress test rules out ischemia, noncontact recreational sports allowed.	Annual follow-up with echocardiogram ± electrocardiogram ± chest X-ray ± additional electrocardiogram at 6-month intervals. For patients in first decade of life, pharmacologic stress testing should be considered.	Angiography, if stress testing or echocardiography suggests stenosis. Elective catheterization may be done in certain circumstances.
V (coronary artery obstruction)	Long-term aspirin (3 to 5 mg/kg per day) ± warfarin. Use of calcium channel blockers should be considered to reduce myocardial oxygen consumption.	Contact sports, isometrics, and weight training should be avoided. Other physical activity recommendations guided by outcome of stress testing or myocardial perfusion scan.	Echocardiogram and electrocardiogram at 6-month intervals and annual Holter and stress testing	Angiography recommended for some patients to aid in selecting therapeutic options. Repeat angiography with new onset or worsening ischemia.

Note: ±, with or without.

Source: Reprinted with permission from AS Dajani, *Circulation*, Vol 89, p 920, © 1994, American Heart Association.

REFERENCES

1. Melish ME. Clinical and epidemiologic aspects of Kawasaki disease. *Clin Cardiol.* 1991;14(suppl II):II-3–II-10.

2. Melish ME. Kawasaki syndrome (the mucocutaneous lymph node syndrome). *Annu Rev Med.* 1982;33:569–585.

3. Kawasaki T, Kosaki F, Okawa S, Shigematsu I, et al. A new infantile acute febrile mucocutaneous lymph node syndrome (MLNS) prevailing in Japan. *Pediatr.* 1974; 54:271–276.

4. Morens DM, O'Brien RJ. News—From the Centers for Disease Control—Kawasaki disease in the United States. *J Infect Dis.* 1978;137:91–92.

5. Mason WH, Schneider T, Takahashi M. The epidemiology and etiology of Kawasaki disease. *Cardio Young.* 1991;1:196–205.

6. Yanagawa H, Nakamura Y. Comments on global epidemiology of Kawasaki disease. In: Kato H, ed. *Kawasaki Disease: Proceedings of the 5th International Kawasaki Disease Symposium.* Fukuoka, Japan, 22–25 May 1995. Amsterdam, the Netherlands: Elsevier; 1995: 90–100, International Congress Series No. 1093.

7. Kato H, ed. *Kawasaki Disease: Proceedings of the 5th International Kawasaki Disease Symposium.* Fukuoka, Japan, 22–25 May 1995. Amsterdam, the Netherlands: Elsevier; 1995. International Congress Series No. 1093.

8. Naoe S, Takahashi K, Masuda H, Tanaka N. Kawasaki disease: with particular emphasis on arterial lesions. *Acta Pathol Jpn.* 1991;41:785–797.

9. Rowley AH, Gonzalez-Crussi F, Shulman ST. Kawasaki syndrome. *Adv Pediatr.* 1991;38:51–74.

10. World Health Organization. *International Statistical Classification of Diseases and Related Health Problems: Tenth Revision.* Geneva, Switzerland: World Health Organization; 1992.

11. Levy M, Koren G. Atypical Kawasaki disease: analysis of clinical presentation and diagnostic clues. *Pediatr Infect Dis J.* 1990;9:122–126.

12. Fukushige J, Takahashi N, Ueda Y, Ueda K. Incidence and clinical features of incomplete Kawasaki disease. *Acta Pediatr.* 1994;83:1057–1060.

13. Yanagawa H, Yashiro M, Nakamura Y, Kawasaki T, et al. Epidemiologic pictures of Kawasaki disease in Japan: from the nationwide incidence survey in 1991 and 1992. *Pediatr.* 1995;95:475–479.

14. Yanagawa H, Nakamura Y, Kawasaki T, Shigematsu I. Nationwide epidemic of Kawasaki disease in Japan during winter of 1985–1986. *Lancet.* 1986;ii:1138–1139.

15. Yanagawa H, Nakamura Y, Yashiro M, Fujita Y, et al. A nationwide survey of Kawasaki disease in 1985–1986 in Japan. *J Infect Dis.* 1988;158:1296–1301.

16. Taubert KA, Rowley AH, Shulman ST. A 10 year (1984–1993) United States hospital survey of Kawasaki disease. In: Kato H, ed. *Kawasaki Disease: Proceedings of the 5th International Kawasaki Disease Symposium.* Fukuoka, Japan, 22–25 May 1995. Amsterdam, the Netherlands: Elsevier; 1995: 34–38, International Congress Series No. 1093.

17. Shulman ST, McAuley JB, Pachman LM, Miller ML, et al. Risk of coronary abnormalities due to Kawasaki disease in urban area with small Asian population. *Am J Dis Children.* 1987;141:420–425.

18. Salo E, Pelkonen P, Pettay O. Outbreak of Kawasaki syndrome in Finland. *Acta Pediatr Scand.* 1986;75: 75–80.

19. Salo E. Kawasaki disease in Finland in 1982–1992. *Scand J Infect Dis.* 1993;25:497–502.

20. Nakamura Y, Hirose K, Yanagawa H, Kato H, et al. Incidence rate of recurrent Kawasaki disease in Japan. *Acta Pediatr.* 1994;83:1061–1064.

21. Fujita Y, Nakamura Y, Sakata K, Hara N, et al. Kawasaki disease in families. *Pediatr.* 1989;84:666–669.

22. Shulman ST, ed. *Kawasaki Disease: Proceedings of the Second International Kawasaki Disease Symposium.* Kauai, Hawaii, November 30–December 3, 1986. New York; Alan R. Liss, Inc; 1987.

23. Dajani AS, Taubert KA, Takahashi M, Bierman FZ, et al. Guidelines for long-term management of patients with Kawasaki disease: report from the Committee on Rheumatic Fever, Endocarditis, and Kawasaki Disease, Council on Cardiovascular Disease in the Young, American Heart Association. *Circ.* 1994;89:916–922.

24. Kato H. Long-term consequences of Kawasaki disease: pediatrics to adults. In: Kato H, ed. *Kawasaki Disease: Proceedings of the 5th International Kawasaki Disease Symposium.* Fukuoka, Japan, 22–25 May 1995. Amsterdam, the Netherlands: Elsevier; 1995: 557–566, International Congress Series No. 1093.

PART V

Achieving the Potential for Cardiovascular Disease Prevention

CHAPTER 28

Implementation of Prevention Policies: Meeting the Global Challenges

SUMMARY

Prevention policies are not being implemented sufficiently at either the population-wide or the individual, high-risk level. Despite a substantial research foundation for such policy in many areas and the formation of appropriate policies and guidelines on this basis, preventive measures are having less than their full potential impact. Several obstacles, at both population-wide and high-risk levels, pose challenges for preventive action in the near and longer-term future. Seen as the last stage in the transition from etiological research to public health application, the implementation of prevention policy is a task requiring commitment by all health professionals but especially by epidemiologists. One example of application and evaluation of preventive measures has been initiated by the International Society and Federation of Cardiology (ISFC) and is being contemplated by a joint United Nations Educational, Scientific, and Cultural Organization (UNESCO)/World Health Organization (WHO)/ISFC task force. It would comprise a series of demonstration projects in one or two sites in each WHO Region designed to show the feasibility of slowing, arresting, or reversing the progression of the major risk factors in several contrasting population settings. The needs and opportunities for effective prevention of the cardiovascular diseases are great, even while further research continues that may still better inform prevention policies of the future.

INTRODUCTION

The topic of this chapter concerns cardiovascular disease prevention on a global scale. In summing up the practical implications of all the preceding chapters, partitioning the challenges for prevention according to the major disease categories adopted earlier is a first step, although it is recognized that some generic issues of policy development and implementation are not specific to any particular disease. Therefore atherosclerotic and hypertensive diseases are discussed first and in greatest detail. Shorter sections on rheumatic fever/rheumatic heart disease, Chagas' disease and other cardiomyopathies, congenital heart disease, and Kawasaki disease follow.

In each case a brief review of the disease problem leads into discussion of current policy and current action, first at the population-wide level and second at the individual, high-risk level. Each section includes comment on major issues concerning implementation of intervention strategies for consideration in the immediate and near term or longer. In conclusion, obstacles and opportunities for policy implementation are addressed. Further research is always a possible recourse, but the intent here is to distinguish between reasonable action needed on the basis of current knowledge and desirable further research, with the potential for even better-informed policy in the future. The first of these is addressed in the present chapter, the second in the final chapter.

ATHEROSCLEROTIC AND HYPERTENSIVE DISEASES

The Problem

Atherosclerosis and hypertension and their several major clinical complications have occurred in epidemic form throughout much of the 20th century in most industrial market economies. This is true even of Japan, Spain, and France, which have experienced relatively low mortality from coronary heart disease but offsetting high rates of stroke. Data for the United States through 1994 suggest that the decline in age-standardized mortality from coronary heart disease and stroke may not continue as in the past two decades. Final mortality data for 1993 showed increases in rates of coronary mortality for the first time in many years for women and men, Blacks and Whites. For 1994, rates were again decreasing in all groups (N Haase, American Heart Association, personal communication, 1997). It will be of interest to observe the trend in rates over the remainder of the 1990s. Whether other countries that have shown similarly marked declines in mortality from the peak rates of the 1960s, such as Finland, have experienced a change in their downward trend of coronary mortality is an important but presently unanswered question. Forthcoming data from the WHO MONICA Project, from the mid-1980s to mid-1990s, are expected to contribute considerable insight.

Regardless of the age-specific mortality, however, when measured by total morbidity the epidemic curve has remained near its peak or has risen, and there are increasing numbers of survivors with previous coronary events or stroke, the former often associated with conges-

tive heart failure. From this point of view, epidemic atherosclerotic and hypertensive diseases continue, even in the countries with already decades-long histories of this process and declining age-adjusted cardiovascular disease mortality. Added to these are the countries with documented or anecdotally reported increases in occurrence of these conditions and the remainder whose demographic, social, and economic development are expected to result in their own cardiovascular disease epidemics in future years. Prevention of these diseases is no less urgent a public health priority in the mid-1990s than was the case at the peak of mortality rates occurring as long as 30 years ago.

The Population-Wide Level

Current Policy in the United States

Prevention policy at the population level is reflected in the United States in such recommendations as those in the Surgeon General's reports on smoking, the several panels of the National Cholesterol Education Program, and the Joint National Committee and Task Force reports from the National High Blood Pressure Education Program. Especially in these latter recommendations concerning blood cholesterol concentrations and blood pressure, population-wide measures are explicitly advocated as the primary strategy for prevention and control of the major risk factors themselves. The US health objectives set forth in *Healthy People 2000* further address not only these risk factors but also underlying behaviors (nutrition and physical activity), school health curricula and food services, and the need to provide preventive programs in the workplace.[1] Recommendations of many other official and voluntary organizations and agencies such as the American Heart Association are consistent with the population-wide approach.

Current Policy Globally

Internationally, the WHO, the World Hypertension League, and several agencies concerned with tobacco control have adopted concordant policies with the objective of prevention of cardiovascular and other chronic diseases. While some differences can be found in specific goals such as those for dietary change or maintenance levels for blood pressure and cholesterol concentration, such differences are not major. Both youth and adulthood are addressed, and intervention settings such as schools, worksites, and health care institutions are identified in many of the recommendations and policy statements. The several Expert Reports of the World Health Organization, developed under the auspices of the former Cardiovascular Disease Unit, were landmarks for more than three decades in the progress of scientific review and policy development supporting global efforts to prevent cardiovascular diseases. At this level of consideration, at least, availability of policy guidelines is not a limiting factor in population-wide cardiovascular disease prevention.

It should be noted that in the international arena especially, as clearly found in the policy milieu of the WHO, cardiovascular diseases have increasingly been merged with other major chronic diseases under noncommunicable diseases. The Cardiovascular Disease Unit was itself merged into the Noncommunicable Diseases Division of WHO in 1996. Whatever the rationale for this action, leading causes of death and disability do, in part, reflect common causes. Therefore, modification of these causal factors would have a broader preventive impact than that measured by change in any one chronic condition alone, even cardiovascular diseases. The epidemiologic foundation for this view was advanced, especially recently, by the work of Epstein.[2] This concept underlies the development of the WHO Integrated Programme for Noncommunicable Diseases Prevention and Control (Interhealth), outlined by Shigan in 1988.[3] The basis for amalgamation of disease-specific and risk factor–specific activities into a single program includes the cross-linkages shown in Figure 28–1. The core diseases are heart disease, stroke, diabetes, cancer, and respiratory diseases, and the common risk factors are diet, tobacco, alcohol, physical activity, environment, oral hygiene, blood pressure, lipids, and glucose. The proposed strategies include population-wide interventions to promote health in whole communities through change in individuals' behavior, reorganization of health care, and development of new intersectoral health-oriented enterprises.

Current Action in the United States

Within the United States, action to prevent cardiovascular diseases is reflected in favorable trends in some but not all risk factors, as indicated by data from the National Center for Health Statistics, many of which are summarized in the *Healthy People 2000, Review 1995–96*.[4] Other sources, cited in Chapter 12, demonstrate a downward shift in the whole distribution of systolic blood pressure that is evident in the median values rather than only in the 90th percentile values, which reflect broader influences than treatment effects among high-risk individuals.[5] Cholesterol concentrations have also decreased, although the fact that these recent trends have been reported only in terms of mean values, which are affected by changes at the upper extreme, does not permit discrimination between population-wide and treatment effects as was possible for blood pressure trends.[6] In addition, the proportion of adults who report having had cholesterol determinations at any time or within the past two years has increased for most population groups for whom data have been reported.[4] Prevalence of cigarette smoking has decreased among persons age 18 years and older, although recent data show that teen smoking is increasing in prevalence once again. Dietary fat intake had decreased slightly by the early 1990s, though under one-third of adults met goals of fewer than 30% of calories from fat and 10% from saturated fat. Salt intake has not decreased and may instead have increased. Prevalence of habitual moderate physical activity increased slightly from the 1985 baseline but remained at less than 25% of the adult population as of 1992. Meanwhile, somewhat paradoxically,

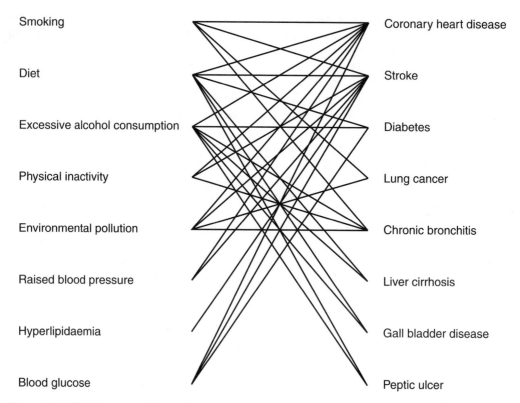

Figure 28–1 Risk Factors and Noncommunicable Diseases—Main Links. *Source:* Reprinted with permission from E Shigan, *World Health Statistics Quarterly*, Vol 41, p 268, © 1988, World Health Organization.

overweight increased in every target group, and for some groups increased markedly, from the late 1970s to the early 1990s.

Although change in nearly every area except overweight has been favorable, many of the goals set for the year 2000 remain distant. Still, population-wide changes in risk factors and behaviors are clearly documented that in the aggregate indicate change in health-related behavior of individuals. Given the many counterinfluences at work, it is reasonable to infer that the prevention policies noted above have had a significant impact.

Current Action Globally

Globally, current action at the population level is not directly measurable in published data as for the United States, although some country-specific data could doubtless be compiled. The WHO MONICA Project will soon report data on trends in major risk factors from the mid-1980s to the mid-1990s from some 40 countries.[7] This unprecedented view of population change in cardiovascular risk factors will be instructive, indicating where prevention policies may have been most effective and where their intensified application is most needed.

In the interim, examples can be cited of organized efforts to implement these policies through both official and voluntary channels. For example, in the WHO Interhealth program cited above, 18 demonstration projects were reported to have been in progress in 15 countries including all WHO Regions, as of 1988.

These were intended to be supplemented by mathematical modeling studies, training activities, and research. Details of the elements of each planned activity are summarized in the report.[3] Currently, further development of a global strategy for integrated prevention of noncommunicable diseases is continuing within WHO.

Another global effort to mobilize action to prevent cardiovascular diseases is represented by the International Heart Health Conferences, inaugurated in Victoria, British Columbia, in 1992. This first conference, with primary sponsorship from private and governmental agencies in Canada and cosponsorship from the WHO, the Pan American Health Organization, and the World Hypertension League, culminated in the adoption of the *Victoria Declaration on Heart Health*, which read as follows:

> Recognizing that both scientific knowledge and widely tested methods exist to prevent most cardiovascular diseases, the Advisory Board of the International Conference on Heart Health calls upon
>
> - health, media, education and social science professionals, and their associations
> - the scientific community
> - government agencies concerned with health, education, trade, commerce, and agriculture
> - the private sector
> - international organizations and agencies concerned with health and economic development
> - community health coalitions
> - voluntary health organizations
> - employers and their organizations
>
> to join forces in eliminating this modern epidemic by adopting new policies, making regulatory changes and implementing health promotion and disease prevention programs directed at entire populations.[8(p iv)]

In the accompanying *Call for Action* and *Policy Framework*, the Advisory Board outlined elements of policy, an implementation process, and partnerships needed for effective action. They presented 59 recommendations for specific actions to be taken. The Implementation Group was charged to pursue the recommended actions, under the leadership of the conference chair, Jack Farquhar.

Following the Second International Heart Health Conference, convened in Barcelona in 1995, *The Catalonia Declaration: Investing in Heart Health* compiled more than 40 case studies to illustrate accomplishments toward improvements in heart health in diverse settings throughout the world.[9] This declaration supplemented the preceding one especially by emphasizing the assets currently available to support improvements in heart health and by outlining methods for use of these assets. The economic benefits as well as the humanitarian effects of successful promotion of heart health were underscored. Recommendations for action by specified types of groups, agencies, and organizations were included, consistent with those presented in the previous declaration. The continuing Implementation Group was charged further to convene conferences at all governmental levels where prevention policy could be considered and to facilitate access to financial and technical assistance for both developing countries and others with especially limited economic resources.

The Individual, High-Risk Level

Persons considered to be at high risk may in principle be defined in four categories: those presently free of risk factors but especially likely to develop major risk factors in the future; those with established risk factors; those already experiencing acute cardiovascular disease events; or those surviving such events or otherwise recognized as having clinically detectable disease. With the possible exception of the first of these categories, recognition of high risk occurs mainly in the context of health care settings or in screening programs, which ideally provide referral for health care. Therefore, policies concerning high risk are closely related to aspects of clinical practice. Because practice conditions may differ widely among countries, including availability of financial and technical resources, it is unclear how broadly the policies elaborated for high-risk intervention in the United States, for example, can be generalized. Use of United States–based policies for illustration therefore has recognized limitations but may serve to represent countries with some of the more fully developed recommendations. They do appear to be broadly applicable in Europe, as discussed below.

Current Policy

As reviewed in Chapter 22, the content of current policy recommendations for prevention of atherosclerotic and hypertensive diseases in high-risk individuals is highly consistent with the advice of the National Health Education Committee Inc., published nearly 40 years ago.[10] Much greater detail is now provided, however, and particular needs of special population groups such as youth, the elderly, women, and minorities are addressed.

Taking the US situation as an example, recommendations concerning the detection and management of the major risk factors—principally, high concentrations of total or low-density lipoprotein cholesterol, high blood pressure, and smoking—provide extensive guidance to health professionals caring for persons from early childhood to advanced age (see Chapter 22). For patients experiencing acute myocardial infarction, guidelines adopted jointly by the American College of Cardiology and the American Heart Association, presented in 1996, also address details of treatment through the first 24 hours, the subsequent hospital stay, preparation for hospital discharge, and the long-term posthospitalization period.[11] For survivors of acute myocardial infarction or those with known coronary artery disease, recommendations for management of 21 risk factors were presented in an extensive report of the 1995

Bethesda Conference of the American College of Cardiology, reviewed in Chapter 22.[12] For the purpose of these latter recommendations, the risk factors were stratified into four classes based on current evidence for the benefit and feasibility of their alteration. Thus, at the high-risk level, potentially comprising groups identified by quite varied criteria, there is no lack of guidance from available policy guidelines.

Current Action

What action is currently being taken to implement these prevention policies? In the United States, there are many indications that practice often fails to match recommendations. For example, *Healthy People 2000, Review 1995–96* reports clinician counseling about physical activity in only 13%–30% of provider categories rather than the year 2000 target of 50% of patients; nutrition assessment and counseling by 15%–53% rather than the target of 75%; smoking cessation counseling, which is to include discussion of strategies to quit among at least 80% of smoking patients, by 19%–50% of clinicians, versus the target of 75%; and controlled high blood pressure by 29% of those with high blood pressure versus the target of 50%.[4] Closest to the year 2000 target was blood cholesterol determination within the past two years, reported by 66% of persons in 1993 versus the target of 75%.

With respect to risk factor management in childhood, surveys reported in 1987 and 1990 revealed substantial lack of action by pediatricians and especially by other primary care providers for children and adolescents.[13,14] Explanations included lack of recognition of the three major risk factors, reservations about the need for early intervention, unpreparedness to provide the needed advice and counseling, and perceived inability to affect blood lipids through dietary changes.

In adulthood also, as suggested by the *Healthy People 2000* update cited above, gaps are found between recommendations and practice. Specifically for interventions on blood pressure and smoking, for example, investigators in the Stanford Five City Project found in 1985 that fewer than 20% of physicians provided health education materials on these risk factors, despite their reported belief that control of these risk factors would have a large effect on coronary heart disease risk.[15] For overweight, sedentary lifestyle, and elevated blood cholesterol, fewer than half of the group of physicians surveyed (and this was after 38% nonresponse) considered potential effects of reduction of these risk factors as important. Generally, specialists were even less likely than primary care physicians to provide educational materials.

Surveys of 1,200–1,600 US physicians in the mid-1980s indicated a marked increase in prevalence of the view that reducing cholesterol concentrations would reduce coronary heart disease risk, from 39% in 1983 to 64% in 1986. This change occurred following the report of the Lipid Research Clinics' Coronary Primary Prevention Trial.[16] Correspondingly, the reported levels of cholesterol at which treatment would be instituted decreased over this interval, especially in the judgment of cardiologists. Over the same period, little change in attitude was reported for other risk factors except

decreased importance of stress and Type A behavior. If the report of the clinical trial had some impact, awareness of a trial in an Oregon courtroom might have reinforced it. In the trial, a jury awarded $400,000 to survivors of a woman dying of myocardial infarction whose known high cholesterol concentration was judged to have been treated inadequately for 15 years before her death.[17] But even persons surviving coronary events, who are at especially high risk of recurrence and death, often fail to receive recommended risk factor intervention, as summarized in the 1995 Bethesda Conference report cited above and shown in Table 28–1.[18]

Central Issues

The central issues in the prevention of atherosclerotic and hypertensive diseases concern not the scientific basis for sound recommendations nor the availability of policy statements and guidelines at both population and high-risk levels but rather the actual implementation of these by the organizations, agencies, or health professionals on whom implementation depends. Policies for population-wide intervention are better supported scientifically than the marketing strategies they are in part designed to counter. The commonplace laissez-faire policy of inaction leaves the latter strategies altogether unopposed. Similarly, it could be argued that both the underlying research and the detailed protocols recommended for addressing individuals at high risk provide better justification for these interventions than for many other common clinical practices. Fuller implementation of current policies at both population and high-risk levels appears to require identifying and addressing the critical obstacles. What these may be, and what opportunities may be available to address them, are considered later in this chapter.

Table 28–1 Estimates of Levels of Risk Factor Management in Patients Surviving Myocardial Infarction

Form of Intervention	% of Patients
Referral to cardiac rehabilitation program	<5%
Smoking cessation counseling	20%
Lipid-lowering drug therapy	25%
Beta-blocker therapy	40%
ACE inhibitor therapy (reduced LV ejection fraction)	60%
Aspirin	70%

Note: ACE, angiotensin-converting enzyme; LV, left ventricular.

Source: Reprinted with permission from the American College of Cardiology, *Journal of the American College of Cardiology*, 1996, Vol 27, p 1040.

OTHER CARDIOVASCULAR DISEASES

For each of the other examples of cardiovascular diseases addressed in Chapters 24–27, much of what is known about their prevention and control is reviewed in the respective chapter. Emphasis is given here to aspects that bear most closely on the potential for their prevention in the immediate future through implementation of currently recognized strategies. Obstacles and opportunities to enhance such implementation are discussed for these conditions later in this chapter as well.

Rheumatic Fever and Rheumatic Heart Disease

The Problem

Rheumatic fever and rheumatic heart disease constitute the major form of cardiovascular disease in some populations, including much of Africa, the Eastern Mediterranean, and Asia. Although newly occurring cases are relatively rare in the United States, localities such as Hawaii and the Intermountain region in the lower Rocky Mountains serve as reminders of the potential for increases in incidence. So far, the pathogenesis of the disease remains obscure, and predictors of individual risk for progression of Group A beta-hemolytic streptococcal infection of the throat to rheumatic fever and carditis remain unknown. Therefore strategies of prevention continue to depend chiefly on long-term administration of penicillin to individuals with known Group A streptococcal pharyngitis or with currently or historically diagnosed acute rheumatic fever.

The Population-Wide Level

Because intervention against rheumatic fever and rheumatic heart disease ultimately requires individual treatment, the high-risk approach is essential for control of this disease. However, population-level components of effective national or regional programs for rheumatic fever and rheumatic heart disease prophylaxis are also needed to support effective implementation at the individual level. As outlined and illustrated in Chapter 24, national programs require laboratory support, personnel training, health education, and statistical reporting, among other elements.[19] In most affected populations, crowding, poor sanitation, and high risks of transmission of communicable disease agents offer potential for population-wide strategies of intervention. These factors are already identifiable as goals for social and economic development, and their attainment would have many specific health implications, including prevention of rheumatic fever and rheumatic heart disease.

The Individual, High-Risk Level

Primary prevention of rheumatic fever and rheumatic heart disease is seen as requiring case detection of Group A beta-hemolytic streptococcal pharyngitis and treatment of those cases. The high attendant costs per prevented case of rheumatic heart disease limit the feasibility of this approach. The high proportion of cases, perhaps 50%, arising from inapparent infections makes primary prevention unavoidably incomplete even where it could in principle be applied. For these reasons, reliance on case detection at the stage of rheumatic fever or already existing rheumatic heart disease remains the more practical approach. For reasons discussed in Chapter 24, immunization is not an immediately promising strategy due to dynamic antigenic properties of the organism.

Central Issues

As identified in the most recent WHO Expert Committee report on rheumatic fever and rheumatic heart disease, several issues warrant continued or renewed attention.[20] These include, among other recommendations: (1) organized, prospective collection of reliable epidemiologic data, emphasizing representation of rural and urban areas and prospective study through school-based programs; (2) development of an improved test for streptococcal antibody; (3) studies to monitor the use and adverse effects of intramuscular benzathine benzylpenicillin, the preferred agent for penicillin prophylaxis; (4) expansion of pilot control programs where such programs have been implemented into long-term health services activities; (5) national resources for implementation of ultrasound examination for assessment of rheumatic heart disease and other heart diseases; and (6) improved health education for persons with rheumatic heart disease to practice appropriate dental hygiene and obtain appropriate prophylaxis against infections from surgical interventions or treatment of intercurrent infections. These and other measures are considered critical for successful implementation of the existing recommendations for prevention of rheumatic heart disease and its late complications.

Chagas' Disease and Other Cardiomyopathies

The Problem

For most of the currently recognized cardiomyopathies, causation is unknown and no means of prevention is yet available. Even the magnitude of the problem has been difficult to estimate, due in part to the absence of standard nomenclature and criteria prior to the publication of the WHO/ISFC Task Force scheme presented in Chapter 25. Some of the "specific heart muscle diseases," according to that classification, do offer possibilities for prevention: alcoholic cardiomyopathy, peripartal heart disease, Keshan disease, and Chagas' disease. Information concerning the first three of these conditions is based on a WHO Expert Committee report from 1984.[21] For Chagas' disease, a more recent report from another Expert Committee provides extensive detail on control measures.[22]

Alcoholic Cardiomyopathy

The Population-Wide Level. Measures to reduce the frequency of long-term high daily intakes of alcohol can reduce the expected frequency of alcoholic cardiomyopathy, which is thought to require 10 years or more of 100 g/day of alcohol consumption.

The Individual, High-Risk Level. The individual who consumes large quantities of alcohol is uniquely at risk for alcoholic cardiomyopathy. Identification of such persons through recognition of other alcohol-related health or social problems or through usual inquiry about health habits would permit instituting preventive measures in such individuals long in advance of disease expression.

Peripartal Heart Disease

The Population-Wide Level. Cardiomyopathy appearing in the mother immediately after birth or in succeeding months, and occasionally before delivery, may in at least one population result from local customs that are potentially amenable to intervention. In northern Nigeria, postpartum practices include excessive body heating and salt intake, which may produce overt cardiomyopathy in women with already-present heart muscle disease. Health education could in principle reduce or eliminate this specific postpartum exposure that appears to trigger the appearance of disease.

The Individual, High-Risk Level. Close monitoring of blood pressure and cardiac status throughout pregnancy would permit early detection of individual cases, and special attention to nutritional status and risk of infection during pregnancy may contribute to prevention of this condition.

Keshan Disease

The Population-Wide Level. Keshan disease is a form of cardiomyopathy found in China, occurring in children below age 15 and in women of childbearing age and geographically confined to a narrow band of rural areas crossing 14 provinces. A relatively high frequency of disease among agricultural families and seasonal variation in its occurrence led to studies of possible dietary factors. It was concluded that selenium deficiency was a prominent contributing factor. Therefore, population-wide measures of health education and provision of selenium supplementation in the diet may have important preventive impact. By the mid-1980s, it appeared that these measures were effective and that few new cases were occurring.

The Individual, High-Risk Level. Individuals thought to be at high risk because of known dietary deficiencies or for whom family members were affected would constitute high-risk persons for whom individual intervention would be appropriate.

Chagas' Disease

The Population-Wide Level. Chagas' disease control programs have been conducted with impressive results, as reviewed in Chapter 25. The programs consist essentially of housing improvement, health education, and insecticide applications. Scientific and technical feasibility of control of this disease have been adequately demonstrated.[22] The Expert Committee report outlined necessary steps in development of a Chagas' disease control program. These included situation and resources analysis, definition of appropriate and affordable strategies, phased implementation (preparatory phase, attack phase, and surveillance phase, discussed in Chapter 25), and cost-effectiveness analysis. Coordination with primary health care workers was emphasized as important in establishing effective community participation. Intersectoral collaboration is also required, including aspects of housing and rural development, education, and environment. The breadth of involvement in these areas is considerable. For example, improvement of housing quality involves changes in construction codes; rural development concerns agricultural credits and crop improvements to make rural agriculture more tenable; education includes a range of elements from community health education modules to postgraduate training in scientific and technical areas central to Chagas' disease control; and environmental issues concern the manner of use of insecticides, from production to disposal, in ways that are safe and environmentally sound. At the same time, detailed educational messages are needed for household members to explain house-spraying activities and related matters. An additional population-wide measure important to reduce risk of Chagas' disease in urban areas is screening of blood donors or treatment of infected blood units to prevent transfusion-related cases.

The Individual, High-Risk Level. Individual risks mainly concern the progression from recognized infection to overt cardiac disease and complications of congestive heart failure. Drug treatment in the acute phase, if infection is clinically apparent, can prevent progression to overt cardiomyopathy. Primary prevention of infection can be undertaken, in principle, by follow-up of household contacts of known cases, insecticide treatment of the household and peridomestic area, and use of bed netting to protect household members not yet infected. Each of these approaches requires identification of the individual case. In view of the high proportion of inapparent infections and the rural settings in which most cases occur, high-risk interventions are much less practical than the population-wide measures discussed above.

Central Issues. As noted in the Expert Committee report of 1991 on Chagas' disease, "few countries have started a control program despite the fact that the basic tools and strategies have been available for more than 30 years."[22(p 57)] General knowledge of the disease and its prevention are not the issue, then. However, local epidemiologic surveys are needed in most areas to document the prevalence of infection, the distribution of vectors, and related aspects of the problem. This knowledge, coupled with sufficient priority in national policy, could bring about substantial control of this one form of cardiomyopathy that is especially well understood. For most cardiomyopathies, prevention depends on new knowledge establishing their causation.

Congenital Heart Disease

The Problem

Causation of congenital heart disease, reviewed in Chapter 26, is largely unknown. Therefore, currently available preventive strategies have limited impact on the problem as a whole. In addition, prevalence of congenital heart disease in adulthood is increasing due to successful early surgical correction of many defects. This circumstance poses challenges for prevention of late complications, such as bacterial endocarditis resulting from residual abnormalities. The increased frequency of reaching reproductive age with recognized congenital heart disease also requires consideration of possible heritable factors that could increase the risk of cardiac or other congenital defects in the offspring when one or both parents are affected.

The Population-Wide Level

Two preventive strategies at the population level are widely adopted. One is immunization of women of reproductive age against rubella. The other is advice to women in this age range to avoid a variety of exposures with known or possible risks to the fetus, such as smoking, alcohol consumption, and use of pharmaceuticals or other drugs, especially early in pregnancy. Public education and product labeling are interventions at the population level that reflect these policies.

The Individual, High-Risk Level

Delivery of immunization requires action by a health care provider at the individual level. After recognition of pregnancy and entry into prenatal care, the pregnant woman should receive reinforcement of advice from a health care provider to avoid particular exposures. However, this is often many weeks following conception and therefore much later in gestation than desired. As discussed in Chapter 26, measures taken at later stages in pregnancy do not prevent the occurrence of congenital defects but instead address their consequences, for example, fetal diagnosis to detect congenital defects, palliative or corrective surgery after birth, clinical monitoring of the affected individual, prophylaxis against bacterial endocarditis, and counseling of parents. Still later, the affected offspring require information about risks of recurrence of defects in the next generation. Effective application of such measures as are presently feasible depends on professional education, regionalization of referral and service networks, and financing of preventive and treatment services.

Central Issues

Until the etiology of congenital heart disease, like that of other congenital defects, is more fully known, prevention will be necessarily limited in its impact. Currently available strategies are important, however, and warrant widespread implementation.

Kawasaki Disease

The Problem

Because the causation of Kawasaki disease is unknown, only very limited preventive measures are available to modify its incidence or to reduce the risks of individuals.

The Population-Wide and Individual, High-Risk Levels

At the population level, surveillance to identify periods of rising incidence may be of value by stimulating greater awareness of the diagnosis of this disease. Public education may serve to bring suspected cases to medical attention, and hence treatment, earlier in the course of the disease. The risk of progression may be reduced in such cases.

At the individual level, diagnosis and treatment may reduce the risk of complications. Increased alertness to signs and symptoms of the disease may bring secondary cases in the same household to earlier medical attention.

OBSTACLES TO IMPLEMENTATION OF PREVENTION POLICIES AND OPPORTUNITIES FOR CHANGE

The overall goal of intervention to prevent the cardiovascular diseases is to reduce to the greatest practical extent their resulting limitations in survival, independence, and quality of life. To achieve this goal requires adoption and implementation of policies based on current knowledge. Such policies exist in many countries but are not being implemented fully. Policy development at any given time is incomplete, of course, as this is a dynamic process that evolves with advancing knowledge. In addition, for some cardiovascular diseases prevention policy is quite limited due to the lack of understanding of their causation, as is true for most of the cardiomyopathies and congenital heart diseases, and for Kawasaki disease. Treatment guidelines for these diseases may reduce the rate of progression or frequency of complications but do not bear on prevention of the disease itself.

Atherosclerotic and Hypertensive Diseases

For atherosclerosis and its complications, major causal factors have been recognized for at least four decades. The extensive research conducted over this period has greatly broadened and deepened the scientific foundation for prevention policy and has also provided a wealth of practical knowledge concerning its implementation. Yet in the United States, where there are clearly explicit goals for intervention as illustrated by *Healthy People 2000*, the attainment of even these intermediate objectives remains distant in many respects.[4] In the United States and other industrialized countries, incidence of the major risk factors—the rate at which new "cases" of high blood cholesterol concentration, high blood pressure, and other factors arise in the population—remains high. In developing countries and the historically nonmarket economies, risk factor epidemics are already known or suspected to be in progress and may be expected to continue and intensify until effective intervention is undertaken.

This is paradoxical from the point of view that knowledge derived from scientific research is intended for application to improve the health of the population. Much, of course, is being done in some countries to address the existing risk factors. In the United States, the examples of the National High Blood Pressure Education Program and the National Cholesterol Education Program of the National Heart, Lung and Blood Institute stand out prominently. But when the focus is on what is being achieved toward actual reduction in incidence of the risk factors in the first place, in contrast to detection and treatment of established high risk in individuals, it is not so clear that progress is being made.

What are the obstacles to effective intervention, and what are the opportunities for change? These questions are considered below at both population-wide and individual, high-risk levels, and answers (at least partial ones) are suggested. The primary emphasis in this discussion is on atherosclerotic and hypertensive diseases, and other cardiovascular diseases are addressed at the close of this section.

Obstacles at the Population-Wide Level

The apparent obstacles to full implementation of existing prevention policies include divergent opinions, competing interests, issues of population diversity and heterogeneity, limitations of the policy framework, and failure to commit needed resources. Each of these is discussed briefly.

Divergent Opinions. Opponents of population-wide intervention strategies can cite conflicts of opinion found in the scientific literature. However, these are perhaps among the least important obstacles to effective prevention. For example, Oliver's feature article in *Circulation* in the mid-1980s protested: "Cardiologists and physicians throughout the world are being persuaded by health educationalists, and some epidemiologists who have also assumed this role, that the only really effective way to prevent coronary heart disease (CHD) is to endorse and promulgate changes in lifestyle of the public at large. . . . Much of the faith in the value of changing lifestyles is little more than wishful thinking."[23(p 1)] Oliver mischaracterized the epidemiologic or "health educationalist" approach as exclusively population-wide in its strategy and advocated instead a focus on prevention of precipitating conditions immediately preceding acute coronary events, an approach that is of theoretical interest but has remained unfeasible. He further argued against continued investment in large-scale trials of population-wide interventions, although he identified such trials as the only source of convincing evidence of the effectiveness of preventive measures.

Another example of opinion counter to intervention at the population level is found in a commentary by McCormick and Skrbanek. They argued that coronary heart disease could not be prevented by population interventions.[24] In addition to chiding Hopkins and Williams for their compilation of 246 risk factors for coronary heart disease (see detailed discussion in Chapter 20), the authors suggested that the causation of coronary heart disease, widely termed "multifactorial," was in fact unknown. Results of the Multiple Risk Factor Intervention Trial, among other studies, were cited as evidence that no experimental data were available to support intervention. Potential harm was raised as an argument against intervention, and costs and side effects of antihypertensive and lipid-lowering drugs were offered as bases for objection. However, confusion of the authors between population-wide and high-risk interventions and their short-sighted view of the results of trials (the Multiple Risk Factor Intervention Trial became clearly positive with extended follow-up; see discussion in Chapter 21) detract substantially from the force of their argument.

Rose, in articulating the contrast between population-wide and high-risk strategies, emphasized the view that only those interventions that tended to restore "biological normality," such as improved dietary balance, in-

creased physical activity, and cessation of smoking, could be strongly advocated as elements of the population strategy in the absence of extensive experimental evidence of safety as well as effectiveness.[25] Rose also addressed what he characterized as the "prevention paradox":

> We arrive at what we might call the prevention paradox—"*a measure that brings large benefits to the community offers little to each participating individual.*" It implies that we should not expect too much from individual health education. People will not be motivated to any great extent to take our advice, because there is little in it for each of them, particularly in the short and medium term. Change in behaviour has to be for some the larger and more immediate reward.[25(p 1850)]

From these comments it seems the "educationalists" and epidemiologists cannot fairly be charged with lack of circumspection about the nature of appropriate population interventions or with altogether unrealistic views of what may be achieved. Waiting to rely on intervention among persons already experiencing acute coronary events or their immediate precipitating conditions ignores both the high proportion of persons dying early in the course of the initial event and the inability to reverse the high risk of recurrence and death among those who survive. For these reasons and because of the increasing evidence of the effectiveness of population interventions, these strategies remain widely advocated despite the opinions illustrated here.

Competing Interests. In some areas central to policy development and implementation, competing interests exert strong influence. For example, James and Ralph noted in discussion of strategies for dietary change at the national level, with particular reference to the United Kingdom, "We are now in a position where the public health priorities are clear, but where the food policies of the government and of the farming and food industries are geared to completely different goals."[26(pp 524–528)] The theme of the review was that "informed choice" as the sole determinant of individual action concerning diet is illusory in view of the many pressures on consumers that result in "the consumer's dilemma"—the inability to make an informed "free" choice. The authors rejected as inappropriate the argument that governmental nutrition policy concerning health should be limited to a role of providing information. Governmental policy development is needed that includes food protection, agricultural strategies, nutrition education and food labeling, among other components. According to James and Ralph, "Analyses of different policies suggest that health issues are readily squeezed out of discussion by economic and vested interests unless able promoters of the health issues are involved in the discussions."[26(p 537)] A specific example is the conflict between salt manufacturers and governmental policies in the United Kingdom, illustrated in Chapter 8 by reference to a revealing set of papers and commentaries that appeared in the *British Medical Journal* in May 1996.[27]

In her opening address at the Third International Conference on Preventive Cardiology in Oslo in 1993, Norwegian Prime Minister Brundtland noted:

> No controversy is involved when governments want to increase research and health education activities, nor when they want to establish systematic preventive programs for high risk groups. These are positive endeavors which are applauded by all political groups and by the people themselves.
>
> Controversies arise when restrictive and legislative measures are proposed and introduced which interfere with people's daily life and intervene with economic interests.[28(p 534)]

She went on to suggest governmental use of subsidies and other price mechanisms, taxation and marketing restrictions, and environmental legislation in order to promote more positive dietary habits, discourage tobacco use, and foster increased physical activity. The intensity of the political fights in some of these arenas in Norway's recent past was highlighted, with emphasis on the value of "new knowledge, inspiration and courage"[28(p 534)] to bring about needed change in support of cardiovascular disease prevention.

Population Diversity and Heterogeneity. That populations are diverse in many respects that may be potentially relevant to population-wide intervention seems self-evident. Yet the nature and extent of such diversity and the need for specification of prevention policies for different groups are less clear. In the United States, development of culturally sensitive intervention programs has been advocated. The Stanford Five City Project provided information on responsiveness to community-wide intervention, as measured by change in a composite, multivariate risk score for all-cause mortality among several subgroups of the population.[29] The study identified characteristics at baseline that best predicted changes in risk score among 411 men and women participating in both baseline and final examinations. Within this study population, not selected by prior knowledge of risk factor or disease status, the subgroup with the greatest proportion of persons whose risk scores changed favorably were those older adults (age greater than 55 years) who had the highest perceived risk, greatest health media use, and highest initial cholesterol concentration and blood pressure. The subgroup with the lowest proportion experiencing favorable change was least educated and most likely to be Hispanic. They had also the least health knowledge and confidence in their ability to achieve the intended personal changes ("self-efficacy."). The authors concluded that specific interventions should be developed for different age, socioeconomic, and cultural subgroups.

On the international level, Janus and colleagues recently addressed the impact of modernization in Asia and its implications for the occurrence of coronary heart disease in that region.[30] Population diversity with respect to coronary heart disease and its risk factors was illustrated by examples from Taiwan, the Philippines, Malaysia, Indonesia, and India. The premise of the review was that thorough knowledge of a region is required for development of acceptable and effective prevention programs, and the conclusion was that "a single prevention strategy for all of Asia may be inappropriate."[30(p 2671)] In particular, it was suggested that recommendations developed in Europe, North America, or Australia might require substantial modification for different Asian countries. Importantly, however, "broader statements on exercise, obesity, smoking, and diet and on the prevention and control of diabetes and hypertension might be appropriate."[30(p 2673)] Better epidemiologic data were considered important for the development of specific strategies and monitoring of their impact in each individual country.

Whether policies or recommendations for cardiovascular disease prevention are applicable to particular countries or groups within a country depends on both the specificity of the policy and the population level of concern. Sound judgment is needed regarding the relation between these two considerations. That "broader statements" may be broadly applicable makes sense, as does the view that much more particular recommendations should take account of particular circumstances. However, it would be contrary to the concept of public health and to public policy itself to focus on differences among specific groups or individuals to the neglect of common characteristics that call for and justify broad and inclusive intervention strategies.

At one extreme is the implication of a recent commentary calling for individualization of lipid-lowering therapy on the basis of genetic heterogeneity. A requirement that treatment be based on individual pretreatment genetic typing could undermine public health recommendations altogether.[31] If individual genetic assessment were needed to evaluate potential risks and benefits of all interventions, the population-wide recommendations that remained acceptable could become so nonspecific and narrow in focus as to offer little guidance for practical action. Failure to support population-wide intervention strategies could bring about a conceptual atomization of populations into mere aggregates of individuals for whom no common action could be proposed. Some vigilance may be required in coming years to protect the public's health and public health policy from reduction to this level.

Limitations of the Policy Framework for Intervention. As stated above, prevention policy for the atherosclerotic and hypertensive diseases is well established on the basis of scientific knowledge available 40 years ago and greatly strengthened since then. At the broadest levels, however, as suggested by James's observations concerning food and nutrition policy, the framework is incomplete because many large societal questions have not yet been resolved. Therefore consistency of policies across the spectrum from land use and food production to recommended dietary behaviors of individuals has not yet been attained. Similarly, Roemer's review of tobacco legislation in developing countries cited in Chapter 22 suggests important gaps and implies that these will remain in any particular country until national data are available to provide the needed justification.[32] Thus despite much support for existing policies, further policy development is needed to enhance the implementation of currently proposed interventions.

Failure To Commit Needed Resources. Resource limitations are of course another obstacle to effective action. It might be assumed by some that such limitations would be less serious in the United States than in many other countries. It is of concern therefore that in 1997 the National Center for Chronic Disease Prevention and Health Promotion of the Centers for Disease

Control and Prevention (CDC) reported the following:

> [T]he nation's public health system framework is severely underdeveloped to address the tremendous burden of chronic disease. . . . Coordinated and comprehensive national chronic disease prevention efforts have not been nearly adequately or systematically applied.
>
> Seven years ago, in 1989, only $245 million—less than 3%—of the $9.5 billion spent by state health agencies was directed toward the prevention and control of chronic disease. Of the 48,000 full-time employees in state health agencies that year, only 2% were employed in chronic disease programs. In 1996, the very small percentage of resources reflected in these numbers remains essentially unchanged.
>
> Without strong, well-coordinated state-based programs aimed at chronic disease and supported by essential national elements, state and local health departments, and indeed, this nation, cannot hope to address the current burden of chronic disease, and efforts will increasingly fall short as the population ages.[33(p 12)]

To the extent that investment in cardiovascular disease prevention elsewhere is proportionately less than that in the United States, significant challenges remain to approach the minimum resource requirements for effective public health action.

Opportunities at the Population-Wide Level

The United States. Despite the obstacles reviewed above, some of which are clearly formidable, real opportunities must also be recognized. In the United States, data on many elements of cardiovascular disease risk factors, health-related behaviors, and preventive services are available for several major segments of the population. These data, as illustrated in *Healthy People 2000*, permit identification of gaps and needs that can serve to direct interventions to specifically targeted problems and population groups. The report from the CDC, cited above, articulates national priorities for chronic disease prevention and indicates that heart disease leads the list of chronic diseases in terms of mortality and costs more than $259 billion annually, including health expenditures and lost productivity resulting from disability and death; diabetes adds $92 billion to these costs.[33] The CDC outlines three national priorities to address these and other chronic diseases: programs to be in place in every state to target these diseases and the major risk factors of tobacco use, lack of physical activity, and poor nutrition; essential technical support to be provided by the CDC (including surveillance, scientific and technical expertise, public and professional education, quality assurance of screening, research and evaluation to develop and improve program elements, and other provisions); and pursuit and maintenance of partnerships with other governmental agencies, voluntary and professional organizations, academic institutions, and the private sector.

The state-based programs identified as essential by the CDC were outlined in a plan developed by the Association of State and Territorial Chronic Disease Program Directors, the Association of State and Territorial Directors of Health Promotion and Public Health Education, and the Association of State and Territorial Public Health Nutrition Directors, in conjunction with the American Heart Association, the CDC, and the National Heart, Lung and Blood Institute. Their document, *Preventing Death and Disability from Cardiovascular Diseases, A State-Based Plan for Action,* was published in 1994 with the objective that "to improve the cardiovascular health of all Americans, every state health department will have the commitment, capacity, and resources to implement comprehensive cardiovascular disease prevention and control programs."[34(p iii)] Core functions of the health departments to conduct such programs were identified, and implementation strategies were recommended. The existence of the plan offers the states, at a minimum, a point of departure for use of the one source of federal funds that can be targeted specifically to cardiovascular disease prevention, the Preventive Health and Health Services Block Grants. Nationwide, this is the leading initiative in cardiovascular disease prevention.

The Global Opportunities. WHO, which long exerted leadership in cardiovascular disease prevention policy through its Cardiovascular Disease Unit founded in 1959, reduced its support by dissolving the unit in 1996 and merging a much-reduced staff into its Noncommunicable Diseases Division. The approach of WHO in cardiovascular disease control has undergone a transition to greater dependence on interagency activities, as illustrated recently by a meeting convened under the aegis of the US Institute of Medicine in 1992. The meeting report, *Towards a Global Strategy on Cardiovascular Disease Prevention and Health Promotion in Developing Countries*, outlined priorities in three areas: statistics and epidemiology, prevention, and case management.[35] The product was to be an action plan referred to WHO and an outline for a study to be conducted by the Institute of Medicine addressing these areas. An implementation committee was formed representing several organizations, with WHO staff to serve as the secretariat. These activities were in progress as of the mid-1990s.

Another initiative with potential impact on cardiovascular diseases in developing countries and other countries with special needs, such as the historically nonmarket economies, also involves WHO as a key partner: the Memorandum of Understanding between UNESCO, WHO, and the ISFC.[36] This agreement, executed in 1996, established a scientific task force to develop plans for work in each of three areas: cardiovascular risk factors, rheumatic fever and rheumatic heart disease, and Chagas' disease. By 1997, all three task forces had been constituted and substantial efforts were being organized to raise funds for their programs. It will remain to be seen if the hopes for these efforts—as well as for a parallel task force on other cardiomyopathies, fostered by the ISFC—will be realized, but they are one group of promising international activities among others undertaken under various auspices largely beginning in the early to mid-1990s.

Another major official agency with growing concern about cardiovascular diseases and their prevention, especially in developing countries, is the World Bank, whose assessments of the problem of atherosclerotic and hypertensive diseases worldwide have been cited extensively in preceding chapters.[37,38] The emphasis of the World Bank to date has been on policy development in these countries, which are faced with major shifts in health priorities as demographic transitions and other potent influences on disease patterns progress in the decades immediately ahead. As noted in *Lancet*, "in financial terms the World Bank is the most important actor in world health."[39(p 411)] This distinction, noted in 1996, was on the basis of some $8 billion in health-related loans by the World Bank out of its total lending program of $23 billion annually. The same editorial underscored the pluralism now evident in the world health community, which included the World Bank and other multinational development banks, WHO, United Nations International Children's Emergency Fund, nongovernmental organizations, business, governments, the media, academic institutions, and foundations. Significantly, the editorial posed this closing question: "Who will step forward to provide the strategic and moral leadership that the international health community, which includes the World Bank, now so desperately needs?"[39(p 411)]

One voluntary organization that could perhaps grow to fill this need is represented by the Advisory Committee of the International Heart Health Conferences, convened in Victoria, British Columbia (1992), and Barcelona, Spain (1995). The declarations of these two conferences and the reports that contain them convey in exceptionally positive terms the potential for heart disease prevention throughout the world.[8,9] The *Catalonia Declaration* of 1995 emphasized the assets available in each country to meet this need and pointed to ways in which they can be exploited to produce significant achievements. Another voluntary organization offering potential international leadership in cardiovascular disease prevention is, of course, the ISFC.

Obstacles at the Individual, High-Risk Level

Many obstacles operate at the individual or high-risk level, as at the population level, to impede implementation of prevention policy. In addition to conflicting viewpoints concerning intervention in general, numerous specific barriers have been identified. These obstacles are discussed below.

Divergent Opinions. The idea that health promotion in clinical practice is unethical was advanced in *Lancet* by McCormick in the mid-1990s. His commentary was in opposition to an announced policy for general practice in the United Kingdom that proposed attention to blood pressure, smoking, body mass index, alcohol consumption, family history, diet, and physical activity.[40] His premise was that this activity constituted unsolicited intrusion into the lives of patients and lacked necessary support of "conclusive evidence that screening can alter the natural history of disease in a significant proportion of those screened,"[40(p 390)] a criterion attributed to Cochrane and Holland. He concluded, "Health promotion as encouraged by [the recommendations being addressed] falls far short of meeting the ethical imperatives for screening procedures, and moreover diminishes health and wastes recourse [sic]. General practitioners would do better to encourage people to live lives of modified hedonism, so that they may enjoy, to the full, the only life that they are likely to have."[40(p 391)] This laissez-faire recommendation, of course, also lacks conclusive evidence but was implicitly justified on the basis that any adverse outcomes would not be attributable to interference by physicians.

Limited Influence of Guidelines. The concern that published guidelines for preventive services often have less than intended impact was a special focus of the 1995 Bethesda Conference report cited above.[12,18] One of the eight task forces contributing to that report identified four types of barriers, related to the patient, the physician, health care settings, and the community or society at large (Exhibit 28–1). Some of these, at the level of the patient and the community, are reminiscent of issues addressed in previous chapters: lack of knowledge and motivation, lack of access to care, cultural and social factors, lack of policies and standards, and lack of reimbursement. Other barriers specific to physicians or to health care settings are discussed in greater detail in that report.

Questions of Cost. Increasingly, in the US health care situation of the 1990s, cost-consciousness and evaluation of procedures in terms of cost have intensified sharply. The example of cholesterol lowering has been addressed in numerous reports, especially in the wake of reports of clinical trials that indicate reductions not only in cardiovascular events but in all-cause mortality by use of certain agents. In one such report, concepts of cost-effectiveness analysis were reviewed and applied to cholesterol-lowering interventions among high-risk individuals, those with manifest coronary heart disease or with elevated total cholesterol concentration alone. Population-based interventions were also evaluated. The authors concluded:

> Although preventive care is intuitively appealing and is often advocated as a means to reduce health care costs, formal economic analyses demonstrate that, similar to most preventive care, cholesterol lowering for primary coronary prevention does not "pay for itself." Nonetheless, most analyses suggest that drug treatment for young and middle-aged men with moderate-to-severe elevations

Exhibit 28–1 Barriers to Implementation of Preventive Services

Patient

Lack of knowledge and motivation
Lack of access to care
Cultural factors
Social factors

Physician

Problem-based focus
Feedback on prevention is negative or neutral
Time constraints
Lack of incentives, including reimbursement
Lack of training
   Poor knowledge of benefits
   Perceived ineffectiveness
   Lack of skills
Lack of specialist-generalist communication
Lack of perceived legitimacy

**Health care settings
(hospitals, practices, etc)**

Acute care priority
Lack of resources and facilities
Lack of systems for preventive services
Time and economic constraints
Poor communication between specialty and
   primary care providers
Lack of policies and standards

Community/society

Lack of policies and standards
Lack of reimbursement

Source: Reprinted with permission from the American College of Cardiology, *Journal of the American College of Cardiology*, 1996, Vol 27, p 1040.

of serum cholesterol (>240 mg/dl) and multiple other risk factors for CHD has a cost-effectiveness ratio below $40,000 per year of life saved—similar to federally funded programs such as outpatient hemodialysis and many other widely practiced medical interventions. . . . The appropriateness of cholesterol reduction for other populations, including young men with isolated mild hypercholesterolemia, women, and the elderly is less certain, however.[41(pp 329–330)]

The dependence of these estimates on the costs of lipid-lowering agents was emphasized. The tendency to identify intervention to lower cholesterol with use of drugs often clouds the question of whether intervention is justified in terms of cost or potential risks of side effects. Until more extensive experience is accumulated to indicate that substantial reductions in choles-

terol concentration can be achieved even in high-risk persons by nonpharmacologic means, this issue will likely remain an obstacle to policies for intervention in high-risk persons except, perhaps, those with already-manifest coronary heart disease.

Opportunities at the Individual, High-Risk Level

Prevention programs in worksites have been reviewed to evaluate their impact on cardiovascular risk factors (KR Pelletier, personal communication, 1997). Few of the identified studies met all criteria for purposes of the review, and none was judged to investigate cost-effectiveness adequately. However, the conclusion could be drawn that program effectiveness depended on both individualized intervention for high-risk individuals and a more comprehensive program throughout the work setting as a whole. Programs with these characteristics were most often successful.

Within health care practice settings, according to a second review, another series of studies indicated that education and training programs are most effective when accompanied by features such as office reminders, feedback on compliance with recommended practices, and practice guidelines (Ockene JK et al. Unpublished data). The joint implementation of recommended interventions by physicians and nonphysicians has appeared to be most effective.

In addition to obstacles to intervention in patients with recognized coronary heart disease, the 1995 Bethesda Conference report addressed possibilities for improvement in intervention.[18] A review of studies in which responsibility was placed either on physicians or on nurses and other health professionals examined those studies that addressed barriers in the health care setting and evaluated the conduct of interventions. Several recommendations were made for action and for further research in this area, suggesting some optimism that these obstacles could be overcome if aided by further investigation.

Several trials were in progress in the mid-1990s to test methods for influencing physicians in nonacademic practice settings to implement the 1988 Adult Treatment Panel Guidelines of the National Cholesterol Education Program.[42] Results were expected to lead to widespread improvements in methods of lipid management and to models for implementation of other such guidelines in similar practices.

In the United States, a major program in physician education for cardiovascular diseases was the Preventive Cardiology Academic Award program, established in 1978 and continuing until the early 1990s.[43] Through this program, thousands of medical trainees were exposed to concepts of prevention otherwise typically lacking or only weakly represented in their professional education. Many of the lessons learned through this program, especially in the teaching of physicians to implement preventive practices, are addressed in a report published in 1990. To the extent that these lessons continue to influence academic training, prevention could become increasingly recognized as the foremost goal of practice instead of only detection and management of the patient with already-established cardiovascular disease or high risk.

That the limited implementation of preventive practices in the United States is not unique was observed by Pyörälä, who noted similar concerns in Europe: "The integration of CHD prevention into the practice of physicians, whether in hospitals or in primary care, has been slow; therefore, the three major European scientific societies working in cardiovascular medicine, the European Society of Cardiology (ESC), the European Atherosclerosis Society (EAS), and the European Society of Hypertension (ESH), appointed a joint task force to prepare recommendations that would summarize the aspects of clinical CHD prevention on which there was good agreement."[44(p S26)]

General agreement was found between the joint task force report and that of the Bethesda Conference. One especially important unifying aspect of the two reports was the stratification of high risk into four categories:

> Highest priority goes to patients with established disease. . . . These patients are identified in ordinary clinical work. . . .
>
> The next place goes to symptom-free individuals at high risk—for example, because of severe hypercholesterolemia—Many of these will already have been identified in the context of ordinary clinical practice.
>
> With the progress of preventive activities, action may be extended to the closest relatives of patients with early-onset CHD or other atherosclerotic vascular disease and, similarly, to the closest relatives of symptom-free high-risk individuals.
>
> With further progress preventive action may finally be extended to the offer of risk-status assessment and

advice to individuals not in these priority groups.[44(p S26)]

The impact of this stratification for clinical practice may be to restrict the scope of high risk to a range that practitioners more readily recognize as warranting intervention. To the extent that physicians' beliefs about the justification for intervention and likely efficacy of preventive measures determine their practice behavior, this development could serve to strengthen high-risk intervention, at least at the very highest levels. The remainder of the population would then be wholly dependent on population-wide measures for prevention. The complementary relation between high-risk and population-wide approaches was emphasized: "This definition of priorities in clinical practice is not meant to detract from the primary approach, whereby risk factor levels are addressed in the whole population."[44(p S26)] Further, the engagement of cardiologists in preventive practices and in adaptation of international guidelines into national ones was seen as critical to progress in prevention overall: "Cardiologists are opinion leaders in cardiovascular medicine and their attitude to preventive services is of decisive importance."[44(p S28)]

The appearance of the European task force report is expected to be a positive development, at least in emphasizing areas of agreement among prevention guidelines. The admonition that implementation of the guidelines at the national level requires local adaptation suggests that their impact could only be gradual, and many of the impediments to implementation already discussed would apply equally to these recommendations. However, with growing recognition of the gaps between guidelines and practices for even the highest-risk patients in the United States and Europe, many parties are now engaging in discussions of the problem. Potentially, increasing attention to prevention for those at highest risk will have favorable influence on preventive strategies more generally. This may be especially true for population-wide strategies if the narrower views of what constitutes high risk prevail, leaving a broader range of risk to be addressed through population-wide measures.

Other Cardiovascular Diseases

For the other cardiovascular diseases for which preventive strategies are available, such as rheumatic fever and rheumatic heart disease, Chagas' disease, and some congenital heart disease, some obstacles at the population-wide level resemble those for atherosclerotic and hypertensive diseases. Resource limitations are perhaps the principal factor, which could be due to competing demands both within and beyond the health sector. Important differences in obstacles and opportunities apply, however, in the respect that what is known about causation of these other conditions is agent specific: the Group A beta-hemolytic streptococcus, *T. cruzi,* and rubella or specific environmental exposures. While social and economic conditions are clearly part of the causal complex for these conditions, the availability of a more specific target is obviously important for focused interventions. As a result, it is feasible to conduct demonstration programs that have measurable impact on the disease process within a period of only a few years, such as the eradication of vectors of *T. cruzi* from the peridomestic environment or the establishment of a high prevalence of immunity to rubella virus. However, like the atherosclerotic and hypertensive diseases, these conditions are deeply rooted in social and environmental circumstances that readily foster the resurgence of disease when temporary preventive measures are interrupted or discontinued. Therefore, the most meaningful opportunities for long-term prevention of these diseases are those that reach more deeply into the process and are sustained for many years. These are major challenges for prevention policy.

CONCLUSION

The challenges to implementation of prevention policies against cardiovascular diseases, based on current knowledge of causation and means of prevention, are many. The needs are great. Major secular trends in populations experiencing epidemic coronary heart disease and stroke demonstrate how much event rates, risk factors, and underlying health behaviors can change even within a decade or less. To the extent that population-wide and high-risk preventive strategies together can accelerate favorable change, it is incumbent on health professionals to advocate their fullest achievable implementation.

It is least difficult to argue for preventive measures in countries where cardiovascular disease event rates are historically high or have recently increased and where risk factor distributions are under continuous surveillance, because the burden of disease is readily demonstrable. But more persuasive argument is apparently necessary even where such data are available. This is the lesson in the United States, in view of the incomplete attainment of interim goals to date. The unpreparedness of the US public health establishment to address the problem of cardiovascular and other chronic diseases in a meaningful way, as indicated by the minuscule allocation of resources to this area, is cause for alarm.

Even greater difficulty, and greater challenges, concern populations for whom data remain unavailable, unreliable, or incomplete to the extent that no convincing argument in support of prevention policies can be made based on the local situation. In this case, projections are needed, based on such support as can be found in limited local surveys, nonsystematic statistical information from particular hospitals or other sources with no defined base population, or anecdotal accounts.

Some signs point to new opportunities for the future, such as establishment of the UNESCO/WHO/ISFC Task Forces. Resources for these initiatives are likely to be modest, and the immediate question will be how to invest these resources most productively. One answer is to undertake multiple demonstration projects in carefully selected sites where, with local collaboration and support, a 5- to 10-year project can show benefit in slowing, arresting, or reversing adverse trends in health-related behaviors and cardiovascular risk factors. One or, better, two sites in each of the six WHO Regions (Africa, Americas, Southeast Asia, Europe, Eastern Mediterranean, Western Pacific) could thus offer opportunities for unprecedented demonstration of the ability to impact risk factor epidemics in multiple settings, linked by a common protocol and tailored to local circumstance, as appropriate.

Opportunities for favorable impact on the implementation of cardiovascular disease prevention policies have been alluded to throughout this book, which has outlined progress from initial authoritative opinion to firmly established scientific foundations and community-based experience in support of preventive strategies. A specific challenge to epidemiology in prevention of cardiovascular diseases was posed by Remington, chair of the Institute of Medicine committee that found a need for sweeping changes in American public health.[45] Further, in addressing the symposium gathered in honor of Professor Geoffrey Rose on the occasion of his retirement in 1991, Remington wrote:

> [A]s epidemiology passes from aetiological investigations through longitudinal studies to community intervention programmes and evaluative trials of CHD control programmes, it recapitulates the several stages encompassed in this publication. The concern of this chapter is with the far end of that transition—the role of organized public health in applying the fruits of epidemiological investigation to cardiovascular disease prevention in the community. This transition from research to policy formation to application has received too little attention among epidemiologists and, for that matter, among professional public health workers. Yet the transition itself has much to

do with the uses of epidemiology in improving community health. Put another way, in the language of the Institute of Medicine report, the substance of public health is considered to be "organized community efforts aimed at the prevention of disease and promotion of health. (Public health) links many disciplines and rests upon the scientific core of epidemiology."[46(p 517)]

It is clear that substantial accountability rests with epidemiology to apply what decades of research have established: the major cardiovascular diseases are largely preventable.

REFERENCES

1. US Dept of Health and Human Services. *Healthy People 2000: National Health Promotion and Disease Prevention Objectives: Full Report with Commentary.* Washington, DC: Public Health Service, US Dept of Health and Human Services; 1991. DHHS publication (PHS) 91-50212.

2. Epstein FH. Cardiovascular disease epidemiology: a journey from the past into the future. *Circ.* 1996;93: 1755–1764.

3. Shigan EN. Integrated Programme for Noncommunicable Diseases Prevention and Control (NCD). *World Health Stat Q.* 1988;41:267–273.

4. National Center for Health Statistics. *Healthy People 2000, Review 1995–96.* Hyattsville, Md: Public Health Service; 1996.

5. Burt VL, Cutler JA, Higgins M, Horan MJ, et al. Trends in prevalence, awareness, treatment, and control of hypertension in the adult US population: data from the Health Examination Surveys, 1960–1991. *Hypertens.* 1995;26:60–69.

6. Johnson CL, Rifkind BM, Sempos CT, Carroll MD, et al. Declining serum total cholesterol levels among US adults: the National Health and Nutrition Examination Surveys. *JAMA.* 1993;269:3002–3008.

7. World Health Organization MONICA Project Principal Investigators. The World Health Organization MONICA Project (Monitoring Trends and Determinants in Cardiovascular Disease): a major international collaboration. *J Clin Epidemiol.* 1988;41:105–114.

8. Advisory Board of the International Heart Health Conference. *The Victoria Declaration on Heart Health.* Victoria, British Columbia: Health and Welfare Canada, BC Ministry of Health and Ministry Responsible for Elders, Heart and Stroke Foundation of Canada; 1992.

9. Advisory Board of the Second International Heart Health Conference. *The Catalonia Declaration: Investing in Heart Health.* Barcelona, Spain: Department of Health and Social Security, Autonomous Government of Catalonia; 1995.

10. White PD, Wright IS, Sprague HB, Katz LN, et al. *A Statement on Arteriosclerosis: Main Cause of "Heart Attacks" and "Strokes."* New York: National Health Education Committee, Inc; 1959.

11. Ryan TJ, Anderson JL, Antman EM, Braniff BA, et al. ACC/AHA guidelines for the management of patients with acute myocardial infarction: executive summary. *Circ.* 1996;94:2341–2350.

12. Pearson TA, Fuster V. Executive summary. *J Am Coll Cardiol.* 1996;27:957–1047.

13. Nader PR, Taras HL, Sallis JF, Patterson TL. Adult heart disease prevention in childhood: a national survey of pediatricians' practices and attitudes. *Pediatr.* 1987;79:843–849.

14. Kimm SYS, Payne GH, Lakatoe E, Darby C, et al. Management of cardiovascular disease risk factors in children: a national survey of primary care physicians. *Am J Dis Control.* 1990;144:967–972.

15. Fortmann SP, Sallis JF, Magnus PM, Farquhar JW. Attitudes and practices of physicians regarding hypertension and smoking: the Stanford Five City Project. *Preven Med.* 1985;14:70–80.

16. Schucker B, Wittes JT, Cutler JA, Bailey K, et al. Change in physician perspective on cholesterol and heart disease. *JAMA.* 1987;258:3521–3526.

17. Trujillo L. Woman's death leads to award by jurors. Kaiser: heart attack halts flow of blood to brain. *Oregonian.* May 1, 1996: B1.

18. Pearson TA, McBride PE, Miller NH, Smith SC Jr. Task Force 8: Organization of preventive cardiology service. *J Am Coll Cardiol.* 1996;27:1039–1047.

19. World Health Organization. *Joint WHO/ISFC Meeting on Rheumatic Fever/Rheumatic Heart Disease Control, with Emphasis on Primary Prevention.* Geneva, 7–9 September 1994. Geneva, Switzerland: World Health Organization; 1994. WHO/CVD/94.1.

20. World Health Organization. *Rheumatic Fever and Rheumatic Heart Disease: Report of a WHO Expert Committee.* Geneva, Switzerland: World Health Organization; 1988. WHO Technical Report Series 764.

21. World Health Organization. *Report of a WHO Expert Committee: Cardiomyopathies.* Geneva, Switzerland: World Health Organization; 1984. WHO Technical Report Series 697.

22. World Health Organization. *Report of a WHO Expert Committee: Control of Chagas Disease.* Geneva, Switzerland: World Health Organization; 1991. WHO Technical Report Series 811.

23. Oliver MF. Prevention of coronary heart disease—propaganda, promises, problems, and prospects. *Circ.* 1986;73:1–8.

24. McCormick J, Skrbanek P. Coronary heart disease is not preventable by population interventions. *Lancet.* 1988;11:839–841.

25. Rose G. Strategy of prevention: lessons from cardiovascular disease. *Br Med J.* 1981;282:1847–1851.

26. James WPT, Ralph A. National strategies for dietary change. In: Marmot M, Elliott P, eds. *Coronary Heart Disease Epidemiology: From Aetiology to Public Health.* Oxford, England: Oxford Medical Publications; 1992: 525–540.

27. Godlee F. The food industry fights for salt. *Br Med J.* 1996;312:1239–1240.

28. Brundtland GM. Influencing environmental factors in cardiovascular disease prevention—a global view. *Preven Med.* 1994;23:531–534.

29. Winkleby MA, Flora JA, Kraemer HC. A community-based heart disease intervention: predictors of change. *Am J Public Health.* 1994;84:767–772.

30. Janus ED, Postiglione A, Singh RB, Lewis B, Council on Arteriosclerosis of the International Society and Federation of Cardiology. The modernization of Asia: implications for coronary heart disease. *Circ.* 1996; 94:2671–2673.

31. Omenn GS. Comment: genetics and public health. *Am J Public Health.* 1996;86:1701–1704.

32. Roemer R. *Legislative Action To Combat the World Smoking Epidemic.* Geneva, Switzerland: World Health Organization; 1982.

33. Report of the National Center for Chronic Disease Prevention and Health Promotion, Centers for Disease Control and Prevention. *Unrealized Prevention Opportunities: Reducing the Health and Economic Burden of Chronic Disease.* Bethesda, Md: Public Health Service, US Dept of Health and Human Services; 1997.

34. Association of State and Territorial Chronic Disease Program Directors, Association of State and Territorial Directors of Health Promotion and Public Health Education, Association of State and Territorial Public Health Nutrition Directors, American Heart Association, Centers for Disease Control and Prevention, National Heart, Lung and Blood Institute. *Preventing Death and Disability from Cardiovascular Diseases: A State-Based Plan for Action.* Atlanta: CDC; 1994.

35. WHO Report on the Interagency Meeting. *Towards a Global Strategy on Cardiovascular Disease Prevention and Health Promotion in Developing Countries.* Geneva, Switzerland: World Health Organization; 1992. WHO/CVD/93.

36. UNESCO. Memorandum of Understanding Between the United Nations Educational, Scientific and Cultural Organization, the World Health Organization and the International Society and Federation of Cardiology. UNESCO Headquarters, Paris, 1996.

37. Jamison DT, Mosley WH. Disease control priorities in developing countries: health policy responses to epidemiological change. *Am J Public Health.* 1991;81:15–22.

38. Jamison DT, Mosley WH, Measham AR, Bobadilla JL, eds. *Disease Control Priorities in Developing Countries.* Oxford, England: Oxford University Press; 1993.

39. The World Bank, listening and learning. *Lancet.* 1996; 347:411. Editorial.

40. McCormick J. Health promotion: the ethical dimension. *Lancet.* 1994;344:390–391.

41. Cohen DJ, Goldman L, Weinstein MC. The cost-effectiveness of programs to lower serum cholesterol. In: Rifkind BM, ed. *Lowering Cholesterol in High Risk Individuals and Populations.* New York: Marcel Dekker, Inc; 1995: 311–336.

42. Expert Panel on Detection, Evaluation, and Treatment of High Blood Cholesterol in Adults. Summary of the second report of the National Cholesterol Education Program (NCEP) Expert Panel on Detection, Evaluation, and Treatment of High Blood Cholesterol in Adults (Adult Treatment Panel II). *JAMA.* 1993;269:3015–3023.

43. Stone EJ, Van Citters RL, Pearson TA, eds. Preventive cardiology: perspectives in physician education. *Am J Preventive Med.* 1990;6 (suppl).

44. Pyörälä K. CHD prevention in clinical practice. *Lancet.* 1996;348:S26–S28.

45. Committee for the Study of the Future of Public Health, Division of Health Care Services, Institute of Medicine. *The Future of Public Health.* Washington, DC: National Academy Press; 1988.

46. Remington RD. Role of organized public health in cardiovascular disease prevention. In: Marmot M, Elliot P, eds. *Coronary Heart Disease Epidemiology. From Aetiology to Public Health.* Oxford, England: Oxford Medical Publications; 1992: 515–524.

CHAPTER 29

Advancement of Epidemiologic Research for the Prevention of Cardiovascular Diseases

SUMMARY

The needs and opportunities for research in the epidemiology and prevention of cardiovascular diseases are great and continue to expand with increasing recognition of the global challenges involved. A concept of epidemiology that is appropriate to these tasks and challenges is one in which the community as the fundamental level of concern is only one of several relevant levels of organization and the territory of epidemiology extends across the whole spectrum of biomedical and community health research. The goals of epidemiologic research in the interest of cardiovascular disease prevention are many but can be subsumed under the understanding of causes, identification of means of prevention, and monitoring of populations to assess the burden of disease and the impact of interventions. A great many outstanding questions are opportune for epidemiologic investigation. Some broad research themes and strategic emphases have been proposed, such as those by the recent Task Force on Research in Epidemiology and Prevention of Cardiovascular Diseases of the US National Heart, Lung and Blood Institute. Supplemented by recommendations from international organizations, these questions constitute an extensive agenda for epidemiology in the near future. This chapter addresses resource needs that will require, for their realization, the dedicated effort of those health professionals throughout the world who recognize the needs and opportunities confronting cardiovascular epidemiology.

INTRODUCTION

As stated in the opening of Chapter 1, the epidemiology and prevention of cardiovascular diseases concern the understanding of causes, identification of means of prevention, and monitoring of populations to assess both the burden of these diseases and the impact of interventions to control them. Together these concerns span the "core functions of public health" articulated in the landmark report of the Committee for the Study of the Future of Public Health, published in 1988 by the Institute of Medicine of the US National Academy of Sciences and alluded to at the close of Chapter 28:

MISSION

- The committee defines the mission of public health as fulfilling society's interest in assuring conditions in which people can be healthy.

THE GOVERNMENTAL ROLE IN PUBLIC HEALTH

- The committee finds that the core functions of public health agencies at all levels of government are assessment, policy development, and assurance.

Assessment

- The committee recommends that every public health agency regularly and systematically collect, assemble, analyze, and make available information on the health of the community, including statistics on health status, community health needs, and epidemiologic and other studies of health problems.

Policy development

- The committee recommends that every public health agency exercise its responsibility to serve the public interest in the development of comprehensive public health policies by promoting use of the scientific knowledge base in decision-making about public health and by leading in developing public health policy. Agencies must take a strategic approach, developed on the basis of a positive appreciation for the democratic political process.

Assurance

- The committee recommends that public health agencies assure their constituents that services necessary to achieve agreed upon goals are provided, either by encouraging actions by other entities (private or public sector), by requiring such action through regulation, or by providing services directly.
- The committee recommends that each public health agency involve key policymakers and the general public in determining a set of high-priority personal and com-

munitywide health services that governments will guarantee to every member of the community. This guarantee should include subsidization or direct provision of high-priority personal health services for those unable to afford them.[1(pp 7–8)]

Epidemiologic contributions to the understanding of causes and identification of means of prevention provide the scientific basis for policy development. Epidemiologic monitoring of populations serves the functions of both community assessment and assurance. It does so by evaluating community health needs, the extent to which public health policies and practices are reaching the population, and the actual impact of those policies and practices on the health of communities. As Remington wrote, "the substance of public health is considered to be 'organized community efforts aimed at the prevention of disease and promotion of health.' (Public health) links many disciplines and rests upon the scientific core of epidemiology."[2(p 517)]

From this view of the centrality of epidemiology for public health—that is, for disease prevention and health promotion in communities—two questions appear especially prominent: What are the needs for epidemiologic research for the prevention of cardiovascular diseases, and what is required to advance that research? These questions are addressed in this chapter by consideration of four aspects:

1. a concept of epidemiology appropriate to its tasks and opportunities
2. some broad goals for epidemiologic research on cardiovascular diseases
3. several elements of a strategy for further development of the needed research base
4. resource requirements in terms of qualified investigators, organizational and institutional settings and partnerships, social and political support, and funding

A CONCEPT OF EPIDEMIOLOGY

One dimension of epidemiology or any other scientific discipline is the array of phenomena with which it is concerned. In his 1980 essay, "To Advance Epidemiology," Stallones depicted the biomedical sciences as arrayed across a scale of biological organization, ranging from the phenomena of submolecular particles to those of societies and from the discipline of molecular biology to epidemiology.[3] While noting discontinuities along this spectrum due to specialization in science, he observed that the true underlying continuity "should be an integrating force, not a divisive one, and ultimately the knowledge accrued by different subspecialties must all fit together without internal contradictions."[3(p 70)] The concern of epidemiology was shown in his depiction to reach across four levels of organization, from individuals to families, communities, and societies. The individual, at the midpoint of the spectrum from particles to societies, was seen as the focal point for integration of all of the biomedical sciences, "and the totality of biomedical research should be coherent, with different disciplines sustaining and supporting each other."[3(p 70)]

Developments throughout the ensuing years, to the mid-1990s, suggest some revisions to this scheme, which generally remains a useful device for understanding the scope of epidemiology in the context of cardiovascular or other diseases. For example, Rose argued persuasively for much greater prominence, indeed primacy, of the population level in thinking about the impact of preventive measures.[4] Determinants of differences in rates of disease between populations are, under this argument, the foremost concern of public health, because the impact of interventions at the population level can be far greater than that of individual-level, patient-oriented interventions. Epidemiology that is limited to the individual level may be oblivious to the larger forces of disease causation at the population level and therefore seriously deficient as a basis for attaining the greatest potential public health benefits. Complementarity of population-wide and individual, high-risk intervention strategies has been widely acknowledged in the field of preventive cardiology and underlies a theme emphasized throughout this book. However, from the public health perspective, the community as a whole is the primary point of reference and the principal orientation of its core functions of assessment, policy development, and assurance.

In this respect the positions of societies and communities in the array of the biomedical sciences belong at the beginning and not the end of the sequence. In fact, reliance on the term *biomedical* alone to represent the full array of health research has been questioned, out of concern that the essential roles and contributions of research at the community or population level may be disregarded too easily in an era of exuberant expectations of research in human genetics and molecular biology. Thus, in the report of the first 10 years' experience in a new federal health research program in the United States, the Prevention Research Centers Program of the Centers for Disease Control and Prevention, adoption of the term *biomedical and community health research* was proposed.[4] This is appealing as an explicitly inclusive designation for the spectrum Stallones identified.

A further development of the 1980s and 1990s has been growing recognition that the fragmentation addressed by Stallones and others may be especially imminent for epidemiology, in relation to other disciplines, if the argument is not advanced effectively that anticipated health benefits from the products of laboratory and patient-oriented research depend on population studies for validation and application. That is, assessment of the public health implications of a new finding, such as a particular gene mutation, requires population studies to determine its frequency in the population and actual correspondence to disease risk. For example, the Expert Panel on Genetic Strategies for Heart, Lung, and Blood Diseases recounted the investigation of a particular gene mutation that affects the enzyme, lipoprotein lipase. In one specific genotype, one-half of the molecules of this enzyme were defective in the affected persons.[5] Collaboration, which included a cardiovascular epidemiologist, permitted demonstration of a phenotypic effect of this mutation: an association with high plasma triglycerides and low concentrations of high-density lipoprotein cholesterol, which appeared only after age 40. The report stated, "Much collaborative work will be needed to investigate fully the possible differences in 150 mutations for the LDL receptor gene and to define the degree and mechanisms for the effects of age and obesity on mutations for lipoprotein lipase. Multiply the large effort already needed simply to understand these two genes by the large number of genes we need to investigate and the task is obviously formidable."[5(p 3)]

The risks of fragmentation affecting epidemiology in particular were also cited by Susser and Susser in a two-part essay on the future of epidemiology.[6,7] They argued that: (1) epidemiology in previous eras was rooted in public health; (2) the latter half of the 20th century has been characterized chiefly by a focus on individual risks, out of context of the population as a whole; and, therefore, (3) epidemiology has evolved to be out of touch with public health. They proposed a "different paradigm" that shows striking parallels with the thought of Stallones and Rose and with the evolution of cardiovascular epidemiology in the most recent decades:

> Encompassing many levels of organization—molecular and societal as well as individual—this paradigm, termed *Chinese boxes*, aims to integrate more than a single level in design, analysis and interpretation. Such a paradigm could sustain and refine a public health–oriented epidemiology. But preventing a decline in this new era will require more than a cogent scientific paradigm. Attention will have to be paid to the social processes that foster a cohesive and humane discipline. . . . Without in-

tense socialization and learning, we may well find—because of the natural momentum and narrow focus that specialization generates—that the links between the values of public health and its specialized disciplines dissolve as we watch. In this respect, epidemiology is most certainly at risk.[7(pp 674, 677)]

The Chinese boxes symbolized for the Sussers an advance, or perhaps a recovery, from the "black box" paradigm of recent decades. In this period the authors have seen a profusion of epidemiologic research on "decontextualized risk factors" that has found satisfaction in associations between exposures and outcomes without integration into a larger picture of the social phenomena at issue. The image of a multilevel hierarchy of different levels of organization, represented by nested Chinese boxes, conveys the idea of the new paradigm. In their concept, epidemiology could thus gain breadth from exploitation of modern information systems within and across levels of organization as well as depth from incorporation of new biomedical techniques.

This view of epidemiology, introduced in Chapter 20, is illustrated again in Figure 29–1. The figure incorporates the multilevel concept common to the views of Stallones, Rose, and the Sussers; indicates the preeminent place of whole societies in the array; and shows the territory of epidemiology extending across the whole array as a basic discipline of biomedical and community health research. This is a valid representation of epidemiology as it applies to the challenges and opportunities of cardiovascular diseases.

GOALS

The goals of epidemiology and prevention of cardiovascular diseases can be characterized in terms as broad as those stated in the introduction to this chapter: the understanding of causes, identification of means of prevention, and mon-

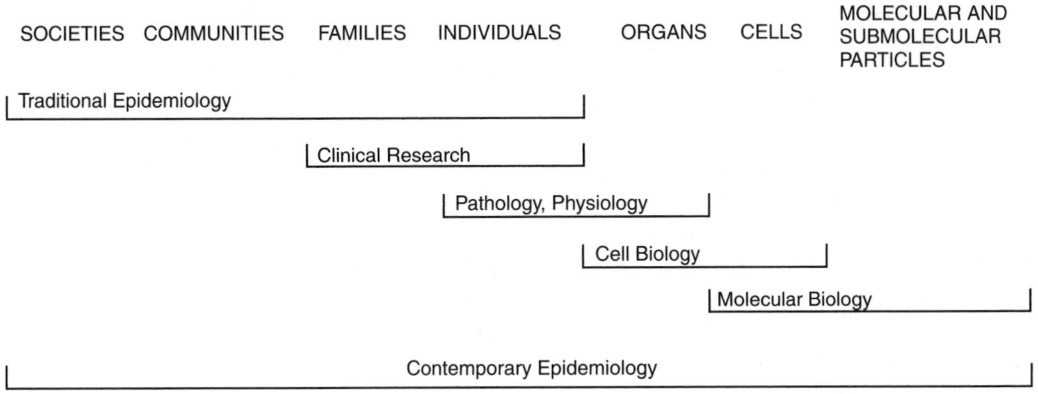

SOCIETIES	COMMUNITIES	FAMILIES	INDIVIDUALS		ORGANS	CELLS	MOLECULAR AND SUBMOLECULAR PARTICLES

Traditional Epidemiology

Clinical Research

Pathology, Physiology

Cell Biology

Molecular Biology

Contemporary Epidemiology

Figure 29–1 A Current View of the Relation of Epidemiology to the Other Biomedical and Community Health Sciences. *Source*: Adapted with permission from the *Annual Review of Public Health*, Vol 1, © 1980, by Annual Reviews, Inc.

itoring of populations to assess the burden of these diseases and the impact of interventions to control them. At the opposite, narrowest extreme, specific research objectives in this field are practically innumerable. Examples could be drawn from pressing questions found in each major report of the recent past, including reports addressing diet, physical inactivity, tobacco use, or any of the other factors or conditions discussed in this book.

A recent effort to formalize a comprehensive research agenda in this field for the United States was presented in the National Heart, Lung and Blood Institute's *Report of the Task Force on Research in Epidemiology and Prevention of Cardiovascular Diseases*, published in 1994.[8] This report is cited extensively in this chapter because it contributes to one view of perceived priority areas for research, considerations of programmatic strategy, and some aspects of the needed resources.

The report addressed the challenge of cardiovascular disease prevention in these terms:

> [T]here are now unequaled opportunities for further reducing CVD within all segments of American society. *The strategic key, and the greatest opportunity in preventing CVD, is to prevent the development of CVD risk in the first place.* . . . The task force thus emphasizes a population-wide strategy aimed at modifying lifestyles and major CVD risk factors beginning in early childhood and continuing throughout the lifespan. Pursuit of this strategy will involve observational and analytical studies, basic epidemiological research, randomized clinical trials, and demonstration projects essential to an effective CVD prevention effort [italics added].[8(pp xiv-xv)]

The great importance of this recommended focus of future research in epidemiology and prevention of cardiovascular diseases is that it makes explicit a fundamental shift from prevention of cardiovascular events to prevention of increased risk. Several implications of this concept have been discussed elsewhere.[9] The chief emphasis is on the concept that the risk factors themselves become the outcome of concern; their precursors (eg, dietary imbalance, physical inactivity, and others) become the focus of intervention; and the target population for research and demonstration projects begins with early childhood (or earlier) and extends throughout mid-adulthood, when a large proportion of the population may still exhibit desirable levels of blood lipids, blood pressure, and other factors related to cardiovascular risks and can therefore continue to benefit from health promotion activities to prevent the risk factors "in the first place."

Beyond this fundamental approach to future research, the Task Force report proposed specific priority areas for research, six of which are listed in Exhibit 29–1. (Two additional priorities concerned resources and research training and are discussed below.) The first priority expresses the overall goal of prevention of the risk factors. The second addresses the control of already-existing risk factors—especially blood pressure, for which greater control should have been achieved through the existing population-wide measures. The third concerns the socioeconomic differences in cardiovascular disease occurrence throughout the United States. The fourth and fifth priorities relate to intervention methods, as well as monitoring strategies, beginning in youth and applied to whole populations. The sixth priority is aimed at clarification of the complex relationships among insulin and glucose regulation, atherosclerosis, and the other major risk factors. In each priority area, a number of more-specific research questions are posed.

Another recent assessment of the need for research on cardiovascular risk factors was undertaken by a World Health Organization (WHO) Scientific Group and was also published in 1994.[10] The specific focus of the review was "new areas for research," which included nutrition; blood lipids; insulin resistance; homocysteine; hemostatic factors; alcohol; physical activity; genetic influences; women and noncontraceptive hormone use; and social, cultural, and psychosocial factors. Many of these recommendations were common to the Task Force and WHO Scientific Group reports. This congruence of recommendations strengthens the argument supporting their adoption.

A still more recent project of the WHO involved a broader scope and generated a more extensive report, *Investing in Health Research and Development*, which appeared in 1996.[11] The report was undertaken as "a review of health needs and related priorities for research and development in the low-income and middle-income countries. . . intended as a resource to assist decision-making by governments, industry and other investors on the allocation of funds to, and within, health R&D."[11(p xxi)] For noncommunicable diseases together, two aspects of research and development were emphasized. First was the need to obtain "reliable basic data on prevalence of and trends in noncommunicable diseases and risk factors"[11(p xxxvii)]:

Exhibit 29–1 Priority Areas for Research

The priority areas—for both basic epidemiological research on causation and enhanced application of already available knowledge—are:

- Prevention of adverse lifestyles and related risk factors
- Control of high blood pressure and other established cardiovascular disease (CVD) risk factors
- Reduction of CVD events, disability, and death associated with socioeconomic differences
- Prevention of hypertension, dyslipidemia, smoking, and atherosclerosis beginning in youth
- Improvement of populationwide prevention strategies
- Clarification of the insulin-glucose-atherosclerosis association

Source: Reprinted from National Heart, Lung and Blood Institute, National Institutes of Health, Bethesda, Maryland.

Faced with rapidly growing burdens of noncommunicable diseases, low-income and middle-income countries should significantly increase their relevant strategic research in epidemiology, behavioural science and health policy with the aim of reliably monitoring the true prevalence and trends of these conditions in their populations, and understanding their determinants. Basic data on morbidity, mortality and disability are currently inadequate in many regions, as are data on the country-specific and region-specific levels and determinants of environmental and behavioural risk factors. Low-cost methods for collecting reliable data, such as the use of disease surveillance points, must therefore be developed. In contrast to the need for epidemiological and behavioural research, biomedical science relevant to these conditions is already comparatively well supported in the established market economies. However, genuine differences in the characteristics of environments and populations will occasionally require additional biomedical research in some regions—as, for example, in seeking explanations for the observed high risk in South Asians of diabetes and heart disease. . . . The development and evaluation of algorithms and policy instruments for the cost-effective prevention, diagnosis, treatment and rehabilitation of noncommunicable diseases is an immediate priority for support by governments and other investors.[11(p xxxvii)]

Clearly, in looking beyond the demands for increased epidemiologic research on cardiovascular diseases within the United States, the immediate needs are virtually limitless.

One further example of research recommendations reflects the viewpoint of the International Heart Health Advisory Committee, whose *Victoria Declaration* and *Catalonia Declaration* were discussed in the preceding chapter.[12,13] The emphasis of the first of these reports was on a wide spectrum of research requirements, ranging from community interventions to risk factor–specific demonstration projects, epidemiologic surveillance and cost-effectiveness evaluation of interventions, heart health education, evaluation methodology, policy research, and etiological and management issues, including genetic research. The approach of the second report shifted to a greater emphasis on action to implement programs and projects, although several specific research emphases were retained or incorporated:

Research agencies should allocate appropriate resources to accomplish the following:

Develop new methods and approaches that facilitate the dissemination and uptake of existing prevention knowledge and interventions by organizations concerned with heart health at all levels.

Carry out organizational and evaluative research studies to learn about the value and cost of alternative methods for organizing, financing, and managing heart health programmes, including options for private sector funding of the delivery of such programmes.

Implement systems for surveillance of risk factors and cardiovascular disease, particularly in sentinel populations, including young people and people undergoing rapid social and economic change.

Implement systems for monitoring and reporting progress and results of both planned and unplanned interventions.[13(p 79)]

STRATEGIES

Apart from specific research priorities, broad strategies were also addressed in the Task Force report recommendations to the National Heart, Lung and Blood Institute.[8] Exhibit 29–2 shows the five characteristics proposed as important considerations for the Institute in its implementation of the recommended research agenda. First, research that has potential for application early in the processes of atherosclerosis and hypertension should be emphasized. Second, a population-wide focus should be an important criterion for selection of research questions and programs by the Institute in planning its research agenda. Third, specific population groups should be addressed for whom special disease burdens or obstacles to prevention are present. (This provision would complement the recently developed policies of the National Institutes of Health for inclusion of women and minorities in clinical and population studies by reinforcing the importance of research in those populations where health concerns are greatest, as determined by socioeconomic status, specific behavioral characteristics, and other significant aspects of populations and not only by gender and ethnicity.) Fourth, studies with potential to bridge the gaps between laboratory or patient-oriented research and prevention in the community should receive high priority in the interest of accelerating the translation of research in these domains as well as in epidemiology in public health practice. Fifth, studies with the potential to build banks of information and materials should be considered especially valuable, since the need for large data sets is increasingly appreciated, as is the utility of long-term follow-up of groups with good documentation of behaviors or risk factors prior to the onset of overt cardiovascular disease.

Exhibit 29–2 Strategies for Research

The nation's research program in epidemiology and prevention of cardiovascular disease (CVD) has the greatest promise of benefiting the public if it is continued *and* expanded to emphasize research that

- *Has potential for early application in CVD prevention* (especially prevention of elevated risk factors) and for discovering other traits amenable to intervention early in the disease process
- *Focuses on the whole population,* as well as on individuals at high risk, in seeking causes and means of prevention of high rates of disease
- *Embraces specific population groups* whose social circumstances (eg, low socioeconomic status), behavioral patterns (eg, diet, smoking, and physical activity), or other characteristics (eg, age, sex, ethnicity, genetics) impose special burdens of disease or special challenges to prevention
- *Incorporates approaches and findings from laboratory and clinical science and from developing technologies* (eg, noninvasive imaging of atherosclerotic lesions) which enhance the potential for population-based studies to accelerate the translation of laboratory, clinical, and epidemiological research results into public health applications
- *Builds banks of information and materials to support future studies* (eg, from large-scale studies, participant rosters maintained to provide later follow-up data on lifestyle characteristics and risk factors for defined populations, frozen samples of serum or DNA and urine, registries of family sets for future studies of postulated genetic-environmental interactions)

Source: Reprinted from National Heart, Blood and Lung Institute, National Institutes of Health, Bethesda, Maryland.

Other contributions to thinking about broad research strategies include the recommendations of the WHO Advisory Committee on Health Research, whose 1993 report included a strategy based on five key elements: control of diseases associated with poverty and environment; control of diseases, both infectious and noncommunicable, specific to the tropics; control of diseases associated with epidemiological and demographic transitions; treatment and care of the sick and disabled; and delivery of health services.[14] The primary emphasis is to be on prevention of disease, toward the short-term objective of Health for All and the long-term mission of achieving health as the state of complete physical, mental, and social well-being.

Research strategies for advancing community intervention activities are also undergoing new appraisals, as studies in various fields are reviewed (see, eg, Chapter 22). Feinleib, for example, has commented on the outcomes of the Stanford, Minnesota, and Pawtucket community intervention studies.[15] He notes observations of others that the scope of the interventions has been modest relative to other influences on the public, that long latent periods occur between the start of intervention and the appearance of their effects, and that the small numbers of community units constitutes an important design limitation in terms of sample size. Feinleib suggests that interventions may need to be targeted to population subgroups with concentrations of adverse risk behaviors rather than to the total community, and that understanding is needed of factors leading to resistance to change at the community level. In addition, effects of community intervention on the population under age 25 years have not been investigated and may differ from the experience of the older generations.

These suggestions, as well as the review of community interventions presented in Chapter 22, raise new possibilities for intervention studies that should be considered thoughtfully. For example, studies that emulate the model of the controlled trial must sacrifice resources in order to preserve intervention-free comparison units.

Those resources could otherwise be invested in intervention. Moreover, the theoretical intervention-free control community may actually be an illusion in many settings, since prevailing trends tend toward beneficial change in behaviors and risk factors independent of structured intervention. If intervention were studied instead in communities with clearly adverse current trends, and if phased implementation were planned in multiple communities, the demonstration of efficacious interventions that slow, arrest, or reverse such trends might be more successful, and more persuasive, than studies conducted to date. Such aspects of strategy for a new generation of intervention studies require full consideration.

RESOURCE REQUIREMENTS

The resource requirements for realization of the research potential in the epidemiology and prevention of cardiovascular diseases include funds, investigators, organizational and institutional bases, and societal and political support.

In the recent past in the United States, funding has received the greatest attention, with training and access to research support for new investigators a distant second. That funding for cardiovascular research has become scarce by historical standards is well recognized by everyone engaged in the competition for research funds at the federal level, and the focus of concern is the National Heart, Lung and Blood Institute. For example, analysis of trends in grant applications received and funded by the Institute from 1964 through 1993 shows that the number of applications increased from 782 to 3073; the success rate decreased from 48.3% to 21.9%; and the number of awards increased from 378 in 1964 to 966 in 1987 but decreased to 673 in 1993.[16] Subsequent success rates have declined, and percentile ranks from peer review of even the best 15% are now no guarantee of an award. Younger applicants represent a smaller proportion of the total; revised and resubmitted applications are more common as initial submissions are less often successful; and levels and duration of funding requests have come under increasing scrutiny.

Much broader concern about the federal appropriations for biomedical and community health research has led to increasingly frequent editorial and journalistic commentary. Concurrently, the scientific community appears to have become more active in the political process of federal appropriations for biomedical research. The American Heart Association has undertaken increased efforts to present members of the United States Congress with information and personal testimony by scientists and celebrities in the cause of heart and stroke research.[17] Nonetheless, the American Heart Association presented data in 1996 indicating a decline in research funding for cardiovascular diseases at the National Heart, Lung and Blood Institute in constant dollars, from 1985 to 1996.[18] The political impetus to reduce federal spending and balance the federal budget by the year 2002 is not an auspicious sign for future research funding.

However, the case for investment in health and health research is being made in terms that emphasize the economic return for the nation, and congressional support for biomedical research is strong in many quarters. If that support extends to biomedical *and community health* research, and to the Centers for Disease Control and Prevention and other key agencies as well as the National Institutes of Health,

prospects may improve for the needed support to implement the nation's health research agenda, through emphasis on the research that is closest to the delivery of effective programs and services for prevention of disease and promotion of health for the population as a whole.

Funding has been addressed in some detail because it is a condition of the other resources needed, especially qualified investigators. Personnel requirements in health research, especially in epidemiology and prevention, have been emphasized, for example, by the Pew Health Professions Commission.[19] In its most recent assessment, *Critical Challenges: Revitalizing the Health Professions for the Twenty-First Century*, the commission concluded that "large numbers of health professionals will require retraining in disease prevention, clinical epidemiology, process and systems analysis and managerial epidemiology."[19(p 55)] Without digressing to contemplation of "managerial epidemiology," it is clear that the need for epidemiologists in cardiovascular disease prevention as in other fields will require training programs in which interdisciplinary approaches to research and program development will be of value.

In this connection, the National Heart, Lung and Blood Institute Task Force report addressed training requirements as shown in Exhibit 29–3.[8] Training opportunities for physicians and other health professionals and researchers should be

Exhibit 29–3 Training for Cardiovascular Epidemiology and Prevention

---

Recommendation: Overcome critical shortages in the training of individuals qualified to pursue needed research in epidemiology and prevention of cardiovascular disease (CVD).

This recommendation includes the following research tasks:

1. Provide expanded, specialized training for practicing health professionals through short-term programs, giving priority to development of physician epidemiologists and cross-disciplinary training in selected, key areas.
2. Expand the current training grant program to attract outstanding students into CVD epidemiology and prevention. Emphasize training in biostatistics, epidemiology, nutrition, clinical trials, health education, health promotion, and research on disease prevention.

Source: Reprinted from National Heart, Lung and Blood Institute, National Institutes of Health, Bethesda, Maryland.

expanded, as these recommendations suggest. Access to both short-term courses and academic degree programs is needed by large numbers of candidates to meet the current and growing demand for qualified investigators. In addition, research funding is critical to permit those entering such careers to obtain needed support and to make the research and other professional contributions for which they have prepared.

Additional technical resources are needed for realization of the research agenda recommended by the Task Force report.[8] As outlined in Exhibit 29–4, these resources include biostatistical developments, follow-up methods for population studies, enhanced standardization and certification procedures for epidemiologic data collection, long-term storage and utilization of biological samples from population studies, a funding mechanism for short-term pilot studies to explore new laboratory findings or for methodologic investigations, and improved methods for large-scale dietary assessment of populations for large samples and long-term follow-up studies. These resources can greatly increase the fruitfulness of the investment in future research projects.

The institutional and organizational bases for the needed research depend, as do individual investigators, on continuity of funding for maintenance of key staff, facilities, and equipment to enable the development and implementation of research proposals. Stability of the research enterprise has been threatened by the funding constraints addressed above and needs to be reestablished so that dissolution of research teams does not progress to an irreversible point. Again, as noted above, a champion of this cause is the American Heart Association, whose incoming president stated in his 1996 address to the annual scientific meeting of the American Heart Association: "We must carry our two-pronged message on the prevalence of cardio-

---

Exhibit 29–4 Resource Requirements for Research in Cardiovascular Epidemiology and Prevention

Recommendation: *Develop technical resources for continuing effective population studies of cardiovascular disease (CVD) epidemiology and prevention.*

This recommendation includes the following research tasks:

1. Develop new biostatistical techniques for analyzing highly correlated variables; studying genetic-environmental interactions; and designing and analyzing the results of community trials, clinical trials, longitudinal studies, and meta-analyses.
2. Evaluate and improve general methods for long-term follow-up of populations in epidemiological studies and specific methods for following unemployed and other low-income or mobile groups, taking advantage of U.S. data linkages that may become possible through health care reform.
3. Develop expanded methods for standardizing and certifying data collection methods for key epidemiological data on CVD, giving specific attention to new techniques.
4. Provide for long-term storage and subsequent utilization of biological specimens and research data files collected in epidemiological studies of CVD.
5. Facilitate short-term pilot studies to investigate new questions and the applicability of new laboratory procedures for population-based studies, and develop procedures that encourage maximum utilization of existing data sets.
6. Refine the methods used to assess dietary intake to improve their suitability for population studies, and clarify the role of diet in CVD risk through population studies using large samples and repeated, comprehensive nutritional assessments.

Source: Reprinted from National Heart, Lung and Blood Institute, National Institutes of Health, Bethesda, Maryland.

vascular disease and scientific opportunities in the field to the three levels in Washington where decisions are made that determine the amount of money that ultimately goes into heart disease and stroke research."[20(p 3022)] The three levels are the White House and Congress, the office of the National Institutes of Health Director, and the National Heart, Lung and Blood Institute itself. Successful communication at these three levels is expected to result in a greater appropriation and greater allocation to support of heart and stroke research at the National Institutes of Health. Similar efforts are needed to support the programs of the Centers for Disease Control and Prevention, including its Prevention Research Centers Program.

Internationally, support for epidemiologic research through the European Community has been noted, and the potential for initiatives from the World Bank has been addressed in earlier chapters. The WHO has undergone recent changes with marked reduction in support specific to cardiovascular diseases, but critical staff remain to sustain key partnerships with other interested organizations and agencies, among them the International Society and Federation of Cardiology.

CONCLUSION

At a time of unprecedented need and opportunity for investment in epidemiology and prevention of cardiovascular diseases, there are mixed signals regarding the readiness of those responsible for funding of research and preventive programs, whether domestically or globally, to make the necessary commitments. This circumstance requires intensified efforts of health professionals to articulate the need and the opportunity for advancing epidemiologic research for cardiovascular disease prevention and to demonstrate the capacity to carry out the significant work that awaits attention. The continued dedication of those around the world who recognize this need and opportunity offers the greatest potential for progress.

REFERENCES

1. Committee for the Study of the Future of Public Health. *The Future of Public Health.* Washington, DC: Division of Health Care Services, Institute of Medicine. National Academy Press; 1988.

2. Remington RD. Role of organized public health in cardiovascular disease prevention. In: Marmot M, Elliott P, eds. *Coronary Heart Disease Epidemiology: From Aetiology to Public Health.* Oxford, England: Oxford Medical Publications; 1992: 515–524.

3. Stallones RA. To advance epidemiology. *Annu Rev Public Health.* 1980;1:69–82.

4. Stoto MA, Green LW, Bailey LA, eds. *Linking Research and Public Health Practice: A Review of CDC's Program of Centers for Research and Demonstration of Health Promotion and Disease Prevention.* Board on Health Promotion and Disease Prevention. Institute of Medicine. Washington, DC: National Academy Press; 1997.

5. *Report of the Expert Panel on Genetic Strategies for Heart, Lung, and Blood Diseases.* Washington, DC: National Heart, Lung, and Blood Institute, National Institutes of Health, Public Health Service, US Dept of Health and Human Services. [Undated].

6. Susser M, Susser E. Choosing a future for epidemiology: I. Eras and paradigms. *Am J Public Health.* 1996; 86:668–673.

7. Susser M, Susser E. Choosing a future for epidemiology: II. From black box to Chinese boxes and eco-epidemiology. *Am J Public Health.* 1996;86:674–677.

8. National Heart, Lung, and Blood Institute. *Report of the Task Force on Research in Epidemiology and Prevention of Cardiovascular Diseases.* Washington, DC: National Institutes of Health, Public Health Service, US Dept of Health and Human Services; 1994.

9. Labarthe DR. Prevention of cardiovascular risk factors in the first place. *J Epidemiol.* 1997;6(suppl):1–5.

10. Report of a WHO Scientific Group. *Cardiovascular Disease Risk Factors: New Areas for Research.* Geneva, Switzerland: World Health Organization; 1994. WHO Technical Report Series 841.

11. Ad Hoc Committee on Health Research Relating to Future Intervention Options. *Report of the Ad Hoc Committee on Health Research Relating to Future Intervention Options: Investing in Health Research and Development.* Geneva, Switzerland: World Health Organization; 1996.

12. Advisory Board of the International Heart Health Conference. *The Victoria Declaration on Heart Health.* Victoria, British Columbia: Health and Welfare Canada, BC Ministry of Health and Ministry Responsible for Elders, Heart and Stroke Foundation of Canada; 1992.

13. Advisory Board of the Second International Heart Health Conference. *The Catalonia Declaration: Investing in Heart Health.* Barcelona, Spain: Department of Health and Social Security, Autonomous Government of Catalonia; 1996.

14. Advisory Committee on Health Research. *Research for Health: Principles, Perspectives and Strategies.* Geneva, Switzerland: World Health Organization; 1993.

15. Feinleib M. New directions for community intervention studies. *Am J of Public Health.* 1996;86:1696–1698.

16. Oparil S. Cardiovascular health at the crossroads: outlook for the 21st century. Presented at the 67th Scientific Sessions of the American Heart Association November 4, 1994, Dallas, Texas. *Circ.* 1995;91:1304–1310.

17. Louis C, Ballin S. AHA's new research initiative. *Circ.* 1995; 92:3369–3370.

18. *Invest in Heart and Stroke Research: Ensure the Future Health of Our Nation, Our Families and Our Children.* Washington, DC: Office of Public Affairs, American Heart Association; 1996.

19. *Critical Challenges: Revitalizing the Health Professions for the Twenty-First Century: The Third Report of the Pew Health Professions Commission.* San Francisco, Calif: Center for the Health Professions, University of California; 1995.

20. Breslow JL. Why you should support the American Heart Association! Presented at the 69th Scientific Sessions of the American Heart Association, November 10, 1996, New Orleans, Louisiana. *Circ.* 1996;94:3016–3022.

Index

Page numbers in *italics* denote figures and exhibits; those followed by "t" denote tables.

A

Acute phase reactants, 371
Adolescents. *See* Children and adolescents
Adulthood, 124–125, 527–529
Aerobics Center Longitudinal Study, 184, 185t, 186t
Age, 119–125
   age adjustment, 123
   alcohol consumption and, 354t
   aortic aneurysm and, 100–101, *101–103,* 103
   ascertainment of, 122–123
   atherosclerosis and, 35–39, *36–38*
   blood pressure and, 121–123, 261, 266, 267t, *271,* 271–272, *272,* 273t
   cardiomyopathy and, 580, *582*
   cardiovascular disease prevention and, 524–529
      adolescence, 527
      birth, 526
      early adulthood, 527–528
      early childhood, 526
      gestation, 525–526
      late adulthood, 528–529
      late childhood, 527
      life span from cardiovascular perspective, 524
      middle adulthood, 528
      middle childhood, 526–527

natural history and opportunities for intervention, 524–525
cholesterol concentration and, 232t–233t, 236t, *237*
congenital heart disease and, 592, 594t, 597–598
congestive heart failure and, 108–111, 109t, *110, 111*
coronary heart disease and, 65t
definitions and categories of, 122
diabetes and, 302, 304, 305t
   gestational, 122
impaired glucose tolerance and, 304, 306t
interpreting health patterns by, 123–125
   childhood and youth, 123–124
   elderly, 124–125
   fetal and neonatal period, 123
   young and middle adulthood, 124
Kawasaki disease and, 611, 617, *619*
peripheral arterial disease and, 96, *96,* 98t
physical inactivity and, 175t, 177t
rheumatic fever/rheumatic heart disease and, 547, *547,* 554, 555t

smoking and, 326–327, 327t, 328t
stroke and, *83, 85, 86,* 87t, 88t
Alcohol consumption, 347–366
   cardiomyopathy induced by, 633
   current issues related to, 365–366
      conflicting attitudes and judgments, 365–366
      question of substance, 366
   definition of, 347–348
      qualitative categories, 347–348, 348t
      quantitative units, 348
   determinants of, 349
   measurement of, 348–349
      ex-drinkers, 349
      general reliability, 348–349
   mechanisms of action of alcohol, 349–353
      blood pressure, 350–351
      genetic factors, 351, 352t
      hemostasis, 351–353
      high-density lipoprotein cholesterol, 349–350, *350*
   peripheral arterial disease and, 98t
   prevalence of, 353–355
      in United States adults, 353, 354t
      in United States youths, 353, *355*

663